Survival Communications
in Illinois: Downstate

ILLINOIS

John E. Parnell, KK4HWX

13 ISBN 978-1-62512-003-8

Cover design by:
Lynda Colón
FREELANCE GRAPHIC DESIGN &
MARKETING COMMUNICATIONS
www.hirelynda.webs.com

I do wish to acknowledge the hard work of **Angie Shirley** in putting together the database required for this book. Without her efforts, this book could not have been done.

Titles available in this series:

Survival Communications in Alabama
Survival Communications in Alaska
Survival Communications in Arizona
Survival Communications in Arkansas
Survival Communications in California
Survival Communications in Colorado
Survival Communications in Connecticut
Survival Communications in Delaware
Survival Communications in Florida
Survival Communications in Georgia
Survival Communications in Hawaii
Survival Communications in Idaho
Survival Communications in Illinois
Survival Communications in Indiana
Survival Communications in Iowa
Survival Communications in Kansas
Survival Communications in Kentucky
Survival Communications in Louisiana
Survival Communications in Maine
Survival Communications in Maryland
Survival Communications in Massachusetts
Survival Communications in Michigan
Survival Communications in Minnesota
Survival Communications in Mississippi
Survival Communications in Missouri

Survival Communications in Montana
Survival Communications in Nebraska
Survival Communications in Nevada
Survival Communications in New Hampshire
Survival Communications in New Jersey
Survival Communications in New Mexico
Survival Communications in New York
Survival Communications in North Carolina
Survival Communications in North Dakota
Survival Communications in Ohio
Survival Communications in Oklahoma
Survival Communications in Oregon
Survival Communications in Pennsylvania
Survival Communications in Rhode Island
Survival Communications in South Carolina
Survival Communications in South Dakota
Survival Communications in Tennessee
Survival Communications in Texas
Survival Communications in Utah
Survival Communications in Vermont
Survival Communications in Virginia
Survival Communications in Washington
Survival Communications in West Virginia
Survival Communications in Wisconsin
Survival Communications in Wyoming

The above titles are available from your favorite online or brick-and-mortar bookstore or directly from the publisher at Tutor Turtle Press LLC, 1027 S. Pendleton St. – Suite B-10, Easley, SC 29642.

TABLE OF CONTENTS

Appendix A – Illinois Ham Radio Clubs

ARRL Affiliated Amateur and Ham Radio Clubs – By City

Appendix B – Illinois: Downstate Ham Licensees by City

Survival Communications in Illinois

Perhaps you have prepared for WTSHTF or TEOTWAWKI with respect to food, water, self-defense and shelter. But what about communication?

Whenever there is a disaster (hurricane, earthquake, economic collapse, nuclear war, EMF, solar eruption, etc.), the normal means of communication that we're all reliant upon (cell phone, land line phone, the Internet, etc.) will probably be, at best, sporadic and at worst, non-existent.

As this author sees it, short of smoke signals and mirrors, there are three options for communication in "trying times": (1) GMRS or FRS radios; (2) CB radios; and (3) ham or amateur radio. Let's consider each of these options to come up with the most acceptable one.

GMRS (General Mobile Radio Service) / FRS (Family Radio Service)

GMRS (General Mobile Radio Service) / FRS (Family Radio Service) radios work optimally over short distances where there is minimal interference. Originally designed to be used as pagers, particularly inside a building or other such confined area, these radios are low-cost and convenient to carry. Unfortunately their small size and light weight comes with a trade-off – short range and short battery life. These radios are supposed to be able to communicate for up to 25-30 miles. Right. That's on level terrain, without buildings or trees getting in the way. While battery life technology is constantly improving, you will need spare batteries to keep communicating or someway of recharging the ones in the radio. In this author's opinion, GMRS/FRS radios are not first choice when concerned with medium or long range communication.

CB (Citizens Band)

CB (Citizens Band) radios operate in a frequency range originally reserved for ham or amateur radio operation. Because of the overwhelming number of people wishing quick, low-cost, regulation-free communication, the FCC (Federal Communication Commission) split off a portion of the frequency spectrum and allowed anyone to purchase a CB radio and start communicating. No test. No license. Just personal/business communication. Today, CB radios are readily available in such outlets as eBay and Craigslist. This author has seen them at yard/garage/tag sales and at flea markets.

CB radios come in a variety of "flavors." Fixed units, sometimes referred to as base units are intended for home use. For the most part, they derive their power from the utility company. In the event of loss of electricity, most base units can also be connected to a 12-volt battery, like that in your car/truck. If you choose to obtain a fixed unit, make sure you know how to connect the unit to the battery – ahead of time. Trying to figure this out when you're under extra stress is not a good situation.

A second type of CB radio is designed to be mobile, that is, installed in your car/truck. It gets its power from the vehicle's battery. You can either attach an antenna permanently to the vehicle or have a removable, magnetic type antenna.

The third type of CB radio is designed for handheld use. They are small and light. Most weigh less than a pound and operate on batteries. Yes, using batteries in a CB poses the same limitations as those by the GMRS/FRS radios, but have the added advantage that most handheld units come with a cigarette lighter adapter. Comes in handy when you are on the move and wish to be able to communicate both from a vehicle and also when you have to abandon it.

While they have a greater range than GMRS/FRS radios, CB radios are, legally, limited to operate on 40 channels, with a power rating of four (4) watts or less. Yes, it is possible to alter CB radios to get around these limitations, but not legally,

Ham/Amateur Radio

Ham/Amateur radio is very appealing. With a ham radio, you are not limited to less than 50 miles, but can communicate with anyone in the world (who also has access to a ham radio, of course).

Standardized Amateur Radio Prepper Communications Plan

In the event of a nationwide catastrophic disaster, the nationwide network of Amateur Radio licensed preppers will need a set of standardized meeting frequencies to share information and coordinate activities between various prepper groups. This Standardized Amateur Radio Communications Plan establishes a set of frequencies on the 80 meter, 40 meter, 20 meter, and 2 meter Amateur Radio bands for use during these types of catastrophic disasters.

Routine nets will not be held on all of these frequencies, but preppers are encouraged to use them when coordinating with other preppers on a routine basis. Routine nets may be conducted by The American Preparedness Radio Net (TAPRN) on these or other frequencies as they see fit. However, TAPRN will promote the use of these standardized frequencies by all Amateur Radio licensed preppers during times of catastrophic disaster. The promotion of this Standardized Amateur Radio Communications Plan is encouraged by all means within the prepper community, including via Amateur Radio, Twitter, Facebook, and various blogs.

Standardized Frequencies and Modes
80 Meters – 3.818 MHz LSB (TAPRN Net: Sundays at 9 PM ET) 40 Meters – 7.242 MHz LSB 40 Meters Morse Code / Digital – 7.073 MHz USB (TAPRN: Sundays at 7:30 PM ET on   CONTESTIA 4/250) 20 Meters – 14.242 MHz USB 2 Meters – 146.420 MHz FM

Nets and Network Etiquette

In times of nationwide catastrophic disaster, the ability of any one prepper to initiate and sustain themselves as a net control may be limited by the availability of power and other resource shortages. However, all licensed preppers are encouraged to maintain a listening watch on these frequencies as often as possible during a catastrophic disaster. Preppers may routinely announce themselves in the following manner:

• This is [Your Callsign Phonetically] in [Your State], maintaining a listening watch on [Standard Frequency] for any preppers on frequency seeking information or looking to provide information. Please call [Your Callsign Phonetically]. Preppers exchanging information that may require follow up should agree upon a designated time to return to the frequency and provide further information. If other stations are utilizing the frequency at the designated time you return, maintain watch and proceed with your communications when those stations are finished. If your communications are urgent and the stations on frequency are not passing information of a critical nature, interrupt with the word "Break" and request use of the frequency.

For More Information

Catastrophe Network: http://www.catastrophenetwork.org or @CatastropheNet on Twitter The American Preparedness Radio Network: http://www.taprn.com or @TAPRN on Twitter

© 2011 Catastrophe Network, Please Distribute Freely

In order to use a ham radio, legally, one must be licensed to do so by the FCC (other countries have analogous governmental bodies to regulate ham radio). To obtain a license is quite easy – take a test and pay your license fee. There are currently three classes of license – Technician, General, and Amateur Extra. With each of these licenses come specific abilities.

Technician class is the beginning level. The exam consists of 35 multiple choice questions randomly drawn from a pool of 395 questions. The question pool is readily available online for free downloading (http://www.ncvec.org/downloads/Revised%20Element%202.Pdf) or in such publications at *Ham Radio License Manual Revised 2nd Edition* (ISBN 978-0-87259-097-7). The current Technician pool of questions is to be used from July 1, 2010 to June 30, 2014. Be sure the question pool you are studying from is current. You will need to score at least 26 correct to pass. (Do not worry, Morse Code is no longer on the test, although many ham operators use it anyway.) You do not need to take a formal class in order to qualify to take the exam. You can learn the material on your own. Most people spend 10-15 hours studying and then successfully take the exam. The cost of taking the exam is under $20. The exam is given in MANY locations throughout the US. Usually the exam is given by area ham clubs. You do not have to belong to the club to take the exam. Check Appendix A for a listing of clubs in Illinois.

Topics for the Technician License in Amateur Radio

The Technician license exam covers such topics as basic regulations, operating practices, and electronic theory, with a focus on VHF and UHF applications. Below is the syllabus for the Technician Class.

Subelement T1 – FCC Rules, descriptions and definitions for the amateur radio service, operator and station license responsibilities

[6 Exam Questions – 6 Groups]

T1A – Amateur Radio services; purpose of the amateur service, amateur-satellite service, operator/primary station license grant, where FCC rules are codified, basis and purpose of FCC rules, meanings of basic terms used in FCC rules

T1B – Authorized frequencies; frequency allocations, ITU regions, emission type, restricted sub-bands, spectrum sharing, transmissions near band edges

T1C – Operator classes and station call signs; operator classes, sequential, special event, and vanity call sign systems, international communications, reciprocal operation, station license licensee, places where the amateur service is regulated by the FCC, name and address on ULS, license term, renewal, grace period

T1D – Authorized and prohibited transmissions

T1E – Control operator and control types; control operator required, eligibility, designation of control operator, privileges and duties, control point, local, automatic and remote control, location of control operator

T1F – Station identification and operation standards; special operations for repeaters and auxiliary stations, third party communications, club stations, station security, FCC inspection

---

Subelement T2 – Operating Procedures

[3 Exam Questions – 3 Groups]

T2A – Station operation; choosing an operating frequency, calling another station, test transmissions, use of minimum power, frequency use, band plans

T2B – VHF/UHF operating practices; SSB phone, FM repeater, simplex, frequency offsets, splits and shifts, CTCSS, DTMF, tone squelch, carrier squelch, phonetics

T2C – Public service; emergency and non-emergency operations, message traffic handling

---

Subelement T3 – Radio wave characteristics, radio and electromagnetic properties, propagation modes

[3 Exam Questions – 3 Groups]

T3A – Radio wave characteristics; how a radio signal travels; distinctions of HF, VHF and UHF; fading, multipath; wavelength vs. penetration; antenna orientation

T3B – Radio and electromagnetic wave properties; the electromagnetic spectrum, wavelength vs. frequency, velocity of electromagnetic waves

T3C – Propagation modes; line of sight, sporadic E, meteor, aurora scatter, tropospheric ducting, F layer skip, radio horizon

Subelement T4 - Amateur radio practices and station setup

[2 Exam Questions – 2 Groups]

T4A – Station setup; microphone, speaker, headphones, filters, power source, connecting a computer, RF grounding

T4B – Operating controls; tuning, use of filters, squelch, AGC, repeater offset, memory channels

Subelement T5 – Electrical principles, math for electronics, electronic principles, Ohm's Law

[4 Exam Questions – 4 Groups]

T5A – Electrical principles; current and voltage, conductors and insulators, alternating and direct current

T5B – Math for electronics; decibels, electronic units and the metric system

T5C – Electronic principles; capacitance, inductance, current flow in circuits, alternating current, definition of RF, power calculations

T5D – Ohm's Law

Subelement T6 – Electrical components, semiconductors, circuit diagrams, component functions

[4 Exam Groups – 4 Questions]

T6A – Electrical components; fixed and variable resistors, capacitors, and inductors; fuses, switches, batteries

T6B – Semiconductors; basic principles of diodes and transistors

T6C – Circuit diagrams; schematic symbols

T6D – Component functions

Subelement T7 – Station equipment, common transmitter and receiver problems, antenna measurements and troubleshooting, basic repair and testing

[4 Exam Questions – 4 Groups]

T7A – Station radios; receivers, transmitters, transceivers

T7B – Common transmitter and receiver problems; symptoms of overload and overdrive, distortion, interference, over and under modulation, RF feedback, off frequency signals; fading and noise; problems with digital communications interfaces

T7C – Antenna measurements and troubleshooting; measuring SWR, dummy loads, feedline failure modes

T7D – Basic repair and testing; soldering, use of a voltmeter, ammeter, and ohmmeter

Subelement T8 – Modulation modes, amateur satellite operation, operating activities, non-voice communications

[4 Exam Questions – 4 Groups]

T8A – Modulation modes; bandwidth of various signals

T8B – Amateur satellite operation; Doppler shift, basic orbits, operating protocols

T8C – Operating activities; radio direction finding, radio control, contests, special event stations, basic linking over Internet

T8D – Non-voice communications; image data, digital modes, CW, packet, PSK31

Subelement T9 – Antennas, feedlines

[2 Exam Groups – 2 Questions]

T9A – Antennas; vertical and horizontal, concept of gain, common portable and mobile antennas, relationships between antenna length and frequency

T9B – Feedlines; types, losses vs. frequency, SWR concepts, matching, weather protection, connectors

Subelement T0 – AC power circuits, antenna installation, RF hazards

[3 Exam Questions – 3 Groups]

T0A – AC power circuits; hazardous voltages, fuses and circuit breakers, grounding, lightning protection, battery safety, electrical code compliance

T0B – Antenna installation; tower safety, overhead power lines

T0C – RF hazards; radiation exposure, proximity to antennas, recognized safe power levels, exposure to others

Once your name and call sign are available in the FCC database, you have the privilege of operating on all VHF (2 m) and UHF (70 cm) frequencies above 30 megahertz (MHz) and HF frequencies 80, 40, and 15 meter, and on the 10 meter band using Morse code (CW), voice, and digital mode. For a Technician license in Illinois, your call sign will consist of a two-letter prefix beginning with K or W, the number nine (9), and a three-letter suffix. The single digit number in the call sign is determined according to which area of the US you obtain your first license. Even though you may move to another state, you keep this number in your call sign. This is also true should you upgrade to a higher license and get a new call sign. The numeral portion of your call sign stays the same.

Call Sign Numbers

Below is a chart showing the various numbers and the state(s) in which you would obtain the number.

Call Sign Number	State(s)
0	CO, IA, KS, MN, MO, NE, ND, SD
1	CT, ME, MA, NH, RI, VT
2	NJ, NY
3	DE, DC, MD, PA
4	AL, FL, GA, KY, NC, SC, TN, VA
5	AR, LA, MS, NM, OK, TX
6	CA
7	AZ, ID, MT, NV, OR, WA, UT, WY
8	MI, OH, WV
9	IL, IN, WI

Residents of Alaska may have any of the following call sign prefixes assigned to them: AL0-7, KL0-7, NL0-7, or WL0-7. Likewise, residents of Hawaii may have the prefix AH6-7, KH6-7, NH6-7, or WH6-7 assigned.

Once you obtain your Technician license, do not stop there. Go and get your General license.

General is the second of three ham license classes. Like the Technician license, to get a General license, you merely have to take a 35-question multiple choice exam and pay your license fee. Passing is still at least 26 correct answers and the fee is the same (less than $20). Again the question pool is available for free online (http://www.ncvec.org/page.php?id=358). It is also available in such print publications as *The ARRL General Class License Manual 7th Edition* (ISBN 978-0-87259-811-9). The current General pool of questions is to be used from July 1, 2011 to June 30, 2015. Be sure the question pool you are using is current. Being a bit more comprehensive than the Technician license, the General license usually requires 15-20 hours of study to learn the material. Check Appendix A for a listing of clubs in Illinois where you might take your exam. Once your name and NEW call sign is listed in the FCC database, you're good to go. For a General license in Illinois, your call sign will consist of a one-letter prefix beginning with K, N or W, the number nine (9), and a three-letter suffix.

Topics for the General License in Amateur Radio

The General license exam covers regulations, operating practices and electronic theory. Below is the syllabus for the General Class.

Subelement G1 – Commission's Rules
(5 Exam Questions – 5 Groups)
G1A – General Class control operator frequency privileges; primary and secondary allocations
G1B – Antenna structure limitations; good engineering and good amateur practice, beacon operation; restricted operation; retransmitting radio signals
G1C – Transmitter power regulations; data emission standards
G1D – Volunteer Examiners and Volunteer Examiner Coordinators; temporary identification
G1E – Control categories; repeater regulations; harmful interference; third party rules; ITU regions

Subelement G2 – Operating procedures
(5 Exam Questions – 5 Groups)
G2A – Phone operating procedures; USB/LSB utilization conventions; procedural signals; breaking into a OSO in progress; VOX operation
G2B – Operating courtesy; band plans, emergencies, including drills and emergency communications
G2C – CW operating procedures and procedural signals; Q signals and common abbreviations; full break in
G2D – Amateur Auxiliary; minimizing interference; HF operations

G2E – Digital operating; procedures, procedural signals and common abbreviations

Subelement G3 – Radio wave propagation

(3 Exam Questions – 3 Groups)
G3A – Sunspots and solar radiation; ionospheric disturbances; propagation forecasting and indices
G3B – Maximum Usable Frequency; Lowest Usable Frequency; propagation
G3C – Ionospheric layers; critical angle and frequency; HF scatter; Near Vertical Incidence Sky waves

Subelement G4 – Amateur radio practices

(5 Exam Questions – 5 Groups)
G4A – Station Operation and setup
G4B – Test and monitoring equipment; two-tone test
G4C – Interference with consumer electronics; grounding; DSP
G4D – Speech processors; S meters; sideband operation near band edges
G4E – HF mobile radio installations; emergency and battery powered operation

Subelement G5 – Electrical principles

(3 Exam Questions – 3 Groups)
G5A – Reactance; inductance; capacitance; impedance; impedance matching
G5B – The Decibel; current and voltage dividers; electrical power calculations; sine wave root-mean-square (RMS) values; PEP calculations
G5C – Resistors; capacitors and inductors in series and parallel; transformers

Subelement G6 – Circuit components

(3 Exam Questions – 3 Groups)
G6A – Resistors; capacitors; inductors
G6B – Rectifiers; solid state diodes and transistors; vacuum tubes; batteries
G6C – Analog and digital integrated circuits (ICs); microprocessors; memory; I/O devices; microwave ICs (MMICs); display devices

Subelement G7 – Practical circuits

(3 Exam Questions – 3 Groups)
G7A – Power supplies; schematic symbols
G7B – Digital circuits; amplifiers and oscillators
G7C – Receivers and transmitters; filters, oscillators

Subelement G8 – Signals and emissions

(2 Exam Questions – 2 Groups)

G8A – Carriers and modulation; AM; FM; single and double sideband; modulation envelope; overmodulation

G8B – Frequency mixing; multiplication; HF data communications; bandwidths of various modes; deviation

Subelement G9 – Antennas and feed lines

(4 Exam Questions – 4 Groups)

G9A – Antenna feed lines; characteristic impedance and attenuation; SWR calculation, measurement and effects; matching networks

G9B – Basic antennas

G9C – Directional antennas

G9D – Specialized antennas

Subelement G0 – Electrical and RF safety

(2 Exam Questions – 2 Groups)

G0A – RF safety principles, rules and guidelines; routine station elevation

G0B – Safety in the ham shack; electrical shock and treatment, safety grounding, fusing, interlocks, wiring, antenna and tower safety

With a General license, you can use all VHF and UHF frequencies and most of the HF frequencies. You would have access to the 160, 30, 17, 12, and 10 meter bands and access to major parts of the 80, 40, 20, and 15 meter bands. Of course, this is in addition to all bands available to Technician license holders.

Amateur Extra is the third of three ham license classes. Like the Technician and General classes, you merely have to pass a test and pay your fee to get your Amateur Extra license. This class of license is more comprehensive than the lower license classes. The exam is longer – 50 questions – and the minimum passing score is higher – 37. However, once you get your Amateur Extra license, all ham frequencies, VHF, UHF and HF are available for your enjoyment. The Extra exam covers regulations, specialized operating practices, advanced electronics theory, and radio equipment design.

Like for the other license classes, the question pool for the Amateur Extra license is available online for downloading (http://www.ncvec.org/downloads/REVISED%202012-2016%20Extra%20Class%20Pool.doc). It is also available in print form in such publications as *The ARRL Extra Class License Manual Revised 9th Edition* (ISBN 978-0-87259-887-4).

Topics for the Extra License in Amateur Radio

Below is the syllabus for the Amateur Extra Class for July 1, 2012 to June 30, 2016.

Subelement E1 – Commission's Rules

[6 Exam Questions – 6 Groups]

E1A – Operating Standards: frequency privileges; emission standards; automatic message forwarding; frequency sharing; stations aboard ships or aircraft

E1B – Station restrictions and special operations: restrictions on station location; general operating restrictions, spurious emissions, control operator reimbursement; antenna structure restrictions; RACES operations

E1C – Station control: definitions and restrictions pertaining to local, automatic and remote control operation; control operator responsibilities for remote and automatically controlled stations

E1D – Amateur Satellite service: definitions and purpose; license requirements for space stations; available frequencies and bands; telecommand and telemetry operations; restrictions, and special provisions; notification requirements

E1E – Volunteer examiner program: definitions, qualifications, preparation and administration of exams; accreditation; question pools; documentation requirements

E1F – Miscellaneous rules: external RF power amplifiers; national quiet zone; business communications; compensated communications; spread spectrum; auxiliary stations; reciprocal operating privileges; IARP and CEPT licenses; third party communications with foreign countries; special temporary authority

Subelement E2 – Operating procedures

[5 Exam Questions – 5 Groups]

E2A – Amateur radio in space: amateur satellites; orbital mechanics; frequencies and modes; satellite hardware; satellite operations

E2B – Television practices: fast scan television standards and techniques; slow scan television standards and techniques

E2C – Operating methods: contest and DX operating; spread-spectrum transmissions; selecting an operating frequency

E2D – Operating methods: VHF and UHF digital modes; APRS

E2E – Operating methods: operating HF digital modes; error correction

Subelement E3 – Radio wave propagation

[3 Exam Questions – 3 Groups]

E3A – Propagation and technique, Earth-Moon-Earth communications; meteor scatter

E3B – Propagation and technique, trans-equatorial; long path; gray-line; multi-path propagation

E3C – Propagation and technique, Aurora propagation; selective fading; radio-path horizon; take-off angle over flat or sloping terrain; effects of ground on propagation; less common propagation modes

Subelement E4 – Amateur practices

[5 Exam Questions – 5 Groups]

E4A – Test equipment: analog and digital instruments; spectrum and network analyzers, antenna analyzers; oscilloscopes; testing transistors; RF measurements

E4B – Measurement technique and limitations: instrument accuracy and performance limitations; probes; techniques to minimize errors; measurement of "Q"; instrument calibration

E4C – Receiver performance characteristics, phase noise, capture effect, noise floor, image rejection, MDS, signal-to-noise-ratio; selectivity

E4D – Receiver performance characteristics, blocking dynamic range, intermodulation and cross-modulation interference; 3rd order intercept; desensitization; preselection

E4E – Noise suppression: system noise; electrical appliance noise; line noise; locating noise sources; DSP noise reduction; noise blankers

Subelement E5 – Electrical principles

[4 Exam Questions – 4 Groups]

E5A – Resonance and Q: characteristics of resonant circuits: series and parallel resonance; Q; half-power bandwidth; phase relationships in reactive circuits

E5B – Time constants and phase relationships: RLC time constants: definition; time constants in RL and RC circuits; phase angle between voltage and current; phase angles of series and parallel circuits

E5C – Impedance plots and coordinate systems: plotting impedances in polar coordinates; rectangular coordinates

E5D – AC and RF energy in real circuits: skin effect; electrostatic and electromagnetic fields; reactive power; power factor; coordinate systems

Subelement E6 – Circuit components

[6 Exam Questions – 6 Groups]

E6A – Semiconductor materials and devices: semiconductor materials germanium, silicon, P-type, N-type; transistor types: NPN, PNP, junction, field-effect transistors: enhancement mode; depletion mode; MOS; CMOS; N-channel; P-channel

E6B – Semiconductor diodes

E6C – Integrated circuits: TTL digital integrated circuits; CMOS digital integrated circuits; gates

E6D – Optical devices and toroids: cathode-ray tube devices; charge-coupled devices (CCDs); liquid crystal displays (LCDs); toroids: permeability, core material, selecting, winding

E6E – Piezoelectric crystals and MMICs: quartz crystals; crystal oscillators and filters; monolithic amplifiers

E6F – Optical components and power systems: photoconductive principles and effects, photovoltaic systems, optical couplers, optical sensors, and optoisolators

Subelement E7 – Practical circuits

[8 Exam Questions – 8 Groups]

E7A – Digital circuits: digital circuit principles and logic circuits: classes of logic elements; positive and negative logic; frequency dividers; truth tables

E7B – Amplifiers: Class of operation; vacuum tube and solid-state circuits; distortion and intermodulation; spurious and parasitic suppression; microwave amplifiers

E7C – Filters and matching networks: filters and impedance matching networks: types of networks; types of filters; filter applications; filter characteristics; impedance matching; DSP filtering

E7D – Power supplies and voltage regulators

E7E – Modulation and demodulation: reactance, phase and balanced modulators; detectors; mixer stages; DSP modulation and demodulation; software defined radio systems

E7F – Frequency markers and counters: frequency divider circuits; frequency marker generators; frequency counters

E7G – Active filters and op-amps: active audio filters; characteristics; basic circuit design; operational amplifiers

E7H – Oscillators and signal sources: types of oscillators; synthesizers and phase-locked loops; direct digital synthesizers

Subelement E8 – Signals and emissions

[4 Exam Questions – 4 Groups]

E8A – AC waveforms: sine, square, sawtooth and irregular waveforms; AC measurements; average and PEP of RF signals; pulse and digital signal waveforms

E8B – Modulation and demodulation: modulation methods; modulation index and deviation ratio; pulse modulation; frequency and time division multiplexing

E8C – Digital signals: digital communications modes; CW; information rate vs. bandwidth; spread-spectrum communications; modulation methods

E8D – Waves, measurements, and RF grounding: peak-to-peak values, polarization; RF grounding

Subelement E9 – Antennas and transmission lines

[8 Exam Questions – 8 Groups]

E9A – Isotropic and gain antennas: definition; used as a standard for comparison; radiation pattern; basic antenna parameters: radiation resistance and reactance, gain, beamwidth, efficiency

E9B – Antenna patterns: E and H plane patterns; gain as a function of pattern; antenna design; Yagi antennas

E9C – Wire and phased vertical antennas: beverage antennas; terminated and resonant rhombic antennas; elevation above real ground; ground effects as related to polarization; take-off angles

E9D – Directional antennas: gain; satellite antennas; antenna beamwidth; losses; SWR bandwidth; antenna efficiency; shortened and mobile antennas; grounding

E9E – Matching: matching antennas to feed lines; power dividers

E9F – Transmission lines: characteristics of open and shorted feed lines: 1/8 wavelength; 1/4 wavelength; 1/2 wavelength; feed lines: coax versus open-wire; velocity factor; electrical length; transformation characteristics of line terminated in impedance not equal to characteristic impedance

E9G – The Smith chart

E9H – Effective radiated power; system gains and losses; radio direction finding antennas

Subelement E0 – Safety

[1 exam question – 1 group]

E0A – Safety: amateur radio safety practices; RF radiation hazards; hazardous materials

Once your new call sign is listed in the FCC database, you are good to go. For an Amateur Extra license in Illinois, your call sign will consist of a prefix of K, N or W, the number nine (9), and a two-letter suffix, or a two-letter prefix beginning with A, N, K or W, the number nine (9), and a one-letter suffix, or a two-letter prefix beginning with A, the number nine (9), and a two-letter suffix.

Ham radio equipment can be expensive or you can do it "on the cheap." The cost will run from a couple hundred dollars to well in the thousands, depending on what you have available. eBay, and Craigslist are good places to start looking. Most ham clubs do some sort of hamfest annually wherein club members or others are willing to part with older equipment. See Appendix A for a list of clubs in Illinois.

Another excellent source of equipment, as well as advice on setting the equipment up and how to use it properly, is current ham operators. In Appendix B, the author has listed all the FCC licensed ham operators in Illinois, listed by city, and then sorted by street and house number on the street. Who knows, maybe someone who lives close to you is a ham operator. Be a good neighbor, stop by and have a chat with him/her.

Like CB radios, ham radios come in three formats – base, mobile, and handheld. They can use the electric company for power, or operate off a car battery. In the opinion of this author, in spite of the slightly higher cost of the equipment and having to take a test to legally use the equipment, ham radio is the way to go when concerned about communication during times of crisis.

Canadian Call Sign Prefixes

Because of our proximity to Canada, many times ham contact is made with our northern neighbors. Below is a chart showing the origin of Canadian call sign prefixes.

Call Sign Prefix	Provence or Territory
CY0	Sable Island
CY9	St. Paul Island
VA1, VE1	New Brunswick, Nova Scotia
VA2, VE2	Quebec
VA3, VE3	Ontario
VA4, VE4	Manitoba
VA5, VE5	Saskatchewan
VA6, VE6	Alberta
VA7, VE7	British Columbia
VE8	North West Territories
VE9	New Brunswick
VO1	Newfoundland
VO2	Labrador
VY0	Nunavut
VY1	Yukon
VY2	Prince Edward Island

Common Radio Bands in the United States

Certain radio bands are more popular with ham radio enthusiasts than others. Below is a chart showing these bands and when they are most popular.

	Band (meter)	Frequency (MHz)	Use
HF	160	1.8 – 2.0	Night
	80	3.5 – 4.0	Night and Local Day
	40	7.0 – 7.3	Night and Local Day
	30	10.1 – 10.15	CW and Digital
	20	14.0 – 14.350	World Wide Day and Night
	17	18.068 – 18.168	World Wide Day and Night
	15	21.0 – 21.450	Primarily Daytime
	12	24.890 – 24.990	Primarily Daytime
	10	28.0 – 29.70	Daytime during Sunspot highs
VHF	6	50 – 54	Local to World Wide
	2	144 – 148	Local to Medium Distance
UHF	70 cm	430 – 440	Local

Common Amateur Radio Bands in Canada

160 Meter Band - Maximum bandwidth 6 kHz

1.800 - 1.820 MHz - CW
1.820 - 1.830 MHz - Digital Modes
1 830 - 1.840 MHz - DX Window
1.840 - 2.000 MHz - SSB and other wide band modes

80 Meter Band - Maximum bandwidth 6 kHz

3.500 - 3.580 MHz - CW
3.580 - 3.620 MHz - Digital Modes
3.620 - 3.635 MHz - Packet/Digital Secondary
3.635 - 3.725 MHz - CW
3.725 - 3.790 MHz - SSB and other side band modes*
3.790 - 3.800 MHz - SSB DX Window
3.800 - 4.000 MHz - SSB and other wide band modes

40 Meter Band - Maximum bandwidth 6 kHz

7.000 - 7.035 MHz - CW
7.035 - 7.050 MHz - Digital Modes
7.040 - 7.050 MHz - International packet
7.050 - 7.100 MHz - SSB
7.100 - 7.120 MHz - Packet within Region 2
7.120 - 7.150 MHz - CW
7.150 - 7.300 MHz - SSB and other wide band modes

30 Meter Band - Maximum bandwidth 1 kHz

10.100 - 10.130 MHz - CW only
10.130 - 10.140 MHz - Digital Modes
10.140 - 10.150 MHz - Packet

20 Meter Band - Maximum bandwidth 6 kHz

14.000 - 14.070 MHz - CW only
14.070 - 14.095 MHz - Digital Mode
14.095 - 14.099 MHz - Packet
14.100 MHz - Beacons
14.101 - 14.112 MHz - CW, SSB, packet shared
14.112 - 14.350 MHz - SSB
14.225 - 14.235 MHz - SSTV

17 Meter Band - Maximum bandwidth 6 kHz

18.068 - 18.100 MHz - CW
18.100 - 18.105 MHz - Digital Modes
18.105 - 18.110 MHz - Packet
18.110 - 18.168 MHz - SSB and other wide band modes

15 Meter Band - maximum bandwidth 6 kHz

21.000 - 21.070 MHz - CW
21.070 - 21.090 MHz - Digital Modes
21.090 - 21.125 MHz - Packet
21.100 - 21.150 MHz - CW and SSB
21.150 - 21.335 MHz - SSB and other wide band modes
21.335 - 21.345 MHz - SSTV
21.345 - 21.450 MHz - SSB and other wide band modes

12 Meter Band - Maximum bandwidth 6 kHz

24.890 - 24.930 MHz - CW
24.920 - 24.925 MHz - Digital Modes
24.925 - 24.930 MHz - Packet
24.930 - 24.990 MHz - SSB and other wide band modes

10 Meter Band - Maximum band width 20 kHz

28.000 - 28.200 MHz - CW
28.070 - 28.120 MHz - Digital Modes
28.120 - 28.190 MHz - Packet
28.190 - 28.200 MHz - Beacons
28.200 - 29.300 MHz - SSB and other wide band modes
29.300 - 29.510 MHz - Satellite
29.510 - 29.700 MHz - SSB, FM and repeaters

160 Meters (1.8-2.0 MHz)

1.800 - 2.000 CW
1.800 - 1.810 Digital Modes
1.810 CW QRP
1.843-2.000 SSB, SSTV and other wideband modes
1.910 SSB QRP
1.995 - 2.000 Experimental
1.999 - 2.000 Beacons

80 Meters (3.5-4.0 MHz)

3.590 RTTY/Data DX
3.570-3.600 RTTY/Data
3.790-3.800 DX window
3.845 SSTV
3.885 AM calling frequency

40 Meters (7.0-7.3 MHz)

7.040 RTTY/Data DX
7.080-7.125 RTTY/Data
7.171 SSTV
7.290 AM calling frequency

30 Meters (10.1-10.15 MHz)

10.130-10.140 RTTY
10.140-10.150 Packet

20 Meters (14.0-14.35 MHz)

14.070-14.095 RTTY
14.095-14.0995 Packet
14.100 NCDXF Beacons
14.1005-14.112 Packet
14.230 SSTV
14.286 AM calling frequency

17 Meters (18.068-18.168 MHz)

18.100-18.105 RTTY
18.105-18.110 Packet

15 Meters (21.0-21.45 MHz)

21.070-21.110 RTTY/Data
21.340 SSTV

12 Meters (24.89-24.99 MHz)

24.920-24.925 RTTY
24.925-24.930 Packet

10 Meters (28-29.7 MHz)

28.000-28.070 CW
28.070-28.150 RTTY
28.150-28.190 CW
28.200-28.300 Beacons
28.300-29.300 Phone
28.680 SSTV
29.000-29.200 AM
29.300-29.510 Satellite Downlinks
29.520-29.590 Repeater Inputs
29.600 FM Simplex
29.610-29.700 Repeater Outputs

6 Meters (50-54 MHz)

50.0-50.1 CW, beacons
50.060-50.080 beacon subband
50.1-50.3 SSB, CW
50.10-50.125 DX window
50.125 SSB calling
50.3-50.6 All modes
50.6-50.8 Nonvoice communications
50.62 Digital (packet) calling
50.8-51.0 Radio remote control (20-kHz channels)
51.0-51.1 Pacific DX window
51.12-51.48 Repeater inputs (19 channels)
51.12-51.18 Digital repeater inputs
51.5-51.6 Simplex (six channels)
51.62-51.98 Repeater outputs (19 channels)
51.62-51.68 Digital repeater outputs
52.0-52.48 Repeater inputs (except as noted; 23 channels)
52.02, 52.04 FM simplex
52.2 TEST PAIR (input)
52.5-52.98 Repeater output (except as noted; 23 channels)
52.525 Primary FM simplex
52.54 Secondary FM simplex
52.7 TEST PAIR (output)
53.0-53.48 Repeater inputs (except as noted; 19 channels)
53.0 Remote base FM simplex
53.02 Simplex
53.1, 53.2, 53.3, 53.4 Radio remote control
53.5-53.98 Repeater outputs (except as noted; 19 channels)
53.5, 53.6, 53.7, 53.8 Radio remote control
53.52, 53.9 Simplex

2 Meters (144-148 MHz)

144.00-144.05 EME (CW)
144.05-144.10 General CW and weak signals
144.10-144.20 EME and weak-signal SSB
144.200 National calling frequency
144.200-144.275 General SSB operation
144.275-144.300 Propagation beacons
144.30-144.50 New OSCAR subband
144.50-144.60 Linear translator inputs
144.60-144.90 FM repeater inputs
144.90-145.10 Weak signal and FM simplex (145.01,03,05,07,09 are widely used for
  packet)
145.10-145.20 Linear translator outputs
145.20-145.50 FM repeater outputs
145.50-145.80 Miscellaneous and experimental modes
145.80-146.00 OSCAR subband
146.01-146.37 Repeater inputs
146.40-146.58 Simplex
146.52 National Simplex Calling Frequency
146.61-146.97 Repeater outputs
147.00-147.39 Repeater outputs
147.42-147.57 Simplex
147.60-147.99 Repeater inputs

1.25 Meters (222-225 MHz)

222.0-222.150 Weak-signal modes
222.0-222.025 EME
222.05-222.06 Propagation beacons
222.1 SSB & CW calling frequency
222.10-222.15 Weak-signal CW & SSB
222.15-222.25 Local coordinator's option; weak signal, ACSB, repeater inputs, control
222.25-223.38 FM repeater inputs only
223.40-223.52 FM simplex
223.52-223.64 Digital, packet
223.64-223.70 Links, control
223.71-223.85 Local coordinator's option; FM simplex, packet, repeater outputs
223.85-224.98 Repeater outputs only

70 Centimeters (420-450 MHz)

420.00-426.00 ATV repeater or simplex with 421.25 MHz video carrier control links and
  experimental
426.00-432.00 ATV simplex with 427.250-MHz video carrier frequency
432.00-432.07 EME (Earth-Moon-Earth)
432.07-432.10 Weak-signal CW
432.10 70-cm calling frequency

432.10-432.30 Mixed-mode and weak-signal work
432.30-432.40 Propagation beacons
432.40-433.00 Mixed-mode and weak-signal work
433.00-435.00 Auxiliary/repeater links
435.00-438.00 Satellite only (internationally)
438.00-444.00 ATV repeater input with 439.250-MHz video carrier frequency and repeater links
442.00-445.00 Repeater inputs and outputs (local option)
445.00-447.00 Shared by auxiliary and control links, repeaters and simplex (local option)
446.00 National simplex frequency
447.00-450.00 Repeater inputs and outputs (local option)

33 Centimeters (902-928 MHz)

902.0-903.0 Narrow-bandwidth, weak-signal communications
902.0-902.8 SSTV, FAX, ACSSB, experimental
902.1 Weak-signal calling frequency
902.8-903.0 Reserved for EME, CW expansion
903.1 Alternate calling frequency
903.0-906.0 Digital communications
906-909 FM repeater inputs
909-915 ATV
915-918 Digital communications
918-921 FM repeater outputs
921-927 ATV
927-928 FM simplex and links

23 Centimeters (1240-1300 MHz)

1240-1246 ATV #1
1246-1248 Narrow-bandwidth FM point-to-point links and digital, duplex with 1258-1260.
1248-1258 Digital Communications
1252-1258 ATV #2
1258-1260 Narrow-bandwidth FM point-to-point links digital, duplexed with 1246-1252
1260-1270 Satellite uplinks, reference WARC '79
1260-1270 Wide-bandwidth experimental, simplex ATV
1270-1276 Repeater inputs, FM and linear, paired with 1282-1288, 239 pairs every 25 kHz, e.g. 1270.025, .050, etc.
1271-1283 Non-coordinated test pair
1276-1282 ATV #3
1282-1288 Repeater outputs, paired with 1270-1276
1288-1294 Wide-bandwidth experimental, simplex ATV
1294-1295 Narrow-bandwidth FM simplex services, 25-kHz channels
1294.5 National FM simplex calling frequency
1295-1297 Narrow bandwidth weak-signal communications (no FM)
1295.0-1295.8 SSTV, FAX, ACSSB, experimental
1295.8-1296.0 Reserved for EME, CW expansion

1296.00-1296.05 EME-exclusive
1296.07-1296.08 CW beacons
1296.1 CW, SSB calling frequency
1296.4-1296.6 Crossband linear translator input
1296.6-1296.8 Crossband linear translator output
1296.8-1297.0 Experimental beacons (exclusive)
1297-1300 Digital Communications

2300-2310 and 2390-2450 MHz

2300.0-2303.0 High-rate data
2303.0-2303.5 Packet
2303.5-2303.8 TTY packet
2303.9-2303.9 Packet, TTY, CW, EME
2303.9-2304.1 CW, EME
2304.1 Calling frequency
2304.1-2304.2 CW, EME, SSB
2304.2-2304.3 SSB, SSTV, FAX, Packet AM, Amtor
2304.30-2304.32 Propagation beacon network
2304.32-2304.40 General propagation beacons
2304.4-2304.5 SSB, SSTV, ACSSB, FAX, Packet AM, Amtor experimental
2304.5-2304.7 Crossband linear translator input
2304.7-2304.9 Crossband linear translator output
2304.9-2305.0 Experimental beacons
2305.0-2305.2 FM simplex (25 kHz spacing)
2305.20 FM simplex calling frequency
2305.2-2306.0 FM simplex (25 kHz spacing)
2306.0-2309.0 FM Repeaters (25 kHz) input
2309.0-2310.0 Control and auxiliary links
2390.0-2396.0 Fast-scan TV
2396.0-2399.0 High-rate data
2399.0-2399.5 Packet
2399.5-2400.0 Control and auxiliary links
2400.0-2403.0 Satellite
2403.0-2408.0 Satellite high-rate data
2408.0-2410.0 Satellite
2410.0-2413.0 FM repeaters (25 kHz) output
2413.0-2418.0 High-rate data
2418.0-2430.0 Fast-scan TV
2430.0-2433.0 Satellite
2433.0-2438.0 Satellite high-rate data
2438.0-2450.0 WB FM, FSTV, FMTV, SS experimental

3300-3500 MHz

3456.3-3456.4 Propagation beacons

5650-5925 MHz
5760.3-5760.4 Propagation beacons

10.00-10.50 GHz
10.368 Narrow band calling frequency 10.3683-10.3684 Propagation beacons
10.3640 Calling frequency

Now that you have your license (you do, don't you?), and your equipment, you are ready to go live. Below is a suggested start.

1) Assuming you have the HT set up to the appropriate frequency, and offset, press the mic button on the HT and say, "KK4HWX listening." Replace the KK4HWX with your own call sign, the one assigned to you by the FCC (it's the law). If no one responds to your call, you may wish to try again. Hopefully someone will respond to your call.

2) Once you get a response, it will be in the form of something like, "KK4HWX this is ??1??? in Eastport returning. My name is Florence. Back to you. ??1???" then a tone. Let us examine the response more closely. She first acknowledged your call sign (KK4HWX), then identified hers (??1???). From the 1 in her call sign, you know that she first got her license in Region 1, meaning she got it while a resident of CT, ME, MA, NH, RI, or VT. She then told you where she's transmitting from (Eastport). The term "returning" means that she is returning your call. Her name is Florence. The phrase, "Back to you" indicates that she is turning over the conversation to you. She then repeats her call sign. The tone indicates to you that it is okay to proceed with your response. BTW if she had used the term "Over" instead of "Back to you," it would mean the same thing, just fewer words.

3) At this point, press the mic button and continue with the conversation. You should restate your call sign often during the conversation (perhaps every 10 minutes or less and whenever you begin transmitting). Don't forget to say, "Over" or "Back to you" whenever you are giving Florence control of the conversation again.

4) When you are ready to stop the conversation, you should say goodbye or use the phrase "73", meaning "best wishes." Your conversation would end something like, "??1??? 73, this is KK4HWX clear and monitoring." The "clear and monitoring" indicates that you are going to continue to monitor the frequency. If you are not going to continue monitoring, you may wish to end the conversation with Florence with, "clear and QRT" instead. The QRT means that you are stopping transmissions.

Call Sign Phonics

Because of different accents of various people, sometimes it is difficult to understand call sign letters when spoken. For this reason, most ham operators verbalize their call sign using phonics. Below is a table listing the accepted phonics for letters and numbers.

A = ALFA		S = SIERRA	
B = BRAVO		T = TANGO	
C = CHARLIE		U = UNIFORM	
D = DELTA		V = VICTOR	
E = ECHO		W = WHISKEY	
F = FOXTROT		X = X-RAY	
G = GOLF		Y = YANKEE	
H = HOTEL		Z = ZULU (ZED)	
I = INDIA		1 = ONE	
J = JULIETT		2 = TWO	
K = KILO		3 = THREE (TREE)	
L = LIMA		4 = FOUR	
M = MIKE		5 = FIVE (FIFE)	
N = NOVEMBER		6 = SIX	
O = OSCAR		7 = SEVEN	
P = PAPA (PA-PA')		8 = EIGHT	
Q = QUEBEC (KAY-BEK')		9 = NINE (NINER)	
R = ROMEO		0 = ZERO	

The words in parentheses are the pronunciation or the alternate pronunciations for the words or numbers, but you will hear both used. With the letter Z, (ZED) is by far the most commonly used. With the number 9, NINER is the most common and easiest to understand ON THE AIR.

If you wish to use Morse code (CW) instead of voice communication, the "conversation" would follow the same steps, with a few modifications. To type out each word would require a lot of typing and translating. If you are like this author, more means more, i.e., more typing means more typos are likely. To help with this situation, CW enthusiasts have developed a language all their own – they use abbreviations for common phrases. Below is a chart showing some of these abbreviations.

Abbreviation	Use
AR	Over
de	From or "this is"
ES	And
GM	Good Morning
K	Go
KN	Go only
NM	Name
QTH	Location
RPT	Report
R	Roger
SK	Clear
tnx	Thanks
UR	Your, you are
73	Best Wishes

Morse Code and Amateur Radio

If you wish to use CW, but are concerned about accuracy, you might consider purchasing a Morse code translator. This is an electronic device that you place in front of your speakers. It takes the CW sounds and translates them into English and displays the transmission on an LCD display. For the reverse, you can pick up a CW keyboard. With the keyboard, you type in your message and it converts the text to Morse code. The translator does not need to be attached to your ham equipment, whereas the keyboard would.

For your convenience, below is a table showing the Morse code signals and their meaning.

Character	Code
A	· —
B	— · · ·
C	— · — ·
D	— · ·
E	·
F	· · — ·
G	— — ·
H	· · · ·
I	· ·
J	· — — —
K	— · —
L	· — · ·
M	— —
N	— ·
O	— — —
P	· — — ·
Q	— — · —
R	· — ·
S	· · ·
T	—
U	· · —
V	· · · —
W	· — —
X	— · · —
Y	— · — —
Z	— — · ·
0	— — — — —
1	· — — — —
2	· · — — —
3	· · · — —
4	· · · · —
5	· · · · ·

6	— · · · ·
7	— — · · ·
8	— — — · ·
9	— — — — ·
Ampersand [&], Wait	· — · · ·
Apostrophe [']	· — — — — ·
At sign [@]	· — — · — ·
Colon [:]	— — — · · ·
Comma [,]	— — · · — —
Dollar sign [$]	· · · — · · —
Double dash [=]	— · · · —
Exclamation mark [!]	— · — · — —
Hyphen, Minus [-]	— · · · · —
Parenthesis closed [)]	— · — — · —
Parenthesis open [(]	— · — — ·
Period [.]	· — · — · —
Plus [+]	· — · — ·
Question mark [?]	· · — — · ·
Quotation mark ["]	· — · · — ·
Semicolon [;]	— · — · — ·
Slash [/], Fraction bar	— · · — ·
Underscore [_]	· · — — · —

An advantage of using Morse Code is that when broadcasting CW, you are using reduced power, thereby saving your battery. Your battery is used only while actually transmitting or receiving.

International Call Sign Prefixes

As was stated earlier, all ham radio call signs begin with letters (or numbers) taken from blocks assigned to each country of the world by the *ITU - International Telecommunications Union,* a body controlled by the United Nations. The following chart indicates which call sign series are allocated to which countries.

Call Sign Series	Allocated to
AAA-ALZ	**United States of America**
AMA-AOZ	Spain
APA-ASZ	Pakistan (Islamic Republic of)
ATA-AWZ	India (Republic of)
AXA-AXZ	Australia
AYA-AZZ	Argentine Republic
A2A-A2Z	Botswana (Republic of)
A3A-A3Z	Tonga (Kingdom of)
A4A-A4Z	Oman (Sultanate of)
A5A-A5Z	Bhutan (Kingdom of)

A6A-A6Z	United Arab Emirates
A7A-A7Z	Qatar (State of)
A8A-A8Z	Liberia (Republic of)
A9A-A9Z	Bahrain (State of)
BAA-BZZ	China (People's Republic of)
CAA-CEZ	Chile
CFA-CKZ	Canada
CLA-CMZ	Cuba
CNA-CNZ	Morocco (Kingdom of)
COA-COZ	Cuba
CPA-CPZ	Bolivia (Republic of)
CQA-CUZ	Portugal
CVA-CXZ	Uruguay (Eastern Republic of)
CYA-CZZ	Canada
C2A-C2Z	Nauru (Republic of)
C3A-C3Z	Andorra (Principality of)
C4A-C4Z	Cyprus (Republic of)
C5A-C5Z	Gambia (Republic of the)
C6A-C6Z	Bahamas (Commonwealth of the)
C7A-C7Z	World Meteorological Organization
C8A-C9Z	Mozambique (Republic of)
DAA-DRZ	Germany (Federal Republic of)
DSA-DTZ	Korea (Republic of)
DUA-DZZ	Philippines (Republic of the)
D2A-D3Z	Angola (Republic of)
D4A-D4Z	Cape Verde (Republic of)
D5A-D5Z	Liberia (Republic of)
D6A-D6Z	Comoros (Islamic Federal Republic of the)
D7A-D9Z	Korea (Republic of)
EAA-EHZ	Spain
EIA-EJZ	Ireland
EKA-EKZ	Armenia (Republic of)
ELA-ELZ	Liberia (Republic of)
EMA-EOZ	Ukraine
EPA-EQZ	Iran (Islamic Republic of)
ERA-ERZ	Moldova (Republic of)
ESA-ESZ	Estonia (Republic of)
ETA-ETZ	Ethiopia (Federal Democratic Republic of)
EUA-EWZ	Belarus (Republic of)
EXA-EXZ	Kyrgyz Republic
EYA-EYZ	Tajikistan (Republic of)
EZA-EZZ	Turkmenistan
E2A-E2Z	Thailand
E3A-E3Z	Eritrea
E4A-E4Z	Palestinian Authority

E5A-E5Z	New Zealand - Cook Islands (WRC-07)
E7A-E7Z	Bosnia and Herzegovina (Republic of) (WRC-07)
FAA-FZZ	France
GAA-GZZ	United Kingdom of Great Britain and Northern Ireland
HAA-HAZ	Hungary (Republic of)
HBA-HBZ	Switzerland (Confederation of)
HCA-HDZ	Ecuador
HEA-HEZ	Switzerland (Confederation of)
HFA-HFZ	Poland (Republic of)
HGA-HGZ	Hungary (Republic of)
HHA-HHZ	Haiti (Republic of)
HIA-HIZ	Dominican Republic
HJA-HKZ	Colombia (Republic of)
HLA-HLZ	Korea (Republic of)
HMA-HMZ	Democratic People's Republic of Korea
HNA-HNZ	Iraq (Republic of)
HOA-HPZ	Panama (Republic of)
HQA-HRZ	Honduras (Republic of)
HSA-HSZ	Thailand
HTA-HTZ	Nicaragua
HUA-HUZ	El Salvador (Republic of)
HVA-HVZ	Vatican City State
HWA-HYZ	France
HZA-HZZ	Saudi Arabia (Kingdom of)
H2A-H2Z	Cyprus (Republic of)
H3A-H3Z	Panama (Republic of)
H4A-H4Z	Solomon Islands
H6A-H7Z	Nicaragua
H8A-H9Z	Panama (Republic of)
IAA-IZZ	Italy
JAA-JSZ	Japan
JTA-JVZ	Mongolia
JWA-JXZ	Norway
JYA-JYZ	Jordan (Hashemite Kingdom of)
JZA-JZZ	Indonesia (Republic of)
J2A-J2Z	Djibouti (Republic of)
J3A-J3Z	Grenada
J4A-J4Z	Greece
J5A-J5Z	Guinea-Bissau (Republic of)
J6A-J6Z	Saint Lucia
J7A-J7Z	Dominica (Commonwealth of)
J8A-J8Z	Saint Vincent and the Grenadines
KAA-KZZ	**United States of America**
LAA-LNZ	Norway
LOA-LWZ	Argentine Republic

LXA-LXZ	Luxembourg
LYA-LYZ	Lithuania (Republic of)
LZA-LZZ	Bulgaria (Republic of)
L2A-L9Z	Argentine Republic
MAA-MZZ	United Kingdom of Great Britain and Northern Ireland
NAA-NZZ	**United States of America**
OAA-OCZ	Peru
ODA-ODZ	Lebanon
OEA-OEZ	Austria
OFA-OJZ	Finland
OKA-OLZ	Czech Republic
OMA-OMZ	Slovak Republic
ONA-OTZ	Belgium
OUA-OZZ	Denmark
PAA-PIZ	Netherlands (Kingdom of the)
PJA-PJZ	Netherlands (Kingdom of the) - Netherlands Antilles
PKA-POZ	Indonesia (Republic of)
PPA-PYZ	Brazil (Federative Republic of)
PZA-PZZ	Suriname (Republic of)
P2A-P2Z	Papua New Guinea
P3A-P3Z	Cyprus (Republic of)
P4A-P4Z	Netherlands (Kingdom of the) - Aruba
P5A-P9Z	Democratic People's Republic of Korea
RAA-RZZ	Russian Federation
SAA-SMZ	Sweden
SNA-SRZ	Poland (Republic of)
SSA-SSM	Egypt (Arab Republic of)
SSN-STZ	Sudan (Republic of the)
SUA-SUZ	Egypt (Arab Republic of)
SVA-SZZ	Greece
S2A-S3Z	Bangladesh (People's Republic of)
S5A-S5Z	Slovenia (Republic of)
S6A-S6Z	Singapore (Republic of)
S7A-S7Z	Seychelles (Republic of)
S8A-S8Z	South Africa (Republic of)
S9A-S9Z	Sao Tome and Principe (Democratic Republic of)
TAA-TCZ	Turkey
TDA-TDZ	Guatemala (Republic of)
TEA-TEZ	Costa Rica
TFA-TFZ	Iceland
TGA-TGZ	Guatemala (Republic of)
THA-THZ	France
TIA-TIZ	Costa Rica
TJA-TJZ	Cameroon (Republic of)
TKA-TKZ	France

TLA-TLZ	Central African Republic
TMA-TMZ	France
TNA-TNZ	Congo (Republic of the)
TOA-TQZ	France
TRA-TRZ	Gabonese Republic
TSA-TSZ	Tunisia
TTA-TTZ	Chad (Republic of)
TUA-TUZ	Côte d'Ivoire (Republic of)
TVA-TXZ	France
TYA-TYZ	Benin (Republic of)
TZA-TZZ	Mali (Republic of)
T2A-T2Z	Tuvalu
T3A-T3Z	Kiribati (Republic of)
T4A-T4Z	Cuba
T5A-T5Z	Somali Democratic Republic
T6A-T6Z	Afghanistan (Islamic State of)
T7A-T7Z	San Marino (Republic of)
T8A-T8Z	Palau (Republic of)
UAA-UIZ	Russian Federation
UJA-UMZ	Uzbekistan (Republic of)
UNA-UQZ	Kazakhstan (Republic of)
URA-UZZ	Ukraine
VAA-VGZ	Canada
VHA-VNZ	Australia
VOA-VOZ	Canada
VPA-VQZ	United Kingdom of Great Britain and Northern Ireland
VRA-VRZ	China (People's Republic of) - Hong Kong
VSA-VSZ	United Kingdom of Great Britain and Northern Ireland
VTA-VWZ	India (Republic of)
VXA-VYZ	Canada
VZA-VZZ	Australia
V2A-V2Z	Antigua and Barbuda
V3A-V3Z	Belize
V4A-V4Z	Saint Kitts and Nevis
V5A-V5Z	Namibia (Republic of)
V6A-V6Z	Micronesia (Federated States of)
V7A-V7Z	Marshall Islands (Republic of the)
V8A-V8Z	Brunei Darussalam
WAA-WZZ	**United States of America**
XAA-XIZ	Mexico
XJA-XOZ	Canada
XPA-XPZ	Denmark
XQA-XRZ	Chile
XSA-XSZ	China (People's Republic of)
XTA-XTZ	Burkina Faso

XUA-XUZ	Cambodia (Kingdom of)
XVA-XVZ	Viet Nam (Socialist Republic of)
XWA-XWZ	Lao People's Democratic Republic
XXA-XXZ	China (People's Republic of) - Macao (WRC-07)
XYA-XZZ	Myanmar (Union of)
YAA-YAZ	Afghanistan (Islamic State of)
YBA-YHZ	Indonesia (Republic of)
YIA-YIZ	Iraq (Republic of)
YJA-YJZ	Vanuatu (Republic of)
YKA-YKZ	Syrian Arab Republic
YLA-YLZ	Latvia (Republic of)
YMA-YMZ	Turkey
YNA-YNZ	Nicaragua
YOA-YRZ	Romania
YSA-YSZ	El Salvador (Republic of)
YTA-YUZ	Serbia (Republic of) (WRC-07)
YVA-YYZ	Venezuela (Republic of)
Y2A-Y9Z	Germany (Federal Republic of)
ZAA-ZAZ	Albania (Republic of)
ZBA-ZJZ	United Kingdom of Great Britain and Northern Ireland
ZKA-ZMZ	New Zealand
ZNA-ZOZ	United Kingdom of Great Britain and Northern Ireland
ZPA-ZPZ	Paraguay (Republic of)
ZQA-ZQZ	United Kingdom of Great Britain and Northern Ireland
ZRA-ZUZ	South Africa (Republic of)
ZVA-ZZZ	Brazil (Federative Republic of)
Z2A-Z2Z	Zimbabwe (Republic of)
Z3A-Z3Z	The Former Yugoslav Republic of Macedonia
2AA-2ZZ	United Kingdom of Great Britain and Northern Ireland
3AA-3AZ	Monaco (Principality of)
3BA-3BZ	Mauritius (Republic of)
3CA-3CZ	Equatorial Guinea (Republic of)
3DA-3DM	Swaziland (Kingdom of)
3DN-3DZ	Fiji (Republic of)
3EA-3FZ	Panama (Republic of)
3GA-3GZ	Chile
3HA-3UZ	China (People's Republic of)
3VA-3VZ	Tunisia
3WA-3WZ	Viet Nam (Socialist Republic of)
3XA-3XZ	Guinea (Republic of)
3YA-3YZ	Norway
3ZA-3ZZ	Poland (Republic of)
4AA-4CZ	Mexico
4DA-4IZ	Philippines (Republic of the)
4JA-4KZ	Azerbaijani Republic

4LA-4LZ	Georgia (Republic of)
4MA-4MZ	Venezuela (Republic of)
4OA-4OZ	Montenegro (Republic of) (WRC-07)
4PA-4SZ	Sri Lanka (Democratic Socialist Republic of)
4TA-4TZ	Peru
4UA-4UZ	United Nations
4VA-4VZ	Haiti (Republic of)
4WA-4WZ	Democratic Republic of Timor-Leste (WRC-03)
4XA-4XZ	Israel (State of)
4YA-4YZ	International Civil Aviation Organization
4ZA-4ZZ	Israel (State of)
5AA-5AZ	Libya (Socialist People's Libyan Arab Jamahiriya)
5BA-5BZ	Cyprus (Republic of)
5CA-5GZ	Morocco (Kingdom of)
5HA-5IZ	Tanzania (United Republic of)
5JA-5KZ	Colombia (Republic of)
5LA-5MZ	Liberia (Republic of)
5NA-5OZ	Nigeria (Federal Republic of)
5PA-5QZ	Denmark
5RA-5SZ	Madagascar (Republic of)
5TA-5TZ	Mauritania (Islamic Republic of)
5UA-5UZ	Niger (Republic of the)
5VA-5VZ	Togolese Republic
5WA-5WZ	Samoa (Independent State of)
5XA-5XZ	Uganda (Republic of)
5YA-5ZZ	Kenya (Republic of)
6AA-6BZ	Egypt (Arab Republic of)
6CA-6CZ	Syrian Arab Republic
6DA-6JZ	Mexico
6KA-6NZ	Korea (Republic of)
6OA-6OZ	Somali Democratic Republic
6PA-6SZ	Pakistan (Islamic Republic of)
6TA-6UZ	Sudan (Republic of the)
6VA-6WZ	Senegal (Republic of)
6XA-6XZ	Madagascar (Republic of)
6YA-6YZ	Jamaica
6ZA-6ZZ	Liberia (Republic of)
7AA-7IZ	Indonesia (Republic of)
7JA-7NZ	Japan
7OA-7OZ	Yemen (Republic of)
7PA-7PZ	Lesotho (Kingdom of)
7QA-7QZ	Malawi
7RA-7RZ	Algeria (People's Democratic Republic of)
7SA-7SZ	Sweden
7TA-7YZ	Algeria (People's Democratic Republic of)

7ZA-7ZZ	Saudi Arabia (Kingdom of)
8AA-8IZ	Indonesia (Republic of)
8JA-8NZ	Japan
8OA-8OZ	Botswana (Republic of)
8PA-8PZ	Barbados
8QA-8QZ	Maldives (Republic of)
8RA-8RZ	Guyana
8SA-8SZ	Sweden
8TA-8YZ	India (Republic of)
8ZA-8ZZ	Saudi Arabia (Kingdom of)
9AA-9AZ	Croatia (Republic of)
9BA-9DZ	Iran (Islamic Republic of)
9EA-9FZ	Ethiopia (Federal Democratic Republic of)
9GA-9GZ	Ghana
9HA-9HZ	Malta
9IA-9JZ	Zambia (Republic of)
9KA-9KZ	Kuwait (State of)
9LA-9LZ	Sierra Leone
9MA-9MZ	Malaysia
9NA-9NZ	Nepal
9OA-9TZ	Democratic Republic of the Congo
9UA-9UZ	Burundi (Republic of)
9VA-9VZ	Singapore (Republic of)
9WA-9WZ	Malaysia
9XA-9XZ	Rwandese Republic
9YA-9ZZ	Trinidad and Tobago

Third-Party Communications and Amateur Radio

If all of this information about ham radios is somewhat intimidating, do not despair. "You" can still use ham radios for communications without being a licensed operator. Yes, you do have to have a ham license in order to legally transmit by ham equipment (or be under the direct supervision of someone else who is licensed), but there is an alternative – third-party communication.

Third-party communications occur when a licensed operator sends either written or verbal messages on behalf of unlicensed persons or organizations. There are two "controls" on third-party communication.

First, the communication must be noncommercial and of a personal nature. Asking a ham operator to contact another ham operator located in an area just hit by tornados and, because of being without power, phones do not work in Grandma Sally's city so you can check up on her, is okay. Asking a ham to send a message out that you have an old Chevy for sale would not be okay.

Second, the message must be going to a permitted area. Transmitting from a US location to another US location is okay, but transmitting from the US to another country may not. Because third-party communications bypass a country's normal telephone and postal systems, many foreign governments forbid such communications. In order to transmit from one country to another, the other country must have signed a third-party agreement with the US. What follows is a list of those countries that do have third-party a communications agreement with the US.

V2	Antigua / Barbuda
LU	Argentina
VK	Australia
V3	Belize
CP	Bolivia
T9	Bosnia-Herzegovina
PY	Brazil
VE	Canada
CE	Chile
HK	Colombia
D6	Comoros (Federal Islamic Republic of)
TI	Costa Rica
CO	Cuba
HI	Dominican Republic
J7	Dominica
HC	Ecuador
YS	El Salvador
C5	Gambia, The
9G	Ghana
J3	Grenada
TG	Guatemala
8R	Guyana
HH	Haiti
HR	Honduras
4X	Israel
6Y	Jamaica
JY	Jordan
EL	Liberia
V7	Marshall Islands
XE	Mexico
V6	Micronesia, Federated States of
YN	Nicaragua
HP	Panama
ZP	Paraguay
OA	Peru
DU	Philippines
VR6	Pitcairn Island

V4	St. Christopher / Nevis
J6	St. Lucia
J8	St. Vincent and the Grenadines
9L	Sierra Leone
ZS	South Africa
3DA	Swaziland
9Y	Trinidad / Tobago
TA	Turkey
GB	United Kingdom
CX	Uruguay
YV	Venezuela
4U1ITUITU	Geneva
4U1VICVIC	Vienna

Remember, before TSHTF, keep your pantry well stocked, your powder dry, and your batteries fully charged. 73

34

APPENDIX A

American Radio Relay League

Affiliated Amateur Radio Clubs in

Illinois

ARRL Affiliated Club	Valley Emergency Communications Association
City:	Aledo, IL
Call Sign:	KB0SAN
Section:	IL
Links:	www.veca.us
ARRL Affiliated Club	Fox River Radio League
City:	Batavia, IL
Call Sign:	W9NE
Section:	IL
Links:	www.frrl.org/, www.frrl.org/index.html
ARRL Affiliated Club	Hamfesters Radio Club
City:	Bedford Park, IL
Call Sign:	W9AA
Section:	IL
ARRL Affiliated Club	St Clair Amateur Radio Club
City:	Belleville, IL
Call Sign:	K9GXU
Section:	IL
Links:	www.scarc.net
ARRL Affiliated Club	Society of Midwest Contesters
City:	Bloomington, IL
Call Sign:	W9SMC
Section:	IL
Links:	www.w9smc.com
ARRL Affiliated Club	Central Illinois Radio Club of Bloomington
City:	Bloomington, IL
Call Sign:	KC9GF
Section:	IL
Links:	www.qsl.net/w9aml
ARRL Affiliated Club	Bolingbrook Amateur Radio Society
City:	Bolingbrook, IL
Call Sign:	K9BAR
Section:	IL
Links:	www.k9bar.org
ARRL Affiliated Club	Six Meter Club of Chicago Inc.
City:	Brookfield, IL
Call Sign:	K9ONA
Section:	IL
Links:	www.k9ona.com

ARRL Affiliated Club	Fulton County Amateur Radio Club
City:	Canton, IL
Call Sign:	K9ILS
Section:	IL
Links:	www.fcarc.com

ARRL Affiliated Club	Southern IL University Amateur Radio Club
City:	Carbondale, IL
Call Sign:	W9UIH
Section:	IL

ARRL Affiliated Club	Macoupin County Amateur Radio Club
City:	Carlinville, IL
Call Sign:	K9MCE
Section:	IL
Links:	www.k9mce.org

ARRL Affiliated Club	Centralia Wireless Assn., Inc.
City:	Centralia, IL
Call Sign:	W9CWA
Section:	IL
Links:	www.w9cwa.net/

ARRL Affiliated Club	Twin City Amateur Radio Club
City:	Champaign, IL
Call Sign:	W9SEH
Section:	IL
Links:	www.w9seh.org

ARRL Affiliated Club	Big Thunder Amateur Radio Club
City:	Cherry Valley, IL
Call Sign:	WA9GWM
Section:	IL
Links:	www.wa9gwm.org

ARRL Affiliated Club	University of Chicago Amateur Society
City:	Chicago, IL
Call Sign:	N9UC
Section:	IL

ARRL Affiliated Club	Suburban Amateur Repeater Assn.
City:	Chicago, IL
Call Sign:	K9GFY
Section:	IL
Links:	www.sararadio.com

ARRL Affiliated Club	DuPage Amateur Radio Club (DARC)
City:	Clarendon Hills, IL
Call Sign:	W9DUP
Section:	IL
Links:	www.W9DUP.org

ARRL Affiliated Club	Vermilion County Amateur Radio Association (VCARA)
City:	Danville, IL
Call Sign:	W9MJL
Section:	IL
Links:	www.vcara.org

ARRL Affiliated Club	Kishwaukee Amateur Radio Club
City:	De Kalb, IL
Call Sign:	WA9CJN
Section:	IL
Links:	www.karc-club.org

ARRL Affiliated Club	Cenois Amateur Radio Club
City:	Decatur, IL
Call Sign:	K9HGX
Section:	IL
Links:	www.cenois.com

ARRL Affiliated Club	Rock River Amateur Radio Club
City:	Dixon, IL
Call Sign:	W9DXN
Section:	IL

ARRL Affiliated Club	Green River Valley Amateur Radio Society
City:	East Moline, IL
Call Sign:	K9WM
Section:	IL
Links:	www.forret.org/grvars/

ARRL Affiliated Club	National Trail Amateur Radio Club
City:	Effingham, IL
Call Sign:	K9UXZ
Section:	IL

ARRL Affiliated Club	York Radio Club, Inc.
City:	Elmhurst, IL
Call Sign:	W9YRC
Section:	IL
Links:	yorkradioclub.com

ARRL Affiliated Club	Evanston Amateur Radio Community
City:	Evanston, IL
Call Sign:	KC9OAS
Section:	IL
Links:	www.evanstonhams.org

ARRL Affiliated Club	Western Lake County Amateur Radio Society
City:	Fox Lake, IL
Call Sign:	W9WLC
Section:	IL
Links:	www.welcars.org

ARRL Affiliated Club	Area Amateur Radio Operators
City:	Galva, IL
Call Sign:	AA9RO
Section:	IL
Links:	www.aa9ro.com

ARRL Affiliated Club	Lewis & Clark Radio Club, Inc.
City:	Godfrey, IL
Call Sign:	K9HAM
Section:	IL
Links:	www.k9ham.org

ARRL Affiliated Club	Egyptian Radio Club Inc.
City:	Granite City, IL
Call Sign:	W9AIU
Section:	IL
Links:	www.w9aiu.org

ARRL Affiliated Club	Mt. Frank Contesters
City:	Hampshire, IL
Call Sign:	K9NS
Section:	IL
Links:	www.k9ns.com/

ARRL Affiliated Club	Illinois Valley Radio Assn.
City:	Hennepin, IL
Call Sign:	K9AVE
Section:	IL

ARRL Affiliated Club	North Shore Radio Club
City:	Highland Park, IL
Call Sign:	NS9RC
Section:	IL
Links:	www.ns9rc.org

ARRL Affiliated Club	Montgomery County A R E C
City:	Hillsboro, IL
Call Sign:	W9BXR
Section:	IL

ARRL Affiliated Club	Tri-Town Radio Amateur Club
City:	Homewood, IL
Call Sign:	W9VT
Section:	IL
Links:	www.w9vt.org/

ARRL Affiliated Club	Jacksonville Amateur Radio Society, Inc.
City:	Jacksonville, IL
Call Sign:	K9JX
Section:	IL
Links:	www.k9jx.com

ARRL Affiliated Club	W.H.E.R.E. Amateur Radio Club
City:	Johnsonville, IL
Section:	IL
Links:	www.whereradio.com

ARRL Affiliated Club	Kankakee Area Radio Society
City:	Kankakee, IL
Call Sign:	W9AZ
Section:	IL
Links:	www.w9az.com

ARRL Affiliated Club	Northern Illinois DX Assn.
City:	La Grange, IL
Call Sign:	W9BZW
Section:	IL
Links:	www.nidxa.org

ARRL Affiliated Club	Starved Rock Radio Club
City:	Leonore, IL
Call Sign:	W9MKS
Section:	IL
Links:	www.qsl.net/w9mks

ARRL Affiliated Club	Lake County RACES/ARES Group
City:	Libertyville, IL
Call Sign:	K9IQP
Section:	IL
Links:	www.races.org

ARRL Affiliated Club   Central IL/St. Louis Area TV Club
City: Litchfield, IL
Call Sign: K9ATV
Section: IL

ARRL Affiliated Club   Moultrie Amateur Radio Klub
City: Lovington, IL
Call Sign: W9BIL
Section: IL
Links: www.qsl.net/mark/

ARRL Affiliated Club   Mount Ava Repeater Association, Inc.
City: Marion, IL
Call Sign: K9GOX
Section: IL

ARRL Affiliated Club   Midwest Amateur Radio Club
City: Metropolis, IL
Call Sign: W9MID
Section: IL

ARRL Affiliated Club   Picorams
City: Monticello, IL
Call Sign: K9IYP
Section: IL
Links: www.piatthamradio.org

ARRL Affiliated Club   Metro DX Club
City: Morris, IL
Call Sign: W9TY
Section: IL
Links: www.metrodxclub.com

ARRL Affiliated Club   Chicago FM Club
City: Norridge, IL
Call Sign: WA9ORC
Section: IL
Links: www.chicagofmclub.org

ARRL Affiliated Club   Chicago Suburban Radio Assn.
City: Oak Park, IL
Call Sign: N9BAT
Section: IL

ARRL Affiliated Club	Metro Amateur Radio Club
City:	Park Ridge, IL
Call Sign:	W9LYA
Section:	IL
Links:	www.metroarc.org, www.metroarc.org/

ARRL Affiliated Club	Pals Repeater Group
City:	Peoria, IL
Section:	IL

ARRL Affiliated Club	Peoria Area Amateur Radio Club
City:	Peoria, IL
Call Sign:	W9UVI
Section:	IL
Links:	www.w9uvi.org/

ARRL Affiliated Club	Society Radio Operators
City:	Prospect Heights, IL
Call Sign:	W9SRO
Section:	IL
Links:	www.W9SRO.org

ARRL Affiliated Club	Western Illinois Amateur Radio Club
City:	Quincy, IL
Call Sign:	W9AWE
Section:	IL
Links:	www.w9awe.org

ARRL Affiliated Club	Rockford Amateur Radio Association
City:	Rockford, IL
Call Sign:	W9AXD
Section:	IL
Links:	www.w9axd.org

ARRL Affiliated Club	Stoned Monkey VHF Amateur Radio Club
City:	Round Lake Beach, IL
Call Sign:	N9UHF
Section:	IL
Links:	www.stonedmonkey.org

ARRL Affiliated Club	Schaumburg Amateur Radio Club
City:	Schaumburg, IL
Call Sign:	N9RJV
Section:	IL
Links:	www.n9rjv.org

ARRL Affiliated Club	Motorola Amateur Radio Club
City:	Schaumburg, IL
Call Sign:	K9MOT
Section:	IL
Links:	www.qsl.net/k9mot/marc/index.html

ARRL Affiliated Club	Shawnee Amateur Radio Assn.
City:	Sesser, IL
Call Sign:	W9RNM
Section:	IL
Links:	www.kc0rnp.net/SARA/

ARRL Affiliated Club	Sangamon Valley Radio Club
City:	Springfield, IL
Call Sign:	W9DUA
Section:	IL
Links:	www.svrc.org

ARRL Affiliated Club	Little Egypt Amateur Radio Society
City:	Thompsonville, IL
Call Sign:	KB9ADK
Section:	IL
Links:	www.learsradio.com

ARRL Affiliated Club	Suburban Technical Amateur Radio System
City:	Tinley Park, IL
Call Sign:	W9SRC
Section:	IL
Links:	www.w9src.org, www.starsradio.org

ARRL Affiliated Club	Iroquois County Amateur Radio Club
City:	Watseka, IL
Call Sign:	W9RWX
Section:	IL
Links:	www.icarc.com

ARRL Affiliated Club	Cortek Radio Association
City:	Wauconda, IL
Call Sign:	W9CA
Section:	IL

ARRL Affiliated Club	Wheaton Community Radio Amateurs
City:	Wheaton, IL
Call Sign:	W9CCU
Section:	IL
Links:	www.w9ccu.org, wcra@w9ccu.org

ARRL Affiliated Club	McHenry County Wireless Assn.
City:	Woodstock, IL
Call Sign:	K9RN
Section:	IL
Links:	mcwa.org

APPENDIX B

Amateur Radio License Holders

in

Illinois: Downstate
(by City)

Call Sign: K9BTI
John A Bowman
Rr 1 Box 46
Abingdon IL 61410

Call Sign: K9BTJ
Marjorie H Bowman
Rr 1 Box 46
Abingdon IL 61410

Call Sign: KA9JNI
William G Robinson Jr
303 Cedar
Abingdon IL 61410

Call Sign: N9ZGD
William D Downer
207 E Snyder St
Abingdon IL 61410

Call Sign: N9OFZ
Paul V Palmer
216 Knox Hwy 5
Abingdon IL 61410

Call Sign: WB9WSL
Harry J Emert Jr
208 Legion Ln
Abingdon IL 61410

Call Sign: KA0STD
Dale E Fuller
407 N Maple St
Abingdon IL 61410

Call Sign: KB9KBB
William G Mathias
800 N Monroe
Abingdon IL 61410

Call Sign: WD9FBE
Stuart A Schrodt
600 N Monroe St
Abingdon IL 61415

Call Sign: KB9JSV

Aaron M Ennis
203 Pennsylvania St
Abingdon IL 61410

Call Sign: N9XOC
Bobby G Cox
303 S Washington St
Abingdon IL 61410

Call Sign: KA9CZN
Kenneth H Durbin
205 W Givens
Abingdon IL 61410

Call Sign: WA9J
David G Sutton
405 W Meek St
Abingdon IL 61410

FCC Amateur Radio
Licenses in Adair

Call Sign: W9PFD
David E Lattan
23820 N 950th Rd
Adair IL 61411

FCC Amateur Radio
Licenses in Addieville

Call Sign: N4TFF
Donald K Moeser Sr
7578 Jimtown Rd
Addieville IL 62214

Call Sign: WB6TWT
Lindsay E Smith
9254 Sleepy Hollow Ln
Addieville IL 62214

Call Sign: N9IXT
Kent W Flach
8257 Weaver Creek Rd
Addieville IL 62214

FCC Amateur Radio
Licenses in Albany

Call Sign: WJ9D

Robert C Quade
202 2nd Ave S Box 504
Albany IL 612300504

Call Sign: N9OIC
James L Haigwood
507 7th Ave S
Albany IL 61230

Call Sign: N2KMA
Frances Striegl
10915 Fuller Rd
Albany IL 61230

Call Sign: K2DRH
Robert J Striegl
10915 Fuller Rd
Albany IL 61230

Call Sign: W0CS
Clinton ARC
10915 Fuller Rd
Albany IL 61230

Call Sign: KC9LLT
Jason J Robbins
103 Riverview Dr
Albany IL 61230

Call Sign: WA9PHF
Claribelle I Traxler
203 S Main
Albany IL 61230

Call Sign: KC9QNV
Ian E Anglese
502 S Main
Albany IL 61230

FCC Amateur Radio
Licenses in Albers

Call Sign: WD9IQN
Ronald A Kehder
502 Opossum Box 152
Albers IL 62215

Call Sign: KC9HZX
Jeffrey R Wallace

109 Timberlake
Albers IL 62215

Albion IL 62806

Albion IL 62806

FCC Amateur Radio Licenses in Albion

Call Sign: KA0JUW
James E Trible Jr
Rt 1 Box 136
Albion IL 62806

Call Sign: WB9ZDB
Kevin R Leslie
Rt 3 Box 146
Albion IL 62806

Call Sign: KC9MFK
Dustin M Brokaw
Rr 3 Box 187
Albion IL 62806

Call Sign: WB9UXD
Charles N Denbo
Rr 5 Box 6
Albion IL 62806

Call Sign: W9IKT
Stanley E Greatline
Rr 1 Box90
Albion IL 62806

Call Sign: KC9JSU
Robert N Southerland II
199 CR 1000 N
Albion IL 62806

Call Sign: AB9NH
James E Trible Jr
1607 CR 300 E
Albion IL 62806

Call Sign: WB9ZND
Charles J Collins
107 Flower Dr
Albion IL 62806

Call Sign: KB9MMW
Kenneth H Butterick
305 N 2nd

Call Sign: W9XI
Greg B Spiller
139 N 4th St
Albion IL 62806

Call Sign: WA9BRC
Billy R Conley
144 N 8th St
Albion IL 62806

Call Sign: N9VYK
Jerry J Henson
226 S 5th
Albion IL 62806

Call Sign: KB9LVA
Lisa D Henson
226 S 5th
Albion IL 62806

Call Sign: KC9CVJ
Bradley Weber
490 S 8th St
Albion IL 62806

Call Sign: N9TKI
Carl E Bunting
64 Terminal St
Albion IL 62806

Call Sign: KB9TXU
Flava I Bunting
64 Terminal St
Albion IL 628061101

Call Sign: KE9NI
Clifford C Brake
229 W Main
Albion IL 62806

Call Sign: N9ZPQ
Robert D Bunting
64 W Terminal
Albion IL 62806

Call Sign: KE4VKQ
Duane A Lear

Albion IL 62806

FCC Amateur Radio Licenses in Aledo

Call Sign: N0FFZ
Cedric E Van Pelt
Rr 3 Box 152
Aledo IL 61231

Call Sign: KA9PNF
David E Kurtz
Rt 3 Box 261
Aledo IL 61231

Call Sign: KC9VGU
David A Dawson
609 NW 4th Ave Apt 203
Aledo IL 61231

Call Sign: W9EOR
David A Dawson
609 NW 4th Ave Apt 203
Aledo IL 61231

Call Sign: W9CTU
Arthur C Johnson
807 NW 4th St
Aledo IL 61231

Call Sign: KC9HDD
Keith A Clark
801 NW 9th Ave
Aledo IL 61231

Call Sign: W9EBH
Frank H Carlson
317 SE 5th St
Aledo IL 61231

Call Sign: KB7OZH
Darlene E Sunken
402 SW 2nd Ave
Aledo IL 61231

Call Sign: KC9QNZ
Nicole L Rush
511 SW 5th
Aledo IL 61231

Call Sign: WA9SCH
Leonard F Ringle
804 SW 8th Aave
Aledo IL 612312152

Call Sign: KA9HSW
Marilyn A Ringle
804 SW 8th Ave
Aledo IL 61231

Call Sign: N6NRR
Hirofumi Oishi
507 SW 9th St
Aledo IL 61231

Call Sign: N2DUP
Chuck Gysi
Aledo IL 612310004

Call Sign: KB0SSQ
Gysi Amateur Group Usa
Aledo IL 612310004

Call Sign: KB0SAN
Valley Emergency
Communications Assn
Aledo IL 612310004

FCC Amateur Radio Licenses in Alexander

Call Sign: KA9HXV
Harry W Hunter
2916 Old SR
Alexander IL 62601

Call Sign: KA9VXU
Mary L Hunter
2916 Old SR
Alexander IL 62601

FCC Amateur Radio Licenses in Alexis

Call Sign: N9BOM
William E Caslin
305 N Henderson Rd
Alexis IL 61412

Call Sign: N9UKB
Loren N Zachmeyer
110 N Hollaway
Alexis IL 61412

Call Sign: W9RMS
Errol G Zachmeyer
305 S McKnight
Alexis IL 61412

Call Sign: WB9BEV
Dorance D Howarter
Alexis IL 61412

FCC Amateur Radio Licenses in Alhambra

Call Sign: N9KHV
Scott A Reeves
Rr 2 Box 195
Alhambra IL 62001

Call Sign: KB9ENT
Walter E Reeves
Rr 2 Box 195
Alhambra IL 62001

Call Sign: N9MND
Bruce P Allen
5925 Conn Rd
Alhambra IL 62001

Call Sign: KC9NJK
William K Fallis
4840 Dauderman Rd
Alhambra IL 62001

Call Sign: K9WKF
William K Fallis
4840 Dauderman Rd
Alhambra IL 62001

Call Sign: KF4NBG
James P Thibeault
6214 SR 160
Alhambra IL 62001

FCC Amateur Radio Licenses in Allendale

Call Sign: KC9CIU
Dale I Buchanan
20440 E 1300 Rd
Allendale IL 62410

Call Sign: N9UIG
Aaron C Ritchey
202 Marshall
Allendale IL 62410

Call Sign: N9NCD
Donald W Bauman
102 N State St
Allendale IL 62410

Call Sign: N9TZT
Robert R Garrett
105.5 S Division St
Allendale IL 62410

Call Sign: N9PNC
Michael J Marcotte
201 W Oak
Allendale IL 62410

Call Sign: N9XEJ
Brad W Garner
18514 Wabash 18 Ave
Allendale IL 62410

Call Sign: KB9JRB
Loraine M Garner
18514 Wabash 18 Ave
Allendale IL 62410

Call Sign: KB9AIN
Joe B Boyd
Allendale IL 62410

FCC Amateur Radio Licenses in Allerton

Call Sign: K9LOF
Bruce E Thompson
Rr 1 Box 82
Allerton IL 61810

Call Sign: W9KAY
Shirley K Thompson
Allerton IL 61810

FCC Amateur Radio Licenses in Alma

Call Sign: KB9VKV
Jeanette G Carter
7884 Brimberry Rd
Alma IL 62807

Call Sign: KB9TRM
Marvin R Carter
7884 Brimberry Rd
Alma IL 62807

Call Sign: KB9TTJ
William P Mallett
310 Broadway
Alma IL 62807

Call Sign: KB9SWN
Richard A Davis
7770 Hoard Ln
Alma IL 62807

Call Sign: KB9VJX
Spencer G Peto
601 Illinois
Alma IL 62807

Call Sign: KC9CZB
Paul W Neff
4803 Kinoka Rd
Alma IL 62807

Call Sign: W9DGX
Marion E Brimberry
719 Railroad St
Alma IL 62807

Call Sign: KA9THG
Marion E Brimberry
719 Railroad St Box 111
Alma IL 62807

Call Sign: N9FUP

Arthur W Rowe
Alma IL 62807

FCC Amateur Radio Licenses in Alpha

Call Sign: KA9DGP
Robert E Mentzer
108 E Dee St
Alpha IL 61413

Call Sign: KC9OTV
Blane E Shields
210 N Park Box 274
Alpha IL 61413

FCC Amateur Radio Licenses in Alsey

Call Sign: K9OIC
Samuel L Wallace
Alsey IL 62610

FCC Amateur Radio Licenses in Altamont

Call Sign: KB9QGZ
Timothy C Suckow
Rr 1 Box 213 M
Altamont IL 62411

Call Sign: KA9SIU
Clinton L Merkel
8515 Country View Ln
Altamont IL 62411

Call Sign: N9RFB
Albert L Higgs
6594 E 600th Ave
Altamont IL 62411

Call Sign: KC9HHO
Benjamin J Voelker
717 E Cumberland Rd
Altamont IL 62411

Call Sign: KC9MBU
Aaron M White
548 E US Hwy 40

Altamont IL 62411

Call Sign: N9ORT
Duane L Guffey
7622 E US Rt 40
Altamont IL 62411

Call Sign: KB9SSQ
Christopher G Guffey
7622 E US Rt 40
Altamont IL 62411

Call Sign: KA9HVP
Richard M Hagler
1 Jays Way
Altamont IL 62411

Call Sign: KB9GIO
Daniel A Lutz
707 Meadows St
Altamont IL 62411

Call Sign: KC9DDW
Travis J Blair
16071 N 250th St
Altamont IL 62411

Call Sign: KB9WUH
Patricia A Childress
8473 N 300th St
Altamont IL 62411

Call Sign: KC9VFI
Douglas L Neller
7366 N 500th St
Altamont IL 624112426

Call Sign: KB9GTY
Lannie A Morris
116 N Bond
Altamont IL 62411

Call Sign: KC9JIV
Judy K Shumaker
312 N Edward St
Altamont IL 62411

Call Sign: KC9MBP
Jaz M Sain

101 S Coles St
Altamont IL 62411

Call Sign: KC9KXD
Edward W Wojnar
10 S Ewing St
Altamont IL 62411

Call Sign: KC9NPK
Patricia A Wojnar
10 S Ewing St
Altamont IL 62411

Call Sign: KE9QD
Byrle E Lister
809 S Main
Altamont IL 624119689

Call Sign: KC9JIZ
Gene L Dye
605 W Jackson St
Altamont IL 62411

Call Sign: KC9EZZ
Bradley L Miller
604 W John Adams
Altamont IL 624111365

Call Sign: KB9COI
Richard G Smith
718 W Prairie St
Altamont IL 62411

Call Sign: KC9HHQ
David E Zumwalt Jr
Altamont IL 62411

FCC Amateur Radio Licenses in Alto Pass

Call Sign: N9HIT
Jeffrey A Yarmola
7275 Rt 127 N
Alto Pass IL 629053220

Call Sign: K9LTO
Joseph E Bennett
2770 Skyline Dr
Alto Pass IL 62905

FCC Amateur Radio Licenses in Alton

Call Sign: WD9GSQ
Joseph W Jackson
4116 Aberdeen
Alton IL 62002

Call Sign: WB9EWI
Walter R Hamel
4208 Aberdeen
Alton IL 62002

Call Sign: KC9NWH
Walter L Blackledge Jr
6505 Alpha Dr
Alton IL 62002

Call Sign: KB9LZJ
Robert L Dancy
2301 Amelia St
Alton IL 62002

Call Sign: W9LWH
Robert E Nowlan
3315 Badley Ave
Alton IL 62002

Call Sign: N9IGH
Gerald E Robertson
2523 Bloomer Dr
Alton IL 62002

Call Sign: KC9TQV
Maurice H Armstead
1951 Brown St
Alton IL 62002

Call Sign: W5TKA
Wilma F Wenzel
3115 Burton
Alton IL 62002

Call Sign: KC9TGY
Christopher K Grieve
3418 California
Alton IL 62002

Call Sign: N9LBI
William H Stogsdill Jr
4625 Camellia Pl
Alton IL 62002

Call Sign: KB9WCT
Jerald T Hampshire
5104 Candy Ln
Alton IL 62002

Call Sign: AG9M
Jerald T Hampshire
5104 Candy Ln
Alton IL 62002

Call Sign: NM9N
Robert G Marchal
409 Cherry St
Alton IL 62002

Call Sign: N9XKJ
Eric R Watkins
3032 College Ave
Alton IL 62002

Call Sign: AE9C
Devereux H Murphy Jr
4500 College Ave
Alton IL 620025059

Call Sign: K9WSU
Dittmar W Merkle
1121 Danforth St
Alton IL 62002

Call Sign: N9ADJ
Ronald E Wright
3807 Davis Ln
Alton IL 62002

Call Sign: WA9YAW
Gilbert J Weyhaupt
3824 Davis Ln
Alton IL 62002

Call Sign: KB9ZPM
Franz-Joseph J Nolan
2503 Della Ave
Alton IL 62002

Call Sign: N9HXC
Dennis R Knight Sr
622 Division St
Alton IL 62002

Call Sign: KG9NE
Rick L Taylor
325 E 3rd St Apt 4
Alton IL 62002

Call Sign: N9YKU
Lawrence R Edwards
614 E 7th St
Alton IL 62002

Call Sign: KB9TBS
Robert S Gills
304 E 7th St Apt C
Alton IL 62002

Call Sign: KB9FXF
Jerry C Smith
603 E 8th St
Alton IL 62002

Call Sign: AG4RO
David A Rix
984 Echo Ln
Alton IL 62002

Call Sign: KA9TOZ
Daniel C Engdale
3020 Edwards St
Alton IL 62002

Call Sign: N9YHN
Lawrence O Sitton
3210 Fernwood
Alton IL 62002

Call Sign: N9KYQ
William S Knight
2304 Fontaine Dr
Alton IL 62002

Call Sign: KB9GPF
Jeffery P Borman
2323 Fontaine Dr

Alton IL 62002

Call Sign: WB9YJV
Larry D Borman
2323 Fontaine Dr
Alton IL 62002

Call Sign: KC9AAU
Lana Edwards
4434 Friarwood Dr
Alton IL 62002

Call Sign: K9LBE
Lana Edwards
4434 Friarwood Dr
Alton IL 62002

Call Sign: KB9VRM
Robert S Edwards
4434 Friarwood Dr
Alton IL 62002

Call Sign: K9RSE
Steve Edwards
4434 Friarwood Dr
Alton IL 62002

Call Sign: KC9STU
Thomas C Andrews
2901 Gilbert Ln
Alton IL 62002

Call Sign: N9SYB
Harrison A Henderson Sr
1315 Harold St
Alton IL 62002

Call Sign: KB9TCQ
Richard A Boschert
3128 Hawthorne Blvd
Alton IL 620024309

Call Sign: KC9ELY
Melinda K Boyd
3211 Hawthorne Blvd
Alton IL 62002

Call Sign: AB9UB
Hugh D Watson

2734 Hillcrest
Alton IL 62002

Call Sign: K9ZVD
Albert J Belanger
15 Holly Hill Dr
Alton IL 620025225

Call Sign: KD9M
Robert L Gray
3829 Horn Ave
Alton IL 62002

Call Sign: KC9JCT
David L Hargiss
8966 Ingersoll Ln
Alton IL 62002

Call Sign: K9TTU
Gail P Kerr
2702 Judson St
Alton IL 62002

Call Sign: K9ORV
William F Haper
2614 Krum St
Alton IL 62002

Call Sign: KB9WFU
Jamie L Overton
2428 Lasalle Dr
Alton IL 62002

Call Sign: KC9RBI
Joshua J Nolan
625 Leonard St
Alton IL 62002

Call Sign: KB9VAM
Keith E Patterson
819 Liberty St
Alton IL 62002

Call Sign: N9JC
John T Cronn
1401 Liberty St
Alton IL 62002

Call Sign: KE9RG

William T Merkle
1202 McPherson
Alton IL 62002

Call Sign: KA9RSC
Geoffrey S Wiegand
2513 Merchant St
Alton IL 62002

Call Sign: KB9CDI
Richard D Gum
3423 Meridocia
Alton IL 62002

Call Sign: KB9YHI
Mark J Kivett
3425 Meridocia
Alton IL 62002

Call Sign: KA9WUF
Alexander Mackenzie
3427 Meridocia
Alton IL 62002

Call Sign: N9WDQ
Dennis C Tuchalski
2300 Morning Star Dr
Alton IL 62002

Call Sign: N9ZJQ
Rebecca C Tuchalski
2300 Morning Star Dr
Alton IL 62002

Call Sign: KB9TCR
Clinton C Followell
2300 Morning Star Dr
Alton IL 620025623

Call Sign: KB9LZG
Jackson S Holland
2303 Morningstar Dr
Alton IL 62002

Call Sign: KC9NPD
David W Preis
3213 Myrle
Alton IL 62002

Call Sign: N9SYA
Eddie F Irvin
9015 Oakridge Dr
Alton IL 62002

Call Sign: KA9LRH
Cecil W Newberry
3400 Oakwood Ave
Alton IL 62002

Call Sign: KC9JZW
James A Mcdermott Sr
220 Patterson Pl
Alton IL 62002

Call Sign: K2BZZ
Orlando E Panfile
2331 Pebble Creek Ln
Alton IL 62002

Call Sign: KC9RBJ
Randall J Uphold
312 Poppins Pl
Alton IL 62002

Call Sign: KB9CWM
James A Embry Sr
2728 Residence St
Alton IL 62002

Call Sign: N9TMC
Terry A Bratton
1206 Rock Spring Dr
Alton IL 62002

Call Sign: K9GNK
Roy C Gunter
1637 Rock Spring Dr
Alton IL 62002

Call Sign: KB9CVT
Henry S Rhetta
Box 608 Rt 1
Alton IL 62002

Call Sign: KB9LFK
Mark D Voumard
1993 Sadie Ln
Alton IL 62002

Call Sign: K9PPT
Emil A Kittel
1536 Seiler Rd
Alton IL 62002

Call Sign: KA9SQQ
Ronald L Denother
2093 Seiler Rd
Alton IL 62002

Call Sign: KC9TWJ
Sue A Williams
1123 Seiler St
Alton IL 62002

Call Sign: K9SD
Sammie H Effinger
8480 Seiler Ter
Alton IL 62002

Call Sign: N9IYB
Catherine L Effinger
8480 Seiler Ter
Alton IL 62002

Call Sign: KC9FIW
Walt Johler Memorial ARC
8480 Seiler Ter
Alton IL 62002

Call Sign: W9FD
Walt Johler Memorial ARC
8480 Seiler Ter
Alton IL 62002

Call Sign: N9XKI
Kevin Michael F Strasser
2820 Seminary
Alton IL 62002

Call Sign: N9FTA
John D Nell
1122 State St
Alton IL 62002

Call Sign: N9IRK
Renee L Bauer
1122 State St

Alton IL 62002

Call Sign: KB9TOI
Paul M Vetter
1309 State St
Alton IL 620023025

Call Sign: KC9JLG
Frederick F Hornsey Jr
1604 State St
Alton IL 62002

Call Sign: K9TBI
Martin Golob
4903 Storeyland Dr
Alton IL 62002

Call Sign: WV9Q
Richard E Blevens Jr
4449 Thatcher Rd
Alton IL 62002

Call Sign: KC9SGH
Michael A Bagwill
3248 Theresa Ave
Alton IL 62002

Call Sign: KC0KD
Patrick E Murphy
3425 Thomas Ave
Alton IL 620024118

Call Sign: KC9STR
Jennifer L Hutchins
1249 W 9th St
Alton IL 62002

Call Sign: KB9FXG
Francis J Hogan
2130 W Dell Dr
Alton IL 62002

Call Sign: KC9RBH
John H Mcclain
1031 Wallace
Alton IL 62002

Call Sign: KC9DZB
Gregory S Sheary

1214 Washington Ave
Alton IL 62002

Call Sign: N9USV
Jennifer A Drake
2010 Washington Ave
Alton IL 62002

Call Sign: KB0UIU
Gregory A Sims
2701 Watalee
Alton IL 62002

Call Sign: AB9LC
Gregory A Sims
2701 Watalee
Alton IL 62002

Call Sign: N9OCH
William A Martin
3633 Western Ave
Alton IL 62002

Call Sign: KD6QKX
Jules J King Jr
3637 Western Ave
Alton IL 62002

Call Sign: N9KRK
Christopher S Carstens
3645 Western Ave
Alton IL 62002

Call Sign: N9LBF
Mari B Carstens
3645 Western Ave
Alton IL 62002

Call Sign: KC9USU
Robert L Christeson
612 Wilson Ave
Alton IL 62002

Call Sign: N9HXK
Fred D Garris Sr
1201 Wise
Alton IL 62002

Call Sign: KA9WZT

Linda S Garris
1201 Wise
Alton IL 62002

Call Sign: KB9STN
Robert A Dossett
4311 Wood Burn Rd
Alton IL 62002

Call Sign: KC9DAU
Nyla R Dossett
4311 Woodburn Rd
Alton IL 620027813

Call Sign: KB9JVZ
Russell E Leggett
7661 Woodstation Rd
Alton IL 62002

Call Sign: KE9WL
William G Korte Jr
1834 Worden
Alton IL 62002

Call Sign: W9YZE
Harry A Turner
1718 Worden Ave
Alton IL 62002

Call Sign: N9OUY
Bryan L Rollins
Rr 1 Box 165
Altona IL 61414

Call Sign: KC9FCY
Michael J Stone
409 E Main St
Altona IL 61414

Call Sign: WA9YUJ
Ronald W Sheeley
104 Walnut Box 28
Altona IL 61414

Call Sign: KC9BSO
Richard M Roller
Altona IL 61414

FCC Amateur Radio Licenses in Alvin

Call Sign: KB9EYT
Donald L Miller
15312 E 2820 N Rd
Alvin IL 61811

Call Sign: N9WTO
Leslie J Miller
15312 E 2820 N Rd
Alvin IL 61811

Call Sign: KD5GPR
Georgia K Tucker
21677 E SR 119
Alvin IL 61811

Call Sign: KM5UE
Robert L Wittig
21677 E SR 119
Alvin IL 61811

Call Sign: KC9KZC
Larry L Trimble
21323 E St Rt 119
Alvin IL 61811

Call Sign: N9JYK
Larry L Trimble
21323 E St Rt 119
Alvin IL 61811

Call Sign: WA9LBV
Neil R Andrews
29638 SR 1
Alvin IL 61811

FCC Amateur Radio Licenses in Amboy

Call Sign: KB9VQE
Joseph M Fenwick
952 Amboy Rd
Amboy IL 61310

Call Sign: KA9PZB
Jim E Feith
324 E Main St

Amboy IL 61310

Call Sign: KC9FJS
Angeline R Taormina
369 Il Rt 26
Amboy IL 61310

Call Sign: K9ANG
Angeline R Taormina Ms
369 Il Rt 26
Amboy IL 61310

Call Sign: N9YFD
Diane L Johnson
369 Il Rt 26
Amboy IL 61310

Call Sign: KC9HBM
Kelly E Dicaro
369 Il Rt 26
Amboy IL 61310

Call Sign: K9KEL
Kelly E Dicaro
369 Il Rt 26
Amboy IL 61310

Call Sign: KA9MCC
Sam S Taormina Jr
369 Il Rt 26
Amboy IL 61310

Call Sign: N9TXN
Eva C Crothers
809 McCoy Rd
Amboy IL 61310

Call Sign: WA9OMJ
Gerald L Crothers
809 McCoy Rd
Amboy IL 61310

Call Sign: WA9SVB
John A Goerlitz
222 N Jones
Amboy IL 61310

Call Sign: KB9FYG
Robert A Bumpus

307 N Mason Ave
Amboy IL 61310

Call Sign: KC9KYT
Edward L Morrissey
649 Rt 26
Amboy IL 61310

Call Sign: N9JWI
Francis C Lachat
307 S Locust
Amboy IL 61310

Call Sign: KC9RPC
Candise S Lachat
231 S Locust Ave
Amboy IL 61310

Call Sign: KC9HFG
Priscilla C Lachat
231 S Locust Ave
Amboy IL 61310

Call Sign: KC9SFO
Lee County ARC
231 S Locust Ave
Amboy IL 61310

Call Sign: WX9LE
Lee County ARC
231 S Locust Ave
Amboy IL 61310

Call Sign: KB5QDA
Wayne A Lachat
231 S Locust Ave
Amboy IL 61310

Call Sign: K9QDA
Wayne A Lachat
231 S Locust Ave
Amboy IL 613101838

Call Sign: N9PYX
Dean A Lachat
307 S Locust Ave
Amboy IL 61310

Call Sign: N9EMK

Donald H Feith
309 S Madison
Amboy IL 61310

Call Sign: KB9KHH
Clay W Taylor
1666 Sterling Rd
Amboy IL 61310

Call Sign: W9OAM
David F Winter
107 Stroble Ave
Amboy IL 61310

Call Sign: KB9ZGX
Keith L Shaw
35 W Main
Amboy IL 61310

Call Sign: N9KVQ
Francis D Lachat
311 W Pieronnet St
Amboy IL 61310

Call Sign: KC9RPA
Kelsie J Lachat
311 W Pieronnet St
Amboy IL 61310

Call Sign: KB9KHK
Keri L Lachat
311 W Pieronnet St
Amboy IL 61310

Call Sign: KA9DVW
Carl E Tucker
16 W Wasson Rd Lot 245
Amboy IL 61310

Call Sign: KB9FZV
Gary R Harper Jr
Amboy IL 61310

FCC Amateur Radio Licenses in Anchor

Call Sign: KC9AXV
Mark D Humphrey
411 1st St

Anchor IL 617200157

Call Sign: KC9MVT
Matthew W Maffett
519 1st St
Anchor IL 61720

FCC Amateur Radio Licenses in Andalusia

Call Sign: WB9RPP
Cecil F Casey
532 7 St W
Andalusia IL 61232

Call Sign: WB9TCJ
Dennis W Martens
334 7th St W
Andalusia IL 61232

Call Sign: KA9BSY
Ernest E Masengarb
320 W 4 Ave Box 533
Andalusia IL 61232

Call Sign: KB9WTK
John R Bald
Andalusia IL 61232

FCC Amateur Radio Licenses in Andover

Call Sign: K9PXC
Eugene W Carlson
639 6th St
Andover IL 61233

Call Sign: KA9PHS
Thomas C Long
106 Sherwood Dr
Andover IL 61233

FCC Amateur Radio Licenses in Anna

Call Sign: N9TWN
William A Full
508 Anna Vista
Anna IL 629061244

Call Sign: N9OWK
Margaret M Jones
370 Body Barn Rd
Anna IL 62906

Call Sign: KB9GIB
Michael W Jones
370 Body Barn Rd
Anna IL 62906

Call Sign: KB9LJS
Rebecca J Loomis
Rr 1 Box 244
Anna IL 62906

Call Sign: N9NOT
James E Flach
Rr 2 Box 272
Anna IL 62906

Call Sign: KA9LFX
Carroll O Loomis
1865 Boyd Dr
Anna IL 629063453

Call Sign: N9OFT
Robert D Carter
2700 Campground Rd
Anna IL 629063315

Call Sign: KA9THF
Wanda K Jones
520 Christian Chapel Rd
Anna IL 62906

Call Sign: WB9D
Robert J Jones Jr
520 Christian Chaple Rd
Anna IL 62906

Call Sign: WB9HEB
John L Kraatz
425 Dog Walk Rd
Anna IL 62906

Call Sign: KC9RJR
Charles L Smithey
3210 Dogwalk Rd

Anna IL 62906

Call Sign: KB9MQH
Robert M Hansil
208 B E Vienna St
Anna IL 62906

Call Sign: W0JWW
Robert A Vitt
118 East Ave
Anna IL 62906

Call Sign: AA9MH
Denny R Lawson
208 Forest St
Anna IL 62906

Call Sign: WA9ZCK
James E Honey
204 Kohler Ave
Anna IL 62906

Call Sign: KC2WPZ
Dustin R Poole
209 Lime Kiln Rd
Anna IL 62906

Call Sign: KC9DJD
Paul C Page
605 N Main St
Anna IL 62906

Call Sign: N9MVT
Jan E Schroth
304 Roberts
Anna IL 62906

Call Sign: KC9CJC
Shawn D Peshoff
200 Roberts St
Anna IL 62906

Call Sign: KB9GEH
Derrill R Schroth
304 Roberts St
Anna IL 62906

Call Sign: KC9SLA
Rebecca L Matuszewich

503 Sharp Rd
Anna IL 62906

Call Sign: KC9SKZ
Timothy J Matuszewich
503 Sharp Rd
Anna IL 62906

Call Sign: KA9EYS
Thomas D Maske
375 Shawnee Meadows Ln
Anna IL 62906

Call Sign: N9KQY
Matthew A Wettig
516 South St
Anna IL 62906

Call Sign: K9TFY
Earl L Edmonds
130 Turner Ave
Anna IL 62906

Call Sign: K0OVD
Gene R Myers
107 W Lewis
Anna IL 629062122

Call Sign: N9SXM
Bill J Stairs
Anna IL 62906

Call Sign: N9UGW
Paula D Stairs
Anna IL 62906

FCC Amateur Radio Licenses in Annapolis

Call Sign: WB9WCT
Charles D Stephens
21751 N 400th St
Annapolis IL 624132207

Call Sign: KC9FPR
Garry A Young
17719 N 700th St
Annapolis IL 62413

FCC Amateur Radio Licenses in Annawan

Call Sign: N9LNL
Bryan E Niemeier
26071 N 1600 Ave
Annawan IL 61234

Call Sign: N9ZAW
Willis D Ufheil
Box 173 Rt 78
Annawan IL 61234

Call Sign: WB9TUT
Alan F Streicher
403 W Patey
Annawan IL 61234

FCC Amateur Radio Licenses in Apple River

Call Sign: KB9NGX
Steven P Hippchen
304 1st N St
Apple River IL 61001

Call Sign: WA9BUZ
Charles R Chadwick Jr
7A11 Broken Lance Ln
Apple River IL 61001

Call Sign: N4GTX
Charles R Chadwick Jr
7A11 Broken Lance Ln
Apple River IL 61001

Call Sign: N9ZLK
John R Mc Fadden
6955 E Stagecoach Trl Box 83
Apple River IL 61001

Call Sign: KB9SJC
Thomas A Lauraitis
105 E Walnut St
Apple River IL 610019411

Call Sign: WA9BMZ
Richard J Potempa
12A203 Eisenhower Dr

Apple River IL 61001

Call Sign: N9HEC
William J Kolacek Jr
7A Lookout Dr 72
Apple River IL 61001

Call Sign: N9NQG
Victor J Burmeister
11A97 Putter Ln
Apple River IL 61001

FCC Amateur Radio Licenses in Arcola

Call Sign: KB9JLK
Ben J Wood
1140 CR 400N
Arcola IL 61910

Call Sign: WB9URK
James W Wood
1140 E CR 400N
Arcola IL 61910

Call Sign: N9OHD
Robert W Guennewig
310 E Main
Arcola IL 61910

Call Sign: WA9WOB
William F Guennewig Jr
310 E Main
Arcola IL 619101512

Call Sign: W9QNE
John W Parker
Arcola IL 61910

FCC Amateur Radio Licenses in Arenzville

Call Sign: KA9YBH
Billy H Kinsey
Rr 1 Box 67
Arenzville IL 62611

FCC Amateur Radio Licenses in Argenta

Call Sign: KC9ATE
Mark D Traxler
143 E Prairie
Argenta IL 62501

Call Sign: W9AXX
Mark D Traxler
143 E Prairie
Argenta IL 62501

FCC Amateur Radio Licenses in Arlington

Call Sign: KC9IZN
Jacob A Pratt
32267 1800 N Ave
Arlington IL 61312

Call Sign: KC9IZP
Sue E Pratt
32267 1800 N Ave
Arlington IL 61312

Call Sign: KC9IZM
Timothy K Pratt
32267 1800 N Ave
Arlington IL 61312

Call Sign: KC9IZO
Zachary J Pratt
32267 1800 N Ave
Arlington IL 61312

Call Sign: KC9HZR
Jeff L Buttke
35292 2100 N Ave
Arlington IL 61312

Call Sign: KD9CG
George T Casford
209 Pleasant St
Arlington IL 61312

FCC Amateur Radio Licenses in Armington

Call Sign: K9TR
Mark A Shaum

29276 Armington Rd
Armington IL 617219400

Call Sign: KB9OTK
Michael J Dull
1423 Dale Rd
Armington IL 61721

Call Sign: ND9V
George T Israel
3113 McLean Rd
Armington IL 617219351

Call Sign: N9GMO
Tammy A Israel
3113 McLean Rd
Armington IL 617219351

Call Sign: KC9JKJ
Brian E Tackett
109 N Monroe St
Armington IL 61721

Call Sign: KC9JKH
Patrick A Hancock
110 North St
Armington IL 61721

Call Sign: KA9UKR
Michael M Noble
108 S Washington
Armington IL 61721

Call Sign: KC9ICE
Charles R Clothier
Armington IL 61721

FCC Amateur Radio Licenses in Arrowsmith

Call Sign: KB9YSG
Michael L Klintworth
Rr 1 Box 43
Arrowsmith IL 61722

Call Sign: KC0WER
Lee C Skinner
32591 E 750 N Rd
Arrowsmith IL 61722

Call Sign: K9SBH
Richard E Willis
301 S Walnut St
Arrowsmith IL 61722

FCC Amateur Radio Licenses in Arthur

Call Sign: KV9Q
Charles R Oye
406 Bonn Ct
Arthur IL 61911

Call Sign: WB9TDB
Daniel W Perrine
219 Chaise Ln
Arthur IL 61911

Call Sign: N9EXN
Richard E House
451N CR 275E
Arthur IL 61911

Call Sign: WD9ICK
Max E Carey
534 Dogwood Dr
Arthur IL 61911

Call Sign: KB9STT
John C Peck
420 E Lincoln
Arthur IL 61911

Call Sign: KC9ALS
Georgia L Peck
420 E Lincoln St
Arthur IL 61911

Call Sign: WB9YIK
Marvin C Reeves
818 Lincoln Pl
Arthur IL 61911

Call Sign: K9MCR
Marvin C Reeves
818 Lincoln Pl
Arthur IL 61911

Call Sign: KA9EVA
Daniel T Brosend
312 N Beech
Arthur IL 61911

Call Sign: WA9PGQ
Eli J Plank
218 S Ash
Arthur IL 61911

Call Sign: N9WGL
Russell L Perrine
222 Taylor Ln
Arthur IL 61911

Call Sign: KA9AHP
Kenneth W Winings
Arthur IL 619110114

FCC Amateur Radio Licenses in Ashland

Call Sign: K9LTI
Thomas E Glossop
2082 Crazyhorse Rd
Ashland IL 62612

Call Sign: K9GXT
Paul F Williams
605 Mechanic St
Ashland IL 62612

Call Sign: KC9VEZ
Kristina L Gardner
2878 Panther Grove Rd
Ashland IL 62612

Call Sign: KB9UWZ
William M Hart
316 S Athens St
Ashland IL 62612

Call Sign: KC9TVB
Matt M Kline
401 W Topeka St
Ashland IL 62612

Call Sign: W9KZD
Homer C Butler

Ashland IL 62612

FCC Amateur Radio Licenses in Ashley

Call Sign: N9MZG
Carole J Mannhard
7370 County Hwy 23
Ashley IL 62808

Call Sign: W5KLC
Kenneth L Cramer
7370 County Hwy 23
Ashley IL 62808

Call Sign: KB9FCQ
Lendell M Panzier Jr
3810 E Bakerville Rd
Ashley IL 62808

Call Sign: KD9UI
Charles L Lentz
184 N Wentworth St
Ashley IL 62808

Call Sign: KA9UXJ
Kathryn L Lentz
184 N Wentworth St
Ashley IL 62808

Call Sign: K9CNR
John B La Busier
22540 SR 15
Ashley IL 62808

Call Sign: WB9DSP
Shirley A La Busier
22540 SR 15
Ashley IL 62808

FCC Amateur Radio Licenses in Ashmore

Call Sign: KC9TOI
Robert L Leach III
20336 Arrowhead Rd
Ashmore IL 61912

Call Sign: KA9BPI

Diane R Wiman
Rt 1 Box 223
Ashmore IL 61912

Call Sign: KB2RWH
David J Mc Kenney
104 E Charleston Rd
Ashmore IL 61912

Call Sign: KC9ECE
David J Mc Kenney
104 E Charleston Rd
Ashmore IL 61912

Call Sign: N9ACX
Ivan L Gunter
409 Kentucky St
Ashmore IL 61912

Call Sign: K9TLK
William T Brannon
Box 296 Rt 1
Ashmore IL 61912

Call Sign: KC9QMI
Rick L Ford
Ashmore IL 61912

Call Sign: KA9WZB
Frederick A Reisinger
1765 Brooklyn Rd
Ashton IL 610069729

Call Sign: KB9NVE
Randall W Albrecht
904 Hick Ave
Ashton IL 61006

Call Sign: KC9LYO
Jerry G Scherer
1503 Middlebury Rd
Ashton IL 61006

Call Sign: KB9UQW
Dale R Tulk
2191 Pipeline Rd

Ashton IL 61006

Call Sign: KB9WSJ
Mark D Wooden
7082A S Hoosier Rd
Ashton IL 61006

Call Sign: N9RFF
Patty A Smith
Ashton IL 61006

Call Sign: KB9NFS
Steen A Albrecht
Ashton IL 61006

Call Sign: KE9EZ
Joseph E Demascal
112 S Poplar
Assumption IL 62510

Call Sign: KC9MXM
Colon N Lawrence
321 W Samuel
Assumption IL 62510

Call Sign: KA9AQW
William D Connolly
217 E State
Astoria IL 615010135

Call Sign: WB9OJR
Roger D Schneider
3648 N Bucher Rd
Astoria IL 61501

Call Sign: W9FF
Roger D Schneider
3648 N Bucher Rd
Astoria IL 61501

Call Sign: KB9NHW
Darel L Baum
22440 Athen Blacktop
Athens IL 62613

Call Sign: KB9ZIU
Kenneth L Litchfield
Rr 2 Box 447 C
Athens IL 62613

Call Sign: KC9IOA
Philip L Tinsley
22005 Cantrall Rd
Athens IL 62613

Call Sign: KA9BQA
Maynard A Anderson Jr
17 Rainbow Dr
Athens IL 62613

Call Sign: AA9ZF
Maynard A Anderson Jr
407 Rainbow Dr
Athens IL 62613

Call Sign: N9WVQ
Jeffrey A Wiker
411 S Mill
Athens IL 62613

Call Sign: KC9EGQ
Lester W Cain
814 W Monroe
Athens IL 62613

Call Sign: KC9PBN
Adam L Hughes
506 W Washington St
Athens IL 62613

Call Sign: KB9CEQ
Andrea N Thomason
Athens IL 62613

Call Sign: N9PWY
Lambert P Fleck III
Athens IL 62613

FCC Amateur Radio Licenses in Atkinson

Call Sign: KB9UPY
Timothy J Roman
22581 N 2120th Ave
Atkinson IL 61235

Call Sign: KC9PVX
Winfred L Gentry
420 W Margaret St
Atkinson IL 61235

FCC Amateur Radio Licenses in Atlanta

Call Sign: KB9ZQS
Devin R Vannoy
2425 1350th Ave
Atlanta IL 61723

Call Sign: WM9N
Larry W Collins
2190 1900th Ave
Atlanta IL 61723

Call Sign: N9BVG
Byron J Jodlowski
2201 2237th St
Atlanta IL 61723

Call Sign: KA9CNC
Robert E Johnson
2274 2237th St
Atlanta IL 61723

Call Sign: K9LN
Rodney A Harmon
1664 2375th St
Atlanta IL 61723

Call Sign: KB9MZP
Susan H Smith
Rr 2 Box 139
Atlanta IL 61723

Call Sign: W9JQ
John D Quiram
103 NE 2nd

Atlanta IL 61723

Call Sign: KC9SUL
David N Roy
107 SW 3rd St
Atlanta IL 61723

Call Sign: KB9RAA
Troy A Howie
803 W North St
Atlanta IL 61723

Call Sign: KB9WLI
Everette P Bateman
Atlanta IL 61723

Call Sign: KB9PJH
John H Swearingen
Atlanta IL 617230356

Call Sign: K9JHS
John H Swearingen
Atlanta IL 617230356

Call Sign: KB9QLM
Susan M Swearingen
Atlanta IL 617230356

Call Sign: K9SMS
Susan M Swearingen
Atlanta IL 617230356

FCC Amateur Radio Licenses in Atwater

Call Sign: KC9HQC
Dustin L Weller
25757 Stead Rd
Atwater IL 62572

FCC Amateur Radio Licenses in Atwood

Call Sign: KC9RUF
Shawn A Robinson
206 Camelot Dr
Atwood IL 61913

Call Sign: KB9IUP

Randy C Long
Rr 1 G79
Atwood IL 61913

Call Sign: KB9TIP
Justin M Rotramel
187 N 1385 E Rd
Atwood IL 619133547

Call Sign: KA9CNV
Bruce G Gregory
325 N Iowa
Atwood IL 61913

Call Sign: KB9IPC
Matt L Jones
202 N Kentucky
Atwood IL 61913

Call Sign: KB9LBQ
Atwood Hammond
Community Unit 39
424 N Missouri Box 507
Atwood IL 61913

Call Sign: KA9EMC
Thomas E Warner
107 S 1st St
Atwood IL 61913

Call Sign: KB9ZDQ
Lisa C Schrad
107 W Magnolia
Atwood IL 61913

Call Sign: KC9KZG
Cassie D Lee
Atwood IL 61913

FCC Amateur Radio Licenses in Auburn

Call Sign: K9CNP
Harold J Dunn
17 Barbara Ln
Auburn IL 626159444

Call Sign: KC9NSQ

Capital Area Amateur Radio
Emergency Response Team
17 Barbara Ln
Auburn IL 626159444

Call Sign: N4ITN
Vincent J Speranza
26 Barbara Ln
Auburn IL 62615

Call Sign: KB9NYZ
Donald C Ihlenfeldt
Rr 1 Box 145
Auburn IL 62615

Call Sign: KB9OAS
Amy M Ihlenfeldt
Rr1 Box 145 Red Bud Ln
Auburn IL 62615

Call Sign: KA9QDB
Michael S Woods
1216 Comanche Rd
Auburn IL 62615

Call Sign: WD9CTO
Mark K Huff
1 Conestoga Dr
Auburn IL 62615

Call Sign: KB9TZS
Richard R Marx
16 Conestoga Dr
Auburn IL 62615

Call Sign: KC9IGN
Trevor L White
312 E Adams St
Auburn IL 62615

Call Sign: N9JQD
Ryan D Funk
416 E Jefferson
Auburn IL 62615

Call Sign: K9UCC
Fred J Manship
264 E Monroe
Auburn IL 62615

Call Sign: WB0SEN
Eugene B Affolter
900 Lincolin St
Auburn IL 62615

Call Sign: N9ZIX
Steven W Mc Near
820 Lincoln Ave
Auburn IL 62615

Call Sign: KD7PLE
Justin R Graves
212 N 6th St
Auburn IL 62615

Call Sign: KC9ACA
Steven Beckwith
430 N 7th St
Auburn IL 62615

Call Sign: KC9AMA
John F Cribbett
400 S 5th St
Auburn IL 62615

Call Sign: KC9KMG
Christopher A Licht
14 Santa Fe Dr
Auburn IL 62615

Call Sign: K9NNC
Christopher A Licht
14 Santa Fe Dr
Auburn IL 62615

Call Sign: KC9POX
Roy E Griffitts
14 Santa Fe Dr
Auburn IL 62615

Call Sign: KC9VPT
Jim A Mcguire
4635 Timberview Dr
Auburn IL 62615

Call Sign: KC9LSK
Jill B Ball
2045 Union School Rd

Auburn IL 62615

Call Sign: KB9ESC
Jeffrey H Ball
12045 Union School Rd
Auburn IL 62615

Call Sign: WA9KCI
David G Sokol
4625 W Divernon Rd
Auburn IL 62615

Call Sign: KC9MXN
Robert L Howard
927 W Jackson St
Auburn IL 62615

Call Sign: KC9HLL
Stephanie M Haney
1013 W Madison
Auburn IL 62615

Call Sign: WB9SVD
Robert J Clotfelter Sr
516 W Madison St
Auburn IL 62615

FCC Amateur Radio Licenses in Augusta

Call Sign: KA9AJH
Doris E Kerr
314 Orchard St
Augusta IL 62311

Call Sign: KB9RKW
Mark E Thompson
711 Prarie St
Augusta IL 62311

Call Sign: KB9CEO
Alan J Holmes
708 Washington St
Augusta IL 62311

Call Sign: KB9CET
Nancy L Holmes
708 Washington St
Augusta IL 62311

FCC Amateur Radio Licenses in Ava

Call Sign: WD9HMD
David A Guenther
11196 Ava Rd
Ava IL 62907

Call Sign: K9UF
David A Guenther
11196 Ava Rd
Ava IL 62907

Call Sign: KB9LIJ
Kathy A Van Zandt
101 E Public
Ava IL 62907

Call Sign: KB9LUY
Sandra E Wentworth
1434 Marlboro Rd
Ava IL 62907

Call Sign: KA9SHY
James B Wentworth Jr
1434 Marlboro Rd
Ava IL 62907

Call Sign: N9LAF
Linda K Hoyt
503 McClure Rd
Ava IL 62907

Call Sign: KE9WR
Paul J Hoyt
503 McClure Rd
Ava IL 62907

Call Sign: N9LAC
Allen L Hoyt
Ava IL 62907

FCC Amateur Radio Licenses in Aviston

Call Sign: KC9DDM
Larry G Wolters
79 E 3rd St Apt 3
Aviston IL 62216

Call Sign: N9MZH
Joyce A Eacho
651 E 4th St
Aviston IL 62216

Call Sign: KD4PS
William D Eacho
651 E 4th St
Aviston IL 62216

Call Sign: N9GJA
Richard P Mueller
E 4th St & CR
Aviston IL 62216

Call Sign: KB9SCN
Thomas E Iler
3432 Highline Rd
Aviston IL 622161016

Call Sign: KC9IYX
Aaron J Schrage
4515 Lee Rd
Aviston IL 62216

Call Sign: KC9UJR
Ronald P Williamson
298 Redwood Dr
Aviston IL 62216

Call Sign: KC9UPC
Timothy J Rapp
449 Redwood Dr
Aviston IL 62216

Call Sign: K9XWX
Timothy J Rapp
449 Redwood Dr
Aviston IL 62216

Call Sign: KB9ATM
Kevin L Zeeb
48 Regal Dr
Aviston IL 62216

Call Sign: KC9TUM
Vincent J Huelsmann

15003 Schumacher Ln
Aviston IL 622163808

Call Sign: KA9TED
Ted L Long
662 W 1st St
Aviston IL 62216

Call Sign: N9JWP
Dennis R Fears
448 W Oak St
Aviston IL 62216

FCC Amateur Radio Licenses in Avon

Call Sign: KA9OVJ
Steve W Whittemore
105 Chestnut St
Avon IL 61415

Call Sign: K9KWG
James R Mitchell
4205 E Smokey Rd
Avon IL 61415

Call Sign: K9LOR
Ruby C Mitchell
4205 E Smokey Rd
Avon IL 61415

Call Sign: KB9JSX
Jeffrey K Luper
208 S Main St
Avon IL 61415

Call Sign: N9LYT
Dannie J Lester
609 W Wood St
Avon IL 61415

FCC Amateur Radio Licenses in Baileyville

Call Sign: N9ZCQ
John M Kaney
11382 Bluff Rd
Baileyville IL 61007

Call Sign: N9KMI
James C Tankersley
718 E Montague Rd
Baileyville IL 61007

Call Sign: WD9EJM
Richard L Dehahn
6132 S Clover Rd
Baileyville IL 61007

FCC Amateur Radio Licenses in Baldwin

Call Sign: KB9KUF
Mark A Theobald
10318 Cheridan Rd
Baldwin IL 62217

Call Sign: W9KUF
Mark A Theobald
10318 Cheridan Rd
Baldwin IL 62217

Call Sign: K9TFB
Elbert E Wehrheim
211 S 5th St
Baldwin IL 62217

FCC Amateur Radio Licenses in Barry

Call Sign: WA9EFV
Carol E Bartlett
32559 250th St
Barry IL 62312

Call Sign: KC9MMO
John O Potter
24742 330th Ave
Barry IL 62312

Call Sign: KB9ZFJ
Jessica R Pederson
Rr 1 Box 31B
Barry IL 62312

Call Sign: KA9QIY
Kathy E Dixon
780 Brown St

Barry IL 62312

Call Sign: KA9KOB
Edward G Doran
29001 County Hwy 4
Barry IL 62312

Call Sign: KA9VIQ
Patricia A Doran
29001 County Hwy 4
Barry IL 62312

Call Sign: KA0RTZ
Russ E Martin
562 Main St
Barry IL 62312

Call Sign: KC9ELE
William J Saflarski Jr
2757 N 1st Ave
Barry IL 62312

Call Sign: N9KGW
Thomas J Deitzman
Rt 2 Pob 39
Barry IL 62312

FCC Amateur Radio Licenses in Barstow

Call Sign: KA9UBR
Steven L Arnold
Barstow IL 61236

FCC Amateur Radio Licenses in Bartelso

Call Sign: KA5TBM
Marty W Rogers
9915 Pioneer Rd
Bartelso IL 62218

Call Sign: KB9IWE
Robert B Boeckmann
203 Wash St Box 26
Bartelso IL 62218

FCC Amateur Radio Licenses in Bartonville

Call Sign: KC9UTQ
Nicholas V Sturm
213 Buena Vista
Bartonville IL 61607

Call Sign: N9PTU
Howard F Magnuson
1013 De Soto Dr
Bartonville IL 61607

Call Sign: KB9YFV
David E Burton
909 Desoto Dr
Bartonville IL 61607

Call Sign: KB9FMD
Dennis R Oedewaldt
1000 Desoto Dr
Bartonville IL 61607

Call Sign: KA9SXJ
Harold L Kaufman
205 Eaton St
Bartonville IL 61607

Call Sign: KC9QMY
Stephen R Gill
1 Foster Ct
Bartonville IL 61607

Call Sign: N9GUE
Fred A Darrah
430 Garfield Ave
Bartonville IL 61607

Call Sign: KC9DBD
Richard L Stambaugh Jr
6300 Monroe
Bartonville IL 61607

Call Sign: WB8HVC
Matthew S Daugherty
124 Paradise Ct
Bartonville IL 61607

Call Sign: KA9AYA
Loydd W Thurman Sr
4219 Paramount Rd

Bartonville IL 61607

Call Sign: WD9EGT
James E Corey
18 Rutledge
Bartonville IL 61607

Call Sign: AB9BO
James E Corey
18 Rutledge
Bartonville IL 61607

Call Sign: AB9BT
James E Corey
18 Rutledge
Bartonville IL 61607

Call Sign: K9RUN
Ron Hill
3810 S Airport Rd
Bartonville IL 616071757

Call Sign: WB3I
Steven S Popovich
1805 S Airport Rd
Bartonville IL 616071312

Call Sign: N9KUJ
Bradley L Day
2008 S Airport Rd
Bartonville IL 61607

Call Sign: N9XHK
John W Stein
4411 S Baker Ln
Bartonville IL 61607

Call Sign: N9GCT
Jeffrey E Cusey
4227 S Fairview Dr
Bartonville IL 61607

Call Sign: N9TYL
Larry L Day
2403 S Harrison Ct
Bartonville IL 61607

Call Sign: WD9GCL
I Joanne Krus

4201 S Lafayette Ave
Bartonville IL 61607

Call Sign: WD9EGM
Peter H Krus
4201 S Lafayette Ave
Bartonville IL 61607

Call Sign: N9QVA
Kristin A Adams
5720 S Lafayette Ave
Bartonville IL 616079212

Call Sign: WB9RVR
Charles D Tharp
8215 S McCumber Rd
Bartonville IL 61607

Call Sign: N9JPE
John L Smith
3935 S Paramount Dr
Bartonville IL 61607

Call Sign: W9GPM
Gordon P Meyers
4126 S Paramount Rd
Bartonville IL 61607

Call Sign: N9HCE
Jill M Meyers
4126 S Paramount Rd
Bartonville IL 61607

Call Sign: KB9UMT
Donald L Hobson Jr
3905 S Sheffield Rd
Bartonville IL 61607

Call Sign: WA9LFN
Donald E Callaway
18 Sherry Ln
Bartonville IL 61607

Call Sign: KB9ABW
Valerie D Meyers
5012 W Burns
Bartonville IL 61607

Call Sign: N9EFL

Gene D Mangis
304 W Garfield Ave
Bartonville IL 616071916

Call Sign: WA9SCD
Donald G Tjarks
311 W Garfield Ave
Bartonville IL 61607

Call Sign: KA9AXU
Ronald E Lavish
4704 W Wanda Ave
Bartonville IL 61607

Call Sign: KF4AFS
Steven H Fruendt
Bartonville IL 61607

FCC Amateur Radio Licenses in Basco

Call Sign: KB9PLP
Leonard C Chase
1430 E CR 600 N
Basco IL 623132140

Call Sign: KB9UFI
Larry J Dittmer
845 N CR 1100
Basco IL 623132113

Call Sign: KA9PUZ
Stanley L Davidson
Basco IL 62313

Call Sign: N9YUU
James D Damron
Basco IL 62313

FCC Amateur Radio Licenses in Batchtown

Call Sign: N1JO
Jeffrey T Oldham
Batchtown IL 620060064

FCC Amateur Radio Licenses in Bath

Call Sign: KB9QNJ
George A Richardson
Bath IL 62617

Call Sign: KB9QNK
Vera B Richardson
Bath IL 62617

FCC Amateur Radio Licenses in Baylis

Call Sign: N9AEB
Kenneth W Smith
Rr 1 Box 87
Baylis IL 62314

Call Sign: KB9WFC
Donald R Owens
70 E 2900th St
Baylis IL 62310

Call Sign: WA9AMG
William R Whitaker
36094 Perry Fishhook Rd
Baylis IL 62314

FCC Amateur Radio Licenses in Beardstown

Call Sign: KA9YHJ
Jamie S Daniels
1405 Adams St
Beardstown IL 62618

Call Sign: N9UHA
Nancy J Trone
7466 Arenzville Rd
Beardstown IL 62618

Call Sign: KB9PPZ
Robert L Frazier
Rr 1 Box 114
Beardstown IL 62618

Call Sign: KB9QEG
Sanders M Frazier
Rr 1 Box 114
Beardstown IL 62618

Call Sign: KB9FAY
Guy E Trone Sr
Rr 1 Box 300
Beardstown IL 62618

Call Sign: KB9WWW
Linda Bailey
1101 Clay
Beardstown IL 62618

Call Sign: W9HCI
Linda L Bailey
1101 Clay
Beardstown IL 62618

Call Sign: W9HUX
Charles D Bailey Jr
1101 Clay St
Beardstown IL 62618

Call Sign: KD9UL
Bruce M Boston
815 E 3rd St
Beardstown IL 62618

Call Sign: W9EVA
Spaceage Radio Society
815 E 3rd St
Beardstown IL 62618

Call Sign: KB9KCQ
Illinois Valley ARC
815 E 3rd St
Beardstown IL 62618

Call Sign: KA9WCR
Phyllis F Boston
815 E 3rd St
Beardstown IL 626181248

Call Sign: KC9IDY
Ronald E Tribble
119 E 4th St
Beardstown IL 62618

Call Sign: KB9OGS
Ryan A Mcgill
901 Edwards
Beardstown IL 62618

Call Sign: KA9JJD
James H Page
1001 Elm St
Beardstown IL 62618

Call Sign: KB9KVE
Bernard F Coil
Frank Wessel Dr Apt 9G
Beardstown IL 62618

Call Sign: KA9SGZ
Donald L Hiles
802 Grand Ave
Beardstown IL 62618

Call Sign: KD9L
Ralph A Sabetti
22 N Deerpath Dr
Beardstown IL 626189501

Call Sign: KD9P
David L Wilcox
9 Oak Grove Dr
Beardstown IL 62618

Call Sign: KB9JQP
Barbara A Knous
317 W 12th
Beardstown IL 62618

Call Sign: KA9ZLR
Charles R Knous II
317 W 12th
Beardstown IL 62618

Call Sign: KB9KRK
Larry L Spoon
1606 Wall St
Beardstown IL 62618

FCC Amateur Radio Licenses in Beaverville

Call Sign: KC9FAO
Terry L Wisniewski
Beaverville IL 60912

Call Sign: K9WIZ

Terry L Wisniewski
Beaverville IL 60912

FCC Amateur Radio
Licenses in Beckemeyer

Call Sign: KB9CXO
Paul F Zinschlag
190 Louis St
Beckemeyer IL 62219

Call Sign: KC9TWH
Gary T Whitlow
230 McKinley St
Beckemeyer IL 62219

Call Sign: KC9TWI
Rachael E Whitlow
230 McKinley St
Beckemeyer IL 62219

Call Sign: KB9IEQ
John C Feldman
Beckemeyer IL 62219

FCC Amateur Radio
Licenses in Beecher

Call Sign: N9JUR
Raymond D Wurl
Rr 2 Box 70
Beecher City IL 62401

Call Sign: N9JUQ
Brian L Carlson
Rr 2 Box 70
Beecher City IL 62414

Call Sign: WD9DPE
Lex K Hopper
Rr 2 Box 96
Beecher City IL 62414

Call Sign: N9IVU
Daniel B Brandenburger
Beecher City IL 62414

FCC Amateur Radio
Licenses in Belknap

Call Sign: KC9UXS
Hudson Pearcy
6248 New Columbia Rd
Belknap IL 62908

Call Sign: KC9UXP
Sherri J Pearcy
6248 New Columbia Rd
Belknap IL 62908

Call Sign: KC9UXQ
Timothy R Pearcy
6248 New Columbia Rd
Belknap IL 62908

Call Sign: KC9UXO
Tim S Pearcy
6248 New Columbia Rd
Belknap IL 62908

Call Sign: KC9UXR
Emma G Pearcy
6298 New Columbia Rd
Belknap IL 62908

FCC Amateur Radio
Licenses in Belle Rive

Call Sign: N9QXA
Amy T Holmes
Rt 1 Box 30 9th & Hickory
Belle Rive IL 62801

Call Sign: N9RNO
Mark A Taylor
20115 E Saddle Club Rd
Belle Rive IL 62810

Call Sign: KC9ADO
Edwin E Miller
6745 N Abbott Ln
Belle Rive IL 62810

Call Sign: NO9Y
James R Threatt
Belle Rive IL 62810

Call Sign: K9GHD

Sammy L Bourland
Belle Rive IL 62810

FCC Amateur Radio
Licenses in Belleville

Call Sign: W9QNC
David A Varnum
1115 4th Ave
Belleville IL 622266825

Call Sign: KC9RJG
David F Kenyon
52 Acorn Lake Dr
Belleville IL 62221

Call Sign: K1POP
David F Kenyon
52 Acorn Lake Dr
Belleville IL 62221

Call Sign: KB9EDW
Paul R Hollansworth
24 Andora Dr
Belleville IL 62221

Call Sign: N9NKH
Donna S Burnett
302 Anna St
Belleville IL 62221

Call Sign: N9NKI
John A Burnett Sr
302 Anna St
Belleville IL 62221

Call Sign: KB9UED
Thomas A Childress
1033 Belle Valley Dr Apt 3
Belleville IL 622203439

Call Sign: KC9JCW
Shelly K Sullivan
524 Benton St
Belleville IL 62220

Call Sign: W9GKA
Kevin C Kaufhold
21 Berrywood Dr

Belleville IL 62223

Call Sign: KB9BGY
Kevin B Duffy
45 Beth Ann Dr
Belleville IL 62221

Call Sign: W9LFN
Robert E Anderson Jr
201 Bittersweet Ln
Belleville IL 62221

Call Sign: KC9RUS
Donnie R Gross Jr
710 Blair Ave
Belleville IL 62220

Call Sign: WD0BHD
Walter L Beaver
109 Blue Grass Ln
Belleville IL 62221

Call Sign: WA9MRH
Richard H Hochstetler
1108 Bristow St
Belleville IL 62221

Call Sign: K9KWH
Larry G Matysik
8 Brittany Ln
Belleville IL 62223

Call Sign: KF6GUX
Dale L Clay
113 Brittany Ln
Belleville IL 62223

Call Sign: W3POP
Dale L Clay
113 Brittany Ln
Belleville IL 62223

Call Sign: KA9FHW
Dallas G Musgrove
224 Brittany Ln
Belleville IL 62223

Call Sign: WA9SQE
James V Musgrove

224 Brittany Ln
Belleville IL 62223

Call Sign: KC9TVW
Michael W Ceule
2829 Brook Meadow Dr
Belleville IL 62221

Call Sign: N1UFG
Vincent D Williams
240 Brookmanor Ct
Belleville IL 62221

Call Sign: N9NOD
Peter W Cervasio
1048 Brookshire Ct Apt 1
Belleville IL 62220

Call Sign: N9SWR
Edward W Finlay
261 Caballeros Blvd
Belleville IL 62221

Call Sign: KC9LIX
Robert L Arndt
21 Cambridge Dr
Belleville IL 62226

Call Sign: KD5KKY
Jaffery L Hansell
322 Carlyle E
Belleville IL 62221

Call Sign: KA0QOC
Brian W Dougherty
408 Carlyle E
Belleville IL 62221

Call Sign: KC9SZA
Jeff E Daum
15 Carr Park Rd
Belleville IL 62223

Call Sign: W9PUG
Krone W Tremaine
210 Carson Dr
Belleville IL 62223

Call Sign: N9NKG

Jerry L Hurst
312 Cascade Dr
Belleville IL 62223

Call Sign: N9NKF
Nancy J Hurst
312 Cascade Dr
Belleville IL 62223

Call Sign: AA2KF
Julio E Reyes
762 Cedar Mill Dr
Belleville IL 62221

Call Sign: KC9LXK
David M Hoffman
769 Cedar Mill Dr
Belleville IL 622213468

Call Sign: KC4TPG
Gary W Streeter
500 Centreville Ave
Belleville IL 62220

Call Sign: WB9KDY
Von C Deeke
925 Centreville Ave
Belleville IL 62220

Call Sign: WX9SVR
Christopher A Musso
1314 Centreville Ave
Belleville IL 62220

Call Sign: W9PAM
William R Burke
20 Chaucer Dr
Belleville IL 622265908

Call Sign: KB9EOV
Elmer V Smith III
412 Chevy Chase Dr
Belleville IL 62223

Call Sign: W9JUM
Nelson E Burbank
1425 Christina
Belleville IL 62223

Call Sign: N9NJX
John A Fulton
40 Christine Dr
Belleville IL 62221

Call Sign: KB9CYY
Floyd H Hoffmann Sr
717 Clay St
Belleville IL 62220

Call Sign: KC9AUK
Stephen Romanik II
7515 Clayman Ct 4
Belleville IL 622232213

Call Sign: N9PZZ
Karen A Jenkins
100 Clearview Dr
Belleville IL 62223

Call Sign: W8CQH
Kenneth E Kellogg
2123 Cloverleaf School Rd
Belleville IL 62223

Call Sign: KB9TNR
Diane R Rasp
3150 Cloverleaf School Rd
Belleville IL 62223

Call Sign: KB9SIB
Martin J Rasp
3150 Cloverleaf School Rd
Belleville IL 62223

Call Sign: KC9IBI
Scott D Carlson Sr
209 Columbus Dr
Belleville IL 62226

Call Sign: KB9AAC
Christy L Mealy
6 Concord Dr
Belleville IL 62223

Call Sign: N9MSU
Marcus C Bauer
8787 Concordia
Belleville IL 62223

Call Sign: N9AZY
Mark A Bauer
8787 Concordia Rd
Belleville IL 622236950

Call Sign: N1PAK
Jon C Wayne
944 Cool Valley Dr
Belleville IL 622203453

Call Sign: W9FPM
Marshall I Alperin
5 Cottonwood Ct
Belleville IL 622232902

Call Sign: KC9FIA
Jp Penet
417 Court St
Belleville IL 62220

Call Sign: KI9A
Albert C Schneebeli Jr
29 Crest Haven Dr
Belleville IL 62221

Call Sign: KB9PNL
Christopher A Musso
104 Crest Haven Dr
Belleville IL 62221

Call Sign: N9PBC
Steven K Flach
5 Cron Dr
Belleville IL 62223

Call Sign: W0NXX
Alan S Christinsin
1201 Dawn Dr
Belleville IL 62221

Call Sign: N9YMT
Donna E Mc Bride
1221 Dawn Dr
Belleville IL 62220

Call Sign: WA9CEO
George W Hawk
1429 Della

Belleville IL 62223

Call Sign: N9KNO
Michael S Staublin
3217 Denvershire Dr
Belleville IL 62221

Call Sign: WB9AJW
Lee R Schofield
637 Devonshire Dr
Belleville IL 622235909

Call Sign: KD9S
Leonard B Paris
3301 Dovershire Dr
Belleville IL 622216668

Call Sign: N9OQL
Michael H Wallace
3305 Dovershire Dr
Belleville IL 62221

Call Sign: KB9OJR
Edward V Callico
613 E A St
Belleville IL 62220

Call Sign: KA9DUL
Bernard A Gola
1800 E B St
Belleville IL 62221

Call Sign: KB9NXX
Jeffrey A Tucker
619 E C St
Belleville IL 622204069

Call Sign: W9SAY
Charles K Zarek
409 E D St
Belleville IL 622204036

Call Sign: KB2HUT
Joseph A Ferri
612 E Garfield St
Belleville IL 62220

Call Sign: N0WVV
John D Simpson

2100 E Main St
Belleville IL 62221

Call Sign: KC9JDD
Velma P Rice
2500 E Main St 42
Belleville IL 62221

Call Sign: KB9JAV
Nathan L Harris
209 E Monroe
Belleville IL 62220

Call Sign: KB9NIE
Chris H Kuberg
517 E Waters Edge
Belleville IL 62221

Call Sign: K9TEJ
Jack M Sullivan
101 Eiler Rd
Belleville IL 62223

Call Sign: KB0JOP
Timothy J Flynn
113 El Cerrito
Belleville IL 62221

Call Sign: KC9AUO
Cecil E Crites
141 El Cerrito
Belleville IL 62221

Call Sign: KB9PTS
Lance Q Lehr
201 Elizabeth Dr
Belleville IL 62223

Call Sign: N9ZTR
David E Reeves Sr
715 Emma
Belleville IL 62220

Call Sign: KB9QBG
Tammie L Reeves
715 Emma
Belleville IL 62220

Call Sign: KC9JUV

Kevin P Gasawski
1564 Erica Renee Ct
Belleville IL 622203257

Call Sign: KA9SXQ
Michael J Neiner
6209 Erie Station Rd
Belleville IL 62223

Call Sign: N9ZWB
Donald L Wilkerson
1405 Express Dr
Belleville IL 62223

Call Sign: N3NMW
John F Hilbing
2720 Fairway Dr
Belleville IL 62220

Call Sign: KC9LJB
Margaret L Riddell
9 Farthing Ln
Belleville IL 62223

Call Sign: KB9CZS
Larry G Massey
617 Fern Dr
Belleville IL 62223

Call Sign: N9TTO
Paul J Ames
7320 Foley Dr
Belleville IL 62223

Call Sign: N9KSU
Alan P Wittlich
715 Forest Ave
Belleville IL 62220

Call Sign: KE9RJ
Geoffrey L Buechler
713 Foster Dr
Belleville IL 62226

Call Sign: N9JYY
Robert S Johnson II
3304 Frank Scott Pkwy W
Belleville IL 62223

Call Sign: WA6ZCI
Ralph A Pyle
2907 Fredericka St
Belleville IL 62226

Call Sign: N9ANY
Timothy W Mc Hugh
316 Garden Blvd
Belleville IL 62220

Call Sign: N9BDK
Henry M Mihelcic
522 Garden Blvd
Belleville IL 622203658

Call Sign: KE6EVR
Donald J Dishong
2312 Greenfield Dr
Belleville IL 62221

Call Sign: KE9RH
Howard M Woodrow
6 Hanley Dr
Belleville IL 622266429

Call Sign: N8OX
Charlie R Hopkins
119 Harbor Pointe
Belleville IL 62221

Call Sign: K9RJN
John E Hickman
7 Harmony Dr
Belleville IL 62223

Call Sign: N8MAD
Richard J Hehmann
237 Hickory Ridge
Belleville IL 62223

Call Sign: KB9RKT
James C Hall
5 High Forest Dr
Belleville IL 62226

Call Sign: W9JMY
Clemence P Mudd Jr
12 High Forest Dr
Belleville IL 622264810

Call Sign: K9RKJ
Clyde R Saul
29 Hilda Ann Dr
Belleville IL 622204741

Call Sign: N9SPW
Erin L Sears
640 Hoffmann Ln
Belleville IL 62223

Call Sign: N9QHC
Eric A Sears
640 Hoffmann Ln
Belleville IL 622266962

Call Sign: WE9A
Steven H Sears
640 Hoffmann Ln
Belleville IL 622266962

Call Sign: N9PXR
John A Firse
2A Hollyhock Ln
Belleville IL 62221

Call Sign: N9HHV
Stanley B Kramkowski
144 Jardin Ct
Belleville IL 622261062

Call Sign: WB9LIJ
Doris J Seper
3400 Joyce Dr
Belleville IL 62223

Call Sign: WB9LIK
Joseph E Seper
3400 Joyce Dr
Belleville IL 62223

Call Sign: KG9LE
Wayne A Cornick
410 Kansas Ave
Belleville IL 622214944

Call Sign: KA9OLA
Helen L Pulliam
3 Kim Berlin

Belleville IL 62221

Call Sign: KA9OKZ
Robert D Pulliam
3 Kimberlin Ln
Belleville IL 62220

Call Sign: KC9SSX
Rebecca S Reed
22 Kingsten Dr
Belleville IL 62223

Call Sign: KC9MZB
James A Reed
22 Kingston Dr
Belleville IL 62223

Call Sign: KC9STZ
Kelly R Reed
22 Kingston Dr
Belleville IL 62223

Call Sign: KC9RSZ
Nancy S Reed
22 Kingston Dr
Belleville IL 62223

Call Sign: AA9C
Andrew L Fellner
1910 La Salle St
Belleville IL 62221

Call Sign: W0FAB
Jeffrey S Fabrizio
46 Lake Forest Dr
Belleville IL 62220

Call Sign: N9HOL
Richard D Friederich
131 Lake Hickory Cir
Belleville IL 62223

Call Sign: WB9GZZ
Steven G Westlund
2608 Lake Lucerne Dr
Belleville IL 622213358

Call Sign: N9VOE
Robert C Mc Bride

124 Lakeview Dr
Belleville IL 62223

Call Sign: KC9AUH
Samuel D James
15 Lakewood Dr
Belleville IL 622233156

Call Sign: W9BPN
Joseph B Otto
24 Lakewood Dr
Belleville IL 622233119

Call Sign: K9GLP
Dennis H Stroot
229 Lebanon Ave
Belleville IL 62221

Call Sign: KC9TE
Paul W Stauder
2620 Lebanon Ave
Belleville IL 62221

Call Sign: KC9JCO
Joseph D Popham
3 Lindberg Cir
Belleville IL 62221

Call Sign: N9NYD
Thomas L Becherer
12 Lindenwood Dr
Belleville IL 62220

Call Sign: N9OCQ
Carol L Becherer
12 Lindenwood Dr
Belleville IL 62223

Call Sign: KE6FDS
Jennifer J Bearden
3270 Linwood Ln
Belleville IL 62221

Call Sign: KE6FDR
Roy D Bearden
3270 Linwood Ln
Belleville IL 62221

Call Sign: KA0IXI

Spencer T Branham
63 Magnolia Dr
Belleville IL 62221

Call Sign: KB9BMM
Vincent J Saia
710 Mascoutah Ave
Belleville IL 622203727

Call Sign: W9QK
Ray D Rushing
2616 Mathilda Dr
Belleville IL 62226

Call Sign: WN9V
Don P Wittlich
55 Meadowview Dr
Belleville IL 62220

Call Sign: KC9LJA
Christopher M Wallace
5735 Memory Ln
Belleville IL 62226

Call Sign: KC9LIY
Zackary A Dickerson
5735 Memory Ln
Belleville IL 62226

Call Sign: K9LXV
Russell A Beard
1824 Menard Dr
Belleville IL 62221

Call Sign: KA9NDX
Judith A Beard
1824 Menard Dr
Belleville IL 62221

Call Sign: KD9DI
Robert A Huffman
3317 Mill Springs Rd
Belleville IL 62221

Call Sign: WA9DYY
Charles K Worley
15 Millstone Ct
Belleville IL 62221

Call Sign: N9STL
Joyce A Wilhelm
2845 Mulligan Ln
Belleville IL 62220

Call Sign: K9HUH
Ted E Wilhelm
2845 Mulligan Ln
Belleville IL 62220

Call Sign: NC9C
Douglas School ARC
2845 Mulligan Ln
Belleville IL 62220

Call Sign: W9DUG
Douglas School ARC
2845 Mulligan Ln
Belleville IL 62220

Call Sign: W9HUZ
Southern Illinois Dx Contest
Club
2845 Mulligan Ln
Belleville IL 62220

Call Sign: KC9LRO
Samuel M Williams
19 N 10th St
Belleville IL 62220

Call Sign: KB9UEB
Phillip J Sawyer
515 N 28th
Belleville IL 62226

Call Sign: AA9UB
Thomas A Hegeman
22 N 28th St
Belleville IL 62226

Call Sign: WB0RAU
Ken P Rapini
101 N 31st St
Belleville IL 62226

Call Sign: KB9VZR
Deborah A Dale
136 N 45th St

Belleville IL 62226

Call Sign: KF9PA
Gene A Pinkerton
136 N 45th St
Belleville IL 62226

Call Sign: KB9MYB
Michael V Woolard
207 N 70th St
Belleville IL 622233123

Call Sign: WB9IFR
Roy H Bischoff
200 N 72nd St
Belleville IL 62223

Call Sign: KG0QM
John M Isabella
109 N 74th 4
Belleville IL 62223

Call Sign: N9HLP
John E O Bryan
222 N 7th St
Belleville IL 62221

Call Sign: KC9RVG
Leia K Smith
901 N Allerton Rd
Belleville IL 62221

Call Sign: K9UZE
Harry E Jasper
6020 N Belt W
Belleville IL 622234225

Call Sign: N9XTQ
Thomas D Halterman
205 N Charles St
Belleville IL 622204002

Call Sign: KE9PD
August J Licourt
415 N Illinois St
Belleville IL 62220

Call Sign: WK9H
Larry J Call

32 N Indiana Ave
Belleville IL 62221

Call Sign: KB9JYB
Bryan S Miller
214 N Jackson St 17
Belleville IL 62220

Call Sign: KB9NID
Howard F Kurtz
38 N Missouri Ave
Belleville IL 62220

Call Sign: N9ZGK
Richard A Perkins
308 N Virginia Ave
Belleville IL 62220

Call Sign: KC9TVR
Brent V Bingham
412 N Virginia Ave
Belleville IL 62220

Call Sign: KA9WTL
John S Hipskind
9 Oakwood Dr
Belleville IL 62223

Call Sign: W3ED
John R Maurais
4445 Old Caseyville Rd
Belleville IL 62223

Call Sign: WA9MW
Michael H Wallace
3500 Old Collinsville Rd
Belleville IL 62226

Call Sign: W5DTR
Curtis R Williams
8900 Old St Louis Rd
Belleville IL 62223

Call Sign: KB9AAG
Theophil W Ross
1440 Optimist Ct
Belleville IL 62220

Call Sign: KB9DEQ

Ivan L Carwell Sr
110 Orchard Dr
Belleville IL 62221

Call Sign: KC5IEM
Michael P West
803 Oxen Dr
Belleville IL 62221

Call Sign: W9OFZ
Gustav H Kuether
536 Pebble Brook Ln
Belleville IL 622217604

Call Sign: W9MIQ
Gary W Byers
805 Penhurst Pl
Belleville IL 62221

Call Sign: N9XJL
Erik D Tinney
61 Periwinkle Cir
Belleville IL 62220

Call Sign: WA9MGX
Paul W Becker
1126 Pine Dr
Belleville IL 622203131

Call Sign: KE0YI
John E Sullivan
2612 Pipers Ct
Belleville IL 62221

Call Sign: N9NJY
Marcel Bechtoldt
2749 Plum Hill School Rd
Belleville IL 62221

Call Sign: KC0WVH
Tim E Periman
1413 Prairie Ave
Belleville IL 62220

Call Sign: KB9ZKJ
Rick A Johnson
2500 Richland Prairie Blvd
Belleville IL 62221

Call Sign: KB9SIA
Paul R Hertel
325 Ring Of Kerry Dr
Belleville IL 62221

Call Sign: KA9QAM
Robert J Snook
104 Roberta Ln
Belleville IL 62223

Call Sign: KC9CXV
Mark E Thurman
32 Robin Hill Ln
Belleville IL 62221

Call Sign: N9LVO
Rita D Wolff
20 Rockingham
Belleville IL 62223

Call Sign: K9TDX
Raymond A Hilmes
3315 Roland Ave
Belleville IL 62223

Call Sign: WA4YSJ
Keith D Blankenship
3701 Rolling Meadows
Belleville IL 62221

Call Sign: N3MFX
Charles F Abernathy Jr
3820 Rolling Meadows Dr
Belleville IL 622210407

Call Sign: N9GFX
Joseph L Sandy
109 Rose Marie Dr
Belleville IL 622203237

Call Sign: W9RQR
Edwin Matysik
204 S 11th St
Belleville IL 62220

Call Sign: KB9HYY
Aaron W Kenney
906 S 11th St
Belleville IL 62220

Call Sign: KC9RUI
Frank C Adams
2201 S 11th St
Belleville IL 62226

Call Sign: KB9HIW
Charles L Miller
300 S 19th St
Belleville IL 62226

Call Sign: N9NJT
Jeffery A Fears
422 S 1st St
Belleville IL 62220

Call Sign: KB9JJA
Dale F Wentz Jr
263 S 27th St
Belleville IL 62226

Call Sign: KB9PNQ
Mitzi G Wentz
263 S 27th St
Belleville IL 62226

Call Sign: WA9YQA
Melburn E Labruyere
802 S 29th St
Belleville IL 62236

Call Sign: KC9PTQ
Jason M Rumpf
19 S 30th St
Belleville IL 62226

Call Sign: N9NHN
Jeffrey E Jones
147 S 33rd St
Belleville IL 62223

Call Sign: KA9NJE
Ruth B Dehne
149 S 34th St
Belleville IL 62223

Call Sign: KB9TOZ
Walter E Sewell
135 S 35th St

Belleville IL 62226

Call Sign: N9XBU
Steve M Helwig
110 S 37th
Belleville IL 62223

Call Sign: N9WSD
Dawn M Harrison
23 S 53rd St Apt 16
Belleville IL 62223

Call Sign: KB2ARN
Thomas G Vallow
405 S 59th St Apt 5
Belleville IL 62223

Call Sign: N9FXB
David N Bowman
1006 S 5th St
Belleville IL 62220

Call Sign: KC9MZ
Randall W Bastian
1712 S Illinois St
Belleville IL 62220

Call Sign: WB0UFZ
Paul A Rickman
310 S McKinley Dr
Belleville IL 62220

Call Sign: KB9VTP
Sam R Pessin
421 S Missouri Ave
Belleville IL 62220

Call Sign: N9VCY
Michael D Owens
4306 S Park Dr
Belleville IL 62223

Call Sign: KB9VNV
Douglas School ARC
519 S Pennsylvania
Belleville IL 62220

Call Sign: KB9VOL
Douglas School ARC

519 S Pennsylvania
Belleville IL 62220

Call Sign: KE9MXV
Terry L Miller
408 S Virginia
Belleville IL 62221

Call Sign: KC9GQI
Allan C Marlow
532 S Virginia Ave
Belleville IL 62220

Call Sign: KC9UIZ
Anthony Belline
1308 Salem Dr
Belleville IL 62221

Call Sign: WB9MAL
Anthony Belline
1308 Salem Dr
Belleville IL 62221

Call Sign: N9BPK
Charles Sarkisian
2 Sandwedge Dr
Belleville IL 622203216

Call Sign: WA9TUG
G Robert Thurgood
5 Seven Iron Ct
Belleville IL 62220

Call Sign: W9GDB
Kenneth L Vaughn
1 Shady Ln
Belleville IL 62221

Call Sign: N9NJW
Janice L Peak
108 Sheffield Dr
Belleville IL 62223

Call Sign: N9HKG
Leonard A Peak
108 Sheffield Dr
Belleville IL 62223

Call Sign: KB9PNW

Martin M Bertulis
1005 Shepherd Dr
Belleville IL 62223

Call Sign: AB9SF
David S Penney
2628 Sierra Dr Apt B
Belleville IL 62221

Call Sign: KA0KOS
Richard G Engel
20 Signal Point
Belleville IL 622231234

Call Sign: K9RGE
Richard G Engel
20 Signal Point
Belleville IL 622231234

Call Sign: KC9DEW
James N Lougeay
10 Smalling Ct
Belleville IL 622232124

Call Sign: KC9MYX
Bonnie R Naylor
2811 Smokehouse Way
Belleville IL 62221

Call Sign: K9JHQ
Carl B Sigler
420 Springdale Dr
Belleville IL 62223

Call Sign: KC5NIO
John E Davis
1239 State St Rd
Belleville IL 62220

Call Sign: KC0DDS
Jerome V Ray Jr
1430 State St Rd
Belleville IL 622202854

Call Sign: KG9CD
Bruce E Reppert
956 Stone Creek Ln
Belleville IL 62223

Call Sign: KC9RUR
Gwen L Goodrich
241 Summers Trace
Belleville IL 62220

Call Sign: KB9AAF
Robert O Lee
336 Sumter Dr
Belleville IL 62221

Call Sign: N9HCD
Phyllis F Lee
336 Sumter Dr
Belleville IL 622215748

Call Sign: N9VDL
Christopher S Musselman
500 Sunrise Dr Apt 500
Belleville IL 62220

Call Sign: KB9CII
La Donne M Portell
23 Superior Dr
Belleville IL 62223

Call Sign: KB9CIJ
Ronald L Mayberry
23 Superior Dr
Belleville IL 62223

Call Sign: N0UQC
Dennis L Myracle
19 Superior Dr
Belleville IL 62223

Call Sign: NR6U
Frederick O Edgar
30 Terrace Dr
Belleville IL 62223

Call Sign: KA9KAY
Leslie E Welch
616 Valencia Dr
Belleville IL 62223

Call Sign: W9QDM
Clarence E Streck
52 Van Rue Dr
Belleville IL 62220

Call Sign: WI9S
Richard L Joy
217 Voss Pl
Belleville IL 62220

Call Sign: KC9OCB
Prime Ara
217 Voss Pl
Belleville IL 62220

Call Sign: WA9TVJ
Charles M Pulliam
3401 W A St
Belleville IL 622236213

Call Sign: WA9TVM
Mary M Pulliam
3401 W A St
Belleville IL 622236213

Call Sign: N9IPG
Delmar T Hug
607 W Adams St
Belleville IL 62220

Call Sign: WC9AAE
Belleville St Clair Co Il Cd
321 W F St
Belleville IL 62220

Call Sign: KC9PTF
John M Brendel
3204 W Main St
Belleville IL 62226

Call Sign: KA9VKE
Howard D Mize
4107 W Main St
Belleville IL 62223

Call Sign: N9UDY
Michael S Beuckman
7920 W Washington
Belleville IL 62223

Call Sign: KC9RZK
Robert P Mueller Jr
310 Wabash Ave

Belleville IL 62220

Call Sign: K9COT
Robert P Mueller Jr
310 Wabash Ave
Belleville IL 62220

Call Sign: N3YDM
William L Rainbolt
613 Wabash Ave
Belleville IL 62220

Call Sign: KC9RVE
Gary S Rojas
10 Whiteside Dr
Belleville IL 62221

Call Sign: KB4FIO
Larry W Wessels
29 Whiteside Dr
Belleville IL 62221

Call Sign: KB9VTO
Kenneth E Rickert
3140 Wild Flower Ln
Belleville IL 62221

Call Sign: K9VTO
Kenneth E Rickert
3140 Wild Flower Ln
Belleville IL 62221

Call Sign: KC9FHZ
Charles W Marshall
413 Williamsburg Dr
Belleville IL 62221

Call Sign: WB9JVE
Thomas E Downey
5 Willow Brook
Belleville IL 62221

Call Sign: N9WSE
Joseph P Alleca
549 Windrift Dr
Belleville IL 62221

Call Sign: N9WSC
Christopher D Atkins

6 Yorkshire 4
Belleville IL 62221

Call Sign: KB9PSB
Cary M Eschmann
Belleville IL 62222

Call Sign: WB9OLY
Henry R Morris
Belleville IL 62223

Call Sign: KA0WBL
Hilda A Koluch
Belleville IL 622228222

Call Sign: KA0WBM
Stephen C Koluch
Belleville IL 622228222

Call Sign: KB9YYB
Walter J Johnson
528 Schweer Ct
Bellevue IL 61604

FCC Amateur Radio Licenses in Bellflower

Call Sign: KB9BE
Robert C Fairchild
Rr 1 Box 38
Bellflower IL 617243715

Call Sign: AA9UF
John E Gercken
35998 E 400 N Rd
Bellflower IL 617249674

Call Sign: KB9LCD
Scott D W Gercken
35998 E 400 N Rd
Bellflower IL 617249674

Call Sign: KB9ZDR
Charles J Cole
4710 N 3800 E Rd
Bellflower IL 61724

Call Sign: N9XPH
Paul L Neubauer

406 W Center St
Bellflower IL 61724

Call Sign: KC9FJM
Wesley D Schield
Bellflower IL 61724

FCC Amateur Radio Licenses in Bellmont

Call Sign: KC9SKP
Colby C Rigg
Bellmont IL 62811

FCC Amateur Radio Licenses in Belvidere

Call Sign: N9PCK
William W Carder
11222 Abbotsford Pl
Belvidere IL 61008

Call Sign: W9MF
Mark F Bradley
11563 Aberdeen Rd
Belvidere IL 61008

Call Sign: KC9VBU
Audrey S Pearson
2556 Anderson Dr
Belvidere IL 61008

Call Sign: KB9VQF
Timothy R Pearson
2556 Anderson Dr
Belvidere IL 61008

Call Sign: N9OCT
Fred D Sturges
2565 Anderson Dr
Belvidere IL 61008

Call Sign: N9WDP
Patricia P Sturges
2565 Anderson Dr
Belvidere IL 61008

Call Sign: AB9SX
James J Holich

315 Beacon Dr
Belvidere IL 61008

Call Sign: N6ALY
Gene A Rampenthal
336 Beacon Dr
Belvidere IL 61008

Call Sign: W9VOV
Ned A Mc Donald
9112 Beaver Valley Rd
Belvidere IL 61008

Call Sign: N9MXQ
Eugene E Young
10083 Beaver Valley Rd
Belvidere IL 61008

Call Sign: KB9TTD
Scott W Nettgen
11019 Beloit Rd
Belvidere IL 61008

Call Sign: KB9YYG
Todd L Walberg
120 Burgess St
Belvidere IL 61008

Call Sign: K9YG
Todd L Walberg
120 Burgess St
Belvidere IL 61008

Call Sign: KC9BCE
Richard H Nelson
1977 Bus 20 W
Belvidere IL 61008

Call Sign: N9ZO
Richard H Nelson
1977 Bus 20 W
Belvidere IL 61008

Call Sign: N9NGW
Jon A Seymour
2532 Bypass 20
Belvidere IL 61008

Call Sign: KC9VDH

Sather M Ranum
2340 Cairnwell Dr
Belvidere IL 61008

Call Sign: KC9RML
Keith A Tracey
1120 Caswell St
Belvidere IL 61008

Call Sign: N9KUX
Robert S Giesecke
1155 Caswell St
Belvidere IL 61008

Call Sign: KA9CCY
Betty D Grispino
2218 Clearwater Dr
Belvidere IL 61008

Call Sign: WO9F
James G Grispino
2218 Clearwater Dr
Belvidere IL 61008

Call Sign: WD9FIM
David M Nicoloff
2727 Clines Ford Dr
Belvidere IL 610087890

Call Sign: N9XVV
Gregory W Kelm
6042 Dar Mae Ln
Belvidere IL 61008

Call Sign: AB9FS
Dwight A Zeka
2116 Davis Dr
Belvidere IL 61008

Call Sign: KA9ESU
David C Mienert
110 E 4th St
Belvidere IL 61008

Call Sign: KA9QDE
George R Eckelbarger Jr
920 E 4th St
Belvidere IL 61008

Call Sign: WB9PMM
Claude D Horsman
616 E Jackson St
Belvidere IL 61008

Call Sign: N9UHF
John E Mc Gann
1015 E Linoln Ave
Belvidere IL 61008

Call Sign: KC2CFG
John H Anderson
618 East Ave
Belvidere IL 61008

Call Sign: KC9TOC
Nicholas J Hughart
917 East Ave
Belvidere IL 61008

Call Sign: WB9WOM
Kenneth L Robertson
1317 East Ave
Belvidere IL 61008

Call Sign: N9KTM
Lawrence H Orvis
3208 Eastwood Ln
Belvidere IL 61008

Call Sign: K8GGN
Alan A Farlee
3703 Eastwood Ln
Belvidere IL 610087851

Call Sign: KC9MXQ
Charles W Daringer Sr
4420 Genoa Rd
Belvidere IL 61008

Call Sign: K9BUA
Wesley B Oliver
1615 Glen Elms Dr
Belvidere IL 61008

Call Sign: W9JAV
Ervin A Koenig
504 Glenwood Dr
Belvidere IL 61008

Call Sign: KC9QLQ
Kevin W Schauer
9565 Henninger Dr
Belvidere IL 61008

Call Sign: WB9EMS
Kevin W Schauer
9565 Henninger Dr
Belvidere IL 61008

Call Sign: N9FS
Floyd Schmidt
3051 Hiddengreen Dr
Belvidere IL 610089089

Call Sign: KB9VFK
Anthony J Baker
509 Highland St
Belvidere IL 61008

Call Sign: KC9LCF
Roger S Terhune
805 Indian Dancer Trl
Belvidere IL 61008

Call Sign: N9DLO
Michael A Draheim
1553 Ipsen Rd
Belvidere IL 61008

Call Sign: N9VJN
Charles S Libby
615 Jamestown Ave
Belvidere IL 61008

Call Sign: KC9SDQ
Mark R Libby
615 Jamestown Ave
Belvidere IL 61008

Call Sign: WB9YZN
David P Baker Jr
817 Jamestown Ave
Belvidere IL 61008

Call Sign: KC9ONI
Dennis R Marak
918 Johnson Ct

Belvidere IL 61008

Call Sign: K9PK
Richard B Ludwig
1006 Johnson Ct
Belvidere IL 61008

Call Sign: KB9JEB
Raymond A Hippard
2892 Karr Rd
Belvidere IL 61008

Call Sign: KB9DXC
Victor S Moore
214 Lynne Ln
Belvidere IL 61008

Call Sign: WA9YRF
Kenneth F Irwin
11171 Meadowlark Ln
Belvidere IL 61008

Call Sign: KC9QFB
Jeffrey S Lightfoot
230 N Appleton Rd
Belvidere IL 61008

Call Sign: WR9V
Peter A Knight
424 N Main St
Belvidere IL 61008

Call Sign: KC9KRH
Jeffery S Rubenzer
226 N State St
Belvidere IL 61008

Call Sign: KC9TQP
Sean M Brooks
704 N State St
Belvidere IL 61008

Call Sign: KB9MTL
Joseph T Saenz
925 Nettie St
Belvidere IL 61008

Call Sign: W9FLY
Thomas M Porter

901 Nevin Ct
Belvidere IL 61008

Call Sign: KA9ZUY
Jerolyn J Daringer
1708 Newburg Rd
Belvidere IL 61008

Call Sign: KA9IMY
Harold R Kearney
345 Oak St
Belvidere IL 61008

Call Sign: KB9DJJ
Lee R Peterson III
2010 Oakbrook Dr
Belvidere IL 61008

Call Sign: N9LSH
Bruce J Zediker
1044 Pearl St
Belvidere IL 61008

Call Sign: KB9MCX
Paul E Larsen
3290 Pheasant Ln
Belvidere IL 61008

Call Sign: WA9GWM
Big Thunder ARC
3290 Pheasant Ln
Belvidere IL 61008

Call Sign: KB9VDJ
Derek E Larsen
3290 Pheasant Ln
Belvidere IL 610089683

Call Sign: N9ENA
Jonathan G Fast
424 Royal Ave
Belvidere IL 61008

Call Sign: KI9DX
Jonathan G Fast
424 Royal Ave
Belvidere IL 61008

Call Sign: N9ORM

Mark N Vondrasek
2021 Sawyer Rd
Belvidere IL 61008

Call Sign: KB9ZFS
John E Mueller
3145 Shattuck Rd
Belvidere IL 61008

Call Sign: N9FTY
Howard A Luse
5282 Shattuck Rd
Belvidere IL 61008

Call Sign: N9EYA
Jeanne W Luse
5282 Shattuck Rd
Belvidere IL 61008

Call Sign: KB9SMI
Robert E Ellsworth Jr
411 Spruce Dr
Belvidere IL 61008

Call Sign: KC9UQJ
Craig A Graham
9369 Steeplebush Dr
Belvidere IL 61008

Call Sign: WB9TZX
Ledo B Lucietto
508 Trumans Ct
Belvidere IL 61008

Call Sign: WB9TZW
Elaine E Lucietto
508 Trumans Ct
Belvidere IL 610081487

Call Sign: WA9HLJ
Gerald P Reed
1221 Union Ave
Belvidere IL 61008

Call Sign: N9EYC
Bruce G Spencer Sr
704 W 10th St
Belvidere IL 610085506

Call Sign: KB9ZZZ
Terry Abdelnour
902 W 12th St
Belvidere IL 61008

Call Sign: K9ORU
Michael K George
627 W 8th St
Belvidere IL 610085533

Call Sign: KG4ZKL
Linda M Varga
1780 W Chrysler Dr
Belvidere IL 610086019

Call Sign: N9CFM
Derek H Volk
523 W Lincoln Ave
Belvidere IL 61008

Call Sign: N9OJR
Erik C Morse
526 W Madison St
Belvidere IL 61008

Call Sign: N9SIA
James D Reynolds
950 Walnut St
Belvidere IL 61008

Call Sign: K9FRP
James E Baker
2295 West Ct
Belvidere IL 61008

Call Sign: KB9VZA
Duane A Powell
722 Whitney Blvd
Belvidere IL 61008

Call Sign: KA9LML
Charlotte A Robertson
Belvidere IL 61008

Call Sign: N9KUZ
David R Babb
Belvidere IL 61008

Call Sign: W9VMO

Charles M Wyndham
Belvidere IL 610080954

Call Sign: KC5BRQ
Charles M Wyndham IV
Belvidere IL 610080954

FCC Amateur Radio Licenses in Bement

Call Sign: KB9WEU
Shawn M Bartley
20 Carriage Pl
Bement IL 61813

Call Sign: KB9WFA
Jason W Crowley
21 Carriage Pl
Bement IL 61813

Call Sign: K9SZ
Joseph E Wittmer
101 E Mansfield St
Bement IL 61813

Call Sign: KB9SIZ
Joseph E Wittmer
649 N High
Bement IL 61813

Call Sign: KC9KND
Jason M Shumard
449 N Sangamon
Bement IL 61813

Call Sign: KB9GLL
Clara K York
449 S Morgan
Bement IL 61813

Call Sign: WA9GBB
Lynn M Crook
265 W Moultrie St
Bement IL 61813

Call Sign: KB9HCW
Marc A Manint
233 W William
Bement IL 61813

Call Sign: KC9UET
Robyn J Lyons
364 W Wilson St
Bement IL 61813

Call Sign: KB9VSI
Bruce K Nesset
364 W Wilson St
Bement IL 618131256

Call Sign: KC9BAA
Burr Nelson
Bement IL 61813

Call Sign: KC9AZZ
Virginia A Dahms
Bement IL 61813

Call Sign: KD9E
Virginia A Dahms
Bement IL 61813

FCC Amateur Radio Licenses in Benld

Call Sign: K9MYQ
Stephen Pollo
108 N Eight St
Benld IL 62009

Call Sign: N9YHM
Preston S Morse
712 N Main
Benld IL 62009

Call Sign: KB9VXQ
Tracy S Lambeth
404 S 4th St
Benld IL 62009

FCC Amateur Radio Licenses in Benson

Call Sign: N9JPB
Timothy W Smith
109 W Tr 116
Benson IL 61516

FCC Amateur Radio Licenses in Benton

Call Sign: KC9PCH
Darrell L Roberts
9364 Aden St
Benton IL 62812

Call Sign: KB9UCX
Judith A Rose
18592 Akin Blacktop
Benton IL 62812

Call Sign: KB9ADK
Jerry L Clayton Sr
800 Aubert St
Benton IL 62812

Call Sign: KB9VIX
Carla K Clayton
800 Aubert St
Benton IL 628123454

Call Sign: KB5VDF
John S Brown
8817 Baxter Rd
Benton IL 62812

Call Sign: KC9SXA
Brent M Mclain
13036 Benton Camp Rd
Benton IL 62812

Call Sign: N9XLK
Phillip A Laurent
Rr 3 Box 119 Bl
Benton IL 62812

Call Sign: WA9CFT
Kenneth E Williams
Rr 3 Box 143
Benton IL 62812

Call Sign: WA9BWW
Roger A Whobrey
R 3 Box 201B
Benton IL 62812

Call Sign: KB9DZH

Peter J Cunningham
R 3 Box 291A
Benton IL 62812

Call Sign: KC9AYE
Alex D Barnfield
209 Brinley St
Benton IL 62812

Call Sign: KC9SWZ
Melonie K Winemiller
213 Brinley St
Benton IL 62812

Call Sign: KC9EHG
Richard E Logsdon
715 Carbon
Benton IL 62812

Call Sign: KC9BBS
Jeremy L Richardson
509 Clearview Pl
Benton IL 62812

Call Sign: KC9RLM
Randy L Mitchell
13249 E Illinois St
Benton IL 62812

Call Sign: KC9LVW
Lena S Bennett
530 E Main
Benton IL 62812

Call Sign: KC9LUA
Billy G Bennett
530 E Main
Benton IL 62812

Call Sign: KA9ADA
Fred R Gulley
202 E Webster Ave
Benton IL 62812

Call Sign: W9PJF
Paul Swearingen
704 E Webster St
Benton IL 62812

Call Sign: KC9OJB
Wayne A Little John
1004 E Webster St
Benton IL 62812

Call Sign: KB9WDI
David D Kinsey
10837 Eakin Grove Rd
Benton IL 62812

Call Sign: KC9LUC
William T Tennison
1029 Enterprise
Benton IL 62812

Call Sign: N9YPJ
Dennis L Kinkade
1402 Espy St
Benton IL 62812

Call Sign: KC9RKR
Amy B Dollins
7539 Hill City Rd
Benton IL 62812

Call Sign: KC9TPS
Mackenzi A Dollins
7539 Hill City Rd
Benton IL 62812

Call Sign: KC9RCG
Michael L Dollins
7539 Hill City Rd
Benton IL 62812

Call Sign: KC9UAZ
Michaela L Dollins
7539 Hill City Rd
Benton IL 62812

Call Sign: KC9IRW
Lori L Robertson
13959 Hwy 14
Benton IL 62812

Call Sign: W9FX
Bradley A Pioveson
301 Kirsch St
Benton IL 62812

Call Sign: KC9RZG
Illinois Ecom Group
301 Kirsch St
Benton IL 62812

Call Sign: NC9IL
Illinois Ecom Group
301 Kirsch St
Benton IL 62812

Call Sign: KC9SQP
Matthew D Hall
15410 Lake Moses Ln
Benton IL 62812

Call Sign: KC9SCX
Terrence J Hall
15410 Lake Moses Ln
Benton IL 62812

Call Sign: KC9RYN
Betty A Batts
707 Lickliter St
Benton IL 62812

Call Sign: KC9IDV
Connie S Sample
11326 Lincoln Rd
Benton IL 62812

Call Sign: KA9VBB
Fredrick L Sample
11326 Lincoln Rd
Benton IL 62812

Call Sign: N9FEY
Ira B Ashby
904 Madison St
Benton IL 62812

Call Sign: WD9APY
Joseph H Hayes
400 Marshal
Benton IL 62812

Call Sign: KC9OJD
Chet S Head
401 McFall Ave

Benton IL 62812

Call Sign: KB9ZZL
Donnie R Cogdill
610 N 8th St
Benton IL 62812

Call Sign: WA0OTU
Thomas J Dickerson
203 N 9th St
Benton IL 62812

Call Sign: W9GAR
Gary D Richardson
402 N 9th St
Benton IL 62812

Call Sign: N9ITW
Ricky A Robinson
12426 N Benton Rd
Benton IL 62812

Call Sign: KC9EYI
Edward L Richardson II
12506 N Benton Rd
Benton IL 62812

Call Sign: KC9BIE
Shannon D Hearst
4720 N Deering Rd
Benton IL 62812

Call Sign: KC9HCC
Christina R Barger
1409 N Della Apt D
Benton IL 62812

Call Sign: KC9UDB
Charles A Green
507 N Grand
Benton IL 62812

Call Sign: KC9KCF
Mark A Hall
1101 N Hickman
Benton IL 62812

Call Sign: N9TPV
Ricky A Fitzpatrick

1102 N Hickman
Benton IL 62812

Call Sign: KC9KCE
Sherry L Hall
1101 N Hickman St
Benton IL 62812

Call Sign: KC9TBN
David A Hartline
1409 N Lincoln Dr
Benton IL 62812

Call Sign: AB9ZC
David A Hartline
1409 N Lincoln Dr
Benton IL 62812

Call Sign: W9KAC
George W Lockin
9871 N Stuyvesant Rd
Benton IL 628125911

Call Sign: KC9LSB
Charles I Prior Jr
18101 Prior Ln
Benton IL 62812

Call Sign: KA9F
Charles I Prior Jr
18101 Prior Ln
Benton IL 62812

Call Sign: KC9RYM
Teri E Rice
1125 Rt 14 W
Benton IL 62812

Call Sign: KC9KWJ
John D Owens
413 S Aiken St
Benton IL 62812

Call Sign: KB9PVP
Randy L Mitchell
207 S Duquoin St
Benton IL 62812

Call Sign: KB9BKG

Christopher D Smith
407 S Layman St
Benton IL 62812

Call Sign: KC9FVJ
David H Rotolo
1207 S Main
Benton IL 62812

Call Sign: KE4GSS
Barry C Choisser
1301 S Main Apt A
Benton IL 62812

Call Sign: WD9CHU
David F Daisy
1002 S Pope St
Benton IL 61843

Call Sign: KC9EHF
Robbie T Wyant
412 S Stotlar
Benton IL 62812

Call Sign: KC9FVK
Garret K Robertson
13959 State Hwy 14
Benton IL 62812

Call Sign: KC9OIK
Southern Illinois Long Wire
Association
13959 State Hwy 14
Benton IL 62812

Call Sign: K9SIL
Southern Illinois Long Wire
Association
13959 State Hwy 14
Benton IL 62812

Call Sign: KC9LSC
Butch L Carter
1405 Vale St
Benton IL 62812

Call Sign: AB9XB
Butch L Carter
1405 Vale St

Benton IL 62812

Call Sign: KC9UEX
Crystal M Carter
1405 Vale St
Benton IL 62812

Call Sign: KC9BZX
Al Shemonia
1420 Vale St
Benton IL 62812

Call Sign: W9SFA
Al Shemonia
1420 Vale St
Benton IL 62812

Call Sign: AA9AZ
Al Shemonia
1420 Vale St
Benton IL 62812

Call Sign: W9GC
Al Shemonia
1420 Vale St
Benton IL 62812

Call Sign: KC9VRX
Raymond T Powell Jr
1420 Vale St
Benton IL 62812

Call Sign: N4FAA
Daniel N Peek
19380 W Bobtail
Benton IL 62812

Call Sign: KC9LUB
Carl W Stipes
408 W Church St
Benton IL 62812

Call Sign: WD9DSA
David E Stowers
513 W Washington St
Benton IL 628121384

Call Sign: KC9GVS
Timothy S Hammond

730 W Webster St
Benton IL 62812

Call Sign: KC9OJC
Arthur C Dobrzynski
Benton IL 62812

Call Sign: KC9UUP
Erik D Phelps
Benton IL 62812

Call Sign: KC9UYR
Erik D Phelps
Benton IL 62812

Call Sign: KC9OJA
Patricia J Dobrzynski
Benton IL 62812

FCC Amateur Radio Licenses in Berwick

Call Sign: WD9IWN
Dan P Massingill
920 140th St
Berwick IL 61417

FCC Amateur Radio Licenses in Bethalto

Call Sign: KC9RIL
Holly M Hugghins
619 2nd St
Bethalto IL 62010

Call Sign: W9HUG
Holly M Hugghins
619 2nd St
Bethalto IL 62010

Call Sign: W4HUG
Benjamin B Hugghins
619 2nd St
Bethalto IL 62010

Call Sign: N9YRH
Charles H Lunceford Jr
4800 2nd St
Bethalto IL 62010

Call Sign: KB9OJQ
Sherri S Lunceford
4800 2nd St
Bethalto IL 62010

Call Sign: N9QEA
Daniel W Lowe
833 Albers Ln
Bethalto IL 62010

Call Sign: KA0OOA
Dennis M Weaver
808 Briarwood Dr
Bethalto IL 62010

Call Sign: K9HAM
Lewis And Clark Radio Club
109 Canterbury St
Bethalto IL 620101707

Call Sign: WA9RD
Dennis D Hutchins
109 Canterbury St
Bethalto IL 620101707

Call Sign: N9UJM
Michael D Bond
417 Georgia St
Bethalto IL 62010

Call Sign: KB0NNN
Eugene K Seibel
816 Homm
Bethalto IL 62010

Call Sign: KC9KKV
Justin M Proctor
902 Kansas St
Bethalto IL 62010

Call Sign: K9QME
Lyndel L Helmkamp
215 Lakeside Dr
Bethalto IL 620102011

Call Sign: WA9AXO
Richard L Largen
4353 McCoy Rd

Bethalto IL 62010

Call Sign: WD9E
Elmer R Zitzman
610 Montana
Bethalto IL 62010

Call Sign: N1NYQ
Alan H Gaffney
401 Montana St
Bethalto IL 62010

Call Sign: N9THE
Russell L Gentry
443 Park Ave
Bethalto IL 62010

Call Sign: WB9FQU
Robert L Stricklin
122 Pickett
Bethalto IL 620101243

Call Sign: KC9BCL
Jan C Harmon
308 Sanders St
Bethalto IL 62010

Call Sign: K2KFW
Richard J Mersinger
821 Sequoia
Bethalto IL 62010

Call Sign: W9RJJ
Richard J Mersinger
821 Sequoia
Bethalto IL 62010

Call Sign: N9HYC
Gordon S Kivett
1110 W Corbin
Bethalto IL 62010

Call Sign: N9VHL
Christopher N Wewetzer
4618 Wood Rd
Bethalto IL 62010

Call Sign: KC9PAT
Patrick P Roth

500 Wyoming
Bethalto IL 62010

Call Sign: KB9BEN
Jason C Travis
Bethalto IL 62010

FCC Amateur Radio Licenses in Bethany

Call Sign: KB9OAT
Lisa M Perry
36 Chickadee Ct E
Bethany IL 61914

Call Sign: N9VAG
Lawrence R Dunlap
Bethany IL 61914

Call Sign: AE5JF
Wava E Owens
Bethany IL 61914

FCC Amateur Radio Licenses in Biggsville

Call Sign: N5AXQ
Darrell R Elsea
Rr 1 Box 118
Biggsville IL 61418

Call Sign: KC9PJD
Robert D Hill
Rr 1 Box 266
Biggsville IL 61418

Call Sign: K9DVP
Robert D Hill
Rr 1 Box 266
Biggsville IL 61418

Call Sign: N9TLH
Greg S Smith
Rr 1 Box 366 Biggsville
Biggsville IL 61418

FCC Amateur Radio Licenses in Bingham

Call Sign: KC9LEI
Karen S Hicks
Rr 1 Box 27
Bingham IL 62011

FCC Amateur Radio Licenses in Bismarck

Call Sign: KB9AEK
Charles E Cauley
21535 E 2300 N Rd
Bismarck IL 61814

Call Sign: KB9AEL
Julia A Cauley
21535 E 2300 N Rd
Bismarck IL 61814

Call Sign: KB9DAZ
Ronald J Spicer
Box 115 Illinois St
Bismarck IL 61814

FCC Amateur Radio Licenses in Blandinsville

Call Sign: KT9Z
Sanderson I Keithley
Box 164 Chestnut St
Blandinsville IL 61420

Call Sign: K9HLT
John E Morrison
715 W Adams St
Blandinsville IL 61420

Call Sign: K9IEA
Everett E Luster
Blandinsville IL 61420

FCC Amateur Radio Licenses in Bloomington

Call Sign: N9FHT
Martha I Revis
1243 12th St Hilltop Ct
Bloomington IL 61704

Call Sign: W9NOE

Steven M Noe
711 7th St Hilltop
Bloomington IL 61704

Call Sign: KA9WCH
Robert A Breen
2206 Altoona Rd
Bloomington IL 61704

Call Sign: N9HCB
Julie A Wilcoxson
2313 Anchor Dr
Bloomington IL 61701

Call Sign: KB9CAY
Adam N Lieberman
705 Arcadia Dr Apt 4
Bloomington IL 61704

Call Sign: W9TI
Steven D Snyder
2705 Ark Dr
Bloomington IL 61704

Call Sign: KF9P
Charles E Justice
3504 Armstrong Dr
Bloomington IL 61704

Call Sign: N9PSV
James L Altshue
301 Ave F Hilltop Tr Ct
Bloomington IL 61704

Call Sign: KC9NHL
Jonathan D Maurer
3708 Baldocchi Dr
Bloomington IL 61704

Call Sign: KB7UM
Howard W Mammen
1008 Barker St
Bloomington IL 61701

Call Sign: KT4SO
Troy A Shealy
210 Beacon Cir
Bloomington IL 61704

Call Sign: KC9PWJ
Andrea J O'Brien
1327 Beverly Ln
Bloomington IL 61701

Call Sign: KA9ESQ
Glenn E Beyer
19 Boardwalk Cir
Bloomington IL 61701

Call Sign: KA9RTW
Adrienne O Ives
Rr 1 Box 104
Bloomington IL 61704

Call Sign: N9FUG
Timothy R Ives
Rr 1 Box 104
Bloomington IL 61704

Call Sign: WA9TIQ
Martin Ohler
Rr 4 Box 104
Bloomington IL 61704

Call Sign: KB9JTI
Eugene C Sauley
Rr 1 Box 143
Bloomington IL 61704

Call Sign: WA9GCF
Leonard M Wrice
Rr 13 Box 155
Bloomington IL 61704

Call Sign: W9AUO
Ben F Frish
R 20 Box 338
Bloomington IL 61701

Call Sign: NF9X
Carl L Baines
14543 Brian Dr
Bloomington IL 61704

Call Sign: K8CMJ
James R Johnson
20 Brickyard Dr J 7
Bloomington IL 61701

Call Sign: W9CMJ
James R Johnson
20 Brickyard Dr J 7
Bloomington IL 61701

Call Sign: KB8YGY
Alana J Bourgond
2713 Brighton Ln
Bloomington IL 617048231

Call Sign: N9OIE
Bonnie J Shadid
1002 Broadmoor Dr
Bloomington IL 61704

Call Sign: WB9LQX
James H Isom
1203 Broadmoor Dr
Bloomington IL 61704

Call Sign: KB9PJR
Ole N Ibsen II
1211 Broadmoor Dr
Bloomington IL 61704

Call Sign: KC9ILA
David B Philipsen
13 Brookridge Ct
Bloomington IL 61704

Call Sign: K1DBP
David B Philipsen
13 Brookridge Ct
Bloomington IL 61704

Call Sign: KC9ILA
David B Philipsen
13 Brookridge Ct
Bloomington IL 61704

Call Sign: N9PE
Paul E Hammond
22 Brookshire
Bloomington IL 61704

Call Sign: WA9BJU
Gary L Frankeberger
15B Brookshire Green St

Bloomington IL 61704

Call Sign: N9EKZ
Leland S Hickman
15 B Brookshire Grn
Bloomington IL 61704

Call Sign: N9BZL
Rodney A Fowler
109 Buttercup Way
Bloomington IL 61704

Call Sign: KB9DUW
Kathryn S Fowler
109 Buttercup Way
Bloomington IL 617047264

Call Sign: KC9ERO
Raymond S Webb
1224 Cadwell Dr
Bloomington IL 617043682

Call Sign: AB9IA
Raymond S Webb
1224 Cadwell Dr
Bloomington IL 617043682

Call Sign: AC9H
Raymond S Webb
1224 Cadwell Dr
Bloomington IL 617043682

Call Sign: N9VIV
Russell P Sauve
24 Cameron Ct
Bloomington IL 61704

Call Sign: WD9IED
Richard K Utter
2811 Capen Dr
Bloomington IL 61704

Call Sign: NX9M
Kenneth G Teutsch
2923 Capen Dr
Bloomington IL 617046217

Call Sign: N9CGF
Linda S Teutsch

2923 Capen Dr
Bloomington IL 617046217

Call Sign: N9ZSA
Perry D Walker
9571 Challenger Dr
Bloomington IL 61704

Call Sign: KB9QLE
Jean F Jackman
1314 Challis Ct
Bloomington IL 61704

Call Sign: KB9SUT
Tami M Jackman
1314 Challis Ct
Bloomington IL 61704

Call Sign: N9JRH
Kathleen S Peelman
1202 Challis Dr
Bloomington IL 61704

Call Sign: N9JRF
Paul E Peelman
1202 Challis Dr
Bloomington IL 61704

Call Sign: K0FMK
Steven V Davis
4 Chatsford Ct
Bloomington IL 61704

Call Sign: N9YUQ
Donald A Pehlke
8772 Cherokee Cir
Bloomington IL 61704

Call Sign: KB0MGB
Lori M Clemens
2 Christopher Way Apt 11
Bloomington IL 61704

Call Sign: N9RBM
Kevin J Page
2509 Clearwater Ave
Bloomington IL 61704

Call Sign: KC9EIE

Kevin J Page
2509 Clearwater Ave
Bloomington IL 61704

Call Sign: KC9HGI
Jonathan C Dassow
3004 Clearwater Ave Apt 5
Bloomington IL 61704

Call Sign: KA9RQX
Regina L Fernandez
1409 Cloud
Bloomington IL 61701

Call Sign: KC9GF
Edward J Deutsch
1409 Cloud St
Bloomington IL 61701

Call Sign: KB9YSH
Michael S Reid
1214 Colonial Ave
Bloomington IL 61701

Call Sign: NB9X
Daniel K Prescott Sr
115 Conley Cir
Bloomington IL 61701

Call Sign: K9OPQ
Andrew M Kraut
1904 Cottage Ave
Bloomington IL 617011419

Call Sign: KX9TS
Troy A Shealy
15919 Crestwicke Dr
Bloomington IL 61705

Call Sign: N0ZOZ
Eric B Hodges
27 Crosswinds Ct
Bloomington IL 61704

Call Sign: N9XAQ
Thomas P Ledgerwood
1317 Crown Ct
Bloomington IL 61704

Call Sign: W9LSI
H Paxton Bowers
606 Delmar Ln
Bloomington IL 617012105

Call Sign: KC9ELL
Douglas L Curtis
312 Deville Dr
Bloomington IL 61704

Call Sign: KA9ROY
Becky S Baker
1217 Dianne Dr
Bloomington IL 61704

Call Sign: WB9EDL
James A Baker
1217 Dianne Dr
Bloomington IL 61704

Call Sign: KA9ZMZ
Theodore S Rossiter
1315 Dianne Dr
Bloomington IL 61704

Call Sign: KM9L
Denny R Chestney
1212 Dogwood
Bloomington IL 61701

Call Sign: N9JNS
Sharon R Chestney
1212 Dogwood Ln
Bloomington IL 61701

Call Sign: N9ETZ
Stacy R Barton
1212 Dogwood Ln
Bloomington IL 61704

Call Sign: KC9HXQ
Stephen A Newbold
1503 Dover Rd
Bloomington IL 61704

Call Sign: N9GIT
Janice D Talkington
9 Downing Cir
Bloomington IL 61704

Call Sign: KC9DCN
Jeffrey E Telling
806 Durham Dr
Bloomington IL 61704

Call Sign: WB9TCS
Walter J Tatar Jr
23800 E 1300 N N Rd
Bloomington IL 61704

Call Sign: KC9SUJ
Kathy A Grimes
14231 E 850 N Rd
Bloomington IL 617055660

Call Sign: WA9BKB
Barbara B Dillingham
1508 E Emerson
Bloomington IL 61701

Call Sign: W9LMJ
L Everett Dillingham
1508 E Emerson
Bloomington IL 617012056

Call Sign: WD9FTV
General Telephone Employees
ARC
1312 E Empire St
Bloomington IL 61701

Call Sign: KC9RIN
Anthony J Sholtis
605 E Front St Apt 1A
Bloomington IL 61701

Call Sign: NF9O
Gerald L Hamlow
510 E Graham
Bloomington IL 61701

Call Sign: N9COI
Michael O Keist
418 E Grove
Bloomington IL 61701

Call Sign: K0VOM
Drexel H Turner

1512 E Grove
Bloomington IL 61701

Call Sign: KA3BQE
Alexandre Polozoff
1401 E Grove St
Bloomington IL 61701

Call Sign: KB9HXS
Brad S Kraft
2023 E Jackson Apt 3
Bloomington IL 61701

Call Sign: KB9ZUL
Griffin J Hammond
1505 E Jackson St
Bloomington IL 61701

Call Sign: WA9ZXZ
Terry L Dewasme
1209 E Jefferson
Bloomington IL 61701

Call Sign: KC9JDL
Scott D Hume
1007 E Jefferson St
Bloomington IL 61701

Call Sign: KA9RSN
Cindy J Lovell
1810 E Lafayette
Bloomington IL 61701

Call Sign: KA9BPV
Jeffrey L Lovell
1810 E Lafayette
Bloomington IL 61701

Call Sign: KB9YJ
Gene Studley
1016.5 E Lafayette St
Bloomington IL 61701

Call Sign: WD9IEQ
Robert E King
1023 E Lafayette St
Bloomington IL 61701

Call Sign: W7FON

Harry A Hale
2025 E Lincoln
Bloomington IL 61701

Call Sign: KC7ET
Evelyn H Cavallo
2012 E Lincoln Apt 109
Bloomington IL 61701

Call Sign: WA9FZL
Glenn V Gill
2025 E Lincoln Apt 3215
Bloomington IL 61701

Call Sign: W9KR
Charles A Walters
2025 E Lincoln St
Bloomington IL 61701

Call Sign: W9PSL
Kenneth E Fuller
2025 E Lincoln St Apt 3106
Bloomington IL 61701

Call Sign: WB9WJA
John H Lighthall
1001 E Marion
Bloomington IL 61701

Call Sign: KB9ANP
Mark L Cook
1408 E Oakland Ave
Bloomington IL 61701

Call Sign: KA9OXO
Patricia M Cook
1408 E Oakland Ave
Bloomington IL 61701

Call Sign: K9MBS
Byron S Tucci
3001 E Oakland Ave
Bloomington IL 61704

Call Sign: KA0FXS
Kenneth N Tridle
1404 E Olive
Bloomington IL 61701

Call Sign: KC9HLS
Les V Mc Calip
1607 E Taylor
Bloomington IL 61701

Call Sign: KB9YSF
Paul Whiteland
711 E Walnut St
Bloomington IL 61701

Call Sign: W7EDT
Delmar W Rowe
2501 E Washington 1
Bloomington IL 61704

Call Sign: K9RYP
William M Goebel
1311 E Washington St
Bloomington IL 61701

Call Sign: KC9JDM
David A Milam
104 E Wood 1210
Bloomington IL 61701

Call Sign: K9GGN
Charles R Tarbox
1225B Eastport Dr
Bloomington IL 61704

Call Sign: KC9TAL
Andrew D Blessing
2015 Ebo Ln
Bloomington IL 61704

Call Sign: N9TDD
Tim M Hendrickson
706 Eddy Rd
Bloomington IL 617041279

Call Sign: N9NHQ
Daniel S Hagberg
2710 Essington St
Bloomington IL 617046531

Call Sign: N9PQS
Jody L Hagberg
2710 Essington St
Bloomington IL 617046531

Call Sign: KA9ZZF
Mary E Howard
2914 Essington St
Bloomington IL 617046539

Call Sign: N9BOK
Morris A Howard
2914 Essington St
Bloomington IL 617046539

Call Sign: KC9HLT
Mark A Snyder
1317 Ewing
Bloomington IL 61701

Call Sign: AB9MP
Mark A Snyder
1317 Ewing
Bloomington IL 61701

Call Sign: WB9NMP
Larry E Venezia
102 Fairway Dr
Bloomington IL 617012107

Call Sign: N9KQS
Wayne L Barton
1504 Fell Ave
Bloomington IL 61701

Call Sign: KB9ZDV
Matt H Hatch
524 Florence
Bloomington IL 61701

Call Sign: K9ONI
Ole N Ibsen II
9 Fountain Lake Ct
Bloomington IL 61704

Call Sign: WA9BJY
Frank W Emmert
307 Garfield Dr
Bloomington IL 61701

Call Sign: N9GOD
Donald F Weissgerber Jr
1103 Gettysburg Dr Unit 2

Bloomington IL 61704

Call Sign: WR9I
David M Crull
2815 Grandview Dr
Bloomington IL 61704

Call Sign: KC9PIN
Thomas R Hazlett
1907 Hackberry Rd
Bloomington IL 617042779

Call Sign: KA9RLS
Rodney M Sabick
29 Harbor Pointe Cir
Bloomington IL 61704

Call Sign: KC9NHN
Christopher A Burkiewicz
2 Harrison Ct
Bloomington IL 61704

Call Sign: N9PEV
Dave R Altshue
9 Harry Dr
Bloomington IL 61701

Call Sign: N9QAZ
Nancy J Altshue
9 Harry Dr
Bloomington IL 61701

Call Sign: K9HOQ
Donald J Geigner
14 Heartland Dr Apt 103
Bloomington IL 617047773

Call Sign: WB9TOO
James W Nelden
2105 Hedgewood Dr
Bloomington IL 61704

Call Sign: N9CRL
Joe M Crosno
1902 Herbert St
Bloomington IL 61701

Call Sign: N1SF
N1sf Radio Club

9679 Heron Bay Rd
Bloomington IL 61704

Call Sign: AB9M
Gary L Huber
9679 Heron Bay Rd
Bloomington IL 61705

Call Sign: WX9WX
N1sf Radio Club
9679 Heron Bay Rd
Bloomington IL 61705

Call Sign: WX9RSO
Noble A Stubblefield
503 Highland Dr
Bloomington IL 61704

Call Sign: K9EMA
Noble A Stubblefield
503 Highland Dr
Bloomington IL 61704

Call Sign: N9FDC
Paula Stubblefield
503 Highland Dr
Bloomington IL 61704

Call Sign: WX9FDC
Paula B Stubblefield
503 Highland Dr
Bloomington IL 61704

Call Sign: WX9ZOO
Paula B Stubblefield
503 Highland Dr
Bloomington IL 61704

Call Sign: KC9PQR
Mclean County Ares
503 Highland Dr
Bloomington IL 61704

Call Sign: WX9EOC
Mclean County Ares
503 Highland Dr
Bloomington IL 61704

Call Sign: W9OBN

Clifford C Horine
1104 Hilltop Ct
Bloomington IL 617047429

Call Sign: WA1UCO
John P Moretto
2818 Huntington Rd
Bloomington IL 617048418

Call Sign: K9IKR
Andrew S Washburn
2013 Interurban Rd
Bloomington IL 61704

Call Sign: KC9CSW
Douglas A Ward
19287 Inverness Ct
Bloomington IL 61705

Call Sign: KB9ZJY
N1sf Radio Club
2702 Ireland Grove Rd
Bloomington IL 617090001

Call Sign: KB9UGY
Michael P Nolan Jr
8 Joslin Ct
Bloomington IL 61704

Call Sign: KC9PUK
Mickey L Hart
1527 Julie Dr
Bloomington IL 61701

Call Sign: N9RYR
Gregory H Shepherd
2012 Juniper Ln
Bloomington IL 61701

Call Sign: K9CYW
Gary L Lenhardt
9331 Kensington Ct
Bloomington IL 617045206

Call Sign: KQ9D
Pamela S Rice
11 Knottingham Ct
Bloomington IL 617048205

Call Sign: KB9QLA
John K Swearingen
1013 Laesch Ave Apt D
Bloomington IL 61704

Call Sign: W9XJ
John K Swearingen
1013 Laesch Ave Apt D
Bloomington IL 61704

Call Sign: N9CIT
Bernard C Dietz
10 Lake Bluff Ct
Bloomington IL 61701

Call Sign: KA9OTY
James W Johnston
805 Lake Fork Rd
Bloomington IL 61704

Call Sign: W9ZST
Arthur E Colvin
5 Lake Pointe Ct
Bloomington IL 61701

Call Sign: KC5FB
Kurt F Bock
19 Lavender Ln
Bloomington IL 61704

Call Sign: WD9FVI
Russell W Murray
1804 Lawndale Way
Bloomington IL 61704

Call Sign: KB9CVD
Wendy S Wilmarth
114 Lucern
Bloomington IL 61701

Call Sign: W9CJL
Lester H Garber
601 Lutz Rd Apt 2204
Bloomington IL 61704

Call Sign: N9VXX
Elinor L Horine
101 Magoun St
Bloomington IL 61701

Call Sign: KC9PIQ
Roger C Fitchorn
706 Marshall Ln
Bloomington IL 61701

Call Sign: KQ9E
Connie J Rice
1013 McGregor Ave
Bloomington IL 61701

Call Sign: N9DZD
Mary F Rice
1013 McGregor Ave
Bloomington IL 61701

Call Sign: N9DXL
William E Rice
1013 McGregor Ave
Bloomington IL 61701

Call Sign: K9GRO
Alan J Brook
115A Meadow Ridge Dr
Bloomington IL 61704

Call Sign: N9OSN
Lonnie R Butler
26 Melissa Dr
Bloomington IL 61704

Call Sign: N9CEF
Lonnie R Butler
26 Melissa Dr
Bloomington IL 61704

Call Sign: KC9JER
Paul D Kimbrel
1405 Mill Creek Rd
Bloomington IL 61704

Call Sign: KB9UBP
John L Archibald
1634 MLK Dr
Bloomington IL 61701

Call Sign: N9BXI
Gary H Wilcoxson
2512 Monica Ln

Bloomington IL 61704

Call Sign: N9KQR
Wade M Kaiser
3302 Monterey Rd
Bloomington IL 61704

Call Sign: WD9B
Joseph I Babb Jr
1316 Mt Vernon Dr
Bloomington IL 61701

Call Sign: KB9SJR
Bradley M Dearing
16410 N 800 E
Bloomington IL 61705

Call Sign: KB9CVE
Kathleen A Shank
14473 N 900 E Rd
Bloomington IL 61705

Call Sign: WD9JBS
William E Shank
14473 N 900 E Rd
Bloomington IL 61705

Call Sign: N9RJL
John F Ruby
1301 N Center St
Bloomington IL 61701

Call Sign: KG9IW
Kyle R Alberts
1404 N Center St
Bloomington IL 61701

Call Sign: N9VTC
Janice E Sleeter
1005 N East St
Bloomington IL 61701

Call Sign: N9GNL
Murleen K Swafford
515 N Lee St
Bloomington IL 61701

Call Sign: KA9ZMX
H Robert Lanham

1318 N Mason St
Bloomington IL 61701

Call Sign: WB9BOS
Joe C Bair
1109 N McLean
Bloomington IL 61701

Call Sign: K9CWX
Willis B Weaver
1224 N Oak St
Bloomington IL 61701

Call Sign: N9XSV
Patricia J Williamson
710 N Roosevelt
Bloomington IL 617012932

Call Sign: KC9LCE
Michael M Hansen
1005 N Roosevelt
Bloomington IL 61701

Call Sign: KG9ICE
Michael M Hansen
1005 N Roosevelt
Bloomington IL 61701

Call Sign: W9OOH
Adolph A Zalucha
606 N Roosevelt Ave
Bloomington IL 61701

Call Sign: KB9RUT
Chad K Phillips
2505 Norton Rd
Bloomington IL 61704

Call Sign: WB9GTK
Jeffrey D Wilcox
13766 Oak Hill Rd
Bloomington IL 61704

Call Sign: AC9S
Keith R Hanson
19848 Oakwood Dr
Bloomington IL 61705

Call Sign: KB9MZ

Arthur H Unwin
15394 Old Colonial Rd
Bloomington IL 61704

Call Sign: K9ZO
Ralph A Bellas Jr
2508 Old Peoria Ct
Bloomington IL 61704

Call Sign: NW9Y
Rumen V Gechev
2508 Old Peoria Ct
Bloomington IL 61704

Call Sign: KB9HTF
Vassil R Gechev
2508 Old Peoria Ct
Bloomington IL 61704

Call Sign: W9SMC
Society Of Midwest Contesters
2508 Old Peoria Ct
Bloomington IL 61704

Call Sign: KB9ZSN
Eric K Bellas
2508 Old Peoria Rd
Bloomington IL 61704

Call Sign: AA9LC
Grant A Zehr
9781 Old Sawmill Rd
Bloomington IL 61704

Call Sign: KD9KZ
Michael Craig
1 Park City S
Bloomington IL 61704

Call Sign: KC9QQM
Jeffrey Lovell
27 Parkshores Dr
Bloomington IL 61701

Call Sign: N9LIO
Ian P Goldsmith
50 Parkshores Dr
Bloomington IL 61701

Call Sign: K9OAT
Daniel W Harms
107 Parkview Dr
Bloomington IL 61701

Call Sign: WA1SVT
James C Liston II
3 Pembrook Cir
Bloomington IL 61704

Call Sign: N9CKL
Richard N Suhadolc
2816 Phillip Pl
Bloomington IL 61704

Call Sign: KC9TMG
Matthew J Suhadolc
2816 Phillip Pl
Bloomington IL 61704

Call Sign: KB9UTA
Ruth A Laverty
18850 Pioneer St
Bloomington IL 617055826

Call Sign: N9KFM
Michael R Pape
8406 Prairie Trl
Bloomington IL 61705

Call Sign: N9FSB
Greta D Mortenson
8431 Prairie Trl
Bloomington IL 61704

Call Sign: KC9NHO
Eric J Baxter
3510 Prescher Pointe
Bloomington IL 61704

Call Sign: KC9CZM
Jeffrey L Thompson
315 Providence Dr
Bloomington IL 61704

Call Sign: KI4CRP
Evan M Russo
1128 Rader Run
Bloomington IL 61704

Call Sign: WD9IID
Gary L Mc Candless
2507 Rainbow Ave
Bloomington IL 61704

Call Sign: KC9SUN
Darrel D Vinson
2412 Rainbow Ave Apt 1B
Bloomington IL 61704

Call Sign: AB9PP
Donald F Weissgerber Jr
1102 Redwood Ave
Bloomington IL 61701

Call Sign: KB9ZQP
Luke M Chubick
811 Reinthaler Rd
Bloomington IL 61701

Call Sign: KC9LOZ
Brian E Adams
2103 Ridge Creek Dr
Bloomington IL 61705

Call Sign: KB9LNS
John A Chubick
2701 Ridge Rd
Bloomington IL 61704

Call Sign: K9XL
Raymond G Myers
9599 Ridgewood Ct
Bloomington IL 61705

Call Sign: KA9KNC
Mary J Myers
9599 Ridgewood St
Bloomington IL 61705

Call Sign: KB9QLB
John D Swearingen
3 Riser Ave
Bloomington IL 61701

Call Sign: KA9BZI
A James Brook
216 Robinhood Ln

Bloomington IL 61701

Call Sign: WB9VKL
Robert D Gray
605 S Clinton St
Bloomington IL 617015450

Call Sign: KC9CSV
Roxanne R Able
507 S Florence Ave
Bloomington IL 61701

Call Sign: N9HBW
Bonnie R Troxel
209 S Hershey Rd
Bloomington IL 61701

Call Sign: KC9MFO
Marilana M Hurst
1104 S Hinshaw
Bloomington IL 61701

Call Sign: KB9QBT
Daniel G May
1104 S Hinshaw Ave
Bloomington IL 61701

Call Sign: KA9KEY
Ray W Wahlstrom
504 S Kreitzer Ave
Bloomington IL 61701

Call Sign: KC9SUM
James H Thomas
803 S Low St
Bloomington IL 61701

Call Sign: N9GCC
Douglas J Walsh
1016 S Main St
Bloomington IL 61701

Call Sign: N9KIU
Karen J Beach
1016 S Main St
Bloomington IL 61701

Call Sign: N9GCD
Tammy L Walsh

1016 S Main St
Bloomington IL 61701

Call Sign: N9FON
Thomas A Guttschow
1613 S Main St
Bloomington IL 61701

Call Sign: N9FGL
Carl J Guhlstorf
606 S McClun
Bloomington IL 61701

Call Sign: WI6A
Donna P Willke
812 S Mercer
Bloomington IL 61701

Call Sign: N9LYR
Charles M Payne
808 S Mercer Ave
Bloomington IL 61701

Call Sign: N9ULP
Duane A Westhoff
1318 S Oak St
Bloomington IL 61701

Call Sign: WB9CTP
Ronald R Ross
805 S Summit St
Bloomington IL 61701

Call Sign: K9UCD
Billy E Smith
605 S Vale St
Bloomington IL 61701

Call Sign: WB9WVZ
Dorothy A Mc Laughlin
716 S Vale St
Bloomington IL 61701

Call Sign: KC8LFR
Patrick B Bak
2414 Savanna Rd
Bloomington IL 61705

Call Sign: KB7VPI

Darren R Erickson
8 Sequoia Ct 166
Bloomington IL 61704

Call Sign: KC9ZU
James W Moberly
2701 Sheffield Dr
Bloomington IL 61704

Call Sign: KE9BA
Alvie D Roberts
207 Sherwood Way
Bloomington IL 61115

Call Sign: KB9ABS
Scott E Evans
1517 Six Points Rd
Bloomington IL 61701

Call Sign: KC9EBM
Bryan M Fogler
104 Snow Ln Willowcreek
Bloomington IL 61701

Call Sign: KB9ZVW
Alexanderq K Coffman
15 Somerset Ct
Bloomington IL 61701

Call Sign: N9UFD
S Hagberg
2702 Southlawn Dr
Bloomington IL 61704

Call Sign: KB9AIM
Jonathan M Gibson
11 Spiria Ct
Bloomington IL 61701

Call Sign: N9GCB
Vernon K Veal
15 Spring Ridge Cir
Bloomington IL 617049114

Call Sign: NV1V
Vernon K Veal
15 Spring Ridge Cir
Bloomington IL 617049114

Call Sign: KA9YMJ
Zona M Guttschow
1810 Springfield Rd
Bloomington IL 61701

Call Sign: K9SIX
Daniel J Meyer
1714 Springfield Rd Apt 7
Bloomington IL 61701

Call Sign: AB9XA
Douglas E Graham
413 Standish Dr
Bloomington IL 61704

Call Sign: WB9QCJ
Wayne L Hicks
419 Standish Dr
Bloomington IL 61701

Call Sign: KC9AQQ
N1sf Radio Club
1 State Farm Plaza C4
Bloomington IL 61701

Call Sign: N9PE
N1sf Radio Club
1 State Farm Plaza C4
Bloomington IL 61701

Call Sign: KA0CPV
Gregory L Hayward
3215 Suffolk Way
Bloomington IL 61704

Call Sign: N9CTK
Jeffrey E Switzer
8417 Surrey Cir
Bloomington IL 61704

Call Sign: N9LVI
David A Henderson
2 Tatiana Ct
Bloomington IL 617048260

Call Sign: KC9NHM
Dennis J Devine
6 Timberlake Rd
Bloomington IL 61704

Call Sign: WB9QDW
Janet E Jumper
1405 Towanda Ave
Bloomington IL 61701

Call Sign: WB9CEB
Richard A Jumper
1405 Towanda Ave
Bloomington IL 61701

Call Sign: KB9BOJ
Robert F Risser
1906 Tracy Dr 210
Bloomington IL 61704

Call Sign: WB9OSO
Loy Macchini
2004 Tracy Dr 3
Bloomington IL 61704

Call Sign: KN9X
Dan M Ausili
18788 US Hwy 150
Bloomington IL 617055817

Call Sign: KC9SKF
Kathleen Kiifner Huber
19266 US Hwy 150
Bloomington IL 61705

Call Sign: N9ZKS
Norman I Huber
19266 US Hwy 150
Bloomington IL 617055855

Call Sign: KB0RUZ
Daniel F Smith
1815 Vladimir Dr
Bloomington IL 61704

Call Sign: WX9DAN
Daniel F Smith
1815 Vladimir Dr
Bloomington IL 61704

Call Sign: KB9NPH
Larry G Mays
1406 W Forrest St

Bloomington IL 61701

Call Sign: KB9WHG
Craig W Ohmart
926 W Grove
Bloomington IL 617014950

Call Sign: KB9YTA
Sam W Hawk
925 W Grove St
Bloomington IL 61701

Call Sign: W9OUF
Lyman E Hill
1304 W Jackson St
Bloomington IL 61701

Call Sign: W9NUP
Ronald W Purkey
2519 W Market
Bloomington IL 61704

Call Sign: KB4WSS
Agnes M Carby
1010 W Mill St
Bloomington IL 61701

Call Sign: W9MNR
Helen M Zalucha
1312 W Mulberry St
Bloomington IL 61701

Call Sign: KB9DXZ
Elizabeth M Chestney
503 W Scott
Bloomington IL 61701

Call Sign: KA9VVO
Steven B Chestney
503 W Scott St
Bloomington IL 61701

Call Sign: KB9RAB
Charles D Hinshaw
925 W Wood
Bloomington IL 61701

Call Sign: WD9HRU
Richard R Kempf

13904 Wagner Dr
Bloomington IL 61704

Call Sign: W9AML
Central Illinois Radio Club Of
Blmngtn Inc
13904 Wagner Dr
Bloomington IL 61704

Call Sign: KC9QKG
Inc Central Illinois Radio Club
Of Bloomington
13904 Wagner Dr
Bloomington il 61705

Call Sign: W9EX
Inc Central Illinois Radio Club
Of Bloomington
13904 Wagner Dr
Bloomington il 61705

Call Sign: KB9IGS
Omar G Lehr
105 Warner
Bloomington IL 61701

Call Sign: KC9LKG
Brian E Adams
308 Waterford Estates Dr
Bloomington IL 61704

Call Sign: KC9FWL
Michael R Sallee
403 Watford Dr
Bloomington IL 61704

Call Sign: N9XSY
Ernest G Lambert
2909 Wellington Way
Bloomington IL 61704

Call Sign: KB9CTI
Carolyn M Jarvis
15 White Pl
Bloomington IL 61701

Call Sign: WR9E
Fred H Knoth
67 White Pl

Bloomington IL 61701

Call Sign: N9LWA
Donna C Brownell
59.5 Whites Pl
Bloomington IL 61701

Call Sign: WB8QXK
Chris A Swisher
13757 Whitetail Ct
Bloomington IL 61705

Call Sign: KB9FKU
Amanda G Tanner
104 Wildflower Pl
Bloomington IL 61704

Call Sign: KB9EIS
James R Bowling
285 Willow Creek Village
Bloomington IL 61701

Call Sign: N9HBV
Roger A Troxel
3411 Windmill Rd
Bloomington IL 61704

Call Sign: N9NSN
Daniel J Beer
3106 Wisteria Ln
Bloomington IL 61704

Call Sign: KC9HLU
Greg J Beer
3106 Wisteria Ln
Bloomington IL 61704

Call Sign: K9ZJ
Thomas R Mc Nabb
214.5 Woodland Ave
Bloomington IL 61701

Call Sign: KC9VAC
Josiah G Husk
19286 Woodland Trl
Bloomington IL 61705

Call Sign: WA9ONH
Eugene Kaufman

Rr 2 Woodrig Rd
Bloomington IL 61701

Call Sign: N9NOE
Lawrence L Noe
4 Zweng Ave
Bloomington IL 61704

Call Sign: WA9GCK
Glenn D Hill
Bloomington IL 61702

Call Sign: W9MTR
Marvin W Nichols
Bloomington IL 61702

Call Sign: WB9UUS
Charles A Henderson
Bloomington IL 61702

Call Sign: KB9LNT
Jerral R Kessinger
Bloomington IL 61702

Call Sign: KB9IWC
Nicholas J Butzirus
Bloomington IL 61702

Call Sign: K9EMA
Noble A Stubblefield
Bloomington IL 617021272

Call Sign: N9FDC
Paula J B Stubblefield
Bloomington IL 617021272

Call Sign: KB9WNK
Steven J Busick
Bloomington IL 617021888

Call Sign: W9SJB
Steven J Busick
Bloomington IL 617021888

FCC Amateur Radio Licenses in Blue Mound

Call Sign: KC9JPR
Mark M Solberg

1849 E 2850 N Rd
Blue Mound IL 62513

Call Sign: N9NWG
Steven W Canaday
325 E Dunbar St Rr 2
Blue Mound IL 62513

Call Sign: AA9H
James C Switzer
118 Kathy Ct
Blue Mound IL 62513

Call Sign: KC9AWG
Carolynn F Carter
102 N Lewis
Blue Mound IL 62513

Call Sign: KB9UKF
Charles J Carter
102 N Lewis
Blue Mound IL 62513

Call Sign: WD9III
Brent D Payne
309 Territim Dr
Blue Mound IL 62513

Call Sign: N9LVW
Spencer A Carter
Blue Mound IL 62513

FCC Amateur Radio Licenses in Bluffs

Call Sign: KB9WHR
Jeremiah J Hawkins
228 N Pine St
Bluffs IL 62621

Call Sign: N9NUD
Jeremiah J Hawkins
228 N Pine St
Bluffs IL 62621

FCC Amateur Radio Licenses in Bluford

Call Sign: N9MPQ

Lee R Craig
Rr 1 Box 164
Bluford IL 62814

Call Sign: KB9QED
Kay S Miller
Rt 1 Box 269
Bluford IL 62814

Call Sign: KC9QIV
Leonard L Wood
Rr 2 Box 306 W
Bluford IL 62814

Call Sign: KB9UXB
Jack White
712 E North St
Bluford IL 62814

Call Sign: KC9RBK
Cory Arnett
15153 N Falcon Ln
Bluford IL 62814

Call Sign: KC9QIU
Bradley P Jackson
13318 N January Ln
Bluford IL 62814

Call Sign: K9JXN
Bradley P Jackson
13318 N January Ln
Bluford IL 62814

Call Sign: WB9KWC
Truman L Wood
Bluford IL 62814

Call Sign: WA9QAY
Harold V Stover
Bluford IL 62814

FCC Amateur Radio Licenses in Bondville

Call Sign: KB9NXF
Jerry L Wells
Cooper Trailer Park 14
Bondville IL 618150062

FCC Amateur Radio Licenses in Bonfield

Call Sign: N9IOQ
Cindy L Melhorn
122 Country Ln
Bonfield IL 60913

Call Sign: N9IO
Clay E Melhorn
122 Country Ln
Bonfield IL 60913

Call Sign: W9IOU
Crystal E Melhorn
122 Country Ln
Bonfield IL 60913

Call Sign: W9ILL
Jonathan D Slack
7300 Landing Ln
Bonfield IL 60913

Call Sign: KA9AMS
Audrey J Naese
10083 W 1000 S Rd
Bonfield IL 60913

Call Sign: KD9QK
Kenneth L Naese Jr
10083 W 1000 S Rd
Bonfield IL 60913

Call Sign: N9OQD
Rollin E Riegel
10080 W 2000 N Rd
Bonfield IL 60913

Call Sign: WB9WEC
Raymond E Norrick
1359C N 7000 W Rd
Bonfield IL 60913

FCC Amateur Radio Licenses in Bonnie

Call Sign: N9PFT
Susan D May

3547 N Reardon Ln
Bonnie IL 62816

Call Sign: WB9PRN
Kirby L Adams
3737 N Spring Garden Ln
Bonnie IL 62816

Call Sign: KC9JGN
Gregory D Lievers
365 N Water Tower Rd
Bonnie IL 62816

Call Sign: KC9JGO
Vicky M Lievers
365 N Water Tower Rd
Bonnie IL 62816

Call Sign: WB9RAS
William E May
3547 Reardon Ln
Bonnie IL 62816

Call Sign: N9QKZ
Roger A Marcum
195 W 3rd St
Bonnie IL 62816

FCC Amateur Radio Licenses in Boody

Call Sign: N9ENB
Larry J Lorton
106 Katie Dr
Boody IL 62514

FCC Amateur Radio Licenses in Bourdonnais

Call Sign: W9VCR
Vernon C Reed Jr
141 Anita Dr
Bourbonnais IL 609141077

Call Sign: KB9NYW
Scott A Martin
1534 Brassie
Bourbonnais IL 60914

Call Sign: KB9GRA
Paul Z Vakselis
8 Cambridge Ct
Bourbonnais IL 60914

Call Sign: KC9MZQ
Dean A Lohrbach
787 Cherokee Dr
Bourbonnais IL 60914

Call Sign: W9JGB
Gerald D Smith
3 Cherry Ln
Bourbonnais IL 60914

Call Sign: WA9NYT
Mildred A Smith
3 Cherry Ln
Bourbonnais IL 60914

Call Sign: KB9IPJ
Norman L Beyer
17 Cherry Ln
Bourbonnais IL 60914

Call Sign: KC9KUC
Caleb C Fisher
281 E Beaudoin
Bourbonnais IL 60914

Call Sign: KB9MLJ
Michael T Higgins
1436 E Cap Cir
Bourbonnais IL 60914

Call Sign: N9TQG
Scott F Williams
225 E John Casey Rd
Bourbonnais IL 60914

Call Sign: KA9OBG
Everett J Baldridge
695 Edwin Dr
Bourbonnais IL 609141303

Call Sign: KC9OQL
Tiffany L Neukomm
854 Gettysburg Dr 5
Bourbonnais IL 60914

Call Sign: K9IOC
John R Moore
528 Highpoint Cir N
Bourbonnais IL 60914

Call Sign: K9SAT
Robert A Nemitz
830 Independence Dr
Bourbonnais IL 60914

Call Sign: KC9VOE
Ham Radio Podcast Radio
Club
830 Independence Dr
Bourbonnais IL 60914

Call Sign: W9HRP
Ham Radio Podcast Radio
Club
830 Independence Dr
Bourbonnais IL 60914

Call Sign: KB9VXC
Thomas J Dunn
3 Inverness
Bourbonnais IL 60914

Call Sign: W9TJD
Thomas J Dunn
3 Inverness Dr
Bourbonnais IL 609141539

Call Sign: WB9RCA
Ray C Flesher
100 Jones Dr Apt 241
Bourbonnais IL 60914

Call Sign: N9EFT
Robert G Bishop
35 Karen Dr
Bourbonnais IL 60914

Call Sign: KB9LXA
Friends Of Amateur Radio
Group
311 Kathy
Bourbonnais IL 60914

Call Sign: N9LCX
Calvin E Smith
311 Kathy Dr
Bourbonnais IL 60914

Call Sign: KB9ZSV
Andy W Martin
7 Kim Dr
Bourbonnais IL 60914

Call Sign: KC9MZT
Clinton A Yale
3539 Linda Dr
Bourbonnais IL 60914

Call Sign: KC9MZO
Michael A Lambert
1589 Mid Ct Dr
Bourbonnais IL 60914

Call Sign: K9LYI
James E Follkie Sr
1335 Millpond Rd
Bourbonnais IL 609141525

Call Sign: KC9UNQ
Adam J Beedle
3366 N 2320 W Rd
Bourbonnais IL 60914

Call Sign: KB9TWD
Patricia B Follkie
4243 N 3000 W Rd
Bourbonnais IL 60914

Call Sign: KG9PS
Frank P Dal Canton
2642 N 4000 E Rd
Bourbonnais IL 60914

Call Sign: AA9XM
Frank P Dalcanton
2642 N 4000 E Rd
Bourbonnais IL 60914

Call Sign: K9XM
Frank P Dalcanton
2642 N 4000 E Rd
Bourbonnais IL 60914

Call Sign: N9OQC
Kyle A Buente
2474 N Osage Dr
Bourbonnais IL 60914

Call Sign: KB9WPQ
Keegan C Crosby
1436 N West Ave
Bourbonnais IL 60914

Call Sign: KB9WPS
Kevin C Crosby
1436 N West Ave
Bourbonnais IL 60914

Call Sign: KB9GLG
Eugene R Schwanbeck IV
597 Olde Lyme Turn
Bourbonnais IL 60914

Call Sign: KB9IVK
Daniel M Young
1311 Plum Creek Dr
Bourbonnais IL 60914

Call Sign: N9ISC
Melody J Orth
1313 Potomac 5
Bourbonnais IL 60914

Call Sign: K9BBJ
Michael E Reeves
420 S Cleveland
Bourbonnais IL 60914

Call Sign: WA9HSN
Timothy J Mercer
180 Spencer Ct
Bourbonnais IL 60914

Call Sign: N9RUB
Allen R Zebrauskas
78 St Peters
Bourbonnais IL 60914

Call Sign: KC9MZR
Mark Thiesen
1035 Stratford Dr E Apt 5

Bourbonnais IL 60914

Call Sign: N9OQE
James A Shanks
275 Tomagene Dr
Bourbonnais IL 60914

Call Sign: KC9QXV
Kevin C Mansberger
1346 W Cap Cir
Bourbonnais IL 60914

Call Sign: W9LCQ
Jay K Seyler
581 W Drummond Dr
Bourbonnais IL 60914

Call Sign: K9KOC
John W Reader
221 W Marsile St
Bourbonnais IL 60914

Call Sign: WC9B
Gerald R Giguere
142 W Ray St
Bourbonnais IL 60914

Call Sign: KB6KEE
Scott A Riley
709 W River St
Bourbonnais IL 60914

Call Sign: KC9LZZ
Scott A Riley
709 W River St
Bourbonnais IL 60914

Call Sign: KX9SAR
Scott A Riley
709 W River St
Bourbonnais IL 60914

Call Sign: WA9WAQ
Dan L Loftus
771 Washington Ave
Bourbonnais IL 60914

Call Sign: WA9QQI
Tom F Eagan

840 Washington Ave
Bourbonnais IL 60914

Call Sign: WB9KTI
Larry D Vail
880 Washington Ave
Bourbonnais IL 60914

Call Sign: KA9UMT
Thomas E Dexter
630 Washington Rd
Bourbonnais IL 60914

Call Sign: AA9IW
Cliff Carr
1864 Yorktown Dr
Bourbonnais IL 60914

FCC Amateur Radio Licenses in Bowen

Call Sign: N9HGD
Ted W Knorr
Rr 1 Box 59A
Bowen IL 62316

Call Sign: KC9FST
Philip A Parker
2010 E CR 150
Bowen IL 62316

Call Sign: KA9EKK
Mary J Knorr
481 N CR 2100 E
Bowen IL 62316

Call Sign: KB9BI
Terry W Knorr
481 N CR 2100E
Bowen IL 62316

FCC Amateur Radio Licenses in Braceville

Call Sign: N9ARK
Jesse E Colvin
3180 S Broadway
Braceville IL 60407

Call Sign: KB9VOY
Fists Of Illinois
3180 S Broadway
Braceville IL 60407

Call Sign: W9FFF
Fists Of Illinois
3180 S Broadway
Braceville IL 60407

Call Sign: AI9L
Jesse E Colvin
3180 S Broadway
Braceville IL 60407

Call Sign: AF9H
Patricia A Colvin
3180 S Broadway
Braceville IL 60407

Call Sign: K9WJL
William J Leib Jr
315 W Division St
Braceville IL 60407

FCC Amateur Radio Licenses in Bradley

Call Sign: WD9AYI
John R Arrington
621 Bishop Ct
Bradley IL 60915

Call Sign: WB9RUE
Dale R Monty
671 Bishop Ct
Bradley IL 609151955

Call Sign: KE9MG
Francis A Giguere
326 Douglas Dr
Bradley IL 60915

Call Sign: N9JES
James L Landry
955 E Broadway
Bradley IL 60915

Call Sign: KB9RNA

Roy A Combs
1116 E Broadway
Bradley IL 60915

Call Sign: KC9FAV
Brian L Erwin
525 Evergreen Ln
Bradley IL 60915

Call Sign: KD9YU
Robert A Ritenour
646 Evergreen Ln
Bradley IL 60915

Call Sign: KC9UNR
John J Mazzuchi
1041 Mallard
Bradley IL 60915

Call Sign: N0ONH
Robert C Haas
1050 Mallard Dr
Bradley IL 60915

Call Sign: NN9T
Robert C Haas
1050 Mallard Dr
Bradley IL 60915

Call Sign: WB9STR
Gregory L Hart
495 N Center
Bradley IL 609151607

Call Sign: WR9L
Gregory L Hart
495 N Center
Bradley IL 609151607

Call Sign: KB9CDS
Mark E Howard
412 N Clevland Ave
Bradley IL 60915

Call Sign: KC9GNI
Brandon A Campbell
229 N Clinton
Bradley IL 60915

Call Sign: K9BAC
Brandon A Campbell
229 N Clinton
Bradley IL 60915

Call Sign: N9VVM
Darrell J Scheppler
524 N Grand
Bradley IL 60915

Call Sign: KC9RKU
Wesley Woo
218 N Lasalle
Bradley IL 60915

Call Sign: KF9PI
Gary R Hawkins
108 N Van Buren
Bradley IL 60915

Call Sign: W9FST
Gary R Hawkins
108 N Van Buren
Bradley IL 60915

Call Sign: KX9J
Thomas J Skube
430 N Van Buren Ave
Bradley IL 60915

Call Sign: KB9FOZ
James R Fitzjarrell Jr
864 Quail Dr
Bradley IL 60915

Call Sign: KC9JKD
Marc E Cote
888 Quail Dr
Bradley IL 60915

Call Sign: K9IXI
Marc E Cote
888 Quail Dr
Bradley IL 60915

Call Sign: KC9KBR
Jeremy M Lathrop
224 S Euclid Ave
Bradley IL 60915

Call Sign: N9NAG
Bruce R Belard Jr
259 S Euclid Ave
Bradley IL 60915

Call Sign: WD9DVW
Richard I Hecht
501 S Michigan Ave
Bradley IL 60915

Call Sign: KC9BCU
James P Schreiner
436 S Prairie
Bradley IL 60915

Call Sign: K9BIG
James P Schreiner
436 S Prairie
Bradley IL 60915

Call Sign: KB9ZQU
Duane L Erwin
335 S Wabash Ave
Bradley IL 60915

Call Sign: KC9MZM
Rodney J Pena Jr
540 W Congress
Bradley IL 60915

Call Sign: K9UNO
Rodney J Pena Jr
540 W Congress
Bradley IL 60915

Call Sign: KC9FDN
Bradley - Bourbonnais High
School ARC
700 W North St
Bradley IL 60915

Call Sign: K9BHS
Bradley - Bourbonnais High
School ARC
700 W North St
Bradley IL 60915

Call Sign: KB9YLW

Andrew S Ball
730 W South St
Bradley IL 60915

Call Sign: WA9QCW
Thomas J Lindsay
Bradley IL 60915

Call Sign: N9UMU
Andrew L Stewart
Bradley IL 60915

FCC Amateur Radio Licenses in Breese

Call Sign: KA9VPT
Ted L Long
12110 Linden Grove
Breese IL 62230

Call Sign: KC9EWZ
Ted L Long
12110 Linden Grove
Breese IL 62230

Call Sign: KD0CLZ
Gary J Holzinger
1180 Meadowlark Ln
Breese IL 62230

Call Sign: W9GJH
Gary J Holzinger
1180 Meadowlark Ln
Breese IL 62230

Call Sign: KC9RZT
Corey B Darr
941 Pioneer Ct
Breese IL 62230

Call Sign: KR9O
Corey B Darr
941 Pioneer Ct
Breese IL 62230

Call Sign: KB9LVE
James A Boeckmann
630 S 6th St
Breese IL 62230

Call Sign: KC9RUQ
Daniel P Dust
14210 St James Ln
Breese IL 62230

**FCC Amateur Radio
Licenses in Bridgeport**

Call Sign: N9SWU
Harry L Griesemer Jr
238 Jefferson St
Bridgeport IL 62417

Call Sign: KB9VPR
Steven L Williams
38 North St
Bridgeport IL 62417

Call Sign: KA9EJH
Merle P Wagner
725 Washington Ave
Bridgeport IL 62417

Call Sign: K9TNR
Rae K Duncan
Bridgeport IL 62417

Call Sign: N9QCX
Rosemary G Roark
Bridgeport IL 62417

Call Sign: W9CFB
Meredith E Atkins
Bridgeport IL 62417

Call Sign: AA9OR
Tony M Roark
Bridgeport IL 62417

**FCC Amateur Radio
Licenses in Brighton**

Call Sign: N9UEW
Valerie R Roach
104 Belvedere
Brighton IL 62012

Call Sign: KC0FRF

Charles P Van Doren
202 Belvedere
Brighton IL 62012

Call Sign: N9VZM
William R Roach
409 Belvedere
Brighton IL 62012

Call Sign: KG9DD
William G Roach
104 Belvedere Pl
Brighton IL 62012

Call Sign: KA9SQR
Daniel P Laslie Sr
1628 Brighton Bunker Hill Rd
Brighton IL 62012

Call Sign: N9RGB
Marsha E Chamberlain
2948 Brighton Bunker Hill Rd
Brighton IL 62012

Call Sign: N9STO
Michael L Morgan
34120 Canoe Ct
Brighton IL 62012

Call Sign: KG9ME
Wayne D Hoxsie Jr
34231 Catfish Ct
Brighton IL 620124035

Call Sign: K9KC
Wayne D Hoxsie Jr
34231 Catfish Ct
Brighton IL 620124035

Call Sign: WB9CNB
Robert J Young
216 Cindy
Brighton IL 62012

Call Sign: N9FYH
Barbara J Young
216 Cindy St
Brighton IL 62012

Call Sign: KG9PL
Jeffrey L Curtis
9 Cottonwood Rd
Brighton IL 62012

Call Sign: KC9TVZ
Julia R Eddington
34030 Craig Lake Rd
Brighton IL 62012

Call Sign: KA9JYU
Jack W Rhodes
303 David Ln
Brighton IL 62012

Call Sign: KC9HOE
Dennis R Lucker
34699 Gotten Rd
Brighton IL 520123609

Call Sign: KB9GNG
Joseph T Jorden
18907 Grange Hall Rd
Brighton IL 62012

Call Sign: KD9ST
John A Laslie Jr
19022 Grange Hall Rd
Brighton IL 62012

Call Sign: KB9EXE
Matt T Laslie
19022 Grange Hall Rd
Brighton IL 62012

Call Sign: N9SNF
Jacqueline T Schmidt
215 Greenwood Ave
Brighton IL 62012

Call Sign: N9OFW
Kenneth O Schmidt
215 Greenwood Dr
Brighton IL 62012

Call Sign: KC9DZE
Curtis J Paulfrey II
34448 Gun Club Rd
Brighton IL 62012

Call Sign: KC9DZD
Joe C Paulfrey
34448 Gun Club Rd
Brighton IL 62012

Call Sign: KC9HOH
Katherine E Paulfrey
34448 Gun Club Rd
Brighton IL 62012

Call Sign: KC9JCJ
Moroni H Escalante
16922 Lageman Ln
Brighton IL 62012

Call Sign: KC9JCK
Rebecca M Escalante
16922 Lageman Ln
Brighton IL 62012

Call Sign: KC9JCL
Tracey D Escalante
16922 Lageman Ln
Brighton IL 62012

Call Sign: KA9SQS
John A Laslie III
514 Marion St
Brighton IL 62012

Call Sign: WY9D
John A Laslie III
514 Marion St
Brighton IL 62012

Call Sign: KA9ZAT
Brenda K Mitchell
123 Mustang Dr
Brighton IL 62012

Call Sign: KD9WC
Clarence L Mitchell
123 Mustang Dr
Brighton IL 62012

Call Sign: N9WDS
Ted E Lohr
9103 N Humbert Rd

Brighton IL 62012

Call Sign: KC9ETC
Metro East Search And Rescue
9103 N Humbert Rd
Brighton IL 62012

Call Sign: KC9QAE
Bruce W Muenstermann
203 North St
Brighton IL 62012

Call Sign: KC9QAD
Cade C Muenstermann
203 North St
Brighton IL 62012

Call Sign: KB9QXF
William G Miller
211 Oak St
Brighton IL 62012

Call Sign: KC9PGM
Raymond R Walter III
31566 Oak Trl
Brighton IL 62012

Call Sign: N9YDY
Mark A Rigsbey
16384 Pine Hurst
Brighton IL 62012

Call Sign: KB9BAT
Jeffrey M Jorden
Box 142 Rr 2
Brighton IL 62012

Call Sign: KC9NPG
Clayton L Cope
61 Seminary Rd
Brighton IL 62012

Call Sign: KF9KJ
James R Shaw
2442 Seminary Rd
Brighton IL 62012

Call Sign: KB9OWP
Manuel T Wense

34138 Teakwood Pl
Brighton IL 62012

Call Sign: N9ECR
Scott A Webb
125 Virginia Ave
Brighton IL 62012

Call Sign: KC9PNA
Vickey G Lewis
34510 Voorhees Ln
Brighton IL 62012

Call Sign: KB0PSA
Donn R Boltz
4 Willow Way
Brighton IL 62012

**FCC Amateur Radio
Licenses in Brimfield**

Call Sign: N9PIY
Dennis A Peck
315 E Knoxville Box 294
Brimfield IL 61517

Call Sign: KA9VUS
Garold S Keithley
509 N Monroe
Brimfield IL 61517

Call Sign: N9LFB
Shirlee R Keithley
509 N Monroe
Brimfield IL 61517

Call Sign: KA9MHF
Francis D Fussner
8529 N Penn Rd
Brimfield IL 61517

Call Sign: WB9CRB
Shirley E Fussner
8529 N Penn Rd
Brimfield IL 61517

Call Sign: KB9NBG
Eugene E Lalicker
110 S Adams

Brimfield IL 61517

Call Sign: WB9UDB
Jerry W Simmons Sr
207 S Washington Box 134
Brimfield IL 61517

Call Sign: W1JWS
Jerry W Simmons Sr
207 S Washington Box 134
Brimfield IL 61517

Call Sign: WB9DSZ
Stephen E Lehnert
17415 W Brimfield Jubilee Rd
Brimfield IL 61517

Call Sign: KB0QWH
Matthew W Dames
132 W Calhoun
Brimfield IL 61517

Call Sign: KC9QNA
Richard A Marshall
14821 W Carlton Ct
Brimfield IL 61517

Call Sign: N0ORE
Michael D Liese
228 W Clay St
Brimfield IL 615170297

Call Sign: W9NWE
James L Plack
16906 W Martin Rd
Brimfield IL 61517

Call Sign: W9DLS
Donald L Stedman
16700 Whittaker Rd
Brimfield IL 61517

FCC Amateur Radio Licenses in Bristol

Call Sign: KC0NBF
Gloria J Brady
Bristol IL 60512

FCC Amateur Radio Licenses in Brocton

Call Sign: N9QYZ
James W Brooks
Brocton IL 61917

FCC Amateur Radio Licenses in Brookport

Call Sign: N9WZF
Kenneth W Walker
R1 Box 252
Brookport IL 62910

Call Sign: KC9UVO
Eddy F Sobkowiak Sr
Rr 1 Box 272 D
Brookport IL 62910

Call Sign: KF4LQJ
Llana D Call
213 E 3rd St
Brookport IL 62910

Call Sign: N9VYA
Raymond M Hollis
114 Ferry St
Brookport IL 62910

Call Sign: KC9FDD
James M Favre
3052 Henderson Rd
Brookport IL 62910

Call Sign: KC9MDU
Mickey R Jacobs
1404 Mt Sterling Rd
Brookport IL 62910

Call Sign: KC9DBA
Bruce E Buchanan
2930 Strawberry Rd
Brookport IL 62910

Call Sign: N9XQP
Matthew C Quint
6733 Unity School Rd
Brookport IL 62910

Call Sign: KB9QFB
Cindy L Forthman
Brookport IL 62910

Call Sign: KD6UNL
Larry D Call
Brookport IL 62910

Call Sign: KB9PPT
Robert T Forthman
Brookport IL 62910

FCC Amateur Radio Licenses in Broughton

Call Sign: WD9JDC
Thomas R Mc Kinnis
Rt 1 Box 95
Broughton IL 628179756

FCC Amateur Radio Licenses in Browning

Call Sign: KA9UFX
James F Dunham
Rr 1 Box 232
Browning IL 62624

Call Sign: W9ACU
Francis F Walton
Rr 1 Box 65
Browning IL 62624

Call Sign: KB9BIJ
Brenda R Doolin
Rr 1 Box 70
Browning IL 62624

Call Sign: AA9FX
Jerry E Gilson
Browning IL 62624

Call Sign: KC9SVF
Jeffrey J Boyd
Browning IL 62624

Call Sign: K9TMG
Jeffrey J Boyd

Browning IL 62624

Call Sign: KC9SVG
Russel P Reedy
Browning IL 62624

Call Sign: K9RPR
Russel P Reedy
Browning IL 62624

FCC Amateur Radio Licenses in Browns

Call Sign: KA9TOA
Christy L Kieffer
11910 E 170 Rd
Browns IL 62818

FCC Amateur Radio Licenses in Brownstown

Call Sign: N9TXA
Edward J Durbin
Rr 1 Box 194A
Brownstown IL 62418

Call Sign: KB9VKQ
Brian J Kramer
210 W Cumberland Rd
Brownstown IL 62418

FCC Amateur Radio Licenses in Brussels

Call Sign: KC9UST
Timothy C Lemmon
Hc 82 Box 20 B
Brussels IL 62013

Call Sign: KC9USR
Heidi M Lemmon
Hc 82 Box 20B
Brussels IL 62013

FCC Amateur Radio Licenses in Buckingham

Call Sign: WD9FGX

Walter J Wehlauch
15335 W 7000 S Rd
Buckingham IL 60917

FCC Amateur Radio Licenses in Buckley

Call Sign: N9COF
Tom O Misenhelter
Rr 1 Box 161
Buckley IL 60918

Call Sign: KC9HGK
Matthew A Young
947 E 700 N Rd
Buckley IL 60918

Call Sign: KA9MET
Mary W Misenhelter
446 E 950 N Rd
Buckley IL 60918

Call Sign: KA9FRQ
Oran C Misenhelter
446 E 950 N Rd
Buckley IL 60918

FCC Amateur Radio Licenses in Buckner

Call Sign: N9PRQ
Ronald D Murray
307 S McDyby
Buckner IL 62819

Call Sign: N9VQH
Rickey G Kondoudis
109 Silkwood St
Buckner IL 62819

FCC Amateur Radio Licenses in Buda

Call Sign: WD9CWU
Eldon R Eigsti
6958 1000 E St
Buda IL 61314

Call Sign: WD9GMH

Ronald K Scott
11069 Kentville Rd
Buda IL 61314

FCC Amateur Radio Licenses in Buffalo

Call Sign: KA9BMN
James L Waggoner
15485 Bullard Rd
Buffalo IL 62515

FCC Amateur Radio Licenses in Bulpitt

Call Sign: N9RBR
Donald A Denning
459 Edwards St
Bulpitt IL 62517

Call Sign: N9ZWQ
Anne M Denning
108 James St
Bulpitt IL 62517

FCC Amateur Radio Licenses in Buncombe

Call Sign: N9QPB
Audrey L Henard
9060 Lick Creek Rd
Buncombe IL 62912

Call Sign: KB9BAD
John R Henard
9060 Lick Creek Rd
Buncombe IL 62912

Call Sign: KC9BRG
Norman D Hinkle
890 Mt Pisgah
Buncombe IL 62912

Call Sign: KC9HXD
Dennis W Newman
1925 Schlenker Rd
Buncombe IL 62912

FCC Amateur Radio Licenses in Bunker Hill

Call Sign: KB9BEX
Linda L Poynter
Rr 2 Box 201B
Bunker Hill IL 62014

Call Sign: KB9BEY
Brandi L Poynter
Rr 2 Box 201B
Bunker Hill IL 62014

Call Sign: KB9BEW
Donald E Poynter
Rr 2 Box 201B
Bunker Hill IL 62014

Call Sign: KA9YCK
Floda B Polacek
R 2 Box 202B
Bunker Hill IL 62014

Call Sign: K9AWP
Charles E Eaker
Rr 2 Box 203A
Bunker Hill IL 62014

Call Sign: N9PPG
Earl E Sauerwein
Rr1 Box 297A
Bunker Hill IL 62014

Call Sign: N9NTZ
Robert R Golike
403 E Grant Box 6
Bunker Hill IL 62014

Call Sign: KB9HWL
Marilae M Golike
403 E Grant St Box 6
Bunker Hill IL 62014

Call Sign: WB4PFQ
Harold E Becker
831 E Morgan
Bunker Hill IL 62014

Call Sign: KA9HEA

Clinton M Spickerman
202 E Warren Box 4
Bunker Hill IL 62014

Call Sign: N9UAZ
Brian D Large
6261 Miles Station Rd
Bunker Hill IL 62014

Call Sign: N9GZO
Mary J Arzuagas
201 S Brighton St
Bunker Hill IL 62014

Call Sign: KB9PNT
Luana M Emery
801 W Wilbur
Bunker Hill IL 62014

Call Sign: KA9YCL
Thomas E Polacek
Bunker Hill IL 62014

Call Sign: WD9T
Carlos Arzuagas
Bunker Hill IL 62014

Call Sign: N9LVY
Charles L Baker
Bunker Hill IL 62014

FCC Amateur Radio Licenses in Bureau

Call Sign: WB9VKU
Harold L Hart
119 N North St
Bureau IL 61315

Call Sign: KA9FDB
Jerry L Yarrington
104 North St
Bureau IL 61315

Call Sign: KB9TVN
Matthew L Wagner
302 W Nebraska St
Bureau IL 61315

FCC Amateur Radio Licenses in Burnside

Call Sign: WB9MCF
Ronald L Priebe
2171 N CR 1700
Burnside IL 623305108

FCC Amateur Radio Licenses in Bushnell

Call Sign: KB9JSU
Juanita F Bryan
459 E Barnes St
Bushnell IL 61422

Call Sign: WB9GQW
Ed S Neel
186 N Crafford
Bushnell IL 61422

Call Sign: W9GQW
Ed S Neel
186 N Crafford
Bushnell IL 61422

Call Sign: KB9JSW
Robert J Heath
765 N Washington St
Bushnell IL 61422

Call Sign: AA9KV
Robert A Wilt
924 Rile St
Bushnell IL 61422

Call Sign: KC9HGJ
Mark A Richardson
350 S Dean St
Bushnell IL 61422

Call Sign: KD9EB
John A Douglas
290 S Green St Apt 2
Bushnell IL 61422

Call Sign: KF4TKY
Lenora M Smith
290 S Jackson St

Bushnell IL 61422

Call Sign: KF4JED
Ronald L Smith
290 S Jackson St
Bushnell IL 61422

Call Sign: W0RBH
Dean F Head
505 W Hail
Bushnell IL 61422

Call Sign: N9WZB
Kimberly D Walter
645 W Main
Bushnell IL 61422

Call Sign: K9JIU
George D Stephens
490 W Osborn
Bushnell IL 61422

Call Sign: KA9FLV
Lynn B Hocraffer
924 Walnut
Bushnell IL 61422

Call Sign: KB9PSG
Larry R Shumaker
573 Washington St
Bushnell IL 614221261

Call Sign: W9ESS
Gayle D Zickefoose
Bushnell IL 61422

FCC Amateur Radio Licenses in Butler

Call Sign: WB0RCA
Michael D Maccanelli
6405 Mullins Trl
Butler IL 62015

Call Sign: KC2ZPQ
Clark H Jillson
17046 Rendering Rd
Butler IL 62015

Call Sign: N9MOJ
James W Woolard
Butler IL 62015

Call Sign: KC9QAO
James H Gaither Jr
Butler IL 62015

FCC Amateur Radio Licenses in Byron

Call Sign: W9JWB
John W Beltz Jr
617 Allison Cir Dr Apt 3
Byron IL 61010

Call Sign: KA9BRW
Geraldine B Dorsey
8614 Byron Hills Dr
Byron IL 61010

Call Sign: KC9HLN
Scott A Ramage
260 Creekside Dr
Byron IL 61010

Call Sign: WA9SLQ
Dennis L Foulke
1965 E Water Rd
Byron IL 61010

Call Sign: K9VFS
Lynn D Lewis
5244 German Church Rd
Byron IL 61010

Call Sign: KC9BCD
George R Macri
813 Kingsway Ln
Byron IL 61010

Call Sign: KC9ETW
Heather M Schumacher
5363 Kufalk Ln
Byron IL 61010

Call Sign: WB9KVI
Joseph T Edom
9686 N Blaine Dr

Byron IL 61010

Call Sign: WA9SWS
James A Lapinski
10960 N Kennedy Hill Rd
Byron IL 61010

Call Sign: W9SWS
James A Lapinski
10960 N Kennedy Hill Rd
Byron IL 61010

Call Sign: N9ZBI
Gerald R Anderson
417 N Peru St
Byron IL 61010

Call Sign: KB9LJX
Adam P Larsen
749 Old Hunter Run
Byron IL 61010

Call Sign: K9AST
Duane L Schuldt
1016 Old Hunter Run
Byron IL 61010

Call Sign: NS9P
Russell R Cline
142 S Fox Run Ln
Byron IL 61010

Call Sign: KC9KCD
Michael W Noga
114.5 S Franklin St
Byron IL 61010

Call Sign: N9NQB
Llewelyn R Ellis
225 S Lafayette St
Byron IL 61010

Call Sign: KC9HMH
Gregory J Kuczek
1406 Southfield Ln
Byron IL 61010

Call Sign: W9VOX
Gregory J Kuczek

1406 Southfield Ln
Byron IL 61010

Call Sign: K9SB
Timothy R Tomljanovich
1918 Southfield Ln
Byron IL 61010

Call Sign: KC9NVP
David B Stein
6779 Summit Dr
Byron IL 61010

FCC Amateur Radio Licenses in Cabery

Call Sign: KC9SQG
David R Bolt
208 S State St
Cabery IL 60919

FCC Amateur Radio Licenses in Cache

Call Sign: N9OWO
Paul R Pittman
Rt 1 Box 1A
Cache IL 62913

FCC Amateur Radio Licenses in Cahokia

Call Sign: WB9HIE
Wayne L Baur
218 Annunication
Cahokia IL 62206

Call Sign: KB5COJ
Matthew M Seher
22 Cir Creek Dr
Cahokia IL 62206

Call Sign: WB9TNR
Allen F Coy
2051 Doris Ave
Cahokia IL 62206

Call Sign: KB9WBH
Donald C Odum Jr

809 Ester
Cahokia IL 62206

Call Sign: N9MDI
Robert M Brown
19 Fox Meadow Ln
Cahokia IL 62206

Call Sign: KC9CXR
Robby L Gordon
1812 Harvest Ave
Cahokia IL 62206

Call Sign: KC9KTP
Brian R Lavallee
730 Howell Ave
Cahokia IL 62206

Call Sign: KC9KTO
Bob K Lavallee
730 Howell Ave
Cahokia IL 622061902

Call Sign: W9KTO
Bob K Lavallee
730 Howell Ave
Cahokia IL 622061902

Call Sign: KB9VQN
Karl E Schumacher
224 Julian Ave
Cahokia IL 62206

Call Sign: KC0NIF
Wayne C Chang
265 Kazilek Dr
Cahokia IL 622062208

Call Sign: KB9WLJ
Vernon A Egert
251 Kazilek Dr Apt 2
Cahokia IL 62206

Call Sign: KE6NTG
Norman J Musselman
131 Kinder
Cahokia IL 62206

Call Sign: KB9DGN

Steven A Hoffman
221 Kinder Dr
Cahokia IL 62206

Call Sign: WA9RJO
Corene Himmer
2445 Lorraine Dr
Cahokia IL 62206

Call Sign: KB9DRA
Buddy G Gillan
2029 Maple Tree
Cahokia IL 622061439

Call Sign: KB9LBC
Jason C Cato
2334 Maynor Dr
Cahokia IL 62206

Call Sign: KC9HUH
Mitchell A Guetterman
1323 Morning Star
Cahokia IL 62206

Call Sign: KC9NTF
Trisha M Guetterman
1323 Morning Star
Cahokia IL 62206

Call Sign: WB9JRH
Trisha M Guetterman
1323 Morning Star
Cahokia IL 62206

Call Sign: KB9DES
James W Bernachi Sr
1765 Park Ln Dr
Cahokia IL 62206

Call Sign: WA9FNJ
Richard A Hamilton
803 Preston Ln
Cahokia IL 622062037

Call Sign: KB9SCP
Richard L Alexander Sr
1305 Richard Dr
Cahokia IL 62206

Call Sign: WD9EQP
James A Markins
327 Rieber Dr
Cahokia IL 62206

Call Sign: W0QAC
Murrel S Perry
1167 Smith St
Cahokia IL 62206

Call Sign: N9USW
Joseph E Flanagan
306 St Leonard
Cahokia IL 62206

Call Sign: N0CUS
Joseph F Messerly Jr
1204 St Michael Dr
Cahokia IL 622062216

Call Sign: KC9NUL
Christopher Jackson Jr
310 W 3rd St
Cahokia IL 62206

Call Sign: KC9NUK
Lucas A Carroll
307 W 4th St
Cahokia IL 62206

Call Sign: KC9NUJ
William M Carroll
307 W 4th St
Cahokia IL 62206

Call Sign: KC9CIJ
Rebecca J Carroll
307 W 4th St
Cahokia IL 62206

Call Sign: KC9CIK
William L Carroll
307 W 4thst
Cahokia IL 622061013

Call Sign: KA9UOM
Donald Wilson
2409 White St
Cahokia IL 62206

FCC Amateur Radio Licenses in Cairo

Call Sign: KC9SPZ
Calvin S Watson
616 26th St
Cairo IL 62914

Call Sign: K9EXH
Donald R Mc Ginness
414 28th St
Cairo IL 629141338

Call Sign: K9ZID
Fred E Lehning
416 28th St
Cairo IL 62914

Call Sign: N9VXC
Rodney Dennis
516 28th St
Cairo IL 62914

Call Sign: KG9ED
Michael R Coleman
428 32nd St
Cairo IL 62914

Call Sign: KB9MLY
Nicci M Coleman
428 32nd St
Cairo IL 62914

Call Sign: N9XZQ
Christopher M Coleman
428 32nd St
Cairo IL 62914

Call Sign: KB9OAU
James T Hinman
520 33rd St
Cairo IL 62914

Call Sign: N9TSM
Fred E Schubert Jr
411 34th St
Cairo IL 62914

Call Sign: N9QJY
Herbert A Vinson
413 34th St
Cairo IL 62914

Call Sign: N9QJX
Manuel W Liong Jr
309 8th St
Cairo IL 62914

Call Sign: KA9NFP
Ralph E Sasseen
Rt 1 Box 282
Cairo IL 62914

Call Sign: KB9NCW
John S Ronnebeck
2 Edgewood Park
Cairo IL 629141043

Call Sign: N9TET
Ronald W Sutton
2501 Holbrook St
Cairo IL 62914

Call Sign: N9XNF
Mary L Moreland
2501 Park Ave
Cairo IL 62914

Call Sign: N9DBL
John G Wild
3101 Park Ave
Cairo IL 62914

Call Sign: KB9SP
Ronald E Hornberger
14952 Seven Mile Rd
Cairo IL 62914

Call Sign: NE9D
Henry Carlton
2210 Washington Ave
Cairo IL 62914

Call Sign: AA9HC
Joseph A Morin
2613.5 Washington Ave
Cairo IL 62914

Call Sign: N9TWZ
Wayne E Thomas
Cairo IL 62914

Call Sign: N9NFN
Elizabeth D Shackles
Cairo IL 62914

Call Sign: KA9SKT
Rickey S Shackles
Cairo IL 62914

Call Sign: KC9CEC
Rikki D H Shackles
Cairo IL 62914

Call Sign: N9ONV
Richard T Kearney
Cairo IL 629140323

FCC Amateur Radio Licenses in Caledonia

Call Sign: KI4NMV
Scott W Evans
6321 Blyth Rd
Caledonia IL 61011

Call Sign: KT9P
Dale F Mather
12357 Cameron Ct
Caledonia IL 610119120

Call Sign: KG9OQ
Nancy A Clark Mather
12357 Cameron Ct
Caledonia IL 610119120

Call Sign: KC9UQK
Matt A Mlsna
1259 Krupke Rd
Caledonia IL 61011

Call Sign: KC9FAI
Robert J Rosander
5286 Lake Crest Rd
Caledonia IL 61011

Call Sign: WF9C
Martin T Bowyer
8570 Perth Ln
Caledonia IL 61011

FCC Amateur Radio Licenses in Calhoun

Call Sign: N9QZA
Jackson M Clodfelter
1860 N Meridan Rd
Calhoun IL 62419

Call Sign: KB9QVD
Mary L Clodfelter
1860 N Meridian
Calhoun IL 62419

Call Sign: KC9QJF
Deanna J Newlin
105 S Jasper St
Calhoun IL 62419

Call Sign: N9TZU
Deanna J Newlin
105 S Jasper St
Calhoun IL 62419

Call Sign: KC9QOU
Kayla M Newlin
107 S Jasper St
Calhoun IL 62419

Call Sign: KC9QJE
Tim E Newlin
107 S Jasper St
Calhoun IL 62419

Call Sign: N9TZU
Wallace E Croslow
107 S Jasper St
Calhoun IL 62419

FCC Amateur Radio Licenses in Camargo

Call Sign: KB9OTP
Larry E Lamasters
1725 E CR 725 N

Camargo IL 61919

Call Sign: KC9KGJ
Jeremy A Lamb
Camargo IL 61919

FCC Amateur Radio Licenses in Cambria

Call Sign: KA9WOK
Henry F Varner
416 W Madison St
Cambria IL 629150153

Call Sign: KD7SIN
Benito J Sanchez
Cambria IL 629150346

FCC Amateur Radio Licenses in Cambridge

Call Sign: KA9UGJ
Christopher W Young
Rr 1 Box 43
Cambridge IL 61238

Call Sign: KB9LRI
Ronald F Franck
8843 E 1200th St
Cambridge IL 61238

Call Sign: KB9LIS
Joyce A Sizek
216 S Holmes
Cambridge IL 61238

Call Sign: KB9LDA
Le Moyne J Sizek
216 S Holmes
Cambridge IL 61238

Call Sign: KB9UPZ
William R Powell
602 West Ct
Cambridge IL 61238

FCC Amateur Radio Licenses in Cameron

Call Sign: KB9QXA
Stephen W Johnson
1455 160th Ave
Cameron IL 61423

Call Sign: KB9QXB
Beverly R Johnson
1455 160th Ave
Cameron IL 61423

Call Sign: K9OST
Theodore E Tinkham
1715 160th St
Cameron IL 61423

Call Sign: W9JV
Edward F Hanson
Rr 1 Box 13
Cameron IL 61423

FCC Amateur Radio Licenses in Camp Point

Call Sign: KA9ZSB
Donald M Sharow
1842 E 2200th St
Camp Point IL 62320

Call Sign: KC9NYN
Amber L Clevenger
106 E Prairie St
Camp Point IL 62320

Call Sign: WA9CIX
George A Mc Nutt
606 E Wood St
Camp Point IL 62320

Call Sign: KC3ZQ
David W Cripe
2202 N 1200 Ave
Camp Point IL 62320

Call Sign: KB9ZEN
Gilbert R Housewright
300 N Ill
Camp Point IL 62320

Call Sign: KB9ZFG

Laura J Housewright
300 N Ill
Camp Point IL 62320

Call Sign: KC9ITO
Steven H Miller
329 N Vermont St
Camp Point IL 62320

Call Sign: K9SHM
Steven H Miller
329 N Vermont St
Camp Point IL 62320

Call Sign: AB6KF
Harry D Mills
208 NE Vermont
Camp Point IL 62320

Call Sign: WB9JQW
Richard O Mensendike
108 W School St
Camp Point IL 62320

Call Sign: NG9R
Danny R Pease
Camp Point IL 62320

Call Sign: KC9MXH
James T Clevenger
Camp Point IL 62320

Call Sign: AB9QW
James T Clevenger
Camp Point IL 62320

Call Sign: KC9LCI
Steven M Eicken
Camp Point IL 62320

Call Sign: KA9VIM
Zuda G Pease
Camp Point IL 62320

FCC Amateur Radio Licenses in Campbell Hill

Call Sign: KC9SCY
Tad R Lee

Campbell Hill IL 62916

FCC Amateur Radio Licenses in Canton

Call Sign: KB9WNJ
Roscoe W Bickel
618 Baxter Ct
Canton IL 61520

Call Sign: KA3GGT
Bruce F Stake
576 Dean Ct
Canton IL 61520

Call Sign: NA9RB
Randal L Burnham
1306 E Ash St
Canton IL 61520

Call Sign: N9BVW
Arnold G Allison
24642 E Baker Dr
Canton IL 61520

Call Sign: KB9DMH
Adam D Swope
8 E Cedar
Canton IL 61520

Call Sign: WB9KEW
Everett G Phillips
23724 E Co Hwy 27
Canton IL 61520

Call Sign: KB9SOD
Daniel G Walters II
20016 E County 21 Hwy
Canton IL 61520

Call Sign: N9IZX
Jeremy B Cole
21236 E County Hwy 17
Canton IL 61520

Call Sign: KB9YBO
Chad A Droll
26867 E Cypress Rd
Canton IL 61520

Call Sign: WA0EFD
Darrell L Bobo
55 E Cypress St Apt 304
Canton IL 61520

Call Sign: N9MJX
Donald S Taylor
554 E Elm St
Canton IL 61520

Call Sign: N9KUL
Richard C Nelson
855 E Elm St
Canton IL 61520

Call Sign: KC9ICW
Marcellus J Brockman
896 E Elm St
Canton IL 61520

Call Sign: KB9KAZ
Aaron M Child
1218 E Elm St
Canton IL 61520

Call Sign: KB9ZMV
William E Moyers
27743 E Il 9 Hwy
Canton IL 61520

Call Sign: KB9ZWU
Andrew W Moyers
27743 E Il 9 Hwy
Canton IL 61520

Call Sign: KA9THI
Anna L Haggerty
21117 E McLouth Rd
Canton IL 61520

Call Sign: KA9THJ
Robert L Haggerty
21117 E McLouth Rd
Canton IL 61520

Call Sign: KB9NKQ
George H O Donnell
221 E Olive

Canton IL 61520

Call Sign: W9GHO
George H O Donnell
221 E Olive
Canton IL 61520

Call Sign: KA9MMW
Michael D Carrier
1219 E Olive St
Canton IL 61520

Call Sign: WD9IGD
Gayle H Ellis
30 E Shamrock
Canton IL 61520

Call Sign: W9GHE
Gayle H Ellis
30 E Shamrock
Canton IL 61520

Call Sign: KC9CID
Dale R Coleno
1110 E Sycamore
Canton IL 61520

Call Sign: KB9NKT
Jimmie M Smith Sr
1240 E Sycamore St
Canton IL 615201427

Call Sign: N9TTC
Patrick A Mc Cabe
22279 E Texas Rd
Canton IL 61520

Call Sign: N9PAM
Patrick A Mc Cabe
22279 E Texas Rd
Canton IL 61520

Call Sign: KA9MMC
Gregory S Zobac
45 Edmar Dr
Canton IL 615202420

Call Sign: KC9MFL
Bruce A Courtney

157 Fairview Plc
Canton IL 61520

Call Sign: KC0TPJ
Shawn L Newlan
271 Fulton Pl
Canton IL 61520

Call Sign: KB9UXL
Edward E Keeran
251 Haffner Blvd
Canton IL 61520

Call Sign: KA9MUI
Henry C Meads
317 Harvester Ln
Canton IL 61520

Call Sign: KE9IJ
Christopher S Kennedy
1211 Juniper St
Canton IL 61520

Call Sign: KC9LDH
Allen K Savegnago
40 Laurel Dr
Canton IL 61520

Call Sign: W9BLP
Barton C Matthews
70 Middle Park Dr
Canton IL 61520

Call Sign: KB9WLM
Larry A Bishop
1350 Montello Ct
Canton IL 61520

Call Sign: KB9UQD
James E Diden
500 N 10th
Canton IL 61520

Call Sign: N9VIR
David A Thompson
700 N 10th Ave Apt 1
Canton IL 61520

Call Sign: WD9IBX

Allistair R Mc Pherson
315 N 11th Ave
Canton IL 61520

Call Sign: KS9A
Colin T Adams
419 N 3rd Ave
Canton IL 61520

Call Sign: N9PJZ
Carl Zaborac Jr
245 N 7th Ave
Canton IL 61520

Call Sign: N9YOS
Richard G Zaborac
245 N 7th Ave
Canton IL 61520

Call Sign: KB9LJJ
Carl W Burnham
756 N 7th St
Canton IL 61520

Call Sign: K9LFP
George S Frank
875 N 9th Ave
Canton IL 61520

Call Sign: AB9QE
Amos A Anderson
258 N Ave D
Canton IL 61520

Call Sign: N9XJW
Candice S Lalwson
139 N Ave F
Canton IL 61520

Call Sign: N9QMA
Ernest E Burchett
435 N Ave F
Canton IL 61520

Call Sign: K9MPX
Harold D Pschirrer
1410 N Main St
Canton IL 61520

Call Sign: N9DXN
David L Butler
2081 N Main St
Canton IL 61520

Call Sign: N9TTF
Phil L Miller
25801 N Pin Oak Dr
Canton IL 61520

Call Sign: KC9BWG
Thomas L Oppe
29192 N Roberson Ln
Canton IL 61520

Call Sign: KC9BVO
Tyler M White
158 N Rogers Park Dr
Canton IL 61520

Call Sign: KD9OX
Linda R Adams
35 N Sycamore Ter
Canton IL 615201222

Call Sign: N9GA
Gary L Adams
35 N Sycamore Ter
Canton IL 615201222

Call Sign: WM9C
Jeremy D Ruck
221 S 1st Ave
Canton IL 61520

Call Sign: N9XJV
Linda S Evans
734 S 1st Ave
Canton IL 61520

Call Sign: N9TYR
Maurice E Phillips Jr
734 S 1st Ave
Canton IL 61520

Call Sign: N9TTD
Jack R Tomlianovich
1161 S 6th Ave
Canton IL 61520

Call Sign: AA9YA
Jack R Tomlianovich
1161 S 6th Ave
Canton IL 61520

Call Sign: WZ9O
Jack R Tomlianovich
1161 S 6th Ave
Canton IL 615203449

Call Sign: KB9SOC
Allen L Herrick
257 S 9th Ave
Canton IL 615202905

Call Sign: N9XKE
Robert E Looser
325 S Bridge St
Canton IL 61520

Call Sign: N9OFQ
Larry D Avery
433 S Main St
Canton IL 61520

Call Sign: KB9KAV
Robert E Shockency Sr
509 S Main St
Canton IL 61520

Call Sign: WA9AFC
Dale A Woods
250 S Main St Apt 405
Canton IL 61520

Call Sign: K9SQA
John Ronketto Jr
250 S Main St Apt 411
Canton IL 61520

Call Sign: KB9HKA
Douglas C Denham
355 Sycamore
Canton IL 61520

Call Sign: K9ILS
Fulton County ARC
35 Sycamore Ter

Canton IL 615201222

Call Sign: N9HWO
Philip B Fleming
149 Van Dyke Dr
Canton IL 61520

Call Sign: KB9JP
Daniel W Corey
165 Van Dyke Dr
Canton IL 615201152

Call Sign: N9PJA
Munjal N Parikh
232 W Chestnut St 8
Canton IL 61520

Call Sign: N9PKA
Randy L Jump
453 W Elm
Canton IL 61520

Call Sign: KC9UTP
Anthony F Nidiffer
1156 W Hickory
Canton IL 61520

Call Sign: N9WJR
William A Nidiffer
1156 W Hickory
Canton IL 61520

Call Sign: KC9ICG
John C Davis
1019 W Locust
Canton IL 61520

Call Sign: KC9MAU
James A Heaton
46 W Maple St
Canton IL 61520

Call Sign: W9OOJ
Herchel D Plotts
540 W Myrtle Ave
Canton IL 61520

Call Sign: KB9LRS
Charles A Shockency

241 W Oak
Canton IL 61520

Call Sign: KC9RNG
Steven L Bowton
450 W Railroad St
Canton IL 61520

Call Sign: KC9FGB
Joseph D Morrow
399 W Walnut
Canton IL 61520

Call Sign: KB9NKR
Benjamin J P Wroblewski
447 Walling Ct
Canton IL 61520

Call Sign: KB9JQF
Cory P Hart
1407 Wheeler
Canton IL 61520

Call Sign: NK9C
Cory P Hart
1407 Wheeler
Canton IL 61520

Call Sign: KB9YKW
David B Bell
Canton IL 61520

Call Sign: WA9AFJ
Jo Ann Block
Canton IL 61520

Call Sign: N9NEV
Phyllis A Walljasper
Canton IL 61520

FCC Amateur Radio Licenses in Cantrall

Call Sign: KB9IPE
Lawrence E Wooley
Rr 1 Box 38B
Cantrall IL 62625

Call Sign: N9MQN

John J Gibbons Jr
2248 Gabbert Rd
Cantrall IL 62625

Call Sign: KA9UBJ
Joyce I Cary
4020 Irwin Bridge Rd
Cantrall IL 62625

Call Sign: WX9DX
James M Cary
4020 Irwin Bridge Rd
Cantrall IL 62625

Call Sign: WA9IAF
Brian D Morgan
5405 S Cantrall Creek Rd
Cantrall IL 626258703

Call Sign: KD9DX
Brian D Morgan
5405 S Cantrall Creek Rd
Cantrall IL 626258703

Call Sign: KA9EVE
Dale E Ingram
Cantrall IL 62625

Call Sign: N9EUO
James M Cary
Cantrall IL 62625

FCC Amateur Radio Licenses in Capron

Call Sign: KC9DHC
Gregory J Kolacinski
7744 Edson Rd
Capron IL 61012

Call Sign: N9INC
Henry J Szmuc
16215 Mill Rd
Capron IL 61012

Call Sign: KB9KQM
Marlowe R Dronen
185 Rainbow Dr
Capron IL 610129588

Call Sign: N9JZR
John M Gray
Capron IL 61012

Call Sign: KB9MWV
Bijan Pashaie
121 4th
Carbondale IL 62901

Call Sign: KC9FDH
Brad J Sata
408 Allen Ii
Carbondale IL 62901

Call Sign: K9JTS
Clifford L Coleman
2971 Alveria Dr
Carbondale IL 62901

Call Sign: KC9SED
Michelle R Thomas
114 Archelle Dr
Carbondale IL 62901

Call Sign: KC9PYU
Alex D Hopkins
79 Bobette Ln
Carbondale IL 62901

Call Sign: KC9SOH
Jacob S Jackson
192 Bobette Ln
Carbondale IL 62901

Call Sign: KC9JPM
Leland A Jackson
192 Bobette Ln
Carbondale IL 62901

Call Sign: AB9OT
Leland A Jackson
192 Bobette Ln
Carbondale IL 62901

Call Sign: K9GDV

Marvin M Hamilton
538 Boskydell Rd
Carbondale IL 62901

Call Sign: K5AAK
Jefferson F Lindsey III
2609 Boskydell Rd
Carbondale IL 629017718

Call Sign: KB9OWG
Julia S Throgmorton
Rr3 Box 253
Carbondale IL 62901

Call Sign: KA9SST
Jon E Hartley
Rt 1 Box 324
Carbondale IL 62901

Call Sign: N9CXE
David P Smeltzer
Rr 1 Box 455
Carbondale IL 62901

Call Sign: KC9JPP
Thomas F Thibeault
904 Brairwood Dr
Carbondale IL 62901

Call Sign: KC9GKP
Kirk R Thirtyacre
1000 Brehm Ln Apt J 2
Carbondale IL 62901

Call Sign: WD9ARU
Thomas M Kalvaitis
2300 Broken Handle Ln
Carbondale IL 62902

Call Sign: N6ASY
Harry J Nelson III
417 Brush Hill Rd
Carbondale IL 62901

Call Sign: WT9D
Shannon L Collins
4995 Collins Ln
Carbondale IL 62901

Call Sign: KC9JPK
Brenda L Bartholemew
1709 Colonial Dr
Carbondale IL 62901

Call Sign: N9JML
Frankie D Payne
1713 Colonial Dr
Carbondale IL 62901

Call Sign: KC9BOW
Robert J Heren
2999 Country Club Rd
Carbondale IL 62901

Call Sign: KA9EWN
Knute R Bleyer
3152 Country Club Rd
Carbondale IL 62901

Call Sign: NR9T
Knute R Bleyer
3152 Country Club Rd
Carbondale IL 62901

Call Sign: K9SIU
Knute R Bleyer
3152 Country Club Rd
Carbondale IL 62901

Call Sign: KC9SZM
Hayden E Smith
152 Court Rd
Carbondale IL 62901

Call Sign: KB5PSN
Catherine J Porter
463 Deerfield Ln
Carbondale IL 62901

Call Sign: N5UMW
Charlie T Porter
463 Deerfield Ln
Carbondale IL 62901

Call Sign: KC9UYX
Christopher D Rogers
3546 Dillinger Rd Apt A
Carbondale IL 62901

Call Sign: KB9FTK
Kenneth M Johnson
2525 Dogwood Rd
Carbondale IL 62902

Call Sign: N9VDK
Kimberly A Talley
170 E Clayton
Carbondale IL 62901

Call Sign: KC9SEG
Robb J Smith
210 E College St
Carbondale IL 62901

Call Sign: KC9VDS
Waylon A Smeathers
800 E Grand Ave Apt 13A
Carbondale IL 62901

Call Sign: KC9FDI
Nicholas J Torres
800 E Grand Ave Apt 36D
Carbondale IL 62901

Call Sign: KC9SEC
Marcus E Randall
322 E Hester St Apt 1
Carbondale IL 62901

Call Sign: KC9SEF
Shawn Strauther
900 E Park St
Carbondale IL 62901

Call Sign: KC9JMW
Richard J Niemeyer
506 E Sycamore St
Carbondale IL 62901

Call Sign: KC9AWF
Anna L Luxion
1181 E Walnut St Apt 5 6
Carbondale IL 62901

Call Sign: W9UIH
Southern Illinois Univ ARC
D47 Engineering S Il Univ

Carbondale IL 629016603

Call Sign: KB9CIB
Vivek Prasad
197 8 Evergreen Ter
Carbondale IL 62901

Call Sign: KC9NJG
Jung W Park
1962 Evergreen Ter Dr E 4
Carbondale IL 62901

Call Sign: KC9BMS
Seok Choo Han
1985 Evergreen Ter Dr E Apt 7
Carbondale IL 62901

Call Sign: WA9PDT
Leonard G Wood
1527 Gary Dr
Carbondale IL 629015062

Call Sign: KC9JPL
Rosemary L Paul
2093 Grammer Rd
Carbondale IL 62903

Call Sign: KC9JPN
Bradley C Paul
2093 Grammer Rd
Carbondale IL 62903

Call Sign: KC9KFG
Rosa A Paul
2093 Grammer Rd
Carbondale IL 62903

Call Sign: KB9PKK
Bertha L Riddle
6896 Hayton School Rd
Carbondale IL 62901

Call Sign: KB9SB
Milburn Riddle
6896 Hayton School Rd
Carbondale IL 629010809

Call Sign: K9TCK

Gordon L Hansen
512 Kennicott
Carbondale IL 62901

Call Sign: KB9WUT
Michael C Riley
920 Kira Ct
Carbondale IL 62901

Call Sign: KC9ULR
Paul B Juergens
364 Lake Indian Hills Cir
Carbondale IL 62902

Call Sign: N9LNU
Bradley W Dillard
11574 Laurelwood Ln
Carbondale IL 62901

Call Sign: AK9J
Lee Rogers
67 Loblolly Ln
Carbondale IL 62902

Call Sign: KC9JNX
Bruce S Stewart
1655 Logan Dr Apt 6
Carbondale IL 62901

Call Sign: KC9UUW
Luke T Tolley
91 Lois Ln
Carbondale IL 62902

Call Sign: W9OW
John S Mead
78 Magnolia Ln
Carbondale IL 62903

Call Sign: KA9BSA
Bsa Troop 66
78 Magnolia Ln
Carbondale IL 629037665

Call Sign: KA9GIS
Candace A Davis
1001 N Bridge St
Carbondale IL 62901

Call Sign: WA9SAC
John R Davis
1001 N Bridge St
Carbondale IL 62901

Call Sign: KB9VES
Nathan P Gibson
1017 N Carico
Carbondale IL 62901

Call Sign: KB9UYT
Paul T Gibson
1017 N Carico
Carbondale IL 629011222

Call Sign: KC9URZ
Aaron C Savka
11288 N County Line Rd
Carbondale IL 62901

Call Sign: KA9TTP
William H Hertter
11795 N Hwy 51
Carbondale IL 62901

Call Sign: KA9PEZ
James R Miller
704 N James
Carbondale IL 62901

Call Sign: N9RIO
Kimberly A Miller
704 N James
Carbondale IL 62901

Call Sign: KA9UUR
Mary E Miller
704 N James
Carbondale IL 62901

Call Sign: KC9FIP
Tod J Policandriotes
1850 N New Era Rd
Carbondale IL 62901

Call Sign: KB9GFK
Walter B Lookofsky
303 N Poplar St
Carbondale IL 62901

Call Sign: N9AAT
Scott A Manthe
403.5 N Poplar St
Carbondale IL 62901

Call Sign: KC9SKW
Mary J Johnson
112 N Rod Ln
Carbondale IL 62901

Call Sign: KC9SKX
Stephen E Johnson
112 N Rod Ln
Carbondale IL 62901

Call Sign: KC9GYE
Nick A Darr
805 N Springer
Carbondale IL 62035

Call Sign: KC9KD
Curtis R Trammel
618 N Springer St
Carbondale IL 62901

Call Sign: KC9DEU
Michael A Nalogin
102 N Violet Apt D
Carbondale IL 62901

Call Sign: W9AAE
Riley P Tucker
355 Neely Dr
Carbondale IL 62901

Call Sign: KC9QVQ
Amanda S Nash
2000 New Era Rd Apt A3
Carbondale IL 62901

Call Sign: KC9QVN
Christopher S Nash
2000 New Era Rd Apt A3
Carbondale IL 62901

Call Sign: KC9NWG
William D Shoup
15 Pine Lake Dr

Carbondale IL 62901

Call Sign: KC9GBC
Derek A Misener
183 Pineview Rd
Carbondale IL 62901

Call Sign: K9DAM
Derek A Misener
183 Pineview Rd
Carbondale IL 62901

Call Sign: KB9DDW
Wilson R Scott
6 Pinewood
Carbondale IL 62901

Call Sign: W9GCO
Morton P Levine
8 Pinewood
Carbondale IL 62901

Call Sign: KB9IUZ
Larry S Briggs
7 Pinewood Dr
Carbondale IL 62901

Call Sign: KB9IQT
Maria M Pereira
305 Robinson Cr Ac
Carbondale IL 62901

Call Sign: WA9QXW
Thomas H Beebe
69 Roosevelt Rd
Carbondale IL 629015719

Call Sign: KC9AYD
William C Stevens
84 Roosevelt Rd
Carbondale IL 62901

Call Sign: K9YP
William C Stevens
84 Roosevelt Rd
Carbondale IL 62901

Call Sign: KB9ANK
Robin M Hanus

Pleasant Hill W 5 Rr 5
Carbondale IL 62901

Call Sign: KF9XP
Glenn D Keneipp
323 Russell Rd
Carbondale IL 62901

Call Sign: W9GDK
Glenn D Keneipp
323 Russell Rd
Carbondale IL 62901

Call Sign: KC9BMP
Etienne M Witte
509 S Ash St Apt 16
Carbondale IL 62901

Call Sign: WD9GVD
William E Byrnes
1453 S County Line Rd 89
Carbondale IL 62901

Call Sign: AB9BD
William E Byrnes
1383 S County Line Rd Lot 24
Carbondale IL 62902

Call Sign: KC9CGU
Robert A Davis
208 S Dixon Ave
Carbondale IL 62901

Call Sign: KC9CVS
Reba K Davis
208 S Dixon Ave
Carbondale IL 629012310

Call Sign: KB9WL
William A Thornburg
932 S Giant City Rd
Carbondale IL 62901

Call Sign: N9EDT
Gaylin D Fligor
3614 S Illinois Ave
Carbondale IL 62903

Call Sign: KC9JPO

Michelle L Stewart
905 S Johnson Ave
Carbondale IL 62901

Call Sign: KA9TQK
Gerald F Zimmerman
700 S Lewis Ln Apt 1305
Carbondale IL 629013362

Call Sign: KC9KNP
Michael E Allen
515 S Lincoln St
Carbondale IL 62901

Call Sign: KC9VDT
Brendan J Mccoy
401 S Logan
Carbondale IL 62901

Call Sign: KC9HXC
Kay M Purcell
1012 S Oakland Ave
Carbondale IL 629012559

Call Sign: K9IE
Kay M Purcell
1012 S Oakland Ave
Carbondale IL 629012559

Call Sign: KC9BMR
Frances J Harackiewicz
107 S Parrish Ln
Carbondale IL 62901

Call Sign: KB9NQP
Nancy S Heuer
701 S Poplar St Th 3
Carbondale IL 62901

Call Sign: KC9BBR
Develon J Robinson
516 S Rawlings Apt A408
Carbondale IL 62901

Call Sign: KA9KCP
Kurt A Feiste
104 S Rod Ln
Carbondale IL 62901

Call Sign: KC9BMO
Sudheer Bhogadi
510 S University Ave Apt 11
Carbondale IL 62901

Call Sign: KC9BMN
Kiyun Han
510 S University Ave Apt 21
Carbondale IL 62901

Call Sign: KC9BBT
John M Bell
716 S University Ave Apt 27
Carbondale IL 62901

Call Sign: KC9BMQ
Adriano P Raiva
509 S Wall St Apt 12
Carbondale IL 62901

Call Sign: KC9UFW
Alan B Selander
514 S Wall St Apt 7
Carbondale IL 62901

Call Sign: KC7QYF
Lindell E Barrell
3488 Sneed Rd
Carbondale IL 62901

Call Sign: WD9DVZ
Sheryl A Hinchcliff
81 Spring Arbor Dr
Carbondale IL 62901

Call Sign: WB9ZHK
William E Hinchcliff Jr
81 Spring Arbor Dr
Carbondale IL 62901

Call Sign: KG9HA
Christopher J Midden
3493 Springer Ridge Rd
Carbondale IL 62901

Call Sign: W9WHH
Terry R Thalman
2609 Sunset
Carbondale IL 62901

Call Sign: N9HOB
Julius A Nolting
611 Surrey Ln
Carbondale IL 62901

Call Sign: KB9SPJ
Chih Liang Huang
707 W College Apt 6
Carbondale IL 62901

Call Sign: KC9BBQ
Lakshmanan Veerappan
820 W Freeman 106
Carbondale IL 62901

Call Sign: KC9SAK
Yi Hsin Chiu
820 W Freeman St
Carbondale IL 62901

Call Sign: KB9RCZ
Wilma E Reese
1206 W Hill
Carbondale IL 62901

Call Sign: KB9ZRI
James Hathaway
1809 W Main 299
Carbondale IL 62901

Call Sign: N6WCB
Karen L Hathaway
1809 W Main 299
Carbondale IL 62901

Call Sign: KB9ZHL
Liesl K Hathaway
1809 W Main 299
Carbondale IL 62901

Call Sign: KB9ZRJ
John C Hathaway
1809 W Main St 299
Carbondale IL 62901

Call Sign: W9DRP
Herman F Ebbs
1052 W No Name Rd

Carbondale IL 62901

Call Sign: K9QW
Thomas H Beebe
2004 W Sunset
Carbondale IL 629012038

Call Sign: WD8NRM
John P Mc Nally
1709 W Sycamore St
Carbondale IL 62901

Call Sign: KA9CSP
Bruce L Cline
1400 W Taylor Dr
Carbondale IL 62901

Call Sign: WI9G
Mamoru Okawara
510 W Walnut 7
Carbondale IL 62901

Call Sign: KC9LJH
Niquita T Lee
910 Walnut 12
Carbondale IL 62901

Call Sign: KB9PAZ
Dennis R Hannon
29 Weatherford Ln
Carbondale IL 629027779

Call Sign: W9JPQ
Harry P Burns
221 Wood Rd
Carbondale IL 62901

Call Sign: KC9ENR
Howard A Underwood
808 Woodland Ct
Carbondale IL 62901

Call Sign: KC9KOI
Harry W Treece II
Carbondale IL 62902

Call Sign: K1MBE
Ray Kelly
Carbondale IL 62902

Call Sign: N9OPQ
W Paul Woolard
Carbondale IL 62903

Call Sign: KB9DBC
Gregg L Sperling
Carbondale IL 629023264

Call Sign: KB9E
Gregg L Sperling
Carbondale IL 629023264

Call Sign: WA9YHX
Robyn M Sperling
Carbondale IL 629023264

FCC Amateur Radio Licenses in Carlinville

Call Sign: WA9STA
Maurice B Madden
113 Alton
Carlinville IL 62626

Call Sign: KA9LVH
John N Wood
Rr 4 Box 102
Carlinville IL 62626

Call Sign: KC9HAT
Macoupin County ARC
129 E 1st St
Carlinville IL 626260253

Call Sign: K9MCE
Macoupin County ARC
129 E 1st St
Carlinville IL 626260253

Call Sign: N9RGA
Mark D Kaiser
702 E 2nd S St
Carlinville IL 62626

Call Sign: KB9WHY
Anthony C Graham
335 Ellison
Carlinville IL 62626

Call Sign: N9UBA
Benjamin M Graham
335 Ellison
Carlinville IL 62626

Call Sign: K9MDQ
Michael D Graham
335 Ellison
Carlinville IL 62626

Call Sign: WD0BTI
Peggy S Graham
335 Ellison
Carlinville IL 62626

Call Sign: K9AUB
Gary R Huff
321 Ellison St
Carlinville IL 62626

Call Sign: N9ZZO
Katherine E Graham
335 Ellison St
Carlinville IL 62626

Call Sign: N9OFV
Thomas E Huson
9726 Hettick Rd
Carlinville IL 62626

Call Sign: W9PPR
Carl Hook
141 Hoehn
Carlinville IL 62626

Call Sign: KB9KZU
Donald M Challans
619 Johnson St
Carlinville IL 626261436

Call Sign: N0AP
William J Ogle
104 Lakeview Dr
Carlinville IL 62626

Call Sign: W9FJ
William J Ogle
104 Lakeview Dr

Carlinville IL 626261552

Call Sign: KC9OHE
George W Emmons
11688 Liberty Church Ln
Carlinville IL 62626

Call Sign: KC9OHD
Jennifer M Emmons
11688 Liberty Church Ln
Carlinville IL 62626

Call Sign: N9TPN
Francis W Snodgrass
308 Minton
Carlinville IL 62626

Call Sign: N9UJF
Doris A Falter
436 N East St
Carlinville IL 62626

Call Sign: N9RQB
Edgar J Falter
436 N East St
Carlinville IL 62626

Call Sign: N9USX
Devin R Kaiser
16328 Nicholas Rd
Carlinville IL 62626

Call Sign: KC9LIC
David E Emmons
210 Pershing Ave
Carlinville IL 62626

Call Sign: KC9OHF
Lisa A Sanders
210 Pershing St
Carlinville IL 62626

Call Sign: KC9KNK
Gregg L Laws
45 Pheasant Ln
Carlinville IL 62626

Call Sign: AB9NU
Gregg L Laws

45 Pheasant Ln
Carlinville IL 62626

Call Sign: KI9Z
Gregg L Laws
45 Pheasant Ln
Carlinville IL 62626

Call Sign: KB9TOG
Delores J Bouillon
16711 Rt 108
Carlinville IL 62626

Call Sign: W9OT
Dennis D Goesmann
16711 Rt 108
Carlinville IL 62626

Call Sign: N9LQC
Dennis D Goesmann
115 S Center St
Carlinville IL 62626

Call Sign: KC9HQA
Tim A Coonrod
18512 Shipman Rd
Carlinville IL 62626

Call Sign: WA9OXH
George E Klaus
1209 Streamwood Ln
Carlinville IL 62626

Call Sign: WD9EOB
Barbara M Hershey
1213 Streamwood Ln
Carlinville IL 62626

Call Sign: WD9ENU
William R Hershey
1213 Streamwood Ln
Carlinville IL 62626

Call Sign: KB9WHZ
Scot L Bouillon
237 Sue St
Carlinville IL 62626

Call Sign: KB9TOH

Sara J Bouillon
237 Sue St
Carlinville IL 62626

Call Sign: KC9QHJ
Edward L Kallbrier
717 Sumner St
Carlinville IL 62626

Call Sign: N9UJH
Aaron J Shipley
821 Sumner St
Carlinville IL 62626

Call Sign: N9JIL
Stephen W Arnett
16751 Tonga Ln
Carlinville IL 62626

Call Sign: KC9OUC
Bill L Crawford
607 W 2nd S
Carlinville IL 62626

Call Sign: KJ9Y
Bill L Crawford
607 W 2nd S
Carlinville IL 62626

Call Sign: N9MFD
Darren R L Schmedeke
123 W Buchanan
Carlinville IL 62626

FCC Amateur Radio Licenses in Carlock

Call Sign: KB9EIM
Michael D Gravitt
1799 CR 75 N
Carlock IL 61725

Call Sign: W9MDG
Michael D Gravitt
1799 CR 75 N
Carlock IL 61725

Call Sign: KC9PIL
Michael J Gravitt

1799 CR 75 N
Carlock IL 61725

Call Sign: W9MJG
Michael J Gravitt
1799 CR 75 N
Carlock IL 61725

Call Sign: WB9CAR
Patrick D Hill
106 N Perry St
Carlock IL 617250127

Call Sign: N9KNZ
Duane M Holliger
Carlock IL 61725

FCC Amateur Radio Licenses in Carlyle

Call Sign: KB9UEA
David D Riddle
790 5th St
Carlyle IL 622311501

Call Sign: KW9V
James M Hooper
1530 Abbott St
Carlyle IL 62231

Call Sign: KC9JDF
Madelyn C Mooth
9360 Brinkman Rd
Carlyle IL 62231

Call Sign: KC9NEZ
David C Mooth
9360 Brinkman Rd
Carlyle IL 62231

Call Sign: KC9FIK
Nathanael D Mooth
9360 Brinkman Rd
Carlyle IL 62231

Call Sign: KC9RVB
John J Rhiner
9480 Brinkman Rd
Carlyle IL 62231

Call Sign: KB9CXP
Urban H Kampwerth
1711 Clinton St
Carlyle IL 62231

Call Sign: K9UK
David P Davis
16221 Emerald Rd
Carlyle IL 62231

Call Sign: N9MEY
Walter Sanders Jr
750 Franklin
Carlyle IL 62231

Call Sign: KC9FGE
Lloyd R Hammel
10707 Huey Rd
Carlyle IL 62231

Call Sign: N9ERC
Vernon R Wheeler
1490 Jefferson
Carlyle IL 62231

Call Sign: KA9CAT
Ferdinand J Gehrs
830 Livingston St
Carlyle IL 62231

Call Sign: KC9RTX
Jack D Hamburg Jr
411 Main St
Carlyle IL 62231

Call Sign: N9DKX
Leo E Ohms
18832 Maple St
Carlyle IL 62231

Call Sign: KC9TUN
Alma C Quick
1421 Methodist St
Carlyle IL 62231

Call Sign: KC9RTY
Warren J Ilges
1711 Methodist St

Carlyle IL 62231

Call Sign: KC9NFA
September Mc Adoo
10790 Slate Dr
Carlyle IL 62231

Call Sign: KC9MYW
Eugene A Mcadoo
14790 State Dr
Carlyle IL 62231

Call Sign: N9NHM
Robert N Mc Quade
19912 Walker Rd
Carlyle IL 62231

Call Sign: KC9HVO
Charles A Simms
1691 Washington St
Carlyle IL 62231

Call Sign: WB9ZEY
H Jay Flanders
Carlyle IL 62231

Call Sign: KB9LHA
Steve F Howell
Carlyle IL 62231

**FCC Amateur Radio
Licenses in Carman**

Call Sign: WD0DYS
Walter D Hoelzen
Box 174 Rr 1
Carman IL 614259744

Call Sign: KN9LKP
Robert H Davilla
Carman IL 61425

**FCC Amateur Radio
Licenses in Carmi**

Call Sign: KC0FWN
Dennis J Bridgeman
202 7th St
Carmi IL 628211303

Call Sign: N9TTS
Margaret E Logan
545A Abelson Dr
Carmi IL 62821

Call Sign: KB9GLN
Michael D Hetzel
Rr 2 Box 119
Carmi IL 62821

Call Sign: KB9GJM
Daniel E Kendrick
1687 CR 1450 N
Carmi IL 62821

Call Sign: KB9WAA
Kenneth D Linzy
1133 CR 695 E
Carmi IL 62821

Call Sign: KC9JKQ
Donald J Paynter
616 Crebs Ave
Carmi IL 62821

Call Sign: K9DWD
Donald J Paynter
616 Crebs Ave
Carmi IL 62821

Call Sign: WB9IYP
William D Mc Ghee
902 Elm
Carmi IL 62821

Call Sign: KB9DAU
Jack W Foster
1619 Hwy 14 W
Carmi IL 62821

Call Sign: WA9MZD
Jacqueline S De Lawter
407 Iris Ln
Carmi IL 62821

Call Sign: N9PDM
Gary L Wagner
610 N 6th St

Carmi IL 62821

Call Sign: N9JJV
Luther O Vaupel
509 N 9th St
Carmi IL 62821

Call Sign: KB9HMF
Dwight C Thomas
907 N 9th St
Carmi IL 62821

Call Sign: WA4HPH
Gregory D Cathcart
703 B Oak St
Carmi IL 62821

Call Sign: W9DO
Gregory D Cathcart
703 B Oak St
Carmi IL 62821

Call Sign: KB9FAZ
Joseph C Maughan
209 Pleasant St
Carmi IL 62821

Call Sign: WQ9L
Wayne L Gibbs
310 S 4th St
Carmi IL 62821

Call Sign: N9OXU
Joe Knight
403 S Walnut St
Carmi IL 62821

Call Sign: KC9IOC
Blake Dimaggio
1631 Saunders Ave
Carmi IL 62821

Call Sign: N9JYG
Kenneth R Pettijohn
206 SE 1st
Carmi IL 62821

Call Sign: KB9FED
Bertis G Knight

1018 Smith
Carmi IL 62821

Call Sign: KB9DCX
Edward L Hon
205 Stevan St
Carmi IL 62821

Call Sign: N9JJY
Carl F Gibbs
1110 Stewart St
Carmi IL 62821

Call Sign: K9HLH
Morris R Burris
201 W Webb St
Carmi IL 62821

Call Sign: WA9NKQ
Leonard R Burgess
514 Webb
Carmi IL 62821

Call Sign: KB9IKV
James H Evans
1106 West Dr
Carmi IL 62821

Call Sign: KB9GGY
Donald R James
Carmi IL 62821

Call Sign: KB9CXE
Don A Colson
Carmi IL 62871

Call Sign: K9RZO
Wayne E Sailer
Carmi IL 628219753

Call Sign: KB9RCY
Charles J Martin
307 Miller St
Carrier Mills IL 62917

Call Sign: N4ZIN

Dana R Dooley
440 Mitchellsville Rd
Carrier Mills IL 62917

Call Sign: KA9YCB
George E Hardesty Jr
621 N Friend
Carrier Mills IL 62917

Call Sign: KC9LJL
Cheryl L Clore
602 N Mill St
Carrier Mills IL 62917

Call Sign: WB9F
Larry W Clore
602 N Mill St
Carrier Mills IL 62917

Call Sign: KC9UXD
Randy R King
655 Providence Rd
Carrier Mills IL 62917

Call Sign: KB9NSK
Russell D Baker
Carrier Mills IL 62917

Call Sign: KB9QZH
Kimberly J Martin
Carrier Mills IL 62917

Call Sign: KB9YBM
Marylin R Dawkins
Carrier Mills IL 62917

Call Sign: N9SCP
Joey K Harpole
Rr 1 Box 128B
Carrollton IL 62016

Call Sign: AI4GZ
Mark A Pace
Rr3 Box 132Bc
Carrollton IL 62016

Call Sign: KB9NRY
Stephen A Field
Rr 3 Box 18
Carrollton IL 62016

Call Sign: N9GMX
Paul D Scroggins
202 E Locust
Carrollton IL 62016

Call Sign: N9MNB
James H Kincade
125 N 6th St
Carrollton IL 62016

Call Sign: WA9DUO
James E Midkiff
R2 Southgate Ests
Carrollton IL 620160066

Call Sign: WA9ZEH
Charles E Schmidt
105 Arbor Dr
Carterville IL 62918

Call Sign: KC9KRT
Andrew T Craig
201 Arbor Dr
Carterville IL 62918

Call Sign: KC9HLP
Walter B Steele
6206 Bayer Cir 231
Carterville IL 62918

Call Sign: N9JFU
Jeffrey G Cottingham
Rt 3 Box 166
Carterville IL 62418

Call Sign: K9WBS
Walter B Steele
306 Brown St
Carterville IL 62918

Call Sign: KB9KZR

Ernie L Murphy
416 Brown St
Carterville IL 62918

Call Sign: KC9KWI
Victor L Turner
1304 Charles Ave
Carterville IL 62918

Call Sign: N9JQY
Mark A Speraneo
15205 Clifford Rd
Carterville IL 62918

Call Sign: N9KVG
Sheryl A Speraneo
15205 Clifford Rd
Carterville IL 62918

Call Sign: WB9UHR
Gregory Chambers
1410 Country Aire Dr
Carterville IL 629185120

Call Sign: KA9MZJ
Roy R Eades
2929 Crescent Ln
Carterville IL 62918

Call Sign: KC9TXF
Grant N James
611 E Illinois Ave
Carterville IL 62918

Call Sign: WA9YIL
Donald R Beer
306 E Vermont St
Carterville IL 62918

Call Sign: KC9NDZ
Janet L Uglum
202 Earl Ct
Carterville IL 62918

Call Sign: N9OCN
Lee E Johnson
12 Executive Ln
Carterville IL 62918

Call Sign: K9TFK
James P Lenz
807 Farris
Carterville IL 62918

Call Sign: KB9VLD
Marsha A Talley
11794 Greenbriar Rd
Carterville IL 62918

Call Sign: WA9APQ
William B Talley
11794 Greenbriar Rd
Carterville IL 62918

Call Sign: KA9ZLE
Larry D Hunter
12285 Hunter Dr
Carterville IL 62918

Call Sign: K9LDH
Larry D Hunter
12285 Hunter Dr
Carterville IL 62918

Call Sign: KC9AOW
Steven P Smiley
503 Jackson St
Carterville IL 62918

Call Sign: KC9AQP
Michael S Gregory
309 Lakeshore Dr
Carterville IL 62918

Call Sign: KB9LNV
Jeffrey A Stopa
100 Lyndsey Ln
Carterville IL 62918

Call Sign: WA9YEE
Ralph F Tate
108 Lyndsey Ln
Carterville IL 62918

Call Sign: WA9FPF
Robert K Wortham
252 McNeil
Carterville IL 62918

Call Sign: KB9ADV
Sandra K Schlager
1017 Meadowlark Dr
Carterville IL 62918

Call Sign: KB9ADW
Stephen C Schlager
1017 Meadowlark Dr
Carterville IL 62918

Call Sign: WD9GFC
Vernie N Redmon III
1106 Meadowlark Dr
Carterville IL 62918

Call Sign: KC9GOH
Vernie N Redmon IV
1106 Meadowlark Dr
Carterville IL 62918

Call Sign: KC9EYJ
Clyde L Bundren
506 Missouri Ave
Carterville IL 62918

Call Sign: AB9LN
Clyde L Bundren
506 Missouri Ave
Carterville IL 62918

Call Sign: N9CPT
George B Muir
1502 Muir Rd
Carterville IL 62918

Call Sign: KC9AYB
Michael A Curry
16362 N Bend Rd
Carterville IL 62918

Call Sign: KC9KWK
Amy L Curry
16362 N Bend Rd
Carterville IL 62918

Call Sign: KC9ATW
Kenneth M Curry
16396 N Bend Rd

Carterville IL 62918

Call Sign: AB9GX
Kenneth M Curry
16396 N Bend Rd
Carterville IL 62918

Call Sign: KB9KC
Kenneth M Curry
16396 N Bend Rd
Carterville IL 62918

Call Sign: KC0RNP
Richard N Piper IV
506 N Dent St
Carterville IL 62918

Call Sign: W0CXN
Sue C Speers
908 N Division St
Carterville IL 62918

Call Sign: KB6IWC
Donnie D Ennis
102 Norton
Carterville IL 62918

Call Sign: N9JMD
James M Dillon
401 Pennsylvania
Carterville IL 62918

Call Sign: KB9UGK
Barry E Cupp
506 S Division St
Carterville IL 62918

Call Sign: KA9JZM
Lynn C Elston
1112 Sycamore Rd
Carterville IL 62918

Call Sign: KC6KCP
Roderic H Uglum
1215 Trails End
Carterville IL 62918

Call Sign: KB9TF
Ronald W Britton

1322 Trails End Rd
Carterville IL 62918

Call Sign: KE4MDX
Stephen A Smith
110 Van Wyck Sq
Carterville IL 62918

Call Sign: KC9HAF
Annuvon D Garavalia
3283 Vermont Rd
Carterville IL 62918

Call Sign: N9LTV
Rod L Sievers
313 Virginia Ave
Carterville IL 62918

Call Sign: KC9PYQ
Lavon K Donley-Cornett
413 W Grand
Carterville IL 62918

Call Sign: W4JBA
Otho Warner
1007 W Grand Rd
Carterville IL 62918

Call Sign: WB9UPA
Alexander M Fine
Carterville IL 62918

Call Sign: KC9SOI
James F Campanella
Carterville IL 62918

Call Sign: KB9VUW
T J Liddell
Carterville IL 62918

Call Sign: K9TJL
T J Liddell
Carterville IL 62918

**FCC Amateur Radio
Licenses in Carthage**

Call Sign: WA9PFY
Robert C Curtis

107 Ash St
Carthage IL 62321

Call Sign: N0FXU
Marvin O Boyer
825 Augusta Rd
Carthage IL 62321

Call Sign: KA9PSB
Bonnie M Mc Farland
Rr 3 Box 142A
Carthage IL 62321

Call Sign: N9JWR
Marshall L Gillenwater
Rr 1 Box 49
Carthage IL 62321

Call Sign: KC9VCE
Robert F Stephens
2606 E C Rd 1400 N
Carthage IL 62321

Call Sign: WA9REQ
Glen B Dickinson
2175 E CR 1250
Carthage IL 62321

Call Sign: KC9JAG
David L Smashey
2135 E CR 1300
Carthage IL 62321

Call Sign: KB9GKF
Donald K Carle
2761 E CR 1900
Carthage IL 62321

Call Sign: WA2WGY
Richard N Conklin
242 Main St
Carthage IL 62321

Call Sign: WA2SJU
Susan Conklin
242 Main St
Carthage IL 62321

Call Sign: KA9UNU

Gary J Smith
627 Main St
Carthage IL 62321

Call Sign: N9GU
Johnny T Ison
606 Maple St
Carthage IL 62321

Call Sign: N9XEG
Brian L Dougherty
740 Miller St
Carthage IL 62321

Call Sign: N9BLD
Brian L Dougherty
740 Miller St
Carthage IL 62321

Call Sign: KC9LRY
Mary Lisa Miller
1486 N CR 1500 E
Carthage IL 62321

Call Sign: KC9LRQ
David Miller
1486 N CR 1500 E
Carthage IL 62321

Call Sign: KC9LRP
Kenneth L Miller
1486 N CR 1500 E
Carthage IL 62321

Call Sign: KB0V
Matthew G Dickinson
1110 N CR 2350
Carthage IL 62321

Call Sign: N0YLQ
Rebecca A Dickinson
1110 N CR 2350
Carthage IL 62321

Call Sign: W9BUA
Oliver F Kirchner Sr
39 N Madison
Carthage IL 62321

Call Sign: K9JPQ
Daryl L Waite
33 N Washington
Carthage IL 62321

Call Sign: KC9VCF
Sarah K Russell
320 N Washington
Carthage IL 62321

Call Sign: W9EE
Floyd A Timberlake
328 S Marion
Carthage IL 62321

Call Sign: KC9OVJ
Robert D Wisehart
211 S Washington St
Carthage IL 62321

Call Sign: W9RDW
Robert D Wisehart
211 S Washington St
Carthage IL 62321

Call Sign: N9MTI
August C Horn
821 Wabash
Carthage IL 62321

Call Sign: KC9OVK
Kody R Horn
821 Wabash Ave
Carthage IL 62321

Call Sign: N9OVF
Synthia J Horn
821 Wabash Ave
Carthage IL 62321

Call Sign: W9FNW
Hubert W Merideth
1321 Wabash Box 152
Carthage IL 62321

Call Sign: WB9VIU
Roger A Lawson
712 Wabash St
Carthage IL 62321

Call Sign: KB9YRB
Dan C Bryan
Carthage IL 62321

Call Sign: KC9LMF
Big Bend ARC
Carthage IL 62321

Call Sign: KB9LOA
Rodney L Walton
Carthage IL 62321

Call Sign: N9MTM
James W Bolton
Carthage IL 62321

FCC Amateur Radio Licenses in Casey

Call Sign: N9ZZS
Patrick W Mullen
5306E 900Rd
Casey IL 62420

Call Sign: WA9EUH
Orville F Yelton
Rr 3 Box 234
Casey IL 62420

Call Sign: KB9GQJ
Shawn A Stifal
Rr 3 Box 349
Casey IL 62420

Call Sign: N9UAD
Larry E Henderson
267 CR 2400 E
Casey IL 62420

Call Sign: N9UBN
Howard L Henderson
267 CR 2400 E
Casey IL 62420

Call Sign: N0BBC
Frank S Campbell
207 E Adams
Casey IL 624201705

Call Sign: N9UBM
Cecil Wright Jr
1000 E Alabama St
Casey IL 62420

Call Sign: W9YVG
Cleone L Markwell
513 E Main
Casey IL 62420

Call Sign: KC9MHQ
Greg L Aldrich
310 E Main St
Casey IL 62420

Call Sign: K9HQF
Richard B England
3495 E Washington Rd
Casey IL 62420

Call Sign: N9UAO
Ronald D Williams
3649 E Washington Rd
Casey IL 62420

Call Sign: KB9AFC
Jack R Connelly
12879 N 320th St
Casey IL 62420

Call Sign: WA9OPZ
Paul R Handley
10671 N 450th St
Casey IL 62420

Call Sign: WA4VBS
Dennis K Richardson
100 NE 15th St
Casey IL 62420

Call Sign: N9UAE
Donna J Nichols
306 NW 5th St
Casey IL 62420

Call Sign: AA9OH
Jerry R Nichols
306 NW 5th St

Casey IL 62420

Call Sign: K9YIN
Don A Littlejohn
Box 73 Rfd 1
Casey IL 62420

Call Sign: KB9GQZ
Kevin A Comer
201 W Florida
Casey IL 62420

Call Sign: KC9NX
Larry E Comer
201 W Florida
Casey IL 62420

Call Sign: KB9GNQ
Aaron P Partlow
Casey IL 62420

Call Sign: KB9GNP
Phillip R Partlow
Casey IL 62420

**FCC Amateur Radio
Licenses in Caseyville**

Call Sign: KB9UMC
Micah W Stephens
62 Acardi Dr
Caseyville IL 62232

Call Sign: WI9X
James R Stoeber
8829 Bermuda Ave
Caseyville IL 62232

Call Sign: K9JHQ
Prime Amateur Radio
Association
8829 Bermuda Ave
Caseyville IL 62232

Call Sign: KA8PMI
Kenneth R Magill
14 Charles Dr
Caseyville IL 62232

Call Sign: KA9KYW
George E Bruner Sr
120 Circle Dr
Caseyville IL 62232

Call Sign: KC9AUI
Susan C Rezabek
850 E Ofallon Dr Lot 1
Caseyville IL 62232

Call Sign: WB9YNE
Joseph P Bator
36 Eberhart Dr
Caseyville IL 62232

Call Sign: KC9MYM
Daniel M Allen Jr
658 Hill Rd
Caseyville IL 62232

Call Sign: KC9MYN
Daniel M Allen Sr
658 Hill Rd
Caseyville IL 62232

Call Sign: KC9RVI
Madelyn K Waidmann
395 Hillside Dr
Caseyville IL 62232

Call Sign: KB9TH
Norman J Wasser
406 Hollywood Heights Rd
Caseyville IL 62232

Call Sign: N9HIH
Dianne L Rossy
1102 Hollywood Heights Rd
Caseyville IL 62232

Call Sign: N9VII
David W Myers
508 Hollywood Hgts Rd
Caseyville IL 62232

Call Sign: KB9RDY
Paula D Mullins
430 Hollywood Htgs Rd
Caseyville IL 62232

Call Sign: KB9LBB
Jerry L Mullins
430 Hollywood Hts Rd
Caseyville IL 62232

Call Sign: N9NKE
Lucille M Skibinski
8730 Maple Ave
Caseyville IL 62232

Call Sign: N9DSY
William G Saul
7337 N Illinois
Caseyville IL 62232

Call Sign: WD9CKY
Larry L Haluch
7925 N Illinois
Caseyville IL 62232

Call Sign: KA9WQD
Wesley A Pracht
7823 N Illinois St
Caseyville IL 622322058

Call Sign: KB9PTW
James E Alvarez Jr
111 N Long
Caseyville IL 62232

Call Sign: W9PHD
Charles L Cunningham
200 N Long St
Caseyville IL 62232

Call Sign: KC9FHS
Joseph L Reed
12 N Oakland Dr
Caseyville IL 62232

Call Sign: N9YMR
Ted L Gibson
8705 Parkdale Dr
Caseyville IL 62232

Call Sign: N9NXU
Nelson C Matter
22 S Main St

Caseyville IL 62232

Call Sign: AA9ZV
Howard D Mize
804 S Main St
Caseyville IL 62232

Call Sign: N9BNR
Ronald S Browne
842 S Main St
Caseyville IL 62232

Call Sign: N9BVD
Fred L Schmedeman
313 W Washington
Caseyville IL 62232

Call Sign: KB9NDO
Mark J Toennies
830 Wells Ave
Caseyville IL 62232

Call Sign: K9KJK
Kenneth J Koski
1959 Witte Rd
Caseyville IL 622320301

Call Sign: K9KEN
Kenneth J Koski
1959 Witte Rd
Caseyville IL 622320301

FCC Amateur Radio Licenses in Catlin

Call Sign: WD9FBC
Betty K Lomax
206 Buckingham
Catlin IL 61817

Call Sign: KC9LQU
Thomas A Peach
7910 Catlin Indianola Rd
Catlin IL 61817

Call Sign: KB9VOV
Randal L Simonson
121 Coronado Dr
Catlin IL 61817

Call Sign: KA9HMS
Charles F Mc Gee
13850 McGee Rd
Catlin IL 61817

Call Sign: N0VXX
Russell W Cottrill
104 Meadowlane Dr
Catlin IL 61817

Call Sign: KB9RMV
Steven J Lovett
15659 N 1250 E Rd
Catlin IL 61718

Call Sign: KC9LDI
Scott A Dowers
602 W Vermilian St Box 614
Catlin IL 61817

Call Sign: WA9PDS
W David Baird
824 W Vermillion
Catlin IL 61817

Call Sign: WB9EVM
Frederick F Kessler Sr
104 W Wayne Dr
Catlin IL 618179769

Call Sign: KQ9C
Craig W Cruppenink
401 Westwood Dr
Catlin IL 618179652

Call Sign: KB9LLH
James R Walker
Catlin IL 61817

Call Sign: WD9FJI
Gerald E Mc Masters
Catlin IL 618170635

FCC Amateur Radio Licenses in Cave In Rock

Call Sign: KC9MA
Carol D Beavers Sr

Rr 1 Box 148
Cave In Rock IL 629199732

Call Sign: WA9NEU
Walter D Bowlby
330 N Canal St
Cave In Rock IL 62919

FCC Amateur Radio Licenses in Cedarville

Call Sign: N9TYA
Allen G Love
177 Mill St
Cedarville IL 61013

Call Sign: N9LXS
Russell L Love Sr
177 Mill St
Cedarville IL 61013

Call Sign: KC9QBS
Alfred G Mcintosh
330 Oak Ridge Dr
Cedarville IL 61013

Call Sign: KB9OLF
Ruben D Dowman
115 Tiffany Ln
Cedarville IL 61013

Call Sign: KA9RCL
David E Southwick
568 W Cedarville Rd Box 164
Cedarville IL 61013

Call Sign: KA9YMV
Don L Ferro
Cedarville IL 61013

Call Sign: KA9YMW
Linda K Ferro
Cedarville IL 61013

FCC Amateur Radio Licenses in Centralia

Call Sign: N9PRN
Anthony C Eovaldi Jr

418 Airport Rd
Centralia IL 62801

Call Sign: W9TRW
Thomas R White
21 Arline Dr
Centralia IL 62801

Call Sign: KB9KX
Thomas R White
21 Arline Dr
Centralia IL 62801

Call Sign: KA9EGM
Jim J Brueggeman
2549 Barker Rd
Centralia IL 62801

Call Sign: KB9HNA
Phyllis E Hawkins
Rr 7 Box 62
Centralia IL 62801

Call Sign: N9LPA
Darrell L Parrish
Rt 7 Box 69
Centralia IL 62801

Call Sign: KG9JZ
Mark A Bone
204 Bruce Ct
Centralia IL 62801

Call Sign: WB9C
James N Brown
235 Bruce Ct
Centralia IL 62801

Call Sign: KC9QWS
Ronald G Sanders
635 Burge Rd
Centralia IL 62801

Call Sign: W9AEG
Ronald G Sanders
635 Burge Rd
Centralia IL 62801

Call Sign: AA9ER

Mary L Vandeveer
839 Burge Rd
Centralia IL 62801

Call Sign: WA9T
Lester D Vandeveer
839 Burge Rt
Centralia IL 62801

Call Sign: AA9FB
Mary M Niepoetter
1022 Cheyenne Rd
Centralia IL 62801

Call Sign: N9FUR
Dale G Roberts Sr
922 Chipwood Ln
Centralia IL 62801

Call Sign: KB9HMZ
Bradley F Webber
900 Cody Rd
Centralia IL 62801

Call Sign: K9KWD
Gerald E Spear Jr
20 Crestwood Ln
Centralia IL 628016701

Call Sign: KA9SNN
Donald D Korstad
438 Davis Ave
Centralia IL 62801

Call Sign: KC9BNE
Harry S Dillingham
32 Devonia Dr
Centralia IL 62801

Call Sign: KB9WFX
Garren E King
48 Devonia Dr
Centralia IL 62801

Call Sign: N9OPB
Gary E Hall
239 Douglas
Centralia IL 62801

Call Sign: KB9OGM
Nancy A Hensley
323.5 Douglas
Centralia IL 62801

Call Sign: KC9RCC
Mark A Zack
324 Douglas
Centralia IL 62801

Call Sign: KF9OB
Michael R Hollingsead
1907 Dunbar Ln
Centralia IL 62801

Call Sign: W9SBK
James T Sanders
639 E 11th St
Centralia IL 62801

Call Sign: KB9LLL
Jennifer L Watson
1201 E 2nd
Centralia IL 62801

Call Sign: WD9DSR
Melvin A Gambill
1100 E 2nd St
Centralia IL 62801

Call Sign: KB9LII
Jerry M Watson
1201 E 2nd St
Centralia IL 628013608

Call Sign: WC9L
Jerry M Watson
1201 E 2nd St
Centralia IL 628013608

Call Sign: KB9WDE
James A Davis
1225 E 3rd St
Centralia IL 62801

Call Sign: N9SJT
Richard A Lee
329 E Broadway Apt 1
Centralia IL 62801

Call Sign: KB9OGN
Stephen G Hensley
1111 E Jonas St
Centralia IL 62801

Call Sign: KB9DBJ
Deana M Hiltibidal
514.5 E McCord
Centralia IL 62801

Call Sign: KB9HPM
Carl S Denzler
1615 E McCord
Centralia IL 62801

Call Sign: KE9XE
James M Mc Clain
1943 E McCord St
Centralia IL 62801

Call Sign: KA9TEC
Samuel L Powe
706 E Rexford
Centralia IL 62801

Call Sign: KA9WPX
Jack S Forth
423 Easthaven
Centralia IL 62801

Call Sign: KB9OPJ
Robin C Cimera
5 Echo Ln
Centralia IL 62801

Call Sign: KF9AO
Jerry E Clifton
2130 Farthing Rd
Centralia IL 62801

Call Sign: KC9PDW
Ralph J Niederhofer
8 Gayla Ave
Centralia IL 62801

Call Sign: K9RJN
Ralph J Niederhofer
8 Gayla Ave

Centralia IL 62801

Call Sign: WD9CYA
Jasper R Donoho
220 High St
Centralia IL 628012046

Call Sign: KC9SMJ
Bill H Wimpy
1418 Holly Ave
Centralia IL 62801

Call Sign: WD9HBD
John F Whipps
1020 Jonas St
Centralia IL 62801

Call Sign: KF6FPV
Boyd T Harrell
18825 Juniper Rd
Centralia IL 628016639

Call Sign: KC9RGL
Dale G Roberts Sr
2191 Lakeshore Rd
Centralia IL 62801

Call Sign: KC9MUW
Larry E Hoffman
40 Lakewood Dr
Centralia IL 62801

Call Sign: KC9MUX
Marcia E Hoffman
40 Lakewood Dr
Centralia IL 62801

Call Sign: N9ZCN
Jon L Logullo
218 Leafland
Centralia IL 62801

Call Sign: KB9DWC
Jerry E Garner
111 Marilyn Ave
Centralia IL 62801

Call Sign: KA9TFX
Edward L Connelly

128 Mitchell Ln
Centralia IL 62801

Call Sign: KB9AIG
Michael D Meyer
29530 Monroe
Centralia IL 628015642

Call Sign: KC9OEY
Bobby M Kell Jr
1723 Mt Moriah Rd
Centralia IL 62801

Call Sign: N9WZM
Robert E Dailey
1800 Mt Moriah Rd
Centralia IL 62801

Call Sign: KB9BFO
Frank A Augustine
1201 N Elm
Centralia IL 62801

Call Sign: N9KJE
Tony K Robinson
1132 N Gary Ave
Centralia IL 62801

Call Sign: N9RUH
Timothy A Faust
304 N Harrison
Centralia IL 62801

Call Sign: KC9VJM
Lonny W Silvey
102 N Jefferson St
Centralia IL 62801

Call Sign: KB9OWZ
Shawn M Davis
1304 N Sycamore
Centralia IL 62801

Call Sign: W9SAG
Revis E Miller
515 Oakdale Dr
Centralia IL 62801

Call Sign: KC9CAH

Clifton A Curtis
69 Park Forest
Centralia IL 62801

Call Sign: K9BYS
Thomas A Simmons
71 Parkforest
Centralia IL 62801

Call Sign: KA9FVA
Bert L Mc Donal
1000 Pine
Centralia IL 628010242

Call Sign: N9PBI
William H Bryant
137 Pullen Blvd
Centralia IL 62801

Call Sign: N9TFM
Clarence E Rasmussen
147 Pullen Blvd
Centralia IL 62801

Call Sign: KB9SJO
Marian Co Emergency
Services & Disaster Agcy
780 Race Track Rd
Centralia IL 62801

Call Sign: KC9UMK
Joseph R Donoho
815 Race Track Rd
Centralia IL 62801

Call Sign: KB9KES
John C Mearns
405 Randolph Dr
Centralia IL 62801

Call Sign: WD9DKN
Billy J Carter
300 S Beech
Centralia IL 628010120

Call Sign: WB9KMB
William A Marsh
333 S Broadway Apt 2
Centralia IL 62801

Call Sign: KD9OT
Carroll D Conder
213 S Cherry
Centralia IL 62801

Call Sign: KB9RKG
James A Bryant
302 S Commercial
Centralia IL 62801

Call Sign: KB9BPZ
Johnny B Koch
430 S Elm
Centralia IL 62801

Call Sign: N9KKB
Donald R Copple
425 S Hickory
Centralia IL 62801

Call Sign: KA9LSY
John M Heggemeier
435 S Hickory St
Centralia IL 62801

Call Sign: KC9LTT
Todd A Johnson
531 S Lincoln Blvd
Centralia IL 62801

Call Sign: KB9KEQ
Stephen L Whitelow
1405 S Lincoln Blvd
Centralia IL 62801

Call Sign: KB9KHN
Lois J Hays
1413 S Locust
Centralia IL 62801

Call Sign: N9RNN
Robert Q Day
2109 S Perrine
Centralia IL 62801

Call Sign: WA9GUU
Larry E Tooley
1424 S Perrine Ave

Centralia IL 62801

Call Sign: WA9G
Larry E Tooley
1424 S Perrine Ave
Centralia IL 62801

Call Sign: KC9BNF
Richard L Davis
126 S Pullen Blvd
Centralia IL 62801

Call Sign: KC9PKX
Joe H Mcnelly
529 S Sycamore
Centralia IL 62801

Call Sign: W9SSB
Joe H Mcnelly
529 S Sycamore
Centralia IL 62801

Call Sign: KC9IJX
Mark D Wilson
8 Spruce Dr
Centralia IL 62801

Call Sign: KC9KTS
Marsha K Wilson
8 Spruce Dr
Centralia IL 62801

Call Sign: NY0Y
Raleigh B Stelle III
26709 SR 161
Centralia IL 62801

Call Sign: KA9FIA
Ronald G Sanders
635 Surge Rd
Centralia IL 62801

Call Sign: KB9ALA
Robert L Selle
27101 W 10th St Rd
Centralia IL 62801

Call Sign: KC9TWO
Jimmy D Robinett III

515 W 6th St
Centralia IL 62801

Call Sign: WD9FJH
Linda J Donoho
802 W Green St
Centralia IL 62801

Call Sign: WB9TFP
Lucy J Ervin
310 W McCord
Centralia IL 62801

Call Sign: KB9VTL
Charles W Waggoner
1626 W McCord
Centralia IL 62801

Call Sign: N9XPG
Ronnie G Smith
1423 Walnut Hill Rd
Centralia IL 62801

Call Sign: N9XPF
Vickie L Smith
1423 Walnut Hill Rd
Centralia IL 62801

Call Sign: KC9SAL
Scott D Cottone
150 Washington Blvd
Centralia IL 62801

Call Sign: KB9VLZ
Laura L Bauer
1453 Woods Ln
Centralia IL 628016771

Call Sign: N9KNI
John M Heggemeier
Centralia IL 62801

Call Sign: WB9KKT
Stephen R Hatfield
Centralia IL 62801

Call Sign: KB9HRC
Charles E Biggs
Centralia IL 62801

Call Sign: W9QC
Glendall O Bush
Centralia IL 62801

Call Sign: KA9RMI
John M Hutchins
Centralia IL 62801

Call Sign: N0QBF
Michael C Musick
Centralia IL 62801

Call Sign: N9ZIQ
Richard L Pugh
Centralia IL 62801

Call Sign: W9CWA
Centralia Wireless Assn Inc
Centralia IL 62801

Call Sign: KB9ALB
Corey R Selle
Centralia IL 62801

Call Sign: W9WGQ
Kenneth R Bauer
Centralia IL 628019113

Call Sign: W9EET
Laura L Bauer
Centralia IL 628019113

**FCC Amateur Radio
Licenses in Cerro Gordo**

Call Sign: KB9WUC
Florence J Keller
203 Carmi
Cerro Gordo IL 61818

Call Sign: WA9SHR
Roy W Hufford
11605 Cerro Gordo Blacktop
Cerro Gordo IL 618183031

Call Sign: N2SJB
Richard B Robrock
112 E 1045 N Rd

Cerro Gordo IL 61818

Call Sign: N9VVN
Earl R Smith
314 N Jefferson St
Cerro Gordo IL 61818

Call Sign: KA9VAI
Thomas G Brockman
111 S Jackson Str
Cerro Gordo IL 61818

Call Sign: KB9SLU
Doug M Clark
517 S Jefferson Apt 301
Cerro Gordo IL 61818

Call Sign: KB9QKN
Bethany J Bolduc
Cerro Gordo IL 61818

FCC Amateur Radio Licenses in Chadwick

Call Sign: K9OEC
Ron I Rendleman
22095 Clark Rd
Chadwick IL 61014

Call Sign: NK9Y
Chester D Peugh
24459 Clark Rd
Chadwick IL 61014

Call Sign: W9ILN
Edward A Mc Daniel
18221 Fairhaven Rd
Chadwick IL 61014

Call Sign: KB9SWH
Nathaniel A Davis
26596 Fairhaven Rd
Chadwick IL 61014

Call Sign: KC9DTS
Bryan E Rockwell
314 Il Rt 40
Chadwick IL 61014

Call Sign: N9PEG
Russell B Greene
23139 Illinois Rt 40
Chadwick IL 61014

Call Sign: KB9WLZ
Jason M Schmitt
218 Marion Ave
Chadwick IL 61014

Call Sign: KC9NEO
Donald L Kness
218 Snow Ave
Chadwick IL 61014

Call Sign: KC9BJU
Jeffrey P Seidel
22057 Tampico Rd
Chadwick IL 61014

Call Sign: KC9BPG
Jeffrey P Seidel
22057 Tampico Rd
Chadwick IL 61014

FCC Amateur Radio Licenses in Champaign

Call Sign: KC0IGX
Jeffrey S Zahos
4010 Aberdeen Dr
Champaign IL 61822

Call Sign: KR4S
Stephen C Zahos
4010 Aberdeen Dr
Champaign IL 61822

Call Sign: N9ZCR
Devin Gengelbach
4011 Aberdeen Dr
Champaign IL 61822

Call Sign: KB9OTQ
Lisa A Gengelbach
4011 Aberdeen Dr
Champaign IL 61822

Call Sign: KA9HGY

J Marlowe Slater
1513 Alma Dr
Champaign IL 61820

Call Sign: KA9QZO
Scott W Henson
208 Arcadia Dr
Champaign IL 61820

Call Sign: W9JX
Stanley W Henson
208 Arcadia Dr
Champaign IL 61820

Call Sign: N9GKM
John W Frizzell
2509 Arden Dr
Champaign IL 61821

Call Sign: KB9VAF
John L Fileccia
2702 Arden Dr
Champaign IL 61821

Call Sign: N9XDB
Matthew L Simeone
2310 Aspen Dr
Champaign IL 61821

Call Sign: WB9NPZ
James P Wentz
701 Balboa
Champaign IL 61820

Call Sign: KB9ODU
Jonathan R Stevens
1908 Barberry Cir
Champaign IL 61821

Call Sign: KB9PVT
John K Hunt
1805 Barrington Dr
Champaign IL 61821

Call Sign: KA0BZP
James B Hebert
1010 Baytowne Dr 23
Champaign IL 61821

Call Sign: KC8OLR
Amanda C Rosenow
1055 Baytowne Dr Apt 25
Champaign IL 61822

Call Sign: KC9PPX
Justin Smith
802 Bellepark Dr
Champaign IL 61821

Call Sign: KC9PPW
Sheena N Smith
802 Bellepark Dr
Champaign IL 61821

Call Sign: N9ZYI
Colin P A Kennedy
1307 Belmeade Dr
Champaign IL 61821

Call Sign: N9ZUV
Christopher M Webber
2007 Bentbrook
Champaign IL 61821

Call Sign: KB9SIY
James M Obyrne
1902 Bentbrook Dr
Champaign IL 61821

Call Sign: N9KVE
Donna M Curtin
2507 Berniece
Champaign IL 61821

Call Sign: N9GOC
Patrick W Curtin
2507 Berniece Dr
Champaign IL 61821

Call Sign: WB9SCP
Louis J Braghini
2308 Blackthorn St
Champaign IL 61821

Call Sign: KE5FNM
Nathan M King
1424 Bluegrass Ln
Champaign IL 61822

Call Sign: WD9CIJ
Stephen S Karnes
1401 Bonnie Blair Dr
Champaign IL 61821

Call Sign: N9SYV
Joan B Lund
515 Bonnymeade
Champaign IL 61821

Call Sign: N9PFC
Thomas J Lund
515 Bonnymeade Dr
Champaign IL 61821

Call Sign: W9KQL
Thomas J Lund
515 Bonnymeade Dr
Champaign IL 61821

Call Sign: N9PFC
Thomas J Lund
515 Bonnymeade Dr
Champaign IL 61821

Call Sign: KB9ODT
Ryan C Standerfer
2405 Brett Dr
Champaign IL 61821

Call Sign: KB9LWS
Christine L Majers
12 Briar Hill Cir
Champaign IL 618226137

Call Sign: W6TRI
Fred J German IV
1309 Broadmoor Dr
Champaign IL 61821

Call Sign: KC9TOG
Jay B Manning
402 Brookwood Dr
Champaign IL 61820

Call Sign: KK9JAY
Jay B Manning
402 Brookwood Dr

Champaign IL 61820

Call Sign: WB9TOM
William H Whetstone
2105 Campbell Dr
Champaign IL 61821

Call Sign: W9IUW
Loyed H Redenbaugh
2200 Campbell Dr
Champaign IL 61820

Call Sign: AB9KQ
Robert E West
2202 Campbell Dr
Champaign IL 618211143

Call Sign: KC9CEI
Bridget D Wille
2410 Cherry Hill Dr
Champaign IL 61822

Call Sign: WA9CYK
Marshall A Lipscomb
2702 Cherry Hills Dr
Champaign IL 61822

Call Sign: WB9JHU
Teresa A Lipscomb
2702 Cherry Hills Dr
Champaign IL 61822

Call Sign: KB9ZDP
James G Runyan
1614 Chevy Chase Dr
Champaign IL 61821

Call Sign: N9QGZ
Paul A Whalen
3205 Clayton Rd
Champaign IL 61821

Call Sign: K9CMI
Paul A Whalen
3205 Clayton Rd
Champaign IL 61821

Call Sign: KB9VQI
Raymond N Sumers

509 Clearwater Dr
Champaign IL 61822

Call Sign: K9RNS
Raymond N Summers
509 Clearwater Dr
Champaign IL 61822

Call Sign: N9UWH
Justin M Martin
2002 Clover Ct E
Champaign IL 61821

Call Sign: KS9I
Kenneth W Sartain
1512 Cobblefield Rd
Champaign IL 618229270

Call Sign: WA5WXZ
Paul R Wilson
2502 Coppertree Rd
Champaign IL 61821

Call Sign: WA7AZ
Matthew Sakiestewa Gilbert
1508 Coral Cove Dr
Champaign IL 61821

Call Sign: KC9LMG
David C Klein
1722 Coronado Dr
Champaign IL 61820

Call Sign: K9LMG
David C Klein
1722 Coronado Dr
Champaign IL 61820

Call Sign: KA9AVB
David L Burns
1408 Country Lake Dr
Champaign IL 61821

Call Sign: KG9BF
John T Bandy
1913 Crescent Dr
Champaign IL 61821

Call Sign: W9WHE

Jonathan S Gunn
4320 Crossgate Dr
Champaign IL 61822

Call Sign: W9FKI
Kenneth P Billings
1805 Cynthia Dr
Champaign IL 618211406

Call Sign: KC9TFG
Kihwal Lee
3209 Cypress Creek Rd
Champaign IL 61822

Call Sign: K9SUL
Kihwal Lee
3209 Cypress Creek Rd
Champaign IL 61822

Call Sign: N0ORX
Alison B Champion
1906 Cypress Dr
Champaign IL 618215819

Call Sign: N9AVG
Jason A Davis
1812 Cypress Dr
Champaign IL 61821

Call Sign: N9PLZ
Jeremy K Look
704 Devonshire
Champaign IL 61820

Call Sign: KB9VIZ
James M O Brien
504 Dogwood Dr
Champaign IL 618213447

Call Sign: KC9EWQ
Serene Ow
307 E Armory Ave 201
Champaign IL 61820

Call Sign: KC9AZY
Sudha Krishnamurthy
309 E Clark St 12
Champaign IL 61820

Call Sign: KC9NMU
Patrick F Shannon
410 E Green St Apt 308
Champaign IL 61820

Call Sign: KB0DIP
Aaron D Lanterman
55 E Healey St Apt 102
Champaign IL 61820

Call Sign: N9LNQ
James T Summers Sr
57 E John Ln
Champaign IL 618229481

Call Sign: KC9EOK
Chihyung D Cheng
108 E Stoughton 8
Champaign IL 61820

Call Sign: KC9OMI
David F Rockwood Jr
508 E Stoughton St Apt 208
Champaign IL 61820

Call Sign: KC9LBH
Joe J Matthesius
506 E White Apt 22
Champaign IL 61820

Call Sign: KC9CEH
Paulus Yulianto
504 E White St 21
Champaign IL 61820

Call Sign: KB9YPJ
Sidney A Cammeresi IV
605 E White St D 37
Champaign IL 61820

Call Sign: K7OEX
Steven H Packard
2205 Edgewater Pl
Champaign IL 618227658

Call Sign: N9JZE
Lester R Rabe
2104 Emerald Dr
Champaign IL 61822

Call Sign: AB9WN
Lester R Rabe
2104 Emerald Dr
Champaign IL 61822

Call Sign: KB9JUB
Errol S Packard
1809 Emerson Dr
Champaign IL 61821

Call Sign: KE9OD
Jeffrey T Kouzmanoff
1809 Emerson Dr
Champaign IL 61821

Call Sign: KA9UTD
Lori D Bianchini
4107 Englewood Dr
Champaign IL 61822

Call Sign: WA9ZXV
Marc A Bianchini
4107 Englewood Dr
Champaign IL 61822

Call Sign: KC9QPA
Brandon D Gillen
2416 Fields S Dr 207
Champaign IL 61822

Call Sign: KC9PTL
Matthew E Crisman
3304 Florence Dr
Champaign IL 61822

Call Sign: KC9PVQ
Brian E Crisman
3304 Florence Dr
Champaign IL 61822

Call Sign: KC9SKB
Michael E Crisman
3304 Florence Dr
Champaign IL 61822

Call Sign: N9AJV
James E Crisman
3304 Florence Dr

Champaign IL 61822

Call Sign: W9KQ
Ralph W Goering
1009 Frank Dr
Champaign IL 618214231

Call Sign: KC9UMG
Charles M Davis
2109 Galen Dr
Champaign IL 61821

Call Sign: W9MDO
Charles W Kelly Jr
2110 Galen Dr
Champaign IL 61821

Call Sign: W9RPU
Manuela Eudes B Kelly
2110 Galen Dr
Champaign IL 61821

Call Sign: N9WKD
Andrew F Kopec
2203 Galen Dr
Champaign IL 61821

Call Sign: W9UEZ
Francis E Merrifield
7 Genevieve Ln
Champaign IL 61820

Call Sign: WZ9O
Richard B Selander
1714 Georgetown Dr
Champaign IL 61820

Call Sign: W9BBI
Richard L Fisher
2221 Georgetown Dr
Champaign IL 61821

Call Sign: KE9NF
Reece S Joyner
410 Ginger Bend Apt 103
Champaign IL 618213556

Call Sign: KC9APK
Daniel T Wright

402 Ginger Bend Dr Apt 310
Champaign IL 61822

Call Sign: K0OJR
Frederic G Kovell
2316 Greenwood Ct
Champaign IL 61821

Call Sign: N9SGS
Larry D Eubank
615 Haines Blvd
Champaign IL 61820

Call Sign: K9NOR
Chad E Peiper
2513 Hallbeck Dr
Champaign IL 61822

Call Sign: WD0ADC
Brad L Booton
1206 Harrington
Champaign IL 61821

Call Sign: N0CDI
Debra S Booton
1206 Harrington
Champaign IL 61821

Call Sign: W9PCM
Elwood N Begley
2506 Hathaway Dr
Champaign IL 61820

Call Sign: KB9PXI
Sharon A Coopoer
9 Hedge Ct
Champaign IL 61821

Call Sign: KB9JUD
Stephen D Cooper
9 Hedge Ct
Champaign IL 61821

Call Sign: WB8BPM
William J Goodman
2602 Heritage Dr
Champaign IL 618227378

Call Sign: KC9DCQ

Matthew E Richards
213 Hessel Blvd
Champaign IL 61820

Call Sign: KC9EON
Joshua Berry
309 Hessel Blvd
Champaign IL 61820

Call Sign: AC9AI
Joshua Berry
309 Hessel Blvd
Champaign IL 61820

Call Sign: K9AZS
Michael E Garrett
1016 Holiday Dr
Champaign IL 61821

Call Sign: KA9SMV
Finley R Provine
1417 Holly Hill Dr
Champaign IL 61821

Call Sign: KB9UJV
Christopher R Heller
1101 Hollycrest
Champaign IL 61821

Call Sign: KC9CVH
Steven J Taylor
1015 Hollycrest Dr
Champaign IL 61821

Call Sign: N9ULO
John F Boch
703 Hollycrest Dr 4
Champaign IL 61821

Call Sign: KB9PXH
Matt B Pontifex
4314 Ironwood Ln
Champaign IL 61821

Call Sign: KC9CIT
Derek J Kouzmanoff
1709 Joanne Ln
Champaign IL 61821

Call Sign: KE9EC
John P Reay Sr
1209 Julie Dr
Champaign IL 61821

Call Sign: KB9LNO
Robert W Lindsey
1908 Kenny Ave
Champaign IL 61821

Call Sign: KB9ZZT
Elizabeth L Hess
3205A Kirby Ave
Champaign IL 61822

Call Sign: KB9NBH
Gregory T Abbott
701 La Sell Dr
Champaign IL 618206817

Call Sign: KC9FYO
Michael L Trautman
2704 Lakeview Dr
Champaign IL 61822

Call Sign: K9MLT
Michael L Trautman
2704 Lakeview Dr
Champaign IL 61822

Call Sign: KC9CYJ
Timothy R Beck
2901 Lawndale Dr
Champaign IL 61821

Call Sign: N9OQU
Robert A Mcgarry
512 Luria Ln
Champaign IL 618221152

Call Sign: KB9QQX
Richard D Furr
1403 Manchester Dr
Champaign IL 61821

Call Sign: KA9YWQ
Jack L Ribelin
42 Maple Ct
Champaign IL 61821

Call Sign: W8EQB
Frank N Ulrich
1516 Marigold Ln
Champaign IL 61821

Call Sign: KC9GRV
Harry G Osoff
1204 Mayfair Rd
Champaign IL 61821

Call Sign: N9GAK
Thomas A Muehling
1813 Maynard Dr
Champaign IL 61821

Call Sign: KC9SIO
Steven T Reiners
7 McDonald Ct
Champaign IL 61821

Call Sign: KC9HSB
Mary E Belding
3111 Meadow Brook Dr
Champaign IL 61822

Call Sign: N9GPA
Mark J Belding
3111 Meadow Brook Dr
Champaign IL 618226148

Call Sign: N9RCT
Paula J Kesler
2127C Melrose
Champaign IL 61820

Call Sign: W9EWL
Whitson L Daily
4 Moraine Ct
Champaign IL 61822

Call Sign: KB9LCJ
Zane Ziegler
1907 N Duncan Rd
Champaign IL 618228912

Call Sign: KA9FWR
Edward J Ziegler
508 N Edwin

Champaign IL 61820

Call Sign: N9XAP
Charles E Riley
809 N Harris
Champaign IL 61820

Call Sign: N9WXH
Deborah F Riley
809 N Harris
Champaign IL 61820

Call Sign: K9UWF
Jerry E Rine
316 N Miller Ave
Champaign IL 61820

Call Sign: W9MBX
Lee G Hickok
504 N Rising Rd
Champaign IL 61821

Call Sign: WB9JCJ
Renae R Hickok
504 N Rising Rd
Champaign IL 61821

Call Sign: KB9JTW
Edwin D Williams
602 N Russell St
Champaign IL 618212635

Call Sign: N9PQT
Webb L Wilkey
1005 N Willis
Champaign IL 61821

Call Sign: WD9EPL
James R Burger
1118 Northwood Dr S
Champaign IL 61820

Call Sign: KC9QQK
Timothy O Hodson
2011 O Donnell Dr
Champaign IL 61821

Call Sign: WA9KGU
Robert G Minton

902 Oakcrest Dr
Champaign IL 61821

Call Sign: KC9GIV
Michael J Dabrowski
1406 Old Farm Rd Unit B
Champaign IL 61821

Call Sign: KC9EOI
Nicholas D Cassavaugh
2320 Osage Dr
Champaign IL 61821

Call Sign: N9DPK
Charles C Gibson
410 Park Ln Dr
Champaign IL 61820

Call Sign: KC9UNN
Bradley S Luhrsen
1824 Parkdale Dr
Champaign IL 61821

Call Sign: K9BSL
Bradley S Luhrsen
1824 Parkdale Dr
Champaign IL 61821

Call Sign: KF4JAQ
Daniel J Bornt
313 Paul Ave
Champaign IL 61822

Call Sign: N3FDF
Melanie B Dankowicz
2706 Pine Valley Dr
Champaign IL 61822

Call Sign: WA9PDV
Harold V Edwards
2515 Prairie Ridge Pl
Champaign IL 61822

Call Sign: KC9BSG
Joel M Schwaab
2712 Rachel Rd
Champaign IL 61822

Call Sign: N9XDG

Kristina L Daily
610 Richards Ln
Champaign IL 61820

Call Sign: KB9GBA
Dina M Nelson
3316 Ridgewood Dr
Champaign IL 61821

Call Sign: KB9ZZM
Thomas B Yu
2908 Robeson Park Dr
Champaign IL 61822

Call Sign: N9HXL
Henry T Wilkinson
2901 Rolling Ac Dr
Champaign IL 61822

Call Sign: KG4CCK
Adam J Cohen
2305 S 1st St 203
Champaign IL 61820

Call Sign: KC9ITF
Samuel S Shea
2319 S 1st St Apt 103
Champaign IL 61820

Call Sign: KB9YXJ
Andrew J Mannix
902 S 2nd St
Champaign IL 61820

Call Sign: KB9LGE
Donald S Phillips
624.5 S 5th St Apt 1
Champaign IL 618208116

Call Sign: KC9AIE
Daniel O Gonshorek
34 S Ashley Ln
Champaign IL 61820

Call Sign: KC9CPE
Keith I Gonshorek
34 S Ashley Ln
Champaign IL 61820

Call Sign: N9WKE
Andrew B Pea
506 S Elm St
Champaign IL 61820

Call Sign: KB9USC
Douglas Armstrong
702 S Lynn St
Champaign IL 61820

Call Sign: KB9JTX
Gary R Stitt
905 S Mattis Ave 5
Champaign IL 61821

Call Sign: KB9RXP
Lane D Broadbent
909 S McKinley Ave
Champaign IL 61821

Call Sign: WA9HZQ
Adrian L Lipscomb
724 S New
Champaign IL 61820

Call Sign: KC9EWS
Jake Reynolds
305 S New St
Champaign IL 618204712

Call Sign: AC9G
Jake Reynolds
305 S New St
Champaign IL 618204712

Call Sign: KC9LMJ
Max P Walker
507 S Pine
Champaign IL 61820

Call Sign: KC9KTC
Douglas D Walker
507 S Pine St
Champaign IL 61820

Call Sign: K9DDW
Douglas D Walker
507 S Pine St
Champaign IL 61820

Call Sign: K9FZK
Donald E Holthoff
807 S Prairie
Champaign IL 61820

Call Sign: KC9CEJ
David J Wheeler
513 S Prairie St
Champaign IL 61820

Call Sign: W9DJW
David J Wheeler
513 S Prairie St
Champaign IL 61820

Call Sign: KB9NBI
Katherine S Lin
1714 S Prospect Ave
Champaign IL 618207006

Call Sign: WA8VZC
David E Goldberg
511 S Ridgeway Ave
Champaign IL 61821

Call Sign: W9RWZ
Oral E Gardner
311 S Russell St
Champaign IL 61821

Call Sign: W9NUV
Virginia M Gardner
311 S Russell St
Champaign IL 61821

Call Sign: WB9TWS
Robert M Anderson
707 S State St
Champaign IL 61820

Call Sign: K9HUD
Elwood S Peterson
803 S State St
Champaign IL 61820

Call Sign: KB6MNC
Brad L Henley
1009 S Victor St

Champaign IL 61821

Call Sign: KA9BRG
Laurel M Henley
1009 S Victor St
Champaign IL 61821

Call Sign: KB9UBN
John W Sias
201 S Wright St Apt 204
Champaign IL 618204545

Call Sign: KA9BDJ
Eric L Meyer
1704 Sandcherry Ct
Champaign IL 61822

Call Sign: KC9UNM
Colleen S Gorman
2006 Sangamon Dr
Champaign IL 61821

Call Sign: KE5YIT
Anne M Thompson
2005 Savanna Dr
Champaign IL 61822

Call Sign: KE5YHX
Will C Lauer
2005 Savanna Dr
Champaign IL 61822

Call Sign: N9UWG
Ryan W Slack
1813 Scottsdale Dr
Champaign IL 61821

Call Sign: WA4CDE
Everette C Burdette II
2115 Seaton Ct
Champaign IL 61821

Call Sign: K9KUN
Richard T Borovec
2303 Seaton Ct
Champaign IL 61821

Call Sign: N9XDE
Matthew C Terry

2407 Southwood Dr
Champaign IL 61821

Call Sign: KB9LCM
Daniel B Kennedy
2513 Southwood Dr
Champaign IL 61821

Call Sign: KC9IHW
David R Pike
808 Stratford Dr
Champaign IL 61821

Call Sign: KC9JEN
David R Pike
808 Stratford Dr
Champaign IL 61821

Call Sign: AB9MK
David R Pike
808 Stratford Dr
Champaign IL 61821

Call Sign: KB9PXO
Gene L Hilberg
1911 Stratford Dr
Champaign IL 61821

Call Sign: KB9TEV
Steven D Hilberg
1911 Stratford Dr
Champaign IL 61821

Call Sign: N7TGI
Margaret L Crisman
2007 Sumac Dr
Champaign IL 61821

Call Sign: KB9JUF
Michael L Ackerman
2317 Sumac Dr
Champaign IL 61821

Call Sign: KC9SIE
Francis B Mandamuna
3723 Summer Sage Ct
Champaign IL 61822

Call Sign: WB9WHE

Jonathan S Gunn
1404 Sussex Ct
Champaign IL 61821

Call Sign: N9OHA
Douglas L Buttry
912 Switchgrass Ln
Champaign IL 61822

Call Sign: N4OCW
Gary S O Neal
4012 Tallgrass Dr
Champaign IL 61822

Call Sign: W9LMC
John D Hathaway
2109 Tamarack Ct
Champaign IL 61821

Call Sign: KC9LMI
Norman G Myers
1712 Tara Dr
Champaign IL 61821

Call Sign: KC1ES
John S Lewis Jr
2605 Trafalgar Sq
Champaign IL 61821

Call Sign: KC9ISP
Larry M Mohr
5314 Traut Lake Dr
Champaign IL 61822

Call Sign: K9LMM
Larry M Mohr
5314 Traut Lake Dr
Champaign IL 61822

Call Sign: W9UID
Merwin E Jervis
611 Union
Champaign IL 61820

Call Sign: KC9DEO
Matthew W Skaj
3114 Valerie Dr
Champaign IL 61822

Call Sign: N9HDQ
Mitch Kazel
3301 Valerie Dr
Champaign IL 61821

Call Sign: KB9RON
Matthew J Braun
2911 Valley Brook Dr
Champaign IL 61822

Call Sign: AB9MC
Yukinori Nishiki
1715 Valley Rd D
Champaign IL 618207168

Call Sign: KC9UWD
James L Mcclellan
610 Ventura Rd
Champaign IL 61820

Call Sign: KF9AI
William H Applegate
510 Victor St
Champaign IL 61821

Call Sign: WA9NEO
Dillon C Farmer
1101 W Beardsley Ave
Champaign IL 61821

Call Sign: KC9GRU
Andrezej Pukniel
307 W Birch St 7
Champaign IL 61820

Call Sign: KB9MHC
Lucky Harvey
1402 W Bradley
Champaign IL 61821

Call Sign: N9VOP
Thomas G Swann
1600 W Bradley Ave Apt
P293
Champaign IL 61821

Call Sign: KB9VJA
William C Osborn
924 W Bradley Ste 2

Champaign IL 61821

Call Sign: K9BSA
Boy Scout Troop 7
807 W Charles St
Champaign IL 61820

Call Sign: K9QZI
Milton L Forsberg
807 W Charles St
Champaign IL 618205801

Call Sign: K0UCH
James R Anderson
1107 W Charles St
Champaign IL 61820

Call Sign: KB9REZ
Douglas L Jones
1214 W Church St
Champaign IL 61821

Call Sign: KB9FMI
Christopher J Pyle
1216 W Church St Apt B
Champaign IL 61821

Call Sign: KC9MVU
Ian S Mcinerney
1306 W Clark St
Champaign IL 61821

Call Sign: KC9MVV
Michael K Mcinerney
1306 W Clark St
Champaign IL 618213156

Call Sign: N9LHI
Gregory D Smith
917 W Columbia Ave
Champaign IL 61821

Call Sign: KB9DLS
Timothy M Combs
1007 W Columbia Ave
Champaign IL 61821

Call Sign: KC9JVV
Marilyn L Cochran

1014 W Columbia Ave
Champaign IL 61821

Call Sign: N9TNA
Andy A Robinson
905 W Green
Champaign IL 61821

Call Sign: N9TNB
Howard H Robinson III
905 W Green
Champaign IL 61821

Call Sign: KC9BFV
Ranald C Wahlfeldt
1012 W Green
Champaign IL 61821

Call Sign: KF9JL
Eric E Hoerner
1220 W Green
Champaign IL 61821

Call Sign: KB9ETR
Ke Wang
108 W Green 210
Champaign IL 61820

Call Sign: W9DEA
Philip C Mitchell
410 W Green St
Champaign IL 61820

Call Sign: KB9PXN
Zak Y Robinson
905 W Green St
Champaign IL 61821

Call Sign: KA9KEF
Eric W Sink
3413 W Hensley Rd
Champaign IL 61822

Call Sign: N9XDD
Eric Hilberg
3108 W John St
Champaign IL 61821

Call Sign: K4FQJ

Eugene H Wilbur
2000 W John St Apt 214
Champaign IL 61820

Call Sign: KC9DSS
Michael L Spinar
1711 W John St Apt 4
Champaign IL 618213746

Call Sign: KC9KTD
Nicolae Popa
2314 W John St Apt B
Champaign IL 61821

Call Sign: WA9EVK
Marc S Roderick
3501 W Kirby Ave
Champaign IL 61822

Call Sign: KB9YGJ
Duncan H Lawrie
1409 W Old Church Rd
Champaign IL 61822

Call Sign: KB9YSY
Linda K Lawrie
1409 W Old Church Rd
Champaign IL 61822

Call Sign: N9XDK
Danny L Hughes
1707 W Park Ave
Champaign IL 61821

Call Sign: WB9DPW
Patrick F Zeglin
1116 W Springfield Ave
Champaign IL 61821

Call Sign: KG9JO
Darren D Taylor
1207 W Springfield Ave
Champaign IL 61821

Call Sign: KB2NIE
Heather L Cawlfield
2403 W Springfield Ave Apt
W 4
Champaign IL 61821

Call Sign: KA8WSW
Stephanie A Mabry
2503 W Springfield Ave B6
Champaign IL 61821

Call Sign: KA9OWL
Robert C Eubank
510 W St Charles
Champaign IL 61820

Call Sign: KB9CZG
William E Folts
1005 W Union St
Champaign IL 61821

Call Sign: W9JPN
William W Cochran
1204 W Union St
Champaign IL 61821

Call Sign: KB9JUG
Donald F Schultz
1207 W University
Champaign IL 61821

Call Sign: KC9FJL
Chad M Siegler
1605 W University
Champaign IL 61821

Call Sign: KC9OMJ
Brock Angelo
1301 W University Ave
Champaign IL 61821

Call Sign: K9JBA
Brock Angelo
1301 W University Ave
Champaign IL 61821

Call Sign: KI4CMS
David J Massey
605 W University Ave Apt 5
Champaign IL 61820

Call Sign: KC9TBU
Joshua J Zirbel
210 W Vine St

Champaign IL 61820

Call Sign: KA9YWK
John B Melby III
1002 W Washington
Champaign IL 61821

Call Sign: K9TGT
Richard E Slavens
207 W Washington 1
Champaign IL 61820

Call Sign: WB8NOS
Paul F Nelson
1009 W Washington St
Champaign IL 61821

Call Sign: KC9OAC
Nicholas C Karr
1104 W Washington St
Champaign IL 61821

Call Sign: KC9PAA
Steve C Karr
1104 W Washington St
Champaign IL 61821

Call Sign: KC9QQL
Michael H Davis
504 W Washington St 3
Champaign IL 61820

Call Sign: K9LJQ
Thomas L Stewart
1100 W Westlawn
Champaign IL 61821

Call Sign: W9BXY
Dean F Schwenk
804 W White St
Champaign IL 61820

Call Sign: KA9WMP
Stephen E Lemmon
1308 W White St
Champaign IL 61821

Call Sign: AA9YF
Darren D Taylor

1708 W White St
Champaign IL 61821

Call Sign: KF9Z
Darren D Taylor
1708 W White St
Champaign IL 61821

Call Sign: KB9VEU
Kevin M Kennedy
508 W White St Apt 31
Champaign IL 61820

Call Sign: NX9W
James G Carrubba
915 W William
Champaign IL 61821

Call Sign: KC9JVY
Adam A Joseph
1013 W William
Champaign IL 61821

Call Sign: KB9WSU
Sheryl C Fisher
1408 W William
Champaign IL 61821

Call Sign: N9DOG
Sheryl C Fisher
1408 W William
Champaign IL 61821

Call Sign: N9EOC
Mary C Price
1614 W William
Champaign IL 61821

Call Sign: N9ETT
Timothy E Price
1614 W William
Champaign IL 61821

Call Sign: KB9QZY
Holly E Husinga
1804 W William 2
Champaign IL 61821

Call Sign: WA9WJP

Michael P Thompson
504 W William St
Champaign IL 61820

Call Sign: KC9DUU
Mark Joseph
1013 W William St
Champaign IL 61821

Call Sign: K9BF
Benjamin J Fisher
1408 W William St
Champaign IL 61821

Call Sign: KB9WTV
Twin City ARC Contesters
Tcarcc
1408 W William St
Champaign IL 61821

Call Sign: KB9LVJ
Lori L Lund
4809 W Windsor Rd D17
Champaign IL 61821

Call Sign: W9LOC
Richard W Rice
1001 Waters Edge Rd
Champaign IL 61822

Call Sign: KC9EKJ
Aaron K Reffett
2703 Wedgewood Dr
Champaign IL 618227545

Call Sign: K9XMG
Aaron K Reffett
2703 Wedgewood Dr
Champaign IL 618227545

Call Sign: KB9PZ
Nancy Anderson
1111 Westfield Dr
Champaign IL 61821

Call Sign: WB9WFP
Leon T Stewart
1100 Westlawn
Champaign IL 61820

Call Sign: N9SQF
Joel F Ward Jr
2809 Willow Bend Rd
Champaign IL 61822

Call Sign: KB9PMT
Angel A Medina
2006 Winchester Dr
Champaign IL 61821

Call Sign: W9MAP
Mary M Twigg
612 Yalow Dr
Champaign IL 61822

Call Sign: N9OQT
Patrick J Twigg
612 Yalow Dr
Champaign IL 61822

Call Sign: N9GKA
Charles M Driskell
3312 York Dr
Champaign IL 61821

Call Sign: N9ICT
Victoria A Driskell
3312 York Dr
Champaign IL 61821

Call Sign: N9XDA
Asad A Husain
1519 Yorkshire Dr
Champaign IL 61821

Call Sign: WB9ULS
Francis S Olson
Champaign IL 61824

Call Sign: WB9VFW
Roberta J Olson
Champaign IL 61824

Call Sign: N9KFJ
Janet G Cains
Champaign IL 61826

Call Sign: KC9PTJ

Daniel Bernstein
Champaign IL 61824

Call Sign: K9JDI
Daniel Bernstein
Champaign IL 61824

Call Sign: KC9PKD
Neil Bernstein
Champaign IL 61824

Call Sign: K9PIX
Neil Bernstein
Champaign IL 61824

Call Sign: KC9HXX
Bruce W Prothe
Champaign IL 61825

Call Sign: K9CU
Twin City ARC Contesters
Tcarcc
Champaign IL 61825

Call Sign: KB9KHJ
Kim R Schutterle
Champaign IL 61826

Call Sign: W9ULS
Francis S Olson
Champaign IL 618241122

Call Sign: K9VFW
Roberta J Olson
Champaign IL 618241122

Call Sign: KB9YBU
Stan E Olson
Champaign IL 618241122

Call Sign: K9SWX
Stan E Olson
Champaign IL 618241122

Call Sign: KC9HUJ
Lionel D Lusardi
Champaign IL 618241421

Call Sign: KC9HPB

Chris M Anderson
Champaign IL 618252325

Call Sign: W9CMA
Chris M Anderson
Champaign IL 618252325

Call Sign: N8SXL
Melissa E Neubauer
Champaign IL 618267102

FCC Amateur Radio Licenses in Chana

Call Sign: KC9NU
Thomas M Bemis
5246 Husking Peg Rd
Chana IL 61015

Call Sign: KA9DXH
Brenda K Anderson
2120 S Knoll Rd
Chana IL 61015

FCC Amateur Radio Licenses in Chapin

Call Sign: N9AYQ
Linda S Hurst
Rr 1 Box 77
Chapin IL 62628

Call Sign: KC9THW
Chip L Evans
213 Oak
Chapin IL 62628

FCC Amateur Radio Licenses in Charleston

Call Sign: KB9ALJ
William R Davis
760 10th St
Charleston IL 61920

Call Sign: KB9MSW
Roger N Brinkley
114 12th Ave
Charleston IL 61920

Call Sign: KA9ZJA
John F Frazier
1815 12th St 3
Charleston IL 61920

Call Sign: KC9INA
Steve M Mcnamer
1415 14th St
Charleston IL 61920

Call Sign: N9QBC
Johnathon C Morgan
1305 18th St Apt 16
Charleston IL 61920

Call Sign: KC9KRA
Coles County Emergency
Management ARC
846 4th St
Charleston IL 61920

Call Sign: KC9MZU
Christina J Miller
761 8th St
Charleston IL 61920

Call Sign: KB9UBO
Robert P Pratte
2218 8th St Cir
Charleston IL 61920

Call Sign: W9LYN
William S James
2237 Andover Pl
Charleston IL 61920

Call Sign: KC9QMH
Gary M Mikel
1310 Audrey Ln
Charleston IL 61920

Call Sign: KA9EVB
Bennie L Easton
Rt 4 Box 184
Charleston IL 61920

Call Sign: N9FJG
Earl O Hoff

Rr 2 Box 184B
Charleston IL 61920

Call Sign: K9LDM
Mildred K Kirk
Rr 4 Box 238
Charleston IL 61920

Call Sign: N9SKW
Jonathan E Bates
Rr 4 Box 86A
Charleston IL 61920

Call Sign: KE9QI
Harold D Fildes
407 Cedar Dr
Charleston IL 61920

Call Sign: WA9EVM
Larry W Rennels
304 Chamberlin Dr
Charleston IL 61920

Call Sign: W9OTJ
Robert L Whittenbarger
6088 Chicory Knoll
Charleston IL 61920

Call Sign: KA9WGA
Marlaine L Francis
2312 Cortland Dr
Charleston IL 61920

Call Sign: KC9TKO
Norman A Garrett
8282 Country Club Rd
Charleston IL 61920

Call Sign: K9NAG
Norman A Garrett
8282 Country Club Rd
Charleston IL 61920

Call Sign: KC9AXW
Matthew M Klarich
1032 Division
Charleston IL 61920

Call Sign: W9HUY

Norman A Strader
887 Division St
Charleston IL 61920

Call Sign: WD9ICG
James A Wiman
1216 Douglas Dr
Charleston IL 61920

Call Sign: W8AQ
Jack K Neal
15157 E CR 1400 N
Charleston IL 61920

Call Sign: KC9QMJ
Eric D Cresap
14109 E CR 300N
Charleston IL 61920

Call Sign: KC9REH
Tonicia M Smith
18305 E CR 400 N
Charleston IL 61920

Call Sign: KC9QMB
Gary W Hanebrink
13020 E CR 720N
Charleston IL 61920

Call Sign: KC9QMC
Karen S Hanebrink
13020 E CR 720N
Charleston IL 61920

Call Sign: AG9W
Emerson G Kinnaman
700 East St
Charleston IL 61920

Call Sign: N9BZQ
Patricia A Kinnaman
700 East St
Charleston IL 61920

Call Sign: KC9QMF
Adam J Due
16470 Forest View Dr
Charleston IL 61920

Call Sign: N9SME
Richard M Stewart
1811 Grant Ave
Charleston IL 61920

Call Sign: KD9AC
James D Riddle
210 Jackson
Charleston IL 61920

Call Sign: N0WYK
William L Hay
1817 Madison
Charleston IL 61920

Call Sign: KC9QME
Thomas C Watson
2200 Madison Ave
Charleston IL 61920

Call Sign: WB9GRA
John C Looby
1818 McComb
Charleston IL 61920

Call Sign: W9JVW
Giles L Henderson
75 McLeod
Charleston IL 61920

Call Sign: KB9SGA
Howard S Eads
2125 Meadowlake Dr
Charleston IL 61920

Call Sign: K9HSE
Howard S Eads
2125 Meadowlake Dr
Charleston IL 61920

Call Sign: KC9QMD
William J Warmoth
31 Miller Ave
Charleston IL 61920

Call Sign: KC9VQL
Alfred E Schlotmann Jr
310 N B St
Charleston IL 61920

Call Sign: WA9MHY
Charles R Maris
13210 Old SR
Charleston IL 619207650

Call Sign: N9GIF
Ronald D Amyx
791 Reynolds Dr
Charleston IL 61920

Call Sign: K3BY
Samuel A Guccione
2127 Seneca Dr
Charleston IL 61920

Call Sign: WA9OWY
Roger D Rice
111 W Fillmore
Charleston IL 61920

Call Sign: N9LPY
Richard D Woodard
305 W Pierce Ave
Charleston IL 61920

Call Sign: N9NNP
Robert D Blagg
409 W Pierce Ave
Charleston IL 619202547

Call Sign: W9HOH
Norman J Weddell
500 W Polk Apt 138
Charleston IL 61920

Call Sign: KB9ATA
Leonard Durham
2725 Whippoorwill Dr
Charleston IL 61920

Call Sign: N9FSI
David W Pottle
510 Wilson Ave
Charleston IL 61920

Call Sign: N9WZZ
Deidra L Pottle
510 Wilson Ave

Charleston IL 61920

Call Sign: KB9QOK
Diana L Pottle
510 Wilson Ave
Charleston IL 61920

Call Sign: KB9LUA
Danielle L Bradford
510 Wilson Ave
Charleston IL 61920

Call Sign: KB9RJP
Dana L Pottle
510 Wilson St
Charleston IL 61920

Call Sign: N4OVL
Joseph T Barron Jr
Charleston IL 61920

FCC Amateur Radio Licenses in Chatham

Call Sign: N9VAC
Jason E Triyonis
69 Axline
Chatham IL 62629

Call Sign: N9KJC
Kenneth M Gorda
29 Bonniebrook Rd
Chatham IL 62629

Call Sign: KB9IUF
Alayna D Kopp
Rr 1 Box 344
Chatham IL 62629

Call Sign: KB9IUG
Kara D Kopp
Rr 1 Box 344
Chatham IL 62629

Call Sign: KB9IUH
Paula E Kopp
Rr 1 Box 344
Chatham IL 62629

Call Sign: WD5BMG
Stephen E White
326 Breckenridge Rd
Chatham IL 62629

Call Sign: KC9CSD
Curtis E Barmes
11 Buckingham
Chatham IL 62629

Call Sign: N9CEB
Curtis E Barmes
11 Buckingham
Chatham IL 62629

Call Sign: KC9FUY
Eric S Barmes
11 Buckingham
Chatham IL 62629

Call Sign: K9ESB
Eric S Barmes
11 Buckingham
Chatham IL 62629

Call Sign: KC9FUW
Karen M Barmes
11 Buckingham
Chatham IL 62629

Call Sign: K9KMB
Karen M Barmes
11 Buckingham
Chatham IL 62629

Call Sign: W9BPX
Samuel B Williams
14 Buckingham Rd
Chatham IL 62629

Call Sign: KA9NQT
J I Kutzler
44 Chukar Dr
Chatham IL 62629

Call Sign: WA9OFO
Louis J Kutzler
44 Chukar Dr
Chatham IL 62629

Call Sign: KB9WEZ
Louis W Kutzler
44 Chukar Dr
Chatham IL 62629

Call Sign: KC9MOW
Carl C Johnson
726 Deerfield Rd
Chatham IL 62629

Call Sign: KB9IUI
Dana L Neumann
202 Diane Dr
Chatham IL 62629

Call Sign: KC9JAH
Ernest H Goetsch
224 Dover Dr
Chatham IL 62629

Call Sign: N9JWK
David L Harrison
520 E Mulberry St
Chatham IL 62629

Call Sign: K9CIL
Errol N Workman
106 E Spruce St
Chatham IL 62629

Call Sign: KB9UWV
William D Fehring
10128 Gilreath Rd
Chatham IL 62629

Call Sign: WB9QXW
James L Smith
5930 Iron Bridge Rd
Chatham IL 62629

Call Sign: W9PLS
James L Smith
5930 Iron Bridge Rd
Chatham IL 62629

Call Sign: KA9QCZ
John S Stout
6880 Ironbridge Rd

Chatham IL 62629

Call Sign: N9GEL
Frederick L Crawford Jr
13 Lake Knolls Dr
Chatham IL 62629

Call Sign: N9FSG
James D Jones
23 Lake Knolls Dr
Chatham IL 62629

Call Sign: AI9E
David W Cripe
224 Manor Hill Dr
Chatham IL 62629

Call Sign: WA9PLT
Robert D Mcinerney
6929 Mansion Rd
Chatham IL 626299750

Call Sign: KC9LAM
Peter A Mayoral
32 Meander Pike
Chatham IL 62629

Call Sign: KB9ZVD
Edward E Conboy
202 N College
Chatham IL 62629

Call Sign: KC9LTV
Edward E Conboy
202 N College
Chatham IL 62629

Call Sign: KC9JFN
Steve D Ogden
650 N Park Ave
Chatham IL 626291136

Call Sign: K9YCF
William H Busch
9781 Old Indian Trl Rd
Chatham IL 626298611

Call Sign: KE4FGT
Jeffrey S Whitehouse

330 Osteen Ln
Chatham IL 62629

Call Sign: KC9GAO
Susan J Duke
10 Parkview
Chatham IL 62629

Call Sign: KC9QEA
Jesse L Hunter III
10 Parkview Ln
Chatham IL 62629

Call Sign: KC9APD
Randy J Kuhl
210 Plains Dr Apt 6
Chatham IL 62629

Call Sign: WB9YNV
Keith L Mahan
401 S Grand
Chatham IL 62629

Call Sign: W9WGP
Edgar H Brandon
500 S Grand
Chatham IL 62629

Call Sign: N9GTU
Krail N Lattig
4774 Spaulding Orchard Rd
Chatham IL 62629

Call Sign: WA9JOP
Carl D Dufner
525 Teal
Chatham IL 62629

Call Sign: KB9IUJ
Chad L Patton
45 Teal Dr
Chatham IL 62629

Call Sign: KB9IUK
Kyle B Patton
45 Teal Dr
Chatham IL 62629

Call Sign: KB9IUL

Pamela J Patton
45 Teal Dr
Chatham IL 62629

Call Sign: KC9MOU
Andrew G Sivertsen
796 Titan Ct
Chatham IL 62629

Call Sign: KC9OJZ
Robert A Jacobs
309 W Chestnut St
Chatham IL 62629

Call Sign: N9OHC
Christopher L Morrow
507 W Chestnut St
Chatham IL 626291221

Call Sign: KF8RS
Clarence O Rogers III
1127 White Birch Dr
Chatham IL 626295026

FCC Amateur Radio Licenses in Chatsworth

Call Sign: KB9YHY
Ferrell W Rich
404 E Cherry St
Chatsworth IL 60921

Call Sign: KG9EO
Bruce A Perring
503 S 7th St
Chatsworth IL 60921

FCC Amateur Radio Licenses in Chebanse

Call Sign: KC9MZN
Susan K Neukomm
6478 S Rt 45 52 B4
Chebanse IL 60922

Call Sign: KC9GWE
Joseph M Renollet
6478 S Rt 45 52 Lot B 3
Chebanse IL 60922

Call Sign: N9LAH
Philip J Snyder
590 S Walnut
Chebanse IL 60922

Call Sign: KB9OYG
Douglas E Webber
423 Crittenden St
Chenoa IL 61726

Call Sign: WB9DUC
Daryl D Haney
31631 E 3100 N Rd
Chenoa IL 61726

Call Sign: KC9AUS
Duane E Haney
800 Grant St
Chenoa IL 61726

Call Sign: KC9AUR
John C Boyd
722 Lincoln St
Chenoa IL 61726

Call Sign: N6LFO
Richard K Myrvold
33489 Maple St
Chenoa IL 61726

Call Sign: K9VQ
Richard K Myrvold
33489 Maple St
Chenoa IL 61726

Call Sign: N9OSU
Doreen R Roeder
421 N 2nd Ave
Chenoa IL 61726

Call Sign: KB9FPY
Ronald A Roeder
421 N 2nd Ave
Chenoa IL 61726

Call Sign: KB9EZL
Dennis L Petersen
31061 N 3360 E Rd
Chenoa IL 61726

Call Sign: WA9BTF
Lewis R Estes
725 S McClellan
Chenoa IL 61726

Call Sign: KC9AUT
Stephen R Macom
124 Scott St
Chenoa IL 61726

Call Sign: KC9GKG
David E Coomer
621 York
Chenoa IL 61726

Call Sign: KA9PKF
Pamela L Haney
Chenoa IL 61726

Call Sign: KB9APA
Aaron M Vogel
3957 Arborlace Ct
Cherry Valley IL 61016

Call Sign: KD5VTN
Arthur Y Tsubaki
7319 Brimmer Way
Cherry Valley IL 61016

Call Sign: KC9MGV
Jessica S Moore
7248 Cornflower Rd
Cherry Valley IL 61016

Call Sign: KA9LMK
Joseph A Moore
7248 Cornflower Rd
Cherry Valley IL 61016

Call Sign: N9TJB
Jeremy D Lierman

119 East St
Cherry Valley IL 61016

Call Sign: KB9ANG
Bryan D Holliday
7466 Farmhome Ln
Cherry Valley IL 61016

Call Sign: KC9MMK
Donald R Layng
310 Grove St
Cherry Valley IL 61016

Call Sign: KB9POH
Jared D Wickam Jr
1726 Irene Rd
Cherry Valley IL 61016

Call Sign: K9BTX
Edward J Slaga
7572 N Cherryvale Blvd Apt
206
Cherry Valley IL 61016

Call Sign: WD9FVB
Ronald E Beiersdorff
6852 River Rd
Cherry Valley IL 61016

Call Sign: KB9DBU
David D Neumann
8910 Sultana Ct
Cherry Valley IL 61016

Call Sign: KA9TKY
James M Alsbury
149 Van Buren St
Cherry Valley IL 61016

Call Sign: KC9NZS
Michael A Holt
7108 Wheatland Ter
Cherry Valley IL 61016

Call Sign: N9TIZ
Robert L Lierman Sr
Cherry Valley IL 61016

FCC Amateur Radio Licenses in Chester

Call Sign: KB9EWD
Margaret K Pierce
Rr 2 Box 354B
Chester IL 62233

Call Sign: W9TAX
Elliott E Reiman
410 Chester St
Chester IL 62233

Call Sign: KB9YLV
Roger L Lautertung
124 Clifford Dr
Chester IL 62233

Call Sign: WB9ONO
Robert H Dickson
210 Dixie Dr
Chester IL 622332106

Call Sign: WA9VAV
Robert C Franklin
6 Greenbriar Ln
Chester IL 62233

Call Sign: KB9MUO
Bertram I Schirmer
2281 Old Plank Rd
Chester IL 62233

Call Sign: KB9LRN
Linda G Young
3837 Palestine Rd
Chester IL 62233

Call Sign: N9RIU
Gene E Young
3837 Palestine Rd
Chester IL 62233

Call Sign: KB9LRM
Travis G Young
3837 Palestine Rd
Chester IL 62233

Call Sign: KB9MGW

Orville H Rinne
Chester IL 62233

Call Sign: AA9ZN
Orville H Rinne
Chester IL 62233

Call Sign: AA9QV
Robert Kotva
Chester IL 62233

FCC Amateur Radio Licenses in Chesterfield

Call Sign: K9RWB
Harry J Giffin
18692 R111
Chesterfield IL 62630

FCC Amateur Radio Licenses in Chestnut

Call Sign: KC9HET
Timothy W Daugherty
993 2120th Ave
Chestnut IL 62578

Call Sign: K9ZM
Gregory C Gobleman
208 N Mulberry
Chestnut IL 625180012

FCC Amateur Radio Licenses in Chillicothe

Call Sign: KB9KBI
David W Mathias
129 2nd St
Chillicothe IL 61523

Call Sign: KG0BF
Charles J Cameron
1217 Chestnut St Apt 7
Chillicothe IL 61523

Call Sign: KA9CIA
Lisa L Ferry
4224 Cloverdale Rd
Chillicothe IL 61523

Call Sign: KA9IKY
Walter E Schaufelberger
4122 E Cloverdale Rd
Chillicothe IL 61523

Call Sign: KA9IKX
Lynn Schaufelberger
4122 E Cloverdale Rd
Chillicothe IL 615239568

Call Sign: KE9WS
Jack E Frank
5008 E Lawrence
Chillicothe IL 61523

Call Sign: KC9EUO
Conrad D Halden
5313 E Marquette St
Chillicothe IL 61523

Call Sign: WB9UCP
Franklin L Brinson
5113 E Richland Ave
Chillicothe IL 61523

Call Sign: K9ILA
Patrick J Pratt
5223 E Richland Ave
Chillicothe IL 61523

Call Sign: KC9DJC
Josh P Oathout
1211 Finney St
Chillicothe IL 61523

Call Sign: KB9PPR
Mark W Sefried
100 Hazle St
Chillicothe IL 61523

Call Sign: N9JHR
Dale E Pope
3522 Hidden Valley
Chillicothe IL 61523

Call Sign: KC9TAO
Jed S Fancher
1619 Holland Ct

Chillicothe IL 61523

Call Sign: KC9IFO
Joe J Merdian
220 Hollybrook
Chillicothe IL 61523

Call Sign: KC9UCQ
Adam M Molohon
16012 N 2nd St
Chillicothe IL 61523

Call Sign: KB9LJG
Kevin L Case
508 N 4th St
Chillicothe IL 61523

Call Sign: WD9BJU
Max E Trumbold
822 N 4th St
Chillicothe IL 61523

Call Sign: N9UQO
Wilvin E Magee Sr
1114 N 5th St
Chillicothe IL 61523

Call Sign: K9OOE
Maynard M Duffy Jr
1720 N 6th St
Chillicothe IL 61523

Call Sign: KC9FQI
Matthew R Church
15204 N 7th St
Chillicothe IL 61523

Call Sign: WA9VLA
Elmer A Scherer
1020 N Benedict
Chillicothe IL 61523

Call Sign: N9RPL
Kevin N Sill
13431 N Bridle Ln
Chillicothe IL 61523

Call Sign: N9VIO
Linda J Sill

13431 N Bridle Ln
Chillicothe IL 61523

Call Sign: KB9VVG
Travis E Cage
1423 N Cutright
Chillicothe IL 61523

Call Sign: KB9OSR
Jonathan W Ward
1216 N Cutright St
Chillicothe IL 61523

Call Sign: KE9IK
Michael E Ward
1216 N Cutright St
Chillicothe IL 615231414

Call Sign: KB8WBO
Andrew C Heebink
20714 N Deer Bluffs
Chillicothe IL 61523

Call Sign: WB9RBZ
Clifford E Wilcox
14632 N Grandview Dr
Chillicothe IL 615239777

Call Sign: WD9HVX
Chris D Williamson
1603 N Hoyt
Chillicothe IL 61523

Call Sign: WA9EDF
Robert M Carroll
19828 N Isaacson Dr
Chillicothe IL 615239184

Call Sign: WB9GYI
Thomas M Albright
19907 N Isaacson Dr
Chillicothe IL 61523

Call Sign: WB9GYH
Robert W Coppernoll
20109 N Isaacson Dr
Chillicothe IL 61523

Call Sign: N9DUQ

Enid E Stratton
105 N Louise St
Chillicothe IL 615231907

Call Sign: KC9YO
Frank L Stratton
105 N Louise St
Chillicothe IL 615231907

Call Sign: KC9OJN
Rodney A Davis
18103 N Old Galena
Chillicothe IL 61523

Call Sign: KC9QND
Wesley T Williamson
13739 N River Beach Dr
Chillicothe IL 61523

Call Sign: W9FRO
Robert S Nelson
13933 N Riverbeach Dr
Chillicothe IL 61523

Call Sign: KT9TB
Terry R Beachler
11850 N Riverview Rd
Chillicothe IL 615239119

Call Sign: KC9PZQ
Frank H High
13705 N Wayne Rd
Chillicothe IL 61523

Call Sign: KF9JR
Darrell D Stedman
1405 N Wilson
Chillicothe IL 61523

Call Sign: KC9PRT
Christian M Papach
27 Pinewood Est
Chillicothe IL 61523

Call Sign: N9JXE
Clarence I Breed
14820 Riverview Rd
Chillicothe IL 61523

Call Sign: N9VDB
Andrea M Mc Cullough
20915 Stephanie Ct
Chillicothe IL 61523

Call Sign: N9RPK
Gary L Mc Cullough
20915 Stephanie Ct
Chillicothe IL 61523

Call Sign: N9XAE
Joe G Mc Cullough
20915 Stephanie Ct
Chillicothe IL 61523

Call Sign: N9VDD
Marjorie A Mc Cullough
20915 Stephanie Ct
Chillicothe IL 61523

Call Sign: KF9RZ
David C Hale
1129 Sunnyside
Chillicothe IL 61523

Call Sign: N9AUT
James L Martin
719 Taylor Dr
Chillicothe IL 615231376

Call Sign: KB9OMQ
James E Watters
611 W Matthews St Lot 11
Chillicothe IL 61523

Call Sign: N9YDL
John L Gray Jr
415 W Truitt Ave
Chillicothe IL 61523

Call Sign: KA9YRZ
Henry A Salter
619 B W Truitt Ave
Chillicothe IL 61523

Call Sign: KB9MTU
Steven B Reginald
1117 W Walnut
Chillicothe IL 61523

Call Sign: KC9ULV
Nathaniel B Reginald
1117 W Walnut St
Chillicothe IL 61523

Call Sign: KC9KEK
Brandon M Cutright
221 White Clover Dr
Chillicothe IL 615231911

FCC Amateur Radio Licenses in Chrisman

Call Sign: KC9PHR
Brian G Martin
16857 E 1700th Rd
Chrisman IL 61924

Call Sign: K9IGY
Walter R Ingram
20876 E 2300th Rd
Chrisman IL 619247853

Call Sign: WA9ATU
Lester W Grissom
520 E Madison Ave
Chrisman IL 61924

Call Sign: K9AJK
Lloyd F Mc Cauley
222 N Colorado St
Chrisman IL 619241011

Call Sign: N7GEH
Thomas J Wheatley
421 N Indiana Ave
Chrisman IL 61924

Call Sign: KB9EYS
Joseph H Techau
111 Woodlawn Dr
Chrisman IL 61924

FCC Amateur Radio Licenses in Christopher

Call Sign: KF9TX
James E Johnson

401 E Washington St
Christopher IL 62822

Call Sign: KB9VOP
Christopher J Snyder
211 Elm
Christopher IL 62822

Call Sign: N8PZP
Chris A Webb
207 S State St
Christopher IL 62822

Call Sign: KC9RVH
Donna K Todd
808 S Victor St
Christopher IL 62822

Call Sign: KC9POI
Anthony C Amato
8646 Stone St
Christopher IL 62822

Call Sign: KB9PJI
Elizabeth J Shurtz
305 W Helen Ave
Christopher IL 62822

Call Sign: K9IRA
John W Ensinger
407 W Ray Ave
Christopher IL 628221423

FCC Amateur Radio Licenses in Cisco

Call Sign: KA9RGJ
James C Leischner
125 E 1200 N Rd
Cisco IL 61830

FCC Amateur Radio Licenses in Cisne

Call Sign: KC9QJP
Tyler A Brooker
Rr 1 Box 102 C
Cisne IL 62823

Call Sign: KB9MWK
Henry S Linder
Rt 1 Box 11 A
Cisne IL 62823

Call Sign: KC9LGV
Joshua S Perry
Rr2 Box 17Aa
Cisne IL 62823

Call Sign: K9BBA
Anthony P Wheeler
Rr2 Box 180
Cisne IL 62823

Call Sign: KC9QBU
Aaron C Barnard
Rr 2 Box 209
Cisne IL 62823

Call Sign: KC9MIW
Bobby J Hill
Cisne IL 62823

FCC Amateur Radio Licenses in Cissna Park

Call Sign: KB9LCI
Paul B Moffat
110 S 1st St
Cissna Park IL 60924

Call Sign: WB9SSO
Robert L Reece Jr
101 W Railroad
Cissna Park IL 60924

Call Sign: K9LPI
Joseph J Lisciandra
Cissna Park IL 60924

FCC Amateur Radio Licenses in Claremont

Call Sign: KA9AEY
Richard E Hesler
4422 N Amity Rd
Claremont IL 62421

Call Sign: WB9FYY
Forrest J Koertge II
5261 N Stringtown Rd
Claremont IL 62421

Call Sign: N9MWK
Dennis R Poland
Claremont IL 62421

FCC Amateur Radio Licenses in Clay City

Call Sign: KC9BUQ
Richard L Schnepper
536 S Illinois St
Clay City IL 62824

Call Sign: N9XPC
Douglas E Weiler
538 Wilcox Bridge Ln
Clay City IL 62824

Call Sign: KC9CGT
Eric U Lake
Clay City IL 62824

FCC Amateur Radio Licenses in Clayton

Call Sign: KB9THK
Greg J Ahsell
Rr 1 Box 204 A
Clayton IL 62334

Call Sign: KC9LCK
Jack R Tubaugh
1548 E 2775 St
Clayton IL 62324

Call Sign: N9IRT
Karen L Oberling
2995 N 1100th Pl
Clayton IL 62324

FCC Amateur Radio Licenses in Cleveland

Call Sign: K9YGA
John R Banks

301 Jackson St
Cleveland IL 61241

Call Sign: K9VB
Thomas J Van Belle
601 Main St
Cleveland IL 61241

Call Sign: KA9WVU
David J Stewart
1008 Main St
Cleveland IL 61241

Call Sign: WD9HEI
Carole A Stewart
1008 Main Strett
Cleveland IL 61241

FCC Amateur Radio Licenses in Clifton

Call Sign: WA9EGI
Robert D Berns
490 E 2950 N Rd
Clifton IL 60927

Call Sign: KB9MDL
Mac A English
250 Henderson Ave
Clifton IL 60927

Call Sign: K9ZHD
Paul Bogomolow
250 Jensen Ave
Clifton IL 60927

Call Sign: KG6GJO
Douglas M Pickett
2906 N 1500 E Rd
Clifton IL 60927

Call Sign: KC9CZQ
Jane A Pickett
2906 N 1500 E Rd
Clifton IL 60927

Call Sign: WD9BHD
Leo V Hoaglund
385 S Locust St

Clifton IL 609270937

Call Sign: WA9CFO
Robert W Zigtema
480 W Lincoln
Clifton IL 609279670

Call Sign: KA9CVS
Tana E Hoaglund
Clifton IL 609270937

| **FCC Amateur Radio Licenses in Clinton** |

Call Sign: W9ZWT
William E Martin
16340 Airport Rd
Clinton IL 61727

Call Sign: KB9WCJ
Gregory A Lux
103 Aspen Dr
Clinton IL 617272400

Call Sign: KB9DVT
Rita A Mills
Rr 2 Box 147
Clinton IL 61727

Call Sign: N9RYQ
Karen L Murphy
Rfd 2 Box 155
Clinton IL 61727

Call Sign: KA9KEI
Marvin D Murphy
Rr 2 Box 155
Clinton IL 61727

Call Sign: K9HRC
Claude S Cain
Rr 1 Box 175
Clinton IL 61727

Call Sign: K9QGR
Hazel V Cain
Rr 1 Box 175
Clinton IL 61727

Call Sign: KA9OHK
Joel White
Rr 1 Box 203
Clinton IL 61727

Call Sign: KB9LNW
Kathleen A White
Rural Rt 1 Box 203
Clinton IL 61727

Call Sign: KC9REG
Fred J Loeffler
Rt 3 Box 223
Clinton IL 61727

Call Sign: KB9GEB
Stephen B Moore
Rr3 Box 235N
Clinton IL 617279316

Call Sign: KB9JLN
Keith E Wright
Rr 2 Box 260
Clinton IL 61727

Call Sign: KA9ETM
Michael D Tindill
Rt 2 Box 263r
Clinton IL 61727

Call Sign: N9GVW
Robert B Farris
R 4 Box 269
Clinton IL 61727

Call Sign: N9GWB
Wanda L Farris
Rr 4 Box 269
Clinton IL 61727

Call Sign: WB4PRR
Charles K Johnston
Rr 3 Box 290F
Clinton IL 67127

Call Sign: KC9ZR
Gertrude E Clark
Rr 2 Box 293
Clinton IL 61727

Call Sign: KC9ZQ
James W Clark
Rr 2 Box 293
Clinton IL 61727

Call Sign: K0MBA
Richard O Snelson
Rr 3 Box 295
Clinton IL 61727

Call Sign: KA9YPK
John G Huisinga
Rr 4 Box 321
Clinton IL 617272714

Call Sign: N9DXX
Terri E Williams-Teutsch
Rr 4 Box 332B
Clinton IL 61704

Call Sign: KB9QKK
Billy R Irvin
Rr 1 Box 341
Clinton IL 61721

Call Sign: W9KXN
James R Lane
918 E Macon St
Clinton IL 61727

Call Sign: N9PYZ
Marvin E Stewart
1419 E Main
Clinton IL 61727

Call Sign: KC9NPW
Thomas L Goodwin Sr
1700 E Main St Apt 119
Clinton IL 61727

Call Sign: K9TZX
Robert L Bradd
1006 E South St
Clinton IL 61727

Call Sign: KB9ZDX
Philip B Kahn
926 E Washington St

Clinton IL 617271770

Call Sign: AB9KC
Philip B Kahn
926 E Washington St
Clinton IL 617271770

Call Sign: N9VIF
Lyle J Gill
1622 E Washington St
Clinton IL 61727

Call Sign: KC9FYP
Frederick A Zacher
9 Fairlawn Dr
Clinton IL 617272525

Call Sign: WA9LHU
James F Dunakey
719 N Elizabeth
Clinton IL 61727

Call Sign: K9LJR
Louis J Rempe
720 N Monroe St
Clinton IL 61727

Call Sign: KC9GAW
John T Reid
122 N Water
Clinton IL 61727

Call Sign: KL7IPW
Nicholas J Waddock Jr
Box 132 Rr 21 Sunset Dr
Clinton IL 61727

Call Sign: KA8TBI
Ronald L Jones
702 S Grant
Clinton IL 61727

Call Sign: N9RYT
Wayne A Clymer
507 S Madison
Clinton IL 61727

Call Sign: KB9UJS
Daniel K Taylor

209 S Portland Pl
Clinton IL 61727

Call Sign: W9JTG
Jerome T Gribbins
514 S Quincy St
Clinton IL 617271880

Call Sign: N9PFB
Patricia A Huisinga
17476 Shiloh Rd
Clinton IL 61727

Call Sign: K9BJJ
Ronald D Martin
5631 State Hwy 54
Clinton IL 617279377

Call Sign: KC9PBO
John M Scharff
12978 State Hwy 54
Clinton IL 61727

Call Sign: KE4WN
Frederick J Richmond
110 W Clay St
Clinton IL 61727

Call Sign: KC9PWU
Christopher D Ware
621 W Leander
Clinton IL 61727

Call Sign: KB9FPG
Daryl V Reiser
624 W Leander Apt 24
Clinton IL 61727

Call Sign: KC9GMN
Robert D Henning II
706 W Main St
Clinton IL 61727

Call Sign: N9IUA
Calvin K Lunny
121 W South St
Clinton IL 61727

Call Sign: N9YTQ

Mel R Lunny
121 W South St
Clinton IL 61727

Call Sign: WB9HZV
Guinevere R Reed
209 W South St
Clinton IL 61727

Call Sign: KB9WES
Keith C Gardner
501 Wright Dr
Clinton IL 61727

Call Sign: KE4TAF
Robert Aber
Clinton IL 61727

**FCC Amateur Radio
Licenses in Coal City**

Call Sign: KA9ZJZ
James I Newman Jr
1155 E 3rd St
Coal City IL 60416

Call Sign: KD0HCI
Keith L Mason
430 E Division St
Coal City IL 60416

Call Sign: KC9ULU
Keith L Mason
430 E Division St
Coal City IL 60416

Call Sign: N9OBF
Elyn A Pogliano
915 E Division St
Coal City IL 60416

Call Sign: K9EEW
Edward E Wendler Jr
5070 E Mcardle Rd
Coal City IL 60416

Call Sign: KC9QGA
Robert M Ellison
150 E Park St

Coal City IL 60416

Call Sign: AB9VN
Robert M Ellison
150 E Park St
Coal City IL 60416

Call Sign: KA9DOD
Robert D Bleifield
215 E Park St
Coal City IL 604161742

Call Sign: WD9BAR
Eugene P Bianchetta
7730 E Spring Rd
Coal City IL 60416

Call Sign: K9EJE
Joseph K Jasnosz
6155 Hilltop Dr
Coal City IL 60416

Call Sign: KC9HLV
George L Hanson
480 Mazon St
Coal City IL 60416

Call Sign: KB9RZ
Edwin D Cairy
590 N 1st Ave
Coal City IL 60416

Call Sign: WD9JFO
Joyce M Corbin
900 N Jugtown Rd
Coal City IL 604169516

Call Sign: KC9QGU
David J Moschetti Sr
1074 S Black Diamond Dr
Coal City IL 60416

Call Sign: KB9GWN
David J Moschetti Sr
1074 S Black Diamond Dr
Coal City IL 60416

Call Sign: KB9GWN
David J Moschetti

695.5 S Broadway
Coal City IL 60416

Call Sign: AF9C
Daniel D Burba
625 W Daisy Pl
Coal City IL 60416

Call Sign: KC9ANQ
William L Galanos
80 W Elm St
Coal City IL 60416

Call Sign: W6GQ
William L Galanos
80 W Elm St
Coal City IL 60416

Call Sign: AB9LX
William L Galanos
Coal City IL 60416

FCC Amateur Radio Licenses in Coal Valley

Call Sign: N9QQU
Brian C Stokes
7309 120th Ave
Coal Valley IL 61240

Call Sign: K9MGR
Norman A Anselmi
10814 120th Ave
Coal Valley IL 61240

Call Sign: KC9MAT
Robert L Pitford
108 1st St
Coal Valley IL 61240

Call Sign: KB9MOT
Alfred J Spaude
8224 50th St
Coal Valley IL 61240

Call Sign: KC9TEC
Rebecca L Cady
8316 50th St
Coal Valley IL 61240

Call Sign: KC9TCN
Roger M Cady
8316 50th St
Coal Valley IL 61240

Call Sign: KA9YMN
Robert E Hollenback
8510 50th St
Coal Valley IL 61240

Call Sign: KC9GJQ
Crystina Mayfield
9027 72nd St
Coal Valley IL 61240

Call Sign: KC9REW
Kaitlyn M Mayfield
9027 72nd St
Coal Valley IL 61240

Call Sign: W9BPK
Gilbert E Leech
1 Deer Hollow
Coal Valley IL 61240

Call Sign: WB9DTJ
Max C Lelonek III
307 E 22nd Ave
Coal Valley IL 61240

Call Sign: K9SEA
Larry E Shumaker
209 E 3rd Ave
Coal Valley IL 61240

Call Sign: KB9LEY
Geraldine L Borkhart
203 E 5th St
Coal Valley IL 61240

Call Sign: KB9CSR
Richard G Reed
1806 E 5th St
Coal Valley IL 61240

Call Sign: N9KGY
Richard J Larson
401 E 9th Ave

Coal Valley IL 61240

Call Sign: KC9QNY
Lisa A Duncan
12201 Niabi Zoo Rd
Coal Valley IL 61240

Call Sign: KC0OQN
Gerald D Higdon
8 Red Oak Dr
Coal Valley IL 61240

Call Sign: KB9IGB
Roger J Borkhart
304 W 1st Ave
Coal Valley IL 61240

Call Sign: KA9YKF
Jonathan C De Crane
125 W 28th Ave
Coal Valley IL 61240

Call Sign: K9MVJ
Leo F Williams
105 W 2nd St
Coal Valley IL 61240

FCC Amateur Radio Licenses in Coatsburg

Call Sign: KA9IWL
William J Mansperger
1870 N 1850th Pl
Coatsburg IL 62325

FCC Amateur Radio Licenses in Cobden

Call Sign: KC9NEI
Lynne Weller
1745 Bell Hill Rd
Cobden IL 62920

Call Sign: KC9NEK
Larry F Weller
1745 Bell Hill Rd
Cobden IL 62920

Call Sign: W9TO

James B Ricks
Rt 1 Box 350
Cobden IL 62920

Call Sign: KB9LHS
Rachel Y Mc Calla
Rr 1 Box 76
Cobden IL 62920

Call Sign: KB9LGK
Robert A Mc Calla
Rt 1 Box 76
Cobden IL 62920

Call Sign: K9IUQ
Stanley J Shestokes
109 Casper Ave
Cobden IL 62920

Call Sign: KB9OQQ
James F Hartsock
935 Cedar Bluff Ln
Cobden IL 629203143

Call Sign: KC9PYS
Earnest E Newton
2395 Cobden School Rd
Cobden IL 62920

Call Sign: KC9NGM
Roger D Turner
1435 Giant City Pk Rd
Cobden IL 62920

Call Sign: KB9IMK
Michael A Tally
4128 Old Hwy 51 N
Cobden IL 62920

Call Sign: KB9OAX
Carroll G Walker
75 Stubbs Ln
Cobden IL 62920

Call Sign: KC9FIQ
Robert W Finster
585 Winstead Rd
Cobden IL 62920

FCC Amateur Radio Licenses in Coffeen

Call Sign: N9GNZ
Cindy L Hill
Rr 1 Box 31
Coffeen IL 62017

Call Sign: N9LJN
Heather C Hill
Rr 1 Box 31
Coffeen IL 62017

Call Sign: KB9ENP
Heidi C Hill
Rr 1 Box 31
Coffeen IL 62017

Call Sign: KB9MGV
Charles E Dowdy
6003 E 18th Rd
Coffeen IL 62017

FCC Amateur Radio Licenses in Colchester

Call Sign: WB9YKH
Robert L Williams
11640 E 700th St
Colchester IL 62326

Call Sign: WB9MWQ
Lloyd E Lefler
310 E South St
Colchester IL 62326

Call Sign: WA9ELK
William H Mourning
313 E South St
Colchester IL 62326

Call Sign: KF9YM
Roger G Brown
207 Jean St
Colchester IL 62326

Call Sign: KB9TMA
Jesse L Risley
614 Macomb St

Colchester IL 62326

Call Sign: K9JLR
Jesse L Risley
614 Macomb St
Colchester IL 62326

Call Sign: N9MKQ
Kevin M Kleinkopf
5176 N 1300th Rd
Colchester IL 62326

Call Sign: KA9CFD
Jay T Hainline
4305 N 1550th Rd
Colchester IL 62326

Call Sign: KC9FSU
Michelle M Hainline
4305 N 1550th Rd
Colchester IL 62326

Call Sign: KB9WAK
Michael A Fross
7730 N 450th Rd
Colchester IL 62326

Call Sign: KB9OML
James F Scrivener
5625 N 800th Rd
Colchester IL 62326

Call Sign: WA2SAM
Samuel M Waldo
814 W Market St
Colchester IL 62326

Call Sign: KA9ASA
Gary M Flynn
Colchester IL 62326

Call Sign: KB9KSV
Phillip R Inmon
Colchester IL 62326

Call Sign: W9MSO
Richard J Mc Court
Colchester IL 62326

FCC Amateur Radio Licenses in Coleta

Call Sign: KA9QYQ
Gerald L Borgmann
108 N Main St
Coleta IL 610815105

FCC Amateur Radio Licenses in Colfax

Call Sign: KA9VJE
John E Moss
Rr 2 Box 183
Colfax IL 61728

Call Sign: KB9MRS
Gregory J Briddick Jr
15747 N 3500 E Rd
Colfax IL 61728

Call Sign: KC9SWL
Michael J Kerber
204 N Brook St
Colfax IL 61728

Call Sign: KC9GAZ
James K Legrand
202 W Fifer
Colfax IL 61728

Call Sign: K9HKA
Donald L Wilber
132 W Main St
Colfax IL 61722

Call Sign: KC9RLQ
Albert J Preston
109 W Wood
Colfax IL 61728

Call Sign: KC9RMB
Roberta L Preston
109 W Wood St
Colfax IL 61728

FCC Amateur Radio Licenses in Collinsville

Call Sign: KB9KMP
Mark T Haberer
602 Arrowhead
Collinsville IL 62234

Call Sign: N9PYV
Frances E Coziar
1413 Beltline
Collinsville IL 62234

Call Sign: KB9HIM
Darold D Coziar
1413 Beltline Rd
Collinsville IL 62234

Call Sign: WA9BTR
James S Kolda
309 Bill Lou
Collinsville IL 62234

Call Sign: WD5ABV
Charley E Westbrook
805 Braidwood Ct
Collinsville IL 622341545

Call Sign: KC9PCN
Jayne R Stuart
106 Bridle Ridge Rd
Collinsville IL 62234

Call Sign: KA9RYP
Alan R Lacquement
308 Brown Ave
Collinsville IL 62234

Call Sign: KB9WZT
David R Stopher
1045 California Ave
Collinsville IL 622344204

Call Sign: N9GUI
Sherolyn G Goetz
99 Chapel Dr
Collinsville IL 62234

Call Sign: N9KDH
Steven C Goetz
99 Chapel Dr
Collinsville IL 622344355

Call Sign: KA9DSQ
Matthew J Cleland
12 Cherry Hills Dr
Collinsville IL 62234

Call Sign: K9RKU
Matthew J Cleland
12 Cherry Hills Dr
Collinsville IL 62234

Call Sign: KB9PGX
Brian P Schaefer
300 Chesapeake Ln
Collinsville IL 622344344

Call Sign: W9UH
Dennis I Mc Cann
300 Chesapeake Ln
Collinsville IL 622344344

Call Sign: N9IRE
Ethel M Mc Cann
300 Chesapeake Ln
Collinsville IL 622344344

Call Sign: KC9OTK
Roger W Wright
311 Chesapeake Ln
Collinsville IL 62234

Call Sign: W9WRW
Roger W Wright
311 Chesapeake Ln
Collinsville IL 62234

Call Sign: KB9HIE
Johnny A Murray
514 Clarence
Collinsville IL 62234

Call Sign: KB9HJL
Travis J Murray
514 Clarence
Collinsville IL 62234

Call Sign: KA9BJV
James V Stogsdill
7079 Clay School Rd

Collinsville IL 62234

Call Sign: KC9UFC
Michael T Kerner
1214 Clifton St
Collinsville IL 62234

Call Sign: WA9GQT
Rodney C Koch
102 Crestmoor Dr
Collinsville IL 62234

Call Sign: KC9MYT
Mary S Griffiths
122 David Dr
Collinsville IL 62234

Call Sign: NG9Q
Charles L Fowler
200 Debbie Dr
Collinsville IL 62234

Call Sign: K9FGO
John E Carlton
1500 Douglas
Collinsville IL 622344442

Call Sign: KA9YAR
Mary L Crites
101 E Wickliffe
Collinsville IL 62234

Call Sign: N9FNA
Milford F Crites
101 E Wickliffe
Collinsville IL 62234

Call Sign: KA9EYB
Donald K Nevinger
1539 Franklin
Collinsville IL 62234

Call Sign: KC9QXB
Ronald T Mcdonald
5927 Galli Ln
Collinsville IL 62234

Call Sign: N9TRQ
Ray H Bohnenstiehl

102 Garan Ju Manor
Collinsville IL 62234

Call Sign: N9YPZ
Brian E Kohl
313 Garnet
Collinsville IL 62234

Call Sign: KC9FHP
Benjamin R Nevin
8125 Gass Ln
Collinsville IL 62234

Call Sign: KC9FZI
Kathleen C Nevin
8125 Gass Ln
Collinsville IL 62234

Call Sign: W9EUS
Wayne F Augsburger Sr
2003 Golfview Dr
Collinsville IL 62234

Call Sign: N9BRG
Louis M Morello
808 Henry
Collinsville IL 62234

Call Sign: N9QCJ
Corey A Simon
506 High School Ave
Collinsville IL 622344052

Call Sign: WA9TMR
David C Schroeder
103 Highland Pl
Collinsville IL 62234

Call Sign: KC9KTQ
Michael P Carnahan
12 Hillside Dr
Collinsville IL 62234

Call Sign: WB9NNG
Sandra C Murray
10A Holloway Ct
Collinsville IL 62234

Call Sign: N9LJQ

Mary J Charney
6 Huntington Ct
Collinsville IL 62234

Call Sign: K9IBP
Lorraine Kebel
713 Johnson Hill Rd
Collinsville IL 62234

Call Sign: WA9DGO
Edward A Kirst Sr
107 Julia
Collinsville IL 62234

Call Sign: K9KXP
Everett Anderson
1712 Keebler Rd
Collinsville IL 622344705

Call Sign: N9MX
Max W Boyd
2446 Keebler Rd
Collinsville IL 62234

Call Sign: AC7C
James L Skinner
3070 Keebler Rd
Collinsville IL 62234

Call Sign: N0AMT
Alex M Tarsha
136 Kenwood Ln
Collinsville IL 62234

Call Sign: KA9KCY
Robert J Mc Ateer
11 Lakeview Ln
Collinsville IL 62234

Call Sign: KA9JRC
Verda K Gauldin
2 Langan Dr
Collinsville IL 62234

Call Sign: WD9GCV
James R Walker
7055 Lebanon Rd
Collinsville IL 62234

Call Sign: KE9AI
Joseph J Italiano
1964 Lemontree
Collinsville IL 62234

Call Sign: K9RKU
James N Cleland
4 Lexington Ct
Collinsville IL 62234

Call Sign: KC0JG
Roy V Glasscock
841 Longhi Rd
Collinsville IL 62234

Call Sign: N9QS
Roy V Glasscock
841 Longhi Rd
Collinsville IL 62234

Call Sign: KC9NEV
Ibsa-Drc
841 Longhi Rd
Collinsville IL 62234

Call Sign: K9IDR
Ibsa-Drc
841 Longhi Rd
Collinsville IL 62234

Call Sign: WB9KHU
Arthur C Hartman
2017 Maple Leaf
Collinsville IL 62234

Call Sign: N9IZE
Paul S Harner
125 March Dr
Collinsville IL 62234

Call Sign: K0KHJ
Paul S Harner
125 March Dr
Collinsville IL 62234

Call Sign: KD9MW
Paul F Manning
523 Mary Ave
Collinsville IL 62234

Call Sign: WA9ZNB
Melvin J Doyle
100 Moffett
Collinsville IL 622342017

Call Sign: KC9LIE
Jeff Hanratty
5747 Old Keebler Rd
Collinsville IL 62234

Call Sign: W9EYJ
Kenneth L Reichert
810 Oran St
Collinsville IL 622345228

Call Sign: N9WXG
Gregory E Becker
11 Pat Dr
Collinsville IL 62234

Call Sign: K9ZYW
Thomas J Bingham Jr
29 Pat Dr
Collinsville IL 62234

Call Sign: N9YDW
Steven K Haislar
36 Pat Dr
Collinsville IL 62234

Call Sign: WB9VAU
Michael D Avett
63 Pat Dr
Collinsville IL 62234

Call Sign: KB9RUD
Raymond E Chandler Jr
541 Pennsylvania St
Collinsville IL 62234

Call Sign: N9DCE
Robert E Breihan Jr
100 Pine Lake Rd
Collinsville IL 62234

Call Sign: KB9RZW
Buzz C Borders
290 Pine Lake Rd

Collinsville IL 62234

Call Sign: KC9SQA
Thomas B Brueggemann
1912 Pinehurst Ct
Collinsville IL 62234

Call Sign: KD6IBW
Richelle L Wiley
403 Plum
Collinsville IL 62234

Call Sign: KD6TVP
Ronald L Wiley
403 Plum
Collinsville IL 62234

Call Sign: KB9PHX
Sheryl A Ireland
492 Portland Ave
Collinsville IL 62234

Call Sign: KB9PLS
Stacey L Kohl
1207 Portland Ave
Collinsville IL 62234

Call Sign: KC9DBY
Charles T Lust
102 Rex Dr
Collinsville IL 62234

Call Sign: N9FDA
Lawrence W Kolo
33 Rickhaven Dr
Collinsville IL 62234

Call Sign: KB9SFK
Lori A Batchelor
1251 Ridgewood Ct
Collinsville IL 62234

Call Sign: KC9CFT
Scott ARS
1251 Ridgewood Ct
Collinsville IL 62234

Call Sign: K9SRS
Scott ARS

1251 Ridgewood Ct
Collinsville IL 62234

Call Sign: KB9TX
Joseph C Wightman
361 Rolek Rd
Collinsville IL 62234

Call Sign: KC9CQ
Virginia C Wightman
361 Rolek Rd
Collinsville IL 62234

Call Sign: W9KRI
Alvah W Mac Donald
224 S Aurora St
Collinsville IL 62234

Call Sign: KC9JXQ
David A Carruba Sr
150 S Aurora St Apt 312
Collinsville IL 62234

Call Sign: KA9MDA
George T Kroder
320 S Jefferson
Collinsville IL 62239

Call Sign: KA9FFD
Rudolph B Spanholtz
4 Scotch Pine
Collinsville IL 62234

Call Sign: W9EKI
Charles P Fischer
912 St Clair Ave
Collinsville IL 62234

Call Sign: KC9GBQ
George D Smith
847 St Louis Rd
Collinsville IL 62234

Call Sign: WA9IMJ
George D Smith
847 St Louis Rd
Collinsville IL 62234

Call Sign: N9HXZ

Doris E Wider
119 St Louis Rd Apt 5
Collinsville IL 62234

Call Sign: KC9AFT
David S Bohnenstiehl
13 Sugar Ln
Collinsville IL 62234

Call Sign: W9ATF
Elmer A Pintar
810 Summit Ave
Collinsville IL 62234

Call Sign: WD9D
Daren W Carstens
120 Timberwood Ln
Collinsville IL 62234

Call Sign: KB0VSQ
Heather J Fettig
20 Valley View Dr
Collinsville IL 62234

Call Sign: AB9HT
Ray H Bohnenstiehl
305 W Juda Ave
Collinsville IL 62234

Call Sign: KB9MJJ
William R Denny
1310 W Main
Collinsville IL 62234

Call Sign: KB9ODZ
Daniel A Toennies
120 W Washington
Collinsville IL 62234

Call Sign: WB9AYO
Robert R Bovinett
104 W Woodcrest
Collinsville IL 62234

Call Sign: K9GUA
George M Lacy Jr
207 Woodridge Ct
Collinsville IL 62234

Call Sign: N9BAA
Thomas E Ashcroft
214 Woodridge Ct
Collinsville IL 62234

Call Sign: N9SQN
William D Anderson
712 3rd St
Colona IL 61241

Call Sign: KA9ISD
Richard A Marsyla
814 4th St
Colona IL 61241

Call Sign: KB9JMC
William W Tuman II
616 8th St
Colona IL 61241

Call Sign: KB9HGW
Dennis E Sullivan
8 Cir O
Colona IL 61241

Call Sign: N9TFW
Paula A Denger
209 Clover Dr
Colona IL 61241

Call Sign: KC9VPJ
Alexis L Saddoris
824 Cypress Dr
Colona IL 61241

Call Sign: KC9QHY
Sarah L Mays
824 Cypress Dr
Colona IL 61241

Call Sign: KC9BEM
Scott A Harris
23365 E 750 St
Colona IL 612418954

Call Sign: N9DQS
Nancy L Beedlow
741 Greenway Ave
Colona IL 612419337

Call Sign: NN9K
Peter E Beedlow
741 Greenway Ave
Colona IL 612419337

Call Sign: KC9RGY
Charles C Hiatt
743 Greenway Ave
Colona IL 61241

Call Sign: KB9JRF
Erma D Arrasmith
Box 77 Kershaw Trailer Ct
Colona IL 61241

Call Sign: K9WA
James A Rounds
1055 Melodie Ln
Colona IL 61241

Call Sign: W9FOC
Downstate Foc Chapter
1055 Melodie Ln
Colona IL 61241

Call Sign: KC9TYC
Louis C Mccarthy Sr
140 Rustic Lake Dr
Colona IL 61241

Call Sign: KA9ISC
Juanita E Marsyla
70 Spruce Dr
Colona IL 612418811

Call Sign: W9ROS
Jeffrey M Wros
94 Spruce Dr
Colona IL 61241

Call Sign: K9JGH
Richard D Frison
254 Wilshire Dr
Colona IL 61241

Call Sign: N9GVX
Kenneth R Robinson
901 Mayor Caliper Dr
Colp IL 62921

Call Sign: KB4PLA
Vickie J Craig
Colp IL 62921

Call Sign: KC9TKC
Gretchen I Conerly
5 Berry Patch Ln
Columbia IL 62236

Call Sign: WA9YDK
Timothy E Smith
268 Bradington Dr
Columbia IL 62236

Call Sign: AI9K
Timothy E Smith
268 Bradington Dr
Columbia IL 62236

Call Sign: KC9MUG
Scott D Bierman
454 Brellinger St
Columbia IL 62236

Call Sign: KA9GGQ
Richard J Coffee II
812 Charlotte Ave
Columbia IL 622361982

Call Sign: N9WJT
Kathy M Richey
1609 Daleview Dr
Columbia IL 62236

Call Sign: KE9WD
Virgil B Keller
8754 Denison Dr
Columbia IL 622364366

Call Sign: N9THM
Royal J Bondie Jr
457 Dianne Dr
Columbia IL 62236

Call Sign: KB0VTH
Hugh B Sorrells
418 E Locust
Columbia IL 62236

Call Sign: KC9FLM
Scott B Zerban
2613 Elmwood Ct
Columbia IL 62236

Call Sign: KC9GFZ
Charles T Melton Jr
9882 Gilmore Lake Rd
Columbia IL 62236

Call Sign: K9QVV
Carl E Upchurch
243 Good Haven
Columbia IL 62236

Call Sign: KC8ALO
Johnny F De Rossett
105 Lookout Dr
Columbia IL 622364539

Call Sign: KC9SLI
Dennis W Auer
215 Micahs Way
Columbia IL 62236

Call Sign: N9EBO
Dennis W Auer
215 Micahs Way
Columbia IL 62236

Call Sign: KA0JNN
Robert K Goddard
307 Micahs Way
Columbia IL 62236

Call Sign: KD9ID
Joseph L Lepp
221 N Beaird

Columbia IL 62236

Call Sign: KC9UQC
Justine Y Young
633 N Briegel
Columbia IL 62236

Call Sign: KA9PCQ
Marilee K Meyer
718 N Briegel
Columbia IL 62236

Call Sign: K9TNA
Justine Y Young
633 N Briegel St
Columbia IL 622361639

Call Sign: K9RJY
Robert J Young
633 N Briegel St
Columbia IL 622361639

Call Sign: W9MO
Robert J Young
633 N Briegel St
Columbia IL 622361639

Call Sign: KC9BJC
St Paul'S Radio Club
227 N Goodhaven
Columbia IL 62236

Call Sign: N0RZW
Mark J Hasler
811 N Main St
Columbia IL 62236

Call Sign: KC9ELZ
Stephen T Krebel
818 N Main St
Columbia IL 622361410

Call Sign: KC9GNE
William J Seibel
721 N Metter Ave
Columbia IL 62236

Call Sign: K9RSJ
Clarence H Schueler

318 Riebeling St
Columbia IL 62236

Call Sign: KC9TWK
Brendan S Beyer
321 S Riebeling St
Columbia IL 62236

Call Sign: KC9RWB
Marilee J Beyer
321 S Rieberling St
Columbia IL 62236

Call Sign: KC9RWC
Martin L Beyer
321 S Rieberling St
Columbia IL 62236

Call Sign: KB9YYK
Richard C Smith
301 Westridge Dr
Columbia IL 62236

Call Sign: KC9JUW
Christopher P Riedy
114 Wierschem
Columbia IL 62236

**FCC Amateur Radio
Licenses in Compton**

Call Sign: WD9COP
Darold L Pasley
2915 Beemerville Rd
Compton IL 61318

**FCC Amateur Radio
Licenses in Concord**

Call Sign: N9RDE
Max L Flavio
East St Box 61
Concord IL 62631

**FCC Amateur Radio
Licenses in Congerville**

Call Sign: KC9NXX
Justin D Zobrist

206 1st St
Congerville IL 61729

Call Sign: WB9YHV
Lois A Hartwig
R 1 Box 27
Congerville IL 61729

Call Sign: WB9YMV
Daryl F Hartwig
Rt 1 Box 27
Congerville IL 61729

Call Sign: KE9VP
Douglas A Knepp
299 County Hwy 8
Congerville IL 61729

Call Sign: WB9VMK
Samuel J Kohler
1905 CR 400 N
Congerville IL 61729

Call Sign: N9LOC
Harold Satterfield
300 E Kauffman
Congerville IL 61729

Call Sign: KC9UCG
Daniel J Craig
206 Reaba Ave
Congerville IL 61729

Call Sign: KG9N
Charles G Van Hoorn
1514 Timberline Rd
Congerville IL 61729

FCC Amateur Radio Licenses in Cooksville

Call Sign: WA5QGM
Nathan L Axton
15807 N 2850 E Rd
Cooksville IL 61730

Call Sign: K9IKG
Arthur W Caldwell
Cooksville IL 61730

FCC Amateur Radio Licenses in Cordova

Call Sign: AA9BU
Kenneth L Wishmeyer
312 12th Ave A
Cordova IL 61242

Call Sign: N9MZB
Leland T Nelson
24304 157th Ave N
Cordova IL 61242

Call Sign: N9PSI
Janice K Rutenbeck
21614 River Rd N
Cordova IL 61242

Call Sign: N9OOF
James A Rutenbeck
21614 River Rd N
Cordova IL 61242

FCC Amateur Radio Licenses in Cottage Hills

Call Sign: KB9MGY
Ronnie D Wolford
1328 13th St
Cottage Hills IL 62018

Call Sign: N9RLM
Richard L Sawyer
1349 9th St
Cottage Hills IL 62018

Call Sign: N9YHP
Dean M Mabb
1353 9th St
Cottage Hills IL 62018

Call Sign: KB9MOO
Harold R Brown Jr
1402 Lee St
Cottage Hills IL 62018

Call Sign: N9RGC
Eva M Cedra

133 S Oak Ave
Cottage Hills IL 62018

Call Sign: KB9GIL
Brenda K Busse Bauman
353 Thumper Ct
Cottage Hills IL 62018

Call Sign: KB9GJA
Michael L Bauman
353 Thumper Ct
Cottage Hills IL 62018

Call Sign: KB9EYP
Jessie F Busse
631 Virginia Ave
Cottage Hills IL 62018

Call Sign: N9JYT
Roy L Busse
631 Virginia Ave
Cottage Hills IL 62018

Call Sign: N9USY
Alan L Sweeney
656 W Virginia
Cottage Hills IL 62018

Call Sign: N9YDX
Kevin S Mosley
656 W Virginia
Cottage Hills IL 62018

FCC Amateur Radio Licenses in Coulterville

Call Sign: KB9FZI
Stanley L Raney
6 Poplar
Coulterville IL 62237

Call Sign: K9SLR
Stanley L Raney
6 Poplar
Coulterville IL 62237

Call Sign: KA9IUY
Peggy S Raney
608 Poplar

Coulterville IL 62237

Call Sign: WA9TCA
Robert H Rust
1101 Roxie Ln
Coulterville IL 62237

Call Sign: KB9VXK
Floyd O Morgan
611 SR 13
Coulterville IL 62237

Call Sign: KB9HDX
Peter J Hubbard
107 W Maple
Coulterville IL 62237

Call Sign: W9MDJ
Douglas J Gallagher
Coulterville IL 62237

FCC Amateur Radio Licenses in Cowden

Call Sign: W9TUL
William J Hill Jr
301 Elm St
Cowden IL 62422

Call Sign: KC9MTI
Fred W Wheeler Jr
237 S 3rd
Cowden IL 62422

FCC Amateur Radio Licenses in Creal Springs

Call Sign: KB9CHJ
Shelby L Lyerla
Rt 2 Box 100B
Creal Springs IL 62922

Call Sign: WA9FOA
Mason M Wheeler
R 2 Box 468
Creal Springs IL 62922

Call Sign: W9PZD
Edward C Dannenhold

200 Faith Dr
Creal Springs IL 629223862

Call Sign: AA9ET
C Ken Mausey
5183 Mauseyville Rd
Creal Springs IL 62922

Call Sign: N9OAB
Sharon K Mausey
5183 Mauseyville Rd
Creal Springs IL 62922

Call Sign: KB4ALU
Virginia W Shepard
13681 S Egypt Shores Dr
Creal Springs IL 62922

Call Sign: N9KMU
Vern K Lemasters
3451 Saraville Rd
Creal Springs IL 62922

Call Sign: N3VL
Vern K Lemasters
3451 Saraville Rd
Creal Springs IL 62922

Call Sign: WA9EIF
William D Ray
5495 Stonefort Rd
Creal Springs IL 62922

Call Sign: KB9WSH
Laquetta C Ray
Creal Springs IL 62922

FCC Amateur Radio Licenses in Crescent City

Call Sign: W9QCD
Richard W Harwood
Crescent City IL 60928

Call Sign: WB9Z
Jerry W Rosalius
Crescent City IL 60928

FCC Amateur Radio Licenses in Creve Coeur

Call Sign: KC9UUC
Jerald A Day
104 Apple Ct
Creve Coeur IL 61610

Call Sign: W9DAY
Jerald A Day
104 Apple Ct
Creve Coeur IL 61610

Call Sign: KB9RHW
Andrew J Baker
333 Carola St
Creve Coeur IL 61610

Call Sign: KB9DPR
Robert F Thatcher
568 Carola St
Creve Coeur IL 61611

Call Sign: KB9KAY
Robert E Shockency Jr
113 Castleman Ct
Creve Coeur IL 61610

Call Sign: WB9UXO
Glenda C Ulrich
652 Dempsey
Creve Coeur IL 61610

Call Sign: N9ZQX
Benjamin Camacho
132 Elm Ridge Pl Apt 1
Creve Coeur IL 61610

Call Sign: K9TZC
Guy J Bauer
100 Gerber Ct
Creve Coeur IL 61610

Call Sign: K9QEX
Clifford E Hopwood
416 Glendale St
Creve Coeur IL 616103242

Call Sign: KC9GGC

Lawrence A Powers
109 Gottlieb Ct
Creve Coeur IL 61610

Call Sign: N9RMG
Richard M Goins
313 Lawndale Ave
Creve Coeur IL 61610

Call Sign: KC9MXO
Richard M Goins
313 Lawndale Rd
Creve Coeur IL 61610

Call Sign: KB9DMG
Charles A Palmer
447 Maplewood St
Creve Coeur IL 61611

Call Sign: KB9GST
Steven A Tennant
329 Margaret Dr
Creve Coeur IL 61610

Call Sign: N9VIH
David A Hilton
141 Maywood Ave
Creve Coeur IL 61611

Call Sign: WB9OGQ
William F Erickson
1009 Pekin Ave
Creve Coeur IL 61611

Call Sign: N9HHU
James F Williams
102 Rainbow Ct
Creve Coeur IL 616104269

Call Sign: KB9LNM
Donald S Mcpheeters
116 Riverview Dr
Creve Coeur IL 61610

Call Sign: KB9ZRE
Cecil L King
313 Roberts St
Creve Coeur IL 61610

Call Sign: KC9JQC
Austin J Grant
512 Roosevelt St
Creve Coeur IL 61610

Call Sign: KB9MIL
Austin J Grant
512 Roosevelt St
Creve Coeur IL 61610

Call Sign: KB9GZS
Darel A Dixon
316 Rusche
Creve Coeur IL 61610

Call Sign: KC9AET
Ralf J Isaac Jr
814 S Creve Coeor Ave
Creve Coeur IL 61610

Call Sign: KB9VIT
Ray L Miller
220 S Highland Ave
Creve Coeur IL 616104018

Call Sign: N9HYN
Chris F Tennant
218 S Stewart Ave
Creve Coeur IL 61611

Call Sign: WA9KFK
Ruby M Zick
313 S Stewart Ave
Creve Coeur IL 61611

Call Sign: KC9VEW
Bradley D Broadfield
708 S Stewart St
Creve Coeur IL 61610

Call Sign: KB9UET
Robert L Van Ness
104 Skyline Dr
Creve Coeur IL 61610

Call Sign: KB9YBS
Scott C Lehman
331 Smith St
Creve Coeur IL 61610

Call Sign: KB9VVH
Gary L Spencer
412 Zessin
Creve Coeur IL 61611

Call Sign: WN9JMY
Gary L Spencer
412 Zessin St
Creve Coeur IL 61610

FCC Amateur Radio Licenses in Crossville

Call Sign: KB9FYQ
William R Pennington
Crossville IL 628270353

FCC Amateur Radio Licenses in Cuba

Call Sign: N9PIZ
Deacon G Thompson
Rr2 Box 173
Cuba IL 61427

Call Sign: KB9NTP
Frances R Gordon
8882 E St Rt 95
Cuba IL 61427

Call Sign: KB9YBL
Mark D Buffum
18205 N Buffum Rd
Cuba IL 61427

Call Sign: N9BUF
Mark D Buffum
18205 N Buffum Rd
Cuba IL 61427

Call Sign: KB9IQF
Clifford E Phillips
402 S 9th St
Cuba IL 61427

FCC Amateur Radio Licenses in Cutler

Call Sign: KC9LJJ
Christopher J Epplin
7586 County Line Rd
Cutler IL 62238

Call Sign: KB9UCD
Everette J Rieckenberg
224 W Mill
Cutler IL 62238

Call Sign: N9UJG
David R Van Ausdoll
Cutler IL 62238

FCC Amateur Radio Licenses in Cypress

Call Sign: KB9VKY
John D Wells
1920 Bethany Rd
Cypress IL 62923

Call Sign: N9OWM
James D Mc Clellan
4495 W Eden Rd
Cypress IL 62923

FCC Amateur Radio Licenses in Dahinda

Call Sign: W9BBP
John R Lindberg
95 Birch Ct
Dahinda IL 61428

Call Sign: KA9GXW
John R Healey
367 Charter Oak Pl
Dahinda IL 61428

Call Sign: KA9GXX
Margaret S Healey
367 Charter Oak Pl
Dahinda IL 61428

Call Sign: KA0QQX
Wilber D Smith
411 Crabtree Ln
Dahinda IL 614289386

FCC Amateur Radio Licenses in Dahlgren

Call Sign: N9KES
Gregory B Karcher
Rt 1 Box 183
Dahlgren IL 62828

Call Sign: KB9BCY
Lesley H Vaughn
Rr2 Box 64
Dahlgren IL 62828

Call Sign: KT9D
Charles P Blades
Dahlgren IL 62828

FCC Amateur Radio Licenses in Dakota

Call Sign: KB9QDA
George H Hoefer Jr
301 Center St
Dakota IL 61018

Call Sign: KB9RZC
Ervin L Kincannon
6990 Henderson Rd
Dakota IL 61018

Call Sign: KC9JKZ
Karen E Hoefer
Dakota IL 61018

FCC Amateur Radio Licenses in Dale

Call Sign: KB9OYF
James C Thorpe
Dale IL 628290045

FCC Amateur Radio Licenses in Dallas City

Call Sign: KA9OGZ
Marilyn F Melton
Rr 1 Box 132A

Dallas City IL 62330

Call Sign: KA9JFS
Kathleen G Hart
Rt 1 Box 23B
Dallas City IL 62330

Call Sign: KA9OZN
Mario A Gualtieri
211 Cherry St
Dallas City IL 62330

Call Sign: K9HQG
Jesse F Foglesong Sr
314 E 1st St
Dallas City IL 623301005

Call Sign: KB9TOM
Martin J Sparrow
1846 E St Hwy 9
Dallas City IL 623309529

Call Sign: KA9JNG
Martin J Sparrow
1846 E St Hwy 9
Dallas City IL 623309529

Call Sign: WF0RT
Fort Madison ARC
1846 E St Hwy 9
Dallas City IL 623309529

Call Sign: K9III
Charles A Faul Sr
620 Orchard St
Dallas City IL 62330

Call Sign: KB9VWV
Raymond E Rutledge
615 W 1st
Dallas City IL 62330

Call Sign: N9NME
John F Olenick
810 W 4th St
Dallas City IL 62330

Call Sign: K9ATJ
Charles G Miller

Dallas City IL 62330

Call Sign: KA0CCC
William C Hart
Dallas City IL 62330

Call Sign: KC9JIC
Keith A Durand
Dallas City IL 62330

FCC Amateur Radio Licenses in Dalton City

Call Sign: KA9HHP
Mary M Henneberry
Rt 1 Box 60
Dalton City IL 61925

Call Sign: KC9POV
Rodger W Koester
5145 Goodwin Ct
Dalton City IL 61925

Call Sign: KC9KEB
William R Settle Sr
Dalton City IL 61925

FCC Amateur Radio Licenses in Damiansville

Call Sign: N5GQN
William R Bell Sr
127 Timberlake Dr
Damiansville IL 62215

FCC Amateur Radio Licenses in Dana

Call Sign: KB9YUV
Robert S Sechrest
107 E Jefferson St
Dana IL 61321

Call Sign: KC9JQE
Peter M Ramsey
Dana IL 61321

FCC Amateur Radio Licenses in Danforth

Call Sign: KK9R
Richard A Sparenberg
Danforth IL 60930

Call Sign: KB9WQR
Thomas M Harnen
Danforth IL 609300042

FCC Amateur Radio Licenses in Danvers

Call Sign: KB9WKF
Thaddeus A Meizelis
Rr 2 Box 325
Danvers IL 61732

Call Sign: N7MB
Michael L Bill
206 E Park
Danvers IL 61732

Call Sign: KA9WAP
David W Zaring
4 Kimberly Ct
Danvers IL 61732

Call Sign: N9QOW
Nora R Zaring
4 Kimberly Ct
Danvers IL 61732

Call Sign: W9MBO
Jack L Hall
16720 King Rd
Danvers IL 61732

Call Sign: KB1DWA
Joseph M Mahoney
37 Park St
Danvers IL 61732

Call Sign: KA9UFT
Charles J Jackson
1048 S Gap
Danvers IL 617329049

Call Sign: KB9YPN
Randall F Zychowski
103 W Winslow
Danvers IL 61732

FCC Amateur Radio Licenses in Danville

Call Sign: N9OQW
David W Starwalt
1313 2nd Ave
Danville IL 61832

Call Sign: WD9AFD
William A Baker
1316 2nd Ave
Danville IL 61832

Call Sign: KA9GEZ
David R Semonick
114 Arlington Dr
Danville IL 61832

Call Sign: K9KEM
John Clark Sr
406 Ave B
Danville IL 61832

Call Sign: WA9DBO
Richard E Harris
2015 Batestown Rd
Danville IL 61832

Call Sign: KA9SLV
Joseph E Evans Sr
310 Blackford Lot 1
Danville IL 61832

Call Sign: WK9Y
Ronald G Stonecipher
Rr 3 Box 117 Potters Woods
Rd
Danville IL 61832

Call Sign: N9JYK
Larry L Trimble
R3 Box 147
Danville IL 61832

Call Sign: N9WTP
Bryan L Wallace
Rr 5 Box 228
Danville IL 61832

Call Sign: WB9NPY
Joseph S Pelszynski Jr
Rr 3 Box 363
Danville IL 61832

Call Sign: KC9PDX
Kevin A Perdue
3726 Brairwood
Danville IL 61832

Call Sign: KA9PCN
Robert E Knight
Rr 5 Brewer Rd Box 94
Danville IL 61832

Call Sign: KC9KKN
Hariharan Subramanian
3510 Cambridge Ct Unit 201
Danville IL 61832

Call Sign: KC9KNH
Vidya Sundaramoorthy
3510 Cambridge Ct Unit 201
Danville IL 61832

Call Sign: KC9SUG
Kenneth D Allison
14851 Catlin Tilton Rd
Danville IL 61834

Call Sign: WD9AEX
James M Stovall
426 Chandler St
Danville IL 61832

Call Sign: N9PLX
Philip W Johnson
3117 Cobblestone Ln
Danville IL 61832

Call Sign: KC9VND
Robert E Mitchell
50 Columbus St
Danville IL 61832

Call Sign: KA9JZK
Glenna J Verhoeven
709 Commercial St
Danville IL 61832

Call Sign: KC9KRC
Donald E Miller
804 Commercial St
Danville IL 61832

Call Sign: KA9AUG
Kenneth L Parsons
3144 Cottle Ln
Danville IL 618345819

Call Sign: KB9YRZ
Barry L Thompson
29 Country Club Dr
Danville IL 61832

Call Sign: KA9UIL
John J Davis
3103 Daisy Ct
Danville IL 61832

Call Sign: K9JLC
Julius V Bobrosky
16 Dale Ave
Danville IL 61832

Call Sign: K9RKV
Walter P Barnes
433 Dawn Ave
Danville IL 61832

Call Sign: KB9WYB
Harry R Miller
1710 Deerwood
Danville IL 61832

Call Sign: K9BSJ
John A Rains
26 Delaware Ave
Danville IL 61832

Call Sign: WA9EQK
Danny L Bunting
33 Delaware St

Danville IL 618326109

Call Sign: KB9PMS
Lloyd A Webb
721 Douglas
Danville IL 61832

Call Sign: K9HZF
Steve M Dyskievicz
218 E 11th St
Danville IL 61832

Call Sign: KC9VNB
Ronald D Bolser Jr
20462 E 1280 Rd
Danville IL 61834

Call Sign: WD9AEZ
Keith K Klett
203 E 13th St
Danville IL 61832

Call Sign: WD9EWW
Arthur W Haskins
205 E 13th St
Danville IL 61832

Call Sign: N9ZIV
Larry D Warner
124 E 14th St
Danville IL 61832

Call Sign: KC9VMZ
Wendy M Pascual
124A E 14th St
Danville IL 61832

Call Sign: KC9BZH
William D White
124A E 14th St
Danville IL 61832

Call Sign: KB9ZMF
David M Cline
14105 E 2100 N Rd
Danville IL 61834

Call Sign: KC9RMY
Juanita M Fischer

14105 E 2100 N Rd
Danville IL 61834

Call Sign: WC9ABO
Danville Vermilion County
Esda
1470 E 2750 N
Danville IL 618345610

Call Sign: KA9SKS
Gary S Denison
14704 E 2750 N Rd
Danville IL 618345610

Call Sign: N9GGP
Lyell A Denison
14704 E 2750 N Rd
Danville IL 618345610

Call Sign: K9JZM
Arthur G Collatz
16047 E 2750 N Rd
Danville IL 61834

Call Sign: N9TIB
Earl H Setser
10 E Bridge
Danville IL 61832

Call Sign: WD9AFB
Edward J Gielow
105 E Hegeler Ave
Danville IL 61832

Call Sign: KF9ZW
Gene R Bostwick Sr
2311 E Main St
Danville IL 61832

Call Sign: N9HJY
Kenneth R Fairchild
932 E Polk
Danville IL 61832

Call Sign: KC9VJX
New Experiment In Radio
Danville
204 E Roselawn St
Danville IL 61832

Call Sign: NE9RD
New Experiment In Radio
Danville
204 E Roselawn St
Danville IL 61832

Call Sign: WA9EIC
Donald R Russell
204 E Roselawn St
Danville IL 61832

Call Sign: KC9MMZ
David F Bealer
2411 East Rd
Danville IL 61832

Call Sign: N9XLH
Morris C Starkey
1602 Eastview Ave
Danville IL 61832

Call Sign: WA9IPT
Walter W Hershberger
606 Forrest
Danville IL 61832

Call Sign: KC9TAM
Ronald D Johnson
501 Forrest St
Danville IL 61832

Call Sign: WD9IAT
William A Spicer
311 Francis
Danville IL 61832

Call Sign: N9EVE
Evelyn B Miller
807 Franklin
Danville IL 61832

Call Sign: NF9T
Tuck Miller
807 Franklin
Danville IL 61832

Call Sign: W9FVC
Wesley W Brooks

3137 Golf Cir
Danville IL 61832

Call Sign: K9CDD
Joseph E Scott
1417 Golf Ter
Danville IL 61832

Call Sign: KC9GRT
Daniel W Stine
118 Grace St
Danville IL 61832

Call Sign: W9HGM
Richard H Smither
1548 Greenwood Cemetery Rd
Danville IL 61832

Call Sign: KB9YZG
Richard A Copass
2102 Greenwood Cemetery Rd
Danville IL 61834

Call Sign: K9CVP
John M Allen Sr
809 Harmon St
Danville IL 61832

Call Sign: WA9FQV
Bruce W Oliver
504 Harvey
Danville IL 61832

Call Sign: KA9EGG
Charles A Cappello
40 Henderson St
Danville IL 61832

Call Sign: KB9DAY
Harold F Woodard
70 Henderson St
Danville IL 61832

Call Sign: KC9NWX
Sven E Munck
19545 Henning Rd
Danville IL 61834

Call Sign: K9HLB

J L Fairchild
25313 Henning Rd
Danville IL 618345600

Call Sign: KC9RMZ
Charles Yount
546 Highland Pk Rd
Danville IL 61834

Call Sign: KC9RNA
Thomas G Eble
548 Highland Pk Rd
Danville IL 61834

Call Sign: KA9FKQ
Nicklas B Moody
1007 Holiday Dr
Danville IL 61832

Call Sign: K9ERP
George W Egger
3221 B Independence Dr
Danville IL 618327933

Call Sign: KI4FXK
Jack L Russell
909 James
Danville IL 61832

Call Sign: KA9LNJ
Quinten L Rouse
1106 James Pl
Danville IL 61832

Call Sign: KB9REE
Russell T Powell
51 Juliana Dr
Danville IL 61832

Call Sign: KB9VDG
Ruth E Powell
51 Juliana Dr
Danville IL 61832

Call Sign: KC9TQG
Michael D Reed
112 Kentucky Ave
Danville IL 61832

Call Sign: KA9IOC
John I Williamson
1112 Koehn Dr
Danville IL 61832

Call Sign: W9AFX
Harold W Betz
72 Lake
Danville IL 61832

Call Sign: KB9VED
Matt J Jordan
28 Lakeshore Dr
Danville IL 61832

Call Sign: KG4GYR
Tonya K Jordan
28 Lakeshore Dr
Danville IL 61832

Call Sign: KA9IUP
Al Ramage
134 Lakeside Dr
Danville IL 61832

Call Sign: KA9IUQ
Colette Ramage
134 Lakeside Dr
Danville IL 61832

Call Sign: KB9ORS
Linda K Osborn
30 Lamm St
Danville IL 61832

Call Sign: W9FNK
Norman E Sanders
601 Lawndale
Danville IL 61832

Call Sign: KA9MXT
John L Shaffer
510 Lawndale Dr
Danville IL 61832

Call Sign: WA9DNF
Estil N Carter
3205 Liberty Ct
Danville IL 61832

Call Sign: KB9CMV
Paul L Boswell
1701 Lincoln St
Danville IL 61832

Call Sign: K9HEQ
George E Moulton
909 Loraine St
Danville IL 61832

Call Sign: KA9IBS
Dennis L Gray
25 Maplewood Dr
Danville IL 61832

Call Sign: KB9WST
Ted A Fisher
123 Marlowe
Danville IL 61832

Call Sign: KC9TAN
Henry F Hooker
3 Maywood Dr
Danville IL 61832

Call Sign: K9SXF
Susan C Hooker
3 Maywood Dr
Danville IL 61832

Call Sign: N9YYI
Patricia R Farnsworth
1219 McKinley Ave
Danville IL 61832

Call Sign: KC9AFN
William E Cronkhite
105 Michigan Ave
Danville IL 61832

Call Sign: KA9EIG
Edward L Trimble
920 Myers
Danville IL 61832

Call Sign: WA9IAC
Alan D Woodrum
1513 Myrtle Dr

Danville IL 61832

Call Sign: WD9IFM
Rebecca W Woodrum
1513 Myrtle Dr
Danville IL 61832

Call Sign: KB9LUD
Jeff R Pryle
23624 N 1530 E Rd
Danville IL 61832

Call Sign: KB9OJO
David R Owens
1204 N Bowman
Danville IL 61832

Call Sign: WD9IAU
Charles R Beagle
1008 N Daisy Ln
Danville IL 61834

Call Sign: W9VB
Martin A Perry
1403 N Gilbert St
Danville IL 61832

Call Sign: KC9TCK
East Central Illinois Amateur
Radio Association
1502 N Gilbert St
Danville IL 61832

Call Sign: NU9R
Thomas H Mills
1502 N Gilbert St
Danville IL 61832

Call Sign: KA9KRK
Karl E Anderson
1127 N Griffin
Danville IL 61832

Call Sign: W9MJL
Vermilion County Amatr Rad
Assn Inc
2403 N Jackson
Danville IL 61832

Call Sign: N9WEW
Josh D Kittle
2403 N Jackson St
Danville IL 61832

Call Sign: N9CTM
Gerald L Oaks
29 5 N Jefferson St
Danville IL 61832

Call Sign: KA9SMT
Richard M Scarlett
3721 N Lake Blvd
Danville IL 61832

Call Sign: KB9YZH
Michael D Swider
3742 N Lake Blvd
Danville IL 61832

Call Sign: K9ZH
Michael D Swider
3742 N Lake Blvd
Danville IL 61832

Call Sign: KF9YD
Michael L Meeker
3832 N Lake Blvd
Danville IL 618321016

Call Sign: KA9VMN
Christina Wells
1309 N Logan Ave
Danville IL 61832

Call Sign: WD9AFG
Lowell T Wells
1309 N Logan Ave
Danville IL 61832

Call Sign: KC9VDK
Mike Orr
1406 N Sherman
Danville IL 61832

Call Sign: KC9IHV
Kevin J Reifsteck
1613 N Vermilion
Danville IL 61832

Call Sign: KA9ANG
T Randal Reed
2200 N Vermilion Apt 103
Danville IL 61832

Call Sign: KC9HZN
Daniel W Stine
1129 N Walnut
Danville IL 61832

Call Sign: KA9GYK
Garry J Kirk
911 N Washington
Danville IL 61832

Call Sign: WD9IBR
Don C Koenig
1514 N Washington
Danville IL 61832

Call Sign: KA9DSA
William R Wright
2304 Oakwood Ave
Danville IL 61832

Call Sign: N9UDR
Linda A Spicer
510 Orchard St
Danville IL 61832

Call Sign: WF9S
Todd A Spicer
510 Orchard St
Danville IL 61832

Call Sign: W9EZ
Todd A Spicer
510 Orchard St
Danville IL 61832

Call Sign: KC9CIS
Kenneth J Knight
122 Oregon
Danville IL 61832

Call Sign: WB9FYH
James D Jones
3025 Park Haven Blvd

Danville IL 61832

Call Sign: N9KVK
Stephen R Myers
3305 Park Haven Blvd
Danville IL 618321220

Call Sign: KC9QJH
James A Miguel
1800 Perrysvill Rd Lot 35
Danville IL 61834

Call Sign: KB9LAF
Jason E Wheaton
1097 Perrysville Rd
Danville IL 61832

Call Sign: KC9OFM
William E Barnes
1800 Perrysville Rd 54
Danville IL 61834

Call Sign: W9CMX
Herbert W Fullerton
119 Rhea
Danville IL 61832

Call Sign: K9PQN
Mildred Langley
311 Ridgeview
Danville IL 61832

Call Sign: K9HMM
Clarence Langley
311 Ridgeview Rd
Danville IL 61832

Call Sign: N9IHD
David M Kouzmanoff
1400 Rivercrest Rd
Danville IL 61832

Call Sign: K9KUZ
James T Kouzmanoff
1400 Rivercrest Rd
Danville IL 61832

Call Sign: KB9ZBJ

Vermilion County War
Museum
1400 Rivercrest Rd
Danville IL 61832

Call Sign: W9VFW
Vermilion County War
Museum
1400 Rivercrest Rd
Danville IL 61832

Call Sign: WA9CVB
Victor E Vanesse
703 Roselawn
Danville IL 61832

Call Sign: N3RVY
Jeffrey A Heaton
22 S Buchanan
Danville IL 61832

Call Sign: WX9EMA
Curtis Lee Chambers
134 S Crawford
Danville IL 61832

Call Sign: KC7EOK
Morgan Bs Williamson
134 S Daisy Ln
Danville IL 61834

Call Sign: KA9JZI
Alonzo D Parker
25 S Kansas
Danville IL 61832

Call Sign: KA9AWA
William M Ryan
15019 S Markley Rd
Danville IL 61834

Call Sign: N9NPT
Brian D Bridges
507 Shadowlawn
Danville IL 61832

Call Sign: KB9SK
James W Wilson
4 Shady Ln

Danville IL 61832

Call Sign: KC9DCB
Gary Gray
27043 Shake Rag Rd
Danville IL 61834

Call Sign: N9YCH
Janet I Aug
7 Sheral Dr
Danville IL 61832

Call Sign: KB9GYF
Michael W Ferris
921 Skyline Dr
Danville IL 61832

Call Sign: N9EVT
Clinton E Hartley
300 Spelter Ave 68
Danville IL 61832

Call Sign: WA9YXQ
Robert R Wittig
127 Sportsman Club Rd
Danville IL 618321327

Call Sign: KA9CEX
Gary B Moody
17518 Stable Ln
Danville IL 61834

Call Sign: KA9EPZ
Donald F Collins
1303 Thomas St
Danville IL 61832

Call Sign: KC9DTN
Joseph L Smith
2730 Townway Rd G82
Danville IL 61832

Call Sign: WA9YPA
Donald L Huff
3816 Tuttle St
Danville IL 618321040

Call Sign: KA9POR
Richard L England

105 Vance Ln
Danville IL 61832

Call Sign: KA9POQ
Russell L England
105 Vance Ln
Danville IL 61832

Call Sign: KC9KZB
Francis L Dearth
215 Vance Ln
Danville IL 61832

Call Sign: KC9VNE
Donald W Demoss
2706 Vine St
Danville IL 61834

Call Sign: KB9ANF
Randall J Wilkinson
11 Vinson St
Danville IL 61832

Call Sign: KC9DCA
Randall J Wilkinson
11 Vinson St
Danville IL 61832

Call Sign: K9ANF
Randall J Wilkinson
11 Vinson St
Danville IL 61832

Call Sign: N9RIV
William R Mc New
106 W 5th St
Danville IL 61832

Call Sign: W9ARX
James A Reynolds
1227 W Voorhees St
Danville IL 61832

Call Sign: KB9GEP
John M Hershberger
1950 W Williams St
Danville IL 61832

Call Sign: AB9IX

John M Hershberger
1950 W Williams St
Danville IL 61832

Call Sign: KA9UEC
Leland L Black Jr
1601 Westview Dr
Danville IL 61832

Call Sign: KB4NAM
David F Meador
21 Westwood Pl
Danville IL 61832

Call Sign: KB9YZJ
Wesley O Grimes
19254 Woodbury Hill Rd
Danville IL 618345421

Call Sign: WB9YJE
Louis H Reik Jr
916 Woodlawn Ct
Danville IL 61832

Call Sign: KA9EVO
Chris R Rediehs
1425 Woodridge Dr
Danville IL 61832

Call Sign: KA9EVP
Cathy R Schaefer
1425 Woodridge Dr
Danville IL 61832

Call Sign: W9NMI
Robert E Rediehs
1425 Woodridge Dr
Danville IL 61832

Call Sign: KB9LKA
James R Matthews
Danville IL 61834

Call Sign: KC9VNA
Jason E Wallis
Danville IL 61834

Call Sign: KC9OHN
Steve T Ridge

Danville IL 61834

Call Sign: KG4DQJ
Thomas H Mills
Danville IL 61834

Call Sign: KI4TQQ
Sandra D Mills
Danville IL 61834

Call Sign: N9YUN
Doris M Mc Intyre
Danville IL 618340326

FCC Amateur Radio Licenses in Davis

Call Sign: KC9LQI
Allen B Long
14742 Best Rd
Davis IL 61019

Call Sign: KC9GOB
Jeffrey A Board
1313 Chadbourne Dr
Davis IL 61019

Call Sign: KC9JAB
Jeffrey A Board
1313 Chadbourne Dr
Davis IL 61019

Call Sign: KC9MBD
Gary L Woodruff
10860 E Farmschool Rd
Davis IL 610199321

Call Sign: KA9CHQ
James L Ryder
2091 Lake Summer Set Rd
Davis IL 61019

Call Sign: N9GXI
Peter J Jakl
138 Lake Summerset Rd
Davis IL 61019

Call Sign: KA9NJZ
Ruth A Ryder

2091 Lake Summerset Rd
Davis IL 61019

Call Sign: WB0BFG
Robert L Diepenbrock
2147 Lake Summerset Rd
Davis IL 61019

Call Sign: N9ECA
Alan W Hukle
2315 Lake Summerset Rd
Davis IL 61019

Call Sign: N9WZC
Christine M Philips
908 Lk Summerset Rd
Davis IL 61019

Call Sign: KB9YRW
Scott B Allshouse
484 Orleans Dr
Davis IL 61019

Call Sign: K9MFQ
Glen R Harting
1424 Pier Dr
Davis IL 61019

Call Sign: KB9MUS
Lynn B Cuddy
412 Primrose Ln
Davis IL 61019

Call Sign: KC9IOZ
Renzy L Stepp Sr
760 Westmore Rd
Davis IL 61019

FCC Amateur Radio Licenses in Davis Junction

Call Sign: KB9AGE
Timothy M Hess
15850 E Timberlane
Davis Junction IL 61020

Call Sign: KA9BQR
Lawrence J Sabella
15642 Rt 72

Davis Junction IL 61020

Call Sign: KB9JEV
Daniel R Dailey
15685 Rt 72
Davis Junction IL 61020

Call Sign: N4ISK
Thomas E Simpson
600 Willow Bend Dr
Davis Junction IL 61020

FCC Amateur Radio Licenses in Dawson

Call Sign: WD9GGT
Jessie P Jones
350 Blane Ct
Dawson IL 625203324

Call Sign: W9LOH
Byron P Liles
412 Blane Ct
Dawson IL 62520

Call Sign: KB9INN
Robin K Downing
Rr 1 Box 17C
Dawson IL 62520

Call Sign: KB9KAD
Charles P Hermes
10988 Darnell Rd
Dawson IL 62520

Call Sign: KB9EYN
Jack H Loyd
9082 Mechanicsburg Rd
Dawson IL 625203363

Call Sign: KB9KZV
James E Parrish
501 N Ledlie
Dawson IL 62520

Call Sign: N9GTE
Wayne S Bridgwater
300 S Tower Rd
Dawson IL 62520

Call Sign: N9YCA
Katherine M Ward
1656 Webb Ct
Dawson IL 62520

Call Sign: KB9EYB
Ronald J Ward
1656 Webb Ct
Dawson IL 62520

FCC Amateur Radio Licenses in De Land

Call Sign: WB9CDX
Robert K Hintz
401 6th St
De Land IL 618390048

Call Sign: N9UEE
Gaylord N Madden
330 6th St Box 243
De Land IL 61839

Call Sign: KA9GST
Carolanne Hager
2573 N 550 E Rd
De Land IL 61839

Call Sign: WD9IUT
Michael T Hager
2575 N 550 E Rd
De Land IL 618399733

Call Sign: KC9CPN
Thomas M Olson
De Land IL 61839

Call Sign: KB9CUC
Yvonne C Olson
De Land IL 61839

FCC Amateur Radio Licenses in De Soto

Call Sign: K9RWI
William D West Sr
107 E Douglas
De Soto IL 62924

Call Sign: KC9PII
Charles A Colp
16075 Key Rd
De Soto IL 62924

Call Sign: KC9TVI
Sandra R Colp
16075 Key Rd
De Soto IL 62924

Call Sign: KC9RTQ
Carol A Hofbauer
358 Lavern Rd
De Soto IL 62924

Call Sign: WG9Z
Gerald L Hofbauer
358 Lavern Rd
De Soto IL 62924

Call Sign: W9EBE
Emerson A Cox
300 Reed Station Rd
De Soto IL 62924

Call Sign: N9FLJ
Ed M Riddle
101 S Locust St
De Soto IL 62924

Call Sign: KC9FVG
Larry R Chew
1425 Waldron Ln
De Soto IL 62924

FCC Amateur Radio Licenses in Decatur

Call Sign: WA9VZO
Carl E Vollmer
12 3rd Dr
Decatur IL 62521

Call Sign: KB9WGE
Edward D Imboden
3 6th Dr
Decatur IL 625215291

Call Sign: KA9OGW
Donald E Hudson
8 6th Dr
Decatur IL 62521

Call Sign: KA9TWE
Jean A Mc Cullough
29 7th Dr
Decatur IL 62521

Call Sign: KA9TWF
Robert L Mc Cullough Sr
29 7th Dr
Decatur IL 62521

Call Sign: KC9IGL
Dennis L Anderson
4492 Adams Dr
Decatur IL 62526

Call Sign: N9DUP
James H Gaither Jr
1209 Andrea Dr
Decatur IL 62521

Call Sign: KC9JCE
Randall J Dastrup
5607 Arrowhead Ct
Decatur IL 62521

Call Sign: KD7IWM
Brent S Daines
2350 Baker Ln
Decatur IL 62526

Call Sign: KD7IWL
Rosemary W Daines
2350 Baker Ln
Decatur IL 62526

Call Sign: KA9WIG
Dale A Yeske
20 Barclay Ct
Decatur IL 62526

Call Sign: N9DWW
Phillip D Ernst
1685 Barrington Ave
Decatur IL 62526

Call Sign: KB9SAH
Phillip R Anello
5255 Bentonville Rd
Decatur IL 62521

Call Sign: KC9BHS
Macon County Ares
3195 Beth Blvd Apt 311
Decatur IL 62526

Call Sign: KB9GDQ
Phyllis A Stoffer
Rr 8 Box 108 Bear Rd
Decatur IL 62522

Call Sign: KB9GDO
Stanley D Stoffer
Rr 8 Box 108 Bear Rd
Decatur IL 62522

Call Sign: N9AXR
Robert W Jones
Rr 6 Box 165E
Decatur IL 62521

Call Sign: KA9JDW
Paul J Martin
Rr 6 Box 173A
Decatur IL 62521

Call Sign: N9EMS
Jack W Bledsaw
Rr 1 Box 45Aa
Decatur IL 62526

Call Sign: K9JGA
James M Waters
1 Brownlow Dr
Decatur IL 62521

Call Sign: KA9WQM
Amy L Richards
Rr 4 Brozio Ln
Decatur IL 62521

Call Sign: WA9HUY
Edward R Houchins Sr
9446 Bruce Rd

Decatur IL 62526

Call Sign: N9DPW
Donald G Hampton
1030 Buckeye Ln
Decatur IL 62521

Call Sign: N4QOM
Ronald K Pittman
3910 Camalot Cr 104
Decatur IL 62526

Call Sign: WD9JLY
Robert F Teague
2841 Cardinal Dr
Decatur IL 62526

Call Sign: N9JUM
Beverly A Van Rheeden
19 Carroll Dr
Decatur IL 62521

Call Sign: KB9HVB
Jason E Van Rheeden
19 Carroll Dr
Decatur IL 62521

Call Sign: N9JFZ
Russell E Van Rheeden
19 Carroll Dr
Decatur IL 62521

Call Sign: N9VVY
Roger S Priestley
14 Colorado Dr
Decatur IL 62526

Call Sign: WD9IXF
William L Steenblock
620 Country Manor Dr
Decatur IL 62521

Call Sign: KC9EGP
Ralph M Ray
715 Country Manor Dr
Decatur IL 625212524

Call Sign: KB9WGJ
George E Tate

3070 Danny Dr
Decatur IL 62521

Call Sign: KC8OKO
Paul T Lineen
1118 Delray Ct
Decatur IL 62526

Call Sign: KA9UDY
Richard E Jenkins
3226 Desert Inn Rd
Decatur IL 62526

Call Sign: KA9BYB
Terry L Mc Coy
2017 Dickinson Pl
Decatur IL 62521

Call Sign: KB9UKJ
Linda L Beanland
4160 Doneta Ave
Decatur IL 62526

Call Sign: KB9UKI
Roger W Beanland
4160 Doneta Ave
Decatur IL 62526

Call Sign: WA9BGH
Dennis R White
2950 Doral Ct
Decatur IL 62521

Call Sign: K9MGE
James F Hunsley
3286 Dove Dr
Decatur IL 62526

Call Sign: NN9O
Earl E Pape
3965 E Cantrell
Decatur IL 62521

Call Sign: N9KWE
Dolores K Pape
3965 E Cantrell St
Decatur IL 62521

Call Sign: KB9MQI

James F Weeks
788 E Clay
Decatur IL 62521

Call Sign: WD9DDX
Albert R Bowen
2290 E Clay
Decatur IL 62521

Call Sign: N9RQN
Allen L Mc Coy
2185 E Clay St
Decatur IL 62521

Call Sign: KC9JCB
Jason W Dion
772 E Condit St
Decatur IL 62521

Call Sign: WD9FIY
Walter D Zilz
4220 E Corman
Decatur IL 62521

Call Sign: N7AJJ
Earl Sexton
2025 E Dickinson Ave
Decatur IL 62521

Call Sign: KD9MJ
Carson R Gaston
1445 E Division St
Decatur IL 62526

Call Sign: KA9OWI
Joseph V Robling
1005 E Elmhurst St
Decatur IL 62526

Call Sign: KB9HHW
Stanley P Boland
3150 E Fulton
Decatur IL 62521

Call Sign: K9GSZ
Mel E Drozs
3705 E Fulton
Decatur IL 62521

Call Sign: KB9SAG
Paul M Hanks
4040 E Hickory
Decatur IL 62526

Call Sign: WB9JCD
Meridith L Burgess
7195 E Hwy 36
Decatur IL 62521

Call Sign: KA9AQS
Harold E Peer
2371 E Johns
Decatur IL 62521

Call Sign: KB9NEF
Luther E Swift Jr
1105 E Johns Ave
Decatur IL 62521

Call Sign: N9DJC
William E Francisco Sr
1440 E Johns Ave
Decatur IL 62521

Call Sign: N9PGC
Lorraine S Peterson
855 E Lakeshore Dr
Decatur IL 625213386

Call Sign: K9AWG
Jesse F Jolly
1414 E Lawrence St
Decatur IL 62521

Call Sign: WB9VIR
Beverly A Burgess
1851 E Main
Decatur IL 62521

Call Sign: N9DKY
Jimmy A Frank
904 E Marlin Dr
Decatur IL 625215549

Call Sign: N9XWU
Archie D Mc Lean
4755 E Maryland St
Decatur IL 62521

Call Sign: N9ULQ
Bert R Ruble
4985 E Melwood Ave
Decatur IL 62521

Call Sign: N9ES
Charles L Hayes
1515 E North St
Decatur IL 62521

Call Sign: KC9NPV
Thomas W Gadberry
2595 E Olive St
Decatur IL 62526

Call Sign: KA9WDU
Robert E Bumpus
404 E Perkins
Decatur IL 62864

Call Sign: KC9CAC
David M Marler
333 E Pierson
Decatur IL 62526

Call Sign: W9HTR
Jack Strong
540 E Pierson Ave
Decatur IL 62526

Call Sign: KC9RVD
Buis E Roger
3202 E Prairie St
Decatur IL 62521

Call Sign: KC9BOM
Timothy R Schrishuhn
1410 E Sedgewick
Decatur IL 62521

Call Sign: N9PFA
Jeffrey D Krause
2901 E Wallace
Decatur IL 62526

Call Sign: W5REF
William C Medlock
3237 E Wallace

Decatur IL 62526

Call Sign: WD9AMK
Jerry K Fargusson
717 E Whitmer St
Decatur IL 62521

Call Sign: KB9JLL
David A Nolte
1430 E Willard Ave
Decatur IL 62521

Call Sign: KC9AGI
Wendy J Sherman
1755 E William St
Decatur IL 62521

Call Sign: N9IJI
Kenneth M Melhorn
2501 E William St
Decatur IL 62521

Call Sign: N9CYC
Douglas H Spensley
3250 E William St
Decatur IL 625211645

Call Sign: N9CDN
Carroll E Caine
5574 E William St Rd
Decatur IL 62521

Call Sign: W9TLL
Jack D Gollahon
955 E Wood
Decatur IL 62521

Call Sign: KB9LVC
Dennis L Kreher
2556 E Wood
Decatur IL 62521

Call Sign: KC9PTK
Sue E Justice
1845 E Wood St
Decatur IL 62521

Call Sign: KA9NMU
Dearld E Justice

1845 E Wood St
Decatur IL 62526

Call Sign: N9HLQ
Larry D Feller
2117 Evandale Dr
Decatur IL 62526

Call Sign: W9KUK
Joseph B Connelly
2506 Fairway Ct
Decatur IL 62521

Call Sign: N9AUC
Marjorie P Robinson
3405 Faries Pkwy
Decatur IL 62526

Call Sign: KA9UHQ
Donald C Robinson
3405 Faries Pkwy
Decatur IL 62526

Call Sign: KA9WNB
Cheryl L Bacon
2205 File Dr
Decatur IL 62521

Call Sign: KZ9J
Mark R Bacon
2205 File Dr
Decatur IL 62521

Call Sign: KB9GZE
Jack R Hathaway
1265 Florida Ave
Decatur IL 62521

Call Sign: KE4HVD
David R Stout
1111 Green Meadow
Decatur IL 62521

Call Sign: N9QHO
Edward L Johnson
3637 Greenhill Rd
Decatur IL 62521

Call Sign: W9EHR

Michael E Wehr
4130 Helen Ct
Decatur IL 62521

Call Sign: KO9I
Michael E Wehr
4130 Helen Ct
Decatur IL 62521

Call Sign: N9FNT
Vicki L Wehr
4130 Helen Ct
Decatur IL 62521

Call Sign: W9EHR
Vicki L Wehr
4130 Helen Ct
Decatur IL 62521

Call Sign: KC9TMP
Christopher M Hahn
4545 Hilltop Blvd
Decatur IL 62521

Call Sign: N9HVK
Charles R Reynolds
1663 Hinsdale Ave
Decatur IL 62526

Call Sign: N9NV
Charles R Reynolds
1663 Hinsdale Ave
Decatur IL 62526

Call Sign: N9XWW
Ray E Ashley Jr
3176 Holly Dr
Decatur IL 62526

Call Sign: N9IEZ
Eldred K Graybill
3195 Holly Dr
Decatur IL 62526

Call Sign: KB9UJQ
Wanda J Thompson
2132 Hoyt Dr
Decatur IL 62526

Call Sign: KB9PGB
James R Thompson
2132 Hoyt Dr
Decatur IL 625263015

Call Sign: KB9QKM
Andrew J Tempel
1123 Illinois Cir
Decatur IL 62526

Call Sign: WA9SYU
Harry L Carlson
19 Isabella Dr
Decatur IL 62521

Call Sign: K9QEW
Daryl G Hurst
3333 Ivywood Ct
Decatur IL 62522

Call Sign: KA9WQO
Sue A Hurst
3333 Ivywood Ct
Decatur IL 62522

Call Sign: N9KCG
James B Hood Jr
214 Karen Dr
Decatur IL 62526

Call Sign: N9AHK
Burton E Ranney
919 Karen Dr
Decatur IL 62526

Call Sign: N9CKP
Todd C Ranney
919 Karen Dr
Decatur IL 62526

Call Sign: W9EQT
Dan M Mc Kee
2435 Knollwood
Decatur IL 62521

Call Sign: N9QBG
Walter J Babcock
64 La Salle Dr
Decatur IL 62521

Call Sign: N9LDY
Charlie L Brown
1814 Lynnwood Ct
Decatur IL 62521

Call Sign: KC9CWL
Louis W Wood
3859 Marietta St
Decatur IL 62526

Call Sign: N9OQV
David H James
236 Marlene Ave
Decatur IL 62526

Call Sign: N9FNR
Charles A Niebrugge
1670 Martin Dr
Decatur IL 62521

Call Sign: WA9RTI
Gary D Goeken
1394 Masters Ln
Decatur IL 625219088

Call Sign: N9OPD
Alberta M Mc Geehon
60 Meadow Ter
Decatur IL 62521

Call Sign: K9IQH
Robert C Mc Geehon
60 Meadow Terr
Decatur IL 62521

Call Sign: KB9IJF
Michael R Plotzke
2150 Melrose Dr
Decatur IL 62526

Call Sign: K9PKK
Carl P Birk Jr
2 Memorial Dr Ste 200
Decatur IL 62526

Call Sign: WB4MKN
Helen T Briehler
261 Michael Ave

Decatur IL 62526

Call Sign: WA4MGB
Donald J Briehler
261 Micheal Ave
Decatur IL 62526

Call Sign: N9ECX
George L Lauderdale
1666 Midland Rd
Decatur IL 62521

Call Sign: WA6CWS
Louis S Canady
2725 Mill River Pl
Decatur IL 62521

Call Sign: KA9ZMI
Larry L Mason
1820 Montrose
Decatur IL 62521

Call Sign: WA9NHT
Harlie C Miller
3746 Moundford Ave
Decatur IL 62526

Call Sign: KB9WPK
Teddy L Summers
1790 N 33rd St
Decatur IL 62526

Call Sign: KE9TED
Teddy L Summers
1790 N 33rd St
Decatur IL 62526

Call Sign: N9SXI
Dale P Baker
536 N 35th St
Decatur IL 625211705

Call Sign: WB9TMK
Frank Delgado
3823 N Burchard Dr
Decatur IL 62526

Call Sign: KC9QWB
Norman J Johnson

4045 N Cambridge Dr
Decatur IL 62526

Call Sign: N9LQE
Russell L Banks
1325 N Church St
Decatur IL 62526

Call Sign: KC9EOG
Jacob A Smith
2719 N Church St
Decatur IL 62526

Call Sign: KA9EWC
James A Hayes
21 N Country Club Rd
Decatur IL 62521

Call Sign: N4PEB
Jill B Rosenstein
92 N Country Club Rd
Decatur IL 62521

Call Sign: WD4CNV
Robert S Rosenstein
92 N Country Club Rd
Decatur IL 62521

Call Sign: KB9WFE
Steven E Rosenstein
92 N Country Club Rd
Decatur IL 62521

Call Sign: N9SAL
David K Staff
227 N Dennis Ave
Decatur IL 62522

Call Sign: KC9BWD
David L Rempe
731 N Excelsior
Decatur IL 62521

Call Sign: N9NHP
John D Lamb II
986 N Fairview Ave
Decatur IL 62522

Call Sign: KB9ZMY

Alfred H Hexum
354 N Fairway Ave
Decatur IL 625221106

Call Sign: KB9JLO
Danny L Reynolds
415 N Glendale Ave
Decatur IL 62521

Call Sign: KB9GOP
William E Heer
1746 N Graceland
Decatur IL 62526

Call Sign: KC9SGX
Robert M Austin
2794 N Hill Ave
Decatur IL 62526

Call Sign: KC9NVW
John D Brand
602 N Houseland Ave
Decatur IL 62521

Call Sign: N9QBH
Dale L Urquhart Jr
340 N Lake Shore Dr
Decatur IL 62521

Call Sign: KB9NEG
Sherman M Taylor
2067 N Maple Ave
Decatur IL 62526

Call Sign: KA9PBH
Charles J Martin
2182 N Maple Ave
Decatur IL 62526

Call Sign: WB9PIN
Gerald C Barnstable
1032 N Monroe St
Decatur IL 62522

Call Sign: W9RMI
James C Wood
4287 N Neely
Decatur IL 62526

Call Sign: KA9NBQ
Connie Stoutenborough
3951 N Neely Ave
Decatur IL 62526

Call Sign: N9DHL
Douglas H Stoutenborough
3951 N Neely Ave
Decatur IL 62526

Call Sign: NN9S
Douglas H Stoutenborough
3951 N Neely Ave
Decatur IL 62526

Call Sign: K9CRT
Douglas H Stoutenborough
3951 N Neely Ave
Decatur IL 62526

Call Sign: N9ZSC
Jason E Jones
1063 N Oakdale
Decatur IL 62522

Call Sign: N9QQT
Vicki L Jones
1063 N Oakdale
Decatur IL 62522

Call Sign: KC9JCF
Sean A Maxey
3204 N Oakland Ave
Decatur IL 62526

Call Sign: K9UZJ
Charles N Connelley
3205 N Oakland Ave
Decatur IL 625261611

Call Sign: N9TID
Horace F Kepler
1108 N Summit Ave
Decatur IL 62522

Call Sign: N9GRM
Terry W Jones
1335 N Summit Ave
Decatur IL 62526

Call Sign: WT9J
Terry W Jones
1335 N Summit Ave
Decatur IL 62526

Call Sign: KC9JCD
Robert M Buchen
1950 N Sunnyside Rd
Decatur IL 62526

Call Sign: WA9FRU
Gerald L Lukens
1960 N Sunnyside Rd
Decatur IL 62526

Call Sign: WA9WTC
Dorothy J Nadenbush
2710 N University
Decatur IL 62526

Call Sign: WA9NUL
Phillip R Nadenbush
2710 N University
Decatur IL 62526

Call Sign: K9RZD
Robert W Kubow
3435 N University Ave
Decatur IL 62526

Call Sign: KC9QEY
Galen W Arnold
2215 N Water
Decatur IL 62526

Call Sign: KC9QEZ
Terri L Arnold
2215 N Water
Decatur IL 62526

Call Sign: KC9REY
Terri L Arnold
2215 N Water
Decatur IL 62526

Call Sign: N9QHF
Joseph L Prosser
4133 N Water St

Decatur IL 62526

Call Sign: N9XWR
Brett J Thomas
3005 N Weastlawn Ave
Decatur IL 62526

Call Sign: KB9ZDM
Don Wright
134 N Westdale Pl
Decatur IL 62522

Call Sign: KC9AWH
Julia A Wright
134 N Westdale Pl
Decatur IL 62522

Call Sign: KC9CNU
Samantha J Wright
134 N Westdale Pl
Decatur IL 62522

Call Sign: KG9MQ
David B Brinkley
1126 N Westlawn
Decatur IL 625221372

Call Sign: W9HQE
Michael E Siegmund
928 N Wilder
Decatur IL 62522

Call Sign: KB9DST
Kenneth Cole
3750 N Woodford 1404
Decatur IL 62526

Call Sign: KD9YV
Donald J Petri Sr
403 Newcastle Dr
Decatur IL 62526

Call Sign: KB9UPE
Amy J Robinson
3709 Northhaven Ct Apt 3F
Decatur IL 62526

Call Sign: N9WBX
Robert E Jacobs

3093 Norwood Ave
Decatur IL 62526

Call Sign: K9GPX
Russell S Koch
1691 NW Rt 121
Decatur IL 625261324

Call Sign: N9ACA
Duane E Beals
330 Oak Ln
Decatur IL 62526

Call Sign: N9KVM
Ilene E Beals
330 Oak Ln
Decatur IL 62526

Call Sign: K9PCJ
Carl P Birk Sr
10 Oak Ridge Dr
Decatur IL 62521

Call Sign: KA9IFA
William L Budds
86 Oriole Dr
Decatur IL 62526

Call Sign: KA9WAH
Arthur Sweet
245 Park Pl
Decatur IL 62522

Call Sign: KA9NFO
Jack B Mc Kinley
4 Peggy Ann Dr
Decatur IL 62521

Call Sign: KD5WZO
Larry A Curtis
3090 Peru Rd
Decatur IL 62522

Call Sign: KC9LKH
Larry A Curtis
3090 Peru Rd
Decatur IL 62522

Call Sign: KB9HHS

Wilfred E Reeves
127 Phillips Dr
Decatur IL 62521

Call Sign: N9ZUU
Mark A Murphy
3666 Plover Dr
Decatur IL 62526

Call Sign: N9DPD
David G Martin
115 Point Bluff Dr
Decatur IL 625215505

Call Sign: K9RED
Mary K Martin
115 Point Bluff Dr
Decatur IL 625215505

Call Sign: NJ9Q
John E Schwalbach
530 Powers Ln
Decatur IL 62522

Call Sign: N9HIF
Darrell K Bartholomew
1765 Race Dr
Decatur IL 625215812

Call Sign: N9HGL
Duan J Bartholomew
1765 Race Dr
Decatur IL 625215812

Call Sign: N9DR
Richard S Rose
2050 Ramsey Dr
Decatur IL 62526

Call Sign: KA9QDU
Sharon E Welch
1735 Ravina Park Rd
Decatur IL 62526

Call Sign: WB9LGJ
Loren C Hollman
4774 Redbud Ct
Decatur IL 625269325

Call Sign: KB9NQS
Edward T Govro
28 Ridge Dr
Decatur IL 62521

Call Sign: N9OQS
David A Brooks
81 Ridge Ln Dr
Decatur IL 62521

Call Sign: N9DDC
Stephen M Mc Guire
89 Ridge Ln Dr
Decatur IL 62521

Call Sign: KB9PUQ
John P O Brien
27 Ridgedale
Decatur IL 62521

Call Sign: KA9YAP
Brad E Wright
23 Ridgeway Dr
Decatur IL 62521

Call Sign: N9FNP
Patrick Stowell
5393 Roderick Ave
Decatur IL 625211831

Call Sign: KB9WCH
Kathy K Fronk
138 S 18th
Decatur IL 62521

Call Sign: KB9WCF
Jody D Fronk
138 S 18th St
Decatur IL 62521

Call Sign: KI6YZZ
Gregory P Melikian
139 S 44th St
Decatur IL 62521

Call Sign: KA9NAF
James M Moran
215 S 44th St
Decatur IL 62521

Call Sign: KC9KPH
Eric D Linn
2587 S Baltimore
Decatur IL 62521

Call Sign: KB9POR
Joshua D Wilson
1765 S Baltimore Ave
Decatur IL 625215017

Call Sign: K9MCA
Macon County Ares
1765 S Baltmore Ave
Decatur IL 62521

Call Sign: KB9YEL
Arletta M Schrishuhn
265 S Camp St
Decatur IL 62522

Call Sign: KA9CCA
Kenneth L Schrishuhn
265 S Camp St
Decatur IL 62522

Call Sign: KN9S
Kenneth L Schrishuhn
265 S Camp St
Decatur IL 62522

Call Sign: KC9AGJ
Justin S Vanderlaan
1705 S Country Club Rd Apt
106
Decatur IL 62521

Call Sign: KB9GID
Michael L Smith
664 S Crea
Decatur IL 62522

Call Sign: KC9CAD
Christopher M Vail
2135 S Decatur St
Decatur IL 62521

Call Sign: WB9VCF
Gerald K Bayless

316 S Delmar
Decatur IL 62522

Call Sign: N9ZR
Brent D Payne
1525 S Fairview Ave
Decatur IL 62521

Call Sign: N9QAN
Donald E Jack
1843 S Fairview Ave
Decatur IL 62521

Call Sign: KB9ZMX
Donald Glenn
1740 S Fairview Ave 11
Decatur IL 625214045

Call Sign: N9GVQ
Donald Glenn
1740 S Fairview Ave 11
Decatur IL 625214045

Call Sign: N9ZMA
Joanne C Sebok
2397 S Franklin St Rd
Decatur IL 62521

Call Sign: N9RBQ
Jerald P Sebok
2397 S Franklin St Rd
Decatur IL 625215303

Call Sign: KC9BIT
Lee A Sharp
601 S Gravel Pit Rd
Decatur IL 62522

Call Sign: KB9UWU
Matthew R Comerford
366 S Linder Ave
Decatur IL 62522

Call Sign: KC9AWI
Joshua A Rich
3378 S Long Creek Rd
Decatur IL 62521

Call Sign: KB9UKH

Allen D Myers
1385 S Maffit St
Decatur IL 62521

Call Sign: KC9KYV
Michael L Niemeyer
628 S Oakland Ct
Decatur IL 625222833

Call Sign: KB9GEG
John K Fischer
2260 S Rainwater Dr
Decatur IL 62521

Call Sign: KB9MVA
Debra L Ellison
3227 S Sprinter Dr
Decatur IL 62521

Call Sign: N9ULL
Douglas K Ellison
3227 S Sprinter Dr
Decatur IL 62521

Call Sign: WD9P
Larry G Sullivan
238 S Sunnyside Rd
Decatur IL 62522

Call Sign: W9ISI
Michael W Atwood
635 S Wyckles Rd
Decatur IL 625221047

Call Sign: KC9VCB
Lyle B Clary
2568 Saddle Trek Rd
Decatur IL 625219360

Call Sign: KD9TB
Clarissa H Holcomb
810 Sarah Dr
Decatur IL 62526

Call Sign: K9TBX
Alvin L Birch
352 Shoreline Pl
Decatur IL 62521

Call Sign: KC9IBP
William F Boss
260 Shutter Dr
Decatur IL 62526

Call Sign: KA9VMA
Richard O Allison
3 Sickles Dr
Decatur IL 625215304

Call Sign: K9IHR
M Eleanor Duncan
13 Southern Dr
Decatur IL 62521

Call Sign: KC9SGF
Gary L Wiley
3108 Southland Rd
Decatur IL 62521

Call Sign: K9MQL
Thomas W Samuels Jr
168 Southmoreland Pl
Decatur IL 62521

Call Sign: KC9GAU
Kent B Dixson
3106 St Andrews Dr
Decatur IL 62521

Call Sign: W9JHD
Kenneth E Landreth
4920 Stewart Dr
Decatur IL 62521

Call Sign: K9CIS
Frank M Wiesenmeyer
2181 Summit Ct
Decatur IL 625263049

Call Sign: N9GKD
Randall B Young
3043 Tempe Dr
Decatur IL 62521

Call Sign: N9BXJ
J Drew Watson
3333 Tropicana Rd
Decatur IL 62526

Call Sign: N9XQC
Stukart P Young
270 Victoria
Decatur IL 62522

Call Sign: KB9KLK
Daniel P Hursh
3241 Vining Dr
Decatur IL 62521

Call Sign: K9UZI
Michael V Cooprider
6755 W Cantrell Rd
Decatur IL 62522

Call Sign: KB9ZDJ
David G Martin
2209 W Center
Decatur IL 62526

Call Sign: KC9BIV
Mary K Martin
2209 W Center
Decatur IL 625263320

Call Sign: KC9BYJ
Eric F Martin
2209 W Center St
Decatur IL 62526

Call Sign: N9ZMB
Mark F Troxel
560 W Decatur
Decatur IL 62522

Call Sign: KB9VQJ
Walter A Coltrin
1361 W Decatur St
Decatur IL 62522

Call Sign: K9HNM
Don Adcock
635 W Elm
Decatur IL 62522

Call Sign: KA9PIQ
Lynn R Oxendale
864 W Forest Ave

Decatur IL 62522

Call Sign: KC9EMZ
Jack L Gordy
2424 W Forest Ave
Decatur IL 62522

Call Sign: KB9VIY
Shara L Le Beau
1825 W Grand Ave
Decatur IL 62522

Call Sign: N9EGK
Lester E Gordy
1087 W Green
Decatur IL 62522

Call Sign: KC9BOL
Jennifer E Sharp
612 W Harrison Ave
Decatur IL 62526

Call Sign: ND9R
Louis W Mollohan
852 W Hazel Ave
Decatur IL 62526

Call Sign: K9QO
Louis W Mollohan
852 W Hazel Ave
Decatur IL 62526

Call Sign: WB9TXY
Steven M Dill
2160 W Hickory Pt Rd
Decatur IL 62526

Call Sign: KC9ALR
Jason A Manley
185 W Hickory Pt Rd Apt 5
Decatur IL 62526

Call Sign: WA9VEV
William J Bohner
2315 W Hunt
Decatur IL 62526

Call Sign: K9IGZ
Eugene L Ragan

1424 W Huston Ave
Decatur IL 62526

Call Sign: KG9JY
Brian T Mc Namara
761 W Karen Ct
Decatur IL 62526

Call Sign: NN9IS
Brian T Mc Namara
761 W Karen Ct
Decatur IL 62526

Call Sign: K9SWR
Bryant J Baum
1705 W Leafland
Decatur IL 625221315

Call Sign: WA9FEQ
Arthur L Ortman
1037 W Leafland Ave
Decatur IL 625221537

Call Sign: KC9LWG
Michael R Craft
5511 W Lindale Dr
Decatur IL 62522

Call Sign: KA9MMJ
Kenneth W Smith
2205 W Macon
Decatur IL 62522

Call Sign: KD9D
David O Peckham
430 W Main St
Decatur IL 62522

Call Sign: AG9H
Dale J Travis
5701 W Main St
Decatur IL 62522

Call Sign: KB9WUB
Holly Duncan
1840 W Marietta
Decatur IL 62522

Call Sign: WA9RNI

Earl W Oyler
1455 W Mound Apt 110
Decatur IL 62526

Call Sign: N9PO
George R Garrett
1005 W Olive St
Decatur IL 62526

Call Sign: KB9BQQ
Martha A Park
1020 W Packard St
Decatur IL 62522

Call Sign: N9IGI
Ronald L Park
1020 W Packard St
Decatur IL 62522

Call Sign: WA9DCZ
Donald D David
2134 W Packard St
Decatur IL 62522

Call Sign: K9BYM
William H Requarth
158 W Prairie
Decatur IL 62523

Call Sign: N9RMM
Calvin R Warden Jr
1009 W Prairie Ave
Decatur IL 62522

Call Sign: KC9FLD
Paul A Mariman
402 W Southhampton Dr
Decatur IL 62526

Call Sign: KC9AGH
Tim L Baker
1563 W Sunset
Decatur IL 62522

Call Sign: WA9RVU
Michael L Hammon
1575 W Sunset
Decatur IL 62522

Call Sign: KA9CTM
Daniel T Landers
2095 W Sunset Ave
Decatur IL 62522

Call Sign: WB9SGK
Douglas D Dunker
559 W William Apt 1
Decatur IL 62522

Call Sign: KC9TET
John A Weibull
1500 W William St
Decatur IL 62522

Call Sign: W9ROL
John A Weibull
1500 W William St
Decatur IL 62522

Call Sign: KA9UDF
Daniel E Groves
2040 W William St
Decatur IL 625221825

Call Sign: KV0ICE
Sean A Maxey
531 W William St
Decatur IL 62522

Call Sign: KC9JCC
Gordon R Schrishuhn
7595 W Wood St
Decatur IL 625229580

Call Sign: KC9DOT
Gordon R Schrishuhn
7595 W Wood St
Decatur IL 625229580

Call Sign: KB9HLJ
Brian L Clanton
2921 Wasson Way
Decatur IL 62521

Call Sign: N9KVR
Ronald D Clanton
2921 Wasson Way
Decatur IL 62521

Call Sign: N9KGZ
Lynn R Cole
1437 Watson Ct
Decatur IL 62522

Call Sign: WB9QLE
Robert G Wittig
338 Wayside Ave
Decatur IL 625215315

Call Sign: KB9WIF
Evett A Martin
4652 White Oak Ln
Decatur IL 62521

Call Sign: KB9GU
James D Shank
4621 Willow Brook Ln
Decatur IL 62521

Call Sign: N9KIC
Lori A Shank
4621 Willow Brook Ln
Decatur IL 62521

Call Sign: N9KIE
Michele M Shank
4621 Willow Brook Ln
Decatur IL 62521

Call Sign: KA9ERP
Rosalee A Shank
4621 Willow Brook Ln
Decatur IL 62521

Call Sign: KC9IBQ
Nicolas Calleja
2123 Windsor Rd
Decatur IL 62521

Call Sign: KB9POT
Wilbur J Jahr
2123 Windsor Rd
Decatur IL 62521

Call Sign: K9VQA
Wilbur J Jahr
2123 Windsor Rd

Decatur IL 62521

Call Sign: WA9RSK
Sharon S Goeken
725 Wolf Rd
Decatur IL 62526

Call Sign: K9HLZ
Paul G Ording
Decatur IL 62524

Call Sign: K9HGX
Cenois ARC
Decatur IL 62525

Call Sign: N9PN
Patrick Stowell
Decatur IL 625243163

Call Sign: WB4GNI
Ronald T Dean
Decatur IL 625250917

FCC Amateur Radio Licenses in Deer Creek

Call Sign: KA9FLG
Max G Bernauer
32348 Bernauer Rd
Deer Creek IL 61733

Call Sign: N9XKA
Bruce E Stortzum
22202 Dee Mack Rd
Deer Creek IL 61733

Call Sign: KC9OJO
Bryan A Collett
28936 Harding Rd
Deer Creek IL 61733

Call Sign: KC9AEU
Aaron D Schlupp
29867 Lakeland Rd
Deer Creek IL 61733

Call Sign: KB9JOZ
Andrew A Knitt
111 N Jackson St

Deer Creek IL 61733

Call Sign: KN1TT
Andrew A Knitt
111 N Jackson St
Deer Creek IL 61733

Call Sign: KB9YVN
Nicolas E Mishler
215 N Main St
Deer Creek IL 61733

Call Sign: KC9NBC
Justin R Hippen
111 W 1st St
Deer Creek IL 61733

Call Sign: NX9H
Justin R Hippen
111 W 1st St
Deer Creek IL 61733

Call Sign: N5LMC
James B Smith
307 W 2nd Ave
Deer Creek IL 617330238

Call Sign: KB9RTR
Roy Phillips
29248 Deer Rd
Deer Grove IL 61243

FCC Amateur Radio Licenses in Delevan

Call Sign: KB9SRG
William F Heaton
110 B St
Delavan IL 61734

Call Sign: W3EOS
James L Reese
819 Cedar St
Delavan IL 61734

Call Sign: KA9FBF
James E Horath
903 Chestnut
Delavan IL 61734

Call Sign: KB9RAO
Anthony W York
1002 Linden Ave
Delavan IL 61734

Call Sign: KB9OEM
Robert D Folsom
7979 Morris Mill Rd
Delavan IL 61734

Call Sign: KB9NOQ
Floyd A Folsom
7979 Morris Mill Rd
Delavan IL 61734

Call Sign: KB9HXM
David W Loy
6956 Venado Dr
Delavan IL 61734

Call Sign: KB9TLA
Robert A Roper
806 W 4th St
Delavan IL 61734

Call Sign: KB9TKU
Sherry L Roper
806 W 4th St
Delavan IL 61734

FCC Amateur Radio Licenses in Delong

Call Sign: N9WRG
Keith E Gray
720 West St
Delong IL 61436

FCC Amateur Radio Licenses in Dennison

Call Sign: KC9MLK
David B Farris
25242 E 2250 Rd
Dennison IL 62423

Call Sign: KA8EER
Eric R Anderson

25543 E Alan Ln
Dennison IL 62423

FCC Amateur Radio Licenses in Dewey

Call Sign: N9GLC
Robert S Camp
3095 CR 1100 E
Dewey IL 61840

Call Sign: WB9ZDO
Paul S Kohler
572 CR 2400 N
Dewey IL 61840

Call Sign: KC9OVE
Joseph G Mccullough
562A CR 2400 N
Dewey IL 61840

Call Sign: N9XAE
Joseph G Mccullough
562A CR 2400 N
Dewey IL 61840

Call Sign: N9FJB
Frank J Bellafiore
588B CR 2400 N
Dewey IL 61840

Call Sign: KC9TOJ
Frank J Bellafiore
588B CR 2400 N
Dewey IL 61840

Call Sign: KC9UVD
Gregory S Elliott
588C CR 2400 N
Dewey IL 61840

Call Sign: N9CRT
Merlin E Howell
2546 CR 600 E
Dewey IL 61840

Call Sign: N9DBT
Carolyn J Howell
2546 CR 600E

Dewey IL 61840

Call Sign: KB9KAI
Mark T Rayburn
2428 CR 700 E
Dewey IL 61840

Call Sign: KC9RHJ
Cynthia M Rayburn
2428 CR 700 E
Dewey IL 61840

FCC Amateur Radio Licenses in DeWitt

Call Sign: W9FWT
James M Forbes
801 Bloomington St
DeWitt IL 61735

Call Sign: KB9BPD
Donald W Waddell
Rr 1 Box 48
DeWitt IL 61735

Call Sign: KB9WGG
Charles Fricker
1101 Chicago St
DeWitt IL 61735

Call Sign: N9NYU
Kenneth L Trone
DeWitt IL 617350191

FCC Amateur Radio Licenses in Diamond

Call Sign: KC9LHV
Jon Collier
3 Balmoral Dr
Diamond IL 60416

Call Sign: KC9NWT
Michael W Mcgowan
2358 Cherry Tree Ln
Diamond IL 60416

Call Sign: KC9QOH
Charles W Faurot

2065 E Stellon St
Diamond IL 60416

Call Sign: KB9QNI
Jeannine M Pelletier
210 N Calkey St
Diamond IL 60416

Call Sign: KB9NPI
David A Pelletier
210 N Calkey St
Diamond IL 60416

Call Sign: N9ZZK
Arthur L Bertheaume
60 S Calkey St
Diamond IL 60416

Call Sign: KC9GLV
Donna K Bertheaume
60 S Calkey St
Diamond IL 60416

FCC Amateur Radio Licenses in Dieterich

Call Sign: KB9KTI
Mark A Feldhake
Rt 2 Box 178
Dieterich IL 62424

Call Sign: KC9JIP
Rick A Bannick
5974 N 2100 St
Dieterich IL 62424

Call Sign: WA9BVH
Floyd D Barlow
Dieterich IL 62424

FCC Amateur Radio Licenses in Divernon

Call Sign: KB9QZ
Lewis B Martin
167 Bobby Dr
Divernon IL 62530

Call Sign: KA9ETP

Edmund F Gaffney Jr
13997 Frazee Rd
Divernon IL 62530

Call Sign: KA9WSY
Mary E Gaffney
13997 Frazee Rd Box 14A
Divernon IL 625309012

Call Sign: N9IKZ
John C Bunting
1075 Horse Farm Rd
Divernon IL 62530

Call Sign: KE5CXJ
James L Burg
303 S 3rd St
Divernon IL 62530

Call Sign: KB9TGZ
Jody L Bonds
127 W Lewis
Divernon IL 62530

Call Sign: N9IWR
Edward A Burg
Divernon IL 62530

FCC Amateur Radio Licenses in Dix

Call Sign: KC9RFG
James B Burnes
8706 E Campbell Rd
Dix IL 62830

Call Sign: KC9SDZ
Benton L Fitzjerrells
8120 E Dix Irvington Rd
Dix IL 62830

Call Sign: KB9HQ
Robert D Hutton
7911 E Matthew Rd
Dix IL 62830

Call Sign: AA9KW
Floyd J Brown
10980 E Rileyville Rd

Dix IL 62830

Call Sign: N9WUH
Shirley L Brown
10980 E Rileyville Rd
Dix IL 62830

Call Sign: N9XTC
Thomas Hester
400 N Main St
Dix IL 62830

Call Sign: N9CNE
Gary E South
120 W Madison St
Dix IL 62830

FCC Amateur Radio Licenses in Dixon

Call Sign: WA9NAA
Wayne Harshman
1020 Ann Ave
Dixon IL 61021

Call Sign: W9LDU
Charles W Randall
1414 Ann Ave
Dixon IL 61021

Call Sign: WB9GQF
Richard R Kuter
315 Autumnwood
Dixon IL 61021

Call Sign: N9DDV
Charles L Miller
1501 Bonnie Ave
Dixon IL 61021

Call Sign: N9ZAS
John R Gewecke
1613 Bonnie Ave
Dixon IL 61021

Call Sign: N9AKC
Glenn A Kastner
813 Chestnut
Dixon IL 610213802

Call Sign: N9ZAV
Alan A Pfeifer
815 Chicago Ave
Dixon IL 61021

Call Sign: KA9SXX
Robert L Kinn
1824 Clark St
Dixon IL 61021

Call Sign: N9VRT
Charles P Faivre
410 Clover Ct
Dixon IL 61021

Call Sign: KC9TUK
Lawrence J Weinreich
708 Cottonwood Ct
Dixon IL 61021

Call Sign: N9JJT
Kathy A Bolen
612 Douglas Ave
Dixon IL 61021

Call Sign: K9PUV
Mary E Webb
109 E 6th St
Dixon IL 61021

Call Sign: KB9MTD
Aaron R Webb
112 E Ells Ave
Dixon IL 61021

Call Sign: KB9PAR
Ceasar L Arellano
122 E Fellows St Apt 8
Dixon IL 61021

Call Sign: KC9ASR
Laurence G Hoyle Jr
513 E McKenney St
Dixon IL 610211653

Call Sign: KC9AHD
Matthew O Hoyle
513 E McKenney St

Dixon IL 610211653

Call Sign: N9UEI
Eugene A Boyd
722 E Morgan St
Dixon IL 61021

Call Sign: WD9GWX
Martin L Boos
226 Eells Ave
Dixon IL 61021

Call Sign: KE9QQ
Dirk E Van Dam
324 Fox Trot
Dixon IL 610210324

Call Sign: KE9MM
Dirk E Van Dam
324 Fox Trot
Dixon IL 610210324

Call Sign: KB9PAQ
Robert L Weed
201 Foxtrot Ln
Dixon IL 61021

Call Sign: N9PEE
John J Tate Jr
1540 Freedom Wlk Apt G5
Dixon IL 61021

Call Sign: K9KNV
Edward S Berard
318 Grant Ave
Dixon IL 61021

Call Sign: WD9JCP
Ralph C Pierson
704 Heights Rd
Dixon IL 610219558

Call Sign: KB9KRJ
Sauk Valley College ARC
173 Il Rt 2
Dixon IL 61021

Call Sign: KC9VRJ
William E Studer

466 Il Rt 2
Dixon IL 61021

Call Sign: N0AE
Brion C Gilbert
2087 Il Rt 2
Dixon IL 61021

Call Sign: WA9RSD
John S Weaver
617 Institute
Dixon IL 61021

Call Sign: KC9MND
Kevin E Lalley
1924 Jaguar Ct
Dixon IL 61021

Call Sign: W9MZJ
Henry E Malone
910 Jaydee Ave
Dixon IL 61021

Call Sign: KB9JGT
Patricia L Frey
531 Kilgore Rd
Dixon IL 61021

Call Sign: WN9B
Burton R Lorenzen
1957 Larod Dr
Dixon IL 610219235

Call Sign: KC9HFF
Andrew J Pepper
1964 Lenox Rd
Dixon IL 61021

Call Sign: K9HFF
Andrew J Pepper
1964 Lenox Rd
Dixon IL 61021

Call Sign: W9PX
James J Pepper
1964 Lenox Rd
Dixon IL 61021

Call Sign: KB9PAS

Frederick John Milens III
601 Logan Ave
Dixon IL 61021

Call Sign: KB9IOY
Robert A Boyd
922 Logan Ave
Dixon IL 61021

Call Sign: WD9AVN
Robert A Boyd
922 Logan Ave
Dixon IL 61021

Call Sign: KB9AYB
Duane T Hermes
1102 Lost Nation Rd
Dixon IL 61021

Call Sign: KA9HQG
Max J Thomas
2060 Lowell Park Rd
Dixon IL 61021

Call Sign: WD9IXN
Dale M Newman
915 Mary Ave
Dixon IL 61021

Call Sign: NU9N
John M Anning
1973 Mound Hill Rd
Dixon IL 61021

Call Sign: N9TNP
Karen B Anning
1973 Mound Hill Rd
Dixon IL 61021

Call Sign: KB9JDI
William J Moser
833 Murphy
Dixon IL 61021

Call Sign: N9FOQ
Donald A Vaughan
907 Myrtle Ave
Dixon IL 61021

Call Sign: N9HPF
Lauren E Cook
718 N Dixon Ave
Dixon IL 61021

Call Sign: K2CAV
Michael Irwin
1006 N Hennepin Ave
Dixon IL 61021

Call Sign: KC9THO
Michael A Irwin
1006 N Hennepin Ave
Dixon IL 61021

Call Sign: KA9ZMS
Fred W Billeb Sr
223 N Lincoln Ave
Dixon IL 61021

Call Sign: N9ZAQ
Matthew A Milby
617 N Ottawa Ave
Dixon IL 61021

Call Sign: WD9CJB
Clarence E Webb
618 Orchard St
Dixon IL 61021

Call Sign: KA9MOE
Clarence E Webb Jr
618 Orchard St
Dixon IL 61021

Call Sign: KA9HGZ
Shirley A Webb
618 Orchard St
Dixon IL 61021

Call Sign: KA9MOZ
Steven C Potter
616 Palmyra Ave
Dixon IL 61021

Call Sign: KB9NFU
Thomas L Kanzler Jr
643 Palmyra Rd
Dixon IL 61021

Call Sign: N9FQN
Richard V Trafny
1308 Prescott
Dixon IL 61021

Call Sign: KC9UHD
Joseph E Searls
632 Reynoldswood Rd
Dixon IL 61021

Call Sign: WD9JCO
Donald E Rogers
572 River Ln
Dixon IL 61021

Call Sign: WB9JCF
Richard L Kuecker
333 Rockside Dr
Dixon IL 61021

Call Sign: K9DXI
Richard L Kuecker
333 Rockside Dr
Dixon IL 61021

Call Sign: KC9IXH
Clinton I Casey
406 S Dixon Ave
Dixon IL 61021

Call Sign: N9GEV
Betty J Higby
1016 S Hill Dr
Dixon IL 61021

Call Sign: W9JMT
James H Higby
1016 S Hill Dr
Dixon IL 61021

Call Sign: W9DHS
Dixon High School ARC
1016 S Hill Dr
Dixon IL 61021

Call Sign: KC9CM
Curtis L Chamness
1110 S Hill Dr

Dixon IL 610211836

Call Sign: WA9UEW
Byron V Gilbert
1111 S Ottawa
Dixon IL 61021

Call Sign: KB9EMC
Michael J Farster
817 S Ottawa Ave
Dixon IL 61021

Call Sign: N9LJZ
Mark A Staley
917 S Ottawa Ave
Dixon IL 61021

Call Sign: K9LJZ
Mark A Staley Sr
917 S Ottawa Ave
Dixon IL 61021

Call Sign: WB9LJZ
Mark A Staley Sr
917 S Ottawa Ave
Dixon IL 61021

Call Sign: WD9AIE
Robert W Logsdon
7317 S Ridge Rd
Dixon IL 61021

Call Sign: KC9HEO
Steve Lyons
123 Sherman Ave
Dixon IL 61021

Call Sign: KA9DVP
John A Wolfe
511 Spruce
Dixon IL 61021

Call Sign: KB9IZT
Steven J Arntzen
938 Stony Point Rd
Dixon IL 61021

Call Sign: KB9EMB
William V Bearden Jr

1217 Tee St
Dixon IL 61021

Call Sign: KB9JMF
Chad A Straw
148 Timber Creek Rd
Dixon IL 61021

Call Sign: N9UNZ
Walter B Miller Jr
407 Van Buren Ave
Dixon IL 61021

Call Sign: KC9RST
Donald G Mcguire Sr
916 W 1st
Dixon IL 61021

Call Sign: KC9FQK
Paula A Portner
1302 W 2nd St
Dixon IL 61021

Call Sign: KC9FMI
Peter A Portner Sr
1302 W 2nd St
Dixon IL 61021

Call Sign: KA9MPC
Edward T Higby
1214 W 3rd St
Dixon IL 61021

Call Sign: KB9ELX
Peggy L Higby
1214 W 3rd St
Dixon IL 61021

Call Sign: KC9IXF
Vincent L Hoyle
1411 W 3rd St
Dixon IL 61021

Call Sign: KC9KYW
Zachary R Woods
2403 W 3rd St
Dixon IL 61021

Call Sign: KC9ABA

Robert L Hunter
1011 W 8th St
Dixon IL 61021

Call Sign: KA9HIP
Bernice I Burrs
1407 W 9th St
Dixon IL 61021

Call Sign: KA9DVT
Larry L Burrs
1407 W 9th St
Dixon IL 61021

Call Sign: W9KZ
Randall S Renne
4909 W Edgewood Rd
Dixon IL 61021

Call Sign: N9YXN
Michael V Welker
4125 W Timber Ln
Dixon IL 61021

Call Sign: KC9EDX
Michael M Stahl
1598 Wadsworth Way
Dixon IL 61021

Call Sign: W9HOC
Wayne W Whitmore
7929 Walnut
Dixon IL 61021

Call Sign: K9CZB
Gary E Myers
1110 White Rock Dr
Dixon IL 61021

Call Sign: KB9SWL
Raymond W Albert
1611 Winnetka
Dixon IL 61021

Call Sign: K9JBX
Darrell E Webb
Dixon IL 61021

Call Sign: WB9EBS

Claud L Ensinger Sr
Dixon IL 61021

Call Sign: W9DXN
Rock River ARC Inc
Dixon IL 61021

FCC Amateur Radio Licenses in Dongola

Call Sign: KG9FT
Jeffrey S Mc Clellan
1918 Cypress Rd
Dongola IL 62926

Call Sign: KC9DKO
Richard L Gates
760 Gates Ln
Dongola IL 62926

Call Sign: WD4SGV
Richard M Gates
760 Gates Ln
Dongola IL 62926

Call Sign: KC9UBM
Vincent E Roberts
114 Housing Cir
Dongola IL 62926

FCC Amateur Radio Licenses in Donnellson

Call Sign: N9PVN
Todd W Krummel
Rr 1 Box 83
Donnellson IL 62019

Call Sign: N9TYY
James E Burris
1991 Elk Rd
Donnellson IL 62019

Call Sign: N9UAY
Rebecca S Burris
1991 Elk Rd
Donnellson IL 62019

FCC Amateur Radio Licenses in Dorsey

Call Sign: K9HAL
Hilary G Knight
7 S Deer Park Dr
Dorsey IL 62021

Call Sign: KC9DYZ
Bruce A Kuethe
4658 Seiler Rd
Dorsey IL 62021

FCC Amateur Radio Licenses in Dover

Call Sign: KB9KHL
Tammy S Lachat
109 N Main St
Dover IL 61323

FCC Amateur Radio Licenses in Dow

Call Sign: WB1GOG
G Robert Burns
Rr 1 Box 127
Dow IL 620229721

Call Sign: KC9PTH
David A Cornelius
14854 Cornelius Ln
Dow IL 62022

Call Sign: N9TME
Harry V Fuguitt
Dow Rd Box 64
Dow IL 62022

Call Sign: N9VDJ
Carolyn G Burns
23850 Green Acres Rd
Dow IL 62022

Call Sign: K9BR
Stephen D Line
Dow IL 62022

FCC Amateur Radio Licenses in Downs

Call Sign: KA9OBU
David L Ashley
8143 N 2200 E Rd
Downs IL 61736

Call Sign: KB9JTK
Donald J Jones Sr
19710 Nottingham Dr
Downs IL 617369371

Call Sign: KA9VJF
Jennie A Moss
22192 Ridgewood Dr
Downs IL 61736

Call Sign: NO9V
John L Moss
22192 Ridgewood Dr
Downs IL 61736

Call Sign: NO9W
Roxann Moss
22192 Ridgewood Dr
Downs IL 61736

Call Sign: KB9PXL
Eldon M Bricker
303 W Washington St
Downs IL 61736

Call Sign: N9SOG
Candy A Gibson
Downs IL 61736

FCC Amateur Radio Licenses in Du Quoin

Call Sign: W9YRY
August A Campanella
8060 SR 14
Du Quoin IL 62832

Call Sign: KF9TZ
Lester D Bilderback
146 Arrowwood Estates Rd
Du Quoin IL 628324059

Call Sign: WB9UJY
George R Bailey
3240 Branch St
Du Quoin IL 62832

Call Sign: KB9SPI
David H Searby Jr
516 E Franklin St
Du Quoin IL 62832

Call Sign: KC9SIF
Jeremy P Troutt
417 E Park St
Du Quoin IL 62832

Call Sign: KB9QKL
Shannon L Clark
321 E Poplar
Du Quoin IL 62832

Call Sign: W9WED
Buster F Alongi
220 N Line St
Du Quoin IL 62832

Call Sign: W9WCN
James Fiorino
10 N Maple St
Du Quoin IL 62832

Call Sign: W9CXH
James C Harris
424 N Summers St
Du Quoin IL 62832

Call Sign: KB9RSN
David H Kennedy
201 S Illinois Ave
Du Quoin IL 628322624

Call Sign: K9DK
David H Kennedy
201 S Illinois Ave
Du Quoin IL 628322624

Call Sign: KC9PZU
Ted G Harsha
200 SR 13 And 127

Du Quoin IL 62832

Call Sign: KC9OEZ
Cody A Bailey
395 US Rt 51
Du Quoin IL 62832

Call Sign: WA9OBJ
David R Allabastro
488 US Rt 51
Du Quoin IL 628320139

Call Sign: KB9LJZ
Elias W Kellerman
Du Quoin IL 62832

FCC Amateur Radio Licenses in Dundas

Call Sign: N9TZS
Chad A Marks
R 1 Box 111
Dundas IL 62425

Call Sign: KC9HWT
Micah J Obrien
7178 N Il 130
Dundas IL 62425

FCC Amateur Radio Licenses in Dunfermline

Call Sign: KC9IOQ
Harold R Carpentier
Dunfermline IL 61524

FCC Amateur Radio Licenses in Dunlap

Call Sign: KE4CFJ
Vincent A Stubbs
116 Castle Dr
Dunlap IL 61525

Call Sign: W9WVA
Michael J Sullivan
13102 Crater Ln Rr 1
Dunlap IL 615250296

Call Sign: KB9RX
Richard B Erickson
613 Hickory Grove Ct
Dunlap IL 61525

Call Sign: N9LR
Lawrence A Reiser
119 N Castle Dr
Dunlap IL 61525

Call Sign: N9EAR
Trude Reiser
119 N Castle Dr
Dunlap IL 61525

Call Sign: KB9NGV
Bart Mol
12627 N Colony Rd
Dunlap IL 61525

Call Sign: KC9EBN
Christina M Mol
12627 N Colony Rd
Dunlap IL 61525

Call Sign: KB9URO
Jack B Long
12627 N Colony Rd
Dunlap IL 61525

Call Sign: KC9PH
Thomas P Long
12627 N Colony Rd
Dunlap IL 61525

Call Sign: N9EIO
Willis G Triplett
12808 N Crescent Dr
Dunlap IL 61525

Call Sign: KC9TCQ
Matthew W Schoedel
10604 N Fieldgrove Dr
Dunlap IL 61525

Call Sign: N9KFO
Harvey E Blanden
12311 N Lake Forrest
Dunlap IL 61525

Call Sign: K9RIE
John M Bailey
13105 N SR 91
Dunlap IL 61525

Call Sign: N9QLY
Alan L Ferguson
10809 N Trail View Dr
Dunlap IL 61525

Call Sign: KB9FUT
Ronald E Sumner
300 Pines
Dunlap IL 61525

Call Sign: KA9VCN
Pat K Rennich
11313 Rte 91
Dunlap IL 61525

Call Sign: WA9UKV
Earnest D Hills
4513 W Alta Ln
Dunlap IL 61525

Call Sign: KA9NFE
Ronald D Hills
4513 W Alta Ln
Dunlap IL 61525

Call Sign: W9MYS
Thomas O Williams
1326 W Bristol Hollow Rd
Dunlap IL 61525

Call Sign: WB9OGS
John J Groezinger
1816 W Bristol Hollow Rd
Dunlap IL 61525

Call Sign: KB0YLD
Rebecca S Fontes
1621 W Cedar Hills Dr
Dunlap IL 61525

Call Sign: KI0EB
Kevin A Fontes
1621 W Cedar Hills Dr

Dunlap IL 61525

Call Sign: KC9PQW
G A Sansom
1624 W Country Oaks Ct
Dunlap IL 61525

Call Sign: N9JXK
Cheryl S Miller
6909 W Deford Ln
Dunlap IL 61525

Call Sign: N9HUZ
Marcel H Truong
1406 W Hickory Trace
Dunlap IL 61525

Call Sign: WD9GWE
Timothy S Hungate
2313 W Jubilee Ln
Dunlap IL 61525

Call Sign: KC9MSE
Roger A John
6927 W Legion Hall Rd
Dunlap IL 61525

Call Sign: WA8NWG
Thomas M Hunt
1531 W Meadowview Dr
Dunlap IL 61525

Call Sign: N9TYN
Marna P Tate
1417 W Timberdale Dr
Dunlap IL 61525

Call Sign: WB9ZLM
William J Tate
1417 W Timberdale Dr
Dunlap IL 61525

Call Sign: KC9GUT
Breckinridge Thomas
12202 Wood Ridge Ct
Dunlap IL 61525

Call Sign: W9GAO

Heart Of Illinois Fm Repeater
Club Inc
Dunlap IL 61525

Call Sign: W9HOI
Heart Of Illinois Fm Repeater
Club Inc
Dunlap IL 61525

Call Sign: W9UFF
Heart Of Illinois Fm Repeater
Club Inc
Dunlap IL 61525

FCC Amateur Radio Licenses in Dupo

Call Sign: KB4CH
Everett B Cotton Jr
420 Edwin
Dupo IL 62239

Call Sign: KG9PZ
Byron S Cobb
329 Miranda Dr
Dupo IL 62239

Call Sign: KB9NIF
Gilbert V Hofstetter
8651 Mollins Rd
Dupo IL 62239

Call Sign: KB9ODC
Sue H Hofstetter
8651 Mullins Rd
Dupo IL 62239

Call Sign: N9VWE
Deborah S Wyrick
412 N 3rd St
Dupo IL 62239

Call Sign: N9WSG
Jeff A Wyrick
412 N 3rd St
Dupo IL 62239

Call Sign: N9RVY
Michael S Wyrick

412 N 3rd St
Dupo IL 622391139

Call Sign: N9EGM
James R Hamann
508 N 3rd St
Dupo IL 62239

Call Sign: N0UHK
Keith J Stephens
105 N 6th St
Dupo IL 62239

Call Sign: N9EGL
Mark W Griffith
2004 N 7th St
Dupo IL 62239

Call Sign: KB9BHP
Mervin C Bauchens
130 N Main
Dupo IL 62239

Call Sign: WB9LPR
Randy R Hamilton
520 S Main
Dupo IL 62239

Call Sign: W9HBF
Robert M Brown
8470 Triple Lakes Rd
Dupo IL 62239

Call Sign: NP4B
Robert K Zimmerman Jr
8554 Triple Lakes Rd
Dupo IL 62239

FCC Amateur Radio Licenses in Duquoin

Call Sign: KB9FOO
Dorothy S Morgan
135 Arrowood Est
Duquoin IL 62832

Call Sign: KB9FON
Harold D Morgan
135 Arrowood Est

Duquoin IL 62832

Call Sign: KC9OLG
Sherry A Wertz
915 E Olive St
Duquoin IL 62832

Call Sign: KD9ER
Stephen R Sinxhorn
119 N Chestnut Appt B
Duquoin IL 62832

Call Sign: KB9ZBL
Roger D Neal
530 S Division St
Duquoin IL 62832

Call Sign: KC9OLI
Daniel W Epplin
3391 US Rt 51
Duquoin IL 62832

Call Sign: KB9SDP
Charles N Genesio
210 W North Ave
Duquoin IL 62832

Call Sign: WB9UEA
Hughes Herman
Duquoin IL 62832

Call Sign: KE9ZZK
William Odom
Duquoin IL 62832

FCC Amateur Radio Licenses in Durand

Call Sign: N9HYE
Nanette A Hendler
1101 Cameron Dr
Durand IL 61024

Call Sign: N9HYG
Les Hendler
1101 Cameron Dr
Durand IL 61024

Call Sign: K9OS

Steven D Otwell
505 E Main St
Durand IL 61024

Call Sign: N9IJM
Lee A Rodewald
506 Fairview St
Durand IL 610249400

Call Sign: KC9SDP
Bryan E Holder
14311 Rowley Rd
Durand IL 61024

Call Sign: W9BDJ
James A Kufahl
402 S Center St 306
Durand IL 610249590

Call Sign: K9SAN
Charles T Derwent
13810 Trask Bridge Rd
Durand IL 610249620

Call Sign: N9LXN
Edwin D Muderlak
16453 Waller Rd
Durand IL 61024

Call Sign: KF9EM
James M Parks
Durand IL 61024

Call Sign: N9YDI
Walter E Postava II
Durand IL 61024

**FCC Amateur Radio
Licenses in Dwight**

Call Sign: WB9VEL
James A Watters
28695 E 2900 N Rd
Dwight IL 60420

Call Sign: KA9ECT
Margaret M Watters
28695 E 2900 N Rd
Dwight IL 60420

Call Sign: KC9LXZ
J Alex Mcwilliams
103 E Chippewa St
Dwight IL 604200218

Call Sign: KA9UPV
Michael Montalbano
211 E James St
Dwight IL 60420

Call Sign: W9PXS
John B Fitzpatrick
214 E North St
Dwight IL 60420

Call Sign: KB9STS
Alan D Metzke
217 E North St
Dwight IL 604201051

Call Sign: N9RLY
Michele L Brant
300 E Spencer St Lot 64
Dwight IL 60420

Call Sign: N9WXA
Gayle M Carman
208 E Waupansie
Dwight IL 60420

Call Sign: N9OAY
Jason M Carman
208 E Waupansie
Dwight IL 60420

Call Sign: KB9MGM
Robert L Simmons
300 E Williams
Dwight IL 604200242

Call Sign: KE9YT
Joseph E Kurowski
116 Morgan St
Dwight IL 60420

Call Sign: KC9IPC
Ronald L Haga
29086 N 3400 E Rd

Dwight IL 60420

Call Sign: W9APP
Ronald L Haga
29086 N 3400 E Rd
Dwight IL 60420

Call Sign: KA9NLP
Timothy J Watters
111 S Clinton St
Dwight IL 60420

Call Sign: WA9ZBW
John J Hoffman
11440 S Johnny Run Rd
Dwight IL 60420

Call Sign: WD9FGD
Joel A Francis
507 S Union St
Dwight IL 60420

Call Sign: KA9YEU
Renee E Erickson
104B Susan Dr
Dwight IL 60420

Call Sign: KA9YET
Ronald E Erickson Jr
104B Susan Dr
Dwight IL 60420

Call Sign: KA9VUZ
Larry D Little
302 W Chippewa
Dwight IL 60420

Call Sign: K9TXR
Joshua D Jahn
316 W Chippewa St
Dwight IL 60420

Call Sign: KB9NPJ
John R Price
412 W Chippewa St
Dwight IL 60420

Call Sign: WD9FGT
Gary L Kratochvil

407 W Delaware
Dwight IL 60420

Call Sign: WA9VKT
Oliver K Zivney
323 W Delaware St
Dwight IL 614200284

Call Sign: N9RJG
Duane E Brant
411 W James St Unit A
Dwight IL 60420

Call Sign: KC9SSI
Elizabeth R Dewaard
124 W Waupansie St
Dwight IL 60420

Call Sign: KC9PIK
Dustin J Campbell
322 W William
Dwight IL 60420

FCC Amateur Radio Licenses in Earlville

Call Sign: N9VFP
Gaylon D Mc Allister
127 Benld Rd
Earlville IL 62023

Call Sign: W9RXP
Gerald R Smith
3452 Cyclone Rd
Earlville IL 60518

Call Sign: K9YMH
Judy E Breuer
4624 E 1175th Rd
Earlville IL 605186214

Call Sign: KB9WJZ
Seth T Hoffman
4279 E 12th Rd
Earlville IL 605186079

Call Sign: KC9DNN
Timothy L Peterson
213 E Brown St

Earlville IL 60518

Call Sign: WA9DJR
Joseph A Kramer
518 S 4th
Earlville IL 60518

Call Sign: KC9OCT
Steven A Miller
905 Sunset Ave
Earlville IL 60518

Call Sign: N9XUF
Earl J Mills
621 W Winthrop St
Earlville IL 60518

Call Sign: KB9WJT
Walter T Grimm Jr
906 Warren St
Earlville IL 605188166

FCC Amateur Radio Licenses in East Alton

Call Sign: N9HXB
Duane K Davis
215 6th
East Alton IL 62024

Call Sign: KC9DZA
Michael D Johns
136 Avalon
East Alton IL 62024

Call Sign: W9AI
Gary W Carstens
3 Beatrice Ct
East Alton IL 62024

Call Sign: WA0UNY
James J Patterson
601 Brookwood Dr
East Alton IL 62024

Call Sign: N9ECI
Jo A Bishop
514 California
East Alton IL 62024

Call Sign: N9CYY
Lloyd E Bishop
514 California
East Alton IL 62024

Call Sign: N9UEV
Dennis D Baumgarden
7 Carolee Ct
East Alton IL 62024

Call Sign: KB9HJK
George R Smith
507 Crestview Dr
East Alton IL 62024

Call Sign: N9SCO
Robert E Reid
156 E Haller Dr
East Alton IL 62024

Call Sign: N9STN
Jeffrey K Pinkerton
1819 E Rock Hill Rd
East Alton IL 62024

Call Sign: WA9JNW
Harold J Perkins
225 Eastmoor
East Alton IL 62024

Call Sign: KB9BDD
Sheridan E Carroll
214 Goulding
East Alton IL 62024

Call Sign: KC9HAI
Canine Emergency Response
Team
212 Grand Ave
East Alton IL 62024

Call Sign: KC4SAR
Canine Emergency Response
Team
212 Grand Ave
East Alton IL 62024

Call Sign: KB9WYH

Norma L Richter
205 Greenbriar Dr
East Alton IL 62024

Call Sign: KB9FOI
Christopher J Hicks
115 Irwin St
East Alton IL 62024

Call Sign: KB9FNZ
Teresa A Hicks
115 Irwin St
East Alton IL 62024

Call Sign: KC9BOY
David B Gaines
330 Job
East Alton IL 62024

Call Sign: KC9TJY
William L Meunier
422 Job St
East Alton IL 62024

Call Sign: KA9PFT
Thomas R Drake
385 Kendall Dr
East Alton IL 62024

Call Sign: KB9LVB
Brian D Rain
1011 Linden Ave
East Alton IL 62024

Call Sign: N9ZPT
Christopher K Grieve
249 Lindenwood Dr
East Alton IL 62024

Call Sign: KB9JVX
Janice K Eaton
324 Oak St
East Alton IL 62024

Call Sign: KA9VZQ
Linda E Kusmanoff
408 Oak St
East Alton IL 62024

Call Sign: KF4WOO
Brenda L Prestenback
414 Ohio St
East Alton IL 62024

Call Sign: AE4TZ
Robert L Prestenback
414 Ohio St
East Alton IL 62024

Call Sign: KB9EXW
Richard W Schneider
1025 Rhondell
East Alton IL 62024

Call Sign: N9SCN
Lawrence B Barth
3411 Rock Hill Rd
East Alton IL 62024

Call Sign: KA9VYV
Steven M Dawson
257 S 9th St
East Alton IL 62024

Call Sign: KC9GMZ
Rosewood Heights Dx Club
257 S 9th St
East Alton IL 62024

Call Sign: K9DNT
Rosewood Heights Dx Club
257 S 9th St
East Alton IL 62024

Call Sign: K9DD
James E Dawson
257 S 9th St
East Alton IL 62024

Call Sign: WW9L
John M Dvorchak
105 S Circle Dr
East Alton IL 62024

Call Sign: N9UJJ
Mark E Cox
148 S Pence
East Alton IL 62024

Call Sign: WB9YXA
Andrew J Hoffman
212 S Pence
East Alton IL 620241144

Call Sign: N9HTD
Woodrow W Davis
152 S Pence Ave
East Alton IL 62024

Call Sign: KL0LB
Cora C Miller
250 Shady Ln
East Alton IL 620241656

Call Sign: K0RJL
David C Miller
250 Shady Ln
East Alton IL 620241656

Call Sign: N9VZP
Mildred E Ballard
609 Sitze Dr
East Alton IL 62024

Call Sign: KB9LZI
Robert E Ballard
609 Sitze Dr
East Alton IL 62024

Call Sign: KC9CHO
Murrel L French Sr
23 Tall Oak Dr
East Alton IL 62024

Call Sign: W9MLF
Murrel L French Sr
23 Tall Oak Dr
East Alton IL 62024

Call Sign: W9PWI
Richard E Rice
444 Valley View Dr
East Alton IL 62024

Call Sign: N9SII
William E Janes III
132 W Airline Dr

East Alton IL 62024

Call Sign: KC9KY
Jack R Leverich
217 W Haller
East Alton IL 62024

Call Sign: KC9KKW
Michael J Hall
375 W Spruce St
East Alton IL 62024

Call Sign: N9KFU
David J Wiegand
406 Washington Ave
East Alton IL 62024

Call Sign: N9YHQ
Murrel L French Jr
428 Washington Ave
East Alton IL 62024

Call Sign: KB9OJS
John D Bunyan
710 Will O Way
East Alton IL 62024

Call Sign: K7WAZ
Robert W Burroughs
East Alton IL 62024

Call Sign: KC9VJP
Robert W Burroughs
East Alton IL 62024

FCC Amateur Radio Licenses in East Carondelet

Call Sign: N9QXU
William B Harris
2906 Adams Dr
East Carondelet IL 62240

Call Sign: KB9BHY
Milan A Warren
R 1 Box 226
East Carondelet IL 62240

Call Sign: KA9POW

Deanna M Hand
Rr 1 Box 259
East Carondelet IL 62240

Call Sign: KC9AUJ
Christopher K Kuni
2312 Old SR 3
East Carondelet IL 62240

Call Sign: WD8CNS
Jack D Strang
1770 Wooded Oak Trl
East Carondelet IL 622401546

FCC Amateur Radio Licenses in East Dubuque

Call Sign: KC9BFX
Donald F Hanley
1050 Hiawatha Dr
East Dubuque IL 61025

Call Sign: KB9WQQ
Scott D Prochaska
441 Montgomery
East Dubuque IL 61025

Call Sign: KC0MOO
John J Einck
3851 N Circle Dr
East Dubuque IL 61025

Call Sign: KA9IVP
Loran L Schonhoff
5710 N Menominee Rd
East Dubuque IL 61025

Call Sign: NM0F
Donald W Kinnaird
219 Park Ln
East Dubuque IL 61025

Call Sign: KA0AGL
James F Delaney
13 Remington Park Cir
East Dubuque IL 61025

Call Sign: KB0SVM
Gerald L Vanderah

49 Remington Park Cir
East Dubuque IL 61025

Call Sign: KB9CYJ
Charles W Finch
430 Sidney St
East Dubuque IL 61025

Call Sign: KC9VTO
Michael B Moser
14442 W Walnut Rd
East Dubuque IL 61025

FCC Amateur Radio Licenses in East Galesburg

Call Sign: N9HYD
Carol K Curry
109 E 2nd
East Galesburg IL 61430

Call Sign: N9HGO
Amanda R Schwabe
109 E 2nd
East Galesburg IL 61430

FCC Amateur Radio Licenses in East Moline

Call Sign: KB9MVF
Michael L Hodshire
3042 10th St
East Moline IL 61244

Call Sign: K9UQI
Richard K Williams
4245 10th St
East Moline IL 61244

Call Sign: KC5WUF
Arnold L Kieffer
223 12th St
East Moline IL 612441518

Call Sign: KA9JYZ
John R Bell Sr
3500 12th St
East Moline IL 612443711

Call Sign: N9QC
John R Bell Sr
3500 12th St
East Moline IL 612443711

Call Sign: KB9CXU
John A Douglas
187 16th Ave
East Moline IL 61244

Call Sign: KB9VHE
Stacey A Bollinger
915 16th Ave
East Moline IL 61244

Call Sign: KB9SVO
Diana K Bayer
4120 180th St N
East Moline IL 612449742

Call Sign: KA3YEB
Adrienne M Donatelli
2126 18th St
East Moline IL 61244

Call Sign: N9MZU
Ray Guyton
3901 1st St
East Moline IL 61244

Call Sign: KB9XD
Craig D Crippen
330 20th St N
East Moline IL 612441136

Call Sign: KC9RJH
Paul L Cummings
721 25th St
East Moline IL 61244

Call Sign: N9TWJ
De Wayne M Mc Creery
238 28th Ave
East Moline IL 61244

Call Sign: WD0FMW
Timothy C Ritter Sr
348 28th Ave
East Moline IL 61244

Call Sign: KA9LNI
Mary J Huber
633 28th Ave
East Moline IL 61244

Call Sign: KB9CLH
Lloyd W Carlson
427 32 Ave
East Moline IL 61244

Call Sign: KB9DPL
James F Coussens
312 33rd Ave
East Moline IL 612443124

Call Sign: N9BIL
Timothy C Rogerwall
611 34th Ave
East Moline IL 61244

Call Sign: K9WM
Green River Valley ARS
611 34th Ave
East Moline IL 61244

Call Sign: KF4FPJ
Thomas W Horton
916 34th Ave
East Moline IL 61244

Call Sign: KC9NLG
Thomas W Horton
916 34th Ave
East Moline IL 61244

Call Sign: N9TGE
David E Apple
3539 3rd St C
East Moline IL 61244

Call Sign: K9JL
Jeffrey A Lindberg
3564 3rd St C
East Moline IL 61244

Call Sign: KB9ALT
Leonard C Leech
1167 45th Ave

East Moline IL 61244

Call Sign: WD9DFX
Lloyd Fletcher Sr
1203 46 Ave
East Moline IL 61244

Call Sign: KA9PWA
Joyce A Fletcher
1203 46th Ave
East Moline IL 61244

Call Sign: KG9IE
Todd E Forret
3332 4th St
East Moline IL 61244

Call Sign: KA9TVM
Lora M Pappas
3916 5th St
East Moline IL 61244

Call Sign: AB9W
Larry M Dickinson
4321 5th St
East Moline IL 612444212

Call Sign: W9SNU
David J Griffith
2641 6th St
East Moline IL 61244

Call Sign: KC9SWT
Michael D Prine
2169 6th St Ct
East Moline IL 61244

Call Sign: N9EHP
Gerald L Rounds
306 7th St
East Moline IL 61244

Call Sign: KA8SSB
Charles S Riechers
3622 7th St
East Moline IL 61244

Call Sign: KA0BZN
Everett G Christensen

4329 7th St
East Moline IL 61244

Call Sign: N9DIZ
Frank L Whitmore
2849 8th St
East Moline IL 61244

Call Sign: KB0OUP
Jill A Whitmore
2849 8th St
East Moline IL 612443212

Call Sign: KB9FNP
Michael R Austin
3633 8th St Ct
East Moline IL 612443524

Call Sign: W9LGS
Richard B Van Zanten
2956 9 1/2 St
East Moline IL 61244

Call Sign: KC9QOA
John W Eaves
2561 9 1/2 St
East Moline IL 61244

Call Sign: NI1Q
John W Eaves
2561 9 1/2 St
East Moline IL 612443226

Call Sign: KA9TUX
Dennis M Chatterton
Rr 3 Box 454A
East Moline IL 61244

Call Sign: N9ILR
Franklin L Stanforth
4021.5 Friendship Rd
East Moline IL 61244

Call Sign: KA9CSF
Rudolph J Fath
350 Island Ave
East Moline IL 61244

Call Sign: K9AZL

Edwin R Spurr Jr
2806 Kennedy Dr
East Moline IL 61244

Call Sign: KC9OTQ
Brett A Hart
2116 Lincolnwood Dr
East Moline IL 61244

Call Sign: N9KXC
Edward A White
2148 Lincolnwood Dr
East Moline IL 61244

Call Sign: N9SQK
Ronald P Larvenz
106 Rt 5 & 92
East Moline IL 61244

Call Sign: KB9SVI
Mary L Tyner
17422 Rt 84 N
East Moline IL 61244

FCC Amateur Radio Licenses in East Peoria

Call Sign: KC9FNL
James B Stolin
312 Baylor St
East Peoria IL 61611

Call Sign: KB9GSS
Charles S Simms
427 Bloomington Rd
East Peoria IL 61611

Call Sign: W9GSS
Charles S Simms
427 Bloomington Rd
East Peoria IL 61611

Call Sign: KG9BQ
Douglas P Schulzki
1720 Bloomington Rd
East Peoria IL 61611

Call Sign: WB9AOV
John W Trobaugh

111 Brentwood Dr
East Peoria IL 616114409

Call Sign: KA9YSH
Melvin R Morger
125 Brentwood Dr
East Peoria IL 61611

Call Sign: KC9ELJ
Chris K Brainerd
401 Briarbrook Dr
East Peoria IL 61611

Call Sign: KB9ZMR
Daniel G Dimitroff
105 Campanile Dr
East Peoria IL 61611

Call Sign: N9YZX
Charles D Heathcoat
1195 Carolyn Ct
East Peoria IL 61611

Call Sign: W0RKF
Fred A Krabbe
105 Carriage Ct
East Peoria IL 616114320

Call Sign: W9ICC
Illinois Central College
Electronics Club
1 College Dr
East Peoria IL 61635

Call Sign: WA9WZZ
Robert D Bloompott
220 Coventry Ln
East Peoria IL 61611

Call Sign: KC9OQR
Michelle P Bodily
105 Cracklewood Ln
East Peoria IL 61611

Call Sign: KB9ZRF
Phil J Thomas
101 District Ct
East Peoria IL 616111410

Call Sign: KC5CWE
Steven E Flinn
203 District Ct
East Peoria IL 61611

Call Sign: WA9DHE
Walter J Kamp
233 E Acorn Dr
East Peoria IL 616111020

Call Sign: KB9ZWW
David F Zalar
159 E N Lakeview Dr
East Peoria IL 61611

Call Sign: KC9VRM
Steven R Dean
212 E N Lakeview Dr
East Peoria IL 61611

Call Sign: KB9UXK
William A Staelens
202 E Sunset Way
East Peoria IL 61611

Call Sign: WX9U
Philip C Rice
3410 E Washington Rd
East Peoria IL 61611

Call Sign: WB9LQT
East Peoria Comm Hs Rad
Club
1401 E Washington St
East Peoria IL 61611

Call Sign: WA9MYW
Gary G Wooley
211 Fenestra Ln
East Peoria IL 616111104

Call Sign: WD9DUF
George H Riegelein
125 Field Grove Ct
East Peoria IL 61611

Call Sign: KC9LNL
Rodger E Graves Jr
140 Field Grove Ct

East Peoria IL 61611

Call Sign: W9FOZ
Robert A Flinn
1105 Fon Du Lac Dr
East Peoria IL 61611

Call Sign: KA9DND
Harold D Rock
107 Fraser St
East Peoria IL 61611

Call Sign: K9RM
Robert F Miller
206 Gardena
East Peoria IL 61611

Call Sign: KB9NW
Ronald G Morgan
114 Herman St
East Peoria IL 61611

Call Sign: W9MEV
Herbert E Sandstrom Jr
136 Highview Ter
East Peoria IL 61611

Call Sign: K9ZGJ
George B Bolton
221 Hillside Rd
East Peoria IL 61611

Call Sign: KA9KZZ
James D Miller
308 Indian Cir
East Peoria IL 61611

Call Sign: KB9SEO
Ryan P Allgaier
405 Indian Cir
East Peoria IL 61611

Call Sign: KC9UKC
Robert F Sims
115 James Ct
East Peoria IL 61611

Call Sign: K9PIG
Max D Snyder

203 Justice Dr
East Peoria IL 616115501

Call Sign: KB9RJK
Gregory J Dekeyser
206 Kerfoot St
East Peoria IL 61611

Call Sign: K9VZW
Raymond D Purdue
113 Lafayette Ln
East Peoria IL 61611

Call Sign: W9QEM
Otto Torre Jr
100 Lawndale Ct
East Peoria IL 61611

Call Sign: N9YDM
Richard C Stoneburner
252 Leadley
East Peoria IL 61611

Call Sign: KC9LNH
Frank J Olivito
307 Liberty Ave
East Peoria IL 61611

Call Sign: K9TIE
Frank J Olivito
307 Liberty Ave
East Peoria IL 61611

Call Sign: WD9FZW
Allan W Campbell
1214 Maple Ln
East Peoria IL 61611

Call Sign: WD9FQO
William N Williamson
112 Mary Pl
East Peoria IL 61611

Call Sign: WB9NKP
Mark K Kupferschmid
130 Mt Aire Dr
East Peoria IL 616111707

Call Sign: K9YUG

Barry K Redenbo
104 N Maple Ln
East Peoria IL 61611

Call Sign: N9AER
Richard M Roedell
1212 N Old Trl Rd
East Peoria IL 616111212

Call Sign: K9RVF
James W Hagemann
1235 N Rim Rd
East Peoria IL 61611

Call Sign: WD9GPF
Stephen N Knobeloch
204 Oakbrook Dr
East Peoria IL 61611

Call Sign: K9VJH
Milton P Stanley
813 Oakwood Rd
East Peoria IL 61611

Call Sign: ND9E
William H Axelrod
297 Old Germantown Rd
East Peoria IL 61611

Call Sign: K3WA
William H Axelrod
297 Old Germantown Rd
East Peoria IL 61611

Call Sign: KB9CQU
Janet L Kavelman
343 Old Germantown Rd
East Peoria IL 61611

Call Sign: N9HSN
Lynn F Kavelman
343 Old Germantown Rd
East Peoria IL 61611

Call Sign: N9YUX
Lisa P Nguyen
127 Orchard
East Peoria IL 61611

Call Sign: N9YUT
Cynthia N Tackmann
127 Orchard St
East Peoria IL 61611

Call Sign: K9VZL
Daniel C Bright
117 Ottawa Ct
East Peoria IL 61611

Call Sign: WB9UCT
James J Henkel
351 Park Ave
East Peoria IL 61611

Call Sign: WD9AAY
William M Petefish Jr
108 Patricia
East Peoria IL 61611

Call Sign: KB9VVM
Daniel W Majors
119 Putnam St
East Peoria IL 61611

Call Sign: KB9ZMT
Andrew M Kraut
113 Rentsch Dr
East Peoria IL 616111231

Call Sign: KB9ZRD
Robert L Crist
220 Reutter Ct
East Peoria IL 61611

Call Sign: WA9CCU
Robert Swadener
200 Ritchie St
East Peoria IL 61611

Call Sign: KC9UTR
Craig E Worrick
101 S Inglewood Dr
East Peoria IL 61611

Call Sign: K9CEW
Craig E Worrick
101 S Inglewood Dr
East Peoria IL 61611

Call Sign: N9FLS
Arvid H Nelson
108 S Pleasant Hill Rd
East Peoria IL 61611

Call Sign: KB9VQG
Andrew S Debelak
133 Shoshone Dr
East Peoria IL 61611

Call Sign: WO9W
William E Cusack
22500 Spring Creek Rd
East Peoria IL 61611

Call Sign: KB9DML
Eugene B Shults
1401 Springbay Rd
East Peoria IL 61611

Call Sign: N9PSU
Donald C Bell Jr
1101 Springfield Rd
East Peoria IL 61611

Call Sign: N9SVO
James A Moyer
1515 Springfield Rd
East Peoria IL 61611

Call Sign: WL7AJM
La Verle Mabeus
1009 Sunset Dr
East Peoria IL 61611

Call Sign: KC9RWD
Andrew D Johnson
1214 Upper Spring Bay Rd
East Peoria IL 61611

Call Sign: KB9UXI
Nate C Reutter
108 Vonachen Ct
East Peoria IL 61611

Call Sign: N9KTY
Judith A Coker
133 Vonachen Ct

East Peoria IL 61611

Call Sign: N9FAM
John M Coker
133 Vonachen Ct
East Peoria IL 616111578

Call Sign: WB9VFS
Jeffrey C Ribak
141 Vonachen Ct
East Peoria IL 61611

Call Sign: N9PSY
Kenneth N Decker
108 W Forrest Ave
East Peoria IL 61611

Call Sign: WB9RNP
Mark A Causey
102 W Glen Rt 5
East Peoria IL 61611

Call Sign: KC9KAI
Richard F Ritchey
210 W Muller Rd
East Peoria IL 616114850

Call Sign: N9LVH
Gary D Grose
104 Walnut Dr
East Peoria IL 61611

Call Sign: WZ9BS
Robert G Siegwarth
East Peoria IL 61611

Call Sign: KC9AHN
Aaron J Schneblin
East Peoria IL 61611

FCC Amateur Radio Licenses in East Saint Louis

Call Sign: W9OBT
Armand J Rolle
7701 Bunkum Rd
East Saint Louis IL 62204

Call Sign: AF3US

Bernard M Lavezza
5110 Collinsville Rd
East Saint Louis IL 62201

Call Sign: N8VGP
Warren D Qualls Jr
5598 Collinsville Rd Lot 2
East Saint Louis IL 62201

Call Sign: WF0F
William A R Daniel Jr
5100 Collinsville Rd Lot 43
East Saint Louis IL 62201

Call Sign: KB9AHS
Mary V Clark
1220 Freeman
East Saint Louis IL 62203

Call Sign: KA9LFB
Herbert A Jackson Jr
1714 Gaty Ave
East Saint Louis IL 622051630

Call Sign: KA9QNC
Walter Hughes
1636 Missouri Ave
East Saint Louis IL 62205

Call Sign: KA9LVU
Walter S Moore
832 N 33rd St
East Saint Louis IL 62205

Call Sign: KA9HDY
James E Hurtz
2349 N 61st
East Saint Louis IL 62204

Call Sign: KB9HRF
Guy M Price
6786 Watts Ave
East Saint Louis IL 62204

FCC Amateur Radio Licenses in Easton

Call Sign: KC9OFS
Walter Shawgo Jr

20503 E Kreiling Rd
Easton IL 62633

Call Sign: K9LOE
Walter Shawgo Jr
20503 E Kreiling Rd
Easton IL 62633

Call Sign: N9JPD
Alan C Wichner
Easton IL 62633

Call Sign: KB9WTU
William R Collander
Easton IL 62633

FCC Amateur Radio Licenses in Eddyville

Call Sign: K9YTO
Vertle E Blair
Eddyville IL 62928

FCC Amateur Radio Licenses in Edelstein

Call Sign: KB9AUF
Jeffrey A Wilson
201 E Swords Dr
Edelstein IL 61526

Call Sign: W9OM
John G Prentiss
Hallock Hills Farm
Edelstein IL 61526

Call Sign: KB9AUE
Darrin K Kamman
526 Horseshoe Trl
Edelstein IL 61526

Call Sign: KB9ANM
Kenneth R Kamman
526 Horseshoe Trl
Edelstein IL 61526

Call Sign: KB9LWW
Todd A Stark
353 La Prairie Rd

Edelstein IL 61526

Call Sign: KB9ES
Harold R Hodges
15914 N Centerville Rd
Edelstein IL 61526

Call Sign: N9KOA
James M Miller
149 N Miller Rd
Edelstein IL 61526

Call Sign: KB9AVF
Loren J Baird
611 Shady Oaks
Edelstein IL 61526

Call Sign: KB9AVD
Michael J Baird
611 Shady Oaks
Edelstein IL 61526

Call Sign: AA9VB
Gerald G Horst
2825 W Lake Shore Dr
Edelstein IL 61526

Call Sign: KB9YBZ
John D Sinks
3006 W Main St
Edelstein IL 61526

FCC Amateur Radio Licenses in Edgewood

Call Sign: KC9IYL
Betty J Mcelyea
Rr 1 Box 177
Edgewood IL 62426

Call Sign: KA9YBT
Clarence L Rutledge
Rt 1 Box 370
Edgewood IL 62426

Call Sign: KA9KSI
Ronald L Caraway
Rr 1 Box 405
Edgewood IL 62426

Call Sign: K0JPH
Noel C Hyde Jr
3961 E 25th Ave
Edgewood IL 62426

Call Sign: KC9BVD
Darin A Koelm
407 Hickory Box 27
Edgewood IL 62426

Call Sign: NE9M
Robert L Brewer
75 Magpie Dr
Edgewood IL 62426

Call Sign: W4CKF
Debra D Yingst
5407 Ridge Rd
Edgewood IL 62426

Call Sign: W9DDY
Debra D Yingst
5407 Ridge Rd
Edgewood IL 62426

Call Sign: W4CKI
Victor L Yingst
5407 Ridge Rd
Edgewood IL 62426

Call Sign: W9VLY
Victor L Yingst
5407 Ridge Rd
Edgewood IL 62426

Call Sign: KB9IYP
Tim A Rush
Edgewood IL 62426

FCC Amateur Radio Licenses in Edinburg

Call Sign: KB9KAG
Alva R Womack
Rr2 Box 91
Edinburg IL 62531

Call Sign: KC9KMC

Barbara A Galloway
301 E Franklin
Edinburg IL 62531

Call Sign: KC9KRB
Patrick D Galloway
301 E Franklin
Edinburg IL 62531

Call Sign: KC9KMD
Tim B Smith
301 E Franklin
Edinburg IL 62531

Call Sign: KC9CPP
Patrick D Galloway
115 E Lincoln
Edinburg IL 62531

Call Sign: N9TUG
Michael A Mc Kinnon
414 Foggit
Edinburg IL 62531

Call Sign: KB9UME
Michael D Dunkirk
308 N Grant
Edinburg IL 62531

Call Sign: W9RIV
Michael D Dunkirk
308 N Grant
Edinburg IL 62531

Call Sign: KA9JLT
George A Ortman
421 W Lincoln St
Edinburg IL 62531

Call Sign: KB9KGO
William A Saunders
702 W Masonic
Edinburg IL 62531

FCC Amateur Radio Licenses in Edwards

Call Sign: WB9UKL
Daniel E Counsil

6501 Kickapoo Edwards Rd
Edwards IL 61528

Call Sign: KC9EUQ
David F Schings
6016 N Gilles Rd
Edwards IL 61528

Call Sign: WD9HBC
Vaclav G Ujcik
7016 N Grand Fir Dr
Edwards IL 61528

Call Sign: KB9CPH
Robert V Mc Garrah
8501 N Trigger Rd
Edwards IL 61528

Call Sign: N9YVA
Kenneth A Scovil
9910 W Chestnut
Edwards IL 61528

Call Sign: K9BWY
Eugene A Nelson
6222 W US Hwy 150
Edwards IL 61528

Call Sign: N9HUT
Keith Atkinson
110 Wagner Ln
Edwards IL 62025

```
FCC Amateur Radio
Licenses in Edwardsville
```

Call Sign: N9STM
Phillip W South
101 4th Ave
Edwardsville IL 62025

Call Sign: KC9KMQ
Sachin H More
123 4th Ave
Edwardsville IL 62025

Call Sign: K9GET
Charles F Fink Jr
221 5th Ave

Edwardsville IL 62025

Call Sign: KB9PQW
Gregory W Coffey
820 Amherst Pl
Edwardsville IL 620252640

Call Sign: N9PTO
Roland D Hurt
5001 Barnes Ln
Edwardsville IL 62025

Call Sign: N9XMY
Clifford E Wisser
51 Birdie Ct
Edwardsville IL 62025

Call Sign: N9KCB
Gearld L Mc Connell
1360 Biscay
Edwardsville IL 62025

Call Sign: KC9MDC
Charlotte J Wilson
4273 Bohm School Rd
Edwardsville IL 62025

Call Sign: N9OPW
Richard A Foreshee Sr
Rr 6 Box 237A
Edwardsville IL 62025

Call Sign: KB9GGX
Burl E Schmidt
R Rt 8 Box 293
Edwardsville IL 62025

Call Sign: N9MWS
Dennis J Svoboda
Rr 4 Box 424
Edwardsville IL 62025

Call Sign: WD9AJI
Thomas E Bannon
97 Burns Farm Blvd
Edwardsville IL 62025

Call Sign: N9QAM
James R Nickerson

517 Cass Ave
Edwardsville IL 62025

Call Sign: N4JQG
Wayne S Eastby
125 Chattanooga Ct
Edwardsville IL 62025

Call Sign: KE4HTR
Byron L Morgan
1808 Cloverdale Dr
Edwardsville IL 62025

Call Sign: KC0LKF
Laticia M Georgie
430 Cougar Village Apt 1C
Edwardsville IL 62025

Call Sign: KC9TGA
Laticia M Georgie
430 Cougar Village Apt 1C
Edwardsville IL 62025

Call Sign: KC9JWP
Jackie E Wilson III
518 Cougar Villiage 2B
Edwardsville IL 62026

Call Sign: K9DQM
Nathan T Colgate
33 Country Club View
Edwardsville IL 62025

Call Sign: W9IWA
Donald W Sherman
290 Deep Cove
Edwardsville IL 62025

Call Sign: KC9JTZ
Anggit O Liek Subroto
19 Devon Ct Apt 6
Edwardsville IL 62025

Call Sign: WD9IVD
Dallas R Dalton
8001 Donna Ln
Edwardsville IL 62025

Call Sign: KB9JVT

Joyce A Dalton
8001 Donna Ln
Edwardsville IL 62025

Call Sign: KA0IRA
Ezra M Tebben
2411 Doral Ct
Edwardsville IL 62025

Call Sign: KC9KTN
Steven B Wolfe
109 Dunwoody Dr
Edwardsville IL 62034

Call Sign: N9SCL
Edward R Williams
409 E Lake Dr
Edwardsville IL 62025

Call Sign: WB9WAS
Steven M Mc Rae
1225 E Liberty Prairie Ln
Edwardsville IL 62025

Call Sign: KC9JDE
Laura J Barnard
421 E Schwarz St
Edwardsville IL 62025

Call Sign: W9CJW
Michael Hoshiko
7754 El Pine Est
Edwardsville IL 62025

Call Sign: KA9VKT
Peyton R House
1255 Emerson Ave
Edwardsville IL 62025

Call Sign: KC9KMR
Naveen K Mangu
1419 Esic Dr Apt 1
Edwardsville IL 62025

Call Sign: KC9KIU
Pradeep Tadakamalla
1419 Esic Dr Apt 4
Edwardsville IL 62025

Call Sign: KC9KMN
Harshitha Digumarthi
1419 Esic Dr Apt 7
Edwardsville IL 62025

Call Sign: KC9KIV
Praveen Kumar Mallempati
1425 Esic Dr Apt 7
Edwardsville IL 62025

Call Sign: KC9KMO
Chandrashekar Parvatharaju
N 1425 Esic Dr Apt 7
Edwardsville IL 62025

Call Sign: WA8YOL
Jack W Grieves
13 Forest Hill Ln
Edwardsville IL 62025

Call Sign: WB0DRH
William J Schmidt II
6617 Fox View Dr
Edwardsville IL 62025

Call Sign: KC9EXM
Naqro-Central Division Club
6617 Fox View Dr
Edwardsville IL 62025

Call Sign: N9FUV
Michael J Berner
6911 Gebhart Ln
Edwardsville IL 62025

Call Sign: KC9DSF
Brian L Gebhardt
914 Grand Ave
Edwardsville IL 62025

Call Sign: KB0ZLY
Leonard A Bringer
1030 Grand Ave
Edwardsville IL 620251328

Call Sign: KB9JE
Robert C Madoux
1577 Grand Ave
Edwardsville IL 620251337

Call Sign: N9GXE
Thomas H Rehg
905 Hale Ave
Edwardsville IL 62025

Call Sign: KB9FLS
Roscoe H Mayberry
6011 Hamel Dr
Edwardsville IL 62025

Call Sign: W9LVA
Roscoe H Mayberry
6011 Hamel Dr
Edwardsville IL 62025

Call Sign: KB9WPZ
Michael E Lohrum
5417 Hazel Rd
Edwardsville IL 62025

Call Sign: KB9WPY
Suzanne R Lohrum
5417 Hazel Rd
Edwardsville IL 62025

Call Sign: N9IRW
Thomas J Hayes
4 Hidden Acres
Edwardsville IL 62025

Call Sign: KC9JQF
Michael L Wibben
413 High Pt Dr
Edwardsville IL 62025

Call Sign: KC9TPA
Brady A O Brien
329 Highpoint Dr
Edwardsville IL 62025

Call Sign: W9EKP
Hartley G Smith
628 Hill Ln
Edwardsville IL 62025

Call Sign: KB9HBR
William B Brown Jr
729 Hillsboro

Edwardsville IL 62025

Call Sign: KC9KBD
Benjamin R Spiller
532 Hilsboro Ave
Edwardsville IL 62025

Call Sign: K0ATC
Scott A Ramage
425 Home Ave
Edwardsville IL 62025

Call Sign: KX4CTO
Stephen D Anderson
5017 Indian Hills Dr
Edwardsville IL 62025

Call Sign: N9BHW
James A Duffey
505 Jaime Lynn Ct
Edwardsville IL 62035

Call Sign: W9CES
Ralph P Anderson
1263 Jamaica Dr
Edwardsville IL 620255184

Call Sign: WH6YK
Richard L Beach
516 Jamie Lynn
Edwardsville IL 62025

Call Sign: W9NWG
Le Roy A La Bardi
625 Jamie Lynn Ct
Edwardsville IL 62025

Call Sign: N9SIJ
Jack L Nothdurft
1476 Ladd
Edwardsville IL 62025

Call Sign: KE4PLU
Douglas E Frey
1349 Lee Dr
Edwardsville IL 62025

Call Sign: KB9DQA
Michael F Schlueter

17 Leverett Ln
Edwardsville IL 62025

Call Sign: N9JWZ
Norma L Richter
1510 Lincoln Knolls Dr
Edwardsville IL 620254119

Call Sign: KB9DXM
Lindley A Renken
406 Lindley Ave
Edwardsville IL 62025

Call Sign: WB8WWE
Gary M Goossens
2400 Little Round Top Dr
Edwardsville IL 62205

Call Sign: KB9AXW
Lance C Beard
19 Madena
Edwardsville IL 62025

Call Sign: N9RCW
Darrel H Lony
860 Madison Ave
Edwardsville IL 62025

Call Sign: N9XMX
Jerry L Cato II
1707 Madison Ave
Edwardsville IL 62025

Call Sign: AB9YM
Brian R Robertson
8615 Maple Grove Rd
Edwardsville IL 62025

Call Sign: KA9KKP
Brian R Robertson
8615 Maple Grove Rd
Edwardsville IL 62025

Call Sign: KC9TMF
Daniel L Halcom
6641 Moro Rd
Edwardsville IL 62025

Call Sign: NP2FK

Matthew E Rodina Jr
21 N Cherry Hills
Edwardsville IL 62025

Call Sign: N5GJH
Deryl W Wilhite
1214 Nassau Dr
Edwardsville IL 62025

Call Sign: W0MTG
Dean C Keune
854 Newport Bay Dr
Edwardsville IL 620255121

Call Sign: N9ZZQ
John E Lopez
712 Notre Dame Ave
Edwardsville IL 62025

Call Sign: WA9KJB
Robert S Lynch
547 Olive St
Edwardsville IL 62025

Call Sign: K2CPU
Thomas E Hall
539 Overlook Dr
Edwardsville IL 62025

Call Sign: N9NYE
Thomas E Hall
539 Overlook Dr
Edwardsville IL 62025

Call Sign: W9AIU
Egyptian Radio Club Inc
2905 Pentacostal Rd
Edwardsville IL 62025

Call Sign: AA9RT
Francis L Cassady
2905 Pentecostal Rd
Edwardsville IL 62025

Call Sign: KE9NZ
Willie C Carpenter Sr
315 Pine St
Edwardsville IL 62025

Call Sign: AA9QM
Katherine A Ledford
1110 Prickett
Edwardsville IL 62025

Call Sign: KB9AXX
Donald R Mc Bride
1304 Randle
Edwardsville IL 62025

Call Sign: N9YEQ
Jeffrey M Lewis
725 Randle St
Edwardsville IL 62025

Call Sign: KB9UDC
Wanda L Mc Bride
1304 Randle St
Edwardsville IL 62025

Call Sign: WA9KQS
Edward F Bauer
514 Roanoke Dr
Edwardsville IL 62025

Call Sign: N9LBG
Larry J Miller
721 Roanoke Dr
Edwardsville IL 620252613

Call Sign: N9UQR
Gregory J Czaczkowski
52 Rottingham Ct
Edwardsville IL 62025

Call Sign: W9JPT
Helen A Thompson
Box 56 Rr 1
Edwardsville IL 62025

Call Sign: KB9CHM
Timothy J Bennett Sr
1165 San Juan Dr
Edwardsville IL 62025

Call Sign: KB9LUT
Jean A Mc Cullough
3559 Sand Rd
Edwardsville IL 620257523

Call Sign: AI9G
Jerry W Mc Cullough
3559 Sand Rd
Edwardsville IL 620257523

Call Sign: N9PPJ
Martin W Schultz III
312 Scott St
Edwardsville IL 62025

Call Sign: N9PYU
Lawrence M Costello
104 Seminole St
Edwardsville IL 62025

Call Sign: N9WPV
Michael L Mc Grew
104 Seminole St
Edwardsville IL 62025

Call Sign: N3ANH
Francis I Coppage Jr
1327 St Louis St
Edwardsville IL 620251309

Call Sign: WD9ETP
Irene M Mezzano
315 State
Edwardsville IL 62025

Call Sign: KB9TCS
Gayle E Boschert
4834 Stcar Rd
Edwardsville IL 620257530

Call Sign: W9RDA
Ronald D Ashby Jr
1607 Stonebrooke Dr
Edwardsville IL 620254220

Call Sign: KC9ODN
Donald C Bush
613 Sunset Dr
Edwardsville IL 62025

Call Sign: KC9JLE
John P Brockus
7401 Swamp Oak Ln

Edwardsville IL 62025

Call Sign: KB9DMZ
George A Marshall
445 Tamarach
Edwardsville IL 62025

Call Sign: KC9GKO
Michael C Farrara
218 Thomas Ter
Edwardsville IL 62025

Call Sign: KB9JPL
Treefon J Siampos
22 Timber Meadows Pl
Edwardsville IL 62025

Call Sign: KC9KQE
David J Sill
30 Tranquility Ridge
Edwardsville IL 62025

Call Sign: KB9ENI
Mark A Muckensturm
991 University Dr
Edwardsville IL 62025

Call Sign: KC9KMP
Anita Sundaram
1317 University Dr Apt 11
Edwardsville IL 62025

Call Sign: KC9KIT
Sandeep Mandarapu
1070 University Dr Apt 12
Edwardsville IL 62025

Call Sign: KD9O
Ray W Eberhart
215 W Franklin
Edwardsville IL 62025

Call Sign: WB9VFU
Ronald D Ashby Jr
205 W Franklin Ave
Edwardsville IL 620252332

Call Sign: KF9BN
Larry G Wofford

6778 W Liberty Prairie
Edwardsville IL 62025

Call Sign: W9LGW
Larry G Wofford
6778 W Liberty Prairie
Edwardsville IL 62025

Call Sign: KC9KBB
Donald W Clements
6737 W Liberty Prairie Ln
Edwardsville IL 62025

Call Sign: W9PAT
Patrick J Riley
258 W Union St
Edwardsville IL 62025

Call Sign: KB9ZZC
Leslie A Archer
417 Warren St
Edwardsville IL 62025

Call Sign: KC9ICQ
Andy G Lozowski
6817 White Oak Ct
Edwardsville IL 62025

Call Sign: W0PH
Andy G Lozowski
6817 White Oak Ct
Edwardsville IL 62025

Call Sign: KC9INQ
Emma S Lozowski
6817 White Oak Ct
Edwardsville IL 62025

Call Sign: KC9GGT
Richard H Townsend
5938 Wooded Est Ln
Edwardsville IL 62025

Call Sign: N9HAQ
Darren W Wright
3 Yorkshire Ct
Edwardsville IL 62025

Call Sign: N9CCK

Robert L Onori
4480 Zika Ln
Edwardsville IL 62025

**FCC Amateur Radio
Licenses in Effingham**

Call Sign: N9EIQ
Gerald D Holley
16 Bluebird Dr
Effingham IL 62401

Call Sign: KB9SSM
Robert A Lidster
Rr 1 Box 162
Effingham IL 62401

Call Sign: KB9TCK
Matthew J Roedl
Rr 4 Box 199 A
Effingham IL 62401

Call Sign: KB9SVB
Linda L Linley
Rt 4 Box 235
Effingham IL 62401

Call Sign: N9RGO
Calvin W Mitchell
R 1 Box 249
Effingham IL 62401

Call Sign: N9LRL
William E Krueger
Rr 2 Box 380
Effingham IL 62401

Call Sign: KB9RYD
Effingham Composite
Squadron Cap
12 Cadillac Dr
Effingham IL 62401

Call Sign: WA9TRK
Harry W Gilbert
23 Court Six
Effingham IL 62401

Call Sign: KB9TCL

Jonathan P Wente
10 Court Ten
Effingham IL 62401

Call Sign: N9XWK
Carol A Perkins
10606 E 1175th Ave
Effingham IL 62401

Call Sign: KB9WUP
James R Perkins
10606 E 1175th Ave
Effingham IL 62401

Call Sign: KB9WUQ
Jonathan A Perkins
10606 E 1175th Ave
Effingham IL 62401

Call Sign: N9XWI
Kevin E Perkins
10606 E 1175th Ave
Effingham IL 62401

Call Sign: KC9MBN
Mary E Perkins
10606 E 1175th Ave
Effingham IL 62401

Call Sign: KB9WUR
Thomas M Perkins
10606 E 1175th Ave
Effingham IL 62401

Call Sign: WB9UVG
Douglas P Mc Devitt
11084 E 1260th Ave
Effingham IL 62401

Call Sign: KB9WUO
James R Fleshner
14094 E 1800th Ave
Effingham IL 62401

Call Sign: KD7LMC
John O Laue
9768 E 1900th Ave
Effingham IL 62461

Call Sign: N9PUY
Dale E Roedl
15182 E 890th Ave
Effingham IL 62401

Call Sign: K9DER
Dale E Roedl
15182 E 890th Ave
Effingham IL 62401

Call Sign: KB9WDR
Bryan R Peters
14186 E 935th Ave
Effingham IL 62401

Call Sign: KC9MGZ
Andrew R Miller
9470 E 975th Ave
Effingham IL 62401

Call Sign: N9XPI
Debbie J Roedl
9337 E 975th Ave
Effingham IL 62401

Call Sign: KB9OCI
Rich B Martin
10569 E Aminoff Dr
Effingham IL 62401

Call Sign: WA9HUH
Paul L Askew Sr
1103 E Fayette Ave
Effingham IL 62401

Call Sign: W9MLS
Don L Roedl
725 E Jefferson Ave
Effingham IL 62401

Call Sign: KB9QGY
William L Binder
9394 E Nees Ave
Effingham IL 62401

Call Sign: N9XWL
Juanita B Perkins
10261 E US Hwy 40
Effingham IL 62401

Call Sign: N9XWH
Kenneth E Perkins
10261 E US Hwy 40
Effingham IL 62401

Call Sign: KB9WUL
Steven D Endebrock
809 Edgar
Effingham IL 62401

Call Sign: WA9HMT
Joe M Willenborg
607 Gordon
Effingham IL 62401

Call Sign: KB9WUN
James R Sullivan
1600 Hillside Dr Apt 10
Effingham IL 62401

Call Sign: AA9HB
Robert W George
606 Holiday Dr
Effingham IL 62401

Call Sign: KC9JIS
Eric L Mcgee
908 Lynn Dr
Effingham IL 62401

Call Sign: W9KVZ
Bill M Oliver
1 Majestic Cir
Effingham IL 62401

Call Sign: KC9MNB
Effingham County Ares
311 Miracle Ave
Effingham IL 62401

Call Sign: KB9RSK
Effingham County Esda
311 Miracle Ave
Effingham IL 62401

Call Sign: KC9JIU
Fred J Gaca
9435 N 1000th Rd

Effingham IL 62401

Call Sign: KB9QGW
Andrew J Linley
10901 N 1000th Rd
Effingham IL 62401

Call Sign: KB9QGV
James R Linley
10901 N 1000th Rd
Effingham IL 62401

Call Sign: KC9MBM
Josh M Perkins
12036 N 1000th Rd
Effingham IL 62401

Call Sign: KB9EKH
Keith E Perkins
12036 N 1000th Rd
Effingham IL 62401

Call Sign: KC9MBQ
Kimberly A Perkins
12036 N 1000th Rd
Effingham IL 62401

Call Sign: N9NJL
Michele R Perkins
12036 N 1000th Rd
Effingham IL 62401

Call Sign: KB9ZML
Donald J Johnson
12264 N 1450th St
Effingham IL 62401

Call Sign: KB9UVL
Terry L Dalton
8825 N 1550th Rd
Effingham IL 62401

Call Sign: N9KHW
Donald H Johnson
703 N 1st St
Effingham IL 62401

Call Sign: KC9RWK
Jerry R Jansen

1310 N 3rd St
Effingham IL 62401

Call Sign: KB9WDS
Daniel G Hille
10062 N 900th St
Effingham IL 62401

Call Sign: KB9SAC
American Red Cross
Effingham County Chapter
202 N Banker
Effingham IL 62401

Call Sign: AB9PI
Brian P Armstrong
15742 N Bluebird Dr
Effingham IL 62401

Call Sign: KC9MST
Patrick A Armstrong
15742 N Bluebird Dr
Effingham IL 62401

Call Sign: KZ6K
Lawrence Leventhal
13220 N Country Club Rd
Effingham IL 62401

Call Sign: KB9QHC
Larry L Stroud
15181 N Dendron
Effingham IL 62401

Call Sign: N9EAH
Larry L Stroud
15181 N Dendron St
Effingham IL 62401

Call Sign: KB9ZMM
R.J. Teets
610 N Henrietta St Apt 306
Effingham IL 62401

Call Sign: N0NOD
David M Walterscheid
202 N Hernrietta St
Effingham IL 62401

Call Sign: KC9JIO
Joshua Jamison
604 N Keller
Effingham IL 62401

Call Sign: KB9WUS
Mary J Tucker
15805 N Lakeview Pl
Effingham IL 62401

Call Sign: KC9HGH
Effington County Search &
Rescue
15805 N Lakeview Pl
Effingham IL 624016279

Call Sign: K9EFF
Effington County Search &
Rescue
15805 N Lakeview Pl
Effingham IL 624016279

Call Sign: KC9HHN
Kevin W Bullard
16111 N Lynn Acres
Effingham IL 62401

Call Sign: KB9QGS
Stephanie A Barker
1018 N Martin
Effingham IL 62401

Call Sign: KC9MBS
Andrew S Barker
1018 N Martin St
Effingham IL 62401

Call Sign: W9BZP
Jacob W Ousley
1113 N Martin St
Effingham IL 62240

Call Sign: N9TXD
T Keith Bishop
906 N Oceola
Effingham IL 62401

Call Sign: KB9HWF
T Kent Bishop

906 N Oceola St
Effingham IL 62401

Call Sign: WS9Y
Larry W Braun
910 N Oceola St
Effingham IL 62401

Call Sign: KB9IYK
Melissa L Jeffries
905 N Pembroke
Effingham IL 62401

Call Sign: KB9QHA
Benny D Bourland
906 N Pembroke
Effingham IL 624013258

Call Sign: KB9IYM
Fred A Katz
1028 N Penguin St
Effingham IL 62401

Call Sign: N9YQH
Lawrence A Wolfert
2301 N Raney
Effingham IL 62401

Call Sign: KC9CHV
Josaphine N Riley
14123 N S Shore Dr
Effingham IL 62401

Call Sign: KG9GK
Larry E Riley
14123 N South Shore Dr
Effingham IL 62401

Call Sign: N9UFQ
Kenneth O Walker
1014 N Taylor St
Effingham IL 62401

Call Sign: KC9MBT
Alex C Jeffries
808 Park Hills Dr
Effingham IL 62401

Call Sign: KB9SSR

Brad E Jeffries
808 Park Hills Dr
Effingham IL 62401

Call Sign: KB9TCJ
Brian D Jeffries
808 Park Hills Dr
Effingham IL 62401

Call Sign: N9KDJ
David M Jeffries
808 Park Hills Dr
Effingham IL 62401

Call Sign: KC9SPB
Alex A Wolters
1002 Penguin St
Effingham IL 62401

Call Sign: KB9EKI
Morris E Webb
2000 Red Oak St
Effingham IL 62401

Call Sign: WB9UUQ
Charles W Medlin
605 Richland Ave
Effingham IL 62401

Call Sign: K9PCT
John T Fennessey
14 Rollin Hills Blvd
Effingham IL 62401

Call Sign: W9JWW
Vernon F Thompson
1403 S 4th St
Effingham IL 62401

Call Sign: KB9FNF
John D Sills
1510 S 4th St
Effingham IL 62401

Call Sign: WA9M
H Edwin Lightfoot
308 S 5th 5
Effingham IL 62401

Call Sign: N9NJN
Jeffrey W Hardig
709 S Cherry
Effingham IL 62401

Call Sign: WB9TXZ
John F Fisher
6 S Circle Dr
Effingham IL 624015059

Call Sign: KC9SPD
William B Bennett
605 S Linden St
Effingham IL 62401

Call Sign: WI9B
Russell D Thomas
706 S Park
Effingham IL 62401

Call Sign: KF9LW
Jo A Thomas
706 S Park St
Effingham IL 62401

Call Sign: AA9YT
Jo A Thomas
706 S Park St
Effingham IL 62401

Call Sign: KB9QGT
Stephanie A Leftwich
706 S Park St
Effingham IL 62401

Call Sign: KB9CSV
James W Wood
1104 S Willow
Effingham IL 62401

Call Sign: N9YJY
Jerrod L Wood
809 S Willow St
Effingham IL 62401

Call Sign: AA9DB
Robert L Scybert
100 Santa Barbara
Effingham IL 62401

Call Sign: KC9BGH
Jack L Ellis
1006 Shiloh Ave
Effingham IL 62401

Call Sign: KC9QXS
Jack L Ellis
1006 Shiloh Ave
Effingham IL 62401

Call Sign: KB9HUV
Kenneth G Larimore
2407 Veterans Dr
Effingham IL 62401

Call Sign: NG9O
Larry D Wade
506 W Clinton Ave
Effingham IL 62401

Call Sign: KB9YJV
Amanda M Fleshner
705.5 W Edgar
Effingham IL 62401

Call Sign: KB9YJU
David A Craig
705 W Edgar Apt 2
Effingham IL 62401

Call Sign: N9XWJ
Justin C Thomas
810 W Flamingo
Effingham IL 62401

Call Sign: KB9VKR
Vernon L Eskew
304 W Hawthorne Ave
Effingham IL 62401

Call Sign: KC9MBR
Gary L West Sr
907 W St Anthony Ave
Effingham IL 62401

Call Sign: KB9HUL
Moris D Sowers
206 W Wabash Ave

Effingham IL 62401

Call Sign: KB9VKS
Justin R Dalton
306 W Wernsing
Effingham IL 62401

Call Sign: WA9VGW
Arthur P Hinson
1018 Wenthe
Effingham IL 62401

Call Sign: KB9BKD
Annette M Loy
Effingham IL 62401

Call Sign: WB9SNK
Teddy G Keller
Effingham IL 62401

Call Sign: KB9ZMN
Chris H Kinkelaar
Effingham IL 62401

Call Sign: KB9WUJ
Gary L Le May
Effingham IL 62401

Call Sign: KB9HVY
K Darlene Bishop
Effingham IL 62401

Call Sign: KB9WUK
Patricia J Parmly
Effingham IL 62401

Call Sign: K9UXZ
National Trail ARC Inc
Effingham IL 62401

Call Sign: N9MPL
Kathryn A Thomas
Effingham IL 624010352

FCC Amateur Radio Licenses in Egan

Call Sign: KB9WOA
Jeremy W Davis

4899 Spielman Rd
Egan IL 61047

FCC Amateur Radio Licenses in El Paso

Call Sign: KB9KXU
Hollie R Kaufman
Rr 2 Box 182
El Paso IL 61738

Call Sign: KA9IRI
George E Thomas
Rr 1 Box 49
El Paso IL 61738

Call Sign: N9WFT
Daniel T Rhodes
79 E 1st St
El Paso IL 617381142

Call Sign: KC0VHN
Ronald A Cooper Jr
295 E 3rd
El Paso IL 61738

Call Sign: N9NEX
Jerry S Gunnerson
403 E 5th St
El Paso IL 61738

Call Sign: N9CAJ
Allen C Drake
561 Fairway Dr
El Paso IL 61738

Call Sign: KB9CDE
Rita M Drake
561 Fairway Dr
El Paso IL 61738

Call Sign: KC9HBG
Sharon L Long
14980 Kappa Rd
El Paso IL 61738

Call Sign: KC9GZK
Thomas D Long
14980 Kappa Rd

El Paso IL 61738

Call Sign: KB9VTD
David W Buck
301 Lovejoy
El Paso IL 61738

Call Sign: N9DOA
Eric E Lowery
98 N Walnut
El Paso IL 61738

Call Sign: KA9BLL
Lee A Bonos II
266 S Chestnut St
El Paso IL 617381586

FCC Amateur Radio Licenses in Eldena

Call Sign: KC9DEY
Michael A Starr
1281 Ash St
Eldena IL 61324

FCC Amateur Radio Licenses in Eldorado

Call Sign: KA9QVQ
Teresa E Moye
1321 1st St
Eldorado IL 62930

Call Sign: KA9LOZ
Timothy W Moye
1321 1st St
Eldorado IL 62930

Call Sign: N9TWG
Allan C Ninness
865 Bourland Rd
Eldorado IL 62930

Call Sign: KB9VBX
Patricia L Grant
704 Bramlet
Eldorado IL 62930

Call Sign: W9AKW

Gayland W Grant
704 Bramlet
Eldorado IL 62930

Call Sign: KC9VOK
Bryce L Winters
709 Bramlet St
Eldorado IL 62930

Call Sign: KB9QAP
Francis E Mc Claughry
708 Briddick St
Eldorado IL 629302416

Call Sign: KC9AYC
Jerry R Givan
603 Bruner St
Eldorado IL 62930

Call Sign: W9YFA
Robert E Carter
1701 Burnett St
Eldorado IL 62930

Call Sign: WB9SPA
Brittain A Blair
910 College Rd
Eldorado IL 62930

Call Sign: KB9EDI
Ronald M Bauer
1862 Fisk St
Eldorado IL 629302123

Call Sign: WB9NVW
Henry E Walters
2504 Glenwood
Eldorado IL 62930

Call Sign: KS0V
Larry E Davies
100 Grayson Rd
Eldorado IL 62930

Call Sign: KB9YRN
Lee E Allen
1901 Illinois Ave
Eldorado IL 62930

Call Sign: KB9KWR
Mark A Fairburn
1912 Jackson St
Eldorado IL 629301515

Call Sign: KC9TMA
Dale A Broadway
1705 Jefferson
Eldorado IL 62930

Call Sign: KB9LOX
Edward L Baugher
1101 Lincoln St
Eldorado IL 62930

Call Sign: KB9BNM
R J Tolbert
2100 Locust St
Eldorado IL 62930

Call Sign: KB9YWJ
George H Mahaffey
115 Mahaffey Rd
Eldorado IL 62930

Call Sign: WA9JBC
Curtis L Healy
2304 N Main St
Eldorado IL 62930

Call Sign: KB9QIL
Ruth E Murphy
2110 Old Broughton Rd
Eldorado IL 62930

Call Sign: KB9QIM
Terry W Murphy
2110 Old Broughton Rd
Eldorado IL 629302012

Call Sign: N9WFL
Harold E Mills
1380 Perkins Rd
Eldorado IL 62930

Call Sign: N9ZCM
Patricia S Mills
1380 Perkins Rd
Eldorado IL 62930

Call Sign: KB9YRO
Matthew D Whyte
3680 Raleigh Rd
Eldorado IL 62930

Call Sign: KC9MEV
Derak J Rash
4190 Raleigh Rd
Eldorado IL 62930

Call Sign: KB9JKB
Kathleen J Tompkins
1963 Roosevelt Ave
Eldorado IL 62930

Call Sign: N9JJI
Tommy W Tompkins
1963 Roosevelt Ave
Eldorado IL 62930

Call Sign: N9WUE
Ronnie D Wallace
Eldorado IL 62930

Call Sign: KC9MDP
David A Morris
Eldorado IL 62930

Call Sign: WB9SKB
Gayland W Grant
Eldorado IL 62930

**FCC Amateur Radio
Licenses in Elizabeth**

Call Sign: KF9KP
Thomas R Veysey
4 Galena Oaks Dr
Elizabeth IL 61028

Call Sign: KC9EBX
Kim D Griffith
64 Galena Oaks Dr
Eliabeth IL 610280069

Call Sign: KA9PPP
Lawrence J Doyle
313 Vine St

Elizabeth IL 61028

Call Sign: N9ZLP
Roy R Havens
317 W Sycamore St
Elizabeth IL 61028

FCC Amateur Radio Licenses in Elizabethtown

Call Sign: WB9KHY
Bill L Bryan
Rr 1 Box 146
Elizabethtown IL 62931

FCC Amateur Radio Licenses in Elkart

Call Sign: KC9BKH
Justin L Camp
967 700 St
Elkhart IL 62634

Call Sign: KB9EPA
James B Wallace
103 Lanterman St
Elkhart IL 62634

FCC Amateur Radio Licenses in Elkville

Call Sign: N9MWW
David A Mc Clure
Rt 1 Box 109
Elkville IL 62932

Call Sign: KB9OTL
Janice E Lestz
1003 Martie Rd
Elkville IL 62932

Call Sign: N9QQS
Luna I Lestz
1003 Martie Rd
Elkville IL 629322615

Call Sign: KF9UD
Moses J Lestz Sr
1003 Martie Rd

Elkville IL 629322615

Call Sign: WD9AHL
Mark B Hill
Elkville IL 62932

Call Sign: KT9C
Marvin L Hill
Elkville IL 62932

Call Sign: KB9UZU
Cindy L Pierce
Elkville IL 629320475

FCC Amateur Radio Licenses in Ellery

Call Sign: KA9EHO
Earl Grieb
Rr 1 Box 152
Ellery IL 62833

Call Sign: KA9OPY
Irene Fisher
Rt 1 Box 153
Ellery IL 62833

FCC Amateur Radio Licenses in Elliott

Call Sign: K9QDM
Charles R Simmons
301 N Main
Elliott IL 60933

FCC Amateur Radio Licenses in Ellsworth

Call Sign: KB9GUL
Stanley E Nelson
Rr 1 Box 15
Ellsworth IL 61737

Call Sign: N9ZVK
Dennis C Stott
Ellsworth IL 61737

Call Sign: N9ZVL
Jacob Stott

Ellsworth IL 61737

FCC Amateur Radio Licenses in Elmwood

Call Sign: KE9IU
Leonard C Glenn
501 E Main
Elmwood IL 61529

Call Sign: N9KUI
Kurt F Whais
6104 N Eden Rd
Elmwood IL 61529

Call Sign: K9FUR
Richard W Meredith
202 N Laurel St
Elmwood IL 61529

Call Sign: W9NVX
Walter D Blackford
1610 N Stone School Rd R 2
Elmwood IL 61529

Call Sign: N9KDS
Gale R Stafford
Elmwood IL 61529

FCC Amateur Radio Licenses in Elsah

Call Sign: KC9NVL
Bryce D Wampole
24175 Crescent Dr
Elsah IL 62028

Call Sign: KC9DYY
Angela D Hartshorn
12772 Deer Trl
Elsah IL 62028

Call Sign: KC9HCT
National ARS
12772 Deer Trl Ln
Elsah IL 62028

Call Sign: WD4SAR
National ARS

12772 Deer Trl Ln
Elsah IL 62028

Call Sign: KC9DDZ
Christopher J Hartshorn
12772 Deer Trl Ln
Elsah IL 62028

Call Sign: WD9RSQ
Christopher J Hartshorn
12772 Deer Trl Ln
Elsah IL 62028

Call Sign: KC9QLL
Robin Burns
1 Dogwood Ln
Elsah IL 62028

Call Sign: N9PLD
Robin S Burns
1 Dogwood Ln
Elsah IL 62028

Call Sign: KC9LOG
Glenn L Ford
25578 Elsah Hills Dr
Elsah IL 62028

Call Sign: AB9TF
Glenn L Ford
25578 Elsah Hills Dr
Elsah IL 62028

Call Sign: KC9GEE
Nicholas H Johnson
25782 Elsah Hills Dr
Elsah IL 62028

Call Sign: KC9GED
Chris B Churchill
1 Maybeck Pl
Elsah IL 62028

Call Sign: KC9JZV
Everett L Brown
1 Maybeck Pl
Elsah IL 62028

Call Sign: W9ELB

Everett L Brown
1 Maybeck Pl
Elsah IL 62028

Call Sign: KC9JQH
Gideon E Setordzie
1 Maybeck Pl
Elsah IL 62028

Call Sign: KC9KGX
Schuyler P Onderdonk
1 Maybeck Pl
Elsah IL 62028

Call Sign: KC9JYO
Alison J Reid
1 Maybeck Pl
Elsah IL 62028

Call Sign: KC9JYN
Byron A Walter
1 Maybeck Pl
Elsah IL 62028

Call Sign: KC9JQI
Feli Zulhendri
1 Maybeck Pl
Elsah IL 62028

Call Sign: KC9JQJ
Iain P Bruce
1 Maybeck Pl
Elsah IL 62028

Call Sign: N9YN
Principia Amateur Wireless
Society
1 Maybeck Pl
Elsah IL 62028

Call Sign: KC9KGY
Justin A Wayne
1 Maybeck Pl 337
Elsah IL 62028

Call Sign: KC9KHA
Pathik Evan Bollaidlaw
1 Maybeck Pl 436
Elsah IL 62028

Call Sign: KC9KGZ
Drew Safronoff
1 Maybeck Pl 794
Elsah IL 62028

Call Sign: KC9GEC
Oli Jobe
1 Maybeck Pl 90
Elsah IL 62028

Call Sign: KC9GEG
Bryce R Littlejohn
1 Maybeck Pl 9777
Elsah IL 62028

Call Sign: KA9ZRX
George R Dean Sr
8 Mill St Box 3
Elsah IL 62028

Call Sign: KB9QVI
Linda J Cornell
2 Oakwood
Elsah IL 62028

Call Sign: WA9NYN
Principia College ARC
2 Oakwood Dr
Elsah IL 62028

Call Sign: KC0THU
Linda E Cunningham
7 Oakwood Dr
Elsah IL 62028

Call Sign: KC9JYP
Thomas H Fuller
11640 Piasa Dr
Elsah IL 62028

Call Sign: N9UF
Thomas H Fuller
11640 Piasa Dr
Elsah IL 62028

Call Sign: KC9INN
Sara M Brown
11680 Piasa Dr

Elsah IL 62028

Call Sign: KC9BZA
Esmeralda N Yitamben
Principia College 777
Elsah IL 62028

Call Sign: KA8REY
William B Hoey
Elsah IL 62028

Call Sign: KA9ZQY
Robin S Burns
Elsah IL 62028

Call Sign: KB9QVJ
Arno S List
Elsah IL 62028

FCC Amateur Radio Licenses in Emden

Call Sign: KC9BJV
Edward R Houchins
675 2650th St
Emden IL 62635

FCC Amateur Radio Licenses in Energy

Call Sign: KC9BBP
David T Williams
317 E Alexander
Energy IL 62933

Call Sign: W9ALA
Tim N Griffith
118 McGinnis St
Energy IL 62933

Call Sign: KB9UYP
David E Mason
401 Shannon Ave
Energy IL 62933

Call Sign: KC9HDF
Anthony J Wilcheski IV
Energy IL 62933

Call Sign: K9SAA
Paul T Hillman
Energy IL 62933

FCC Amateur Radio Licenses in Enfield

Call Sign: WD9EML
Gerald J Van Paassen
301 Gowdy St
Enfield IL 62835

Call Sign: KA9MDH
Wanda D Van Paassen
301 Gowdy St
Enfield IL 62835

Call Sign: KA9IDB
Benjamin R Gates
302 N Brockett
Enfield IL 62835

Call Sign: KA9IDM
J B Gates
302 N Brockett St
Enfield IL 628350289

Call Sign: KA9LHS
James C Johnson
406 W Johnson St
Enfield IL 62835

Call Sign: KB9GPT
Ruth J Gates
Enfield IL 62835

FCC Amateur Radio Licenses in Equality

Call Sign: K9IRB
Freeman B Dempsey
292 E Jackson St
Equality IL 62934

Call Sign: KA9DTS
Tenney D Tarlton
4725 Eagle Creek Rd
Equality IL 62934

Call Sign: KC9MFU
Janet M Cremeens
Equality IL 62954

FCC Amateur Radio Licenses in Erie

Call Sign: KC9TMQ
John T Wirth
29572 E 1900th St
Erie IL 61250

Call Sign: WA9YOV
David P Verkruysse
1009 Main St
Erie IL 61250

FCC Amateur Radio Licenses in Essex

Call Sign: KB9OFH
Michael P Janczak
120 E Main St
Essex IL 60935

Call Sign: KB9SGJ
Richard A Kennedy
380 Pine
Essex IL 609350235

Call Sign: N9NMF
Charles L Reardanz
311 S East St
Essex IL 60935

FCC Amateur Radio Licenses in Eureka

Call Sign: N9FIR
Susan M Stafford
Rr 2 Box 495
Eureka IL 61530

Call Sign: K9IHF
Frank T Supan
Rt 3 Box 85 E G
Eureka IL 61530

Call Sign: N9LOB

Randy R Duncan
222 Carolyn Ln Apt 24
Eureka IL 61530

Call Sign: KC9LNM
Michael B Brady
901 Cedar Ct
Eureka IL 61530

Call Sign: WX9MDT
Michael B Brady
901 Cedar Ct
Eureka IL 61530

Call Sign: N9JDD
Dennis L Schumacher
1424 Church Rd
Eureka IL 61530

Call Sign: W9CJX
John W Green
1466 Church Rd
Eureka IL 615309440

Call Sign: N8MY
Michael J Yonka
1185 Country Rd 600 N
Eureka IL 61530

Call Sign: KC9ICC
Kevin R Garman
1478 CR 1200 N
Eureka IL 61530

Call Sign: KC9RNF
Bryce Wieland
1460 CR 475 N
Eureka IL 61530

Call Sign: KB9YCA
Erik J Van Etten
410 E Bullock
Eureka IL 61530

Call Sign: KB9TBP
Chad T Vanetten
410 E Bullock
Eureka IL 61530

Call Sign: AI9B
James M Ulrich
707 E Bullock St
Eureka IL 61530

Call Sign: K9EAR
James R Teel
310 E James St
Eureka IL 61530

Call Sign: N9VNO
Gary L Adams
409 E James St
Eureka IL 61530

Call Sign: KB9SE
Larry G Fillman
804 N Main St
Eureka IL 61530

Call Sign: KI5AU
Fred M Kamp
700 N Main St Apt 254
Eureka IL 61530

Call Sign: N9JDC
Dale R Schumacher
1616 S Adams Rd
Eureka IL 61530

Call Sign: N9CJN
Leon E Fenwick
502 S Henry
Eureka IL 61530

Call Sign: KB9CPA
Keith E Knepp
606 S Main St
Eureka IL 61530

Call Sign: N9AGM
Robert L Ulrich
902 S Vennum
Eureka IL 61530

Call Sign: K9VGC
Alan R Gerber
208 S Walnut St
Eureka IL 61530

Call Sign: N9JHL
Darrell E Dies
106 W Burton
Eureka IL 61530

Call Sign: KA9WEI
Charles E Bush
505 W Crestwood Dr
Eureka IL 615301319

Call Sign: KF9HC
Richard W Frank
610 W Cruger Apt 115
Eureka IL 615300128

Call Sign: KB9PFU
Stephen M Bock
503 W Sunset Dr
Eureka IL 61530

Call Sign: KA9KKR
Mavis E Herbst
505 W Sunset Dr
Eureka IL 61530

Call Sign: WA9DOD
Mary E Hayward
Eureka IL 61530

Call Sign: KB9LNJ
Adam L Schenk
Eureka IL 61530

**FCC Amateur Radio
Licenses in Evansville**

Call Sign: N9YMS
Charles A Kisro
7092 Buttercreek Rd
Evansville IL 62242

Call Sign: N9LUC
Paul K Joiner
201 Cedar St
Evansville IL 62242

Call Sign: KB9MAF
Nick W Schoenberger

1001 Gross St
Evansville IL 62242

Call Sign: K9MEH
James H Malott
8341 SR 3
Evansville IL 62242

**FCC Amateur Radio
Licenses in Ewing**

Call Sign: KB9UYQ
Dale E Wilson
17720 Logcabin Rd
Ewing IL 62836

Call Sign: N0NGK
Thomas J Satterfield
18157 Tick Ridge Rd
Ewing IL 62836

Call Sign: WB9PJX
Gordon G Pryor
31 W 3rd St
Ewing IL 62836

Call Sign: KA9TQH
Darell D Wyatt
408 W Main St
Ewing IL 62836

**FCC Amateur Radio
Licenses in Exeter**

Call Sign: KC9UZI
William R Kemp
61 Center St
Exeter IL 62621

**FCC Amateur Radio
Licenses in Fairbury**

Call Sign: W9JZE
Kenneth E Headley
100 E Amber Dr
Fairbury IL 61739

Call Sign: KC9FWK
Robert C Nussbaum

---

307 E Hickory St
Fairbury IL 61739

Call Sign: WD9CKO
Gene A Denick
308 N 2nd St
Fairbury IL 61739

**FCC Amateur Radio
Licenses in Fairfield**

Call Sign: KC9CBO
Lawrence E Lindner Jr
6 Ash St
Fairfield IL 62837

Call Sign: WA9IZV
Len K Mason
Rr 1 Box 119
Fairfield IL 62837

Call Sign: KC9KLQ
Patrick J Workman
Rr 4 Box 134
Fairfield IL 62837

Call Sign: KB9RQU
Larry S Anderson
Rt 5 Box 377
Fairfield IL 62837

Call Sign: KB9JKA
Steve R Barbre
Rr 3 Box 433
Fairfield IL 62837

Call Sign: KB9RQY
Wesley C Weber
Rr 4 Box 55
Fairfield IL 62837

Call Sign: KC9CBQ
Aaron W Vandengraph
Rt 4 Box 554 C
Fairfield IL 62837

Call Sign: KC9MIX
Ben A Weedon
Rr 2 Box 617

Fairfield IL 62837

Call Sign: K9IT
Ray L Fansler
Rr 3 Box 878
Fairfield IL 62837

Call Sign: KE9HT
Bradley J Sheraden
1509 Cumberland Dr
Fairfield IL 62837

Call Sign: N9JKL
Arthur E Nation
308 E Center St 6
Fairfield IL 62837

Call Sign: KC9LVD
Chris D Miller
902 E Main
Fairfield IL 62837

Call Sign: KC9CBN
Melvin G Kemplen
1203 Il Ave
Fairfield IL 62837

Call Sign: KB9RQV
Jeffrey R Jake
710 Laurel
Fairfield IL 62837

Call Sign: KB9RQW
Tommy A Windland
601 NE 4th
Fairfield IL 62837

Call Sign: N9YPK
Nolan C Warren
708 NE 4th St
Fairfield IL 62837

Call Sign: KA9EEX
Jerry D Gill
510 NW 9th
Fairfield IL 62837

Call Sign: K9GKR
John W Dilges

407 SE 3rd St
Fairfield IL 62837

Call Sign: KB9KVR
Floyd J Harris
514 SE 3rd St
Fairfield IL 62837

Call Sign: KC9QJO
Galen A Esmon
500 SE 4th St
Fairfield IL 62837

Call Sign: KB9LPD
Missy S Harris
506 Shoreway Dr
Fairfield IL 62837

Call Sign: WA9BVA
Orville D Clagg
806 Summer St
Fairfield IL 62837

Call Sign: KC9TON
Wayne County E M A
505 SW 10th St
Fairfield IL 62837

Call Sign: N9UIF
Andrew D Miller
205 Union St
Fairfield IL 62837

Call Sign: KC9RCR
Barry J Shreve
113 W College St
Fairfield IL 62837

Call Sign: WA9MBQ
Marshall H Tucker
1000 W Main
Fairfield IL 62837

Call Sign: N9QJL
Jeffery A Miller
403 Wilson Ave
Fairfield IL 62837

Call Sign: KB9JMM

Ivan E Holler
505 Windsor Ln
Fairfield IL 62837

Call Sign: K9UE
Roy L Fansler
Fairfield IL 62837

Call Sign: K9IQY
Bradley F Dye
Fairfield IL 62837

Call Sign: KB9BZY
Bruce A Stephens
Fairfield IL 62837

FCC Amateur Radio Licenses in Fairmont City

Call Sign: N9TWP
Richard A Boyer
5504 Delmar
Fairmont City IL 62201

Call Sign: KC9IRM
Scott E Penny
2949 N 63rd St
Fairmont City IL 62201

FCC Amateur Radio Licenses in Fairmount

Call Sign: KB9KUE
Robert D Redmond
Rr 1 Box 330
Fairmount IL 61841

Call Sign: KA9BUA
Olive J Lomax
14700 N 875 E Rd
Fairmount IL 618416311

Call Sign: WD9IOL
Oscar D Lomax
14700 N 875 E Rd
Fairmount IL 618416311

Call Sign: N0CUJ
Tony A Nash

13806 N 920 E Rd
Fairmount IL 61841

Call Sign: WD9AFI
Darold J Street
Fairmount IL 618410151

FCC Amateur Radio Licenses in Fairview

Call Sign: N9WYV
Edward E Cozart
28456 N Co Hwy 16
Fairview IL 61432

Call Sign: KB9LLX
David A Anderson
Fairview IL 61432

FCC Amateur Radio Licenses in Fairview Heights

Call Sign: KA9RFA
Edward T Childers
10 Alice Ln
Fairview Heights IL 62208

Call Sign: KA9GYU
James C Stinnett
115 Bountiful Dr
Fairview Heights IL
622082403

Call Sign: KE0SG
Allen L Pennington
223 Brittany Dr
Fairview Heights IL 62208

Call Sign: KC9TWB
Adam J Gaines
9918 Bunkum Rd
Fairview Heights IL 62208

Call Sign: KC9TWC
Sandra L Gaines
9918 Bunkum Rd
Fairview Heights IL 62208

Call Sign: KB9UEF

Louis R Stark
10 Carlin Dr
Fairview Heights IL
622082301

Call Sign: KE9BV
Jeffrey A Nettleton
70 Circle Dr
Fairview Heights IL
622083303

Call Sign: N9SZI
Albert W Mester Jr
175 Circle Dr
Fairview Heights IL 62208

Call Sign: W3LSA
John B Boysha Sr
11 Concord Dr
Fairview Heights IL 62208

Call Sign: N9YMU
Marilyn R Thornton
11 Countryside Ln
Fairview Heights IL 62208

Call Sign: KC9QHM
Jeffrey M Smith
224 Crystal Ln
Fairview Heights IL 62208

Call Sign: KA9HNT
Michael J Petz
7 Deerwood Trl
Fairview Heights IL 62208

Call Sign: KC9RZU
David A Butler
637 Deppe Ln
Fairview Heights IL 62208

Call Sign: W9PRX
Vernie N Redmon Jr
105 Durley Rd
Fairview Heights IL
622083766

Call Sign: KK9N
Kenneth E Norris

5406 East Dr
Fairview Heights IL 62208

Call Sign: KA9IML
Mary E Neal
205 Edding Ln
Fairview Heights IL 62208

Call Sign: KA9IMM
Michael A Neal
205 Edding Ln
Fairview Heights IL 62208

Call Sign: KE9UV
William Swacil Jr
212 Elm Dr
Fairview Heights IL 62208

Call Sign: KC9HIW
Karl A Gee
213 Elm Dr
Fairview Heights IL 62208

Call Sign: KC9JCS
Eneida Gee
213 Elm Dr
Fairview Heights IL 62208

Call Sign: KC9HIV
Matthew Gee
213 Elm St
Fairview Heights IL 62208

Call Sign: N9LIX
Larry E Kreissler
28 Fairview Dr
Fairview Heights IL 62208

Call Sign: KA9IKM
Beatrice L Miller
9165 Forest Dr
Fairview Heights IL 62208

Call Sign: K9CNB
Curtis N Blake
872 Foxgrove Dr
Fairview Heights IL 62208

Call Sign: WD9GSP

Sidney E Hepp
108 Joseph Dr
Fairview Heights IL 62208

Call Sign: WA9IUF
William S Keller
313 Joseph Dr
Fairview Heights IL 62208

Call Sign: KB9TMD
Brian S Schifferdecker
521 Joseph Dr
Fairview Heights IL 62208

Call Sign: WB9DRR
William V Bell
31 Judy Ln
Fairview Heights IL 62208

Call Sign: N9TIL
John W Cooper
9 Keelan Dr
Fairview Heights IL 62208

Call Sign: KC9KMT
Lionel L Chambers
405 Kim Dr
Fairview Heights IL 62208

Call Sign: WA0DDQ
Charles V Peterson
413 Kim Dr
Fairview Heights IL 62208

Call Sign: WB9TGB
Malcolm G Anson
100 Lakeland Hills Dr
Fairview Heights IL 62208

Call Sign: KA0CTH
Robert E Sapp
505 Lemans Way
Fairview Heights IL 62208

Call Sign: N9NKA
Edward S Omelson
14 Leo Dr
Fairview Heights IL 62208

Call Sign: KB9QVM
Joseph V Vaughn
457 Liberty Rd
Fairview Heights IL 62208

Call Sign: W9EKQ
Earl J Chapman
10303 Lincoln Trl
Fairview Heights IL 62208

Call Sign: KB9MYD
Robert S Chapman
31 Marilyn Cir
Fairview Heights IL 62208

Call Sign: W9EKQ
Chapman ARS
31 Marilyn Cir
Fairview Heights IL 62208

Call Sign: KB9PTG
Chapman ARS
31 Marilyn Cir
Fairview Heights IL 62208

Call Sign: N9IPM
John L Fischer
228 Merriweather Ln
Fairview Heights IL 62208

Call Sign: KG9PP
Michael W Stephens
221 Monticello Pl
Fairview Heights IL
622081320

Call Sign: KB9SNI
Stacie L Stephens
221 Monticello Pl
Fairview Heights IL
622081320

Call Sign: KC9TPD
Alexander W Grudzinski
21 Mt Vernon Dr
Fairview Heights IL 62208

Call Sign: KC9LCG
Curtis N Blake

17 N Brook Cir Apt 32
Fairview Heights IL 62208

Call Sign: W9MLT
Hillory W Still
9750 N Holy Cross Rd
Fairview Heights IL 62208

Call Sign: K9EID
Robert G Heil
5800 N Illinois
Fairview Heights IL 62208

Call Sign: KB0WIP
Angela D Turner
215 N Point Rd
Fairview Heights IL 62208

Call Sign: KI0HZ
James E Turner
215 N Point Rd
Fairview Heights IL 62208

Call Sign: KC9ICB
Sean P Bell
64 Pasadena Dr
Fairview Heights IL 62208

Call Sign: KB9WO
Leslie J Spainhower
11 Peachtree Ln
Fairview Heights IL 62208

Call Sign: KC9DHT
Fred R Hensler Jr
27 Peachtree Ln
Fairview Heights IL 62208

Call Sign: KC9TWF
Gwendolyn M Musick
230 Pleasant Ridge Rd
Fairview Heights IL 62208

Call Sign: KT4GG
Barry L Johnson
9604 Richfield Rd
Fairview Heights IL 62208

Call Sign: WA9FLX

Richard F Wohlschlag
117 Richmond Dr
Fairview Heights IL 62208

Call Sign: KA9MPY
Erick J Tejkowski
319 Ryan Dr
Fairview Heights IL 62208

Call Sign: W9CPJ
Erick J Tejkowski
319 Ryan Dr
Fairview Heights IL 62208

Call Sign: N2RXH
Robert H Benton III
109 S Embassy Dr
Fairview Heights IL 62208

Call Sign: N9OQK
William D Dusenbery
10 Sherry
Fairview Heights IL 62208

Call Sign: KA9ZSJ
Sherry S Gatewood
132 St Clair Dr
Fairview Heights IL 62208

Call Sign: KC5IBZ
Orin R Champlin III
505 St Clair Rd
Fairview Heights IL 62208

Call Sign: KC9JCP
Karol A Walker
1000 St Clair Rd
Fairview Heights IL 62208

Call Sign: N9WWH
Robert J Whitcomb
115 Stacy Dr
Fairview Heights IL 62208

Call Sign: KB9PNP
Robert H Pinkerton III
8 Susan Ct
Fairview Heights IL 62208

Call Sign: KC9RUJ
Judy M Allen
1722 Sycamore
Fairview Heights IL 62208

Call Sign: KC9RUK
Randy R Allen
1722 Sycamore
Fairview Heights IL 62208

Call Sign: KB9ZMQ
Paul D Jackson
111 C Union Hill Rd
Fairview Heights IL 62208

Call Sign: KB9UEE
Paul S Schlachter
7 Voss Dr
Fairview Heights IL 62208

Call Sign: KA9IED
C Edward Way
9119 Wedgewood Dr
Fairview Heights IL 62208

Call Sign: K9WAY
C Edward Way
9119 Wedgewood Dr
Fairview Heights IL 62208

Call Sign: K6QKL
Charles W Hines
4 Weinel Dr
Fairview Heights IL
622081709

Call Sign: KC9SKI
Matthew J Rygelski
713 Willow Spring Hill Dr
Fairview Heights IL 62208

Call Sign: KC9MYR
Sonia Chavez
22 Wilshire Dr
Fairview Heights IL 62208

Call Sign: KC9JDJ
Cesar D Chavez
22 Wilshire Dr

Fairview Heights IL 62208

Call Sign: KA9HVI
Ronnie J Boesch Dc
17 Windmill Ct
Fairview Heights IL 62208

Call Sign: KC9NAX
William V Mcdonald
7345 Wolf Lake Ct
Fairview Heights IL 62208

Call Sign: KD0MZY
James D Egbert
264 Wonchester Pl
Fairview Heights IL 62208

Call Sign: N9UCQ
Frederick W Clark Jr
Fairview Heights IL 62208

Call Sign: WA3TDR
Jerry J Coombs
Fairview Heights IL
622080264

**FCC Amateur Radio
Licenses in Farina**

Call Sign: KB9YRQ
James R Mahon
Rt 2 Box 140
Farina IL 62838

Call Sign: KB9HUN
Douglas T Aderman
Rr 2 Box 144
Farina IL 62838

Call Sign: KB9HUM
Julie D Aderman
Rr 2 Box 144
Farina IL 62838

Call Sign: KB9GKZ
Calvin D Byers
Rr 1 Box 218
Farina IL 62838

Call Sign: KB9UYO
Kenneth L Wilson
Rr 1 Box 232
Farina IL 62838

Call Sign: KC9JIY
Bill J Walters
355 Gull Ln
Farina IL 62838

Call Sign: KC9IYM
Allen L Smith
204 Jenny Haley Dr
Farina IL 62838

Call Sign: W9FIU
Roger P Ries
2275 Raven Rd
Farina IL 62838

**FCC Amateur Radio
Licenses in Farmer City**

Call Sign: AB9TQ
Matthew Marcinkowski
25661 Hillcrest Dr
Farmer City IL 61842

Call Sign: KB9GQV
Joshua M Kettleson
718 N John St
Farmer City IL 61842

Call Sign: KB9HCU
Fern N Satterfeal
402 N Plum
Farmer City IL 61842

Call Sign: KC9KFD
Bobbi L Battleson
215 W Market
Farmer City IL 61842

Call Sign: KC9LEJ
Richard A Walsh
504 W Water St
Farmer City IL 618421354

Call Sign: K9PXA

Joseph D Bealor
315 Washington Ave
Farmer City IL 61842

Call Sign: KB9QQV
William J Whitworth
206 5th St
Farmersville IL 62533

Call Sign: KB9ZWV
Joshua J Robb
567 E Court
Farmington IL 61531

Call Sign: WB9AUO
Audrey M Roberts
700 E Court St
Farmington IL 615311359

Call Sign: K9DGX
Leo O Roberts
700 E Court St 18
Farmington IL 61531

Call Sign: N9VIG
Todd C Guidi
290 E Fort St
Farmington IL 61531

Call Sign: N9TYK
Simon J Maccanelli
19449 E Sugar Rd
Farmington IL 61531

Call Sign: K9OTX
Jimmy A Perry
353 E Vine St
Farmington IL 61531

Call Sign: N9QOY
James W Bearden
Gypsy Ln Acres Rr 1
Farmington IL 61531

Call Sign: N9VIE
Jack A Davis

443 Idlewhile
Farmington IL 61531

Call Sign: KB9OSZ
Gordon R Wright
154 N East St
Farmington IL 61531

Call Sign: KC9NBB
Terry L Benedict
43 N Hickory St
Farmington IL 61531

Call Sign: N9PSZ
Carlyle R Bennett
159 N West St
Farmington IL 61531

Call Sign: N9PJX
Linda L Bennett
159 N West St
Farmington IL 61531

Call Sign: N9OBE
Daniel J Hartman
153 S Apple St
Farmington IL 615311404

Call Sign: KB9QFL
Ronald E Pensinger
194 S Main
Farmington IL 61531

Call Sign: KC9IHK
Robert T Sherrod
8310 Turkey Hill Ct
Fenton IL 61251

Call Sign: KB9FCK
Ryan R King
22 Walnut
Ferris IL 62336

Call Sign: KC9HOI
Robin L Plunkett
13438 Mallard Dr
Fieldon IL 62031

Call Sign: N9LJO
Jason R Miles
Rr 1 Box 83
Fillmore IL 62032

Call Sign: KC9GLO
Lori A Hopwood
797 Settles Trl
Fillmore IL 62032

Call Sign: KC9IYK
Amy S Stewart
2996 Wonder Trl
Fillmore IL 62032

Call Sign: KA9BTD
Donald E Whitten
Fillmore IL 62032

Call Sign: KB9KXG
Ralph A Rickett
Fillmore IL 62032

Call Sign: K9JVI
Paul E Enoch
306 E Division
Findlay IL 62534

Call Sign: K9BML
Jean S West
305 E N 2nd
Findlay IL 62534

Call Sign: W9UFR
Robert W West

305 E N 2nd
Findlay IL 62534

Call Sign: WA9WFT
Richard O Waggoner
Box 202 Rr 1
Findlay IL 62534

Call Sign: K9FYY
Clark Mode
320 S Main Box 36
Findlay IL 62534

Call Sign: WC9J
Charles B Doerr
Findlay IL 62534

FCC Amateur Radio Licenses in Fisher

Call Sign: NA8K
Michael M Siegel
701 CR 3300 N
Fisher IL 61843

Call Sign: KC9AGZ
Theresa L Siegel
701 CR 3300 N
Fisher IL 61843

Call Sign: K9INI
Chester L Zehr
3020 CR 400 E
Fisher IL 61843

Call Sign: KC9GBA
Kevin M Douglas
25 Crestview Ct
Fisher IL 61843

Call Sign: KC9RIQ
Jacob K Stockle
6 Elmwood Dr
Fisher IL 61843

Call Sign: K9GJJ
Gerald D Heiser
404 W Sangamon St
Fisher IL 61843

Call Sign: KA9DAU
Patricia A Heiser
404 W Sangamon St Box 425
Fisher IL 61843

Call Sign: WD9DQQ
David D Heiser
Fisher IL 61843

FCC Amateur Radio Licenses in Fithian

Call Sign: K9IDI
James A Rittis
Rt 1 Box 17
Fithian IL 61844

Call Sign: KA9EES
Edward L Dowdy
304 E Webster
Fithian IL 61844

Call Sign: KB9RDU
Lester A Walz
22360 N 620 E Rd
Fithian IL 61844

FCC Amateur Radio Licenses in Flanagan

Call Sign: KA9IRL
Ray G Chumbley
Chumbley
Flanagan IL 617409038

Call Sign: KC9KEI
Charles J Wheeler
400 Goldenrod Dr
Flanagan IL 61740

Call Sign: WA9SGJ
Charles J Wheeler
400 Goldenrod Dr
Flanagan IL 61740

Call Sign: KA9NAQ
David L Peters
105 N Harison

Flanagan IL 61761

Call Sign: KB6ODI
Barbara M Tuftie
200 N Monroe
Flanagan IL 61740

Call Sign: WB9YLI
Arlan D Koopman
103 N Park St Box 553
Flanagan IL 61740

Call Sign: W9UXL
Lois E Zehr
200 N Tina Dr Apt G
Flanagan IL 617400543

Call Sign: W9OQI
Richard S Zehr
200 N Tina Dr Apt G
Flanagan IL 617400543

Call Sign: AA9TN
Paul M Lellelid
18035 N 100 E Rd
Flanagon IL 61740

FCC Amateur Radio Licenses in Flat Rock

Call Sign: N9XUA
John W Brown
202 1st & Pine
Flat Rock IL 62427

Call Sign: KC9TDP
Robert B Baker
Rt 2 Box 175 B
Flat Rock IL 62427

Call Sign: W9BLZ
Robert B Baker
Rt 2 Box 175 B
Flat Rock IL 62427

Call Sign: WD9BOB
Robert D Inboden
11970 E 400th Ave
Flat Rock IL 62427

Call Sign: N6DHD
Richard P Clark
16282 E Lawrence Av
Flat Rock IL 624272800

Call Sign: KB6OXI
Jeannine L Clark
16282 E Lawrence Ave
Flat Rock IL 62427

Call Sign: NF9Y
Don R Weger
Flat Rock IL 62427

FCC Amateur Radio Licenses in Flora

Call Sign: KC9PES
James S Lane
327.5 Austin Ave
Flora IL 62839

Call Sign: KB9MWJ
Martin E Johns
Rr 3 Box 14
Flora IL 62839

Call Sign: KB9PJJ
Gregory S Summerville
1087 Cherry Bark Ln
Flora IL 62839

Call Sign: KB9PBB
Burghard Hanisch
8 Cir Dr Apt 8
Flora IL 62839

Call Sign: KC9EKH
Farrell L Trousdale
560 E North Ave
Flora IL 62839

Call Sign: K9XXX
Farrell L Trousdale
560 E North Ave
Flora IL 62839

Call Sign: KC9AXY

Pamela S Huff
432 East Dr
Flora IL 62839

Call Sign: W9HUF
Pamela S Huff
432 East Dr
Flora IL 62839

Call Sign: K9HUF
Pamela S Huff
432 East Dr
Flora IL 62839

Call Sign: KE9DK
Alan M Huff
432 East Dr
Flora IL 62839

Call Sign: AI9F
Alan M Huff
432 East Dr
Flora IL 62839

Call Sign: KB9MWL
Jerry L Ellis
345 Fair Ave
Flora IL 62839

Call Sign: KC9AGC
Clay County ARC
345 Fair Ave
Flora IL 628392237

Call Sign: KA9NXN
Edith M Colclasure
307 Flora Ave
Flora IL 62839

Call Sign: KA9NXM
Everett E Colclasure
307 Flora Ave
Flora IL 62839

Call Sign: KE7YWP
James W Vastbinder
102 Flora Ave
Flora IL 62839

Call Sign: KC9LSR
Clifford W Smith
893 Meadowview Dr Apt
Flora IL 62839

Call Sign: N9LPX
John M Phillips
7961 Old Hwy 50
Flora IL 628394106

Call Sign: KA9ZRA
Sam L Senters
832 Rio Grand
Flora IL 62839

Call Sign: KA9OZB
Timothy L Frye
1003 S Mill St
Flora IL 62839

Call Sign: WA8WEP
Robert E Greer
111 Shady St
Flora IL 62839

Call Sign: K9IVD
Gerald B Griffith
426 W 6th St
Flora IL 62839

Call Sign: KC9PHK
Michael E Dickerson
539 W 6th St
Flora IL 62839

Call Sign: KB9MWM
Randy P Ferguson
203 W Washington
Flora IL 62839

Call Sign: KE9KS
Steven W Mc Cormick
Flora IL 62839

Call Sign: KB9UQH
Steven D Lewis
Flora IL 629390365

Call Sign: N9TND
Denise R Risley
3125 CR 175 E
Foosland IL 61845

Call Sign: KB9GQW
Samuel J Risley
3125 CR 175E
Foosland IL 61845

Call Sign: K9GKP
Jack B Miller
3406 CR 300 E
Foosland IL 61845

Call Sign: KJ4QXQ
Chris A De Roo
263 CR 3200N
Foosland IL 61845

Call Sign: KD9CB
Philip L Peterson
418 E 80N Rd
Foosland IL 618459503

FCC Amateur Radio Licenses in Forest City

Call Sign: N9VIL
Kevin A Robb
Rr 3 Box 4
Forest City IL 61532

Call Sign: N9OSR
David J Dosier
30547 E CR 1900 N
Forest City IL 61532

Call Sign: KB9MJE
Lisa D Dosier
30547 E CR 1900 N
Forest City IL 61532

Call Sign: KC9QNB
Charles E Meiner
19951 N Bishop Rd

Forest City IL 61532

Call Sign: KA9BDP
Richard J Fuller
500 S Broadway
Forest City IL 61532

Call Sign: N9RJF
Richard J Fuller
500 S Broadway
Forest City IL 61532

FCC Amateur Radio Licenses in Forest

Call Sign: AC9W
Robert L Mayo
318 E Bullard
Forrest IL 617410095

Call Sign: KB9ECL
Aldine R Blunier
101 W North St
Forrest IL 61741

Call Sign: KB9DYW
Scott M Blunier
101 W North St
Forrest IL 61741

FCC Amateur Radio Licenses in Forreston

Call Sign: WB9VEG
Eric C Welch
7289 Columbine Rd
Forreston IL 61030

Call Sign: KC9RMG
Erik E Cavazos Jr
7067 N Mile Rd
Forreston IL 610309221

Call Sign: K9DUG
Carroll M Cooley
411 S Walnut St
Forreston IL 61030

Call Sign: K9EYI

Michael K Meyers
13320 W Springdale Rd
Forreston IL 610309503

Call Sign: KA9ZSL
Irwin J Rysdam
Forreston IL 61030

FCC Amateur Radio Licenses in Forsyth

Call Sign: K9DAG
James R Current
160 Home Ave
Forsyth IL 625350332

Call Sign: KB9PGC
William G Grieve
5223 Navajo Dr
Forsyth IL 62535

Call Sign: N9CKF
Kevin J Adlaf
729 Phillip Cir
Forsyth IL 62535

Call Sign: KB9KNX
Roy H Johnson
452 S Washington St
Forsyth IL 625350405

Call Sign: W9KNX
Roy H Johnson
452 S Washington St
Forsyth IL 625350405

Call Sign: KA9RHP
John D Milliman
402 Tyrone Dr
Forsyth IL 62535

Call Sign: N9OPE
Melenie J Milliman
402 Tyrone Dr
Forsyth IL 62535

Call Sign: KB9OHF
Michael O Lane
1120 W Weaver Rd

Forsyth IL 62535

FCC Amateur Radio Licenses in Fowler

Call Sign: KB9WCY
Jason A Wollbrink
Rri Box99C
Fowler IL 62338

Call Sign: KC9MXD
Terry M Bauer
1460 E 1500th St
Fowler IL 62338

Call Sign: KC0MZV
Pamela D Garner
119 Lakeshore Hills
Fowler IL 62338

Call Sign: KB9TQA
Tammy L Brown
1345 N 1720th Ave
Fowler IL 62338

Call Sign: KB9ZEK
Karen F Taylor
1378 N 1750th Ave
Fowler IL 62338

Call Sign: N9KFT
Karen F Taylor
1378 N 1750th Ave
Fowler IL 62338

Call Sign: N9DT
Darell W Taylor
1378 N 1750th Ave
Fowler IL 62338

Call Sign: KA9HAH
Timothy M Brecht
1271 N 1925th Ave
Fowler IL 62338

Call Sign: KB9SPF
Heather D Sohn
Fowler IL 62338

FCC Amateur Radio Licenses in Franklin

Call Sign: WB9BZX
Allen G Gerberding
383 Gerberding Ln
Franklin IL 626389741

Call Sign: WA9VWM
Harvey M Smith
420 Main St
Franklin IL 62638

FCC Amateur Radio Licenses in Franklin Grove

Call Sign: K9VRL
John Babich Sr
408 E Lincoln Way
Franklin Grove IL 61031

Call Sign: KC9RXA
Frank D Bonnell III
334 Hillside Dr
Franklin Grove IL 610319454

Call Sign: N9EEX
Roy B Conibear
502 N State
Franklin Grove IL 61031

Call Sign: KC9ROZ
Randall L Williams
1486 Rockyford Rd
Franklin Grove IL 61031

Call Sign: KB9MFA
Michael S Albrecht
126 S Walnut St
Franklin Grove IL 61031

Call Sign: WA9MQD
Frank W Faivre
201 W Stone Barn Rd
Franklin Grove IL 61031

Call Sign: KB9OUT
Herbert C White
Franklin Grove IL 61031

FCC Amateur Radio Licenses in Frederick

Call Sign: KC9SKO
Illinois Valley ARC
Rr 1 Box 31 B
Frederick IL 62639

Call Sign: W9ACU
Illinois Valley ARC
Rr 1 Box 31 B
Frederick IL 62639

Call Sign: AA9GK
Keith L Chapman
Rr 1 Box 48
Frederick IL 62639

Call Sign: KB9LZP
Norman E Tritsch
Rr1 Box31B
Frederick IL 62639

FCC Amateur Radio Licenses in Freeburg

Call Sign: N9LVG
Leonard W Schultz
8520 Da Nang Dr
Freeburg IL 62243

Call Sign: KG9IR
Thomas J Cassady Sr
54 Deerfield Ct
Freeburg IL 62243

Call Sign: K9VFA
James T Munn Jr
6200 Douglas Rd
Freeburg IL 62243

Call Sign: KA2BEB
Douglas S Rajski
305 E Meadow Brook Dr
Freeburg IL 62243

Call Sign: KB9QKR
Jeffrey T Vernier

12 Lakeview
Freeburg IL 62243

Call Sign: W9VOU
James E Siemens
208 N Alton
Freeburg IL 62243

Call Sign: WB9CUB
James D Huffman
412 N Railroad
Freeburg IL 62243

Call Sign: WB9TKC
Titania Miller
108 N Vine St
Freeburg IL 62243

Call Sign: WI9Y
Ronald R Humphries
712 Pine Tree Ln
Freeburg IL 62243

Call Sign: N9YAJ
Cynthia D Antry
511 S Edison St
Freeburg IL 62243

Call Sign: WD9HBA
David L Antry Jr
511 S Edison St
Freeburg IL 62243

Call Sign: WA9TZL
Eugene G Kramer
611 S Elizabeth Dr
Freeburg IL 62243

Call Sign: KC9NPN
St Clair Co Amateur Radio
Emergency Aux
Communications Group
611 S Elizabeth Dr
Freeburg IL 62243

Call Sign: KC9CXW
John J Dittmann
202 S Walnut St
Freeburg IL 62243

Call Sign: KE9PC
Frank L Bowen
112 Southgate Dr
Freeburg IL 62243

Call Sign: KA9AEE
Richard L Harper
3922 SR 15
Freeburg IL 62243

Call Sign: N9XS
Robert J Noles
412 Telluride Dr
Freeburg IL 62243

Call Sign: KB9FQR
Robert D Evans
570 W Phillips
Freeburg IL 62243

FCC Amateur Radio Licenses in Freeport

Call Sign: K9UIY
Victor A Shields
2009 Bedford Rd
Freeport IL 61032

Call Sign: N6WPD
Donald L Harju
1408 Bolkinwood Dr
Freeport IL 61032

Call Sign: AA9YB
Donald L Harju
1408 Bolkinwood Dr
Freeport IL 61032

Call Sign: KC9NVN
Norman E Heyen
1032 Burke Dr
Freeport IL 61032

Call Sign: N9TYB
Robert H Huisinga
2076 Chelsea Ave
Freeport IL 61032

Call Sign: N9LHF
Ray E Matthews
703 Chelsea Ct
Freeport IL 610329114

Call Sign: KC9BUU
Steven K Tellefson
811 Cheshire Ct Apt 6
Freeport IL 61032

Call Sign: W9SKT
Steven K Tellefson
811 Cheshire Ct Apt 6
Freeport IL 61032

Call Sign: KB9MUR
Jason M Kerlin
933 E Clinton St
Freeport IL 61032

Call Sign: KC9ROD
Patrick M Flannery
803 E Shawnee St
Freeport IL 61032

Call Sign: N9QQG
Melvin O Wright Jr
905 E Stephenson St
Freeport IL 61032

Call Sign: W9RQY
Robert E Hartman
2113 Eagle Dr
Freeport IL 61032

Call Sign: W9RAN
Robert A Nickels
2645 East Dr
Freeport IL 61032

Call Sign: KC9BVF
James B Winker
2219 Farmdale Ln
Freeport IL 61032

Call Sign: W9JBW
James B Winker
2219 Farmdale Ln
Freeport IL 61032

Call Sign: KC9GKL
Daniel L Bowman
101 Fieldcrest Dr
Freeport IL 61032

Call Sign: K9DLB
Daniel L Bowman
101 Fieldcrest Dr
Freeport IL 61032

Call Sign: KC9GKM
Mildred J Bowman
101 Fieldcrest Dr
Freeport IL 61032

Call Sign: K9MJB
Mildred J Bowman
101 Fieldcrest Dr
Freeport IL 61032

Call Sign: KC9ERA
Timothy K Urquhart
1502 Frances St
Freeport IL 61032

Call Sign: W9NEA
Thomas R Pinner
818 Hamilton St
Freeport IL 61032

Call Sign: W9FN
Thomas Pinner
818 Hamilton St
Freeport IL 610326227

Call Sign: KC9JLA
Eldora M Welch
6226 High St
Freeport IL 61032

Call Sign: N9RPN
Melvin C Welch
6226 High St
Freeport IL 61032

Call Sign: KB9RNT
Stephenson County Repeater
Association

6226 High St
Freeport IL 61032

Call Sign: KC9LZD
William A Rosemeier
2662 Il Rt 26 N
Freeport IL 61032

Call Sign: KD9CR
Carl C Plaster
1356 Ill Rt 75 E
Freeport IL 61032

Call Sign: KE9HO
Charles L Maltry Sr
2080 Lancaster Hts Rd
Freeport IL 61032

Call Sign: W9SJS
Thomas E Greene
1921 Mesa Dr
Freeport IL 61032

Call Sign: N9TOE
Barton J Blocklinger
2143 Middle Ct
Freeport IL 61032

Call Sign: KB9BUO
Terry D Millam
405 N Apple
Freeport IL 61032

Call Sign: N9WSN
Clarence D Wilken
40 N Bailey
Freeport IL 61032

Call Sign: W9TNL
Robert J Castle
102 N Bailey Ave
Freeport IL 61032

Call Sign: WB9YSL
Steven J Gorham
2063 N Flansburg Rd
Freeport IL 61032

Call Sign: KC9DMJ

Anna F Erwin
109 N Greenfield 3
Freeport IL 61032

Call Sign: W9KGY
Keith E Le Baron
550 N Greenfield Dr
Freeport IL 61032

Call Sign: KC9GCR
James B Dorsey
320 N Harlam Ave N 6
Freeport IL 61032

Call Sign: KB9SEW
Alvin J Retzlaff
320 N Harlem Ave Apt 209
Freeport IL 61032

Call Sign: KC9HZM
Marlene K Allshouse
329 N Park Blvd
Freeport IL 61032

Call Sign: K9MKA
Marlene K Allshouse
329 N Park Blvd
Freeport IL 61032

Call Sign: W9SBA
Scott B Allshouse
329 N Park Blvd
Freeport IL 61032

Call Sign: W9MSL
Erwin D Toerber
115 N Stewart
Freeport IL 61032

Call Sign: AD9DE
David G Ewing
2973 N Tower Rd
Freeport IL 610328962

Call Sign: KC9AJV
Rod L Beverley
458 N Trunck Ave
Freeport IL 61032

Call Sign: WB9PHQ
David G Ewing
705 N Warren Ave
Freeport IL 61032

Call Sign: KB9OLG
Susan L Bouvia
525 N Winnebago
Freeport IL 61032

Call Sign: KC9UGH
Robert T Baker
415 N Winnebago Ave
Freeport IL 61032

Call Sign: KC9PPH
Robert T Baker
415 N Winnebago Ave
Freeport IL 610323318

Call Sign: N9WSQ
David L Bouvia
525 N Winnebago Ave
Freeport IL 61032

Call Sign: N9DLB
David L Bouvia Sr
525 N Winnebago Ave
Freeport IL 61032

Call Sign: KC9IOY
Benjamin J Thompson
1303 Oakdale Pl
Freeport IL 610326629

Call Sign: W9EIP
Charles W Price
1655 Pearl City Rd
Freeport IL 61032

Call Sign: KB9PWK
Roy C Ragan
9 Pleasant Ln
Freeport IL 61032

Call Sign: KC6MGX
John H Thomas
1841 Revere St
Freeport IL 61032

Call Sign: KC6MGW
Sharon I Thomas
1841 Revere St
Freeport IL 61032

Call Sign: KB0WPR
John E Nichols
107 Round Tree Dr
Freeport IL 61032

Call Sign: N9DDY
Marvin G Robey
2635 Royal Oaks Dr
Freeport IL 61032

Call Sign: KB9FIZ
William T Stauffer
1431 S Bidwell Ave
Freeport IL 61032

Call Sign: KC9IET
Jacob P Backus
1300 S Browns Mill Rd
Freeport IL 61032

Call Sign: W9KHV
Lawrence R Kant
2301 S Bunker Hill Rd
Freeport IL 61032

Call Sign: KB9ZZB
Tina M Scheuning
706 S Chicago Ave
Freeport IL 61032

Call Sign: KB9LJW
Roger L Wienk
706 S Chicago Ave
Freeport IL 610325631

Call Sign: KC9DFX
James L Endriss
712 S Chippewa Ave
Freeport IL 61032

Call Sign: KB9JHT
Dennis J Shade
737 S Float Ave

Freeport IL 61032

Call Sign: W9SJW
John R Greene
1444 S Float Ave
Freeport IL 610326516

Call Sign: N9LXX
Ronald Blaine Fox
1210 S Homestead Ave
Freeport IL 61032

Call Sign: KA9HBT
Kevin B Randall
1204 S Maple Ave
Freeport IL 61032

Call Sign: N9TIY
Lloyd I Love
58 S Mary St
Freeport IL 61032

Call Sign: KC9EIL
Mary J Guthrie
924 S Oak Ave
Freeport IL 61032

Call Sign: KB9LLK
William A Beamish
924 S Oak Ave
Freeport IL 61032

Call Sign: KC9SBR
David G Knight
1650 S Rawleigh Ave
Freeport IL 61032

Call Sign: W9DGK
David G Knight
1650 S Rawleigh Ave
Freeport IL 61032

Call Sign: KD9WU
Jesse D Watson
1236 S Van Brocklyn Rd
Freeport IL 61032

Call Sign: K9JES
Jesse D Watson

1236 S Van Brocklyn Rd
Freeport IL 61032

Call Sign: KC9MMI
Kristina M Buisker
1390 S Van Brocklyn Rd
Freeport IL 61019

Call Sign: KC9MGS
Joel D Schroer
1390 S Van Brocklyn Rd
Freeport IL 61032

Call Sign: NW9J
Joel D Schroer
1390 S Van Brocklyn Rd
Freeport IL 61032

Call Sign: KA9LUV
Daniel F Massie
1252 S Walnut
Freeport IL 61032

Call Sign: KB9IQG
Craig J Miller
446 S West
Freeport IL 61032

Call Sign: KC9CWO
William S Backus
424 S West Ave
Freeport IL 61032

Call Sign: KB9HVN
Dale W Sievert
2642 Shepard Dr
Freeport IL 610329267

Call Sign: W9RB
Robert E Bicking
2648 Shepard Dr
Freeport IL 61032

Call Sign: N9DHR
Elbert D Barrett
3723 US Bus 20 W
Freeport IL 61032

Call Sign: W9EDB

Elbert D Barrett
3723 US Bus 20 W
Freeport IL 61032

Call Sign: KA9WGG
David S Wing
651 W American St
Freeport IL 61032

Call Sign: KB9WVK
Jon M Miccolis
1227 W American St
Freeport IL 61032

Call Sign: N9HRE
James C Spaide
1406 W American St
Freeport IL 610324706

Call Sign: W9JS
James C Spaide
1406 W American St
Freeport IL 610324706

Call Sign: KE9Q
Jesse D Watson
1240 W American St
Freeport IL 61032

Call Sign: N9LHE
Ronald K Brattrud
650 W Avon St
Freeport IL 61032

Call Sign: KC9JZC
Peter W Frey
5464 W Beaver
Freeport IL 61032

Call Sign: W9PWF
Peter W Frey
5464 W Beaver
Freeport IL 61032

Call Sign: N9WFX
Donald G Mc Nabb
3120 W Cedarville Rd
Freeport IL 61032

Call Sign: KB9KCI
Julianne M Mc Nabb
3120 W Cedarville Rd
Freeport IL 61032

Call Sign: KA9ZSO
Stephen J Postma
416 W Chestnut
Freeport IL 61032

Call Sign: KB9VDK
Greg J Munda
841 W Cleveland
Freeport IL 61032

Call Sign: K9VDK
Greg J Munda
841 W Cleveland
Freeport IL 61032

Call Sign: N9VK
Greg J Munda
841 W Cleveland
Freeport IL 61032

Call Sign: WB9YJZ
Reginald A Morton
1231 W Crestwood Dr
Freeport IL 61032

Call Sign: KD0IZB
David G Knight
426.5 W Exchange St
Freeport IL 61032

Call Sign: N9PEC
Jeffrey S Bouray
416 W Garfield
Freeport IL 61032

Call Sign: N9FVH
Shirley J Watson
535 W Garfield
Freeport IL 61032

Call Sign: WB9RYX
Gregory J Zeigler
1720 W Harrison St
Freeport IL 61032

Call Sign: K6TCZ
Vernon F Sprague
1614 W Laurel St
Freeport IL 61032

Call Sign: W9HAF
Kenneth R Meyer
1264 W Logan
Freeport IL 61032

Call Sign: N9HVA
Scott A Maher
1101 W Meadows Dr
Freeport IL 61032

Call Sign: KA9TIU
Keith E Pasch
422 W Moseley
Freeport IL 61032

Call Sign: N9JCJ
Marvin H Klemm
5228 W Pearl City Rd
Freeport IL 61032

Call Sign: N9WN
Marvin H Klemm
5228 W Pearl City Rd
Freeport IL 610328101

Call Sign: KB9ZDD
Michael A Backus
816 W Pleasant St
Freeport IL 61032

Call Sign: W9QGT
Charles L Heuser
5737 W Preston Rd
Freeport IL 61032

Call Sign: N9ZXK
Robert M Harris
206 W Ringold
Freeport IL 61032

Call Sign: K9YRF
Russell L Hartman
1205 W Staver

Freeport IL 61032

Call Sign: KC9BPA
Daniel S Barron
941 W Stephenson St 4
Freeport IL 61032

Call Sign: W9DSB
Daniel S Barron
941 W Stephenson St 4
Freeport IL 61032

Call Sign: KB9PLB
Steven W Garner
6807 W Stephenson St Rd 25
Freeport IL 61032

Call Sign: KC9RMH
James L Colbert
6807 W Stephenson St Rd Lot
92
Freeport IL 61032

Call Sign: KA9WIT
Joseph S Cannova
1409 W Stover St
Freeport IL 61032

Call Sign: K9WIT
Joseph S Cannova
1409 W Stover St
Freeport IL 61032

Call Sign: KE9K
Joseph S Cannova
1409 W Stover St
Freeport IL 61032

Call Sign: KA9WVS
John A Mitchell
1421 W Stover St
Freeport IL 61032

Call Sign: W9ELT
Donald F Straub
1244 W Violet
Freeport IL 61032

Call Sign: KC9NSC

Grant W Hasting
900 Woodside Terr
Freeport IL 61032

Call Sign: KC9FQL
Timothy L Baker
Freeport IL 61032

FCC Amateur Radio Licenses in Fulton

Call Sign: KA9TAU
Perry L Thompson
1100 11th Ave
Fulton IL 612521110

Call Sign: N0TXK
Howard M Paysen
1113 11th Ave
Fulton IL 612521109

Call Sign: KA9ZKD
G Scott Vogel
1201 15th Ave
Fulton IL 61252

Call Sign: KB9KUZ
Randy C Swemline
408 21st Ave
Fulton IL 612521763

Call Sign: KB9ZGP
Randy C Swemline
408 21st Ave
Fulton IL 612521763

Call Sign: KC9HQX
Joseph M Zipprich
1223 3rd Ave
Fulton IL 612521004

Call Sign: KB9JJT
Randolph A Lewis
410 8th Ave
Fulton IL 61252

Call Sign: KB9WGY
Jacob L Pence
718 8th Ave

Fulton IL 61252

Call Sign: KA9NRK
James J Evans
1100 8th Ave
Fulton IL 61252

Call Sign: KC9MQE
Russell K Widener
1126 8th Ave 2
Fulton IL 61252

Call Sign: N0RXF
Steven L Ketelsen Jr
3829 Balk Rd
Fulton IL 61252

Call Sign: AB9HM
Steven L Ketelsen Jr
3829 Balk Rd
Fulton IL 61252

Call Sign: K9YW
Steven L Ketelsen Jr
3829 Balk Rd
Fulton IL 61252

Call Sign: N9FQY
Evelyn L Ege
5200 Benson Rd
Fulton IL 61252

Call Sign: W9EGE
William E Ege
5200 Benson Rd
Fulton IL 61252

Call Sign: N0RDX
Gerald E Johannsen Jr
17400 Diamond Rd
Fulton IL 612529704

Call Sign: K9STP
Gerald E Johannsen Jr
17400 Diamond Rd
Fulton IL 612529704

Call Sign: N9PYW
Rickey A Bonnell

14820 Elk Rd
Fulton IL 61252

Call Sign: N9PSH
Tina L Bonnell
14820 Elk Rd
Fulton IL 61252

Call Sign: KB9PDQ
Robert D Stone
14831 Elk Rd
Fulton IL 61252

Call Sign: KB9MAA
Kenneth D Vanderploeg
6924 Indian Hills Dr
Fulton IL 61252

Call Sign: KC9OVC
Ernest H Eads
15001 Kennedy Rd
Fulton IL 61252

Call Sign: N9XBG
Guy R Plumley
105 N 11th St
Fulton IL 61252

Call Sign: KA9UKU
Lisa M Davis
4264 Palmer Rd
Fulton IL 61252

Call Sign: N9TEL
David P Starbuck
6324 Penrose Rd
Fulton IL 61252

Call Sign: N9VGY
Marcia R Starbuck
6324 Penrose Rd
Fulton IL 61252

Call Sign: KB0FIU
James L Westerhof
14930 Sand Rd
Fulton IL 61252

Call Sign: W9EVG

Walter D White
15624 Waller Rd
Fulton IL 61252

FCC Amateur Radio Licenses in Galatia

Call Sign: KB9JDQ
J Chris Watson
Rt 1 Box 52A
Galatia IL 62935

Call Sign: KB9RUE
Clifford W Blum
102 E Walker
Galatia IL 62935

Call Sign: N9WFK
James R Baker
207 E Walker
Galatia IL 62935

Call Sign: KB9YRL
Luke A Johnson
5335 Galatia Rd
Galatia IL 629352057

Call Sign: KB9KPN
Billy R Vantrease
300 Illinois Ave
Galatia IL 62935

Call Sign: KC9ATV
Ben E Williams
308 McKinley
Galatia IL 62935

Call Sign: KB9SHZ
Johnnie L Peyton
Galatia IL 62935

FCC Amateur Radio Licenses in Galena

Call Sign: KC9VTP
Quentin T Petraitis
373 Blackjack Rd
Galena IL 61036

Call Sign: KA9QVW
Howard C Barch Jr
25 Cameron Rd
Galena IL 61036

Call Sign: KA9NAP
Keith J Kouzmanoff
13447 Clipper Ln
Galena IL 61036

Call Sign: W9OBW
Melvin Mendelsohn
248 Council Fire Cir
Galena IL 61036

Call Sign: WB9OHQ
Rollin D Porter
113 Country View Ct
Galena IL 610368114

Call Sign: KC9DTR
John P Myers
1712 Field St
Galena IL 61036

Call Sign: N9MDG
Kay E Outcalt
901 Hill St
Galena IL 61036

Call Sign: KA9NJW
Arthur G Arand Sr
Rr 2 Hwy 20 W
Galena IL 61036

Call Sign: KC9VIZ
Benjamin C Petitgout
708 N Division St
Galena IL 61036

Call Sign: KC9NSH
Steven J Holland
47 N Rocky Hill Rd
Galena IL 61036

Call Sign: KC9NSI
Douglas C Duplessis
157 N Rocky Hill Rd
Galena IL 61036

Call Sign: WB9NXJ
Forest View High School
Amat Radio Clb Dist 214
14 Pond Ct
Galena IL 61036

Call Sign: KA9WMS
John A Myers
10862 Rt 20 W
Galena IL 61036

Call Sign: W6KRY
Philip W Cornelius
269 S Irish Hollow Rd
Galena IL 61036

Call Sign: N9AEV
Robert D Funderburk
833 Shadow Bluff Dr
Galena IL 610369090

Call Sign: K9OI
Lawrence A Galer
3 Timberon Trl
Galena IL 61036

Call Sign: AA9KZ
Richard E Weimer
9636 W Buckhill Rd
Galena IL 610368941

Call Sign: N9VRR
Robert R Weimer
9636 W Buckhill Rd
Galena IL 610368941

FCC Amateur Radio Licenses in Galesburg

Call Sign: KB9BQU
Glenn A Carr
2595 155th St
Galesburg IL 61401

Call Sign: WB9LKT
Stephen D Squires
649 Arnold St
Galesburg IL 61401

Call Sign: KA9YUG
Richard E Pearson
936 Bateman St
Galesburg IL 614012827

Call Sign: K9MEI
William D Strong
1519 Bateman St
Galesburg IL 61401

Call Sign: KC9CBZ
George D Schultz
953 Beecher Ave
Galesburg IL 61401

Call Sign: W9GXT
Robert E Mitchell
1604 Beecher Ave
Galesburg IL 61401

Call Sign: W9SLO
Peter J Polillo
1170 Brown Ave
Galesburg IL 61401

Call Sign: N9QBE
Janet A Heller
1436 Brown Ave
Galesburg IL 61401

Call Sign: KA9PCU
Larry E Heller
1436 Brown Ave
Galesburg IL 61401

Call Sign: WD0SFT
Santa Fe Trail Club
1436 Brown Ave
Galesburg IL 614012064

Call Sign: WD9FBD
Michael T Hurst
2397 Carol Dr
Galesburg IL 61401

Call Sign: KC9JBT
Donald F Axcell
29 Chestnut St

Galesburg IL 61401

Call Sign: WA9USO
John M Symmonds
1582 Clay St
Galesburg IL 61401

Call Sign: K9BEI
James B Osborn
423 Columbus Ave
Galesburg IL 61401

Call Sign: WB9OQL
Robert F Gruba
511 Columbus Ave
Galesburg IL 61401

Call Sign: WD9GAG
Donald L Holman
258 Duffield Ave
Galesburg IL 61401

Call Sign: KB9EVW
Sandra J Guild
497 E 2nd
Galesburg IL 61401

Call Sign: KB9NBN
Danny C Clarke
246 E 3rd St
Galesburg IL 61401

Call Sign: N9QHN
Gary M Egan
1127 E Brooks St
Galesburg IL 61401

Call Sign: WB9QEY
Christopher A Zost
98 E Carl Sandburg Dr
Galesburg IL 614011246

Call Sign: K9HWJ
Donald Greenwell
550 E Carl Sandburg Dr
Galesburg IL 61401

Call Sign: WA9OFM
Chauncey R Brown

550 E Carl Sandburg Dr Apt
131
Galesburg IL 61401

Call Sign: KA9NWC
Ernest E Caves
927 E Knox St
Galesburg IL 61401

Call Sign: KC9GWR
Charles A Bennett
311 E Simmons St 611
Galesburg IL 61401

Call Sign: W9OFE
Charles A Bennett
311 E Simmons St Apt 602
Galesburg IL 61401

Call Sign: KA9FCA
Donald W Ascher Sr
866 E South St
Galesburg IL 61401

Call Sign: N9OGB
Calhoun G Thomas
1548 Edgebrook Dr
Galesburg IL 61401

Call Sign: WB9BIX
Thomas G Calhoun
1548 Edgebrook Dr
Galesburg IL 61401

Call Sign: W9DNE
Edwin A Crowell
356 Fair Acres Dr
Galesburg IL 61401

Call Sign: K9FLS
Howard G Cole Jr
932 Florence Ave
Galesburg IL 614012943

Call Sign: KA9FIZ
Raymond F Armstrong
1343 Florence Ave
Galesburg IL 61401

Call Sign: KA9FHM
Robert E Johnson
1411 Florence Ave
Galesburg IL 61401

Call Sign: N9RL
Rick A Lawsha
106 Fulton St
Galesburg IL 61401

Call Sign: KB9LNN
Christopher D Cooley
110 Garfield Ave
Galesburg IL 61401

Call Sign: W9UBS
Kenneth K Hartman
242 Hawkinson Ave
Galesburg IL 61401

Call Sign: N9FYV
Kenneth L Raymer
401 Hawkinson Ave
Galesburg IL 61401

Call Sign: KF9RP
Michael L Whitman
563 Hawkinson Ave
Galesburg IL 61401

Call Sign: KA9NRT
Harold L Wensel
136 Highland Ave
Galesburg IL 61401

Call Sign: K9GCI
Jerry J Nelson
513 Hillbrook Ests
Galesburg IL 61401

Call Sign: N9YSW
William F Bonner III
1387 Hollycrest Cir
Galesburg IL 614012257

Call Sign: W9ATX
Paul W Morgan
1666 Indiana Dr
Galesburg IL 61401

Call Sign: WA9HYD
Henry A Chesko
1038 Johnston
Galesburg IL 61401

Call Sign: N9OGA
Eugene S Mc Ghee
586 Kenwick Dr
Galesburg IL 61401

Call Sign: WB0USS
Marlowe E Lawnsdale
1770 Knox Hwy 9
Galesburg IL 61401

Call Sign: N9VPT
Cheryl M La Follette
2242 Knox Rd 200 E
Galesburg IL 61401

Call Sign: N9CYO
James T Ralston
65 Locust St
Galesburg IL 61401

Call Sign: W9YEV
Hugh W Reno
808 Locust St
Galesburg IL 61401

Call Sign: K9SHK
Ruby G Reno
808 Locust St
Galesburg IL 61401

Call Sign: N9WYW
Bradley W Harrell
972 Lombard
Galesburg IL 61401

Call Sign: N9XXO
Brenda D Harrell
972 Lombard
Galesburg IL 61401

Call Sign: N9XZZ
George L Chadderdon
1083 Macomb Rd

Galesburg IL 61401

Call Sign: KB9KSY
T Nolan Purtell
108 Madison St
Galesburg IL 61401

Call Sign: W9NEK
Theodore W Lindberg
1142 Maple Ave
Galesburg IL 614012634

Call Sign: K9GCO
Michael J Howerter
4262 Maple Dr
Galesburg IL 61401

Call Sign: KA9WZE
Rosetta C Howerter
4262 Maple Dr
Galesburg IL 61401

Call Sign: W9BUD
Lloyd A Noel
4351 Maple Dr
Galesburg IL 61401

Call Sign: W9PTL
Lloyd A Noel
4351 Maple Dr
Galesburg IL 61401

Call Sign: KF9FE
Glenn R Baldwin
4287 Maple Dr W
Galesburg IL 61401

Call Sign: KB3HIF
Eric S Pavloff
1592 Meadow Lark Dr
Galesburg IL 61401

Call Sign: N9SB
Stephen M Boos
1675 Meadow Lark Dr
Galesburg IL 61401

Call Sign: K9BAZ
Brent A Zhorne

2798 Montague
Galesburg IL 61401

Call Sign: AA9AS
Paul V Jobe
1599 Moshier Ave
Galesburg IL 61401

Call Sign: N9SQP
Scott C Wurzburger
1622 Moshier Ave
Galesburg IL 614013404

Call Sign: KC9CLE
Jack L Roller
1056 Mulberry St
Galesburg IL 61401

Call Sign: WA9HJY
Donald E Lundquist
1269 N Academy St
Galesburg IL 61401

Call Sign: KB9TYM
Dale D Peterson
1723 N Academy St
Galesburg IL 61401

Call Sign: KC9EFO
Elizabeth A Peterson
1723 N Academy St
Galesburg IL 61401

Call Sign: KB9OZY
James F Wayne
188 N Arthur Ave
Galesburg IL 61401

Call Sign: N9XAY
Daniel E Murphy
1162 N Broad
Galesburg IL 61401

Call Sign: N9SPC
Clarence A Clark
1273 N Cedar St
Galesburg IL 61401

Call Sign: AC9AH

Richard P Lotz
220 N Chambers St
Galesburg IL 61401

Call Sign: N3LIO
Andrew S Leahy
1187 N Cherry St
Galesburg IL 61401

Call Sign: WD9BKG
Fred T Reinschmidt
1289 N Cherry St
Galesburg IL 61401

Call Sign: KA9MFY
Wesley B Wilson
208 N Elm St
Galesburg IL 61401

Call Sign: KA9RIM
Charles L Luallen Sr
124 N Farnham
Galesburg IL 61401

Call Sign: KA9IWV
Thomas M Carithers
219 N Henderson
Galesburg IL 61401

Call Sign: N9UVZ
Laura J Appell
1017 N Kellogg St
Galesburg IL 61401

Call Sign: N9WRH
Richard L Waldorf
1017 N Kellogg St
Galesburg IL 61401

Call Sign: N9VXZ
Roger L Appell
1017 N Kellogg St
Galesburg IL 61401

Call Sign: N9SPB
Richard D Hobbs
1649 N Kellogg St
Galesburg IL 61401

Call Sign: W9OBG
Walter H Boller
182 N Pearl
Galesburg IL 61401

Call Sign: N9RXN
Jeffrey L Holman
725 N Prairie St
Galesburg IL 61401

Call Sign: KA9VHE
Richard L Heath
1336 N Prairie St
Galesburg IL 61401

Call Sign: KA9ZIO
Randolph E Trautvetter
1470 N West St Apt 41
Galesburg IL 61401

Call Sign: N9HSZ
William G Conroy Jr
248 N Whitesboro St
Galesburg IL 614013937

Call Sign: KA9QIL
Connie L Brown
446 Oak St
Galesburg IL 61401

Call Sign: KA9FCB
Ralph W Brown Sr
446 Oak St
Galesburg IL 61401

Call Sign: W9FCX
Lyle W Dunlap
442 Oakwood Dr
Galesburg IL 61401

Call Sign: N9WZA
Julie L Waldorf
350 Olive St
Galesburg IL 61401

Call Sign: WB9QVY
Mike A Hammer
7 Parkside Hill Lake Brachen
Galesburg IL 61401

Call Sign: KA9TBW
Jeffrey B Hammer
7 Parkside Hill Lake Bracken
Galesburg IL 61401

Call Sign: WA9JFL
Richard L Turpin Sr
1111 Parkview Rd
Galesburg IL 614011337

Call Sign: N9NPX
Thomas J Stone
807 Phillips St
Galesburg IL 61401

Call Sign: N9JVP
Patricia I Goldsmith
364 Pine St
Galesburg IL 61401

Call Sign: KB9EVU
Ryan A Goldsmith
364 Pine St
Galesburg IL 61401

Call Sign: N9HEB
Terrence L Stallings
1252 Rock Island Ave
Galesburg IL 61401

Call Sign: N9XRJ
Julia L Baughman
1480 Rock Island Ave
Galesburg IL 61401

Call Sign: W9IYC
Richard L Baughman
1480 Rock Island Ave
Galesburg IL 61401

Call Sign: N9VPU
Benjamin K Derry
768 Ruby St
Galesburg IL 61401

Call Sign: KB9UPX
Joshua R O Frievalt
729 S Academy St

Galesburg IL 61401

Call Sign: N9JVT
Ralph J Rogers
1021 S Chambers
Galesburg IL 61401

Call Sign: W9DTL
Charles R Miller
144 S Farnham St
Galesburg IL 61401

Call Sign: N9OAT
Ralph S Benejam
1440 S Lake Storey Rd
Galesburg IL 61401

Call Sign: N9KIS
James W Rowe
1839 S Lake Storey Rd
Galesburg IL 61401

Call Sign: KB9EFF
Larry R Palmer
2540 S Lake Storey Rd
Galesburg IL 61401

Call Sign: WT9O
Larry R Palmer
2540 S Lake Storey Rd
Galesburg IL 61401

Call Sign: KC9TCM
Sean Bonner
348 S Pearl St
Galesburg IL 61401

Call Sign: N9MIV
Charles S Gaylord
374 S Pearl St
Galesburg IL 61401

Call Sign: KB9NBO
Roger L Baughman
61 S Pleasant Ave
Galesburg IL 61401

Call Sign: KA9MGO
Carl O Hamilton

1146 S Seminary St
Galesburg IL 61401

Call Sign: N9DH
Robert D Houlihan
170 S West St Apt 816
Galesburg IL 61401

Call Sign: KB9NRZ
Clarence O Greenstreet
2081 Soperville Rd
Galesburg IL 61401

Call Sign: AA3OG
Robert R Migliorino
1074 Spoden Ln
Galesburg IL 61401

Call Sign: AB9QV
Robert R Migliorino
1074 Spoden Ln
Galesburg IL 61401

Call Sign: KV0M
Robert R Migliorino
1074 Spoden Ln
Galesburg IL 61401

Call Sign: K9YXH
Lewis W Ralston
248 Sumner St
Galesburg IL 61401

Call Sign: K9FML
Stephen M Finn
1019 Sunnyknoll Dr
Galesburg IL 61401

Call Sign: KA9MTM
Richard D Morton
204 Sunnyview Dr
Galesburg IL 61401

Call Sign: WB9UEV
Carl D Kennett Jr
1048 W Losey St
Galesburg IL 61401

Call Sign: KD9FN

Richard A Withrow II
74 W North St
Galesburg IL 61401

Call Sign: N9MXS
Merle L Strong
1151 W North St
Galesburg IL 61401

Call Sign: N9QOX
Demond D Crider
1086 W South St
Galesburg IL 61401

Call Sign: N9SPD
Carey J Anderson
581 W Tompkins St
Galesburg IL 61401

Call Sign: KC9NSR
Jeremy T Johnson
979 Washington Ave
Galesburg IL 61401

Call Sign: W9DQF
Dennis M Little Sr
1647 Willard St
Galesburg IL 614011938

Call Sign: KA9TRQ
George F Glavas
1126 Windcrest Acres
Galesburg IL 61401

Call Sign: K9TRQ
George F Glavas
1126 Windcrest Acres
Galesburg IL 61401

Call Sign: N9CGO
David C Adcock
1624 Woodbine Cir S
Galesburg IL 61401

Call Sign: N8VVN
Mario Di Biase
582 Yates St
Galesburg IL 61401

Call Sign: N9VPV
Kevin E Gray
Galesburg IL 61402

Call Sign: KX9T
Steven L Thurman
Galesburg IL 61402

Call Sign: K9ZRN
William E Fowler Jr
Galesburg IL 61402

Call Sign: N9PHV
Robert M Cooper
Galesburg IL 614020422

Call Sign: K9RMC
Robert M Cooper
Galesburg IL 614020422

FCC Amateur Radio Licenses in Galt

Call Sign: WD9EHR
Rodney T Cushman
Galt IL 61037

FCC Amateur Radio Licenses in Galva

Call Sign: WB9ATU
Paul H Collinson
Rr 2 Box 84
Galva IL 61434

Call Sign: KC9HKX
Olof S Collinson
Rt 2 Box 84
Galva IL 61434

Call Sign: KB9WHF
Glen A Ketchum
17756 N 200 Ave
Galva IL 61434

Call Sign: KB9LLW
Ashley J Garcia
1107 N Center Ave
Galva IL 61434

Call Sign: KA9AEU
David A Peterson
403 NE 2nd St
Galva IL 61434

Call Sign: WB9WQJ
Dale H De Smith
25 NE 4 St
Galva IL 61434

Call Sign: KC9SQE
Ronald A Modesto II
511 NW 11th St
Galva IL 61434

Call Sign: KB9LFE
Robert I Johnson
209 NW 1st Ave
Galva IL 614341303

Call Sign: KC9HNO
Cathryn H Ren
710 NW 2nd St
Galva IL 61434

Call Sign: WB9ELT
Lawrence A Swanson
112 NW 6th Ave
Galva IL 614341257

Call Sign: KC9SIM
Michael C Lind
706 NW 7th Ave
Galva IL 614340010

Call Sign: W9KHE
Michael C Lind
706 NW 7th Ave
Galva IL 614340010

Call Sign: WD9EKG
Thomas S Hulsey
417 SE 2nd St
Galva IL 61434

Call Sign: KB9WTC
Area Amateur Radio
Operations

920 W Division St
Galva IL 61434

Call Sign: KB9WZU
Area Amateur Radio Operators
920 W Division St
Galva IL 61434

Call Sign: AA9RO
Area Amateur Radio
Operations
30 Wallace St
Galva IL 61434

Call Sign: N9ZK
Area Amateur Radio Operators
30 Wallace St
Galva IL 61434

Call Sign: KC9IQN
Area Amateur Radio Operators
30 Wallace St
Galva IL 61434

Call Sign: WB9WQJ
Area Amateur Radio Operators
30 Wallace St
Galva IL 61434

Call Sign: WA9BA
William L Anderson
30 Wallace St
Galva IL 61434

Call Sign: W9YPS
Area Amateur Radio Operators
30 Wallace St
Galva IL 614341641

FCC Amateur Radio Licenses in Garden Prairie

Call Sign: KB9KQR
Jeannie D Sharp
4348 County Line Rd
Garden Prairie IL 61038

Call Sign: KB9KEY
Kevin Sharp

4348 County Line Rd
Garden Prairie IL 61038

Call Sign: KC9PDE
Kenneth G Jaeger
11875 Orth Rd
Garden Prairie IL 61038

Call Sign: KA9ZOT
John J Dini
11122 Station St
Garden Prairie IL 61038

Call Sign: N9OGT
Alice P Marquis
Garden Prairie IL 61038

Call Sign: KC9TIL
Franky R Chappel
Garden Prairie IL 61038

Call Sign: WC9P
William F Marquis
Garden Prairie IL 61038

FCC Amateur Radio Licenses in Gardner

Call Sign: WD9FGG
Richard D Morgan
Rr 2 Box 149 104N Center St
Gardner IL 60424

Call Sign: KB9TNS
George E Davis
4780 E Grinter Rd
Gardner IL 60424

Call Sign: W9GEO
George E Davis
4780 E Grinter Rd
Gardner IL 60424

Call Sign: KC9HXA
William R Yuras
102 N East St
Gardner IL 60424

Call Sign: KB9DEZ

Jeanne A Hnetkovsky
105 North St
Gardner IL 60424

Call Sign: KA9EBD
Harold R Patton
201 Parker St
Gardner IL 60424

Call Sign: KA9QLR
Margaret L Patton
201 Parker St
Gardner IL 60424

Call Sign: KC9HWZ
Christopher D Himes
102 S Jackson St
Gardner IL 60424

FCC Amateur Radio Licenses in Gays

Call Sign: WB9WIT
Joy E Hortenstine
Rr 1 Box 67
Gays IL 61928

Call Sign: K9JH
John T Hortenstine
Rr 1 Box 67
Gays IL 619289726

Call Sign: KA9PRC
Scott J Mayer
Rr 2 Box 75
Gays IL 61928

FCC Amateur Radio Licenses in Geff

Call Sign: KB9RQX
Dale E Lampley
Rt 1 Box 112
Geff IL 62842

Call Sign: N9PDI
Scott A Hubble
Rr 1 Box 173 B
Geff IL 62842

Call Sign: KF9YY
Richard L Attebery
Rr 1 Box 18A
Geff IL 62842

Call Sign: AA9RP
Jerry C Withrow
R 1 Box 314
Geff IL 62842

Call Sign: KC9RHF
Leif M Mccarthy
Rr 1 Box 94B
Geff IL 62842

Call Sign: KC9GMX
Steven R Hamilton
207 S Washington St
Geff IL 62842

Call Sign: WA9TEC
Dennis E Vaughan
Geff IL 62842

FCC Amateur Radio Licenses in Genesco

Call Sign: N9WYX
Charles W Kriegermeier
26016 Ridge Rd
Genesco IL 61254

Call Sign: WD9ICE
Stephen K Hawkins
806 Bluebird Ct
Geneseo IL 61254

Call Sign: N9HCN
Larry F Rasko
Rte 3 Box 157
Geneseo IL 61254

Call Sign: KB9NTR
Hannah J Cryder
714 Cardinal Ct
Geneseo IL 61254

Call Sign: KC9FLK

William G Radicic
23031 Dorchester Dr
Geneseo IL 61254

Call Sign: NS0A
William G Radicic
23031 Dorchester Dr
Geneseo IL 61254

Call Sign: WB9ECA
James W Weisser
18895 E 1500 St
Geneseo IL 61254

Call Sign: KA9WGK
David R Johnson
23341 E 1680th St
Geneseo IL 612549094

Call Sign: KC9BJE
Joshua W Anderson
235 E North St
Geneseo IL 61254

Call Sign: KB9MFR
Nicholas J Ashley
615 E Wells St
Geneseo IL 61254

Call Sign: W9ZXT
Nicholas J Ashley
615 E Wells St
Geneseo IL 61254

Call Sign: KD0FHY
Kyle R Goldsmith
42 Estate Rd
Geneseo IL 61254

Call Sign: N9HUO
Anthony W Goldsmith
42 Estate Rd
Geneseo IL 61254

Call Sign: K9TO
Lawrence H Flaherty
25 Green Acres
Geneseo IL 61254

Call Sign: WA9ZAS
William T Lamont
24760 Hazelwood W Rd
Geneseo IL 61254

Call Sign: N9WFO
Richard M Sheets
228 Hillcrest Dr
Geneseo IL 61254

Call Sign: N9WML
Roger M Sheets
228 Hillcrest Dr
Geneseo IL 61254

Call Sign: N9YMI
Catherine L Sheets
228 Hillcrest Dr
Geneseo IL 612541934

Call Sign: N9YMH
Eddielea H Sheets
228 Hillcrest Dr
Geneseo IL 612541934

Call Sign: KB9EBI
Laura L Hecht
213 Longview Dr
Geneseo IL 61254

Call Sign: KA9KQA
Brian P Burghgrave
77 Lynwood Ave
Geneseo IL 61254

Call Sign: N9QMH
Robert C Ahlgren
824 Mulberry Dr
Geneseo IL 612541167

Call Sign: KB9PQJ
Donald V Detloff Jr
13035 N 1700 Ave
Geneseo IL 61254

Call Sign: N9BOL
William R Schopp
420 N Hill St
Geneseo IL 61254

Call Sign: N9JCB
James L Smith
616 N State
Geneseo IL 61254

Call Sign: KC9OKZ
Scott J Teerlinck
30 Prairie Dawn Dr
Geneseo IL 61254

Call Sign: NO9X
Leslie E Conrad
920 S Chicago St Apt 21
Geneseo IL 61254

Call Sign: KA9GZM
Ellis Fenical
215 S Russell St
Geneseo IL 61254

Call Sign: KA6DSQ
John T Greenwood
111 S Stewart Ave
Geneseo IL 61254

Call Sign: WB9BVE
Dale M Gradert
319 S Stewart St
Geneseo IL 61254

Call Sign: KB9CTW
Katherine L Lodge
209 S Vail St
Geneseo IL 61254

Call Sign: N9QQC
Lisa L Mc Millan
72 Spruce Ct Hz Ht
Geneseo IL 612549567

Call Sign: KC9JHF
James W Mason
206 Sylvan Ln
Geneseo IL 61254

Call Sign: KF9LM
Patrick E Monahan
6766 US Hwy 6

Geneseo IL 61254

Call Sign: W7COK
Sims Memorial Repeater
Group
9600 Wolf Rd
Geneseo IL 61254

Call Sign: KA9YQG
Henry J Mc Millan
9600 Wolf Rd
Geneseo IL 612549039

Call Sign: K9ZK
Phillip H Mc Millan
9600 Wolf Rd
Geneseo IL 612549039

Call Sign: W9MVG
Shafer Memorial Repeater
Group
9600 Wolf Rd
Geneseo IL 612549039

Call Sign: K9DHS
Maurice L Ver Brugge
11096 Wolf Rd
Geneseo IL 612548364

Call Sign: N9OVC
Nancy L Holling
13 Woodcrest Dr
Geneseo IL 61254

Call Sign: N9MZP
Walter E Holling
13 Woodcrest Dr
Geneseo IL 61254

Call Sign: WA9LT
Walter E Holling
13 Woodcrest Dr
Geneseo IL 61254

FCC Amateur Radio Licenses in Georgetown

Call Sign: K9FEA
Franklin E Stokes

Rr 2 Box 21
Georgetown IL 61846

Call Sign: KC9KTB
Leighton T Starwalt
5270 Cedar St
Georgetown IL 61846

Call Sign: KC9SBG
Logan R Starwalt
5270 Cedar St
Georgetown IL 61846

Call Sign: KA9DZR
Dennis M Semonick
15245 College Ave
Georgetown IL 61846

Call Sign: KB9NBF
Donald R Roeder
312 E 11th
Georgetown IL 61846

Call Sign: KB4QZF
James M Ewing
5 Kings Dr
Georgetown IL 61846

Call Sign: KC9TVD
Jonathan A Collins
309 Logan Ave
Georgetown IL 61846

Call Sign: K9CND
Louis M Zamberletti
5074 N 1500 E Rd
Georgetown IL 618466614

Call Sign: KB9DMR
Jean A Hayward
5199 N 1500 E Rd
Georgetown IL 61846

Call Sign: W9DDU
John A Hayward
5199 N 1500 E Rd
Georgetown IL 61846

Call Sign: KA9SUE

Joseph L Hayward
5222 N 1500 E Rd
Georgetown IL 61846

Call Sign: N9YYS
Steve T Hayward
5310 N 1500 E Rd
Georgetown IL 61846

Call Sign: KA9TLV
Stephanie A Augustus
8364 N 2100 E Rd
Georgetown IL 61846

Call Sign: KB9AZA
James R Kiser
25 Ramey Ct
Georgetown IL 61846

Call Sign: KB9RDV
Diane Smith
200 S Seminary
Georgetown IL 61846

Call Sign: N9XQS
Philip P Smith
200 S Seminary St
Georgetown IL 61846

Call Sign: WD9AFF
Barbara J Tolson
201 W 12th
Georgetown IL 61846

Call Sign: KC9IZC
Charlie A Tintorri
312 Whittier St
Georgetown IL 61846

Call Sign: KW9CAT
Charlie A Tintorri
312 Whittier St
Georgetown IL 61846

FCC Amateur Radio Licenses in German Valley

Call Sign: KB9ZCU
Karl A Larson

46 S Bunker Hill Rd
German Valley IL 61039

Call Sign: W9UIJ
Karl A Larson
46 S Bunker Hill Rd
German Valley IL 61039

FCC Amateur Radio Licenses in Germantown

Call Sign: N9WDR
Richard P Frerker
404 Elm
Germantown IL 62245

Call Sign: WB0JRK
Patrick A Wilson
1207 Hermeling Ln
Germantown IL 62245

Call Sign: KB9SCO
Peggy R Iler
3432 Highline Rd
Germantown IL 63245

Call Sign: KC9TTT
Danny D Johnson
101 Holly Ave
Germantown IL 622450048

Call Sign: KC9TUL
Joshua A Shubert
9507 Wesclin Rd
Germantown IL 62245

FCC Amateur Radio Licenses in Gibson City

Call Sign: KB9GQT
Gerald E Merritt
Rr 2 Box 126
Gibson City IL 60936

Call Sign: KU9T
Earl Hendrickson
520 Carriage Ln
Gibson City IL 60936

Call Sign: WD9FOX
Darrel L Steele
380 E 150 N Rd
Gibson City IL 60936

Call Sign: KB9PWU
Stanley D Frieburg
477 E 300 N Rd
Gibson City IL 60936

Call Sign: WG9S
Robert J Benefiel
327 E 9th St
Gibson City IL 60936

Call Sign: N9AO
Lynn A Anliker
630 N 800 E Rd
Gibson City IL 60936

Call Sign: KA9EPR
Ellis W Unzicker
410 N Lott Blvd
Gibson City IL 60936

Call Sign: KB9JTJ
Brady T Peters
206 S Church St
Gibson City IL 60936

Call Sign: WB9QQA
Randall P Berger
220 S Sangamon St
Gibson City IL 609361559

Call Sign: KC9JJN
Robert H Wilson
404 S West St
Gibson City IL 60936

FCC Amateur Radio Licenses in Gifford

Call Sign: WB9GZW
Michael B Busboom
2316 CR 2800 N
Gifford IL 61847

Call Sign: N9MNT

Joe H Kerr Jr
302 W Summit
Gifford IL 61847

FCC Amateur Radio Licenses in Gillespie

Call Sign: WB9KKM
Charles R Heyen
Rr 2 Box 101A
Gillespie IL 62033

Call Sign: WD9CZO
Collis C Stauffer
Rr 2 Box 106A
Gillespie IL 62033

Call Sign: KA9WEW
Philip G Adcock
Rri Box 156
Gillespie IL 62033

Call Sign: WB9QFJ
Thomas A Bauer
Rr 2 Box 96
Gillespie IL 62033

Call Sign: KA9WRX
Norman J Sherman
15 Circle Dr
Gillespie IL 620332226

Call Sign: WA9WZB
Jenny L James
525 Dorsey Rd
Gillespie IL 62033

Call Sign: KC9PIU
Montemac Amateur Repeater Club Inc
525 Dorsey Rd
Gillespie IL 62033

Call Sign: WA9FDP
Montemac Amateur Repeater Club Inc
525 Dorsey Rd
Gillespie IL 62033

Call Sign: N9FNG
Jill R Secoy
500 E Chestnut
Gillespie IL 62033

Call Sign: KA9JPB
Jennie M Wilson
810 Easton
Gillespie IL 62033

Call Sign: KA9NQZ
John D Wilson
810 Easton
Gillespie IL 62033

Call Sign: KF9GT
David C Hasquin
609 Francis
Gillespie IL 62033

Call Sign: N9GZJ
Jo Ann Tallman
108 Frey St
Gillespie IL 62033

Call Sign: N9QIF
John J Weidner
308 Fulton St
Gillespie IL 62033

Call Sign: W9BPG
David E Decobert
609 Henrietta
Gillespie IL 62033

Call Sign: N9VQV
Shirlene L South
317 Henry St
Gillespie IL 62033

Call Sign: WB9VJG
Martin L Taylor
511 Henry St
Gillespie IL 62033

Call Sign: WM9R
James R Wright
108 Madison St
Gillespie IL 620331517

Call Sign: WB9JBC
Gary L Bauer
8296 N Dorchester Rd
Gillespie IL 620333320

Call Sign: N9JYH
Bernadette K Hasquin
609 N Francis
Gillespie IL 62033

Call Sign: N9MMH
Gary R Visintin
708 N Frey
Gillespie IL 62033

Call Sign: K9KXK
Gary R Visintin
708 N Frey
Gillespie IL 62033

Call Sign: KB9RZV
Larry D Cooke
322 N Macoupin
Gillespie IL 62033

Call Sign: N9MAD
George M Holesko
420 Park Ave
Gillespie IL 62033

Call Sign: KF9KS
Joann Pomatto
15767 Pump House Rd
Gillespie IL 62033

Call Sign: K9YY
Ronald M Pomatto
15767 Pump House Rd
Gillespie IL 62033

Call Sign: KS9R
Black Hole Dxers
15767 Pump House Rd
Gillespie IL 62033

Call Sign: WB9QXG
Harold E Valerio
15793 Pump House Rd

Gillespie IL 62033

Call Sign: WB9YGJ
Lori A Valerio
15793 Pump House Rd
Gillespie IL 62033

Call Sign: N9HRB
Paul R Koschak
407 S Jersey St
Gillespie IL 62033

Call Sign: KB9EPE
Lanny R Cloud
1003 S Madison St
Gillespie IL 62033

Call Sign: KB9MIV
Anthony S Pollo
2267 Staunton Rd
Gillespie IL 62033

Call Sign: KF9GB
Ruth A Pomatto
206 W Henrietta
Gillespie IL 62033

Call Sign: KA9VIZ
David L Davis
215 W Oak St
Gillespie IL 62033

Call Sign: KC9GEW
Midwest Grid Chasers
Association
309 W Spruce St
Gillespie IL 62033

Call Sign: KS9Z
Midwest Grid Chasers
Association
309 W Spruce St
Gillespie IL 62033

Call Sign: WA9FDP
James H Heyen
417 W Walnut St
Gillespie IL 62033

Call Sign: WB9QHK
Marsha L Heyen
417 W Walnut St
Gillespie IL 62033

Call Sign: N9NFM
Catherine C Visintin
705 Western St
Gillespie IL 62033

Call Sign: W9TV
Peter G Visintin
705 Western St
Gillespie IL 62033

Call Sign: K9GTB
Herbert M Hildebrand
Gillespie IL 62033

FCC Amateur Radio Licenses in Gilson

Call Sign: KC9KWT
Kathryn B Palmer
1026 Roberts
Gilson IL 61436

FCC Amateur Radio Licenses in Girard

Call Sign: KC9NTC
Gloria J Pitchford
18303 Blackhawk Dr
Girard IL 62640

Call Sign: N9LQF
James W Pitchford
18303 Blackhawk Dr
Girard IL 626409574

Call Sign: N9MZE
Lori A Pitchford
Rr 2 Box 151
Girard IL 62640

Call Sign: KB5RLS
Michele D Speckhart
515 E Center
Girard IL 62640

Call Sign: AL7II
Scott A Speckhart
515 E Center
Girard IL 62640

Call Sign: AK9I
Scott A Speckhart
515 E Center
Girard IL 62640

Call Sign: WB4CHN
Bobby L Cantrell
330 E Madison St
Girard IL 62640

Call Sign: WD9GKV
Kenneth J Bricker
18856 Finney Rd
Girard IL 62640

Call Sign: KA9PVW
Eva L Jacoby
186 Hickory Ln
Girard IL 62640

Call Sign: KA9PVV
Russell A Jacoby
186 Hickory Ln
Girard IL 62640

Call Sign: KC9NDN
James M Matuska
202 N 1st St
Girard IL 62640

Call Sign: KB9CIK
Allen A Schroll
18 N 34 Ave
Girard IL 62640

Call Sign: KB9PZE
Allen A Schroll Jr
18 N 34 Ave
Girard IL 62640

Call Sign: KC9ULA
Debra D Nichols
218 N 3rd St

Girard IL 62640

Call Sign: N9TRN
Lynn M Jones
218 N 4th St
Girard IL 62640

Call Sign: KA9VIV
Timothy T Jones
218 N 4th St
Girard IL 62640

Call Sign: KC9OUD
Phillip A Hall
335 S Sherman St
Girard IL 62640

Call Sign: WA9OJC
Norman E Champion
13438 Stamper Rd
Girard IL 62640

Call Sign: K9OKI
Nathan E Jones
174 W Center St
Girard IL 62640

Call Sign: WB9DTF
William D Lynch
816 W Center St
Girard IL 62640

FCC Amateur Radio Licenses in Glasford

Call Sign: KC9DHK
Stephen D Fischer
212 N Fahnestock Ave
Glasford IL 61533

Call Sign: KG9DH
Edward A Fischer
7621 S Martin Weber Rd
Glasford IL 61533

Call Sign: KC0TOT
Seth R Isaacs
15118 W Glasford Canton Rd
Glasford IL 61533

Call Sign: KA9YMG
Kendall D Charlier
16827 W Todd School Rd
Glasford IL 615339732

Call Sign: WD9FQL
Charles T Naylor
Glasford IL 61533

**FCC Amateur Radio
Licenses in Glen Carbon**

Call Sign: KC9ILS
John C Freeman
128 Appletree Ln
Glen Carbon IL 62034

Call Sign: K9WHC
William E Newman
175 Birger Ave
Glen Carbon IL 62034

Call Sign: KA0HFE
Daniel L Glasscock
2219 Bunkum Pl
Glen Carbon IL 62034

Call Sign: KC9CGP
Dustin E Frey
9B Cougar Rd
Glen Carbon IL 62034

Call Sign: NK9X
Dustin E Frey
9B Cougar Rd
Glen Carbon IL 62034

Call Sign: KC5WPB
Robert A Schwartz
54 E 30 Mhc
Glen Carbon IL 62034

Call Sign: KC9KYQ
Mark E Cox
36 Ernst Dr
Glen Carbon IL 62034

Call Sign: N9ATT

Mark E Cox
36 Ernst Dr
Glen Carbon IL 62034

Call Sign: AB9CP
Elmer V Smith III
34 Foreman Dr
Glen Carbon IL 62034

Call Sign: KB9WNQ
Robert D Blankenship Jr
114 Forest Grove Dr
Glen Carbon IL 62034

Call Sign: KC9SUD
Robert D Blankenship Jr
114 Forest Grove Dr
Glen Carbon IL 62034

Call Sign: WA9NBB
Maurice H Miller
5 Ginger Wood Estate
Glen Carbon IL 62034

Call Sign: KF0XY
Thomas E Chapman
11 Glen Hollow
Glen Carbon IL 62034

Call Sign: N9MAE
Terry M Weatherford Jr
229 Glen Lake Dr
Glen Carbon IL 620341112

Call Sign: WX9SAR
Terry M Weatherford Jr
229 Glenlake Dr
Glen Carbon IL 620341112

Call Sign: KC9MYU
Camille Hawk
8 Jason Dr
Glen Carbon IL 62034

Call Sign: KC9MYV
Matthew J Hawk
8 Jason Dr
Glen Carbon IL 62034

Call Sign: WB9GLY
Keith F Scobbie
332 Jo Lee Ln
Glen Carbon IL 62034

Call Sign: KB9HKK
Kevin T Gebeau
1 Kaman Dr
Glen Carbon IL 62034

Call Sign: KA9AKM
Scott E Kuether
205 Lake Hillcrest
Glen Carbon IL 62034

Call Sign: N9WNB
James T Murphey
232 Lake Hillcrest Dr
Glen Carbon IL 62034

Call Sign: W9ITM
Harry K Windland
106 Lakewood Dr
Glen Carbon IL 620342986

Call Sign: KB9YBH
Claudia A Perozzi
44 Larkmoor
Glen Carbon IL 62034

Call Sign: KB9YBG
William T Perozzi
44 Larkmoor
Glen Carbon IL 62034

Call Sign: KG9OV
Anthony F Contratto
18 Lou Juan Dr
Glen Carbon IL 62034

Call Sign: KB9QXS
John D Rezabek
18 Lou Juan Dr
Glen Carbon IL 62034

Call Sign: AA9BW
Patricia S Brown
209 Matterhorn Ct
Glen Carbon IL 62034

Call Sign: WB9FLW
Peter J Eaton
35 Norspur Rd
Glen Carbon IL 620342910

Call Sign: N9IPL
Harry P Mc Quinn
41 Old Orchard Ln
Glen Carbon IL 620343025

Call Sign: KC9KMS
Stephen A Daniels
18 Pepperwood Ct
Glen Carbon IL 62034

Call Sign: W0HAG
Leon P Mace
34 S Meadow Ln
Glen Carbon IL 620342762

Call Sign: W9CUN
Kenneth A Anderson
300 S Station Rd Apt 105
Glen Carbon IL 620342739

Call Sign: KC9MZA
Kenneth G Rawson
135 Savannah Ct
Glen Carbon IL 62034

Call Sign: KC9MYZ
Patrice Ranson
135 Savannah Ct
Glen Carbon IL 62034

Call Sign: WB9TUN
Joseph R Floeter
12 Shingle Oaks
Glen Carbon IL 620342912

Call Sign: KD7FXG
Eric J Marler
9 Sierra Dr
Glen Carbon IL 62034

Call Sign: N9JVR
Edita D Mercado
37 Sierra Dr

Glen Carbon IL 62034

Call Sign: N9OMC
Marilyn M Bautista
37 Sierra Dr
Glen Carbon IL 62034

Call Sign: KB9ICU
Rhonda J Mercado
37 Sierra Dr
Glen Carbon IL 62034

Call Sign: WG9N
Isabelo J Mercado
37 Sierra Dr
Glen Carbon IL 62034

Call Sign: K9FHV
Robert P Graff
2 Squire Dr
Glen Carbon IL 620344016

Call Sign: K0YQU
Edward K Wolfe
43 Summit Dr
Glen Carbon IL 62034

Call Sign: KB9TEG
Jim W Howard
201 W Glen Dr
Glen Carbon IL 62034

Call Sign: N9JIJ
Scott T Cullen
33 Windermere Dr
Glen Carbon IL 620341477

Call Sign: KC9MCP
Melvin E Mathenia
7 Wintergreen
Glen Carbon IL 62034

Call Sign: WA9BRQ
Walter L Wise
Glen Carbon IL 62034

**FCC Amateur Radio
Licenses in Glenarm**

Call Sign: N0GTI
Craig A Campbell
11941 Clearspring Dr
Glenarm IL 62536

Call Sign: KB9KOS
Fred A Morgan
4 Sugar Creek Ests
Glenarm IL 62536

Call Sign: WB6SJT
Richard P Falzone
1266 W Glenarm Rd
Glenarm IL 62536

**FCC Amateur Radio
Licenses in Godfrey**

Call Sign: K9DTH
Ronald A Aldridge
300 Admiral Dr
Godfrey IL 62035

Call Sign: W9PLD
Joseph R Barnard
13 Alpha Dr
Godfrey IL 62035

Call Sign: WB9AYU
Robert E Barnard
6523 Alpha Dr
Godfrey IL 62035

Call Sign: KC9DYW
John F Gaskill
1902 Arrowhead Ln
Godfrey IL 62035

Call Sign: N9TC
Joseph A Russo
5201 Asbury Ave Apt 115
Godfrey IL 62035

Call Sign: W9NYD
Robert E Tripp
1709 Aster Ln
Godfrey IL 62035

Call Sign: KD7RPB

Teresa S Tripp
1709 Aster Ln
Godfrey IL 62035

Call Sign: KC9FZC
Teresa S Tripp
1709 Aster Ln
Godfrey IL 62035

Call Sign: WB9IRJ
Andy J Hogue
5711 Barbara Pl
Godfrey IL 62035

Call Sign: KA9OKB
Carroll D Jones
704 Beltline
Godfrey IL 62035

Call Sign: KC9SGI
Noel C Powers
114 Bethany Ln
Godfrey IL 62035

Call Sign: KB9BPF
Bradley C Andrews
805 Chestnut Dr
Godfrey IL 62035

Call Sign: KB9EXF
Andrew J Allen
5101 Clifton Ter
Godfrey IL 62035

Call Sign: W9ENT
William D Allen
5101 Clifton Ter
Godfrey IL 62035

Call Sign: N9VZO
Philip C Seitzinger
1509 Colonial Dr
Godfrey IL 62035

Call Sign: KC9JCM
Candice L Cope
5002 Crystal Lake Dr
Godfrey IL 62035

Call Sign: N9FOB
Gordon L Admire
5908 Deer Trl
Godfrey IL 62035

Call Sign: KB9BEF
Richard L Trobaugh
5129 Dixon Dr
Godfrey IL 62035

Call Sign: N9VZN
Evelyn M Elmore
5203 Dixon Dr
Godfrey IL 62035

Call Sign: N9HE
Harold E Elmore
5203 Dixon Dr
Godfrey IL 62035

Call Sign: N9QDD
Carla L Wainright
5303 Dixon Dr
Godfrey IL 62035

Call Sign: N9XCV
Joseph F Kettelhake
5315 Dixon Dr
Godfrey IL 62035

Call Sign: N9IRA
Hector M Hernandez
3210 Doral Dr
Godfrey IL 62035

Call Sign: W9MXC
Larry H Roberts
5319 Dover Dr
Godfrey IL 62035

Call Sign: KC9DYX
Aubrey J Goers
1304 Duval Dr
Godfrey IL 62035

Call Sign: KC9USV
Thomas E Walter
17 Frontenac Pl
Godfrey IL 62035

Call Sign: KB9LZF
David F Fiola
2820 Godrey Rd
Godfrey IL 62035

Call Sign: KB9PAH
John L Mcdaniels
3208 Greenwood Ln
Godfrey IL 620351815

Call Sign: N9MGX
George B Corzine
3306 Greenwood Ln
Godfrey IL 62035

Call Sign: N9MNF
Steven C Brown
2804 Grovelin St
Godfrey IL 62035

Call Sign: K9FNM
Charles G Vandegriff
360 Hand Dr
Godfrey IL 62035

Call Sign: KA9UCW
Kevin J Botterbush
369 Hand Dr
Godfrey IL 62035

Call Sign: KA9RLK
Raymond W Botterbush
369 Hand Dr
Godfrey IL 62035

Call Sign: KA9TBH
Wilmer J Botterbush
369 Hand Dr
Godfrey IL 62035

Call Sign: KC9TVO
Timothy B Anderson
6115 High Meadow Dr
Godfrey IL 62035

Call Sign: KA9YTR
Noble F Watkins
4917 Hill Dr

Godfrey IL 620351344

Call Sign: WD9GMO
Edgar A Wilson
3501 Hillview Pl
Godfrey IL 620351157

Call Sign: N9HII
Darwin E Gill
5713 Humbert Rd
Godfrey IL 62035

Call Sign: K9ANP
Harry R Nickens
7709 Humbert Rd
Godfrey IL 62035

Call Sign: KC9JCU
Glenn Milton
3113 Illini Trl
Godfrey IL 62035

Call Sign: N9ZJR
Edna M Sommars
7218 Ingham Ln
Godfrey IL 62035

Call Sign: KA9TQA
Louis E Sommars
7218 Ingham Ln
Godfrey IL 62035

Call Sign: KC9UES
Terry J Wooten
7000 Ivy Ln
Godfrey IL 62035

Call Sign: KE9DV
Vic V Amschler
5115 Jerome Dr
Godfrey IL 620351425

Call Sign: N9UJI
John D Wilson
5503 Ladue Dr
Godfrey IL 62035

Call Sign: KB9QEO
Fred L Sevier

803 Lafayette
Godfrey IL 620352547

Call Sign: K0EAA
Marion E Free
713 Lexington Ests Dr
Godfrey IL 62035

Call Sign: KC9UEQ
Scott A Hovey
26582 Lockhaven Hill
Godfrey IL 62035

Call Sign: KB9GKN
Jerry O King
217 Lorretta Ln
Godfrey IL 62035

Call Sign: N9GQE
Don K Mc Kinney
4821 Manitou Trl
Godfrey IL 62035

Call Sign: N9GGE
John M Mc Kinney
4821 Manitou Trl
Godfrey IL 62035

Call Sign: KB9BIL
Julie A Harris
3329 McKee Ln
Godfrey IL 62035

Call Sign: KA9TOY
William C Harris
3329 McKee Ln
Godfrey IL 62035

Call Sign: WD9GNG
Kenneth E Wigger
113 Meadowlark
Godfrey IL 62035

Call Sign: KA9YKC
Ronnie L Gill
4518 N Alby
Godfrey IL 62035

Call Sign: K9UOU

Ronald W Kessler
3809 N Enos Ln
Godfrey IL 62035

Call Sign: KF9F
Richard C Morgan
329 Neptune Ln
Godfrey IL 62035

Call Sign: N8GIL
Garry L Valentine
4707 Otterbein Ct
Godfrey IL 620354804

Call Sign: KA9SYG
Walter H Effinger
1820 Paris Dr
Godfrey IL 62035

Call Sign: KC9BXW
Troy A Ware
310 Pearl St
Godfrey IL 62035

Call Sign: KB9CUE
Patti S Stark
5700 Piasa Trl
Godfrey IL 62035

Call Sign: KA9VZK
Karl C Fiedler
6006 Prairie St
Godfrey IL 62035

Call Sign: KC9TWG
Rosalie E Payne
1212 Preis Ln 4
Godfrey IL 62035

Call Sign: K9RIR
Lawrence G Pohlman Jr
7708 Redbird Ln
Godfrey IL 62035

Call Sign: KB9ZMO
Christina M Kallal
7740 Redbird Ln
Godfrey IL 62035

Call Sign: K9CMO
Arvid C Engdale
2707 Ridgedale Dr
Godfrey IL 62035

Call Sign: KC9PFF
Jeffrey A Auston
1314 Ridgefield Dr
Godfrey IL 62035

Call Sign: WB9CIA
Alice F Preis
3400 Riverview Ct
Godfrey IL 62035

Call Sign: K9KE
William J Preis
3400 Riverview Ct
Godfrey IL 62035

Call Sign: N9HCI
Mark A Walker
5925 Roach Rd
Godfrey IL 62035

Call Sign: N9UAV
Harry E Williams
3520 Rosenberg Ln
Godfrey IL 62035

Call Sign: N9YHO
Linda S Morgan
1809 Seminole Dr
Godfrey IL 62035

Call Sign: N9ZUQ
Susan M Morgan
1809 Seminole Dr
Godfrey IL 62035

Call Sign: KG5UC
Glenn D Roberson
1309 Sir Galahad Ln
Godfrey IL 62035

Call Sign: KA9YTT
Patricia L Blizzard
409 St Anthony Dr
Godfrey IL 62035

Call Sign: N9HSU
Sally A Jacobs
626 St Peter Dr
Godfrey IL 62035

Call Sign: WB9V
Stanley A Jacobs
626 St Peter Dr
Godfrey IL 62035

Call Sign: KA9QOS
John D Schweitzer
3918 Stanka Ln
Godfrey IL 62035

Call Sign: KC9JCZ
Victoria M Mc Claine
26549 State Hwy 3
Godfrey IL 62035

Call Sign: WD9EYT
Dennis J Plebanek
7819 Straube Ct
Godfrey IL 62035

Call Sign: KC9JLH
Ernest L Kautz
6415 Sunset
Godfrey IL 62035

Call Sign: KG0HA
Richard J Belt
1233 Surrey Ct Apt 2
Godfrey IL 62035

Call Sign: N9UEY
Brenda S Oehler
1808 Sycamore Hill Dr
Godfrey IL 62035

Call Sign: KA9TOV
Dean E Oehler
1808 Sycamore Hill Dr
Godfrey IL 62035

Call Sign: KA9CWY
John W Galbreath
4803 Terrace Ln

Godfrey IL 620351116

Call Sign: N9HAX
David A Barringer
6614 Vollmer Ln
Godfrey IL 62035

Call Sign: KD5ON
Steven R Brown
4904 W Hill Dr
Godfrey IL 62035

Call Sign: N9QEE
Darrin L Floyd
5669 W Mil Spring
Godfrey IL 62035

Call Sign: KA9WBJ
Robert J Perkins
6810 Wadlow Ct
Godfrey IL 62035

Call Sign: W9NQU
Earl D Smith
2723 Walters St
Godfrey IL 62035

Call Sign: KC9OGP
David E Sturm
7208 Westwind Dr
Godfrey IL 62035

Call Sign: N9KBN
William G Almonroeder Jr
1401 White Oak Trl
Godfrey IL 62035

Call Sign: KB9OWO
Kevin L Gibbs
5315 Williams Pl
Godfrey IL 62035

Call Sign: N9HAT
Lawrence G Burch
Godfrey IL 62035

Call Sign: KH6BC
Lloyd R Collins
Godfrey IL 62035

Call Sign: WA4BNZ
Ray M Shell
Godfrey IL 62035

Call Sign: N9UJN
Virginia M Fiedler
Godfrey IL 62035

Call Sign: WB9GXC
Brenda S Barnard
Godfrey IL 62035

Call Sign: KB9ZVK
Gregg T Jameson
Godfrey IL 62035

Call Sign: KB9WCV
Jason M Shell
Godfrey IL 62035

Call Sign: KC9NPE
Julianna M Richie
Godfrey IL 62035

Call Sign: WB4MJD
Nita L Shell
Godfrey IL 62035

Call Sign: KB9JVY
Charles A Richie
Godfrey IL 620355187

Call Sign: KB9TSX
Charles A Richie II
Godfrey IL 620355187

Call Sign: KB9OWQ
Donna M Richie
Godfrey IL 620355187

FCC Amateur Radio
Licenses in Golconda

Call Sign: WB9VVN
Aletha L Judd
Rr I Box 189
Golconda IL 62938

Call Sign: WB9VVO
Jay L Judd
Rt 2 Box 189
Golconda IL 62938

Call Sign: N9MWL
Weldon C Rorer
R 1 Box 24
Golconda IL 62938

Call Sign: WD9DFR
Roy L Owens
R 1 Box 31
Golconda IL 62938

Call Sign: K9GJK
Prentice R Board
R 1 Box 99A
Golconda IL 62938

Call Sign: AD4FJ
Edward B Barger Jr
213 E Chatham St
Golconda IL 62938

Call Sign: KE4CKX
Sharon L Barger
213 E Chatham St
Golconda IL 62938

Call Sign: KB9NXQ
Donald L Millis
607 Raum Park Dr
Golconda IL 62938

Call Sign: N9EX
Jack D Hendricks
132 Rosebud Rd
Golconda IL 62938

Call Sign: N9VCS
Kenneth A Baldeser
Golconda IL 62938

Call Sign: K9QPV
Curtis O Broadway
Golconda IL 62938

Call Sign: N6BDA

John T Crabb
Golconda IL 62938

Call Sign: KA9ZIH
Steve E Crabb
Golconda IL 62938

Call Sign: KB9SFL
Mark E Broadway
Golconda IL 629380112

FCC Amateur Radio
Licenses in Golden

Call Sign: KB9TBW
Heather L Whitaker
503 Albers
Golden IL 62339

Call Sign: KB0EVK
Arlyn V Robbins
1102 Hayes St
Golden IL 62339

Call Sign: KA3JUY
Craig A Mackrides
2168 Hwy 61
Golden IL 62339

Call Sign: N9LDR
Joseph D Barlow
903 Prairie Mills Rd
Golden IL 62339

Call Sign: W9JLG
Jerry L Golden
301 W 4th St
Golden IL 62339

Call Sign: WJ9G
Jerry L Golden
401 W 4th St
Golden IL 62339

FCC Amateur Radio
Licenses in Golden Eagle

Call Sign: N9IAN
Michael R Halemeyer

Rr 1 Box 136B
Golden Eagle IL 62036

Call Sign: K9BVE
Billy J Rogers
Rr 1 Box 238A
Golden Eagle IL 62036

FCC Amateur Radio Licenses in Golden Gate

Call Sign: KB9OLS
Michelle R Butts
205 Factory
Golden Gate IL 62843

Call Sign: KB9LKK
Margo M Eyman
1 Rigg St
Golden Gate IL 62843

Call Sign: KB9JVV
Ronald G Eyman
1 Rigg St
Golden Gate IL 62843

FCC Amateur Radio Licenses in Good Hope

Call Sign: KC9NYA
David R Hainline
19525 E 1100th St
Good Hope IL 61438

FCC Amateur Radio Licenses in Goodfield

Call Sign: KC9UCF
Richard A Stevens
518 E Robinson St
Goodfield IL 61742

Call Sign: KC9GMU
Bruce R Wyss
10 Maple Dr
Goodfield IL 61742

Call Sign: K9KKK
Robert J Hoffer

650 Oak Ct
Goodfield IL 61742

Call Sign: KB9NOT
John R Worthen
1470 US Hwy 150
Goodfield IL 61742

Call Sign: KC9HNL
Jeffrey A Klaus
501 W Martin Dr
Goodfield IL 61742

Call Sign: N9IPR
Deborah K Ulrich
215 W Peoria St Box 305
Goodfield IL 61742

Call Sign: KB9INJ
Glennis D Smith
Goodfield IL 61742

Call Sign: N9PSX
Ray H Smith Jr
Goodfield IL 61742

Call Sign: K9HHO
Lenn S Hunt
Goodfield IL 61742

FCC Amateur Radio Licenses in Goreville

Call Sign: N9THZ
Philip W Phillips
Rr 2 Box 121
Goreville IL 62939

Call Sign: N9OW
Michael A Hood
120 E Gore St
Goreville IL 62939

Call Sign: KC9BZS
William C Ahrendt
345 Janeal Dr
Goreville IL 62939

Call Sign: KC9OLV

Michael K Mighell
1430 Lake Shore Dr S
Goreville IL 62939

Call Sign: WA9AME
Keith L Meadows
430 Lakeshore Dr S
Goreville IL 62939

Call Sign: KC9OLU
Derek R Hanson
150 Mark Dr
Goreville IL 62939

Call Sign: KC9SRY
Derek R Key
302 N Ferne Clyffe Rd
Goreville IL 62939

Call Sign: KC9MIH
Ronald G Hancock
308 S Hubbard
Goreville IL 62939

Call Sign: KB9JCY
Michael R Craig
216 S Hubbard Ave
Goreville IL 62939

Call Sign: KB9JNR
Lily L Craig
216 S Hubbard Box 122
Goreville IL 62939

Call Sign: KF9TD
Dennis L Brenningmeyer
410 Sugar Creek Rd
Goreville IL 62939

Call Sign: N9WND
Sheryl A Brenningmeyer
410 Sugar Creek Rd
Goreville IL 62939

Call Sign: KC9OMD
Kenneth S Maze
775 Sullivan Rd
Goreville IL 62939

Call Sign: N9RZT
Donald E Hood
160 Sunset Ln
Goreville IL 62939

Call Sign: WA9RLI
Nathan I Gross
565 Toler Ln
Goreville IL 62939

Call Sign: N9TPT
Susan M King
124 W Side St
Goreville IL 62939

Call Sign: KB9TWP
Philip E Jones
Goreville IL 629390272

FCC Amateur Radio Licenses in Gorham

Call Sign: KA9YIP
John W Few
106 Park St
Gorham IL 62940

Call Sign: W9WLA
Melvin E Hopfer
Gorham IL 62940

FCC Amateur Radio Licenses in Grafton

Call Sign: KB9PZH
Christopher P Zimmerman
Rr 1 Box 35
Grafton IL 62037

Call Sign: KC9QWO
Ross C Crowson Sr
15308 Liberty Ridge Rd
Grafton IL 62037

Call Sign: WU9V
Wesley C Townzen
17157 Liberty Ridge Rd
Grafton IL 62037

FCC Amateur Radio Licenses in Grand Chain

Call Sign: KJ9T
Jimmy J Isom
Grand Chain IL 62941

Call Sign: KC9NJL
John W Harp
Grand Chain IL 62941

Call Sign: KJ9H
John W Harp
Grand Chain IL 62941

FCC Amateur Radio Licenses in Grand Ridge

Call Sign: KA9YPD
Richard K Munter
3 Clover Ct
Grand Ridge IL 61325

Call Sign: WD9DVS
John H Scifers
155 Poundstone Ave
Grand Ridge IL 613250176

Call Sign: N9QIK
Ronald E Wilson
230 W Penn
Grand Ridge IL 61325

Call Sign: KB9EQD
Carol A White
Grand Ridge IL 61325

FCC Amateur Radio Licenses in Grand Tower

Call Sign: K9SYB
William E Golliher Sr
616 3rd Ave 10
Grand Tower IL 62942

FCC Amateur Radio Licenses in Granite City

Call Sign: KC9KGL
Timothy A Wimberly
714 26th Pl
Granite City IL 62040

Call Sign: N9RLS
Ruby Sullivan
1940 Adams
Granite City IL 62040

Call Sign: N9LS
Lawrence R Sullivan
1940 Adams St
Granite City IL 62040

Call Sign: KB9KXH
Randall A Hall Sr
2004 Amos Ave
Granite City IL 620405915

Call Sign: WA9EYQ
Clarence E Schiber
3228 Aubrey
Granite City IL 62040

Call Sign: N9BSL
Michael W Clements
1935 Benton St
Granite City IL 62040

Call Sign: KB9KDV
Tonya M Miller
2589 Boyle Ave
Granite City IL 62040

Call Sign: WU9J
Lloyd L Johnson
4129 Braden St
Granite City IL 62040

Call Sign: N9HSY
Grover H Pace Sr
131 Braircliff Dr
Granite City IL 62040

Call Sign: KC9RIM
Mike S Robbins
4220 Breckenridge Ln
Granite City IL 62040

Call Sign: W9NVW
Theodore Kawula
3232 Carlson Ave
Granite City IL 62040

Call Sign: K9RUV
Joseph H Burmeister
2565 Center St
Granite City IL 62040

Call Sign: KC9BXF
Jeffrey E Dill
617 Chouteau Ave
Granite City IL 62040

Call Sign: KC9CFY
Jeffrey E Dill
617 Chouteau Ave
Granite City IL 62040

Call Sign: KC9LXJ
Garen D Carroll
1342 Chouteau Pl Rd
Granite City IL 62040

Call Sign: N9PBX
David W Foreshee
1736 Chouteau Pl Rd
Granite City IL 62040

Call Sign: N9JGU
Roger D Foreshee Sr
1736 Chouteau Pl Rd
Granite City IL 62040

Call Sign: N9REL
Vickie L Foreshee
1736 Chouteau Pl Rd
Granite City IL 62040

Call Sign: KA9BGT
James M Noeth
2209 Cleveland
Granite City IL 62040

Call Sign: WA9KJV
Lawrence J Unfried
2226 Cleveland Blvd

Granite City IL 62040

Call Sign: KB9YWS
Darrin R Hutson
2407 Cleveland Blvd
Granite City IL 62040

Call Sign: KB9ZCG
Jill E Hutson
2407 Cleveland Blvd
Granite City IL 62040

Call Sign: KA9FVF
Charles R Simon
7 Cobblestone Ct
Granite City IL 62040

Call Sign: N9LDT
Vahog Matoesian
3226 Colgate Pl
Granite City IL 62040

Call Sign: WB9TUO
John F Ropac Jr
3300 Colgate Pl
Granite City IL 62040

Call Sign: KA9WVI
Ryan L Bramm
1061 Cote Brilliant
Granite City IL 62040

Call Sign: WD9IJH
John W Headrick
2013 Cottage Ave
Granite City IL 62040

Call Sign: K9JDM
Paul D Simon
3208 Davis Ave
Granite City IL 62040

Call Sign: KC9MYQ
William E Carruba
2238 Delmar
Granite City IL 62040

Call Sign: KC9RVF
Jeffrey B Smith

2254 Delmar Ave
Granite City IL 62040

Call Sign: KB9QGQ
Eric D Jaycox
2454 Delmar Ave
Granite City IL 620403426

Call Sign: KB9MXB
Marion D Whitehead
2833 Dogwood
Granite City IL 62040

Call Sign: KB9MHB
Terry L Rumpf
2433 E 25th
Granite City IL 62040

Call Sign: K7AAB
Collin A Dvorak
2426 E 25th St
Granite City IL 62040

Call Sign: KD7AVO
Tiffany L Dvorak
2426 E 25th St
Granite City IL 62040

Call Sign: WA9ZWW
Ray L Williams
2545 E 27th St
Granite City IL 62040

Call Sign: K9ZTF
Alfred F Johnson
7 Eduardo Dr
Granite City IL 62040

Call Sign: AA9KC
John F Knipping
27 Eduardo Dr
Granite City IL 62040

Call Sign: KB9MHA
Kevin M Knipping
27 Eduardo Dr
Granite City IL 62040

Call Sign: W4FCW

The Old Freewheelers
Amateur Radio Transmitter
Society
27 Eduardo Dr
Granite City IL 62040

Call Sign: W9AUE
Floyd A Converse
2827 Edwards
Granite City IL 62040

Call Sign: N9UQA
Elden L Craft Jr
2432 Edwards St
Granite City IL 62040

Call Sign: KA9FFJ
Robert D Bridges
2323 Emert
Granite City IL 62040

Call Sign: KA9PWM
James L Graham Sr
627 Fleming
Granite City IL 62040

Call Sign: KB9CQX
Dale R Newberry
528 Fleming Pl
Granite City IL 62040

Call Sign: N9GNI
Louis A Wienhoff
1712 Garfield Ave
Granite City IL 62040

Call Sign: N9HSP
Stephen D Line II
2619 Grand Ave
Granite City IL 62040

Call Sign: KB9BFD
William D Line
2619 Grand Ave
Granite City IL 62040

Call Sign: K9YQJ
Phillip F Szymarek
2633 Grand Ave

Granite City IL 62040

Call Sign: W9RXT
Frank J Draganich
2713 Grand Ave
Granite City IL 62040

Call Sign: KA9IHC
William H Grammer
3325 Harvard Pl
Granite City IL 62040

Call Sign: KA9BGI
Joseph H Decker
2313 Hodges Ave
Granite City IL 62040

Call Sign: N9YXO
Roland M Ernst
240 Holiday MHP
Granite City IL 62040

Call Sign: N9IBM
Robert S York
4281 Hwy 162
Granite City IL 62040

Call Sign: K9IYC
Herbert J Gillham
2700 Hwy 67
Granite City IL 620402029

Call Sign: W0MX
Timothy M Boyd
2248 Iowa
Granite City IL 620405418

Call Sign: KC9NLY
Dennis E Mize
2802 Iowa St
Granite City IL 62040

Call Sign: KC9QXC
Mark E Thomas
35 Janine Ct
Granite City IL 62040

Call Sign: WA9F
Tommy L Manis

2472 Kilarney
Granite City IL 62040

Call Sign: AA9UX
Royal E Hurt
3231 Kilarney
Granite City IL 620405143

Call Sign: KB9FCX
Harold R Denson
3420 Lake Dr
Granite City IL 62040

Call Sign: KB9VCZ
Anne E Losito
3836 Lake Dr
Granite City IL 62040

Call Sign: KB9SQB
Michael J Losito
3836 Lake Dr
Granite City IL 620404326

Call Sign: KB9TWN
Sharon E Losito
3836 Lake Dr
Granite City IL 620404326

Call Sign: KB9OHJ
Jesse S Johnson
4488 Lake Dr
Granite City IL 62040

Call Sign: KZ9G
Jesse S Johnson
4488 Lake Dr
Granite City IL 62040

Call Sign: KC9DRV
Janneth L Hall
4488 Lake Dr
Granite City IL 62040

Call Sign: KC9AFP
Jadie L Johnson
4728 Lake Dr
Granite City IL 62040

Call Sign: KB9PKL

Kevin S Johnson
4728 Lake Dr
Granite City IL 62040

Call Sign: KZ9D
Kevin S Johnson
4728 Lake Dr
Granite City IL 62040

Call Sign: KC9EMU
Mollie M Johnson
4728 Lake Dr
Granite City IL 62040

Call Sign: KJ9H
Roy B Johnson
3801 Lake Dr Box 359
Granite City IL 62040

Call Sign: KF9UQ
Curtis A Russell
4510 Lakeshore Dr
Granite City IL 62040

Call Sign: N9TWO
Jason E Johnson
2426 Lincoln Ave
Granite City IL 62040

Call Sign: N9TTG
Jerome D Johnson Sr
2426 Lincoln Ave
Granite City IL 62040

Call Sign: KC9NTG
Marion S Fisk Sr
2438 Lincoln Ave
Granite City IL 62040

Call Sign: KF9EV
David A Miller
2440 Lincoln Ave
Granite City IL 62040

Call Sign: KA9PMP
Janet L Stoppkotte
2440 Lincoln Ave
Granite City IL 62040

Call Sign: KB0AKW
Lawrence R Wienhoff
48 Lockhaven Dr
Granite City IL 62040

Call Sign: KA9NEM
Larry W Hutchison
53 Lockhaven Dr
Granite City IL 62040

Call Sign: W9DXY
William W Broadwater
2616 Logan Ave
Granite City IL 62040

Call Sign: KF9UA
Bryan S Poole
2237 Lynch
Granite City IL 62040

Call Sign: K9IVN
Edward B Nichols
3014 Madison Ave
Granite City IL 62040

Call Sign: N9AHJ
Thomas C Walker
2012 Manley
Granite City IL 62040

Call Sign: KB9IAL
Robin E Thurston
1827 Maple St
Granite City IL 62040

Call Sign: N9CZN
Karl G Fulmer
601 Margaret
Granite City IL 62040

Call Sign: KC9GYP
Vance E Kelley
2712 Maryville Rd
Granite City IL 62040

Call Sign: KC9IRB
Brian A Ladig
847 Mcintosh Dr
Granite City IL 62040

Call Sign: NE9R
Glen E Hommert
4108 Melrose Ave
Granite City IL 620402207

Call Sign: KB9PGW
Clarence O Linton Jr
2133 Miracle
Granite City IL 62040

Call Sign: N9QYB
Dennis L Culver
2245 Miracle
Granite City IL 62040

Call Sign: N9VPS
Sheryl L Culver
2245 Miracle Ave
Granite City IL 62040

Call Sign: KB9GBP
Randall S Morgan
3019 Myrtle St
Granite City IL 62040

Call Sign: N9IWY
Dorothy R Spiller
2819 Nameoki Dr
Granite City IL 62040

Call Sign: KU9R
James L Spiller
2819 Nameoki Dr
Granite City IL 62040

Call Sign: KA9LWW
Kenneth D Simon
24 Oaklawn Dr
Granite City IL 62040

Call Sign: KC9VHW
Daniel L Whitaker
5745 Old Alton Rd
Granite City IL 62040

Call Sign: N9SNO
Kelly L Bowen
6239 Old Alton Rd

Granite City IL 62040

Call Sign: N9YDT
Linda M Bowen
6239 Old Alton Rd
Granite City IL 62040

Call Sign: KB9YGC
Fayetta S Williamson
205 Paradise Ln
Granite City IL 62040

Call Sign: KB9YGB
Jason D Durrett
205 Paradise Ln
Granite City IL 62040

Call Sign: W9CHV
Albert T Howards
2572 Parkview Dr Apt 304
Granite City IL 62040

Call Sign: KA9LSM
Cloyd E Burris
2357 Paul Ave
Granite City IL 62040

Call Sign: WA9SDT
Everett E Watson Jr
2360 Paul Ave
Granite City IL 62040

Call Sign: KC9VHV
Tyler W Schooley
2540 Pine St
Granite City IL 62040

Call Sign: N9DJG
Leslie A Hall
1621 Primrose
Granite City IL 62040

Call Sign: N9UJV
John W Alsop
3420 Princeton Dr
Granite City IL 62040

Call Sign: N9BRD
Terrell E Nichols

4913 Redwood Ln
Granite City IL 620402651

Call Sign: KG9JF
Martin L Davis
2408 Roney Dr
Granite City IL 62040

Call Sign: WB9RXO
Michael W Lipe
3717 Ruth Dr
Granite City IL 62040

Call Sign: N9VQU
Earl C Voss Jr
2916 Saratoga Ave
Granite City IL 62040

Call Sign: AA9JF
Forrest L Borror
5112 Sheila Dr
Granite City IL 62040

Call Sign: K9BHA
Gene H Cassy
2191 Shirlene Dr
Granite City IL 62040

Call Sign: KC9HAG
Vincent L Sigite
4100 South Dr
Granite City IL 62040

Call Sign: KC9UJA
Katherine D Simon
1733 Spring Ave
Granite City IL 62040

Call Sign: WB9SMG
Marsha L Acord
1614 Spruce St
Granite City IL 62040

Call Sign: KB9SFV
David A Bast
1949 St Clair Ave
Granite City IL 62040

Call Sign: KB9QQP

Philip J Bast
1949 St Clair Ave
Granite City IL 62040

Call Sign: KB9RDX
Susan B Bast
1949 St Clair Ave
Granite City IL 62040

Call Sign: NU9T
John E White
2469 St Clair Ave
Granite City IL 62040

Call Sign: WB9IPN
Lillian L Delps
961 St Thomas Rd
Granite City IL 62040

Call Sign: N9MQV
James R Mersinger
2594 Stratford
Granite City IL 62040

Call Sign: KE9OM
Roy G York
2204 Terminal Ave
Granite City IL 62040

Call Sign: W9JZM
Walter L Bruch
4 Terrace Ln
Granite City IL 62040

Call Sign: N9PPM
Fred T Mc Cauley
536 Thorngate Dr
Granite City IL 620407148

Call Sign: KD9RX
Kerry T Green Sr
540 Thorngate Dr
Granite City IL 62040

Call Sign: WB9SHJ
Gary R Marcum
1637 Venice Ave
Granite City IL 62040

Call Sign: W9GRM
Gary R Marcum
1637 Venice Ave
Granite City IL 62040

Call Sign: KC9OV
James L Winters
3321 Village Ln
Granite City IL 62040

Call Sign: KB9VJI
Michael W Scannell
187 Voight Pl
Granite City IL 62040

Call Sign: K9AOS
Michael W Scannell
187 Voight Pl
Granite City IL 62040

Call Sign: KA0CBG
Al Smoot
3113 W Chain Of Rocks Rd
12
Granite City IL 62040

Call Sign: KB9UGP
David J Heck
3315 Wabash
Granite City IL 62040

Call Sign: K9BTR
Patrick Hall
3112 Wabash Ave
Granite City IL 62040

Call Sign: N9SIN
Mary F Wallace
3006 Warren Ave
Granite City IL 62040

Call Sign: N9KMW
Harold D Howard
2318 Washington Ave
Granite City IL 62040

Call Sign: KB9ZSW
Richard H Matthews
2721 Washington Ave

Granite City IL 62040

Call Sign: K9BGY
Charles J Dickey
2901 Washington Ave
Granite City IL 62040

Call Sign: KA9NFL
John J Von Nida Jr
3033 Washington Ave
Granite City IL 62040

Call Sign: KA9PKM
Gary L Pfroender
3275 Westchester
Granite City IL 62040

Call Sign: KB9BGM
Shannon S Allen
9 William John Ct
Granite City IL 62040

Call Sign: WA9RSJ
Ewing L Andrews
3230 Wilshire Dr
Granite City IL 62040

Call Sign: KC9GBS
Frank C Mehrtens
2300 Wilson Ave
Granite City IL 62040

Call Sign: K9QMD
Harold E Stiverson II
2801 Yale Dr
Granite City IL 62040

Call Sign: KA9YIG
Janice G Stiverson
2801 Yale Dr
Granite City IL 62040

Call Sign: N9EHG
Mark W Brand
Granite City IL 62040

Call Sign: N9HZI
Max J Aubuchon
Granite City IL 62040

Call Sign: N9PFI
Beryl L Foreshee Jr
Granite City IL 62040

FCC Amateur Radio Licenses in Grant Park

Call Sign: W9SRV
Tom W Gunderson
17477 E 10500 N Rd
Grant Park IL 60940

Call Sign: KC9HKL
Waldofar Repeater Club
17477 E 10500 N Rd
Grant Park IL 60940

Call Sign: WA9WLN
Waldofar Repeater Club
17477 E 10500 N Rd
Grant Park IL 60940

Call Sign: KC9KGK
Matthew King
9087 E 5000 N Rd
Grant Park IL 60940

Call Sign: N9LVQ
Michael W Schaefer Jr
8496A E 700N Rd
Grant Park IL 60940

Call Sign: KC9NLB
Gary W Kole
17706 E Rt 17
Grant Park IL 60940

Call Sign: W9GUN
Gary W Kole
17706 E SR 17
Grant Park IL 609405441

Call Sign: N9TQI
Donald P Cantway
47 Lake Metonga Trl
Grant Park IL 60940

Call Sign: N9CYD

William E Stone
6161 N 15000 E
Grant Park IL 60940

Call Sign: W9IEY
Paul T Kwiatkowski
4708 W County Line Rd
Grant Park IL 60940

Call Sign: KB9ONT
Christopher R Gordon
308 W Curtis
Grant Park IL 609400387

FCC Amateur Radio Licenses in Grantsburg

Call Sign: KB9APC
James L Manier
2045 Central Hill Rd
Grantsburg IL 62943

Call Sign: N9YDU
Kimberly A Manier
2045 Central Hill Rd
Grantsburg IL 62943

FCC Amateur Radio Licenses in Granville

Call Sign: KI6OIB
Tennille K Bregar
305 E Silverspoon
Granville IL 61326

Call Sign: K9LK
David J Giudici
203 Elm St
Granville IL 61326

Call Sign: KB9HNQ
Daniel J Serafini
418 Hennepin St
Granville IL 61326

Call Sign: W9CP
Daniel J Serafini
418 Hennepin St
Granville IL 61326

Call Sign: K9CRW
Dorothy V Novak
310 S Church St
Granville IL 61326

Call Sign: K9CSC
Edward J Novak Sr
310 S Church St
Granville IL 61326

Call Sign: KI4EVD
Emerson L Fandel Jr
502 S McCoy St
Granville IL 61326

Call Sign: N9TNZ
Earle G Rice
Granville IL 61326

Call Sign: K9BDQ
Gerald R Masini
Granville IL 61326

Call Sign: KB9LNX
Walter R Waligora
Granville IL 61326

Call Sign: KB9FZM
Steve M Lyons
Granville IL 61326

FCC Amateur Radio Licenses in Grayville

Call Sign: N9HBT
Curry J Baker
612 Lake St
Grayville IL 62844

Call Sign: KC9HCA
Scott M Henson
819 N 1st
Grayville IL 62844

Call Sign: KC9NPI
Amy M Henson
819 N 1st
Grayville IL 62844

Call Sign: KB9RBU
Seth A Summers
819 N 1st St
Grayville IL 62844

Call Sign: N9FTJ
James O Funkhouser
2150 N 1st St
Grayville IL 62844

Call Sign: N9BJE
Gerald A Pollard Sr
304 N 5th St
Grayville IL 62844

Call Sign: N9TKE
Bobby L Paschal
1625 N Court
Grayville IL 62844

Call Sign: KF9UY
Dale E Cox
413 S 1st St
Grayville IL 62844

Call Sign: KB9PQS
Larry A Perry
309 S Main
Grayville IL 62844

Call Sign: KB9NQK
Jerry M Taylor
721 S Water St
Grayville IL 62844

Call Sign: KB9BMU
James W Buckman
813 S Water St
Grayville IL 62844

Call Sign: KA9OFT
William L Walling
409 W North St
Grayville IL 62844

Call Sign: WB9YUA
Finis W Mc Comas
533 W North St

Grayville IL 62844

Call Sign: KC9HVZ
Bruce Ekstrom
1270 Guerin Rd
Green Oaks IL 60048

Call Sign: WB9YCF
Donald R Jacobs
2219 Irondale
Green Oaks IL 60048

Call Sign: WB6LBK
Adrian G Slikkers
2050 Palmer Ln
Green Oaks IL 60048

Call Sign: W9MHJ
Milton I Levenberg
31057 Prairie Ridge Rd
Green Oaks IL 60048

Call Sign: KC9BTZ
John Watkins
14856 Rt 176
Green Oaks IL 60048

Call Sign: KB9NDV
Adam M Stanford
105 Coriell St
Green Valley IL 61534

Call Sign: KB9NDU
Jason K Stanford
105 Coriell St
Green Valley IL 61534

Call Sign: KB9NLO
Paul K Stanford
105 Coriell St
Green Valley IL 61534

Call Sign: N9ITA

Rick W Rynerson
209 Eagle Dr
Green Valley IL 61534

Call Sign: KG9PH
Robin J Miller
16900 Goeken Rd
Green Valley IL 61534

Call Sign: KA9FLC
Debra J Jackson
112 N Maple St
Green Valley IL 61534

Call Sign: KB9MJB
Edward F Mensen
112 N Maple St
Green Valley IL 61534

Call Sign: W9FHB
Gene E Mensen
112 N Maple St
Green Valley IL 61534

Call Sign: KB9PPV
James R Kleiber
6155 Rt 29
Green Valley IL 61534

Call Sign: KC9QXZ
Christopher J Harmon
13613 Tobaggan Rd
Green Valley IL 61534

Call Sign: N9BVH
Robert G Mensen
Green Valley IL 61534

Call Sign: KA9ARH
Wanda J Mensen
Green Valley IL 61534

Call Sign: KC9NIX
Carol A Jones
1005 Chestnut
Greenfield IL 62044

Call Sign: KC9MWN
Dawn E Knotts
901 Chestnut St
Greenfield IL 62044

Call Sign: W9ZMF
Nile E Smith
705 S Main St
Greenfield IL 62044

Call Sign: KC9GIK
Joseph E Tuley
338 CR 1900 E
Greenup IL 62428

Call Sign: W9YKO
David W Dillman
228 CR 2100E
Greenup IL 62428

Call Sign: WD9HNH
Jerry A Feltner
1801 Hazel Dell Rd
Greenup IL 62428

Call Sign: WD9DPA
Raymond D Bowman
404 N Cincinnati
Greenup IL 62428

Call Sign: K9VJI
Ted R Latta
201 S Mill St
Greenup IL 62428

Call Sign: K9WXR
William J Wylde
Greenup IL 62428

Call Sign: N9TXB
Jerry L Ellis
Greenup IL 62428

Call Sign: W9LFO
C Richmond Thayer Jr
151 Alkire St Box 177
Greenview IL 62642

Call Sign: WB9STS
Donald B Baker
Rr 1 Box 170
Greenview IL 62642

Call Sign: W9MFZ
James L Beloungy
Rr 1 Box 175
Greenview IL 62642

Call Sign: KB7H
Kenneth L Hunter
22216 Peoria St
Greenview IL 62642

Call Sign: KC5CDY
Rose A Hunter
22216 Peoria St
Greenview IL 62642

Call Sign: KC9EWR
Douglas L Thayer
151 S Alkire
Greenview IL 626420177

Call Sign: N4RSK
Richard D Lunsford
313 W Van Buren St
Greenview IL 62642

**FCC Amateur Radio
Licenses in Greenville**

Call Sign: KC9PPG
Helen D Bare
1524 7th Rd
Greenville IL 62246

Call Sign: KC9UBC
David P Bare
1524 7th Rd
Greenville IL 62246

Call Sign: KC9VBJ
Karen E Bare
1524 7th Rd
Greenville IL 62246

Call Sign: KC9PBS
Amelia A Vaughn
501 Alice Ave
Greenville IL 62246

Call Sign: W9ATS
Gerald B Todd
901 Allen St
Greenville IL 62246

Call Sign: KB9MKT
Stephen C Ross
325 Asbury
Greenville IL 62246

Call Sign: WB9SLM
Kristine A Hickerson
707 Ash St
Greenville IL 62246

Call Sign: N9NFI
Thad R Bice
934 Beaumont Ave
Greenville IL 62246

Call Sign: KB9SFU
John C Turley
Rt 1 Box 12
Greenville IL 62246

Call Sign: N9KCF
Brenda J Trible
Rr 2 Box 127
Greenville IL 62246

Call Sign: KB0CS
Wesley M Ray
Rt 2 Box 183
Greenville IL 62246

Call Sign: WB0TKQ
Oneda R Ray
Rt 2 Box 183
Greenville IL 62246

Call Sign: KB9ENU
Edwin R Bowen
Rr 3 Box 78
Greenville IL 62246

Call Sign: KB9ENV
Barbara J Oney
Rr 3 Box 94
Greenville IL 62246

Call Sign: N9PKZ
Larry J Schaffner
702 Charles
Greenville IL 62246

Call Sign: KC9PPF
Kayla R Dannaman
522 Charles Ave
Greenville IL 62246

Call Sign: N9PLD
James G Fisher
905 Chicago St
Greenville IL 62246

Call Sign: KC9SHX
Logan Hilmes
884 Cottonwood Ave
Greenville IL 62246

Call Sign: KB0KIJ
Howard M Harris
1076 Cottonwood Ave
Greenville IL 62246

Call Sign: KC9TOY
James D Harris
901 Coyote Ave
Greenville IL 622463209

Call Sign: W9GRN
James D Harris
901 Coyote Ave
Greenville IL 622463209

Call Sign: K39RKF
James D Harris
901 Coyote Ave

Greenville IL 622469748

Call Sign: KC9SHZ
Kaitlynn Smith
727 Deerwood Trl
Greenville IL 62246

Call Sign: N0BFT
David J Harper
744 Deerwood Trl
Greenville IL 62246

Call Sign: N0HOX
Debra L Spitzer-Ford
861 Dolls Orchard Ave
Greenville IL 62246

Call Sign: KC9JZX
James L Ford
861 Dolls Orchard Ave
Greenville IL 62246

Call Sign: KC9UBH
Katelyn R Thomason
1015 E Asbury St
Greenville IL 62246

Call Sign: KC9PBC
Samantha L Siefken
904 E Beaumont
Greenville IL 62246

Call Sign: WB9DRW
Kathryn J Wise
717 E Beaumont Ave
Greenville IL 62246

Call Sign: N9GEQ
Howard S Wise
717 E Beaumont Ave
Greenville IL 622461219

Call Sign: KC9IDR
Boyd K Turley
849 E College Ave
Greenville IL 62246

Call Sign: WB9HHV
Clifford L Seale

603 E Harris Ave
Greenville IL 622460126

Call Sign: KC9RPF
Michael D Huff
948 E Main St
Greenville IL 62246

Call Sign: KC9SID
Allison Confer
1201 E Main St
Greenville IL 62246

Call Sign: WB9YVG
Robert L Kirkman
1111 E Oak
Greenville IL 62246

Call Sign: KC9SIK
Justin Rieke
1206 E Oak
Greenville IL 62246

Call Sign: WD9JDM
James C Keaster
1210 E SR 140
Greenville IL 62246

Call Sign: KA9NRX
Thelma A Keaster
1210 E SR 140
Greenville IL 62246

Call Sign: KC9PBE
Camden N Wall
801 E Vine St
Greenville IL 62246

Call Sign: KB9PVK
Kent L Corrington
911 E Ward
Greenville IL 62246

Call Sign: KA9YMR
Barbara J Marbut
810 E Winter
Greenville IL 62246

Call Sign: KA9NQL

Charley R Marbut
810 E Winter
Greenville IL 62246

Call Sign: KA9YTV
Dennis A Warren
111 E Winter Av
Greenville IL 62246

Call Sign: KC9SIB
Tyler Bryant
13304 Eagle Dr
Greenville IL 62246

Call Sign: W9HOT
Adrian Z Hodson
406 Eastern
Greenville IL 622461414

Call Sign: KC9PAX
Abigail L Barber
626 Eastern Ave
Greenville IL 62246

Call Sign: KB9EST
Stephen P Weller
909 Finch Rd
Greenville IL 62246

Call Sign: KC9UBF
Jacqueline R Forys
1432 Hillcrest Dr
Greenville IL 62246

Call Sign: N9USJ
Charlotte A Turley
Rt 1 Hillsboro Rd Box 12
Greenville IL 62246

Call Sign: KB9HUU
Ronald L Neer
1528 Hueter Rd
Greenville IL 62246

Call Sign: KC9UBI
Emily R Unterbrink
1528 Hunter School Ave
Greenville IL 62246

Call Sign: KC9KQD
Jon M Chasteen
339 Il Rt 127
Greenville IL 62246

Call Sign: N9LIS
Marc A Seale
1402 Il Rt 140
Greenville IL 62246

Call Sign: KC9PBB
Delaney N Rogier
1426 Il Rt 140
Greenville IL 62246

Call Sign: WB9YVF
George W Hentz
795 Il Rt 146
Greenville IL 62246

Call Sign: KC9PAH
Andrew T Warchol
883 Il Rte 140
Greenville IL 62246

Call Sign: KC9PAZ
Austin L Hathaway
2 Illini E
Greenville IL 62246

Call Sign: KC9SPA
Irene C Seale
1402 Illinois Rt 140
Greenville IL 62246

Call Sign: KC9SIC
Madeline Balducci
1307 Irongate Trl
Greenville IL 62246

Call Sign: KA9NQK
Kimberly J Gan
1321 Irongate Trl
Greenville IL 62246

Call Sign: KA9NYF
Donna S Walker
1322 Irongate Trl
Greenville IL 62246

Call Sign: KA9NRW
Hope H Walker Jr
1322 Irongate Trl
Greenville IL 62246

Call Sign: KC9SHF
Cameryn Gan
1327 Irongate Trl
Greenville IL 62246

Call Sign: KC9SIA
Joshua Brannon
1350 Irongate Trl
Greenville IL 62246

Call Sign: KB9EEO
Donald A Speraneo
1397 Kingsbury Ln
Greenville IL 62246

Call Sign: KC9VAK
Alexis A James
407 Ladue
Greenville IL 62246

Call Sign: KC9OXD
Justin R Hildreth
704 Ladue Pl
Greenville IL 62246

Call Sign: KC9PBD
Matthew W Timmermann
1318 Lakeview Dr
Greenville IL 62246

Call Sign: KC9UFF
Michael W Timmermann
1318 Lakeview Dr
Greenville IL 62246

Call Sign: KC9UBG
George M Timmermann
1318 Lakeview Dr
Greenville IL 62246

Call Sign: KC9PBA
Kimberly D Lovatto
1272 Miller Ln

Greenville IL 62246

Call Sign: KC9UBE
Francis H Feaster
1225 Mt Tabor Ave
Greenville IL 62246

Call Sign: KB9GJL
John W Donnell
915 N Elm St
Greenville IL 62246

Call Sign: N9FVJ
Robert J W Dergan
915 N Elm St
Greenville IL 62246

Call Sign: WE9YVD
Gerald K Ketten
703 N Hena
Greenville IL 62246

Call Sign: KA9SBO
Cary L Holman
521 N Locust
Greenville IL 62246

Call Sign: W4GRN
Cary L Holman
521 N Locust
Greenville IL 62246

Call Sign: KC9SHW
Cody Finley
331 N Prairie
Greenville IL 62246

Call Sign: N9FHN
Daniel P Rohrs
865 Paradise Ln
Greenville IL 62246

Call Sign: N9FTE
William R Hargan
700 Pecan
Greenville IL 62246

Call Sign: KC9PAG
Meghan E Thies

116 Quail Hollow Rd
Greenville IL 62246

Call Sign: KC9PAF
Lucas M Carlson
118 Quail Hollow Rd
Greenville IL 62246

Call Sign: KC9OYI
Lyndsey A Carlson
118 Quail Hollow Rd
Greenville IL 62246

Call Sign: KC9LEG
Donna L Carlson
118 Quale Hollow Rd
Greenville IL 62246

Call Sign: N5ZDJ
Jim F Horton III
822 Rc Cardinal Ln
Greenville IL 62246

Call Sign: N5ZEO
Kelly L Horton
822 Rc Cardinal Ln
Greenville IL 62246

Call Sign: KC9PPE
Taylor M Mayes
1209 Ridge Ave
Greenville IL 62246

Call Sign: KC9DGB
Eric E Bennett
603 S 1st St
Greenville IL 62246

Call Sign: KE4FQF
William H Bowman
1318 S 2nd St
Greenville IL 62246

Call Sign: KC9PAY
Jarett S Barnes
418 S 4th St
Greenville IL 62246

Call Sign: N9ILF

Van Loyd
1603 S 4th St
Greenville IL 62246

Call Sign: N9OJM
Sandra K Loyd
1603 S 4th St
Greenville IL 62246

Call Sign: N9DAN
Rex E Catron
406 S 5th
Greenville IL 62246

Call Sign: KC9SHG
Travis S Neer
412 S Elm St
Greenville IL 62246

Call Sign: KB9WRM
Cathy M Neer
766 Samboro Ln
Greenville IL 62246

Call Sign: N9YFO
Rickey A Vaughn
766 Samboro Ln
Greenville IL 62246

Call Sign: WA9RAV
Rickey A Vaughn
766 Samboro Ln
Greenville IL 62246

Call Sign: KC9OYJ
Hannah M Gaffner
852 Shady Grove Ave
Greenville IL 62246

Call Sign: KC9OXC
Tommy J Chapman
606 Shannon Dr
Greenville IL 62246

Call Sign: KA9NQN
Joanne E Ketten
212 Vine
Greenville IL 62246

Call Sign: AB9WY
Orren W Wilcox
915 Vine St
Greenville IL 62246

Call Sign: N9TLG
Daniel A Hahn
609 W College Ave
Greenville IL 62246

Call Sign: KB9EGI
Donald H Stover
515 W Main
Greenville IL 62246

Call Sign: KB9NOK
Patrick Franzke
316 W Main St
Greenville IL 62246

Call Sign: N9VQJ
William E Donnell
203 W Oak
Greenville IL 62246

Call Sign: KC9UBD
Anne E Ennen
524 W Spring
Greenville IL 62246

Call Sign: KB9HYJ
Robert H Neer
525 W Winter St
Greenville IL 62246

Call Sign: KC9UDO
Brandon J Reeves
814 Willard Ave
Greenville IL 62246

Call Sign: KB9AJK
Anthony R Brooks
1506 Willow St
Greenville IL 62246

Call Sign: KC9SIJ
Alexander Moeller
423 Wyatt Ave
Greenville IL 62246

Call Sign: KC9UDN
Chloe E Matute
505 Wyatt Ave
Greenville IL 62246

Call Sign: KB9SLT
Bruce C Volkers
803 Wyatt Ave
Greenville IL 62246

Call Sign: W9KXQ
John K King
Greenville IL 62246

Call Sign: WB9YVE
Allan L Davis
Greenville IL 62246

Call Sign: N9USK
Travis C Turley
Greenville IL 62246

Call Sign: K9RDC
Charles A Bunting
Greenville IL 62246

Call Sign: KA9DEO
Stephen R Neer
Greenville IL 62246

FCC Amateur Radio Licenses in Gridley

Call Sign: KB9VFT
James H Baltz
Rr 1 Box 104
Gridley IL 61744

Call Sign: WB9RSO
Noble A Stubblefield
Rr 1 Box 126 E
Gridley IL 61744

Call Sign: KA9ZEQ
Robert G Fairburn
301 Pkwy Ct
Gridley IL 61744

Call Sign: WF9Y
Mark W Steffen
410 W 7th St
Gridley IL 61744

Call Sign: KA9WQS
Bernard J Ferneau Sr
412 W 7th St
Gridley IL 61744

Call Sign: KC9PZ
Hugh L Mc Broom
Gridley IL 61744

FCC Amateur Radio Licenses in Griggsville

Call Sign: KB9SWD
Kevin R Henthorn
32349 443rd St
Griggsville IL 62340

Call Sign: KB9DQ
Randall V Zimmerman
Rr 1 Box 147
Griggsville IL 62340

Call Sign: KC9ATY
Patrick S Allen
Rr 2 Box 2A1
Griggsville IL 62340

Call Sign: KB9WAL
Larry C White
Apt 21 E Chestnut Box 178
Griggsville IL 62340

Call Sign: KC9BIH
Chris J Lightle
Griggsville IL 62340

Call Sign: KC9BXE
Fred C Slight
Griggsville IL 62340

Call Sign: KC9RFO
Wendel W White
Griggsville IL 62340

FCC Amateur Radio Licenses in Groveland

Call Sign: KC9MKG
Gerald N Braley II
8 Lakeview Dr
Groveland IL 61535

Call Sign: WA9WTS
Clifford E Easden
22 Lakeview Dr
Groveland IL 61535

Call Sign: KD9JN
James A Nation
304 Northern Oaks Dr
Groveland IL 61535

Call Sign: K9JN
James A Nation
304 Northern Oaks Dr
Groveland IL 61535

Call Sign: KC2LBN
Mark A Oram
624 Northern Oaks Dr
Groveland IL 61535

Call Sign: KA9SFH
William S Blackman
288 Sheffield Rd
Groveland IL 61535

Call Sign: N9ELK
Edward L Kline
405 Towne Rd
Groveland IL 61535

Call Sign: KB9EUU
Alan L Legel
17663 Unsicker Rd
Groveland IL 61535

Call Sign: KA9FBJ
Charles R Smith
Box 92 West St
Groveland IL 61535

Call Sign: KB9WAM

Edward L Kline
Groveland IL 61535

Call Sign: KC9ELK
Michael D Christman
Groveland IL 61535

Call Sign: KC9MDD
Gregory A Gresham
Rr 1 Box 116 A
Hamburg IL 62045

Call Sign: KC9AFO
Jeffrey D Eggemeyer
26 Meyer Ave
Hamel IL 62046

Call Sign: N9ZZY
Brian K Weiler
109 Wolf Ave
Hamel IL 62046

Call Sign: KA9HLO
John Morgando
17 Wolf St
Hamel IL 62046

Call Sign: N9TTI
Matthew S Gordon
Hamel IL 62046

Call Sign: KA9YCE
Richard D Riley
1410 Casley Dr
Hamilton IL 62341

Call Sign: KB9KBQ
Robert R Campbell
1281 Elm St
Hamilton IL 62341

Call Sign: KC9UGY
Thomas M Morris
101 Hillcrest Dr
Hamilton IL 62341

Call Sign: KA9VBG
Richard L David
1531 Laurel St
Hamilton IL 62341

Call Sign: N9UOS
Ricky J Wieprecht
531 Main St
Hamilton IL 62341

Call Sign: AB9TW
Ricky J Wieprecht
531 Main St
Hamilton IL 62341

Call Sign: N9JWQ
Arlyn R Hopkins
140 N 20 St
Hamilton IL 62341

Call Sign: N9GR
Greg R Ruhs
1405 N Country Rd 900
Hamilton IL 62341

Call Sign: KA0WJY
Ross D Boyer
1595 N Country Rd 900
Hamilton IL 62341

Call Sign: KB9YBX
Nicholas P Ruhs
1405 N CR 900
Hamilton IL 62341

Call Sign: KB9YBW
Joan E Ruhs
1405 N CR 900
Hamilton IL 62341

Call Sign: KC9LRU
Robin C Crider
1830 Oak St

Hamilton IL 62341

Call Sign: W9HDC
Glenn E Peikett
1660 School St
Hamilton IL 62341

Call Sign: KA9PGL
Robert E Beck
Rt 1 Box 133Y
Hammond IL 61929

Call Sign: KC9DSU
Lindsay D Demark
502 D St
Hammond IL 61929

Call Sign: N9BQD
Lois R Wolfe
600 D St
Hammond IL 61929

Call Sign: W0PDI
Leo M Severe
109 W 7th St
Hammond IL 61929

Call Sign: WA9IVM
Samuel G Osborne
Hammond IL 61929

Call Sign: K9HEZ
Robert B Wolfe
Hammond IL 61929

Call Sign: KA9EVX
William H Bradshaw
Hammond IL 61929

Call Sign: N9FPR
Richard F Bideaux Sr
315 2nd Ave
Hampton IL 61256

Call Sign: KA9KFY
Joseph L De Baker
620 4H Ave
Hampton IL 61256

Call Sign: N9TCL
Thomas L Carmack
1008 7th
Hampton IL 61256

Call Sign: KS9T
Charles W Carmack
1008 7th St
Hampton IL 61256

Call Sign: N9TGJ
Toby L Carmack
1008 7th St
Hampton IL 61256

FCC Amateur Radio Licenses in Hanna City

Call Sign: KB9TLF
John G Torset
12923 Court St
Hanna City IL 61536

Call Sign: WA9NMD
Leo C Klute Jr
11323 Farmington Rd
Hanna City IL 61536

Call Sign: WD9BJI
Patricia J Krause
620 N Main Box 51
Hanna City IL 61536

Call Sign: N9VIQ
Wayne A Satterfield
1207 S Murphy Rd
Hanna City IL 61536

Call Sign: N9HUW
Timothy J Ylinen
12816 W Center St
Hanna City IL 61536

Call Sign: KT9Y
Timothy J Ylinen
12816 W Center St
Hanna City IL 61536

Call Sign: K9IDK
Robin L Ylinen
12816 W Center St
Hanna City IL 61536

Call Sign: WA9SCA
Earl R Kimzey
13925 W Farmington Rd
Hanna City IL 61536

Call Sign: WB9REV
Richard C Vogel
8822 W Plank Rd
Hanna City IL 61536

Call Sign: KC9FQJ
Bradley R Isbell
Hanna City IL 61536

Call Sign: KC9MFS
Robin L Ylinen
Hanna City IL 61536

FCC Amateur Radio Licenses in Hanover

Call Sign: WA9RYZ
Norman L TRUE
98 Blackhawk
Hanover IL 61041

Call Sign: K9DLI
Richard W Jones
8620 Fisher Rd
Hanover IL 61041

Call Sign: N9PED
Roy G Nance
Box 222 Jefferson St
Hanover IL 61041

Call Sign: W9ITV
Joseph E Unfried
704 Monroe St

Hanover IL 61041

FCC Amateur Radio Licenses in Hardin

Call Sign: W9CWU
Rex E Nichols
Hc 61 Box 21A
Hardin IL 62047

Call Sign: AC9AS
Lawrence G Burch
Hardin IL 62047

Call Sign: N9HAT
Lawrence G Burch
Hardin IL 62047

FCC Amateur Radio Licenses in Harmon

Call Sign: N9QFK
David C Smith
739 Hoyle Rd
Harmon IL 61042

Call Sign: KA9VRI
Jeanette M Sutton
Harmon IL 61042

Call Sign: KC9AAB
Dale R Smith
Harmon IL 61042

Call Sign: N9FIS
David G Sutton
Harmon IL 61042

Call Sign: KB9JZH
James M Jordan
Harmon IL 610420116

FCC Amateur Radio Licenses in Harrisburg

Call Sign: K9TSI
David L Stilley
1412 Barnett Rd
Harrisburg IL 62946

Call Sign: N9BRI
Karen R Stilley
1412 Barnett Rd
Harrisburg IL 62946

Call Sign: KC9CQG
Southern Counties Amateur
Network
1412 Barnett St
Harrisburg IL 62946

Call Sign: WS9CAN
Southern Counties Amateur
Network
1412 Barnett St
Harrisburg IL 62946

Call Sign: KB9MFX
Curtis E Mills
1300 Blue Hole Rd
Harrisburg IL 62946

Call Sign: K9JFN
Lanora P Lawson
Rt 3 Box 260
Harrisburg IL 62946

Call Sign: W9RVG
Marshall V Pochay
Rt 3 Box 260
Harrisburg IL 62946

Call Sign: KC9HGQ
Casey M Boone
1765 Briar Creek Rd
Harrisburg IL 62946

Call Sign: WA9MPF
Carl D Mallady
101 E College St
Harrisburg IL 62946

Call Sign: KA9HTK
Rose Stocker
109 E Raymond St
Harrisburg IL 62946

Call Sign: KE9KJ

Larry W Clore
202 E Rose St Apt 6
Harrisburg IL 62946

Call Sign: KB9MLC
Marshall H Watkins
2 E Sloan St
Harrisburg IL 62946

Call Sign: W9BPY
Harvey H Slaton
23 Ford St
Harrisburg IL 62946

Call Sign: KC9EYK
Carl L Banks
915 Hwy 145 S
Harrisburg IL 62946

Call Sign: KC9MMN
Robert D Romonosky
150 Jones Rd
Harrisburg IL 62946

Call Sign: AB9QQ
Robert D Romonosky
150 Jones Rd
Harrisburg IL 62946

Call Sign: KB9RSM
Julius T Lumpkin
355 Ledford Rd
Harrisburg IL 62946

Call Sign: KB9IFH
Steven K Mitchell
455 Ledford Rd
Harrisburg IL 62946

Call Sign: KA8GEM
James E Shover
222 Missouri St
Harrisburg IL 62946

Call Sign: KB9ZBK
Angela K Milligan
6100 Mt Moriah Rd
Harrisburg IL 62946

Call Sign: KB9TYF
Jeffery L Milligan
6100 Mt Moriah Rd
Harrisburg IL 62946

Call Sign: KA9YCX
John L Feazel
400 N Main
Harrisburg IL 62946

Call Sign: KC9OLY
Brian V Casteel
806 N Main
Harrisburg IL 62946

Call Sign: WB9QFK
Jane H Gillen
207 N McKinley
Harrisburg IL 62946

Call Sign: KC9SMM
William R Culkin
612 N Webster St
Harrisburg IL 62946

Call Sign: KB9KZT
Randall K Futch
3200 Old Hwy 13 W
Harrisburg IL 62946

Call Sign: N9YRK
Edward A Moore
380 Puckett Rd
Harrisburg IL 62946

Call Sign: KA9RPJ
Roger L Clark
1130 S Cheney
Harrisburg IL 62946

Call Sign: KB9VFC
Russell E Simmons
121 S Jackson St
Harrisburg IL 62946

Call Sign: KB9ROO
Kimberley S Glasscock
1011 S Ledford St
Harrisburg IL 62946

Call Sign: KB9ORF
Roy B Glasscock
1011 S Ledford St
Harrisburg IL 62946

Call Sign: KB9ROR
Jeffrey K Oestreich Sr
1201 S Ledford St
Harrisburg IL 62946

Call Sign: KC9LXV
Charles E Hamlin Jr
13 S McKinley St
Harrisburg IL 62946

Call Sign: KC9MEU
Patrick A Higgins
1025 S Roosevelt St
Harrisburg IL 62946

Call Sign: KB9KPO
Alice E Clark
411 S Shaw St
Harrisburg IL 62946

Call Sign: N9YUK
Gary D Hooten
801 Sahara Apt G1
Harrisburg IL 62946

Call Sign: KC9CAX
Lyndell B Haney
1240 Somerset Rd
Harrisburg IL 62946

Call Sign: N9DNH
John W Kearns
213 Southwest Dr
Harrisburg IL 62946

Call Sign: KC9VTF
James R Wilkerson III
216 Southwest Dr
Harrisburg IL 62946

Call Sign: N9WUI
Ronnie L Crank
306 St Mary Dr

Harrisburg IL 62946

Call Sign: WB9QAN
Betty J Myers
5840 US 45 S
Harrisburg IL 62946

Call Sign: KC9PV
Dennis E Myers
5840 US Hwy 45 S
Harrisburg IL 62946

Call Sign: KC9QVM
Steven E Stricklin
710 W Charleston St
Harrisburg IL 62946

Call Sign: WB9TQR
Paul E Welling
840 W Church St
Harrisburg IL 62946

Call Sign: KA9HRA
Carl J Hauptmann
14 W Lincoln Ave
Harrisburg IL 62946

Call Sign: AA9TD
Charles R Bybee Sr
2416 W North St
Harrisburg IL 62946

Call Sign: KC9HXB
Henry L Dooley
204 W Raymond St
Harrisburg IL 62946

Call Sign: N9EBN
Richard P Hicks Sr
212 W Raymond St
Harrisburg IL 62946

Call Sign: N9HNA
David L Hicks Sr
212 W Raymond St Box 97
Harrisburg IL 62946

Call Sign: K5AAC
Charles D Harrington

713 W South St
Harrisburg IL 62946

Call Sign: KB9KCV
Charles L Conwell
2530 Wasson Rd
Harrisburg IL 62946

Call Sign: W9UBD
Harry L Isom Sr
Harrisburg IL 62946

Call Sign: N9RAI
Vickie A Woolard
Harrisburg IL 62946

FCC Amateur Radio Licenses in Harristown

Call Sign: WA9KJP
John H Kaufman
1160 N Meridian
Harristown IL 62537

Call Sign: KA9YOD
Sue J Buxton
8130 W 2nd
Harristown IL 62537

Call Sign: NR9I
William H Buxton
8130 W 2nd St
Harristown IL 62537

FCC Amateur Radio Licenses in Hartford

Call Sign: N9IRL
Edward L File
120 W 4th St
Hartford IL 62048

Call Sign: KB9YYJ
Matthew W Harrison
122 W Cherry St
Hartford IL 62048

Call Sign: AB9TJ
Matthew W Harrison

122 W Cherry St
Hartford IL 62048

FCC Amateur Radio Licenses in Harvel

Call Sign: KB9MPN
Roy L Young Jr
225 Fraley
Harvel IL 62538

Call Sign: KA9TGG
Elmer R Bails
Harvel IL 62538

Call Sign: KB9MXC
Tiara S Young
Harvel IL 62538

FCC Amateur Radio Licenses in Havava

Call Sign: KC9MKI
Philip D Shore
16061 CR 1810 N
Havana IL 62644

Call Sign: WB9YWE
David M Kimbrel
17184 CR 1900 E
Havana IL 626440617

Call Sign: KB9PES
John A Zebroski
16510 E 1850 N
Havana IL 62644

Call Sign: W9KVJ
Karl B Arundale
309 E Adams St
Havana IL 62644

Call Sign: KA9HLT
Lawrence L Ginglen
19948 E Ct Rd 1500 N
Havana IL 62644

Call Sign: KC9VHJ
Michael F Schroeder

501 E Main
Havana IL 62644

Call Sign: KC9LCD
Ted E Snider Jr
212 E Mound
Havana IL 62644

Call Sign: KB9ZNR
Gerald M Smith
17024 Hcr 1840 E
Havana IL 62644

Call Sign: KB9NYS
David W Smith
322 N Orange
Havana IL 62644

Call Sign: N9TRR
William J Smith
322 N Orange
Havana IL 62644

Call Sign: N9QLZ
Richard L Lewis
326 N Orange St
Havana IL 62644

Call Sign: W2HND
Robert B Flint
411 N Orange St
Havana IL 626441122

Call Sign: KB9OMS
Kevin S Irons
616 N Pearl
Havana IL 62644

Call Sign: KB9QKU
Richard J Fliege
716 N Plum
Havana IL 62644

Call Sign: KB9DAK
Thomas P Moore
15641 N SR 78
Havana IL 62644

Call Sign: KB9OBS

Alice L Lewis
326 Orange St
Havana IL 62644

Call Sign: K9UF
Stephen D Specketer
18214 Quiver Beach Rd
Havana IL 62644

Call Sign: N9UB
Stephen D Specketer
18214 Quiver Beach Rd
Havana IL 62644

Call Sign: KB9PLO
Bradley J Landry
725 S Coleman
Havana IL 62644

Call Sign: KB9CUD
David E Johnson Sr
215 S Pearl St
Havana IL 62644

FCC Amateur Radio Licenses in Hecker

Call Sign: WD9AQE
Richard S Kaiser
230 W Washington
Hecker IL 62248

Call Sign: KC9EXN
Shawn P Eagan
Hecker IL 62248

FCC Amateur Radio Licenses in Hennepin

Call Sign: KN9T
Michael J O Connor
7th And High St
Hennepin IL 61327

Call Sign: W9SP
Roy K Fearman
7553 Audubon Dr
Hennepin IL 61327

Call Sign: K9ERM
Harvey D Brown
510 E Court St
Hennepin IL 613270107

Call Sign: N9RLZ
Kenneth A Brown
710 E Court St
Hennepin IL 613270092

Call Sign: WB9YWR
Robert C Myers
922 E Market St
Hennepin IL 613270346

Call Sign: KA9WXX
Norman K Raffety
619 E Mulberry St
Hennepin IL 61327

Call Sign: N9NEZ
Norma J Brown
702 E Mulberry St
Hennepin IL 61327

Call Sign: N9OBC
Linda J De Mattia
9044 Henning Ln
Hennepin IL 613275094

Call Sign: N9OBB
Daniel J De Mattia
9044 Henning Ln
Hennepin IL 613275094

Call Sign: KC9SAM
Douglas M Anzlovar
8069 Urnikis Dr
Hennepin IL 61327

Call Sign: KA9YQK
Linda L Litwiler
8069 Urnikis Dr
Hennepin IL 61327

Call Sign: N9CZW
Richard L Seibert
Hennepin IL 61327

Call Sign: K9GRG
Floyd J Brown
Hennepin IL 61327

Call Sign: KC9DLB
Paul H Miller
Hennepin IL 61327

**FCC Amateur Radio
Licenses in Henry**

Call Sign: KB9PUN
Debra D Young
515 2nd St Apt 4
Henry IL 61537

Call Sign: KB9KOW
Robert H Foster
526 CR 1150 N
Henry IL 61537

Call Sign: N9UQM
Ronald L Foster
526 CR 1150 N
Henry IL 61537

Call Sign: KB9KOV
Janet L Foster
526 CR 1150 N
Henry IL 615379746

Call Sign: W9BIN
Charles H Perdew
902 Front St Box 69
Henry IL 61537

Call Sign: N9ODN
John S Mooberry
625 Gateway Dr
Henry IL 61537

Call Sign: KB9PUW
Charles D Young III
313 Jefferson St
Henry IL 61537

Call Sign: K9KOB
Norman A Hoover
409 Lincoln Ave

Henry IL 615371105

Call Sign: K9CAW
Val M Johnson
104 Railroad Ave
Henry IL 61537

Call Sign: KD6NFJ
Claude J Cook
515 School St
Henry IL 61537

Call Sign: KC9BQU
Harrison L Eaves
1043 Warren St
Henry IL 61537

Call Sign: W9SNG
Donald Serpette
Henry IL 61537

Call Sign: KC9QCP
Donald L Serpette
Henry IL 61537

Call Sign: KC9QKC
Donald L Serpette
Henry IL 61537

Call Sign: KB9RKR
Nicole O Bren
Henry IL 61537

**FCC Amateur Radio
Licenses in Herod**

Call Sign: KB8LOH
Leon W Gauthier
Rt 1 Box 144
Herod IL 62947

**FCC Amateur Radio
Licenses in Herrick**

Call Sign: KB9LZ
Robert E Chamberlain
Rr 1 Box 496
Herrick IL 62431

Call Sign: KA9DZO
Norman B Wilson
Rr 1 Box 533
Herrick IL 62431

Call Sign: KB9YJR
Andrea L Schoonover
Rr 1 Box 553
Herrick IL 62431

Call Sign: KB9YJS
Randy W Schoonover
Rr 1 Box 553
Herrick IL 62431

Call Sign: KC9TDN
Randy W Schoonover
Rr 1 Box 553
Herrick IL 62431

Call Sign: KA9YVK
John K Mascher
403 S Adams Ave
Herrick IL 62431

FCC Amateur Radio Licenses in Herrin

Call Sign: KC9OPE
Chris M Cornell
14437 Allen Rd
Herrin IL 62948

Call Sign: KC9HGR
Scott A Sims
9 B Ln
Herrin IL 62948

Call Sign: KC9KIA
Robert W Owsley
2400 Blue Blaze Trl Lot E4
Herrin IL 62948

Call Sign: WA9BAG
Russell L Watson Sr
Rr 2 Box 277
Herrin IL 62948

Call Sign: WA9ZUU

Roland R Walden
Rt 2 Box 346
Herrin IL 62948

Call Sign: KA9VYL
Carl J Knerr
220 Circle Dr
Herrin IL 62948

Call Sign: KB9JCZ
John E Crespi
3206 Corsair Dr
Herrin IL 62948

Call Sign: WB9CZU
Robert L Oakley
908 E Clark Trl
Herrin IL 62948

Call Sign: KB9YNZ
Michael L Bottiaux
322 Evergreen Dr
Herrin IL 62948

Call Sign: W9RF
Joseph H Hayes
18114 Freeman Spur Rd
Herrin IL 62948

Call Sign: KC9SAJ
Jason M Buchanan
607 James Ct
Herrin IL 62948

Call Sign: KB9SDN
Murle M Hill
208 N 11th Ave
Herrin IL 62948

Call Sign: N9XZN
Denise A Wade
1613 N 13th
Herrin IL 62948

Call Sign: N9TWI
Michael R Wade
1613 N 13th
Herrin IL 62948

Call Sign: KC9OLN
Patrick A Creek
1001 N 14th St
Herrin IL 62948

Call Sign: KA9ZIY
Steven C Shafer
101 N 16th B
Herrin IL 62948

Call Sign: KC9POJ
John R Yates
2904 N 17th St
Herrin IL 62948

Call Sign: N9SMX
Dan C Cox
712 N 18th
Herrin IL 62948

Call Sign: KB9MFV
Earl H Todd
401 N 18th St
Herrin IL 62948

Call Sign: W9PQB
Robert W Starnes
601 N 19th St
Herrin IL 629481212

Call Sign: KB9UGJ
Lucas E Childers
715 N 23 St
Herrin IL 62948

Call Sign: KC9OLL
Edward F Wallace
200 N 32nd St
Herrin IL 62948

Call Sign: W9ORI
Edward F Wallace
200 N 32nd St
Herrin IL 62948

Call Sign: KB9TTM
Adam J Faulkner
509 N 6th St
Herrin IL 62948

Call Sign: KB9IOU
Joshua J Dunnigan
420 N 7th St
Herrin IL 62948

Call Sign: KA9ALJ
Martin H Stout
213 N 9th St
Herrin IL 62948

Call Sign: AA9EZ
Michael E Townzen
621 N 9th St
Herrin IL 62948

Call Sign: N9XUC
Charles L Cline Jr
721 B N Park Ave
Herrin IL 62948

Call Sign: KC9OPD
Ronda M Koch
3012 Pine Ridge Dr
Herrin IL 62948

Call Sign: WB8SXT
Dienard D Koch
3024 Pine Ridge Dr
Herrin IL 629483758

Call Sign: N9BOA
Ralph E Hudson
109 S 10th St
Herrin IL 62948

Call Sign: KC9MFW
Bradley A Campbell
917 S 10th St
Herrin IL 62948

Call Sign: KC9KWM
April D Bennett
325 S 12th St
Herrin IL 62948

Call Sign: N9AJI
Larry L Miles
1221 S 14th St

Herrin IL 62948

Call Sign: KC9OLJ
Richard A Yancey
1416 S 14th St
Herrin IL 62948

Call Sign: KB9HNO
Edward J Helleny
600 S 16th St
Herrin IL 62948

Call Sign: K9QX
Edward J Helleny
600 S 16th St
Herrin IL 62948

Call Sign: N9GYL
James M Dillon
1607 S 22 St Apt A
Herrin IL 62948

Call Sign: WB9TEL
G W Watson
519 S 25th St
Herrin IL 62948

Call Sign: KA9YPH
Jerry L Lewis
601 S 25th St
Herrin IL 62948

Call Sign: W9MXM
Raymond E Melhorn
512 S 27th
Herrin IL 62948

Call Sign: KJ7EN
Allen J Knuth
100 S 43rd St
Herrin IL 62948

Call Sign: KA9ETE
Donna M Knuth
100 S 43rd St
Herrin IL 62948

Call Sign: KC9OHZ
Alice M Waldron

213 S 8th St
Herrin IL 62948

Call Sign: KC9NEA
Ricky J Waldron
213 S 8th St
Herrin IL 62948

Call Sign: KC9DEV
Ernest E Sadovnikov
215 S Park Ave
Herrin IL 62948

Call Sign: AA7OL
Hidenori Takahashi
215 S Park Ave
Herrin IL 62948

Call Sign: W9PYL
Louis A French Jr
821 S Park Ave
Herrin IL 62948

Call Sign: KC9LJI
Jimmy A Finney
1704 W Adams St
Herrin IL 62948

Call Sign: KC9OPC
Melinda L Howard
1501 W Cherry St
Herrin IL 62948

Call Sign: W9JGN
Carl J Scarlette
308 W Clark Trl
Herrin IL 62948

Call Sign: K9SQM
Dorothy L Scarlette
308 W Clark Trl
Herrin IL 62948

Call Sign: WB9CZT
William D Oakley
709 W Madison
Herrin IL 62948

Call Sign: KC9ESZ

Raymond L Mileur
812 W Madison
Herrin IL 62948

Call Sign: N9VKM
Timothy D Follis
516 W Monroe
Herrin IL 62948

Call Sign: W9DEF
Donald E Fout
107 W Smith St
Herrin IL 62948

Call Sign: N9XZO
Larry J Giovanetti
1212 W Tyler Ave
Herrin IL 629481322

Call Sign: KC9OLM
Denise G Ewing
Herrin IL 62948

Call Sign: WB9VJF
Don L Smith
Herrin IL 62948

FCC Amateur Radio Licenses in Herscher

Call Sign: K9EMX
Gordon J Feige
231 S Main
Herscher IL 60941

FCC Amateur Radio Licenses in Hettick

Call Sign: WD9EBQ
David E Lattan
7771 Hettick Rd
Hettick IL 62649

Call Sign: N9CNQ
Mary E Lattan
7771 Hettick Rd
Hettick IL 62649

Call Sign: K4DNN

Stanley E Dunn
236 Oak St
Hettick IL 62649

FCC Amateur Radio Licenses in Heyworth

Call Sign: KA9SHU
Art L Molinar
Rr 1 Box 223
Heyworth IL 61745

Call Sign: WB9RQN
Harvey W Toon
Rr 1 Box 309
Heyworth IL 61745

Call Sign: WB9WQL
Garth D Nicholas
Rr 1 Box 434A
Heyworth IL 61745

Call Sign: WD9ADI
Joseph D Necessary
4675 Circle Dr
Heyworth IL 61745

Call Sign: KG9DW
Michael D Brown
16469 E 200 N Rd
Heyworth IL 61745

Call Sign: K9GUN
William T Suttle
16824 E 400 N Rd
Heyworth IL 61745

Call Sign: KB9VVJ
William T Suttle
16824 E 400 N Rd
Heyworth IL 61745

Call Sign: KD9XL
Harold L Freeman
410 E Main
Heyworth IL 61745

Call Sign: W9TXU
Joe L Reda

107 E Sullivan St
Heyworth IL 617459226

Call Sign: KC9HRF
Uhacc
107 E Sullivan St
Heyworth IL 617459226

Call Sign: KC9FWM
Tanya S Leahy
4362 N 1700 E Rd
Heyworth IL 61745

Call Sign: K9HKF
Ernest W Mountjoy
5598 N 1800 E Rd
Heyworth IL 61745

Call Sign: WB9JAR
Carolyn L Van Winkle
106 N Poland
Heyworth IL 61745

Call Sign: N9CME
Baxter D Rogers
403 N Vine St
Heyworth IL 61745

Call Sign: KB9RUF
Larry E Raglan
603 Tomahawk Ct
Heyworth IL 617459346

Call Sign: W9LIQ
Wilbur F Yates
310 W Clarke
Heyworth IL 61745

Call Sign: W8SM
Barry A Bourgond
1104 Wakefield Dr
Heyworth IL 617459669

Call Sign: NZ9C
Barry A Bourgond
1104 Wakefield Dr
Heyworth IL 617459669

Call Sign: W8SM

Barry A Bourgond
1104 Wakefield Dr
Heyworth IL 617459669

**FCC Amateur Radio
Licenses in Hidalgo**

Call Sign: KC9DUQ
Brian M Evans
14363 E 1800 Ave
Hidalgo IL 62432

Call Sign: WA9WRD
Floyd E Clark
302 E Harrison St
Hidalgo IL 62432

**FCC Amateur Radio
Licenses in Highland**

Call Sign: KC9KBC
Bradley R Wheeler
1201 12th St
Highland IL 62249

Call Sign: N9PVS
Thelo M Jenny
1416 8th St
Highland IL 62249

Call Sign: KB9PTV
Nicholas A Kampwerth
2580 Becker Rd
Highland IL 62249

Call Sign: K2SGS
Lance Greve
12772 Buckeye Rd
Highland IL 62249

Call Sign: KC9PXN
Lance Greve
12772 Buckeye Rd
Highland IL 62249

Call Sign: K2SGS
Lance Greve
12772 Buckeye Rd
Highland IL 62249

Call Sign: KA9JFW
Timothy D Adair
2905 Candytuft
Highland IL 62249

Call Sign: N9JJ
Ronald J Murray
55A Crimson Ct
Highland IL 62249

Call Sign: W9TCB
Floyd J Basler
805 Dolphin Dr W
Highland IL 62249

Call Sign: KC9GQJ
Frank T Lipski
170 Falcon Dr
Highland IL 62249

Call Sign: KC9VBK
Monica L Rensing
1002 Helvetia Dr
Highland IL 62249

Call Sign: KG5EG
Harry R Ward
4748 Hill Rd
Highland IL 62249

Call Sign: KB5LPD
Patricia A Ward
4748 Hill Rd
Highland IL 62249

Call Sign: KB5MUC
Thomas J Ward
4748 Hill Rd
Highland IL 62249

Call Sign: KB9SOT
Donald C Crosby
13847 Klaus Lake Rd
Highland IL 62249

Call Sign: W9RRX
Dennis E Mejia
13336 Koch Rd

Highland IL 62249

Call Sign: KV9F
Everett K Hubbard
10850 Lake Rd
Highland IL 62249

Call Sign: KX9K
Thomas E Stewart
2424 Lakeshore Dr
Highland IL 62249

Call Sign: KC9FHI
Mark D Boekhout
2720 Lemon St Rd
Highland IL 62249

Call Sign: KB9SCQ
Steven Long
56 Lexington
Highland IL 622493937

Call Sign: K9WLR
James M Johnson
20 Meadowlark Ln
Highland IL 62249

Call Sign: KC9RDK
Patrick E Gauen
30 Meadowlark Ln
Highland IL 62249

Call Sign: N9RQZ
Dennis R Sievers
15 Memorial Dr
Highland IL 62249

Call Sign: KB9MYE
Karen S Frey
2004 Olive St
Highland IL 62249

Call Sign: KB9NIH
Michelle A Frey
2004 Olive St
Highland IL 62249

Call Sign: KB9MYC
Stanley D Frey

2004 Olive St
Highland IL 62249

Call Sign: KC9LIB
Darrin Starks
1815 Papin St
Highland IL 62249

Call Sign: W9RUZ
Waldo J Frierdich
1609 Paradise Dr
Highland IL 62249

Call Sign: K9WDL
Jon L Sugg
700 Porpoise Dr
Highland IL 62249

Call Sign: N9BVE
Leonard F Loebel
700 Porpoise Dr
Highland IL 62249

Call Sign: KC9PSW
Thomas E Brockman
11 Rialto
Highland IL 62249

Call Sign: W9LRA
Merle M Weber
2111 S St Michael
Highland IL 62249

Call Sign: KA9VPS
Fred J Schwappach
919 SR 160
Highland IL 62249

Call Sign: N9ASN
Deanna F Lentz
3847 SR 160
Highland IL 62249

Call Sign: W9RL
Russell R Lentz
3847 SR 160
Highland IL 62249

Call Sign: W9JHE

Dewey F Noles
60 Sunflower Dr
Highland IL 62249

Call Sign: KB0JTV
Robert W Zink
290 Sunflower Dr
Highland IL 62249

Call Sign: WL7CPW
Loren J Chassels Do
Highland IL 62249

FCC Amateur Radio Licenses in Hillsboro

Call Sign: WA9ETI
Kenneth W Degg
78 Bandor Cir
Hillsboro IL 62049

Call Sign: WB9OVF
Sharon K Mc Farlin
638 Beal St
Hillsboro IL 62049

Call Sign: KF4MAQ
Timothy P Elliot
202 Birch St
Hillsboro IL 620491119

Call Sign: KB9LRU
Roger G Myers
Rr2 Box 185
Hillsboro IL 62049

Call Sign: WA9OEX
David W Reynolds
620 Chase St
Hillsboro IL 62049

Call Sign: KA9ACM
Judith L Reynolds
620 Chase St
Hillsboro IL 62049

Call Sign: N9IDD
Lucas W Funk
619 E Tremont

Hillsboro IL 62049

Call Sign: W9EOP
John H Parry
405 E Tremont St
Hillsboro IL 62049

Call Sign: KB9ZAP
Jennifer J Funk
619 E Tremont St
Hillsboro IL 62049

Call Sign: KF9MQ
Terry L Baker
310 E Water St
Hillsboro IL 62049

Call Sign: N9QIJ
Madeline I Baker
310 E Water St
Hillsboro IL 62049

Call Sign: K9AXS
Goldie F Hoover
401 E Wood St
Hillsboro IL 62049

Call Sign: KA9TRM
Carroll D Lewey
2213 Frey Ave
Hillsboro IL 62049

Call Sign: N9KUM
Roy A Burris
8410 Hilltop Trl
Hillsboro IL 62049

Call Sign: N9MXH
Susan M Burris
8410 Hilltop Trl
Hillsboro IL 62049

Call Sign: W9SUP
David C Wells
106 Hunt Ave
Hillsboro IL 62049

Call Sign: W9LZE
Richard A Hewitt

10197 Il Rte 16
Hillsboro IL 62049

Call Sign: KB9PXY
Amy Mullins Ceney
525 Kinkead Rd
Hillsboro IL 62049

Call Sign: K9HYZ
Frank A Ceney Jr
525 Kinkead Rd
Hillsboro IL 62049

Call Sign: KB9PWC
James M Ceney
525 Kinkead Rd
Hillsboro IL 62049

Call Sign: WA9CSU
Cecil R Cope
Rr 2 Kinkead Rd 363
Hillsboro IL 62049

Call Sign: KE6HEM
Donna M Cravens
107 Lakewood Dr
Hillsboro IL 62049

Call Sign: KE6IAK
Ronald L Cravens
107 Lakewood Dr
Hillsboro IL 62049

Call Sign: KC9QHE
Michael Wilcox
212 Lakewood Dr
Hillsboro IL 62049

Call Sign: NF9M
Michael Wilcox
212 Lakewood Dr
Hillsboro IL 62049

Call Sign: N9HAP
Kelli S Smith
22 Lakewood Ests
Hillsboro IL 62049

Call Sign: K9JFE

Harold G Markos
210 Lands End Rd
Hillsboro IL 62049

Call Sign: WB9ZFU
Richard W Mc Carty
120 Larkin
Hillsboro IL 62049

Call Sign: K9KYK
Max W Page
318 Mechanic St
Hillsboro IL 62049

Call Sign: N9TOP
Sue I Goodin
705 Mechanic St
Hillsboro IL 62049

Call Sign: N9PVM
Charles L Goodin
705 Mechanic St
Hillsboro IL 62049

Call Sign: N9FKS
John S Tallman Sr
225 N Douglas
Hillsboro IL 62049

Call Sign: WB9QYT
Harold D Thomas
400 N Douglas
Hillsboro IL 62049

Call Sign: N9OWV
Brian C Talley
1610 Oakbrook Dr
Hillsboro IL 62049

Call Sign: WA9KKM
Vernon L Terneus Jr
4 Old Oaks Dr
Hillsboro IL 62049

Call Sign: N0HEJ
Marlyn E Uri
400 S Hamilton Apt 3
Hillsboro IL 62049

Call Sign: WA9RUM
Valle M Funk
625 S Main St
Hillsboro IL 62049

Call Sign: W9VEY
W9Vey Memorial Amateur
Society
625 S Main St
Hillsboro IL 62049

Call Sign: KC9ITY
John D Stretch
630 S Oak St
Hillsboro IL 62049

Call Sign: W9KHQ
John D Stretch
630 S Oak St
Hillsboro IL 62049

Call Sign: WB9OIN
Karen E Osborn
1515 Seymour Ave
Hillsboro IL 62049

Call Sign: WA9SXK
Mark E Osborn
1515 Seymour Ave
Hillsboro IL 62049

Call Sign: KB9WAS
Melissa K Osborn
1515 Seymour Ave
Hillsboro IL 62049

Call Sign: W9BXR
Montgomery Co Ar Emer
Corps Inc
1515 Seymour Ave
Hillsboro IL 62049

Call Sign: KB9TZQ
James L Riley
9 Shelbyville Rd
Hillsboro IL 62049

Call Sign: KB9QBP
Bill L Hefley

913 St Louis
Hillsboro IL 62049

Call Sign: K9GXP
Charles W Tritt
1007 Vandalia Rd
Hillsboro IL 62049

Call Sign: KC9SRZ
Edward L Boyd
422 W Fairground Av
Hillsboro IL 62049

Call Sign: K9WUA
Mary E Ceney
525 W Kinkead Rd
Hillsboro IL 62049

Call Sign: W9KHQ
Dale D Stretch
635 W Kinkead Rd
Hillsboro IL 62049

Call Sign: N9KFN
Kelly D Marcolini
618 W Wood St
Hillsboro IL 62049

Call Sign: KC9NJT
Jason W Pieper
909 Walnut St
Hillsboro IL 62049

Call Sign: N9AWE
Phyllis D Altenberger
55 Westwood Dr
Hillsboro IL 62049

Call Sign: W9DAN
Daniel P Altenberger
55 Westwood Dr
Hillsboro IL 62049

Call Sign: KC9UPZ
Larry Terneus
Hillsboro IL 62049

Call Sign: KB9KZN
Thomas E Simpson Jr

Hillsboro IL 62049

FCC Amateur Radio Licenses in Hillsdale

Call Sign: WB4RSY
Oval E Vernia
2700 290th St N
Hillsdale IL 61257

Call Sign: N9XBH
Diane N Larvenz
127 Butzer St
Hillsdale IL 61257

Call Sign: N9TPS
James A Larrenz
127 Butzer St
Hillsdale IL 61257

Call Sign: KB9ELZ
Sheryl A Bridges
410 Jackson St
Hillsdale IL 61257

Call Sign: WB9WSO
Judith D Brown
Hillsdale IL 61257

Call Sign: KY9C
Stanley L Brown
Hillsdale IL 61257

FCC Amateur Radio Licenses in Hoffman

Call Sign: KB9GPD
William A Guile
128 W 5th St
Hoffman IL 62250

FCC Amateur Radio Licenses in Holcomb

Call Sign: KB9ACT
Vernon L Wolfe
204 2nd Ave
Holcomb IL 61043

Call Sign: KB9OPB
Cameron F Young
105 W Main St
Holcomb IL 61043

FCC Amateur Radio Licenses in Homer

Call Sign: N9XDM
Ryan L Adkins
Rr 1 Box 82
Homer IL 61849

Call Sign: KB9VFZ
Kyle L Webb
303 E South St
Homer IL 61849

Call Sign: WB9PAT
Patricia J Butler
310 S Carolina St
Homer IL 61849

Call Sign: WB9KMD
William T Butler
310 S Caroline St
Homer IL 618491403

Call Sign: N9XDC
Steven D Hilberg
2666 S Homer Lake Rd
Homer IL 61849

Call Sign: KB9OTM
Mari L Hilberg
2666 S Homer Lake Rd
Homer IL 618499756

Call Sign: WB9PRY
Daniel W Gordon
108 S Josephine
Homer IL 61849

FCC Amateur Radio Licenses in Hoopeston

Call Sign: N9FBM
Terry J Flesher
601 E Penn St

Hoopeston IL 609421537

Call Sign: KC9IWZ
James F Eyrich
402 E Seminary Ave
Hoopeston IL 60942

Call Sign: KB9SOK
Shawn K Hack
603 Judson Ave
Hoopeston IL 60942

Call Sign: W5VPH
Robert D Pittman
221 N 4th St
Hoopeston IL 60942

Call Sign: K9BJM
Lawrence W Petry
318 S 4th St
Hoopeston IL 60942

Call Sign: AA1BZ
D Michael Mc Farland
701 Trego Dr
Hoopeston IL 60942

Call Sign: AB9ES
D Michael Mc Farland
701 Trego Dr
Hoopeston IL 60942

Call Sign: WD9CRA
Larry L Powley
515 W Chestnut St
Hoopeston IL 609421732

Call Sign: KI4GCN
Michael P Poole
710B W Main St
Hoopeston IL 60942

Call Sign: N9ARW
Ronald L Lacy
709 W Washington
Hoopeston IL 60942

Call Sign: KC9DBZ
Carey A Green

Hoopeston IL 60942

Call Sign: KB9YZI
Jeremy Z Green
Hoopeston IL 60942

Call Sign: K9DXR
Russell P Hibma
Hoopeston IL 60942

Call Sign: KC9JRU
Illiana Skywarn Group
Hoopeston IL 60942

**FCC Amateur Radio
Licenses in Hopedale**

Call Sign: KC9VEV
Robert J Bortolussi Jr
6070 Angus Ln
Hopedale IL 61747

Call Sign: NJ9A
Justin D Nelson
801 Elm St
Hopedale IL 61745

Call Sign: K9PPZ
Joel L Nafziger
119 Hittle Rd
Hopedale IL 61747

Call Sign: KB9ZXO
Joseph R Gibbens
8712 N Wildlife Dr
Hopedale IL 61747

Call Sign: KC9UQS
Terrance A Fairburn II
317 NW Monroe St
Hopedale IL 61747

Call Sign: KC9JSJ
William R Bush
138 SE Main
Hopedale IL 61747

Call Sign: W9WTF
William R Bush II

138 SE Main
Hopedale IL 61747

Call Sign: WD9IXU
Robert K Prather
23912 Toboggan Ave
Hopedale IL 61747

Call Sign: KC9EUR
Terry J Wilson
822 Walnut
Hopedale IL 61747

Call Sign: W9ZMZ
Paul V Thomas
Hopedale IL 61747

Call Sign: KC9EUS
Yvonne D Wilson
Hopedale IL 617470536

**FCC Amateur Radio
Licenses in Hopewell**

Call Sign: KC9LVZ
John P Hays
196 Cahokia Ct
Hopewell IL 61565

Call Sign: KC9DRH
Britt M Fidler
196 Cahokia Ct
Hopewell IL 61565

Call Sign: KC9OOP
Britt M Fidler
196 Cahokia Ct
Hopewell IL 61565

Call Sign: N9VIM
Tracy A Ruble
37 Hopewell Dr
Hopewell IL 61565

Call Sign: KD8DMG
Jay H Cline
19 Tecumseh Ct
Hopewell IL 61565

Call Sign: KB8BXU
Kenneth M Towne
19 Tecumseh Ct
Hopewell IL 61565

Call Sign: N9SMZ
Sandy J Robinett
131 E Oak St
Hoyleton IL 62803

Call Sign: KG9PJ
Paul J Davis
313 E St Louis St
Hoyleton IL 62803

Call Sign: K9CI
Coram J Davis
295 N Main
Hoyleton IL 62803

Call Sign: KA9LXO
Coram W Davis
295 N Main
Hoyleton IL 62803

Call Sign: KA9EYZ
Thurman M Conrey
Hoyleton IL 62803

Call Sign: N9PGI
Jimmy D Robinett
Hoyleton IL 62803

Call Sign: W9PRV
Floyd J Sakemiller
Rt 1 Box 301
Hudson IL 61748

Call Sign: KB9UEU
Ronald L Stanley
Rr 1 Box 98C
Hudson IL 61748

Call Sign: W9JCR
John C Rediger
15084 E 2100 N Rd
Hudson IL 617489280

Call Sign: KC9ITD
Russell L Symington
17466 Pleasant View Dr
Hudson IL 61748

Call Sign: WB9UWV
Alma J Walters
202 S East St
Hudson IL 61748

Call Sign: KA9ZNJ
Holly A Slappey
404 S East St
Hudson IL 61748

Call Sign: W9CHM
James J Hamm
Hudson IL 61748

Call Sign: KB9VIS
Brian S Dunker
17879 County Hwy 57
Hull IL 62343

Call Sign: KC9AEO
Gilbert D Haistings
890 S Elm St
Hull IL 62343

Call Sign: KB9VIR
Thomas J Eddingfield
Hull IL 62343

Call Sign: N9SPP
John O Trimble
14959 CR 400 E
Humboldt IL 61931

Call Sign: N9YFH
Neil J Hoover
Rr 1 Box 69
Huntsville IL 62344

Call Sign: K9SCT
Frank H Decker
210 E Lincoln St
Hurst IL 62949

Call Sign: KC9MFX
Leslie H Hall Jr
127 N Hubbs St
Hurst IL 62949

Call Sign: KC9LDF
Walter E Tackitt
115 N Williamson St
Hurst IL 62949

Call Sign: KC9PIH
Danielle L Hillman
Hurst IL 62949

Call Sign: N9NEB
Dewayne D Hillman
Hurst IL 62949

Call Sign: AB9YI
Dewayne D Hillman
Hurst IL 62949

Call Sign: KB9CEH
Michael L Lingle
Hurst IL 62949

Call Sign: KB9QMY
Michael O Holland
Hurst IL 62949

Call Sign: N9YJU
Kathryn G Bloomer
103 Cherry
Hutsonville IL 62433

Call Sign: K9FYL
David P Freeland
10079 E 1700th Ave
Hutsonville IL 62433

Call Sign: KA9PIA
Christeen A Gurley
11232 E 2000 Ave
Hutsonville IL 624332115

Call Sign: WA9RZK
Bradley N Gurley
11232 E 2000th Ave
Hutsonville IL 62433

Call Sign: N9FCX
Roy D Bousley
500 Mill St
Hutsonville IL 62433

Call Sign: N9PTP
Sidney A O Dell
16781 N 1600th St
Hutsonville IL 62433

Call Sign: KC9TCY
Moreena L Powell
301 N Main St
Hutsonville IL 62433

Call Sign: AB9QG
William M Gray
503 S Rose St
Hutsonville IL 62433

Call Sign: KC9PAQ
James Powell
Hutsonville IL 62433

Call Sign: WD9L
James Powell
Hutsonville IL 62433

FCC Amateur Radio Licenses in Illinois City

Call Sign: WB9YFN
Neal P Thirtyacre
25201 124th Ave W
Illinois City IL 61259

Call Sign: KA9AQR
Steven R Fowler
26819 190th Ave W
Illinois City IL 612599713

Call Sign: KC9NLH
Carl L Goodrick
10103 207th St W
Illinois City IL 61259

Call Sign: KC9NLI
Linda D Fox
10103 207th St W
Illinois City IL 61259

Call Sign: KD0BFY
Collin S Morehouse
11122 300th St W
Illinois City IL 61259

FCC Amateur Radio Licenses in Illiopolis

Call Sign: WB9YJO
Terry L Blakeman
449 6th St
Illiopolis IL 62539

Call Sign: N9MWO
Adam W Hawkins
103 E Matilda St
Illiopolis IL 62539

Call Sign: N9DZ
Rex E Perry
314 W Matilda St
Illiopolis IL 62539

Call Sign: KC9CCA
Sandra S Perry
Illiopolis IL 62539

Call Sign: KB9YCB
Timothy S Wood
Illiopolis IL 62539

Call Sign: KB9PFZ
Rex E Perry
Illiopolis IL 62539

FCC Amateur Radio Licenses in Ina

Call Sign: N9XLO
Charles L Minor
602 E Tamaroa Rd
Ina IL 62846

Call Sign: KB9VKT
Gordon P Pryor
Ina IL 62846

Call Sign: N9XLN
Seasida J Minor
Ina IL 62846

FCC Amateur Radio Licenses in Indianola

Call Sign: KA9IDR
Thomas R Belton
8787 E 850 N Rd
Indianola IL 61850

FCC Amateur Radio Licenses in Industry

Call Sign: K9SPD
Keith E Ushman
Rr 1 Box 106
Industry IL 61440

Call Sign: N9FTZ
Timothy A Eifert
Rr 1 Box 148H
Industry IL 61440

Call Sign: KC9NQQ
Ronald E Lindsey
Industry IL 61440

FCC Amateur Radio Licenses in Ingraham

Call Sign: KB9UFK
Chandra H Fulk
1217 E 50th Ave
Ingraham IL 62434

Call Sign: KB9UBI
Tim D Fulk
1217 E 50th Ave
Ingraham IL 62434

FCC Amateur Radio Licenses in Ipava

Call Sign: KC9BVK
Wayne N Covedill
Rr 1 Box 64
Ipava IL 61441

Call Sign: KC9BVM
Timothy A Grzanich
9753 US 24 Hwy
Ipava IL 61441

FCC Amateur Radio Licenses in Iroquois

Call Sign: KC9OQQ
Gery A Johnston
101 SE Chestnut
Iroquois IL 60945

FCC Amateur Radio Licenses in Irving

Call Sign: KB9KVO
Doris A Bryce
113 Central St
Irving IL 62051

Call Sign: KB9KVP
Mark G Bryce
113 Central St
Irving IL 62051

Call Sign: KC9PVA
Kurt F Fenton
201 McCords Trl
Irving IL 62051

Call Sign: KB9SNZ
David D Dowdy
416 McCords Trl
Irving IL 62051

Call Sign: WD9DBB
Cena M Keen
594 McCords Trl
Irving IL 62051

Call Sign: KC9FKN
Nedra S Bryce
205 N Pine St
Irving IL 62051

Call Sign: KG9CO
Ricky L Bryce
205 N Pine St
Irving IL 62051

Call Sign: KC9UFE
Adam J Schmitt
213 N Vine St
Irving IL 62051

Call Sign: KC9TDV
Andrew T Schmitt
Irving IL 62051

FCC Amateur Radio Licenses in Irvington

Call Sign: KB9BFN
Rickey L Ruhl
615 Superior St
Irvington IL 62848

FCC Amateur Radio Licenses in Iuka

Call Sign: WB9UTO
Ivan N Wooley
620 Deerfield St
Iuka IL 62849

Call Sign: KB9VJW
Jerry M Beard
5339 Foster Ln
Iuka IL 62849

Call Sign: N9MNO
Richard W Brockschmidt
8009 Green Rd
Iuka IL 62849

Call Sign: KC9FGD
Zachary W Simmons
9336 Green Rd
Iuka IL 62849

Call Sign: KB9YPV
Mike B Simmons
9336 Green Rd
Iuka IL 62849

Call Sign: K7LAX
Barbara J Hodgins
4512 Kirby Rd
Iuka IL 62849

Call Sign: K7CP
Libby N Hodgins
4512 Kirby Rd
Iuka IL 62849

Call Sign: NG9I
Kirk E Myers
4914 Kirby Rd
Iuka IL 62849

Call Sign: KC9CZA
John M Thomas
4029 Landmark Rd
Iuka IL 62849

Call Sign: KB9VOK
Ross E Klier
2570 Nickelson Cir
Iuka IL 62849

Call Sign: N9EAH
Gorman E Stroud
1314 Old Bell Rd

Iuka IL 628492842

Call Sign: WD9IKH
Carl D Shinall
2059 Baldwin Rd
Jacksonville IL 62650

Call Sign: KC9JFO
Jim L Patterson
9 Baxter Pl
Jacksonville IL 62650

Call Sign: W9GHB
Lorenz S Kehl Jr
1 Book Ln
Jacksonville IL 62650

Call Sign: W9ZIT
Willard A Prewitt
30 Briarwyck
Jacksonville IL 62650

Call Sign: KB9SWW
Brain A Hoots
544 Brooklyn Ave Lot 10
Jacksonville IL 62650

Call Sign: KB2TVR
James Cook
121 Coral Verry Dr
Jacksonville IL 62650

Call Sign: WA9OXF
Billy E Hart
947 E College
Jacksonville IL 62650

Call Sign: N9UPD
Chad M Myers
4 E Lake Dr
Jacksonville IL 62650

Call Sign: N9PCT
Claude A Curry
1042 E Morton Unit 2
Jacksonville IL 62650

Call Sign: WA9OXN
Clifford Litwiller
727 E State
Jacksonville IL 62650

Call Sign: N9WRA
Kenneth W Kolberer
699 E State St
Jacksonville IL 62650

Call Sign: KB9IXO
Richard E Tavender
721 E State St
Jacksonville IL 62650

Call Sign: WA9GUJ
Helen M Mayberry
222 E Superior
Jacksonville IL 626503322

Call Sign: N9OFP
Mike Myers
1064 E Vandalia Rd
Jacksonville IL 62650

Call Sign: K9RVK
Richard B Blough
915 Goltra Ave
Jacksonville IL 62650

Call Sign: KB9LCB
Carlin R Anderson
1107 Hall Dr
Jacksonville IL 62650

Call Sign: KC9VPQ
Teresa E Rust
104 Harbor Ct
Jacksonville IL 62650

Call Sign: KB0URS
Charles E Jenkins Jr
1007 Hardin Ave
Jacksonville IL 62650

Call Sign: WA9DSU
Ralph O Sullivan
10 Havendale Ct

Jacksonville IL 62650

Call Sign: KB9KHP
Margo A Gilmore
800 Hoagland Blvd 502
Jacksonville IL 62650

Call Sign: KB9QYJ
Danny R Van Hyning
800 Hoagland Blvd Apt 219
Jacksonville IL 62650

Call Sign: KC9NRA
James T Settles
800 Illinois Ave 27
Jacksonville IL 62650

Call Sign: W9NRA
James T Settles
800 Illinois Ave 27
Jacksonville IL 62650

Call Sign: KB9KHQ
Catherine E Green
27 Ivy Wood Dr
Jacksonville IL 62650

Call Sign: KB9KHR
John F Green
27 Ivy Wood Dr
Jacksonville IL 62650

Call Sign: KD6ITT
James G Jones
4 Jacob Ln
Jacksonville IL 62650

Call Sign: WD9DNB
James E Lumos
5 Janet Pl
Jacksonville IL 62650

Call Sign: WD9FVO
Marian C Brim
1110 King St
Jacksonville IL 62650

Call Sign: W9SBV
Arthur Hipkins Jr

1171 King St
Jacksonville IL 62650

Call Sign: WB9WYU
Edith C Hipkins
1171 King St
Jacksonville IL 62650

Call Sign: W9BGM
William B Ricks
203 Leland Lake Dr
Jacksonville IL 62650

Call Sign: KD9PQ
Marc D Marino
1225 Lincoln Ave 306
Jacksonville IL 62650

Call Sign: KB9TZR
Chad N Morrison
1225 Lincoln Ave Apt 212
Jacksonville IL 62650

Call Sign: KB9OOK
James T Streib
601 Locust St
Jacksonville IL 62650

Call Sign: WB9LWO
James T Streib
601 Locust St
Jacksonville IL 62650

Call Sign: KC9FXZ
Danny R Van Hyning
72 Main St
Jacksonville IL 62650

Call Sign: K9AGA
Elmer J Tuma
12 Mound Pl
Jacksonville IL 62650

Call Sign: KB9HSN
Merton H Abbott
2007 Mound Rd
Jacksonville IL 62650

Call Sign: KF4AHI

Jennifer L Smith
2022 Mound Rd
Jacksonville IL 62650

Call Sign: KC9MLI
Larry K Lewis
412 N Church St
Jacksonville IL 62650

Call Sign: WA9GMM
Donald E Mayberry
607 N Fayette
Jacksonville IL 62650

Call Sign: KB9KHT
Gary L Vanbebber
1006 N Fayette
Jacksonville IL 62650

Call Sign: KA9PVQ
Stephen H Oakes
415 N Laurel Dr
Jacksonville IL 62650

Call Sign: KA9ADQ
Norman G Higgerson II
919 N Main
Jacksonville IL 62650

Call Sign: W9NGH
Norman G Higgerson II
919 N Main
Jacksonville IL 62650

Call Sign: N9ZSB
Jerry A Wade
1010 N West Ave
Jacksonville IL 62650

Call Sign: N9WJL
John H Adcock
2076 New Lake Rd
Jacksonville IL 62650

Call Sign: WA7AVC
Gordon L Cady
2099 New Lake Rd
Jacksonville IL 62650

Call Sign: W9AVC
Gordon L Cady
2099 New Lake Rd
Jacksonville IL 62650

Call Sign: N9EGX
Mary E Jarvis
1701 Nita Ln
Jacksonville IL 62650

Call Sign: KB9ZBS
Michael D Meyer
704 Park St
Jacksonville IL 62650

Call Sign: K9VEN
John A Hays
1 Passavant Ct
Jacksonville IL 62650

Call Sign: N9OGK
Jack W Doyle
243.5 Pine St
Jacksonville IL 62650

Call Sign: KA9QLF
Steven K Wenger
803 S Church St
Jacksonville IL 62650

Call Sign: W9QLF
Steven K Wenger
803 S Church St
Jacksonville IL 62650

Call Sign: KB9KOU
Albert H Harris
431 S Clay Ave
Jacksonville IL 62650

Call Sign: KB9LLY
Edward R Horton
658 S Diamond
Jacksonville IL 62650

Call Sign: KC9UFZ
Gregory L Ketcham
1335 S Diamond St Apt 232
Jacksonville IL 62650

Call Sign: KB9KOT
Jack W Trumbo Sr
215 S East
Jacksonville IL 62650

Call Sign: KB9DZE
Bonny J Biggs
1020 S East St
Jacksonville IL 62650

Call Sign: K9VPX
Coy R Burnett
1338 S East St
Jacksonville IL 62650

Call Sign: WB9LUX
Donna M Edwards
1236 S East St Apt C
Jacksonville IL 62650

Call Sign: WB9LUY
Herbert Edwards Jr
1236 S East St Apt C
Jacksonville IL 62650

Call Sign: KB9RUG
Nigel S Haynes
3 Sherwood Eddy Dr Apt C
Jacksonville IL 62650

Call Sign: N9QJM
Russell A Ward
5 Southview Dr
Jacksonville IL 62650

Call Sign: WB9RNY
Mike D Mayberry
411 Southville
Jacksonville IL 62650

Call Sign: W9RNY
Mike D Mayberry
411 Southville
Jacksonville IL 62650

Call Sign: K9LUO
George M Strawn
2389 Swain Rd

Jacksonville IL 62650

Call Sign: W9UFL
Joseph F O Reilly Jr
1319 Tendick St 3
Jacksonville IL 62650

Call Sign: K9YDG
Steve A Mc Carty
15 Victoria Ln
Jacksonville IL 62650

Call Sign: KB9DLZ
Scott E Shade
301 W Beecher Apt 307
Jacksonville IL 62650

Call Sign: W9CMR
Charles I Calvin
861 W Chambers
Jacksonville IL 62650

Call Sign: WB9TOP
Jerome D Sommer
1131 W Lafayette Ave
Jacksonville IL 62650

Call Sign: N9ZPJ
Timothy D Thurston
841 W Morton Ave Lot 58
Jacksonville IL 62650

Call Sign: KB9FBI
Timothy C Childers
107 W Point Dr
Jacksonville IL 62650

Call Sign: K9JX
Jacksonville ARS
107 W Point Dr
Jacksonville IL 62650

Call Sign: K9PN
James E Lumos
309 W Vandalia Rd
Jacksonville IL 62650

Call Sign: KB9FRR
Timothy A Staker

318 W Walnut
Jacksonville IL 62650

Call Sign: KA9WRW
James R Aggertt
12 Wadsworth Dr
Jacksonville IL 62650

Call Sign: WD9FYZ
John W Corder
248 Webster
Jacksonville IL 62650

Call Sign: KB9IEW
Daniel L Jones
5 Westgate Cir
Jacksonville IL 62650

Call Sign: N9OVB
Michael L Jones
5 Westgate Cir
Jacksonville IL 62650

Call Sign: N9WQJ
Kenneth E Mayner Sr
Jacksonville IL 62650

Call Sign: KC9KLV
Richard Talkington Jr
Jacksonville IL 62651

FCC Amateur Radio Licenses in Jerseyville

Call Sign: N9ZJS
John D Fox
Rr 2 Box 318
Jerseyville IL 62052

Call Sign: KB9RHD
Lois K Sharos
Rr 4 Box 347
Jerseyville IL 62052

Call Sign: KF6HAH
Todd M Fallin
1240 Brookshire Pl Apt 801
Jerseyville IL 62052

Call Sign: K9UOT
Irene K Kessler
222 CR
Jerseyville IL 62052

Call Sign: KB9BAV
Patrick E Tucker
403 E Fairgrounds
Jerseyville IL 62052

Call Sign: N9IAP
Michael L Bowman
207 E Pearl St
Jerseyville IL 62052

Call Sign: KC9MCO
Joseph R Landon
23351 Glenda Ave
Jerseyville IL 62052

Call Sign: N9TMU
Virgil C Noah Jr
23309 Glenda Ave
Jerseyville IL 62052

Call Sign: N9JDP
Michael L Bizaillion
405 Henry St
Jerseyville IL 62052

Call Sign: KB9QHJ
Robert M Albrecht
18893 Jones Rd
Jerseyville IL 62052

Call Sign: K9KG
John P Newgent
19405 Jones Rd
Jerseyville IL 62052

Call Sign: WB9IUL
Milton V Ruyle
110 Kirby St
Jerseyville IL 62052

Call Sign: N9UEX
Loretta A Williams
400 N State
Jerseyville IL 62052

Call Sign: KB9NWJ
Robert L Early
103A North State
Jerseyville IL 62052

Call Sign: N9UJC
Leslie L Flautt
3 Oakwood Pl
Jerseyville IL 62052

Call Sign: KC9UJJ
Raymond A Sinclair
20306 Otterville Rd
Jerseyville IL 62052

Call Sign: KB9LZH
Bobby J Kyle
1809 Palimino Dr
Jerseyville IL 62052

Call Sign: K9TLB
Fred H Wallace Sr
105 Pleasant
Jerseyville IL 62052

Call Sign: N9UUH
Lawrence E Reeves Sr
1001 S State St
Jerseyville IL 62052

Call Sign: WQ3L
Gary F Brunnworth
24114 State Hwy 16 W
Jerseyville IL 62052

Call Sign: KC9OGN
Michael W Beiermann
28848 Victory School Rd
Jerseyville IL 62052

Call Sign: WA9OQW
Lee A Jones Jr
415 W Barr Ave
Jerseyville IL 62052

Call Sign: KA9TOU
Omar A Snider
421 W Fletcher

Jerseyville IL 62052

Call Sign: K9LUP
Wayne E Dugger
1005 W Mulbery St
Jerseyville IL 62052

Call Sign: KF6AGW
Carole E Fallin
303 W Pine St
Jerseyville IL 62052

Call Sign: KE6KZV
Kenneth D Fallin
303 W Pine St
Jerseyville IL 62052

Call Sign: N9JII
Edward E Goetten
401 W Prairie
Jerseyville IL 62052

Call Sign: N9LIH
Harold R Blackorby
205 Walton
Jerseyville IL 62052

Call Sign: KC9USS
Keith A Skipper
24612 Witt Mill Rd
Jerseyville IL 62052

Call Sign: KA9UAM
Alvin R Hinman
Jerseyville IL 62052

Call Sign: K9KMH
Charles W Knauel
Jerseyville IL 62052

FCC Amateur Radio Licenses in Johnsonville

Call Sign: KB9YVR
Crystal G Kelly
Rr 1 Box 22
Johnsonville IL 62850

Call Sign: KB9YVS

David M Kelly Jr
Rr 1 Box 22
Johnsonville IL 62850

Call Sign: KC9FPE
Hollie A Kelly
Rt 1 Box 23 A
Johnsonville IL 62850

Call Sign: KC9JOE
Hollie A Kelly
Rt 1 Box 23 A
Johnsonville IL 62850

Call Sign: KC9FPF
Jack L Kelly
Rt 1 Box 23 A
Johnsonville IL 62850

Call Sign: KC9JIQ
Jesse D Weaver
Rr 1 Box 23B
Johnsonville IL 62850

Call Sign: W9VER
Jesse D Weaver
Rr 1 Box 23B
Johnsonville IL 62850

Call Sign: KC9DUO
Pat L Kelly
Rr 1 Box 25
Johnsonville IL 62850

Call Sign: KC9FMT
David M Kelly Sr
Rr 1 Box 26
Johnsonville IL 62850

Call Sign: KC9NPJ
Jarrett A Weaver
Rr 1 Box 38
Johnsonville IL 62850

Call Sign: KC9UDP
Where ARC
Rr 1 Box 50
Johnsonville IL 62850

Call Sign: N9SQO
Brenda P Heifner
Rt 1 Box 50
Johnsonville IL 62850

Call Sign: WT9H
Ronald J Heifner
Rt 1 Box 50
Johnsonville IL 62850

Call Sign: KC9NKF
Daniel W Brown
Rt 1 Box 96A
Johnsonville IL 62850

Call Sign: AA9LJ
Tim R Brown
Rt 1 Box 96A
Johnsonville IL 62850

FCC Amateur Radio Licenses in Johnston City

Call Sign: WA9WXO
John W Shadowens Sr
906 Barham
Johnston City IL 62951

Call Sign: K9VR
Richard D Smith
Rr 1 Box 10B
Johnston City IL 62951

Call Sign: K9UH
David T Williams
9994 Champaign Rd
Johnston City IL 62951

Call Sign: KC9BIG
Joan D Williams
9994 Champaign Rd
Johnston City IL 62951

Call Sign: N9KCI
Dennis W Perry
16090 Collins Rd
Johnston City IL 62951

Call Sign: K9CIN

Cynthia A Carner
16385 Collins Rd
Johnston City IL 62951

Call Sign: KB9IOA
Randall L Carner
16385 Collins Rd
Johnston City IL 62951

Call Sign: N9DQ
Randall L Carner
16385 Collins Rd
Johnston City IL 62951

Call Sign: KC9MFV
Roy N Rogers
14111 Corinth Rd
Johnston City IL 62951

Call Sign: KC9ROY
Roy N Rogers
14111 Corinth Rd
Johnston City IL 62951

Call Sign: N9XLL
Lisa K Childers
1203 Davis Ave
Johnston City IL 62951

Call Sign: KC9AGB
Edward R Cash
1206 Davis St
Johnston City IL 62951

Call Sign: W9ERC
Edward R Cash
1206 Davis St
Johnston City IL 62951

Call Sign: N9XZP
Larry D Giovanetti
803 E 9th St
Johnston City IL 62951

Call Sign: KC9NWF
Daven L Edwards
625 E Broadway Ave
Johnston City IL 62951

Call Sign: N9WNP
Edward E Barger
10874 Ferges Rd
Johnston City IL 62951

Call Sign: K9DZ
Edward E Barger
10874 Ferges Rd
Johnston City IL 62951

Call Sign: KA9HTL
Doris A Smith
13813 Fowler School Rd
Johnston City IL 62959

Call Sign: KB9QEC
Gary A Sullivan
1302 Hazel Ln
Johnston City IL 62951

Call Sign: KA9ALH
Dora R Roach
1310 Jefferson Ave
Johnston City IL 62951

Call Sign: KC9FDC
Diana K Cash
13876 Jeffery Mine Rd
Johnston City IL 62951

Call Sign: KC9AJR
Scott E Cash
13876 Jeffery Mine Rd
Johnston City IL 62951

Call Sign: W9FLJ
George P Hammond
16426 Log Cabin Rd
Johnston City IL 629512841

Call Sign: W9PPK
Kenneth M Hill
805 Monroe
Johnston City IL 629511560

Call Sign: W9AJF
Savino Giacomelli
1112 Monroe Ave
Johnston City IL 62951

Call Sign: WB9VDW
Bradford L Buckner
1611 N Follis St
Johnston City IL 629510115

Call Sign: KC9KRU
Marvin D Bundren
1208 N Grand
Johnston City IL 62951

Call Sign: N9TWH
Matthew A Chestosky
14334 Prosperity Rd
Johnston City IL 62951

Call Sign: WV9I
Matthew A Chestosky
14334 Prosperity Rd
Johnston City IL 62951

Call Sign: KB9LKJ
Douglas A Smith
12377 Villa Way
Johnston City IL 62951

Call Sign: AA9VA
John C Rembold
805 W 14th St
Johnston City IL 62951

Call Sign: KA9GUU
Johnie C Winstead
311 W 17th
Johnston City IL 62951

Call Sign: WO7K
David L Pier
713 W 4th St
Johnston City IL 62951

Call Sign: K9UNF
Gene E Lloyd
204 W 8th
Johnston City IL 62951

Call Sign: KC9TEO
John P Moore
102 W 9th St

Johnston City IL 62951

Call Sign: K9CWL
John P Moore Teo
102 W 9th St
Johnston City IL 62951

FCC Amateur Radio Licenses in Jonesboro

Call Sign: KA9QMN
Loyce J Livesay
Rr 2 Box 226
Jonesboro IL 62952

Call Sign: WB9UPV
Gary R Faire
205 E Whitlock St Box 309
Jonesboro IL 62952

Call Sign: KB9ZMW
Bobby Jackson
145 Follis Dr
Jonesboro IL 62952

Call Sign: N9MVR
Toni S Leggans
355 Lingle Creek Rd
Jonesboro IL 62952

Call Sign: KB9ISZ
Donald A Leggans
355 Lingle Creek Rd
Jonesboro IL 62952

Call Sign: N9DWC
Jacqueline Mowery
505 Mowery Valley Ln
Jonesboro IL 62952

Call Sign: K9DMG
Perry V Mowery
505 Mowery Valley Ln
Jonesboro IL 62952

Call Sign: KA9ZFB
Roger D Gardner
103 N Jasper St
Jonesboro IL 629521707

Call Sign: KA9CRB
Andrew L Acklin
214 N John St
Jonesboro IL 62952

Call Sign: K9GOX
Melvin L Skelton
104 S J St
Jonesboro IL 62952

Call Sign: KA9WDP
Gaylen J Holden
324 S Orange
Jonesboro IL 62952

Call Sign: WB9HLC
Carrell E O Daniell
111 Willard Ferry Rd Box 391
Jonesboro IL 62952

Call Sign: N9MBC
Gary A Noble
406 Williford Rd
Jonesboro IL 62952

Call Sign: WB9YFH
Sharon L O Daniell
Jonesboro IL 62952

Call Sign: AA9DP
Donald J Leggans
Jonesboro IL 62952

FCC Amateur Radio Licenses in Joppa

Call Sign: KB9UMB
Lacy C Arrison
Joppa IL 62953

FCC Amateur Radio Licenses in Junction City

Call Sign: N9RUG
Connie S De Boer
1300 Jefferson
Junction City IL 62882

FCC Amateur Radio Licenses in Kangley

Call Sign: KG9FU
Donald D Lemler
Kangley IL 61364

FCC Amateur Radio Licenses in Kankakee

Call Sign: WB9WOC
Jerome W Whalen
3872n 5000W Rd
Kankakee IL 60901

Call Sign: WB9UDM
Dennis L Kerouac
18 Baker
Kankakee IL 60901

Call Sign: WD9EEE
Ruth L Kinnersley
633 Beckman Dr
Kankakee IL 60901

Call Sign: WD9FBF
Clarence L Williamson
R 6 Box 127
Kankakee IL 60901

Call Sign: KA9WLB
Gordon K Wolterstorff
Rr 3 Box 289
Kankakee IL 60901

Call Sign: AK9F
Howard S Dybedock
1455 Budd Blvd
Kankakee IL 609014505

Call Sign: WB9SFL
Ely A Pratt
19 Croydon Pl
Kankakee IL 60901

Call Sign: KB9JHA
Robert V Houde
483 Dudleys Grove Rd
Kankakee IL 60901

Call Sign: KC9OZZ
Roland J Hertz
2627 E 1000N Rd Apt B
Kankakee IL 60901

Call Sign: N9RJM
Roland J Hertz
2627 E 1000N Rd Apt B
Kankakee IL 60901

Call Sign: K9QT
Billie L Kerouac
6311 E Flora St
Kankakee IL 60901

Call Sign: KF9IF
Billie L Kerouac
6311 E Flora St
Kankakee IL 60901

Call Sign: K9NR
Donald L Kerouac
6311 E Flora St
Kankakee IL 60901

Call Sign: KC9SVU
Kankakee Iroquois Dx &
Contesting Group
6311 E Flora St
Kankakee IL 60901

Call Sign: KF9IK
Sheri L Clifford
6311 E Flora St
Kankakee IL 60901

Call Sign: KA9PSI
Jerry A Burgard
1770B E Maple
Kankakee IL 60901

Call Sign: N9LCR
Jay G Bainbridge
2217 E Maple St
Kankakee IL 60901

Call Sign: KB9SKL
Kankakee Ares

470 E Merchant St
Kankakee IL 60901

Call Sign: N9YNZ
Leslie A Longtin
300 E River
Kankakee IL 609015167

Call Sign: WB9WPS
Frances M Norrick
300 E River St
Kankakee IL 60901

Call Sign: NI9I
Charles E Dubie
1534 E Sheridan
Kankakee IL 60901

Call Sign: WD9CLX
Lawrence A Sebby
1118 Justine Dr
Kankakee IL 60901

Call Sign: WD9AZK
Christopher R Tarlini
800 N 2750E Rd
Kankakee IL 609018025

Call Sign: WB9WXW
Joan M Tarlini
800 N 2750E Rd
Kankakee IL 609018025

Call Sign: K9OZY
William J Paskowicz
126 N 3530 E Rd
Kankakee IL 60901

Call Sign: K9CWF
Robert C Mehrer
334 N 4000 E Rd
Kankakee IL 609018034

Call Sign: KT9J
Albert L Morris
250 N Hammes Ave
Kankakee IL 609012712

Call Sign: KB9SGI

Wallace Dean Hereth
760 N Kennedy Ave
Kankakee IL 60901

Call Sign: KB9JZJ
Matthew L Janusauskas
656 N Kennedy Dr
Kankakee IL 60901

Call Sign: N2UCL
Dennis B Nolan
884 N Main Ave
Kankakee IL 60901

Call Sign: KB9N
Clifford J Donovan
156 N Monterey
Kankakee IL 60901

Call Sign: W9EL
Clifford J Donovan
156 N Monterey
Kankakee IL 60901

Call Sign: KA9AHR
Venita K Donovan
156 N Monterey
Kankakee IL 60901

Call Sign: W9KK
Clifford J Donovan
156 N Monterey Dr
Kankakee IL 609017781

Call Sign: K9DI
Wayne M Scace
818 N Rosewood Ave
Kankakee IL 60901

Call Sign: KA9BZS
Karron L Hartley
2028 N Springview Dr
Kankakee IL 60901

Call Sign: KC9HHU
John W Mcgarey
1069 N Terrace Ave
Kankakee IL 60901

Call Sign: K9BYT
John W Mcgarey
1069 N Terrace Ave
Kankakee IL 60901

Call Sign: K5NMX
Frederick M Swaim
1472 N Terrace Ave
Kankakee IL 60901

Call Sign: K9XZ
Frederick M Swaim
1472 N Terrace Ave
Kankakee IL 60901

Call Sign: W9YNI
Kenneth A Buser
32 Norman Ave
Kankakee IL 60901

Call Sign: W9IE
Kenneth A Buser
32 Norman Ave
Kankakee IL 60901

Call Sign: KA9VHH
Jan C Parcell
40 Norman Ave
Kankakee IL 60901

Call Sign: KF9DM
Ronald E O Connell
7 Park Pl
Kankakee IL 60901

Call Sign: KC9MZS
Daney L Ferguson
8 River Ln
Kankakee IL 60901

Call Sign: KC9OCS
Duane T Harwood
3020 River Rd
Kankakee IL 60901

Call Sign: KA9BWX
Duane F Phillips
3081 River Rd
Kankakee IL 60901

Call Sign: N9RUC
Scott W Kuchel Sr
8444 C Rt 17 W
Kankakee IL 60901

Call Sign: N9QQP
Ronald E Brown
390 S 3000 W Rd
Kankakee IL 60901

Call Sign: KB9OJC
Lydia M Brown
3905 S 3000 Wrd
Kankakee IL 60901

Call Sign: KB9KZP
Phillip J Leppert
371 S 3rd Ave
Kankakee IL 60901

Call Sign: KB9MRT
Sandra L Leppert
371 S 3rd Ave
Kankakee IL 60901

Call Sign: KN0Z
John M Mclean
1035 S 3rd Ave
Kankakee IL 60901

Call Sign: KC9RKW
Lance E Marczak
1639 S 5th Ave
Kankakee IL 60901

Call Sign: KC9RKV
Van L Wegner
940 S 7th Ave
Kankakee IL 60901

Call Sign: K1VLW
Van L Wegner
940 S 7th Ave
Kankakee IL 60901

Call Sign: N9OKX
William A Doran
454 S Alma

Kankakee IL 60901

Call Sign: N9LCZ
Ronald B Johnson Jr
440 S Alma Ave
Kankakee IL 60901

Call Sign: KB9MJY
Scott D Dubois
299 S Barbara Dr
Kankakee IL 60901

Call Sign: KC9OET
Henry F Terrell
289 S Greenwood Ave
Kankakee IL 60901

Call Sign: KB9EI
David R Mazza
366 S McKinley
Kankakee IL 60901

Call Sign: KB9TWC
James T Mercede
659 S Nelson
Kankakee IL 60901

Call Sign: KC9UPL
Don C Papineau
141 S Oakdale
Kankakee IL 60901

Call Sign: KB9LIL
Randy L Iliff
692 S Osborn Ave
Kankakee IL 609015628

Call Sign: N9PGZ
Keith A Floriant
243 S Sibley
Kankakee IL 60901

Call Sign: N9MAJ
Francisco S Jones
791 S Wildwood Ave
Kankakee IL 60901

Call Sign: KT4VH
Louis L Benoche

959 S Yates
Kankakee IL 60901

Call Sign: KE9YO
Norman S Palow
205 Shaftsbury Rd
Kankakee IL 60901

Call Sign: WB9CDE
Boyd M Shade
52 Strasma Dr W
Kankakee IL 60901

Call Sign: WD9FYF
Harry G Seyfert
1477 Sunset Ln
Kankakee IL 609014542

Call Sign: KC9KZZ
Keith A Floriant
145 W Broadview Apt 700
Kankakee IL 60901

Call Sign: WB9QQP
Arthur G Lay
1478 W Hawkins
Kankakee IL 60901

Call Sign: N9REG
Kevin H Norden
3429 W Hwy 115
Kankakee IL 60901

Call Sign: N9MWA
Thomas J Higgins
1117 W Station
Kankakee IL 60901

Call Sign: KC9ELW
Brian J Kirk
851 W Stone
Kankakee IL 60901

Call Sign: KC9BPU
Bradley A Kirk
851 W Stone St
Kankakee IL 60901

Call Sign: KA9BWZ

David J Kaufman
1864 W Tampa Ln
Kankakee IL 60901

Call Sign: KC9NIA
Mark A Lanting
403 W Water St
Kankakee IL 60901

Call Sign: K9NIA
Mark A Lanting
403 W Water St
Kankakee IL 60901

Call Sign: WB9MPP
Vern A Weiss Sr
719 W Water St
Kankakee IL 60901

FCC Amateur Radio Licenses in Kansas

Call Sign: KB9PIF
Gary R Burns
3235 E 700th Rd
Kansas IL 61933

Call Sign: KC9UDK
Jess A Cannoy
9365 Il Hwy 49
Kansas IL 61933

Call Sign: N9VWQ
Jessica D Spesard
109 N Center St
Kansas IL 61933

FCC Amateur Radio Licenses in Karbers Ridge

Call Sign: KC9KWP
Donald D Ozee
Karbers Ridge IL 62955

FCC Amateur Radio Licenses in Karnak

Call Sign: KB9QXK
Leslie M Bradley

705 E 8th St
Karnak IL 62956

Call Sign: KD9MS
Craig A Bradley
705 E 8th St
Karnak IL 629560016

Call Sign: KC9DAZ
Johnathan R Arrison
1342 Rolling Hills Rd
Karnak IL 62956

FCC Amateur Radio Licenses in Keenes

Call Sign: WB9NYW
Robert T Woods
Rr1 Box 109
Keenes IL 62851

Call Sign: KB9RKI
Jerry D Peeples
Rt 1 Box 26
Keenes IL 62851

Call Sign: KC9OKX
Jason P Nelson
Rr 1 Box 55A
Keenes IL 62851

FCC Amateur Radio Licenses in Keensburg

Call Sign: W9MR
Kenneth R Martin
9616 E Market
Keensburg IL 628520124

Call Sign: KB9TAW
Stephen C Sutton
9422 Jackson St
Keensburg IL 62852

Call Sign: N9IMG
Lee F Lewis
1806 Jackson St
Keithsburg IL 61442

Call Sign: W9KBG
Michael W Tweed
Keithsburg IL 61442

Call Sign: K9GZH
John W Stewart
Keithsburg IL 61442

FCC Amateur Radio Licenses in Kell

Call Sign: KC9OWN
Lisa M Beasley
5003 Cartter Rd
Kell IL 62853

Call Sign: KB9TRH
Micheal J Mc Cray
111 E 2nd St
Kell IL 62853

Call Sign: WD9CHW
John P Buffat
827 S Jefferson
Kell IL 628531821

FCC Amateur Radio Licenses in Kempton

Call Sign: K9JLK
Lawrence A Gardner
3548 N 1700 E Rd
Kempton IL 609464011

Call Sign: WB9QYF
Carol L Gardner
3548 N 1700E Rd
Kempton IL 609464011

FCC Amateur Radio Licenses in Kenney

Call Sign: KC9EUP
Stephen J Lighthall
201 N Alexander St
Kenney IL 61749

FCC Amateur Radio Licenses in Kent

Call Sign: N9GTN
Terry L Flickinger
14804 E Airport Rd
Kent IL 61044

FCC Amateur Radio Licenses in Kewanee

Call Sign: KB9RIP
Robert M Davis
215 Community Sq 144
Kewanee IL 61443

Call Sign: KC9HWM
Thomas J Weston
319 Dwight St
Kewanee IL 61443

Call Sign: KB9OZZ
Thomas L Tracy
10370 E 2300 St
Kewanee IL 61443

Call Sign: WZ9D
Frank E De Clerk
6744 E 2480 St
Kewanee IL 61443

Call Sign: N9KYK
Tommie S Newman
13017 E 2520 St
Kewanee IL 61443

Call Sign: KC9HYE
Kewanee Esda
401 E 3rd St
Kewanee IL 61443

Call Sign: K9KPD
Kewanee Esda
401 E 3rd St
Kewanee IL 61443

Call Sign: KG9KO
Gerhard Jensen
326 E Church St

Kewanee IL 61443

Call Sign: KB9YWM
Byron J Hendrix
438 E Church St
Kewanee IL 61443

Call Sign: KB9WXW
Andrew D Bullock
419 E College St
Kewanee IL 61443

Call Sign: KB9TIO
Matthew D Bullock
419 E College St
Kewanee IL 61443

Call Sign: W9SIX
Matthew D Bullock
419 E College St
Kewanee IL 61443

Call Sign: KB9NXU
Michael E Hovey
608 E Prospect Ave
Kewanee IL 61443

Call Sign: KA9VXZ
John P Blankenbehler
523 Franklin
Kewanee IL 61443

Call Sign: KC9LOP
Alan J Abbott
203 Hillcrest Dr
Kewanee IL 61443

Call Sign: KB9VFV
Ronald L Price
1210 Lake St
Kewanee IL 61443

Call Sign: AA9AX
Ronald L Price
1210 Lake St
Kewanee IL 61443

Call Sign: N9UVY
Rodney E Johnson

1316 Lake St
Kewanee IL 61443

Call Sign: KF9OT
Bryon D Vigor
27659 N 570 Ave
Kewanee IL 61443

Call Sign: KF9ZC
Bradley D Leggett
820 N Tremont St
Kewanee IL 61443

Call Sign: AB9DX
Bradley D Leggett
820 N Tremont St
Kewanee IL 61443

Call Sign: KB9PUH
Betty J Peed
720 N Union St
Kewanee IL 61443

Call Sign: WB5ORU
Patricia J Seawright
418 N West St
Kewanee IL 61443

Call Sign: WA5WQC
Tommie K Seawright
418 N West St
Kewanee IL 61443

Call Sign: WB9WKE
Josef Novak
608 Page St
Kewanee IL 61443

Call Sign: KC9MN
Donald F Jenkins
115 Payson St
Kewanee IL 614433441

Call Sign: N4DUU
John G Humphreys
540 Pine St
Kewanee IL 61443

Call Sign: KB9WLL

William H Gordon Jr
707 Rockwell St
Kewanee IL 61443

Call Sign: K9RWT
William H Gordon Jr
707 Rockwell St
Kewanee IL 61443

Call Sign: N9OSP
Thomas E Davis
802 Rose St
Kewanee IL 61443

Call Sign: KC9PGU
Kenneth F Hampton Jr
1023 Roseview Ave
Kewanee IL 61443

Call Sign: KC9HNN
Kenneth F Hampton Sr
1023 Roseview Ave
Kewanee IL 61443

Call Sign: KB9RKX
Donald E Wilkie
1109 Roseview Ave
Kewanee IL 61443

Call Sign: K9DEW
Donald E Wilkie
1109 Roseview Ave
Kewanee IL 61443

Call Sign: W9NCZ
Mary B Oberlander
1113 Roseview Ave
Kewanee IL 61443

Call Sign: KB9TFL
Eric R Bellemore
314 S Park St
Kewanee IL 61443

Call Sign: N0ZDN
Keith G Edwards
700 S Tremont St
Kewanee IL 61443

Call Sign: W9JEO
Milton W Nicholas Jr
611 Shadycrest Dr
Kewanee IL 61443

Call Sign: KC9HKY
Roy G Dunn
1409 W 2nd St
Kewanee IL 61443

Call Sign: KB9FH
Warren R Peed
1309 W 4th St
Kewanee IL 61443

Call Sign: KE6JOJ
Mario B Massens
403 W Central Blvd
Kewanee IL 61443

Call Sign: KC9HKZ
Dennis L Lindstrom
216 Whitney Ave
Kewanee IL 61443

Call Sign: N9UKD
Leon S Kennaugh
333 Willard Ave
Kewanee IL 61443

Call Sign: WD9IRE
Phillip A Imes
908 Zang Ave
Kewanee IL 61443

Call Sign: KB9TBQ
Pammila A Phillis
Kewanee IL 61443

FCC Amateur Radio Licenses in Keyesport

Call Sign: KB9GKO
Joseph O Emery
3rd St
Keyesport IL 62253

Call Sign: KB9WLF
Carl G Paoletti

411 Republican St
Keyesport IL 62253

Call Sign: W0XE
John W Morgan
604 W Davis St
Keyesport IL 62253

Call Sign: W9YX
John W Morgan
604 W Davis St
Keyesport IL 62253

Call Sign: KB9BEA
Robin Roberts
Keyesport IL 62253

Call Sign: KD9DE
Florence E Emery
Keyesport IL 62253

Call Sign: N9IHK
Mc Kinley Sizemore
Keyesport IL 62253

FCC Amateur Radio Licenses in Kilbourne

Call Sign: KB9PFR
Kimmie J Brewer
107 W Walnut St
Kilbourne IL 626550033

Call Sign: KB9PFT
Michael L Brewer
107 W Walnut St
Kilbourne IL 626550033

FCC Amateur Radio Licenses in Kincaid

Call Sign: N9XRE
Anthony F Mollusky Sr
202 Ebison St
Kincaid IL 62540

Call Sign: N9WWZ
Wilbert H Griffin
119 Elm St

Kincaid IL 62540

Call Sign: KB9HRP
Patric J Grafton
209 Richardson
Kincaid IL 62540

Call Sign: KC9GFG
Charles F Connor
Kincaid IL 62540

Call Sign: KC9CAE
Howard J Davis
Kincaid IL 62540

Call Sign: KB9KBE
Dennis M House
Kincaid IL 625400872

Call Sign: KB9QCX
Jenniffer J House
Kincaid IL 625400872

FCC Amateur Radio Licenses in Kinmundy

Call Sign: N9OLI
Darrell D Chance
9150 Ford Rd
Kinmundy IL 62854

Call Sign: N9PFV
Dorothy L Chance
9150 Ford Rd
Kinmundy IL 62854

Call Sign: KB9ISC
Lorelei E Brimberry
101 Goodwin St
Kinmundy IL 62854

Call Sign: N9UPK
Mark A Brimberry
101 Goodwin St
Kinmundy IL 62854

Call Sign: KB9TTH
William A Hawkey Jr
6141 Lowe Rd

Kinmundy IL 62854

Call Sign: KB9HOG
Larry L Mulvaney Sr
6044 McCarty Rd
Kinmundy IL 62854

Call Sign: KB9HOF
Sheryl R Mulvaney
6044 McCarty Rd
Kinmundy IL 62854

Call Sign: KC9CXP
Richard D Schoreck
211 N Madison St
Kinmundy IL 62854

Call Sign: KC9CVV
Nathel L Halterman
414 N Monroe St
Kinmundy IL 62854

Call Sign: KB9TRG
Bradley W Hawkey
6048 Robb Rd
Kinmundy IL 62854

Call Sign: KB9TRF
Stephanie D Hawkey
6048 Robb Rd
Kinmundy IL 62854

Call Sign: KB9WHS
Cindy A Rose
7215 Rose Rd
Kinmundy IL 62854

Call Sign: KB9UBH
Vernon L Rose
7215 Rose Rd
Kinmundy IL 62854

Call Sign: N9RSQ
Jacob L White
304 S Porter St
Kinmundy IL 62854

Call Sign: KB9YJO
Mack A Myers Sr

310 W 2nd St
Kinmundy IL 62854

Call Sign: KB9TTL
Richard G Schoreck
Kinmundy IL 62854

FCC Amateur Radio Licenses in Kinsman

Call Sign: KC9LYT
Jim L Dunning
Kinsman IL 60437

FCC Amateur Radio Licenses in Kirkwood

Call Sign: KD9J
Aaron T Winski
140 Knoll Dr
Kirkwood IL 61447

Call Sign: KM9Z
Mac A English
140 Knoll Dr
Kirkwood IL 614479245

Call Sign: N9QOZ
Thomas E Winski
425 N Broadway
Kirkwood IL 614470043

Call Sign: KC4EI
William A Shumate
325 S Irvine
Kirkwood IL 61447

Call Sign: KA9GGU
Edward L Chewning
420 W Peach St
Kirkwood IL 61447

FCC Amateur Radio Licenses in Knoxville

Call Sign: KA9RZK
Max H Kassera
Rr 2 Box 172
Knoxville IL 61448

Call Sign: WB9WLE
Robert A Mattson
Rr 2 Box 54 A
Knoxville IL 61448

Call Sign: KA9CZV
Neil A Ruhl
Rr 1 Box 65
Knoxville IL 61448

Call Sign: KA9HHW
Lloyd W Tenneson
1217 Knox Hwy 8
Knoxville IL 614489350

Call Sign: WA9BNZ
William H Pelton
1292 Kreigh Ln
Knoxville IL 61448

Call Sign: KC5QOR
Alan M Wilt
104 Mill St
Knoxville IL 61448

Call Sign: KA9PJG
Charles N Burdette
820 S Market
Knoxville IL 61448

Call Sign: KB9TPH
Kevin A Poulson
209 W South
Knoxville IL 61448

Call Sign: WB9DDF
William F Johnson
307 Walnut St
Knoxville IL 61448

Call Sign: W9GFD
Knox County ARC
307 Walnut St
Knoxville IL 61448

FCC Amateur Radio Licenses in Lacon

Call Sign: KC9ALA
William J Starry
403 N Fulton St
Lacon IL 61540

Call Sign: KC9CAN
Robert C Brown
205 N Ida St
Lacon IL 61540

Call Sign: N8HRO
Lane L Knouse
216 N Ida St
Lacon IL 61540

Call Sign: N9XUM
James Moreland
927 S Washington Box 44
Lacon IL 61540

FCC Amateur Radio Licenses in Ladd

Call Sign: WB9YOE
Mark W Baker
3445 E Cleveland St
Ladd IL 61329

Call Sign: KA9WRZ
Bradley K Nicholson
3460 E Spring Creek Dr
Ladd IL 61329

Call Sign: K9RTL
James J Theodore
3485 E Spring Creek Dr
Ladd IL 61329

Call Sign: KB9TLY
Jerry P Funfsinn
111 N Western Ave
Ladd IL 61329

Call Sign: KC9QIM
Timothy M Oswald
116 S Peru Ave
Ladd IL 61329

Call Sign: KC9TIM

Timothy M Oswald
116 S Peru Ave
Ladd IL 61329

Call Sign: W9PZT
Rudy A Marusich
Ladd IL 61329

Call Sign: W9FF
Paul A Freeland
Ladd IL 61329

Call Sign: KC9JEP
Diane L Wozniak
Ladd IL 613290223

FCC Amateur Radio Licenses in LaFayette

Call Sign: KB9OUF
David M Krans
Rr 1 Box 44
LaFayette IL 61449

Call Sign: KB9OUG
Henry F Pease
Rr 1 Box 85A
LaFayette IL 61449

Call Sign: KG9CC
James P Rowley
611 Hodgson St
LaFayette IL 61449

FCC Amateur Radio Licenses in LaHarpe

Call Sign: N9PGW
Kenneth L Brown
107 Monmouth Rd
LaHarpe IL 61450

Call Sign: N9PGV
Thomas D Todd
205 W 3rd Ave
LaHarpe IL 61450

Call Sign: K9YIR
Henry R Hallowell

309 W Main
LaHarpe IL 61450

Call Sign: KB9ODV
Kendall J Beals
LaHarpe IL 61450

FCC Amateur Radio
Licenses in Lake Carroll

Call Sign: WB9NLQ
John J Grotto
2023 Hideout Ct
Lake Carroll IL 61046

Call Sign: WB9YFX
Justina M Grotto
2023 Hideout Ct
Lake Carroll IL 61046

FCC Amateur Radio
Licenses in Lake Fork

Call Sign: KB9JCE
John H Buckner Sr
Lake Fork IL 62541

FCC Amateur Radio
Licenses in LaMoille

Call Sign: KC9AWB
Elliott G Gebhardt
32910 2300 N Ave
LaMoille IL 61330

Call Sign: K9ZQ
Mark Gebhardt
32910 2300 N Ave
LaMoille IL 61330

Call Sign: KB9ZQQ
Diane S Gebhardt
32910 2300 N Ave
LaMoille IL 613309204

Call Sign: KB9JTL
Richard M Gebhardt
32910 2300 N Ave
LaMoille IL 61330

Call Sign: KB9ZGZ
Neil C Gebhardt
32910 2300 W Ave
LaMoille IL 61330

Call Sign: W9JPM
Robert J Boulay
706 Park Ave
LaMoille IL 613300496

Call Sign: KC9OCU
Edward L Zimmerlein
302 Wade Dr
LaMoille IL 61330

FCC Amateur Radio
Licenses in Lanark

Call Sign: WD9JFK
Ryland B Smith
Rr 2 Box 184
Lanark IL 61046

Call Sign: N9CJO
Jack E Welch
508 Crestview Ct
Lanark IL 61046

Call Sign: KA9UOO
Duane K Brown
11786 Grange Rd
Lanark IL 61046

Call Sign: KA9UPT
Jacqueline A Brown
11786 Grange Rd
Lanark IL 61046

Call Sign: W9AN
Alan R Ahasic
28 81 Highland Ct
Lanark IL 610469684

Call Sign: K9CRX
George W Cleary
21 37 Marina Ct
Lanark IL 610469204

Call Sign: KC9HP
Robert L Johnson
129 W Claremont
Lanark IL 61046

Call Sign: KC9NEY
Arnold L Owens
327 W Franklin St
Lanark IL 61046

Call Sign: AK9W
Arnold L Owens
327 W Franklin St
Lanark IL 61046

Call Sign: KB9TRD
Brian L Kruse
106 W Lanark Ave
Lanark IL 61046

Call Sign: N9ZLZ
David A Short
Lane IL 61750

FCC Amateur Radio
Licenses in LaPlace

Call Sign: KB5SRU
Kevin M Moser
87 N 100 E Rd
LaPlace IL 619360212

Call Sign: N9OUS
Timothy S Sanders
105 N Main St
LaPlace IL 619360153

Call Sign: KB9MR
William Bradshaw Jr
LaPlace IL 61936

FCC Amateur Radio
Licenses in LaSalle

Call Sign: KA9NSG
John W Ryba
435 11th St
LaSalle IL 61301

Call Sign: WB9FLB
Joseph T Assalley
813 1st St
LaSalle IL 61301

Call Sign: N9QPW
Todd D Warden
1040 2nd St 407
LaSalle IL 61301

Call Sign: KB9PUX
Michael A Young
206 2nd St Upper
LaSalle IL 61301

Call Sign: KB9LNK
Cecil G Atwell Jr
1317 4th St
LaSalle IL 61301

Call Sign: W9ACJ
Francis S Pyrz
845 5th St
LaSalle IL 61301

Call Sign: W9IZY
Walter A Pyszka
627 6th St
LaSalle IL 61301

Call Sign: KC9IH
Keith C Kerchner
549 7th St
LaSalle IL 613011803

Call Sign: WB9VBW
James M Brown
142 9th St
LaSalle IL 61301

Call Sign: KD9IC
Robert A Jensen
1352 Bucklin Ave
LaSalle IL 61301

Call Sign: WA9CEG
John A Gedraitis
1759 Campbell Ave
LaSalle IL 61301

Call Sign: KC9HZQ
Jerry D Friend Sr
1530 Chartres
LaSalle IL 61301

Call Sign: WD9GHU
Dwight A Redders
1600 Chartres
LaSalle IL 61301

Call Sign: KB9LSL
Michael E Barry
1070 Chartres St
LaSalle IL 61301

Call Sign: NO9Q
Donald G Selbrede
1314 Creve Coeur St
LaSalle IL 61301

Call Sign: N9QAL
Kathryn M Selbrede
1314 Creve Coeur St
LaSalle IL 61301

Call Sign: N9ZVN
Charles E Davis
2135 Creve Coeur St
LaSalle IL 61301

Call Sign: KC9UMZ
Michael J Pienta
2961 E 419th Rd
LaSalle IL 61301

Call Sign: K9UMZ
Michael J Pienta
2961 E 419th Rd
LaSalle IL 61301

Call Sign: KB9VVI
Harold L Deacon
2898 E 5th Rd
LaSalle IL 61301

Call Sign: KB9ZGY
Jacob L Deacon
2898 E 5th Rd

LaSalle IL 61301

Call Sign: K9MUJ
John A Biggs
608 Joliet St
LaSalle IL 61301

Call Sign: W9AGB
June L Russel
1435 Lafayette St
LaSalle IL 61301

Call Sign: N9XSW
John H Urbanowski
144 N 31st Rd
LaSalle IL 61301

Call Sign: KB9ZGV
Bernhard Ernst
1015 Oconor Ave
LaSalle IL 61301

Call Sign: W9OWT
Floyd A Sarwinski
Illinois Veterans Home W
Wing Rm 28B 1015 Oconor
Ave
LaSalle IL 61301

Call Sign: KB9NPG
Robert J Dunn
2709 St Vincent Ave 5
LaSalle IL 61301

Call Sign: KC9OTI
Steven Smith
736 Tonti St
LaSalle IL 61301

Call Sign: KB9OEP
David J Gedraitis
1332 Tonti St
LaSalle IL 61301

Call Sign: KC9IZR
Clinton J Kapinski
51 Victoria Dr
LaSalle IL 61301

Call Sign: WD9HEZ
Charles E Elsasser
Latham IL 62543

Call Sign: N9FG
Charles E Elsasser
Latham IL 62543

Call Sign: KA9MYB
Sandra J Elsasser
Latham IL 62543

FCC Amateur Radio
Licenses in Lawrenceville

Call Sign: K9YSL
George L Wells
1504 10th St
Lawrenceville IL 62439

Call Sign: WB9WQW
Kevin B Borden
1619 11th St
Lawrenceville IL 62439

Call Sign: KA9LDC
Steven B Miner
504 20th St
Lawrenceville IL 624391905

Call Sign: KB9KRS
Steven R Allender
1309 8th St
Lawrenceville IL 62439

Call Sign: WD9AFA
Brenda A Hartley
1312 8th St
Lawrenceville IL 62439

Call Sign: KB9PCS
David L Wright II
1114 9th St
Lawrenceville IL 62439

Call Sign: WD8RNI

Jackson C Archibald
1506 Ash St
Lawrenceville IL 62439

Call Sign: WB9HED
Marilyn A Finley
Rr 1 Box 208
Lawrenceville IL 62439

Call Sign: N8OOU
Walter M Meek
R R 3 Box 258
Lawrenceville IL 62439

Call Sign: KA9VWV
Michael E Frederick
R 2 Box 279
Lawrenceville IL 62439

Call Sign: KB9OEG
David L Risley
Rr 2 Box 311A
Lawrenceville IL 62439

Call Sign: KC8BNO
Joseph A Meek
R R 4 Box 50
Lawrenceville IL 62439

Call Sign: N9XXJ
Brad L Volkman
Rr 3 Box 7
Lawrenceville IL 62439

Call Sign: KB9YAJ
George D Nuttall
1606 Lexington
Lawrenceville IL 62439

Call Sign: KC9GIF
Carlton L Crasher
706 Lexington Av
Lawrenceville IL 62439

Call Sign: N9KJL
Peter C Crasher
706 Lexington Ave
Lawrenceville IL 62439

Call Sign: WD9FHH
J W Dollahan
1810 State St
Lawrenceville IL 62439

Call Sign: KB9YAH
John D Secrest
Lawrenceville IL 62439

FCC Amateur Radio
Licenses in Le Roy

Call Sign: N9PFG
Kyle A White
1 Blue Jay Ct
Le Roy IL 61752

Call Sign: N9XWS
Thomas A Harpenau
15828 Rosewood Rd
Le Roy IL 617529710

Call Sign: N9IAD
Joe E Harbison
409 Samuel Dr
Le Roy IL 61752

Call Sign: AB9DB
David R Tancig
411 Sunset Dr
Le Roy IL 61752

Call Sign: KA9UIY
John R Monical
304 W Cedar St
Le Roy IL 61752

Call Sign: N9XWT
Gerald L Williamson Jr
612 W Vine Lot 11
Le Roy IL 61752

FCC Amateur Radio
Licenses in Leaf River

Call Sign: KA9QES
Joseph C Gremba
3093 Lightsville Rd
Leaf River IL 61047

Call Sign: N9IIF
John W Beltz Jr
7194 Truimp Rd
Leaf River IL 61047

Call Sign: KA8IUY
Melody L Ashcraft
5504 W Town Line Rd
Leaf River IL 61047

Call Sign: W9JJT
Richard G Wood
Leaf River IL 61047

Call Sign: KC9LQW
Paul C Detmer
Leaf River IL 610470028

**FCC Amateur Radio
Licenses in Lebanon**

Call Sign: AA9VK
Lawrence A Galer
912 Belleville St
Lebanon IL 62254

Call Sign: KC9LTX
Russell P Jarvis
26 Bernhardt Rd
Lebanon IL 62254

Call Sign: KC7TTU
Daniel J Ely
106 Cavins Run
Lebanon IL 62254

Call Sign: KC7WPN
Dixie M Ely
106 Cavins Run
Lebanon IL 62254

Call Sign: WB9VAJ
Catherine T Davis
620 Clover Dr
Lebanon IL 62254

Call Sign: N9NKC
Frank L Tempia

1232 College Rd
Lebanon IL 62254

Call Sign: KC9PTG
Douglas R Dyher
10101 Faust Rd
Lebanon IL 62254

Call Sign: WA9JMG
Roger D Smalley
105 Florence St
Lebanon IL 62254

Call Sign: KB9OGI
Joscelyn Russell
11261 Fox Lake Dr
Lebanon IL 62254

Call Sign: WA9ZYE
Thurman D Carver
33 Harmon Dr
Lebanon IL 62254

Call Sign: KE4UVG
James L Tempus
208 N Herman St
Lebanon IL 62254

Call Sign: KC9LIZ
Thomas L Myers
7 Roger Dr
Lebanon IL 62254

Call Sign: KA9MEP
Pierre J Ferendzo
125 Roger Dr
Lebanon IL 62254

Call Sign: KC9UFD
Gary M Myers
129 Roger Dr
Lebanon IL 62254

Call Sign: AA9RU
Stanley R Schellenbach
520 Roger Dr
Lebanon IL 62254

Call Sign: KB9FNU

Harry E Vink
680 Scott Troy Rd
Lebanon IL 622541906

Call Sign: KF7MA
Larry D Magnuson
544 Shady Ln
Lebanon IL 62254

Call Sign: W0KXP
Harrison L Church
10940 SR 4
Lebanon IL 62254

Call Sign: WB9UDL
Stephen J Mueller
10212 US Hwy 50
Lebanon IL 62254

Call Sign: N9FDJ
Fred R Hensler Jr
318 W Center St
Lebanon IL 62254

Call Sign: N9AOR
Barbara E Cohen
424 W Main St
Lebanon IL 62254

Call Sign: N9RGE
Wilbert R Warke
438 W Main St
Lebanon IL 62254

Call Sign: KZ0Z
Thomas D Blackburn Jr
703 W St Louis St
Lebanon IL 62254

**FCC Amateur Radio
Licenses in Lee**

Call Sign: KC9FMG
Erik D Swanson
391 Erickson Gate
Lee IL 60530

Call Sign: KC9FMN
Jonathan J Swanson

391 Erickson Gate
Lee IL 60530

Call Sign: KC9QJI
Christian W Ponall
1167 Paw Paw Rd
Lee IL 60530

Call Sign: KA9WLS
William P Ponall
1167 Paw Paw Rd
Lee IL 60530

Call Sign: KC9YJ
William A Springer
1426 Paw Paw Rd
Lee IL 60530

Call Sign: KC9AFH
Steven R Gogol
13801 Tower Rd
Lee IL 60530

Call Sign: N9XFM
Jeffrey M Henderson
251 W Hardanger Gate
Lee IL 60530

Call Sign: WB9OGY
Thomas H Noon Jr
Lee Center IL 613310006

Call Sign: KC9OSX
Don T Head
995 Benson Rd
Leland IL 60531

Call Sign: KE9ES
Frederick C Mangold
4585 E 18th Rd
Leland IL 60531

Call Sign: KC9KX

David L Rodgers
560 Indian Creek Dr
Leland IL 60531

Call Sign: K9UX
David L Rodgers
560 Indian Creek Dr
Leland IL 60531

Call Sign: KC9IBY
Richard A Johnson
621 Deer Trl Dr
Lena IL 61048

Call Sign: W9KCN
Arnold R Johnson
418 Grove Ave
Lena IL 61048

Call Sign: KC9JLB
Richard T Reid
3977 N A Y P Rd
Lena IL 61048

Call Sign: N9CAL
Ivan R Broaddus
403 S Center St
Lena IL 61048

Call Sign: N9OGU
Michael A Dimiceli
10208 W Dameier Rd
Lena IL 61048

Call Sign: W9SRX
Dale E Schmertman
529 W Fairway Dr
Lena IL 61048

Call Sign: WB9WGQ
James E Odlin
11501 W Howardsville Rd
Lena IL 61048

Call Sign: W9GDE
Gordon D Edler

11803 W Mound Rd
Lena IL 61048

Call Sign: W9MKS
Starved Rock Radio Club Inc
100 Tabor St
Leonore IL 61332

Call Sign: KA9WEA
David M Greenwood
1144 CR 1400 N
Lerna IL 62440

Call Sign: WA9CUE
Keith E Tucker
7872 E CR 225 N
Lerna IL 624409703

Call Sign: WA9HNE
Virginia L Tucker
7872 E CR 225 N
Lerna IL 624409703

Call Sign: W9CUE
Keith E Tucker
7872 E CR 225N
Lerna IL 624402510

Call Sign: KB9AUV
John F Protz
Lerna IL 62440

Call Sign: KB9QIG
Joshua L Van Middlesworth
Rr 2 Box 247
Lewistown IL 61542

Call Sign: KD6QII
Gregory S Juergens
13398 E Duncan Mills Rd

Lewistown IL 61542

Call Sign: KB9LVM
Garrett A Ginglen
509 E Euclid
Lewistown IL 61542

Call Sign: AA9BX
William L Bath
16051N Il 78 Hwy
Lewistown IL 61542

Call Sign: K9OL
William L Bath
16051N Il 78 Hwy
Lewistown IL 61542

Call Sign: KC9RCT
Darold D Richardson
14976 N Ic Hwy 78
Lewistown IL 61542

Call Sign: N9MTZ
Agnes M Bath
16051 N Ill 78 Hwy
Lewistown IL 61542

Call Sign: N9UFE
Montye L Jolliff
403 N Main St
Lewistown IL 651421140

Call Sign: KC9MFP
Montye L Jolliff
403 N Main St
Lewistown IL 651421140

Call Sign: KE9DG
William G Breckenridge
17132 N State Hwy 100
Lewistown IL 61542

Call Sign: KA9GFJ
Donald R Hall
920 S Jefferson
Lewistown IL 61542

Call Sign: N9FDG
George J Gillis

403 S Main St
Lewistown IL 61542

Call Sign: WA9RLG
Laverne E Zook
803 W Ave E
Lewistown IL 615420108

Call Sign: KA9MXH
Cheryl A Hall
410 W Ave J
Lewistown IL 61542

FCC Amateur Radio Licenses in Lexington

Call Sign: KC9BWE
Girard C Steichen
26136 E 2200 N Rd
Lexington IL 61753

Call Sign: KC9KWB
James F Bakaitis
208 E Wall St
Lexington IL 61753

Call Sign: KC9KWD
Megan C Bakaitis
208 E Wall St
Lexington IL 61753

Call Sign: KC9JXO
Rachael C Bakaitis
208 E Wall St
Lexington IL 61753

Call Sign: KC9KWC
Benjamin M Bakaitis
208 E Wall St
Lexington IL 61753

Call Sign: KF9PE
Charles E Justice
3 Patricia Ct
Lexington IL 61753

Call Sign: N9LYW
James R Wisdom
22533 Pj Keller Hwy

Lexington IL 61753

FCC Amateur Radio Licenses in Liberty

Call Sign: KB9GBZ
Dawn E Matheina
Rr 1 Box 173
Liberty IL 62347

Call Sign: KB9FCM
Forrest E Waters
Rr 1 Box 209
Liberty IL 62347

Call Sign: N9ATT
Kenneth C Thomas
Rr 1 Box 32A
Liberty IL 62347

Call Sign: KB9SWB
Troy E Irvin
Rr 3 Box 65
Liberty IL 62347

Call Sign: KB9RZJ
Robert N Claus
Rt 2 Box 7B
Liberty IL 62347

Call Sign: K9GZO
Alfred G Maple Sr
Rr 2 Box 8C
Liberty IL 62347

Call Sign: KC9LCL
Mark A Morrison
1102 E 1900th St
Liberty IL 62347

Call Sign: KA1DYD
Gerald P Fleming
535 E 2050th St
Liberty IL 623473006

Call Sign: N9OFO
David P Bigelow
400 E 2533rd Ln
Liberty IL 623472832

Call Sign: KA9CNR
Duane P Leech
567 E 2553 Ln
Liberty IL 62347

Call Sign: KB9UNQ
Ryan A Lockett
Rr 1 Marian Acres Box 7D
Liberty IL 62347

Call Sign: KB9JIZ
Charlyn C Funk
2742 N 230 Ave
Liberty IL 62347

Call Sign: N9MTX
Darren W Funk
2742 N 230 Ave
Liberty IL 62347

Call Sign: N9JF
James L Funk
2742 N 230 Ave
Liberty IL 62347

Call Sign: KB9CES
Melba L Funk
2742 N 230 Ave
Liberty IL 62347

Call Sign: KR9L
Liberty Radio Explorers
2742 N 230 Ave
Liberty IL 62347

Call Sign: KB9TGY
Amy J Claus
707 Talbot St
Liberty IL 62347

Call Sign: KB9GYE
Paul P Clark
311 W SR
Liberty IL 62347

Call Sign: KB9EYY
Ian D Henning
Liberty IL 62347

FCC Amateur Radio Licenses in Lima

Call Sign: WB2JSC
Robert W Butler
523 S Range Line
Lima IL 62348

FCC Amateur Radio Licenses in Lincoln

Call Sign: N9XHY
David J Morrow
310 11th St
Lincoln IL 62656

Call Sign: W9ERF
John R Berker
1192 1250th Ave
Lincoln IL 626565390

Call Sign: KB0WUP
Thomas J Wachtel
1035 1450th Ave
Lincoln IL 62656

Call Sign: KA9TMO
Betty F Peacock
905 1575th St
Lincoln IL 62656

Call Sign: WB9RJY
Earl M Schultz
904 21st 33
Lincoln IL 62656

Call Sign: N9GNB
Glen N Bonaparte
309 21st St
Lincoln IL 62656

Call Sign: N9WGT
Michael K Roos
348 5th St
Lincoln IL 62656

Call Sign: KA9PMM
Brian S Martens

634 6th St
Lincoln IL 62656

Call Sign: KA9BMQ
James W Bailey
1111 7th
Lincoln IL 62656

Call Sign: W9QVK
Robert N Woll
1360 Airport Rd
Lincoln IL 62656

Call Sign: W9JSQ
Gerald L Fargusson
502 College Ave
Lincoln IL 62656

Call Sign: KB9SIW
Russell F Flynn Jr
27 Community Dr
Lincoln IL 62656

Call Sign: KC0KOS
Llyle J Barker III
107 Crestwood Dr
Lincoln IL 62656

Call Sign: K9RVS
Edward J Malkowski
1029 Delavan St
Lincoln IL 62656

Call Sign: WB9QMO
William L Bradley
142 Foley
Lincoln IL 62656

Call Sign: WD9JAN
Michael D Jones
155 Half Moon
Lincoln IL 62656

Call Sign: KA9DAL
William F Breen Jr
33 Illini Dr
Lincoln IL 62656

Call Sign: WB9UVH

Terry L Storer
121 Keokuk St
Lincoln IL 626561625

Call Sign: K9TLS
Terry L Storer
121 Keokuk St
Lincoln IL 626561625

Call Sign: KC9NPU
Terry R Baker
619 Lincoln Ave
Lincoln IL 62656

Call Sign: KE9DA
Marvin S Robinson
208 Maple
Lincoln IL 62656

Call Sign: KB9OWY
David M Hurley
1000 N College St Apt B 4
Lincoln IL 62656

Call Sign: N9EZJ
Donald R Begolka
410 N Elm St
Lincoln IL 62656

Call Sign: KA9DSC
Richard T Sullivan
929 N Hamilton
Lincoln IL 626561815

Call Sign: KB9OXT
Margo L Hudson
1715 N Jefferson St
Lincoln IL 62656

Call Sign: K9VH
Virgil L Hudson IV
1715 N Jefferson St
Lincoln IL 62656

Call Sign: W9RIX
Edward J Pelc
1307 N Kankakee St
Lincoln IL 62656

Call Sign: KB9NXS
John S Grimsley
516 N Logan
Lincoln IL 62656

Call Sign: K9UIA
Virgil W Mc Cann
1036 N Monroe St
Lincoln IL 62656

Call Sign: WA9PAZ
Brayton V Danner
435 N Union St
Lincoln IL 62656

Call Sign: KD9GN
David P Lolling
611 N Union St
Lincoln IL 62656

Call Sign: N9HKU
Jack Schwalbach
24 Oak Hill Dr
Lincoln IL 62656

Call Sign: W9MYN
Arthur F Briggs
107 Portland Ave
Lincoln IL 62656

Call Sign: W9LHS
Jack V Hart
925 Primm Rd Apt 107
Lincoln IL 62656

Call Sign: WB9ZAA
Fred W Cook
1210 Pulaski Ave
Lincoln IL 62656

Call Sign: KC9UMY
Austin M Hopp
1501 Pulaski St
Lincoln IL 62656

Call Sign: K9AMH
Austin M Hopp
1501 Pulaski St
Lincoln IL 62656

Call Sign: KB9PCB
Jay F Gaydosh
307 S Hamilton
Lincoln IL 62656

Call Sign: KB9NKW
Glen N Bonaparte
503 S Madison
Lincoln IL 62656

Call Sign: WA9DND
Gene W Talley
290 Southgate Dr
Lincoln IL 62656

Call Sign: KB9UKG
Sherry A Davis-Dodd
604 SR 10
Lincoln IL 62656

Call Sign: KC9IGV
Lincoln Weather ARC
1362 SR 10
Lincoln IL 62656

Call Sign: WX9ILX
Lincoln Weather ARC
1362 SR 10
Lincoln IL 62656

Call Sign: N9CEH
Glenn F Michaelis
607 Tremont St
Lincoln IL 62656

Call Sign: W9LDV
Larry D Voyles
206 Willard Ave
Lincoln IL 62656

Call Sign: WB9GYJ
Gary L Stanford
926 Woodlawn Rd
Lincoln IL 62656

Call Sign: AB9XN
Gary L Stanford
926 Woodlawn Rd

Lincoln IL 62656

FCC Amateur Radio Licenses in Lindenwood

Call Sign: KG9JU
Ralph F Pullin Jr
14579 Lindenwood Rd
Lindenwood IL 610491063

Call Sign: N9GZH
Bernice P Holtman
211 Lynnville Rd
Lindenwood IL 61049

Call Sign: W9BKW
Clarence W Holtman Sr
211 Lynnville Rd
Lindenwood IL 61049

FCC Amateur Radio Licenses in Litchfield

Call Sign: KC9VPP
Josh A Snow
23248 Airport Trl
Litchfield IL 62056

Call Sign: N9VFQ
Richard D Wilson Jr
Rr 3 Box 169
Litchfield IL 62056

Call Sign: N9UVX
Mary A Bishop
Rr 3 Box 269
Litchfield IL 62056

Call Sign: KA9OIM
Dolores M Taylor Marley
Rr 2 Box 97
Litchfield IL 62056

Call Sign: W9YXC
George J Taylor
Rr 2 Box 97
Litchfield IL 62056

Call Sign: N9QCG
Karen K Presnell
1118 E Hauser
Litchfield IL 62056

Call Sign: AC9P
Charles E Presnell Sr
1118 E Hauser St
Litchfield IL 620562803

Call Sign: N9GQO
James A Wright
604 E Ryder
Litchfield IL 62056

Call Sign: N9ZVW
Larry E Smoot
1350 E Ryder
Litchfield IL 62056

Call Sign: KB9MPO
Tammy K Young
1350 E Ryder
Litchfield IL 62056

Call Sign: K9DNH
J P Sisson
901 E Tyler
Litchfield IL 62056

Call Sign: KA9VGH
Marilyn J Sisson
901 E Tyler
Litchfield IL 62056

Call Sign: KC9PGN
Gary A Law
520 E Union
Litchfield IL 62056

Call Sign: KC9NJW
Isaac J Pizzo
3398 Honey Bend Ave
Litchfield IL 62056

Call Sign: WD9DOA
Merlin W Vancil
25 Howard St
Litchfield IL 62056

Call Sign: WD9EYS
Jane M Taylor
11209 Litchfield Trl
Litchfield IL 62056

Call Sign: WB9DAS
Joseph F Taylor
11209 Litchfield Trl
Litchfield IL 62056

Call Sign: KC9BSR
Steve J Taylor
11209 Litchfield Trl
Litchfield IL 62056

Call Sign: N9WWG
Dale L Bishop
2224 N 14th Ave
Litchfield IL 62056

Call Sign: N9ZBY
Rebecca J Bishop
2224 N 14th Ave
Litchfield IL 62056

Call Sign: KB9NVC
Gerald W Lane
103 N Douglas
Litchfield IL 62056

Call Sign: N9UJE
Darin R Mc Bride
1326 N Franklin
Litchfield IL 62056

Call Sign: K9KOD
William Conlon
1315 N Franklin Ave
Litchfield IL 62056

Call Sign: AA9WC
William Conlon
1315 N Franklin Ave
Litchfield IL 62056

Call Sign: N9KK
William Conlon
1315 N Franklin Ave

Litchfield IL 62056

Call Sign: WA9WC
William Conlon
1315 N Franklin Ave
Litchfield IL 62056

Call Sign: WB9JFS
Betty J Driscoll
812 N Harrison
Litchfield IL 62056

Call Sign: WB9HRC
Joseph P Driscoll
812 N Harrison
Litchfield IL 62056

Call Sign: KB9VXR
Mark E Hammond
401 N Illinois
Litchfield IL 62056

Call Sign: N9ANX
David C Hendricks
628 N Illinois
Litchfield IL 62056

Call Sign: WB9QLY
Kathryn L Millick
222 N Jackson
Litchfield IL 62056

Call Sign: WD9DKU
Thomas E Bradburn
911 N Jackson
Litchfield IL 62056

Call Sign: WB9WAU
Dwight H Wright
1909 N Jackson
Litchfield IL 62056

Call Sign: N9RTI
Kevin L Wright
1909 N Jackson
Litchfield IL 62056

Call Sign: WB9WAV
Theresa M Wright

1909 N Jackson
Litchfield IL 62056

Call Sign: K9SM
Scott C Millick
222 N Jackson St
Litchfield IL 62056

Call Sign: K9ATV
Central Illinois St Louis Area
Amateur Tv Club
222 N Jackson St
Litchfield IL 62056

Call Sign: KB9MHL
James S Heslop
610 N Locust
Litchfield IL 62056

Call Sign: KC9DYN
Earl T Brown
416 N Madison St
Litchfield IL 62056

Call Sign: KC9BSS
Mary J Weeks
1504 N Monroe
Litchfield IL 62056

Call Sign: N9JLM
Carol A York
1917 N Monroe
Litchfield IL 62056

Call Sign: KB9AAP
Mark A York
1917 N Monroe
Litchfield IL 62056

Call Sign: KC9IKJ
Matthew D Weber
420 N Monroe Apt 207
Litchfield IL 62056

Call Sign: KC9WEB
Matthew D Weber
420 N Monroe Apt 207
Litchfield IL 62056

Call Sign: KC9PGL
David W Sumpter
1602 N State St
Litchfield IL 620561112

Call Sign: KB9MIU
Linda J Dowdy
1425 N Van Buren
Litchfield IL 62056

Call Sign: KB9SNY
Brandon M Hicks
1425 N Van Durean
Litchfield IL 62056

Call Sign: N9QMY
Janice M Leonard
820 S State
Litchfield IL 62056

Call Sign: KB9HOS
Danny C Leonard
820 S State St
Litchfield IL 62056

Call Sign: WA9HEP
Paul M Ashmore
407 S Walnut
Litchfield IL 62056

Call Sign: K9KYW
Robert C Cranford
215 W Ferdon St
Litchfield IL 62056

Call Sign: KB9LGL
Shawna R Burke
900 W Tyler Ave
Litchfield IL 62056

Call Sign: KC9POZ
Darin R Mcbride Jr
900 W Tyler Ave
Litchfield IL 62056

Call Sign: W9GQ
Albert C Lattig
54 Woodlawn Dr
Litchfield IL 62056

Call Sign: KA9OMN
George M Taylor
Litchfield IL 62056

Call Sign: W9YXC
George M Taylor
Litchfield IL 62056

Call Sign: N9OWS
Jeremy A Graham
Litchfield IL 620560277

FCC Amateur Radio
Licenses in Little York

Call Sign: KB9VLY
Nick R Williamson
Rr 1 Box 58
Little York IL 61453

Call Sign: KB9VVO
Dane R Williamson
Rr 1 Box 58
Little York IL 61453

FCC Amateur Radio
Licenses in Littleton

Call Sign: KA9IZI
Jimmy A Pierce
Rr 1 Box 116
Littleton IL 61452

Call Sign: N9UGZ
Steve E Spencer
R 1 Box 31
Littleton IL 61452

Call Sign: N9UHB
Barbara J Spencer
Rr 1 Box 31
Littleton IL 61452

Call Sign: WD9AJL
Carroll D Noland
129 E Broadway
Littleton IL 61452

Call Sign: WD9AJM
Mary E Noland
129 E Broadway
Littleton IL 61452

Call Sign: KC9MXE
Danny L Engelbrecht
Littleton IL 61452

FCC Amateur Radio
Licenses in Livingston

Call Sign: WZ9V
William L Call
Box 384 Cora St
Livingston IL 62058

Call Sign: KC9FHL
Lewis F Harty
527 Rodenberg
Livingston IL 62058

FCC Amateur Radio
Licenses in Loami

Call Sign: N9DS
Duston C Suits
13500 Maxwell Hall Rd
Loami IL 626613129

Call Sign: K9QFO
Lyle E Devore
203 N East St
Loami IL 62661

FCC Amateur Radio
Licenses in Loda

Call Sign: N9EWS
Stephen D Farrington
106 Dakota Dr
Loda IL 60948

Call Sign: K9TA
Stephen D Farrington
106 Dakota Dr
Loda IL 60948

Call Sign: K9UXC

Allen J Gharst
205 N Elm St
Loda IL 609480151

Call Sign: W9FDP
Laddie J Konas
230 Ocala Dr
Loda IL 60948

Call Sign: W9NKX
Iroquois Ford ARS
Loda IL 60948

Call Sign: WA9BVU
Marvin F Dale
Loda IL 60948

FCC Amateur Radio
Licenses in Logan

Call Sign: KD6QJP
Frederick H Deer
6267 Washington St
Logan IL 62856

Call Sign: KC9CSN
Zachary D Ozbourn
Logan IL 62856

FCC Amateur Radio
Licenses in Lomax

Call Sign: K0RW
John C Lenahan Jr
Rr 1 Box 123B
Lomax IL 61454

Call Sign: WB9SVE
Larry K Moreland
Rr 1 Box 13A
Lomax IL 61454

FCC Amateur Radio
Licenses in London Mills

Call Sign: KA9ZOL
Bryan L Rice
208 Elm
London Mills IL 61544

Call Sign: KB9KAW
Rodney A Brady
302 W Elm St
London Mills IL 61544

Call Sign: KB9KAX
Donavon J Tinder
London Mills IL 61544

FCC Amateur Radio
Licenses in Long Point

Call Sign: WA9VCT
Leroy H Albertson
502 Morgan St
Long Point IL 61333

FCC Amateur Radio
Licenses in Longview

Call Sign: KB9ZZP
Donna E Sanders
110 W Church St
Longview IL 61852

Call Sign: KB9JJN
Thomas W Sanders
110 W Church St
Longview IL 61852

FCC Amateur Radio
Licenses in Loraine

Call Sign: KB9MXO
Rosemary E Jenkins
Rr 1 Box 195
Loraine IL 62349

Call Sign: KC9LCN
Gary E Dittmer
1430 E CR 0
Loraine IL 62349

Call Sign: N9AYP
Louis L Irvin
Log Home
Loraine IL 623490386

FCC Amateur Radio
Licenses in Lostant

Call Sign: N9OBD
Frank L Hartenbower
215 N 17th Rd
Lostant IL 61334

Call Sign: WB9ZFO
Kenneth J Stasiak
106 N Seigel St
Lostant IL 61334

FCC Amateur Radio
Licenses in Louisville

Call Sign: K9AAF
Andrew R Ehrlicher
1285 Bible Grove Ln
Louisville IL 628589525

Call Sign: KC9OZK
Mark A Feldhake
4481 Bible Grove Ln
Louisville IL 62858

Call Sign: KB9QGX
Celeste S Hale
Rt 1 Box 195
Louisville IL 62858

Call Sign: KB9PDY
Thomas J Hale
Rt 1 Box 195
Louisville IL 62858

Call Sign: N9CIB
Raymond A Grundy
Rt 1 Box 237
Louisville IL 628589778

Call Sign: KB9KOQ
Donald L Zink
Rt 2 Box 33
Louisville IL 62858

Call Sign: KB9WDT
Mark D Strange
Rr 1 Box10A

Louisville IL 62858

Call Sign: N9UIH
Vaughn R Moore
1100 Church
Louisville IL 62858

Call Sign: N9PB
Mark A Feldhake
700 Leopard Dr
Louisville IL 62858

Call Sign: KB9YJT
Laura L Hale
685 Palm Ln
Louisville IL 62858

Call Sign: KC9EKM
Dana J Jones
325 S Green St
Louisville IL 62858

Call Sign: KC9ERD
Mark C Leonberger
1275 Skimmer Dr
Louisville IL 62858

Call Sign: KB0OWV
Gene R Keller
121 Tanner St
Louisville IL 62858

Call Sign: W8KKZ
Perry A Wiley
348 Woods Ln
Louisville IL 62858

Call Sign: W9DBI
Victor A Hale
Louisville IL 62858

FCC Amateur Radio
Licenses in Loves Park

Call Sign: N9MCR
Paul J Walder
6039 Basin Dr
Loves Park IL 61111

Call Sign: K9RUK
Marvin D Smith
5846 Beechwood Dr Apt C
Loves Park IL 61111

Call Sign: K9GMS
Larry W Denhart
5417 Bennett St 12
Loves Park IL 61111

Call Sign: KA9DNQ
Jo Ann M Landis
7709 Bufalo Grove Rd
Loves Park IL 61111

Call Sign: KB9WD
Dale D Landis
7709 Buffalo Grove Rd
Loves Park IL 61111

Call Sign: KD9MQ
Roger V Sawvell
7158 Cauletti Dr
Loves Park IL 611115314

Call Sign: KA9PUM
Timothy M Gragg
7158 Cauletti Dr
Loves Park IL 611115314

Call Sign: KE8ES
William J King
825 Clifford Ave
Loves Park IL 61111

Call Sign: N0NNK
Patrick M Griffith
540 Clifford Ave 112
Loves Park IL 611114672

Call Sign: KB9RHP
Ronald L Evans
6401 Commonwealth Dr
Loves Park IL 61111

Call Sign: WB9JFF
John J Tewell Jr
2014 Coronet Rd
Loves Park IL 61111

Call Sign: WA9AXG
Francis J Delmore
6071 Durrington Dr
Loves Park IL 61111

Call Sign: W9SON
Jack C Chancellor
6021 Durrington Dr Mulford
Hills
Loves Park IL 61111

Call Sign: N9VJU
Thomas E Shouler
5236 East Dr
Loves Park IL 61111

Call Sign: N9KOV
Calvin P Spruit
5413 East Dr 3
Loves Park IL 61111

Call Sign: KC9DTT
Jeffrey J Schroeder
7075 Equestrian Cir
Loves Park IL 61111

Call Sign: KC9RUG
Jason E Halbrader
1621 Evans Ave
Loves Park IL 61115

Call Sign: N9ZXJ
Emmeran R Geyer
5295 Gettysburg Dr
Loves Park IL 61111

Call Sign: N9JRD
Kim K Kirkpatrick
5336 Gettysburg Dr
Loves Park IL 61111

Call Sign: NZ9N
John J Kimberly
129 Grand Blvd
Loves Park IL 61111

Call Sign: KA9NZK
Thomas R Fernandez

6632 Hayfield Ln
Loves Park IL 61111

Call Sign: KB9IJL
David A Mayhew
5719 Hollis Ave
Loves Park IL 61111

Call Sign: KB9YX
Steven H Pash
4979 Hummingbird Trl
Loves Park IL 61111

Call Sign: KB8GOO
Sandra L Mc Bride
5019 Hummingbird Trl
Loves Park IL 61111

Call Sign: N8IRC
Richard H Mc Bride
5019 Hummingbird Trl
Loves Park IL 611111967

Call Sign: K5SY
Milton E Otwell
4619 Illinois St
Loves Park IL 61111

Call Sign: KA9VSV
Harley D Beebe
4827 Illinois St
Loves Park IL 611115847

Call Sign: WA9GNU
John S Edwards
4953 Illinois St
Loves Park IL 61111

Call Sign: KC9QPL
Paul R Spencer
2216 Maple Ave
Loves Park IL 61111

Call Sign: KA9MOQ
William A Best
5423 Marble Dr
Loves Park IL 61111

Call Sign: KB9KCK

Lawrence P Alex
6309 Material Ave
Loves Park IL 61111

Call Sign: N9IAF
Geoffrey A Driebusch
5126 Morning Glory Ln
Loves Park IL 611300072

Call Sign: W9SS
Dennis G Eksten
5006 N 2nd St
Loves Park IL 61111

Call Sign: KB9OPE
George O Pepke
5696 Peachstone Pl
Loves Park IL 61111

Call Sign: KD9WW
Ralph L Peterson
5044 Pine Rock Ave
Loves Park IL 61111

Call Sign: KB9Y
Kenneth S Rorheim
4975 Rolex Pkwy
Loves Park IL 61111

Call Sign: N9WHW
Adam P Faber
5296 Sandpiper
Loves Park IL 611117034

Call Sign: N9YOP
Dennis E Politic
5675 Shale Dr
Loves Park IL 611118306

Call Sign: KC9ISC
Richard T Jensen
4164 Split Leaf Dr
Loves Park IL 61111

Call Sign: KC9GRN
Lorne E Hoover
427 Theodore St
Loves Park IL 61111

Call Sign: N9KJN
Norman M Stilphen Jr
7483 Thomas
Loves Park IL 61111

Call Sign: KC9BYB
Ruth M Stilphen
7483 Thomas Dr
Loves Park IL 61111

Call Sign: KF9CL
Willard D Dembinski
6527 Timberleaf Ct Apt 1
Loves Park IL 61111

Call Sign: N9ZKR
F Duane Ingram
6382 Torch Lite Trl
Loves Park IL 61111

Call Sign: KD9CA
Alfred O Fischer
6220 Torchlite Trl
Loves Park IL 61111

Call Sign: N9AMV
Billy E Keen
6297 Valhalla Dr
Loves Park IL 611113460

Call Sign: N9TJA
Joseph M Lierman
7717 Venus St
Loves Park IL 61111

Call Sign: KC9VAD
Timothy C Karr
706 W Hampton Ave
Loves Park IL 61111

Call Sign: KB9TQR
Pamela L Watson
5614 Walker Ave
Loves Park IL 61111

Call Sign: K9KLB
Kelly L Bunge
5624 Walker Ave
Loves Park IL 61111

Call Sign: W9MUT
Patrick A Bunge
5624 Walker Ave
Loves Park IL 61111

Call Sign: N9ZRB
Edward C Vanderbosch
5206 Wil Acre Dr
Loves Park IL 61111

Call Sign: N9ZRC
Jeanette B Vanderbosch
5206 Wil Acre Dr
Loves Park IL 61111

Call Sign: AA9G
Bradley S Smith
7133 Windsor Lake Pkwy
Loves Park IL 61111

Call Sign: WW2D
Bradley S Smith
7133 Windsor Lake Pkwy
Loves Park IL 61111

Call Sign: KB9VRC
Douglas G Rix
4705 Winford Ln
Loves Park IL 61111

Call Sign: NN8M
Bradley S Smith
Loves Park IL 61111

Call Sign: WB9HNJ
Arthur A Nelson
Loves Park IL 61130

Call Sign: KB9YYH
Jason S Myers
Loves Park IL 611322474

Call Sign: K9JSM
Jason S Myers
Loves Park IL 611322474

Call Sign: N9LHK
Thomas P Myers

Loves Park IL 611325321

Call Sign: KC0AVM
Thomas F Wisner
Loves Park IL 611326076

Call Sign: KB0MXB
Aaron L Bowers
Rt 1 Box 13
Lovington IL 61937

Call Sign: KB9TIS
Robert M Brinkley Jr
Rr 2 Box 29
Lovington IL 61937

Call Sign: KZ9I
Ronald R Hurst Sr
Rr 1 Box 44
Lovington IL 61937

Call Sign: W9KPI
Thomas G Schuetz
R 2 Box 61
Lovington IL 61937

Call Sign: WC9V
Ralph Zancha
340 E Addition St
Lovington IL 61937

Call Sign: KC9MXR
Ronald R Hurst
575 E Doratownship Rd
Lovington IL 61937

Call Sign: W9ADG
Donald G Hampton
5279 Prairie Hall Rd
Lovington IL 61937

Call Sign: N9GRL
Gregory L Hill
108 S Logan
Lovington IL 61937

Call Sign: KR9X
Gregory L Hill
108 S Logan
Lovington IL 61937

Call Sign: KX9K
Robert K Frantz
315 S Panther Dr
Lovington IL 619370136

Call Sign: KC9CNV
Harold L White
Lovington IL 61937

Call Sign: KC9UAV
Moultrie Amateur Radio Klub
Lovington IL 61937

Call Sign: W9MBD
Moultrie Amateur Radio Klub
Lovington IL 61937

Call Sign: W9BIL
Moultrie Amateur Radio Klub
Inc
Lovington IL 61937

Call Sign: KB9URN
Robert K Frantz
Lovington IL 619370136

Call Sign: K9UTK
John L Bowers
Lovington IL 619379708

Call Sign: KC9HNK
Kris C Heins
686 Bricktown Rd
Lowpoint IL 61545

Call Sign: W9ALU
Harley L Christ
1903 CR 905 E
Lowpoint IL 61545

Call Sign: KB9TLG

Paul D Force
Lowpoint IL 61545

Call Sign: W9PGE
Ralph C Cox
133 N Locust St
Ludlow IL 60949

Call Sign: KC9UBR
David W Mcpherson
320 Orange St
Ludlow IL 60949

Call Sign: WB9PGE
Ralph C Cox
Ludlow IL 60949

Call Sign: KB9KHD
Matthew T Gerrity
17929 Moline Rd
Lyndon IL 61261

Call Sign: KB9KHE
Micah E Gerrity
17929 Moline Rd
Lyndon IL 61261

Call Sign: N9ZAT
Thomas E Gerrity
17929 Moline Rd
Lyndon IL 61261

Call Sign: KA9WAG
Mary C Conrad
Lynn Center IL 61262

Call Sign: KC9OMA
Donald E Darnell
Rr 1 Box 143
Macedonia IL 62860

Call Sign: KF9OJ
George W Kuhn
Rr1 Box 206
Macedonia IL 62860

Call Sign: KB9TDU
Sheila A Plamowski
22757 Heifner Rd
Macedonia IL 62860

Call Sign: KC9RYP
Judith A Courter
14562 N Thompsonville Rd
Macedonia IL 62860

Call Sign: KC9SWY
Lee S Winemiller
8853 Winemiller Rd
Macedonia IL 62860

FCC Amateur Radio Licenses in Machesney Park

Call Sign: WA9AAG
John R Hutchison
4703 Apollo Dr
Machesney Park IL
611152265

Call Sign: N9HLU
John E Kelsey
1309 Arvidson Dr
Machesney Park IL 61115

Call Sign: K9VMY
Dennis R Johanson
10444 Baederwood Dr
Machesney Park IL
611151278

Call Sign: KB9OXS
Brian K Doherty
529 Blossom Ct
Machesney Park IL 61115

Call Sign: KB9PHC
Karen C Doherty
529 Blossom Ct
Machesney Park IL 61115

Call Sign: KB9QNC
Michael W Heckel
8222 Cadet Rd
Machesney Park IL 61115

Call Sign: K9OMG
Michael W Heckel
8222 Cadet Rd
Machesney Park IL 61115

Call Sign: KA9OYS
John W Neese
7812 Coopers Hawk Trl
Machesney Park IL 61115

Call Sign: KU9S
Gerald L Alberts
914 Crystal Ct
Machesney Park IL 61115

Call Sign: N9KIR
Benjamin T Schoepski
9932 Debbie Ln
Machesney Park IL 61115

Call Sign: N9YTY
Steven M Palm
11308 Debussey Dr
Machesney Park IL
611151270

Call Sign: KB9AYF
Donald R Russell Jr
11707 Dorothea Ave
Machesney Park IL 61115

Call Sign: N9GYN
Duane H Shallcross
1004 Emerald
Machesney Park IL 61115

Call Sign: N9OCW
Jonathan C Schwarz

8715 Emerald Ln
Machesney Park IL 61115

Call Sign: N9YBH
Ralph L Hull
316 Gilbert Ter
Machesney Park IL 61115

Call Sign: N9AXD
Robert J Glazier
1137 Glen Forest
Machesney Park IL 61115

Call Sign: WD9JEH
Arthur C Miller
827 Glen Forest Dr
Machesney Park IL 61115

Call Sign: N9JOL
Edmund L Borman
1524 Hackberry
Machesney Park IL 61111

Call Sign: KB9SLK
Richard W Kelm
1602 Harlem Rd
Machesney Park IL 61115

Call Sign: KC9MBZ
Timothy W Murphy
1709 Jennie Dr
Machesney Park IL 61115

Call Sign: KB9MBM
Robert D Jozsa
1005 Knightsbridge Dr
Machesney Park IL 61115

Call Sign: KB9IHJ
Wade M Forster
55 Liberty Blvd
Machesney Park IL 61115

Call Sign: KB9THB
Clarence R Izydorski
9120 Longfellow Ln
Machesney Park IL 61115

Call Sign: W9AOR

Robert J Szuch
4520 Luna Dr
Machesney Park IL 61115

Call Sign: N0GKX
Timothy A Moffitt
4639 Meteor Ct
Machesney Park IL 61115

Call Sign: KB9NBD
Shawn E Rundblade
7602 Mildred Rd
Machesney Park IL 61115

Call Sign: KC9BPB
Justin T Rogers
1622 Millicent Dr
Machesney Park IL 61115

Call Sign: N9MP
Murry M Page
4718 Minns Dr
Machesney Park IL
611151929

Call Sign: KB9GVE
Terry W Myers
5078 Minns Dr
Machesney Park IL
611151978

Call Sign: KC9OYZ
Steven W Twigg
941 Minns Dr Apt 1
Machesney Park IL
611153215

Call Sign: W9SWT
Steven W Twigg
941 Minns Dr Apt 1
Machesney Park IL
611153215

Call Sign: WB9LXO
David W Lefavour
7877 Nesting Eagles Rd
Machesney Park IL 61115

Call Sign: KB9ZCV

William J Lilly
231 Northway Park Rd 12
Machesney Park IL 61115

Call Sign: N5EEA
Roger W Sellers
849 Ramona Ter
Machesney Park IL 61115

Call Sign: KC9QPK
Richard J List
7903 Randy Rd
Machesney Park IL 61115

Call Sign: KC0DEH
Timothy D Hosmann
1336 Sandy Point Dr
Machesney Park IL
611038867

Call Sign: KC9FMA
Thomas C Freeman
5160 Seaton Hall Dr Apt 3
Machesney Park IL 61115

Call Sign: KB9BJQ
Pete P Bianchi Jr
9601 Shore Dr
Machesney Park IL 61111

Call Sign: N9UQQ
Floyd H Fox
314 Shoreland Park
Machesney Park IL 61115

Call Sign: KC9IEF
Albert Walker
525 Superior Ave
Machesney Park IL 61115

Call Sign: N9LHH
Paul H Mitkusevitch
709 Sycamore Ln
Machesney Park IL 61111

Call Sign: KE4CLD
Bret B Krebeck
476 Symphony Cove
Machesney Park IL 61115

Call Sign: KE4ORF
Martha A Krebeck
476 Symphony Cove
Machesney Park IL 61115

Call Sign: KB9LBT
James D Warren
808 Tampa Dr
Machesney Park IL 61115

Call Sign: KA9LAG
Sarah J Arend
8313 Tetterhall
Machesney Park IL 61115

Call Sign: KA9GNR
Susan A Peters
8312 Tetterhall Ln
Machesney Park IL
611157929

Call Sign: WB9MCZ
William R Peters
8312 Tetterhall Ln
Machesney Park IL
611157929

Call Sign: KC9SLB
Robert A Fitch
12814 Ventura Blvd
Machesney Park IL 61115

Call Sign: NB9G
Robert A Fitch
12814 Ventura Blvd
Machesney Park IL 61115

Call Sign: KA9BXA
Shawn P Harlan
135 Wilson Ave
Machesney Park IL 61115

Call Sign: WB9PYU
John A Ruud
1024 Windbourne Dr
Machesney Park IL 61115

Call Sign: WA6NPG

James F Schutt
222 Winona Dr
Machesney Park IL 61115

FCC Amateur Radio Licenses in Mackinaw

Call Sign: WD9EGV
James M Roach Jr
29511 Allentown Rd Box 342
Mackinaw IL 61755

Call Sign: WA9YTV
Richard L Luttrell
206 E Franklin
Mackinaw IL 61755

Call Sign: K9KTR
Jeffrey A Imig
395 Heritage Dr
Mackinaw IL 61755

Call Sign: N9UFF
Jack W Means
444 Heritage Dr
Mackinaw IL 61755

Call Sign: WA9GCG
Walter R Williams
402 S Monroe
Mackinaw IL 61755

Call Sign: KA0YEG
Benjamin W Griggs
209 Westminster Dr
Mackinaw IL 61755

Call Sign: KC9TLI
Bruce W Weise
29976 Woodfield Dr
Mackinaw IL 61755

Call Sign: W0FFY
Bruce W Weise
29976 Woodfield Dr
Mackinaw IL 61755

Call Sign: KB9SFZ
David G Pierce

Mackinaw IL 61755

FCC Amateur Radio Licenses in Macomb

Call Sign: W5YNT
Charles E Neblock
65 Arlington Dr
Macomb IL 61455

Call Sign: KC9AHI
Joshua S Andrews
101 Barsi Blvd
Macomb IL 61455

Call Sign: KC9CLC
Stephem C Andrews
101 Bavsi Blvd
Macomb IL 61455

Call Sign: N9VWM
Kenneth C Keudell
40 Briarwood Pl
Macomb IL 61455

Call Sign: KC9CRU
Randall L Roberts
1025 Derry Ln Apt 10
Macomb IL 61455

Call Sign: N9OWH
Walter E Derry
11235 E 1000 St
Macomb IL 61455

Call Sign: W9COP
David E Nissen
4340 E 1050th St
Macomb IL 61455

Call Sign: KA9VJT
Anna M Miller
7770 E 1100 St
Macomb IL 61455

Call Sign: N0OSH
Martha L Phoenix
10030 E 1200th St
Macomb IL 61455

Call Sign: N9BA
Ronald L Phoenix
10030 E 1200th St
Macomb IL 61455

Call Sign: WB9FHQ
Robert W Cook
14991 E 1400 St
Macomb IL 61455

Call Sign: KB9ZBE
Raoul E Reinertsen
14400 E 850th St
Macomb IL 61455

Call Sign: KA9SZX
Mark A Garrett
9885 E 950 Th St
Macomb IL 61455

Call Sign: K1MOD
Jeffrey M Kadet
1143 E Adams St
Macomb IL 61455

Call Sign: W9MFC
William H Welty
729 E Bobby Ave
Macomb IL 61455

Call Sign: KC9ERB
Kenneth A Betz
627 E Calhoun
Macomb IL 61455

Call Sign: KC9NSE
Mellisa M Hays
1124 E Carrol St
Macomb IL 61455

Call Sign: KA9MOT
Steven L Hays Sr
1124 E Carroll St
Macomb IL 61455

Call Sign: N9BKP
Bernard A Hightower
1200 E Grant Apt 102

Macomb IL 61455

Call Sign: KG4LDT
Joel B Craig
203 E Jackson 3
Macomb IL 61455

Call Sign: KC9BNW
William S Taylor
1601 E Jackson St Lot 248
Macomb IL 61455

Call Sign: N9MCW
Michelle S Rossmiller
232 E Jefferson
Macomb IL 61455

Call Sign: KB9YXI
Lamoine Emergency ARC
232 E Jefferson
Macomb IL 61455

Call Sign: AG9Y
Joseph L Rossmiller
232 E Jefferson
Macomb IL 614552204

Call Sign: KC9RCS
Jeffrey J Bennett
1225 E Rebecca Ln
Macomb IL 61455

Call Sign: KA9OUM
Joan G Keithley Lindsey
100 Holden Ter
Macomb IL 61455

Call Sign: N9EWQ
Richard R Sample
417 Hurst Dr
Macomb IL 61455

Call Sign: N9RMF
Sharon A Sample
417 Hurst Dr
Macomb IL 61455

Call Sign: W9SSP
Lamoine Emergency ARC

417 Hurst Dr
Macomb IL 61455

Call Sign: WB9TEA
Lamoine Emergency ARC
417 Hurst Dr
Macomb IL 61455

Call Sign: KA9VPJ
Thomas B Frazier
32 Indian Trl
Macomb IL 61455

Call Sign: KB9RKY
Charles E Neblock
255 Jamestown Rd
Macomb IL 61455

Call Sign: KC9LDG
Christopher D Fitzgerald
232 Jana Rd
Macomb IL 61455

Call Sign: N9PSR
Wayne M Scace
3 104 Lamoine Vlg
Macomb IL 61455

Call Sign: AB9BM
Wayne M Scace
3 104 Lamoine Vlg
Macomb IL 61455

Call Sign: W9CY
John R Harvey
400 Meadow Dr
Macomb IL 61455

Call Sign: KC9EQD
Western Illinois Univ ARC
449 Memorial Hall 1 Univ Cir
Macomb IL 61455

Call Sign: W9WIU
Western Illinois Univ ARC
449 Memorial Hall 1 Univ Cir
Macomb IL 61455

Call Sign: W9YOL

Western Illinois Univ Ama
Rad Club
449 Memorial Hall 1 Univ Cir
Macomb IL 61455

Call Sign: KC9AHT
Charles M Stark
10395 N 1200 Rd
Macomb IL 61455

Call Sign: KC9QMW
Mark A Arnold
8021 N 1450th Rd
Macomb IL 61455

Call Sign: KC9AEN
David J Lutz
5522 N 1700th Rd
Macomb IL 61455

Call Sign: WB9ETT
Marvin E Cook
806 N Madison
Macomb IL 61455

Call Sign: W9SSP
Charles L Gill
603 N McArthur
Macomb IL 61455

Call Sign: KC9SIW
Scott A Wheelhouse
327 N Monroe
Macomb IL 61455

Call Sign: KC9BVL
Timothy D Formhals
721 N Pearl St
Macomb IL 61455

Call Sign: N9FWK
Stanley G Mercer
700 N Western Ave
Macomb IL 61455

Call Sign: KI6CZD
Walter J Burnett
103 Oakland Ln
Macomb IL 61455

Call Sign: N9LBC
John C Carson
1316 Parkview Dr
Macomb IL 61455

Call Sign: N9RGF
Lewis L Mc Entire
938 Penny Oaks Dr
Macomb IL 61455

Call Sign: W9SNL
Jack A Frost
1601 River View Dr
Macomb IL 61455

Call Sign: KA9EHQ
Eldon R Stambaugh
Box 186 Rr 1
Macomb IL 61455

Call Sign: KA9MWN
Margaret E Ellis
930 S Garfield
Macomb IL 61455

Call Sign: KA9YWN
William J Davenport
603 S Lafayette
Macomb IL 61455

Call Sign: KA9KHQ
Bruce E Holdcroft
420 S Lafayette St
Macomb IL 61455

Call Sign: KB9ABN
John P De Volder
806 S Pearl
Macomb IL 61455

Call Sign: KB9NAB
Anthony S Coniglio
30 S Quail Walk Rd
Macomb IL 61455

Call Sign: N9FCT
Maurice R Riggins
326 S Randolph

Macomb IL 61455

Call Sign: N9RDF
Robert F Rippey
409 S Randolph
Macomb IL 61455

Call Sign: KA9SSA
Habibollah Atarodi
821 3 S Ward
Macomb IL 61455

Call Sign: KB9KEO
Stanley R Clayton
700 S Ward Lot 24
Macomb IL 61455

Call Sign: N9RDD
Cindy D Clayton
700 S Ward St Raintree Lot 24
Macomb IL 61455

Call Sign: N9XMZ
Paula J Mc Clellan
145 S Yorktown Rd
Macomb IL 61455

Call Sign: KC9ILN
Brandon T Sullivan
14585 US Hwy 67
Macomb IL 61455

Call Sign: KC9SIY
Michael K Bornkamp
1209 W Calhoun St
Macomb IL 61455

Call Sign: KC9SIX
Stephanie B Bonds
1209 W Calhoun St
Macomb IL 61455

Call Sign: KB9QFM
James P Bloom
1218 W Calhoun St
Macomb IL 61455

Call Sign: KB9MRN
Paul J Strasma

1218 W Calhoun St
Macomb IL 61455

Call Sign: KB9WZX
Monica M Livingston
244 W Fisk St
Macomb IL 61455

Call Sign: KC9QEB
Kerry L Lemaster
1517 W Jackson 12
Macomb IL 61455

Call Sign: KC9VIB
Mark Clough
1543 W Jackson St
Macomb IL 61455

Call Sign: WO0V
Melvin E Ellis
100 W Jefferson Apt 605
Macomb IL 61455

Call Sign: NK9E
Melvin E Ellis
100 W Jefferson Apt 605
Macomb IL 61455

Call Sign: KC9LRC
Dustin S Forman
503 W Kelly St
Macomb IL 61455

Call Sign: WB9HVD
Rolla Hightower Jr
827 W McDonough
Macomb IL 61455

Call Sign: W5FOX
Lisa A Allyn
322 W Piper St Apt 904
Macomb IL 61455

Call Sign: KC9QIA
Donald H Johnson
702 W Washington St
Macomb IL 61455

Call Sign: K9SQB

Donald H Johnson
702 W Washington St
Macomb IL 61455

Call Sign: KA9SQB
Donald H Johnson
702 W Washington St
Macomb IL 614552023

Call Sign: N9FDB
George L Mulvin
717 W Washington St
Macomb IL 61455

Call Sign: KA9RMX
Laureen S Mulvin
717 W Washington St
Macomb IL 61455

Call Sign: KC9VIA
Bethanie A Brooks
9385 Wigwam Hollow Rd
Macomb IL 61455

Call Sign: KC9AHM
Andrea M Ratermann
224 Woodchuck Ln
Macomb IL 61455

Call Sign: KA9RFF
Charles D Rebman
Macomb IL 61455

Call Sign: K9IUM
Thomas K Pennington
Macomb IL 61455

Call Sign: KA9TMI
Robert E Robinson
Macomb IL 61455

Call Sign: KC9EES
Tom K Depauw
Macomb IL 61455

Call Sign: N9MCV
Kristy J Reagor
Macomb IL 61455

Call Sign: KA9HRW
Larry V Reagor
Macomb IL 61455

Call Sign: KC9EER
Darryl L Roberts
Macomb IL 614550665

FCC Amateur Radio Licenses in Macon

Call Sign: N9PLE
Mark Hilvety
5175 Jackson Rd
Macon IL 62544

Call Sign: K9LPA
Mark Hilvety
5175 Jackson Rd
Macon IL 62544

Call Sign: K9VPK
Richard L Coombe
485 N Shaw St
Macon IL 62544

Call Sign: KB9JLJ
James R Wiles
325 S Wiles St
Macon IL 62544

FCC Amateur Radio Licenses in Madison

Call Sign: KC9RTA
Joyce M Marini
1939 3rd St
Madison IL 62060

Call Sign: KC9JDA
Michelle A Marini
1939 3rd St
Madison IL 62060

Call Sign: KA9ORG
Kathy E Parker
1537 4th St
Madison IL 62060

Call Sign: W9CRY
Terry Parker
1537 4th St
Madison IL 62060

Call Sign: KC9FVB
Bobby G Butler
2008 4th St
Madison IL 62060

Call Sign: KC9NEQ
Neal A Mize
1815 5th St
Madison IL 62060

Call Sign: KA9CBG
Beryl L Foreshee
824 Alton Ave
Madison IL 62060

FCC Amateur Radio Licenses in Magnolia

Call Sign: KC9IZX
Noah M Roberts
257 E Evans Rd
Magnolia IL 61336

Call Sign: KC9MIV
Isaiah P Roberts
2573 Evans Rd
Magnolia IL 61336

Call Sign: KA9VAU
Paul M Roberts
2573 Evans Rd
Magnolia IL 61336

FCC Amateur Radio Licenses in Mahomet

Call Sign: KB9GQU
Ryan A Belscamper
Rr 5 Box 133
Mahomet IL 61853

Call Sign: KC9SVQ
David P Maria
583 Bureau St

Mahomet IL 61853

Call Sign: K9DPM
David P Maria
583 Bureau St
Mahomet IL 61853

Call Sign: KB9ZZN
James G Simpson
612 Bureau St
Mahomet IL 61853

Call Sign: KB9GAX
Beverly J Paquin
87 Carroll
Mahomet IL 61853

Call Sign: KB9LCH
Cathy S Peterson
120 Carroll
Mahomet IL 61853

Call Sign: KB9JUA
James G Peterson
120 Carroll
Mahomet IL 61853

Call Sign: KB9EFS
Ralph W Paquin Sr
87 Carroll Candlewood Est
Mahomet IL 61853

Call Sign: K9GTI
Joseph Plowick III
1105 Charter Oaks Cir
Mahomet IL 61853

Call Sign: KC9FLL
Andrew P Geil
2060 B CR 125 E
Mahomet IL 61853

Call Sign: W9HQE
Robert E Durst
459 CR 2425 N
Mahomet IL 61853

Call Sign: KC9VHI
John D Schmale

505C CR 2500 N
Mahomet IL 61853

Call Sign: KC9M
James G Eden
314 CR 2650N
Mahomet IL 61853

Call Sign: KC9HVD
Ann Leininger
416 Dorchester Dr
Mahomet IL 61853

Call Sign: W9EML
Ann Leininger
416 Dorchester Dr
Mahomet IL 61853

Call Sign: KC9EKF
David M Leininger I
416 Dorchester Dr
Mahomet IL 61853

Call Sign: W9DML
David M Leininger I
416 Dorchester Dr
Mahomet IL 61853

Call Sign: KC9MAC
4 L R C
416 Dorchester Dr Ste A
Mahomet IL 61853

Call Sign: KC0UU
John W Mc Cain
1905 E Katherine Ct
Mahomet IL 61853

Call Sign: N0GYD
Rebecca L Mc Cain
1905 E Katherine Ct
Mahomet IL 61853

Call Sign: KA9NPN
James J Schmidt
1906 Katherine Ct
Mahomet IL 61853

Call Sign: KB9LLE

Dwayne A Julin
430 Kendall
Mahomet IL 61853

Call Sign: KC9RC
Gerald A Fox
101 Marcella Dr
Mahomet IL 61853

Call Sign: KB9FIF
Ronald D Edmison
317 McLean Rd
Mahomet IL 61853

Call Sign: KD4JCM
Joseph Plowick III
2002 C Middletown Dr
Mahomet IL 61853

Call Sign: KB9SZV
Robert M Laboyteaux
1605 Mitchell Dr
Mahomet IL 61853

Call Sign: KB9WSV
David D Nelson
2659 N CR 350 E
Mahomet IL 61853

Call Sign: W1FGN
David D Nelson
2659 N CR 350 E
Mahomet IL 618539797

Call Sign: N9RLV
John C Horton
703 N Craig Box 109
Mahomet IL 61853

Call Sign: N9YJA
David J Marshall
1005 N Hillside Ln
Mahomet IL 61853

Call Sign: KB9LCN
Edgar E Hutchins
603 N Raymond Ct
Mahomet IL 61853

Call Sign: K9ODX
Harry J Guymon
511 N Ridge Rd
Mahomet IL 61853

Call Sign: K9KYY
Andrew S Kirk
1105 Olen Dr
Mahomet IL 61853

Call Sign: N9PEZ
Joseph F Guenther Jr
2203 Olen Dr
Mahomet IL 61853

Call Sign: WB4YVJ
Raymond S Wilck III
1712 Phillippe Dr
Mahomet IL 61853

Call Sign: K9ALD
Roger H Taylor
1106 Rayburn Ct
Mahomet IL 61853

Call Sign: KC9SVP
Steve B Gauze
1107 Riverside Ct
Mahomet IL 61853

Call Sign: KC9HND
Adam M Carlson
802 Riverside Dr
Mahomet IL 61853

Call Sign: W9LLC
Adam M Carlson
802 Riverside Dr
Mahomet IL 61853

Call Sign: KD4LP
Larry W Powell
805 S Amy Dr
Mahomet IL 61853

Call Sign: KB9LGM
Andrew A Ziegler
1106 S Center
Mahomet IL 61821

Call Sign: KB9JR
George R Howe
305 S Turner Dr
Mahomet IL 61853

Call Sign: W9GRH
George R Howe
305 S Turner Dr
Mahomet IL 61853

Call Sign: K9HHW
William R Ferguson
106 Sharon Dr
Mahomet IL 618539023

Call Sign: KC9UNO
Lon A Westfall
1007 Timber
Mahomet IL 61853

Call Sign: KB9VSJ
Bryan A Gerber
606 W Dianne Ln
Mahomet IL 61853

Call Sign: WA9AGU
Michael J Williams
807 W James Ct
Mahomet IL 61853

Call Sign: W9WQ
Michael J Williams
807 W James Ct
Mahomet IL 61853

Call Sign: N9KVS
David M Smalley
1706 W N Shore Dr
Mahomet IL 618538922

Call Sign: KA9FWD
Carolyn K Brown
307 Weathering Dr
Mahomet IL 61853

Call Sign: WD8QJB
Stephen E Brown
307 Weathering Dr

Mahomet IL 61853

Call Sign: W9HC
Stephen E Brown
307 Weathering Dr
Mahomet IL 61853

Call Sign: AA9DH
Robert A Hoffswell
Mahomet IL 61853

FCC Amateur Radio Licenses in Makanda

Call Sign: KC9TJW
Steven M Blair
346 Church Camp Rd
Makanda IL 62958

Call Sign: K9SXD
Jerry L Kline
1989 Grassy Rd
Makanda IL 62958

Call Sign: KC9OLS
Alan Gordon
109 Honeysuckle Rd
Makanda IL 62958

Call Sign: KC9KCH
Kara A Dunkel
2643 Old US Hwy 51
Makanda IL 62958

Call Sign: KC9KCI
William A Dunkel
2643 Old US Hwy 51
Makanda IL 62958

Call Sign: KC9TEM
George S Trifon
400 Old US Hwy 51 Apt B
Makanda IL 62958

Call Sign: K9ABZ
Arthur L Houseman
180 Pitts Rd
Makanda IL 62958

Call Sign: KB9SLN
Lillie L Houseman
180 Pitts Rd
Makanda IL 62958

Call Sign: KB9QBL
Gary D Childers
8 Private Rd Pqq
Makanda IL 62958

Call Sign: N9ZSE
Rustomji H Vania
305 Pump Station Rd
Makanda IL 62901

Call Sign: AI4X
Kevin C Wise
205 Rock Springs Rd
Makanda IL 62958

Call Sign: KC9NEJ
Lesley R Sales
2 Ty Rd
Makanda IL 62958

Call Sign: N9UUV
John P Dunn
340 White Deer Run
Makanda IL 629582619

FCC Amateur Radio Licenses in Malden

Call Sign: KA9RTK
Doris L Johnson
102 Spruce St
Malden IL 61337

Call Sign: W0KPS
Lavern L Johnson
102 Spruce St
Malden IL 61337

Call Sign: KA9RRN
Gregory P Johnson
102 Spruce St
Malden IL 61337

Call Sign: KC9OJR

Jeremy F Maynard
500 W Main St
Malden IL 61337

Call Sign: KC9NTA
Howard Buckels
Malden IL 61337

Call Sign: KC9GHC
Natesha O Woolley
Malden IL 61337

Call Sign: KC9YLU
Natesha O Woolley
Malden IL 61337

FCC Amateur Radio Licenses in Manchester

Call Sign: N9UPE
Darren S Johnson
Manchester IL 62663

FCC Amateur Radio Licenses in Manito

Call Sign: KB9DBM
Walman G Campbell
913 Collins
Manito IL 61546

Call Sign: KB9LIY
Bryce E Hoover
1005 Collins St
Manito IL 61546

Call Sign: KC0SLE
Lilly M Litz
95 Crest Ln
Manito IL 61546

Call Sign: KC0ROM
Scott A Litz
95 Crest Ln
Manito IL 61546

Call Sign: KC9TSG
Steven P Dirst
33413 E CR 2400 N

Manito IL 61546

Call Sign: KB9QDV
William W Olsen
103 E Glendale Rr 3
Manito IL 61546

Call Sign: KB9UFN
Donald K Lippert Jr
10484 Evergreen Dr
Manito IL 61546

Call Sign: KC9FWP
Douglas G Carrol
14255 Grand View Dr
Manito IL 61546

Call Sign: WA9DKO
William R Nowlin
3752 Grandview Ct
Manito IL 61546

Call Sign: KB9PYR
Esther G Bennett
74 Maple Ln
Manito IL 61546

Call Sign: KA9WGD
Larry D Lay
218 Meadow Lawn
Manito IL 61546

Call Sign: WD9AQJ
Hollis R Daniels
7429 Myrtle St
Manito IL 61546

Call Sign: NN9M
Donald C Hinkel
21830 N CR 3300 E
Manito IL 61546

Call Sign: KC9JKF
Carol J Eggers
11088 N Manito Rd
Manito IL 61546

Call Sign: KC9JKG
Randle E Eggers Sr

11088 N Manito Rd
Manito IL 61546

Call Sign: N9SPY
John C Smock
506 N Park Ave
Manito IL 61546

Call Sign: KB9LJE
Ronald G Handke
202 N Washington
Manito IL 61546

Call Sign: K9EOC
Ronald G Handke
307 S Arthur Ave
Manito IL 61546

Call Sign: KB9LRV
Mason County ARC
209 S Park Ave
Manito IL 61546

Call Sign: KB9PYQ
William W Olsen
204 S Washington Box 253
Manito IL 61546

Call Sign: WA9YFA
Gary Lalock
11124 Sky Ranch Rd
Manito IL 61546

Call Sign: WD9HSW
Patricia A Lalock
11124 Sky Ranch Rd
Manito IL 61546

Call Sign: N9CYV
Clifford D Eldert
1966 Tomahawk Trl
Manito IL 61546

Call Sign: KB9VZC
Douglas W Herrman
9117 Townline Rd
Manito IL 61546

Call Sign: KB9VVK

Daniel L Kleiber Sr
Manito IL 61546

Call Sign: KB9LNI
Jimmy Y Kim
Manito IL 61546

Call Sign: K9HH
Robert L Mc Kinney
Manito IL 61546

Call Sign: KB9QDW
Robert W Simmons
Manito IL 61546

FCC Amateur Radio Licenses in Manlius

Call Sign: KB9KHG
Ernie Rutledge
310 E Pine
Manlius IL 61338

Call Sign: W9PCY
Joe D Graham
211 Nelson St
Manlius IL 61338

FCC Amateur Radio Licenses in Mansfield

Call Sign: KA9PJU
Norman K Clapper
1205E 2500N
Mansfield IL 61854

Call Sign: KB9ETO
Walter E Pryke
Rr 1 Box 116
Mansfield IL 61854

Call Sign: K9VFH
Charles J Schrock
404 McKinley
Mansfield IL 61854

Call Sign: KB9ETP
Linda L Schrock
404 McKinley

Mansfield IL 61854

Call Sign: KB9GAU
John W James
2728 N 1000 E Rd
Mansfield IL 61854

Call Sign: KB9PXJ
Brandon J Tobias
2997 N 1350 E Rd
Mansfield IL 61854

Call Sign: N9RZC
Allen J Hall
2 Sangamor Bluffs
Mansfield IL 61801

Call Sign: K9BV
William B Vokac
Mansfield IL 61854

Call Sign: KC9CRK
Earl M Bragg Jr
Mansfield IL 61854

Call Sign: W9SQR
James W Ponsler
Mansfield IL 61854

FCC Amateur Radio Licenses in Manteno

Call Sign: KC9OAL
Craig R Cahan
46 Alan Ave
Manteno IL 60950

Call Sign: KC9OQP
Daniel A Tobbe
1111 Aspen Dr
Manteno IL 60950

Call Sign: WD9ETO
Daniel A Tobbe
1111 Aspen Dr
Manteno IL 60950

Call Sign: N8CH
Charles D Harding Sr

881 Banyan
Manteno IL 60950

Call Sign: W9VWZ
Richard H Granger
Rr 2 Box 21
Manteno IL 60950

Call Sign: N9OQF
Kent A Ponton
155 E Baker St
Manteno IL 60950

Call Sign: N9FD
Craig R Cahan
7 Franklin Dr
Manteno IL 60950

Call Sign: N9YAB
James C Ailes
1067 Lincoln Dr
Manteno IL 609509393

Call Sign: K9SAE
David R Evely
55 Maple Ridge Pk
Manteno IL 60950

Call Sign: N9GI
Dr. Mikeal R Hughes
8857 N 4000 E
Manteno IL 60950

Call Sign: W9RCH
Reba C Hughes
8857 N 4000 E
Manteno IL 60950

Call Sign: WD9BAI
John A Meyer Jr
8631 N 5000 W Rd
Manteno IL 609503550

Call Sign: KC9GDP
Ronald L Creek
9754 N 6000 W Rd
Manteno IL 60950

Call Sign: KC9DBO

Roger K Cast
9082 N 6030 E Rd 10
Manteno IL 60950

Call Sign: KC9VDI
Jamison P Wheeler
368 N Spruce St
Manteno IL 60950

Call Sign: N9BFJ
Darrell L Bewsey
40 Norway Dr
Manteno IL 60950

Call Sign: KB9SQP
Terri M Geeding
368 S Oak Ave
Manteno IL 60950

Call Sign: KB9WIK
William J Crane
240 S Oak St
Manteno IL 60950

Call Sign: N9YSE
Timothy H Geeding
368 S Oak St
Manteno IL 60950

Call Sign: KC9OSS
Thomas Piunti
146 Scarlet Dr
Manteno IL 60950

Call Sign: KC9NWU
Robert A Nemitz
4 Todd Ct Apt 2
Manteno IL 60950

Call Sign: KA9HMM
David W Roberts
177 W 5th St
Manteno IL 60950

FCC Amateur Radio
Licenses in Manville

Call Sign: KA9PIE
John A Fairburn

7095 E 3000 N Rd
Manville IL 61319

FCC Amateur Radio
Licenses in Mapleton

Call Sign: W9JXZ
Daniel C Borneman
10200 Kingston Mines Rd
Mapleton IL 61547

Call Sign: KB9OSV
Dale B Herget
5315 S Acre Rd
Mapleton IL 61547

Call Sign: N9FW
Frank A Willis
3910 S Autumn Dr
Mapleton IL 61547

Call Sign: N9XHN
David W Mc Mullen
4027 S Walnut Pt Dr
Mapleton IL 61547

Call Sign: N9GUV
Marshall J Leeper
8520 W 1st St
Mapleton IL 61547

Call Sign: KB9SVC
Paul F Carpenter
7423 W Pfeiffer Rd
Mapleton IL 61547

Call Sign: KC9ELM
Mark D Miller
7601 W Sportsman
Mapleton IL 61547

Call Sign: N9SS
David S Miller
7601 W Sportsman Dr
Mapleton IL 61547

FCC Amateur Radio
Licenses in Maquon

Call Sign: KB1FUA
Dean W Stoner
214 E 4th St
Maquon IL 61485

Call Sign: WD9FUO
Danny L Thomas
E 5th St
Maquon IL 61458

Call Sign: KB9KSW
Kim J Morris
281 Knox Hwy 8
Maquon IL 61458

Call Sign: N9ZZE
Robert T Morris
281 Knox Hwy 8
Maquon IL 61458

**FCC Amateur Radio
Licenses in Marine**

Call Sign: KK9W
James W Lumley
405 E Alton
Marine IL 62061

Call Sign: NT9AA
James W Lumley
405 E Alton
Marine IL 620610063

Call Sign: KB9VZQ
Anita M Lumley
405 E Alton
Marine IL 620611401

Call Sign: KC9NAY
Sherry J Chase
11412 Pocahontas Rd
Marine IL 62061

Call Sign: K9SJC
Sherry J Chase
11412 Pocahontas Rd
Marine IL 62061

Call Sign: KB9SVT

William J Chase
11412 Pocahontas Rd
Marine IL 620610446

Call Sign: K9WJC
William J Chase
11412 Pocahontas Rd
Marine IL 620611246

Call Sign: KB9VZP
Betty J Lorance
300 S Duncan
Marine IL 62061

Call Sign: N9KCC
De Anne C Mc Connell
108 Savannah Ct
Marine IL 62061

Call Sign: KC9UZX
Gerhard W Tscheschlok
938 Virginia Dr
Marine IL 62061

**FCC Amateur Radio
Licenses in Marion**

Call Sign: N9RU
Thomas P Costa
4796 Andrew Rd
Marion IL 62959

Call Sign: KA4SIR
Deborah A Bartle
4963 Andrew Rd
Marion IL 62959

Call Sign: K9HR
Dennis F Doelitzsch
1411 Augusta Dr
Marion IL 62959

Call Sign: KB9GHW
Michael B Wiemken
416 Bainbridge Rd
Marion IL 62959

Call Sign: KC9TZU
Thomas H Frey

14329 Balsa Ln
Marion IL 62959

Call Sign: KA9ZIZ
Lori R Power
900 Boston Rd
Marion IL 62959

Call Sign: N9BCB
Daniel J Graff
Rt 2 Box 106
Marion IL 62595

Call Sign: KA9CUD
Clifford E Owen
Rr 6 Box 276
Marion IL 62959

Call Sign: N9LNV
Darrell D James
Rt 1 Box 310
Marion IL 62959

Call Sign: N9QJK
Gary W Mausey
R 2 Box 400
Marion IL 62959

Call Sign: KB5RWL
Paul R Roth
2105 Bristol Dr
Marion IL 62959

Call Sign: K9ILD
Wendel B Arms
511 Candy Ln
Marion IL 62959

Call Sign: K9FHD
William H Rogers
601 Candy Ln
Marion IL 62959

Call Sign: KC9TXJ
Kristopher E Lowe
1705 Castleberry Dr
Marion IL 62959

Call Sign: KC9QDR

Timothy A Lehner
403 Charlotte Rd
Marion IL 62959

Call Sign: N9FLM
Harry L Engledow
3210 Cherokee Dr
Marion IL 62959

Call Sign: KB9VUZ
Robert L Ray
19302 Coal Valley St
Marion IL 62959

Call Sign: KB9MFY
Eugene F Parker
707 College St
Marion IL 62959

Call Sign: KB9MFZ
Darlene S Choate
18859 Crab Orchard Rd
Marion IL 629597305

Call Sign: KB9LRL
John W Choate
18859 Crab Orchard Rd
Marion IL 629597305

Call Sign: KB9NKX
Brian K Choate
1212 E Boyton
Marion IL 62959

Call Sign: KC9NJF
Brent R Hemrich
1508 E Boyton St Apt C
Marion IL 62959

Call Sign: N9IOU
Elwin E Stowers
1002 E Carter
Marion IL 62959

Call Sign: K9YHN
Robert D Ramsey
408 E College
Marion IL 62959

Call Sign: KC4ZZW
Carl C Davis
304 E College St
Marion IL 62959

Call Sign: KB9YOB
Victoria L Corzine
407 E College St
Marion IL 62959

Call Sign: N9UEH
Ryan C Ollis
1111 E Reeves St
Marion IL 62959

Call Sign: KC9AXF
Lois A Hanks
908 Fairlane Dr
Marion IL 62959

Call Sign: K9AGA
Lois A Hanks
908 Fairlane Dr
Marion IL 62959

Call Sign: KC9AGA
Raymond L Young
908 Fairlane Dr
Marion IL 62959

Call Sign: KC9SML
Robert L Pennock Jr
3811 Grange Hall Rd
Marion IL 62959

Call Sign: KC9ULX
James H Byassee
802 Gregory Ave
Marion IL 62959

Call Sign: W9LOY
Loy R Smith
906B Independence Ave
Marion IL 62959

Call Sign: KD4CAE
Richard J George Jr
11562 Julie Ln
Marion IL 62959

Call Sign: AK9O
William G Fuller
657 Lake Harbor Dr
Marion IL 62948

Call Sign: N9SNZ
William G Fuller
600 Lake Harbor Pl
Marion IL 62959

Call Sign: N9SXK
Ronald G Bernhard
3200 Lakeview Rd
Marion IL 62959

Call Sign: KC9KWG
Stephen K Land
11330 Lamaster Rd
Marion IL 62959

Call Sign: N6YRI
Thomas W Wood
11687 Lamaster Rd
Marion IL 62959

Call Sign: K9IVV
John J Emery
1006 Laura Ln
Marion IL 62959

Call Sign: W4DIN
Joseph H Ziglinski
2103 Lerin Ln
Marion IL 62959

Call Sign: AA9VF
Mayo W Schaede
10274 Limb Branch Ln
Marion IL 62959

Call Sign: K9WV
Brent L Stroud
16906 Log Cabin Rd
Marion IL 62959

Call Sign: AA9QK
Brent L Stroud
16906 Log Cabin Rd

Marion IL 62959

Call Sign: KB9WMA
Kimberly D Stroud
16906 Log Cabin Rd
Marion IL 62959

Call Sign: W9HJW
Stephen J Beyers
12121 Malibu Ln
Marion IL 62959

Call Sign: KB9VIG
Clara A Avery
1706 Marcella Dr
Marion IL 62959

Call Sign: W9RGA
Rickey G Avery
1706 Marcella Dr
Marion IL 62959

Call Sign: KC9MFY
Bobby W Whitledge
12150 Marina Rd
Marion IL 62959

Call Sign: KC9JUQ
Jason D Swisher
4932 Market Rd
Marion IL 62595

Call Sign: KA9KSW
Brenda F Swisher
4932 Market Rd
Marion IL 62959

Call Sign: N9BAY
Jerry D Swisher
4932 Market Rd
Marion IL 62959

Call Sign: KB9WFT
Jessica D Coyle
4932 Market Rd
Marion IL 62959

Call Sign: KB9WTA
Jeffrey D Swisher

4932 Market Rd
Marion IL 62959

Call Sign: W9RV
Albert N Novara
5188 Market Rd
Marion IL 629599421

Call Sign: N9VIJ
James D Parris
1248 Midway Ct
Marion IL 62959

Call Sign: W9DFH
Joe A Fasig
7528 Moake School Rd
Marion IL 62959

Call Sign: KB9NKY
Howard L Lee
1407 N Bentley St
Marion IL 62959

Call Sign: KC9MFT
Robert J Deaton
13261 N Casey Rd
Marion IL 62959

Call Sign: N9MVW
Steven G Taylor
203 N Hamlet Apt 4
Marion IL 62959

Call Sign: WA9FKV
Lewis E Odum
1204 N Logan
Marion IL 62959

Call Sign: KA9BQT
Lawrence L Radcliffe
1006 N Radcliffe St
Marion IL 62959

Call Sign: N9ECG
Vernon L Ferguson Sr
208 N Spillertown
Marion IL 62959

Call Sign: KB9TDT

Larry E Clayton
1606 N State St
Marion IL 629595300

Call Sign: KB9JDC
Steven K Durfee
1206 N Van Buren St
Marion IL 62959

Call Sign: KC9AHG
Billy D Swan
604 N Washington St
Marion IL 62959

Call Sign: KA9LEE
William J Daniel
703 N Washington St
Marion IL 629593457

Call Sign: W0PHJ
David R Neuman
1002 N Whitman Dr
Marion IL 62959

Call Sign: KC9IRD
Cathryn N Tate
11821 Norman Rd
Marion IL 62959

Call Sign: KC9PYT
Joann K St Pierre
7463 Norris Dr
Marion IL 62959

Call Sign: W9PBL
Joann K St Pierre
7463 Norris Dr
Marion IL 62959

Call Sign: KE1IN
David M St Pierre
7463 Norris Dr
Marion IL 62959

Call Sign: NG9W
David M St Pierre
7463 Norris Dr
Marion IL 62959

Call Sign: KC9SIV
Derek L Key
7547 Norris Dr
Marion IL 62959

Call Sign: N9XWM
Alan R Pritchett
1908 Park Ln
Marion IL 62959

Call Sign: N9WNC
Edward E Nicholson Sr
1606 Peabody St
Marion IL 62959

Call Sign: KC9OLO
Marianne L Guskos
1402 Primrose Ln
Marion IL 62959

Call Sign: WB9VWR
Charles G Thetford
12198 Prosperity Rd
Marion IL 62959

Call Sign: WA4YZF
Charles E Daum
15066 Remington Rd
Marion IL 62959

Call Sign: KA9HTN
Joann F Doelitzsch
12338 Rt 37
Marion IL 62959

Call Sign: W9AIB
Ray Browder
510 S 1st
Marion IL 62959

Call Sign: KA9TRP
Bruce Rainey
501 S 1st St
Marion IL 62959

Call Sign: KA9ZIX
Brian C Shafer
327 S 3rd St
Marion IL 62959

Call Sign: N9KMV
Cecil D Emery
601 S Buchanan
Marion IL 62959

Call Sign: KC9KWQ
Brian D Kennedy
617 S Calumet
Marion IL 62959

Call Sign: N9LTW
Louis E Childers
111 S Carbon St
Marion IL 629591242

Call Sign: W9WPO
George W Dodds
1006 S Carbon St
Marion IL 62959

Call Sign: KB9MWU
Bobby J Owens
1005 S Duncan
Marion IL 62959

Call Sign: N9WFJ
David M Rady
706 S Duncan St
Marion IL 62959

Call Sign: KB9MIX
Ricky J Bennett
206 S Future St
Marion IL 62959

Call Sign: KB9MWT
Tommy Valentine
1007 S Griggs St
Marion IL 62959

Call Sign: KA9MEU
Wendell G Kilpatrick
703 S Hadfield
Marion IL 62959

Call Sign: KC9CAW
Robret D Aldridge
1101 S Hadfield

Marion IL 62959

Call Sign: K9NSS
Garrett C Carter
1202 S Hadfield
Marion IL 62959

Call Sign: KV9L
Leland E Wright
700 S Virginia Ave
Marion IL 62959

Call Sign: KC9KWO
David A Lindley
11762 Scraville Rd
Marion IL 62959

Call Sign: KC9UAY
Robert G Oleary
19722 Shed Church Rd
Marion IL 62959

Call Sign: KC9JUS
Mike B Uselton
11550 Simon
Marion IL 62959

Call Sign: K8SIW
James A Wades
810 Skyline Dr
Marion IL 62959

Call Sign: WB8SIW
James A Wades
810 Skyline Dr
Marion IL 62959

Call Sign: KA9IEE
Francis M Boyd
424 South Ct
Marion IL 62959

Call Sign: WD0CYP
Harold G Landwehr
2008 Spring Garden Rd
Marion IL 62959

Call Sign: AB9TG
Daven L Edwards

105 Stotlar
Marion IL 62959

Call Sign: N9CDB
Emory D Rutherford
703 Toby Dr
Marion IL 62959

Call Sign: W9ROJ
John T Anderson
504 Tower Square
Marion IL 62959

Call Sign: KA9IEN
Harmon E Davis
8450 Valley View Rd
Marion IL 62959

Call Sign: KC9AHH
Mark B Taylor
610 Vinewood Ln
Marion IL 62959

Call Sign: KC9URG
Jarrod V Travelstead
309 W Blvd
Marion IL 62959

Call Sign: WB9UIC
Forrest W Richardson
312 W Blvd
Marion IL 62959

Call Sign: W9LQZ
Merle D Mecord
1613 W Cherry
Marion IL 62959

Call Sign: N9CPS
Henry D Mitchell
912 W Chestnut
Marion IL 62959

Call Sign: KB9YFX
Robert W Barclay
812 W Chestnut St
Marion IL 62959

Call Sign: K0YGO

Robert W Barclay
812 W Chestnut St
Marion IL 62959

Call Sign: KB9KWT
John W Parker
707 W College
Marion IL 62959

Call Sign: N9VSY
William A Norton
1716 W Dewey
Marion IL 62959

Call Sign: W9DLA
Frank P Geraci
1606 W Dewey St
Marion IL 62959

Call Sign: KB3PAW
Carolyn B Loving
3206 W Lakeview Rd
Marion IL 62959

Call Sign: KC2HJR
Michael R Ladwig
3311 W Lakeview Rd
Marion IL 62959

Call Sign: N9VKL
David B Bronecke
809 W Main
Marion IL 62959

Call Sign: KF8OX
Bennie D Manion Jr
1100 W Malden St
Marion IL 62959

Call Sign: W9BDM
Bennie D Manion Jr
1100 W Malden St
Marion IL 62959

Call Sign: KC9QNF
Gregory G Lambert
809 W Maplewood
Marion IL 62959

Call Sign: WB0VTM
Jon S Bivin
1711 W Maplewood St
Marion IL 62959

Call Sign: KC9OLR
Eric L Johns
201 W Reid St
Marion IL 62959

Call Sign: KB9QZI
Anthony J Heneghan
835 Wargo Ln
Marion IL 62959

Call Sign: KB9HOV
Robert L Copeland
206 Westernaire Dr
Marion IL 62959

Call Sign: KC9VBC
Maurice R Sprague
507 Whippoorwil Ln
Marion IL 62959

Call Sign: W8RG
Robert W Mowery
3114 Williamson County
Pkwy Apt 16
Marion IL 62959

Call Sign: W9AKW
Clifford E Arnold
Marion IL 62959

Call Sign: KC9KWL
Alan M Gower
Marion IL 62959

Call Sign: KC9PBF
Larry D Johnson
Marion IL 62959

Call Sign: KA9PSS
Deanna B Doelitzsch
Marion IL 62959

Call Sign: KA9PST
Dinah J Doelitzsch

Marion IL 62959

FCC Amateur Radio Licenses in Marissa

Call Sign: KB9FZR
Charles R Bird
178 Green St
Marissa IL 62257

Call Sign: KC9CXQ
Bobby E Gregory
234 Green St
Marissa IL 62257

Call Sign: K9ZQK
Bobby E Gregory
234 Green St
Marissa IL 62257

Call Sign: N9BJJ
Ervin D Geralds Sr
105 Hotz St
Marissa IL 62257

Call Sign: WA9RJT
Le Roy W Behnke
3211 Marissa Rd
Marissa IL 62257

Call Sign: WD9HHN
Lawrence E Kilman
125 Pinckneyville Rd
Marissa IL 62257

Call Sign: KG9NR
Richard E Smith
102 S Bess Ave
Marissa IL 622571507

Call Sign: KB9DCP
William D Finch Sr
808 S Euclid Ave
Marissa IL 62257

Call Sign: KA9TZP
Judy M Heil
411 S Main
Marissa IL 62257

Call Sign: KC9DFT
Fred H Lewis
603 South Dr
Marissa IL 62257

Call Sign: KB9YOA
Terry R Blank
501 SR 13
Marissa IL 62257

Call Sign: K9TRB
Terry R Blank
501 SR 13
Marissa IL 62257

FCC Amateur Radio Licenses in Mark

Call Sign: KB9ZDK
Keenan D Campbell
106 N Milwaukee St
Mark IL 61340

Call Sign: WB9UBT
Richard Serafini
211 N Saint Paul St
Mark IL 61340

Call Sign: KC9OGX
Steven C Faletti
508 S Milwaukee St
Mark IL 61340

Call Sign: KA9UGL
Gilbert J Serafini
115 S St Paul St
Mark IL 61340

Call Sign: W9LIG
Hugh R Borri
Mark IL 61340

FCC Amateur Radio Licenses in Maroa

Call Sign: KB9WUI
James D Kuhlman
123 Montgomery Ct

Maroa IL 61756

Call Sign: AB9WS
James D Kuhlman
123 Montgomery Ct
Maroa IL 61756

Call Sign: KA9OAW
William D Keyes III
416 N Wood
Maroa IL 61756

Call Sign: KB9SAI
Bruce D Wells
602 N Wood St
Maroa IL 61756

Call Sign: KA9OAX
Rose M Keyes
201 S Walnut
Maroa IL 61756

Call Sign: KA9OAY
Howard D Keyes
201 S Walnut St
Maroa IL 617569638

Call Sign: W9GJL
W Dayton Keyes Jr
317 W Main Rt 1 Box 203
Maroa IL 61756

FCC Amateur Radio Licenses in Marquette Heights

Call Sign: KB9TLB
Mark E York
201 Kaskaskia Rd
Marquette Heghts IL 61554

Call Sign: KB9LJC
Robert J Sherwood
204 Algonquin Rd
Marquette Heights IL 61554

Call Sign: KC9PUM
Mark T Valentine
203 Beloit

Marquette Heights IL 61554

Call Sign: KC9BQQ
Hal M Burdin
109 Calumet
Marquette Heights IL 61554

Call Sign: KC9QKE
Jeff B Wabel
208 Craig Rd
Marquette Heights IL 61554

Call Sign: N9XJZ
James R Bolander
230 Douglas Rd
Marquete Heights IL 61554

Call Sign: WB9UCU
Walker V Fox
200 Frontenac Rd
Marquette Heights IL 61554

Call Sign: WC9N
Everett L Wright
404 Grant Rd
Marquette Heights IL 61554

Call Sign: W9VLZ
Virgil R Taylor Sr
406 Grant Rd
Marquette Heights IL 61554

Call Sign: N9RBO
John W Smith Jr
212 Kaskaskia Rd
Marquette Heights IL 61554

Call Sign: K9BRZ
Jack L Montgomery
909 Lincoln Rd
Marquette Heights IL 61554

Call Sign: KC9OXL
R Bruce Clifton
205 Radisson
Marquette Heights IL 61554

Call Sign: K9RBC
R Bruce Clifton

205 Radisson
Marquette Heights IL 61554

FCC Amateur Radio Licenses in Marseilles

Call Sign: KC9EMQ
John M Taylor
817 Bel Air Ct
Marseilles IL 61341

Call Sign: KB9HEV
Roger A Enrico
1015 Bluff Pl
Marseilles IL 61341

Call Sign: W9EQS
Howard A Brower
1018 Catalpa St
Marseilles IL 61341

Call Sign: KB9WJV
Laura E Zeedyk
741 Clark St
Marseilles IL 61341

Call Sign: KB9HEU
Gerald W Stevenson
2468 E 22nd Rd
Marseilles IL 61341

Call Sign: KC9VHY
David S Alexander
2482 E 22nd St
Marseilles IL 61341

Call Sign: N9JNK
Weldon E Oetken
3483 E 2350 Rd
Marseilles IL 61341

Call Sign: KA9FER
William L Kraus Sr
2806 E 2575th Rd
Marseilles IL 61341

Call Sign: KB9HET
Howard G Spicer
392 E Bluff

Marseilles IL 61341

Call Sign: K9BGD
Ronald L Johnson
850 E Bluff St
Marseilles IL 61341

Call Sign: KB9HGG
Danny J Mathews
2631 E US Hwy 6
Marseilles IL 61341

Call Sign: AA9CJ
Thomas L Kewley Sr
1089 Lakin Ave
Marseilles IL 61341

Call Sign: KC9HJG
William J Durdan
444 Lawrence Ave
Marseilles IL 61341

Call Sign: KC9WJD
William J Durdan
444 Lawrence Ave
Marseilles IL 61341

Call Sign: N9BES
Frederick W Krause
623 Lincoln St
Marseilles IL 61341

Call Sign: K9SON
Vernon H Meyer Sr
914 Magnolia St
Marseilles IL 61341

Call Sign: KC9NL
J Burton Hayes
2295 N 2453 Rd
Marseilles IL 61341

Call Sign: WB5RRP
Michael S Mc Natt
2563 N 2879 Rd
Marseilles IL 61341

Call Sign: KB9LFJ
Angelo L Daghi

2614 N 28th Rd
Marseilles IL 61341

Call Sign: K9PHW
Joseph J Elzer
2337 N 30th Td
Marseilles IL 61341

Call Sign: KC9KVZ
Bonny L Combs
755 Opal St
Marseilles IL 61341

Call Sign: N9DRU
Debra L Burton
1080 Orange Ave Apt 1
Marseilles IL 61341

Call Sign: W9MAD
Jack V O Keefe
858 Union Jaruski Tax Ser
Marseilles IL 61341

Call Sign: WA9UHS
Richard A Peddicord
419 Union St
Marseilles IL 613411513

Call Sign: KU9A
Bruce W Burton
1153 Union St
Marseilles IL 61341

Call Sign: KA9QFX
Jeffrey P Wiebe
598 Walnut Lt 58
Marseilles IL 61341

**FCC Amateur Radio
Licenses in Marshall**

Call Sign: KB9YKH
Donald R Pine
56 Archer Ave
Marshall IL 62441

Call Sign: WB0LJF
Annah M Smith
101 Archer Ave

Marshall IL 62441

Call Sign: N9YRX
John W Van Sandt
1302 Beech St
Marshall IL 62441

Call Sign: KB9QCB
Robert O Stout
Rr 2 Box 267A
Marshall IL 62441

Call Sign: KC9GNN
Annah M Smith
202 Cherry
Marshall IL 62441

Call Sign: N9WEO
Raymond A Quinn
25754 E 1750th Rd
Marshall IL 62441

Call Sign: WA9WJJ
Ray A Luth
13964 E Clark Center Rd
Marshall IL 624419558

Call Sign: K9DRP
Donald R Pine
23345 E Iron Bridge Rd
Marshall IL 62441

Call Sign: KB9YNO
Jane C Pine
23345 E Iron Bridge Rd
Marshall IL 62441

Call Sign: N9NVS
David M Dery
803 Elm
Marshall IL 62441

Call Sign: N9BRW
Debra K Moore
320 Fox Run Ln
Marshall IL 624413977

Call Sign: KB9JD
Steven J Moore

320 Fox Run Ln
Marshall IL 624413977

Call Sign: AI9T
Steven J Moore
320 Fox Run Ln
Marshall IL 624413977

Call Sign: WA9LZN
George A Hasten
17221 N 1800th St
Marshall IL 624413912

Call Sign: WD9FEF
Darrell B Ligget
18855 N 2200 St
Marshall IL 62441

Call Sign: KC9NJE
Clark County Ema
207 N 5th St
Marshall IL 62441

Call Sign: KB9RGR
Ray A Neff
514 N 8th St
Marshall IL 62441

Call Sign: N9AK
Kenneth E Snedeker
14378 N Amacher St
Marshall IL 62441

Call Sign: KC9UYV
Amanda R Evinger
19250 N Livingston Rd
Marshall IL 62441

Call Sign: N9TRS
Charla K Evinger
19250 N Livingston Rd
Marshall IL 62441

Call Sign: KC9ODB
Dean A Evinger Jr
19250 N Livingston Rd
Marshall IL 62441

Call Sign: KC9FDF

Nicole M Long
19250 N Livingston Rd
Marshall IL 62441

Call Sign: WD9EKA
Robert A Evinger
19250 N Livingston Rd
Marshall IL 62441

Call Sign: N9YUH
David L Mira
15265 N State Hwy 1
Marshall IL 62441

Call Sign: KE9XG
Glen A Duzan
615 S 10th St
Marshall IL 62441

Call Sign: KC9BHQ
Jeffrey A Carpenter
420 S 9th St
Marshall IL 62441

Call Sign: K9IFR
Lewis E Goekler
121 Tarble Rd
Marshall IL 62441

Call Sign: N9YEA
Frank Wells
Marshall IL 62441

FCC Amateur Radio Licenses in Martinsville

Call Sign: N9XQU
Brian E Martin
Rr 2 Box 95
Martinsville IL 62442

Call Sign: KA9ILL
Bryan P Chrysler
9304 E 1400th Rd
Martinsville IL 62442

Call Sign: W9GWF
Eastern Illinois Hamateurs
9304 E 1400th Rd

Martinsville IL 62442

Call Sign: WD9EJU
Ernest R Shotts
10433 N 1200th St
Martinsville IL 62442

Call Sign: KC9BBJ
Charles H Shotts Jr
12824 N 1330th St
Martinsville IL 62442

Call Sign: AA9BM
David C Morgan
18011 N 850th St
Martinsville IL 624422107

Call Sign: WA9OQC
Carl N Morgan
18011 N 850th St
Martinsville IL 624422108

Call Sign: KC9VFQ
Donnie L Barlow
205 N Elm St Apt 3B
Martinsville IL 62442

Call Sign: WD9EKK
Helen E Lee
310 N Mill St
Martinsville IL 62442

Call Sign: WA9VNS
James O Lee
310 N Mill St
Martinsville IL 62442

Call Sign: AC5UD
James F Cunningham
14021 N Ridgelawn Rd
Martinsville IL 624422546

Call Sign: K9YHW
Joseph Hawker
211 W Webster
Martinsville IL 62442

Call Sign: NT9X
Joseph Hawker

211 W Webster
Martinsville IL 62442

Call Sign: KC9RBD
Austin J Stamis
Martinsville IL 62442

FCC Amateur Radio Licenses in Martinton

Call Sign: W9SQX
Leonard R Wisniewski
2838 N SR 1
Martinton IL 60951

FCC Amateur Radio Licenses in Maryville

Call Sign: NK9Z
Terry W Phillips
72 Annebriar Dr
Maryville IL 62062

Call Sign: KC9KTR
Suzanne Bullard
201 B Anthony
Maryville IL 62062

Call Sign: KB9KLC
Gregory G De Chiara
201 B Anthony Dr
Maryville IL 62062

Call Sign: KB9KLD
Jeffrey R Uchitjil
9 Barbarotto Ln
Maryville IL 62062

Call Sign: KA9EXM
Jimmy K Hallowell
404 Bauer Ln
Maryville IL 62062

Call Sign: KC9TKB
Anthony S Wilshire
509 Birch Ln
Maryville IL 62062

Call Sign: KC9NVK

Gary C Wright
8 Bonnie Ct
Maryville IL 62062

Call Sign: K9NVK
Gary C Wright
8 Bonnie Ct
Maryville IL 62062

Call Sign: N9CWK
Patrick R Zantow
1 Forest Dr
Maryville IL 62062

Call Sign: KC9RUX
Kevin W James
7 Frontenac Lae
Maryville IL 62062

Call Sign: KC9RUW
Colleen A James
7 Frontenac Ln
Maryville IL 62062

Call Sign: WA4AQW
Carl F Freeman
28 Gary Ave
Maryville IL 62062

Call Sign: WA0GQT
Gary G Fogleman
2879 Keebler Rd
Maryville IL 620626841

Call Sign: AB9YL
Kevin L Melcher
7008 Magona Ct
Maryville IL 62062

Call Sign: KZ2S
Kevin L Melcher
7008 Magona Ct
Maryville IL 62062

Call Sign: KB9TAG
Joseph B Frerker Jr
6845 Manchester Dr
Maryville IL 62062

Call Sign: N9XV
Kevin L Gibbs
8 Nassau Dr
Maryville IL 620625618

Call Sign: N9VCE
Brad W Clarkson
716D Patty Dr Box 582
Maryville IL 62062

Call Sign: KB9BNZ
Larry E Kolling
28 Rosewood Dr
Maryville IL 62062

Call Sign: WA9SOF
Ricky L Acuncius
152 Stonebridge Bluff Dr
Maryville IL 62062

Call Sign: N0UHI
Richard T Conley
7607 Stonebridge Golf Dr
Maryville IL 62062

Call Sign: K9RKT
Terry L Clayton
2023 Vadalabene Dr
Maryville IL 62062

Call Sign: KC9TJZ
Scott E Young
1818 Vaughn Ln
Maryville IL 62062

Call Sign: WD9ITK
Steven M Crabb
Maryville IL 62062

Call Sign: N9PH
Joseph J Italiano
Maryville IL 62062

Call Sign: WB9YRI
Joseph J Italiano
Maryville IL 62062

Call Sign: N0WOP
Joseph J Italiano

Maryville IL 62062

FCC Amateur Radio Licenses in Mascoutah

Call Sign: KA9MGL
Betty J Schmidt
1200 Antique Ln
Mascoutah IL 622582748

Call Sign: AA9BL
Wallace J Schmidt
1200 Antique Ln
Mascoutah IL 622582748

Call Sign: WY9S
Wallace J Schmidt
1200 Antique Ln
Mascoutah IL 622582748

Call Sign: N9HHS
Carl G Kraske
Rr 2 Box 78
Mascoutah IL 62258

Call Sign: KA9ZNR
Kurt A Kraske
Rr 2 Box 78
Mascoutah IL 62258

Call Sign: N0NKA
Mark T Hatcher
9920 Cessna Ct
Mascoutah IL 62258

Call Sign: N9RWZ
Richard L Chausse
10121 Chaussee Ln
Mascoutah IL 62258

Call Sign: N9PYL
Ryan M Connolly
13 Cheryl Dr
Mascoutah IL 62258

Call Sign: W9JGC
Jerome G Cohen
202 E Phillips St
Mascoutah IL 62258

Call Sign: KB9MGT
Christopher G Treff
607 E Poplar
Mascoutah IL 622581522

Call Sign: KB9YQZ
Amber N Roof
402 E South St
Mascoutah IL 62258

Call Sign: KD5INX
Edward L Barbour
516 Falling Leaf Way
Mascoutah IL 62258

Call Sign: KC9MYS
Rose A Jones
208 Impala Dr
Mascoutah IL 622581225

Call Sign: KC9GBR
Gary L Jones
208 Impala Dr
Mascoutah IL 622581225

Call Sign: KC9CFX
Lance E Wood
400 Impala Dr
Mascoutah IL 62258

Call Sign: N9HZD
James C Wescoat Sr
315 Jackson St
Mascoutah IL 62258

Call Sign: N9MAU
Raymond Force Jr
10500 Jefferson Rd
Mascoutah IL 62258

Call Sign: KB9MXY
Michael S Purdy
1236 Lincoln Blvd
Mascoutah IL 62258

Call Sign: KC9CIL
Curtis A Fisher
404 N August St

Mascoutah IL 62258

Call Sign: N9SWQ
Garry L Haruska
4 N Levanon
Mascoutah IL 622580174

Call Sign: KA9RYR
Dennis H Knobeloch
10143 Perrin Rd
Mascoutah IL 62258

Call Sign: KA9RYQ
Pamela A Knobeloch
10143 Perrin Rd
Mascoutah IL 62258

Call Sign: KB9GVO
Raymond Force Jr
5853 Pintail Dr
Mascoutah IL 62258

Call Sign: KA9JVJ
Robert W Zerkle
22 Quail Point
Mascoutah IL 62258

Call Sign: W8WUD
Gary H Laakko
35 Quail Point
Mascoutah IL 62258

Call Sign: KC9OGO
Jeffrey D Rhoderick
1125 Quail Pt
Mascoutah IL 62258

Call Sign: KC9HCU
Richard A Sturgill
31 S CR Apt 17
Mascoutah IL 62258

Call Sign: W9ARJ
Richard A Sturgill
31 S CR Apt 17
Mascoutah IL 62258

Call Sign: KB9LIC
Rose A Groves

11416 Schlichter Rd
Mascoutah IL 62258

Call Sign: K9ZHN
David P Bobzin
11555 Schlichter Rd
Mascoutah IL 622584427

Call Sign: N9THN
Deborah L Schneidewind
6100 SR 15
Mascoutah IL 62258

Call Sign: KB9MXX
Janice L Harpstrite
10144 SR 161
Mascoutah IL 62258

Call Sign: K9BGL
Karl C Bretz
10633 SR 161
Mascoutah IL 62258

Call Sign: AA9ME
Richard K Schneidewind
6100 Stat Rt 15
Mascoutah IL 62258

Call Sign: N9MVX
Tipton E Klamberg
6419 Timber Ln Dr
Mascoutah IL 62258

Call Sign: WD9DDW
Ken J Kilian
503 W Church St
Mascoutah IL 62258

Call Sign: KC9VHU
Thomas A Griffin
35 W Green St
Mascoutah IL 62258

Call Sign: KB9JJW
Linda F Gilkerson
613 W Main St
Mascoutah IL 62258

Call Sign: N9YAL

Michael D Gilkerson
613 W Main St
Mascoutah IL 62258

Call Sign: KB9JYA
Wilma C Groves
811 W Main St
Mascoutah IL 62258

Call Sign: WB9SNX
Jerome G Cohen
918 W State St
Mascoutah IL 62254

Call Sign: KC9RET
Gary V Schanz
719 Westsouth St
Mascoutah IL 62258

Call Sign: KC9RUO
Anne J Draper
9702 Winchester St
Mascoutah IL 62258

Call Sign: KC9RUP
Randon H Draper
9702 Winchester St
Mascoutah IL 62258

Call Sign: N9ZQJ
Andrea R Blackmer
1180 Windshire Dr
Mascoutah IL 62258

Call Sign: KC9RUU
Cheyenne L Hughes
1188 Windshire Dr
Mascoutah IL 62258

Call Sign: KC9RUV
Jeffrey F Hughes
1188 Windshire Dr
Mascoutah IL 62258

Call Sign: WB1CDG
David J Di Censo
Mascoutah IL 62258

| FCC Amateur Radio |
| Licenses in Mason |

Call Sign: KB9PWI
George J Buening
R 1 Box 220
Mason IL 62443

Call Sign: KB9PWH
Ann E Buening
Rt 1 Box 220
Mason IL 62443

Call Sign: KA9SXM
Alan R Bell
Rt 1 Box 231
Mason IL 62443

Call Sign: KC9VDQ
Tyler J Budde
16709 E 100th Ave
Mason IL 62443

Call Sign: KB9WDU
Artie A Warner
13067 E 300 Ave
Mason IL 62443

Call Sign: KB9WDO
Gae A Warner
12897 E 300th Ave
Mason IL 62443

Call Sign: KB9WDP
Virgil E Warner
12897 E 300th Ave
Mason IL 62443

Call Sign: KB9SSO
Jesse D Warner
13067 E 300th Ave
Mason IL 62443

Call Sign: KB9WRF
Effingham High School ARC
13067 E 300th Ave
Mason IL 62443

Call Sign: KD4HFG

Thomas E Denton
3392 E 500th Ave
Mason IL 62443

Call Sign: WR9N
Douglas R Bishop
951 E Pearl St
Mason IL 62443

Call Sign: KB9UVM
Richard L Wells Jr
5563 N 950th Rd
Mason IL 62443

Call Sign: KB9COH
Brenda K Bishop
1 Pearl St
Mason IL 62443

Call Sign: KB9HWJ
Carol S Ullrich
Mason IL 62443

Call Sign: N9UAQ
Elizabeth K Mc Whorter
Mason IL 62443

Call Sign: N9OAL
Frank T Mc Whorter
Mason IL 62443

| FCC Amateur Radio |
| Licenses in Mason City |

Call Sign: W7CMY
Leonard W Burleson
29600 E CR 1150N
Mason City IL 62664

Call Sign: KO2R
Douglas E Bergeron
35956 E CR 800 N
Mason City IL 62664

Call Sign: W1BAH
Douglas E Bergeron
35956 E CR 800 N
Mason City IL 62664

Call Sign: KB9KCJ
Lesa M Bergeron
35956 E CR 800 N
Mason City IL 62664

Call Sign: KB9OZS
Jerome A Roemer
32241 E CR 930 N
Mason City IL 62664

Call Sign: WB9ZAG
David L Bergman
521 E Walnut
Mason City IL 62664

Call Sign: KC9JFL
Michael J Skaggs
111 N Keefer
Mason City IL 62664

Call Sign: KA9JLX
Gary L Hilst
519 N Tonica
Mason City IL 62664

Call Sign: K9UWC
Donald L Windsor
310 NW Ave
Mason City IL 62664

Call Sign: K9VGH
Vernalee Windsor
310 NW Ave
Mason City IL 62664

Call Sign: KR5TX
Clifford J Bills
702 W Arch
Mason City IL 62664

Call Sign: KR9TX
Clifford J Bills
702 W Arch
Mason City IL 62664

Call Sign: KA9CFI
Clarence E Sheary
624 W Pine St
Mason City IL 62664

Call Sign: AK9TX
Cliff J Bills
Mason City IL 62664

FCC Amateur Radio Licenses in Matherville

Call Sign: KC9HDC
Aron M Benner
103 B St
Matherville IL 612630672

Call Sign: K9FYU
Aron M Benner
103 B St
Matherville IL 612630672

Call Sign: KC9OEN
George C Herrman
Matherville IL 61263

Call Sign: KC9MUU
Catherine I Benner
Matherville IL 612630672

FCC Amateur Radio Licenses in Mattoon

Call Sign: KA9BRJ
Daniel C Horn
1400 Annis
Mattoon IL 61938

Call Sign: KB9SGD
Kevin D Howard
901 Bell Ave
Mattoon IL 61938

Call Sign: N9TYZ
Robbie A King
Rr2 Box 354
Mattoon IL 61938

Call Sign: KA9HAL
Vernon W Shirley
3012 Cedar
Mattoon IL 61938

Call Sign: KA9WEB
Debra K Greenwood
1005 Champaign
Mattoon IL 61938

Call Sign: KF9NB
David A Duggins
1009 Champaign
Mattoon IL 61938

Call Sign: NG9P
Dale E Connor
1613 Charleston Apt 308
Mattoon IL 61938

Call Sign: W9JY
Dale E Connor
1613 Charleston Ave
Mattoon IL 61938

Call Sign: KB9RFQ
Steven P Chapman
2517 Commercial Ave
Mattoon IL 61938

Call Sign: N9XPD
Phillip A Thompson
Country Acres 7
Mattoon IL 61938

Call Sign: KB9REF
Verl J Tryon
N 6 Country Garden
Mattoon IL 61938

Call Sign: KC9HUZ
Craig E Frantz
28 Country Gardens
Mattoon IL 61938

Call Sign: KC9EPR
Julie A Frantz
28 Country Gardens
Mattoon IL 61938

Call Sign: N9JJG
Michael J Morris
436 CR 1400 N
Mattoon IL 61938

Call Sign: KB9GEO
George P Beason
417 Crestmore Ave
Mattoon IL 61938

Call Sign: KB0LMN
David K Reynolds
600 Crestview Dr
Mattoon IL 61938

Call Sign: KB9LCK
Christopher Freshwater
720 Dakota Ave
Mattoon IL 61938

Call Sign: WA9YFR
Frank H Decker
2105 Dewitt Ave
Mattoon IL 61938

Call Sign: KC9SHV
Jason D Taylor
7 Dogwood Ln
Mattoon IL 61938

Call Sign: KB0DBA
Charles G Lunceford
1394 E CR 250 N
Mattoon IL 619389529

Call Sign: KA9ZJB
Kevin K Kilman
1313 Edgar Apt 1
Mattoon IL 61938

Call Sign: KB9QCQ
Jon K Anderson
2504 Essex Ave
Mattoon IL 61938

Call Sign: N9UUU
Robert H Janes
304 Hickory Ln
Mattoon IL 61938

Call Sign: KB9RGQ
James E Gravil
413 Illnois Ave

Mattoon IL 61938

Call Sign: KC9MNA
Joyce D Zschau
800 Lafayette
Mattoon IL 61938

Call Sign: KB9PXK
Robert A Zschau Sr
800 Lafayette
Mattoon IL 61938

Call Sign: N9VUT
James J J Stone
1312 Lafayette Apts
Mattoon IL 61938

Call Sign: KC9GAV
Bradley R Emel
905 Lafayette Ave
Mattoon IL 61938

Call Sign: WX9RFD
Bradley R Emel
905 Lafayette Ave
Mattoon IL 61938

Call Sign: KB9OWJ
Donna R Crites
1201 Lafayette Ave
Mattoon IL 61938

Call Sign: KB9LVD
Bruce E Wilson Sr
1217 Lakeland Blvd
Mattoon IL 61938

Call Sign: WA9VDI
Bernard H White
5261 Lerna Rd
Mattoon IL 61938

Call Sign: KB9IMG
Douglas R Mc Kibben
721 Lincoln Ave
Mattoon IL 61938

Call Sign: KB9KRL
William L Kercheval Jr

1817 Maple Ave
Mattoon IL 61938

Call Sign: KB9KOP
Christopher M Miller
1609 Moultrie Ave
Mattoon IL 61938

Call Sign: KC8DGF
Ronald B Gillis
916 N 13th St
Mattoon IL 61938

Call Sign: KB9YEP
David W Laue
1100 N 16th St
Mattoon IL 61938

Call Sign: KA9FTW
Nick C Stokes
1107 N 19th St
Mattoon IL 61938

Call Sign: N9JSH
Dale R Williams
905 N 21 St
Mattoon IL 61938

Call Sign: N9PLB
Thomas A Gover
204 N 22
Mattoon IL 61938

Call Sign: N9PKT
Daniel E Lewis
308 N 23rd
Mattoon IL 61938

Call Sign: KC9QFM
Brian L Kirby
713 N 27th St
Mattoon IL 61938

Call Sign: KB9OKF
Nicole C Schmid
913 N 28th
Mattoon IL 61938

Call Sign: KB9OHG

Daniel Schmid
913 N 28th St
Mattoon IL 61938

Call Sign: KB9PXM
George P Beason
800 N 31st
Mattoon IL 61938

Call Sign: KK9U
Kenneth C Dodson
828 N 33rd
Mattoon IL 61938

Call Sign: N9VLD
Charles L Howard
2793 N CR 330 E
Mattoon IL 61938

Call Sign: KB9QKC
John K Stafford
Lot 125 O Sv
Mattoon IL 61938

Call Sign: N9YFU
Nancy A Edersheim
Old St Village MHP
Mattoon IL 61938

Call Sign: N9VHB
Stewart A Edersheim
Old St Village MHP 2
Mattoon IL 61938

Call Sign: KC9REF
Don A Kaley
109 Prairie Ave
Mattoon IL 61938

Call Sign: KB9REG
Gary W Gravil
2209 Prairie Ave
Mattoon IL 61938

Call Sign: KC9FQM
Gerald G Fuller
2608 Richmond Ave
Mattoon IL 61938

Call Sign: AB9IW
Gerald G Fuller
2608 Richmond Ave
Mattoon IL 61938

Call Sign: WA9OCV
Russell G Wiley
933 Rudy
Mattoon IL 619386032

Call Sign: AA9WA
Dale E Connor
821 S 23rd St
Mattoon IL 61938

Call Sign: W9OGV
Randall G O Dell
1620 S 9th
Mattoon IL 61938

Call Sign: KC9TVE
Gary D Cohoon
1220 S 9th St
Mattoon IL 61938

Call Sign: KB9PXP
Thomas A Williams
1504 S 9th St
Mattoon IL 61938

Call Sign: KB9SUI
James G Giberson
3021 Shelby
Mattoon IL 61938

Call Sign: W9AYT
James S Campbell
3012 Shelby Ave
Mattoon IL 61938

Call Sign: KA9LRZ
Robert M Olson
6430 Stockton Rd
Mattoon IL 61938

Call Sign: N9OVP
Charles A Ormsby
11 Sugar Creek Ln
Mattoon IL 61938

Call Sign: KA9FID
William R Rauwolf
1120 Wabash
Mattoon IL 61938

Call Sign: N9RIT
Charles A Truhlar
Mattoon IL 61938

Call Sign: KB9PZD
Edward L Gardner
Mattoon IL 619381821

FCC Amateur Radio Licenses in Mazon

Call Sign: N9HFK
L Stanley Wilber
Rr 1 Box 73B
Mazon IL 60444

Call Sign: KB9KI
Leo J Fonck
3225 E Rt 113
Mazon IL 60444

Call Sign: N9UCP
James E Lutz
500 Front St
Mazon IL 60444

Call Sign: KC9HRY
Joshua D Jahn
1170 S Higgins Rd
Mazon IL 604446148

Call Sign: KC9PZZ
Brenda A Lutz
Mazon IL 60444

FCC Amateur Radio Licenses in McClure

Call Sign: N0JTV
Regina M Spier
Rt 1 Box 380
McClure IL 62957

Call Sign: N0YII
Michael C Schildt
66 Chickasaw St
McClure IL 62957

Call Sign: AD4FT
Sherman E Hill
51 Eastwood Dr
McClure IL 62957

Call Sign: KC9TXH
Brandon W Peters
32000 Grape Vine Trl
McClure IL 62957

FCC Amateur Radio Licenses in McConnell

Call Sign: KC9RMI
Robert L Englert
7275 W McConnell Rd
McConnell IL 61050

FCC Amateur Radio Licenses in McLean

Call Sign: KD9LU
Charles A Shoemaker
Rr 1 Box 139
McLean IL 61754

Call Sign: KA9RQQ
Daniel D Freeman
Rr 1 Box 70
McLean IL 61754

Call Sign: K9LMY
Fred S Leach
200 E North St
McLean IL 61754

Call Sign: N9EUY
Lawrence L Noe
114 Main St Box 91
McLean IL 61754

Call Sign: KB9YSE
Lawrence E Funk
4445 N 800 E Rd

McLean IL 617547603

Call Sign: W9EHX
Lawrence W Mc Guire
213 SW St
McLean IL 61754

Call Sign: WB9SNS
Robert S Craig
517 W Charles St
McLean IL 61754

FCC Amateur Radio Licenses in McLeansboro

Call Sign: W9MPM
Kenneth P Mitchell
Rr 1 Box 104
McLeansboro IL 62859

Call Sign: KE9ZO
Mark S Epperson
Rt 1 Box 12A
McLeansboro IL 62859

Call Sign: WB9SQY
Jimmie T Moles
Rr 4 Box 192
McLeansboro IL 62859

Call Sign: W9ZX
John S Epperson
Rr 4 Box 194
McLeansboro IL 62859

Call Sign: KA9CPO
Ralph E Shay
Rr 3 Box 197
McLeansboro IL 62859

Call Sign: KB9CBK
William D Glenn
Rr 5 Box 23B
McLeansboro IL 62859

Call Sign: KC9BIF
John C Lasswell
Rr 3 Box 245D Maple St
McLeansboro IL 62859

Call Sign: N9KMT
John A Drew
Rr 3 Box 85
McLeansboro IL 62859

Call Sign: N9KMX
Melvin A Drew
Rr 3 Box 85
McLeansboro IL 62859

Call Sign: KF9GV
Edward D Souden
605 E Broadway
McLeansboro IL 62859

Call Sign: KB9ZHM
Robert J Souden
605 E Broadway
McLeansboro IL 62859

Call Sign: WA9BPJ
W E Shuster
500 E Main
McLeansboro IL 62859

Call Sign: WA9NBR
Evert Moles
500.5 E Randolph
McLeansboro IL 62859

Call Sign: W9MWK
Lloyd M Epperson
Rfd 1 Epperson Dr
McLeansboro IL 62859

Call Sign: KC9NNO
Justin W Epperson
705 Foote St
McLeansboro IL 62859

Call Sign: W9MWK
Justin W Epperson
705 Foote St
McLeansboro IL 62859

Call Sign: N9NHO
Darlene K Souden
400 Heard St

McLeansboro IL 62859

Call Sign: AD9N
Bradley K Cross
106 Meadow Hills Dr
McLeansboro IL 62859

Call Sign: KB9BCZ
Gary D Lynn
307 N Pearl St
McLeansboro IL 62859

Call Sign: KA9BLH
Daniel L Dare
5 Redbud Ln
McLeansboro IL 62859

Call Sign: WB9IBO
Gary J Nelson
605 S Hancock St
McLeansboro IL 62859

Call Sign: WA9NDW
Carl L Nelson
605 S Hancock St
McLeansboro IL 62859

Call Sign: WD9GIL
Rodney S Lescalleet
410 W Main St
McLeansboro IL 62859

Call Sign: N9RBC
Tara V Arview
McLeansboro IL 62859

Call Sign: WA9EQW
Marion J Drew
McLeansboro IL 62859

Call Sign: N9SGY
John L Arview
McLeansboro IL 62859

Call Sign: N9SGX
Rosemary Arview
McLeansboro IL 62859

Call Sign: N9SGZ

Tiffany L Arview
McLeansboro IL 62859

Call Sign: KA9CXV
Jack D Hays
McLeansboro IL 62859

FCC Amateur Radio Licenses in McNabb

Call Sign: N9VQS
Michael J Harris
Rr 1 Box 14
McNabb IL 61335

Call Sign: K9BDR
Gary R Borri
3898 E Fishnfun Rd
McNabb IL 61335

Call Sign: N9GZ
Michael A Schrowang
4026 Swaney Rd
McNabb IL 61335

Call Sign: N9VIP
Tamara S Schrowang
4026 Swaney Rd
McNabb IL 61335

Call Sign: N9RJH
Paul A Hebel
McNabb IL 61335

FCC Amateur Radio Licenses in Mechanicsburg

Call Sign: KC9PWG
Keegan Huston
628 E 2675 N Rd
Mechanicsburg IL 62545

Call Sign: KB9YFZ
Tad J Ferratier
204 E South St Box 263
Mechanicsburg IL 62545

Call Sign: WB9RLZ
Dale W Barnstable

1775 Young Rd
Mechanicsburg IL 62545

FCC Amateur Radio Licenses in Media

Call Sign: KA9ZSU
Everett E Heap
Rr 1 Box 5
Media IL 61460

Call Sign: KA9ZST
Everett B Heap
Media IL 61460

FCC Amateur Radio Licenses in Medora

Call Sign: KB9RDD
Stephen W Yurick
34469 Ryan Rd
Medora IL 620633059

Call Sign: N9GGF
Thomas L Brinkman
117 S Railroad St
Medora IL 62063

FCC Amateur Radio Licenses in Mendon

Call Sign: KB9FLI
Michael W Koch
Rr 1 Box 196
Mendon IL 62351

Call Sign: N9RXV
Jody A Reid
Rt 1 Box 28
Mendon IL 62351

Call Sign: N9WSL
Conrad C Blackburn
Rr 2 Box 76
Mendon IL 62351

Call Sign: N9REK
Cynthia D Rigsbee
327 Church

Mendon IL 62351

Call Sign: N4RIH
Ethel S Wilkerson
2138 E 1050th St
Mendon IL 623512018

Call Sign: W4QLT
Ethel S Wilkerson
2138 E 1050th St
Mendon IL 623512018

Call Sign: WM4D
Kenneth L Wilkerson
2138 E 1050th St
Mendon IL 623512018

Call Sign: WA9YAS
David K Rigsbee
329 E Church Rd
Mendon IL 623510243

Call Sign: KC9OJQ
Christopher D Schulz
136 E Collins St
Mendon IL 62351

Call Sign: AB9XD
Christopher D Schulz
136 E Collins St
Mendon IL 62351

Call Sign: NR9Q
Christopher D Schulz
136 E Collins St
Mendon IL 62351

Call Sign: KC9JBD
Heartland Repeater Group
136 E Collins St
Mendon IL 62351

Call Sign: KC9KHZ
Ben P Robinson
1744 Hwy 61
Mendon IL 62351

Call Sign: WM9DX
Ben P Robinson

1744 Hwy 61
Mendon IL 62351

Call Sign: N9PDH
Leslie K Hoener
335 Washington Ave
Mendon IL 62351

FCC Amateur Radio Licenses in Mendota

Call Sign: KB9WCN
Gina L Madden
100 1st Ave
Mendota IL 61342

Call Sign: N9ZAL
Joeomie C Winfree
100 1st Ave
Mendota IL 61342

Call Sign: KC9DIA
Thomas A Maloy
408 3rd Ave
Mendota IL 61342

Call Sign: KB9KSD
T G P ARC
1205 3rd St
Mendota IL 61342

Call Sign: N9ZJK
Gerald D Hagemann
1107 4th Ave
Mendota IL 61342

Call Sign: N9HON
William R Chenneour
609 4th St
Mendota IL 61342

Call Sign: W9ZTK
Calvin J Sondgeroth
800 5th Ave
Mendota IL 61342

Call Sign: KB9AFM
Paul A Wagner
1200 5th St

Mendota IL 61342

Call Sign: K9KBP
Willis M Snyder
1218 Burlington St
Mendota IL 61342

Call Sign: K9HAW
Gerald G Whitmore
1610 Char Lu Dr
Mendota IL 61342

Call Sign: WD9DZE
Jeffrey L Spanier
107 E 6th St
Mendota IL 61342

Call Sign: KB9KQU
Geoffrey L Smith
1708 Hillcrest Ct
Mendota IL 61342

Call Sign: N9OVE
Douglas K Jackson
24 N 4179th Rd
Mendota IL 61342

Call Sign: N0STX
Howard L Demoret
1102 Oak Ct
Mendota IL 61342

Call Sign: KC9PXJ
Thomas P Kerns
708 Pennsylvania Ave
Mendota IL 61342

Call Sign: KB9RKU
Kurt H Clausen
111 S 13th Ave Lot C2
Mendota IL 61342

Call Sign: W9FID
Dallas W Wulf
1004 Wisconsin Ave
Mendota IL 613421543

Call Sign: N9ZVP
Kenneth L Jones

711 Wiscosin Ave
Mendota IL 61342

FCC Amateur Radio Licenses in Meredosia

Call Sign: N9WQK
Craig R Schmitz
Rr 1 Box 64
Meredosia IL 62665

Call Sign: KC9TNE
Seth T Schmitz
218 Forest Ln
Meredosia IL 62665

Call Sign: KB9FOG
Lester P Bowen
616 Ojer St
Meredosia IL 62665

Call Sign: W9LUW
Kermit A Muntman
529 Spunky Ridge Rd
Meredosia IL 62665

FCC Amateur Radio Licenses in Metamora

Call Sign: KB9NOW
Chris J Campen
1202 Arthur Ln
Metamora IL 61548

Call Sign: KC9AUU
Albert C Wilson
408 Ashland Cir
Metamora IL 61548

Call Sign: KB9RVK
Richard L Hosbrough Sr
Rr 7 Box 113
Metamora IL 615488408

Call Sign: N9SKC
Shawn C Passwater
Rr 2 Box 424
Metamora IL 61548

Call Sign: KB9MXL
Matthew L Boggs
860 Cardinal Cir
Metamora IL 61548

Call Sign: K9PDF
Paul D Force
383 Claytons Way
Metamora IL 61548

Call Sign: N9FGJ
Beth E Rocke
1018 Country Rd 1200 N
Metamora IL 615487506

Call Sign: K9UQF
Curtis V Rocke
1018 CR 1200 N
Metamora IL 615487506

Call Sign: KC9VMU
Keith D Turner
867 CR 1500 N
Metamora IL 61548

Call Sign: WB9IFL
Gary L Knepp
886 CR 1500 N
Metamora IL 61548

Call Sign: WA9VJW
Thomas W Herrick
421 Crestview Dr
Metamora IL 61548

Call Sign: WA9TH
Thomas W Herrick
421 Crestview Dr
Metamora IL 61548

Call Sign: WA9WEO
Irvin L Guth
721 E Partridge
Metamora IL 61548

Call Sign: W9FST
Wilson D Speight
1200 E Partridge 13B
Metamora IL 61548

Call Sign: WB9YPO
Sidney L Crank
1200 E Partridge Ln Lot 58A
Metamora IL 615488718

Call Sign: KB9LNR
James E Copes
372 E Ten Mile Creek Rd
Metamora IL 61548

Call Sign: KF4IQA
Ashok K Srinivasan
502 Fandel Rd
Metamora IL 61548

Call Sign: N9VOG
Matthew P Wilmot
604 Fandel Rd
Metamora IL 61548

Call Sign: KA9HDM
Gregory L Williamson
1278 Hickory Hills Rd
Metamora IL 61548

Call Sign: WD8OQY
Lowell E Baker
1508 Hickory Point Rd
Metamora IL 61548

Call Sign: KC9UMX
Dorothy J Caho
1577 Hickory Point Rd
Metamora IL 61548

Call Sign: N9ZBD
Robert J Herrick
107 Hollyhock Ln
Metamora IL 61548

Call Sign: KC9KXE
Randall S Charlier
511 Justa Rd
Metamora IL 61548

Call Sign: W9RVH
John R Rauh
1304 Killdeer Ln

Metamora IL 615480587

Call Sign: KB9LJI
Kurt A Blickenstaff
Rr 5 Lake Sant Fe
Metamora IL 61548

Call Sign: KB9LNY
Diane Geurin
1319 Lourdes Rd
Metamora IL 61549

Call Sign: KB9LNQ
Ronald E Geurin
1319 Lourdes Rd
Metamora IL 61549

Call Sign: W9GCE
John F Sauer
1415 Lourdes Rd
Metamora IL 61548

Call Sign: KE9LS
Joseph A Wernsman
1296 N Forrest Dr
Metamora IL 61548

Call Sign: KA9VVS
Diane L Higgins
1338 N Forrest Dr
Metamora IL 615489440

Call Sign: KB9YJX
James D Johnson
1331 Paradise Dr
Metamora IL 61548

Call Sign: KB9RVJ
Kenneth Stonecipher
101 Peach Tree Ln
Metamora IL 61548

Call Sign: WD9HYY
Paul R Coltrin Jr
510 Ponds Ct
Metamora IL 61548

Call Sign: N9NSM
Yvonne E Coltrin

510 Ponds Ct
Metamora IL 61548

Call Sign: K9YUR
Herbert J Silldorff
506 S Menard
Metamora IL 61548

Call Sign: KC9VTE
Woodford County Repeater
Association
213 S Tazewell St
Metamora IL 61548

Call Sign: KC9GQR
Bradley D Haney
213 S Tazewell St
Metamora IL 61548

Call Sign: NT9H
Thomas W Herrick
755 Santa Fe Trl
Metamora IL 61548

Call Sign: WC9Y
David J Smith
506 Settlers Way
Metamora IL 61548

Call Sign: KB9KCC
Mike R Purfield
26080 Tazewood Rd
Metamora IL 61548

Call Sign: KA9IJI
Homer A Gundy
28601 Tazwood Rd
Metamora IL 61548

Call Sign: KB9OSS
Ashley L Copes
372 Ten Mile Creek Rd
Metamora IL 61548

Call Sign: K9JHP
Eli Tepovich Jr
Rr 4 Timberlain Rd
Metamora IL 61548

Call Sign: K9RQT
Robert E Wagner
Tuckaway Tr Pk
Metamora IL 61548

Call Sign: KA9HFK
Paul F Mitchell
116 W Mt Vernon
Metamora IL 615480147

Call Sign: KC9GPS
David A Evans
244 Whispering Oaks Dr
Metamora IL 61548

Call Sign: KC4MOC
Richard H Greene
341 Whispering Oaks Dr
Metamora IL 61548

Call Sign: KB9JKX
Matthew D Shertz
1627 Wiedman Rd
Metamora IL 61548

Call Sign: N9CRP
William H Jenkins
Metamora IL 61548

Call Sign: K9KZP
Stanley W Rush
Metamora IL 61548

Call Sign: KC9ELN
Michael J Owens
Metamora IL 61548

Call Sign: K9ZQW
Willis B Hodel
Metamora IL 61548

Call Sign: AA9GU
Donald M Watts
Metamora IL 615480890

Call Sign: KC9RN
Ansel L Burditt
Metamora IL 615480927

Call Sign: KA9LGG
Kerry M Burditt
Metamora IL 615480927

FCC Amateur Radio Licenses in Metcalf

Call Sign: N9YEU
Earnest R Gilkerson Jr
208 Douglas St
Metcalf IL 61940

Call Sign: KB9LLC
Rosalind K Gilkerson
208 Douglas St
Metcalf IL 61940

Call Sign: N9WZY
Lee R Barth
24210 N 1050th St
Metcalf IL 61940

Call Sign: N9WZX
Michael J Haddix
217 W Douglas
Metcalf IL 61940

Call Sign: KB9OJN
Robert L Burns
502 West St
Metcalf IL 61940

FCC Amateur Radio Licenses in Metropolis

Call Sign: KB9ALU
Margaret M Harrison
774 Airport Rd
Metropolis IL 629603059

Call Sign: N9NYB
Mylon R Hulsey
212 Baker Dr
Metropolis IL 62960

Call Sign: N9VQI
Michael J Hicks
Rt 3 Box 188
Metropolis IL 62960

Call Sign: N9KHQ
Odell Allbritten
Rt 1 Box 202
Metropolis IL 62960

Call Sign: N9XWN
John R Bowman
Rr 3 Box 258
Metropolis IL 62960

Call Sign: KD9EK
William C Anderson
Rt 1 Box 655
Metropolis IL 62960

Call Sign: KB9NXP
Laura E Dresser
1307 Catherine
Metropolis IL 62960

Call Sign: N9SPX
Patrick J Dresser
1307 Catherine St
Metropolis IL 62960

Call Sign: N9DIV
Patrick J Dresser
1307 Catherine St
Metropolis IL 62960

Call Sign: KB9KGK
Robert A Pergande Jr
1414 Catherine St
Metropolis IL 629601334

Call Sign: N9WOR
James O Phelps
941 Country Club Rd
Metropolis IL 62960

Call Sign: KA8TER
Anne E Parmley
1123 Country Club Rd
Metropolis IL 62960

Call Sign: KR8L
William A Parmley
1123 Country Club Rd

Metropolis IL 62960

Call Sign: N9KHL
James E Borum
1322 Country Club Rd
Metropolis IL 62960

Call Sign: W9NFM
Charles A Taylor
4180 Crestwood Rd
Metropolis IL 62960

Call Sign: N9HZB
John L Mc Corkle
209 Dorris Dr
Metropolis IL 62960

Call Sign: N9WZH
Edward M Hollis
1100 E 2nd St
Metropolis IL 62960

Call Sign: KB9AJX
Norval R Kelley
307 E 5th St
Metropolis IL 62960

Call Sign: N9IBS
Keith E Davis
811 E 5th St
Metropolis IL 62960

Call Sign: N9MJY
Lisa A Davis
811 E 5th St
Metropolis IL 62960

Call Sign: KB9TNT
Kevin L Meyers
2119 E 5th St
Metropolis IL 62960

Call Sign: KA9UGZ
Randall W Lampley
212 E 8th St
Metropolis IL 62960

Call Sign: WB7PNC
William A Harrison

10 Eastland Dr
Metropolis IL 62960

Call Sign: KC9ECM
Charles R Arrison
1509 Ferry St
Metropolis IL 62960

Call Sign: KB9VUY
Donna J Young
418 Girad
Metropolis IL 62960

Call Sign: KB9VVX
James E Young
418 Girard
Metropolis IL 62960

Call Sign: KB9PPU
James D Sumner
27 Grace Dr
Metropolis IL 62960

Call Sign: N9XUD
Cheryl M Green
19 James Dr
Metropolis IL 62960

Call Sign: N9XWP
Gary W Green
19 James Dr
Metropolis IL 62960

Call Sign: KB9ZAC
David W Bowman
4630 Kommer Rd
Metropolis IL 62960

Call Sign: KB9ZAB
Tammie M Bowman
4630 Kommer Rd
Metropolis IL 62960

Call Sign: WB9PVX
Milburn C Johnson
5038 Kommer Rd
Metropolis IL 62960

Call Sign: KB9FPZ

Charles A Taylor
211 Lindsey St
Metropolis IL 62960

Call Sign: N9TSL
Robert J Woolard
312 Lindsey St
Metropolis IL 62960

Call Sign: KB9YWV
Patrick L Kennedy
1324 Magnolia Ln
Metropolis IL 62960

Call Sign: KB9QFV
David W Mc Coy
4387 Maple Rd
Metropolis IL 62960

Call Sign: KB9QFC
Elijah N Mc Coy
4387 Maple Rd
Metropolis IL 62960

Call Sign: KF9J
Ray R Frasher
3448 Massac Creek Rd
Metropolis IL 62960

Call Sign: KC9OFT
Brian D Lagore
1810 McCrary St
Metropolis IL 62960

Call Sign: K9HIX
Robert L Trieglaff
1815 North Ave
Metropolis IL 62960

Call Sign: K4LG
William R Ashley
3014 North Ave
Metropolis IL 62960

Call Sign: KB9VKZ
Cory A Trovillion
301 Oak Dr
Metropolis IL 62960

Call Sign: N9ANT
Eugene Beasley
111 Oak Ln
Metropolis IL 62960

Call Sign: N9OWG
Douglas A Westermann
1051 Old Joppa Rd
Metropolis IL 62960

Call Sign: KG4HSF
James L Gurley
4847 Old Marion Rd
Metropolis IL 62960

Call Sign: N9HQM
Durwood D Eleam
3250 Riverview Rd
Metropolis IL 62960

Call Sign: N9HYF
Gerald E Lamb
3547 Riverview Rd
Metropolis IL 62960

Call Sign: KC9VFV
Rob A Larrison
3474 Rocky Branch Rd
Metropolis IL 62960

Call Sign: N9WZG
John F La Veau
4402 Rosebud Rd
Metropolis IL 62960

Call Sign: W9NRM
Omer N Bremer
5941 Rosebud Rd
Metropolis IL 62960

Call Sign: KB9BNB
Gregory V Krempasky
3927 Shady Grove Rd
Metropolis IL 62960

Call Sign: N9TSN
Lee A Krempasky
3927 Shady Grove Rd
Metropolis IL 62960

Call Sign: KX9B
Fred W Reed
216 Shawnee Ln
Metropolis IL 62960

Call Sign: KC9HHA
Bobby K Norwood
2516 Strawberry Rd
Metropolis IL 62960

Call Sign: KB9OAW
William J Davidson Jr
409 W 7th St
Metropolis IL 62960

Call Sign: WB9JFT
Leonard L Potterbaum
502 W 8th
Metropolis IL 62960

Call Sign: KC9ILR
William K Stokes
512 W 9th St
Metropolis IL 62960

Call Sign: KB9QFD
Ambus W Bradley Jr
517 W 9th St
Metropolis IL 62960

Call Sign: KB9ZAD
Rhonda G Shales
14 Westland Dr
Metropolis IL 62960

Call Sign: NW9W
Stephen R Harrison
7 White Oak Ln
Metropolis IL 62960

Call Sign: KG9OM
Donald J Snodgrass
5 Woodhaven Estates
Metropolis IL 62960

Call Sign: N9PXJ
Randy S Horstman
Metropolis IL 62960

Call Sign: KB9VUX
Debbie J Miller
Metropolis IL 62960

Call Sign: K9TIG
Debbie J Miller
Metropolis IL 62960

Call Sign: KC9GHX
Jesse E Paschal
Metropolis IL 62960

Call Sign: KI4YHP
Midwest ARC
Metropolis IL 62960

Call Sign: W9MID
Midwest ARC
Metropolis IL 62960

Call Sign: K9OWU
Joseph V Miller Jr
Metropolis IL 629600596

FCC Amateur Radio Licenses in Michael

Call Sign: NW9M
Mark B White
Rr 1 Box 3
Michael IL 62065

Call Sign: ND2D
Dare To Dream Radio Club
Rt 1 Box 3
Michael IL 62065

Call Sign: N9OHS
Mark B White
Michael IL 62065

FCC Amateur Radio Licenses in Middletown

Call Sign: N9VAD
Ronald D Alexander
1230 200th Ave
Middletown IL 62666

Call Sign: WD9HFH
Theodore A Leach
207 N Grove
Middletown IL 62666

Call Sign: KC9QOZ
Judith A Jennings
600 S Main
Middletown IL 62666

Call Sign: KC9OUA
William A Jennings Sr
600 S Main St
Middletown IL 62666

Call Sign: N9OQ
William A Jennings Sr
600 S Main St
Middletown IL 62666

Call Sign: K9KYZ
Raymond T Estill
406 S Main St Box 247
Middletown IL 62666

FCC Amateur Radio Licenses in Milan

Call Sign: K9PXU
Wayne J Blick
2526 113 Ave Ct W
Milan IL 61264

Call Sign: KB9JCS
William L Conner
2524 113th Ave Ct W
Milan IL 61264

Call Sign: WA9CHD
Sidney K Sisson
5707 120th Ave W
Milan IL 61264

Call Sign: K9YDE
Clarence L Johnson
2425 127th Ave
Milan IL 61264

Call Sign: N0ATS
Cory W Leland
2617 136th Ave Ct W
Milan IL 61264

Call Sign: KB9MVG
Ralph J Raisbeck
3206 143 Ave Ct W
Milan IL 612644753

Call Sign: KC9RQE
Michael A Duke
407 18th Ave E
Milan IL 61264

Call Sign: WD9HZU
Marlin D Webb
301 19th Ave Ct W
Milan IL 61264

Call Sign: KC9VPL
Craig S Scharer Sr
9530 27th St
Milan IL 61264

Call Sign: KC5OSZ
Matthew D Hall
8917 28th St Ct
Milan IL 61264

Call Sign: KC9OTW
Daniel E Olson
1149 4th St W
Milan IL 61264

Call Sign: KB9SVL
Katherine L Schumaker
6622 52nd St
Milan IL 61264

Call Sign: KB9NTT
Peter D Schumaker
6622 52nd St
Milan IL 61264

Call Sign: WB9UAA
Donald M Turner
11419 6th St
Milan IL 61264

Call Sign: WD9IDZ
Michael B Hoefle
4328 78th Ave W
Milan IL 61264

Call Sign: WO9T
Robert W King
12008 9th St
Milan IL 61264

Call Sign: KB9DO
Alex P Aldrian
522 Bruce Ave
Milan IL 61264

Call Sign: KB9SKN
Joan D Aldrian
522 Bruce Ave
Milan IL 61264

Call Sign: N9TGF
Bill J Capps
200 E 17th St
Milan IL 61264

Call Sign: AA0VD
Nobuyuki Makabe
929 E 32nd Ave
Milan IL 61264

Call Sign: WD9IRZ
Daniel F Mack
437 E 6 St
Milan IL 61264

Call Sign: N9XAL
Paul E West
401 E 6th St
Milan IL 61264

Call Sign: N9TGC
Cleo M Freeman
11 Hillcrest
Milan IL 61264

Call Sign: N9TGB
Edmund R Freeman
11 Hillcrest Rd

Milan IL 61264

Call Sign: N9VYH
Amy J Miller
1233 Hilltop Dr
Milan IL 61264

Call Sign: N9VYI
Richard E Miller
1233 Hilltop Dr
Milan IL 61264

Call Sign: KC9NSS
Christopher D Liedtke
13926 Knoxville Rd
Milan IL 61264

Call Sign: KZ9Q
Robert H Cawley
704 North Ave
Milan IL 61264

Call Sign: N9KHB
Kristine M Cawley
704 North Ave
Milan IL 61264

Call Sign: KB9EWV
Gary G Coon
11121 Ridgewood Rd
Milan IL 61264

Call Sign: WD9HJF
Richard A Nowack
3206 Rt 67
Milan IL 61264

Call Sign: WY9Z
James H Brown
317 W 12th Ave
Milan IL 61264

Call Sign: KA9SDW
Richard J Moses
811 W 12th St
Milan IL 61264

Call Sign: KB9SVK
Erin M Shaffer

1628 W 3rd St Ct
Milan IL 61264

Call Sign: WB0UZT
Richard H Moeller
Milan IL 61264

Call Sign: KC9IVX
Lawrence J Tucker Jr
Milan IL 61264

Call Sign: W9LJT
Lawrence J Tucker Jr
Milan IL 61264

FCC Amateur Radio Licenses in Milford

Call Sign: KC9OVF
Paul W Wilson
2064 E 1200 N Rd
Milford IL 60953

Call Sign: WA9GGU
Theodore W Boehm
403 E Irving St
Milford IL 609531139

FCC Amateur Radio Licenses in Mill Shoals

Call Sign: KC9VDR
Isaac S Etheridge
2495 CR 175E
Mill Shoals IL 62862

FCC Amateur Radio Licenses in Milledgeville

Call Sign: W9FRC
John J Sluce
4192 Eagle Rd
Milledgeville IL 610519224

Call Sign: N4VSK
Harry W Pettenger
313 W 6th St
Milledgeville IL 61051

Call Sign: N9HWS
Andrew J Shaw
213 W 8th St
Milledgeville IL 61051

FCC Amateur Radio Licenses in Miller City

Call Sign: N9XDZ
Charles E Bonifield Jr
21591 Miller City Rd
Miller City IL 62962

FCC Amateur Radio Licenses in Millstadt

Call Sign: N9FYF
Bruce A Conley
128 Benham Dr
Millstadt IL 62260

Call Sign: W9TJ
Thomas E Johns
1 Blackburn Manor
Millstadt IL 62260

Call Sign: WB9PWH
Steven P Walden
Rr 1 Box 299
Millstadt IL 62260

Call Sign: KB9BTO
Jeri L Walden
Rt 1 Box 299
Millstadt IL 62260

Call Sign: WD9CRR
Raymond A Nobe
38 Coachlite Dr
Millstadt IL 62260

Call Sign: KB9WQV
Judy A Hassard
44 Coachlite Dr
Millstadt IL 62260

Call Sign: KB9MRZ
Michael R Laing
6158 Floraville Rd

Millstadt IL 62260

Call Sign: N9DBI
Alva J Eaton Jr
2913 Imbs Station Rd
Millstadt IL 62260

Call Sign: WB9QPL
Elige D Fortenberry
8624 Lepere School Rd
Millstadt IL 62260

Call Sign: KC9OFD
Anderson J Manly
619 Manor Ln
Millstadt IL 62260

Call Sign: KC9UAW
Troy R Baldwin
7549 Nelson Ln
Millstadt IL 62260

Call Sign: N9NOB
Kathleen A Hoeffken
19 Rhineland Pl
Millstadt IL 622602257

Call Sign: WB9QYY
Russell W Hoeffken
19 Rhineland Pl
Millstadt IL 622602257

Call Sign: KA9YZP
Charles L Cobillas
2336 Spring Valley Farm
Millstadt IL 62260

Call Sign: K9ISM
Leslie G Procasky
6904 SR 163
Millstadt IL 62260

Call Sign: N9YSD
Genevieve J Hall
7404 SR 163
Millstadt IL 62260

Call Sign: N9UPF
Lawrence D Loiseau

8412 Tebby Ln
Millstadt IL 62260

Call Sign: K0PWS
Chesley F Poole Sr
409 W Washington
Millstadt IL 62260

Call Sign: KE9GL
Harvey C Kohlenberger
210 W White St
Millstadt IL 62260

Call Sign: W9IFR
Michael G Hoff
3178 Zingg Rd
Millstadt IL 62260

FCC Amateur Radio Licenses in Milmine

Call Sign: KC9DEL
Austin H Brandenburg
403 E 800 N Rd
Milmine IL 61855

Call Sign: KC9DEK
Rosemary A Brandenburg
403 E 800 N Rd
Milmine IL 61855

Call Sign: KA9VHQ
Samuel W Brandenburg
403 E 800 N Rd
Milmine IL 618559505

FCC Amateur Radio Licenses in Minier

Call Sign: N9JJQ
Georgia S Singley
5087 MacKinaw Rd
Minier IL 61759

Call Sign: WQ9E
Rodger B Singley
5087 MacKinaw Rd
Minier IL 61759

Call Sign: N9GYD
Morris E Peine
412 S Eastern
Minier IL 61759

Call Sign: W9ROK
Ronald W Asbill
Minier IL 61759

Call Sign: KB9WIA
Maureen L Brunsdale
Minier IL 61759

FCC Amateur Radio Licenses in Minonk

Call Sign: N8NVV
Tony R Jones
3019 CR 1600N
Minonk IL 61760

Call Sign: N9YDG
Ralph W Ford
635 E 6th St
Minonk IL 617601334

Call Sign: K9VVP
Roger A Spires
527 Lincoln St
Minonk IL 61760

Call Sign: K9OAU
John A Schuster
110 W 1st
Minonk IL 61760

Call Sign: K9TGX
Joseph G Vallow
830 W 6th
Minonk IL 61760

Call Sign: N9IGW
Glenn H Barth
719 W 6th St
Minonk IL 61760

Call Sign: N9NGU
Paul A Alpiser
602 Washington St

Minonk IL 61760

FCC Amateur Radio Licenses in Mitchell

Call Sign: N9WDU
William E Smith
128 Cynthia Ln
Mitchell IL 62040

Call Sign: N9FUE
Timothy P Nichols
529 English Pl
Mitchell IL 62040

Call Sign: WA9REW
Monta J Newberry
528 Fleming Pl
Mitchell IL 62040

FCC Amateur Radio Licenses in Modesto

Call Sign: WD9HBF
Mark A Kerhlikar
32795 Otten Rd
Modesto IL 62667

FCC Amateur Radio Licenses in Moline

Call Sign: KC9GLP
Scott D Coborn
4117 10th Ave
Moline IL 61265

Call Sign: WD9CYH
Don M Eastman
1308 11th St
Moline IL 61265

Call Sign: W9UD
James M Roseman
2131 11th St
Moline IL 612654747

Call Sign: KB9ATT
Christopher S Benner
811 12th Ave

Moline IL 61265

Call Sign: KB9CDW
Talbert L Widick
1427 12th St
Moline IL 61265

Call Sign: KB9OLH
Joyce A Eder
1812 12th St
Moline IL 61265

Call Sign: N9VLE
William J Peiffer
1932 12th St
Moline IL 61265

Call Sign: K9AKS
Curtis C Roseman
2120 12th St
Moline IL 61265

Call Sign: KB9BFU
Richard L Scherer
1835 14th Ave
Moline IL 61265

Call Sign: WA9SBV
Frank E Drake Jr
3629 14th Ave
Moline IL 61265

Call Sign: N9BUD
Frank E Drake Jr
3629 14th Ave
Moline IL 61265

Call Sign: WA9FBJ
Barbara L Henson
2029 14th St
Moline IL 61265

Call Sign: K9SDQ
Ronald L Henson
2029 14th St
Moline IL 61265

Call Sign: N9OUU
Kenton L Mc Lain

512 15th Ave
Moline IL 61265

Call Sign: W0MJW
Richard E Whitaker
3705 15th Ave
Moline IL 612653415

Call Sign: N9FFB
Harry R Impens
3002 15th St
Moline IL 61265

Call Sign: N9WWC
Dennis J Mc Donald
3715 15th St D
Moline IL 61265

Call Sign: KE4ONK
Kenneth W Helmers
1504 16th St
Moline IL 61265

Call Sign: K9ONK
Kenneth W Helmers
1504 16th St
Moline IL 61265

Call Sign: KC9IDW
Sims Memorial Repeater
Group
4343 16th St 108
Moline IL 61265

Call Sign: W9WOP
William A Woehr
4322 17th Ave
Moline IL 61265

Call Sign: N9NWF
Joseph D Laird
5413 17th Ave
Moline IL 61265

Call Sign: KC9LTU
Frank D Fisher
1862 18th Ave
Moline IL 61265

Call Sign: KC9MJX
Adam G Jones
1715 18th Ave A
Moline IL 61265

Call Sign: KC9NGN
Wendell Sullivan
2327 18th St C
Moline IL 612654883

Call Sign: WD9DHA
James M Osborn
1650 19th Ave
Moline IL 61255

Call Sign: KA9ACF
Jeffry M Osborn
1650 19th Ave
Moline IL 61265

Call Sign: WA9WUR
Gene D Cowdery
1180 22nd St
Moline IL 61265

Call Sign: W9THY
Alfred H Bohy
3108.5 23rd Ave
Moline IL 61265

Call Sign: KC9BAN
Shaun M Debow
3711 23rd Ave 211
Moline IL 612654423

Call Sign: KB9SAJ
Kenneth L Rangen
1940 23rd St A
Moline IL 612654144

Call Sign: N9KLR
Kenneth L Rangen
1940 23rd St A
Moline IL 612654144

Call Sign: KA9RWM
Marion Hook
2723 24th Ave
Moline IL 61265

Call Sign: WB9ETU
Joe E Waite
4110 24th Ave
Moline IL 61265

Call Sign: KB9NED
Mark H Hendricks
1916 24th St
Moline IL 61265

Call Sign: KB9IMJ
Joyce A Moon
1428 25 Ave
Moline IL 61265

Call Sign: N9XEC
Robert J Moon III
1428 25th Ave
Moline IL 61265

Call Sign: N9XBC
Robert J Moon Jr
1428 25th Ave
Moline IL 61265

Call Sign: W9DNT
Merle E Reynolds
710 25th Ave Ct
Moline IL 61265

Call Sign: W9TFZ
Harold M Morse Sr
4025 26 Ave
Moline IL 61265

Call Sign: WB9OOS
Charles N Jones
4120 26th Ave
Moline IL 61265

Call Sign: KC9RJJ
Donald W Fulscher
4120 26th Ave
Moline IL 61265

Call Sign: WB9WBH
Robert L Ross
5102 26th Ave A Ct

Moline IL 61265

Call Sign: WR9B
Larry P Granell
1155 26th St
Moline IL 61265

Call Sign: K9ZFK
Orville J Vogelbaugh
3704 26th St
Moline IL 61265

Call Sign: KA9PYA
William J Rasmussen
3705 26th St
Moline IL 61265

Call Sign: N9AAV
William E Mosher
4100 27 St Lot A2
Moline IL 612656384

Call Sign: N0TQH
Kevin S Sneed
1410 27th Ave
Moline IL 61265

Call Sign: KB9HSO
William H Diedrich
2924 27th Ave A
Moline IL 61265

Call Sign: K9URE
Tom P Serandos
528 28th Ave
Moline IL 61265

Call Sign: N9CLR
Jewell R Engstrom
4917 28th Ave
Moline IL 61265

Call Sign: N9DNY
Robert E Engstrom Jr
4917 28th Ave
Moline IL 61265

Call Sign: W9REE
Robert E Engstrom Jr

4917 28th Ave
Moline IL 61265

Call Sign: WD9IWO
Glenn D Rogerson
2437 28th St
Moline IL 61265

Call Sign: KB9ATU
George S Johnson
1900 29th St
Moline IL 61265

Call Sign: N9UZH
Douglas E Greene
2508 2nd St
Moline IL 61265

Call Sign: N9TPQ
Robert E Cannon
2801 2nd St
Moline IL 61265

Call Sign: KC9HGP
Douglas C Decherd
2520 30th Ave Ct
Moline IL 61265

Call Sign: N9TFZ
William H Dailey
1330 30th St
Moline IL 61265

Call Sign: W9UC
Charles P Alter
2505 31st Ave Ct
Moline IL 61265

Call Sign: W9NUB
Charles P Alter
2505 31st Ave Ct
Moline IL 61265

Call Sign: KB9SVM
Bradi M Kipper
1020 31st St
Moline IL 61265

Call Sign: K9MIG

Adrian R Brundage
2335 31st St
Moline IL 61265

Call Sign: K9FFC
Viril E Dulaney
3710 33rd Ave
Moline IL 61265

Call Sign: KA9KCK
John E Davis
1908 33rd St
Moline IL 61265

Call Sign: K9KCK
John E Davis
1908 33rd St
Moline IL 61265

Call Sign: WA9QBC
Duane Churchwell
2452 33rd St
Moline IL 61265

Call Sign: K6XZ
Robert G Craig
1171 33rd St Ct
Moline IL 61265

Call Sign: KB9EGT
Cyril E White
6147 34 Ave
Moline IL 61265

Call Sign: KB9ING
William R Crouch
1309 34 Ave A
Moline IL 61265

Call Sign: KA9LJC
Hugh E Saunders
4224 34 Ave Pl
Moline IL 61265

Call Sign: N9VOU
William C Van Brunt
2407 34 St Apt 9
Moline IL 61265

Call Sign: K6STV
Walter R Keller
1620 34th St Dr
Moline IL 61265

Call Sign: KK4DC
Elizabeth V Keller
1620 34th St Dr
Moline IL 61265

Call Sign: N9OUX
Donald A Breivogel
1901 35 St
Moline IL 61265

Call Sign: KB9NTU
Victor S Hanger
1104 35 St Ct
Moline IL 61265

Call Sign: KB9NTS
David R Hanger
1104 35th St Ct
Moline IL 61265

Call Sign: KB9JVO
Betty J Scrogham
1514 36th Ave
Moline IL 61265

Call Sign: WC9M
Thomas N Laird
7101 36th Ave A Ct
Moline IL 61265

Call Sign: W9QI
Thomas N Laird
7101 36th Ave A Ct
Moline IL 61265

Call Sign: N9CRC
Judith A Laird
7101 36th Ave A Ct
Moline IL 61265

Call Sign: KB9SKQ
Jeff V Kircher
4110 36th Ave Apt 9
Moline IL 61265

Call Sign: WB9JWH
Richard L Hawotte
5902 36th Ave Ct
Moline IL 612656632

Call Sign: WB9UGQ
Robert E Gardner
1020 38th St
Moline IL 61265

Call Sign: N9RVE
George F Palmer
3117 38th St
Moline IL 61265

Call Sign: N9SQU
James S Larvenz
3306 38th St
Moline IL 61265

Call Sign: N9SQL
Carl L Larvenz
3306 38th St
Moline IL 61265

Call Sign: N9TFX
Phyllis J Larvenz
3306 38th St
Moline IL 61265

Call Sign: KC9GON
Charles M Leland
3520 38th St
Moline IL 61265

Call Sign: K9JI
Granville J Jordan Jr
2502 3rd St
Moline IL 61265

Call Sign: KB9SVN
Timothy J Harris
1301 3rd St A
Moline IL 61265

Call Sign: KB5WOM
Jeffrey M Wros
1019 41st St

Moline IL 61265

Call Sign: AA9GQ
Joseph E Palmer
2424 41st St Apt 137t
Moline IL 61265

Call Sign: N9KJD
James E Pauletti Jr
1815 43rd St
Moline IL 61265

Call Sign: W9QYD
Earl C Dennis
2129 43rd St
Moline IL 61265

Call Sign: KB0TKQ
Hilary A Sheets
3630 43rd St Apt 105
Moline IL 61265

Call Sign: N9SQJ
Robert F Lazenby
2615 44th St Ct
Moline IL 61265

Call Sign: KC9QPG
Jessie L Fiebig
2824 44th St Trlr 3
Moline IL 61265

Call Sign: KB9OEU
Matthew L Wainman
5025 45th Ave Ct
Moline IL 61265

Call Sign: KA9ISA
Daniel H Hanson
1818 46th St
Moline IL 61265

Call Sign: KC9UUJ
Weerawat Thesprayool
1831 46th St
Moline IL 61265

Call Sign: K9PUM
William H Matters

1825 47 St Ct
Moline IL 61265

Call Sign: K0OFY
Eugene E Bartosh
1914 47th St Ct
Moline IL 61265

Call Sign: W9PWM
Richard V Shrader
3411 50th St
Moline IL 61265

Call Sign: WB9WSQ
Ina J Morehouse
1213 53 St
Moline IL 61265

Call Sign: WB9HEU
Paul E Whitaker
1116 53rd
Moline IL 61265

Call Sign: KA9VCV
Kenneth L Gregory
2103 53rd St
Moline IL 61265

Call Sign: WB0TNO
Lee B Bughman
3010 53rd St
Moline IL 61265

Call Sign: KB9IMM
William O Serre
1809 54 St Ct
Moline IL 61265

Call Sign: W3CR
Charles E Ralph
3005 54th St
Moline IL 61265

Call Sign: K9CHZ
William M Coopman Jr
1711 55th St Pl
Moline IL 61265

Call Sign: KB9LOB

Stephen B Darling
1528 6th Ave
Moline IL 61265

Call Sign: K7VAJ
Bruce C Crosby
2011 6th Ave 6
Moline IL 61265

Call Sign: KB9BNR
Crystina K Mayfield
1821 7 St
Moline IL 61265

Call Sign: W0DEH
Donald E Henry
3709 72nd St Ct
Moline IL 61265

Call Sign: WB9FJR
Jesse P Gradel
3614 73rd St
Moline IL 612658021

Call Sign: KA9TWG
Randy L Erickson
2415 7th Ave
Moline IL 61265

Call Sign: WO9DX
James D Boddie Sr
1817 7th St
Moline IL 61265

Call Sign: KZ4DX
James D Boddie Sr
1817 7th St
Moline IL 61265

Call Sign: N9LZG
Cynthia K Mayfield
1821 7th St
Moline IL 61265

Call Sign: W9WRL
James D Mayfield
1821 7th St
Moline IL 61265

Call Sign: KB9BNR
James D Mayfield
2205 Barnard Ct
Moline IL 61265

Call Sign: N9WWD
Robert A Roden
3700 N Shore Dr
Moline IL 61265

Call Sign: N9FDM
Eric R Trimble
Moline IL 61265

FCC Amateur Radio Licenses in Momence

Call Sign: N9IIO
Kris L Mathers
Rt 3 Box 217
Momence IL 60954

Call Sign: N9SVP
Basu Basu
13643 E 2000 S Rd
Momence IL 60954

Call Sign: KC9SVO
Gene A Anderson
16081 E 5000 N Rd
Momence IL 60954

Call Sign: KC9MZL
Gerhardt F Schultz
12152 E Gregg Blvd
Momence IL 609543422

Call Sign: W9GFS
Gerhardt F Schultz
12152 E Gregg Blvd
Momence IL 609543422

Call Sign: N9WYR
Steven L Aicher
117 Elm St
Momence IL 60954

Call Sign: KC9ANJ
John W Martin

3146 N 17120 E Rd
Momence IL 60954

Call Sign: KO9L
Glenn A Morrison
3141 N 17120E Rd
Momence IL 609543060

Call Sign: NI9H
Peter Nikolic Jr
216 N Franklin St
Momence IL 60954

Call Sign: KB9JRD
Robert M Kondrot
219 N Locust
Momence IL 609541231

Call Sign: K9IFO
Willis E Bowser
1210 N Riverside Dr
Momence IL 60954

Call Sign: K9FO
Willis E Bowser
1210 N Riverside Dr
Momence IL 60954

Call Sign: W9AZ
Kankakee Area Radio Society
Inc
1210 N Riverside Dr
Momence IL 60954

Call Sign: N9LZD
Terry D Sharkey
203 S Gladiolus Ave
Momence IL 60954

Call Sign: KA9TZU
John M Sokol
Momence IL 60954

Call Sign: K9JMS
John M Sokol
Momence IL 60954

FCC Amateur Radio Licenses in Monica

Call Sign: AA9IG
Jon R Symmonds
14505 W Southern
Monica IL 61559

Call Sign: KF9RF
Valerie J Symmonds
14505 W Southern Ave
Monica IL 61559

FCC Amateur Radio Licenses in Monmouth

Call Sign: KC9SQO
James W Watson
618 200th Ave
Monmouth IL 61462

Call Sign: WA0YKL
Gary N Mallonee
1362 200th Ave
Monmouth IL 61462

Call Sign: N9BOH
David L Gillen
161 210th Ave
Monmouth IL 61462

Call Sign: W9XYZ
Gary G Kitchin
632 210th Ave
Monmouth IL 61462

Call Sign: KA9IMR
Terri L Kitchin
632 210th Ave
Monmouth IL 61462

Call Sign: KC9JUC
John A O'Daniel
2193 55th St
Monmouth IL 61462

Call Sign: N9ABB
Lawrence R Penn
723 E 1st Ave
Monmouth IL 614622303

Call Sign: KC9NMX
Charlotte E Young
1043 E 1st Ave
Monmouth IL 61462

Call Sign: KC9NMY
Rodney L Young
1043 E 1st Ave
Monmouth IL 61462

Call Sign: KC9OHO
Michael T Young
1043 E 1st Ave
Monmouth IL 61462

Call Sign: KC9JUF
Christopher G Fasano
718 E 2nd Ave
Monmouth IL 61462

Call Sign: KC9JUD
Patrick J Fasano
718 E 2nd Ave
Monmouth IL 61462

Call Sign: KC9OYM
Cedar Creek ARS
718 E 2nd Ave
Monmouth IL 61462

Call Sign: WB9TEU
Don R Josephson
1033 E Boston
Monmouth IL 61462

Call Sign: KC9MQJ
Douglas Hoelscher
402 E Euclid
Monmouth IL 61462

Call Sign: KB9FMC
Aaron T Winski
60 Lake Warren Dr
Monmouth IL 61462

Call Sign: N9WYY
Henry L Myers
221 N G St
Monmouth IL 61462

Call Sign: KD9ZE
John D Smallwood
87 N Side Sq
Monmouth IL 61462

Call Sign: KB9QWE
Todd Tinkham
933 S 2nd
Monmouth IL 61462

Call Sign: N9IVH
Patricia L Johnson
308 S 6th St
Monmouth IL 61462

Call Sign: KB9KSX
Stan V Presswood
501 S 7th
Monmouth IL 61462

Call Sign: KC0REY
Steven L Hays Sr
815 S 7th St
Monmouth IL 61462

Call Sign: N9GZS
Charles T Murphy
320 S C St
Monmouth IL 61462

Call Sign: W9SYF
Fred C Hoy
820 S Sunny Ln
Monmouth IL 61462

Call Sign: WQ9T
Richard S Clark
900 S Sunny Ln
Monmouth IL 61462

Call Sign: KA9EEM
Charles E Mc Geehon
2080 US Hwy 67
Monmouth IL 61462

Call Sign: N0VHK
Constance A Mc Geehon
2080 US Hwy 67 N

Monmouth IL 61462

Call Sign: KA9EEN
Constance A Mc Geehon
2080 US Hwy 67 N
Monmouth IL 61462

Call Sign: W9RJH
Robert N L Forman
Monmouth IL 61462

Call Sign: WD9IVS
David R Lefort
Monmouth IL 61462

FCC Amateur Radio Licenses in Monroe Center

Call Sign: KA9MHZ
Timothy J Weltzer
15731 Royster
Monroe Center IL 61052

Call Sign: WB9VLL
William J Mc Guire
Monroe Center IL 61052

FCC Amateur Radio Licenses in Monticello

Call Sign: N9TWR
Bonita K Amenda
701 Adams St
Monticello IL 61856

Call Sign: N9SKX
Jeffrey L Amenda
701 Adams St
Monticello IL 61856

Call Sign: KC9BSD
Ken Keller
3015 Appletree Dr
Monticello IL 61856

Call Sign: WA9AVN
Richard H Grant
2129 Bonnie Ln
Monticello IL 61856

Call Sign: W9RG
Richard H Grant
2129 Bonnie Ln
Monticello IL 61856

Call Sign: N9KEJ
Donna A Parkinson
Rr 1 Box 143A
Monticello IL 61856

Call Sign: N9IXQ
Harl R Parkinson
Rte 1 Box 143A
Monticello IL 61856

Call Sign: KC9BAF
Harry T Coleman
1094 Bucks Pond
Monticello IL 61856

Call Sign: K9AQQ
Harry T Coleman
1094 Bucks Pond
Monticello IL 61856

Call Sign: KC9CEK
Amelia J Coleman
1094 Bucks Pond Rd
Monticello IL 61856

Call Sign: K5AQQ
Amelia J Coleman
1094 Bucks Pond Rd
Monticello IL 61856

Call Sign: KA6A
James J Coleman
1094 Bucks Pond Rd
Monticello IL 61856

Call Sign: N9ESA
Teresa A Coleman
1094 Bucks Pond Rd
Monticello IL 61856

Call Sign: K9USA
Ivesdale Radio Club
1094 Bucks Pond Rd

Monticello IL 61856

Call Sign: W9SEH
Twin City ARC
1094 Bucks Pond Rd
Monticello IL 61856

Call Sign: KB9OXE
Michael W Donaldson
28 Coachman
Monticello IL 61856

Call Sign: K9IYP
Piatt County Radio Amateurs
774 County Farm Rd
Monticello IL 61856

Call Sign: KB9DMI
Katherine R Look
774 County Farm Rd
Monticello IL 618568232

Call Sign: KA9SZW
Stephen R Look
774 County Farm Rd
Monticello IL 618568232

Call Sign: KB9ZAM
Ubiquitous Radio Club
774 County Farm Rd
Monticello IL 618568232

Call Sign: KF9XI
William B Taylor
442 E 1300 N Rd
Monticello IL 61856

Call Sign: KC9HNC
James E Donaldson
807 E Center
Monticello IL 61856

Call Sign: KC9BAD
Andy T Chase
1402 E Center St
Monticello IL 61856

Call Sign: KA9LXL
Stanley E Dawson

317 E Lafayette
Monticello IL 61856

Call Sign: KB9WCG
Alan L Sprinkle
624 E Livingston
Monticello IL 61856

Call Sign: KC9VDJ
David P Marshall
829 E Old Rt 47
Monticello IL 61856

Call Sign: KA9YJT
Douglas D Uphoff
901 E Washington
Monticello IL 61856

Call Sign: AA9BQ
Lynn A Peterson
2000 E Washington Box 55
Monticello IL 61856

Call Sign: N9WGO
Robert E Jorgensen
5 Foothill Rd
Monticello IL 618561063

Call Sign: KC9BAB
Gregory K Crawford
14 Foothill Rd
Monticello IL 61856

Call Sign: K9CFH
Gregory K Crawford
14 Foothill Rd
Monticello IL 61856

Call Sign: KA9YPJ
Dorothy G Martin
907 Hillside Ct
Monticello IL 61856

Call Sign: KC9BAC
Robert W Rennels
702 Hillside Dr
Monticello IL 618562216

Call Sign: WA9QEO

David L Brown
800 Hillside Dr
Monticello IL 618562218

Call Sign: KB9ODF
Phillip T Dickinson
1167 Karen Dr
Monticello IL 61856

Call Sign: WB9TVD
Donald A Nay
907 Lincoln Dr
Monticello IL 61856

Call Sign: WA9SVZ
Kenneth R Bauman
708 Madison St
Monticello IL 61856

Call Sign: KC9GIE
Thomas A Gardner
402 Maple Ln
Monticello IL 61856

Call Sign: N3FPG
Thomas M Gordon
1513 N 1000 E Rd
Monticello IL 61856

Call Sign: KA9NQE
Michael D Wileaver
1517 N 1000 E Rd
Monticello IL 61856

Call Sign: N9GQL
Roy J Kleven
1317 N 300 E Rd
Monticello IL 61856

Call Sign: AB4XY
Michael W Mullvain Jr
850 N Front St
Monticello IL 61856

Call Sign: WB9HYQ
Samuel R Strawn
1101 N Union Dr
Monticello IL 61856

Call Sign: KC9PCQ
Melea J Fombelle
1104 N Union Dr
Monticello IL 61856

Call Sign: KC9BAE
Harry D Munster
1934N Old Rt 47
Monticello IL 61856

Call Sign: W9HDM
Harry D Munster
1934N Old Rt 47
Monticello IL 61856

Call Sign: K9HY
Stephen S Karnes
4014 Orchard Ln
Monticello IL 61856

Call Sign: KC9CWK
Carlos T Miranda
1007 Park Dr
Monticello IL 61856

Call Sign: KC9CWJ
Eda S Flores-Miranda
1007 Park Dr
Monticello IL 61856

Call Sign: KB9WGF
Stanley R Eades
1009 Poplar Ln
Monticello IL 61856

Call Sign: WA9JHE
Leland D Riggins
601 Robert Webb
Monticello IL 61856

Call Sign: N9RTF
Kevin P Osborne
507 S Chaucer Blvd
Monticello IL 61856

Call Sign: WA9IVM
Kevin P Osborne
507 S Chaucer Blvd
Monticello IL 61856

Call Sign: WD9EED
Donald J Sprinkle
519 S Hamilton
Monticello IL 61856

Call Sign: KB9EAW
Wilma J Castang Ms
101 Surrey Ct Apt 8
Monticello IL 61856

Call Sign: KA0TRW
Steven J Sparenberg
11 Turtle Creek
Monticello IL 61856

Call Sign: K9GWT
George W Henry Jr
3 Turtle Creek Rd
Monticello IL 61856

Call Sign: WA9JBI
Harry R Gale
621 W Blaine
Monticello IL 61856

Call Sign: KA9NNH
Bruce A Hammerschmidt
318 W Bond St
Monticello IL 61856

Call Sign: KC9AHL
Charles E Kammin
707 B W Marion
Monticello IL 61856

Call Sign: AB9PT
William D Kirkland
6 Walnut Point Ct
Monticello IL 61856

Call Sign: AB9WK
William D Kirkland
6 Walnut Point Ct
Monticello IL 61856

Call Sign: KB9WGI
Frederick W Seibold
Monticello IL 61856

Call Sign: N9XDL
Anthony J Stuckey
Rr 1 Box 153
Montrose IL 62445

Call Sign: KC9JIR
Calvin E Hamann
6296 E 1800th Ave
Montrose IL 62445

Call Sign: KC9DHU
Brad J Horton
1523 E 2160th Ave
Montrose IL 62445

Call Sign: KC9DHV
Franklin L Fearington
3364 E 2160th Ave
Montrose IL 62445

Call Sign: KC9DHW
James P Burgess
3364 E 2160th Ave
Montrose IL 62445

Call Sign: WA9HLC
Robert D Harris
328 S Spring Creek Rd
Montrose IL 62445

**FCC Amateur Radio
Licenses in Moro**

Call Sign: WD9GVB
Don S Arnold
120 Dee St
Moro IL 62067

Call Sign: KB9MON
Ross C Crowson Sr
110 Fairway Dr
Moro IL 62067

Call Sign: KC9HNQ
Brian C Stacks

22 Hickory Point
Moro IL 62067

Call Sign: KB9QHK
Andrew M Bruza
5909 Moro Rd
Moro IL 62067

Call Sign: KB9QHI
Homer L Smith
5933 Moro Rd
Moro IL 62067

Call Sign: KA9VKC
Nolan R Zobrist
6952 N Rt 159
Moro IL 62067

Call Sign: WA9VCE
Robert H Pape
6820 N SR 159
Moro IL 62067

Call Sign: N9YHL
Brian M Pape
6820 N SR 159
Moro IL 620671616

Call Sign: KA9LXF
Raymond L Hunt Jr
7576 N SR 159
Moro IL 620671408

Call Sign: KA9IXB
Bonnie C Hutchison
6873 West Dr
Moro IL 62067

Call Sign: KA9IXA
Danny R Hutchison
6873 West Dr
Moro IL 62067

Call Sign: N5INX
Sherman L Burwell Jr
104 Westwood Dr
Moro IL 620671024

Call Sign: KB9RTF

R Neil Adams Jr
Moro IL 620670257

**FCC Amateur Radio
Licenses in Morris**

Call Sign: KC9QXH
Richard J Allen
1275 Alicia Dr
Morris IL 60450

Call Sign: KC9GCK
Christopher R Kindelspire
428 Armstrong St
Morris IL 60450

Call Sign: WB9HUR
Horace J Helgeson
929 Armstrong St
Morris IL 60450

Call Sign: N9AWI
Robert G Wren
5675 Barrington Rd
Morris IL 60450

Call Sign: KB9NPF
Thomas A Wilkinson
5730 Barrington Rd
Morris IL 60450

Call Sign: KA9FIY
James J Vejr
3580 Beth Dr
Morris IL 60450

Call Sign: WD9AZN
Richard L Leach
1814 Charles St
Morris IL 60450

Call Sign: KC9TWR
Michael D Harrill
118 Crabapple Ln
Morris IL 60450

Call Sign: KB9KTM
Aaron S Heck
862 Douglas

Morris IL 60450

Call Sign: KB9RJQ
Erik Garriott
604 Douglas St
Morris IL 60450

Call Sign: KB9ZWH
Robert W Cockream
829 Douglas St
Morris IL 60450

Call Sign: AB9EE
Robert W Cockream
829 Douglas St
Morris IL 60450

Call Sign: WA9YNS
Gordon K Vaksdal
1016 Dupont Ave
Morris IL 604501264

Call Sign: KB9LST
Darlene A Orsini
1305 E Alicia Dr
Morris IL 604508902

Call Sign: KG9EI
Joseph F Orsini
1305 E Alicia Dr
Morris IL 604508902

Call Sign: WB9JPP
Wilfred K Robinson
2617 E Holderman Rd
Morris IL 60450

Call Sign: W9AKM
Robert W White
603 E Jefferson
Morris IL 60450

Call Sign: KC9STD
Selena M Visser
624 E Jefferson St
Morris IL 60450

Call Sign: N9TJX
Jonathan S Visser

624 E Jefferson St
Morris IL 60450

Call Sign: KB9ZL
Rita Burba
731 E North St
Morris IL 60450

Call Sign: N9WNM
Wayne J Oleson
5945 E Peart Rd
Morris IL 60450

Call Sign: KC9CUG
Charles E Roseland
603 E Washington St
Morris IL 60450

Call Sign: AB9HJ
Charles E Roseland
603 E Washington St
Morris IL 60450

Call Sign: KC9JYZ
Thomas J Schroeder
804 E Washington St
Morris IL 60450

Call Sign: WD9FFZ
Roger W Breitwieser
165 Jacqueline St
Morris IL 60450

Call Sign: KC9DNQ
William D Morris
6435 Junebug Ln
Morris IL 60450

Call Sign: KC9LZL
Brandon T Kindelspire
613 Lake Shore Ct
Morris IL 60450

Call Sign: K9ILX
Bruce W Blanchard
909 Lakewood Dr
Morris IL 60450

Call Sign: KC9ENE

Daniel L Lyon
1621 Lisbon Rd
Morris IL 60450

Call Sign: KC9CQL
Donald L Lyon
1621 Lisbon Rd
Morris IL 60450

Call Sign: N9XSZ
Joseph A Barracca
7495 Lisbon Rd
Morris IL 60450

Call Sign: WB9BYV
Gerald J Le Vault Sr
2330 Lynwood St
Morris IL 60450

Call Sign: W9NWQ
Richard J Meadows
3630 N Beth Dr
Morris IL 60450

Call Sign: W9ILY
John R Holmes
3810 N Chamlin Dr
Morris IL 60450

Call Sign: W9TY
Metro Dx Club
3810 N Chamlin Dr
Morris IL 60450

Call Sign: W9JI
Arthur W Hacker
3515 N Jugtown Rd
Morris IL 60450

Call Sign: KB9MLK
William N Rakes
6050 N Nettle School Rd
Morris IL 60450

Call Sign: KB9FTF
Charles D Skelton
3780 N Prairie Ln
Morris IL 60450

Call Sign: WB9LPW
William M Capper
3865 N Prairie Ln
Morris IL 60450

Call Sign: KC9SFH
Jeffrey D Jackson
732 Old Stage Rd
Morris IL 604501669

Call Sign: W9LVT
Jeffrey D Jackson
732 Old Stage Rd
Morris IL 604501669

Call Sign: WB9JMK
Francis A Donnelly
221 Ottawa Bend Dr 104C
Morris IL 60450

Call Sign: KC9JZL
Robert L Houlne
2345 Parklake Dr
Morris IL 60450

Call Sign: KC9EQH
Phillip T Orr
1721 Parklake Dr 1 B
Morris IL 60450

Call Sign: K9NYX
Phillip T Orr
1721 Parklake Dr 1 B
Morris IL 60450

Call Sign: KC9VRO
Michael C Moss
1026 Partridge Ln
Morris IL 60450

Call Sign: W4OBF
Charles R Gibbs
5735 Peart Rd
Morris IL 60450

Call Sign: W9HDB
Charles R Gibbs
5735 Peart Rd
Morris IL 60450

Call Sign: N9XBT
Mary E Oleson
5945 Peart Rd
Morris IL 60450

Call Sign: AA9FT
Gilbert G Jones
3755 Primrose Ln
Morris IL 60450

Call Sign: N9USH
Paul M Barajas
105 Redbud Ln
Morris IL 60450

Call Sign: KB9FOC
Beth I Brooks
217 Robinson Dr
Morris IL 60450

Call Sign: N9KIZ
Steven Y Brooks
217 Robinson Dr
Morris IL 60450

Call Sign: N9USL
Linda F Barajas
105 Rosebud Ln
Morris IL 604501632

Call Sign: WB9YWW
Robert Wojtas
5375 Sand Ridge
Morris IL 60450

Call Sign: KB9VXP
Jessica R Leffelman
5375 Sand Ridge Rd
Morris IL 60450

Call Sign: KC9MKN
Raymond E Hemmersbach
1240 Susan Cir
Morris IL 60450

Call Sign: KB8JYS
Joseph O Pavich
2500 Sycamore Dr 106

Morris IL 60450

Call Sign: KB9SZK
Grundy County ARC
1320 Union St Rm E 01
Morris IL 60450

Call Sign: AC9X
Robert W Malmquist
605 Vine St
Morris IL 60450

Call Sign: N9MMA
Steve M Marvick Sr
1703 W Anne Ln
Morris IL 60450

Call Sign: KA9SBW
Carmelo C Ruiz Sr
725 W Jackson St
Morris IL 60450

Call Sign: WA9QAR
James V Leonard
410 W Southmor Rd
Morris IL 60450

Call Sign: KB9TKM
Wanda G Steele
515 W Washington St
Morris IL 60450

Call Sign: N0NNA
Wanda G Steele
515 W Washington St
Morris IL 60450

Call Sign: KE9SZ
William L Steele
515 W Washington St
Morris IL 60450

Call Sign: KB9GX
William L Steele
515 W Washington St
Morris IL 60450

Call Sign: KX9A
William L Steele

515 W Washington St
Morris IL 60450

Call Sign: KC9RKX
Steven L Gorham
3385 W Wauponsee Rd
Morris IL 604508141

Call Sign: KC9KKO
John P Watters
108 Woodland Rd
Morris IL 60450

Call Sign: KC9UEI
Charles H Mathews IV
Morris IL 60450

Call Sign: W9LGB
Van L Hicks
Morris IL 60450

FCC Amateur Radio
Licenses in Morrison

Call Sign: KD9YK
John R Cooley
15750 Bishop Rd
Morrison IL 61270

Call Sign: KA9GNZ
Edna I Reynolds
514 Christopher
Morrison IL 61270

Call Sign: K9TCC
William C Rice Sr
17870 Clove Rd Rr 4
Morrison IL 61270

Call Sign: N9SQI
Victor L Roggendorf
23581 Crosby Rd
Morrison IL 61270

Call Sign: W9ALW
Robert L Van Osdol Sr
401 E Main St
Morrison IL 61270

Call Sign: N9SRE
Aaron L Johnson
107 E Park
Morrison IL 61270

Call Sign: N9SRD
Judith K Johnson
107 E Park
Morrison IL 61270

Call Sign: KA9ULJ
Elmer L Schipper
19645 Fellows Rd
Morrison IL 61270

Call Sign: KB9MOU
Gary L Fritz
21226 Fulfs Rd
Morrison IL 61270

Call Sign: KC9FMQ
Christopher A Nye
15831 Hazel Rd
Morrison IL 61270

Call Sign: K9STP
Albert R Turner
14879 Henry Rd
Morrison IL 61270

Call Sign: N9FQX
Ronald O Williams
1008 Hilltop Dr
Morrison IL 61270

Call Sign: KC9OTT
Elizabeth A Myers
18025 Holly Rd
Morrison IL 61270

Call Sign: KC9OTX
Terry L Myers
18025 Holly Rd
Morrison IL 61270

Call Sign: KA9QYR
Nancy L Shank
14245 Lister Rd
Morrison IL 61270

Call Sign: KA9QYS
Ronald K Shank
14245 Lister Rd
Morrison IL 61270

Call Sign: KC9KBV
Leland L Waters
12347 Loron Rd
Morrison IL 61270

Call Sign: K9IJP
George O James
17440 Malvern Rd
Morrison IL 61270

Call Sign: W9OVQ
John G Stoudt
504 Maple Ave
Morrison IL 612702938

Call Sign: N9EXI
David F Hanson
12880 Masters Dr
Morrison IL 61270

Call Sign: KA9WUS
Arthur N Dykema
442 N Jackson St
Morrison IL 61270

Call Sign: WA9ZHP
Roger F Huisman
12197 Nelson Rd
Morrison IL 61270

Call Sign: WB9UAZ
Yvonne C Huisman
12197 Nelson Rd
Morrison IL 61270

Call Sign: WB9PAC
George D Berridge
15344 Norrish Rd
Morrison IL 61270

Call Sign: W9PAC
George D Berridge
15344 Norrish Rd

Morrison IL 61270

Call Sign: N9SQH
Mervin P Fitzwater
11360 Prairie Center Rd
Morrison IL 61270

Call Sign: KA9ULT
Phillip E Benson
205 S Grape St
Morrison IL 61270

Call Sign: KB9CZC
Doug Seelye
205 S Heaton
Morrison IL 61270

Call Sign: N9OOG
Marion T Petersen
504 S Jackson St
Morrison IL 61270

Call Sign: KA9ULL
Renee R Temple
605 S Jackson St
Morrison IL 61270

Call Sign: KA9ULK
Scott D Temple
605 S Jackson St
Morrison IL 61270

Call Sign: KC9IXD
August F Ufkin
1355 S Treva Dr
Morrison IL 61270

Call Sign: N9XBK
Bruce E Unger Jr
13901 Sawyer Rd
Morrison IL 61270

Call Sign: KD9WM
Michael Knapp
21208 Smit Rd
Morrison IL 61270

Call Sign: KC9IXG
Lisa K Boles

13231 W Covell Rd
Morrison IL 61270

Call Sign: KC9HFD
Mitchell L Boles
13231 W Covell Rd
Morrison IL 61270

Call Sign: N9XBI
Robert M Fulton
503 W Lincoln Way
Morrison IL 61270

Call Sign: W9CIW
Donald S Fulton
503 W Lincolnway
Morrison IL 61270

Call Sign: KC9FMF
Jeffrey L Bramm
204 W Morris St
Morrison IL 61270

Call Sign: KB9JJU
Terry J Vogel
20690 White Oaks Rd
Morrison IL 61270

Call Sign: K9TER
Terry J Vogel
20690 White Oaks Rd
Morrison IL 61270

FCC Amateur Radio Licenses in Morrisonville

Call Sign: KA9TGE
Paul B Pomeroy
300 Dey St
Morrisonville IL 62546

Call Sign: KA9TGD
Wayne B Mitchell
700 W North St
Morrisonville IL 62546

Call Sign: KG9FI
Kevin L King
207 Wyandotte St

Morrisonville IL 62546

Call Sign: KA9TEM
H B Wolf
Morrisonville IL 62546

Call Sign: KA9TEL
I K Wolf
Morrisonville IL 62546

FCC Amateur Radio Licenses in Morton

Call Sign: WB4MOR
Gary S Nace
1212 Autumn Ridge Ct
Morton IL 61550

Call Sign: KA9TWS
Larry S De Long
105 Beverly Ave
Morton IL 61550

Call Sign: KB9CPF
Paul B Choberka
1200 Brentwood St
Morton IL 61550

Call Sign: K9UJN
Ronald F Bieber Sr
108 Buckeye Dr
Morton IL 61550

Call Sign: WA9ENC
Marvin C Hoyt
19722 Chaffer Rd
Morton IL 615509434

Call Sign: WD9DRU
Donald L Moore
310 Circle Dr
Morton IL 61550

Call Sign: KC9ERN
David W Johnson
1852 Copperfield Dr
Morton IL 61550

Call Sign: W9DWJ

David W Johnson
1852 Copperfield Dr
Morton IL 61550

Call Sign: KB9OSW
Eric J Zimmerman
215 Delwood
Morton IL 61550

Call Sign: W9ZF
Robert L Bundy
239 Delwood
Morton IL 61550

Call Sign: WA9JVT
Ronald J Strelecky
109 Dietrich Ct
Morton IL 615502101

Call Sign: N9HRG
Rudy S Mason
113 Durant Mayfair Adn
Morton IL 61550

Call Sign: KC9QNR
Abigail K Marten
401 E Delwood St
Morton IL 61550

Call Sign: KC9QCQ
Anna A Marten
401 E Delwood St
Morton IL 61550

Call Sign: KC9SPY
Katie Marten
401 E Delwood St
Morton IL 61550

Call Sign: W9FSW
Claire H Brooner
440 E Delwood St
Morton IL 61550

Call Sign: N9YOQ
John A Olson
809 E Dunne
Morton IL 61550

Call Sign: N9VDC
Eric P Musselman
815 E Dunne St
Morton IL 61550

Call Sign: K9YCD
Edward H Simanek
318 E Forestwood
Morton IL 61550

Call Sign: WD9EGU
Philip D Farwell
331 E Forestwood
Morton IL 61550

Call Sign: KC9GRQ
Steven O Hart
386 E Forestwood St
Morton IL 615502544

Call Sign: W9JRO
Joseph R Oyer
349 E Greenwood St
Morton IL 61550

Call Sign: KB9YPM
Lawrence G Leary II
120 E Hazelwood St
Morton IL 61550

Call Sign: AB9DJ
Lawrence G Leary II
120 E Hazelwood St
Morton IL 61550

Call Sign: K9QPU
Theodore L Stahler
143 E Idlewood
Morton IL 61550

Call Sign: KC9KUO
Billy R Ousley
160 E Idlewood
Morton IL 61550

Call Sign: N9USO
Bruce G Howell
396 E Idlewood St
Morton IL 615503102

Call Sign: KC9LVF
Michael D Edie
609 E Jackson St
Morton IL 61550

Call Sign: AA9WO
Daniel R Petersen
1325 E Jefferson Box 444
Morton IL 61550

Call Sign: KB9TFM
David S Petersen
1325 E Jefferson Box 444
Morton IL 61550

Call Sign: KB9TFP
Joy R Petersen
1325 E Jefferson Box 444
Morton IL 61550

Call Sign: KB9TFN
Kathy M Petersen
1325 E Jefferson Box 444
Morton IL 61550

Call Sign: KB9TFO
Nathaniel R Petersen
1325 E Jefferson Box 444
Morton IL 61550

Call Sign: KA9RKQ
Raymond F Funk
924 E Kay
Morton IL 615502250

Call Sign: N9WFU
Paul J Hoehne
132 E Lakewood
Morton IL 61550

Call Sign: KC9HES
Calvin J Stidman Jr
201 E Lakewood
Morton IL 61550

Call Sign: KB9SEP
Nick J Sherrill
922 E Madison St

Morton IL 61550

Call Sign: N9ILP
William E Little
120 E Queenwood Rd D3
Morton IL 61550

Call Sign: KA9VFK
Paul D Arnett
102 Elm
Morton IL 61550

Call Sign: N9TWM
Joseph P Leibold
110 Elm St
Morton IL 61550

Call Sign: N9VNN
Denise J Galesky
751 Fillmore St
Morton IL 61550

Call Sign: K9OOW
Robert L Albright
41 Forest View Ave
Morton IL 61550

Call Sign: N9CCF
Nadiene D Backlund
633 Glen
Morton IL 61550

Call Sign: N9GCV
Deborah J Cusey
345 Glen St
Morton IL 61550

Call Sign: K9QZ
James E Cusey
345 Glen St
Morton IL 61550

Call Sign: W9OI
Clifford L Shoemaker
45 Grey Wolf Ct
Morton IL 615507800

Call Sign: KA4DEB
Deb J Suhs

108 Hampton Way
Morton IL 61550

Call Sign: W9WGN
Mark E Suhs
108 Hampton Way
Morton IL 61550

Call Sign: WA9WYC
Richard R Burritt
53 Hyde Park Dr
Morton IL 61550

Call Sign: N9ZBC
Maxine J Lalock
143 Jadewood
Morton IL 61550

Call Sign: KB9GSQ
Richard A Crandell
1025 Johnson
Morton IL 61550

Call Sign: KC9VEX
Robert C Brunke
34 Maple Ridge Dr
Morton IL 61550

Call Sign: KC9CZI
Russell L Bensel
122 Mulberry
Morton IL 61550

Call Sign: KA9RAD
Beno E Echerd
101 Mulberry Dr
Morton IL 61550

Call Sign: KB9RHX
Ruth M Echerd
101 Mulberry Dr
Morton IL 61550

Call Sign: KC9FWO
Carol L Bensel
122 Mullberry
Morton IL 61550

Call Sign: KC9PUL

Lisa C Schock
309 N 3rd Ave
Morton IL 61550

Call Sign: N9JOZ
William A Schock
309 N 3rd Ave
Morton IL 61550

Call Sign: KC9IGQ
Jeffrey A Teel
428 N 3rd Ave
Morton IL 61550

Call Sign: W1HTA
Michael D Wesner
640 N 3rd Ave
Morton IL 61550

Call Sign: KC9RHI
Crystal A Speed
119 N 4th Ave
Morton IL 61550

Call Sign: N9TYF
William D Mitchell
213 N 4th St
Morton IL 61550

Call Sign: KB9OIG
Jason A Smith
462 N Bauman
Morton IL 61550

Call Sign: KB9YDO
Peter C Ackerman
308 N Illinois
Morton IL 61550

Call Sign: KB9BMK
John E Pryor
304 N Illinois St
Morton IL 61550

Call Sign: WB9CIS
John J Harper
413 N Indiana Ave
Morton IL 61550

Call Sign: W9EEB
Morton Radio Club
413 N Indiana Ave
Morton IL 61550

Call Sign: KC9UCO
Jeffrey B Ogden
212 N Louisiana Ave
Morton IL 61550

Call Sign: KC9UCP
Lisa R Ogden
212 N Louisiana Ave
Morton IL 61550

Call Sign: KC9UCN
Stuart R Ogden
212 N Louisiana Ave
Morton IL 61550

Call Sign: N9JRK
Craig D Garber
509 N Main St
Morton IL 61550

Call Sign: KC9GMS
Craig D Garber
509 N Main St
Morton IL 61550

Call Sign: KC9GMT
Jacob A Garber
509 N Main St
Morton IL 61550

Call Sign: KC9FWQ
William J Delameter
514 N Main St
Morton IL 61550

Call Sign: N9JPA
Robert A Gorrie
142 N Maple Ave
Morton IL 61550

Call Sign: AB9BY
Robert A Gorrie
142 N Maple Ave
Morton IL 61550

Call Sign: N9JPC
Tony F Gorrie
142 N Maple Ave
Morton IL 61550

Call Sign: KC9CDI
Drew D Bazil
300 N Missouri
Morton IL 61550

Call Sign: KC9CDH
Connie Bazil
300 N Missouri Ave
Morton IL 61550

Call Sign: KB9ECM
Gail V Hodel
522 N Ohio Ct
Morton IL 61550

Call Sign: N9ZZL
Marvin A Hodel
522 N Ohio Ct
Morton IL 61550

Call Sign: KB9GES
Timothy J Hodel
522 N Ohio Ct
Morton IL 61550

Call Sign: N9ZQV
Benjamin J Hodel
522 N Ohio St
Morton IL 61550

Call Sign: KA9RYV
Stig T Ruxlow
736 N Oregon Ave
Morton IL 61550

Call Sign: KB9THI
William C Mount
117 Northshore Dr
Morton IL 61550

Call Sign: KC9EE
Gary L Hunt
22304 Oak Ln

Morton IL 61550

Call Sign: KB9KBF
Andrew D Canopy
103 Oak St
Morton IL 61550

Call Sign: AC4YM
Maria T Wefer
22202 Oaklane
Morton IL 61550

Call Sign: W9BDN
Stephen G Conrad
22382 Oaklane
Morton IL 61550

Call Sign: KA9EQE
Larry D Lelm
29290 Queenwood Rd
Morton IL 61550

Call Sign: N9PVB
Terry E Wiseman
29654 Queenwood Rd
Morton IL 61550

Call Sign: W9AO
Elton E Heubach
1015 S 1st
Morton IL 61550

Call Sign: W9KIR
Lowell I Schroeder
1318 S 2nd St
Morton IL 61550

Call Sign: WX9TVS
Mark W Sefried
500 S 4th Ave Apt B10
Morton IL 61550

Call Sign: N9EYR
David P Jones
765 S Columbus
Morton IL 61550

Call Sign: KV9A
Robert R Backlund

633 S Glen Ave
Morton IL 615502411

Call Sign: N9TRT
Matthew R Miller
1240 S Main St Apt 121G
Morton IL 61511

Call Sign: WB9VAP
Michael D Lucas
300 S Minnesota
Morton IL 61550

Call Sign: WD9EEO
Bernard E Pierceall
115 S Mississippi
Morton IL 61550

Call Sign: N8TA
John L Mori
112 S Mississippi Ave
Morton IL 61550

Call Sign: KC9GYS
Oval D Stephens
364 S Mississippi Ave
Morton IL 61550

Call Sign: KA9CEL
Lindsey R Block
133 S Nebraska
Morton IL 61550

Call Sign: WA9RNE
Wallace F Strow Jr
412 S Nebraska Ave
Morton IL 615502748

Call Sign: KC9TAK
Turner A Holcombe
27 Sapphire Pt
Morton IL 61550

Call Sign: KB9HML
Anthony W Mohns
21989 Springer Ct
Morton IL 61550

Call Sign: K9MFI

Stanley B Pope
216 Sycamore
Morton IL 61550

Call Sign: KA9RAF
Matthew D Brown
21 Tamarack Ct
Morton IL 61550

Call Sign: W9KBK
Gerald R Custer
530 Taylor
Morton IL 61550

Call Sign: N9TYE
Curtis D Wesner
558 Taylor
Morton IL 61550

Call Sign: KA9SXL
Anna M Wesner
658 Taylor St
Morton IL 615501764

Call Sign: KA9QNS
Merle D Fairley
557 Taylorn St
Morton IL 615501763

Call Sign: W9FSW
Michael L Volle
122 Tuscany Ct
Morton IL 61550

Call Sign: N9SJX
Michael L Volle
122 Tuscany Ct
Morton IL 61550

Call Sign: KB9GLT
Raymond J Kolesar
128 W Adams St
Morton IL 61550

Call Sign: KC9BGT
Jim M Brasfield
605 W Jefferson
Morton IL 61550

Call Sign: W9RGH
Russell M Planck
730 W Jefferson St Apt 50
Morton IL 61550

Call Sign: KB9GSU
Tony D Phan
219 W Wagler
Morton IL 61550

Call Sign: KB9VVN
Brian E Thames
315 White Oak Dr
Morton IL 61550

Call Sign: W9VJN
Clifford E Schick
407 White Oak Dr
Morton IL 615501248

Call Sign: N9WIA
Lucas E Huber
Morton IL 61550

Call Sign: K9WLE
Donald E Litwiller
Morton IL 61550

**FCC Amateur Radio
Licenses in Mossville**

Call Sign: KC9MK
Eugene A Krause
10701 Moss St
Mossville IL 61552

Call Sign: W9UAW
Darwin G Winter
Mossville IL 61552

Call Sign: WA9W
Darwin G Winter
Mossville IL 61552

Call Sign: KC9PQV
John G Offutt
Mossville IL 61552

Call Sign: KB9YYC

Lisa K Offutt
Mossville IL 61552

Call Sign: KC9QFA
Taylor A Layton
Mossville IL 61552

Call Sign: KC9PZP
William T Offutt
Mossville IL 61552

Call Sign: KB9YYD
Peter W Offutt
Mossville IL 615520222

FCC Amateur Radio Licenses in Mounds

Call Sign: N9XWQ
Alan W Moreland
Rt 1 Box 1600
Mounds IL 62964

Call Sign: N9XDY
Harry L Moreland
2705 Lufkin Rd
Mounds IL 62964

Call Sign: KB9CMZ
Stephen D Hayes
324 N Oak
Mounds IL 62964

Call Sign: N9LEC
James A Flummer
202 N Spencer
Mounds IL 629640007

Call Sign: KB9CNA
Larry E King Jr
702 S Reader
Mounds IL 62964

Call Sign: K9IM
904 ARC Inc
Mounds IL 62964

FCC Amateur Radio Licenses in Mount Carmel

Call Sign: N9UQJ
Ray C Parker
519 Ash St
Mount Carmel IL 62863

Call Sign: KC9PWQ
Ray C Parker
519 Ash St
Mount Carmel IL 62863

Call Sign: AB9UO
Ray C Parker
519 Ash St
Mount Carmel IL 62863

Call Sign: W9LB
Larry G Benham
917 Bainum St
Mount Carmel IL 62863

Call Sign: WA9TJE
Eugene P Collins
1202 Bainum St
Mount Carmel IL 62863

Call Sign: N9WFP
John M Beauchamp
823 Boradmoor Dr
Mount Carmel IL 62863

Call Sign: KB9KKE
Marc G Hudson
Rt 1 Box 163
Mount Carmel IL 62863

Call Sign: N9XLQ
Timothy L Beauchamp
Rr 3 Box 218B
Mount Carmel IL 62863

Call Sign: N9RIP
George F Beckerman
Rr 2 Box 248
Mount Carmel IL 62863

Call Sign: KB9AJJ
Michael L Etheridge
126 Cherry Hill Dr

Mount Carmel IL 62863

Call Sign: KB9LOV
William W Wood
318 Cherry Hills Dr
Mount Carmel IL 62863

Call Sign: KB9RXY
Wabash Valley College
Electronics Club
2200 College Dr
Mount Carmel IL 62863

Call Sign: KC9OCJ
Philip A Coleman
102 Deeridge Crossing
Mount Carmel IL 62863

Call Sign: WD9BGX
Marion E Glenn
20805 E 1000 Rd
Mount Carmel IL 62863

Call Sign: KC9TKI
Kendall C Cunningham
11582 E 1020 Ln
Mount Carmel IL 62863

Call Sign: KC9CIW
Brad J Winter
18361 E 1200 Rd
Mount Carmel IL 62863

Call Sign: KC9CVK
Eunice S Carwile
17842 E 1220 Rd
Mount Carmel IL 62863

Call Sign: KC9BGE
Harvey J Calvin
12200 E 500 Rd
Mount Carmel IL 62863

Call Sign: KC9FIE
William D Calvin
12200 E 500 Rd
Mount Carmel IL 62863

Call Sign: N9LGN

Barry M Roberts
430 E 8th St
Mount Carmel IL 62863

Call Sign: KB9GKK
Francis E Richards
431.5 E 8th St
Mount Carmel IL 62863

Call Sign: N9ZPU
William C Mc Gillem
411 E 9th
Mount Carmel IL 62863

Call Sign: KB9FI
William R Mc Gillem
411 E 9th
Mount Carmel IL 62863

Call Sign: N9WCC
Robert L Carwile Jr
427 E 9th St
Mount Carmel IL 62863

Call Sign: KC9SNT
Beverley A Eckiss
208 Forio Ave
Mount Carmel IL 62863

Call Sign: KC9OCK
Richard R Eckiss
208 Forio Ave
Mount Carmel IL 62863

Call Sign: KF9W
Kenneth F Wood
110 Froman Dr
Mount Carmel IL 62863

Call Sign: KB9IVO
Renee Wood
110 Froman Dr
Mount Carmel IL 62863

Call Sign: WO0DE
Thick Of The Wood ARC
110 Froman Dr
Mount Carmel IL 62863

Call Sign: KB9QYE
Thick Of The Wood ARC
110 Froman Dr
Mount Carmel IL 62863

Call Sign: KC9LJE
Charles J Sundstrom
116 Froman Dr
Mount Carmel IL 62863

Call Sign: N9CJS
Charles J Sundstrom
116 Froman Dr
Mount Carmel IL 62863

Call Sign: KB9PQT
Donald F Meier
37 Lambert Dr
Mount Carmel IL 62863

Call Sign: KB9KKD
Larry R Worlow
1114 Landes St
Mount Carmel IL 62863

Call Sign: KC9MDG
Larry R Worlow
1114 Landes St
Mount Carmel IL 62863

Call Sign: K9LRW
Larry R Worlow
1114 Landes St
Mount Carmel IL 62863

Call Sign: KC9PLB
Andrew T Bailey
1202 Landes St
Mount Carmel IL 62863

Call Sign: WA9THM
Linda S Effland
1422 Lisa Ln
Mount Carmel IL 628631829

Call Sign: AI9H
Robert E Effland
1422 Lisa Ln
Mount Carmel IL 628631829

Call Sign: W9GH
Radio Amateur Downstate Ill
Orgn
1422 Lisa Ln
Mount Carmel IL 628631829

Call Sign: KC9HVS
Betty J Effland
1422 Lisa Ln
Mount Carmel IL 62863

Call Sign: K9BJE
Betty J Effland
1422 Lisa Ln
Mount Carmel IL 62863

Call Sign: KC9MAK
Wabash County Emergency
Management Agency
930.5 Market St
Mount Carmel IL 62863

Call Sign: N9PIU
Kenneth W Terry
1210 Market St
Mount Carmel IL 62863

Call Sign: N9TKJ
Timothy W Luker
722 Mulberry
Mount Carmel IL 62863

Call Sign: KB9SJ
Glen W Luker
722 Mulberry St
Mount Carmel IL 62863

Call Sign: N9XEI
Rigoberto A Caceres
1131 Mulberry St
Mount Carmel IL 62863

Call Sign: W9JDC
Dennis B Alka
6861 N 1220 Blvd
Mount Carmel IL 62863

Call Sign: WA9MEO

Linda S Kolb
10394 N 1400 Blvd
Mount Carmel IL 62863

Call Sign: KB9VPS
Sharon A Majors
8174 N 1600 Blvd
Mount Carmel IL 62863

Call Sign: KB9KHB
Charles W Skidmore
4424 N 1850 Blvd
Mount Carmel IL 62863

Call Sign: KE6KMM
Randy W Bender
8464 N 880 Ln
Mount Carmel IL 62863

Call Sign: KC9CBP
Clayton P Merrick
1318 N Cherry
Mount Carmel IL 62863

Call Sign: K4HHN
James E Neigh
822 N Cherry St
Mount Carmel IL 62863

Call Sign: KC9ICX
Matthew E Carroll
1226 N Cherry St
Mount Carmel IL 62863

Call Sign: KC9OLE
Jeffrey D Titzer
7599 N Mesa Lake Dr
Mount Carmel IL 62863

Call Sign: KA9EUY
Robert C Fearheiley
121.5 Park Rd
Mount Carmel IL 62863

Call Sign: KB9MMX
Craig E Lane
1207 Parrish
Mount Carmel IL 62863

Call Sign: KC9OWO
Douglas W Garrett
1006 Parrish St
Mount Carmel IL 62863

Call Sign: N9TZT
Douglas W Garrett
1006 Parrish St
Mount Carmel IL 62863

Call Sign: KF9YB
Jason M Beauchamp
127 Pin Oak St
Mount Carmel IL 62863

Call Sign: KB9PQQ
Stephan G Wasion
707 Plum St
Mount Carmel IL 628632060

Call Sign: N9TKD
Thomas J Perillo
1225 Poplar St
Mount Carmel IL 62863

Call Sign: KC9PLA
Bradley L Osmon
203 S Pear St
Mount Carmel IL 62863

Call Sign: N9KJ
John J Reburn
125 Southview Dr
Mount Carmel IL 62863

Call Sign: KB9SRP
Amna L Majors
720 W 10th St
Mount Carmel IL 62863

Call Sign: KB9QLJ
Mark A Majors
720 W 10th St
Mount Carmel IL 62863

Call Sign: KC9PRF
Dale L Fisher
814 W 11th Ave
Mount Carmel IL 62863

Call Sign: AB9UK
Dale L Fisher
814 W 11th Ave
Mount Carmel IL 62863

Call Sign: W9PNE
Brice Anderson
301 W 11th St Unit C
Mount Carmel IL 62863

Call Sign: KB9PQR
Joseph A Thompson Jr
118 W 1st St
Mount Carmel IL 62863

Call Sign: KC9CNY
James A Bergman II
124 W 2nd St
Mount Carmel IL 62863

Call Sign: KC9CIV
Edgar E Fortner
1149 W 3rd 17
Mount Carmel IL 62863

Call Sign: N9XEK
Dean W Hillyard
611 W 4th St
Mount Carmel IL 62863

Call Sign: KB9LTK
Vicki L Hillyard
611 W 4th St
Mount Carmel IL 62863

Call Sign: N9XRD
Duane C Smith
515 W 5th St
Mount Carmel IL 62863

Call Sign: N9LDI
Marvin L Jones
530.5 W 5th St
Mount Carmel IL 62863

Call Sign: KB9HOW
Kenneth A Cook
827 W 5th St

Mount Carmel IL 62863

Call Sign: KC9BGF
Allen L Byrns
9673 Wabash 10
Mount Carmel IL 62863

Call Sign: KC9PRG
Curtis A Brown
9255 Wabash 17 Ave
Mount Carmel IL 62863

Call Sign: KB9KZS
Judy A Reburn
1019 Westwood
Mount Carmel IL 62863

Call Sign: KA9ZXR
Robert A Siverly
Mount Carmel IL 62863

Call Sign: N9WFQ
Farrell L Youngman
Mount Carmel IL 62863

Call Sign: W9NBW
Dorothy I Mc Williams
Mount Carmel IL 62863

Call Sign: KC9BEK
Elizabeth K Banks
Mount Carmel IL 62863

Call Sign: KC9BEL
Glenda K Banks
Mount Carmel IL 62863

FCC Amateur Radio Licenses in Mount Carroll

Call Sign: KB9GMN
Matthew T Magill
Rr 1 Box 119
Mount Carroll IL 61053

Call Sign: K9AUA
Roger E Miner
11508 E Loran Rd
Mount Carroll IL 610539545

Call Sign: N9DLD
Joseph E Mc Cray
207 E Market St
Mount Carroll IL 61053

Call Sign: NA9VY
Joseph E Mc Cray
207 E Market St
Mount Carroll IL 61053

Call Sign: W9IW
James E Fecke
13611 Loran Rd
Mount Carroll IL 61053

Call Sign: W9BPT
Palisades ARC And 90 West
Dx Assn
13611 Loran Rd
Mount Carroll IL 61053

Call Sign: WA9KIG
Earl R Warfield
207 N Clay St Apt 2
Mount Carroll IL 61053

Call Sign: KA9LYY
Michael E Martin
106 S Clay St
Mount Carroll IL 61053

Call Sign: AA9ZY
Michael E Martin
106 S Clay St
Mount Carroll IL 61053

Call Sign: KB9WVZ
Thomas A Disher
215 S Clay St
Mount Carroll IL 61053

Call Sign: W9KKJ
Earl J Martin
407 S Clay St
Mount Carroll IL 610531307

Call Sign: KC9IYE
Thomas R Charles

102 S East St
Mount Carroll IL 610531444

Call Sign: KB9WFR
Michael C Whitmarsh
17644 Vinegar Hill Rd
Mount Carroll IL 61053

Call Sign: K9UFA
Alfred C Mc Intosh Jr
120 W Cole
Mount Carroll IL 61053

Call Sign: KA9SRH
Susan M Simpson
12594 W Point Rd
Mount Carroll IL 61053

Call Sign: K9TI
Kenneth R Simpson
12727 W Point Rd
Mount Carroll IL 61053

Call Sign: K9KUP
Thomas A Disher
805 Washington Ave
Mount Carroll IL 61053

Call Sign: N9WMF
Glenn L Nutter
901 Washington Ave
Mount Carroll IL 61053

Call Sign: KB9GNK
John L Clifford
Mount Carroll IL 61053

FCC Amateur Radio Licenses in Mount Morris

Call Sign: KC9FQZ
Brian L Buzard
301 E Brayton Rd
Mount Morris IL 61054

Call Sign: AB9UM
Brian L Buzard
301 E Brayton Rd
Mount Morris IL 61054

Call Sign: K9ZIL
Harold N Wright
306 E Center
Mount Morris IL 61054

Call Sign: KC9PGV
Richard A Sweeney
302 E Front St
Mount Morris IL 61054

Call Sign: KB9KHF
William D Howey
6 E Hitt St
Mount Morris IL 61054

Call Sign: W9WPJ
James A Baker
109 E Lincoln
Mount Morris IL 61054

Call Sign: KB9YBY
Vanessa E Schumann
13 Emily Bsmt
Mount Morris IL 61054

Call Sign: KB9CFB
Donald N Sofolo
109 N Hannah
Mount Morris IL 61054

Call Sign: WA9PTN
Allen D Ryan
400.5 N Hannah
Mount Morris IL 61054

Call Sign: KC9HMI
Gerald M Stauffer
11 N McKendric Ave
Mount Morris IL 61054

Call Sign: N9AUW
Gary J Melvin
5964 N Mt Morris Rd
Mount Morris IL 610540181

Call Sign: KF6TKP
Joy R Angelbeck
1849 N Weller Dr

Mount Morris IL 61054

Call Sign: W9KZM
James L Isenhart
302 N Wesley Ave
Mount Morris IL 61054

Call Sign: KC9BGJ
Harold L Root
408 S McKendrie Apt 244
Mount Morris IL 61054

Call Sign: W9HLR
Harold L Root
408 S McKendrie Ave Apt 244
Mount Morris IL 61054

Call Sign: K9CZR
Paul C Detmer
124 S Wesley Ave
Mount Morris IL 61054

Call Sign: N4PZ
Stephen R Gross
602 W 1st St
Mount Morris IL 61054

Call Sign: W9OJI
Mount Morris Radio Club
602 W 1st St
Mount Morris IL 61054

Call Sign: KB9MAD
Duane D Linscott
113 W 1st St
Mount Morris IL 61054

Call Sign: N9KJH
Donna L Cope
107 W Front St
Mount Morris IL 61054

Call Sign: W9KYC
Robert E Buser
318 W Hitt St
Mount Morris IL 61054

Call Sign: KB9MYK
Erik W Page

7139 W Lowell Park Rd
Mount Morris IL 61054

Call Sign: K9CEV
Ivan E Hess
104 W Main St
Mount Morris IL 61054

Call Sign: N9KKY
David G Brink
403 W Main St
Mount Morris IL 61054

Call Sign: K9FFN
Alan S Hall
8602 W Northwest Rd
Mount Morris IL 61054

Call Sign: WD9EJN
James D Lindvall
8253 W Rt 64
Mount Morris IL 61054

FCC Amateur Radio Licenses in Mount Olive

Call Sign: WB9ALD
Mary A Hagerman
2750 Adden Rd
Mount Olive IL 620692908

Call Sign: KA9WVE
Henry B Carlile
Rr 1 Box 17G 1
Mount Olive IL 62069

Call Sign: N9DIB
William A Kuzia
Rr 1 Box 74
Mount Olive IL 62069

Call Sign: N9XTR
David D Groves
6890 Deepwater Cove
Mount Olive IL 62069

Call Sign: KB9BQZ
James M Williams
404 E 5th N

Mount Olive IL 62069

Call Sign: KC9UPX
Zachary V Taylor
4669 Litchfield Trl
Mount Olive IL 62069

Call Sign: KC9UPW
Michael H Taylor
9669 Litchfield Trl
Mount Olive IL 62069

Call Sign: KC9UPY
Michael R Taylor
9669 Litchfield Trl
Mount Olive IL 62069

Call Sign: N9NFL
Jeff W Friesner
311 S Cherry
Mount Olive IL 62069

Call Sign: N9RQC
Timothy M Friesner
311 S Cherry
Mount Olive IL 62069

Call Sign: KC0QLW
Gerard A Wnuk
8289 S Panther Creek
Mount Olive IL 62069

Call Sign: KB9VIQ
Kara J Wilson
205 W 1st N
Mount Olive IL 62069

Call Sign: N9JNE
Albert L Bly
401 W 3rd S
Mount Olive IL 62069

FCC Amateur Radio Licenses in Mount Pulaski

Call Sign: N9ULN
Delbert F Horn
200 E German Ave
Mount Pulaski IL 62548

Call Sign: N9YBD
Clint M Pollock
8 Lakewind Dr
Mount Pulaski IL 62548

Call Sign: N9KIV
Audrey J Martin
507 N Scott
Mount Pulaski IL 62548

Call Sign: N9NWH
Bradley C Aylesworth
420 N Washington St
Mount Pulaski IL 62548

Call Sign: K9BHT
Harvey M Davis
880 SR 121
Mount Pulaski IL 62548

Call Sign: N9EXL
Lyndel L Emrick
121 W Harry St
Mount Pulaski IL 62548

Call Sign: N9NWI
Richard A Volle
Mount Pulaski IL 62548

FCC Amateur Radio Licenses in Mount Sterling

Call Sign: KC9LCH
Eugene J Zackey
Rr 4 Box 124D
Mount Sterling IL 62353

Call Sign: KC9QAN
Jeff L Rigg
Rr 4 Box 161A
Mount Sterling IL 62353

Call Sign: KC9MXF
Bob P Heffren
Rr 3 Box 49
Mount Sterling IL 62353

Call Sign: N9CDS

Richard L Young
Rt 3 Box 53
Mount Sterling IL 62353

Call Sign: WB9DJC
John M Hogan
211 E Washington
Mount Sterling IL 62353

Call Sign: N9WQL
Brian L Luthy
228 W North Ave
Mount Sterling IL 62353

Call Sign: KA9BBK
Larry E Moorman
217 W Union St
Mount Sterling IL 62353

Call Sign: W9LEM
Larry E Moorman
217 W Union St
Mount Sterling IL 62353

Call Sign: KA9EZO
Rosemary E Moorman
217 W Union St
Mount Sterling IL 62353

Call Sign: KA9BDA
Alan L Koch
Mount Sterling IL 62353

Call Sign: W9CJR
Robert E Koch
Mount Sterling IL 62353

FCC Amateur Radio Licenses in Mount Vernon

Call Sign: N9MWT
Sharon M Wiseman
1515 5th 12th
Mount Vernon IL 62064

Call Sign: N6ONG
Donald R Linville
3103 Apricot
Mount Vernon IL 62864

Call Sign: KA9EFN
Donald E Lewis
190 Aspen
Mount Vernon IL 62864

Call Sign: KC9UUV
Dennis R Riley Jr
727 Barton St
Mount Vernon IL 62864

Call Sign: KB9LIK
Dale E Crawford
Rt 4 Box 164
Mount Vernon IL 62864

Call Sign: KB9ROQ
David O Williams
Rr 6 Box 165
Mount Vernon IL 62864

Call Sign: KB9UBJ
Edith I Williams
Rr 6 Box 165
Mount Vernon IL 62864

Call Sign: WD9CHV
Harold D Boyd
Rr 5 Box 192
Mount Vernon IL 62864

Call Sign: KB9RWP
Leslie A Hayes
Rt 3 Box 264
Mount Vernon IL 62864

Call Sign: N9OXJ
Matthew S Hoyt
Rr 6 Box 373
Mount Vernon IL 62864

Call Sign: W9BHI
Robert Schultz
Rfd 7 Box 412
Mount Vernon IL 62864

Call Sign: N9JHA
Chris G Weatherly
Rr 6 Box 85

Mount Vernon IL 62864

Call Sign: KC9IGU
John E Clements
5 Brookhaven Est
Mount Vernon IL 62864

Call Sign: KB9VJJ
Casimir S Sakowicz
415 Casey Ave
Mount Vernon IL 62864

Call Sign: KB0VGM
Ricky L Hicks
2025 Casey Ave
Mount Vernon IL 62864

Call Sign: KC9IUR
Ricky L Hicks
2025 Casey Ave
Mount Vernon IL 62864

Call Sign: N1ZW
Robin L Ward
211 Castleton Ave
Mount Vernon IL 62864

Call Sign: KB9HQI
Gerald L Merritt
2816 Cherry
Mount Vernon IL 62864

Call Sign: KF9KN
Franklin W Kone
28 Cherry Dr
Mount Vernon IL 62864

Call Sign: WK9W
Le Roy C Mc Duffie Sr
33 Cherry Dr
Mount Vernon IL 62864

Call Sign: KB9BIG
Robert J Loughmiller Jr
65 Cherry Dr
Mount Vernon IL 62864

Call Sign: KB9JKD
Larry G Hoffman

2808 College St
Mount Vernon IL 62864

Call Sign: N9WDX
Robert W De Young
73 Cottonwood Dr
Mount Vernon IL 62864

Call Sign: W9HAB
Raymond J Millmaker
1708 Derry Ln Apt 2
Mount Vernon IL 62864

Call Sign: N9GHB
Orville E Kerr
10151 E Bakerville Rd
Mount Vernon IL 62864

Call Sign: KB9IYA
Kenneth D Sisk
10735 E Bakerville Rd
Mount Vernon IL 62864

Call Sign: KC9MZE
Keith L Wilcox
15691 E Country Meadows
Mount Vernon IL 62864

Call Sign: KC9MZD
Tracey Wilcox
15691 E Country Meadows Rd
Mount Vernon IL 62864

Call Sign: N9UQD
Bruce E Venters
15625 E Fairfield Rd
Mount Vernon IL 62864

Call Sign: W9TZB
Glen R Wall
15674 E Fairfield Rd
Mount Vernon IL 628647797

Call Sign: WA9RSO
Paul M Wall
15698 E Fairfield Rd
Mount Vernon IL 628647797

Call Sign: KC9IWP

Wayne E Sampson
15838 E Fairfield Rd
Mount Vernon IL 62864

Call Sign: AB9VW
Wayne E Sampson
15838 E Fairfield Rd
Mount Vernon IL 62864

Call Sign: WB9IYG
Mark Busse
17603 E Fairfield Rd
Mount Vernon IL 628648099

Call Sign: KB9MLP
Stephen L Modert
12670 E Il 148
Mount Vernon IL 62864

Call Sign: KC9SRX
John T Locke
12358 E Lakeview Rd
Mount Vernon IL 62864

Call Sign: WD9DKT
Daryl L Kennedy
11795 E Sunflower Rd
Mount Vernon IL 62864

Call Sign: AA9EM
Cheryl L Hertenstein
12 Evergreen
Mount Vernon IL 62864

Call Sign: KA9TAZ
Thomas A Bain
1700 Franklin
Mount Vernon IL 62864

Call Sign: KB9TWG
James R Laughmiller
1102 Gaskin Ave 8
Mount Vernon IL 62864

Call Sign: N9NIY
Julie M Mitchell
1118 Gaskins
Mount Vernon IL 62864

Call Sign: KC9LLV
Hallin B Burgan
3 Grant Pl
Mount Vernon IL 62864

Call Sign: N9KVB
John M Steffy
723 Harrison
Mount Vernon IL 62864

Call Sign: KB9FJW
Crile Doscher
10 Hawthorne Hills
Mount Vernon IL 62864

Call Sign: WO9V
Cranston D Crawford
8 Indian Trl Dr
Mount Vernon IL 62864

Call Sign: W9BFO
John A Warren
2908 Jamison
Mount Vernon IL 62864

Call Sign: KC9LPZ
Steven N Peeples
3116 Jamison Blvd
Mount Vernon IL 62864

Call Sign: KC9GVQ
Gregory P Schroeder
3200 Jamison Blvd
Mount Vernon IL 62846

Call Sign: KC9MZC
Frank L Todd
3213 Jamison Blvd
Mount Vernon IL 62864

Call Sign: WD9DAO
Clifford R Fields
708 Lake Pk
Mount Vernon IL 62864

Call Sign: KC9MYY
Brian A Ouellette Sr
4337 Lilac Ln
Mount Vernon IL 62864

Call Sign: KB9TXJ
Robert G Weisz
4201 B Lincolnshire Dr
Mount Vernon IL 62864

Call Sign: KB9DTV
Robert G Tomlin
717 Magnolia
Mount Vernon IL 62864

Call Sign: WA9DNL
Vernois ARC
717 Magnolia
Mount Vernon IL 62864

Call Sign: KB9VTM
James E Boyd
836 McCauley Ln
Mount Vernon IL 62864

Call Sign: KC5IQW
Donald R Bigham
14327 McRaven Ln
Mount Vernon IL 62864

Call Sign: KA5UHN
Gary E Myers
813 Meadowbrook Rd
Mount Vernon IL 62864

Call Sign: W9KM
Kenneth C Mudd
1006 Mulligan Pl
Mount Vernon IL 62864

Call Sign: K9JOG
Marjorie B Mudd
1006 Mulligan Pl
Mount Vernon IL 62864

Call Sign: KD9IB
Joel W Avery
110 N 7th St
Mount Vernon IL 62864

Call Sign: AA9GH
Harold R Mc Intyre
1016 N 7th St

Mount Vernon IL 62864

Call Sign: KB9JKC
Rhonda R Delaney
10504 N Delaney Ln
Mount Vernon IL 62864

Call Sign: WU9C
Robert M Delaney
10504 N Delaney Ln
Mount Vernon IL 62864

Call Sign: KC9PZT
Cody M Moss
10518 N Delaney Ln
Mount Vernon IL 62864

Call Sign: KA9UVY
Robert L Delaney
10630 N Delaney Ln
Mount Vernon IL 62864

Call Sign: N9WZJ
Marty D Mills
16318 N Hawthorne Dr
Mount Vernon IL 62864

Call Sign: KC9TSB
Charles W Meads
8443 N Il Hwy 148
Mount Vernon IL 62864

Call Sign: KC9CZC
Louis P Helsing
16499 N Il Hwy 37
Mount Vernon IL 62864

Call Sign: KA9CPS
Nuncio L Raffa
16499 N Il Hwy 37
Mount Vernon IL 62864

Call Sign: KB9LKN
Randy J Henderson
16750 N Il Hwy 37
Mount Vernon IL 62864

Call Sign: AB9FI
Randy J Henderson

16750 N Il Hwy 37
Mount Vernon IL 62864

Call Sign: KC9SDY
Michael S Cook
16584 N Il Hwy 37 Lot 25
Mount Vernon IL 62864

Call Sign: KG9EG
Donald G Summers
12752 N Liebengood Ln
Mount Vernon IL 62864

Call Sign: KB9KWQ
Luke Crawford
15208 N Loyola Ln
Mount Vernon IL 62864

Call Sign: KC9CCP
Luke Crawford
15208 N Loyola Ln
Mount Vernon IL 62864

Call Sign: N9PRO
Donald B Hoyt
14390 N McCauley Ln
Mount Vernon IL 62864

Call Sign: KB9ITA
David R Leggans
19202 N Miller Lake Ln
Mount Vernon IL 62864

Call Sign: AA9EE
Edward G Hayes
9193 N Monmouth Ln
Mount Vernon IL 62864

Call Sign: KA9JJX
Wilma J Hayes
9193 N Monmouth Ln
Mount Vernon IL 62864

Call Sign: KA9JJS
Douglas J Hayes
9237 N Monmouth Ln
Mount Vernon IL 62864

Call Sign: KA9JJW

Leslie A Hayes
9237 N Monmouth Ln
Mount Vernon IL 62864

Call Sign: KB9YVQ
Harold E Coleman
133601 N Sandburg Ln
Mount Vernon IL 62864

Call Sign: W9RJN
Robert J Newman
15030 N Tundra Ln
Mount Vernon IL 62864

Call Sign: KB9HBL
Kendra S Peterson
15130 N Valley St
Mount Vernon IL 62864

Call Sign: AA9KF
Noel L Smith
1109 Oakland Ave
Mount Vernon IL 62864

Call Sign: KD9GV
Samuel L Shaw
2403 Pace
Mount Vernon IL 62864

Call Sign: N9HWF
Nealy R Glenn
705 Pavey Ave
Mount Vernon IL 62864

Call Sign: KB9SNF
Wayne E Pettit
605 S 10th
Mount Vernon IL 62864

Call Sign: KB9YJN
Donald C Laughmiller
505 S 20th St
Mount Vernon IL 62864

Call Sign: KB9QXR
Robert O Edwards
1002 S 20th St
Mount Vernon IL 62864

Call Sign: N9OQZ
Karen S Delaney
1102 S 22nd
Mount Vernon IL 62864

Call Sign: KC9TVX
Jeremy A Clutter
810 S 24th St
Mount Vernon IL 62864

Call Sign: KC9TVY
Theresa J Clutter
810 S 24th St
Mount Vernon IL 62864

Call Sign: N9SWP
David G Smith
1203 S 25 St
Mount Vernon IL 62864

Call Sign: WD9GHG
Alan C Jolly
302 S 28th St
Mount Vernon IL 62864

Call Sign: KA9YTQ
Ben G Fryar
326 S 2nd
Mount Vernon IL 62864

Call Sign: KC9SDA
Becky S Hart
413 S 32nd St
Mount Vernon IL 62864

Call Sign: KC9JAJ
Mark A Hart
413 S 32nd St
Mount Vernon IL 62864

Call Sign: KC9RVA
Terry L Mezo
6 Southbrook Dr
Mount Vernon IL 62864

Call Sign: KC9JEO
Darrell W Mezo
6 Southbrook Dr
Mount Vernon IL 628642732

Call Sign: KA9RLX
Danny R Davis
401 Spruce
Mount Vernon IL 62864

Call Sign: W9DRD
Danny R Davis
401 Spruce
Mount Vernon IL 62864

Call Sign: KC9RFI
Steven L Lueker
1516 Triangle St
Mount Vernon IL 62864

Call Sign: N9AYS
Guy W Baker
4202 Westwood Dr 10
Mount Vernon IL 62864

Call Sign: AA9KE
Bill E Shoemaker
620 White Ave
Mount Vernon IL 62864

Call Sign: K9MER
James A Mc Kenzie
3232 Wild Rose Dr
Mount Vernon IL 62864

Call Sign: N0BMR
Robert J Korchik
1313 Wilshire Dr
Mount Vernon IL 62864

Call Sign: WA6DRB
Donald E Wilson
414 Wren Dr
Mount Vernon IL 628642250

Call Sign: KB9DTU
Charles A Bruce
Mount Vernon IL 62864

Call Sign: KB9CJV
Patricia W Shaw
Mount Vernon IL 62864

Call Sign: KB9HOC
Anthony K Hertenstein
Mount Vernon IL 62864

Call Sign: WT9K
James R Hertenstein
Mount Vernon IL 62864

Call Sign: KF5EKG
Bartholomew Stavisky
Mount Vernon IL 62864

Call Sign: KB9MBT
Jerry H Towns
Mount Vernon IL 62864

Call Sign: KB9NDX
Paul W Widicus
Mount Vernon IL 62864

Call Sign: KB9KDE
ARC Of Mount Vernon
Mount Vernon IL 62864

Call Sign: WA9PTE
George A Haynes
Mount Vernon IL 62864

FCC Amateur Radio Licenses in Mount Zion

Call Sign: N9SXH
Jonathan E Proesel
713 Antler Dr
Mount Zion IL 62549

Call Sign: WA9PYO
Denny R Benner
740 Bell St
Mount Zion IL 62549

Call Sign: KA9RUH
Ronald R Hurst Jr
330 Debby Dr
Mount Zion IL 62549

Call Sign: KC9BIU
Corey M Wicker
1564 Dogwood Dr

Mount Zion IL 62549

Call Sign: KC9JEM
Donald G Hampton
501 E Florian Ave
Mount Zion IL 62549

Call Sign: KB9JSE
Robert A Rucker
705 Fawn Ct
Mount Zion IL 62549

Call Sign: KA9WMZ
Bryan D Mc Ghee
1215 Florian Ave
Mount Zion IL 62549

Call Sign: KA9IHM
Ivan D Williams
4637 Highcock Dr
Mount Zion IL 625492749

Call Sign: KA9WMY
Leonhard G Mau
520 Lawrence Dr
Mount Zion IL 62549

Call Sign: KA9QDV
Edward W Welch
675 Maple St
Mount Zion IL 62549

Call Sign: KB9POS
Ruth E Welch
675 Maple St
Mount Zion IL 62549

Call Sign: N9OPC
Paul W Nixon
535 Mintler Dr
Mount Zion IL 62549

Call Sign: KC9SGE
Grif W Dunakey
600 Mintler Dr
Mount Zion IL 62549

Call Sign: N9SKY
Russell J Proesel

713 N Antler Dr
Mount Zion IL 62549

Call Sign: K9ARQ
Joseph G Moran
23 Prairie Rose Ct
Mount Zion IL 62549

Call Sign: KA9VAH
William G Elliott
1610 Ridgewood Ct
Mount Zion IL 62549

Call Sign: KB9GBO
Robert D Walker
320 Rt 121
Mount Zion IL 62549

Call Sign: WA9KCN
Roger V Van Rheeden
330 Spitler Park Dr
Mount Zion IL 625491218

Call Sign: W9MMM
Darrell E Statzer
908 State Hwy 121
Mount Zion IL 62549

Call Sign: KC9JRV
Timothy D Niebrugge
1675 Westside Dr
Mount Zion IL 62549

Call Sign: KN9H
Bob T Burns
602 Woodland Ct
Mount Zion IL 62549

Call Sign: KA9JNZ
Mary E Burns
602 Woodland Ct
Mount Zion IL 62549

Call Sign: W9KXZ
Stephen H Eyer
Mount Zion IL 62549

**FCC Amateur Radio
Licenses in Moweaqua**

Call Sign: KC9FYR
Marion L Mcvey
Rr 1 Box 18 B
Moweaqua IL 62550

Call Sign: KB9AAO
Dixie L Shewmaker
Rr 1 Box 203
Moweaqua IL 62550

Call Sign: N9VWA
David R Hogan
Rr 2 Box 203
Moweaqua IL 62550

Call Sign: N9XWX
Ronald R Hogan
Rr 2 Box 203
Moweaqua IL 62550

Call Sign: KC9GFF
David R Nave
Rr 2 Box 81
Moweaqua IL 62550

Call Sign: W9DRN
David R Nave
Rr 2 Box 81
Moweaqua IL 62550

Call Sign: KC9SGG
Brett E Mcvey
2276 E 1800 N Rd
Moweaqua IL 62550

Call Sign: KC9FYT
Kevin M Waggoner
2433 E 1900 N Rd
Moweaqua IL 62550

Call Sign: KC9FYS
Michelle D Waggoner
2433 E 1900 N Rd
Moweaqua IL 62550

Call Sign: KC9FYU
Paderic O Waggoner
2433 E 1900 N Rd

Moweaqua IL 62550

Call Sign: N9TZA
Charles R Stout
210 E Cherry
Moweaqua IL 62550

Call Sign: KB9PGA
Ida L Mc Donald
223 E Main St
Moweaqua IL 62550

Call Sign: KC9FYQ
Kolton W Minott
3 Hunter Ct
Moweaqua IL 62550

Call Sign: KB9NPM
Michael L Simmons
2499 N 900 E Rd
Moweaqua IL 62550

Call Sign: KB9LIQ
Benjamin E Manley
119 W Madison
Moweaqua IL 62550

FCC Amateur Radio Licenses in Muddy

Call Sign: AA9UN
Edgar Devous
175 Maple St
Muddy IL 62965

FCC Amateur Radio Licenses in Mulberry Grove

Call Sign: N9PPH
Ida A Dooly
Rt 2 Box 264
Mulberry Grove IL 62262

Call Sign: KB9SOQ
John A Street
R 2 Box 371
Mulberry Grove IL 62262

Call Sign: KA9YOG

David A Dooly
842 Mulberry Gr Rd
Mulberry Grove IL 62262

Call Sign: KB9BEB
Clareen D Dunn
826 Mulberry Grove Rd
Mulberry Grove IL 62262

Call Sign: KB9BDZ
Thomas C Dooly
833 Mulberry Grove Rd
Mulberry Grove IL 62262

Call Sign: KB9ELI
Linda A Dooly
833 Mulberry Grove Rd
Mulberry Grove IL 62262

Call Sign: KB9SVA
Rachel A Dooly
833 Mulberry Grove Rd
Mulberry Grove IL 62262

Call Sign: KB9JPK
Denise Terry
1360 Mulberry Grove Rd
Mulberry Grove IL 62262

Call Sign: N9LIT
Robert W Terry
1360 Mulberry Grove Rd
Mulberry Grove IL 62262

Call Sign: K9YER
Fred L Hall
1655 Old Park Ave
Mulberry Grove IL 62262

FCC Amateur Radio Licenses in Mulkeytown

Call Sign: W9OXQ
Leslie E Berner
7541 Arkansas Rd
Mulkeytown IL 62865

Call Sign: KB9DGQ
Glen D Hobbs

Rt 1 Box 35
Mulkeytown IL 62685

Call Sign: W9QYX
Norman W Swisher
9099 Swisher St
Mulkeytown IL 62865

FCC Amateur Radio Licenses in Muncie

Call Sign: KC9JVT
Chad D Wahls
Muncie IL 61857

FCC Amateur Radio Licenses in Murphysboro

Call Sign: N9ZOH
William L Schuh
9 Amethyst
Murphysboro IL 62966

Call Sign: KB9KIM
Laurie K Schuh
9 Amethyst Rd
Murphysboro IL 62966

Call Sign: KC9PAW
Marc L Johnson
5261 Ava Rd
Murphysboro IL 62966

Call Sign: WA9VVH
Herbert L Elbrecht
6966 Ava Rd
Murphysboro IL 629664015

Call Sign: AA9V
Darryl R Huppert
Rt 5 Box 264
Murphysboro IL 62966

Call Sign: N9VKN
Rex E Fager
Rr 3 Box 323A
Murphysboro IL 62966

Call Sign: N9UQB

Daryl R Grammer
Rt 3 Box 88
Murphysboro IL 62966

Call Sign: WC9W
Andrew A Wist
77 Brock Ln
Murphysboro IL 62966

Call Sign: N9DXI
Michelle A Wist
77 Brock Ln
Murphysboro IL 62966

Call Sign: KA9WXM
David M Swetland
2229 Bus Hwy 13
Murphysboro IL 62966

Call Sign: KC9HXT
Shawnee Hills Int'L Telegraph
Society
181 Caraway Rd
Murphysboro IL 62966

Call Sign: K9QG
Shawnee Hills Int'L Telegraph
Society
181 Caraway Rd
Murphysboro IL 62966

Call Sign: N5RP
Charles R Perring
181 Caraway Rd
Murphysboro IL 62966

Call Sign: WB9EBD
William E Brown
1908 Clarke St
Murphysboro IL 62966

Call Sign: KB9KZK
Matthew W Schuh
2331 Clay St
Murphysboro IL 62966

Call Sign: KC9OMC
Oliver Flatt
90 Devan Dr

Murphysboro IL 62966

Call Sign: KC9NWY
Brian P Mclaughlan
1903 Division
Murphysboro IL 62966

Call Sign: WA9GYH
Ronald W Hunter
1839 Edith St
Murphysboro IL 62966

Call Sign: KA9LLU
Robert A Fisher
64 Everest Rd
Murphysboro IL 62966

Call Sign: KA9UTF
Charles L Glasser Sr
1924 Gartside
Murphysboro IL 62966

Call Sign: WA9DWQ
Jack H Miller
2136 Gartside St
Murphysboro IL 62966

Call Sign: N9RCY
Jo Ann Haney
40 Helm Rd
Murphysboro IL 629669668

Call Sign: N9KRL
Raymond A Haney Jr
40 Helm Rd
Murphysboro IL 629669668

Call Sign: KA9IVC
Dennis R Ebersohl
113 Hide A Way Acres Rd
Murphysboro IL 629669745

Call Sign: KA9VYW
Nancy L Ebersohl
113 Hide A Way Acres Rd
Murphysboro IL 629669745

Call Sign: KC9JTG
Rick G Fletcher

1284 Hoffman Rd
Murphysboro IL 62966

Call Sign: KC9KIB
Joshua A Brown
7168 Hwy 127
Murphysboro IL 62966

Call Sign: K9KZC
Oliver Grammer
7206 Hwy 127
Murphysboro IL 62966

Call Sign: KA9SSR
Daniel D Lecocq
10068 Hwy 149
Murphysboro IL 62966

Call Sign: W9LLF
Harold O Maerker
2108 Illinois Ave Box 1269
Murphysboro IL 62966

Call Sign: KC9KNQ
Stevan E Burtnett
1075 Jenkins Rd
Murphysboro IL 62966

Call Sign: K9EZZ
Stevan E Burtnett
1075 Jenkins Rd
Murphysboro IL 62966

Call Sign: KC9TXI
Bryan J Brown
100 Lambs Ln
Murphysboro IL 62966

Call Sign: W9LEN
Charles A Ford
473 Logan Run Rd
Murphysboro IL 62966

Call Sign: KA9NEW
Daniel W Ellison
2028 McCord
Murphysboro IL 62966

Call Sign: N9TAK

Dennis E Karnes
2104 McCord St
Murphysboro IL 62966

Call Sign: KA9EJL
Jeffrey D Carver
2304 McCord St
Murphysboro IL 62966

Call Sign: K9LRE
Jerry R Giffin
138 McDowell Rd
Murphysboro IL 62966

Call Sign: KC9ERX
Mount Ava Repeater
Association
138 McDowell Rd
Murphysboro IL 62966

Call Sign: K9GOX
Mount Ava Repeater
Association
138 McDowell Rd
Murphysboro IL 62966

Call Sign: K9WZH
Joseph L Godar Jr
287 Melody Ln
Murphysboro IL 629664511

Call Sign: KC9KFF
Brian J Lambert
604 Mulberry Apt 7
Murphysboro IL 67960

Call Sign: KC9SZL
Neil A Reitenbach
118B Murdale Gardens Rd
Murphysboro IL 62966

Call Sign: N9HKC
Dan J Chavez
617 Murphysboro Lake Rd
Murphysboro IL 62966

Call Sign: AC7CT
Alden T Arbon
117 N 18th St Apt B

Murphysboro IL 62966

Call Sign: K9IZE
Leonard Novara
227 N 22nd St
Murphysboro IL 62966

Call Sign: N9OWL
Randy L Wood
909 N 6th St
Murphysboro IL 62966

Call Sign: KC9QXT
Kenneth R Cline
322 N 9th St
Murphysboro IL 62966

Call Sign: N9KDY
Wesley W Will
519 N 9th St
Murphysboro IL 629661841

Call Sign: N9RRA
John J Bochantin
943 N Jungle Rd
Murphysboro IL 62966

Call Sign: W0TPO
Thomas D Laase
2520 New Era Rd 85
Murphysboro IL 62966

Call Sign: KC9TZQ
Landon A Beasley
504 North St
Murphysboro IL 62966

Call Sign: N9FSS
Rob Roy Ellett
114 Old Kimmel Bridge Rd
Murphysboro IL 62966

Call Sign: KC9KFE
John J Jehle
27 Paper Ln
Murphysboro IL 62966

Call Sign: KJ6IP
Paul A Farrell

221 Pine Ln
Murphysboro IL 62966

Call Sign: K9KZD
William P Munson
2229 Pine St
Murphysboro IL 62966

Call Sign: KC9QVP
Pam Fleming
556 Pump House Rd
Murphysboro IL 62966

Call Sign: KC9NEM
Gary C New
28 R Eugene Kennedy Ln Unit
1B
Murphysboro IL 62966

Call Sign: KB9IQS
Francisco J Pereira
1103 B Sandra Ct
Murphysboro IL 62966

Call Sign: WA9HAB
Robert R Morefield
2020 Spruce
Murphysboro IL 62966

Call Sign: KC9OMB
James R Mcminn III
1133 Stave Mill Rd
Murphysboro IL 62966

Call Sign: KC9NEL
Rebekah E Teel
410 Walnut St
Murphysboro IL 62966

Call Sign: W9HWL
Robert S Mc Cormick
2020 Walnut St
Murphysboro IL 62966

Call Sign: K9MB
Michael D Burke
389 Wells St
Murphysboro IL 62966

Call Sign: KB9MUH
Raymond A Whiteside
41 Westwood Ln
Murphysboro IL 62966

Call Sign: K9FXG
Carl E Stoker
44 Westwood Ln
Murphysboro IL 62966

Call Sign: AE9KY
Carl E Stoker
44 Westwood Ln
Murphysboro IL 62966

Call Sign: K9FXG
Carl E Stoker
44 Westwood Ln
Murphysboro IL 62966

Call Sign: AE9KY
Carl E Stoker
44 Westwood Ln
Murphysboro IL 62966

Call Sign: K9FXG
Carl E Stoker
44 Westwood Ln
Murphysboro IL 62966

Call Sign: AE9KY
Carl E Stoker
44 Westwood Ln
Murphysboro IL 62966

Call Sign: W1RJ
Ralph J Henry
138 Worthen Rd
Murphysboro IL 62966

Call Sign: KB9RTW
Benjamin D Connor
Murphysboro IL 62966

Call Sign: KC9QVO
Dora E Hayes
Murphysboro IL 62966

FCC Amateur Radio Licenses in Murrayville

Call Sign: KB9SWX
Linda V Van Bebber
Rr 2 Box 113
Murrayville IL 62668

Call Sign: KB9KHV
Wayne L Van Bebber
Rr 2 Box 113
Murrayville IL 62668

Call Sign: N9WJM
George R Mellor Sr
R 1 Box 286
Murrayville IL 62668

Call Sign: W9KGM
Charles L Wyatt
106 Cottage Ln
Murrayville IL 62668

Call Sign: WB9ROC
David L Robson
517 Happy Hollow Rd
Murrayville IL 62668

Call Sign: KB9GEE
Joseph C Enochs Jr
574 S Smokey Ln
Murrayville IL 62668

Call Sign: KB9KHU
Roy L Van Bebber
Murrayville IL 62668

Call Sign: KB9YWR
Dale E Van Bebber
Murrayville IL 62668

Call Sign: K9WDX
Herbert H TRUE
Murrayville IL 62668

FCC Amateur Radio Licenses in Naplate

Call Sign: N9YLY

Albert P Bailey
2112 Center St
Naplate IL 61350

FCC Amateur Radio Licenses in Nashville

Call Sign: KC9JKN
Marilyn S Stevenson
826 E Adams
Nashville IL 62263

Call Sign: WD9IMK
Gerald Krueger
242 E Lebanon St
Nashville IL 62263

Call Sign: WB9VJA
Byron L Meade
14 Mallard Dr
Nashville IL 62263

Call Sign: W9BUD
Byron L Meade
14 Mallard Dr
Nashville IL 62263

Call Sign: KC9OLH
Timothy J Heckman
22056 Phillips St
Nashville IL 62263

Call Sign: K9VZI
Michael R Hogan
773 S Heaman Dr
Nashville IL 622632009

Call Sign: AA9EQ
Bradley D Lietz
774 S Mill
Nashville IL 62263

Call Sign: KB9PNU
John B Labusier
1640 S Sunrise
Nashville IL 62263

Call Sign: KB9NGK
Bradley D Lietz

15509 SR 15
Nashville IL 62263

Call Sign: KB9BCU
Gene A Hackstadt
710 W Adams St
Nashville IL 62263

Call Sign: KB4TOZ
Bonita J Pryor
173 W Lebanon St
Nashville IL 62263

Call Sign: KC9MVA
Bradley R Criley
224 W Lebanon St
Nashville IL 62263

Call Sign: KB9QXU
James B Hale
1076 W St Louis St
Nashville IL 62263

FCC Amateur Radio Licenses in Nauvoo

Call Sign: N9ISS
Clifford M Trapp
125 Barnett St
Nauvoo IL 62354

Call Sign: KC9PNR
Jesse W Evans
1050 E CR 1900 N
Nauvoo IL 62354

Call Sign: KC9LRR
Phyllis A Andersen
40 Fields Cir
Nauvoo IL 62354

Call Sign: N7JC
Glen L Andersen
40 Fields Cir
Nauvoo IL 62354

Call Sign: KC9AOT
William J Bloomberg
Hwy 96S

Nauvoo IL 62354

Call Sign: KC9NQP
Franklin T Rahman
2045 Knight St
Nauvoo IL 62354

Call Sign: KC9LRS
Jack J Stossel
1295 Knight St Box 275
Nauvoo IL 62354

Call Sign: KC9LRX
William R Snyder
335 N Page St
Nauvoo IL 62354

Call Sign: KA9FAJ
Gary L Shanks
125 N Winchester
Nauvoo IL 623540341

Call Sign: KC9EQU
Hans S Smith
1 Riverview Dr
Nauvoo IL 62354

Call Sign: K9STL
Hans S Smith
1 Riverview Dr
Nauvoo IL 62354

Call Sign: KB0KDQ
Ruth Ann S Smith
1 Riverview Dr
Nauvoo IL 62354

Call Sign: WB7P
David C Smith
1 Riverview Dr
Nauvoo IL 62354

Call Sign: WB9YHS
Kris L Priebe
68 Riverview Dr
Nauvoo IL 62354

Call Sign: KD4CBO
Martin J Daly

290 S Fulmer St
Nauvoo IL 62354

Call Sign: KI6TYW
Josef A Blunier
455 S Gordon St
Nauvoo IL 62354

Call Sign: N7VSL
Evan L Ivie
300 S Wilcox St
Nauvoo IL 62354

Call Sign: N7VRB
Peter A Ivie
300 S Wilcox St Box 116
Nauvoo IL 62354

Call Sign: KC9LRV
Clive D Moon
Nauvoo IL 62354

Call Sign: KC9AAA
Clive D Moon
Nauvoo IL 62354

Call Sign: KC9LRW
Leslie Graham
Nauvoo IL 62354

Call Sign: K1GRG
Glen R Gabler Md
Nauvoo IL 62354

FCC Amateur Radio Licenses in Nebo

Call Sign: KC9BVC
Debra L Grimes
42938 170th Ave
Nebo IL 62355

Call Sign: KC9RFP
David E Hill
12206 440th St
Nebo IL 62355

Call Sign: KC9KEJ
Bradley S Guthrie

340 W Middle St
Nebo IL 62355

Call Sign: KB9YBP
Bradley G Guthrie
Nebo IL 62355

Call Sign: KB9YBQ
Wendy Z Guthrie
Nebo IL 62355

**FCC Amateur Radio
Licenses in Neoga**

Call Sign: KB9PWJ
Randal R Albin
Rr 1 Box 173
Neoga IL 62447

Call Sign: KB9QGR
Dawn J Albin
Rr1 Box 173
Neoga IL 62447

Call Sign: KA9ZLM
William S Himes
Rr 1 Box 198
Neoga IL 62447

Call Sign: K9UYI
Harry D Bailey
R 2 Box 94
Neoga IL 62447

Call Sign: KC9PLN
David F Foster
48 Clear Creek Dr
Neoga IL 62447

Call Sign: WA9PTY
Donald K Baker
1148 CR 400 E
Neoga IL 62447

Call Sign: WA9PTZ
Joan L Baker
1148 CR 400 E
Neoga IL 62447

Call Sign: KE9QC
Michael A May
377 E 5th
Neoga IL 62447

Call Sign: WA9EYS
David P Gallivan
15 Prahls Dr
Neoga IL 624472003

Call Sign: WA9IGA
Thomas L Clearwater
Shorts Subdivision
Neoga IL 624470294

Call Sign: N9NPR
Patrick M Manley
Neoga IL 62447

Call Sign: W9BPP
Robert C Queen
Neoga IL 624470246

**FCC Amateur Radio
Licenses in Neponset**

Call Sign: KB9INL
William G Currier
105 W Norton St
Neponset IL 61345

**FCC Amateur Radio
Licenses in New Athens**

Call Sign: KB9FLC
Gary W Longanecker
2223 Lake Dr
New Athens IL 62264

Call Sign: KE9NK
John E Brewer
403 N Johnson
New Athens IL 62264

Call Sign: KC9PXT
Rose M Thomas
3473 Old Sand Rd
New Athens IL 62264

Call Sign: KC9OBZ
Sandy M Ramage
3473 Old Sand Rd
New Athens IL 62264

Call Sign: KB9ZQN
Mark E Causey
7501 Peacock Site Rd
New Athens IL 62264

Call Sign: AB9MG
Mark E Causey
7501 Peacock Site Rd
New Athens IL 62264

Call Sign: W9CKT
Curt C Lindauer Jr
2717 SR 13
New Athens IL 622640434

Call Sign: KB9FX
David O Vogler
New Athens IL 62264

**FCC Amateur Radio
Licenses in New Baden**

Call Sign: N9WDT
Robert M Rittis
49 Bluebell
New Baden IL 62265

Call Sign: N9ADB
James E Denny
1013 Court Rd
New Baden IL 62265

Call Sign: N9KWC
Herman H Heierman
194 Mary Irene
New Baden IL 622651902

Call Sign: WD0GHI
Jimmie R Crank
601 Thouvenot Ln
New Baden IL 622651145

Call Sign: KC9AEC
Robert W Riddell

3 W Birch St
New Baden IL 62265

Call Sign: KC9OTS
Howard W Ferris
403 W Hanover St
New Baden IL 62265

Call Sign: N9TIK
Kevin D Woods
103 W Poplar
New Baden IL 62265

FCC Amateur Radio Licenses in New Bedford

Call Sign: KA0PSG
Eddie T Craig
New Bedford IL 61346

FCC Amateur Radio Licenses in New Berlin

Call Sign: N9EDB
Raymond N Lloyd
1357 Annandale Rd
New Berlin IL 626706796

Call Sign: WD9HKT
Lea M Kaydus
Rr 1 Box 142C
New Berlin IL 62670

Call Sign: AF9D
Clarence E Peecher
Rr 1 Box 205
New Berlin IL 62670

Call Sign: KA9EQJ
Matthew L Peecher
Rr 1 Box 205
New Berlin IL 62670

Call Sign: N9GTT
Larry M Gorski
9 Constitution
New Berlin IL 62670

Call Sign: WD9EMK

James L Clink
506 E Illinois St
New Berlin IL 626700362

Call Sign: KC9LSH
Alfred P Lairo
2242 Haven Ln
New Berlin IL 62670

Call Sign: KA9DXI
Mildred E Denson
6329 Moffet
New Berlin IL 62670

Call Sign: AG9T
Paul D Denson
6329 Moffet St
New Berlin IL 62670

Call Sign: WA9PFB
Edward F Clink
1285 New Salem Church Rd
New Berlin IL 62670

Call Sign: KC9LSM
Walter W Rudolph
16657 Old Jackson Rd
New Berlin IL 62670

Call Sign: KC9KLW
Cynthia E Bridges
2152 S Farmingdale Rd
New Berlin IL 62670

Call Sign: KB9PHF
David E Bridges
2152 S Farmingdale Rd
New Berlin IL 62670

Call Sign: W9SCA
Elmer L Armstrong
401 S Oak St
New Berlin IL 62670

Call Sign: N9AHN
Darvin K Munter
320 Shenandoah
New Berlin IL 62670

Call Sign: KC9VCL
Daniel P Summers
6245 W Iles Ave
New Berlin IL 52670

Call Sign: KB5AKW
Gail L Summers
6245 W Iles Ave
New Berlin IL 526706648

Call Sign: WR5C
Willard R Summers
6245 W Iles Ave
New Berlin IL 626706648

FCC Amateur Radio Licenses in New Boston

Call Sign: KB9PBV
Ava S Bluedorn
525 120th Ave
New Boston IL 61272

Call Sign: KB9PBU
Hans W Bluedorn
525 120th Ave
New Boston IL 61272

Call Sign: KB9PBW
Helena Y Bluedorn
525 120th Ave
New Boston IL 61272

Call Sign: KB9PBT
Johannah L Bluedorn
525 120th Ave
New Boston IL 61272

Call Sign: KB9PBR
Laurie M Bluedorn
525 120th Ave
New Boston IL 61272

Call Sign: KB9PBS
Nathaniel P Bluedorn
525 120th Ave
New Boston IL 61272

Call Sign: N9NEH

Stephen P Louck
458 145th Ave
New Boston IL 61272

Call Sign: KF9GO
Norman L Baggett
101 Blackhawk St
New Boston IL 61272

Call Sign: KF9DD
Robert R Burger
1249 Burger Bluff Rd
New Boston IL 61272

Call Sign: KF9DC
Rose M Burger
1249 Burger Bluff Rd
New Boston IL 61272

Call Sign: KB9TLX
John E Butler Sr
930 Cottage Rd
New Boston IL 61272

Call Sign: KF9VL
Pamela M Nelson
611 Locust St
New Boston IL 61272

Call Sign: KF9MZ
Ronald C Nelson
611 Locust St
New Boston IL 61272

Call Sign: K9WXE
Howard W Bridger
851 Mannon Rd
New Boston IL 61272

Call Sign: KB9NHO
Melvin D Lilly
763 Pumping Station Ln
New Boston IL 61272

Call Sign: K9HP
Herb C Mikel Jr
New Boston IL 61272

Call Sign: KB9NHN

Ricky L Wakeland
New Boston IL 61272

**FCC Amateur Radio
Licenses in New Burnside**

Call Sign: KC9OLT
Keith E Teal
350 Belville Rd
New Burnside IL 62967

Call Sign: WB9WIR
Larry G Flannell
260 Maple St Box 43
New Burnside IL 62967

Call Sign: KB9OWF
Rebecca A Mercer
New Burnside IL 62967

**FCC Amateur Radio
Licenses in New Douglas**

Call Sign: WA0LIS
John L Sundstrom Sr
8776 Heinz Rd
New Douglas IL 620741002

Call Sign: K9GXU
Saint Clair ARC
8776 Heinz Rd
New Douglas IL 620741002

Call Sign: KC9CIM
David L Ragsdale
83 Mettlerville Ln
New Douglas IL 62074

Call Sign: N0SCC
Paul D Ragsdale Jr
83 Mettlerville Ln
New Douglas IL 62074

Call Sign: AG9R
Paul D Ragsdale Jr
83 Mettlerville Ln
New Douglas IL 62074

Call Sign: KC9GZH

Tri State Search And Rescue
83 Mettlerville Ln
New Douglas IL 62074

Call Sign: WD9SAR
Tri State Search And Rescue
83 Mettlerville Ln
New Douglas IL 62074

Call Sign: N9YQA
Billie J Ferguson
523 S 5th St
New Douglas IL 62074

Call Sign: KC9UER
Dennis W Harris Jr
123 S Main St
New Douglas IL 62074

Call Sign: KA9ZTJ
Mary E Harris
123 S Main St
New Douglas IL 62074

**FCC Amateur Radio
Licenses in New Haven**

Call Sign: KC9TAR
Robert S Gmerek Jr
121 Franklin St
New Haven IL 62867

Call Sign: WA9LZI
John B Barnett
Vine St NW
New Haven IL 62867

**FCC Amateur Radio
Licenses in New Holland**

Call Sign: N9GIA
Randall R Conklen
1753 100th Ave
New Holland IL 62671

Call Sign: KB9HDM
Joseph G Eimer Jr
169 1550th St
New Holland IL 62671

FCC Amateur Radio Licenses in New Memphis

Call Sign: N9JDF
Cornelius A Santel
209 Mill St Box 154
New Memphis IL 62266

FCC Amateur Radio Licenses in New Salem

Call Sign: KA9TKV
Wyvetta M Davis
Rr 1 Box 56
New Salem IL 62357

FCC Amateur Radio Licenses in Newman

Call Sign: WA9GJN
George E Hicks
322 Hopkins St
Newman IL 61942

Call Sign: KC9PPY
Matthew H Davis
721 N CR 2560 E
Newman IL 61942

Call Sign: W3WCT
William C Thompson
305 S Hopkins St
Newman IL 61942

FCC Amateur Radio Licenses in Newton

Call Sign: KC9QJG
John A Smith Jr
8360 1650th Ave
Newton IL 62448

Call Sign: AA9IJ
Mark W Calvert
Rr 6 Box 182
Newton IL 62448

Call Sign: KA9APZ
Herschel L Little
Rfd 4 Box 5
Newton IL 62448

Call Sign: WB9AZO
Francella E Dhom
Rt 5 Box 71
Newton IL 62448

Call Sign: WB9IFJ
Thomas M Taylor
9523 E 300th Ave
Newton IL 62448

Call Sign: N9PZ
Robert L Copper
7340 E 800th Ave
Newton IL 62448

Call Sign: N9HWM
Eric Barkley
309 E Decatur
Newton IL 62448

Call Sign: K9ZN
Robert H Dhom
13817 E Lake Jasper S Ave
Newton IL 624483661

Call Sign: KB9BVC
Lee A Vanderhoof
305 E Morgan St
Newton IL 62448

Call Sign: KB9RIC
Matt A Rubsam
704 Fairground St
Newton IL 62448

Call Sign: KC9FMO
Andrew G Zuber
5 Jeffery Ln
Newton IL 62448

Call Sign: KC9ENA
Greg F Zuber
5 Jeffrey Ln
Newton IL 62448

Call Sign: KB9WOM
Michelle D Einhorn
202 Martin St
Newton IL 62448

Call Sign: WB9AZN
Robert H Dhom
10409 N 1600th St
Newton IL 624488846

Call Sign: KB9CQP
Loren L Poe
404 S Jackson St
Newton IL 62448

Call Sign: N9MCC
Leonard E Dickey
102 Sycamore
Newton IL 62448

Call Sign: N9JCO
Robert L Copper
306 W Reynolds
Newton IL 62448

FCC Amateur Radio Licenses in Niantic

Call Sign: KB9KAJ
Valle S Funk
531 Lee Sturgis Dr
Niantic IL 62551

Call Sign: KB9LRR
Janice M Funk
531 Lee Sturgis Dr
Niantic IL 625510374

Call Sign: WA9HUY
Norman A Meador
Niantic IL 62551

FCC Amateur Radio Licenses in Nilwood

Call Sign: KB9OXH
Charles M Ritter
30 Judd St

Nilwood IL 62672

Call Sign: KB9MZB
Leslie O Walden
Nilwood IL 62672

FCC Amateur Radio Licenses in Niota

Call Sign: KD0HIA
Jesse J Molyneux
1195 E CR 2920
Niota IL 62358

Call Sign: KC9LRT
Ben A O'Dell II
Niota IL 62358

Call Sign: KC9ACB
Christi L Dochterman
Niota IL 62358

FCC Amateur Radio Licenses in Noble

Call Sign: KC9BUP
Casey M Fulk
1345 E Calhoun Ln
Noble IL 62868

Call Sign: KA9JYN
Kelly D Gibson
550 E Countryside Ln
Noble IL 62868

Call Sign: KC0HJI
Kathleen A Voigt
1379 E Il 250
Noble IL 62868

Call Sign: KC0EZK
Steven L Voigt
1379 E Il 250
Noble IL 62868

Call Sign: KB9ULP
Amy R Rose
2314 E Il 250
Noble IL 62868

Call Sign: KB9OTJ
Benny J Rose
2314 E Il 250
Noble IL 62868

Call Sign: KQ9DX
Benny J Rose
2314 E Il 250
Noble IL 62868

Call Sign: KB9DII
Amy E Fulk
696 E Old Illinois 250
Noble IL 62868

Call Sign: W9LJM
Donald D Schnell
415 E Small Ln
Noble IL 62868

Call Sign: K9QAT
ARC Of Olney
415 E Small Ln
Noble IL 62868

Call Sign: KB9PAY
Ryan M Taulbee
2291 Jesse Rd
Noble IL 62868

Call Sign: WB9JAP
Walter R Rosenberg
219 Locust St
Noble IL 62868

Call Sign: KC9MEB
Ricky S Huffman
424 N Noble Ave
Noble IL 62868

Call Sign: KB9SRS
Jeremy L Berger
2169 N Schnell Creek Rd
Noble IL 62868

Call Sign: WB9WGT
Melvin K Stanley
115 W Elm St
Noble IL 62868

Call Sign: KB9SRO
Benjamin L Morgan
Noble IL 62868

Call Sign: KC9RHH
Jesse A Weiss
Noble IL 62868

Call Sign: KC9RHG
Judith Anderson
Noble IL 62868

Call Sign: KB9SRM
Martin P Seessengood
Noble IL 62868

Call Sign: WZ9B
Alfred Berger
Noble IL 628680073

FCC Amateur Radio Licenses in Nokimis

Call Sign: N9JEM
Richard D Hensley
619 S Union St
Nokimis IL 62075

Call Sign: KB9RKQ
Rita A Schmidt
1345 E 000 N Rd
Nokomis IL 62075

Call Sign: KB9UGO
Jimmy L Pease
17278 E 28th Rd
Nokomis IL 62075

Call Sign: N9MZD
Albert M Gatton
219 E Front
Nokomis IL 62075

Call Sign: KC9CIZ
Karrie M Tosetti
815 E Union
Nokomis IL 62075

Call Sign: N9TZ
Todd B Tosetti
815 E Union
Nokomis IL 62075

Call Sign: W9COS
Chris L Coss
216 Lena
Nokomis IL 62075

Call Sign: N9VOF
Charles R Whitlow
25127 N 16th Ave
Nokomis IL 620754417

Call Sign: KC9SZH
Jason M Brummet
26116 N 17th Ave
Nokomis IL 62075

Call Sign: KC9IRX
Kenneth L Carlock
23206 N 21st Av
Nokomis IL 62075

Call Sign: KB9TZU
Matt A Casey
171 N Western Ave
Nokomis IL 62075

Call Sign: KA9VYO
Gene E Schneider
209 S Elm St
Nokomis IL 62075

Call Sign: KB9UWW
Jeff J Bapst Jr
306 S Oak St
Nokomis IL 620751315

Call Sign: KC9BCX
Jeffrey J Bapst Sr
306 S Oak St
Nokomis IL 620751315

Call Sign: KC9TJH
Jeremiah T Ruppert
219 W South St

Nokomis IL 62075

**FCC Amateur Radio
Licenses in Normal**

Call Sign: KB9QLD
Royce C Kraft
17143N 2000E Rd
Normal IL 61761

Call Sign: K9CEU
Charles W Thompson
514 5th St Northmedow Vilg
Normal IL 61761

Call Sign: KC9LYU
Justin D Nelson
1828 A St
Normal IL 61761

Call Sign: N9DKK
Charles W Riley
715 Angela Dr
Normal IL 61761

Call Sign: KB9ZDW
Robert S Lassiter
214 Arlington Dr
Normal IL 61761

Call Sign: KA9TYR
D N Bussan
217 Arlington Dr
Normal IL 61761

Call Sign: KA9TYS
D W Bussan
217 Arlington Dr
Normal IL 61761

Call Sign: N4ZPN
Jay L Drew
1004 Asbury Farms Ct
Normal IL 61761

Call Sign: W9ZPN
Jay L Drew
1004 Asbury Farms Ct
Normal IL 61761

Call Sign: N6JNS
Glen L Mays
512 Bantam Ln
Normal IL 61761

Call Sign: KD6ZAF
Helen J Mays
512 Bantam Ln
Normal IL 61761

Call Sign: KE9UA
Sherrill D Mills
1615 Barton Dr
Normal IL 61761

Call Sign: N9FZF
William D Blomgren
1612 Baumgart Dr
Normal IL 61761

Call Sign: N9KSN
Glenell E Forbes
1009 Beech St
Normal IL 61761

Call Sign: N9CZO
James P Dady
370 Beechwood Ct
Normal IL 61761

Call Sign: KC9BSE
Sara B Mieczkowski
219 Belview Ave
Normal IL 61761

Call Sign: KA9FXY
George W Baker
1617 Bensington Ct
Normal IL 61761

Call Sign: N9JNA
Mollie E Castleman
7 Birch Ct
Normal IL 61761

Call Sign: K9TSR
Timothy S Renollet
3192 Blue Bird St

Normal IL 61761

Call Sign: KB9PKF
Jon P Rice
900 Bull St
Normal IL 61761

Call Sign: KJ9P
Thomas E Planer
2354 Callard Ln
Normal IL 61761

Call Sign: W8JHB
Satoru Aonuma
F70 Cardinal Ct
Normal IL 61761

Call Sign: W9SE
John A Flinn
207 Concord Dr
Normal IL 61761

Call Sign: KB7ISP
Margaret R Flinn
207 Concord Dr
Normal IL 61761

Call Sign: N9PEX
Roger L Altshue
217 Concord Dr
Normal IL 61761

Call Sign: W9YYT
Charles B Porter
1004 Crescent Ln
Normal IL 61761

Call Sign: N9KOX
Robert J Shaw
1105 Crooked Stick
Normal IL 61761

Call Sign: KB9HXQ
James M Carroll
1007 Dillon Dr
Normal IL 61761

Call Sign: KA9ZMO
Christopher A Otto

1464 E College Ave Apt 2
Normal IL 61761

Call Sign: K9UJ
John F Shumaker
1323 E Vernon Ave
Normal IL 61761

Call Sign: KA9CYJ
Dwight A Baker
140 Eastview Dr
Normal IL 61761

Call Sign: KI4YJE
Joshua T Golladay
212 Edwards Dr
Normal IL 61761

Call Sign: KC9UJS
Joshua T Golladay
212 Edwards Dr
Normal IL 61761

Call Sign: K9DCW
E Donald Chrisman
1408 Essex Ct
Normal IL 61761

Call Sign: WB9ZDR
Jean J Kauffman
338 Fieldcrest Ct
Normal IL 61761

Call Sign: K9ILP
Loren L Graber
901 Franklin
Normal IL 61761

Call Sign: W9SZP
Walter H Sparf
1010 Franklin Ave
Normal IL 617613512

Call Sign: N9EUU
Charles A Simmons
1820 Ft Jesse Rd
Normal IL 61761

Call Sign: WB9UKK

James A Smith
501 Grandview
Normal IL 61761

Call Sign: W9JSS
James A Smith
501 Grandview Dr
Normal IL 617613140

Call Sign: KD4OW
Michael A Pope
101 Hammitt Dr
Normal IL 61761

Call Sign: N9VXY
Earla M Shaffer
1310 Hanson
Normal IL 61761

Call Sign: WB9UWA
Earl J Shaffer
1310 Hanson Dr
Normal IL 61761

Call Sign: K0VT
Timothy A Iannone
1101 Harmony Way
Normal IL 61761

Call Sign: WA8MCD
Gary R Wightman
2264 Heather Ridge Dr
Normal IL 61761

Call Sign: N1DPT
Danny P Tidaback
104 Highpoint Rd
Normal IL 61761

Call Sign: K8VRX
Charles E Francis
117 Highpoint Rd
Normal IL 61761

Call Sign: KE9XI
Joseph M Crull
1824 Hoover Dr
Normal IL 61761

Call Sign: KA9ZZW
Karen E Crull
1824 Hoover Dr
Normal IL 617612246

Call Sign: AA9BS
Richard D Lacy
1003 Howard
Normal IL 61761

Call Sign: WB9UUR
Sherry L Rider
4 Hundman Ct
Normal IL 61761

Call Sign: KC9RHL
Christopher J Coffman
1570 Hunt Dr Apt F1
Normal IL 61761

Call Sign: K0HML
Ralph O Bolt
1314 Ironwood Dr
Normal IL 617615228

Call Sign: WA9VKW
Harry R Hill
1302 Joan Way
Normal IL 61761

Call Sign: KA9ZNA
Debra A Ziemkowski
1803 Johnson Dr
Normal IL 61761

Call Sign: KC9LEK
Louis W Burghgrave Jr
1826 Johnson Dr
Normal IL 617612249

Call Sign: KA9CJA
Ellen C Hardy
1104 Karin Dr
Normal IL 617613149

Call Sign: N9QYO
Michael R Zink
2004 Kennedy
Normal IL 61761

Call Sign: WA9ZRP
Eric S Johnson
1015 Kings Mill Rd
Normal IL 617614889

Call Sign: KA9IVX
Fada R Titterton
102 Lawrence St
Normal IL 61761

Call Sign: WD9GAL
Alanson G Titterton
102 Lawrence St
Normal IL 61761

Call Sign: KB9YSC
Anthony J Meizelis
21 Linda Ln
Normal IL 61761

Call Sign: K9ED
Robert D Edwards
801 Livingston Dr
Normal IL 61761

Call Sign: AD9E
William K Dunbar
1101 Maplewood Dr
Normal IL 61761

Call Sign: KC9QEX
Joe D Beier
1401 N Beech
Normal IL 61761

Call Sign: N9EOO
Jon M Mc Casky
703 N Golfcrest Rd Unit B
Normal IL 61761

Call Sign: WA9NWE
John P Mc Curdie
1423 N Linden Ave
Normal IL 61776

Call Sign: W9FXK
George F Mc Intosh
611 N Main St

Normal IL 61761

Call Sign: N9RGG
Donald E Pratt
304 N Parkside Rd
Normal IL 61761

Call Sign: W9EX
Floyd N Hofmann
1102 N Walnut St
Normal IL 61761

Call Sign: KI9D
Joseph H Neeves
1209 N Walnut St
Normal IL 61761

Call Sign: KB9CDF
Eugene A Arbuckle
710 Normal Ave
Normal IL 61761

Call Sign: KB9GNN
Gary L Max
1004 Norwood
Normal IL 61761

Call Sign: KB9EIQ
Daniel T Painter
214 Orlando Ave
Normal IL 61761

Call Sign: N9JYF
David W Painter
214 Orlando Ave
Normal IL 61761

Call Sign: KB9TAV
Marie F Sage
707 Orlando Ave Apt F
Normal IL 61761

Call Sign: KJ6EIU
Sean M O Brien
701 Phaeton Pl
Normal IL 61761

Call Sign: KA9YNC
Pamela M Russell

909 Randall Dr
Normal IL 61761

Call Sign: N9HEE
Morgan J Bullard II
110 Riss Dr
Normal IL 61761

Call Sign: WA9CGW
Raymond F Coker
119 Riss Dr
Normal IL 61761

Call Sign: KC9LEL
Jon M Ropp
2245 Ropp Rd
Normal IL 61761

Call Sign: KC9OK
Earl E Miller
1203 Russell St
Normal IL 61761

Call Sign: KC9CAO
Patrick S Sullivan
216 S Coolidge
Normal IL 61761

Call Sign: N9CUQ
Donald D Swigart
210 S Grove St
Normal IL 61761

Call Sign: KB9EIR
Tim L Hansen
600 S Linden
Normal IL 61761

Call Sign: KE9KI
Dennis M Huette
916 S Linden
Normal IL 61761

Call Sign: NQ9M
Paul F Felth
1312 S Linden
Normal IL 61761

Call Sign: KA9WHG

Karen Huette
916 S Linden St
Normal IL 61761

Call Sign: W7ZJ
Thomas R Mc Nabb
1301 S Linden St
Normal IL 61761

Call Sign: N9VQE
Nathan L Deitch
109 S Orr Dr
Normal IL 61761

Call Sign: KB9BBJ
Rand H Veerman
205 S Orr Dr
Normal IL 61761

Call Sign: WB9VXI
Deborah A Franson
704 Samantha
Normal IL 61761

Call Sign: WB9JNB
Bruce A Franson
704 Samantha St
Normal IL 61761

Call Sign: KA9FND
Lynden E Harms
1314 Schroeder Dr
Normal IL 61761

Call Sign: KC9HXP
Thomas I Rutherford
1001 Sheridan Rd
Normal IL 617614050

Call Sign: K9DW
Donald G Mc Lean
809 Spear Dr
Normal IL 61761

Call Sign: KB9OMK
Jeffrey B Mays
301 Stanhope Ln
Normal IL 61761

Call Sign: KB9ZQO
Jamie R Theis
1826 Taft Dr
Normal IL 61761

Call Sign: K9GIL
John L Johnston
816 W College Ave
Normal IL 61761

Call Sign: KC9EFQ
Erik A Costlow
606 W Hovey Apt 12
Normal IL 61761

Call Sign: N9GGI
Steven M Noe
1219 W Hovey Lot 7
Normal IL 61761

Call Sign: N9RPE
Richard E Sage Jr
623 W Orlando Apt 206
Normal IL 61761

Call Sign: KA9ZNB
Andrew D Sutton
1410 Westview Dr
Normal IL 61761

Call Sign: N9HAZ
Patricia E Sutton
1410 Westview Dr
Normal IL 61761

Call Sign: WD9EMP
Donna M Dobson
408 Whispering Pines Cc Dr
Normal IL 61761

Call Sign: KG9MU
David O Dobson
408 Whispering Pines Cc Dr
Normal IL 61761

Call Sign: AB9BQ
David O Dobson
408 Whispering Pines Cc Dr
Normal IL 61761

Call Sign: KA9VHB
Braxton S Slappey Jr
Normal IL 61761

Call Sign: KC0CSB
Zachariah D Winchester
Normal IL 61761

Call Sign: KC9PIR
Gayle E Lane Jr
Normal IL 617610006

FCC Amateur Radio Licenses in Norris City

Call Sign: K9JOA
Carl R Whipple
205 Barnes St
Norris City IL 62869

Call Sign: K9CXG
Vern O Holland
Rt 1 Box 232
Norris City IL 62869

Call Sign: KB9LXT
Eugene L Forster
Rr 2 Box 81
Norris City IL 62869

Call Sign: KB9KVU
David P Wright
1080 CR 600 E
Norris City IL 62869

Call Sign: KB9OKC
Sherry E Wright
1080 CR 600 E
Norris City IL 62869

Call Sign: K9CON
Robert J Beam
507 E 2nd St
Norris City IL 62869

Call Sign: KB9TWF
John L Wright
211 N Conger St
Norris City IL 62869

Call Sign: KC9ULF
Ginger G Clark
408 W Main
Norris City IL 62869

Call Sign: KC9RYO
Michael R Johnson
304 W Main St
Norris City IL 62869

Call Sign: KC9SDR
Michael R Johnson
304 W Main St
Norris City IL 62869

Call Sign: AB9YX
Michael R Johnson
304 W Main St
Norris City IL 62869

Call Sign: KC9TPG
Timothy M Bumoskey
408 W Main St
Norris City IL 62869

Call Sign: K3TED
Betsy L Williamson
Norris City IL 62869

Call Sign: K5TED
Theodore L Williamson
Norris City IL 62869

FCC Amateur Radio Licenses in North Henderson

Call Sign: KB9PAC
Brian L Meeker
3256 15th Ave
North Henderson IL 61466

Call Sign: KB9PAB
Bruce G Meeker
North Henderson IL
614660128

FCC Amateur Radio Licenses in North Pekin

Call Sign: K9TPT
Kenneth R Simmons
205 Lincoln Blvd
North Pekin IL 61554

Call Sign: KB9TFK
Richard E Brooks
101 N Main St
North Pekin IL 61554

Call Sign: KC9CPQ
Jason A Bader
130 Sunset Blvd
North Pekin IL 61554

Call Sign: N9OAZ
Roger A Bader
130 Sunset Blvd
North Pekin IL 61554

Call Sign: KB9YBV
Michael W Powell
131 Sunset Blvd
North Pekin IL 61554

FCC Amateur Radio Licenses in Oakdale

Call Sign: KA9SHI
Veron S Auld
122 E Main
Oakdale IL 62268

Call Sign: N9KRE
Daniel R Arens
6859 Harding Rd
Oakdale IL 62268

Call Sign: WB9TIA
William E Ray
12625 Perry County Line Rd
Oakdale IL 62268

FCC Amateur Radio Licenses in Oakland

Call Sign: W9XAA
Andrew R Ehrlicher
650N CR 2360E
Oakland IL 61943

Call Sign: KC9REE
Michael J Gronsky
21790 E CR 1720 N
Oakland IL 61943

Call Sign: KC9ILJ
Robert J Southworth
212 Logan St
Oakland IL 61943

Call Sign: W9YN
Andrew R Ehrlicher
650 N CR 2360E
Oakland IL 619438608

Call Sign: W9LW
Andrew R Ehrlicher
650 N CR 2360E
Oakland IL 619438608

Call Sign: W9YN
Andrew R Ehrlicher
650 N CR 2360E
Oakland IL 619438608

Call Sign: AB9UP
Andrew R Ehrlicher
650 N CR 2360E
Oakland IL 619438608

Call Sign: K9AAB
Andrew R Ehrlicher
650 N CR 2360E
Oakland IL 619438608

Call Sign: W6YH
Andrew R Ehrlicher
650 N CR 2360E
Oakland IL 619438608

Call Sign: KC9APA
James K Mauzy
204 N Walnut
Oakland IL 61943

Call Sign: KC9QMG
Gregg D Baker
Oakland IL 61943

FCC Amateur Radio Licenses in Oakley

Call Sign: KA9MNW
Walter L Morganthaler
Rfd 1 Box 108
Oakley IL 62552

Call Sign: N9PLQ
Gary L Simms
180 Illini Rd
Oakley IL 62501

Call Sign: W9DMD
Gary L Simms
180 N Illini Rd
Oakley IL 62501

Call Sign: WB9WGN
Richard L Scales
4079 N Prairie View Rd
Oakley IL 625017033

Call Sign: W9ZMH
Thomas E Fulk
4074 Ruch Rd
Oakley IL 62501

Call Sign: KB9MSV
James C Bush
8674 Sheets Rd
Oakley IL 62501

FCC Amateur Radio Licenses in Oakwood

Call Sign: KB9LLF
Arlo J Raim
11455 Kickapoo Park Rd
Oakwood IL 618586227

Call Sign: KC9HTS
Ronald W Fermon
247 Lee St

Oakwood IL 61858

Call Sign: KC9VNC
Matthew P Thomas
18346 N 1000 E
Oakwood IL 61858

Call Sign: KB9YNC
Robert H Graves
18270 N 1000 E Rd
Oakwood IL 61858

Call Sign: KB9YKY
Joseph L Mc Kenzie
19202 N 900 E Rd
Oakwood IL 61858

Call Sign: K9ADL
Anthony D Lawson
20294 Newtown Rd
Oakwood IL 61858

Call Sign: KB9MYS
Rita J Baker
Oakwood IL 61858

Call Sign: KB9AEM
Jacob G Baker
Oakwood IL 618580491

FCC Amateur Radio Licenses in Oblong

Call Sign: KB9QLH
Francis G Schalasky
Rr 1 Box 15B
Oblong IL 62449

Call Sign: KB9QAE
Jack N Cunningham
2996 E 1350th Ave
Oblong IL 62449

Call Sign: KC9KDM
Amber M Waldrop
219 E 1980th St
Oblong IL 62449

Call Sign: KC9FPQ

James L Weaver
5250 E 600th Ave
Oblong IL 62449

Call Sign: KA9IXE
Rondel L Boyd
408 E Illinois St
Oblong IL 62449

Call Sign: WA9OUH
Merdith L Cook
306 E Main
Oblong IL 62449

Call Sign: KB9QBV
Lewis L Henry
11063 N 200th St
Oblong IL 62449

Call Sign: KB9QAG
Daniel E Schalasky
1274 N 2150th St
Oblong IL 62449

Call Sign: KC9VDU
Branden L Littlejohn
11860 N 450th St
Oblong IL 62449

Call Sign: KA9IXI
Myrl E Littlejohn
601 N Harrison
Oblong IL 62449

Call Sign: KB9RHI
Brian L Smith
303 N Harrison St
Oblong IL 62449

Call Sign: KA9IXH
Jack D Gallion
701 N Range
Oblong IL 62449

Call Sign: KA9IXK
Richard A Ralston
505 N Range St
Oblong IL 62449

Call Sign: KA5MVV
Jack M Gabbert
202 S Taylor Ave
Oblong IL 62449

Call Sign: KC9EKE
Daniel J Fritchie
301 W Ohio
Oblong IL 62449

Call Sign: W9DJF
Daniel J Fritchie
301 W Ohio
Oblong IL 62449

Call Sign: WN9DOG
Phillip A Herman
Oblong IL 62449

Call Sign: KA9UYP
Ronald L Hinterscher
Oblong IL 62449

FCC Amateur Radio Licenses in Odell

Call Sign: WB0PPB
Edward J Speer III
355 S Wabash
Odell IL 604600432

Call Sign: KB9YSD
Margueritte J Stadel
210 W Elk
Odell IL 60460

FCC Amateur Radio Licenses in Odin

Call Sign: WA9IYD
Alice E Poole
Rt 1 Box 12
Odin IL 62870

Call Sign: KC9MZF
Patricia A Willis
101 E Main St
Odin IL 62870

Call Sign: KC9JDI
Patrick E Willis
101 E Main St
Odin IL 62870

Call Sign: KC9AOZ
Ron A De Clue
104 N Everett
Odin IL 62870

Call Sign: KB9TRE
Randal D Meredith
1480 Red Stripe Rd
Odin IL 62870

Call Sign: KC9FGF
Thomas F Gimbel
1480 Red Stripe Rd
Odin IL 62870

Call Sign: KG9QG
Randal D Meredith
1482 Red Stripe Rd
Odin IL 62870

Call Sign: KB9WHO
Marissa L Meredith
1482 Red Stripe Rd
Odin IL 62870

Call Sign: KB9TYV
Ralph L Jarnagin Jr
7631 Robinett Rd
Odin IL 62870

Call Sign: K9YII
Fred W Rushing Jr
404 S Merritt St
Odin IL 62870

FCC Amateur Radio Licenses in O'Fallon

Call Sign: KB9ZZS
Joel C Jordan
1102 Affirm Dr
O'Fallon IL 62269

Call Sign: KB9WQJ

Michael C Cornwall
311 Agnes Dr
O'Fallon IL 62269

Call Sign: KC9RDR
Todd G Reichelt
630 Aladar Dr
O'Fallon IL 62269

Call Sign: WB0HCL
Leo V Waters
116 Alice Dr
O'Fallon IL 62269

Call Sign: N9GNR
Gerald D Witt
314 Amy Dr
O'Fallon IL 62269

Call Sign: WD0EPG
William A Blanchette
209 Aquarius Dr
O'Fallon IL 62269

Call Sign: KC9RUT
Spencer K Holt
8536 Armsleigh Pl
O'Fallon IL 62269

Call Sign: KC9FHK
Rose Stokes
1793 Bentwater Ln
O'Fallon IL 62269

Call Sign: N9HPQ
Elizabeth J Mc Reaken
704 Bobwhite Cir
O'Fallon IL 62269

Call Sign: KC9EIZ
Christopher C Pixton
1213 Bossler Ln
O'Fallon IL 622697127

Call Sign: KC9FPG
Linda A Pixton
1213 Bossler Ln
O'Fallon IL 62269

Call Sign: KC9SGD
Mid-America Preparedness
Net
1213 Bossler Ln
O'Fallon IL 62269

Call Sign: K9OFL
Mid-America Preparedness
Net
1213 Bossler Ln
O'Fallon IL 62269

Call Sign: WL7LH
Richard J De Trafford
1420 Bristlecone Dr
O'Fallon IL 62269

Call Sign: KC9HIX
Shawn R Miller
714 Carol Ann Dr
O'Fallon IL 622697528

Call Sign: WB8RTD
Brian A Reno
1056 Catalpa Dr
O'Fallon IL 62269

Call Sign: KT7TOM
Thomas R Mitchell
1201 Clarendon Dr
O'Fallon IL 62269

Call Sign: WB7RFE
Peter Clark
729 Country Oaks Ln
O'Fallon IL 62269

Call Sign: KC9BSH
Ie Comm ARC
1818 Crestview Dr
O'Fallon IL 62269

Call Sign: W9EPV
Ie Comm ARC
1818 Crestview Dr
O'Fallon IL 62269

Call Sign: N9ZTQ
Raymond L Methner

1904 Crestview Dr
O'Fallon IL 62269

Call Sign: KB4UW
Joseph T Lee
1002 Dale Ave
O'Fallon IL 62269

Call Sign: KC9BDF
Daniel E Heil
403 Dartmouth
O'Fallon IL 62269

Call Sign: N9XTU
Daniel N Heil
403 Dartmouth
O'Fallon IL 62269

Call Sign: W9EMI
Lance R Holt
510 Dartmouth Dr
O'Fallon IL 62269

Call Sign: KC9RVC
C Daniel Ringo
507 Deer Creek Rd
O'Fallon IL 62269

Call Sign: KB3QYJ
Douglas Handyside
320 Dewitt Ct
O'Fallon IL 62269

Call Sign: KB9LBA
Erwin L Schultze Jr
631 Donna Dr
O'Fallon IL 62269

Call Sign: KB9MXW
Viola M Carson
617 E State
O'Fallon IL 62269

Call Sign: KC9LJC
Herbert Gooch Jr
401 E State St
O'Fallon IL 62269

Call Sign: N9VWD

Kenneth G Carson
617 E State St
O'Fallon IL 62269

Call Sign: N9GQQ
Robert J Muller
507 E Washington
O'Fallon IL 622691508

Call Sign: KC9FHQ
Larry D Shepherd
306 E Wesley Dr
O'Fallon IL 62269

Call Sign: W9BP
Robert J Parrish
1022 Edgewood Dr
O'Fallon IL 62269

Call Sign: N9EQD
Earl E Armstrong
205 Edward St
O'Fallon IL 62269

Call Sign: KC9JDH
Danny P Sitton
1222 Elisabeth
O'Fallon IL 62269

Call Sign: KC9RUN
Dana J Distelhorst
1034 Elisabeth Dr
O'Fallon IL 62269

Call Sign: WA9EZV
Paul E Mc Vickar
1109 Elisabeth Dr
O'Fallon IL 62269

Call Sign: K9HOT
Richard C Gould
1117 Elisabeth Dr
O'Fallon IL 622693534

Call Sign: KA3WLK
Carl E Hordesky
1222 Elisabeth Dr
O'Fallon IL 622697159

Call Sign: KC9FHJ
Jennifer P Sitton
1222 Elisabeth Dr
O'Fallon IL 62269

Call Sign: KC9ISV
Richard A Hair
1317 Engle Creek Dr
O'Fallon IL 62269

Call Sign: KC9JFR
Spencer R Hair
1317 Engle Creek Dr
O'Fallon IL 62269

Call Sign: K9QQ
Brian A Maves
1322 Engle Creek Dr
O'Fallon IL 62269

Call Sign: KB9WSM
Richard F Loderstedt III
310 Fieldspring Ct
O'Fallon IL 62269

Call Sign: KC9ISW
Eric W Nelson
818 Forest Green Dr
O'Fallon IL 62269

Call Sign: KC9JTH
Kenneth L Maness
818 Forest Green Dr
O'Fallon IL 62269

Call Sign: KC9LXX
Saint Louis Area Preparedness
Net (Slap-N)
818 Forest Green Dr
O'Fallon IL 62269

Call Sign: KC9DZC
Kevin J Quade
4 Fox Run
O'Fallon IL 62269

Call Sign: WA5IKB
Rex Forman
1256 Greenfield Pl Apt 106

O'Fallon IL 62269

Call Sign: KF7PL
Carl L Tucker
1224 Greenfield Pl Apt 112
O'Fallon IL 62269

Call Sign: KB9PHY
Timothy R Brown
1202 Hamlin Ct
O'Fallon IL 62269

Call Sign: K9LTA
Timothy R Brown
1202 Hamlin Ct
O'Fallon IL 62269

Call Sign: KF4LAK
James M Norris
207 Hartman Ln
O'Fallon IL 62269

Call Sign: KC9RTR
Joshua L Rolph
1145 Heartstone Dr
O'Fallon IL 62269

Call Sign: K9RLH
Norman R Acker
1 Hill St
O'Fallon IL 62269

Call Sign: N0KRO
Martin R Mullican
153 Hodgens Mill Ln
O'Fallon IL 622696621

Call Sign: KC9JCV
Edward J Pridmore
230 Hodgens Mill Ln
O'Fallon IL 62269

Call Sign: N9KKU
Bernard H Boskamp Jr
107 Homestead
O'Fallon IL 62269

Call Sign: KK4EO
David A Wiederhold

14 Hunters Point
O'Fallon IL 62269

Call Sign: N0CUP
Henry J Wizeman
911 Indian Springs Rd
O'Fallon IL 62269

Call Sign: KD5FCZ
Charles R Phariss II
548 Jeffrey Pine Ct
O'Fallon IL 62269

Call Sign: KB9ZAA
Anthony F Giordano
12 Joshua Dr
O'Fallon IL 62269

Call Sign: N9NFJ
Marsha G Goddard
316 Joy Dr
O'Fallon IL 62269

Call Sign: KC9DAQ
Steven P Pyrdeck
620 Juniper Dr
O'Fallon IL 62269

Call Sign: N9OUO
Kathleen M Rowney
710 Juniper Dr
O'Fallon IL 62269

Call Sign: KC9TWD
Patrick D Hairr
1505 Keck Ridge Dr
O'Fallon IL 62269

Call Sign: KB5VFP
Gary E Brauer
1310 Kim Dr
O'Fallon IL 622692706

Call Sign: N6CTI
Adlai O Breger
1046 Kingbird Ct
O'Fallon IL 62269

Call Sign: KC9AUM

George F Duffield
6 Laurel Heights Ct
O'Fallon IL 62269

Call Sign: KC7JZJ
James E Chaney
536 Maple St
O'Fallon IL 62269

Call Sign: KB9ZSQ
Richard W Kenna
201 B Melissa Ct
O'Fallon IL 62269

Call Sign: KC9FCZ
Matthew J Rygelski
110 Melissa Ct 1
O'Fallon IL 62269

Call Sign: N9XTS
Elmer S Garrett Jr
507 N Cherry St
O'Fallon IL 62269

Call Sign: WB7RIU
Thornton D Phillips Jr
1206 Nancy Dr
O'Fallon IL 62269

Call Sign: KB7FLV
William G Wheeler Sr
1115 Northern Dancer Dr
O'Fallon IL 62269

Call Sign: W4ZVZ
William M Long
1115 Northern Dancer Dr
O'Fallon IL 62269

Call Sign: KC9VOO
Stephen A Gaudin
1002 Oak Tree Ct
O'Fallon IL 62269

Call Sign: KA9QNG
David A Floyd Jr
608 Obernuefemann
O'Fallon IL 62269

Call Sign: WN9E
Eric W Nelson
1148 Ogle Rd
O'Fallon IL 62269

Call Sign: KC9JLJ
Jennifer L Nelson
1148 Ogle Rd
O'Fallon IL 62269

Call Sign: WA0STL
Saint Louis Area Preparedness
Net (Slap-N)
1148 Ogle Rd
O'Fallon IL 62269

Call Sign: KC9BYQ
Charles J Lelko
610 Osage Dr
O'Fallon IL 622693304

Call Sign: N9CHZ
Charles J Lelko
610 Osage Dr
O'Fallon IL 622693304

Call Sign: KC9TVP
Allen K Ayers
912 Paige Ln
O'Fallon IL 62269

Call Sign: KC9TVQ
Julia E Ayers
912 Paige Ln
O'Fallon IL 62269

Call Sign: KC9TVT
Daniel B Bingham
1531 Peach Orchard Ln
O'Fallon IL 62269

Call Sign: KC0ELB
Anthony M Brittingham
415 Ponderosa Ave Apt 4
O'Fallon IL 62269

Call Sign: KC5ENC
Timothy D Geisler
964 Prairie Crossing

O'Fallon IL 62269

Call Sign: N9CPU
Pershing Hicks Jr
1512 Princeton Dr
O'Fallon IL 62269

Call Sign: KA9MIE
Richard L Kelly
403 Rebecca Dr
O'Fallon IL 62269

Call Sign: KB9PTN
Joseph E Kidd
802 Reiss Rd
O'Fallon IL 62269

Call Sign: KB9AAD
Durand D Drumtra
910 Reiss Rd
O'Fallon IL 62269

Call Sign: KC9JDG
Joseph A Young
1717 Rivera Ln
O'Fallon IL 62269

Call Sign: KC9JBH
David M Young
1717 Riviera Ln
O'Fallon IL 62269

Call Sign: K9DMY
David M Young
1717 Riviera Ln
O'Fallon IL 62269

Call Sign: KB9PNO
Jeff W Calog
131 Robert Dr
O'Fallon IL 62269

Call Sign: KB9RGN
Mark A Buchanan
1525 Royal Oak Ct
O'Fallon IL 62269

Call Sign: W9KQK
Lorraine P Place

210 S 2nd St
O'Fallon IL 62269

Call Sign: WB4ACP
Daniel H Casey
1415 S Yale Dr
O'Fallon IL 622692739

Call Sign: N9PBF
Jana L Bechtoldt
1418 S Yale Dr
O'Fallon IL 622692738

Call Sign: WB9FHL
John R Bechtoldt
1418 S Yale Dr
O'Fallon IL 622692738

Call Sign: K9AIR
Society For Preserving
Amateur Radio Comm
1418 S Yale Dr
O'Fallon IL 622692738

Call Sign: N0TNS
Dean S Ford
341 Scott Troy Rd
O'Fallon IL 62269

Call Sign: KB9VTN
Marilyn J Trainor
173 Seibert Rd
O'Fallon IL 62269

Call Sign: N9IGL
Jerry D Hoffman
1202 Shingle Pine Ct
O'Fallon IL 622693481

Call Sign: N9IGK
Lynn C Hoffman
1202 Shingle Pine Ct
O'Fallon IL 622693481

Call Sign: KC9JCQ
Betony R Conte
218 Shoreline Dr 5
O'Fallon IL 62269

Call Sign: N2NNP
Eric E Silbaugh
119 Sugar Pine Ln 8
O'Fallon IL 62269

Call Sign: KB9SRV
William J Hembree
924 Terrace Ct
O'Fallon IL 622693436

Call Sign: N9PBD
Gregory L Horine
1050 Thornbury Pl
O'Fallon IL 622696817

Call Sign: N0BIX
Robert W Fisher
616 W Adams St
O'Fallon IL 62269

Call Sign: KC9TWA
Carl M Fisher
618 W Adams St
O'Fallon IL 62269

Call Sign: AA9NI
Frederick W Clark Sr
1713 W Hwy 50 Lot 90
O'Fallon IL 62269

Call Sign: KC9JCR
William E Graves Jr
805 W Lakeshore Dr
O'Fallon IL 62269

Call Sign: KB9LOD
Alfred James Willmont
904 W Madison
O'Fallon IL 62269

Call Sign: KB9PNX
Karen D Willmont
904 W Madison
O'Fallon IL 62269

Call Sign: KB9PHZ
Joshua M Willmont
904 W Madison St
O'Fallon IL 62269

Call Sign: KB9MGR
Roosevelt F Lavalle
713 W Nixon Dr
O'Fallon IL 62269

Call Sign: N0HFU
Raymond J La Benne
1155 Windermere Run
O'Fallon IL 62269

Call Sign: KC9QJK
Dennis P Mcfadden III
347 Woodford Park Dr
O'Fallon IL 62269

Call Sign: KC9JCN
Malcolm N Goodwin Jr
206 Woodland Ct
O'Fallon IL 62269

Call Sign: KC6EVI
Jon L Demers
O'Fallon IL 62269

Call Sign: KC9FGP
Dennis Miller
O'Fallon IL 62269

Call Sign: KC9IXO
Dennis Miller
O'Fallon IL 62269

Call Sign: KM9O
Dennis Miller
O'Fallon IL 62269

Call Sign: KC9OJT
Amateur Space Telemetry
Radio Operations
O'Fallon IL 62269

Call Sign: KC9TNL
Antenna Builders Guild
O'Fallon IL 62269

Call Sign: W9ABG
Antenna Builders Guild
O'Fallon IL 62269

FCC Amateur Radio Licenses in Ogden

Call Sign: N9HQB
Donita K Osterbur
Rr 1 Box 32
Ogden IL 61859

Call Sign: NO9Z
Lynn D Osterbur
2041 CR 2700 E
Ogden IL 61859

Call Sign: KB9TET
William D Compton
308 Ellen St
Ogden IL 61859

Call Sign: KA9KMI
Russell H Green
103 Marilyn Ave
Ogden IL 61859

Call Sign: WB9JSO
Howard W Redenbaugh
115 Prairie Box 164
Ogden IL 61859

Call Sign: W9CAR
William J Morrison
302 S Willow
Ogden IL 61859

Call Sign: N9VH
William J Morrison
302 S Willow
Ogden IL 618590041

Call Sign: KB1USA
Les L Brooks
Ogden IL 618590321

FCC Amateur Radio Licenses in Oglesby

Call Sign: KI7YN
Jack R Utz
168 E Florence St

Oglesby IL 61348

Call Sign: WU3Z
Jack R Utz
168 E Florence St
Oglesby IL 61348

Call Sign: N9ZAK
John M Mac Leod
466 E SR 351
Oglesby IL 61348

Call Sign: KB9MGN
Dan P Hammerich
233 Elm St
Oglesby IL 61348

Call Sign: KB9LSM
Thomas A Hammerich
233 Elm St
Oglesby IL 61348

Call Sign: KC9CVQ
Derek R Vicich
132 Magnall
Oglesby IL 61348

Call Sign: KA9YFN
Mary E Carlson
342 Maple St
Oglesby IL 61348

Call Sign: KC9NSY
Gary M Corless
918 Mormon St
Oglesby IL 61348

Call Sign: AB9RQ
Gary M Corless
918 Mormon St
Oglesby IL 61348

Call Sign: WK9G
Gary M Corless
918 Mormon St
Oglesby IL 61348

Call Sign: KC9FGU
James L Clapp

921 N 24th Rd
Oglesby IL 61348

Call Sign: W9ZEN
John M Vasicak
124 N Glen Ave
Oglesby IL 61348

Call Sign: KB9YFW
Casey B Mackay
422 N Kenosha Ave
Oglesby IL 61348

Call Sign: KC9IZW
Chris Drewel
2409 N Rt 178
Oglesby IL 61348

Call Sign: KA9LHB
Gerald J Olson
538 N School Ave
Oglesby IL 61348

Call Sign: N9HWA
Louis J Scheri
106 Spring Ave
Oglesby IL 61348

Call Sign: KB9MGO
Jerry J Gruenwald
9 Timberwood Ln
Oglesby IL 61348

Call Sign: KF9C
Charles A Kosciewicz
438 W 2nd St
Oglesby IL 61348

Call Sign: AA9VR
Paul W Meyers
425 W Walnut St Apt 7
Oglesby IL 61348

Call Sign: KC9UPK
Nick Stein
Oglesby IL 61348

Call Sign: AC9AO
Nick Stein

Oglesby IL 61348

FCC Amateur Radio Licenses in Ohio

Call Sign: WB9HRT
Harry F Cassidy
308 W Church St
Ohio IL 61349

Call Sign: N9ZAP
Steven J Keller
Ohio IL 61349

FCC Amateur Radio Licenses in Okawville

Call Sign: WD9CRV
Larry E Pruett
8546 5th St Rd
Okawville IL 62271

Call Sign: KC9GBU
Alice R Frerichs
505 N Sparta St
Okawville IL 62271

Call Sign: KC9MZK
Bryton G Cathcart
211 S Front St
Okawville IL 62271

Call Sign: KA9RYO
Suzanne A La Busier
104 Washington Ave
Okawville IL 62271

Call Sign: K9QYV
Cecil A Robinson
Okawville IL 62271

Call Sign: KC9FHU
Harry P Frerichs
Okawville IL 62271

FCC Amateur Radio Licenses in Olive Branch

Call Sign: WA9JJM

Russell L Dillingham
22621 Old Mill Rd
Olive Branch IL 62969

Call Sign: KC9TXG
Bryant K Fore
Olive Branch IL 62969

Call Sign: KB9LPE
Richard A Wallace
Olive Branch IL 62969

FCC Amateur Radio Licenses in Olmsted

Call Sign: N9HRW
George A Britt
2400 Old Feather Trl
Olmsted IL 62970

Call Sign: AA9CU
Grace M Britt
2400 Old Feather Trl
Olmsted IL 62970

FCC Amateur Radio Licenses in Olney

Call Sign: KC9OVM
Wayne J Kocher
712 E Chestnut St
Olney IL 62450

Call Sign: KC9OVL
Jeffrey L Johnson
5995 E Il 250
Olney IL 62450

Call Sign: KC9LBL
Dean B Smith
1417 E Locust St
Olney IL 62450

Call Sign: KC9FAA
Stephen G Schwartz
4716 E Miller Grove Ln
Olney IL 62450

Call Sign: KC9HEQ

Patrick F Smith
6760 E Montclare Ln
Olney IL 62450

Call Sign: KC9LHZ
Dan R Fuschak
920 E North Ave
Olney IL 62450

Call Sign: KA9TCH
Kevin L Parker
6220 E Pleasant Ridge Ln
Olney IL 62450

Call Sign: KC9TPH
Sandra J Poland
4498 E Radio Tower Ln
Olney IL 62450

Call Sign: AB9YQ
Sandra J Poland
4498 E Radio Tower Ln
Olney IL 62450

Call Sign: KC9OVO
Dennis R Poland
4498 E Radiotower Ln
Olney IL 62450

Call Sign: W9JEM
Walter N Gallagher
812 E South Ave
Olney IL 62450

Call Sign: N9WXT
Richard L Sumner
1260 Hall St
Olney IL 62450

Call Sign: KC9SKQ
Bill W Ellison
601 Henry St
Olney IL 62450

Call Sign: WA8AFM
William A Bates
1129 Keiffer Dr
Olney IL 62450

Call Sign: KC9SKR
Justin Ellison
409 Lee Ave
Olney IL 62450

Call Sign: K9UHR
Robert C Monarch
1703 Mary Ln
Olney IL 62450

Call Sign: WA9TUT
Dirk V Rosenberg
3096 N Big Creek Ln
Olney IL 624500457

Call Sign: WD9FHS
Pascol U Reynolds
812 N Boone
Olney IL 62450

Call Sign: KC9HOU
Nathan A Roberson
5324 N Midway Rd
Olney IL 62450

Call Sign: KC9FMS
Michael A Tovo
211 N Ohio St
Olney IL 62450

Call Sign: N9XQT
Timothy C Tovo
211 N Ohio St
Olney IL 62450

Call Sign: KG9FK
Jackie L Davis
1001 N Silver St
Olney IL 62450

Call Sign: KC9EKI
Dustin L Miller
704 N Van
Olney IL 62450

Call Sign: KC9IDK
William E Jenkins Jr
802 N Van
Olney IL 62450

Call Sign: KB9SGC
Norman F Dvorak
426 N Van St
Olney IL 624503152

Call Sign: KA9PHN
Chester L Tracy
520 N Walnut
Olney IL 62450

Call Sign: KE6BKN
John C Coen
1102 N Walnut St
Olney IL 624501969

Call Sign: KC9GCA
Loren A Urfer
810 Orchard Dr
Olney IL 62450

Call Sign: KG9JW
Dennis R Sivert
811 Orchard Dr
Olney IL 62450

Call Sign: KC9OVQ
Daun M Parker
6220 Pleasant Ridge
Olney IL 62450

Call Sign: N9CXH
John W Robertson
600 S Baltimore St
Olney IL 62450

Call Sign: KA9FCZ
George C Hursta
726 S East St
Olney IL 624502903

Call Sign: K9UIM
David P Smith
906 S Maple Box 81
Olney IL 62450

Call Sign: W9CHW
Stanley Beal
308 S Morgan

Olney IL 62450

Call Sign: WA9FZU
Paul W Sutherland Jr
1212 Shurron St
Olney IL 62450

Call Sign: KC9SCJ
Matthew R Purcell
403 Vance Dr
Olney IL 62450

Call Sign: KA9KDP
James L Gibson
939 W Elm St
Olney IL 62450

Call Sign: KC9OVP
Cecil W Vaughn
104 W Glenwood
Olney IL 62450

Call Sign: KA9EJG
Bobbie L Jarvis
228 W Main St
Olney IL 62450

Call Sign: KA9EJF
Samuel L Jarvis Sr
228 W Main St
Olney IL 62450

Call Sign: KC9HMG
Kendal J Jones
416 W St John
Olney IL 62450

Call Sign: N9ZEN
Carsten Bruch
12 Watergate Dr Schaette
Olney IL 62450

Call Sign: KB9SRN
Garth A Ries
Olney IL 62450

Call Sign: WA9IUG
Glen D Chaplin
Olney IL 62450

Call Sign: N9WYM
Michael R Moye
Rr 2 Box 233
Omaha IL 62871

Call Sign: K9CVL
John T Beam
Omaha IL 62871

Call Sign: KC9JZG
Hargis D Harding
312 E Lincoln
Onarga IL 60955

Call Sign: N9CFP
Norman T Moore
334 E Lincoln Ave
Onarga IL 60955

Call Sign: KB9JJJ
Rolla C Dolph
1359 E SR 49
Onarga IL 60955

Call Sign: KC9VT
Wilbur M Bowman
331 N Knox St
Oneida IL 61467

Call Sign: AA9KS
Martin E Hampton
17981 E Il Hwy 142
Opdyke IL 62872

Call Sign: KB9SDO

Mary A Hampton
17981 E Il Hwy 142
Opdyke IL 62872

Call Sign: KB9KWS
Robert J Patterson
18623 E Lighthouse Rd
Opdyke IL 628722214

Call Sign: KC9EKK
Judith M Richardson
9208 N Log Cabin Ln
Opdyke IL 62872

Call Sign: KA9HFP
Dave L Hucke
Rr 1 Box 159B
Oquawka IL 61469

Call Sign: KA9HFO
Barbara L Hucke
Rr 1 Box 161
Oquawka IL 61469

Call Sign: W3CUL
William A Moody
1006 N Front St
Oquawka IL 61469

Call Sign: N9FUN
William A Moody
1006 N Front St
Oquawka IL 61469

Call Sign: N9BZN
William A Moody
1006 N Front St
Oquawka IL 61469

Call Sign: W9BZN
William A Moody
1006 N Front St
Oquawka IL 61469

Call Sign: KB9RD
Charles R Gibson

Oquawka IL 61469

Call Sign: KC9CNT
Marc J Olson
Oquawka IL 61469

Call Sign: N9BZN
William A Moody
Oquawka IL 61469

FCC Amateur Radio Licenses in Orangeville

Call Sign: KC9UNB
Dion N Fotinakes
13477 N Juda Rd
Orangeville IL 61060

FCC Amateur Radio Licenses in Oreana

Call Sign: N9LQG
Janice P Fisher
Rr 1 Box 30
Oreana IL 62554

Call Sign: KC9RHS
Rex A Fleming
112 E Belle St
Oreana IL 62554

Call Sign: N9HQJ
Richard L Fisher
5321 Kirby Rd
Oreana IL 62554

Call Sign: N9HO
Richard L Fisher
5321 Kirby Rd
Oreana IL 62554

Call Sign: KC9QIR
David P Gerdes
5299 Mayberry Ct
Oreana IL 62554

Call Sign: N9JIN
Rick A Boland
506 N East St

Oreana IL 62554

Call Sign: N9OQG
Jeffrey N Campbell
218 S View St
Oreana IL 62554

Call Sign: N9JNC
Jeffrey N Campbell
218 S View St
Oreana IL 62554

Call Sign: N9SKV
Stuart A Wolken
5930 Timberlane Dr
Oreana IL 62554

Call Sign: KA9STR
Dick L Burger
205 W Plains
Oreana IL 62554

Call Sign: KA9OWM
Samuel C Eubank
R 1 White Oak Ct
Oreana IL 62554

Call Sign: KB9UPD
Stephen T Le Beau
5248 White Oak Ct
Oreana IL 62554

Call Sign: K9KZK
Harold A Wilber
139 Wilber Dr
Oreana IL 62554

Call Sign: KA9AWJ
Ruth A Wilber
139 Wilber Dr
Oreana IL 62554

FCC Amateur Radio Licenses in Oregon

Call Sign: KA9UXK
Frank Babich
1172 Bradley Ln
Oregon IL 61061

Call Sign: KB9FDZ
Chase E Carlson
100 Clay St
Oregon IL 61061

Call Sign: N9ECQ
Brian A Stuart
3004 E Ancient Oak Dr
Oregon IL 61061

Call Sign: KG9HN
John F Ley
4143 E Pine Rock Rd
Oregon IL 61061

Call Sign: KC9FNY
Ryan P Schuster
829 Fairground Cir Dr
Oregon IL 61061

Call Sign: N9ZXM
Donald W Lund
5394 Holcomb Rd
Oregon IL 61061

Call Sign: KV9E
William P Johnston
5709 Il Rt 2 N
Oregon IL 610616323

Call Sign: N9MKI
Mark E Miller
606 Monroe St
Oregon IL 61061

Call Sign: K9PDW
Lorrel J Bruce
103 Moring Ct
Oregon IL 61061

Call Sign: N9CNA
Sidney G Messing
309 N 6th St
Oregon IL 61061

Call Sign: KB9GLW
Matthew A Mc Court
406 N 6th St

Oregon IL 61061

Call Sign: W9RXY
Marjorie S Dickson
300 N 7th St
Oregon IL 61061

Call Sign: W9AAH
Lewis W Dickson
300 N 7th St
Oregon IL 610611312

Call Sign: KB9GKA
Eric M Johnson
883 N Etnyre Ter Rd
Oregon IL 61061

Call Sign: WA6UCA
John H Sorensen
1041 Oak Pointe Dr
Oregon IL 61061

Call Sign: KC9BCI
Spencer O Stich
507 Phelps St
Oregon IL 61061

Call Sign: K9KEK
Spencer O Stich
507 Phelps St
Oregon IL 61061

Call Sign: W9SDO
Conrad Kolpak
807 Rhoads Pl
Oregon IL 61061

Call Sign: N9UQS
Allen E Burd
1618 Ridge Rd
Oregon IL 61061

Call Sign: W9GD
Richard E Duncan
811 S 10th St
Oregon IL 61061

Call Sign: KB9ZLO
Daniel M Root

305 S 4th St
Oregon IL 61061

Call Sign: KA9N
Michael B Ryder
503 S 5th St
Oregon IL 61061

Call Sign: KC9MBC
Benjamin G Rocke
808 S 5th St
Oregon IL 61061

Call Sign: KC5NPD
Laura J Lacy
403 S 6th St
Oregon IL 61061

Call Sign: KB9GKH
Josh R Stone
603 S 6th St
Oregon IL 61061

Call Sign: KB9KAT
Peter R Nagel
401 S 9th St
Oregon IL 610611708

Call Sign: WB9ZPP
Leslie W Taylor
7655 S Carthge Rd
Oregon IL 610619744

Call Sign: N9SHZ
Stanley L Gilkey
2019 S Daysville Rd
Oregon IL 61061

Call Sign: N9QDJ
Charles A Anderson
2115 S Daysville Rd
Oregon IL 61061

Call Sign: WB9VNI
Mervin E Spangler
2239 S Daysville Rd
Oregon IL 610619713

Call Sign: N8IKA

Alice A Conrad
4229 S Daysville Rd
Oregon IL 61061

Call Sign: W8MQ
James O Conrad
4229 S Daysville Rd
Oregon IL 61061

Call Sign: KC9VRI
Dominic A O'Rorke
4197 S Prairie Rd
Oregon IL 61061

Call Sign: N9LHL
Gregory A Wakenight
2647 S Snyder Rd
Oregon IL 61061

Call Sign: KB9BXR
Richard D Kilker
19 Terrace View
Oregon IL 61061

Call Sign: KE9DT
Gordon A Grimm
9 Terrace View Blvd
Oregon IL 61061

Call Sign: WB2FZC
Alan C Gutfrucht
756 W Chinquapin Dr
Oregon IL 61061

Call Sign: N9RJS
Mary C Gutfrucht
756 W Chinquapin Dr
Oregon IL 61061

Call Sign: K9LTN
Robert J Hajek Sr
4024 W Henry Rd
Oregon IL 61061

**FCC Amateur Radio
Licenses in Orient**

Call Sign: W9CKI
Lewis J Gass

201 Bond Ave
Orient IL 62874

FCC Amateur Radio Licenses in Orion

Call Sign: KC9QAY
Carel J Van Der Merwe
1010 10th Ave
Orion IL 61273

Call Sign: KB9EO
Averill H Holloway
1004 12th Ave
Orion IL 61273

Call Sign: KB9BFV
Victoria L Blair
9123 148th Ave
Orion IL 61273

Call Sign: AC0UH
Donald E Achelpohl
1001 14th Ave B
Orion IL 612739636

Call Sign: WD9FFB
Lewis E Burson
1206 3rd St
Orion IL 61273

Call Sign: KB9BHR
Jennifer M Gustafson
910 4th St
Orion IL 61273

Call Sign: KB9HXX
Mary Ann Galliart
1515 8th St Box 95
Orion IL 61273

Call Sign: KC9SOD
Kathleen L Mcdonald
12596 E 200th St
Orion IL 61273

Call Sign: KC9SCW
William D Mcdonald
12596 E 200th St

Orion IL 61273

Call Sign: KC9PFN
Nathan K Truninger
2012 N 1200 Ave
Orion IL 61273

Call Sign: KC9ERC
Dennis M Mrasak
6 Sunny Hill Ln
Orion IL 61273

Call Sign: KB9HAQ
James E Cope
10 Sunnyhill Dr
Orion IL 61273

Call Sign: N9TFY
Vicky R Cope
10 Sunnyhills Dr
Orion IL 61273

FCC Amateur Radio Licenses in Ottawa

Call Sign: KC9OCO
David C Gerding
429 1st Ave
Ottawa IL 61350

Call Sign: KB9PUU
James L Underwood
1834N 2959th Rd
Ottawa IL 61350

Call Sign: KB9EQT
Carl C Mickelson III
515 2nd Ave
Ottawa IL 61350

Call Sign: KB9UKV
Mark C Gretzinger
425 4th Ave
Ottawa IL 61350

Call Sign: KA9YBA
Cecil D Gatewood
620 7th Ave
Ottawa IL 61350

Call Sign: KC9NDY
Bruce A Hucker
510 8th Ave
Ottawa IL 61350

Call Sign: KC9OCP
Dennis C Blackford
730 Adams St
Ottawa IL 61350

Call Sign: K9MSD
Gerald T Williams
803 Adams St
Ottawa IL 61350

Call Sign: KB9KOX
Kathy A Moe
932 Adams St
Ottawa IL 61350

Call Sign: N9JDO
Kevin L Moe
932 Adams St
Ottawa IL 61350

Call Sign: KC9KVW
Kevin L Moe Jr
932 Adams St
Ottawa IL 61350

Call Sign: WB8VBH
Robert C Weagraff
840 Adrienne Ct
Ottawa IL 61350

Call Sign: KC9HAU
George W Zellers
2014 Autumnwood Dr
Ottawa IL 61350

Call Sign: KC9INL
Karen A Trowbridge
2514 Beverly Way
Ottawa IL 61350

Call Sign: KC9QWN
Beth J Chenault
1122 Briarcrest Dr

Ottawa IL 61350

Call Sign: W9EHB
August Freschi
215 Buchanan St
Ottawa IL 61350

Call Sign: N9SXG
Georgiann J Kobiella
2494 Cedar Crest Dr
Ottawa IL 61350

Call Sign: KB9UKW
Jamison W Rappeport
2320 Charles Ct
Ottawa IL 61350

Call Sign: KB9UTF
Austin J Rappeport
2320 Charles Ct
Ottawa IL 61350

Call Sign: K9MDR
William H Kidd
2500 Cherie Ln
Ottawa IL 61350

Call Sign: KB9RMR
Clifford L Ensley
1419 Cherokee Ln
Ottawa IL 61350

Call Sign: KC9QGI
Todd L Hollingsworth
542 Christie St
Ottawa IL 61350

Call Sign: WA9ULB
Robert E Poggi
2451 Circle Dr
Ottawa IL 61350

Call Sign: WB0YNC
Elinore M Grande
1202 Columbus St 313
Ottawa IL 61350

Call Sign: N9OJU
Brian J Scanlon

633 Congress St
Ottawa IL 61350

Call Sign: W9BJS
Brian J Scanlon
633 Congress St
Ottawa IL 61350

Call Sign: K9RQY
Brian J Scanlon
633 Congress St
Ottawa IL 61350

Call Sign: KF9N
Brian J Scanlon
633 Congress St
Ottawa IL 61350

Call Sign: KB9VZH
Matthew S Weaver
319 Desoto St
Ottawa IL 61350

Call Sign: KB9TSK
Kurt J Kleckner
3075 E 16th Rd
Ottawa IL 61350

Call Sign: N9UWQ
Adam C Zeitlin
2737 E 1809th Rd
Ottawa IL 61350

Call Sign: WD9CLY
Kevin R Calhan
2456 E 1859th Rd
Ottawa IL 61350

Call Sign: KC9OCR
Laurie J Bradach
1286 E Il Rt 71
Ottawa IL 61350

Call Sign: W9CAV
Laurie J Bradach
1286 E Il Rt 71
Ottawa IL 61350

Call Sign: WA9HNA

Robert E Mazur
553.5 E Joliet St
Ottawa IL 61350

Call Sign: W9MD
John M Damron
630 E Main St
Ottawa IL 61350

Call Sign: KB9PUK
Lisa M Bond
533 E Marquette St
Ottawa IL 61350

Call Sign: KB9PUL
Randall D Bond
533 E Marquette St
Ottawa IL 61350

Call Sign: KC9QDL
Morgan E Johnson
1286 E SR 71
Ottawa IL 61350

Call Sign: K9QDL
Morgan E Johnson
1286 E SR 71
Ottawa IL 61350

Call Sign: KC9KWA
Michael L Jobst
1513 E US Rt 6
Ottawa IL 61350

Call Sign: N9GYH
Robert D Allen
400 E Washington St Apt 2L
Ottawa IL 613502280

Call Sign: K4WEC
William E Chapman
524 Elm St
Ottawa IL 61350

Call Sign: K9EIF
William H Franklin Jr
2903 Emerald Dr
Ottawa IL 61350

Call Sign: KC9FQE
Walter K Nelson
907 Evans
Ottawa IL 613501361

Call Sign: KB9DSU
Dennis D Connors
805 Evans St
Ottawa IL 61350

Call Sign: WB9ZFT
Donald B Evans
901 Evans St
Ottawa IL 61350

Call Sign: KC9HVX
Daniel G Nelson
907 Evans St
Ottawa IL 61350

Call Sign: KC9HVW
William H Nelson
907 Evans St
Ottawa IL 61350

Call Sign: KC9JE
Fred P Wagner
129 Forest Park Rd
Ottawa IL 613501138

Call Sign: KB9PUR
Dean E Reynolds
639 Gentleman Rd
Ottawa IL 61350

Call Sign: KC9QLE
Thomas M Hillard
1011 Guion St
Ottawa IL 61350

Call Sign: KC9DMW
David L Smith
1115 Illinois Ave
Ottawa IL 61350

Call Sign: KC9VHX
Karen L Keller
1628 Kansas St
Ottawa IL 61350

Call Sign: KC9CIR
Loni J Henderson
822 King Arthur Ln
Ottawa IL 61350

Call Sign: KB9EZZ
Joseph J Tokarz
881 Knottingham Dr
Ottawa IL 613504223

Call Sign: KB9RRY
Veronica R Tokarz
881 Knottingham Dr
Ottawa IL 613504223

Call Sign: KB9WJW
Richard L Leipold
970 Knottingham Dr
Ottawa IL 61350

Call Sign: KB9WJX
Sue Leiopold
970 Knottingham Dr
Ottawa IL 61350

Call Sign: KB9ELR
Arthur B Markwalter
1210 Lincoln Ave
Ottawa IL 61350

Call Sign: WB9NWS
Joseph P Bayer
824 Luke St
Ottawa IL 61350

Call Sign: N9WOL
Timothy J Mc Taggart
733 Marcy St
Ottawa IL 61350

Call Sign: KC9OCQ
Vincent L Czibor Jr
1932 N 2653rd Rd
Ottawa IL 61350

Call Sign: KC9QOX
Brian B Smith
1539 N 2659 Th Rd

Ottawa IL 61350

Call Sign: KC9QOY
Mark S Smith
1539 N 2659th Rd
Ottawa IL 61350

Call Sign: N9TYI
Tom H Rowlee
1436 N 30th Rd 17
Ottawa IL 613509605

Call Sign: N9OWP
Jeffrey A Johnson
2943 N Rt 71
Ottawa IL 61350

Call Sign: WB6KWH
James S Gallops
3460 N SR 23
Ottawa IL 613509651

Call Sign: N7VTF
Alan A Arneson
1407 Navajo Dr
Ottawa IL 61350

Call Sign: N7VJS
Lisa M Arneson
1407 Navajo Dr
Ottawa IL 61350

Call Sign: KB9PUP
Caroline A Daughterity
19 Oaklane
Ottawa IL 61350

Call Sign: KA9UTO
Joseph M Spika
24 OAklane Dr
Ottawa IL 61350

Call Sign: KB9WJS
Joseph M Spika
24 OAklane Dr
Ottawa IL 61350

Call Sign: KB9UPT
Jon R Bryant

1252 Ottawa Ave
Ottawa IL 61350

Call Sign: KB9UPU
Larry C Bryant
1252 Ottawa Ave
Ottawa IL 61350

Call Sign: WN9D
Randall B Williams
1437 Ottawa Ave
Ottawa IL 61350

Call Sign: K9GNW
Donald R Turner
1515 C Pine St
Ottawa IL 61350

Call Sign: W9OPI
Joseph R Vicich
717 Poplar St
Ottawa IL 61350

Call Sign: N9TJO
Susan M Armentrout
1111 Post St
Ottawa IL 61350

Call Sign: KC9QLX
Karl H Hachmuth
211 Prairie St
Ottawa IL 61350

Call Sign: KC9DLA
Jeffrey P Martin
136 Riverview Dr
Ottawa IL 61350

Call Sign: KC9OCM
Lisa M Jung
960 Robinhood Ln
Ottawa IL 61350

Call Sign: K9CGH
James A Renwick
1 Shady Oaks Dr
Ottawa IL 61350

Call Sign: WA9JYW

Marshall S Tisler
2207 Spencer Pl
Ottawa IL 61350

Call Sign: N9TJK
William E Quigley
2510 Sunset Blvd
Ottawa IL 61350

Call Sign: W9AJX
Jack W Rosier
1740 Sycamore St
Ottawa IL 613501358

Call Sign: W9AJZ
Mary M Rosier
1740 Sycamore St
Ottawa IL 613501358

Call Sign: KC9KVV
Roger R Hallowell
413 Thompson St
Ottawa IL 613504335

Call Sign: KC9OCN
Steven M Niemann
833 Thornberry Dr
Ottawa IL 61350

Call Sign: KB9WJU
John W Cowell
710 W Jefferson St
Ottawa IL 61350

Call Sign: W9JID
William F Dunlap
1200 W Lafayette
Ottawa IL 61350

Call Sign: W9VOK
Robert J Calhan Jr
1324 W Lafayette
Ottawa IL 61350

Call Sign: W9KEP
William J Tammen
1434 W Lafayette St
Ottawa IL 613501761

Call Sign: KB9BQB
Danny P Muth
413 W McKinley 10
Ottawa IL 61350

Call Sign: KC9TLP
Terry E Wilson Jr
416 W McKinley Rd
Ottawa IL 61350

Call Sign: KC9OGW
Tom J Hufnagel
1022 W McKinley Rd
Ottawa IL 61350

Call Sign: KB9JVA
Scott E Bunge
708 Webster 10
Ottawa IL 61350

Call Sign: KB9PUM
Robert R Bond
741 Westwood Dr
Ottawa IL 61350

Call Sign: KA9DKF
Ronald R Bond
741 Westwood Dr
Ottawa IL 61350

Call Sign: KC9NKY
Amanda L Wiegmann
Ottawa IL 61350

Call Sign: KB9WJR
Margaret F Reynolds
Ottawa IL 61350

Call Sign: KC9KWE
Rick Koshko
Ottawa IL 61350

Call Sign: KO5HKO
Rick Koshko
Ottawa IL 61350

**FCC Amateur Radio
Licenses in Owaneco**

Call Sign: KC9BJQ
Jason M Klinefelter
624 N 1350 E Rd
Owaneco IL 62555

Call Sign: N9HKB
Theda J Petitt
1094 Rt 29
Owaneco IL 62555

FCC Amateur Radio Licenses in Oark

Call Sign: KC9SSJ
Judith A Kramer
Rr 1 Box 223
Ozark IL 62972

Call Sign: N9OAA
Jeffery A Brown
830 McKinley Ln
Ozark IL 62972

Call Sign: N9OQY
Laura L Brown
830 McKinley Ln
Ozark IL 62972

Call Sign: KC9SGJ
Dexter J Gary
2110 Thunderhawk
Ozark IL 62972

Call Sign: KB0RFS
David C Mohesky
Ozark IL 62972

Call Sign: KB0RFR
Pamela J Mohesky
Ozark IL 62972

FCC Amateur Radio Licenses in Palestine

Call Sign: KC9FPS
Paula R Hilderbrand
15220 E 1400th Ave
Palestine IL 62451

Call Sign: K9CSO
Larry L Hildebrand
15220 E 1400th Ave
Palestine IL 624512819

Call Sign: KC9KDS
Earnie M Mendenhall III
418 E Grand Prairie St
Palestine IL 62451

Call Sign: KE9CA
Ausby L Lowe
13767 N 1775th St
Palestine IL 62451

Call Sign: KB9QAF
Thomas M Brashear
6516 N 1800 Th St
Palestine IL 62451

Call Sign: KC9CCJ
Judith E Hudson
301 S Rush
Palestine IL 62451

Call Sign: KC9AWT
Tony R Hudson
301 S Rush St
Palestine IL 62451

Call Sign: W9PDQ
Tony R Hudson
301 S Rush St
Palestine IL 62451

Call Sign: N9XTZ
Ocie N Seeders
302 W Grand Prairie
Palestine IL 62451

Call Sign: K9SYR
Donald R Winter
605 W La Motte Rd
Palestine IL 624511152

Call Sign: WN9KMA
Phillip A Herman
Palestine IL 624510001

Call Sign: W9TUD
Phillip A Herman
Palestine IL 624510011

Call Sign: KC9EGM
Northwest Amateur Radio
Association Nwara
Palestine IL 624510011

Call Sign: WN9ARA
Northwest Amateur Radio
Association Nwara
Palestine IL 624510011

FCC Amateur Radio Licenses in Palmyra

Call Sign: KB9PBZ
Norma M Funk
Rr 1 Box 20
Palmyra IL 62674

Call Sign: KB9OVL
Victor M Funk
Rr1 Box 20
Palmyra IL 626749611

Call Sign: KB9PCA
Wendell C Funk
Rr 1 Box 22C
Palmyra IL 62674

FCC Amateur Radio Licenses in Paloma

Call Sign: KA9SCS
John D Martin
Paloma IL 62359

FCC Amateur Radio Licenses in Pana

Call Sign: KB9HUI
Avgary G Kehias
Rr 4 Box 37C
Pana IL 62557

Call Sign: KB9HUS
Jack D Stocker

Rt 2 Box 65
Pana IL 62557

Call Sign: W9HLX
Paul L Berroyer
712 Cherry St
Pana IL 62557

Call Sign: KC9VEB
William T Baughman
505 Clay St
Pana IL 62557

Call Sign: KA9TVI
Everett E Wafford
2666 E 200 N Rd
Pana IL 62557

Call Sign: KC9QQD
Kolby D Kroenlein
607 E 5th St
Pana IL 62557

Call Sign: KC9VGD
John D Wright
914 E Jefferson St
Pana IL 62557

Call Sign: N9GYM
Larry R Mc Kittrick
400 E Washington
Pana IL 62557

Call Sign: WA9YZM
James E Jensen
603 Kitchell
Pana IL 62557

Call Sign: W9HQQ
Robert C Simpson
111 Kitchell Ave
Pana IL 62557

Call Sign: WB8WXG
Harvey S Bonser
416 Kitchell Ave
Pana IL 62557

Call Sign: NR9EM

Harvey S Bonser
416 Kitchell Ave
Pana IL 62557

Call Sign: KB9LCE
Terry L Walters
114 MacArthur
Pana IL 62557

Call Sign: WB9AMX
Oliver H Kretzer
134 MacArthur Blvd
Pana IL 62557

Call Sign: KC9MUC
Scott W Savage
709 Monroe St
Pana IL 62557

Call Sign: KA6UTD
Neil Maron
500 N Locust St
Pana IL 62557

Call Sign: AA9LK
Robert W York
202 Park Ave
Pana IL 62557

Call Sign: KC9BJR
Jerry D Jordan
606 S Chestnut St
Pana IL 625571566

Call Sign: KC9TJO
Nathan T Peters
412 S Maple St
Pana IL 62557

Call Sign: N9PGR
Samuel R Grotts Sr
111 S Sheridan Dr
Pana IL 62557

Call Sign: KC9RBM
Pana Schools ARC
203 W 8th St
Pana IL 62557

Call Sign: NQ9P
Pana Schools ARC
203 W 8th St
Pana IL 62557

FCC Amateur Radio Licenses in Panama

Call Sign: N9ND
Dale E Eccles
Panama IL 62077

FCC Amateur Radio Licenses in Paris

Call Sign: KB9DIU
Richard A Rinehart
R 6 Box 195
Paris IL 61944

Call Sign: KA9BVZ
Roberta A Rinehart
R 6 Box 195
Paris IL 61944

Call Sign: W9KYG
James A Wilson
Rr 1 Box 214
Paris IL 61944

Call Sign: N9TKO
Steven L Bradley
Rr 5 Box 24
Paris IL 61944

Call Sign: AA9GX
Shinji Kimura
8 Briar Hill Rd
Paris IL 61944

Call Sign: KC9TBV
Rick D Strange
14 Briar Hill Rd
Paris IL 61944

Call Sign: WF3Q
Rick D Strange
14 Briar Hill Rd
Paris IL 61944

Call Sign: WD9IWW
James E Ogle
713 Buena Vista
Paris IL 61944

Call Sign: WA9TUR
Wilbur E Livesay
16841 Donna Dr
Paris IL 61944

Call Sign: K9WVO
Eugene E Sunkel
12773 E 1100th Rd
Paris IL 61944

Call Sign: KC9AGL
Karen L Burkybile
16448 E 700th Rd
Paris IL 61944

Call Sign: KB9ZVA
Terry L Hackett
16448 E 700th Rd
Paris IL 61944

Call Sign: AA9JE
John W Welch
315 E Edgar
Paris IL 61944

Call Sign: KA6DMK
Carolyn E Steele
407 E Monroe
Paris IL 619442455

Call Sign: KB6TS
Arthur E Bishop
407 E Monroe St
Paris IL 619442455

Call Sign: KB9HYI
James P Tretter
18761 E Terre Haute Rd
Paris IL 61944

Call Sign: W9JPT
James P Tretter
18761 E Terre Haute Rd

Paris IL 61944

Call Sign: N9TIC
Jimmy L Walls
403.5 E Van Buren
Paris IL 61944

Call Sign: KD9SH
Steven V Abbott
516 E Wood St
Paris IL 61944

Call Sign: K9HWP
Arthur A Hand
517 Elm
Paris IL 61944

Call Sign: N9JZU
Donald L Seals
201 Grandview St
Paris IL 61944

Call Sign: KC9PHS
Chris A Drake
18 Janice Ave
Paris IL 61944

Call Sign: KB9KPP
Brian T Bridges
508 Lasalle St
Paris IL 61944

Call Sign: WJ9K
George R Rinehart
605 Munsell
Paris IL 61944

Call Sign: KC9PHQ
Kathy J Drake
12460 N 1200 St
Paris IL 61944

Call Sign: W9OZZ
Kathy J Drake
12460 N 1200 St
Paris IL 61944

Call Sign: KC9PHO
Keith A Drake

12460 N 1200 St
Paris IL 61944

Call Sign: W9KAD
Keith A Drake
12460 N 1200 St
Paris IL 61944

Call Sign: KB9IXE
Harry C Parrish Jr
13512 N 1300th
Paris IL 61944

Call Sign: N9SLT
Donald D Mackessy
219 N Austin Ave
Paris IL 61944

Call Sign: KB9GOG
Joseph E Steffey
100 N High St
Paris IL 61944

Call Sign: KC9NQM
Norman W Eveland
702 N Main St
Paris IL 61944

Call Sign: K9NWE
Norman W Eveland
702 N Main St
Paris IL 61944

Call Sign: W9GHZ
Danely D Mc Cullough
925 N Main St
Paris IL 61944

Call Sign: KC9VMK
John F Griffin IV
16507 Otis Dr
Paris IL 61944

Call Sign: W9UU
Donald R Hollowell
6048 Reynolds Way Dr
Paris IL 61944

Call Sign: W9OAD

Mary L Hollowell
6048 Reynolds Way Dr
Paris IL 61944

Call Sign: KB9ZU
Thomas J Hentz
109 Robinwood Dr
Paris IL 61944

Call Sign: N9POI
Jeffrey W Stuck
1002 S Alexander
Paris IL 61944

Call Sign: KB9QBW
John G Holley
1504 S Main St
Paris IL 619442930

Call Sign: WA9PHI
Margaret A Vestal
413 Sheriff St
Paris IL 61944

Call Sign: WB9ACA
Larry E F Anders
24 Shoot Dr
Paris IL 61944

Call Sign: WO8X
Robert W Nelson
16169 Sulphur Springs Rd
Paris IL 61944

Call Sign: KB9VUF
Christopher L Garner
1402 Ten Broeck
Paris IL 61944

Call Sign: K9QKV
Leonard J Twigg
514 Vance Ave
Paris IL 61944

Call Sign: N9PKX
James A Watkins Jr
327 W Blackburn St
Paris IL 61944

Call Sign: KB9KMA
Kenneth W Winschief
417 W Crawford
Paris IL 61944

Call Sign: N9NVU
Ben J Julian
406 W Edgar St
Paris IL 61944

Call Sign: WD5HNW
Dale A Lindeau
414 W Jackson
Paris IL 61944

Call Sign: W5HNW
Dale A Lindeau
414 W Jackson
Paris IL 61944

Call Sign: KB9LHQ
Thad L Phillips
432 W Washington St Apt E
Paris IL 61944

Call Sign: N9RGH
Ronald E Mackessy
311 W Wood St Apt 4B
Paris IL 61944

Call Sign: K9OZV
Robert A Frey
Paris IL 61944

FCC Amateur Radio Licenses in Parkersburg

Call Sign: KC9GCB
Morgan S Haner
7892 E Wayne Ln
Parkersburg IL 62452

Call Sign: KB9VDQ
Walter L Haner
7892 E Wayne Ln
Parkersburg IL 62452

Call Sign: KC9UKV
Muriel L Cokley

94 N Il 130
Parkersburg IL 62452

Call Sign: KC9TFD
William R Shrode
94 N Il 130
Parkersburg IL 62452

Call Sign: KC9FMR
Atlanta N Cokley
284 N Il 130
Parkersburg IL 62452

Call Sign: KC9DDY
Verlin E Cokley
284 N Il 130
Parkersburg IL 62452

Call Sign: WB9RXG
Frances E Arnold
Parkersburg IL 62452

FCC Amateur Radio Licenses in Patoka

Call Sign: AA9EX
Jack L Ross
Rt 1 Box 43
Patoka IL 62875

Call Sign: AA9EY
Nancy J Ross
Rt 1 Box 43
Patoka IL 62875

Call Sign: N9YZZ
Isaac W Moody
Rr 1 Box 53
Patoka IL 62875

Call Sign: N9WZK
Jon D Harwell
Rr 2 Box 64
Patoka IL 62875

Call Sign: KC9DAT
Samuel D Hester
303 E Clinton
Patoka IL 62875

Call Sign: WA9LHV
William J Gerrish
717 Gerrish Rd
Patoka IL 628751828

Call Sign: W9JDH
Jimmy D Hill
109 N Oak St 1
Patoka IL 62875

Call Sign: K9JAH
Judy A Hill
109 N Oak St 1
Patoka IL 62875

Call Sign: KB9RKH
Richard L Gerrish
309 N Railroad St
Patoka IL 62875

Call Sign: KC9LGU
Gary A Meier
604 Shady Grove Rd
Patoka IL 62875

Call Sign: KC9EC
Erwin L Norris
Patoka IL 62875

FCC Amateur Radio Licenses in Paw Paw

Call Sign: W9SIA
Franklin E Swan Sr
510 Grummon St Box 376
Paw Paw IL 613530376

Call Sign: N9KSM
William H Burnham
210 Peru St
Paw Paw IL 61353

Call Sign: KC9IHJ
Wade P Raymer
441 Wyoming Ave
Paw Paw IL 61353

Call Sign: KB9LBE

Thomas W Ague
444 Wyoming Ave
Paw Paw IL 61353

Call Sign: KC9NXZ
Joel T Bertram
Paw Paw IL 61353

Call Sign: KC9OJF
Samuel G Dunklau
Paw Paw IL 61353

Call Sign: KC9ODJ
Joel T Bertram III
Paw Paw IL 613530188

FCC Amateur Radio Licenses in Pawnee

Call Sign: WD9CHP
William H Rogers
314 10th St
Pawnee IL 62558

Call Sign: KA9YPZ
Kenneth R De Silva
114 13th St
Pawnee IL 62558

Call Sign: KB9SQO
Gregory J Roth
132 13th St
Pawnee IL 62558

Call Sign: KC9BJT
Joshua Roth
132 13th St
Pawnee IL 62558

Call Sign: N9CQL
Robert W Lynch
Rr 2 Box 140C
Pawnee IL 62558

Call Sign: KC9QDS
Christopher C Sprinkel
21 Cahokia Dr
Pawnee IL 62558

Call Sign: N9MAF
Alan M Tabor
1409 Dickey Rd
Pawnee IL 62558

Call Sign: AA9RE
Stanley G Courtney
3892 Dickey Rd
Pawnee IL 62558

Call Sign: KC9HQE
Ernest Pickett
3250 E Boarman Rd
Pawnee IL 62558

Call Sign: KB9FIG
Andreas S Eichenberg
7203 Frisiana Box 806
Pawnee IL 62558

Call Sign: N9OHR
Garth M King
1203 Frisina
Pawnee IL 62558

Call Sign: KA9TEO
Jane L Brown
410 Harrison St
Pawnee IL 62558

Call Sign: WA9ZQM
Richard E White
1109 Madison
Pawnee IL 62558

Call Sign: KC9MOX
Travis S Vreeland
1546 N 175 E Rd
Pawnee IL 62558

Call Sign: KA9CXM
Darrell A Neisler
1101 N 6th St
Pawnee IL 62558

Call Sign: N9UFO
Jackie E Alspaugh
1208 Rutledge
Pawnee IL 62558

Call Sign: N9RAN
James A Smith
Pawnee IL 62558

Call Sign: KE9JR
James L Sharp
1912 E 100 N Rd
Paxton IL 60957

Call Sign: K9CKY
Evelyn L Streff
426 E Franklin St
Paxton IL 60957

Call Sign: N9HTB
James S Swinconos
706 E Orleans
Paxton IL 60957

Call Sign: N9PLV
Franklyn C Crego Jr
606 E Patton St
Paxton IL 609571529

Call Sign: N9YSF
Alfred A Banghart
360 E Prospect St
Paxton IL 60957

Call Sign: KA9WYZ
Ronald A Rasmus
2115 E St Rt 9
Paxton IL 60957

Call Sign: WA9EYW
John L Ryberg
640 E Summer St
Paxton IL 60957

Call Sign: N9RIX
Robert A Steiger Jr
1130 E Summer St
Paxton IL 60957

Call Sign: WA5YCL

Donald L Loudermilk
1175 Eastview Dr
Paxton IL 60957

Call Sign: N9GIJ
Thomas E Scott
486 N 1200 E Rd
Paxton IL 60957

Call Sign: KB9LUB
Gary E Hendricks
247 N Railroad
Paxton IL 60957

Call Sign: K9JWF
Donald L Peters
1010 Park Ter
Paxton IL 60957

Call Sign: KB9LUC
William F Rose
303 S High
Paxton IL 60957

Call Sign: KF9JI
Howard C Rose
303 S High St
Paxton IL 60957

Call Sign: N9NHW
Michael W Rose
303 S High St
Paxton IL 60957

Call Sign: N8ODS
Jerry D Morton
730 S High St Apt F
Paxton IL 60957

Call Sign: WB9JKP
George R Smith
1104 Stockholm Rd
Paxton IL 609579214

Call Sign: KA9MNY
James F Anderson Jr
555 W Franklin St
Paxton IL 60957

Call Sign: WB9NKQ
Bradly D Marshall
242 W Patton St
Paxton IL 609571439

Call Sign: KC9DPX
Brian W Capps
7600 Anna Wall Rd
Payson IL 62360

Call Sign: KB9WDB
David A Remington
Rri Box 119
Payson IL 62360

Call Sign: KB9MOM
Lawrence E Schuermann
407 Briarwood
Payson IL 62360

Call Sign: N9XST
John A Clarkson
115 Hereford Dr
Payson IL 62360

Call Sign: W9GQK
Maurice L Butts
6928 Hwy 96 S
Payson IL 62360

Call Sign: KB9ZKC
Steve A Tucker
521 Magnolia St
Payson IL 62360

Call Sign: KB9CEU
Allen E Scheuermann
419 Sumac
Payson IL 62360

Call Sign: KB9MUV
Gerard V Havermale
432 Willow Dr
Payson IL 62360

Call Sign: KB6OGL

Milo J Zeh
Payson IL 62360

Call Sign: N9TML
Viola L Walker
Payson IL 62360

FCC Amateur Radio Licenses in Pearl

Call Sign: KC9BZD
Larry J Chatfield
Rr 1 Box 8
Pearl IL 62361

Call Sign: KC9BZE
Shawn B Chatfield
Rr 1 Box 8
Pearl IL 62361

FCC Amateur Radio Licenses in Pearl City

Call Sign: KE9BG
George F Flanagan
1382 Rees Rd
Pearl City IL 61062

Call Sign: WD9HWM
Judy L Flanagan
1382 Rees Rd
Pearl City IL 61062

Call Sign: W9YS
Michael L Otte
5001 S Koch Rd
Pearl City IL 61062

Call Sign: KC9MCD
David B Miner
6798 S Loran Rd
Pearl City IL 610629254

Call Sign: K9MBX
Algerd C Churas Jr
15428 W Clay Rd
Pearl City IL 61062

FCC Amateur Radio Licenses in Pecatonica

Call Sign: KC9SDO
Douglas K Abrahamson
16943 Comly Rd
Pecatonica IL 61063

Call Sign: KB9WOD
John T Weltzer
1136 Jackson
Pecatonica IL 61063

Call Sign: K9MFL
Thomas W Moth
702 Main St Box 178
Pecatonica IL 61063

Call Sign: N9IDT
Melvin T Hess
3158 N Jackson Rd
Pecatonica IL 610639222

Call Sign: N9MDQ
Pamela S Hess
3158 N Jackson Rd
Pecatonica IL 610639222

Call Sign: KA9JAX
Todd R Haas
17581 Sumner Rd
Pecatonica IL 61063

Call Sign: N9CCC
Richard L Witherby
214 W 1st St
Pecatonica IL 61063

Call Sign: KB9OPC
William R Spears Jr
Pecatonica IL 61063

FCC Amateur Radio Licenses in Pekin

Call Sign: AA9VE
Lawrence D Kruzan
13785 1st St
Pekin IL 61554

Call Sign: KC9PFR
Michael D Kruzan
13785 1st St
Pekin IL 61554

Call Sign: KB9LNZ
Pearl Cottingham
13548 2nd Ave
Pekin IL 61554

Call Sign: KB9NOR
Audrey C Cottingham
13548 2nd St
Pekin IL 615548639

Call Sign: KA9YMF
Albert A Juergens
2008 Alameda Ct
Pekin IL 61554

Call Sign: N9CVC
Randy J Mingus
2100 Alameda Dr
Pekin IL 61554

Call Sign: KA9JPT
Richard W Waldmeier
2015 Alhambra
Pekin IL 61554

Call Sign: W9JJW
Marvin W Willmoth
915 Amanda St
Pekin IL 61554

Call Sign: N9XLG
Christopher A Yount Sr
1201 Ann Eliza 3
Pekin IL 61554

Call Sign: N9LOD
Stanley P Ehmke
900 Ann Eliza St
Pekin IL 61554

Call Sign: KB9UFO
Timothy A Whiteside
2404 Arlington Cir

Pekin IL 61554

Call Sign: K9GBN
Arthur L Oates Jr
122 Arrow Dr
Pekin IL 61554

Call Sign: KC9DHO
Reinhold H Steckmann
116 Arrow St
Pekin IL 61554

Call Sign: KB9NKP
Craig A Zukowski
2302 Bay Colony Dr
Pekin IL 61554

Call Sign: KB9KCA
Christopher J Meskimen
1010 Black St
Pekin IL 61554

Call Sign: K9IN
John R Reed
R 3 Box 305
Pekin IL 61554

Call Sign: W9EJL
James A Segler
14 Briarcliff Ct
Pekin IL 615545315

Call Sign: KA9IAA
Roger A Stien
2806 Broadway
Pekin IL 61554

Call Sign: KB9JKZ
Aaron D Zuercher
1003 Cambridge Ct
Pekin IL 61554

Call Sign: W9TAZ
Tazewell County Area
Amateur Radio Socie
118 Cape Ann
Pekin IL 61554

Call Sign: AA9MY

Robert E Davis
118 Cape Ann Ct
Pekin IL 61554

Call Sign: KC9NQJ
Casper J Boom
510 Caroline
Pekin IL 61554

Call Sign: N9FXR
Norman D Harding
1027 Caroline St Apt 2
Pekin IL 615543525

Call Sign: KB9BEK
Donald L York
12578 Carter Rd
Pekin IL 615548472

Call Sign: KB9JKV
Steven P York
12871 Carter Rd
Pekin IL 61554

Call Sign: KC9SCB
Andrew D Maddox
1303 Caterine St
Pekin IL 61554

Call Sign: KC9SYO
William A R Maddox
1303 Catherine St
Pekin IL 61554

Call Sign: KC9DHN
Scott M Smith
1508 Center St
Pekin IL 61554

Call Sign: KB9JOW
Wallace L Dennis
1806 Center St
Pekin IL 61554

Call Sign: KB9UFQ
Stephen S Clements
351 Charlotte
Pekin IL 61554

Call Sign: KB9MIY
David A Smith
1314 Chestnut
Pekin IL 61554

Call Sign: W8WLC
Kenneth M Cubilo
1902 Chicory Ed
Pekin IL 61554

Call Sign: KB9MTT
Billy J Merrill
1827 Columbus Dr
Pekin IL 61554

Call Sign: N9CVG
Michael L Carman
2204 Crestview Dr
Pekin IL 61554

Call Sign: WD4MBJ
Robert N Flanagan
6 Cypress Point
Pekin IL 61554

Call Sign: KD4YSG
Frederick L Folsom
1107.5 Dell Ave
Pekin IL 61554

Call Sign: KC9KXZ
Extreme Amateur Radio
Networks
1107.5 Dell Ave
Pekin IL 61554

Call Sign: W9WRJ
Nathan L Voll
510 Derby
Pekin IL 61554

Call Sign: KB9CPE
James R Dully
205 Dogwood Ln
Pekin IL 61554

Call Sign: N9HHQ
Jon L Crank
716 E Shore Dr

Pekin IL 615545221

Call Sign: KC9PZN
Darrell L Jacob Jr
126 Edds St
Pekin IL 61554

Call Sign: WB9CLA
Robert L Ingram
3413 Edgewater Dr
Pekin IL 61554

Call Sign: WB9UCV
Frank M Sanders
3612 Edgewater Dr
Pekin IL 61554

Call Sign: KC9UQT
Michael D Hill
3816 Edgewater Dr
Pekin IL 61554

Call Sign: N9SKB
Douglas W Friedrich
1007 Edison Ct
Pekin IL 61554

Call Sign: KC9PUN
Brian J Valentine
2046 El Camino Dr
Pekin IL 61554

Call Sign: N9VNP
James R Reynolds
1404 Everett Dr
Pekin IL 61554

Call Sign: N9UWP
Richard A Cunningham
2203 Fahnders Dr
Pekin IL 61554

Call Sign: N9ZBE
Allison T Gillespie
1405 Fenley
Pekin IL 615542315

Call Sign: N9YUY
John M Gillespie

1405 Fenley
Pekin IL 615542315

Call Sign: KA9AYF
Rex C Thorpe
1519 Fisher
Pekin IL 61554

Call Sign: N9YVF
Jeffrey L Frailey
1721 Florence Ave
Pekin IL 61554

Call Sign: KD0EKA
Jacqueline R Radetic
1207 Florence Ave Apt 1
Pekin IL 61554

Call Sign: KB9WTJ
Amos A Anderson
1200 Florence Ave Apt 19C
Pekin IL 61554

Call Sign: K9SKJ
Dale E Elliott
4514 Forest Hill Dr
Pekin IL 61554

Call Sign: KE9GE
Harry H Bowen
2207 Glendale Ave
Pekin IL 615545312

Call Sign: K9FMD
Raymond W Schaefer
191 Gunion
Pekin IL 61554

Call Sign: N9DM
David N Meeks
1507 Hamilton St
Pekin IL 61554

Call Sign: KA9GCI
Larry G Gouliard Jr
1509 Hamilton St
Pekin IL 61554

Call Sign: KB9MJC

Christopher R Kinsey
6008 Hartford Dr
Pekin IL 61554

Call Sign: W9SKO
James D Garls
824 Henrietta St
Pekin IL 615543445

Call Sign: WD9EGP
Earl E Melchers
1821 Highwood Ave
Pekin IL 61554

Call Sign: N9RMB
Eric K Tindall
1825 Highwood Ave
Pekin IL 61554

Call Sign: KB9VVP
Scott A Kampas
2124 Highwood Ave
Pekin IL 61554

Call Sign: AB9PL
James A Heaton
1713 Hope Ct
Pekin IL 61554

Call Sign: N9DCX
Verla L Hill
1311 Howard Ct
Pekin IL 61555

Call Sign: KD9CO
Ova P Hill
1311 Howard Ct
Pekin IL 61555

Call Sign: KA9FBU
David J Kasley
1005 Illinois
Pekin IL 61554

Call Sign: KC9GRP
Everett D Hill
337 Illinois St
Pekin IL 61554

Call Sign: K9ICC
Everett D Hill
337 Illinois St
Pekin IL 61554

Call Sign: N9PJY
John F Berra
411 Illinois St
Pekin IL 61554

Call Sign: W9HB
Harry M Mc Cormick
1010 Illinois St
Pekin IL 61554

Call Sign: KC9ICD
Donald Yavorshak Jr
1021 Janssen
Pekin IL 61554

Call Sign: KA9SRW
David J Eldert
1324 Janssen
Pekin IL 61554

Call Sign: KC9IFP
Robert J Stallwitz
1017 Janssen St
Pekin IL 61554

Call Sign: KC9JSI
Donna J Yavorshak
1021 Janssen St
Pekin IL 61554

Call Sign: KC9BQT
William L Duckett
1411 Janssen St
Pekin IL 61554

Call Sign: KB9RHQ
Bryan J Karneboge
315 Knollcrest
Pekin IL 61554

Call Sign: KC9GAE
Larry Lee Moore
221 Koch St
Pekin IL 61554

Call Sign: KC9GHM
Larry Lee Moore
221 Koch St
Pekin IL 61554

Call Sign: KB9GQI
Kim P Nelson
1414 Koch St
Pekin IL 61554

Call Sign: WY4G
Joyce A Bennett
300 Lakeside Dr
Pekin IL 61554

Call Sign: KA9OMQ
Audrey K Voll
1309 Lawndale
Pekin IL 615542222

Call Sign: W9LTF
Donald W Voll
1309 Lawndale Ave
Pekin IL 615542222

Call Sign: KC9OKA
Steven K Hoffman
400 Linden Ln
Pekin IL 61554

Call Sign: KC9LNG
Richard A Gorrie
502 Manor St
Pekin IL 61554

Call Sign: KB9UQF
Jeremiah N Duden
209 Maple Park Dr
Pekin IL 61554

Call Sign: N9VNM
Wallace D Litte
2107 Mariana Dr
Pekin IL 61554

Call Sign: N0GFJ
Clark W Southwell
1301 Market St

Pekin IL 61554

Call Sign: KC9LVY
Gary W Lawson
1409 Market St
Pekin IL 615543713

Call Sign: K9GWL
Gary W Lawson
1409 Market St
Pekin IL 615543713

Call Sign: KC9MCF
Daniel N Reed
1421 Market St
Pekin IL 61554

Call Sign: N9DNR
Daniel N Reed
1421 Market St
Pekin IL 61554

Call Sign: KB9UQC
Amos A Anderson
1915 Market St
Pekin IL 61554

Call Sign: N9DCK
Albert F Hinthorn Sr
1613 Matilda
Pekin IL 61554

Call Sign: KB9VVR
Kay E Haslett
107 Matilda St
Pekin IL 61554

Call Sign: KB9HMG
Charles D Bacon
4427 Meadow Dr
Pekin IL 61554

Call Sign: KA9VAG
Timothy N Reed
1112 Mechanic St
Pekin IL 615544343

Call Sign: KB9TKT
Donovan J Wendell

1519 Mechanic St
Pekin IL 61554

Call Sign: KB9VVF
Ernest B Mahan
716 Monge
Pekin IL 61554

Call Sign: KB8WNE
Michael T Bearden Jr
1302 Morton St
Pekin IL 61554

Call Sign: W9WSM
Joseph R Koonce
1318 Morton St
Pekin IL 615545831

Call Sign: N9ZBL
Roger D Payne
1402.5 Morton St
Pekin IL 61554

Call Sign: WA9NOJ
James W Nash
1505 N 10th St
Pekin IL 61554

Call Sign: N9NMJ
Lois L Sunderland
1407 N 12th St
Pekin IL 61554

Call Sign: KB9MTQ
Ray F Lunsford
1522 N 16th
Pekin IL 61554

Call Sign: KA9YSD
Lewis A Gugliemelli
1612 N 8th St
Pekin IL 61554

Call Sign: KF9DI
Dan C Nelson
1408 N Capitol St
Pekin IL 61554

Call Sign: KB9NOU

Jon S Morrissey
1413 N Pkwy Dr
Pekin IL 61554

Call Sign: KB9PYS
Jessie L Bradshaw
1322 Northgate
Pekin IL 61554

Call Sign: WA9VPD
Owen R Ingram
1500 Norwood
Pekin IL 61554

Call Sign: WA9WPJ
Mary L Ingram
1500 Norwood Pl
Pekin IL 61554

Call Sign: N9SJW
Terry D Lyons
323 Park Ridge Ln
Pekin IL 615543981

Call Sign: W9JRK
Joseph R Koonce
2707 Pine St Apt 19
Pekin IL 61554

Call Sign: KC9CZL
David L Mize
801 Prince St
Pekin IL 61554

Call Sign: KA9LVV
Le Roy C Swanson
62 Rainbow Dr
Pekin IL 615542427

Call Sign: N9XKD
John J Williams
17356 Red Shale Hill Rd
Pekin IL 61554

Call Sign: KB9LJF
Roxanne M Williams
17356 Red Shale Hill Rd
Pekin IL 61554

Call Sign: KE9AJ
Joseph M Werth
1117 Redwood Dr
Pekin IL 61554

Call Sign: N9YVG
Gary M Kelley
813 S 10th
Pekin IL 61554

Call Sign: KB9UOE
Pekin Community High
School Rad & Electrc Clb
1205 S 10th
Pekin IL 61554

Call Sign: KB9GSR
Walter J Greggs
501 S 10th St
Pekin IL 61554

Call Sign: KC9QR
Malcolm J Gillies
1318 S 10th St
Pekin IL 61554

Call Sign: KC9QYA
Lawrence T Reeves
1416 S 12th St
Pekin IL 61554

Call Sign: KB9DLX
Thomas A Blasdel
1716 S 14th
Pekin IL 61554

Call Sign: KA9EYT
John C Nowack
903 S 17th St
Pekin IL 61554

Call Sign: KC8CQQ
Carole A Bearden
1107 S 18th St
Pekin IL 61554

Call Sign: N9ASM
Michael T Bearden Sr
1107 S 18th St

Pekin IL 61554

Call Sign: K9AVF
Jesse L Fahnders
1206 S 18th St
Pekin IL 61554

Call Sign: WA9VWX
Gary R West
1501 S 18th St
Pekin IL 61554

Call Sign: W9FED
Frederick L Folsom
1114 S 2nd St
Pekin IL 61554

Call Sign: WD9IKZ
Albert V Walty
1909 S 2nd St
Pekin IL 615545413

Call Sign: KC9QKD
Robbin P Mock
1114 S 2nd St Ste B
Pekin IL 61554

Call Sign: KC9LN
James E Cohenour
1010 S 3rd St
Pekin IL 61554

Call Sign: W9LN
James E Cohenour
1010 S 3rd St
Pekin IL 61554

Call Sign: N9NSK
Mahala S Mathias
1226 S 4th
Pekin IL 61554

Call Sign: KB9PMK
Dlebert L Atterberry
13722 S 4th
Pekin IL 61554

Call Sign: N9DRC
Lewis D Pollock Sr

1507 S 4th St
Pekin IL 61554

Call Sign: KA9HSJ
Barbara A Harper
915 S 6th Ave
Pekin IL 61554

Call Sign: KA9FBI
Larry G Harper
915 S 6th Ave
Pekin IL 61554

Call Sign: KE9VO
Roy G Cottingham
327 S 6th St
Pekin IL 61554

Call Sign: KB9MIZ
Joseph R Koonce
1310 S 6th St
Pekin IL 61554

Call Sign: W9WSM
Joseph R Koonce
1310 S 6th St
Pekin IL 61554

Call Sign: KB9MIZ
Joseph R Koonce
1310 S 6th St
Pekin IL 61554

Call Sign: N9XKB
Robert L Trowbridge
1516 S 7th
Pekin IL 61554

Call Sign: KB9RAN
Evan J Bonnett
710 S 7th St
Pekin IL 615544622

Call Sign: W9QXX
William J Currie
1201 S 7th St
Pekin IL 61554

Call Sign: N9BAP

Neil C Beiersdorf
506 S 8th
Pekin IL 61554

Call Sign: WA9FDZ
Stephen M Starman
702 S 8th St
Pekin IL 61554

Call Sign: KC9MOV
Bonnie R Opie
1508 S 8th St
Pekin IL 61554

Call Sign: KC9LXY
Ted G Opie
1508 S 8th St
Pekin IL 61554

Call Sign: W9TGO
Ted G Opie
1508 S 8th St
Pekin IL 61554

Call Sign: WB9UCS
Donald G Schoedel
1405 S Capitol St
Pekin IL 61554

Call Sign: N9HXH
James M Byer
1508 S Capitol St
Pekin IL 61554

Call Sign: KC9RNI
James M Byer
1508 S Capitol St
Pekin IL 61554

Call Sign: K9TNT
James M Byer
1508 S Capitol St
Pekin IL 61554

Call Sign: KB9PYT
Donald H Taylor
207 Schramm
Pekin IL 61554

Call Sign: W9PYT
Donald H Taylor
207 Schramm
Pekin IL 61554

Call Sign: KC9ERW
Raleigh W Parrott
115 Schramm Dr
Pekin IL 61554

Call Sign: KB9UFR
Steven D Richards
1932 St Clair Ave
Pekin IL 61554

Call Sign: KB9SEN
Brian J Richards
1932 St Clair Dr
Pekin IL 61554

Call Sign: KB9UFP
Denise D West
804 St Julian St
Pekin IL 61554

Call Sign: KB9UES
James E West
804 St Julian St
Pekin IL 61554

Call Sign: K9PQD
James F Anderson
1321 St Julian St
Pekin IL 615542948

Call Sign: KC9BVN
Michael A Townzen
315 State St
Pekin IL 61554

Call Sign: KB9LJA
Lambert Mantovani
2009 State St
Pekin IL 61554

Call Sign: K9SEJ
Walter W Strader
2220 State St
Pekin IL 61554

Call Sign: K9GHM
Frank W Tidaback
1705 Summit Dr
Pekin IL 61554

Call Sign: K9ROG
Roger R Kidd
223 Sunnyridge Rd Apt C
Pekin IL 61554

Call Sign: WD9EGQ
Glen E Bergerhouse
2213 Sunset Dr
Pekin IL 615545364

Call Sign: KB9VWI
Guy A Tisdale
107 Susannah St
Pekin IL 61554

Call Sign: N9LFD
Robert J Ferrell
14065 Townline Rd
Pekin IL 61535

Call Sign: WD9CLW
Gregory M Williams
1816 Valencia Pl
Pekin IL 61554

Call Sign: WD9HYV
Louis V Compton
2208 Valentine Ave
Pekin IL 61554

Call Sign: KC9SCE
Christopher M Simonsen
2214 Valentine Ave
Pekin IL 61554

Call Sign: W8OB
Kenneth M Cubilo
1300 Windflower
Pekin IL 61555

Call Sign: KC9OXA
Steven B Wabel
1612 Winged Foot Dr

Pekin IL 61554

Call Sign: N9CL
Steven B Wabel
1612 Winged Foot Dr
Pekin IL 61554

Call Sign: WA9QBE
Edwin N Rathbun
Pekin IL 61554

Call Sign: W9EBW
John R Garing
Pekin IL 61555

Call Sign: KB9NOV
Robert A Bundy
Pekin IL 61554

FCC Amateur Radio Licenses in Penfield

Call Sign: KB9ZDO
Lisa J Enloe
3468 CR 2775 E
Penfield IL 61862

Call Sign: KB9TLJ
Colin K Weston
2518 CR 3100 N
Penfield IL 61862

Call Sign: KE9KC
Darryl A Coan
Penfield IL 61862

FCC Amateur Radio Licenses in Peoria

Call Sign: KB9ISN
Jeremy W Block
7211 Benjamin Ct
Peoria IL 61614

Call Sign: AA9X
John L Morton
6007 Bent Oak Ln
Peoria IL 61615

Call Sign: KB9HZV
Paul C Caughey
6811 Bobolink Rd
Peoria IL 61614

Call Sign: KA9UWT
John E Phillips
2324 Cameron Ln
Peoria IL 61607

Call Sign: KA9DNB
Ronald F Kolb
3130 Chartwell Rd
Peoria IL 61614

Call Sign: N9NEY
Angela M Clancy
3708 Dayton Ave
Peoria IL 61614

Call Sign: N9MZS
Geoffrey D Ginzel
4129 Devon
Peoria IL 61614

Call Sign: W9KCB
Allan H Lurie
605 E Armstrong Ave
Peoria IL 61603

Call Sign: W9JVR
Peoria High ARC
605 E Armstrong Ave
Peoria IL 61603

Call Sign: KB9NOP
Charles E Watters
1424 E Beach
Peoria IL 61615

Call Sign: KB9SPP
Bill J Huffman
1437 E Elmhurst Ave
Peoria IL 616031667

Call Sign: N9XHM
Mark D Tolson
1012 E Elmhust Ave
Peoria IL 61603

Call Sign: N9JSW
John C Hall Jr
414 E Forrest Hill
Peoria IL 61603

Call Sign: KB9VQH
Merle A Joiner
705 E Frye Ave
Peoria IL 61603

Call Sign: WD9EGL
Frank R Raschert Sr
1108 E Hazard
Peoria IL 616147622

Call Sign: WD9IYS
Robert L Barbier
1622 E Hendryx Ln
Peoria IL 61615

Call Sign: KB9GMB
Michael F Penca
467 E High Point Dr
Peoria IL 61614

Call Sign: KB9ISG
Catherina J Reith
369 E High Point Rd
Peoria IL 61614

Call Sign: KB9HZU
Mitzi M Mc Cord
556 E High Point Rd
Peoria IL 61614

Call Sign: KC9TFI
George W Mullen III
1312 E Lake Ave
Peoria IL 61614

Call Sign: N9DIT
Melvin Ziedman
1814 E Lake Ave
Peoria IL 61614

Call Sign: N9ZVI
George C Knight
620 E Marietta

Peoria IL 61614

Call Sign: KB9UXH
Charles R Billingsley Sr
726 E McClure
Peoria IL 61603

Call Sign: N9KXN
Scott Friesth
1219 E Moneta Ave
Peoria IL 61615

Call Sign: N9KGX
Alfred W Grupe
1129 E Norwood Ave
Peoria IL 61603

Call Sign: KC9UCS
Clyde O Huffman
1129 E Parkside Ln
Peoria IL 61615

Call Sign: K9QXF
Clyde O Huffman
1129 E Parkside Ln
Peoria IL 61615

Call Sign: KB9KXT
Holli A Cook
601 E Pasadena
Peoria IL 61603

Call Sign: WE9SCB
Dean R Whitely
510 E Pennsylvania
Peoria IL 61603

Call Sign: KB9IYU
James N Slaughter
417 E Republic
Peoria IL 61603

Call Sign: WB9WYY
Donald E Brown
307 E Thrush
Peoria IL 61603

Call Sign: WA9WZX
Donald Trimnell

1101 E Wilson St
Peoria IL 61603

Call Sign: N9VIK
William L Phillips
3125 Freemont St
Peoria IL 61605

Call Sign: WB9UVB
Raymond T Weitzel
626 Haungs Ave
Peoria IL 616032826

Call Sign: KB9TLD
William A Wilcox
710 Haungs Ave
Peoria IL 61603

Call Sign: N9TDF
Gary L Sundberg
4124 Hawthorne Pl
Peoria IL 616147210

Call Sign: N9LFA
David F Ginzel
4645 Heatherwood
Peoria IL 61615

Call Sign: KB9YBT
Moore H Moore II
1622 Hendryx Ln
Peoria IL 61615

Call Sign: N9ENS
Thomas J Cusack
357 High Pt Rd
Peoria IL 61614

Call Sign: K9LFH
Lyle L Bishop
4322 Independence
Peoria IL 61614

Call Sign: N9SJZ
John B Hineman
4212 Keenland
Peoria IL 61614

Call Sign: KB9HWK

Robert P Hougland Jr
858 Kimmoor
Peoria IL 61605

Call Sign: KA9KQW
Bruce E Galletti
4409 Lynnhurst
Peoria IL 61615

Call Sign: KB9HZO
Tasha S Ramsay
912 MacTavish Rd
Peoria IL 61614

Call Sign: KB9IFX
David M Ramsay
912 MacTavish Rd
Peoria IL 61615

Call Sign: KB9HZK
William W Swanson
6905 Michele
Peoria IL 61614

Call Sign: N9WNG
Regina H Dos Santos
3020 N 12 Oaks Dr
Peoria IL 61604

Call Sign: K9SOC
Philip C Mayer
6500 N Allen Rd 60
Peoria IL 616145806

Call Sign: KA9NJX
Frederick C Genge
5819 N Andover Ct
Peoria IL 61615

Call Sign: KB9KBG
Jonathon M Genge
5819 N Andover Ct
Peoria IL 61615

Call Sign: KB9GLZ
Ryan M Daniels
7225 N Benjamin Ct
Peoria IL 61614

Call Sign: KB9UXJ
Philip G Burroughs
5610 N Biltmore
Peoria IL 61614

Call Sign: WD9FQE
James R Lytle Sr
1417 N Bourland
Peoria IL 61606

Call Sign: KB9HZM
Nicole L Bradford
1310 N Bourland Ave
Peoria IL 61606

Call Sign: WB9KFR
Frederick L Gruss Sr
9914 N Broadway
Peoria IL 616159727

Call Sign: KC9CMH
Lisa L Poole
4015 N Brookmont Rd
Peoria IL 61614

Call Sign: KA9WOG
Ronald N Cooke
3216 N California Ave
Peoria IL 61603

Call Sign: KC9RFS
Aaron J Prentice
3128 N Chapel Pl
Peoria IL 61603

Call Sign: N7BYI
Mark T De Cou
6757 N Chateau Pl
Peoria IL 61615

Call Sign: NN9P
Joel R Ingles
10316 N Churchill Dr
Peoria IL 61615

Call Sign: WB9YPL
Ilga Williams
614 N Cooper
Peoria IL 61606

Call Sign: KC9TCO
Jonathan A Eisenmann
1128 N Country Ln
Peoria IL 61604

Call Sign: KB9OMO
Dale A Howard Jr
1301 N Country Ln
Peoria IL 61604

Call Sign: WA9SIT
Charles W Gardner
5001 N Dawn Dr
Peoria IL 61614

Call Sign: KA9JHI
Glenwood B Manning
4010 N Dayton
Peoria IL 61614

Call Sign: KW9J
Mary E Garrett
2312 N Delaware
Peoria IL 616032646

Call Sign: KA9PVS
Kevin S Milleson
3911 N Donna Ln
Peoria IL 61615

Call Sign: K9DRF
Darhal J Wolf
10820 N Dorset St
Peoria IL 61615

Call Sign: KB4PFA
James J Babon
1504 N Douglas St
Peoria IL 61606

Call Sign: NU9E
Charles D Dermody
5702 N Eastvue Ct
Peoria IL 61615

Call Sign: N9TYO
Lon A Carr
5706 N Eastvue Ct

Peoria IL 61615

Call Sign: WB9NWO
John E Lewis
3526 N Elmcroft Ter
Peoria IL 61604

Call Sign: WM9Y
Gary L Brubaker
3115 N Emery Ave
Peoria IL 61604

Call Sign: K9KBJ
Ronald J Schuster
1047 N Emily Pl Apt 209
Peoria IL 61604

Call Sign: KB9FRV
Woody A White
4919 N Everts Ct
Peoria IL 61614

Call Sign: KB9HZX
Daniel S Rossi
5502 N Fairmont Dr
Peoria IL 61614

Call Sign: N9SJY
William E Allen
6927 N Flamingo Ct
Peoria IL 61614

Call Sign: KF9XF
Neal W Rudy
10461 N Forest Tr
Peoria IL 61615

Call Sign: KB9HZW
Heidi R Slaw
6891 N Fox Point Dr
Peoria IL 61614

Call Sign: KC9PQX
James V Boyle
6903 N Fox Point Dr
Peoria IL 61614

Call Sign: KB9ISK
Kristen M Vanek

7017 N Fox Point Dr
Peoria IL 61614

Call Sign: KB9GMA
Jeffery M Vanek
7017 N Foxpoint Dr
Peoria IL 61614

Call Sign: K9JEM
John R Mc Michael Jr
6225 N Frostwood Pky
Peoria IL 61615

Call Sign: WD9IBJ
Kenneth W Jones
6901 N Galena Rd Apt 327
Peoria IL 616143165

Call Sign: W9PJR
Thomas E Kingery
5533 N Galena Rd Box 52
Peoria IL 616144458

Call Sign: KC9UIT
Andrew B Montgomery
1202 N Glenwood Ave
Peoria IL 61606

Call Sign: KZ9DRW
Andrew B Montgomery
1202 N Glenwood Ave
Peoria IL 61606

Call Sign: N9FCS
Pierre C Guerindon
5102 N Gln
Peoria IL 61614

Call Sign: W9DGF
Orrin E Ingles
5004 N Graceland Dr
Peoria IL 616144649

Call Sign: WD9CIR
Stephen S Craig
4112 N Grand Blvd
Peoria IL 61614 .

Call Sign: KB9NSJ

Debra A Craig
4112 N Grand Blvd
Peoria IL 616120763

Call Sign: N9SJ
Debra A Craig
4112 N Grand Blvd
Peoria IL 616120763

Call Sign: KC9UJD
Pals Repeater Group
3615 N Grandview Dr
Peoria IL 61614

Call Sign: WX9PIA
Pals Repeater Group
3615 N Grandview Dr
Peoria IL 61614

Call Sign: N9AMH
Richard A Kutter Sr
5713 N Hamilton Rd
Peoria IL 616143833

Call Sign: W9NS
James L Moon
5714 N Hamilton Rd
Peoria IL 61614

Call Sign: KC9HEV
John F Grimes
3905 N Harmon Ave
Peoria IL 616146632

Call Sign: N9JFG
John F Grimes
3905 N Harmon Ave
Peoria IL 616146632

Call Sign: N9PSD
George P Smith
4110 N Harvard
Peoria IL 61614

Call Sign: N9TYG
Daisy B Sundberg
4124 N Hawthorne Pl
Peoria IL 61614

Call Sign: KB9LIX
William F Peters
1103 N Institute
Peoria IL 61606

Call Sign: KB9FQV
David A Wombacher
5602 N Isabel
Peoria IL 61614

Call Sign: KB9NXT
Liz A Miller
4115 N Keenland
Peoria IL 61614

Call Sign: KB9IAB
Nicholas P Mosser
6919 N Kimberly Ct
Peoria IL 61614

Call Sign: KA9UEY
Waldemar Jaczkowski
1919 N Knoxville
Peoria IL 61603

Call Sign: KB9HZN
Luke A Ulrich
8208 N Knoxville
Peoria IL 61615

Call Sign: KB9NGR
Madhana Gopal Narayanan
5250 N Knoxville Ave 103
Peoria IL 61614

Call Sign: KC9ALV
Daniel A Seagraves
4717 N Knoxville Ave Apt
515
Peoria IL 61614

Call Sign: KC9UCH
Philip L Graves
4121 N Koerner Rd
Peoria IL 61615

Call Sign: WB9YNQ
Duane T Hill
4732 N Laurel Dr

Peoria IL 61614

Call Sign: KA9PFF
Merle H Miller
2106 N Lehman Rd
Peoria IL 61604

Call Sign: N9KIT
William E Gebhards
2429 N Lehman Rd
Peoria IL 61604

Call Sign: KB9KCD
Joel A Kilpack
2321 N Linn St
Peoria IL 61604

Call Sign: KA9KVM
James L Steere Sr
5318 N Longwood Dr
Peoria IL 61614

Call Sign: K9PSA
Jack B Maticka
3915 N Lynnwood Pl
Peoria IL 61614

Call Sign: KB9MJA
Brent A Christians
3909 N Lynnwood Pl
Peoria IL 61614

Call Sign: KB9ISH
Bradley J Christoffersen
7120 N Manning Dr
Peoria IL 61614

Call Sign: KB9ISP
Megan M Smith
7321 N Manning Dr
Peoria IL 61614

Call Sign: WB9VXQ
Margaret E Wright
734 N Maxwell Rd
Peoria IL 61604

Call Sign: WB9YEG
Vernon L Wright

734 N Maxwell Rd
Peoria IL 61604

Call Sign: KC9SSN
Michael A Shook
5125 N Merrimac Ave
Peoria IL 61614

Call Sign: WB9KNF
James A Henderson
5710 N Merrimac Ave
Peoria IL 616143931

Call Sign: KA9JPK
Romona L Henderson
5710 N Merrimac Ave
Peoria IL 616143931

Call Sign: WB9YKA
Alan B Craig
6902 N Michele Ln
Peoria IL 61614

Call Sign: N9ZBB
Michael C Gomes
3304 N Missouri
Peoria IL 61603

Call Sign: KB9AQS
James E Maricle Jr
2007 N Missouri St
Peoria IL 61603

Call Sign: KB9HQJ
Jeffrey A Counsil
10427 N N Forest Tr
Peoria IL 61615

Call Sign: K9QNE
Walter J Wolf
3214 N Parish
Peoria IL 61604

Call Sign: N9WST
Mark L Elliott
8705 N Picture Ridge Rd
Peoria IL 61615

Call Sign: KB9KBZ

Betty A Elliott
8705 N Picture Ridge Rd
Peoria IL 616151736

Call Sign: K9DAB
David A Budzynski
9120 N Pine Tree Rd
Peoria IL 616151438

Call Sign: N9TYM
James D Malone
6301 N Post Oak Rd
Peoria IL 61615

Call Sign: WB9RSS
James T Buchanan
2714 N Prospect Rd
Peoria IL 61603

Call Sign: W9TMI
Michael D Hill
3926 N Prospect Rd
Peoria IL 61614

Call Sign: KA9DNC
Robert J Malone
5631 N Renwood Ave
Peoria IL 61614

Call Sign: KB9QCY
Clifford L Shoemaker
6425 N Robinwood Dr
Peoria IL 61614

Call Sign: N9UTS
Tom A Hendrickson
5231 N Ronald Rd
Peoria IL 61614

Call Sign: K9SZG
James L Hopper
3658 N Sandia Dr
Peoria IL 616041099

Call Sign: KA9YWA
Denise C Bernhard Cooksey
914 N Sheridan Rd
Peoria IL 61606

Call Sign: N9SKA
Paul H Mueller
5110 N Sheridan Rd
Peoria IL 61614

Call Sign: KB9GSV
Theodore Scharle
6310 N Sheridan Rd
Peoria IL 61614

Call Sign: WA9HBX
Lindbergh Middle School
ARC
6327 N Sheridan Rd
Peoria IL 61614

Call Sign: KB9VVS
Brett R Ring
1805 N Sheridan Rd
Peoria IL 61604

Call Sign: KB9AQT
Stephen T Courtney
3218 N Sherwood
Peoria IL 61604

Call Sign: KB9CAL
Ronnie S Cristobal
5603 N Sherwood
Peoria IL 61614

Call Sign: KC9FWT
Debrah M Parsley
10207 N Spring Ln
Peoria IL 61615

Call Sign: KB9VVT
Norman W Parsley
10207 N Spring Ln
Peoria IL 61615

Call Sign: N9KLY
Fred E Julien Jr
5328 N Stephen Dr
Peoria IL 61615

Call Sign: WD9HGC
Martha E Tieber
2720 N Sterling

Peoria IL 61604

Call Sign: WA9FCN
Francis C Tieber
2720 N Sterling Ave
Peoria IL 61604

Call Sign: KC9MGK
Alexander R Cannon
10601 N Strawn Ct
Peoria IL 616151190

Call Sign: N9TOF
Michel A Cox
6608 N Suffolk Dr
Peoria IL 61615

Call Sign: WB9HZI
William R Woolsey
5107 N Sunnybrook Dr
Peoria IL 61614

Call Sign: N9GQR
Frank L Johnson
6827 N Terra Vista Dr 801
Peoria IL 61614

Call Sign: KC9AXO
Thomas E Jerrell
7150 N Terra Vista Dr Apt
101
Peoria IL 61614

Call Sign: K9NWF
Thomas E Jerrell
7150 N Terra Vista Dr Apt
101
Peoria IL 61614

Call Sign: KC9RBS
Sita Rama Sastry Kompella
7150 N Terra Vista Dr Apt
705
Peoria IL 61614

Call Sign: KC9OTZ
David B Rankin
7150 N Terra Vista Dr Apt
804

Peoria IL 61614

Call Sign: WD9EGW
Charles W Kuhn
7005 N Tobi Ln
Peoria IL 616141939

Call Sign: N9YDN
Phyllis A Ackerman
3020 N Twelve Oaks Dr
Peoria IL 61604

Call Sign: N9NTG
Boyd G Harris
5108 N University St
Peoria IL 61614

Call Sign: KD5OOB
Darrell C Norton
6500 N University St Apt 512
Peoria IL 61614

Call Sign: N9RLX
Stephen N Chase
6720 N Upper Skyline Dr
Peoria IL 61614

Call Sign: WB9UCW
Ronald L Anderson Sr
5801 N Wacker Dr
Peoria IL 61615

Call Sign: KB9ISF
Erica D Graves
7233 N Whippoorwill Ln
Peoria IL 69614

Call Sign: KC9QH
Richard E Tompkins
11100 N Wilderness Dr
Peoria IL 61615

Call Sign: KB9RHV
Duane J Libby
1005 N Wildwood Ct
Peoria IL 616044466

Call Sign: WA9RFU
Barbara B Gurtler

6723 N Wilshire Ct
Peoria IL 61614

Call Sign: KB9IAC
Tara K Szold
5704 N Woodlawn Ct
Peoria IL 61614

Call Sign: W9UNB
John E Dahl
2511 NE Adams
Peoria IL 61603

Call Sign: WA9ZTG
Dewey R Brownfield
1947 NE Glendale
Peoria IL 61603

Call Sign: K5USM
Jeffrey A Dale
100 NE Monroe St Ste 42
Peoria IL 61602

Call Sign: N9NLS
John D Alms
1005 NE Perry Ave
Peoria IL 616034041

Call Sign: K9YTI
William E Smothers
4516 Nelson
Peoria IL 61614

Call Sign: KB9KBH
Mike W Elliot
5431 Nottingham
Peoria IL 61614

Call Sign: WA9EAQ
William E Defenbaugh
136 Oak Park Dr
Peoria IL 61614

Call Sign: KB9HZG
Laura K Swisher
1004 Oakglen Dr
Peoria IL 61614

Call Sign: KB9FLP

Colleen A Fast
1830 Park Ave
Peoria IL 61604

Call Sign: KB9FLO
Pablo H Fast
1830 Park Ave
Peoria IL 61604

Call Sign: N9YDF
Ronald R Utter
6713 Parkdale 11
Peoria IL 61614

Call Sign: KC9FA
Eric L Johnson
6223 Post Oak Rd
Peoria IL 61615

Call Sign: KB9HZL
Kirk G Williams
1400 Queens Ct Rd
Peoria IL 61614

Call Sign: KA0KDE
Victoria L Loberg
320 Ravinswood Rd
Peoria IL 61615

Call Sign: KA9ENH
Karen M Bishop
2124 Roosevelt Rd
Peoria IL 61614

Call Sign: KC9CIE
Todd M Moore
2900 Rushford Ct
Peoria IL 61614

Call Sign: N9QDI
Matthew F Elliott
4910 S Airport Rd
Peoria IL 61607

Call Sign: KB9NGT
James W Rodgers
1232 S Apache Ln
Peoria IL 61607

Call Sign: W9CZS
Elmer C Schoch
720 S Blaine St
Peoria IL 616051722

Call Sign: N9YVB
Robert J Hillier
1418 S Crown Dr
Peoria IL 61605

Call Sign: KB9KBA
Kermit L Peterson
1608 S Faraday
Peoria IL 61605

Call Sign: KA9BEK
Efral L Keys Sr
1712 S Kneer
Peoria IL 61605

Call Sign: WA9EBM
Jack M Hiltbold
2015 S Mahark Ln
Peoria IL 616071342

Call Sign: KB9TSZ
Dennis A Jurewicz Jr
5621 S Matt Cody
Peoria IL 61607

Call Sign: KB9TWW
Cindy L Jurewicz
5621 S Mattcody Ct
Peoria IL 61607

Call Sign: W9LVU
Edward R Orr
2701 S Tiara Strip
Peoria IL 61607

Call Sign: KC9SN
Terry R Beachler
3928 Stable Ct
Peoria IL 616146909

Call Sign: KC9BQP
Kara L Bendix
1314 Stella Ct
Peoria IL 61604

Call Sign: KB9HZJ
Candace M D Agnolo
9300 Timberlane Dr
Peoria IL 61615

Call Sign: N6SAL
Michael S Lukich
9828 Townsend Dr
Peoria IL 61615

Call Sign: N9OSS
Michael V Neff
605 Vine
Peoria IL 61603

Call Sign: N9PST
Paul M Elgen
605 Vine
Peoria IL 61603

Call Sign: N9PEJ
Debby L Neff
605 Vine St
Peoria IL 61603

Call Sign: N9RBL
Fern E Elger
605 Vine St
Peoria IL 61603

Call Sign: KB9OMN
Gail M Patton
3009 W Alan Ct
Peoria IL 61615

Call Sign: AA9MK
Michael P Patton
3009 W Alan Ct
Peoria IL 61615

Call Sign: KC9FNJ
Jackie G Crowe
1913 W Albany Ave
Peoria IL 61604

Call Sign: KC9TFH
Tabitha A Buffard
3200 W Alice Ave

Peoria IL 61604

Call Sign: WB9ILU
Craig R Miller
408 W Altorfer Ln
Peoria IL 61615

Call Sign: N9ERS
Mary M Cooley
5309 W Ancient Oak Dr
Peoria IL 61615

Call Sign: N0RIP
Bruce A Stark
4408 W Andover Dr
Peoria IL 616152814

Call Sign: KB9ISQ
Reid T Henrichs
212 W Aspen Way
Peoria IL 61614

Call Sign: KB9ISL
Katie J Kleinow
W Aspen Way
Peoria IL 61614

Call Sign: KB9KLZ
Rayburn P Ellington III
1227 W Barker Ave
Peoria IL 61606

Call Sign: N9BAS
Eugene W Adkins
6218 W Beacon Rd
Peoria IL 61604

Call Sign: N9XAF
Jeffery L Ensinger
3603 W Bennington
Peoria IL 61615

Call Sign: W9DHE
L Ferrel Lytle
2537 W Benton Ct
Peoria IL 616158839

Call Sign: W9JWC
Bradley University ARC

1501 W Bradley Ave
Peoria IL 61625

Call Sign: KC9QMX
Michael L Dafforn
7450 W Branch Dr
Peoria IL 61607

Call Sign: N9MSG
John J Best
4802 W Bridalwood Dr
Peoria IL 616152710

Call Sign: N9MZO
Keith C Claypool
826 W Broadmoor St
Peoria IL 61614

Call Sign: K9KIO
Thomas F Nauman
920 W Butterfield Dr
Peoria IL 61614

Call Sign: KC9NBD
Giovana Valerio
2413 W Cabana Ct
Peoria IL 61614

Call Sign: KC9UCY
James C Miller
2312 W Callender
Peoria IL 61604

Call Sign: WB9UCX
Bliss S Phillips
3417 W Capitol
Peoria IL 61614

Call Sign: KA9VCQ
Robert D Ellingsworth
3205 W Capitol Dr
Peoria IL 61614

Call Sign: KA9VCR
Scott D Ellingsworth
3205 W Capitol Dr
Peoria IL 61614

Call Sign: KB9ESR

Matt S Phillips
3417 W Capitol Dr
Peoria IL 61614

Call Sign: W5UBN
Thalous L Key
4315 W Castleton
Peoria IL 61615

Call Sign: KB9HZT
Michael A Dunn
1036 W Centennial Dr
Peoria IL 61614

Call Sign: KC8HZQ
Jeffery D Deheer
3127 W Chadwick Ln
Peoria IL 61614

Call Sign: KB9HZI
Roger W Friend
2017 W Clarke
Peoria IL 61604

Call Sign: KC0BBM
Shaun M Hassen
5002 W Closen Rd
Peoria IL 61604

Call Sign: KC9KYY
Shaun M Hassen
5002 W Closen Rd
Peoria IL 61604

Call Sign: AB9PW
Shaun M Hassen
5002 W Closen Rd
Peoria IL 61604

Call Sign: WB9USB
Charles W Hicok
521 W Columbia Ter
Peoria IL 61606

Call Sign: N9UOT
Robert D Roach
1417 W Columbia Ter
Peoria IL 61606

Call Sign: KB9TNZ
John A Kujawa
1612 W Columbia Terr
Peoria IL 61606

Call Sign: KC9QHQ
Ayesha Brown
1601 W Coneflower Dr 4115
Peoria IL 61615

Call Sign: W9MI
Wayne R Miller
105 W Crestwood
Peoria IL 61614

Call Sign: N9PFE
Brandon S Miller
627 W Crestwood Dr
Peoria IL 61614

Call Sign: KB9CST
Anthony R Curless
148 W Detweiller Dr
Peoria IL 61615

Call Sign: KC9TLH
Wm L Andrews
611 W Detweiller Dr
Peoria IL 61615

Call Sign: N9KUK
Paul A Tackmann
711 W Eleanor Pl
Peoria IL 61604

Call Sign: KB9HZF
Ryan T Mc Leigh
825 W Fairlawn
Peoria IL 61614

Call Sign: KB9YPF
Nathan D Bayless
2315 W Forrest Hill
Peoria IL 61604

Call Sign: N9VIN
Gregory Rudd
1526 W Forrest Hill Ave
Peoria IL 61604

Call Sign: KA9KEX
Daniel D Bayless
2315 W Forrest Hill Ave
Peoria IL 616041967

Call Sign: N9RBK
Tim D Miller
2705 W Fountaindale
Peoria IL 61614

Call Sign: N9JID
Ryan T Shaff
1301 W Fredonia
Peoria IL 61606

Call Sign: KC9LNI
Paul A Perrilles
1716 W Geneva
Peoria IL 61615

Call Sign: N9MRX
Gene F Collins
906 W Gift Ave
Peoria IL 61604

Call Sign: N9OBA
Mark K Collins
906 W Gift Ave
Peoria IL 61604

Call Sign: KC9UCT
Jill E Harter
1004 W Gift Ave
Peoria IL 61604

Call Sign: KB9HZE
Michael R Sullivan
1121 W Glen Ave
Peoria IL 61614

Call Sign: KB9HZC
Myia M Sullivan
1121 W Glen Ave
Peoria IL 61614

Call Sign: KB9ISJ
Erin L Bradley
1127 W Glen Ave

Peoria IL 61614

Call Sign: KB9ZWT
Brian J Morgan
2022 W Glen Ave
Peoria IL 61614

Call Sign: N9FXS
Mervin L Rennich
5616 W Grande Cir
Peoria IL 61615

Call Sign: KC9NXY
Matthew F Adams
601 W High St
Peoria IL 616061926

Call Sign: KB9SD
Joseph F Kosmicki
1320 W Holly Hedges Dr
Peoria IL 61614

Call Sign: KC9OXB
David M Bryant
1213 W Howett
Peoria IL 61605

Call Sign: WB9YUN
Stephan R Ihnken
517 W Hudson
Peoria IL 61604

Call Sign: KC9SIP
Ricky D Weber
3113 W Humboldt St
Peoria IL 61605

Call Sign: KB9HZQ
Amanda R Turner
1101 W Inverness Dr
Peoria IL 61615

Call Sign: N9EJ
Eric L Johnson
2206 W Kenfield Ct
Peoria IL 61615

Call Sign: KB9HZD
Lindsay A Rose

815 W Kennsigton
Peoria IL 61614

Call Sign: N9CN
Robert F Fahey
903 W Kensington Dr
Peoria IL 61614

Call Sign: KC9UCJ
Dion L Wilson
2506 W Kenwood Ave
Peoria IL 61604

Call Sign: WD9GZW
Jeffrey S Morton
3002 W Kenwood Ave
Peoria IL 61604

Call Sign: KC9CLD
Vernon W Beaty
3413 W King Henry Ct
Peoria IL 61604

Call Sign: KB9HZP
Diana M Hegwood
1415 W Kingsway Dr
Peoria IL 61614

Call Sign: KB9CAO
Sumit P Bhatia
1415 W Kingsway Dr
Peoria IL 61614

Call Sign: KB9HZY
Eric M Cox
1603 W Kingsway Dr
Peoria IL 61614

Call Sign: WD9FQF
Henry R Faubel
2300 W Krause
Peoria IL 61605

Call Sign: K9ZDC
George O Huber Sr
2332 W Krause Ave
Peoria IL 61605

Call Sign: KB9DRG

Alan G Davis
1705 W Lake Ave
Peoria IL 61614

Call Sign: KC9CIG
Sheri L Zalar
3328 W Lexington Ct
Peoria IL 61615

Call Sign: KC9PZS
Nerio J Calgaro
3351 W Lexington Ct
Peoria IL 61615

Call Sign: AB9UN
Nerio J Calgaro
3351 W Lexington Ct
Peoria IL 61615

Call Sign: W9ETC
Yangmin Shen
4433 W Longmeadow Ct
Peoria IL 616158929

Call Sign: W9SVO
Alvin P Gillick Jr
806 W Mac Queen
Peoria IL 61604

Call Sign: N9RBN
Alex J Overend
800 W Mac Queen Ave
Peoria IL 61604

Call Sign: N9YYT
Wilbur N Robinson
8325 W Maple Ridge Rd
Peoria IL 61607

Call Sign: AB9KS
Wilbur N Robinson
8325 W Maple Ridge Rd
Peoria IL 61607

Call Sign: N9RPM
Laura A Pearsall
2615 W Marian Ct
Peoria IL 616143754

Call Sign: KA9YSE
David L Pearsall
2615 W Marian Ct
Peoria IL 61614

Call Sign: N9FUO
Bradley A Weyeneth
2601 W Mass Ave
Peoria IL 61604

Call Sign: WB9BMY
Louis A Rittschof
907 W Meadows Pl
Peoria IL 61604

Call Sign: N9PEF
L James Bridges
4419 W Middle Rd
Peoria IL 61605

Call Sign: KC9QFK
Ashle E Easley
2723 W Millbrook Ct
Peoria IL 61615

Call Sign: K9OJO
Rosella M Dees
5221 W Monroe Rd
Peoria IL 61607

Call Sign: KW5Q
Kevin J Mc Williams
815 W Moss Ave
Peoria IL 61606

Call Sign: WD9FMB
Frederic M Bock
1011 W Moss Ave
Peoria IL 61606

Call Sign: KB9GQL
Wayne W Johnson
1205 W Moss Ave
Peoria IL 61606

Call Sign: K9WFG
Donald L Markley
1802 W Moss Ave
Peoria IL 61606

Call Sign: KB9ISM
Brandon D Blayney
621 W Mt Hawley Ter
Peoria IL 61615

Call Sign: N9OSO
Kenneth G Ball
2122 W N Circle Ct
Peoria IL 61604

Call Sign: KB9FQT
Bryce E Weber
3C1 W N Point Ct
Peoria IL 61615

Call Sign: KC9JKI
David R Ellis
2901 W Nevada
Peoria IL 61605

Call Sign: KB9ZJ
De Wayne L Householter
630 W North Ln
Peoria IL 61615

Call Sign: KB9FQU
Eric L Moreland
831 W North Ln
Peoria IL 61615

Call Sign: KB9HZH
Jamaal A Rehman
121 W Northaven Ct
Peoria IL 61614

Call Sign: W9KUR
Frank E Zerwekh
907 W Northcrest Ave
Peoria IL 61614

Call Sign: AB9WI
Edward A Smith
511 W Northgate Rd
Peoria IL 61614

Call Sign: KC9FWR
James L Hornbaker
1917 W Northmoor Rd

Peoria IL 61614

Call Sign: N9HHW
Bradford Craig
1201 W Northmoor Rd Apt
317
Peoria IL 616143415

Call Sign: KA9ONL
Gary R Hartzler
503 W Northmoor Rd Apt B
Peoria IL 61614

Call Sign: N9AUS
Bruce E Landwehr
935 W Oakview Dr
Peoria IL 61615

Call Sign: N9SKD
Habib G Habib
2215 W Overhill Rd
Peoria IL 61615

Call Sign: N9DYJ
Lynn T Tripp
2721 W Overhill Rd
Peoria IL 61615

Call Sign: NM0O
Jon A Dainty Sr
2721 W Parkridge Dr
Peoria IL 616042117

Call Sign: K9HJZ
Jeffrey L Stangeland
5805 W Parkside Cl
Peoria IL 61615

Call Sign: N9BKF
Thomas F Cummings
1321 W Parkside Dr
Peoria IL 61606

Call Sign: KB9LJB
Scott E Blickenstaff
2408 W Pasmoso 2201
Peoria IL 61614

Call Sign: N9UKC

William I Cusson
2321 W Pintura Ct
Peoria IL 616141406

Call Sign: KA9WAI
C Lyman Monroe
4823 W Pottstown Rd
Peoria IL 61615

Call Sign: KB9ISO
Kristie L Mc Caw
1702 W Queens Ct Rd
Peoria IL 61614

Call Sign: KB9ISI
Erin M Brown
1710 W Queens Ct Rd
Peoria IL 61614

Call Sign: KB9OMH
James L Hamp
1419 W Queenscourt Rd
Peoria IL 61614

Call Sign: KE9KE
Douglas J Loberg
320 W Ravinswood Rd
Peoria IL 616151363

Call Sign: KB9HZS
Matthew F Metzger
614 W Ravinwoods Rd
Peoria IL 61615

Call Sign: KC9HB
John G Lorentz
4811 W Redbud Dr
Peoria IL 61604

Call Sign: K9DCQ
Bert O Briggs
2724 W Reservior Blvd
Peoria IL 61615

Call Sign: KC9CZJ
Michael R Le Crone
4013 W Richards Way
Peoria IL 61615

Call Sign: KB0CHO
Roger W Westerhold
3438 W Richwoods
Peoria IL 61604

Call Sign: KB9MOA
John L Matern
3223 W Richwoods Blvd
Peoria IL 61604

Call Sign: AA9TI
John W Marincic
2302 W Riviera Dr
Peoria IL 61614

Call Sign: N9GLH
Carole M Rogers
4324 W Rockwell
Peoria IL 61615

Call Sign: KB9DNA
James J Kalafut
4307 W Rustic Hollow
Peoria IL 61615

Call Sign: N3VI
James J Kalafut
4307 W Rustic Hollow
Peoria IL 61615

Call Sign: KB9DNA
James J Kalafut
4307 W Rustic Hollow
Peoria IL 61615

Call Sign: KA9IKZ
Larry E Fatheree
3501 W Saymore Ln
Peoria IL 61615

Call Sign: N9HCC
John L Birks
3520 W Saymore Ln
Peoria IL 61615

Call Sign: KB9NGS
Jimette L Beil
3527 W Saymore Ln
Peoria IL 61615

Call Sign: K9ND
Richard C Beil
3527 W Saymore Ln
Peoria IL 61615

Call Sign: KB9MZO
Paul A Conton
1408 W Smith St
Peoria IL 61605

Call Sign: KB9RPO
Billy R Miller
3510 W Sylvan Ln
Peoria IL 61615

Call Sign: N9AAP
John R Sutton
608 W Teton Dr
Peoria IL 61614

Call Sign: KA9ATB
Mary L Sutton
608 W Teton Dr
Peoria IL 61614

Call Sign: N9YUZ
Michael S Whitlow
1853 W Teton Dr
Peoria IL 61614

Call Sign: KB9CAM
Jason R Arndt
1719 W Thames Dr
Peoria IL 61614

Call Sign: KB9HZZ
Jacqueline A Crow
705 W Timber Ridge Dr
Peoria IL 61615

Call Sign: N9BWL
Robert E Melton
1217 W Virginia
Peoria IL 61604

Call Sign: WD9EGN
Michael J Moore
500 W Westwood Dr

Peoria IL 61614

Call Sign: KB9CSS
Nick A Lovier
1020 W Wilshire Dr
Peoria IL 61614

Call Sign: N9ARU
Thomas C Meisel Jr
3211 W Wilshire Dr
Peoria IL 61614

Call Sign: N9HBD
Stephen A Link
5601 W Woodbriar Ln
Peoria IL 61615

Call Sign: W9SRH
Edward J Knebel
1406 Westaire
Peoria IL 61614

Call Sign: KB9LFD
Donald L Stedman
2215 Willow Knolls 410A
Peoria IL 61614

Call Sign: N9YOR
Sally A Link
2314 Wisconsin C
Peoria IL 61603

Call Sign: WD9ATN
Wayne O Kahila
Peoria IL 61612

Call Sign: WA2EDB
John T Brown
Peoria IL 61612

Call Sign: KA9CRT
Mark J Sherman
Peoria IL 61612

Call Sign: KC9UCW
Matthew L Alaksiewicz
Peoria IL 61612

Call Sign: KB9NOS

Wael R Salem
Peoria IL 61612

Call Sign: KC9NCY
Peoria Area ARC
Peoria IL 616123508

Call Sign: KC9NCZ
Peoria Area ARC
Peoria IL 616123508

Call Sign: K9PEO
Peoria Area ARC
Peoria IL 616123508

Call Sign: W9PIA
Peoria Area ARC
Peoria IL 616123508

Call Sign: W9UVI
Peoria Area ARC Inc
Peoria IL 616123508

Call Sign: KB9ZQR
John W Janicke
Peoria IL 616561655

Call Sign: KB9HZR
Michael S Campbell
815 E Division Ave
Peoria Heights IL 61616

Call Sign: KB9KBC
David J Pula
304 E Frances
Peoria Heights IL 61614

Call Sign: KC9NOS
Samuel W Pierce
1501 E Gardner Ln 1604
Peoria Heights IL 61616

Call Sign: KC7KCS
Clifton S Forseth
1109 E Samuel Ave
Peoria Heights IL 61616

Call Sign: KC9QYB
Paul M Shirey
1203 E Samuel Ave
Peoria Heights IL 61616

Call Sign: K9CJS
Dorothy J Segler
2010 E Wren St
Peoria Heights IL 61614

Call Sign: N9NEW
Robert A Hadank
4926 Glen Elm Dr
Peoria Heights IL 61614

Call Sign: KC9CAT
Bfd Repeater Club
5308 Glen Elm Dr
Peoria Heights IL 616165123

Call Sign: W9BFD
Bfd Repeater Club
5308 Glen Elm Dr
Peoria Heights IL 616165123

Call Sign: K9TWV
John P Thornton
5308 Glen Elm Dr
Peoria Heights IL 616165123

Call Sign: NJ9T
John P Thornton
5308 Glen Elm Dr
Peoria Heights IL 616165123

Call Sign: KC9MKZ
By Invitatation Radio Society
5308 Glen Elm Dr
Peoria Heights IL 616165123

Call Sign: AJ4FN
By Invitatation Radio Society
5308 Glen Elm Dr
Peoria Heights IL 616165123

Call Sign: KC9RNE
Andrew J Olson
4728 N Galena Rd

Peoria Heights IL 61616

Call Sign: KF6YPE
John P Caviness
4949 N Grandview Dr
Peoria Heights IL 61616

Call Sign: N9TYQ
Janet D Metzger
3920 N Illinois
Peoria Heights IL 61616

Call Sign: WB9UPS
Merrill W Metzger
3920 N Illinois Ave
Peoria Heights IL 61616

Call Sign: KC9HEU
Cody L Bell
4919 N Ogden Ave
Peoria Heights IL 61616

Call Sign: KC9GPU
Nicholas T Vespa
4810 N Prospect Rd
Peoria Heights IL 61616

Call Sign: KC9NTV
Nicholas T Vespa
4810 N Prospect Rd
Peoria Heights IL 61616

Call Sign: WE9CUX
Lonnie D Atteberry
5701 N Terrace Ct 3
Peoria Heights IL 61616

Call Sign: N9RBD
Robert S Wunderlich
703 E Almond St
Percy IL 62272

Call Sign: KA9RLJ

Gary E Olson
1915 10th St
Peru IL 61354

Call Sign: N9UZD
Michael J Bara
2015 10th St
Peru IL 61354

Call Sign: KB9NFW
Jimmy A Anderson
611 11th St
Peru IL 61354

Call Sign: N9ZPC
Ronald R Reeland
1921 12th St
Peru IL 61354

Call Sign: N9MRG
E Eugene Beck
2114 12th St
Peru IL 61354

Call Sign: KC9VIC
Thomas J Foust
1711 13th St
Peru IL 613541712

Call Sign: KC9IZU
Rita K Mertel
915 14th Ave
Peru IL 61354

Call Sign: K9EWU
Donald G Houde
2411 15th St
Peru IL 61354

Call Sign: WB9ZJH
Lasalle Peru Area Vocational
Center Radio Club
2411 15th St
Peru IL 61354

Call Sign: W9JVC
Ernest A Stuart
1107 31st St 338
Peru IL 61354

Call Sign: KC9PFJ
Illinois Valley Chapter
American Red Cross
1530 4th St
Peru IL 61354

Call Sign: KC9EMP
Illinois Valley Chapter
American Red Cross
1530 4th St
Peru IL 61354

Call Sign: KC9HZP
Richard A Brown
2836 4th St Trlr 36
Peru IL 61354

Call Sign: WB9MMP
Archie G Miller
2715 6th
Peru IL 61354

Call Sign: KC9EXG
Dennis L Bowen
1905 6th St
Peru IL 613542612

Call Sign: KC9VIF
Constance P Brooks
2123 6th St
Peru IL 61354

Call Sign: KC9ROJ
Derek J Martin
2119 6th St
Peru IL 61354

Call Sign: K9REF
Richard W Donahue
2413 7th St
Peru IL 61354

Call Sign: N9OUW
Richard F Grimshaw
2015 8th St
Peru IL 61354

Call Sign: K9REG

Leo A Engelman
2109 9th St
Peru IL 61354

Call Sign: KC9IZT
Bonita L Welch
1412 Buffalo
Peru IL 61354

Call Sign: K9TWZ
Donald L Newburn
705 Calhoun Apt 4D
Peru IL 61354

Call Sign: KJ4IXR
Arland J Pappas
1322 Center St
Peru IL 61354

Call Sign: N9PEI
Michael C Grimshaw
616 Church St
Peru IL 61354

Call Sign: W9DON
Don E Naumann
9435 E 1600th St
Peru IL 61354

Call Sign: N9VD
Mark J Tondi
2375 E 175th Rd
Peru IL 61354

Call Sign: KB9JWA
Pamela S Tondi
2375 E 175th Rd
Peru IL 61354

Call Sign: K9AVE
Illinois Valley Radio Assn Inc
2375 E 175th Rd
Peru IL 61354

Call Sign: NZ9A
Jerome L Wojciechowski
416 E 7th St
Peru IL 613542832

Call Sign: KB9PLJ
Charles S Kwiatkowski
2206 Elmwood Rd
Peru IL 61354

Call Sign: K9BK
Richard M Koscielski
2321 Fifteenth St
Peru IL 613541619

Call Sign: KC9HZO
John J Lindenmeyer
1103 Lincoln Ave
Peru IL 61354

Call Sign: KC9PZO
James P Kristapovich Jr
2530 Main St
Peru IL 61354

Call Sign: N9XSX
Thomas R Rogel
2801 Market St
Peru IL 61354

Call Sign: KC9EMO
Kimberly K Turner
1837 May Rd Apt 22
Peru IL 61354

Call Sign: N9GTI
William T Schweickert
2001 Pine St
Peru IL 61354

Call Sign: KC9EMP
Joseph A Musial
726 Rock St
Peru IL 61354

FCC Amateur Radio Licenses in Pesotum

Call Sign: W9MOO
James H Baltz
1036 CR 0 N
Pesotum IL 61863

Call Sign: KB9UJX

Steven A Bickers
1 Harness Ln
Pesotum IL 61863

Call Sign: WB9ZOY
Jerry H Duke
201 Maple St
Pesotum IL 61863

FCC Amateur Radio Licenses in Petersburg

Call Sign: KB9ZYQ
Edward A Sage
112 E Jackson
Petersburg IL 62675

Call Sign: WB9VEE
William J Davis
15454 Forest Ln
Petersburg IL 62675

Call Sign: KA9FIL
Terry J Coker
18629 Hilltop Rd
Petersburg IL 62675

Call Sign: KB9CKH
Douglas S Pettit
17685 Lone Oak Cir
Petersburg IL 62675

Call Sign: WB9KVM
Wayne M Severns
203 N 13th St
Petersburg IL 62675

Call Sign: KC9HLK
Jens H Haferkamp
15076 New Salem Bluff Rd
Petersburg IL 62675

Call Sign: WA9AQN
John L Swartz
15076 New Salem Bluff Rd
Petersburg IL 62675

Call Sign: WD9JLR
Darrell W Wright

772 Pecan Point
Petersburg IL 62675

Call Sign: KC9LAL
Ronald G Wesley
115 S 7th St
Petersburg IL 62675

Call Sign: KC9SQJ
Charles D Swartz
616 S 8th St
Petersburg IL 62675

Call Sign: W9YYC
Charles D Swartz
616 S 8th St
Petersburg IL 62675

Call Sign: K9IDQ
Benjamin D Kiningham III
13806 State Hwy 97
Petersburg IL 62675

Call Sign: KT9H
John R Eden
17982 State Park Rd
Petersburg IL 626757504

FCC Amateur Radio Licenses in Philo

Call Sign: KB9JTZ
Ray A Pettenger II
1560 CR 1000 N
Philo IL 61864

Call Sign: WB9CAD
Curtis D Rugroden
303 E Eisenhower Dr
Philo IL 61864

Call Sign: K9AL
Albert M Johnston Jr
402 E Jefferson
Philo IL 61864

Call Sign: K9HRO
Donald F Melohn
407 E Madison

Philo IL 61864

Call Sign: K9GVK
Roger P Selle
201 S Harrison
Philo IL 61864

FCC Amateur Radio Licenses in Piasa

Call Sign: N9GUB
Kenneth P Belcher
Rr 1 Box 20
Piasa IL 62079

Call Sign: KC9GVR
Donald C Dubree
34950 Kellwood Ln
Piasa IL 62079

Call Sign: N0OWJ
Herschel E Hall
34173 Prairie Dell Rd
Piasa IL 62079

Call Sign: WA9KIA
Herschel E Hall
34173 Prairie Dell Rd
Piasa IL 62079

FCC Amateur Radio Licenses in Pierron

Call Sign: KC9MKX
Eddie L Tinnea
Pierron IL 62273

FCC Amateur Radio Licenses in Pinckneyville

Call Sign: KC9JMX
Danny L Mcelvain
3976 Apache Cir
Pinckneyville IL 62274

Call Sign: KB9KET
Jeffery L Hubbard
403 Beancoup
Pinckneyville IL 62274

Call Sign: KA9NJD
Martin M Beltz
403 E Chester St
Pinckneyville IL 62274

Call Sign: KB9GCP
Edward G Keller
5 E Ozburn St
Pinckneyville IL 62274

Call Sign: KC9OLW
Billy A Doerflein Jr
210 E Water St
Pinckneyville IL 62274

Call Sign: KC9IGT
Mary H Giacomo
1245 Indiana St
Pinckneyville IL 62274

Call Sign: N9VKO
Robert E Giacomo
1245 Indiana St
Pinckneyville IL 622749595

Call Sign: N9MPP
Darby R Mathis
409 Mason St
Pinckneyville IL 62274

Call Sign: N9LNK
Ronald E Holyfield
6483 Misty Rd
Pinckneyville IL 62274

Call Sign: KB9OGL
Sharon K Holyfield
6483 Misty Rd
Pinckneyville IL 62274

Call Sign: KB9KEU
Geoffrey P Hubbard
403 N Beancoup
Pinckneyville IL 62274

Call Sign: WA9VXX
Kevin G Van Pelt
4535 New Church Rd

Pinckneyville IL 622740265

Call Sign: WD9J
Gladys L Spear
4499 Primrose Rd
Pinckneyville IL 62274

Call Sign: N9IOR
David K Mathis
4427 Private Rd 46
Pinckneyville IL 62274

Call Sign: KB9FFI
Barbara R Williams
112 S Main St
Pinckneyville IL 62274

Call Sign: KA9VGR
Scott A Holt
802 S Walnut St
Pinckneyville IL 62274

Call Sign: WB9WHA
James R Farmer
1505 Shawnee Bend
Pinckneyville IL 62274

Call Sign: KB9DJT
Amanda L Holt
4790 SR 13
Pinckneyville IL 622744145

Call Sign: WG9Q
Gary L Holt Sr
4790 SR 13
Pinckneyville IL 622749570

Call Sign: KC9JOW
Keith J Shasteen
307 W Kaskaskia St
Pinckneyville IL 62274

Call Sign: WA9ORY
Harry W Brown
Pinckneyville IL 62274

Call Sign: KC9OLX
Kevin L Miller
4213 Bethel Church Rd

Pinekneyville IL 62274

Pittsburg IL 62974

FCC Amateur Radio Licenses in Piper City

Call Sign: K9EAX
Richard K Chandler
Piper City IL 60959

Call Sign: KF9HL
Thomas W Mc Mahan
Piper City IL 60959

FCC Amateur Radio Licenses in Pittsburg

Call Sign: KB9JNP
Donna S Simmons
R 1 Box 167A
Pittsburg IL 62974

Call Sign: N9YUI
William L Simmons
Rr 1 Box 167A
Pittsburg IL 62974

Call Sign: K9OYF
Paul E Hillman
14507 Dwina Rd
Pittsburg IL 62974

Call Sign: KD4VJZ
Jessie R Vlastnik
304 S Church St
Pittsburg IL 62974

Call Sign: WB9STX
Gene A Vlastnik
304 S Church St
Pittsburg IL 62974

Call Sign: KC9EQC
Jon D Bain
19843 St Car Rd
Pittsburg IL 62974

Call Sign: AB9LS
Jon D Bain
19843 St Car Rd

FCC Amateur Radio Licenses in Pittsfield

Call Sign: KA9GWM
Larry W Dixon
42316 235th Ave
Pittsfield IL 62363

Call Sign: N9ACT
Danny D Piper
25553 430 Ln
Pittsfield IL 62363

Call Sign: N9JAP
Joyce A Piper
25553 430 Ln
Pittsfield IL 62363

Call Sign: KB9ZKB
Danny D Piper
Rr 1 Box 1558
Pittsfield IL 62363

Call Sign: KB9ZVF
Joyce A Piper
Rr 1 Box 1558
Pittsfield IL 62363

Call Sign: N9XAT
Donald L James
R 3 Box 3083
Pittsfield IL 62363

Call Sign: W9HVR
Leo W Smith Sr
Rr 2 Box 73A
Pittsfield IL 62363

Call Sign: KD9XX
Johnnie B Collins
18002 County Hwy 7
Pittsfield IL 62363

Call Sign: WB9BUU
Gary J White
530 E Griggsville St
Pittsfield IL 62363

Call Sign: WB9HPT
Lewis M Grigsby Jr
815 E Washington
Pittsfield IL 62363

Call Sign: KB9ZT
H Dean Artman
832 E Washington
Pittsfield IL 62363

Call Sign: KC9AJQ
Douglas A White
123 Higbee
Pittsfield IL 62363

Call Sign: KC5GT
Robert L Rowles
203 Janie Ln
Pittsfield IL 62363

Call Sign: KC9GT
Robert L Rowles
203 Janie Ln
Pittsfield IL 62363

Call Sign: N0EOR
Frank L Claus
515 Lowry St
Pittsfield IL 62363

Call Sign: N9CHF
Patrick S Allen
429 N Illinois
Pittsfield IL 62340

Call Sign: WA9NID
Robert L Sievers
534 N Jackson
Pittsfield IL 62363

Call Sign: K9MYT
Cecil R Stauffer
527 N Memorial Ave
Pittsfield IL 62363

Call Sign: N9DO
George E Halpin
1021 Pringle Hgts

Pittsfield IL 62363

Call Sign: WD9DDO
George E Halpin
1021 Pringle Hgts Rr 3
Pittsfield IL 623631503

Call Sign: KB9WFB
Virginia H Halpin
1021 Pringle Hts
Pittsfield IL 62363

Call Sign: K9DUF
William J Belt
356 W Gay St
Pittsfield IL 62363

Call Sign: W9WM
William J Belt
356 W Gay St
Pittsfield IL 62363

Call Sign: KC9QPP
Lyle E Hill
219 W Perry St
Pittsfield IL 62363

Call Sign: KB9KME
Joseph S Di Prizio
Pittsfield IL 62363

FCC Amateur Radio Licenses in Plainview

Call Sign: N8ELY
Frank N Manning
11995 Stagecoach Rd
Plainview IL 62685

FCC Amateur Radio Licenses in Pleasant Hill

Call Sign: KA9PVO
James A Ervin Jr
306 E Clay St
Pleasant Hill IL 623660385

Call Sign: K9RAF
Gillis B Barton

208 E Quincy 143
Pleasant Hill IL 62366

Call Sign: N9YOX
Earl D Hillman
Pleasant Hill IL 62366

FCC Amateur Radio Licenses in Pleasant Plains

Call Sign: KG9BA
Kevin T Hecht
116 Chestnut
Pleasant Plains IL 626779700

Call Sign: WX9CAH
Craig A Held
104 E Church St
Pleasant Plains IL 62677

Call Sign: KC9IGM
Kevin N Kesselring
405 E Main
Pleasant Plains IL 62677

Call Sign: KC9VCM
Jeremy D Jones
15 Hawthorne
Pleasant Plains IL 62677

Call Sign: KF9OH
Richard L Leamons Sr
6116 Main
Pleasant Plains IL 62677

Call Sign: KB9OVN
Carol S Swettman
5656 Richland Rd
Pleasant Plains IL 62677

Call Sign: K9QFR
Alfred E Swettman Jr
5656 Richland Rd
Pleasant Plains IL 62677

Call Sign: W1CTW
Craig T Wadsworth
16067 Sparrow Rd
Pleasant Plains IL 626773431

Call Sign: W9CTW
Craig T Wadsworth
16067 Sparrow Rd
Pleasant Plains IL 626773431

Call Sign: KA9ZLH
Pamela A White
Pleasant Plains IL 62677

FCC Amateur Radio Licenses in Plymouth

Call Sign: KB9HYU
James K Hendricks
Rr 3 Box 108
Plymouth IL 62367

Call Sign: KB9UTJ
Tammy L Huffman
Rr 3 Box 126
Plymouth IL 62367

Call Sign: N9ORP
Gary E Duncan
Rr 2 Box 42
Plymouth IL 62367

Call Sign: N9IPZ
Francis L Hollon
Rt 1 Box 72
Plymouth IL 62367

Call Sign: KB9DHS
Donald F Range
203 E Main
Plymouth IL 62367

Call Sign: KB9LCA
Mark A Clark
4950 N 450th Rd
Plymouth IL 62367

Call Sign: KA9EJY
Brenda L Ussery
216 N Church St
Plymouth IL 62367

Call Sign: N9AYO

Joseph N Johnson
308 N Franklin St
Plymouth IL 62367

Call Sign: K9HMI
Otis A Henry
303 S Liberty St
Plymouth IL 62367

Call Sign: WD9BEO
Richard A Winters
207 S Virginia
Plymouth IL 62367

FCC Amateur Radio Licenses in Pocahontas

Call Sign: N9OUP
David W Ceney
507 Baden Ave
Pocahontas IL 62275

Call Sign: KC9BOZ
Robert B Lewis
531 Baden Ave
Pocahontas IL 62275

Call Sign: KC9HCD
Sandra L Murphy
531 Baden Ave
Pocahontas IL 62275

Call Sign: KC9SHY
Lawton File
952 Bilyeu Rd
Pocahontas IL 62275

Call Sign: KB9VLC
Jerry M Scribner
722 E Shawnee Ln
Pocahontas IL 62275

Call Sign: KC9ITK
Larry L Shenkel
29 Jamestown Rd
Pocahontas IL 62275

FCC Amateur Radio Licenses in Polo

Call Sign: N9JVG
Paul E Shriber
2511 Galena Trl Rd
Polo IL 61064

Call Sign: KB9JZZ
Mark L Ellis
209 N Barber Ave
Polo IL 61064

Call Sign: KA9KDL
Mark L Zeigler
109 N Cherry Ave
Polo IL 61064

Call Sign: KB9DBG
Gerald W Ludewig
1312 N Eagle Creek Rd
Polo IL 61064

Call Sign: KC9LEB
Jacob H Bolen
208 N Franklin Ave
Polo IL 61064

Call Sign: KB9UIT
Jeffery T Bolen
208 N Franklin Ave
Polo IL 61064

Call Sign: WD9COM
Duane L Milhorn
612 S Congress Ave
Polo IL 61064

Call Sign: KB9KRQ
Eugene F Mc Mahon
401 S Franklin Ave
Polo IL 61064

Call Sign: KB1GRJ
Steven A Starr
112 S Prairie Ave
Polo IL 61064

Call Sign: N9JJU
Carolyn L Altenburg
16169 W Hazelview Rd
Polo IL 61064

Call Sign: WD9CON
Kurt H Altenburg
16169 W Hazelview Rd
Polo IL 61064

Call Sign: WD9JJZ
Allan J Wooden
10781 W Judson Rd
Polo IL 61064

FCC Amateur Radio Licenses in Pomona

Call Sign: KB9SPH
Aur J Beckstein
186 Gates Rd
Pomona IL 629752506

Call Sign: KB9TMR
Robert A Strodick
644 Pomona Rd
Pomona IL 62975

FCC Amateur Radio Licenses in Pontiac

Call Sign: WN9F
Ronald E Erickson Sr
21445N 1817E Rd
Pontiac IL 61764

Call Sign: N9EDR
Rosalie A Erickson
21445N 1817E Rd
Pontiac IL 61764

Call Sign: KC9NFB
James R Stewart
216 Bennett
Pontiac IL 61764

Call Sign: KC9IKZ
Martin A Bourgeois
15461 E 1200 N Rd
Pontiac IL 61764

Call Sign: N9MNK

William E Hammond
16704 E 1550 N Rd
Pontiac IL 61764

Call Sign: WB9RLX
Raymond P Pfleeger
206 E Clark St
Pontiac IL 617642774

Call Sign: KC9NPL
William W Stith
800 E Indiana Ave
Pontiac IL 61764

Call Sign: KB9IGT
Constance P Kostelc
113 E Lee St
Pontiac IL 61764

Call Sign: N9RZV
Charles R Kostelc
113 E Lee St
Pontiac IL 617642777

Call Sign: KB9PZA
Eldon G Akers
912 E Madison St
Pontiac IL 61764

Call Sign: KB9RKV
Joshua M Kunkle
520 E Prairie
Pontiac IL 61764

Call Sign: N9UKV
Norman M Kunkle
520 E Prairie St
Pontiac IL 61764

Call Sign: N9RTT
John P Cummins Jr
602 E Washington St
Pontiac IL 61764

Call Sign: WB9GMJ
Stanley W Austin
405 Evenglow Lodge 215 E
Washington
Pontiac IL 61764

Call Sign: N9ODT
Suzanne R Suss
16953 N 1130 E Rd
Pontiac IL 61764

Call Sign: N9JFM
Robert K Freese
17024 N 1900 E Rd
Pontiac IL 61764

Call Sign: KC9OPG
Scott T Harmon
809 N Douglas
Pontiac IL 61764

Call Sign: KC9RFR
Willis D Landrus Jr
920 N Hazel
Pontiac IL 61764

Call Sign: KC9GPT
Mack A Hutchison
1381 S Turtle St
Pontiac IL 61764

Call Sign: K9MAH
Mack A Hutchison
1381 S Turtle St
Pontiac IL 61764

Call Sign: NG9E
James R Jones
842 S Walnut St
Pontiac IL 617642657

Call Sign: N9LOE
Joseph E Stock
1395 Turtle Dr
Pontiac IL 61764

Call Sign: KD9F
Gary L Dearth
634 W Grove St
Pontiac IL 61764

Call Sign: K9ENM
Communicators Radio Club
634 W Grove St

Pontiac IL 61764

Call Sign: W9ZFW
Fred K Steimle
301 W Henry St
Pontiac IL 617642415

Call Sign: W9NGG
Harvey C Lugar
300 W Lowell Ave
Pontiac IL 61764

Call Sign: W9YYE
Paul B Trainor
822 W Moulton
Pontiac IL 61764

Call Sign: K9QOF
Charles T Vose
123 Wabash Ave
Pontiac IL 61764

Call Sign: N9MZK
Ronald D Busing
Pontiac IL 61764

FCC Amateur Radio Licenses in Pontoon Beach

Call Sign: KE7TWT
Roy D Mcmullen
3801 Lake Dr Lot 341
Pontoon Beach IL 62040

Call Sign: KB9RSJ
6M 222 1 2 Preservation
Group
27 Teal St
Pontoon Beach IL 62040

Call Sign: KC9AHA
Bruce A Vinson
103 Wilson Ct
Pontoon Beach IL 62040

Call Sign: KC9AHB
Carolyn A Vinson
103 Wilson Ct
Pontoon Beach IL 62040

Call Sign: KC9FGC
Quite Unusual ARC
107 Abbey Dr
Poplar Grove IL 61065

Call Sign: WD0W
Quite Unusual ARC
107 Abbey Dr
Poplar Grove IL 61065

Call Sign: K0HNM
Larry C Snyder
107 Abbey Dr
Poplar Grove IL 61065

Call Sign: KA9GEU
David W Peterson
207 Boeing Trl
Poplar Grove IL 61065

Call Sign: KC9JDT
Susan C Peterson
207 Boeing Trl
Poplar Grove IL 61065

Call Sign: KC9VZ
Clifford A Stetter
209 Boeing Trl
Poplar Grove IL 61065

Call Sign: KB9JHF
Matthew S Kolberg
506 Bounty Dr NE
Poplar Grove IL 61065

Call Sign: KA9VYC
Anthony M Angell
126 Bullard St
Poplar Grove IL 61065

Call Sign: N9SAU
Kipp M Koenig
609 Candlewick Dr NE
Poplar Grove IL 61065

Call Sign: KC9RFQ
Gary L Engelsen
622 Candlewick Dr NE
Poplar Grove IL 61065

Call Sign: K9MGX
Richard De Vries
674 Candlewick Dr NE
Poplar Grove IL 61065

Call Sign: KC9KCR
Gordon E Morse
1617 Candlewick Dr SW
Poplar Grove IL 61065

Call Sign: N9KPN
Timmy S Naami
218 Carson Dr
Poplar Grove IL 610658410

Call Sign: WA9TTY
Terry J Sellick
3223 Dawson Lake Rd
Poplar Grove IL 61065

Call Sign: KA9YDV
Francis C Pazdzioch III
100 Falcon Way SW
Poplar Grove IL 61065

Call Sign: N9BCS
Robert J Steinhofer
219 Gables Dr Sw
Poplar Grove IL 61065

Call Sign: KB9OXQ
Tall J Shelby
221 Liverpool Dr Se
Poplar Grove IL 61065

Call Sign: W9HRF
James G Grimsby
210 Oak Lawn Ln
Poplar Grove IL 61065

Call Sign: KA9LMJ
Wanda E Grimsby
210 Oak Lawn Ln
Poplar Grove IL 61065

Call Sign: KA9OPC
Richard H Olsen
222 Oak Lawn Ln
Poplar Grove IL 61065

Call Sign: N9IMH
Alan D Shepherd
5825 Orth Rd
Poplar Grove IL 61065

Call Sign: WD9FBR
Linda L Wachsmuth
124 Ray St
Poplar Grove IL 61065

Call Sign: KC9FQY
John M Bednar
410 Redman Way
Poplar Grove IL 61065

Call Sign: KC9KA
George W Barnett
301 Rochester Rd NE
Poplar Grove IL 61065

Call Sign: KA9ITK
Sandra L Barnett
301 Rochester Rd NE
Poplar Grove IL 61065

Call Sign: KB9OSP
Robert B Nilles
612 Sawgrass Close
Poplar Grove IL 61065

Call Sign: KB9YKN
Chad S Dreher
105 Sequoyah Ct Sw
Poplar Grove IL 610658725

Call Sign: KC9RFK
William C Helvey
2704 Stearman St
Poplar Grove IL 61065

Call Sign: WE6S
Ronald S Willke
2726 Stearman St

Poplar Grove IL 610658248

Call Sign: KC9FOF
James S Mac Connell
212 Talladega Dr Sw
Poplar Grove IL 61065

Call Sign: KC9DIY
Wesley H Ganz
209 Thornhill Dr
Poplar Grove IL 61065

Call Sign: KG4JYW
John A Folvig III
164 Titleist Trl
Poplar Grove IL 61065

FCC Amateur Radio Licenses in Port Byron

Call Sign: KB9KCY
Stephen C Sallows
22205 115th Ave N
Port Byron IL 61275

Call Sign: WD9FSH
Jerry D Conner
3403 214th St N
Port Byron IL 61275

Call Sign: KB9LFA
Craig J Wilkins
2507 214th St N Lot 6
Port Byron IL 61275

Call Sign: KW9H
Jerry L Orey
5207 227th St Ct N
Port Byron IL 61275

Call Sign: N9TPR
Henry J Scheff
21008 71st Ave N
Port Byron IL 61275

Call Sign: KA9IYE
Mary A Fick
27101 94th Ave N
Port Byron IL 61275

Call Sign: KA9BSW
George E Rowland
23428 97th Ave N
Port Byron IL 61275

Call Sign: WA9EZY
Wade A Calvert
21114 94 Ave N
Port Byron IL 61275

Call Sign: W9EZY
Wade A Calvert
21114 94 Ave N
Port Byron IL 61275

Call Sign: KA9VDG
Claude M Lohse
4 Deer Trl Ct
Port Byron IL 61275

Call Sign: KC9JHJ
Claude M Lohse
4 Deer Trl Ct
Port Byron IL 61275

Call Sign: WD9GSH
Robert G Thornton
Port Byron IL 61275

Call Sign: W9HSZ
Lawrence G Hutton
Potomac IL 61865

Call Sign: N9LTN
Marigene R Hutton
Potomac IL 61865

FCC Amateur Radio Licenses in Prairie City

Call Sign: N9UVL
Kyle B Walter
21665 E 2100 St
Prairie City IL 61470

Call Sign: KB9DEH
Jerry L Walter
21665 E 2100 St

Prairie City IL 614708441

Call Sign: KB9EBJ
Kevin L Walter
21665 E 2100 St
Prairie City IL 614708441

Call Sign: N9TGA
Sharon K Walter
21665 E 2100th
Prairie City IL 61470

Call Sign: KC9HLA
George R Stolp
625 N Jefferson St
Prairie City IL 61470

FCC Amateur Radio Licenses in Prairie Du Rocher

Call Sign: KC9TPC
Shawn P Behnken
1658 Ames Rd
Prairie Du Rocher IL 62277

Call Sign: KC9DNT
Richard L Derousse
506 Bluff St
Prairie Du Rocher IL 62277

FCC Amateur Radio Licenses in Preemption

Call Sign: W9MGI
John W Watson
1648 US Hwy 67
Preemption IL 61276

FCC Amateur Radio Licenses in Princeton

Call Sign: N9MRW
Carol I M Hassler
19731 1725 E St
Princeton IL 61356

Call Sign: KF9B
Curtis L Hassler

19731 1725 E St
Princeton IL 613569764

Call Sign: WA9UXT
Merle L Purvis
14890 1800 E St
Princeton IL 61356

Call Sign: KA9TOX
De Wight E Johnson
19227 1950 E St
Princeton IL 61356

Call Sign: KA9TPQ
Sherrye K Johnson
19227 1950 E St
Princeton IL 61356

Call Sign: KC9UEW
Todd Drumheller
13539 2800 E St
Princeton IL 61356

Call Sign: KB9JRX
Grace M Frank
427 Anderson 402
Princeton IL 61356

Call Sign: WA9AZB
Fred E Gibbs
460 Anita Ln
Princeton IL 61356

Call Sign: KA9RRM
Sheryl E Harris
Rr 1 Box 328
Princeton IL 613569744

Call Sign: KB9KYP
Justin T Day
715 E Central Av Apt 5
Princeton IL 61356

Call Sign: W9LJS
Larry J Smith
323 E La Salle
Princeton IL 61356

Call Sign: KB9KYT

Christine M Smith
323 E La Salle St
Princeton IL 61356

Call Sign: KB9YLU
Richard D Quevy
441 E Marion Apt 1E
Princeton IL 61356

Call Sign: K9HSK
Richard A Hade
654 E Peru St 2
Princeton IL 61356

Call Sign: WB9MYE
Clifford C Berry
904 E Peru St Apt M
Princeton IL 61356

Call Sign: W9RQO
Joseph E Moran
313 Euclid Ct
Princeton IL 61356

Call Sign: KC9CIF
Eldon A Richards
321 Hideaway Dr 9L
Princeton IL 61356

Call Sign: N9TNO
Francis R Bouxsein II
210 Lake St
Princeton IL 61356

Call Sign: WA9EOB
John R Young
819 Mayfair
Princeton IL 61356

Call Sign: W9IBU
John R Young
819 Mayfair
Princeton IL 61356

Call Sign: WB9NTG
Thomas J Makransky
830 Mayfair Dr
Princeton IL 61356

Call Sign: W9TTK
Lee A Head
422 N 1st St
Princeton IL 61356

Call Sign: WA9VMP
Stanton L Gibbs
1700 N And 2224 E Rt 2 Box
225
Princeton IL 61356

Call Sign: N0SGH
Richard L Mahnke
124 N Fairground Ave
Princeton IL 61356

Call Sign: KB9VZB
Jessica N Hassler
321 N Knox
Princeton IL 61356

Call Sign: KB9SJH
Jason D Hassler
321 N Knox St
Princeton IL 61356

Call Sign: WA9J
Jason D Hassler
321 N Knox St
Princeton IL 61356

Call Sign: KC9MFR
Mark R Williams
625 N Main
Princeton IL 61356

Call Sign: W9CCT
Mark R Williams
625 N Main
Princeton IL 61356

Call Sign: KC9NSZ
Adam D Rabe
620 N Vernon St
Princeton IL 61356

Call Sign: W9ZHB
Adam D Rabe
620 N Vernon St

Princeton IL 61356

Call Sign: KC9PZK
Erica A Rabe
620 N Vernon St
Princeton IL 61356

Call Sign: W9LFD
Erica A Rabe
620 N Vernon St
Princeton IL 61356

Call Sign: KA9JOO
Floyd C Bickett
915 N Vernon St
Princeton IL 61356

Call Sign: N9MRL
Anna M Meyer
19291 Norwood Dr
Princeton IL 61356

Call Sign: N9LOA
James L Meyer
19291 Norwood Dr
Princeton IL 61356

Call Sign: WA2ECC
Robert R Chamberlain Jr
420 Park Ave W
Princeton IL 61356

Call Sign: K9TSV
Stephen W Samet
834 Park Ave W
Princeton IL 61356

Call Sign: WD9GQR
Robert L Burr
904 S 1st
Princeton IL 61356

Call Sign: W9NBY
William R Ollila
935 S Church St
Princeton IL 61356

Call Sign: KB9ZGW
Andrew P Gibson

208 S Euclid Ave
Princeton IL 61356

Call Sign: N9UEJ
Paul M Ham
1427 S Euclid Ave
Princeton IL 61356

Call Sign: WA9PSI
Richard L Heaton
1501 S Euclid Ave
Princeton IL 61356

Call Sign: WC9ABD
Bureau Co Emer Service &
Disaster Agency
1501 S Euclid Ave
Princeton IL 61356

Call Sign: WB9UNY
Donald J Schiff
1026 S Fairway Dr
Princeton IL 61356

Call Sign: W9BMG
Lee R Walters
2104 S Main St
Princeton IL 61356

Call Sign: KB9MGP
John K Thomson
832 S Pleasant St
Princeton IL 61356

Call Sign: KC9INM
Randy J Warren
527 W Central Ave
Princeton IL 61356

Call Sign: N9ZSR
Gail R Frank
824A W Marquette St
Princeton IL 61356

Call Sign: WB9VCK
Louis R Maxwell
1545 W Peru St Apt 7
Princeton IL 61356

Call Sign: N9ZCF
Deborah A Markley
2137 Westmore Dr
Princeton IL 61356

Call Sign: KA9DVX
John D Markley
2137 Westmore Dr
Princeton IL 61356

Call Sign: WA9WBY
Harold I Richards
305 Zearing Ave
Princeton IL 613562615

Call Sign: W9LUY
Arley B Hackney
Princeton IL 61356

Call Sign: W9PWL
Burton E Olin
Princeton IL 61356

Call Sign: KB9EWT
Ryan J Colmone
Princeton IL 61356

FCC Amateur Radio
Licenses in Princeville

Call Sign: WD9AEN
Joseph B Hott
904 E Jane St
Princeville IL 615590385

Call Sign: N9MSF
Steve M Lehmann
11325 Jubilee Ridge Rd
Princeville IL 61559

Call Sign: KC9J
Jerome W Gawthorp
610 N Aten Ave
Princeville IL 61559

Call Sign: KC9UCV
Marisa L Bonomo
16800 N Elliott Rd
Princeville IL 61559

Call Sign: WA9VRH
Larry J Saletzki
11729 N Evans Mill Rd
Princeville IL 61559

Call Sign: KB9SQE
Heart Of Illinois Fm Repeater
Club Inc
11729 N Evans Mill Rd
Princeville IL 61559

Call Sign: KC9MHF
Jonathan P Seyfert
628 N Town Ave
Princeville IL 61559

Call Sign: KE0BE
Michael D Seyfert
628 N Town Ave
Princeville IL 615599772

Call Sign: K9HAE
Armond R Wilson
326 S Wilson Ave
Princeville IL 61559

Call Sign: WD9HCF
Dennis E Doye
10340 Township Rd 62 N
Princeville IL 61559

Call Sign: KB9YBN
Elizabeth A Doye
10340 Township Rd 62 N
Princeville IL 61559

Call Sign: N9BAU
Garrett E Mansfield
515 W Evans
Princeville IL 61559

Call Sign: WD9CWR
David J Stoner
9400 W Oertley Rd
Princeville IL 61559

Call Sign: KB9OMJ
David Smotrilla

7005 W Streitmatter Rd
Princeville IL 61559

Call Sign: N9XKG
Lynn M Momenteller
Princeville IL 61559

Call Sign: N9TZZ
Robert G Momenteller
Princeville IL 61559

FCC Amateur Radio Licenses in Prophetstown

Call Sign: KC9JQ
C Wayne Snyder
13200 Black Hawk Rd
Prophetstown IL 61277

Call Sign: KA9JKC
Earl E Brown
610 E 3rd St
Prophetstown IL 61277

Call Sign: N9SQM
Brad F Kershaw
324 East Ave
Prophetstown IL 61277

Call Sign: K9PFA
Douglas A Jorgensen
408 Maple St
Prophetstown IL 61277

Call Sign: WD9CXW
Robert L Hansen
412 Maple St
Prophetstown IL 61277

Call Sign: WD9CXL
Larry T Frederick
42 Meadow Ln
Prophetstown IL 61277

Call Sign: WD9DJY
Thomas L Frederick
42 Meadow Ln
Prophetstown IL 61277

Call Sign: N9DTN
Bernabe R De La Torre
310 Mosher Dr 101
Prophetstown IL 61277

Call Sign: KC0AOK
Matthew E Ewoldsen
19970 Prophet Rd
Prophetstown IL 61277

Call Sign: W9BIZ
Joseph J Roserski
322 W 3rd St
Prophetstown IL 612771023

Call Sign: KB9AZV
Harold W Cook
501 Washington St
Prophetstown IL 61277

FCC Amateur Radio Licenses in Putnam

Call Sign: KC9JQD
Robert L Shipp
13 Barbados Dr
Putnam IL 61560

Call Sign: W9WOV
George M Bercos
73 Barbados Dr
Putnam IL 61560

Call Sign: N9LW
Larry R Wilson
197 Lake Thunderbird Dr
Putnam IL 61560

Call Sign: N9ABR
Carter J Morrison
15 Wheeler Ct
Putnam IL 61560

FCC Amateur Radio Licenses in Quincy

Call Sign: KB9RNK
Bill J Mc Donald
26 23 Lind

Quincy IL 62301

Call Sign: W9BIQ
Ralph W Hagerbaumer
1026 Adams St
Quincy IL 62301

Call Sign: KC9DD
Bruce A Roberts
925 Anne Ave
Quincy IL 62301

Call Sign: W9AAW
Bruce A Roberts
925 Anne Ave
Quincy IL 62305

Call Sign: WB9VBX
Thomas G Belker
1120 Anne Ave
Quincy IL 62305

Call Sign: K9MRM
Kenneth C Thomas
2837 Bluff Ridge Dr
Quincy IL 62305

Call Sign: KB9YEJ
Michael R Neuliep
2902 Bluff Ridge Dr
Quincy IL 60305

Call Sign: WA9HHI
Louis J Demers
2938 Bluff Ridge Dr
Quincy IL 623051389

Call Sign: KB9QEE
Chad R Mc Clelland
3013 Bluff Ridge Dr
Quincy IL 62305

Call Sign: N9PDG
John C Schuessler
Rr 1 Box 46A
Quincy IL 62301

Call Sign: NM9V
Lester F West

3107 Brentwood Dr
Quincy IL 62301

Call Sign: KA9LMD
Fred B Freeman
527 Broadway Apt 902
Quincy IL 623012758

Call Sign: KC9BNV
Donald C Mann
3905 Catamaran Ct
Quincy IL 62305

Call Sign: KA9NNQ
Douglas F Ebert
4024 Catamaran Ct
Quincy IL 623017143

Call Sign: KC9KZW
Roger W Huner
645 Cedar St
Quincy IL 62301

Call Sign: K9VMW
Rolland J Hastings
1733 Cedar St
Quincy IL 62301

Call Sign: N9MCZ
Jerry M Westberg
3326 Chapel Valley
Quincy IL 62301

Call Sign: KC9QOD
Jerry A Harland
3322 Chapel Valley Dr
Quincy IL 62305

Call Sign: KC9KZV
Nicholas J Doellman
2023 Cherry
Quincy IL 62301

Call Sign: N9GXW
Michael J Mc Cabe
2125 Cherry Ln
Quincy IL 62301

Call Sign: N9QY

Michael J Mc Cabe
2125 Cherry Ln
Quincy IL 62301

Call Sign: KB9VEI
Myles P Mc Cabe
2125 Cherry Ln
Quincy IL 62301

Call Sign: W9EXJ
David A Nagel
2212 Cherry Ln Est W
Quincy IL 623017326

Call Sign: N9IRU
Roger F Cave
2228 Cherry Ln Est W
Quincy IL 623017320

Call Sign: KA9FJN
Lori J Thomas
301 Cherry St
Quincy IL 62301

Call Sign: K9HO
Big Dog Contesting Club
2535 Cherry St
Quincy IL 62301

Call Sign: WA9KRG
Roger E Humke
708 Cheshire Blvd
Quincy IL 62301

Call Sign: W9PQD
Olin G Shuler
909 Christopher Ct
Quincy IL 62305

Call Sign: KB9PH
John R Allen
4135 Coachlight Ct
Quincy IL 62301

Call Sign: W9TRR
John R Allen
4135 Coachlight Ct
Quincy IL 62301

Call Sign: KA9QQY
Donald S Hagood
1600 College Ave
Quincy IL 62301

Call Sign: W9IEA
George A Windolph
1800 College Ave
Quincy IL 623012699

Call Sign: AA9GL
Ronald C Rose
2811 College Ave
Quincy IL 62301

Call Sign: W0IYF
Francis M Shipp
3123 College Ave
Quincy IL 623014611

Call Sign: KA9FMX
Virginia J Williams
17 Country Club Dr
Quincy IL 62301

Call Sign: N9RCM
Kyle S Peterson
812 Country Club Hghts Dr
Apt 100
Quincy IL 62301

Call Sign: N9TMJ
Kenneth G Kuhl
1431 Curtis Creek
Quincy IL 62301

Call Sign: N9KUU
Carl W Proescholdt
2416 Curved Creek
Quincy IL 62301

Call Sign: KD9VA
Johanna L Schutjer
1204 Daniel Ct
Quincy IL 62301

Call Sign: WB9ROZ
Quincy Area Repeater Group
1204 Daniel Ct

Quincy IL 62301

Call Sign: WB9MUO
Kent W Bunte
1173 E 1330th St
Quincy IL 62305

Call Sign: N9QH
Kent W Bunte
1173 E 1330th St
Quincy IL 62305

Call Sign: N9IL
William C Harper
1428 E 1500th St
Quincy IL 62305

Call Sign: KB9UNE
Joe V Prenger
2812 E Bluff Ct
Quincy IL 62301

Call Sign: KB9ZFI
Diane E Prenger
2812 E Bluff Ct
Quincy IL 62301

Call Sign: KC9FSO
Donald A Steinbrecher
2301 Elm
Quincy IL 62301

Call Sign: KB9IPH
Ricki C Goodapple
2315 Elm St
Quincy IL 62301

Call Sign: N9SN
James R Ruxlow
1934 Elmwood Dr E
Quincy IL 62301

Call Sign: WB9KWV
Philip E Reilly Jr
5314 Esther Ave
Quincy IL 62301

Call Sign: W0ROA
Raymond F Taylor

330 Evergreen E
Quincy IL 62301

Call Sign: KB9OGR
Steve K Hull
3230 Fox Run E
Quincy IL 62301

Call Sign: KA9RPD
Karen A Kelly
1209 Fundy Rd
Quincy IL 62301

Call Sign: KB9SEI
Carolyn D Sparks
6320 Gardner Expwy
Quincy IL 62305

Call Sign: AB9DU
Robert G Mitchell
6825 Gardner Expwy
Quincy IL 62305

Call Sign: KB9ZEJ
Susan F Mitchell
6825 Gardner Expwy
Quincy IL 62305

Call Sign: N9KXM
Kevin M Kennedy
1603 Granview
Quincy IL 62301

Call Sign: N9XEN
Curtis B Quist
5517 Greenbriar
Quincy IL 62301

Call Sign: N9XEF
Eric B Quist
5517 Greenbriar
Quincy IL 62301

Call Sign: K0FFY
William D Webster
3110 Gross Gables
Quincy IL 62301

Call Sign: N9UPG

William R Morrison
2000 Grove Ave
Quincy IL 623014334

Call Sign: K9JJD
Glenn W Glessner
1234 Hamann Ln
Quincy IL 62301

Call Sign: KB9PQK
Brian M Prenger
2015 Harison
Quincy IL 62301

Call Sign: WA9HOW
Leland S Hickman
2130 Harrison Cottage 37B
Quincy IL 62301

Call Sign: W9HQW
George A Van De Boe
2125 Harrison St
Quincy IL 62301

Call Sign: KC9NES
Clinton K Stiefel
6201 Hickory Grove N
Quincy IL 62305

Call Sign: KB9FIN
David H Williams
1607 Highland Ln
Quincy IL 62305

Call Sign: N9ZCC
Brenda S Smith
103 Holiday Dr
Quincy IL 62301

Call Sign: KC9POW
Joseph A Fisch
3608 Holiday Dr
Quincy IL 62305

Call Sign: KC9FWB
Matthew M Bruns
7133 Hwy 96 N
Quincy IL 62305

Call Sign: NA9DM
Dana W Myers
1119 Jackson
Quincy IL 62301

Call Sign: W9FGH
John F Schneider
1662 Jersey St
Quincy IL 62301

Call Sign: W9FPN
Richard R Riney
2426 Kentucky Rd
Quincy IL 62301

Call Sign: K9UUD
Paul S Gabriel
1019 Klondike Rd
Quincy IL 62301

Call Sign: N9XXV
Mark W Priepot
2116 Kochs Ln
Quincy IL 62305

Call Sign: N9VYP
Terry L Priepot
2116 Kochs Ln
Quincy IL 62305

Call Sign: KB9OGQ
Jana S Priepot
2116 Kochs Ln
Quincy IL 62305

Call Sign: W9LMT
Charles L Henry
4900 Lakeview Dr
Quincy IL 62305

Call Sign: WA9GBC
David S Soncek
3000 Lantern Ln
Quincy IL 62301

Call Sign: WA9NRO
Joseph B Havermale
630 Lind St
Quincy IL 62301

Call Sign: KE9ZA
Brian K Winking
1117 Lind St
Quincy IL 62301

Call Sign: KB9MUW
Christina L Winking
1117 Lind St
Quincy IL 62301

Call Sign: KB9SPE
Michael D Steinkamp
2233 Lind St
Quincy IL 62301

Call Sign: N9GO
Douglas L Brown
2623 Lind St
Quincy IL 62301

Call Sign: KB9PRK
Trudy K Brown
2623 Lind St
Quincy IL 62301

Call Sign: KB9KVF
Douglas L Brown
2623 Lind St
Quincy IL 62301

Call Sign: W0CTA
Christopher T Ahrens
2735 Linda Ln
Quincy IL 62305

Call Sign: KB9JTO
Greg A Korschot Jr
3501 Lindell Ave
Quincy IL 62301

Call Sign: KB9JXK
Ried R Hollander
2035 Locust St
Quincy IL 62301

Call Sign: KC9AEK
Gary M Bunger
730 Long Dr

Quincy IL 623056191

Call Sign: K9PCF
Gary M Bunger
730 Long Dr
Quincy IL 623056191

Call Sign: KB9ZEH
Robert G Mitchell
816 Long Dr
Quincy IL 62301

Call Sign: KC9FSP
David L Craig
1515 Lorie Dr
Quincy IL 62305

Call Sign: KC9QHZ
Kevin L Hart
1108 Madison
Quincy IL 62301

Call Sign: W9KUG
Harold R Hackbarth
2624 Manor Hill Dr
Quincy IL 62301

Call Sign: KB9KNW
Charles E Cain
1706 Maple
Quincy IL 62301

Call Sign: KB9ZEO
Mary A Wilson
2221 Maple St
Quincy IL 62301

Call Sign: KC9VLY
James L Eyster
709 Meadow Lark Dr
Quincy IL 62305

Call Sign: KC9VLX
Larry L Eyster
709 Meadow Lark Dr
Quincy IL 62305

Call Sign: KB9SPB
Christopher C Trowbridge

2635 Midlan
Quincy IL 62301

Call Sign: W9QMU
Leslie D Gray
4115 Mistletoe Ct
Quincy IL 62301

Call Sign: W9DPC
Myron A Hagerbaumer
1616 Monroe
Quincy IL 62301

Call Sign: WB9WJO
Earl E Weaver
1364 N 1003rd Ln
Quincy IL 623050100

Call Sign: KB9WCZ
David J Stegeman
1415 N 10th
Quincy IL 62301

Call Sign: KB5MDO
Howard W Wilke
1313 N 10th St
Quincy IL 62301

Call Sign: W0IYF
David J Stegeman
1415 N 10th St
Quincy IL 62301

Call Sign: N9GWV
John A Niekamp
1323 N 12th
Quincy IL 62301

Call Sign: N9WGR
Sheela D Chanodia
120 N 12th Apt G
Quincy IL 62301

Call Sign: KB9ZEL
Daniel E Grawe
520.5 N 12th St
Quincy IL 62301

Call Sign: N9KLH

Johnnie L Walker
628 N 12th St
Quincy IL 62301

Call Sign: KF4PB
John E Borg
1707 N 12th St
Quincy IL 62301

Call Sign: W9EQI
Joseph C Caproni
1707 N 12th St
Quincy IL 62301

Call Sign: KB9SEK
Michael T Lenane
717 N 15th St
Quincy IL 62301

Call Sign: N9PDZ
Dustin M Schnelle
1422 N 17th
Quincy IL 62301

Call Sign: KB9HGI
Steven R Baker Sr
1717 N 17th St
Quincy IL 62301

Call Sign: W9QCY
Matthew A Kennedy
208 N 18th St Apt N
Quincy IL 623013112

Call Sign: W9VPW
Joseph F Zimmerman
724 N 20th St
Quincy IL 62301

Call Sign: N9RLW
Melissa R Eberle
1113 N 20th St
Quincy IL 62301

Call Sign: KB9WDA
Frank W Chatten
6309 N 24th
Quincy IL 62301

Call Sign: K9LSD
Matthew A Kennedy
301.5 N 24th St
Quincy IL 62301

Call Sign: N1NER
Christopher G Brocksmith
1026 N 24th St
Quincy IL 62301

Call Sign: KC9DPY
Matthew A Kennedy
1228 N 25th
Quincy IL 623013412

Call Sign: K9TS
Philip E Covert
5915 N 60th
Quincy IL 62305

Call Sign: N9OAK
Harvey E Beers
625 N 66th St
Quincy IL 623058786

Call Sign: N9FBI
W Arthur Clow
627 N 6th St
Quincy IL 62301

Call Sign: KB9VCK
Kenneth W Harmon
1224 N 6th St
Quincy IL 62301

Call Sign: KC9LCM
James R Marthaler
1230 N 6th St
Quincy IL 62301

Call Sign: N9GVQ
Donald Glenn
205.5 N 8th St
Quincy IL 62301

Call Sign: KC9FSN
Brett D Douglas
1417 N 8th St
Quincy IL 62301

Call Sign: W9LKS
Gary D Alexander
301 N 8th St Apt 319
Quincy IL 62301

Call Sign: KC9PGT
Todd S Purdue
435 N 8th St Apt 4
Quincy IL 62301

Call Sign: KC9HIQ
Zane Evans
1131 N 9th St
Quincy IL 62301

Call Sign: KC9KZT
James M Kahs
3121 N College Ave
Quincy IL 62301

Call Sign: KA9UXS
John D Harker
6119 N Hickory Grove
Quincy IL 62305

Call Sign: WD9BLQ
Arlyce A Nowack
2011 N Sheridan Dr
Quincy IL 62301

Call Sign: NA9Q
Michael L Nowack
2011 N Sheridan Dr
Quincy IL 62301

Call Sign: NB9Q
Arlyce A Nowack
2011 N Sheridan Dr
Quincy IL 623058929

Call Sign: WD9GUG
Timothy L Bell
418 Noel Ct
Quincy IL 62305

Call Sign: N9HAW
Jeffrey E Schutte
7 Northwood

Quincy IL 62301

Call Sign: K9FHX
David C Gill
716 Oakland Ave
Quincy IL 62301

Call Sign: KC9FSR
Skyler J Wiegmann
615 Ohio
Quincy IL 62301

Call Sign: KC9BNU
Steven D Hudelson
1616 Ohio St
Quincy IL 62301

Call Sign: KB9ZEI
Scott A Bowen
1904 Ohio St
Quincy IL 62301

Call Sign: WB6FWX
Wardell A Finney
2017 Ohio St
Quincy IL 623015147

Call Sign: KD9YD
John T Inghram IV
2528 Old Orchard Rd
Quincy IL 623060035

Call Sign: WA9EOS
Harold L Pickinpaugh
628 Pawn Ave
Quincy IL 623050802

Call Sign: N0PMK
Louis J Tickus
633 Pawn Ave
Quincy IL 62305

Call Sign: W9TFL
Pansy P Hardin
2040 Payson Ave
Quincy IL 62301

Call Sign: KC9FSS
Ralph L Wiegmann

2307 Payson Ave
Quincy IL 62301

Call Sign: N9IAQ
Kent A Williams
2500 Payson Rd
Quincy IL 62301

Call Sign: NC9E
Kail L Jarvis
2544 Prentiss Ave
Quincy IL 62301

Call Sign: KD9KB
George L Gross
3001 Ray Mar Ct
Quincy IL 62301

Call Sign: N9SEC
Sandra I Gnann
12 Ridgeline Dr
Quincy IL 62301

Call Sign: ND9U
Donald R Cole
711 Ridgewood Dr
Quincy IL 62301

Call Sign: KG9CB
Fred A Chanen
929 Ridgewood Dr
Quincy IL 62301

Call Sign: AA9YG
Fred A Chanen
929 Ridgewood Dr
Quincy IL 62301

Call Sign: KG9W
Fred A Chanen
929 Ridgewood Dr
Quincy IL 62301

Call Sign: K9ZBI
John A Stephenson
118 River View Dr
Quincy IL 623011563

Call Sign: KB9HGH

William E Cole Jr
3006 Riverside Ter
Quincy IL 62305

Call Sign: KB9ZEP
Robert E Sapp
309 S 10 St
Quincy IL 62301

Call Sign: NG9F
David M Campbell
1221 S 12th St
Quincy IL 62301

Call Sign: KB9HLE
Raphael E Padavic
715 S 13th
Quincy IL 62301

Call Sign: W5UBS
Wilmer H Walther
613 S 14th
Quincy IL 62301

Call Sign: WA9VEH
Albert L Woodworth
728 S 15
Quincy IL 62301

Call Sign: KC9PGS
Luan R Sandberg
1220 S 15th St
Quincy IL 62301

Call Sign: KB9ZFK
Norbert Bentele
711 S 16th
Quincy IL 62301

Call Sign: KB9TBA
Brian J Cook
310 S 16th St
Quincy IL 62301

Call Sign: KC9DFR
Garry M Wellman
716 S 16th St
Quincy IL 62301

Call Sign: WD9EYG
Jack J Nauber
834 S 16th St
Quincy IL 62301

Call Sign: KB9USO
Jayme L Irvin
1024 S 16th St
Quincy IL 62301

Call Sign: W9SFT
James M Rhodes
733 S 19th
Quincy IL 62301

Call Sign: KB9TDN
Scott A Speer
1300 S 19th St
Quincy IL 62301

Call Sign: AB9LP
Samuel A Speer Jr
1302 S 19th St
Quincy IL 62301

Call Sign: KB9SPD
Samuel A Speer Jr
1302 S 19th St
Quincy IL 623016647

Call Sign: KB9TDM
Sarah A Speer
1302 S 19th St
Quincy IL 623016647

Call Sign: N9TMT
Francis G Langenburg Jr
625 S 21st
Quincy IL 62301

Call Sign: N9TMM
John W Simon II
1015 S 21st
Quincy IL 62301

Call Sign: W9OAB
John C Fisher
934 S 22nd
Quincy IL 62301

Call Sign: N9PDY
Ronald C Hendrian
727 S 22nd St
Quincy IL 62301

Call Sign: WB9RMI
Albert J Wilson
1003 S 22nd St
Quincy IL 62301

Call Sign: KC9BCW
Michael A Smith
1224 S 22nd St
Quincy IL 62301

Call Sign: K9MAS
Michael A Smith
1224 S 22nd St
Quincy IL 62301

Call Sign: KC9PBT
Harold J Sharp
1626 S 28th St
Quincy IL 62301

Call Sign: KD7DOX
Jason E Sharp
1626 S 28th St
Quincy IL 62301

Call Sign: KB7IDE
Nicole L Sharp
1626 S 28th St
Quincy IL 62301

Call Sign: KD9Q
Douglas E Williams
1717 S 28th St
Quincy IL 62301

Call Sign: WB9EWM
John V Myers II
1222 S 30th
Quincy IL 62301

Call Sign: KB9WDC
Pamela D Myers
1222 S 30th

Quincy IL 62301

Call Sign: W9NOO
Ronald E Fisk
1529 S 30th St
Quincy IL 62301

Call Sign: K2PEY
Joseph A Huie
1910 S 30th St
Quincy IL 62301

Call Sign: KC9JAE
Linda C Huie
1910 S 30th St
Quincy IL 62301

Call Sign: KB9SWC
Gary L Kurfman
2700 S 31st St
Quincy IL 62305

Call Sign: KC9NET
Stephen J Kathmann
1325 S 36th
Quincy IL 62301

Call Sign: KG9MN
Albert P Angerer
2019 S 40th St
Quincy IL 623016071

Call Sign: KC9GBW
Armonio Peter D Banez
1414 S 46th St
Quincy IL 62305

Call Sign: KC9CRT
Manuela Eudes B Kelly
1414 S 46th St
Quincy IL 62305

Call Sign: KC9KUU
Adam C Gibson
110 S 8th
Quincy IL 62301

Call Sign: KB9OIA
Edward W Burger

310 S 8th
Quincy IL 62301

Call Sign: KD9UH
Wendell E Woods
715 S 8th
Quincy IL 62301

Call Sign: KM9K
Kevin M Kennedy
3440 S Glendale Dr
Quincy IL 62301

Call Sign: WB9IMP
Roy E Brooks
1224 S Park Ter
Quincy IL 62301

Call Sign: KB9WHQ
Robert M Crockett
1923 S Sheridan Dr
Quincy IL 62301

Call Sign: N9KXP
Louise A Crockett
1923 S Sheridan Dr
Quincy IL 623018978

Call Sign: N9KUT
Robert J Crockett
1923 S Sheridan Dr
Quincy IL 623018978

Call Sign: W9BC
Robert J Crockett
1923 S Sheridan Dr
Quincy IL 623058978

Call Sign: W9RMC
Robert M Crockett
1923 S Sheridan Dr
Quincy IL 623058978

Call Sign: N9MTK
Clark A Emerick
2000 S Sheridan Dr
Quincy IL 62301

Call Sign: KB9ZEM

Eric R Rand
3021 Schildt Ln
Quincy IL 62301

Call Sign: KB9GZO
Paul D Packard
2929 Selkirk Ln
Quincy IL 62301

Call Sign: KC9LCJ
Dustin A Gorder
1728 Seminary Rd
Quincy IL 62301

Call Sign: KC9RSY
William M Finley
834 Shirlen Dr
Quincy IL 62301

Call Sign: N9BZ
Daryl M Buechting
1520 Silverthorne Dr
Quincy IL 62301

Call Sign: AC9M
Linda R Buechting
1520 Silverthorne Dr
Quincy IL 62301

Call Sign: KB9PLH
Katherine E Dauksch-
Schumacher
2241 Spring St
Quincy IL 62301

Call Sign: KA9JCW
Harold E Lamb
2316 St Charles Dr
Quincy IL 62305

Call Sign: KC9IBL
David L Scranton
1218 State St
Quincy IL 623015040

Call Sign: W9WE
David L Scranton
1218 State St
Quincy IL 623015040

Call Sign: KB9YNW
Michael R Taylor
1635 State St
Quincy IL 62301

Call Sign: K9MRT
Michael R Taylor
1635 State St
Quincy IL 62301

Call Sign: W9MOF
James R Dixon
7201 State St
Quincy IL 623058061

Call Sign: K4MRN
Emily F Robinson
3100 State St Apt C34
Quincy IL 62301

Call Sign: KE9BD
David M Hallow
3100 State St Apt D 54
Quincy IL 623015734

Call Sign: KB3GWJ
Spencer D Smith
3736 Stone Crest Dr
Quincy IL 62305

Call Sign: KC9QWR
Daniel A Steele
1420 Sycamore
Quincy IL 62301

Call Sign: KY9S
Timothy G Jarvis
1426 Sycamore
Quincy IL 67301

Call Sign: N9XL
Michael R Smith
2802 Tamala Ter
Quincy IL 62305

Call Sign: N9MTL
Mark V Emerick
3834 Tiffany

Quincy IL 62301

Call Sign: KA9WTK
John E Helm Jr
3618 Tiffany Ln
Quincy IL 62305

Call Sign: W4HTP
Edward C Westenhaver
2433 Vermont
Quincy IL 62301

Call Sign: KC4YDC
Philip H Langston
1831 Vermont St
Quincy IL 62301

Call Sign: K9VAT
Robert E Norris
1718 W Granview
Quincy IL 62301

Call Sign: W9BIG
Emmett J Griep
20 W Hilltop Dr
Quincy IL 623017216

Call Sign: K9QY
Homer R Stanley
2035 W Wilmar
Quincy IL 623016822

Call Sign: KB9WDD
Larry G Tournear Jr
506 Washington Ave
Quincy IL 62301

Call Sign: KB9ZFH
Adam W Steinkamp
1011 Washington Ave
Quincy IL 62301

Call Sign: WB9YRH
E Mont Robertson
110 West Ave
Quincy IL 62301

Call Sign: KB9JST
Keith A Mullin

1719 Wilmar Dr
Quincy IL 62301

Call Sign: W9OCQ
Theodore R Wahlmann
21 Wilmar Orchard
Quincy IL 62301

Call Sign: W9NTG
Edward W Flowers
2834 Wind Rush Rd
Quincy IL 62301

Call Sign: KB9MIW
Michael F Perry
1305 Winsor Dr
Quincy IL 62305

Call Sign: WB9OTW
James R Garrison
2717 Wisemann Ln
Quincy IL 62301

Call Sign: N9JI
James R Garrison
2717 Wisemann Ln
Quincy IL 62301

Call Sign: N9XEE
Linda L Garrison
2717 Wisemann Ln
Quincy IL 62301

Call Sign: WB9YQW
Ralph S Mc Reynolds
2301 York St
Quincy IL 62301

Call Sign: KA9UKT
William E Mc Reynolds
2301 York St
Quincy IL 62301

Call Sign: N9BCM
William U Mc Reynolds
2301 York St
Quincy IL 62301

Call Sign: N9SEB

Bill W Hannaford
Quincy IL 62301

Call Sign: KA9KDJ
Paul A Lummer
Quincy IL 62306

Call Sign: KC9RSX
Donald W Casper Jr
Quincy IL 62301

Call Sign: KY9E
Gerald W Collins
Quincy IL 62301

Call Sign: N9TMK
William A Hoyt
Quincy IL 62301

Call Sign: KK9Z
Kent A Williams
Quincy IL 62305

Call Sign: N3OWI
Walter C Freeman
Quincy IL 62305

Call Sign: KB9LNP
Jeanette M Turnbull
Quincy IL 62306

Call Sign: KC9FSQ
Joseph W Newkirk
Quincy IL 62306

Call Sign: W9AWE
Western Illinois ARC
Quincy IL 62306

Call Sign: KB9YGL
Western Illinois ARC
Quincy IL 623053132

Call Sign: W9OAB
Western Illinois ARC
Quincy IL 623053132

Call Sign: N9XEP
Stanley E Marquardt

Quincy IL 623053795

Call Sign: KA0SNL
Andrew A Skattebo
Quincy IL 623060110

Call Sign: KC9JYI
Richard M Ehrhart
Quincy IL 623060916

Call Sign: W9RME
Richard M Ehrhart
Quincy IL 623060916

FCC Amateur Radio Licenses in Raleigh

Call Sign: KB9TJY
Christopher T Parks
5125 Hwy 34 N
Raleigh IL 629771400

Call Sign: KB9TPP
H Andrew Cserny
1645 Raleigh Rd
Raleigh IL 62977

Call Sign: WA4KQL
Garrett C Carter
88 S Main St
Raleigh IL 62977

Call Sign: KA9VRF
John P King
Raleigh IL 62977

FCC Amateur Radio Licenses in Ramsey

Call Sign: KB9TDO
Mettie P Hamilton
311 1st St
Ramsey IL 68020

Call Sign: WC9AAV
Fayette Co Vandalia Esda
R 2 Box 12A
Ramsey IL 620809306

Call Sign: KA9K
Nelvin K Wilson
Rt 2 Box 147
Ramsey IL 62080

Call Sign: N9LVX
Darren A Beck
Rr 2 Box 150
Ramsey IL 62080

Call Sign: KB9SIX
David W Bumgardner
Rr 2 Box 170B
Ramsey IL 62080

Call Sign: N9LVZ
David S Challans
Rr 1 Box 192
Ramsey IL 62080

Call Sign: W9DSC
David S Challans
Rr 1 Box 192
Ramsey IL 62080

Call Sign: WD9N
David S Challans
Rr 1 Box 192
Ramsey IL 62080

Call Sign: KB9WAO
Patsy L Challans
Rr 1 Box 192
Ramsey IL 62080

Call Sign: KB9TMS
Dustin W Brewer
Rr 1 Box 198
Ramsey IL 62080

Call Sign: KB9UJP
Leslie A Robinson
R 1 Box 203Aa
Ramsey IL 62080

Call Sign: WB9VND
Norman R England
Rr 1 Box 215A
Ramsey IL 62080

Call Sign: KC9JRB
Jessica D Beck
Rr 2 Box 221 A
Ramsey IL 62080

Call Sign: KB9LR
Rickie J Chamberlain
Rr 1 Box 345
Ramsey IL 62080

Call Sign: WD9ENQ
Janet S Pryor
Rr 1 Box 42
Ramsey IL 62080

Call Sign: WB9NEY
Gerald A Jones
Rr 3 Box 63
Ramsey IL 62080

Call Sign: KC9SPC
Gary L Phelps
Rr 3 Box 7A
Ramsey IL 62080

Call Sign: W9GLP
Gary L Phelps
Rr 3 Box 7A
Ramsey IL 62080

Call Sign: N9KDM
Michael L Pryor
115 E Main
Ramsey IL 62080

Call Sign: KA9UUU
Georgeanne H Finn
Ramsey IL 62080

Call Sign: KA9LDQ
Kenneth S Lay
Ramsey IL 62080

**FCC Amateur Radio
Licenses in Rankin**

Call Sign: KC9AWD
Gary L Amaya

426 E 4th St
Rankin IL 60960

Call Sign: KC9FLW
Minette M Warren
316 N Guthrie
Rankin IL 60960

Call Sign: KB9YWE
Aaron Warren
316 N Guthrie St
Rankin IL 60960

Call Sign: WD9IAS
Reuben T Bradley
309 N Johnson St
Rankin IL 60960

Call Sign: KB9TKS
Andrew C Crowell
220 S Guthrie
Rankin IL 60960

Call Sign: WX9T
Andrew C Crowell
220 S Guthrie
Rankin IL 60960

Call Sign: KB9UWX
Simon P Shak
220 S Guthrie
Rankin IL 60960

Call Sign: KB9TGH
Ronald A Warren
436 S Main St
Rankin IL 60960

Call Sign: N9RON
Ronald A Warren
436 S Main St
Rankin IL 60960

Call Sign: KB9TLH
Carrie L Warren
436 S Main St
Rankin IL 60960

Call Sign: W9EII

Robert W Shaw
Rankin IL 60960

FCC Amateur Radio Licenses in Ransom

Call Sign: KC9BQO
Ronald J Barrett
601 Plumb
Ransom IL 60470

Call Sign: KC9FGV
Ronald J Barrett
601 Plumb
Ransom IL 60470

Call Sign: KB9ETH
William H Koehler
312 S Cartier Box 124
Ransom IL 60470

FCC Amateur Radio Licenses in Rantoul

Call Sign: W9JQA
Benjamin H O Brian
904 4 Juniper Dr
Rantoul IL 61866

Call Sign: KC8RFE
Kevin W Coogan
1109 Ascot St
Rantoul IL 61866

Call Sign: KA9RHZ
David J Bennett
417 Broadmeadow Rd
Rantoul IL 61866

Call Sign: KA9BAJ
Claudia A Nibeck
500 Broadmeadow Rd
Rantoul IL 61866

Call Sign: WB9VKT
Richard L Nibeck
500 Broadmeadow Rd
Rantoul IL 61866

Call Sign: KA9DWJ
Gilbert L Dailey
1968 CR 3000 N
Rantoul IL 61866

Call Sign: K9HNF
Gary L Arbuckle
2015 CR 3000 N
Rantoul IL 618669518

Call Sign: N9AIL
Dale A Kaiser
915 E Congress
Rantoul IL 61866

Call Sign: N9PLU
James A Rusk
607 E Sangamon
Rantoul IL 61866

Call Sign: KA9BAI
Sidney L Morgan
1048 Englewood Dr
Rantoul IL 61866

Call Sign: KF8ZN
Michael J Haydon
1420 Fairway
Rantoul IL 61866

Call Sign: AC2Q
Michael J Haydon
1420 Fairway
Rantoul IL 61866

Call Sign: WD9IXI
Homer D Wright Jr
500 Garden St
Rantoul IL 61866

Call Sign: NS9K
Arthur A Braghini
1525 Gleason Dr
Rantoul IL 61866

Call Sign: N9PMK
Charles H Hensley
389 Highland Dr
Rantoul IL 61866

Call Sign: N6SYT
Timothy E Scott
376 Highland Dr
Rantoul IL 61866

Call Sign: W9ZK
Robert F Junkins
236 Illinois Dr
Rantoul IL 61866

Call Sign: N9SGP
Dwayne M Flenoury
1334 10 Juniper Dr
Rantoul IL 61866

Call Sign: KF9KD
George A Mayberry
1544 Marcia Dr
Rantoul IL 61866

Call Sign: N9PLW
Cindy M Crego
1556 Marcia Dr
Rantoul IL 61866

Call Sign: KC9KQT
Shawn R Bemount
303 Marco Dr
Rantoul IL 61866

Call Sign: W9EPL
Shawn R Bemount
303 Marco Dr
Rantoul IL 61866

Call Sign: KC9DEQ
Heather N Schlesser
405 Marco Dr
Rantoul IL 61866

Call Sign: KC9NRI
Richard W Hurd
660 Morningside Dr
Rantoul IL 61866

Call Sign: KC9TOH
William A Samples
1208 Prairieview Dr

Rantoul IL 61866

Call Sign: KB9VAI
Forest L Poland
1113 Sunset Dr
Rantoul IL 61866

Call Sign: K9FLP
Forest L Poland
1113 Sunset Dr
Rantoul IL 61866

Call Sign: KC9LPX
Bernard Bojanowski
222 W Grove St Apt 6
Rantoul IL 61866

FCC Amateur Radio Licenses in Rapids City

Call Sign: N7MTW
Michael S Holcomb
1200 9th Ave
Rapids City IL 61278

Call Sign: WB4QBF
R Thomas Davey
14 Eagle Pointe Pass
Rapids City IL 61278

FCC Amateur Radio Licenses in Raritan

Call Sign: KE7APG
Christopher L Rodriguez
208 E Main
Raritan IL 61471

Call Sign: WB7BNL
Lewis L Arnold
208 E Main
Raritan IL 614710095

Call Sign: KA7NPR
Lou Ann Arnold
208 E Main
Raritan IL 614710095

FCC Amateur Radio Licenses in Raymond

Call Sign: WB9KJS
Ben B Savage
20042 E Frontage Rd
Raymond IL 62560

Call Sign: N9QII
Brenda J Falter
610 N West St
Raymond IL 62560

Call Sign: N9MGP
David E Falter
610 N West St
Raymond IL 62560

Call Sign: N9TUF
Charles L Falter
Raymond IL 62560

Call Sign: KC9PUZ
Shawn D Allen
Raymond IL 62560

FCC Amateur Radio Licenses in Red Bud

Call Sign: W0KME
Norman C Baetz
5279 Beck Rd
Red Bud IL 62278

Call Sign: KB9ATC
Andrew B Joshu
Rr 1 Box 108
Red Bud IL 62278

Call Sign: KC9NSD
Randy L Blakeslee
111 Catherine Dr
Red Bud IL 62278

Call Sign: KC9TPB
David J Dehne
228 Charles St
Red Bud IL 62278

Call Sign: WB9YCB
Dennis J Malott
900 Hartmann Dr
Red Bud IL 62278

Call Sign: KB9VTZ
Southern Illinois Dx Contest
Club
9694 S Prairie Rd
Red Bud IL 62278

Call Sign: KC9VRP
Paul M Ellner
1341 Tyler Ct
Red Bud IL 62278

Call Sign: KB9BGU
Todd A Burmester
211 Washington Ave
Red Bud IL 62278

FCC Amateur Radio Licenses in Reynolds

Call Sign: N9XXP
William D Bogart Jr
11520 162nd Ave W
Reynolds IL 61279

Call Sign: WB9OAO
David D House
1787 210th St
Reynolds IL 61279

FCC Amateur Radio Licenses in Richview

Call Sign: N9FRP
Victor A Mc Coy
27012 California Rd
Richview IL 62877

Call Sign: N9OTO
James R Connelly
136 S Oak St
Richview IL 62877

FCC Amateur Radio Licenses in Ridge Farm

Call Sign: KB9EFB
James R Wengler Sr
Rr 1 Box 162
Ridge Farm IL 61870

Call Sign: KA9OAT
Richard L Carico Sr
200 E North
Ridge Farm IL 61870

Call Sign: WD9CNI
Jerry Troxel
16 E West St
Ridge Farm IL 61870

Call Sign: K9FJS
James A Wilson Jr
308 N 1st
Ridge Farm IL 61870

Call Sign: W9KYG
James A Wilson Jr
308 N 1st
Ridge Farm IL 61870

Call Sign: KB9YRM
Lyndal D Williams
722 E Main St
Ridgway IL 62979

Call Sign: KC9OIY
Kenneth R Dale
416 S Kimbro St
Ridgway IL 62979

Call Sign: K9YUD
James H Smith
South St
Ridgway IL 62979

Call Sign: W9ONP
Dale E Strohecker

3360 S Rock City Rd
Ridott IL 61067

Call Sign: KC9QBT
Catherine L Drye
106 Washington St
Ridott IL 61067

Call Sign: KB9ZCW
Kenneth W Muto
Ridott IL 61067

Call Sign: K9KWM
Kenneth W Muto
Ridott IL 61067

Call Sign: WD9FGU
Byron E Barr
Rt 1 Box 115
Rinard IL 62878

Call Sign: WD9JFP
Inez F Barr
Rt 1 Box 115
Rinard IL 62878

Call Sign: KA4NNI
Charles L Krueger
105 S Main
Rio IL 614720001

Call Sign: N9ANM
John R Frerkes
2679 US Hwy 150 N
Rio IL 61472

Call Sign: KA9CQQ
Dawn M Thomas
Rr 2 Allen St
Riverton IL 62561

Call Sign: K9FNB
Richard I Osland
45 Devine Dr
Riverton IL 625619627

Call Sign: WB9RAM
Judy M Osland
45 Devine Dr Rt 2
Riverton IL 62561

Call Sign: KA9JWE
Dan L Carter
21 Francis Dr
Riverton IL 62561

Call Sign: N9DFS
Michael A Klever
16 Holiday Ln
Riverton IL 62561

Call Sign: KB9QHY
Ronald H Hughes Jr
37 Jamestown Cir
Riverton IL 62561

Call Sign: KB9VAT
Joann York
34 Mueller Ct
Riverton IL 62561

Call Sign: WX9APG
Andrew P Geil
1014 N 5th St Apt 8
Riverton IL 62561

Call Sign: KA9AKG
James A Caruso
430 N 6th St
Riverton IL 62561

Call Sign: W9EBY
Thomas J Mussatt
804 N 7th St
Riverton IL 625610021

Call Sign: KA9AXJ
David C Thomas
112 N Allen St

Riverton IL 62561

Call Sign: W9RMP
William J Gill
131 Woodland Ave Rr 1
Riverton IL 62561

Call Sign: K9WLG
Donald P White
Riverton IL 62561

Call Sign: KA9KQH
Dwayne J Terry
Riverton IL 62561

Call Sign: KB9SQF
Thomas J Ross
Riverton IL 62561

Call Sign: KC9JPQ
Vicki L Terry
Riverton IL 62561

FCC Amateur Radio Licenses in Roanoke

Call Sign: KB9FPH
Jennifer A Smith
109 Cleveland
Roanoke IL 61561

Call Sign: K9VSK
Roger L Studer
1637 CR 1500 N
Roanoke IL 61561

Call Sign: KA9MFP
Michael J Smith
101 E Placid Dr
Roanoke IL 61561

Call Sign: KC9HNM
Ben J Wagner
205 S Main
Roanoke IL 61561

Call Sign: KA9KBG
John C Onken
711 W Davison St

Roanoke IL 61561

Call Sign: WB9USY
Joe R Rogge
606 W High St
Roanoke IL 61561

Call Sign: KC9DBE
David G Cashion
Roanoke IL 61561

Call Sign: N0NGQ
George H Baumann
Roanoke IL 61561

Call Sign: KC9ICF
Stacy Amigoni
Roanoke IL 61561

FCC Amateur Radio Licenses in Roberts

Call Sign: WB9UZD
Bonnie J Mosier
1250 E 1700 N Rd
Roberts IL 609628108

Call Sign: WB9RIV
William H Mosier
1250 E 1700 N Rd
Roberts IL 609628108

Call Sign: KN9BAM
William W Wood
204 Hickory Dr
Roberts IL 60962

Call Sign: KB9SF
Leland W Geyer
104 W Green Box 203
Roberts IL 60962

FCC Amateur Radio Licenses in Robinson

Call Sign: KC9IMZ
Joshua D Butcher
8906 E 1200th Ave
Robinson IL 62454

Call Sign: KC9SYF
William D Burbank
14037 E 1425th Ave
Robinson IL 62454

Call Sign: WB9VKZ
Francis V De Doming
7891 E 1616th Ave
Robinson IL 62454

Call Sign: KB9TGI
John P Jones III
10329 E 700th
Robinson IL 62454

Call Sign: W9TWJ
Tanner W Jones
10329 E 700th Ave
Robinson IL 62454

Call Sign: WB9SVH
Ray E Everly
310 E Magnolia
Robinson IL 62454

Call Sign: KB9YHJ
T Lee Hess Jr
802 E Orlando Dr
Robinson IL 62454

Call Sign: KA9ANE
James D Mc Kee
403 Loyland Dr
Robinson IL 62454

Call Sign: KC9QHI
Hermon E Johnson
13469 N 1150th St
Robinson IL 62454

Call Sign: KC9NED
Morris H Gosnell
6891 N 1360th St
Robinson IL 62454

Call Sign: N9CLZ
Gladys P Parker
4516 N 575th St

Robinson IL 624546518

Call Sign: KC9GHF
Doug M Pringle
11282 N 725th St
Robinson IL 62454

Call Sign: N9FTI
Curtis S Estep
10938 N 800th St
Robinson IL 62454

Call Sign: N9GEO
Deborah M Price
4723 N 850th St
Robinson IL 624546633

Call Sign: NM9R
Ronald D Price
4723 N 850th St
Robinson IL 624546633

Call Sign: KC9GKJ
Kari E Skaggs
712 N Cross St
Robinson IL 62454

Call Sign: KC9KXV
Carl J Wright
406 N Eagleton
Robinson IL 62454

Call Sign: AB9KO
Roy D Bousley
1105 N Jefferson St
Robinson IL 62454

Call Sign: KB9PKO
Omer F Hartz
1211 N Jefferson St
Robinson IL 624542620

Call Sign: N9KBM
Robert D Ogle
310 N King St
Robinson IL 62454

Call Sign: KC9NCV
Garret M Godwin

1006 N Lincoln Robinson
Robinson IL 62454

Call Sign: KC9PTI
Gerald G Gordy
205 N Reed St
Robinson IL 62454

Call Sign: N9UBL
Keith E Jones
1407 N Walters
Robinson IL 62454

Call Sign: KA9PHH
Kenneth D Pryor
703 Orlando Dr
Robinson IL 624543615

Call Sign: KI9P
Kenneth D Pryor
703 Orlando Dr
Robinson IL 624543615

Call Sign: KA9FPE
Michael L Dorn
1114 Rector Ave
Robinson IL 62454

Call Sign: KA9CIW
Mark L De Doming
905 Rector St
Robinson IL 62454

Call Sign: WA9DDS
Jerry L Underwood
607 Robinwood Dr
Robinson IL 62454

Call Sign: KA9PHO
Nancy C Underwood
607 Robinwood Dr
Robinson IL 62454

Call Sign: KC9ECD
Tom S Beard Sr
806 S Jefferson
Robinson IL 62454

Call Sign: KB9VOX

Lee J Gatton
1610 S Pickford St
Robinson IL 62454

Call Sign: KC9IHY
Jonathan M Cook
205 S Prairie St
Robinson IL 62454

Call Sign: N9EMY
Harold E Alexander
109 S Reed
Robinson IL 62454

Call Sign: KB9FCZ
Edmund C Michl
Lot46 Sacramento St Wstview
Add 50B
Robinson IL 62454

Call Sign: KA9RBG
Jamie L Nethery
308 St Petersburg
Robinson IL 62454

Call Sign: KC9ATF
Jere R Wood
605 W Ash St
Robinson IL 62454

Call Sign: WA9HPA
Warren L Jennings
1203 W Cherry
Robinson IL 62454

Call Sign: KA9PHI
Kenneth D Pryor Jr
506 W Chestnut St
Robinson IL 62454

Call Sign: KC9FPU
Richard L Coulter
804 W Highland Dr
Robinson IL 625451024

Call Sign: N9ZWC
Edith L Cox
1103 W Main Apt 6
Robinson IL 62454

Call Sign: KA9LRG
Darvin L Mc Cloud
806 W Oak
Robinson IL 62454

Call Sign: K9CGG
Otto A Prier O D
804 W Oak St
Robinson IL 624540493

Call Sign: KA9ENU
Mark D Kilburn
Robinson IL 62330

Call Sign: KA9ANC
Dana L Hargis
Robinson IL 62454

Call Sign: KA9ANB
G Max Hargis
Robinson IL 62454

Call Sign: KB9QAH
Walter J Schalasky
Robinson IL 62454

Call Sign: WA9ISV
Crawford Co ARC
Robinson IL 62454

Call Sign: NW9J
Phillip A Herman
Robinson IL 624540224

Call Sign: WN9TUD
Northwest Amateur Radio
Association Nwar
Robinson IL 624540224

**FCC Amateur Radio
Licenses in Rochelle**

Call Sign: N9YKJ
Robert W Guynn
117 7th Ave Apt 15
Rochelle IL 61068

Call Sign: K9YFY

Betty A Barnes
917 8th Ave
Rochelle IL 61068

Call Sign: KA7JQE
Ellen L White
900 Ave B Apt D
Rochelle IL 61068

Call Sign: KA7JQD
James E White
900 Ave B Apt D
Rochelle IL 61068

Call Sign: KB9WEH
James R Frederick
215 Ave C
Rochelle IL 61068

Call Sign: N9VZI
Dennis G Allan
204 Erickson Rd
Rochelle IL 61068

Call Sign: W9GPC
Leslie E Springmire
9554 Fowler Rd
Rochelle IL 61068

Call Sign: KA9IMW
Donald J Hansen
18410 Gillis Rd
Rochelle IL 61068

Call Sign: KA9IMX
Wayne S Hansen
18410 Gillis Rd
Rochelle IL 610689623

Call Sign: WB9NJJ
Lawrence L Raymond
10293 Hickory Ridge Dr
Rochelle IL 61068

Call Sign: KC9DCZ
Dean B Smith
220 Jeffrey Ave Apt A
Rochelle IL 61068

Call Sign: N9SLD
Kenneth H Stol
1227 Lakeview Dr
Rochelle IL 61068

Call Sign: K9BPT
Joseph L Dearth
965 N Caron Rd Apt 3
Rochelle IL 61068

Call Sign: W9FLV
Lloyd A King
329 N Woodlawn Dr Rt2
Rochelle IL 61068

Call Sign: KA9WHC
Frank R Bemis
512 S 2nd St
Rochelle IL 61068

Call Sign: KC9ORM
Michael L Abell
3332 S Kings Rd
Rochelle IL 61068

Call Sign: WA9LCE
William A Patrick
5393 S Mill Pond Rd
Rochelle IL 61068

Call Sign: WD9IYT
Andrew E Reynolds
146 S Washington St
Rochelle IL 61068

Call Sign: KC9FSC
Deborah J Lower
1209 Scott Ave
Rochelle IL 61068

Call Sign: KC9DDA
Thomas P Lower
1209 Scott Ave
Rochelle IL 61068

Call Sign: K9GPC
Thomas P Lower
1209 Scott Ave
Rochelle IL 61068

Call Sign: WD9IFW
Jack B Lovell
1178 SR 38
Rochelle IL 61068

Call Sign: W9NII
Jack B Lovell
1178 SR 38
Rochelle IL 61068

Call Sign: W9QQ
David S Plyman
1211 Sunrise Ct
Rochelle IL 61068

Call Sign: KD0KJB
Matthew S Plyman
1211 Sunrise Ct
Rochelle IL 61068

Call Sign: KD0KJC
Ryan S Plyman
1211 Sunrise Ct
Rochelle IL 61068

Call Sign: KC9CEF
William H Karr III
1500 W Lincoln Ave
Rochelle IL 61068

Call Sign: N9YBB
William H Middaugh
1152 Westview Dr
Rochelle IL 61068

Call Sign: N9AFH
Chester M Slothower
1163 Westview Dr
Rochelle IL 61068

Call Sign: KC9UUK
Samuel M Crago
309 Willis Ave
Rochelle IL 61068

**FCC Amateur Radio
Licenses in Rochester**

Call Sign: N9NWJ
Marty C Ribble
Rr 2 Box 162
Rochester IL 62563

Call Sign: N9YBE
Troy D Tamminga
Rr 1 Box 55
Rochester IL 62563

Call Sign: WD9JKS
Gary W Stout Sr
10843 Buckhart Rd
Rochester IL 62563

Call Sign: KC9THV
Frank P Hughes
5932 Chicken Bristle Rd
Rochester IL 62563

Call Sign: KC9KMB
Patrick A Malone
6469 Country Green
Rochester IL 62563

Call Sign: N9XHZ
John T Hatcher
231 Deer Creek
Rochester IL 62563

Call Sign: KC9MFN
Mitch Hopper
536 E Mill
Rochester IL 62563

Call Sign: K9ZXO
Mitch Hopper
536 E Mill
Rochester IL 62563

Call Sign: WB9WQS
Bradley S Churchill
906 Hillcrest Rd
Rochester IL 62563

Call Sign: K9HDZ
Bradley S Churchill
906 Hillcrest Rd
Rochester IL 62563

Call Sign: N9PLF
Robert H Becker
523 Karen Rose Dr
Rochester IL 62563

Call Sign: WB9QWR
Carole J Churchill
622 Magnolia Dr
Rochester IL 62563

Call Sign: K9HDZ
James R Churchill
622 Magnolia Dr
Rochester IL 62563

Call Sign: KC9RCU
Dwain C Hill
28 Maplehurst Dr
Rochester IL 62563

Call Sign: W9KKN
Dean F Bunger
12 Mishawaka Dr
Rochester IL 625639405

Call Sign: W9WGT
Merlyn H Ranney
33 Mishawaka Dr
Rochester IL 62563

Call Sign: KB9KGY
Mark T Daniels
6060 Mottar Rd
Rochester IL 62563

Call Sign: W9MTD
Mark T Daniels
6060 Mottar Rd
Rochester IL 62563

Call Sign: KB9AXF
Rebecca L Schmidt
321 N Park St
Rochester IL 62563

Call Sign: KB9WNN
Andrew L Hamm
31 Penacook Dr

Rochester IL 62563

Call Sign: KB9VCM
John K Hamm
31 Penacook Dr
Rochester IL 62563

Call Sign: WB9WUG
Richard B Churchill
316 S Walnut
Rochester IL 62563

Call Sign: KC8FZA
Roy T Battle
423 S Walnut
Rochester IL 62563

Call Sign: WA9PTW
Delbert L Penrod
14 Sherry Ln
Rochester IL 62563

Call Sign: N9ETP
Ronald T Mc Donald
3 Swannanoa Dr
Rochester IL 62563

Call Sign: WB2MWY
Warren A Gordon
59 Taft Dr
Rochester IL 62563

Call Sign: KC9KLX
Geoffrey P Mchugh
111 Willow Rd
Rochester IL 62563

FCC Amateur Radio Licenses in Rock City

Call Sign: N9YUP
John L Jeschke
6696 E Rock Grove Rd
Rock City IL 61070

Call Sign: N9ZBK
Karl J Jeschke
6696 E Rock Grove Rd
Rock City IL 61070

Call Sign: KC9LOQ
Donald L Woodruff
Rock City IL 61070

Call Sign: KC9SUO
Jean M Woodruff
Rock City IL 61070

FCC Amateur Radio Licenses in Rock Falls

Call Sign: K9FGD
Everett W Schreiner
1106 10th Ave
Rock Falls IL 61071

Call Sign: KA9ANU
Federico Ramirez
1505 11th Ave
Rock Falls IL 61071

Call Sign: WB9NGF
Carl W Roorda
603 14th Ave
Rock Falls IL 610711048

Call Sign: KA0WBP
Donald E Taylor
503 15th Ave
Rock Falls IL 61071

Call Sign: KB9LRT
Nicholas L Simmer
415 4th Ave
Rock Falls IL 610711225

Call Sign: KC9CVN
Danny A Miller Sr
1101 5 Ave Apt 806
Rock Falls IL 61071

Call Sign: N9ZSS
John M Bell
1101 5th Ave 304
Rock Falls IL 61071

Call Sign: KC9EBY
Joseph W Greer Sr

2915 A St
Rock Falls IL 61071

Call Sign: KB9SJI
Jack R Redell
3406 A St
Rock Falls IL 61071

Call Sign: AA9YD
Jack R Redell
3406 A St
Rock Falls IL 61071

Call Sign: N9ZAN
Shane R Bibby
1109 Arland St
Rock Falls IL 61071

Call Sign: N9ZLN
Melvin E Camden
701 Ave A
Rock Falls IL 61071

Call Sign: KA9GNS
Elmer J Leusby
403 Ave C
Rock Falls IL 61071

Call Sign: KB9UIR
David P Brown
611 Ave D
Rock Falls IL 61071

Call Sign: WA9TTJ
Thomas E Zigler
402 Ave E
Rock Falls IL 61071

Call Sign: WD9S
Michael D Hughes
10400 Calhoun Rd
Rock Falls IL 61071

Call Sign: KC9KYR
Eric M Richmond
501 E 4th St
Rock Falls IL 61071

Call Sign: WD9EHM

George J Welch
503 E 4th St
Rock Falls IL 61071

Call Sign: KA9HQB
James H Van Horne
509 E 4th St
Rock Falls IL 61071

Call Sign: N9ZAJ
Joseph A Forren
402 E 5th St
Rock Falls IL 61071

Call Sign: N9TZX
Karen L Timbs
411 E 5th St
Rock Falls IL 61071

Call Sign: N9SRJ
Ronald W Timbs
411 E 5th St
Rock Falls IL 61071

Call Sign: N9TOD
Tammy L Baldwin
507 E 5th St
Rock Falls IL 61071

Call Sign: N9SRF
Willard E Baldwin II
507 E 5th St
Rock Falls IL 61071

Call Sign: KA9QYT
Fredric E Bramm
31535 E Thome Rd
Rock Falls IL 61071

Call Sign: KB9CZD
Lunda J Bramm
31535 E Thome Rd
Rock Falls IL 61071

Call Sign: KC9FML
Sara J Bramm
31535 E Thome Rd
Rock Falls IL 61071

Call Sign: KC9CVM
Lunda J Bramm
31535 E Thome Rd
Rock Falls IL 610719476

Call Sign: KB9CZD
Lunda J Bramm
31535 E Thome Rd
Rock Falls IL 610719476

Call Sign: KB9CLN
Howard F Richmond
2102 French St
Rock Falls IL 61071

Call Sign: N9ZAX
David A Jacobs
10431 Harper Dr
Rock Falls IL 61071

Call Sign: KB9CLN
Eric M Richmond
425 Haskell Ave
Rock Falls IL 61071

Call Sign: KC9OGV
Michael R Oldenburg
9767 Hickory Hills Rd
Rock Falls IL 61071

Call Sign: N4RR
Roger L Hoffman
709 Hoffman Dr
Rock Falls IL 61071

Call Sign: N9ORQ
Joseph E Baldwin
10304 Hoover Rd
Rock Falls IL 61071

Call Sign: N9TOB
Patricia L Baldwin
10304 Hoover Rd
Rock Falls IL 61071

Call Sign: N9PEB
James M Brown Jr
10464 Hoover Rd
Rock Falls IL 61071

Call Sign: K9MGA
Melvyn W Kinney
26135 Knief Rd
Rock Falls IL 61071

Call Sign: W9BTT
Albert D Woodyatt
27942 Knief Rd
Rock Falls IL 61071

Call Sign: KB9RT
Robert D Francis
809 Le Roy Ave
Rock Falls IL 61071

Call Sign: WA9BIW
Mildred M Ogan
605 Lincoln Ave
Rock Falls IL 61071

Call Sign: KA9DXW
Byron H Grassnickle
27579 Logan Rd
Rock Falls IL 61071

Call Sign: WD9EHN
James B Ordean
28140 Logan Rd
Rock Falls IL 61071

Call Sign: N9HCL
David L Terwelp
438 Martin Rd Apt G
Rock Falls IL 61071

Call Sign: NE9N
David W Mc Laren
432 Martin Rd Apt H
Rock Falls IL 61071

Call Sign: KB9QPO
Ramiro O Garza Sr
1213 Minkle St
Rock Falls IL 610711435

Call Sign: KC9IXI
Thomas E Sheldon
2204 N Humphrey Ave

Rock Falls IL 61071

Call Sign: N9VZQ
Judith A Skates
22802 Prophet Rd
Rock Falls IL 61071

Call Sign: AB9AT
James M Jordan
23723 Prophet Rd
Rock Falls IL 61071

Call Sign: N9SRI
Robert H Wadsworth
25018 Prophetstown Rd
Rock Falls IL 61071

Call Sign: KB9NVF
George D Cheshier
9700 Ridge Rd
Rock Falls IL 61071

Call Sign: KB9PWM
Richard D Van Ausdoll
1205 Riverdale Rd
Rock Falls IL 61071

Call Sign: KC9IEE
Richard D Sandison
1600 Riverdale Rd Lot 93
Rock Falls IL 61071

Call Sign: WA9HOO
Loren W Hume
Riverside Mobile Est Lot 603
Rock Falls IL 61071

Call Sign: W9OKV
Gene L Klock
510 W 12th St
Rock Falls IL 61071

Call Sign: N9BZR
Janie L Johnson
1208 W 16th St
Rock Falls IL 61071

Call Sign: KA9HHC
Roger E Johnson

1208 W 16th St
Rock Falls IL 61071

Call Sign: KB9LDJ
Wayne A Russell
503 W 19th St
Rock Falls IL 61071

Call Sign: WB9ZPR
Donald D Law
300 W 20th St
Rock Falls IL 61071

Call Sign: KC9RPB
Susan R Zies
1213 W Rockfalls Rd
Rock Falls IL 61071

Call Sign: KA9HUK
Regis L Dahlstrom
910 Wiker Dr
Rock Falls IL 61071

Call Sign: WY9G
Robert E Welch
28445 Woodside Dr
Rock Falls IL 61071

Call Sign: KC9RSS
Kimberly A Thompson
Rock Falls IL 61071

Call Sign: N9SRK
Lawrence E Thompson
Rock Falls IL 61071

**FCC Amateur Radio
Licenses in Rock Island**

Call Sign: KB9KTJ
Timothy D Klauer
1308 101 Ave Ct W
Rock Island IL 61201

Call Sign: WA9SBW
Adrian J Arday
3051 10th Ave
Rock Island IL 61201

Call Sign: K9HQU
Lawrence E Apple
3158 10th St
Rock Island IL 61201

Call Sign: N9NEE
Gerald W Epperson
8119 10th St W
Rock Island IL 612017742

Call Sign: K9HHM
Charles F Strayer
3320 11th St
Rock Island IL 61201

Call Sign: WW9CW
Craig J Wilkins
2524 11th St
Rock Island IL 61201

Call Sign: WB9ASG
Mark A Smith
2809 12th Ave 802
Rock Island IL 61201

Call Sign: KC0ENS
Cynthia K Springer
3532 12th St
Rock Island IL 612016007

Call Sign: N3TSC
Eugene R Bocstrom
4529 13th Ave
Rock Island IL 61201

Call Sign: KB9LDC
Amy M Vinzant
9405 13th St W
Rock Island IL 61201

Call Sign: N9OVA
Scott M Vinzant
9405 13th St W
Rock Island IL 61201

Call Sign: N0LYK
Dana L Leonard
1333 14 1/2 St
Rock Island IL 61201

Call Sign: WD9FSP
Edwin J Foss
1642 14th St
Rock Island IL 61201

Call Sign: KC9MQX
Benjamin D Farrar III
3723 14th St
Rock Island IL 61201

Call Sign: WA3KDQ
David R Hawk
1928 15 1/2 St
Rock Island IL 61201

Call Sign: KB9WTL
Jay A Rakus
4321 15th Ave
Rock Island IL 61201

Call Sign: WD6FEV
Todd L Davis
3609 15th St
Rock Island IL 61201

Call Sign: KC9IVO
Harold L Masengarb
2422 18th Ave
Rock Island IL 61201

Call Sign: KC9PGK
Phillip W Traman
3905 18th Ave
Rock Island IL 61201

Call Sign: KC9BCV
Stephen V Wilson
2314 20 1/2 Ave
Rock Island IL 61201

Call Sign: KC9RJI
Faustin B Romero
2427 20th Ave
Rock Island IL 61201

Call Sign: WA9MQJ
Marvin C Bergwall
2937 20th Ave

Rock Island IL 61201

Call Sign: N9IWT
Charles W Musinski Sr
1635 20th St
Rock Island IL 61201

Call Sign: KC9IOU
David J Perry
2533 21st Ave
Rock Island IL 61201

Call Sign: N9KVC
Lewis T Greim
1337 21st Ave 7C
Rock Island IL 61201

Call Sign: KC9MHS
Ladonna S Nurse
2025 21st St Apt 4
Rock Island IL 61201

Call Sign: N9NTE
James J Boudro
3115 22nd Ave
Rock Island IL 61201

Call Sign: KA0GSL
Virgil D Smith
3116 22nd Ave
Rock Island IL 61201

Call Sign: W9ILC
Coy M Bullard
3301 22nd Ave
Rock Island IL 61201

Call Sign: WA6ZMD
Alan P Hillis
2116 23rd Ave
Rock Island IL 61201

Call Sign: KG9LZ
Thomas G Dolph
956 24th Ave
Rock Island IL 61201

Call Sign: W9MFX
Richard A Hillyer

3240 24th Ave
Rock Island IL 61201

Call Sign: WG9X
Lawrence H Hinzman
3601 24th St
Rock Island IL 61201

Call Sign: W9SBD
Richard H Mc Quady
2833 25th Ave
Rock Island IL 61201

Call Sign: K9ZVR
Perry D Mason
4543 25th Ave
Rock Island IL 61201

Call Sign: K9HMA
Raymond Fredrickson
2319 25th St
Rock Island IL 61201

Call Sign: WU9Q
Robert C Christenson
4412 26th Ave
Rock Island IL 61201

Call Sign: KN9O
Jesse W Tennison
2917 28th Ave
Rock Island IL 61201

Call Sign: KB9CUF
John E Walsh
3804 28th Ave
Rock Island IL 61201

Call Sign: KB9CYA
John M Walsh
3804 28th Ave
Rock Island IL 61201

Call Sign: N9YPN
Anthony J Padavich
4019 28th Ave
Rock Island IL 61201

Call Sign: WB9VVQ

Aron L Lumbard Sr
2037 28th St
Rock Island IL 61201

Call Sign: KB9GUB
Christopher B Downs
2041 28th St
Rock Island IL 61201

Call Sign: KC9RDD
Robert C Elder
1527 29 1/2 St
Rock Island IL 61201

Call Sign: KC9RLD
Susan A Elder
1527 29 1/2 St
Rock Island IL 61201

Call Sign: W9JF
Jay T Finn
1700 29 1/2 St
Rock Island IL 612013733

Call Sign: KA9LJD
Irving Sonner
2310 29 1/2 St
Rock Island IL 61201

Call Sign: WB9AAT
Marvilee J Aden
2618 29 1/2 St
Rock Island IL 61201

Call Sign: K9PVZ
E Harold Swanson
2519 29 Ave
Rock Island IL 61201

Call Sign: KC9FRT
Quad City Historical Radio
Society
2519 29th Ave
Rock Island IL 61201

Call Sign: W9RI
Quad City Historical Radio
Society
2519 29th Ave

Rock Island IL 61201

Call Sign: KB9OET
John A Stanford
2052 30th St
Rock Island IL 61201

Call Sign: KB9SVJ
Stephanie J Stanford
2052 30th St
Rock Island IL 61201

Call Sign: WB9NWW
Philip J Lipovac
2042 31st Ave
Rock Island IL 61201

Call Sign: KC9QGS
Brad J Goddard
2507 32nd Ave
Rock Island IL 61201

Call Sign: WX9BJG
Brad J Goddard
2507 32nd Ave
Rock Island IL 61201

Call Sign: KC9IAB
Carl S Davis
2058 32nd St
Rock Island IL 61201

Call Sign: WB9OBB
William J Vancura
9010 33 St W
Rock Island IL 61201

Call Sign: KC9DCX
Loma E Nesbitt
2420 33rd Ave
Rock Island IL 61201

Call Sign: W9OWN
Loma E Nesbitt
2420 33rd Ave
Rock Island IL 61201

Call Sign: KB9LCX
Carol S Kramer

2701 34th St
Rock Island IL 61201

Call Sign: WB9PVW
Richard M Kramer
2701 34th St
Rock Island IL 61201

Call Sign: KC9HUI
Robert W Milas
3311 34th St
Rock Island IL 61201

Call Sign: WD9CMP
Jack R Hartwig
2013 36 St
Rock Island IL 61201

Call Sign: W9RI
John E Greve
3216 37th Ave
Rock Island IL 61201

Call Sign: N9AXH
Steven H Greve
3216 37th Ave
Rock Island IL 61201

Call Sign: N9XGO
James E Maloney
1120 38th St
Rock Island IL 612013156

Call Sign: KB9LDD
Thomas E Maloney
1120 38th St
Rock Island IL 612013156

Call Sign: N9OK
Albert T Broendel
2712 38th St
Rock Island IL 61201

Call Sign: KB9FWY
Ahmad K Bayrakdar
4524 39 Ave
Rock Island IL 61201

Call Sign: K9HCW

Thomas M Jackson Sr
635 39th St
Rock Island IL 61201

Call Sign: N9VLF
John D Perry
1544 40 St
Rock Island IL 61201

Call Sign: KB9NPS
David D Bane
1422 40th Ave
Rock Island IL 61201

Call Sign: W8UGL
Edward M Lieblein
1428 40th Ave
Rock Island IL 612016044

Call Sign: KC9OVD
Kevin K Aunan
1812 40th St
Rock Island IL 61201

Call Sign: KB9RDW
Tonya R Aunan
1812 40th St
Rock Island IL 61201

Call Sign: N9ID
James I Dowie
800 41 St
Rock Island IL 61201

Call Sign: K9AHH
Walter H Geuther
3540 41st Ave
Rock Island IL 61201

Call Sign: KC9FXS
Russell Shropshire
1427 41st St
Rock Island IL 61201

Call Sign: KA9PXD
Gale V Stombaugh
2008 42 St
Rock Island IL 61201

Call Sign: KB9IUA
Kevin L Anderson
819 42nd St
Rock Island IL 612012223

Call Sign: WB9ASF
Robert M Hecht
1325 42nd St
Rock Island IL 61201

Call Sign: KC5MOU
Ernest T Thurston
1519 42nd St
Rock Island IL 61201

Call Sign: WD8RDF
Joseph S Nash
1833 42nd St
Rock Island IL 61201

Call Sign: KB9LCS
John M Saarivirta
910 43rd St
Rock Island IL 61201

Call Sign: AB9QZ
John M Saarivirta
910 43rd St
Rock Island IL 61201

Call Sign: WB9MYT
Robert W Bradford
1130 44 St
Rock Island IL 61201

Call Sign: KC9IVP
Randace L Muse
1112 45th Ave
Rock Island IL 61201

Call Sign: N9JEF
Joseph R Gustafson
4429 46th Ave
Rock Island IL 61201

Call Sign: WA9SBC
Joseph R Holman
1827 46th St
Rock Island IL 61201

Call Sign: WB9WEV
George R Butler Sr
1319 5 1/2 Ave
Rock Island IL 61201

Call Sign: KB9PCL
Melodee L Benner
2300 79th Ave W Lot 125
Rock Island IL 61201

Call Sign: KC9MUV
William D Bogart Jr
2300 79th Ave W Lot 38
Rock Island IL 61201

Call Sign: K9FYV
Sheryl E Benner
2300 79th Ave W Lot125
Rock Island IL 612017468

Call Sign: NG9K
Sheryl E Benner
2300 79th Ave W Lot125
Rock Island IL 612017468

Call Sign: KB9LIR
Kevin A Pauletti
1730 85th Ave W
Rock Island IL 612017626

Call Sign: N9LCW
Mary A Goodell
1730 85th Ave W
Rock Island IL 612017626

Call Sign: KA0STB
Steven C Goodell
1730 85th Ave W
Rock Island IL 612017626

Call Sign: KA9STB
Steven C Goodell
1730 85th Ave W
Rock Island IL 612017626

Call Sign: KB0NBF
Gerald L Nave
1330 8th St

Rock Island IL 61201

Call Sign: KC9MEP
Benjamin L Ziegler
1207 95th Ave W
Rock Island IL 61201

Call Sign: K9HRL
Richard A Gooch
43 Blackhawk Hills Dr
Rock Island IL 61201

Call Sign: N9XGP
Jeffrey J Leech
1 Forest Ct
Rock Island IL 61201

Call Sign: KC9YL
Kenneth L Meeks
8720 Ridgewood Rd
Rock Island IL 61201

Call Sign: KD9KM
Kenneth L Meeks
8720 Ridgewood Rd
Rock Island IL 61201

Call Sign: KB9HEB
Philip P Oliver
Rock Island IL 61204

Call Sign: KB9SKO
Lynn M Craig
Rock Island IL 612043046

FCC Amateur Radio Licenses in Rockbridge

Call Sign: KC9NZV
Alyssa A Blumenberg
Box 27 Locust St
Rockbridge IL 62081

FCC Amateur Radio Licenses in Rockford

Call Sign: KB9TCV
Edwin G Mc Kaughan Jr
710 10th Ave

Rockford IL 61104

Call Sign: KB9RAU
Karon K Miller
6195 11th St
Rockford IL 61109

Call Sign: KB9QGM
Richard E Miller
6195 11th St
Rockford IL 61109

Call Sign: N9IEJ
Randall C Johnson
2013 13th Ave
Rockford IL 61104

Call Sign: KB9CCN
John E Garver
1520 16th Ave
Rockford IL 61104

Call Sign: K9KLY
Rudolph G Benander
1214 17th Ave
Rockford IL 61108

Call Sign: WA9BWK
Dale D Veline
2333 17th Ave
Rockford IL 61104

Call Sign: W9BWK
Dale D Veline
2333 17th Ave
Rockford IL 61104

Call Sign: N9ZXL
David J Larsen
2512 17th Ave
Rockford IL 61108

Call Sign: KB9VDM
Wayne W West
1706 18th Ave
Rockford IL 61104

Call Sign: K9PZZ
John G Olson

2707 18th Ave
Rockford IL 61_085833

Call Sign: W9JGO
John G Olson
2707 18th Ave
Rockford IL 611085833

Call Sign: KC9CYR
James T Thomas III
1514 20th Ave
Rockford IL 61115

Call Sign: KA9ZEJ
Kenneth C Geiger
2912 20th St
Rockford IL 61109

Call Sign: KC9BCG
Kennith D Pope
6152 20th St
Rockford IL 61109

Call Sign: K9KDP
Kennith D Pope
6152 20th St
Rockford IL 61109

Call Sign: KA9YCD
Denise L Burnside
1212 21st St
Rockford IL 61108

Call Sign: N9NQC
Gust C James
1017 22nd Ave
Rockford IL 61104

Call Sign: KT4SJ
Carol H Anderson
2204 22nd St
Rockford IL 61108

Call Sign: KB9ZKX
Jennifer A Birly
1403 24th St
Rockford IL 61108

Call Sign: KC9QBD

Jack A Riverdahl
1804 24th St
Rockford IL 61108

Call Sign: N9OJQ
Janelle L Birly
1403 24th St
Rockford IL 61108

Call Sign: AA9SK
John W Birly
1403 24th St
Rockford IL 61108

Call Sign: KA9NYL
Bertil O Johnson
1517 25th St
Rockford IL 61108

Call Sign: KC9LQB
Joseph A Burchardt
2312 25th St
Rockford IL 61108

Call Sign: KC9UDQ
Winnebago County Ares
Skywarn
2312 25th St
Rockford IL 61108

Call Sign: WX9WAS
Winnebago County Ares
Skywarn
2312 25th St
Rockford IL 61108

Call Sign: KC9VAE
Jeremy M Horn
402 27th St
Rockford IL 61108

Call Sign: WB9PBO
Harold N Cartwright
1420 27th St
Rockford IL 611083633

Call Sign: KB9CDC
Everett L Johnson
1416 28th St

Rockford IL 61108

Call Sign: W9MZW
John R Welsh Jr
312 29th St
Rockford IL 61108

Call Sign: KB9YDE
Fred M Adams
416 29th St
Rockford IL 61108

Call Sign: K9YDD
Fred M Adams
416 29th St
Rockford IL 61108

Call Sign: WA9CCT
Roger O Swanson
2615 2nd Ave
Rockford IL 61108

Call Sign: KC9GGD
Paul C Nordmoe
2026 3rd Ave
Rockford IL 61104

Call Sign: WB9QYV
Vail R Cordell III
1215 41st Ave
Rockford IL 611093044

Call Sign: N9TYC
Jackson W Foster
1513 4th Ave
Rockford IL 61104

Call Sign: WA9IYK
William A Penn
1027 6th St
Rockford IL 61108

Call Sign: KC9JDR
Richard T Jindrich
1006 6th St Apt A
Rockford IL 61104

Call Sign: KB9QGP
Brad A Hieb

620 8th St
Rockford IL 61104

Call Sign: KB9CUI
Joseph B Bukowski
6256 Abington Dr
Rockford IL 61109

Call Sign: AK9I
Emil G Borys Jr
6951 Academy Trl
Rockford IL 611072661

Call Sign: W9NM
Emil G Borys Jr
6951 Academy Trl
Rockford IL 611072661

Call Sign: KC9VLS
Nicholas J Coats
218 Albert Ave
Rockford IL 61101

Call Sign: K9JMW
Othel P Andrews
113 Alder Ave
Rockford IL 61107

Call Sign: N9HEW
Leo Battaglia
3031 Allington Ave
Rockford IL 61103

Call Sign: KB9OHW
Barbara C Quimby
5658 Alma Dr
Rockford IL 61108

Call Sign: KG9ID
Leonard R Quimby
5658 Alma Dr
Rockford IL 61108

Call Sign: K9AMJ
Herbert H Eckstein
5911 Alma Dr
Rockford IL 61108

Call Sign: WB9MMM

Eugene G Harlan
5931 Alma Dr
Rockford IL 61108

Call Sign: KB9SH
Sharon E Harlan
5931 Alma Dr
Rockford IL 61108

Call Sign: N9SH
Sharon E Harlan
5931 Alma Dr
Rockford IL 61108

Call Sign: N9UN
Werner R Steinhauser
5931 Alma Dr Harlan
Rockford IL 61108

Call Sign: KC9VRG
Greg L Geiger
4804 Alpine Park Dr
Rockford IL 61108

Call Sign: KB9HVO
Keith J Gade
6713 Alvina Rd
Rockford IL 61101

Call Sign: WA6UNS
George C Kopecky
5127 Arbutus Rd
Rockford IL 61107

Call Sign: KB9UJD
Bradley S Smith
5235 Arbutus Rd
Rockford IL 61107

Call Sign: WW9WWW
Bradley S Smith
5235 Arbutus Rd
Rockford IL 61107

Call Sign: AB8WD
Bradley S Smith
5235 Arbutus Rd
Rockford IL 611072454

Call Sign: KB9UJD
Bradley S Smith
5235 Arbutus Rd
Rockford IL 611072454

Call Sign: AB9Z
Bradley S Smith
5235 Arbutus Rd
Rockford IL 611072454

Call Sign: KA8N
Bradley S Smith
5235 Arbutus Rd
Rockford IL 611072454

Call Sign: AA9G
Bradley S Smith
5235 Arbutus Rd
Rockford IL 611072454

Call Sign: KB9TCW
Jeff S Bagwell
3020 Arcadia Terr
Rockford IL 61103

Call Sign: KB9EZF
Arthur D Hampton III
1317 Arvidson Dr
Rockford IL 61111

Call Sign: KB9FXD
Stoddard W Wisner
4110 Aspen Cir
Rockford IL 61107

Call Sign: N9WFW
Pankaj K Mahajan
2130 Auburn St 7
Rockford IL 61103

Call Sign: N9JWD
Stephen P Cooper
3517 Balsam Ln
Rockford IL 61109

Call Sign: N9ORB
Steven M Sarna
4677 Bamburg Ave
Rockford IL 611096702

Call Sign: WD9JDY
Elizabeth A Fiduccia
3020 Barrington Pl
Rockford IL 611071902

Call Sign: KB9LOJ
Daniel J Hallstrom
4008 Barrington Rd
Rockford IL 61107

Call Sign: KB9NBE
Bonnie L Moore
2621 Beaumont Pl
Rockford IL 611091516

Call Sign: WB9DFK
Thomas B Moore
2621 Beaumont Pl
Rockford IL 611091516

Call Sign: AI9R
Thomas B Moore
2621 Beaumont Pl
Rockford IL 611091516

Call Sign: N9CHX
David R Brunner
7386 Bell Vista Ter
Rockford IL 61107

Call Sign: KB9ASE
Anne M Glees
1589 Ben Franklin Rd
Rockford IL 61108

Call Sign: KB9ARX
Sabrina A Osowski
1650 Ben Franklin Rd
Rockford IL 61108

Call Sign: KB9UAD
Donald M Fishel
3607 Bently Dr
Rockford IL 61101

Call Sign: KA9VCW
Jaysen P Martin
1325 Benton St

Rockford IL 61107

Call Sign: KB9YGT
Sheri L Martin
1325 Benton St
Rockford IL 61107

Call Sign: W9KOT
Clyde E Aspling
250 Bienterra Trl 105
Rockford IL 61107

Call Sign: N3QOM
Carl D Walthall Jr
311 Bienterra Trl 4
Rockford IL 61107

Call Sign: N1LGZ
Mark R Streed
494 Bienterra Trl Apt 2
Rockford IL 61107

Call Sign: K9YOD
Albert White
906 Blue Lake Ave
Rockford IL 61102

Call Sign: KA9QEQ
Ross L King
634 Bohm Ave
Rockford IL 611074315

Call Sign: KB9TYT
Timothy P Bederka
2186 Bordeaux Dr
Rockford IL 61107

Call Sign: K9LLI
Stephen P Thorne
1105 Brae Burn Ln
Rockford IL 61107

Call Sign: W9ABY
Harold F Quick
2418 Brendenwood Rd
Rockford IL 61107

Call Sign: KC9UNC
Jason R Mcdonough

387 Brett Pl
Rockford IL 61107

Call Sign: N9BZT
Nancy L Korf
6146 Bristlecone Ln
Rockford IL 61109

Call Sign: N9VXJ
George C Vestal
1524 Bruner St
Rockford IL 61103

Call Sign: W9WOQ
Frederick A Miner
2012 Bruner St
Rockford IL 611034421

Call Sign: KC9MQZ
Ronald E Langley
2708 Buckingham Dr
Rockford IL 61107

Call Sign: W9PNP
Ronald E Langley
2708 Buckingham Dr
Rockford IL 61107

Call Sign: KA9ZVF
Charles C Rechtin
3316 Burrmont Rd
Rockford IL 61107

Call Sign: KA9BQX
Donald J Grattelo
4015 Burrmont Rd
Rockford IL 61107

Call Sign: KC9DBW
Jared A Mcquire
7806 Cadet Rd
Rockford IL 61115

Call Sign: KB9PHB
Scott L Williams
810 Camilin Ave
Rockford IL 61103

Call Sign: N9MKD

George A Hagen
1110 Campus Hills Rd
Rockford IL 61103

Call Sign: KB9KAA
Luka Biljeskovic
2237 Canary Dr
Rockford IL 61103

Call Sign: N9CNC
Cheryl A Anderson
947 Candleford Ln
Rockford IL 61108

Call Sign: WD9APQ
Raymond E Anderson
947 Candleford Ln
Rockford IL 61108

Call Sign: N0DIH
Thomas J Martin
6093 Canyon Woods Dr
Rockford IL 61109

Call Sign: WB9UMC
Charles F Liljegren
3787 Capron Dr
Rockford IL 61109

Call Sign: N9PCJ
Dwight D Gail
2620 Carmac Rd
Rockford IL 61101

Call Sign: KB9ARY
Leah N Parker
6534 Carman Dr
Rockford IL 61108

Call Sign: N9UQZ
Patricia A Deuel
1620 Carney Ave
Rockford IL 61103

Call Sign: N5DT
Cecil R Estes
6271 Carriage Green Way
Rockford IL 61108

Call Sign: KA9ZEL
Gregory S Ricketts
3135 Carriage Trl
Rockford IL 61109

Call Sign: WA9WVY
Leland E Gehlhausen
4610 Cayuga Rd
Rockford IL 61107

Call Sign: KC9KVO
Barry M Morris
6893 Cemetery Rd
Rockford IL 61101

Call Sign: W6PAM
William A Staats
10695 Cemetery Rd
Rockford IL 61063

Call Sign: W9MOS
Zygmont A Podgorny
2620 Centerville Rd
Rockford IL 61102

Call Sign: KB9GTN
Joe E Busenbark
5803 Chandler Dr
Rockford IL 61114

Call Sign: KC9OZD
Dennis L Carter
2222 Charles St
Rockford IL 61104

Call Sign: KB9VEC
Lavon E Carlson
4710 Charles St
Rockford IL 61108

Call Sign: WA9NTT
Robert E Davidson
3111 Chateau Ln
Rockford IL 61103

Call Sign: WA9NGR
Sheldon B Silver
904 Chelsea Ave
Rockford IL 61107

Call Sign: WB0JGR
Allen E Hermanson
2241 Chenowith Ct
Rockford IL 61107

Call Sign: KB9TBG
George B Beranek
2882 Cheroakwood Ln
Rockford IL 61114

Call Sign: KE9KL
Edward A Smerke
8225 Cherry N Dr
Rockford IL 61108

Call Sign: KC9ERH
Kevin L Grant
5484 Cheyenne Dr
Rockford IL 61109

Call Sign: W9MG
David R Bond
4571 Cinnamon Ln
Rockford IL 61114

Call Sign: WA0JDT
Murray L Hanson
3603 Clayton Ct
Rockford IL 611011816

Call Sign: N9UVQ
Douglas T Hanna
2137 Clinton St
Rockford IL 61103

Call Sign: N9QBT
Charles H Gooden
8098 Cloverdale Ln
Rockford IL 611072812

Call Sign: W9NCS
George J Bury
5351 Coachlite
Rockford IL 61111

Call Sign: KC9PDF
Dean J Schoff
9096 Cog Hill Fairway

Rockford IL 61103

Call Sign: W9WSG
Arthur V Anderson
2032 Colorado Ave
Rockford IL 61108

Call Sign: KC9CAB
Carmen M Riley
2404 Colorado Ave
Rockford IL 61108

Call Sign: KC9VGF
Jesus L Calvillo
2618 Colorado Ave
Rockford IL 61109

Call Sign: KA9BVG
Peter G Schmitz
4640 Colt Rd
Rockford IL 61109

Call Sign: KE9MH
John R Wacker
1412 Comanche Dr
Rockford IL 61107

Call Sign: N9VPQ
Andrew P Stephenson
2904 Conklin Dr 18
Rockford IL 61101

Call Sign: N9SZX
Bradley E Scudder
3407 Constance Dr
Rockford IL 61108

Call Sign: KB9UGF
George K Kitner
804 Coolidge Pl
Rockford IL 61107

Call Sign: N9QPP
Jimmie A Unger
1140 Coral Cir
Rockford IL 61108

Call Sign: N9IMI
Jeff A Mulrooney

3411 Cornelia
Rockford IL 61102

Call Sign: KK7IW
John C Huntley
1614 Corona Rd
Rockford IL 61108

Call Sign: KB9NMI
Charles E Brown
18 Country Club Beach
Rockford IL 61103

Call Sign: N9ESE
Ralph E Rungren
7130 Crimson Ridge Dr B204
Rockford IL 61107

Call Sign: N1REG
Charles L Dorsett Jr
1044 Crosby St
Rockford IL 61107

Call Sign: KA9BOD
Eugene P Stankiewicz
3531 Cross St
Rockford IL 61108

Call Sign: N9JBB
John S Dobel
2208 Cumberland
Rockford IL 61103

Call Sign: N9QMC
Mark A Carlson
2134 Cumberland St
Rockford IL 61103

Call Sign: KB9OW
Bruce C Hamilton
2603 Custer Ave
Rockford IL 61101

Call Sign: KC9DHX
Geordon M Van Tassle
3029 Custer Ave
Rockford IL 61101

Call Sign: K9PDZ

Harris A Anderson
114 Daisyfield Rd
Rockford IL 61102

Call Sign: N9DRL
Kathryn E Becker
4015 Dakota Ln
Rockford IL 61108

Call Sign: KC9WF
Marvin K Becker
4015 Dakota Ln
Rockford IL 61108

Call Sign: N9DTD
William M Becker
4015 Dakota Ln
Rockford IL 61108

Call Sign: KB9CSN
Christie A Van Hulle
6141 Dana Dr
Rockford IL 61109

Call Sign: WA9GNO
Vernon W Pearson
143 Dawn Ave
Rockford IL 61107

Call Sign: KC9COM
Jonathan K Tyson
403 Dawson Ave
Rockford IL 61107

Call Sign: KB9ARW
Anne M Larsen
4729 Dellview Dr
Rockford IL 61109

Call Sign: N9HVM
David R Yone
1378 Dennis Dr
Rockford IL 61103

Call Sign: W9HL
Randy E Scott
6129 Denwood Dr
Rockford IL 611145814

Call Sign: W9SES
Spencer E Scott
6129 Denwood Dr
Rockford IL 611145814

Call Sign: K9ARC
Meadow Ridge ARC
6129 Denwood Dr
Rockford IL 611145814

Call Sign: N9WEY
Ronald A Canode
571 Donna Dr Apt 1
Rockford IL 61107

Call Sign: KB9BPO
Jon R Cope
5690 Dorchester Dr
Rockford IL 61108

Call Sign: KB9ASD
Jennifer A Jepsen
5841 Dorchester Dr
Rockford IL 61108

Call Sign: N9CWT
Howard A Shallcross
901 Drexel Blvd
Rockford IL 61111

Call Sign: KA9GSF
Jeffrey T Kirk
2521 Driftwood Ln
Rockford IL 61107

Call Sign: W9ZWZ
Edward J Kleczewski
4211 Dunbar Pl
Rockford IL 61114

Call Sign: W9FFQ
Milton R Carlson
1815 E Gate Pky
Rockford IL 61108

Call Sign: WW9WWW
Bradley S Smith
7431 E State St
Rockford IL 61108

Call Sign: AB9LR
Bradley S Smith
7431 E State St 229
Rockford IL 61108

Call Sign: N9JTA
Robert B Hade
7675 E State St A5
Rockford IL 61108

Call Sign: KC9KQH
Maurycy M Sliwowski
3370 E Summerfield Dr
Rockford IL 61114

Call Sign: K9QYY
Jay A C Hart
2406 East Ln
Rockford IL 611071116

Call Sign: KB9GTH
Le Roy Abanes
1210 Eastview Rd
Rockford IL 61108

Call Sign: KA9MYF
Robert M Urbas
1320 Eastview Rd
Rockford IL 61108

Call Sign: K9MIP
Marsha I Plasters
3408 Ed Vera Dr
Rockford IL 61109

Call Sign: K9PEP
Paul E Plasters
3408 Ed Vera Dr
Rockford IL 61109

Call Sign: KC9CKH
Satern Of Rockford
3408 Ed Vera Dr
Rockford IL 61109

Call Sign: K9RSA
Satern Of Rockford
3408 Ed Vera Dr

Rockford IL 61109

Call Sign: N9ZQZ
Jamison T Cook
2813 Edelweiss Rd
Rockford IL 61109

Call Sign: KC9ALP
Ted W Faull
4821 Edgewood Hills Dr
Rockford IL 61108

Call Sign: N9YVL
Jeffrey M Whiteman
2110 Eggleston Rd
Rockford IL 61108

Call Sign: W4JR
James C Miller
5581 Einor Ave
Rockford IL 61108

Call Sign: K9PUR
Arthur C Chomacke
5661 Einor Ave
Rockford IL 61108

Call Sign: N9RBJ
Alek O Buczkowski
1227 Esmond Dr
Rockford IL 61108

Call Sign: KA9VDT
Jason Oldejans
2413 Evanston Dr
Rockford IL 61108

Call Sign: KB9ZXK
Simeon J Bartz
1631 Evergreen St
Rockford IL 61101

Call Sign: KB9NLS
Jean E Anderson
1601 Featherstone Rd
Rockford IL 61107

Call Sign: N9LAN
Michael R Anderson

1601 Featherstone Rd
Rockford IL 61107

Call Sign: N9ZUT
Jeffrey S Anderson
1014 Fieldcrest Dr
Rockford IL 61108

Call Sign: KC9TIN
Gary L Galloway
3663 Flambeau Dr
Rockford IL 61114

Call Sign: AB9YJ
Gary L Galloway
3663 Flambeau Dr
Rockford IL 61114

Call Sign: N9WDN
Mario Calvagna
3520 Fleetwood Dr
Rockford IL 611011832

Call Sign: KC9OJP
William S Calow III
5002 Fletcher Pl
Rockford IL 61108

Call Sign: KE9FW
Earl E Burdick
4211 Florida Dr Apt 203
Rockford IL 61108

Call Sign: K9MFN
Gary W Peterson
1749 Fox Wood Ct
Rockford IL 61107

Call Sign: WB9DME
Joseph M Schuller
1172 Foxtail Ln
Rockford IL 61108

Call Sign: WP4MVQ
Benjamin Velazquez Valentin
6484 Garrett Ln
Rockford IL 61107

Call Sign: KC9AVV

Mark R Streed
6133 Garrett Ln Apt 12
Rockford IL 611076614

Call Sign: KB9MFO
Stephen R Fleeman
1408 Geneva Ave
Rockford IL 61108

Call Sign: KC9FJR
Scott A Dowling
1416 Geneva Ave
Rockford IL 61108

Call Sign: K9DRM
Steven M Berglund
5259 Gingeridge Ln
Rockford IL 61114

Call Sign: WB9PBZ
Byron C Dale
1619 Grant Ave
Rockford IL 61103

Call Sign: N9WSP
Cynthia M Martin
2113 Grant Ave
Rockford IL 61103

Call Sign: K9BHG
Curtis B White
3945 Gray Fox Run
Rockford IL 61114

Call Sign: KB9ARZ
Amy L Di Benedetto
6231 Graydon Rd
Rockford IL 61109

Call Sign: N9OTC
John S Lawrence
2811 Greendale Dr
Rockford IL 61109

Call Sign: N9VGG
Charles R Fiduccia Sr
1912 Greenfield Ln
Rockford IL 61107

Call Sign: W9KIA
Donald V Sjoberg
1612 Greenwood Ave
Rockford IL 61107

Call Sign: KC9SQR
William C Lund
625 Gregory St
Rockford IL 61104

Call Sign: KC9FOG
Kenneth T Poncek
220 Guard St
Rockford IL 61103

Call Sign: KC8UHY
Scott G Kennedy
2818 Guilford Rd
Rockford IL 61107

Call Sign: KB9PC
Gertrude M Kindell
5734 Halley Rd
Rockford IL 61101

Call Sign: KA9OEX
Travis H Kelly
6552 Happy Acres Rd R 3
Rockford IL 61103

Call Sign: KB9WEM
Marcus A Cassady
1065 Harbortown Green
Rockford IL 61103

Call Sign: KB9WEN
Raylene J Cassady
1065 Harbortown Green
Rockford IL 61103

Call Sign: WA9PLW
James J Falzone
1608 Harlem Blvd
Rockford IL 61103

Call Sign: NA9J
Jack R Cook
2511 Harlem Blvd
Rockford IL 61103

Call Sign: K9HDB
Lowell L Wheeler
5220 Harrison Rd
Rockford IL 61101

Call Sign: KC9FIV
Jason D Ackerman
6980 Harrison Rd
Rockford IL 61101

Call Sign: WA9BKR
Jay B Hammell
2323 Hecker Ave
Rockford IL 61103

Call Sign: N8AMC
Bradley A Courter
5801 Heidi Dr
Rockford IL 61109

Call Sign: KA9ZVA
Linda M Hansen
1606 Henry St
Rockford IL 61103

Call Sign: KC9FOC
Mark T Germain
4653 High Pt Dr Unit 29
Rockford IL 61114

Call Sign: WA9GRN
William E Davis
2424 Highcrest Rd
Rockford IL 61107

Call Sign: KT9Q
Lloyd Kissick
1916 Hillcrest Rd
Rockford IL 61108

Call Sign: KA9QZU
Henry A Hallberg
136 Hilton Ave
Rockford IL 61107

Call Sign: WB9JAU
Charles M Oberg
2725 Hooker Ave

Rockford IL 61108

Call Sign: AB9AY
Charles M Oberg
2725 Hooker Ave
Rockford IL 61108

Call Sign: N9LAM
Denise Fell
2746 Horton St
Rockford IL 61109

Call Sign: KB9DFB
Kenneth D Fell
2746 Horton St
Rockford IL 61109

Call Sign: KB9PXR
Mike A Steffen
3033 Horton St
Rockford IL 61109

Call Sign: KB9IPU
Don H Eubanks
10699 Hwy 2 N
Rockford IL 61102

Call Sign: W6UOE
Paul Speciale
5214 Illini Ct
Rockford IL 61107

Call Sign: K9VSE
Robert B Bennett
5305 Indianhead Ave
Rockford IL 61108

Call Sign: KD9GI
Robert J Gustafson
1095 Ingram Rd
Rockford IL 61108

Call Sign: KC9JAW
Michael B Carter
3296 Ironwood Ave
Rockford IL 61109

Call Sign: N9OCV
Tammy L Mulrooney

1105 Iroquois Ave
Rockford IL 61102

Call Sign: KC9NLD
James W Carrell Sr
730 Island Ave
Rockford IL 61102

Call Sign: KC9LLS
Robert D Ditzler
7610 Ivory Ln
Rockford IL 61108

Call Sign: KC9GPO
Joel E Akre
1420 Jackson St
Rockford IL 61107

Call Sign: WB9KOR
Earl L Davis
1694 Jennie Dr
Rockford IL 61111

Call Sign: W9GOW
Lee Jones
1808 Jonathan Ave
Rockford IL 61103

Call Sign: KC9QYY
David K Bailey
1916 Jonathan Ave
Rockford IL 61103

Call Sign: KB9JRV
Krista M Boley
2215 Jonathan Ave
Rockford IL 61103

Call Sign: KB9HCT
Brian C Kostick
2415 Jonathan Ave
Rockford IL 61103

Call Sign: KB9UYV
Cesar R Solares
396 Karls Ct
Rockford IL 61107

Call Sign: K9RNR

Paul J Franklin
722 King St
Rockford IL 61103

Call Sign: WB9QOL
Robert V Gendle
5847 Kirkwood Dr
Rockford IL 61109

Call Sign: KC9LQX
Michael E Sullivan
5651 Knollwood Rd
Rockford IL 61107

Call Sign: W9ADY
Michael E Sullivan
5651 Knollwood Rd
Rockford IL 61107

Call Sign: N9OHT
Bruce A Carlson
5716 Knollwood Rd
Rockford IL 61107

Call Sign: KB9FRI
Donald G Senglaub
3031 La Salle Ave Apt 3
Rockford IL 61111

Call Sign: KA9URK
Monty B Johnson
7524 Lamaine Dr
Rockford IL 61103

Call Sign: KB9ZEQ
Aaron D Kennedy
5402 Lambeth Dr
Rockford IL 611071668

Call Sign: KB9YYF
David L Kennedy
5402 Lambeth Dr
Rockford IL 611071668

Call Sign: W9WXR
David L Kennedy
5402 Lambeth Dr
Rockford IL 611071668

Call Sign: KC9JDP
Steven R Finger
4112 Larson Ave
Rockford IL 61108

Call Sign: K9RFD
Repeater Technology Group
Of Winnebago
3115 Latham St
Rockford IL 61103

Call Sign: N9CCE
Maurice M Bolte Jr
3115 Latham St
Rockford IL 611033036

Call Sign: WR9H
Herbert T Case III
3648 Laura Ln
Rockford IL 61114

Call Sign: N9JOM
Ronald J Thorson
6546 Laurel Cherry Dr
Rockford IL 611084388

Call Sign: KA9SYJ
Robert W Krenek Sr
3076 Laurelhurst Dr
Rockford IL 61114

Call Sign: W9UYB
Charles E Bert
6520 Laurelwood Dr
Rockford IL 611081552

Call Sign: KB9WSK
Bryant J Erickson
1308 Leaman Pl
Rockford IL 61108

Call Sign: K9PHO
James R Millikin
8347 Leesburg Ct
Rockford IL 61114

Call Sign: KC9IJL
Gary L Burgess
3949 Lemans Dr

Rockford IL 61101

Call Sign: KB9LN
Robert J Milhone
1505 Lilac Ln
Rockford IL 61111

Call Sign: W9IGB
Robert W Mitchell
4731 Lincliff Dr
Rockford IL 61109

Call Sign: KB9MTH
Joseph P Perry
3921 Linden Rd
Rockford IL 61109

Call Sign: K9JPP
Joseph P Perry
3921 Linden Rd
Rockford IL 61109

Call Sign: KC9JVI
Regina A Perry
3921 Linden Rd
Rockford IL 61109

Call Sign: WB9KOT
Clyde E Aspling
4970 Linden Rd
Rockford IL 61109

Call Sign: KB9NBP
Edward F Gilligan III
5049 Linden Rd Apt 6206
Rockford IL 61109

Call Sign: KC9VRK
Gregory L Watkins
6112 Lockwood Dr
Rockford IL 61109

Call Sign: W9LSE
Paul W Patton
4250 Lori Dr
Rockford IL 61114

Call Sign: KB9ZKV
Paul D Ross

6178 Lorilynn Ln
Rockford IL 61109

Call Sign: KC9AP
James F Holmes
3010 Lotus Ln
Rockford IL 61111

Call Sign: KA9JSY
Richard L Holmes
3010 Lotus Ln
Rockford IL 61111

Call Sign: KC9ATQ
Bradley J Mckibben
2645 Lund Ave 3
Rockford IL 61109

Call Sign: KB9AOY
Julie A Medernach
6449 Lyndehurst
Rockford IL 61109

Call Sign: KC9IJK
Michael D Ableiter
4691 Marble Mnr
Rockford IL 61102

Call Sign: KB9UNL
Joseph J Mercaitis Jr
4727 Marble Mnr
Rockford IL 611024737

Call Sign: N9ANI
Donald D Feller
4216 Marsh Ave
Rockford IL 61114

Call Sign: WB9ETH
James W Nilson
4412 Marsh Ave
Rockford IL 61114

Call Sign: KB9JM
Donald J Cousins
6936 Meadow Song Trl
Rockford IL 61109

Call Sign: KB9GTO

Rolland O Westra
922 Medford Dr
Rockford IL 61107

Call Sign: KC9PGX
Michael W Virtue
613 Meeker Dr
Rockford IL 61109

Call Sign: W9MWV
Michael W Virtue
613 Meeker Dr
Rockford IL 61109

Call Sign: KC9TLN
Richard M Covert
1826 Melrose St
Rockford IL 61103

Call Sign: KC9ATS
Scott L Fortune
620 Menard Dr
Rockford IL 61109

Call Sign: KB4EFK
Sheila R Hill
2020 Midway Dr
Rockford IL 61103

Call Sign: WB5YNI
Samuel G Williams
7397 Mill Rd
Rockford IL 61108

Call Sign: W9RTQ
Leona Seymour
1711 Mobile Home Ave
Rockford IL 61109

Call Sign: WA9HZX
Roger A Dentandt
3811 Modesto Dr
Rockford IL 61111

Call Sign: KB9KQV
Douglas C Dailing
1206 Mondale Dr
Rockford IL 611084145

Call Sign: N9XUL
David A Milburn
425 Monroe St
Rockford IL 61101

Call Sign: KA9IMZ
Edmund A Schott
2203 Montague Rd
Rockford IL 61102

Call Sign: KA9JEJ
Edmund R Schott
2203 Montague Rd
Rockford IL 61102

Call Sign: KA9NSO
Lindsey A Schott
2203 Montague Rd
Rockford IL 61102

Call Sign: KB9CDD
Anthony De Pasqua
1810 Montague St
Rockford IL 61102

Call Sign: N9MKL
Frances De Pasqua
1810 Montague St
Rockford IL 61102

Call Sign: KA9VDF
Vito Rosolia
6391 Myrtle Ln
Rockford IL 61108

Call Sign: K9LC
Larry J Carlstrom
6712 N 2nd St
Rockford IL 61111

Call Sign: WB6IXZ
Rita J Tomacelli
6712 N 2nd St
Rockford IL 61111

Call Sign: KB9WEO
Willie J Fridell
220 N 4th St Apt 7
Rockford IL 611074042

Call Sign: KB9RSI
Michael J Goodwin
610 N Alpine Rd
Rockford IL 61107

Call Sign: KB9TLU
Jose I Marquez
2213 N Alpine Rd
Rockford IL 61107

Call Sign: WB0QHH
George R Harlan
3650 N Alpine Rd
Rockford IL 611144806

Call Sign: W9GKI
Reginald K Wells Sr
3655 N Alpine Rd
Rockford IL 61114

Call Sign: N9CNW
Mark W Broman
1643 N Alpine Rd 104
Rockford IL 61107

Call Sign: K9CIG
Theodore R Jacob Jr
3655 N Alpine Rd Apt B206
Rockford IL 61114

Call Sign: KI5XZ
Roman L Robles
424 N Calvin Park Blvd
Rockford IL 61107

Call Sign: KC9KVN
Brooke L Williamson
123 N Chicago Ave
Rockford IL 61107

Call Sign: K9WOI
William F Goets
131 N Chicago Ave
Rockford IL 61107

Call Sign: KA9NDQ
Michael L Cartwright
222 N Chicago Ave

Rockford IL 61107

Call Sign: KB9HQQ
James O Hilton
1710 N Church St
Rockford IL 61103

Call Sign: K3ZW
Paul D Hecker
2322 N Church St
Rockford IL 61103

Call Sign: KB9JZS
David A Spataro
3006 N Church St
Rockford IL 61103

Call Sign: KA9ODX
Donald P Campbell
1316 N Court St
Rockford IL 61103

Call Sign: N9VJI
Steven D Strait
1510 N Court St
Rockford IL 61103

Call Sign: KA9OJI
Timothy L Welk
718 N Court St Apt 28
Rockford IL 61103

Call Sign: KC9RUH
Joseph K Wenstrom
1630 N Horace Ave
Rockford IL 61101

Call Sign: N9FBC
Louis M Rossi
837 N Main St
Rockford IL 61103

Call Sign: WB9LHU
Scott Knodle
913 N Main St Apt 606
Rockford IL 61103

Call Sign: KC9AXP
Lloyd A Fulcer Jr

4010 N Meridan Rd
Rockford IL 61101

Call Sign: KC9VHC
Phillip S Gonzalez
2120 N Meridian Rd
Rockford IL 61101

Call Sign: N9PM
Philip T Miner
1784 N Mulford Rd
Rockford IL 611072541

Call Sign: KA9OES
Paul D Grams
2625C N Mulford Rd 131
Rockford IL 61114

Call Sign: N9WFY
Nancy A Mitchell
570 N Mulford Rd Apt 4
Rockford IL 61107

Call Sign: NE9Q
John H Dempster
225 N Prospect St
Rockford IL 61107

Call Sign: WD9EJK
Paul W Lindvall
936 N Prospect St
Rockford IL 61107

Call Sign: KB9IRQ
Forrest E Burris
2227 N Rockton Ave
Rockford IL 61103

Call Sign: N9HPG
Robert P Bloyer
3602 N Rockton Ave
Rockford IL 61103

Call Sign: N9VJ
James W Elkins
5823 N Rockton Ave
Rockford IL 61103

Call Sign: W4GFX

James W Elkins
5823 N Rockton Ave
Rockford IL 61103

Call Sign: WA9TLY
Ervin C Turner
322 N Sunset Ave
Rockford IL 61101

Call Sign: K9VJL
Don E Bissell
127 N Wyman St Apt 2
Rockford IL 611011107

Call Sign: W9AG
James A Siebel
1238 National Ave
Rockford IL 61103

Call Sign: KB9OTB
Angelo Piccione
2307 Nebraska Rd
Rockford IL 61108

Call Sign: N9CWQ
Peter T Nielsen
4517 Newburg Rd
Rockford IL 61108

Call Sign: N9CWQ
Amateur Radio Emergency
Communication As
4517 Newburg Rd
Rockford IL 61108

Call Sign: KB9QYF
Amateur Radio Emergency
Communication As
4517 Newburg Rd
Rockford IL 61108

Call Sign: N9WZD
B Fay Hansen
4517 Newburg Rd
Rockford IL 611086414

Call Sign: N9JRS
Timothy P Kortes
3801 Northline Dr

Rockford IL 61101

Call Sign: N9UVP
Mark A Carlson
1518 Notre Dame Rd
Rockford IL 61103

Call Sign: WB9IED
Richard L Connors
3204 Orleans Ave
Rockford IL 61111

Call Sign: N9HFD
Sharon A Connors
3204 Orleans Ave
Rockford IL 61111

Call Sign: KC9FQH
Robert E Ritchie
3981 Orlydrive
Rockford IL 61101

Call Sign: KD6EEY
Mary C Campbell
4109 Ostrander Rd
Rockford IL 61107

Call Sign: K9KTS
Fredric M Johnson
4712 Ottawa Rd
Rockford IL 61107

Call Sign: WB9PBY
James T Michna
4732 Ottawa Rd
Rockford IL 61107

Call Sign: N9SNY
Joseph F Di Mario Jr
2119 Overdene
Rockford IL 61103

Call Sign: WB9TFX
Henry A Murphy
7609 Owen Center Rd
Rockford IL 61101

Call Sign: KC9IJN
David A Kobler

2011 Oxford St
Rockford IL 61103

Call Sign: KC9OWB
David J Kiefer
6796 Oxtail Ct
Rockford IL 61107

Call Sign: K9UPQ
Frank A Lynn
2625 Pacific Pkwy
Rockford IL 61114

Call Sign: WD9HDU
Edna E Hibbs
3421 Packard Pkwy
Rockford IL 61103

Call Sign: KC9CL
Leland C Groop
5676 Palisades Pkwy
Rockford IL 61109

Call Sign: KB9ERN
Thomas J Southwood
5778 Palisades Pky
Rockford IL 61109

Call Sign: KB9JEU
Darren J Anderson
5980 Palomino Pkwy
Rockford IL 61109

Call Sign: N9AYI
Gilbert M Gratti
2935 Panorama Dr
Rockford IL 611091819

Call Sign: KA9IRA
Shirley J Gratti
2935 Panorama Dr
Rockford IL 611091819

Call Sign: WB5MRY
Ted R Schnetker
410 Paris
Rockford IL 61107

Call Sign: N9JVJ

Barry A Hufstedler
6086 Parish Pl
Rockford IL 61109

Call Sign: WB6EEM
Kenneth K Clarke
570 Parker Woods Dr
Rockford IL 61102

Call Sign: KA9ZUX
Glenn A Craig
3107 Parkside Ave
Rockford IL 61103

Call Sign: WB9JAV
Steven W Donaldson
408 Parkside Dr
Rockford IL 61108

Call Sign: W9OVY
Eric G Frank
508 Parkside Dr
Rockford IL 61108

Call Sign: N9GHM
Howard B Estes
519 Parkside Dr
Rockford IL 61108

Call Sign: WA9BNK
James F Karnes
619 Parkside Dr
Rockford IL 61108

Call Sign: K9PJJ
Urban L Kyburz
1103 Parkwood Ave
Rockford IL 61107

Call Sign: KC9LYP
Thomas J Zerebny
5822 Pathfinder Rd
Rockford IL 61109

Call Sign: N9SIB
Joseph L Peters
4797 Pelley Rd
Rockford IL 61102

Call Sign: N9FSA
Flora J Toth
4979 Pelley Rd
Rockford IL 61102

Call Sign: K9VMI
Francis T Toth
4979 Pelley Rd
Rockford IL 61102

Call Sign: KB9GTM
Albert F Abanes
4915 Pepper Dr
Rockford IL 61111

Call Sign: KB9SWF
Charles S Voyles
5789 Pepper Dr
Rockford IL 61114

Call Sign: KC9BIO
Daniel M Christy
7038 Perrietta Ln
Rockford IL 61107

Call Sign: KA9CDJ
James J Henry Jr
3501 Pheasant Run
Rockford IL 61103

Call Sign: KA9FFH
Ronald E Blahunka
3524 Pheasant Run
Rockford IL 61103

Call Sign: N9HJM
Lawrence M Hill
1819 Pierce Ave
Rockford IL 61103

Call Sign: KC9GVT
Roberto Hernandez
2324 Pierce Ave
Rockford IL 61103

Call Sign: KC9KCQ
Steven C Sproull
3923 Pinecrest Rd
Rockford IL 61107

Call Sign: KE9JB
Bernard R Crittenden
4028 Pinecrest Rd
Rockford IL 61107

Call Sign: KB9NBB
Tony C Turner
603 Pope St
Rockford IL 61104

Call Sign: KA9ZVC
Rowland E Holmertz
1420 Post Dr
Rockford IL 61108

Call Sign: K9VJJ
Paul A Klein
5027 Potomac Dr
Rockford IL 61107

Call Sign: KB9RWM
Barbara J Brown
997 Prescott Dr
Rockford IL 611082590

Call Sign: N9CFE
Robert H Pierce
10747 Quail Hill Cove
Rockford IL 61114

Call Sign: N9WSR
David E Roof
1627 Quentin Rd
Rockford IL 61108

Call Sign: N9LMF
Garth G Miller Jr
3334 Quiet Valley Ln
Rockford IL 61109

Call Sign: N9MKJ
Rhonda R Miller
3334 Quiet Valley Ln
Rockford IL 61109

Call Sign: N9SBJ
Scott M Walter
1343 Randall Dr

Rockford IL 61108

Call Sign: WA9WSR
Milo F Case
2643 Revelation Ln
Rockford IL 61109

Call Sign: WD9BDM
Leon C Raiford Jr
331 Reynolds St
Rockford IL 61103

Call Sign: W9OWK
David H Brill Jr
724 Reynolds St
Rockford IL 61103

Call Sign: N9MKK
Harlan E Meece
710 River Park Dr
Rockford IL 61111

Call Sign: KC9FOD
Nancy A Gilbert
112 Rome Ave
Rockford IL 61107

Call Sign: N9PCI
Brian D Scott
410 Rome Ave
Rockford IL 61107

Call Sign: N9JRT
Shirley M De Witt
1137 Roxbury Rd
Rockford IL 61107

Call Sign: N9HUB
Clayton C De Witt
1137 Roxbury Rd
Rockford IL 611073756

Call Sign: N9JBZ
Derek M Piec Sr
7964 Royal Oaks Rd
Rockford IL 61107

Call Sign: KA0NRZ
Gary E O Neill

4998 Rundquist Ct
Rockford IL 61114

Call Sign: K9IUD
Paul G Willer
3516 Rural St
Rockford IL 61107

Call Sign: KC9GPP
Dennis R Murray
1819 Rural St 3
Rockford IL 61107

Call Sign: N9KEI
Dennis R Murray
1819 Rural St 3
Rockford IL 61107

Call Sign: K9KZT
Lawrence A Lisle
3030 Rutgers Pl
Rockford IL 61109

Call Sign: N9HJB
David G Watson
6785 Rydberg Rd
Rockford IL 61109

Call Sign: KA9ZVH
Diana L Watson
6785 Rydberg Rd
Rockford IL 61109

Call Sign: KA9OLU
Leland L Wolfe
6796 Rydberg Rd
Rockford IL 61109

Call Sign: N9TIX
Stephen A Scarabelli
418 S 1st St
Rockford IL 61104

Call Sign: KC9OWA
Clifton Hill
939 S 3rd
Rockford IL 61104

Call Sign: N9YDJ

Kurt W Geiger
2207 S 6th St
Rockford IL 61104

Call Sign: KC9FOB
Sherman H Buetsch
1923 S Alpine Rd
Rockford IL 611087701

Call Sign: KC9GIO
Alvin O Alexander
523 S Ave
Rockford IL 61109

Call Sign: KC9RMK
Wayne A Snell
408 S Gardiner Ave Apt2
Rockford IL 61104

Call Sign: KB9TIN
Cynthia L Bergsmith
116 S Highland Ave 1
Rockford IL 61104

Call Sign: KB9DXD
Arthur R Gustafson
8826 S Main Rd
Rockford IL 61102

Call Sign: KB9LVN
Robert D Millard
3113 S Main St
Rockford IL 61102

Call Sign: N9RNS
Michael D Sortino
657 S Mulford Rd
Rockford IL 61108

Call Sign: KH6UX
Van A Johnson
4567 S Mulford Rd
Rockford IL 61109

Call Sign: K9QOT
Randy F Sturm
4747 S Mulford Rd
Rockford IL 61109

Call Sign: KA8GQS
Charles A Warner
129 S Phelps Ave Ste 503
Rockford IL 61108

Call Sign: KB9UYW
Pedro T Hernandez
12 S Suclid Ave
Rockford IL 61107

Call Sign: N9KUY
James E Gutshall
927 S Trainer Rd
Rockford IL 611081575

Call Sign: KB9YON
Andrew W Fiduccia
6203 Safford Rd
Rockford IL 61101

Call Sign: K9TLH
Thomas L Hosmann
1336 Sandy Point Dr
Rockford IL 611038867

Call Sign: KC9GIP
James W Webber
2759 Savanah Ln
Rockford IL 61102

Call Sign: N8QKI
Jena K Webber
2759 Savannah Ln
Rockford IL 611023661

Call Sign: KC9JNV
Joanna K Webber
2759 Savannah Ln
Rockford IL 611023661

Call Sign: KF8XC
William H Webber
2759 Savannah Ln
Rockford IL 611023661

Call Sign: KB9TYE
Robert E Houser
508 Sawyer Rd
Rockford IL 61109

Call Sign: KU9G
Russell E Nimocks Jr
8330 Scott Ln
Rockford IL 61115

Call Sign: N9EJB
Duane C Kopecky
1216 Scottswood Rd
Rockford IL 61107

Call Sign: N9HVX
Kurt L Brown
515 Seminary St Apt 205
Rockford IL 61104

Call Sign: N9OCS
Jeff T Lierman
90 Senate Dr
Rockford IL 611091350

Call Sign: N9LJJ
James C Thompson
1756 Sentinel Ct
Rockford IL 61107

Call Sign: WB9PBR
Carl A Cacciatore
127 Shadow Ridge Ln Rr 17
Rockford IL 61107

Call Sign: W9TQ
Carl A Cacciatore
127 Shadow Ridge Ln Rr 17
Rockford IL 61107

Call Sign: W9HH
David A Swanson
2420 Shady Ln
Rockford IL 61107

Call Sign: W9EU
David A Swanson
2420 Shady Ln
Rockford IL 61107

Call Sign: KB9EZB
Nicholas R Clayton
5570 Shagbark Cir

Rockford IL 61109

Call Sign: KA9NYM
David G Mc Christie
5573 Shagbark Cir
Rockford IL 61109

Call Sign: KS9X
Frank J Hirsch
5573 Shagbark Cir
Rockford IL 61109

Call Sign: KA9OYR
Brian C Ahlgren
1907 Sharon Ave
Rockford IL 611033835

Call Sign: KB9FXB
Kenneth D Dean
317 Shaw St
Rockford IL 61104

Call Sign: KB9JZV
Timothy L Mc Dougal
318 Sherman St
Rockford IL 61103

Call Sign: KC9ION
Bruce W Magnuson
3620 Shirley Rd
Rockford IL 61108

Call Sign: N9BWM
Bruce W Magnuson
3620 Shirley Rd
Rockford IL 61108

Call Sign: W2IOS
Willard J Shears Jr
3720 Shirley Rd
Rockford IL 611081948

Call Sign: KC9ICH
Robert A Larson
3911 Shirley Rd
Rockford IL 611081950

Call Sign: KC9QBC
Shannon K Larson

3911 Shirley Rd
Rockford IL 611081950

Call Sign: KA9DNR
William A Schroeder Sr
5385 Shoshoni Trl
Rockford IL 61101

Call Sign: KA9DEE
Donald C Ross Sr
2603 Sierra Dr
Rockford IL 61109

Call Sign: N9KBK
Robert Steinhauser
4610 Skyline Dr
Rockford IL 61107

Call Sign: KA0TCM
James C Williams
202 Smith Ave
Rockford IL 61107

Call Sign: N9NQD
Art M Naud
623 Smith Ave
Rockford IL 61107

Call Sign: KA9LHR
Jon W Mains
820 Soper Ave
Rockford IL 61101

Call Sign: N9HKM
David M Ewaldz
4612 Sovereign Blvd
Rockford IL 61108

Call Sign: KC9HVR
Karl C Auerswald
2511 Spingdale Dr
Rockford IL 61114

Call Sign: K9KCA
Karl C Auerswald
2511 Spingdale Dr
Rockford IL 61114

Call Sign: WB9PIT

Joseph J Krusa
5548 Spring Brook Rd
Rockford IL 61114

Call Sign: KF9AU
James E Zahrndt
10272 Springborough Dr
Rockford IL 61107

Call Sign: KA9SOG
John R Auerswald
2511 Springdale Dr
Rockford IL 61114

Call Sign: KC9AKC
Mary L Auerswald
2511 Springdale Dr
Rockford IL 61114

Call Sign: KC9HVQ
Mikayla E Auerswald
2511 Springdale Dr
Rockford IL 61114

Call Sign: K9MEA
Mikayla E Auerswald
2511 Springdale Dr
Rockford IL 61114

Call Sign: KC9MDV
Austin J Polnow
908 St Andrews Way
Rockford IL 61107

Call Sign: KA9FSK
Ernest H Stark
4708 Stonegate Pl
Rockford IL 611082120

Call Sign: KB9DEO
Jim L De Castris
2742 Stoneham Pky
Rockford IL 61109

Call Sign: N9HEZ
Joseph W Roling
5850 Strathmoor Dr Apt 3
Rockford IL 611075159

Call Sign: KC9BCB
Richard J Fleming
525 Summer St
Rockford IL 61103

Call Sign: N9KCT
Phillip J Calvagna
3356 Sun Valley Ter Apt 2
Rockford IL 61103

Call Sign: KB9PPE
Northern Illinois Digital
Communications Assoc
4547 Sunderman Rd
Rockford IL 61114

Call Sign: N9LHA
Lawrence J Hanneman
2912 Sunnyside Dr
Rockford IL 61114

Call Sign: KC9OVZ
Paul D Branning
2709 Swanson Pkwy
Rockford IL 61109

Call Sign: KC9MIP
Edwin H Colson II
2216 Tacoma Ave
Rockford IL 61103

Call Sign: KB9NGO
Ronald L Lundstrom
2115 Taliesen Ln
Rockford IL 61107

Call Sign: N9YDH
William A Smith
3908 Tallwood Ave
Rockford IL 61114

Call Sign: N9NQA
David R Paton
4003 Tallwood Ave
Rockford IL 61114

Call Sign: K0DST
David C Moore
3606 Teal Ln

Rockford IL 61103

Call Sign: K9DO
David C Moore
3606 Teal Ln
Rockford IL 61103

Call Sign: KB9AWD
Valerie L Anderson
1811 Telemark Dr
Rockford IL 61108

Call Sign: N9NYG
David P Harter
8526 Terry Rd
Rockford IL 61108

Call Sign: KC9JDO
Bradley L Barnhart
6567 Thomas Pkwy
Rockford IL 61114

Call Sign: KB9YXA
James G Wernberg
6073 Thorncrest Dr
Rockford IL 61109

Call Sign: WA9APA
Scott J Francis
6382 Thorncrest Dr
Rockford IL 61109

Call Sign: KG9SF
Scott James Francis
6382 Thorncrest Dr
Rockford IL 61109

Call Sign: W9TBD
Peter Andree
2591 Timber Trl
Rockford IL 61107

Call Sign: KA4IIK
Gary H Winters
8352 Towermont Dr
Rockford IL 61102

Call Sign: N9MJN
Rickey Winders

4824 Treeview Ter
Rockford IL 611094136

Call Sign: KB9YKM
Keith R Owano
4759 Treeview Terr
Rockford IL 61109

Call Sign: KC9BCF
Wendy Owano
4759 Treeview Terr
Rockford IL 611094133

Call Sign: N9UVR
Mark W Snodgrass
4728 Trevor Cir 4
Rockford IL 61109

Call Sign: KB9YHM
John S Erickson
5107 Upland Dr
Rockford IL 61108

Call Sign: WB2ADR
Joseph A Di Caprio
6281 Valley Knoll Dr
Rockford IL 61109

Call Sign: KA9CDI
James W Gent
2012 Van Wie Ave
Rockford IL 61103

Call Sign: W9KIX
Donald E Burchard
4209 Villa Wood Cir
Rockford IL 61107

Call Sign: K9GGA
Fred C Mertz
1604 Virginia Ave
Rockford IL 61101

Call Sign: K9HBT
Kevin B Randall
4201 Virginia Ave
Rockford IL 61101

Call Sign: KC9VRH

Marianne Geiger
2304 Vista Close
Rockford IL 61107

Call Sign: KB9AOZ
Jennifer T Hemmens
4706 Waukegan Dr
Rockford IL 61108

Call Sign: N9QQF
Steven V Knaack
507 Welty Ave
Rockford IL 61107

Call Sign: N9WDO
Theodore H Faber
3201 Wesley Way
Rockford IL 61101

Call Sign: N9VPP
Howard E Stewart
516 Westchester Dr
Rockford IL 61107

Call Sign: W9TZU
Robert L Neumann
5898 Weymouth
Rockford IL 61114

Call Sign: WA9QON
John E Shepler
5653 Weymouth Dr
Rockford IL 61111

Call Sign: WB9TNB
Donald E Wallgren
2613 Whale Ave
Rockford IL 61109

Call Sign: WD9JGH
Michael L Santucci
10852 Whispering Pines Way
Rockford IL 61114

Call Sign: KB9EPZ
David C Vivian
5833 White Cliff Rd
Rockford IL 61109

Call Sign: KA9QEN
Michael P O Brien
4802 White Oak
Rockford IL 61111

Call Sign: KB9CYC
Angela N Blasiola
6168 Whitefriars Way
Rockford IL 61109

Call Sign: KB9CLF
Stacy E Blasiola
6168 Whitefriars Way
Rockford IL 61109

Call Sign: N9BSD
Thomas R Johnson
1307 Widergren Dr
Rockford IL 61108

Call Sign: KA9BBH
Ike J Terhorst
5216 Wilderness Trl
Rockford IL 61114

Call Sign: K9YFZ
Susan B Engebretson
4350 Wildwood Ln
Rockford IL 61101

Call Sign: KB9MJG
Dennis A Gray Jr
1002 Willard Ave
Rockford IL 61101

Call Sign: WB9UHL
John E Gustafson
2231 Wilmette Dr
Rockford IL 61108

Call Sign: KB9ERM
Lynn M Vogel
2828 Windamere Way
Rockford IL 61109

Call Sign: KA9SFP
Connie J Groshans
2016 Winters Dr
Rockford IL 61111

Call Sign: KA9QER
James K Groshans
2016 Winters Dr
Rockford IL 61111

Call Sign: N9KEI
Dennis R Murray
1126 Winthrop Ln
Rockford IL 61107

Call Sign: KB9ANH
Tiffaney K Kress
1846 Witchita Dr
Rockford IL 61108

Call Sign: WA9DXC
Ernest B Johnson
5604 Woodbine Dr
Rockford IL 61108

Call Sign: KC9JDN
Jennie E Beranek
605 Woodridge Dr
Rockford IL 61108

Call Sign: N9TOA
Marion J Pinter
6268 Wynbrook Dr
Rockford IL 61109

Call Sign: N9MCS
Eric B Hultgren
2404 Wyoming Dr
Rockford IL 61108

Call Sign: KC9ISX
N9Mcs Repeater Group
2404 Wyoming Dr
Rockford IL 611087625

Call Sign: WX9MCS
N9Mcs Repeater Group
2404 Wyoming Dr
Rockford IL 611087625

Call Sign: KC9OQG
Robert F Rose
4104 Yale Dr

Rockford IL 61109

Call Sign: W2TQA
William J Michaels
5397 Yellowstone Dr
Rockford IL 61109

Call Sign: N8CDW
Carl D Walthall Jr
3222 Youngfield Dr
Rockford IL 61114

Call Sign: N3QOM
Carl D Walthall Jr
3222 Youngfield Dr
Rockford IL 61114

Call Sign: N8CDW
Carl D Walthall Jr
3222 Youngfield Dr
Rockford IL 61114

Call Sign: KC9DBI
Prairieland ARS
3222 Youngfield Dr
Rockford IL 61114

Call Sign: WW9P
Prairieland ARS
3222 Youngfield Dr
Rockford IL 61114

Call Sign: KD9MX
Jon T Eliason
Rockford IL 61126

Call Sign: KC9FAH
Linda L Hunt
Rockford IL 61104

Call Sign: N9XKH
Dennis A Gray
Rockford IL 61105

Call Sign: KC9ATR
Daniel C Hunt
Rockford IL 61106

Call Sign: KC9LXS

Bill A Jeske
Rockford IL 61110

Call Sign: N4KXH
Kenneth D Windham Sr
Rockford IL 61125

Call Sign: KC9GOL
James H Curtis
Rockford IL 61125

Call Sign: N9UQP
Scot Price
Rockford IL 61125

Call Sign: K9LLL
Austin J Polnow
Rockford IL 61126

Call Sign: W9AXD
Rockford Amateur Radio
Association Inc
Rockford IL 61126

Call Sign: KC9AKD
Janet L Grayum
Rockford IL 611267184

Call Sign: KC9EFU
Rockford Amateur Radio
Association Inc
Rockford IL 611268465

Call Sign: W9ATN
Rockford Amateur Radio
Association Inc
Rockford IL 611268465

FCC Amateur Radio
Licenses in Rockton

Call Sign: WB8PKS
Larry C Schubert
1025 Armstrong Ave
Rockton IL 61072

Call Sign: WE9KXZ
Thomas M Silletti
15758 Cannel Rd

Rockton IL 61072

Call Sign: K9POJ
William K Oliver
707 Center St
Rockton IL 61072

Call Sign: KB9RAV
Mitchell J Eley
228 Dancette Dr
Rockton IL 61072

Call Sign: WA9KSS
David L Eley
228 Dancette Dr
Rockton IL 61072

Call Sign: K9ZHC
Norman L Beck
626 E Warren St
Rockton IL 61072

Call Sign: KC9QPJ
Raymond L Knapp III
13183 Glencree Ln
Rockton IL 61072

Call Sign: N9DAZ
Richard W Mc Glynn
10065 Haas Rd
Rockton IL 61072

Call Sign: WB9KKA
Robert E Pearson
10801 Haas Rd
Rockton IL 61072

Call Sign: W9MX
Allen R Holecek
15929 Hauley Rd
Rockton IL 61072

Call Sign: WD9JBD
Doris E Holecek
15929 Hauley Rd
Rockton IL 61072

Call Sign: KB9JKG
Kurt A Shipman

725 Kelsey Ct
Rockton IL 61072

Call Sign: KB9UJC
Christopher A Wrate
4186 Kensington Way
Rockton IL 61072

Call Sign: KB9SEY
Derek S Hoaglund
748 Kocher St
Rockton IL 61072

Call Sign: K9LJN
Gary H Hilker
3194 Moffett Rd
Rockton IL 610729462

Call Sign: N9XUG
Charles E Blum
1412 N Blackhawk
Rockton IL 61072

Call Sign: N9ZBJ
Woodson S Fuller II
916 N Blackhawk Blvd
Rockton IL 610721502

Call Sign: KB9HBS
Lloyd W Rhodes
9238 N Meridian Rd
Rockton IL 61072

Call Sign: KC9FWN
Kenneth M Olson
12974 Northland Ests Ct
Rockton IL 61072

Call Sign: N9KMO
Kenneth M Olson
12974 Northland Ests Ct
Rockton IL 61072

Call Sign: KB9BEZ
Brad D Scoville
9021 Pomeroy Rd
Rockton IL 61072

Call Sign: KA8FBU

Michael J Powers
18 Sandhurst Dr
Rockton IL 61072

Call Sign: KC9MJV
Lawrance G Glenn
1230 Sandpebble Dr
Rockton IL 61072

Call Sign: KC9MJW
Terri L Glenn
1230 Sandpebble Dr
Rockton IL 61072

Call Sign: KA9HTQ
Charles A Richter
630 Strawbridge Dr
Rockton IL 61072

Call Sign: KG9NV
Stanley F Magrecki
1525 Torch Pine Dr
Rockton IL 61072

Call Sign: KD9KW
Stanley F Magrecki
1525 Torch Pine Dr
Rockton IL 61072

Call Sign: KB9MNL
Jodi L Briscoe
11944 Truman Dr
Rockton IL 61072

Call Sign: AC9V
Robert E Briscoe Jr
11944 Truman Dr
Rockton IL 61072

Call Sign: N9DQU
James R Swanson
833 Valley Forge Trl
Rockton IL 61072

Call Sign: K9AVK
Diane K Busker
571 W Rockton Rd
Rockton IL 61072

Call Sign: K9AVJ
Leroy H Busker
571 W Rockton Rd
Rockton IL 61072

Call Sign: N9IZB
Gale D Lawson
7549 Wishop Rd
Rockton IL 61072

Call Sign: KB9MBN
Myron P Werbowecky
664 Wynstone Way
Rockton IL 61072

Call Sign: W9FDA
David O Lewis
13245 Wynstone Way
Rockton IL 61072

FCC Amateur Radio Licenses in Rockwood

Call Sign: WB9WGA
William C Rendleman Sr
364 Private Rd Fh
Rockwood IL 62280

Call Sign: KC9QDQ
Ricky A Grah
2181 Vinewood Ln
Rockwood IL 62280

FCC Amateur Radio Licenses in Rome

Call Sign: KB9VIU
Stephen E Schlosser
16026 Front St
Rome IL 61562

Call Sign: WX9SS
Stephen E Schlosser
16026 Front St
Rome IL 61562

Call Sign: KA9OPI
Alan E Salz
Rome IL 61562

Call Sign: KD9AT
Cheri K Salz
Rome IL 61562

FCC Amateur Radio Licenses in Roodhouse

Call Sign: KA9AZY
Richard S Lawson
115 Benton Ave
Roodhouse IL 62082

Call Sign: WB9ROB
Eugene R Summers
Rr 3 Box 190
Roodhouse IL 62082

Call Sign: WA9RTK
Wilmer R Burrus
203 E Clay St
Roodhouse IL 62082

Call Sign: KB9TVR
Robin D Haynes
1278 Roger Ln
Roodhouse IL 62082

FCC Amateur Radio Licenses in Rosamond

Call Sign: W3IAL
Wesley W Skelly
Rosamond IL 62083

FCC Amateur Radio Licenses in Roscoe

Call Sign: K9CUQ
Floyd W Spearing
11125 3rd St
Roscoe IL 61073

Call Sign: KA9WSH
Michael J Drost
10825 6th St
Roscoe IL 61073

Call Sign: KB9BRW

Sheryl A Drost
10825 6th St
Roscoe IL 61073

Call Sign: WA9DIM
David W Drake
11718 Banbridge Dr
Roscoe IL 61073

Call Sign: KC9GOA
James T Larson
6525 Barkridge Rd
Roscoe IL 61073

Call Sign: KC9OZP
Michael L Hahn
9610 Belvidere Rd
Roscoe IL 61073

Call Sign: N9KCR
Robert W Sanderson IV
12145 Bend River Rd
Roscoe IL 61073

Call Sign: N9SZY
Richard A Wells
11855 Bowen Pkwy
Roscoe IL 61073

Call Sign: KA0NUH
B Scot Schulz
5938 Broad St
Roscoe IL 61073

Call Sign: WA8FTA
Bruce M Handy
11898 Burnside Ln
Roscoe IL 61073

Call Sign: N9HEA
Robert W Butterworth
6353 Burr Oak Rd Box 505
Roscoe IL 61073

Call Sign: WA9CIY
Dennis G Makovec
12165 Carberry Ln
Roscoe IL 61073

Call Sign: KC9JIA
John R Huddleston
11308 Cedarbrook Rd
Roscoe IL 610738610

Call Sign: K9JRH
John R Huddleston
11308 Cedarbrook Rd
Roscoe IL 610738610

Call Sign: N9EGF
Kevin R Puckett
7685 Chantelle Ln
Roscoe IL 610739769

Call Sign: KC9ILT
Christopher D Warner
5912 Chestnut St
Roscoe IL 61073

Call Sign: WA9YVI
Donald C Wallen
19255 County Line Rd
Roscoe IL 610738407

Call Sign: N9EIM
Robert C Stark
20373 Countyline Rd
Roscoe IL 61073

Call Sign: KB9UR
William W Spires Jr
9230 Crescent Ct
Roscoe IL 61073

Call Sign: KT9X
James M Graff
5069 Edgemere Ct
Roscoe IL 61073

Call Sign: K9EIR
Robert D Ahlberg
6464 Elevator Rd
Roscoe IL 61073

Call Sign: KA9OWG
William A Null
8785 Elevator Rd
Roscoe IL 61073

Call Sign: KC9SLC
Andrew J Mertzenich
10052 Fawn Prairie Dr
Roscoe IL 61073

Call Sign: KB9OTC
Edmond F Mertzenich
10052 Fawn Prairie Dr
Roscoe IL 61073

Call Sign: KB9VRB
Nancy A Mertzenich
10052 Fawn Prairie Dr
Roscoe IL 61073

Call Sign: KC9ORL
Alice J Stoicescu
8674 Grandview Dr
Roscoe IL 61073

Call Sign: KA3KTN
Edward P Titcomb
5655 Gray Eagle Rd
Roscoe IL 610738539

Call Sign: KB9LOI
William J Nealand
11737 Graystone Cir
Roscoe IL 61073

Call Sign: KE9GJ
Curtis A Hagenbuch
12449 Greensview Dr
Roscoe IL 61073

Call Sign: WB9NDH
Vernon J Berg
6818 Gunpowder
Roscoe IL 61073

Call Sign: KC9GDU
Charles E Ingle
5561 Hodges Run
Roscoe IL 61073

Call Sign: AB9KA
Charles E Ingle
5561 Hodges Run

Roscoe IL 61073

Call Sign: KA9NCP
Terry L Makovec
4324 Honey Locust Ln
Roscoe IL 61073

Call Sign: N0LNG
Michael J Krenz
12847 Huntsboro Ln
Roscoe IL 61073

Call Sign: KC9QLS
Linda M Aimers
11091 Jasmine Dr
Roscoe IL 61073

Call Sign: N9SOC
Patrick A Aimers
11091 Jasmine Dr
Roscoe IL 61073

Call Sign: N9HAG
Lyle D Brubaker
11353 Jeremy Ln
Roscoe IL 61073

Call Sign: N9OJT
Craig P Gleason
7521 Joy Ln
Roscoe IL 61073

Call Sign: N9DEM
Loren R Heinzeroth
7258 Kinnikinnick Dr
Roscoe IL 61073

Call Sign: N9MXO
Earl A Ustruck
12314 Legend Lakes Dr
Roscoe IL 61073

Call Sign: KC9KKB
Gerald D Whalen
11130 Lemon Grass Ln
Roscoe IL 61073

Call Sign: KC9CLJ
James D Bunting Jr

10814 Linden Blossom Ln
Roscoe IL 61073

Call Sign: KB9SSV
Michael L Richardson
10877 Linden Blossom Ln
Roscoe IL 61073

Call Sign: N9VGF
David W Hinde
8730 Lovesee Rd
Roscoe IL 61073

Call Sign: N9GYT
John D Milhone
4984 McCurry Rd
Roscoe IL 61073

Call Sign: N9GYS
Peggy L Milhone
4984 McCurry Rd
Roscoe IL 61073

Call Sign: N9EN
Bradley R Anbro
8259 McCurry Rd
Roscoe IL 610738469

Call Sign: KC9SLD
Levi V Orsinger
8362 McCurry Rd
Roscoe IL 61073

Call Sign: KC9UQL
Scott J Orsinger
8362 McCurry Rd
Roscoe IL 61073

Call Sign: WD9FLO
Dean W Livingston
8384 McCurry Rd
Roscoe IL 61073

Call Sign: K9FLO
Dean W Livingston
8384 McCurry Rd
Roscoe IL 61073

Call Sign: N9QER

James L Ambruoso Sr
6741 Meadowbrook
Roscoe IL 61073

Call Sign: KC9UK
Thomas A Daniels
11898 Moore Woods Rd
Roscoe IL 61073

Call Sign: KC9FOE
Anton T Kramer
303 N Creek Rd
Roscoe IL 61073

Call Sign: KA9OFP
David P Johnston
8592 N Creek Rd
Roscoe IL 61073

Call Sign: W9PJ
Paul F Johnston
8592 N Creek Rd
Roscoe IL 61073

Call Sign: W9USA
Illinois Historical Radio
Society
8592 N Creek Rd
Roscoe IL 61073

Call Sign: N9FAJ
William L Stepanek Jr
12612 N Gate
Roscoe IL 61073

Call Sign: N9BLL
William L Stepanek Jr
12612 N Gate
Roscoe IL 61073

Call Sign: N9XJC
Derrick S Rose
12731 N Sec St
Roscoe IL 61073

Call Sign: N9LXR
Christopher D Wells
5688 Oak Village Dr
Roscoe IL 61073

Call Sign: WB8HVW
John T Moore
10558 Pearl St
Roscoe IL 610730466

Call Sign: W1AIP
Jack E Horner
401 Rockton Rd
Roscoe IL 61073

Call Sign: KA6CDE
Nancy A Mason
4703 Rollingford Ln
Roscoe IL 61073

Call Sign: N9CEZ
Brian C Lindquist
5607 Rural Edge Dr
Roscoe IL 61073

Call Sign: N9CNB
Marguerite R Baker
11993 S Gate Rd
Roscoe IL 61073

Call Sign: WB9OGD
Frank R Baker Jr
11993 S Gate Rd
Roscoe IL 61073

Call Sign: KB9LBW
Linda M Mlsna
9462 Sagewood Dr
Roscoe IL 61073

Call Sign: KB9KXC
Matt A Mlsna
9462 Sagewood Dr
Roscoe IL 61073

Call Sign: KC9UNA
Jeffrey T Anderson
6587 Sawmill Dr
Roscoe IL 61073

Call Sign: N9JTA
Jeffrey T Anderson
6587 Sawmill Dr

Roscoe IL 61073

Call Sign: WA9PBQ
Paul A Cox Jr
8587 Secret Way Dr
Roscoe IL 61073

Call Sign: KI9F
James A Milhone
6175 Southdown Ln
Roscoe IL 61073

Call Sign: N9IA
David R Patton
4014 Straw Ln
Roscoe IL 61073

Call Sign: KB9ZXG
Kirk A Johnson
7560 Swanson Rd
Roscoe IL 61073

Call Sign: N9KRK
Kirk A Johnson
7560 Swanson Rd
Roscoe IL 61073

Call Sign: KA9WON
Lonnie W Miller
12618 Thistle Ridge Close
Roscoe IL 61073

Call Sign: KC9FKO
Blackhawk Experimental ARS
(Bears)
12618 Thistle Ridge Close
Roscoe IL 61073

Call Sign: W9EIS
Blackhawk Experimental ARS
(Bears)
12618 Thistle Ridge Close
Roscoe IL 61073

Call Sign: KB9YAC
Ross W Stenberg
7603 Thistle Ridge Rd
Roscoe IL 61073

Call Sign: K9COX
Ross W Stenberg
7603 Thistle Ridge Rd
Roscoe IL 61073

Call Sign: KB9RWL
Robert E Schwarz Sr
5696 Thompson Dr
Roscoe IL 61073

Call Sign: WB9FRD
Norman O Bransky
12245 Tresemer Rd
Roscoe IL 61073

Call Sign: KE9NJ
Kurt C Eversole
13176 Twelve Oaks Dr
Roscoe IL 61073

Call Sign: KE9N
Kurt C Eversole
13176 Twelve Oaks Dr
Roscoe IL 61073

Call Sign: KB9LBX
Sheila A Eversole
13176 Twelve Oaks Dr
Roscoe IL 61073

Call Sign: N9IXU
Eric G Wilkins
9552 Twin Deer Run
Roscoe IL 61073

Call Sign: KB9TOS
Jason G Foster
6665 W Gate Ct
Roscoe IL 60173

Call Sign: KC9BVE
Jacob C Webb-White
11708 Wagon Ln
Roscoe IL 61073

Call Sign: KC9ETQ
Russell D Gilbert
11975 Wagon Ln
Roscoe IL 61073

Call Sign: KC9EWI
Josef R Kurlinkus
13333 White School Rd
Roscoe IL 61073

Call Sign: KB9FOX
Josef R Kurlinkus
13333 White School Rd
Roscoe IL 61073

Call Sign: KB9QNB
Jonathan R Makovec
Roscoe IL 61073

Call Sign: KC9IOO
Phillip A Riley
Roscoe IL 61073

FCC Amateur Radio Licenses in Roseville

Call Sign: KA9KJU
George M Hennenfent
360 S Main
Roseville IL 61473

Call Sign: KA9EAU
Donald L Myers
550 S Main
Roseville IL 614730291

Call Sign: KB9QYI
Chrissy D Page
580 W Penn
Roseville IL 61473

Call Sign: N9KP
Kathleen M Page
580 W Penn
Roseville IL 61473

Call Sign: AC4YH
Max D Hallock
315 W Penn Ave
Roseville IL 61473

Call Sign: N9WYZ
Darrell L Page

580 W Penn Rr 1
Roseville IL 61473

Call Sign: N9VFM
Thomas A Montroy Jr
Roseville IL 61473

FCC Amateur Radio Licenses in Rosiclare

Call Sign: N9ZVO
Tim R Frey
514 4th
Rosiclare IL 62982

Call Sign: N9PVA
Francis E Stengel
Rosiclare IL 62982

Call Sign: K9AIW
Edward Powell
Rosiclare IL 62946

Call Sign: KB1ECZ
Thomas O Maxham
Rosiclare IL 62982

FCC Amateur Radio Licenses in Rossville

Call Sign: KC9AMD
Earl E Eells
37604 B N1900 E Rd
Rossville IL 60963

FCC Amateur Radio Licenses in Roxana

Call Sign: N9SIM
Shawn A Schmidt
233 W Thomas St
Roxana IL 62084

FCC Amateur Radio Licenses in Royalton

Call Sign: KA9YGR
Jon E Brookmyer

105 N Meadow
Royalton IL 62983

Call Sign: KB9MEZ
Thomas J Coffey Sr
810 State Hwy 149
Royalton IL 62983

Call Sign: N1LAR
Larry R Roethe
6423 State Hwy 184
Royalton IL 62983

Call Sign: KB9ULR
Rebekah L Roethe
6423 State Hwy 184
Royalton IL 62983

FCC Amateur Radio Licenses in Rushville

Call Sign: WY9C
Robert J Woodruff
Rr3 Box 181A
Rushville IL 62681

Call Sign: KC9B
Charles W Redshaw
Rr 2 Box 258
Rushville IL 62681

Call Sign: KC9JAF
Lance W Black
Rr 3 Box 43
Rushville IL 62681

Call Sign: KC9NYB
Daniel C Benner
Rr 1 Box 56 Aaa
Rushville IL 62681

Call Sign: N9AQJ
John A Poltawsky
Rr 3 Box 76
Rushville IL 62681

Call Sign: WA9BRZ
E Bart Beatty
123 E Clinton St

Rushville IL 62681

Call Sign: WA9FWL
Erma M Beatty
123 E Clinton St
Rushville IL 62681

Call Sign: N9HGC
Joseph W Redshaw
404 E Jefferson
Rushville IL 62681

Call Sign: KA9PRD
Thomas E Acker
402 E Washington
Rushville IL 62681

Call Sign: N9FDL
Harold E Smith
910 E Washington
Rushville IL 626811539

Call Sign: KA9AES
Carson D Klitz
18 Robinwood Dr
Rushville IL 62681

Call Sign: KB9BHD
Donald K Corbridge
407 Silverleaf Apt 15
Rushville IL 62681

Call Sign: WB9SBT
Charles E Young
211 W Adams St
Rushville IL 62681

Call Sign: KE9BII
Jason L Chute
447 W Clinton
Rushville IL 62681

Call Sign: N9IDN
Joanne Chute
458 W Jefferson
Rushville IL 52681

Call Sign: KE9GU
James R Chute

458 W Jefferson St
Rushville IL 62681

Call Sign: N9HWX
Jeffrey A Chute
451 W Lafayette St
Rushville IL 62681

Call Sign: WA4KJC
Robert W Lauzon
567 W Madison Ext
Rushville IL 62681

Call Sign: KA9PLB
Robert E Cox
Rushville IL 62681

Call Sign: KA9PJS
Cathy S Redshaw
Rushville IL 62681

Call Sign: N9HGB
Leslie J Redshaw
Rushville IL 62681

FCC Amateur Radio Licenses in Rutland

Call Sign: KD9ZT
James D Flynn
2808 CR 400 N
Rutland IL 61358

Call Sign: N9TJM
Kathryn S Flynn
2808 La Rose Rd
Rutland IL 61358

Call Sign: KC9KVX
Duane Knepp
442 Rt 251 N
Rutland IL 61358

Call Sign: KC9KVY
Kathy J Knepp
442 Rt 251 N
Rutland IL 61358

FCC Amateur Radio Licenses in Sadorus

Call Sign: W9FWS
Frederick W Seibold
Sadorus IL 61872

Call Sign: KC9SVR
Jody G Seibold
Sadorus IL 61872

FCC Amateur Radio Licenses in Saint Anne

Call Sign: WB9VII
Edwin A Hedlin
1023 Paul Dr
Saint Anne IL 60964

Call Sign: KC9DBN
Eric P Wendt
4376 S 6000 E Rd
Saint Anne IL 60964

FCC Amateur Radio Licenses in Saint David

Call Sign: KB9NOO
Carl H Burnham
603 Grand Ave
Saint David IL 61563

FCC Amateur Radio Licenses in Saint Elmo

Call Sign: W9YVE
Dorwin E Julius
Rr 1 Box 12
Saint Elmo IL 62458

Call Sign: KC9DQT
Dwight A Newberry
Rr 2 Box 253
Saint Elmo IL 62458

Call Sign: K9DEE
Dwight A Newberry
Rr 2 Box 253

Saint Elmo IL 62458

Call Sign: W9PFE
Dwight A Newberry
Rr 2 Box 253
Saint Elmo IL 62458

Call Sign: WY9J
Harold L Richardson
301 E Cumberland Rd
Saint Elmo IL 62458

Call Sign: KA9JXL
John Maurer
405 E Cumberland Rd
Saint Elmo IL 62458

Call Sign: KA9IKO
Louis E Aldridge
311 N Elm
Saint Elmo IL 62458

Call Sign: W9CFE
Charles G Shively
1015 N Maple St
Saint Elmo IL 624581528

Call Sign: KB9CPM
Regina A Stites
Rr2 Pob 97
Saint Elmo IL 62458

Call Sign: KB9GVI
Michelle L Myers
206 S Pine
Saint Elmo IL 62458

Call Sign: KB9WUM
Xon Hanna
323 W 12th St
Saint Elmo IL 62458

Call Sign: WB9UTW
William E Himes
Saint Elmo IL 62458

FCC Amateur Radio Licenses in Saint Francisville

Call Sign: KA9JTC
Steve S Archibald
R 1 Box 208
Saint Francisville IL 62460

Call Sign: WB9UDJ
Gary L Auerswald
Rr 1 Box 37
Saint Francisville IL 62460

Call Sign: N9NCF
James D Armstrong
416 S 9th
Saint Francisville IL 62460

Call Sign: KC9QHX
A G G A
N 430 St E 1050 Ave
Saint Francisville IL 62460

Call Sign: AG9GA
A G G A
N 430 St E 1050 Ave
Saint Francisville IL 62460

Call Sign: N9XEM
Joseph W Taggart
1873 Taggart Rd
Saint Francisville IL
624603233

Call Sign: KC9SCV
R A D I O
4295 W Circle Rd
Saint Francisville IL 62460

Call Sign: N9QZA
R A D I O
4295 W Circle Rd
Saint Francisville IL 62460

Call Sign: KA9SBY
Estella B Auerswald
4295 W Circle Rd
Saint Francisville IL 62460

Call Sign: N9LKU
Steven R Collins
Saint Francisville IL 62460

Call Sign: N9XEL
Reginold L Padgett
Saint Francisville IL 62460

Call Sign: KA9LRW
Don I Hills
Saint Francisville IL 62460

FCC Amateur Radio Licenses in Saint Jacob

Call Sign: KC9DGC
Richard J Saia
5 David Dr
Saint Jacob IL 62281

Call Sign: KC9QHD
Mark A Polege
10530 Ellis Rd
Saint Jacob IL 62281

Call Sign: KC9CAG
Amy R Ritter
11202 Ellis Rd
Saint Jacob IL 62281

Call Sign: KC9GBT
Bryan R Garrett
8903 Schmolz Rd
Saint Jacob IL 62281

Call Sign: KB9LBD
Virgil W Langford
510 Walnut Rd
Saint Jacob IL 62281

FCC Amateur Radio Licenses in Saint Joseph

Call Sign: W9KLZ
Frank E Romack
Rural Rt 2 Box 234
Saint Joseph IL 61873

Call Sign: KA9MQC
Nicholas W Dalrymple
Rr 1 Box 328
Saint Joseph IL 61873

Call Sign: N9CMI
Harley E Wynn
2377 CR 1500N
Saint Joseph IL 618739741

Call Sign: KD5EOQ
Jay A Kreibich
2372 CR 1550 N
Saint Joseph IL 61873

Call Sign: N9DN
Debra J Fligor
2372 CR 1550N
Saint Joseph IL 61873

Call Sign: KC9TOF
Pierce B Kreibich
2372 CR 1550N
Saint Joseph IL 61873

Call Sign: N9EDT
Pierce B Kreibich
2372 CR 1550N
Saint Joseph IL 61873

Call Sign: KB9RLQ
ARES Of Champaign Co
2372 CR 1550N
Saint Joseph IL 61873

Call Sign: WA9RES
ARES Of Champaign Co
2372 CR 1550N
Saint Joseph IL 61873

Call Sign: W9YR
University Of Illinois Vhf
Experimenters
2372 CR 1550N
Saint Joseph IL 61873

Call Sign: KB9RIG
University Of Illinois Vhf
Experimenters
2372 CR 1550N
Saint Joseph IL 61873

Call Sign: WA9AW

James G Jessup
1252 CR 2125E
Saint Joseph IL 61873

Call Sign: N9DKD
David L Stark
1485 CR 2200 E
Saint Joseph IL 61873

Call Sign: N9RZF
David N Paul
1497 CR 2200 E
Saint Joseph IL 61873

Call Sign: WD9AGO
David P Jones
1752 CR 2200 E
Saint Joseph IL 61873

Call Sign: WB9YKV
David D Sanstrom
2239 Heather Hills
Saint Joseph IL 61873

Call Sign: W9IPV
David D Sanstrom
2239 Heather Hills
Saint Joseph IL 61873

Call Sign: W9KFX
Virgil R Sims
708 B Jeanes Dr
Saint Joseph IL 61873

Call Sign: K9KC
David L Foster
408 Rosewood Dr
Saint Joseph IL 61873

Call Sign: W9AAS
Robert E Patton
104 W Briarcliff Dr
Saint Joseph IL 61873

Call Sign: KC9RHK
John H Gnuechtel
602 Wiltshire Dr
Saint Joseph IL 61873

Call Sign: N9PFD
Robert L Mc Clain
Saint Joseph IL 61873

FCC Amateur Radio Licenses in Saint Libory

Call Sign: W0MSF
Harold E Vitrey Jr
736 St Libory St
Saint Libory IL 62282

Call Sign: KC9NBE
James G Hopkins
7600 Washington St
Saint Libory IL 62282

FCC Amateur Radio Licenses in Saint Marie

Call Sign: N9OHB
Ivan J Falconer
323 Lamot St
Saint Marie IL 624590015

Call Sign: KA9IXJ
John C Michl
Saint Marie IL 62459

Call Sign: KC9OVN
Bruce E Minor
Saint Marie IL 62459

FCC Amateur Radio Licenses in Saint Peter

Call Sign: N9RGN
Della E Pontious
R 1 Box 174
Saint Peter IL 62880

Call Sign: N9TXC
Myron D Pontious
Rr 1 Box 174
Saint Peter IL 62880

Call Sign: KB9SOR
Pete A Taylor
Rr 1 Box 180

Saint Peter IL 62880

Call Sign: N9XWF
Kevin D Jenne
106 W 2nd
Saint Peter IL 62880

FCC Amateur Radio Licenses in Salem

Call Sign: KB9UVO
Jimmy L Bays
508 Airport Rd
Salem IL 628813931

Call Sign: KB9UBT
John J Mc Dermott
2191 Bannister Rd
Salem IL 628817261

Call Sign: WB9QEH
James W Cavins
2919 Boone St Rd
Salem IL 62881

Call Sign: KB9FQO
Robbie M Ritchey
Rr 1 Box 339
Salem IL 62881

Call Sign: N9MVZ
Timothy E Bailey
Rt 6 Box 57
Salem IL 62881

Call Sign: N9XLR
Frank D Barbre
1561 Charelston Rd
Salem IL 62881

Call Sign: AB4WR
John E Nichols
1579 Charleston Rd
Salem IL 62881

Call Sign: KB9VBI
Alan R Hollinshead
209 Chatham Dr
Salem IL 62881

Call Sign: KB9AVL
Dennis R Slater
4543 Church Rd
Salem IL 62881

Call Sign: N9VTK
Lindell Mulvany
4261 County Farm Rd
Salem IL 62881

Call Sign: AB9UD
Tim E Bailey
103 Donoho Dr
Salem IL 62881

Call Sign: KB9WMW
Joshua K White
516 E Clark St
Salem IL 62881

Call Sign: KB9FPJ
Allen E Biggs
321 E Jennings
Salem IL 62881

Call Sign: KB9FMY
Robyn N Biggs
321 E Jennings
Salem IL 62881

Call Sign: N9WZL
Steve A Gordon
1008 E McMackin St
Salem IL 62881

Call Sign: KB9VVE
Eric J Hathaway
4703 England Rd
Salem IL 62881

Call Sign: KB9NSG
Matthew B Harrell
2363 Foxville Rd
Salem IL 62881

Call Sign: N9JUA
Gary G Moore
2363 Foxville Rd

Salem IL 62881

Call Sign: KB9UIV
Derek E Bundy
4551 Harris Rd
Salem IL 62881

Call Sign: KB9TTK
Brenda A Bundy
4551 Harris Rd
Salem IL 628816944

Call Sign: K9RRP
J Ray Young
4630 Hoots Chapel Rd
Salem IL 62881

Call Sign: N9QIH
Patsy E Young
4630 Hoots Chapel Rd
Salem IL 62881

Call Sign: WD9GLP
Walter R Sullivan
3717 Hotze Rd
Salem IL 62881

Call Sign: KB9TRK
Clarence A Wimberly
5030 Kinmundy Rd
Salem IL 62881

Call Sign: KB9TRL
Keith W Kline
5461 Kinmundy Rd
Salem IL 62881

Call Sign: KE9ITH
Keith W Kline
5461 Kinmundy Rd
Salem IL 62881

Call Sign: KB9TRN
Mary Jo Kline
5461 Kinmundy Rd
Salem IL 62881

Call Sign: N9JUC
Kenneth P Moore

3256 Lazy Acres Rd
Salem IL 62881

Call Sign: KE5SSH
John S Williams
5315 Lois Ln
Salem IL 62881

Call Sign: N9WZN
Robert E Travis Jr
Rr 4 Lot 2 Box 3 Smhp
Salem IL 62882

Call Sign: KF9OK
Gregory A Maxey
5339 Maxey Rd
Salem IL 62881

Call Sign: N9FYR
Claude B Williams
900 Meadow Ln
Salem IL 62881

Call Sign: KA9HXB
Claude Cantrell
1701 N Broadway
Salem IL 62881

Call Sign: K9WOQ
Alan P Wilson
415 N Indiana Ave
Salem IL 62881

Call Sign: N9LNT
Ramonda L Wilson
415 N Indiana Ave
Salem IL 62881

Call Sign: KC9OLQ
Marvin R Owens
1320 N Jackson
Salem IL 62881

Call Sign: W9FON
Bryan Davidson
315 N Lakeview Dr
Salem IL 62881

Call Sign: WB2CGY

John J Mc Dermott
431 N Lakeview Dr
Salem IL 628813522

Call Sign: N9VQF
Gary D Smith
3258 Nation Rd
Salem IL 62881

Call Sign: KF9RC
Kathryn J Smith
3258 Nation Rd
Salem IL 62881

Call Sign: AA9EW
Barbara K Tucker
3354 Nation Rd
Salem IL 62881

Call Sign: AA9GS
Jimmy D Tucker
3354 Nation Rd
Salem IL 62881

Call Sign: KB9KVS
Howard D Karrick
3403 Nation Rd
Salem IL 62881

Call Sign: W9HDK
Howard D Karrick
3403 Nation Rd
Salem IL 62881

Call Sign: KC9TEN
Dale R Wood
213 Northwood Ln
Salem IL 62881

Call Sign: KC9NPM
Roger Baker
2110 Old Texas Ln
Salem IL 62881

Call Sign: KB9YRP
Andrew M Howard
2924 Possum Trot Rd
Salem IL 62881

Call Sign: KB9WMO
Candace M Howard
2924 Possum Trot Rd
Salem IL 62881

Call Sign: KB9WDG
Jason A Howard
2924 Possum Trot Rd
Salem IL 62881

Call Sign: KB9WDH
Wayne A Howard
2924 Possum Trot Rd
Salem IL 62881

Call Sign: WB9YZE
Fred L Zurbriggen
3301 Possum Trot Rd
Salem IL 62881

Call Sign: KC9MRT
Eric R Marshall
3567 Purcell Dr
Salem IL 62881

Call Sign: N9VTI
Kathryn L Coatney
3366 Rough Ln
Salem IL 62881

Call Sign: KC9JMP
Justin R Draper
415 S Castle Ave
Salem IL 62881

Call Sign: KE4ESK
Roger G Young
1522 S College
Salem IL 62881

Call Sign: W9RGY
Roger G Young
1522 S College
Salem IL 62881

Call Sign: WD9OEM
City Of Salem Illinois
Emergency Management
201 S Rotan

Salem IL 62881

Call Sign: KB9SFT
City Of Salem Illinois
Emergency Management
201 S Rotan
Salem IL 62881

Call Sign: KB9WHN
Nathan E Howard
224 S Vincent
Salem IL 62881

Call Sign: KB9FKX
Alfred W Moureau Jr
108 Salem Dr
Salem IL 62881

Call Sign: N9WBY
Joshua C Knopp
3329 Selmaville Rd
Salem IL 62881

Call Sign: KB9TTI
Ray J Hollinshead
101 Shingle Oak
Salem IL 62881

Call Sign: WA9HVI
Ray J Hollinshead
101 Shingle Oak
Salem IL 62881

Call Sign: KC8UPQ
David A Baker
1208 Spruce St
Salem IL 62881

Call Sign: N9RRB
Larry L Maxey
3359 Tonti Rd
Salem IL 62881

Call Sign: KA9PQN
Billy R Heflin
1205 W Bennett
Salem IL 628811132

Call Sign: W9RZI

Jack F Holt
105 W Boone St
Salem IL 62881

Call Sign: KB8IAB
James E Boyd
3376 W Boone St
Salem IL 62881

Call Sign: KB9HKI
Paul D Gardner
510 W Bryan
Salem IL 628814225

Call Sign: N9PFU
Lance J Owens
320 W Lake
Salem IL 62881

Call Sign: KA9ZPS
Albert J Long
520 W Schwartz
Salem IL 62881

Call Sign: ND9E
Jimmy D Hill
624 W Schwartz Apt 11
Salem IL 62881

Call Sign: KC9JMQ
Judy A Hill
624 W Schwartz Apt 11
Salem IL 62881

Call Sign: KB9AUJ
Michael M Molenhour
1006 W Spruce
Salem IL 62881

Call Sign: WD0FQM
Randall L Huff
1205 W Spruce
Salem IL 62881

Call Sign: KB9TRJ
Cathy S Harpe
5384 Woodard School Rd
Salem IL 62881

Call Sign: WD9EON
Jerry M Harpe
5384 Woodard School Rd
Salem IL 62881

Call Sign: K9UJX
James E Wheeler
214 Woodland Dr
Salem IL 62881

Call Sign: N9GRH
Frank D Ristick
Salem IL 62881

Call Sign: W3ZMD
Michael E Tucker
Salem IL 62881

FCC Amateur Radio Licenses in Salisbury

Call Sign: N9PCS
Paul R Zerkel
7505 Deer Run Rd
Salisbury IL 62677

Call Sign: KC9LZQ
Dawn A Zerkel
7505 Deer Run Rd
Salisbury IL 62677

FCC Amateur Radio Licenses in San Jose

Call Sign: KC9AHP
George B Skelton
101 Arch St
San Jose IL 62682

FCC Amateur Radio Licenses in Sandoval

Call Sign: WA9U
Alva L King Jr
776 Bethel Rd
Sandoval IL 62882

Call Sign: AA9EK
Daisy F King

776 Bethel Rd
Sandoval IL 62882

Call Sign: N9HRY
Rodney A King
776 Bethel Rd
Sandoval IL 62882

Call Sign: KB9AZC
Carolina B Oliveira
Rr 1 Box 457
Sandoval IL 62882

Call Sign: N9HST
Donald J Hardy
543 Brink Rd
Sandoval IL 62882

Call Sign: N9QPV
William D De Boer
3556 Old 51 Lot 40
Sandoval IL 62882

Call Sign: KB9LZX
Kenneth D Karrick
407 S Maple Ave
Sandoval IL 62882

Call Sign: N9SYQ
Stephanie D Karrick
407 S Maple Ave
Sandoval IL 62882

Call Sign: KF9L
Randal D Meredith
121 S Mulberry St
Sandoval IL 62882

Call Sign: KC9URF
Southern Illinois Dstar
Association
121 S Mulberry St
Sandoval IL 62882

Call Sign: KC9VMT
Southern Illinois Dstar
Skywarn Association
121 S Mulberry St
Sandoval IL 62882

Call Sign: KC9TWN
David W Guidish
304 Van Buren Ave
Sandoval IL 62882

FCC Amateur Radio Licenses in Sauget

Call Sign: WB9SDQ
Michael J Pegg Sr
2702 Falling Springs Rd
Sauget IL 62206

FCC Amateur Radio Licenses in Saunemin

Call Sign: N9GXN
Steven L Schaffer
Rr 1 Box 61
Saunemin IL 61769

Call Sign: N9HKT
Debra A Schaffer
83 E Main
Saunemin IL 61769

FCC Amateur Radio Licenses in Savanna

Call Sign: NR9G
James L Buikema
525 3rd St Apt 306
Savanna IL 610741585

Call Sign: KB9VWH
Michael J Rannow
9933 Airport Rd
Savanna IL 61074

Call Sign: N9FID
Charles C Corey
625 Beech St
Savanna IL 61074

Call Sign: W9MTM
William A Dalacker
502 Beech St Box B2 Lot 30
Savanna IL 61074

Call Sign: WA9OAU
Lawrence G Roemer
101 Diagonal St
Savanna IL 610741508

Call Sign: K9FGH
John L Byrd Jr
1607 E Lawn Dr
Savanna IL 61074

Call Sign: KA9TSQ
Alan E Schroeder
13402 Messmer Rd
Savanna IL 61074

Call Sign: KA9VQF
Thomas C Sorensen
1722 Michigan Ave
Savanna IL 61074

Call Sign: KB9TOJ
David P Hamling
1832 Michigan Ave
Savanna IL 61074

Call Sign: WA9LJZ
Richard A Kline
726 N 4th St
Savanna IL 61074

Call Sign: KB9GMM
Loren L Baker
1759 N Jacobstown
Savanna IL 61074

Call Sign: KC9HNT
Nathan T Green
8134 S Farr St
Savanna IL 61074

Call Sign: KA9QAR
William J Brown
8278 S Hummel St
Savanna IL 61074

Call Sign: N9WLJ
Perry G Myrick
9473 Scenic Bluff Rd

Savanna IL 61074

Call Sign: WA9YLP
Donald A Henderickx
16157 Scenic Ridge Rd
Savanna IL 61074

Call Sign: W4ZHG
Paul J Mayer Jr
10745 Serenity Ln
Savanna IL 61074

Call Sign: KB9RYV
Robert H Hutchison
1418 Sorenson Ln Apt 7
Savanna IL 61074

Call Sign: KA9ZKU
Robert G Mace
1630 Superior Ave
Savanna IL 61074

Call Sign: WD9ENC
Eldon J Shepherd
208 Van Buren
Savanna IL 61074

Call Sign: KA9TZD
Patricia J Shepherd
208 Van Buren
Savanna IL 61074

Call Sign: WD9EMB
Kenneth F Rodda
12245 Wacker Rd
Savanna IL 61074

FCC Amateur Radio Licenses in Savoy

Call Sign: WB9CRA
Frank H Russ
401 Burwash Ave
Savoy IL 61874

Call Sign: W9NLW
Jean M West
302 Burwash Dr
Savoy IL 61874

Call Sign: KB4RJI
Shane T Carlin
407 Buttercup Dr
Savoy IL 61874

Call Sign: N9XDF
Thomas P Scheu
207 Calvin St
Savoy IL 618749443

Call Sign: KB9JTY
Gifford T Smith
303 Ellen Ave
Savoy IL 61874

Call Sign: KC9MVS
John F Boch
19 Evergreen Sq
Savoy IL 61874

Call Sign: W9MH
Nicolae Popa
306 Gentian
Savoy IL 61874

Call Sign: KC9KYZ
Stefania V Popa
306 Gentian
Savoy IL 61874

Call Sign: KC9JVU
Nicholas D Buraglio
809 Indigo Ave
Savoy IL 61874

Call Sign: W9NDB
Nicholas D Buraglio
809 Indigo Ave
Savoy IL 61874

Call Sign: N3QKM
James T Holsberger
810 Lavender Dr
Savoy IL 61874

Call Sign: KB9PXG
James W Daly
107 N Wesley

Savoy IL 61874

Call Sign: KB9YZF
Nathan J Burnside
149 Paddock Dr E
Savoy IL 61874

Call Sign: KI6GBX
Catherine M Cromar
212 Paddock Dr E
Savoy IL 61874

Call Sign: KE6LCU
Scott A Cromar
212 Paddock Dr E
Savoy IL 61874

Call Sign: KB9ZME
Wade E Boyd
104 Sterling Ct Apt 301D
Savoy IL 61874

Call Sign: N0OOO
Richard K Lake
602A Sunflower St
Savoy IL 61874

Call Sign: KC9GIJ
Debbie I Gardner
504 Van Buren
Savoy IL 61874

Call Sign: K0DIG
Debbie I Gardner
504 Van Buren
Savoy IL 61874

Call Sign: KC9GID
Michael G Gardner
504 Van Buren St
Savoy IL 61874

Call Sign: K0MGG
Michael G Gardner
504 Van Buren St
Savoy IL 61874

Call Sign: KC9UNL
Curtis E Gidding

109 W Tomaras Ave Apt B
Savoy IL 61874

Call Sign: KC9DES
David K Tcheng
406 Wesley Ave
Savoy IL 61874

Call Sign: K9DKT
David K Tcheng
406 Wesley Ave
Savoy IL 61874

Call Sign: N9TAU
Kurt M Gimbel
1204 Wesley Ave Apt 1
Savoy IL 61874

FCC Amateur Radio Licenses in Saybrook

Call Sign: W9JHG
Warren W Waters
41611 E 1025 N Rd
Saybrook IL 617709436

Call Sign: W9NBD
Wayne W Wills
201 E Harrison
Saybrook IL 61770

Call Sign: W9KNY
Stanley M Wilson
301 E Jackson St Rr 1
Saybrook IL 61770

Call Sign: N9XUS
Danny R Parma
410 S East St
Saybrook IL 61770

FCC Amateur Radio Licenses in Scales Mound

Call Sign: WD9IBV
Scott A Anderson
6825 N Hill Rd
Scales Mound IL 61075

FCC Amateur Radio Licenses in Scheller

Call Sign: KA9GXT
Charles B Shurtz
3943 E Freeman Rd
Scheller IL 62883

FCC Amateur Radio Licenses in Sciota

Call Sign: KA0FBJ
Robert E Hull
40 10th Ave
Sciota IL 61475

Call Sign: KB9WFD
Teddy J Fross
8270 Il Hwy 9
Sciota IL 61475

FCC Amateur Radio Licenses in Scioto Mills

Call Sign: W9VLI
Fredmont H Engelman Sr
3689 Iris Hill Rd
Scioto Mills IL 61076

FCC Amateur Radio Licenses in Scott AFB

Call Sign: N4KVV
Robert C Chaplin
158S A St
Scott AFB IL 62225

Call Sign: KD4ILG
Jonathan R Slone
4447 A Artemus Dr
Scott AFB IL 62225

Call Sign: N9VAM
Brian J Worth
2385A Ash Creek Dr
Scott AFB IL 62225

Call Sign: KB0RTB

Kevin P Wilson
2169 B Cloverwood Ln
Scott AFB IL 62225

Call Sign: KB9HIX
Andrew W Gillespie
1428D Galaxy
Scott AFB IL 62225

Call Sign: KA9CCO
Mark A Sumwalt
2505A Greenfield Cir
Scott AFB IL 62225

Call Sign: KB3RWR
Joshua D Vanderford
4296 Hercules Rd
Scott AFB IL 62225

Call Sign: N9ZBX
Ramon M Lopez
5303B Hesse Ave
Scott AFB IL 62225

Call Sign: N9WIT
Daniel D Boone
4620 Patrick Henry Cir Unit A
Scott AFB IL 62225

Call Sign: KA5MUS
T Hall Keyes IV
171 S B St
Scott AFB IL 62225

Call Sign: KC9JDC
Jessica Hartzell
4807 B Thomas Paine Cir
Scott AFB IL 62225

Call Sign: KC9TWE
Matthew A Hanks
Psc 2 Unit 116
Scott AFB IL 62225

Call Sign: KB0QCK
Daniel L Hughes
Psc 2 Unit 221
Scott AFB IL 62225

Call Sign: KC7VOF
Benjamin J Gates
2407B Vista Manor
Scott AFB IL 62225

Call Sign: N5IE
Michael S Stough
162 W E Clay St
Scott AFB IL 62225

Call Sign: AA9PE
Larry L Ziegler
Scott AFB IL 622250133

Call Sign: N6BSE
Carlos M Porter
Scott AFB IL 62225

Call Sign: KC9JQG
Glyn Howells Jr
Scott AFB IL 62225

Call Sign: KB9PAU
Scott Composite ARS
Scott AFB IL 62225

FCC Amateur Radio Licenses in Seaton

Call Sign: W9WWE
Marvin J Cook Sr
205 6th St Box 82
Seaton IL 61476

Call Sign: KA9HSX
Denise D Greer
E 3rd St
Seaton IL 61476

Call Sign: KA9HJK
Gary A Strom
E 3rd St
Seaton IL 61476

Call Sign: WD9JKO
Janis M Strom
203 Maple St
Seaton IL 61476

Call Sign: WB9VXD
Bernard H Strom
203 Maple St
Seaton IL 61476

Call Sign: WA9TNG
George S King
Seaton IL 61476

**FCC Amateur Radio
Licenses in Seatonville**

Call Sign: KC9HVV
Gregory D Swanson
101 E 6th St
Seatonville IL 61359

Call Sign: KC9IZQ
Linda S Swanson
101 E 6th St
Seatonville IL 61359

Call Sign: KC9ROL
Wallace D Duncan
608 N Center St
Seatonville IL 61359

**FCC Amateur Radio
Licenses in Secor**

Call Sign: KC9OYO
Donald D Downen
2126 US Hwy 24
Secor IL 61771

**FCC Amateur Radio
Licenses in Seneca**

Call Sign: KC9RTT
Daniel D Ellis
121 Country Ct
Seneca IL 61360

Call Sign: KF9NZ
Francis X Carraro
2428 E 29th Rd
Seneca IL 61360

Call Sign: N9YFL

Raymond J Hansen Sr
366 E Jackson
Seneca IL 61360

Call Sign: N9CLQ
James L Fiedler
456 E Lincoln St
Seneca IL 613600583

Call Sign: N9TQH
Robert P Caron
374 N Market St
Seneca IL 61360

Call Sign: KB9YBK
Wyant L Niswonger
175 Oak St
Seneca IL 61360

Call Sign: KC9VIE
Kathleen J Angelakos
221 Oak St
Seneca IL 61360

Call Sign: KC9DZP
Scott C Peddicord
300 Richards St
Seneca IL 61360

Call Sign: N9PGU
Wyman L Olsen
139 Valley View
Seneca IL 61360

Call Sign: KB9WJY
Robert E Chapman Jr
Seneca IL 61360

Call Sign: WA9WYX
Alvin F Biros
Seneca IL 61360

**FCC Amateur Radio
Licenses in Serena**

Call Sign: KC9NGA
Donald A Rudolph
3984 E 2259th Rd
Serena IL 60549

Call Sign: W9BHI
Donald A Rudolph
3984 E 2259th Rd
Serena IL 60549

**FCC Amateur Radio
Licenses in Sesser**

Call Sign: KB9LUZ
Cyndi L Kirk
R 1 Box 690
Sesser IL 62884

Call Sign: KB9LZY
Charles S Kirk
Rr 1 Box 690
Sesser IL 62884

Call Sign: KB9BPN
Yolanda M Gunter
Rte 1 Box 737
Sesser IL 62884

Call Sign: W9KED
Billy J Needham
6955 Deer Ln
Sesser IL 62884

Call Sign: N9EBV
Tammy D Jewell
212 E Espy St
Sesser IL 62884

Call Sign: KB9DGP
Charles L Eubancks
703 E Murray
Sesser IL 62884

Call Sign: KF9CZ
Jason C Sample
7551 Grammer Rd
Sesser IL 62884

Call Sign: KC9RFU
Little Egypt ARS
7551 Grammer Rd
Sesser IL 62834

Call Sign: W9RNM
Shawnee Amateur Radio
Assoc Inc
7551 Grammer Rd
Sesser IL 62884

Call Sign: N9WUF
William A Bunton
14906 Hwy 148 S
Sesser IL 62884

Call Sign: KA9UWJ
Maureen M Murphy
301 N Davis St
Sesser IL 62884

Call Sign: KC9LVE
Cody A Lingle
6199 Peach Orchard Rd
Sesser IL 62884

Call Sign: N9RNM
John D Lingle
6199 Peach Orchard Rd
Sesser IL 62884

Call Sign: N9QHQ
Jeffrey P Carlson
201 S Broadway
Sesser IL 62884

Call Sign: KF9BO
Robert E Mc Atee
415 S Davis
Sesser IL 62884

Call Sign: W9RZ
Robert E Mc Atee
415 S Davis
Sesser IL 62884

Call Sign: N9RBE
William J Bryant
411 S Locust
Sesser IL 62884

Call Sign: N9SMY
Gloria G Bryant
411 S Locust Box 909

Sesser IL 62884

Call Sign: KB9IEB
Donna M Roberts
711 S Locust St
Sesser IL 62884

Call Sign: KG9EJ
Robert E Harrison
803 S Locust St
Sesser IL 62884

Call Sign: AA9AJ
Cecil G Roberts
714 S Locust St Rr 1
Sesser IL 62884

Call Sign: AA9TJ
David M Shurtz
15743 Vivian St
Sesser IL 62884

Call Sign: KB9QEB
Nancy E Shurtz
15743 Vivian St
Sesser IL 62884

Call Sign: KB9FZZ
Ryan S Curry
506 W Callie
Sesser IL 62884

Call Sign: KB9QQR
Kimberly F Scott
506 W Franklin
Sesser IL 62884

Call Sign: N9OXK
Roy W Pinkston III
504 W Murray St
Sesser IL 62884

Call Sign: WQ9Z
Roy W Pinkston Jr
504 W Murray St
Sesser IL 62884

Call Sign: N9JGZ
Patricia G Pinkston

504 W Murray St
Sesser IL 62884

Call Sign: KI9L
Donald L Doerr
Sesser IL 62884

Call Sign: KB9FZJ
Elmer H Mc Atee
Sesser IL 62884

Call Sign: AA9EP
Michael D Jewell
Sesser IL 62884

Call Sign: KC9LUD
Joshua W Bryant
Sesser IL 62884

Call Sign: N9XBB
William R Bunton
Sesser IL 62884

FCC Amateur Radio Licenses in Seymour

Call Sign: N0QEA
Kathy J Mullins
1251A CR 400E Box 166
Seymour IL 618750166

Call Sign: N0PRN
Michael S Mullins
1251A CR 400E Box 166
Seymour IL 618750166

Call Sign: W3HDH
Douglas R Maddox
144 Oaktree Rd
Seymour IL 61875

Call Sign: KC9BSF
Philip M Mullins
Seymour IL 61875

FCC Amateur Radio Licenses in Shannon

Call Sign: KB9QGO

Andy B Johanneson
113 N Linn
Shannon IL 61078

Call Sign: KB9PXS
Cynthia M Johanneson
113 N Linn St
Shannon IL 61078

Call Sign: KC9T
Craig P Wheeler
17217B Rt 73
Shannon IL 61078

Call Sign: KB9GMO
John F Mitchell
402 S Hickory
Shannon IL 61078

Call Sign: K9LFB
Paul E Rivers
15127 Shannon Rt
Shannon IL 61078

Call Sign: KA9VQD
Sandra K Woodyatt
Shannon IL 61078

Call Sign: WA9LSW
William A Woodyatt
Shannon IL 61078

FCC Amateur Radio Licenses in Shattuc

Call Sign: KB9HPE
Carl D Wadkins
20000 Bud Rd
Shattuc IL 62283

Call Sign: KG9DJ
Kenneth E Norris
607 Main St
Shattuc IL 62283

FCC Amateur Radio Licenses in Shawneetown

Call Sign: KB9OEH

Steven M Green
133 Green Dr
Shawneetown IL 62984

FCC Amateur Radio Licenses in Sheffield

Call Sign: KB9WTW
Hans C Bayer
7927 1850 N Ave
Sheffield IL 61361

Call Sign: KB9OMR
Edith P Mc Laren
503 S Church St
Sheffield IL 61361

FCC Amateur Radio Licenses in Shelbyville

Call Sign: WB9KSE
Lawrence E Stevens
Rt 1 Box 130
Shelbyville IL 62565

Call Sign: KB9CEJ
Leo L Banning
Rr 3 Box 217
Shelbyville IL 62565

Call Sign: KB9TCM
Michael L Hightower
Rr1 Box 247L
Shelbyville IL 62565

Call Sign: KB9UVN
Vicki L Hightower
Rt 1 Box 247L
Shelbyville IL 62525

Call Sign: KC9TJG
Scott E Henne Jr
Rr 3 Box 5
Shelbyville IL 62565

Call Sign: WB9FCZ
Scott E Henne Jr
Rr 3 Box 5
Shelbyville IL 62565

Call Sign: KC9GZL
Ryan D Spain
Rr 4 Box 71C
Shelbyville IL 62565

Call Sign: N9RDS
Ryan D Spain
Rr 4 Box 71C
Shelbyville IL 62565

Call Sign: W9IDD
Philip L Turner II
603 N Broadway
Shelbyville IL 62565

Call Sign: KB9GFI
Christine A Bogart
707 N Chestnut
Shelbyville IL 62565

Call Sign: KB9GFJ
Theodore E Bogart
707 N Chestnut
Shelbyville IL 62565

Call Sign: KA4BRL
Paul F Stevens
915 N Long
Shelbyville IL 62565

Call Sign: N9ZSM
Walter L Gregg
1008 N Long
Shelbyville IL 62565

Call Sign: K9FJI
Ervil W Fisher Sr
920 N Morgan
Shelbyville IL 62565

Call Sign: AB9GR
Walter B Lookofsky
300 N Spruce
Shelbyville IL 62565

Call Sign: WD9HHB
Glenn E Blackwell
815 S 10th St

Shelbyville IL 62565

Call Sign: WB9QPM
James B Hudson Jr
202 S Hickory
Shelbyville IL 62565

Call Sign: KC9TJF
Eric L Banning
205 S Locust
Shelbyville IL 62565

Call Sign: N9XWV
Ken L West
602 S Wood
Shelbyville IL 62565

Call Sign: W9VTQ
Fred A Kurz
908 W 1st St
Shelbyville IL 625651908

Call Sign: K9UZG
Joseph W Wiandt
1305 W Main St
Shelbyville IL 62565

Call Sign: KB9KHA
William N Sluss
501 W N 2nd St
Shelbyville IL 62565

Call Sign: KB9BWT
Richard D Simmering
714 W N 2nd St
Shelbyville IL 62565

Call Sign: KC9GFS
Joshua K Ferguson
808 W S 10th
Shelbyville IL 62565

Call Sign: WB9KES
Clarence H Holley
201 W S 3rd St
Shelbyville IL 62565

Call Sign: KC9TJE
Jennifer S Houck

906 W S 4th St
Shelbyville IL 62565

Call Sign: WB9FCZ
William D Renner
408 W S 9th
Shelbyville IL 625650352

FCC Amateur Radio Licenses in Sheldon

Call Sign: WA9BZB
Raymond A Luhring
125 E Main
Sheldon IL 60966

Call Sign: KA7AHL
Clayton C Christenson
565 N 4th St
Sheldon IL 60966

Call Sign: KC9GNH
Justin R Kaiser
260 S 1st St
Sheldon IL 60966

FCC Amateur Radio Licenses in Sheridan

Call Sign: N9JD
Jess D Holcomb
2476 4203 Rd
Sheridan IL 60551

Call Sign: KA9HSE
Robin D Larson
Rt 1 Box 10A
Sheridan IL 60551

Call Sign: KF9DP
Edward R Seitzinger
Rt 2 Box 118F
Sheridan IL 605519728

Call Sign: KE4NNT
Janet T Sutter
4397 E 2925th Rd
Sheridan IL 60551

Call Sign: KC0GBV
Jonathan L Sutter
4397 E 2925th Rd
Sheridan IL 60551

Call Sign: N9OUT
Hally J Brown
2634 N 3659th Rd
Sheridan IL 60551

Call Sign: WB8VIC
James S Crisp
2721 N 3853 Rd
Sheridan IL 60551

Call Sign: N9JVF
Thomas A Novey
2484 N 4249th Rd
Sheridan IL 60551

Call Sign: W7TAN
Thomas A Novey
2484 N 4249th Rd
Sheridan IL 60551

Call Sign: W9BTO
Franklin D Bishop
2456 N 42nd Rd
Sheridan IL 60551

Call Sign: KA9ANH
Rodney W Hampton
2194 N 4350th Rd
Sheridan IL 60551

Call Sign: NE9V
Dale E Morin
2879 N 4360th Rd
Sheridan IL 60551

Call Sign: KB9FXZ
Howard L Wesley Sr
2931 N 4395 Rd
Sheridan IL 60551

Call Sign: K9REI
Howard L Wesley Sr
2931 N 4395 Rd
Sheridan IL 605519669

Call Sign: KC9HQG
Howard L Wesley Sr
2931 N 4395 Rd
Sheridan IL 605519669

Call Sign: KC9GHW
Amanda M Bartling
525 W Grant St
Sheridan IL 60551

Call Sign: N9OWQ
David E Bartling
525 W Grant St
Sheridan IL 60551

Call Sign: K9QKC
Clifford K Miller
Sheridan IL 60551

FCC Amateur Radio Licenses in Sherman

Call Sign: W3AW
Kirk E Staats
6875 Barclay Rd
Sherman IL 62684

Call Sign: KF9BX
Walter F Black
52 Birch Lake Dr
Sherman IL 62684

Call Sign: KC9OUB
Nathaniel L Harris
2972 E Andrew Rd
Sherman IL 62684

Call Sign: N9PIN
Steven J Doerfler
4738 Fawn Dr
Sherman IL 626848063

Call Sign: KA9MME
David W Thurber
910 Lost Tree Dr
Sherman IL 62684

Call Sign: KA9GDL

Al Cikas
412 Radford Dr
Sherman IL 62684

Call Sign: KB9PCD
Jean M Cikas
412 Radford Dr
Sherman IL 62684

Call Sign: KC9VPS
Jacob N Lord
112 Ramblewood Ln
Sherman IL 62684

Call Sign: W9KF
Monroe Penick
509 St Johns Dr
Sherman IL 62684

Call Sign: W9ZKN
Louis J Brandis Sr
100 Stardust Dr
Sherman IL 62684

Call Sign: KC9VCN
Keith R Spaniol
4900 Turkey Run Rd
Sherman IL 62684

Call Sign: KC9DTW
John E Underfanger IV
4873 Williamsville Rd
Sherman IL 62684

Call Sign: KA9OIW
Steve L Griffin
54 Woodsmill
Sherman IL 62684

FCC Amateur Radio Licenses in Sherrard

Call Sign: KB9LCZ
James A Franks
2962 155th Ave
Sherrard IL 61281

Call Sign: KB9LCY
Linda L Franks

2962 155th Ave
Sherrard IL 61281

Call Sign: KB9MVH
Thomas J Hayden
2980 155th Ave
Sherrard IL 61281

Call Sign: KC9HME
Bill L Holdsworth
2631 160th Ave
Sherrard IL 61281

Call Sign: K9IYM
Hal J Lester
3901 176th Ave
Sherrard IL 61281

Call Sign: KC9JIX
Jonathan W Smith
1546 325th St
Sherrard IL 61281

Call Sign: K1JWS
Jonathan W Smith
1546 325th St
Sherrard IL 61281

Call Sign: KD9NK
William A Smet
18501 81st St
Sherrard IL 61281

Call Sign: KC9DCY
Chad M Sutton
1722 Knoxville Rd
Sherrard IL 61281

Call Sign: K9SFD
Chad M Sutton
1722 Knoxville Rd
Sherrard IL 61281

Call Sign: KA9DEJ
Milton C Box
Sherrard IL 61281

Call Sign: KB9CSQ
Shirley J Box

Sherrard IL 61281

Call Sign: N9RNG
Katherine M Jackson
1458 Cadwell Ct
Shiloh IL 62269

Call Sign: N9REY
Randy M Jackson
1458 Cadwell Ct
Shiloh IL 62269

Call Sign: KB9OQZ
Philip S Cristensen
115 Cornelius Dr
Shiloh IL 62269

Call Sign: KC9CLL
Kyle M Boide
132 Cornelius Dr
Shiloh IL 62269

Call Sign: KA9ZAV
Marlyn L Thorne
522 N Main St
Shiloh IL 622693702

Call Sign: KA9YZS
Terry L Thorne
522 N Main St
Shiloh IL 622693702

Call Sign: KB9ODB
James M Willmont
2332 Rockwood Dr
Shiloh IL 62221

Call Sign: W9GMR
Patrick V Pelland
206 S 2nd St
Shiloh IL 62269

Call Sign: AA9TC
Nicholas R Lambert
217 S 2nd St
Shiloh IL 62269

Call Sign: KE9W
Earl W Stoops
9275 Blues Ln
Shipman IL 62685

Call Sign: N9SCQ
Russell C Clark
Box 13 R 1
Shipman IL 62685

Call Sign: KA9UVB
Mary Lou Stoops
Box 97Es Rr 2 N
Shipman IL 62685

Call Sign: KB9PNS
Dirk A Matuska
5845 Schoeneman
Shipman IL 62685

Call Sign: W9OSI
Dirk A Matuska
5845 Schoeneman
Shipman IL 62685

Call Sign: WB9KRS
James C Murrell
Shipman IL 62685

Call Sign: K9CAB
Charles A Boyer
13731 Boswell
Shirland IL 61079

Call Sign: KB9UNK
Charles A Boyer
13731 Boswell Rd
Shirland IL 61079

Call Sign: N8FCP
Mary H Schnetker
8245 North St

Shirland IL 61079

Call Sign: N9WSM
Colin C Winters
Shirland IL 61079

Call Sign: N9SNX
Andrew H Sneed
Shirland IL 61079

Call Sign: N9GNN
Rita M Cramer
Quinn St
Shirley IL 617720084

Call Sign: W9IJE
Wallace D Bertram
Rr 1 Box 193
Shobonier IL 62885

Call Sign: KC9BUN
Kelly A Taylor
Rr 1 Box 96A
Shobonier IL 62885

Call Sign: KC9BSQ
Shane A Taylor
Rr 1 Box 96A
Shobonier IL 62885

Call Sign: WA9ZTL
John A Taylor
Rt 1 Box 97
Shobonier IL 62885

Call Sign: N9XWG
Patricia A Taylor
Rt 1 Box 97
Shobonier IL 62885

Call Sign: KB9JXM
Carin T Blair
Rr 1 Box 108
Shumway IL 62461

Call Sign: WA9MID
Ray R Sherwood
19132 N State Hwy 32
Shumway IL 62461

FCC Amateur Radio Licenses in Sidell

Call Sign: KA9GBC
James W Housel
606 Chicago St Box 405
Sidell IL 61876

Call Sign: KC9SDW
Guy G Coehran
602 N Gray
Sidell IL 61876

Call Sign: K2ZSD
Larry J Ince
508 S Gray
Sidell IL 618760143

Call Sign: KB9ANE
Larry J Ince
Sidell IL 61876

FCC Amateur Radio Licenses in Sidney

Call Sign: KD9PL
Joseph M Sutton
2151 CR 1100 N
Sidney IL 618779764

Call Sign: KB9TWY
Linda Menner
1037 CR 2200 E
Sidney IL 61877

Call Sign: WA9IVQ
Larry D Schilson
17 Dunlap Woods
Sidney IL 618779750

Call Sign: K9GHK
Loren E Fear Jr
107 Pleasant Dr
Sidney IL 618770335

Call Sign: WB9OIH
Allen L Wolfe
2266 Rd 1200 N
Sidney IL 61877

Call Sign: K9SI
Allen L Wolfe
2266 Rd 1200 N
Sidney IL 61877

Call Sign: KC9IHU
Tyler Sellers
411 S White St
Sidney IL 61877

Call Sign: KB9TWX
Tom L Menner
Sidney IL 61877

FCC Amateur Radio Licenses in Silvis

Call Sign: WB9ZKB
Genevieve M Ditch
1115 10th St
Silvis IL 61282

Call Sign: WB9WST
William H Ditch
1115 10th St
Silvis IL 612821973

Call Sign: KB9CTV
Thomas C Tague
620 11th St
Silvis IL 61282

Call Sign: N9CDX
William T Halse
1503 11th St
Silvis IL 61282

Call Sign: N9NEF

Michael T Huff
151 12th St
Silvis IL 61282

Call Sign: KG9OA
Jerry L Orey
427 12th St
Silvis IL 612821274

Call Sign: KF9TL
Mark W Orey
501 12th St
Silvis IL 61282

Call Sign: KC9KGM
Gerard M Gillcoly
2404 12th St
Silvis IL 61282

Call Sign: W0LSN
Ladonna S Nurse
509 15th St
Silvis IL 61282

Call Sign: W0BDN
Brian D Nurse
509 15th St
Silvis IL 61282

Call Sign: KA9UPG
Michael E Flanagan
325 16th Ave
Silvis IL 61282

Call Sign: K9LMZ
Gerald W Bentley
3304 18th St Em
Silvis IL 61282

Call Sign: KA9VJO
Mary Ann A Scott
1821 27th Ave E M
Silvis IL 61282

Call Sign: N9ULF
Melodie J Beedlow
1009 29th Ave
Silvis IL 61282

Call Sign: KA9BSU
Michael A Beedlow
1009 29th Ave
Silvis IL 61282

Call Sign: W9PZ
Robert C Lundstrom
279 6th St
Silvis IL 61282

Call Sign: KC9VSL
James R Murray
509 9th Ave
Silvis IL 61282

Call Sign: N9RDU
Brian M Smith
215 Cliff Ct
Silvis IL 61282

Call Sign: N9IWE
Larry D Smith
215 Cliff Ct
Silvis IL 61282

Call Sign: WB9HEV
Carl L Sutton
107 Orchard Ct
Silvis IL 61282

Call Sign: KC0DYH
Kevin S Davis
125 Orchard Ct
Silvis IL 61282

Call Sign: W9KSD
Kevin S Davis
125 Orchard Ct
Silvis IL 61282

Call Sign: N9BXR
Walter F Bolte
Silvis IL 61282

**FCC Amateur Radio
Licenses in Simpson**

Call Sign: KB3AAW
Richard N Humes

Rt 1 Box 115A
Simpson IL 62985

Call Sign: KC9MET
Diana L Vaughn
Rt 1 Box 37
Simpson IL 62985

Call Sign: KC9HBE
Michael L Vaughn
Rt 1 Box 37
Simpson IL 62985

Call Sign: AB9PO
Michael L Vaughn
Rt 1 Box 37
Simpson IL 62985

Call Sign: WB9WIS
John A Blatter
Rr 1 Box 5
Simpson IL 62985

Call Sign: KC9ILQ
Mary E Blatter
Rr 1 Box 5
Simpson IL 62985

Call Sign: KC9OLK
Roger D Ditterline
3115 Flatwoods Rd
Simpson IL 62985

Call Sign: KC9OLP
Lee R Duncan
825 Rock Springs Ln
Simpson IL 62985

Call Sign: WA9R
Jerry R Boaz
456 Rt 145 N
Simpson IL 62985

Call Sign: N9XWO
Lou D Spurlin
565 Rushing Rd
Simpson IL 62985

Call Sign: N9VXB

Benjamin J Spurlin
Simpson IL 62985

**FCC Amateur Radio
Licenses in Sims**

Call Sign: KC9QBV
Christopher C Walters
Sims IL 62886

**FCC Amateur Radio
Licenses in Smithboro**

Call Sign: WA9CVW
Guy C Chasey
1819 Pleasant Mound Ave
Smithboro IL 62284

Call Sign: KC0KPD
Paul K Cayo
Smithboro IL 62284

Call Sign: WB9YVH
Dorothy I Chasey
Smithboro IL 62284

**FCC Amateur Radio
Licenses in Smithfield**

Call Sign: KB9UQB
Noel P Lane
6110 E Buckeye Church Rd
Smithfield IL 61477

Call Sign: KB9UQE
John D Lane
6110 E Buckeye Church Rd
Smithfield IL 614779375

Call Sign: KB9DPT
Carla E Lasswell
15868 N County Hwy 14
Smithfield IL 61477

Call Sign: KB9DPU
Gregory H Lasswell
15868 N County Hwy 14
Smithfield IL 61477

Call Sign: KA9KKS
Juanita E Lasswell
15890 N County Hwy 14
Smithfield IL 61477

Call Sign: KA9RPK
Renee L Lasswell
15890 N County Hwy 14
Smithfield IL 61477

Call Sign: N9BBO
Richard L Lasswell
15890 N County Hwy 14
Smithfield IL 61477

Call Sign: KA9KKT
Roger L Lasswell
15890 N County Hwy 14
Smithfield IL 61477

Call Sign: KB9NKS
Daniel R Welch
19016 N Hodgkins Rd
Smithfield IL 61477

Call Sign: KB9HNM
Chad E Ensinger
Smithfield IL 61477

Call Sign: KB9FPE
Glen A Ensinger
Smithfield IL 61477

**FCC Amateur Radio
Licenses in Smithshire**

Call Sign: KC9MXI
Daniel J Anderson
Rr 1 Box 49
Smithshire IL 61478

**FCC Amateur Radio
Licenses in Smithton**

Call Sign: KB9TVG
Chad D Boeving
5561 Blank Rd
Smithton IL 622852525

Call Sign: KB9QBF
Charles H Meyer
4019 Chestnut Oak
Smithton IL 62285

Call Sign: KC9ONB
Brian J Smith
805 Fieldview Dr
Smithton IL 62285

Call Sign: K9SF
Steven S Stryker
203 Jo Mar Ave
Smithton IL 62285

Call Sign: WW9N
Kent A Hollansworth
5157 Live Oak Dr
Smithton IL 62285

Call Sign: KC9VFJ
Steve R Kerley
5757 Palomino Ln
Smithton IL 62285

Call Sign: KB9GWD
Tyler M Spearing
5928 Robinson School Rd
Smithton IL 62285

Call Sign: KC9JBI
Charlie E Parke
405 S Hickory
Smithton IL 62285

Call Sign: WA9OWO
Harold S Barton Sr
4426 Wildhorse Rd
Smithton IL 62285

**FCC Amateur Radio
Licenses in Sorento**

Call Sign: KA9RMQ
Julie J Eschmann
Rt 2 Box 149
Sorento IL 62086

Call Sign: KB9PSA

Julie M Eschmann
Rt 2 Box 149
Sorento IL 62086

Call Sign: KA9RYT
Robert E Towell
Rr 1 Box 52
Sorento IL 62086

Call Sign: KC9LEH
Jackie R Blumer
1688 Dove Rd
Sorento IL 62036

Call Sign: N9SND
Ray C Trimble
663 Pan Estates
Sorento IL 62036

Call Sign: KB9RQR
Kathryn A Trimble
663 Pan Estates Ave
Sorento IL 62086

Call Sign: N9WWI
Val W Crafton
Sorento IL 62086

**FCC Amateur Radio
Licenses in South Beloit**

Call Sign: KC4UVV
Evelyn M Keierleber
1615 Blackhawk Blvd Apt 214
South Beloit IL 61080

Call Sign: N9RHD
Stephen C Vilmin Jr
15573 Bryden Dr
South Beloit IL 61080

Call Sign: KA9HON
Donald D Carlson
14647 Donnalynn Dr
South Beloit IL 610802384

Call Sign: KC9GNZ
Tyler D Peterson
5756 Dusty Ln

South Beloit IL 61080

Call Sign: KK7UN
Samuel J Saladino
911 Gardner St
South Beloit IL 61080

Call Sign: NW9T
Samuel J Saladino
911 Gardner St
South Beloit IL 61080

Call Sign: N9SZV
Ronald G Callahan Jr
1509 Hayes Ave
South Beloit IL 61080

Call Sign: KC9IED
John H Cotner Jr
525 Hemenway Pl
South Beloit IL 610801942

Call Sign: KC9JDS
Jeffrey S Macdonald
14735 Joseph Pkwy
South Beloit IL 61080

Call Sign: KC9QFC
Bradley W Wilson
14159 Kirane Ct
South Beloit IL 61080

Call Sign: KB9QJE
Herbert L Crenshaw
5542 Kutzke Pkwy
South Beloit IL 610802324

Call Sign: KC9FOH
Richard J Schlee
532 Lathrop Ter
South Beloit IL 61080

Call Sign: K9YWQ
Donn Hathaway
1120 Manchester Rd
South Beloit IL 61080

Call Sign: KC9IJM
Michael G Demrow

14164 Nautical Ct
South Beloit IL 61080

Call Sign: AB9WM
Brett A Johnson
15063 Northview Trl
South Beloit IL 61080

Call Sign: K9BY
Brett A Johnson
15063 Northview Trl
South Beloit IL 61080

Call Sign: N9VPO
Kenneth R Wayne Jr
307 Oakland Ave
South Beloit IL 61080

Call Sign: KC9HGZ
Donald H Shaw
5917 Pierce Ln
South Beloit IL 61080

Call Sign: KC9KYX
Donald H Shaw
5917 Pierce Ln
South Beloit IL 61080

Call Sign: W9UG
Donald H Shaw
5917 Pierce Ln
South Beloit IL 61080

Call Sign: N9OEG
Christopher J Green
305 S Bluff St
South Beloit IL 61080

Call Sign: N8XTA
John C Moore
666 S Bluff St Lot 201
South Beloit IL 61080

Call Sign: KA9LQZ
William D Frisbee
229 S Lincoln
South Beloit IL 61080

Call Sign: WB9ZCO

Samuel J Saladino
136 S Lincoln Ave
South Beloit IL 61080

Call Sign: KB8FMF
Curtis D Terpstra
730 S Park
South Beloit IL 61080

Call Sign: KC9CTP
Curtis D Terpstra
730 S Park
South Beloit IL 61080

FCC Amateur Radio Licenses in South Jacksonville

Call Sign: KA9YDB
Richard A Evans
412 Columbian
South Jacksonville IL 62650

Call Sign: WA9NZF
Rodney N Jackson
429 Pendik Rd
South Jacksonville IL 62650

Call Sign: W9OES
Vincent C Berkman
403 W Greenwood Ave
South Jacksonville IL 62650

FCC Amateur Radio Licenses in South Pekin

Call Sign: KC9IGP
Roy E Edwards
310 Minch St
South Pekin IL 61564

Call Sign: KB9OSY
Hal B Harper
214 St Anthony St
South Pekin IL 61564

Call Sign: KB9JKW
Jonathan A York
201 St Marks Dr

South Pekin IL 61564

Call Sign: KC9ERV
Raymond J Hagan Jr
South Pekin IL 615640662

FCC Amateur Radio Licenses in South Roxana

Call Sign: KB9UXG
Frank R Talbott
424 Southard
South Roxana IL 62087

FCC Amateur Radio Licenses in South Streator

Call Sign: WB9DCQ
Joseph A Centko Jr
1509 S Vermillion
South Streator IL 61364

FCC Amateur Radio Licenses in South Wilmington

Call Sign: WD9FGH
Larry D Elliott
135 Monroe St
South Wilmington IL 60474

Call Sign: N9LCG
Charles F Harvey
South Wilmington IL 60474

FCC Amateur Radio Licenses in Sparland

Call Sign: AA9VT
John C Fidler
196 Cahokia Ct
Sparland IL 61565

Call Sign: W9DNI
Steve D Staats
1038 Camp Grove Rd
Sparland IL 61565

Call Sign: K9AH
Charles K Bussell Jr
871 CR 800 E
Sparland IL 61565

Call Sign: KB9YKX
Justin A Lockhart
205 School St
Sparland IL 615659397

Call Sign: KB9TPI
Robert A Lockhart
205 School St
Sparland IL 615659397

Call Sign: KG9DQ
Richard R Starkweather Sr
54 Winnebago
Sparland IL 61565

Call Sign: WB9NNS
Ronald L Barr
Sparland IL 61565

FCC Amateur Radio Licenses in Sparta

Call Sign: WB9REJ
Alan E Ashbrook
1106 Birch Ln
Sparta IL 62286

Call Sign: KC9SDE
Michael S Sykes
237 Debra Ln
Sparta IL 62286

Call Sign: N9MPA
John F Clendenin
604 Fox Run Dr
Sparta IL 62286

Call Sign: K9SGD
Joseph N Hall
7080 Gordon Rd
Sparta IL 62286

Call Sign: KA9RLM
Robert E Barber

9630 Houston Rd
Sparta IL 622863307

Call Sign: KC9NRB
Bryan E Todd
44 Kool Valley Dr
Sparta IL 62286

Call Sign: WB9VWT
John E Shields
720 N James St
Sparta IL 62286

Call Sign: KC9SZ
Michael D Laurent
12760 Roseborough Rd
Sparta IL 62286

Call Sign: KC9OEE
Rickey L Oeth
100 S James 3
Sparta IL 62286

Call Sign: KF9PD
Maurice Nixon
501 S Market St
Sparta IL 62286

Call Sign: AJ9F
Richard A Barber
12291 SR 154
Sparta IL 62286

Call Sign: KA9FTC
Walter H Conners Sr
600 W Bdwy
Sparta IL 62286

FCC Amateur Radio Licenses in Spaulding

Call Sign: KI9I
John E La Croix
5425 Primrose Ln
Spaulding IL 62561

FCC Amateur Radio Licenses in Speer

Call Sign: KA9NIT
David L Gehrt
Rr 1 Box 4
Speer IL 61479

Call Sign: WB9JNC
Rodger D Marshall
106 CR 550 N
Speer IL 61479

FCC Amateur Radio Licenses in Spring Valley

Call Sign: AA9R
Peter N Jacobsen
19 Briarcliff Dr
Spring Valley IL 61362

Call Sign: N9CUT
Sam W Schaumleffel
221 E 2nd St
Spring Valley IL 61362

Call Sign: KB9LSN
Ronald R Kuffel
102 E Cleveland St
Spring Valley IL 61362

Call Sign: KC9NV
Robert L Daugherty
620 E Erie St
Spring Valley IL 61362

Call Sign: KC9TUJ
William Watson
618 E St Paul
Spring Valley IL 61362

Call Sign: K9MIE
Robert W Morrow Jr
406 Elm St
Spring Valley IL 61362

Call Sign: N9VLB
Albeno A Bianchi
620 N Richards
Spring Valley IL 61362

Call Sign: KB9TVO

Albert W Kulupka
105 Prairie St
Spring Valley IL 61362

Call Sign: KC9UEV
Randi Lind
217 W 7th St
Spring Valley IL 61362

Call Sign: KB9JKE
Adam W Lind
217 W 7th St
Spring Valley IL 61362

Call Sign: KA9MDZ
Shanon K Urbanski
612 W Cleveland
Spring Valley IL 61362

Call Sign: KB9PAP
Barbara A Bendkowski
601 W Cleveland St
Spring Valley IL 61362

Call Sign: KB9EWU
Jody M Hicks
508 W Devlin
Spring Valley IL 61362

Call Sign: WA9TGK
Rita K Peterson
700 W Devlin
Spring Valley IL 61362

Call Sign: KC9CVR
Judith M Taylor
218 W Erie St
Spring Valley IL 61362

Call Sign: KB9ZWJ
Christopher R Phelps
218 W Erie St
Spring Valley IL 613621928

Call Sign: KB9API
Michael G Borri
209 W Iowa St
Spring Valley IL 61362

Call Sign: N9SQX
Roger Schrader
214 W Minnesota
Spring Valley IL 61362

Call Sign: N9PLJ
Nils R Barto Jr
405 W St Paul St
Spring Valley IL 61362

Call Sign: WD9CNB
Richard A Jensen
722 W St Paul St
Spring Valley IL 61362

FCC Amateur Radio Licenses in Springerton

Call Sign: WX0A
Robert C York Sr
Rt 1 Box 134
Springerton IL 62887

FCC Amateur Radio Licenses in Springfield

Call Sign: KB9WLW
William L Workman
105 Adloff Ln
Springfield IL 62703

Call Sign: KA9MPO
Ronald L Pratt
1797 Albany St
Springfield IL 627023159

Call Sign: W9RLP
Ronald L Pratt
1797 Albany St
Springfield IL 627023159

Call Sign: KA9MPK
Mike Pratt
1797 Albay
Springfield IL 62702

Call Sign: K9LKI
Jeff R Hamor
31 Anchor Rd

Springfield IL 62707

Call Sign: KC9LKI
Jeffrey R Hamor
31 Anchor Rd
Springfield IL 62707

Call Sign: KF9DW
Joan L Kelly
417 Armor Rd
Springfield IL 627045203

Call Sign: KF4WQH
Carl D Larson
2713 Arrowhead Dr
Springfield IL 62702

Call Sign: WA9ULT
Deloris J Spears
2602 Austin
Springfield IL 62704

Call Sign: K9YNU
Gordon D Murray
4525 Barrington
Springfield IL 62707

Call Sign: W9GDM
Gordon D Murray
4525 Barrington
Springfield IL 62707

Call Sign: KC9FLE
Bryan D Sim
4604 Barrymore Dr
Springfield IL 62711

Call Sign: K0HMO
Richard F Drew
2965 Battersea Pt
Springfield IL 62704

Call Sign: KB9HUE
William P Hopkins III
6 Beachview
Springfield IL 62707

Call Sign: KA9WFI
Thomas P Costa

1105 Bedford Rd
Springfield IL 62704

Call Sign: N9LVV
Jonathan J Trepal
3001 Bennington Dr
Springfield IL 62704

Call Sign: N9OWT
Audrey K South
2913 Biscayne Dr
Springfield IL 62707

Call Sign: N9OWU
John D South
2913 Biscayne Dr
Springfield IL 62707

Call Sign: WD9API
Diana J Skube
714 Bonanza Pass
Springfield IL 627074571

Call Sign: W9API
Diana J Skube
714 Bonanza Pass
Springfield IL 627074571

Call Sign: WD9AQL
Edmund J Skube Sr
714 Bonanza Pass
Springfield IL 627074571

Call Sign: W9AQL
Edmund J Skube Sr
714 Bonanza Pass
Springfield IL 627074571

Call Sign: WD9FPE
Herbert S Woods II
2301 Boysenberry Ln Apt 4
Springfield IL 62707

Call Sign: N9AXU
Irvine A Turley
58 Brookside Pl
Springfield IL 62704

Call Sign: KB7NHD

Jeffrey S Watterson
5242 Buford St
Springfield IL 62703

Call Sign: W9LVG
William R Margetts
3242 Butler St
Springfield IL 62703

Call Sign: WT9WT
William W Tinsley Sr
114 Calvin
Springfield IL 627046112

Call Sign: N9XHW
Eloise A Tinsley
114 Calvin Ave
Springfield IL 627046112

Call Sign: W9LZS
Dan Menghini
2029 Cambridge Rd
Springfield IL 627044129

Call Sign: W9HA
Steven L Tuma
23 Carole Rd
Springfield IL 62711

Call Sign: KC9VCK
William H Long
1245 Carver Rd
Springfield IL 62707

Call Sign: KB9ZVE
Steven M Malnich
3816 Castle Hill Blvd
Springfield IL 627128316

Call Sign: WA9JRT
William L Wheeler
1770 Chatham Rd
Springfield IL 62704

Call Sign: KC9HGW
Robert A Carson
924 Cherokee Dr
Springfield IL 62711

Call Sign: NA9GW
Robert A Carson
924 Cherokee Dr
Springfield IL 62711

Call Sign: KC9POY
Brian M Skeeters
2309 Cherry Hills Dr Apt 201
Springfield IL 62704

Call Sign: KB9BKK
Michael L Burton
2319 Cherryhill Dr Apt 3
Springfield IL 62704

Call Sign: N9SZN
John R Allen
2311 Chesapeake Landing
Springfield IL 62707

Call Sign: AB9OW
Jay C Bartlett
2324 Chesapeake Landing
Springfield IL 62712

Call Sign: N9YF
Jay C Bartlett
2324 Chesapeake Landing
Springfield IL 62712

Call Sign: N9XHV
Richard L Daniel
2421 Chinchilla Ln
Springfield IL 62702

Call Sign: W9LSS
Lawrence M Brooke
141 Circle Dr
Springfield IL 62703

Call Sign: WA9AIQ
James A Newbanks I
273 Circle Dr
Springfield IL 62703

Call Sign: KA9HTZ
Patrick G Tinkham
6 Claire Dr
Springfield IL 62702

Call Sign: KA9WEY
Eric A Adcock
3180 Cobblestone Ln Apt 4
Springfield IL 627078007

Call Sign: KE9LE
Fernando A Ares
4400 Comanche Dr
Springfield IL 62711

Call Sign: N8HF
Adolf E Fullgrabe
35 Crater Lake Dr
Springfield IL 627129140

Call Sign: N8EHU
Portia R Fullgrabe
35 Crater Lake Dr
Springfield IL 627129140

Call Sign: KB9MKC
Daniel R Frasco
4078 Crocus
Springfield IL 62707

Call Sign: N9DKA
John B Jamison
70 Crusaders
Springfield IL 62704

Call Sign: KA9WHR
Neal D Sim
6 Danbury Dr
Springfield IL 62704

Call Sign: N9YXQ
Allison C Laabs
10 Danbury Dr
Springfield IL 62704

Call Sign: N9ZGE
Donald D Wilson
2908 Dartmoor Ct
Springfield IL 627046469

Call Sign: KB9OLC
Linda K Wilson
2908 Dartmoor Ct

Springfield IL 627046469

Call Sign: WA9YXK
Ronald W Steffen
46 De Soto Dr
Springfield IL 62707

Call Sign: KC9DQS
Alan E Broadhurst
2427 Delaware Dr
Springfield IL 62702

Call Sign: AB9HK
Alan E Broadhurst
2427 Delaware Dr
Springfield IL 62702

Call Sign: KB9KAF
Jeffrey S Tucker
1000 Diane Ct
Springfield IL 62702

Call Sign: WA9IHO
Harold W Reno
2505 Dickens Dr
Springfield IL 627117244

Call Sign: K9CFC
Charles F Connor
6 Downing Ln
Springfield IL 62712

Call Sign: KB9QBE
John Blockyou
2232 Dunwich St
Springfield IL 62702

Call Sign: KC9KLU
Kenneth L Crutcher
800 Durkin St 441
Springfield IL 62704

Call Sign: KB9SQM
Guy D Jones
2209 E Black Ave
Springfield IL 62702

Call Sign: KB9TBZ
Marlina K Kellum

116 E Camp Sangamo Rd
Springfield IL 62707

Call Sign: KB9SQJ
Troy S Kellum
116 E Camp Sangamo Rd
Springfield IL 62707

Call Sign: KB9KAL
Anna M Kutzera
3404 E Carpenter St
Springfield IL 62702

Call Sign: KA9ZWL
Bryan S Tate
2166 E Cincinnati
Springfield IL 62702

Call Sign: WA9JWD
Ivan O Crain
2369 E Cincinnati Ave
Springfield IL 62702

Call Sign: KA9NJV
Dallas E Mrasak
2349 E Converse
Springfield IL 62702

Call Sign: K9RXG
Frank T Brock
3535 E Cook St Lot 167
Springfield IL 627032163

Call Sign: W9GIW
Howard P Mc Cormick
915 E Cornell Ave
Springfield IL 62703

Call Sign: KB9KGN
Rex A Jaronske
2322 E Cornell Ave
Springfield IL 62703

Call Sign: KA9ZBM
Mark A Bermel
1522 E Cummins
Springfield IL 62702

Call Sign: KC9JFM

Craig A Held
1832 E Grant St
Springfield IL 62703

Call Sign: KB9EUY
Carolyn A Lee
1317 E Jackson
Springfield IL 62703

Call Sign: WI9I
George W Hinkle
407 E Keys
Springfield IL 62702

Call Sign: KA9CVK
Clarence H Robinson
2224 E Keys Ave
Springfield IL 62702

Call Sign: KC9QVY
Jasen M Staples
2316 E Keys Ave
Springfield IL 62702

Call Sign: KB9WWR
Michael J Gallant
2524 E Keys Ave
Springfield IL 62702

Call Sign: KC9OFY
James R Miller
900 E Linton Ave
Springfield IL 62703

Call Sign: K7CZ
William N Parfitt
2913 E Mason St
Springfield IL 62702

Call Sign: K9YJI
John G Alexander
2157 E Reservoir St
Springfield IL 62702

Call Sign: KC9MAR
Aubrey A Troesch
2120 E Sangamon Ave
Springfield IL 62702

Call Sign: KC9IAN
Mark W Barber
226 E Wilcox
Springfield IL 62707

Call Sign: KC9VCI
Marian K Giaccmini
6113 Elisa Trl
Springfield IL 62711

Call Sign: KC9VCJ
Albert J Giacomini
6113 Elisha Trl
Springfield IL 62711

Call Sign: KA9UCX
Kenneth R Cary
2304 Elmhurst Ct
Springfield IL 627045456

Call Sign: K9UCX
Kenneth R Cary
2304 Elmhurst Ct
Springfield IL 527045456

Call Sign: N9SOF
George L Tucker
2221 Enterprize
Springfield IL 62703

Call Sign: KC9BQR
Scott A Bybee
1804 Fairfield Dr
Springfield IL 62702

Call Sign: KC9TEP
Ronald E Bakunas
1924 Fairfield Dr
Springfield IL 62702

Call Sign: KC9UJC
Matthew C Brown
3100 Falcon Point
Springfield IL 62711

Call Sign: KE9UDW
Richard E Brown
3100 Falcon Pt
Springfield IL 62707

Call Sign: N9UWI
Oliver D Gross
4220 Fort Donelson Dr
Springfield IL 62711

Call Sign: KB9TWE
Cornerstone Radio Club
906 Gabbert Rd
Springfield IL 62707

Call Sign: W9TUN
Robert J Miller
7112 Gardenview Ln
Springfield IL 627128907

Call Sign: KB9OQL
David A Cook
3105 Geneva Ln
Springfield IL 62707

Call Sign: W9GPS
David A Cook
3105 Geneva Ln
Springfield IL 62707

Call Sign: KC9LSJ
Deborah M Bridges
8 Gettysburg Dr
Springfield IL 62702

Call Sign: KC9BZC
William J Bridges
8 Gettysburg Dr
Springfield IL 62702

Call Sign: W9MVQ
Arthur M Grepling
2405 Gillespie
Springfield IL 62704

Call Sign: K9DGK
Darwin T Osmonson
68 Glen Aire Dr
Springfield IL 62703

Call Sign: N9NBA
Charles E Nettles
93 Glen Aire Dr

Springfield IL 62703

Call Sign: KC9CSE
Joe I Lipsey Sr
120 Glenn Air Dr
Springfield IL 62703

Call Sign: KC9BVH
Philip D Moore
74 Golf Rd
Springfield IL 62704

Call Sign: WA9WDJ
Scott E Silliman
177 Golf Rd
Springfield IL 62704

Call Sign: KC9UZJ
Robert J Zeeck
1252 Governor St
Springfield IL 62704

Call Sign: KF9UI
Thomas B Bishop
56 Green Castle Cir
Springfield IL 62707

Call Sign: K9PLR
Steven R Howard
4525 Greenbriar Rd
Springfield IL 62707

Call Sign: KB9VCN
Eric A Adcock
4 Greenview Ct
Springfield IL 627042145

Call Sign: KF9TA
Thomas E Hamilton
2341 Grinnell Dr
Springfield IL 62704

Call Sign: KC9BJS
Lyle M Ahrens
2353 Grinnell Dr
Springfield IL 62704

Call Sign: KC9CSF
Jennifer C Ramm

1117 Harmony Ct
Springfield IL 62703

Call Sign: KC9CSH
Michael T Ramm
1117 Harmony Ct
Springfield IL 62703

Call Sign: WD9HEJ
James A Zick
2129 Hastings Rd
Springfield IL 62702

Call Sign: WA9JZ
James A Zick
2129 Hastings Rd
Springfield IL 62702

Call Sign: KC9QWA
William R Hurt
3313 Haviland Dr
Springfield IL 62704

Call Sign: K9PGM
Jennifer S Johnson
30 Hazel Ln
Springfield IL 62707

Call Sign: K9WLD
Michael A Johnson
30 Hazel Ln
Springfield IL 62707

Call Sign: WA9KRL
John F Sams
2301 Heather Mill Ct
Springfield IL 62704

Call Sign: WB9QXA
Patricia A Sams
2301 Heather Mill Ct
Springfield IL 62704

Call Sign: N9GVP
Thomas M Snyder
2308 Heather Mill Ct
Springfield IL 62704

Call Sign: KD9RZ

Mark W Lipe
2409 Heather Mill Ct
Springfield IL 62704

Call Sign: KE5BSF
David W Mc Connell
909 Helene St
Springfield IL 62702

Call Sign: KB9AFE
Jeanne Perkinton
2042 Henley Rd
Springfield IL 62702

Call Sign: W9HJA
Richard L Perkinton Sr
2042 Henley Rd
Springfield IL 62702

Call Sign: N9RAZ
Abraham P Wood Jr
2109 Henley Rd
Springfield IL 627021913

Call Sign: KB9IUM
Eden E Tallon
4 Hickory Hills Dr
Springfield IL 62707

Call Sign: KB9IUN
Erin M Tallon
4 Hickory Hills Dr
Springfield IL 62707

Call Sign: KB9IUO
Sherry A Tallon
4 Hickory Hills Dr
Springfield IL 62707

Call Sign: WB9IAQ
Dean K Naritoku
5 Hickory Hills Dr
Springfield IL 62707

Call Sign: N9SCM
Brent R Urfer
2075 Hill Meadows Dr Apt 5
Springfield IL 62702

Call Sign: KC9VJL
Charles B Call Jr
1405 Hoechester Rd
Springfield IL 62712

Call Sign: KB9IMD
K L Ross
47 Holiday Rd
Springfield IL 62702

Call Sign: N5NYP
Andrew T Van Deventer
2433 Holmes
Springfield IL 62704

Call Sign: KC9KME
Cathy A Cumpston
1624 Holmes Ave
Springfield IL 62704

Call Sign: KC9KMF
David M Cumpston
1624 Holmes Ave
Springfield IL 62704

Call Sign: K9EI
James W Grubbs III
2120 Holmes Ave
Springfield IL 62704

Call Sign: KB9LYQ
Todd A Rutter
2201 Huntleigh Rd
Springfield IL 62704

Call Sign: KB9KDL
Andrew P Affrunti
2808 Huron Dr
Springfield IL 62707

Call Sign: WA9YBW
Howard J Thomas
839 Independence Ridge
Springfield IL 62702

Call Sign: W9OFP
William G Swan
1133 Indiana
Springfield IL 62702

Call Sign: KA9MCD
Denise A Hesler
1656 Jerome Ave
Springfield IL 62704

Call Sign: KA9PEG
Thomas K Curran
2629 Kent Dr
Springfield IL 62703

Call Sign: WA9EER
Robert J Herron
316 Kenyon Dr
Springfield IL 62704

Call Sign: WD9ALM
Carl W Pietsek
2736 Kipling Dr
Springfield IL 62711

Call Sign: N9YUW
Paul F Kerby
721 Kirkwood Dr Apt 3
Springfield IL 527126848

Call Sign: KC9TPT
Ryan A Stalets
800 Kirkwood Dr Apt 5
Springfield IL 62712

Call Sign: K9LLT
John L Satterlee
6 Lambert Ln
Springfield IL 62704

Call Sign: KB9HRE
Richard D Livingston
78 Lambert Ln
Springfield IL 62704

Call Sign: W9GOJ
J Rolland Lyons
3642 Lancaster Rd
Springfield IL 62703

Call Sign: KC9LSI
Simon M Daniels
4001 Lavender Ln

Springfield IL 62711

Call Sign: N9OXS
Mary I Creedon
Laverna Rd
Springfield IL 627949431

Call Sign: KB9DKH
Maryann Berard
Laverna Rd Box 19431
Springfield IL 627949431

Call Sign: WD9EMH
William C Fifer
2000 Lee St
Springfield IL 62703

Call Sign: KB9LXQ
Etta E Dahlquist
1674 Lick Creek Ln
Springfield IL 62629

Call Sign: KC9INY
Rock E Daniels
3484 Lightfoot Dr
Springfield IL 62707

Call Sign: AB9MB
Rock E Daniels
3484 Lightfoot Dr
Springfield IL 62707

Call Sign: KC9INZ
Rock E Daniels II
3484 Lightfoot Dr
Springfield IL 62707

Call Sign: KA9HLZ
John P Ransdell
2309 Lindbergh Blvd
Springfield IL 627045529

Call Sign: WB9GFT
Karen L Fargusson
3109 Lindenwood Dr
Springfield IL 62704

Call Sign: W9PRN
Edmond A Metzger

1917 Lindsay Rd
Springfield IL 62704

Call Sign: KD9KK
Thomas L Work
1012 Livingston
Springfield IL 62703

Call Sign: N9EBO
Lloyd E Lenhart
56 Locksley Ln
Springfield IL 627045314

Call Sign: WB9RCF
Barbara C Therkildsen
53 Longbow Ln
Springfield IL 62704

Call Sign: W9BVN
Lawrence J Sintay
1 Longview Dr
Springfield IL 62712

Call Sign: N9FME
Gregory A Coady
21 Longview Dr
Springfield IL 62712

Call Sign: WB9LHD
Eugene J Gallant
3009 Louise Ln
Springfield IL 62702

Call Sign: WD9FBZ
Linda K Gallant
3009 Louise Ln
Springfield IL 62702

Call Sign: KA9BKW
Douglas C Lawrence
3016 Louise Ln
Springfield IL 62702

Call Sign: N6SMK
Jack V Dickinson
6205 MacKenzie Pl
Springfield IL 62711

Call Sign: WA9LZH

Wayne M Soule
2200 Makemie Ave
Springfield IL 62704

Call Sign: W9QEQ
Jerry M Waggoner
5408 Manhattan Dr
Springfield IL 627117987

Call Sign: KB9ZWP
Andrew E Scroggin
1008 Marco Ln Apt D
Springfield IL 62712

Call Sign: KA2MZP
Michael Thomas
4012 Marie Dr
Springfield IL 627078830

Call Sign: KC9KLZ
Michael W Rhodes
2032 Marland St
Springfield IL 62702

Call Sign: KC9HDE
William W Bercaw
7 Marshall Ct
Springfield IL 62712

Call Sign: KF9OI
Gary W Britz
1525 Maureen Ct
Springfield IL 62702

Call Sign: WD9HKR
Kerri E Cawley
1613 Maureen Ct
Springfield IL 62702

Call Sign: WB9TZY
Kurt A Taraba
76 Meadowbrook Rd
Springfield IL 62707

Call Sign: N9ADD
Kevin W Cranford
5042 Mechanicsburg Rd
Springfield IL 627126420

Call Sign: KA9NLV
Margaret A Hankins
6505 Mechanicsburg Rd
Springfield IL 62707

Call Sign: WA9SID
Stanley J Hankins
6505 Mechanicsburg Rd
Springfield IL 62707

Call Sign: KB9HOX
David A Henebry
77 Mesa Rd
Springfield IL 62702

Call Sign: K9ATG
Joe W Armstrong
2529 Miami Trl
Springfield IL 627021336

Call Sign: KB9OPY
Joe W Armstrong
2529 Miami Trl
Springfield IL 627021366

Call Sign: KB9TJM
Terrill J Meyer
2909 Mill Pt
Springfield IL 62704

Call Sign: KA9ZBN
William T Culbertson
2601 Montvale Dr Apt 233
Springfield IL 62704

Call Sign: WB9NSJ
Richard C Lahndorff
1217 Mossman
Springfield IL 62702

Call Sign: WD9F
Forrest G Hester III
5109 Mtn View Dr
Springfield IL 62711

Call Sign: KB9NEH
Gregory F Robison Jr
2017 N 11th St
Springfield IL 62702

Call Sign: WB9TLZ
Patrick F O Connell
2431 N 15th St
Springfield IL 62702

Call Sign: KC9KMI
Burley E Daniels Sr
2019 N 17th St
Springfield IL 62702

Call Sign: KA9BDU
Broice E Hill
2020 N 21st St
Springfield IL 62702

Call Sign: KC9QWD
Dale E Simpson
1936 N 24th
Springfield IL 62702

Call Sign: KB9UWY
Elizabeth A Thetford
1131 N 2nd St
Springfield IL 62702

Call Sign: KB9UDV
Michael C Thetford
1131 N 2nd St
Springfield IL 62702

Call Sign: KC9LSN
Deborah L Owens
929 N 3rd Ave
Springfield IL 62702

Call Sign: KA9ZKW
Leroy A Billbe
703 N 4th St
Springfield IL 62702

Call Sign: KB9AFG
Gayle L Meyer
1121 N 5th St
Springfield IL 62702

Call Sign: KC9LSL
George R Lancaster
1529 N 5th St

Springfield IL 62702

Call Sign: N9VBU
Ernest J Gerber
2128 N 5th St
Springfield IL 62702

Call Sign: WB9OEZ
Robert T Dinsmore
2128 N 5th St
Springfield IL 62702

Call Sign: KC9IO
Timothy E Teeter Sr
1941 N 7th St
Springfield IL 62702

Call Sign: W9EMN
Henry A Trapp
2005 N 7th St
Springfield IL 62702

Call Sign: N9ZAC
Douglas J Mummertz
852 N 7th St Apt B
Springfield IL 62702

Call Sign: KC9ITV
Daniel L Powers
1930 N 8th St
Springfield IL 62702

Call Sign: N9XFY
James S Reed
919 N 9th St
Springfield IL 62702

Call Sign: WE9OAT
Samuel E Burgener
1800 N 9th St
Springfield IL 62702

Call Sign: KC9BQS
Olivier E Darbin
700 N Bruns Ln
Springfield IL 62702

Call Sign: W9KMD
Lucille F Falzone

720 N Daniel
Springfield IL 62702

Call Sign: W9MCE
Armand P Falzone
720 N Daniel Ave
Springfield IL 62702

Call Sign: KC9KLS
John C Burris Jr
1021 N Daniels
Springfield IL 62702

Call Sign: KB9JJP
James A Hood
1123 N Frankin
Springfield IL 62702

Call Sign: KD5FPO
Michael J Harnett
1306 N Franklin Ave
Springfield IL 62702

Call Sign: KC9DQU
Keith E Ushman
3617 N Grand Ave E 201
Springfield IL 62702

Call Sign: WB9GBF
Paul G Fargusson
3617 N Grand Ave E 222
Springfield IL 62702

Call Sign: N9JPW
Vernon W Lawrence
527 N Grand Ave W
Springfield IL 62702

Call Sign: N9QIG
David C Smith
2373 N Grand E
Springfield IL 62702

Call Sign: K9TNO
Raymond L Manion
1225 N Grand W
Springfield IL 62702

Call Sign: N9VBV

Kenneth C Hoebbel Sr
1005 N Hill
Springfield IL 62702

Call Sign: N9XHU
Leonard E Mc Whorter
837 N Hill St
Springfield IL 627026229

Call Sign: WB9UBA
Thomas G Micklus
5845 N Lake Rd
Springfield IL 627117372

Call Sign: KC9RCV
John R Buckley
1045 N Osburn
Springfield IL 62702

Call Sign: N9XVI
Melissa S Childers
1025 N Rutledge
Springfield IL 62702

Call Sign: NI9B
Rodney L Jarrard
505 N St Marys Ave
Springfield IL 627026309

Call Sign: KB9JJO
Elmer E Gant
320 N Stephens
Springfield IL 62702

Call Sign: N9OZO
Terry L Jacobs Sr
200 N Wesley
Springfield IL 62702

Call Sign: KC9UJB
Sharon A Robson
820 N Wesley
Springfield IL 62702

Call Sign: N9DPH
Lloyd L Mintz
923 N Wesley St
Springfield IL 62702

Call Sign: WA9ACW
Eldon L Launer
112 Norwalk
Springfield IL 62704

Call Sign: KC9MHG
Ryan T Juhl
5762 Oakdale Dr
Springfield IL 62711

Call Sign: KC9NFE
Azeem Abdul Azeez
2317 Old Jacksonville Rd Apt I
Springfield IL 62704

Call Sign: KA9TSR
Russell L Clay
6005 Old Salem Lnt
Springfield IL 62711

Call Sign: KE9FO
Richard L Fox
7667 Olde Carriage Way
Springfield IL 627076803

Call Sign: KB9VON
Patrick W Kelley
1981 Outer Park Dr
Springfield IL 62704

Call Sign: K9PWK
Patrick W Kelley
1981 Outer Park Dr
Springfield IL 62704

Call Sign: KI9T
Patrick W Kelley
1981 Outer Park Dr
Springfield IL 62704

Call Sign: N9UUK
Ahren J Hartman
3301 Palmer St
Springfield IL 62703

Call Sign: N9VLG
Martin B Pereira
8 Palomino Rd

Springfield IL 62702

Call Sign: KA9GUF
Valle H Funk
1901 Parkview
Springfield IL 62704

Call Sign: KA9LBK
Bob W Roberts
4688 Pec Rd
Springfield IL 62711

Call Sign: WA9PLL
Barbara A Roberts
4688 Pec Rd
Springfield IL 627116045

Call Sign: K9URI
William H Tatro Jr
5729 Pec Rd
Springfield IL 627076056

Call Sign: KC9CGC
Crit J Prichard
1412 Pennsylvania
Springfield IL 62702

Call Sign: W9COM
Crit J Prichard
1412 Pennsylvania
Springfield IL 62702

Call Sign: KB9LSZ
Henry L Wahl
3004 Peoria Rd
Springfield IL 627021257

Call Sign: KB9EYO
Dennis R Rector
3725 Peoria Rd Lot 212
Springfield IL 627021054

Call Sign: N9MFK
Beau C Thompson
6601 Phlox Dr
Springfield IL 62712

Call Sign: N9KLJ
George P Langan Jr

130 Pinehurst
Springfield IL 62704

Call Sign: WB9TWC
John S Lowe
2516 Plateau Dr
Springfield IL 62707

Call Sign: W9YCI
Donald G Thompson
59 Providence Ln
Springfield IL 627078023

Call Sign: KB9UDD
Sharon E Mc Bride
70 B Providence Ln
Springfield IL 62707

Call Sign: KC9ESU
Jeph Bassett
2324 Queensway Rd
Springfield IL 62703

Call Sign: W9RFC
Joseph S Suarez
2421 Queensway Rd
Springfield IL 627035025

Call Sign: N9HHE
Claudia M Pitchford
2504 Queensway Rd
Springfield IL 627035028

Call Sign: W9EBK
Donald D Pitchford
2504 Queensway Rd
Springfield IL 627035028

Call Sign: W9LOK
Edward W Cikas
2505 Queensway Rd
Springfield IL 62703

Call Sign: KE9EB
Leland H Bates
3121 Red Bud Ln
Springfield IL 627078954

Call Sign: KC9KNL

Benjamin J Upchurch
17 Red Fox Ct
Springfield IL 62712

Call Sign: K9WAV
James S Upchurch
17 Red Fox Ct
Springfield IL 62712

Call Sign: KC9CSX
Kimberly A Upchurch
17 Red Fox Ct
Springfield IL 62712

Call Sign: W9DUA
Sangamon Valley Radio Club
Inc
17 Red Fox Ct
Springfield IL 52712

Call Sign: KB0YDD
James S Upchurch
17 Red Fox Ct
Springfield IL 62707

Call Sign: N9ZYM
Todd M Oliver
3101 Red Oak Ln
Springfield IL 62707

Call Sign: KC9HPA
Ronald G Brest
3451 Ridge Ave Trl 46
Springfield IL 62702

Call Sign: N9HPA
Ronald G Brest
3451 Ridge Ave Trl 46
Springfield IL 62702

Call Sign: WD9GPD
Frank R Thornton
30 Ridgeview
Springfield IL 62707

Call Sign: KA9NWB
George W Rompot
900 Roanoke Dr
Springfield IL 62702

Call Sign: N9GMA
Nancy D Clark
928 Roanoke Dr
Springfield IL 62702

Call Sign: K9BJ
Stephen D Clark
928 Roanoke Dr
Springfield IL 62702

Call Sign: K9YL
C Lee Affrunti
3309 Robbins Rd 184
Springfield IL 62704

Call Sign: K9GDS
Erin A Affrunti
3309 Robbins Rd 184
Springfield IL 62704

Call Sign: K9NT
Robert E Affrunti
3309 Robbins Rd 184
Springfield IL 62704

Call Sign: KA9ELI
David D Denson
24 Ross Dr
Springfield IL 62707

Call Sign: KC9OEP
Bradley L Bales
55 Roundtable Rd
Springfield IL 62204

Call Sign: KB9SQN
William J Vaughn
2416 S 10th
Springfield IL 62703

Call Sign: KB9ZFC
William J Vaughn
2416 S 10th
Springfield IL 62703

Call Sign: W9WJV
William J Vaughn
2416 S 10th

Springfield IL 62703

Call Sign: KC9SCK
Nicholas R Skaggs III
2317 S 10th St
Springfield IL 62703

Call Sign: KB9ZVG
David A Vaughn
2416 S 10th St
Springfield IL 62703

Call Sign: KY9D
William J Bermel
3110 S 13th
Springfield IL 627034121

Call Sign: KB9AAX
James W Riba
2404 S 14th
Springfield IL 62703

Call Sign: KB9AAW
Jasen L Riba
2404 S 14th
Springfield IL 62703

Call Sign: KB9HJX
Melissa S Riba
2404 S 14th
Springfield IL 62703

Call Sign: KE9ZU
Harry E Beams Jr
2201 S 14th St
Springfield IL 62703

Call Sign: KB9DPM
Sandra L Riba
2404 S 14th St
Springfield IL 62703

Call Sign: KC9SZT
Jean S Killen
2735 S 14th St Lot 4
Springfield IL 62703

Call Sign: K1SMA
Jean S Killen

2735 S 14th St Lot 4
Springfield IL 62703

Call Sign: KC9ITU
Craig T Wadsworth
1530 S 15th St
Springfield IL 62703

Call Sign: N9PIP
David M Cotner
1627 S 15th St
Springfield IL 62703

Call Sign: KB9SUN
Becky A Hermes
2160 S 15th St
Springfield IL 627033639

Call Sign: KB9SQK
Charles M Hermes
2160 S 15th St
Springfield IL 627033639

Call Sign: KB9PML
Clyde M Hughes
2160 S 19th St
Springfield IL 62703

Call Sign: WD9CZJ
Emily J Compton
1707 S 1st
Springfield IL 62704

Call Sign: W9ADF
Ramon L Taylor
1925 S 1st St
Springfield IL 62704

Call Sign: N9IBN
Karl W Kochman
3157 S 1st St
Springfield IL 62703

Call Sign: KA9UTS
Roland L Marr
1840 S 2nd
Springfield IL 62704

Call Sign: KC9HCI

Kenneth R Gaul
1424 S 2nd St
Springfield IL 62704

Call Sign: AB9HN
Kevin E Gaul
1424 S 2nd St
Springfield IL 62704

Call Sign: N9HHI
Kevin E Gaul
1424 S 2nd St
Springfield IL 62704

Call Sign: WD9GMY
Bradley J Sommer
1716 S 2nd St
Springfield IL 62704

Call Sign: KA9ZZX
Bonnie J Gaul
1424 S 2nd St
Springfield IL 62704

Call Sign: KA9HFS
Steven L Martin
3424 S 4th
Springfield IL 62703

Call Sign: KC9BMT
Shaun P Curry
3024 S 4th St
Springfield IL 62703

Call Sign: KC9LAK
Jefrrey R Hamor
2129 S 5th St
Springfield IL 62703

Call Sign: KB9NXL
Martin S Wilcoxson
2304 S 5th St
Springfield IL 62703

Call Sign: AB9KT
Martin S Wilcoxson
2304 S 5th St
Springfield IL 62703

Call Sign: W9TBZ
Fred H Anderson
3210 S 5th St
Springfield IL 62703

Call Sign: K9CZ
Stephen E Beckwith
3344 S 5th St
Springfield IL 627034730

Call Sign: W9ABI
Edwin P Vaughn
2417 S 7th
Springfield IL 62703

Call Sign: WA9LOU
Theodore J Baer
909 S 8th
Springfield IL 62703

Call Sign: KC9UVC
Adron A Sanders
2304 S 8th
Springfield IL 62703

Call Sign: KA9AYT
Gilbert M Peck
2413 S 8th
Springfield IL 62703

Call Sign: KB9KZW
Pamela J Scott
2444 S 8th St
Springfield IL 62703

Call Sign: KB9OVM
William H Spindel
2444 S 8th St
Springfield IL 62703

Call Sign: KA9JFT
Helen J Ballard
2524 S 8th St
Springfield IL 62703

Call Sign: WD9IOX
Maurice A Ballard Jr
2524 S 8th St
Springfield IL 62703

Call Sign: KB9NQT
James K Zerkle
1526 S Bates
Springfield IL 62704

Call Sign: WA9WKN
James C Suttie III
2621 S College St
Springfield IL 62704

Call Sign: KB9KAC
James M Oliver
1501 S Douglas Ave
Springfield IL 62704

Call Sign: K9LJB
Roger B Whitaker
2944 S Douglas Ave
Springfield IL 62704

Call Sign: KB9MGD
Ralph S Killion
200 S English Ave
Springfield IL 62704

Call Sign: KA9OEH
Frank D Beyer
612 S Glenwood Ave
Springfield IL 62704

Call Sign: W9JSX
Fred N Valerius
2515 S Glenwood Ave
Springfield IL 62704

Call Sign: W9PNO
Herman Hovey
2432 S Grand Ave E
Springfield IL 62703

Call Sign: WB9PID
Charles W Hershey
325 S Illinois Ave
Springfield IL 62704

Call Sign: N9LXI
Michael T Cavanagh
823 S Illinois St

Springfield IL 62704

Call Sign: W9BLG
Raymond E Taylor
2227A S Koke Mill Rd
Springfield IL 62707

Call Sign: KB9RCX
Travis R Scroggin
2800 S Lincoln Ave
Springfield IL 62704

Call Sign: WA9APC
Michael W Becker
1921 S Lowell Ave
Springfield IL 62704

Call Sign: KC9LAJ
Stevie A Roberts
2220 S Lowell Ave
Springfield IL 62704

Call Sign: N9MGW
Pete D Gonzales
2313 S Lowell Ave
Springfield IL 62704

Call Sign: WA9RBX
Donald M Eastep
109 S Mac Arthur Blvd
Springfield IL 62704

Call Sign: W9RBX
Donald N Eastep
109 S Mac Arthur Blvd
Springfield IL 62704

Call Sign: KA9HGJ
David T Nauman
2015 S Noble
Springfield IL 62704

Call Sign: KC9PYP
Teri L Mcdonough
127 S Oaklane Rd
Springfield IL 62712

Call Sign: K9TLM
Teri L Mcdonough

127 S Oaklane Rd
Springfield IL 62712

Call Sign: W9SPI
Capital Area Amateur Radio
Emergency Response Team
127 S Oaklane Rd
Springfield IL 62712

Call Sign: N9PUZ
Timothy P Mc Donough
127 S Oaklane Rd
Springfield IL 62712

Call Sign: WB9KTY
Glenn W Weatherford
650 S Oaklane Rd
Springfield IL 62712

Call Sign: KA9TEN
Russell L Spann
3320 S Park
Springfield IL 62704

Call Sign: KD9QZ
Matthew E Teeter
810 S Park Ave
Springfield IL 62704

Call Sign: KC9EVM
Thomas T Daywalt
3433 S Park Ave
Springfield IL 62704

Call Sign: KC9QWC
Charlene A Falco
1619 S Pasfield
Springfield IL 62704

Call Sign: N9PIM
Steven N White
1722 S Pasfield
Springfield IL 62704

Call Sign: KB9LYK
William B Richards
2822 S Price Ave
Springfield IL 62704

Call Sign: NL7NK
John L Mc Bride
1201 S Spring St
Springfield IL 62704

Call Sign: WD9IFF
Forrest G Hester III
2417 S State
Springfield IL 62704

Call Sign: KB9THX
Jonathan K Myers
1728 S State St
Springfield IL 627044012

Call Sign: K9YMT
H William Lipsmire
1905 S State St
Springfield IL 62704

Call Sign: KC9ABH
Erin A Affrunti
2743 S Veterans Pkwy 184
Springfield IL 62704

Call Sign: KB9LYP
Gustav A J Speder
818 S Walnut
Springfield IL 62704

Call Sign: KC9KLY
Donald A St Lawrence
2028 S Walnut
Springfield IL 62704

Call Sign: KA9CVF
Charles E Harris
2317 S Walnut
Springfield IL 62704

Call Sign: W9YUK
George F Finney
2500 S Walnut
Springfield IL 627044547

Call Sign: N9ZTK
Merle L King
1708 S Walnut St
Springfield IL 627044046

Call Sign: KC9RNH
Stephen S Ingerson
1908.5 S Whittier Ave
Springfield IL 62704

Call Sign: N9SHK
David F Pershing
2601 Sage Ln
Springfield IL 62707

Call Sign: KC9QWE
Chad M Gray
4001 Sandhill Rd 219
Springfield IL 62702

Call Sign: KD9ND
Jerry L Rutledge
41 Sarah Ave
Springfield IL 62703

Call Sign: K9HHQ
Henrietta Bunger
3616 Satinwood Dr
Springfield IL 62712

Call Sign: N9QJP
Mary H Selk
3324 Saxony Rd
Springfield IL 61703

Call Sign: N9PYF
James A Selk
3324 Saxony Rd
Springfield IL 62703

Call Sign: WA9OGI
Alford E Zick Sr
1900 Scarbrough Rd N
Springfield IL 62702

Call Sign: WB9OTV
Ronald E Fargusson
2748 Selkirk Rd
Springfield IL 62702

Call Sign: WB6GYR
Terry D Nitzel
1652 Seven Pines Rd Apt 110

Springfield IL 627045733

Call Sign: N9LJH
James A Young II
1670 Seven Pines Rd Apt 303
Springfield IL 62704

Call Sign: KD4DLL
Daniel O Butzirus
1508 Seven Pines Rd Apt L
Springfield IL 62704

Call Sign: N9ZJL
Joseph L Utter
1528 Seven Pines Rd F
Springfield IL 62704

Call Sign: KA9UQF
Ronald A Bernet
12 Shetland Dr
Springfield IL 62702

Call Sign: W8LFX
David D Hyde
1326 Shiloh Dr
Springfield IL 62704

Call Sign: KC9KMJ
William A Gray
1821 South St Ct
Springfield IL 62703

Call Sign: W9PXP
Frank H Finney Jr
900 Southwind Rd Apt 136
Springfield IL 627035371

Call Sign: W9YCE
Harold M Switzer
900 Southwind Rd Apt 340
Springfield IL 62703

Call Sign: KB9RW
Stephen J Bissler
2500 St James Rd
Springfield IL 627079736

Call Sign: KA9WRR
William Bain

2960 Stanton Ave
Springfield IL 62703

Call Sign: N8UUM
Lawrence M Clair
13 Stelte Ln
Springfield IL 62702

Call Sign: KC9EBW
Edmund L Martin
2904 Stokebridge Rd
Springfield IL 62702

Call Sign: KB9BIV
Dennis W Durnyahn
2617 Stratford Dr
Springfield IL 62704

Call Sign: K9TXH
Howard E Carr
44 Sutton Pl
Springfield IL 62703

Call Sign: K9GHL
Howard W Feldman
154 Tamarisk Dr
Springfield IL 62704

Call Sign: KX9DX
Richard L Pile
620 Tecumseh Trl
Springfield IL 62711

Call Sign: KB9SQL
Tina M Pile
620 Tecumseh Trl
Springfield IL 62711

Call Sign: KA9AWE
Daniel L Stark
275 Trillium Ln Rr 5
Springfield IL 62707

Call Sign: KC9VCO
Steven M Young
7512 Tumbleweed Trl
Springfield IL 62707

Call Sign: KB9NHU

Trever C Trader
4509 Venetian Dr
Springfield IL 62703

Call Sign: KA9UBC
Jeffrey D Palmisano
105 Veneto Villa
Springfield IL 62703

Call Sign: N9XFV
Barry R De Nardo
1819 Vernon
Springfield IL 62704

Call Sign: W9PS
Joseph C Perkinton
3569 Vestige Trl
Springfield IL 62707

Call Sign: WD9ALN
Linda S Perkinton
3569 Vestige Trl Rr 2
Springfield IL 62707

Call Sign: KC9QVZ
Kymberlie Y Hartman
1640 W Adams St
Springfield IL 62704

Call Sign: KC9CSG
Qaisar Khan
418 W Canedy
Springfield IL 62704

Call Sign: KC9KMH
Karen S Dinsmore
1620 W Capitol
Springfield IL 62704

Call Sign: AF9D
Robert T Dinsmore
1620 W Capitol Ave
Springfield IL 62704

Call Sign: KA9VYN
Kenneth W Owens
1045 W Centre St
Springfield IL 62704

Call Sign: WA9ARY
Charles R Brown
111 W Cordelia
Springfield IL 627034646

Call Sign: WA9UBE
Leo Bartelt
422 W Elliott Ave
Springfield IL 62702

Call Sign: KC9BZB
Brad A Taylor
1411 W Fayette Ave
Springfield IL 62704

Call Sign: KC9CWS
David Bruce Jr
1607 W Glen Ave
Springfield IL 62704

Call Sign: WB9YYJ
Robert D Florence
1306 W Glenn Ave
Springfield IL 62704

Call Sign: KB9KAK
David L Bruce Sr
1607 W Glenn Ave
Springfield IL 62704

Call Sign: AB9YG
David L Bruce Sr
1607 W Glenn Ave
Springfield IL 62704

Call Sign: KC9GQQ
Dennis J Brown
1645 W Glenn Ave
Springfield IL 627044824

Call Sign: N9YFP
David B Glass
1021 W Governor 19
Springfield IL 62704

Call Sign: KC9TKQ
Eric Wenthe
1021 W Governor Apt 1
Springfield IL 62704

Call Sign: KC9ALB
Edwin A Holt
37 W Hazel Dell Ln
Springfield IL 62703

Call Sign: KA9HVO
Richard A Mc Connell
4220 W Jefferson
Springfield IL 62711

Call Sign: W9TRC
John P Anderson
1508 W Lake Shore Dr
Springfield IL 627129570

Call Sign: W0ELD
Daniel B Morehead
2115 W Lawrence
Springfield IL 62704

Call Sign: KA9BYG
Janet S Peecher
2119 W Lawrence
Springfield IL 62704

Call Sign: W9TNG
Donald D Broden
2209 W Lawrence Ave
Springfield IL 627041418

Call Sign: N9CNK
Keith E Ushman
808 W Monroe Apt 5
Springfield IL 62704

Call Sign: KC9KFM
Mark D Pitchford
421 W Reynolds
Springfield IL 62702

Call Sign: N9PIO
Michael S Smith
108 W Reynolds Apt B
Springfield IL 62702

Call Sign: W9FSK
Charles Barton
2120 W Washington

Springfield IL 62702

Call Sign: W9FFH
Robert E Eberhardt
2251 W Washington
Springfield IL 62702

Call Sign: N9ONH
Allan G Larson
2430 Westchester Blvd
Springfield IL 62704

Call Sign: KB9SQH
Jackie L Follis
2116 Westview Dr
Springfield IL 627042166

Call Sign: KB9FAA
Jackie L Follis
2116 Westview Dr
Springfield IL 627042166

Call Sign: KB9UDX
Saralyn Follis
2116 Westview Dr
Springfield IL 627042166

Call Sign: KA9LBI
Larry A Lichtenberger
6302 Westwind Dr
Springfield IL 627116157

Call Sign: KB9BHN
Cynthia M Scott
94 White Birch
Springfield IL 62707

Call Sign: KA9CKI
Taylor C Scott III
94 White Birch
Springfield IL 62707

Call Sign: KA9TVH
Carol M Allen
113 White Pine Dr
Springfield IL 62712

Call Sign: WD9IDS
Lee F Davis

130 White Pine Dr
Springfield IL 62712

Call Sign: N9ONI
Avram J Peters
304 Whitefield Rd
Springfield IL 62704

Call Sign: KA9UDT
Philip E Chiles
313 Whitefield Rd
Springfield IL 62704

Call Sign: W9QZJ
Harry C Wilson
2020 Whittier
Springfield IL 62704

Call Sign: WA9NSX
John C Stuemke
1112 Wickford Dr
Springfield IL 627042126

Call Sign: WB0BUF
Karen L Hoelzer
1303 Wiggins
Springfield IL 62704

Call Sign: W9HDA
James C Chapel Jr
2349 Wiggins Ave
Springfield IL 627044372

Call Sign: KB9TMU
Michael J Harris
2218 Wilbur Rd
Springfield IL 62707

Call Sign: KB9KAE
Scott O Phillips
1551 Williams Blvd
Springfield IL 62704

Call Sign: KC9HLM
John T Peters
1115 Willow Brook Dr
Springfield IL 62711

Call Sign: N0NNJ

Debra A Peters
1115 Willowbrook Dr
Springfield IL 62711

Call Sign: WD0CMB
Timothy J Peters
1115 Willowbrook Dr
Springfield IL 62711

Call Sign: W9WHD
Richard W Tutt
3721 Windshire Dr
Springfield IL 62704

Call Sign: KE9LI
Susan J Pike
22 Windsor Rd
Springfield IL 62702

Call Sign: W9YJF
Charles M Barber
2217 Winnebago Dr
Springfield IL 62702

Call Sign: N9XZB
Donald F Fadden
1836 Wolfe
Springfield IL 62702

Call Sign: WD9EEK
Dennis E Grim
1516 Wood Mill Dr
Springfield IL 62704

Call Sign: KB9SQI
Gregory W Davis
3440 Woodhaven Dr
Springfield IL 62707

Call Sign: W9PLS
Robert M Smith
2930 Woodward Ave
Springfield IL 62703

Call Sign: KC9KT
William Sapp Jr
2725 Wordsworth Dr
Springfield IL 62711

Call Sign: K9VWM
Preston H Kidd
2656 Yale Blvd
Springfield IL 62703

Call Sign: KA9BKV
Thomas B Bannon
266 Yeoman Dr
Springfield IL 627045236

Call Sign: KB9ESB
William T Kabisch
Springfield IL 62705

Call Sign: K9DUE
Charles L Richey
Springfield IL 62705

Call Sign: KC9KNJ
David E Risley
Springfield IL 62705

Call Sign: KC9EGO
Edgar J Riley
Springfield IL 62705

Call Sign: N9RPO
Tony A Huddleston
Springfield IL 62707

Call Sign: KA9WFY
Curtis M Swanson
Springfield IL 62708

Call Sign: N9MZL
Paul E Woolsey
Springfield IL 62708

Call Sign: WB6WPQ
Charles J Phillips
Springfield IL 62791

Call Sign: N9ZPD
Debra A Foster
109 6th St
Standard IL 61363

Call Sign: KB9JZX
Denise S Jones
221 8th St
Standard IL 61363

Call Sign: N9TOC
Kenneth L Jones
221 8th St
Standard IL 61363

Call Sign: KC9LZK
Bob Hunter
Standard IL 61363

Call Sign: KC9ANP
Dareck D Otto
12347 N 400 E Rd
Stanford IL 61774

Call Sign: WA9BIX
Carol S Nafziger
405 North St
Stanford IL 61774

Call Sign: W9AHQ
Harry J Greuel
Stanford IL 61774

Call Sign: KD9RS
William E Dodge
Stanford IL 617740045

Call Sign: WH6BBA
Barbara A Brown
9350 Albrecht Rd
Staunton IL 62088

Call Sign: WH6BBB
Leonard W Brown Sr
9350 Albrecht Rd
Staunton IL 62088

Call Sign: NZ9Q
Glenn M Sies
303 E Lafayette
Staunton IL 62088

Call Sign: AB9LM
James R Shrum
705 E Main
Staunton IL 62088

Call Sign: KA9VYH
Steven R Allen
716 E Pearl St
Staunton IL 62088

Call Sign: KB9NDP
Frank A Laurent
219 Harris
Staunton IL 62088

Call Sign: KC9RPE
Frederick W Partridge Sr
852 N Union St
Staunton IL 62088

Call Sign: K9ZC
Naqro-Central Division Club
22751 Ruschaupt Rd
Staunton IL 62088

Call Sign: KC9OTJ
Bradley E Coppedge
807 W 5th St
Staunton IL 62088

Call Sign: KC9ADV
James E Harmer
1145 W 6th
Staunton IL 62088

Call Sign: WA9HSK
William H Morris
229 W Henry St
Staunton IL 62088

Call Sign: KC9FFX
James R Shrum
835 W Myrtle Ave
Staunton IL 62088

Call Sign: KD8KVO
John E Nalezyty
513 W Spring St
Staunton IL 620881743

FCC Amateur Radio Licenses in Steeleville

Call Sign: KA9PDW
Eric L Hamilton
509 N John St
Steeleville IL 62288

Call Sign: KC9GCE
Don Williams ARC
1383 N Sparta St
Steeleville IL 62288

Call Sign: K9BSS
Don Williams ARC
1383 N Sparta St
Steeleville IL 62288

Call Sign: K9SR
Dennis S Ramsey
1383 N Sparta St
Steeleville IL 622881203

Call Sign: KB9KGL
Jeff J Eaton
6064 Oak Grove Rd
Steeleville IL 62288

Call Sign: KB0JD
Alan W Janneke
604 S Charles St
Steeleville IL 622882013

Call Sign: KA0SCX
Donna K Janneke
604 S Charles St
Steeleville IL 622882013

Call Sign: AA9JN
Larry K Kerley
5844 SR 4
Steeleville IL 62288

Call Sign: N9UI
Larry K Kerley
5844 SR 4
Steeleville IL 62288

Call Sign: N9MKV
Vivian W Kerley
5844 SR 4
Steeleville IL 62288

Call Sign: N9CQH
Lex A Kilgore
201 W 1st St
Steeleville IL 62288

FCC Amateur Radio Licenses in Stelle

Call Sign: KC8THF
David C Sanders
116 Crescent Ln
Stelle IL 609195500

Call Sign: KC9FDK
David C Sanders
116 Crescent Ln
Stelle IL 609195500

FCC Amateur Radio Licenses in Sterling

Call Sign: N9SRG
Craig E Aschbrenner
2004 11th Ave
Sterling IL 61081

Call Sign: KB9EEK
Kurt E Glazier
716 12th Ave
Sterling IL 61081

Call Sign: N9MMI
Anita L Little
407 15th Ave
Sterling IL 61081

Call Sign: K9EEH
Richard A Little
407 15th Ave

Sterling IL 61081

Call Sign: N9SEA
Hasmukh P Shah
3302 15th Ave
Sterling IL 61081

Call Sign: KB9EEI
Jigar H Shah
3302 15th Ave
Sterling IL 61081

Call Sign: KB9GIW
Nishu H Shah
3302 15th Ave
Sterling IL 61081

Call Sign: KB9GJG
Vivek O Shah
3302 15th Ave
Sterling IL 61081

Call Sign: N9SRC
Steven E Michel
2510 16th Ave
Sterling IL 61081

Call Sign: KB9GFU
Cynthia L Lasater
405A 16th Ave
Sterling IL 61081

Call Sign: KA9SEO
Robert L Lasater
405 16th Ave Apt A
Sterling IL 61081

Call Sign: KA6VJU
Jerrold V Moore
1603 17th Ave
Sterling IL 61081

Call Sign: WB9ARR
Howard A Clayton
1715 17th Ave
Sterling IL 61081

Call Sign: KA9GPW
Doreen E Gryder

1808 17th Ave
Sterling IL 61081

Call Sign: KA9GPV
James D Gryder
1808 17th Ave
Sterling IL 61081

Call Sign: KA9CWG
Barbara J Hayen
1613 18th Ave
Sterling IL 61081

Call Sign: WD9EHQ
Dale A Hayen
1613 18th Ave
Sterling IL 61081

Call Sign: WB9RVY
Kenneth A Weissenburger
1703 18th Ave
Sterling IL 610811670

Call Sign: KA9GPT
Dolores J Weissenburger
1703 18th Ave
Sterling IL 610811670

Call Sign: K9BEF
Edward P Johnson
111 19th Ave
Sterling IL 610813008

Call Sign: K9HQJ
Pearl M Johnson
111 19th Ave
Sterling IL 610813008

Call Sign: KA9IMF
Barry E Montague Sr
1902 19th Ave
Sterling IL 61081

Call Sign: N9NDJ
Joyce G Mc Murry
1511 1st Ave
Sterling IL 61081

Call Sign: WB9DNR

Warren P Mc Murry
1511 1st Ave
Sterling IL 61081

Call Sign: N9ZAR
Eric H Zigler
1514 1st Ave
Sterling IL 61081

Call Sign: N9ZAU
Paul A Zigler
1514 1st Ave
Sterling IL 61081

Call Sign: N9ZLM
David F Zigler
1514 1st Ave
Sterling IL 61081

Call Sign: WA9YSP
George F Jacobs
1801 22 Ave
Sterling IL 61081

Call Sign: KC9FPK
Steven P Mcpherson
711 2nd Ave
Sterling IL 61081

Call Sign: WD9GTC
Steven P Mcpherson
711 2nd Ave
Sterling IL 61081

Call Sign: KC9FMJ
Andrew P Young
1202 2nd Ave
Sterling IL 61081

Call Sign: K9APY
Andrew P Young
1202 2nd Ave
Sterling IL 61081

Call Sign: N9INY
Bob W Dunsworth
1910 3rd Ave Apt F
Sterling IL 61081

Call Sign: KB9ZWD
Aneela L Qureshi
605 4th Ave
Sterling IL 61081

Call Sign: WA9OJZ
Gary L Hahn
2304 4th Ave
Sterling IL 610811307

Call Sign: N9TCC
Ron Haahr
102 5th Ave
Sterling IL 61081

Call Sign: KB9YGN
Louis A Ramirez Jr
610 6th Ave
Sterling IL 61081

Call Sign: K9RQK
Dale L Smith
2816 6th Ave R3
Sterling IL 61081

Call Sign: K9APD
Edward K Fisher
506 7th Ave
Sterling IL 61081

Call Sign: WB9YQM
Kenneth E Murphy
911 8th Ave
Sterling IL 61081

Call Sign: N9QQV
Timothy J Callahan
402 Ave A Apt 108
Sterling IL 61081

Call Sign: KB9GJF
Nathan C Rahn
309 Ave F
Sterling IL 61081

Call Sign: W9KPT
I Otto Rhoades
1801 Ave G
Sterling IL 61081

Call Sign: N9ZLO
Shelly M Timbs
408 Ave I
Sterling IL 61081

Call Sign: N9LVM
Laurie M Sherman
25873 Capp Rd
Sterling IL 61081

Call Sign: KB9APW
Lloyd C Sherman
25873 Capp Rd
Sterling IL 61081

Call Sign: KC9DEZ
Philip E Hull
27129 Capp Rd
Sterling IL 61081

Call Sign: KC9JAX
Calvin Nutt
24710 Como Rd
Sterling IL 61781

Call Sign: N9AWZ
Donald L Rastede
1014 Crestview Rd
Sterling IL 61081

Call Sign: KC9IXE
Frederick W Rastede
1014 Crestview Rd
Sterling IL 61081

Call Sign: KC9BCA
Lori A Wedekind
1005 Douglas Dr
Sterling IL 61081

Call Sign: KB9SWE
William D Wedekind
1005 Douglas Dr
Sterling IL 61081

Call Sign: WA9KZW
John W Hohler
1401 Douglas Dr

Sterling IL 610811833

Call Sign: N9SRH
John H Wardell
806 E 15th St
Sterling IL 61081

Call Sign: KC9LED
James J Maloney
808 E 15th St
Sterling IL 61081

Call Sign: K9HKS
James A Bellini
817 E 15th St
Sterling IL 61081

Call Sign: KC9HGX
Angel R Sierra
810 E 16th St
Sterling IL 61081

Call Sign: KC9HFC
Roberto A Sierra Sierra
810 E 16th St
Sterling IL 61081

Call Sign: WB9RZQ
Roger M Polzin
1206 E 18th St
Sterling IL 61081

Call Sign: KA0JNK
Jean L Cogdall
1402 E 18th St
Sterling IL 61081

Call Sign: KC9KYU
Dick A Abbas
1406 E 18th St
Sterling IL 61081

Call Sign: KB9TTV
Raymond E Ricklefs
624 E 19th St
Sterling IL 61081

Call Sign: KB9EEJ
Derek J Whiting

1407 E 19th St
Sterling IL 61081

Call Sign: N9SEM
Neal E Shipley
3406 E 19th St
Sterling IL 61081

Call Sign: N9SHO
Elisa J Gatz
1202 E 20th St
Sterling IL 61081

Call Sign: KC9FMM
Nickolaus W Dirks
1401 E 24th Pl
Sterling IL 61031

Call Sign: KA9UKN
Peter A Yoeckel
215 E 25th St Apt 220
Sterling IL 61081

Call Sign: KC9NEP
Peter A Yoeckel
215 E 25th St Apt 220
Sterling IL 61081

Call Sign: K9UWD
Cled R Yochum
1403 E 28th St Rr 5
Sterling IL 61081

Call Sign: N9ZAM
Nick J Schultz
1711 E 2nd St
Sterling IL 61081

Call Sign: KA9NIH
Kelly T Babin
1007 E 4th St
Sterling IL 61081

Call Sign: N9JTF
Timothy M Mangan
1906 E 6th St
Sterling IL 61081

Call Sign: KC9VPK

Michael J Trischan
4313 Emerson
Sterling IL 61081

Call Sign: K9WNU
Stuart Y Keller
23737 Emerson Rd
Sterling IL 610819170

Call Sign: KB9MYJ
Shawn C Bailey
24794 Front St
Sterling IL 61081

Call Sign: WA9BSO
John C Ordean
24869 Front St Como
Sterling IL 61081

Call Sign: N9GEY
Don F Stranberg Jr
27428 Fulfs Rd
Sterling IL 61081

Call Sign: KC9ILC
Salvador Torres
30628 Genesee Rd
Sterling IL 61081

Call Sign: K9LAC
James C Wesner
611 Green Ct
Sterling IL 61081

Call Sign: KC9RSU
Gpaul A Zollinger
804 Greenridge Dr
Sterling IL 61081

Call Sign: KC9ROX
Timothy B Zollinger
804 Greenridge Dr
Sterling IL 61081

Call Sign: KB9GIV
Keith A Potter
702 Gregden Shores
Sterling IL 61081

Call Sign: KC9OYV
Joseph D Henderson Jr
904 Gregdon Shores Dr
Sterling IL 61081

Call Sign: N9FQC
Larry A Horner Sr
1105 Harvey Dr
Sterling IL 61081

Call Sign: KE9EE
Margo A Horner
1105 Harvey Dr
Sterling IL 61081

Call Sign: KA9UJW
Larry A Horner Jr
1111 Harvey Dr
Sterling IL 61081

Call Sign: KB9GIU
George W Matthiessen
21496 Hazel Rd
Sterling IL 61081

Call Sign: KB9LKI
Erin M Dunphy
1723 Heritage Dr
Sterling IL 61081

Call Sign: N9OQQ
Christopher M Mueller
1726 Heritage Dr
Sterling IL 610819694

Call Sign: N9OQP
James M Mueller
1726 Heritage Dr
Sterling IL 610819694

Call Sign: KC9FMH
Ben J Beach
24209 Hillcrest Dr
Sterling IL 61081

Call Sign: K9JZ
Mervin J Zeigler Jr
20261 Hoover Rd
Sterling IL 61081

Call Sign: WA9SJE
Sterling High School ARC
20261 Hoover Rd
Sterling IL 61081

Call Sign: KB9ETA
Kollin J Patten
1501 Howard St
Sterling IL 61081

Call Sign: W0ORW
Nick Geer
24040 Kane Dr
Sterling IL 610819203

Call Sign: N9TNN
Thomas E Anderson
15721 Lakeside Dr
Sterling IL 61081

Call Sign: KB9JQE
Leland J Buntjer
15819 Lakeside Dr
Sterling IL 61081

Call Sign: KB9GJH
Tim L Reynolds
15820 Lakeside Dr
Sterling IL 61081

Call Sign: KA9PYD
William T Cushman
12645 Lawrence
Sterling IL 61081

Call Sign: KC9SSK
Nicholas M Breed
3249 Mineral Springs Rd
Sterling IL 61081

Call Sign: WD9INT
George L Arno
22180 Moline Rd
Sterling IL 610818889

Call Sign: KB9GIX
John T Moore
2202 Moonlight Bay Ln

Sterling IL 61081

Call Sign: N9SRL
Jack E Stout
1784 Mound Hill Rd
Sterling IL 61081

Call Sign: KR9Q
Jack E Stout
1784 Mound Hill Rd
Sterling IL 61081

Call Sign: KB9PWL
Dale E Bertolozzi
807 North St
Sterling IL 61081

Call Sign: KA9ZGK
Thomas J Fredericks
24950 Penrose Rd
Sterling IL 61081

Call Sign: KC9VDG
Alan G Fennell
22417 Polo Rd
Sterling IL 61081

Call Sign: KB9QPN
Bredon R Clay
22417 Polo Rd
Sterling IL 61081

Call Sign: N9PEH
Allan K Johnson
24471 Science Ridge Rd
Sterling IL 61081

Call Sign: KB9MYI
Dennis J Nolan
1308 Sinnissippi Rd
Sterling IL 61081

Call Sign: KI5WF
Stuart H Myster
1719 Timber Dr
Sterling IL 61081

Call Sign: WB9YHC
John J Urbaniak

308 W 13th St
Sterling IL 610812210

Call Sign: KB9JME
Kary L Lukancic
602 W 19th St
Sterling IL 610811168

Call Sign: K9RAR
Kenneth A Girardi
1411 W 21st St
Sterling IL 61081

Call Sign: KC9KYS
Richard C Snyder
1008 W 4th St
Sterling IL 61081

Call Sign: KC9PGW
Dale W Lindsley
1232 W 4th St
Sterling IL 61081

Call Sign: KC9LEC
Brad P Mcclellan
302 W 5th St
Sterling IL 61081

Call Sign: W9MEP
Sterling-Rock Falls Ars
Sterling IL 61081

Call Sign: KB9NGJ
Gregory R Nicol
Sterling IL 610810971

Call Sign: KA9ZII
Robert T Fielding Jr
Sterling IL 610818321

**FCC Amateur Radio
Licenses in Stewardson**

Call Sign: WA9HWH
Richard J Warren
Rr 1 Box 132
Stewardson IL 624639774

Call Sign: W9HWH

Richard J Warren
Rr 1 Box 132
Stewardson IL 624639774

Call Sign: KA9YVY
Daryl G Mc Cormick
Rr 1 Box 23D
Stewardson IL 62463

Call Sign: N9QHE
Shirley M Mc Cormick
R 1 Box 24
Stewardson IL 62463

Call Sign: WD9DOX
Arlyn W Mc Cormick
Rfd 1 Box 24
Stewardson IL 62463

Call Sign: KB9WDQ
Clint R Mc Cormick
Rr 1 Box 25
Stewardson IL 62463

Call Sign: WB0RUJ
Robert E Bennett
314 E S 1st
Stewardson IL 62463

Call Sign: KA9MHW
Keith W Wortham
205 N Cherry St Apt 2
Stewardson IL 624631122

Call Sign: KC9BUO
Tina M Wortham
205 N Cherry St Apt 2
Stewardson IL 624631122

Call Sign: KA9YVU
Ronald E Boldt
402 W North St
Stewardson IL 62463

**FCC Amateur Radio
Licenses in Stillman Valley**

Call Sign: W15B
Terry W Temple

6885 E Bluegrass Trl
Stillman Valley IL 610849001

Call Sign: K9MQG
Bruce C Roe
5719 E Skinner Rd
Stillman Valley IL 61084

Call Sign: WZ9Q
James R Morgart
5881 E Skinner Rd
Stillman Valley IL 61084

Call Sign: N9MQT
Daniel A Drake
8210 Hales Corner Rd
Stillman Valley IL 61084

Call Sign: KA2CNL
Dennis Kent
8487 N Canary Dr
Stillman Valley IL 61084

Call Sign: KC9ETF
Frank W Zimmerman
9640 N Girl Scout Rd
Stillman Valley IL 61084

Call Sign: KC9NEX
Gordon L Seaman
8341 N Pheasant Trl
Stillman Valley IL 61084

Call Sign: KB9EEL
La Dedra L Marcum
6614 O Hare Dr
Stillman Valley IL 61084

Call Sign: KF9CN
Steven J Marcum
6614 Ohare Dr
Stillman Valley IL 61084

Call Sign: N9KX
Steven J Marcum
6614 Ohare Dr
Stillman Valley IL 61084

Call Sign: KB9ULE

Cory M Tveit
Stillman Valley IL 61084

Call Sign: WB9VLK
Diana L White
Stillman Valley IL 610840015

Call Sign: NM9I
Diana L White
Stillman Valley IL 610840015

Call Sign: N9LXO
Robert N White Jr
Stillman Valley IL 610840015

FCC Amateur Radio Licenses in Stockton

Call Sign: KC9LEE
Steve R Holesinger
13211 E Canyon Rd
Stockton IL 61085

Call Sign: KC9HFE
Sharon R Hasting
13216 E Krise Rd
Stockton IL 61085

Call Sign: KE9PS
Galen R Heid
125 N Main St
Stockton IL 61085

Call Sign: KC9VJA
William P Zigmont
505 S Ward St
Stockton IL 61085

Call Sign: N9ZYB
Brian G Gallagher
116 W High Ave
Stockton IL 61085

FCC Amateur Radio Licenses in Stonefort

Call Sign: WD9BAA
Donald E Mathis
300 Beagle Rd

Stonefort IL 629871405

Call Sign: KC9AYF
Noel F Clore
1070 Old Town Rd
Stonefort IL 62987

Call Sign: W9NFC
Noel F Clore
1070 Old Town Rd
Stonefort IL 62987

Call Sign: KB9MWW
Jason W Murphy
10000 US 45 S
Stonefort IL 62987

FCC Amateur Radio Licenses in Strasburg

Call Sign: KC9THP
Daniel E Greuel
Rr 1 Box 260
Strasburg IL 62465

FCC Amateur Radio Licenses in Streator

Call Sign: W9GCQ
Robert J Bonebrake
213 11th St
Streator IL 61364

Call Sign: K9SAA
Stephan A Ahasic
111 7th St
Streator IL 61364

Call Sign: KC9NYW
Steve A Ahasic
111 7th St
Streator IL 61364

Call Sign: N9OUZ
Walter W Shepard
801 Bazore St
Streator IL 61364

Call Sign: W9CWP

John H Fornof
23 Boys Rd
Streator IL 61364

Call Sign: KA9BPW
Gene M Gehrts
1103 Carroll St
Streator IL 613642641

Call Sign: KC0LVE
Christopher A Hallam
1417 Cleveland Ave
Streator IL 61364

Call Sign: N9WXC
John J Renner
1427 Cleveland Ave
Streator IL 61364

Call Sign: W9OLF
Bernard G Mc Gurk
204 Colorado
Streator IL 61364

Call Sign: KC9CXU
Marjorie L Riddell
911 E 12th St
Streator IL 61364

Call Sign: WA9OMG
Myles W Van Duzer
1317 E 12th St
Streator IL 61364

Call Sign: K9CAU
Streator Radio Club
1317 E 12th St R6
Streator IL 61364

Call Sign: AB9XC
Pravinkumar P Anandan
305 E 14th St
Streator IL 61364

Call Sign: WB9ZAT
Theodore F Post
1713 E 1st St
Streator IL 61364

Call Sign: WB9YLJ
Elgie J Long
301 E 4th St
Streator IL 61364

Call Sign: W9JAU
Charles A Burt Jr
1516 E Bridge St
Streator IL 61364

Call Sign: N9PLH
Kurt L Plymire
1007 E Bronson St
Streator IL 61364

Call Sign: KB9VFX
Keith A Risley
1406 E Hickory St
Streator IL 61364

Call Sign: WB9VLY
Fletcher W Culver
508 E La Rue
Streator IL 61364

Call Sign: KA9IYW
Jacqueline L Culver
508 E La Rue
Streator IL 61364

Call Sign: KA9IGU
Andrew J Matas
918 E Lundy St
Streator IL 61364

Call Sign: N4WSH
Ronald A Good
2005 E Main St
Streator IL 61364

Call Sign: KE4MMD
Vickie L Good
2005 E Main St
Streator IL 61364

Call Sign: WB9VUG
Dwayne O Cagley
803 E Wilson St
Streator IL 61364

Call Sign: N9BQE
Jeffrey W Durbin
111 El Camino Ct
Streator IL 61364

Call Sign: N9PLM
James W Morris Jr
1705 Florence St
Streator IL 61364

Call Sign: KB9PUV
Thomas L Vagasky
607 Fuller Ave
Streator IL 61354

Call Sign: W9TLV
Thomas L Vagasky
607 Fuller Ave
Streator IL 61364

Call Sign: N9MVC
Eric A Jonland
1802 Golf View 1
Streator IL 61364

Call Sign: KB9ETI
Brian E Wicks
1004 Hall St
Streator IL 61364

Call Sign: KA9IGV
Michael R Pavlick
1707 Highland Pl
Streator IL 61364

Call Sign: KA9RQI
Margaret B Pavlick
1707 Highland Pl
Streator IL 613641717

Call Sign: WB9TQB
John D Abdnour
15 Imperial Dr
Streator IL 61364

Call Sign: KC9CIP
Brian L Dagraedt
Jefferson Oaks S 4th St Apt 10

Streator IL 61364

Call Sign: KB9ETF
John V Lamango
1106 Jessie Ave
Streator IL 61364

Call Sign: N9HT
Hutch Towner
1536 Little Main St
Streator IL 613642518

Call Sign: W9DKF
Talbert J Ruckman Jr
1305 Lowden Rd
Streator IL 61364

Call Sign: KB9UPQ
Brian C Phillips
1215 Madison St
Streator IL 61364

Call Sign: KA9NJB
Selvin W Trotter
2 Manhattan Dr
Streator IL 61364

Call Sign: K9MPU
Vernon G Pouk
1 Meredith Dr
Streator IL 61364

Call Sign: AA9WB
Robert L Kersmarki
31952 N 100 E Rd
Streator IL 61364

Call Sign: WA9GJI
Burton W Evans
1841 N 12th Rd
Streator IL 61364

Call Sign: KC9LHH
Dustin L Spray
2010 N Bloomington St A6
Streator IL 61364

Call Sign: KB9NPK
Ralph E Reed Jr

811 N Park St
Streator IL 61364

Call Sign: WB9ZBF
Leon Latham
616 N Sterling
Streator IL 61364

Call Sign: N9TYJ
Derek D Carter
1604 N Wasson
Streator IL 61364

Call Sign: WB9VLZ
James R Winn
806 N Wasson St
Streator IL 61364

Call Sign: KC9VID
Fred S Moore
1313 N Wasson St
Streator IL 61364

Call Sign: KA9BHH
Charles A Burt III
902 Painter
Streator IL 61364

Call Sign: W9LQ
John E Eilts
212 S 3rd Ave
Streator IL 61364

Call Sign: N9OUV
John E Eilts
212 S 3rd Ave
Streator IL 61364

Call Sign: KA9NKU
John B Fairburn
1625 S Bloomington St
Streator IL 61364

Call Sign: KB9UIU
Frederick E Beaulac
315 S Bloomington St Apt 8
Streator IL 61364

Call Sign: WB9YJD

Tim L Kmetz
1004 S Park
Streator IL 61364

Call Sign: WB9VLW
Francis S Kmetz
1004 S Park St
Streator IL 61364

Call Sign: KB9ETG
Sandra K Graham
1401 S Park St
Streator IL 61364

Call Sign: KC9RJ
Danny L Hillyer
1515 S Park St
Streator IL 61364

Call Sign: KB9MKU
Dennis L Smith
410 S Sterling St
Streator IL 61364

Call Sign: KA9IGO
Delores I Kenney
927 S Vermillion
Streator IL 61364

Call Sign: WB9TAC
James L Walker
32 Sequoia Dr
Streator IL 61364

Call Sign: KB9NOM
Shelley A Walker
32 Sequoia Dr
Streator IL 61364

Call Sign: KC9VHZ
Mary K Ford
1619 Sharon Rd
Streator IL 61364

Call Sign: KA9RQJ
Valentine P Butz
44 Stanton St
Streator IL 61364

Call Sign: WD9IDR
Chris M Pavlick
1519 Union St
Streator IL 61364

Call Sign: N9SDD
Darrin K Munter
206 W 10th St
Streator IL 61364

Call Sign: K7ZYM
Emmett V Sears
407 W 2nd St
Streator IL 61364

Call Sign: KB9KPQ
Dwayne D Alexander
427 W Frech St Lot 8
Streator IL 61364

Call Sign: KB9UPR
Timothy M Coplin
608 W Grant St
Streator IL 61364

Call Sign: WB9JNV
Delores M Hausaman
Streator IL 61364

Call Sign: N9PFF
Thomas L Talty
Streator IL 61364

Call Sign: KB9JTH
Candis M Zelenak
Streator IL 61364

Call Sign: KB9JTG
Donald E Zelenak Jr
Streator IL 61364

Call Sign: KB0AYA
Teresa M Sorensen
Rr 1 Box 18
Stronghurst IL 61480

Call Sign: N9MZW
Eric R Chockley
Stronghurst IL 61480

Call Sign: N9KKQ
Melvin J Kiper
29384 Bent Twig Trl
Sublette IL 61367

Call Sign: N9LZF
Pearl I Prate
29384 Bent Twig Trl Box 211
Sublette IL 61367

Call Sign: KB9WRU
Clarence E Zapf
341 Penkins Rd
Sublette IL 61367

Call Sign: KB9MAB
Henry L Robinson
1355 Sublette Rd
Sublette IL 613679506

Call Sign: N9KVW
Timothy E Bonnell
312 Virginia St
Sublette IL 61367

Call Sign: W9NTN
Timothy E Bonnell
202 W 1st St
Sublette IL 61367

Call Sign: N9CRI
Ronald B Melzer
604 W Santee
Sublette IL 61367

Call Sign: N9SBM
Dorothy C Bumpus
Sublette IL 61367

Call Sign: W9NTN
Harold L Bonnell Sr
Sublette IL 61367

Call Sign: N9LAR
Richard L Gilliam Sr
Sublette IL 61367

Call Sign: K0SQB
Robert H Le Vin
Sublette IL 61357

Call Sign: N9LPS
William J Bumpus Sr
Sublette IL 61367

Call Sign: N9SPF
Douglas L Elliott
Sublette IL 613670297

Call Sign: N9RAY
Troy E Reed
Rr 1 Box 124
Sullivan IL 61951

Call Sign: WB9ZCN
Ronald D Jack
Rr 1 Box 159D
Sullivan IL 61951

Call Sign: K9DYY
Richard M Montague
Rr 1 Box 284
Sullivan IL 61951

Call Sign: KB9NSL
James R Matthews
Rr 1 Box 307
Sullivan IL 61951

Call Sign: KB9WET
Aaron O Marshall
1221 Ck 750 E
Sullivan IL 61951

Call Sign: KB9BWS
Byron F Abrams
6 Corey Ave Apt D
Sullivan IL 61951

Call Sign: K9BFA
Byron F Abrams
6 Corey Ave Apt D
Sullivan IL 61951

Call Sign: KB9YWD
John W Stewart
1346 CR 1470 E
Sullivan IL 61951

Call Sign: W9WGL
Don A Miller
916 E Jackson
Sullivan IL 61951

Call Sign: KC9S
Clint C Parrish
105 Elim Springs Dr
Sullivan IL 619518001

Call Sign: KA9Z
R. Alan Dickens
291 Elim Springs Dr
Sullivan IL 61951

Call Sign: KB9YEM
Douglas D Moore
130 Elim Springs Park
Sullivan IL 61951

Call Sign: KB4GNI
Frank H Mathews
Illinois Masonic Home
Sullivan IL 61951

Call Sign: K4DRN
James E Harney
Illinois Masonic Home
Sullivan IL 61951

Call Sign: W9YDV
M Warren Clark
Illinois Masonic Home
Sullivan IL 61951

Call Sign: KA9HBR
Jerry L Isaacs
517 N Pierce St

Sullivan IL 61951

Call Sign: KA7SLL
Anders Dillner
212 N Seymour St
Sullivan IL 619511340

Call Sign: WA9QNL
Jane I Compton
6 Northlawn Dr
Sullivan IL 61951

Call Sign: KA9HAK
Roberta L Martin
6 Northlawn Dr
Sullivan IL 61951

Call Sign: N9XPJ
Paul W Knobloch
10 Northlawn Dr
Sullivan IL 61951

Call Sign: KB9GFL
Ronald J Allen
415 S 5th St
Sullivan IL 61951

Call Sign: KB9MJV
Clint C Parrish
909 S Hamilton
Sullivan IL 619512211

Call Sign: N9UWF
Robert D Jordan
316 S Lincoln St
Sullivan IL 61951

Call Sign: WD9IIL
James L Rentfrow
815 S Washington St
Sullivan IL 61951

Call Sign: AA9HM
Robert L Compton
604 Sunrise Dr
Sullivan IL 61951

Call Sign: K9COB
Paul E Hutchcraft

627 Sunrise Dr
Sullivan IL 61951

Call Sign: WD9DKV
Timothy C Waddell
215 W Eden
Sullivan IL 61951

Call Sign: WA9IGG
Carl L Allen
604 W Eden
Sullivan IL 61951

Call Sign: KC9BXQ
David W Welsh
820 W Harrison
Sullivan IL 61951

Call Sign: KY9W
William D Lowe
512 W Harrison St
Sullivan IL 61951

Call Sign: WB9RTZ
Fred H Muxfeldt
415 W Russell
Sullivan IL 61951

Call Sign: K9SWY
Vernon E Jack
916 W Strain St
Sullivan IL 61951

FCC Amateur Radio Licenses in Summerfield

Call Sign: KA1JKP
Wynn J Beattie
303 W Peeples St Box 302
Summerfield IL 62289

FCC Amateur Radio Licenses in Sumner

Call Sign: KA9IHW
James D Moye
Rr 3 Box 912
Sumner IL 62466

Call Sign: KA9PUK
Verna E Bennett
Rr 1 Box 98
Sumner IL 62466

Call Sign: K9YIC
Amy A Heath
100 Chestnut St Apt 4
Sumner IL 62466

Call Sign: N9MWJ
Rod D Poland
1927 Frontage Creek Ln
Sumner IL 62466

Call Sign: KB9QLI
Brent A Perrott
203 Sycamore Ave
Sumner IL 62466

Call Sign: KA9NNX
Gail E Bennett
Sumner IL 62466

FCC Amateur Radio Licenses in Swansea

Call Sign: KD6CVB
Brian K Parrish
513 Abby Ln
Swansea IL 62226

Call Sign: KE9HL
Thomas F Hennessy III
125 Adam Dr
Swansea IL 62226

Call Sign: W9AOM
Raymond B Dienberg
3 Alhambra Ct
Swansea IL 622261650

Call Sign: KD9KV
Jim M Wolff
1772 Ambrose Ter Dr
Swansea IL 62226

Call Sign: N9MFC
Curtis L Geiler

3919 Benington Dr
Swansea IL 62226

Call Sign: KC9SZB
John E Daum
517 Big Bend Blvd
Swansea IL 62226

Call Sign: K1IF
John M Isabella
709 Brackett
Swansea IL 62226

Call Sign: KC9MTF
Karen E Allen
709 Brackett
Swansea IL 62226

Call Sign: KA9RLL
James F Meyer
1463 Cantwell Ln Apt 7
Swansea IL 62226

Call Sign: N9PYM
Kurt Hoerz
10 Dale Crest Manor
Swansea IL 622266484

Call Sign: KB9ZUC
Jared G Macke
5 Deerfield Ct
Swansea IL 62226

Call Sign: N9UPZ
Kurtis A Sleeter
104 E Caroline St
Swansea IL 62226

Call Sign: N9SNN
Lloyd R Wilson
324.5 Gilbert St
Swansea IL 62220

Call Sign: N9MVQ
Dennis R Becker
320 Lake Lorraine Dr
Swansea IL 62221

Call Sign: KC9OBY

Michael W Carl
405 Lake Lorraine Dr
Swansea IL 62226

Call Sign: KE5IB
Charles F Chace
116 Lakeland Blvd
Swansea IL 62226

Call Sign: K9ZA
Carl J Buehler
604 Leighigh
Swansea IL 62226

Call Sign: WB9ZAK
Karen J Buehler
604 Leighigh Dr
Swansea IL 622261004

Call Sign: WB9ZJZ
Lloyd R Mixer Sr
250 Marcella Dr Apt 7
Swansea IL 62221

Call Sign: KB9LIN
James E Pauling
1926 Messinger Trl
Swansea IL 62226

Call Sign: KE5NN
Norbert H Karyer
1604 Pin Oak
Swansea IL 62226

Call Sign: K7CRM
Lawrence B Fuller
1848 Stafford Way
Swansea IL 622267901

Call Sign: WB9IGB
Paul T Sanford
516 Thistle Ln
Swansea IL 622261886

Call Sign: KF9WY
Derek P VanLith
317 Turnbridge Dr
Swansea IL 62226

Call Sign: N9NJV
David A Kozlowski
164 Twin Lake Dr
Swansea IL 62226

Call Sign: N9NJU
Mary L Kozlowski
164 Twin Lake Dr
Swansea IL 62226

Call Sign: KB9KTH
Prime Amateur Radio Assn
164 Twin Lake Dr
Swansea IL 622211952

Call Sign: KN9G
John J Kozlowski
164 Twin Lake Dr
Swansea IL 622261952

FCC Amateur Radio Licenses in Table Grove

Call Sign: N9EM
Theodore L Williamson
13088 County Hwy 34
Table Grove IL 61482

Call Sign: N9EM
Theodore L Williamson
13088 County Hwy 34
Table Grove IL 61482

Call Sign: K5TED
Theodore L Williamson
13088 County Hwy 34
Table Grove IL 61482

Call Sign: KB9EZD
Wilmer N Willis
100 E Grove
Table Grove IL 61482

Call Sign: N9MTN
George R Wilson
1692 E Quarter Rd
Table Grove IL 61482

Call Sign: KC9HMU

Western Illinois Extreme
Amateur Radio Operators Club
13088 N Co Hwy 34
Table Grove IL 61482

Call Sign: N9ENM
Betsy L Williamson
13088 N County Hwy 34
Table Grove IL 61482

Call Sign: W9PIG
Betsy L Williamson
13088 N County Hwy 34
Table Grove IL 61482

Call Sign: NB9V
Betsy L Williamson
13088 N County Hwy 34
Table Grove IL 61482

Call Sign: N9EM
Theodore L Williamson
13088 N County Hwy 34
Table Grove IL 61482

Call Sign: K5TED
Theodore L Williamson
13088 N County Hwy 34
Table Grove IL 61482

Call Sign: N9EM
Theodore L Williamson
13088 N County Hwy 34
Table Grove IL 61482

Call Sign: NU9TS
Western Illinois Extreme
Amateur Radio Operators Club
13088 N County Hwy 34
Table Grove IL 61482

FCC Amateur Radio Licenses in Tallula

Call Sign: KB9WYM
Violet M Gentry
Rr1 Box 82
Tallula IL 62688

Call Sign: K9KGO
Robert E Mc Neal
11236 Richland St
Tallula IL 62688

Call Sign: KB9WAN
Dorothy A Mcneal
11236 Richland St
Tallula IL 62688

Call Sign: KF4CGH
David T Daniel
16869 Rock Creek Ave
Tallula IL 62688

Call Sign: W9HTI
Jon P Gentry
15421 State Hwy 123
Tallula IL 626889542

Call Sign: K5HIV
Violet M Gentry
15421 State Hwy 123
Tallula IL 626889542

Call Sign: KB9PMM
Dalton G Boehm
Tallula IL 62688

Call Sign: AD9GB
Dalton G Boehm
Tallula IL 62688

Call Sign: N9KJB
Sherald D Sherman
Tallula IL 62688

FCC Amateur Radio Licenses in Tamaroa

Call Sign: KC9PCI
Mark A Chaney
215 Broadway
Tamaroa IL 62888

Call Sign: KC9PPB
Sandra B Huggins
426 E Main
Tamaroa IL 62888

Call Sign: KC9JUR
Thomas L Marsh
9016 E Tamaroa Rd
Tamaroa IL 62888

Call Sign: W9JUR
Thomas L Marsh
9016 E Tamaroa Rd
Tamaroa IL 62888

Call Sign: N9LUD
Gary E Nickens
31 Ford St
Tamaroa IL 62888

Call Sign: KC9HFQ
Kasey J Zettler
Gladson Rd
Tamaroa IL 62888

Call Sign: KC9GAH
Kenneth J Zettler
Gladson Rd
Tamaroa IL 62888

Call Sign: N9NJZ
William C Place
Tamaroa IL 62888

FCC Amateur Radio Licenses in Tamms

Call Sign: N9SNI
John C Burke
Rt 2 Box 181
Tamms IL 62988

Call Sign: KB9GMW
Bruce Modicue Sr
Tamms IL 62988

Call Sign: KB9OTR
Jeannie R Beasley
Tamms IL 62988

FCC Amateur Radio Licenses in Tampico

Call Sign: N7SVN
Bart B Thiriot
406 E Market St
Tampico IL 61283

Call Sign: N9NDI
Mark L Mayfield
208 S Benton St
Tampico IL 61283

FCC Amateur Radio Licenses in Taylor Ridge

Call Sign: K9ZFI
Richard D Smith
7429 106th Ave W
Taylor Ridge IL 61284

Call Sign: N9MRC
Don L Mc Manus
11425 108 St W
Taylor Ridge IL 61284

Call Sign: KC9RGZ
Paul A Fisher
8328 114th Ave W
Taylor Ridge IL 61284

Call Sign: KB0WWM
Thomas R Gambucci
10312 136th St W
Taylor Ridge IL 612849329

Call Sign: N9UYJ
Robert J Geiger
9119 143rd St Ct W
Taylor Ridge IL 61284

Call Sign: NS1G
Robert J Geiger
9119 143rd St Ct W
Taylor Ridge IL 61284

Call Sign: KB9AJU
Aron M Benner
8509 147th St W
Taylor Ridge IL 61284

Call Sign: AE9M

James R King
6708 92nd Ave W
Taylor Ridge IL 61284

Call Sign: W9P3Z
Warren J Wilkins Sr
8829 98 W
Taylor Ridge IL 61284

FCC Amateur Radio Licenses in Taylor Springs

Call Sign: N9SNE
Janet L Osborn
714 Park St
Taylor Springs IL 62089

Call Sign: KL0LS
Thomas P Flint
Taylor Springs IL 62089

FCC Amateur Radio Licenses in Taylorville

Call Sign: KA9WIF
Bruce B Harrold
1368N 1900E Box 183
Taylorville IL 62568

Call Sign: N9OD
Bruce B Harrold
1368N 1900E Box 183
Taylorville IL 62568

Call Sign: N9OZN
Claud H Harrold
1368N 1900E Rd
Taylorville IL 62568

Call Sign: N9YMZ
Donna F Buesinger
Rr 3 Box 331
Taylorville IL 62568

Call Sign: KE9KRZ
Christian County ARC
Rt 3 Box 331
Taylorville IL 62568

Call Sign: KB9AKT
Charles O Stephens
Rr 3 Box 356
Taylorville IL 62568

Call Sign: KA9RZZ
Odra E Kirby
1207 Brantley Rd
Taylorville IL 62568

Call Sign: KC9MTJ
Philip A Capaul
610 Chestnut St
Taylorville IL 62568

Call Sign: KC9UTO
Adam M Jeffrey
880 E 1800 N Rd
Taylorville IL 62568

Call Sign: KB9YXO
Richard L Brewer
802 E Franklin
Taylorville IL 62568

Call Sign: WR9X
Robert L Griffin
501 E Franklin Apt 5
Taylorville IL 62568

Call Sign: N9FJJ
Jesse T Franklin
912 E Oak
Taylorville IL 62568

Call Sign: K9GO
Jesse T Franklin
912 E Oak
Taylorville IL 62568

Call Sign: KA9WCL
Lucille Franklin
912 E Oak
Taylorville IL 62568

Call Sign: N9DID
Donald I Dunkirk
705 E Oak St
Taylorville IL 62568

Call Sign: NN9D
David L Maskel
800 E Park
Taylorville IL 62568

Call Sign: KC9MOT
Larry R Wheeler
702 E Stevenson
Taylorville IL 62568

Call Sign: W9MOT
Larry R Wheeler
702 E Stevenson
Taylorville IL 62568

Call Sign: N9VQK
Ronald C Ungerer
214 Fairway Ave
Taylorville IL 62568

Call Sign: KA9MML
Errol A Duni
901 Haner Ave
Taylorville IL 62568

Call Sign: KA9TRO
Barbara K Allen
807 Heights Ave
Taylorville IL 62568

Call Sign: NT9Q
Gary W Allen Sr
807 Heights Ave
Taylorville IL 62568

Call Sign: KB9BUK
Troy A Williams
118 Hillcrest Park
Taylorville IL 62568

Call Sign: KC9SDX
Charles L Duncan
3508 Lake Dr
Taylorville IL 62568

Call Sign: WA9SSG
Alan T Achenbach
601 Lakeside Dr

Taylorville IL 62568

Call Sign: KA9ZYB
Carrie J Milligan
308 Lakeside Dr
Taylorville IL 62568

Call Sign: NG9S
Mark L Milligan
308 Lakeside Dr
Taylorville IL 62568

Call Sign: WB9N
Betty L Bowman
1201 Mark Ln
Taylorville IL 62568

Call Sign: KZ9A
James D Bowman
1201 Mark Ln
Taylorville IL 62568

Call Sign: W9KPS
Dorice L Richardson
2003 N 1200 E Rd
Taylorville IL 625687914

Call Sign: KC9KUN
Christopher W Izatt
305 N Paw Paw St
Taylorville IL 62568

Call Sign: KB9AKK
Kristy L Bowman
518 N Pawnee
Taylorville IL 62568

Call Sign: N9FU
James P Buesinger
797E 1250 N Rd
Taylorville IL 62568

Call Sign: KA9TGF
Robert S Ricci
505 N Silver
Taylorville IL 62568

Call Sign: KA9HAD
Allen H Hamell

1125 N Springfield Rd
Taylorville IL 625686126

Call Sign: W0PNL
Louis L Pulley
630 N Webster St Apt 206
Taylorville IL 62568

Call Sign: K9EHA
Robert F White
520 N West St
Taylorville IL 62568

Call Sign: KB9UGU
Donald E Dunkirk
621 Oak
Taylorville IL 62568

Call Sign: N2HOG
Donald E Dunkirk
621 Oak
Taylorville IL 62568

Call Sign: KC9MML
Stephen A Hansen
906 Oak St
Taylorville IL 62568

Call Sign: W9MML
Stephen A Hansen
906 Oak St
Taylorville IL 62568

Call Sign: W9JLM
Jeromy L Miller
2430 Pinetree Dr
Taylorville IL 62568

Call Sign: KC9OJS
Vincent C Sherman
1805 S Boch St
Taylorville IL 62568

Call Sign: KC9SEJ
Glenn E Sherman
1817 S Boch St
Taylorville IL 62568

Call Sign: KB9SVS

James R Wicker
721 S Houston
Taylorville IL 62568

Call Sign: KC9CPR
James R Wicker
721 S Houston
Taylorville IL 62568

Call Sign: KC9CPS
Annette K Wicker
721 S Houston
Taylorville IL 62568

Call Sign: K9MGF
Robert D Hamell
515 S Shawnee 9
Taylorville IL 62568

Call Sign: N9EMW
John H Winn
517 S Washington St
Taylorville IL 62568

Call Sign: W9INN
John H Winn
517 S Washington St
Taylorville IL 62568

Call Sign: WF9N
Jimmie R Johnson
618 S Webster
Taylorville IL 62568

Call Sign: WB9R
Harold L Simons
805 Samuel
Taylorville IL 62568

Call Sign: KB9HUW
Robin R Simons
805 Samuel
Taylorville IL 62568

Call Sign: W9GK
Jay A Deem
910 W Adams St
Taylorville IL 62568

Call Sign: KC9LTW
Douglas L Schnell
925 W Adams St
Taylorville IL 625682113

Call Sign: N9XFW
Neil J Hoover
1015 W Adams St
Taylorville IL 62568

Call Sign: W9SMD
Donald L Taylor Sr
710 W Elm
Taylorville IL 62568

Call Sign: WA9OUT
Leslie H Black
1310 W Franklin
Taylorville IL 62568

Call Sign: N9CGL
Todd E Daugherty
800 W Main Cross
Taylorville IL 52568

Call Sign: N9KNF
Walter F Harwell
507 W Maple St
Taylorville IL 625682470

Call Sign: N9HW
Walter F Harwell
507 W Maple St
Taylorville IL 625682470

Call Sign: KB9CIL
Robert P Phoenix
1120 W Market
Taylorville IL 62568

Call Sign: W9UIA
Susan J Barnett
922 W Rich St
Taylorville IL 62568

Call Sign: N9BBI
James R Wicker
1103 W Rich St
Taylorville IL 62568

Call Sign: K9WJR
James R Wicker
1103 W Rich St
Taylorville IL 62568

Call Sign: KA9OGN
Charles L Duncan
1003 W Vine St
Taylorville IL 62568

Call Sign: N9XUK
Jerry L Phillips
1023 W Vine St
Taylorville IL 62568

Call Sign: KC9LXG
Charles D Alvey Jr
310 W Wilson
Taylorville IL 62568

Call Sign: KC9NGK
John R Weaver
512 White Ave
Taylorville IL 62568

Call Sign: W9NGK
John R Weaver
512 White Ave
Taylorville IL 62568

FCC Amateur Radio Licenses in Tennessee

Call Sign: KC9AEL
Jay D Lutz
2960 E CR 1500
Tennessee IL 62374

Call Sign: N9SQR
Stepehn F Zdebski
Box 13 Rr 1
Tennessee IL 62374

FCC Amateur Radio Licenses in Teutopolis

Call Sign: KA9YZG
Richard P Hartke

R1 Box 121
Teutopolis IL 62467

Call Sign: KB9IYO
Dennis J Walk
17453 E 1650th Ave
Teutopolis IL 62467

Call Sign: KC9PLM
George D Willis
1425 E Country Ave
Teutopolis IL 62467

Call Sign: KB9TCI
Charles M Percival
406 E Main St
Teutopolis IL 62467

Call Sign: KC9PLL
Matthew B Stead
19808 E St Hwy 33
Teutopolis IL 62467

Call Sign: W0NZW
Theodore G Bracco
203 Main St
Teutopolis IL 62467

Call Sign: K9DCM
Theodore G Bracco
203 Main St
Teutopolis IL 62467

Call Sign: KC9GBG
Brad C Buening
11406 N 1775th Rd
Teutopolis IL 62467

Call Sign: KB9NPL
Scott D Westendorf
304 N Plum
Teutopolis IL 62467

Call Sign: N9YGW
Jerry W Weber
412 W Walnut
Teutopolis IL 62467

Call Sign: KB9KOR

Louise A Weber
412 W Walnut St
Teutopolis IL 62467

Call Sign: KC9ATM
Jay M Ladew
Teutopolis IL 62467

FCC Amateur Radio Licenses in Texico

Call Sign: KB9KEP
Michael J Bullock
16119 E Hershey Rd
Texico IL 62889

Call Sign: KB9KER
Stephen N Dehart
21164 N Tolle Ln
Texico IL 62889

FCC Amateur Radio Licenses in Thawville

Call Sign: KC9JDK
John A Boomgarden
2174 N 1200 E Rd
Thawville IL 60968

FCC Amateur Radio Licenses in Thebes

Call Sign: KC9CEB
John J Holland
29651 State Hwy 3
Thebes IL 62990

Call Sign: WB9WVW
James Caldwell
Thebes IL 62990

FCC Amateur Radio Licenses in Thomasboro

Call Sign: KB9HXW
Robert Swiader
2477 CR 2100 E
Thomasboro IL 61878

Call Sign: KB9NJW
David D Moore
1486 CR 2400 N
Thomasboro IL 618789636

Call Sign: K9CW
Andrew B White
1725 CR 2500 N
Thomasboro IL 618789642

Call Sign: K9IVY
Sally J White
1725 CR 2500 N
Thomasboro IL 618789642

Call Sign: N1JE
Jerry L Eagles
1971 CR 2500 N
Thomasboro IL 618789645

Call Sign: N9PKV
Michael A Bandy
506 W Frederick
Thomasboro IL 61878

Call Sign: KB9OQT
Deborah J Bandy
506 W Fredrick
Thomasboro IL 61878

Call Sign: WB9KYC
Marion K Fargo
507 W Pearl St Rr 1
Thomasboro IL 61878

Call Sign: W9RRY
Warner Q Bandy
507 W Shurbet
Thomasboro IL 61878

Call Sign: N9ZSL
Robert J Harper
Thomasboro IL 61878

**FCC Amateur Radio
Licenses in Thompsonville**

Call Sign: KC8SXX

Matthew R Andrew
3663 1st St
Thompsonville IL 62890

Call Sign: N9MRA
Matthew R Andrew
3663 1st St
Thompsonville IL 62890

Call Sign: KE4AMT
Barry C Fitch
21749 Benton St
Thompsonville IL 62890

Call Sign: AB9XP
Barry C Fitch
21749 Benton St
Thompsonville IL 62890

Call Sign: N9SHA
David D Kinsey
5820 Bolen Store Rd
Thompsonville IL 62890

Call Sign: KC9RYL
Nicholas L Sullivan
Rr 2 Box 112
Thompsonville IL 62890

Call Sign: KB9NWC
Samuel E Barwick
Rt 2 Box 86
Thompsonville IL 62890

Call Sign: KC9PYR
Michael G Motsinger
20965 Corinth Rd
Thompsonville IL 62890

Call Sign: KB9COL
Raymond D Jackson
15364 Dillingham Rd
Thompsonville IL 62890

Call Sign: AA9QZ
Matt Todd
21133 Division St
Thompsonville IL 62890

Call Sign: KB9JEI
Tracy L Todd
21133 Division St
Thompsonville IL 62890

Call Sign: WB9OHN
Francis H Bonnell
21148 Division St
Thompsonville IL 62890

Call Sign: KA9OLR
Margaret C Bonnell
21148 Division St
Thompsonville IL 62890

Call Sign: WD9JLS
Robert M Thackston
16685 Droit City Rd
Thompsonville IL 62890

Call Sign: W7MRB
Michael R Babb
21879 Knob Prairie Rd
Thompsonville IL 62890

Call Sign: WB9WRH
Clarence E Larson
5493 N Thompsonville Rd
Thompsonville IL 62890

Call Sign: KC9ECU
Teresa M Baker
20861 Number 9 Blacktop
Thompsonville IL 62890

Call Sign: KC9SWQ
Michael S Mccormick
3708 Poplar St
Thompsonville IL 62890

Call Sign: AE9XW
Michael S Mccormick
3708 Poplar St
Thompsonville IL 62890

Call Sign: KA7AIQ
William L Worf
3951 Thompson St
Thompsonville IL 62890

FCC Amateur Radio Licenses in Thomson

Call Sign: K0CVG
Eugene J Tack
Rr 1 Box 223B
Thomson IL 61285

Call Sign: KB9TOK
David L Lawton
4041 Il Rt 84
Thomson IL 61285

Call Sign: N9XLE
Steve S Kaufman
4473 Illinois Rt 84
Thomson IL 61285

Call Sign: KB9AZT
Wayne E Rohr
10202 Three Mile Rd
Thomson IL 612859716

FCC Amateur Radio Licenses in Tilden

Call Sign: KB9DCO
Leonard E Mines
Center St
Tilden IL 62292

Call Sign: N9SBN
Dan S Surdyk
430 Lindel
Tilden IL 62292

Call Sign: KC9AUN
Donald E Etling
220 Wilson Ave
Tilden IL 62292

FCC Amateur Radio Licenses in Tilton

Call Sign: KC9GFR
Brian J Schull
511 Dellwood
Tilton IL 61833

Call Sign: N9GAR
William L Moreman
713 Dellwood
Tilton IL 61833

Call Sign: N9YUM
Darrell K Hendricks
709 5 Dellwood St
Tilton IL 61833

Call Sign: KB9YNE
Russell E Deatley
1622 King
Tilton IL 61833

Call Sign: KA9BLE
Martin A Brant
2025 Liberty Ave
Tilton IL 61833

Call Sign: KA9CQP
Stewart M Lorenz
1427 Lincoln Ave
Tilton IL 61833

Call Sign: KB9KBV
David P Ellis
203 S L
Tilton IL 61833

Call Sign: WB9EXC
Raymond L White
1814 S Monroe St
Tilton IL 61833

Call Sign: KA9ZKP
Kathie A Schmitt
1911 S Washington St
Tilton IL 61833

Call Sign: KA9OXP
William H Schmitt
1911 S Washington St
Tilton IL 61833

Call Sign: N9VVJ
Tommy G Mc Intyre
1822 S Washington St
Tilton IL 61833

FCC Amateur Radio Licenses in Timberlane

Call Sign: KB9UXQ
Jonathan A Mensching
2969 Prairie Rd
Timberlane IL 61008

Call Sign: KC9EJJ
Jonathan A Mensching
2969 Prairie Rd
Timberlane IL 61008

FCC Amateur Radio Licenses in Tiskilwa

Call Sign: KC9MQW
Earl L Harman
10933 1890 E St
Tiskilwa IL 61368

Call Sign: W9WIF
Earl L Harman Sr
10933 1890 E St
Tiskilwa IL 61368

Call Sign: W9BOS
Earl L Harman Sr
10933 1890 E St
Tiskilwa IL 61368

Call Sign: KB9MGL
Charles W Hamilton
445 Galena
Tiskilwa IL 61368

Call Sign: WB9CXG
David S Znavor
300 Hill St
Tiskilwa IL 61368

Call Sign: N6OAN
Ronald L Ziegler
18935 1250 North Ave
Tiskilwa IL 613689109

Call Sign: KB9SYN

Randy K Hassler
140 Owen St
Tiskilwa IL 61368

Call Sign: KC9IHT
John P Murphy
Tiskilwa IL 61368

Call Sign: KC9EGB
Thomas B Chromzack
Tiskilwa IL 613680101

Call Sign: K9ML
Thomas B Chromzack
Tiskilwa IL 613680101

FCC Amateur Radio Licenses in Toledo

Call Sign: KA9PYG
Ronald L Drum
907 Adams
Toledo IL 62468

Call Sign: KB9TLK
Isar
Rr 2 Box 148C 463 Cr 850 N
Toledo IL 624683015

Call Sign: N9PLY
Vickie D Swisher
Rr 2 Box 155D
Toledo IL 62468

Call Sign: N9RGP
Brooks R Bridges
Rr 2 Box 163
Toledo IL 62468

Call Sign: W9FVJ
Samuel E Miller
Rr 1 Box 98
Toledo IL 62468

Call Sign: WD9DPD
Mary L Evans
524 CR 1100 E
Toledo IL 624689708

Call Sign: WD9DPC
William L Evans Sr
524 CR 1100 E
Toledo IL 624689708

Call Sign: W9MBD
Howard W Knoebel
674 CR 600 N
Toledo IL 62468

Call Sign: KB9OHI
Carolyn S Drummond
463 CR 850 N
Toledo IL 62468

Call Sign: KB9OHH
Jerry E Drummond
463 CR 850 N
Toledo IL 62468

Call Sign: N9NPS
William B Trimble
501A CR 875 N
Toledo IL 624683031

Call Sign: KB9NUI
Ted A Schnorf
102 E Washington
Toledo IL 62468

Call Sign: WA9FBI
Lloyd F White
200 S Meridian St
Toledo IL 624681225

Call Sign: N9QBD
John T Brewer
Toledo IL 62468

Call Sign: K9EJ
Douglas C Morgan
Toledo IL 62468

Call Sign: N9JUT
Julia A Morgan
Toledo IL 62468

FCC Amateur Radio Licenses in Tolono

Call Sign: KB9WDF
Kenneth R Williams
311 Country Ln
Tolono IL 618809025

Call Sign: KC9TUO
Michael E Siegmund
777 CR 800 N
Tolono IL 61880

Call Sign: KC9TMR
Keith P Schoenefeld
110 E Benham
Tolono IL 61880

Call Sign: KB9AW
Robert R Cicone
808 E Boone
Tolono IL 61880

Call Sign: WD9GCB
Michael D Anderson
307 E Walnut
Tolono IL 61880

Call Sign: N9XDH
Larry D Kearns
102 E Washington St
Tolono IL 61880

Call Sign: N9HPC
Mark B Thomas
417 N Central St
Tolono IL 61880

Call Sign: WA9GWC
William M Wiese
712 N Clifford St
Tolono IL 61880

Call Sign: WB8TYW
John E Malmberg
405 N Condit
Tolono IL 61880

Call Sign: KC9UNP
John A Wiman
606 W Linden St

Tolono IL 61880

Call Sign: KA9QOF
Ronald A Myers
Tolono IL 61880

Call Sign: KG9AG
John L File
Tolono IL 618800566

Call Sign: KC9IZZ
Tayler S Mcgillis
2716 CR 400 W
Toluca IL 61369

Call Sign: KA9IHD
Jeff R Mc Casky
618 E Bennington
Toluca IL 61369

Call Sign: W9QKL
Gordon Mastalio
416 N Locust
Toluca IL 61369

Call Sign: KC9IVW
Mark S Mays
108 S Lincoln St
Toluca IL 61369

Call Sign: KB9JHN
Woodrow C Olson
112 Lasalle St Apt A
Tonica IL 61370

Call Sign: K9KHZ
Jack L Ashley
436 N 1809th Rd
Tonica IL 613709629

Call Sign: KB9TLZ
Jamesf D Dunn
305 N 1st St

Tonica IL 61370

Call Sign: KD0DSL
Candice Barton
107 S 1st St
Tonica IL 61370

Call Sign: KD0DOV
Peter Barton
107 S 1st St
Tonica IL 61370

Call Sign: KB9WPT
Kathleen S Ryan
113 W Elm St
Tonica IL 613700001

Call Sign: KC9SUU
Noah Olson
Tonica IL 61370

Call Sign: KC6VVT
Robert P Ryan
Tonica IL 613700024

Call Sign: KC9UCK
Eric D Thurman
20113 CR 1800 N
Topeka IL 61567

Call Sign: K9EDT
Eric D Thurman
20113 CR 1800 N
Topeka IL 61567

Call Sign: WA9LLR
Dennis R Tunis
26185 Harris Ln
Topeka IL 61567

Call Sign: W9LLR
Dennis R Tunis
26185 Harris Ln
Topeka IL 61567

Call Sign: KB9MIX

Cory L Atterberry
101 Main St
Topeka IL 61567

Call Sign: KC9KLT
Cory L Freeman
101 Main St
Topeka IL 61567

Call Sign: KA9NVI
Delbert L Atterberry
Topeka IL 61567

Call Sign: KB9LZW
Douglas A Bennett
Topeka IL 61567

Call Sign: N9XKC
Tamre E Atterberry
Topeka IL 61567

Call Sign: K9DWW
Jack L Fisher
Rr 1 Box 264
Toulon IL 61483

Call Sign: KA9GVO
Marvin L Shults
Rr1 Box 31
Toulon IL 61483

Call Sign: WB9WQK
Joan C Nicholas
Rd 2 Box 93
Toulon IL 61483

Call Sign: KB0OQY
Michele L Jezierski
224 E Turner Ave
Toulon IL 614839504

Call Sign: AD9Z
David M Krans
3059 Township Rd 292 E
Toulon IL 61483

Call Sign: KC9LTQ
Debra K Rhoades
517 W Thomas St
Toulon IL 61483

Call Sign: K9DKR
Debra K Rhoades
517 W Thomas St
Toulon IL 61483

Call Sign: KA9IJK
Allen D Goins
Toulon IL 61483

Call Sign: WA9SJQ
Anne E Fisher
Toulon IL 61483

Call Sign: WA9AUY
Harry L Swank
Toulon IL 61483

FCC Amateur Radio Licenses in Tovey

Call Sign: N9TOO
Eugene F Gudgel Jr
304 Borah Ave
Tovey IL 62570

Call Sign: KB9IKT
Edward D Bialas
314 Likins
Tovey IL 62570

Call Sign: N9TON
Robert Gudgel
201 Linkins Ave
Tovey IL 62570

Call Sign: WE9W
Ernest L Waite I
305 Linkins Ave
Tovey IL 62570

Call Sign: N9PKW
Lawrence E Coghlan
606 Linkins Ave
Tovey IL 62570

Call Sign: KB9MTN
Joann M Waite
305 Linkins St
Tovey IL 62570

Call Sign: AF4WZ
Aaron W Gatton
614 Mason
Tovey IL 62570

Call Sign: N9WHJ
Michael J Perona
201 Midland Blvd
Tovey IL 62570

Call Sign: AA9II
Patrick J Grafton
713 Midland Blvd
Tovey IL 62570

Call Sign: N9XKF
Wendy L Grafton
713 Midland Blvd
Tovey IL 62570

Call Sign: N9RPP
John W Meikle Sr
Tovey IL 62570

Call Sign: KC9CQH
Sharon M Dain
Tovey IL 62570

FCC Amateur Radio Licenses in Towanda

Call Sign: KB9QZZ
Peter D Cuoco
22416E 1900N Rd
Towanda IL 61776

Call Sign: KC9PIM
Duane R Benjamin
24251 E 1900 N Rd
Towanda IL 61776

Call Sign: N9RKD
Christopher Miller

129 Fincham Way
Towanda IL 61776

Call Sign: KB9ZDZ
John S Payne
309 Hely Rr 1 Box 7
Towanda IL 61776

Call Sign: KB9QLC
Jeffrey A Showalter
123 Hunt St
Towanda IL 61776

Call Sign: N9QEP
Herbert M Beer
20397 N 2050 E Rd
Towanda IL 61776

Call Sign: KC9BRO
Herbert M Beer
20397 N 2050 E Rd
Towanda IL 61776

Call Sign: KE9HB
Craig B Russell
106 North St
Towanda IL 61776

Call Sign: K9JSP
John S Payne
309 W Hely St
Towanda IL 61776

Call Sign: KB9RAC
Bill A Bradford
Towanda IL 61776

Call Sign: KC9KAN
Harlan K Ogan
Towanda IL 61776

Call Sign: W9HKO
Harlan K Ogan
Towanda IL 61776

Call Sign: WB9YRC
Rodney W Parker
Towanda IL 61776

Call Sign: WB9YRD
Sharon C Parker
Towanda IL 61776

FCC Amateur Radio Licenses in Tower Hill

Call Sign: KC9DAA
Adam D Thull
Rr 1 Box 109
Tower Hill IL 62571

Call Sign: KB9UDE
John P Hippard
Rr 2 Box 121
Tower Hill IL 62571

Call Sign: KC9TJN
Todd J Stivers
Rr 1 Box 123
Tower Hill IL 62571

Call Sign: N9ULM
Orval W Miller
Rr 2 Box 179
Tower Hill IL 62571

Call Sign: K9WPK
James E Van Hooser
Tower Hill IL 62571

FCC Amateur Radio Licenses in Tremont

Call Sign: WD9GKS
Kenneth A Koch
10146 Arrow Rd
Tremont IL 61568

Call Sign: N9KKS
Michael J Legel
Rr 1 Box 41
Tremont IL 61568

Call Sign: N9KLP
Tracey J Legel
Rr 1 Box 41
Tremont IL 61568

Call Sign: N9ZBF
Byron L Zuercher
21598 Connell Rd
Tremont IL 61568

Call Sign: KB9QCV
Nick E Kinsey
713 E South St
Tremont IL 61568

Call Sign: KC9BQV
Samuel L Snyder
206 East St
Tremont IL 61568

Call Sign: WB9RZY
Jerry C Zuercher
25747 Iron Mountain Rd
Tremont IL 615689174

Call Sign: KB9PFS
Andy S Ridgeway
14150 N Lake Windermere
Tremont IL 61568

Call Sign: KB9FC
John M Sander
521 N Sampson
Tremont IL 61568

Call Sign: KC9FGX
Beth A Killen
120 W Franklin
Tremont IL 61568

Call Sign: KC9FGY
Devin L Killen
120 W Franklin
Tremont IL 61568

Call Sign: N9RLI
Paul A Reid
Tremont IL 61568

Call Sign: KB9EBG
William C Elliott Jr
Tremont IL 61568

Call Sign: W9RWD

Donald D Reid
Tremont IL 615680773

FCC Amateur Radio Licenses in Trenton

Call Sign: KB9DKO
Dan J Rinderer
Rr 1 Box 78A
Trenton IL 62293

Call Sign: W0YT
Donald S Stalcup Sr
12710 Crackerneck Rd
Trenton IL 622933318

Call Sign: KC9DGS
Charlotte A Reymond
12705 Crestview Ln
Trenton IL 62293

Call Sign: KC9TPJ
Cynthia E Dawson
17 E 2nd St
Trenton IL 62293

Call Sign: KB9PNM
Thomas A Leveling
220 E 2nd St
Trenton IL 62293

Call Sign: WC9AAI
Trenton Emergency
Management Service
220 E 2nd St
Trenton IL 62293

Call Sign: N9KUH
Deborah L Melzer
705 E 5th St
Trenton IL 622931730

Call Sign: KC9DGT
Barbara A Rudy
835 E 5th St
Trenton IL 62293

Call Sign: KB9DKP
John L Rinderer

6716 Lee Rd
Trenton IL 62293

Call Sign: KC9DBP
Howard Burhanna III
109 N Fillmore St
Trenton IL 62293

Call Sign: KB9MXU
Nancy D Frey
11730 N Grove School Rd
Trenton IL 622932114

Call Sign: KB9MXT
Gerard D Frey
11730 N Grove School Rd
Trenton IL 622932114

Call Sign: KC9DGQ
Elizabeth K Zeller
432 N Maple
Trenton IL 622931741

Call Sign: WA9YKO
Clinton County ARC
423 N Olive
Trenton IL 62293

Call Sign: K9BNI
Donald J Wehrle
423 N Olive
Trenton IL 62293

Call Sign: N9SXL
John W Cooper
3427 Old US 50
Trenton IL 62293

Call Sign: N9TTH
Dennis L Gordon
226 Rinderer Rd
Trenton IL 62293

Call Sign: KB9PPQ
Christopher T Miller
9320 Ruth School Rd
Trenton IL 62293

Call Sign: KC9DGR

Kathleen M Hayes
212 S Cedar St
Trenton IL 62293

Call Sign: WA9NE
Wayne A Cornick
635 S Main St
Trenton IL 62293

Call Sign: KB9PNK
Bertram V Jones
25 W 2nd St
Trenton IL 62293

Call Sign: KC9TDU
John F Bauer
205 W Illinois St
Trenton IL 62293

Call Sign: KC9JHX
Trenton Emergency
Management Service
25 W Indiana St
Trenton IL 62293

Call Sign: KC9VOJ
Brian V Ripperda
3020 Wheatfield
Trenton IL 62293

Call Sign: N9RIP
Brian V Ripperda
3020 Wheatfield
Trenton IL 62293

Call Sign: N9MFA
Leslie A Schaefer
Trenton IL 62293

FCC Amateur Radio Licenses in Trilla

Call Sign: KA9HGX
Delno F Hart
Trilla IL 62469

FCC Amateur Radio Licenses in Trivoli

Call Sign: K9CT
Craig A Thompson
1603 N Holiday Ln
Trivoli IL 615699643

Call Sign: W9EGF
E Duane Bitner
3007 N Texas Rd
Trivoli IL 615699506

Call Sign: W9FZO
Duane L Mitchell
16318 Pleasant Grove Rd
Trivoli IL 61569

Call Sign: N9ZQW
Imogene N Mc Guinnis
16614 Pleasant Grove Rd
Trivoli IL 61569

Call Sign: KC9SCD
Douglas M Harman
415 S Stone School Rd
Trivoli IL 61569

Call Sign: KC9SCC
Reid D Harman
415 S Stone School Rd
Trivoli IL 61569

Call Sign: KC9NOT
John R Burton
16212 W Pleasant Grove Rd
Trivoli IL 61569

FCC Amateur Radio Licenses in Troy

Call Sign: KC9LIA
Dustin W Little
304 Arrowhead
Troy IL 62294

Call Sign: W9YHV
Dustin W Little
304 Arrowhead
Troy IL 62294

Call Sign: N9JKD

Richard J Woods
424 Arrowhead Dr
Troy IL 62294

Call Sign: KF9VH
Michael A Vlasich
34 Autumn Cir
Troy IL 62294

Call Sign: WA9SED
Lloyd D Gardner
106 Avalon Dr
Troy IL 62294

Call Sign: WB9GZR
Martha A Gardner
106 Avalon Dr
Troy IL 62294

Call Sign: WA9UTO
Frederick W Wolf
401 Bluebird
Troy IL 62294

Call Sign: N9WF
Frederick W Wolf
401 Bluebird
Troy IL 62294

Call Sign: KF9IJ
Kimberley S Arzuagas
529B Briarwood
Troy IL 62294

Call Sign: KC9UPB
Trenton T Dittmer
203 Camelford Dr
Troy IL 62294

Call Sign: K9TYR
Trenton T Dittmer
203 Camelford Dr
Troy IL 62294

Call Sign: KC9FHN
James J Kagele
920 Carla Dr
Troy IL 62294

Call Sign: N5GPT
Kenneth S Madison
329 Cobblestone Ct
Troy IL 62294

Call Sign: N9OPV
Joseph A Martinez
116 Country Aire Dr
Troy IL 62294

Call Sign: N9OP
Joseph A Martinez
116 Country Aire Dr
Troy IL 62294

Call Sign: KA9JRD
Rita F Nimmo
8801 Country Ln
Troy IL 62294

Call Sign: K9SOY
Rupert L Nimmo
8801 Country Ln
Troy IL 62294

Call Sign: AK9C
David R Stopher
8842 County Ln
Troy IL 62294

Call Sign: KB9GDP
Ricky D Krieb
913 Edwardsvill Rd
Troy IL 62294

Call Sign: KC9FHT
Lynn C Anderson
135 Fairington Dr
Troy IL 62294

Call Sign: KC9HOG
Charles A Burcham
312 Franklin Ave
Troy IL 62294

Call Sign: KB9AIL
Tod A West Sr
709 Gawain
Troy IL 62294

Call Sign: W9YIY
William F Guennewig
316 Hickory St
Troy IL 62294

Call Sign: KB9RCN
Donald G Cook
8434 Hilltop Dr
Troy IL 62294

Call Sign: N5RZG
Cynthia M Crowe
501 Ivy Ln
Troy IL 622942826

Call Sign: N5RZC
Gregory G Crowe
501 Ivy Ln
Troy IL 622942826

Call Sign: KB9PNV
Donna M Druessel
1031 K A Acres Rd
Troy IL 62294

Call Sign: KD9ME
Robert R Druessel Sr
1031 K A Acres Rd
Troy IL 62294

Call Sign: KC5CFJ
Lon Huffman
974 Lakewood Ct
Troy IL 622943155

Call Sign: N9SIO
David G Cook
8435 Lebanon Rd
Troy IL 62294

Call Sign: AA9LO
Glenn L Cook
8435 Lebanon Rd
Troy IL 62294

Call Sign: WB9YDK
Carl E Waller
204 Liberty Sq Dr Apt 21

Troy IL 62294

Call Sign: N9HZC
Keith R Mechler
518 Lone Robin
Troy IL 622942111

Call Sign: KA9YMH
Gary A Rossy
967 Longbranch
Troy IL 62294

Call Sign: KC9RCW
Donald R Phipps
927 Longbranch Rd
Troy IL 62294

Call Sign: KB9WQC
Michael W Crump
108 Mary Dr
Troy IL 62294

Call Sign: KC9UML
Zachary J Konkel
609 Meadowlark Rd
Troy IL 62294

Call Sign: KC9UZR
Zachary J Konkel
609 Meadowlark Rd
Troy IL 62294

Call Sign: KC9ITL
Duane T Fontana
408 Oakwood Dr
Troy IL 62294

Call Sign: W9MH
William Bauer
949 Olde Farm Rd
Troy IL 62294

Call Sign: N9PYT
Norma L Mc Grew
301 Park St
Troy IL 62294

Call Sign: N9MNC
Bryce L Renken

305 Park St
Troy IL 62294

Call Sign: KC5LFD
Tim D Waterhouse
535 Patton Dr
Troy IL 62294

Call Sign: N9KMQ
Robert J Ramsey
411 Reid
Troy IL 62294

Call Sign: KB9TZL
Kevin E Pollock
446 Reid Ave
Troy IL 62294

Call Sign: KC9JLF
Matthew F Hanafin
523 Riggin Rd
Troy IL 62294

Call Sign: N9PPL
Dwayne A Spangler
603 Riggin Rd
Troy IL 62294

Call Sign: WB9KSA
Thomas J Guennewig
318 S Hickory St
Troy IL 62294

Call Sign: AA9MZ
Roger D Clark Sr
1700 Scott Troy Rd
Troy IL 62294

Call Sign: WF9D
Robert L Brennan Sr
1739 Scott Troy Rd
Troy IL 622943001

Call Sign: W9RVT
George A Hendricks
7210 SR 162
Troy IL 62294

Call Sign: KC9JRC

Frederick M Schreiber
8437 Steelecrest Ln
Troy IL 62294

Call Sign: AB9JJ
Craig J Murray
5 Steven Louis Ct
Troy IL 62294

Call Sign: KB9PTT
Kelly R Murray
5 Steven Louis Ct
Troy IL 62294

Call Sign: KC9UYB
Rollin S Reichert
621 Sundance Trl
Troy IL 62294

Call Sign: N9HH
William O Reichert
621 Sundance Trl
Troy IL 62294

Call Sign: KD9SG
Harold M Mathis
2701 Tower Ln
Troy IL 62294

Call Sign: N9END
Reba L Mathis
2701 Tower Ln
Troy IL 62294

Call Sign: KE5BG
Daniel J Pierson
301 Troy O'Fallon Rd
Troy IL 62294

Call Sign: N9ETN
Susan L Wightman
642 Troy O'Fallon Rd
Troy IL 62294

Call Sign: KJ4EG
Johnnie A Lorbacher Jr
1063 Troy O'Fallon Rd
Troy IL 62294

Call Sign: KC9JXR
Jocelyn A Benscoter
1069 Troy O'Fallon Rd
Troy IL 62294

Call Sign: KC9RER
Keith Melton
1578 Troy O'Fallon Rd
Troy IL 62294

Call Sign: KF9AA
Floyd L Bennett
113 Turtle Crk
Troy IL 62294

Call Sign: K9FF
Michael J Breyer
7967 W Mill Creek Rd
Troy IL 62294

Call Sign: WD9JBT
Sharen K Breyer
7967 W Mill Creek Rd
Troy IL 62294

Call Sign: KD5GWJ
Raymond A Forster Jr
311 Wildwood Dr
Troy IL 62294

FCC Amateur Radio Licenses in Tunnel Hill

Call Sign: KD4YGD
Chester A Persinger Jr
230 Colfax St
Tunnel Hill IL 62972

Call Sign: KC9NHI
Chester A Persinger Jr
230 Colfax St
Tunnel Hill IL 62972

Call Sign: KB9JNO
Darwin L Pfaltzgraff
45 Little John Loop
Tunnel Hill IL 62972

Call Sign: KB9MGA

Loris R Pfaltzgraff
45 Little John Loop
Tunnel Hill IL 62972

FCC Amateur Radio Licenses in Tuscola

Call Sign: K9GYI
Howard D Eskridge
424 E CR 1250 N
Tuscola IL 619539302

Call Sign: KB9TIQ
Tony A Borries
503 E Pembroke
Tuscola IL 61953

Call Sign: KB9IUU
Ronald E Korte
107 E Pinzon
Tuscola IL 61953

Call Sign: KB9TDP
John Ehrsam
113 E Sale
Tuscola IL 61953

Call Sign: K9HNQ
John H Frantz
700 E Scott
Tuscola IL 61953

Call Sign: KA9TXE
Terrance R Bassett
208 E Scott St
Tuscola IL 61953

Call Sign: AB9KP
Terrance R Bassett
208 E Scott St
Tuscola IL 61953

Call Sign: W9TRB
Terrance R Bassett
208 E Scott St
Tuscola IL 61953

Call Sign: KB9LNB
Wayne H Seip

606 E Van Allen St
Tuscola IL 61953

Call Sign: KC9JVS
Zachery A Danielson
800 E Wilson St
Tuscola IL 61953

Call Sign: KC9PXI
Douglas County Amateur
Radio Association
908 Glenview Dr
Tuscola IL 61953

Call Sign: KB9ZJW
Lloyd A Murphy
715 Lakeshore Dr
Tuscola IL 61953

Call Sign: KC9APB
Tasha K Carter
701 N Carico Box 37
Tuscola IL 61953

Call Sign: KB9MJW
Elizabeth F Hoel
1140 N CR 625E
Tuscola IL 61953

Call Sign: K9FTJ
Robert L Stallsworth
606 N Niles Ave
Tuscola IL 61953

Call Sign: KG0BX
Henry R Mohn Sr
1010 Pleasant View Dr
Tuscola IL 61953

Call Sign: KC4CJC
James R Hasler Jr
600 S Court St
Tuscola IL 61953

Call Sign: K9TOM
John R Foote
208E Sale St
Tuscola IL 61953

Call Sign: KB9QWI
Julian G Blagg
510 Southland Cir Dr
Tuscola IL 619532033

Call Sign: KC9JVR
Brian A Endres
100 Tayler Ln
Tuscola IL 61953

Call Sign: KC9OEO
Nellie E Endres
100 Tayler Ln
Tuscola IL 61953

Call Sign: KC9JYH
Kevin R Endres
100 Tayler Ln
Tuscola IL 619537526

Call Sign: KC9KRE
Kevin R Endres
100 Tayler Ln
Tuscola IL 619537526

Call Sign: N9BPE
Carl J Humes
114 W Ensey
Tuscola IL 61953

Call Sign: K9EEI
Carl J Humes
114 W Ensey
Tuscola IL 61953

FCC Amateur Radio Licenses in Ullin

Call Sign: KB9MGZ
Shawnee College ARC
Rt 1 Box 53
Ullin IL 62992

Call Sign: N9NFO
Thomas E Haynes
690 Railroad St
Ullin IL 62992

Call Sign: N9YLP

Linda K Haynes
Ullin IL 62992

Call Sign: KC9TQS
Nigel R Phelps
Ullin IL 62992

Call Sign: KC9WOW
Nigel R Phelps
Ullin IL 62992

FCC Amateur Radio Licenses in Urbana

Call Sign: N9CQS
Jeffrey D Mc Pike
276 Apple Tree Dr
Urbana IL 61802

Call Sign: WA9IXS
Virgil J Allen
2710 Arlene Dr
Urbana IL 61801

Call Sign: K9FYP
Champ H Cotton
2017 Boudreau Dr
Urbana IL 61801

Call Sign: KC9UAU
Morgan R Coates
1212 Briarcliff Dr
Urbana IL 61801

Call Sign: KC9VCG
Ursula E Hernandez
1212 Briarcliff Dr
Urbana IL 61801

Call Sign: N9PMA
Judith E Yasunaga
904 Brighton
Urbana IL 61801

Call Sign: AA9FS
Shig Yasunaga
904 Brighton
Urbana IL 61801

Call Sign: WB9RHO
Ronald L Johnston
902 Brighton Dr
Urbana IL 61801

Call Sign: WD9FVR
Gary A Rypski
2010 Brownfield Rd
Urbana IL 61802

Call Sign: KC9IKM
Keith E Kuchenbecker
1602 Bunker Ct
Urbana IL 61802

Call Sign: KB9TWZ
Paul A Spomer
704 Burkwood Dr
Urbana IL 61801

Call Sign: W9RVD
Gerald A Drake
1001 Burkwood Dr
Urbana IL 61801

Call Sign: W9CGZ
Earl F Finder
2011 Burlison
Urbana IL 61801

Call Sign: W9QFV
Albert R Krug
2026 Burlison Dr
Urbana IL 61801

Call Sign: KC9UWC
Dabin Zhang
1002 College Ct
Urbana IL 61801

Call Sign: KF9AK
Albert C Bianchini
2204 Combes
Urbana IL 61801

Call Sign: KA9WFU
Sydney B Bianchini
2204 Combes
Urbana IL 61801

Call Sign: KA9SOO
Timothy A Brumleve
602 Cottage Grove
Urbana IL 61801

Call Sign: KC9TBW
William R Mcgehee
2008 Cureton Dr
Urbana IL 61801

Call Sign: KB9BQO
Kim Han Seok
Urh 419 Daniels 1010 W
Green
Urbana IL 61801

Call Sign: N9ZCS
Mary I Gunawan
Urh 220 Daniels 1010 W
Green St
Urbana IL 61801

Call Sign: KA9OFX
Jeffrey J Fairchild
703 Dodson Dr E
Urbana IL 61801

Call Sign: KC9IHX
Ryan Harden
1914 E Amber Ln 208
Urbana IL 61802

Call Sign: KC9IKL
Josh Reeley
1912 E Amber Ln Apt 203
Urbana IL 61802

Call Sign: K9AN
Steven J Franke
3314 E Anthony Dr
Urbana IL 61802

Call Sign: N9WJP
Patricia M Franke
3314A E Anthony Dr
Urbana IL 61801

Call Sign: N9TNT

Brandon C Bowersox
802 E California
Urbana IL 61801

Call Sign: K9UMI
Carl C Reiner
503 E Colorado Ave
Urbana IL 61801

Call Sign: KF6SFR
Yuxin Zhou
703 E Colorado Ave Apt 109
Urbana IL 61801

Call Sign: W9CW
Donald R Allen
701 E Dodson Dr
Urbana IL 618022109

Call Sign: KF9IR
Gary L Buck
308 E Elm St
Urbana IL 61801

Call Sign: N9KZX
Laura G Kolb
508 E Elm St
Urbana IL 61801

Call Sign: KC9DEM
John J Farney
2504 E Florida Ave
Urbana IL 61802

Call Sign: KE9MQ
Laurence E Kirby
1406 E Ford Harris Rd
Urbana IL 618029785

Call Sign: KC9IOB
Scott R Dossett
501 E High St
Urbana IL 61801

Call Sign: W9KZY
Carl G Jockusch Jr
704 E McHenry St
Urbana IL 61801

Call Sign: N9WPX
Kelly J Griner
406 E Michigan Ave Apt 3
Urbana IL 61801

Call Sign: KI4ZZX
Lucas A Scharf
201 E Mumford Dr
Urbana IL 61801

Call Sign: KB9ZZV
Henry D Fineberg
408 E Oakbrook Cir
Urbana IL 61802

Call Sign: KC9MHP
John C Akers
1905 E Prairie Wind
Urbana IL 618024447

Call Sign: KC9HBH
Gary R Swenson
107 E Sherwin Dr
Urbana IL 61802

Call Sign: KA9ORH
Stephen M Ater
206 E Sherwin Dr
Urbana IL 61802

Call Sign: KB9LCC
Keith W Wessel
902 E Shurts St
Urbana IL 61801

Call Sign: W9SZ
Zachary R Widup
1003 E Washington St
Urbana IL 618014415

Call Sign: WB9QPW
Harold E Stewart
1108 Eastern Dr
Urbana IL 61801

Call Sign: KB9ZZR
Amber L Miles
1107 Eliot Dr
Urbana IL 61801

Call Sign: W9ADS
Andrew J Wadsworth
1107 Eliot Dr
Urbana IL 61801

Call Sign: KB9ZZQ
Teresa L Miles
1107 Eliot Dr
Urbana IL 61801

Call Sign: KB9EKC
Terry Denny
306 Evergreen Ct W
Urbana IL 61801

Call Sign: KC9VGG
John E Stone
108 G H Baker Dr
Urbana IL 61801

Call Sign: W9RXC
Robert B Sandell
205 G H Baker Dr
Urbana IL 61801

Call Sign: N1ZZC
Alex Parga
1903 George Huff
Urbana IL 61801

Call Sign: KC9KAO
Xin Chen
802 Hawthorne Dr
Urbana IL 61801

Call Sign: AB9NC
Xin Chen
802 Hawthorne Dr
Urbana IL 61801

Call Sign: KB9OTO
Daniel T Smith
2911 Haydon Dr
Urbana IL 61802

Call Sign: KK9CK
Gail A Mc Williams
2707 Holcomb Dr

Urbana IL 61802

Call Sign: KC9CK
John A Mc Williams
2707 Holcomb Dr
Urbana IL 61802

Call Sign: N0YHH
Steven L Stanley
1704 Independence Ave
Urbana IL 61802

Call Sign: KC9QFL
Scott Sivers
1304 Jackson Rd
Urbana IL 61802

Call Sign: WB9HFK
Mark A Prather
1804 Jean Lee Ct
Urbana IL 618027056

Call Sign: KC9JJM
Kenneth R Miller
1405 Lincolnwood Dr
Urbana IL 61802

Call Sign: KE9NL
Dennis S Anderson
20 Loral
Urbana IL 61801

Call Sign: KB9UJW
Joshua P Tolbert
404 MacArthur Dr
Urbana IL 61802

Call Sign: KG9OE
Robert P Tolbert
404 MacArthur Dr
Urbana IL 61802

Call Sign: AA9XO
Robert P Tolbert
404 MacArthur Dr
Urbana IL 61802

Call Sign: AA9X
Robert P Tolbert

404 MacArthur Dr
Urbana IL 61802

Call Sign: KC9MJE
Paul W Grindley
1221 Mason Cir
Urbana IL 61802

Call Sign: KC9HBI
Viki L Hawley
602 McGee Rd
Urbana IL 61802

Call Sign: KE9UW
Charles J Hawley Jr
602 McGee Rd
Urbana IL 61802

Call Sign: WB9LQB
Raymond M Fish
801 McHenry
Urbana IL 61801

Call Sign: KC9HXY
Joan M Friedman
101 Meadow Dr
Urbana IL 618015822

Call Sign: W9KMS
James A Aaron
1203A Mitchem Dr
Urbana IL 61801

Call Sign: KC9LMH
Brian M Latimer
1312 Montgomery St
Urbana IL 61802

Call Sign: W9YR
Jay D Gooch
1204 N Berkley
Urbana IL 61801

Call Sign: KB9GAV
Jay W Bennett
309 N Busey 7
Urbana IL 61801

Call Sign: KB9ELJ

Sue A Stone
3211 N Cottonwood Rd
Urbana IL 61801

Call Sign: KB9YSZ
Thomas B Pullyard
6504 N Cunningham Ave
Urbana IL 61802

Call Sign: KC9AZW
Philip J Reiter
1341 N Lincoln Ave 2040
Urbana IL 618011360

Call Sign: K9CFD
Thomas B Yu
1903 Oliver 7
Urbana IL 61802

Call Sign: K9BLG
James G Simpson
1108 Patton Pl
Urbana IL 61801

Call Sign: WB9FAZ
Wayne H Szafranski
1811 Prairie Winds Cir
Urbana IL 61802

Call Sign: N9MSC
Consuelo J Alvarez
423 Ral 1209 W California St
Urbana IL 61801

Call Sign: KC9EOM
Maria C Peters
3106 Ridge Park Rd
Urbana IL 61802

Call Sign: KB9VAE
Jayesh V Shah
1003 S Anderson St
Urbana IL 61801

Call Sign: KB0FOS
Matthew W Olson
407 S Anderson St S Apt
Urbana IL 61801

Call Sign: AB9UJ
Chris Bonnell
703 S Broadway Apt 2
Urbana IL 61801

Call Sign: KA9PYL
Darryl A Pifer
505 S Busey 107
Urbana IL 61801

Call Sign: KC9PPZ
Leslie G Gasser
2009 S Cottage Grove Ave
Urbana IL 61801

Call Sign: AB9UH
Leslie G Gasser
2009 S Cottage Grove Ave
Urbana IL 61801

Call Sign: W9XC
Leslie G Gasser
2009 S Cottage Grove Ave
Urbana IL 61801

Call Sign: N9VVK
Joseph R Rannebarger
205 S Glover Ave
Urbana IL 61802

Call Sign: KC9RHM
Zachary A Brown
311 S Glover Ave
Urbana IL 61802

Call Sign: KC9MVR
Alexander R Ghosh
300 S Goodwin Ave Apt 502
Urbana IL 61801

Call Sign: KA9ZPG
Mike B Dieter
103 S Goodwin St
Urbana IL 61801

Call Sign: KC9GIW
David P Bellmore
1603 S Grove Ave
Urbana IL 61801

Call Sign: KC9HNB
Andrew M Pritchard
1602 S Grove St
Urbana IL 61801

Call Sign: KC9CPM
Paul W Wefel
1603 S Hillcrest
Urbana IL 61801

Call Sign: KC9POT
Benjamin A Sweedler
1502 S Hillcrest St
Urbana IL 61801

Call Sign: KB9ZZX
Jeremy S Bredfeldt
1404 S Lincoln Ave
Urbana IL 61801

Call Sign: KC9CPO
Jon M Dugan
1301A S Maple Ave
Urbana IL 61801

Call Sign: W9BEU
Joseph W Corbett
507 S McCullough
Urbana IL 618013938

Call Sign: KC9FJK
Kathryn A Swiontek
103 S McCullough 3
Urbana IL 61801

Call Sign: KC9MJD
Yih-Chun Hu
1605 S Orchard St
Urbana IL 61801

Call Sign: KA9CAP
Ronald E Berkman
1003 S Philo Rd
Urbana IL 618015372

Call Sign: W9CD
Clement C Constant Jr
2208 S Race St

Urbana IL 61801

Call Sign: WB9ITN
Michael E Berger
1512 S Smith Rd
Urbana IL 61802

Call Sign: N9SAJ
Jamie A Nelson
1003 S Smith Rd Apt A
Urbana IL 618025645

Call Sign: KC9DKF
Lisa A Murphy
1604 S Vine St
Urbana IL 61801

Call Sign: WA9AQG
Daniel R Grayson
2409 S Vine St
Urbana IL 61801

Call Sign: KB9IFV
Paul D Grayson
2409 S Vine St
Urbana IL 61801

Call Sign: KC9TQT
Benjamin T Brem
1007 S Webber St
Urbana IL 61801

Call Sign: NW9N
Benjamin T Brem
1007 S Webber St
Urbana IL 61801

Call Sign: W9KQ
Benjamin T Brem
1007 S Webber St
Urbana IL 61801

Call Sign: KC9HGM
Aaron Dufrene
401 S Webber St Apt B
Urbana IL 61801

Call Sign: N9GAS
Gregory A Smith

809 Scoville Ave
Urbana IL 61801

Call Sign: KC9DDX
Kimberly S Lewis
2413 Sharlyn Dr
Urbana IL 61802

Call Sign: KA9ZPH
Sandy I Helman
2015 Silver Ct W
Urbana IL 61801

Call Sign: KC9ISO
Gregory N Sellers
2607 Somerset Dr
Urbana IL 61802

Call Sign: KB9QBU
Diane E Ditzler
31 Toni Ln
Urbana IL 61802

Call Sign: NB9F
Chris Bonnell
103 W California Ave
Urbana IL 61801

Call Sign: KB9UBQ
Alijeet S Bains
1009 W Clark St 102
Urbana IL 61801

Call Sign: KB9YND
Curry B Taylor
808 W Clark St 4
Urbana IL 61801

Call Sign: AB9BG
Curry B Taylor
808 W Clark St 4
Urbana IL 61801

Call Sign: N9RZB
Nicolas S Dade
405 W Delaware
Urbana IL 61801

Call Sign: N9XDN

Paul A Toth
911 W Eads St
Urbana IL 61801

Call Sign: KF9FF
Charles V Kline
306 W Florida Ave
Urbana IL 61801

Call Sign: WA9DNH
Robert W Anderson
209 W Green
Urbana IL 61801

Call Sign: KB9USB
David A Iffland
803 W Green 7
Urbana IL 61801

Call Sign: KC9JSB
Nick Giannopoulos
806 W Green St 205
Urbana IL 61801

Call Sign: N9RRD
Joseph J Tien
1010 W Green St 314
Urbana IL 61801

Call Sign: KC9MAH
Jun-Soo Park
1107 W Green St 335
Urbana IL 61810

Call Sign: KC9JRZ
Michael Qin
806 W Green St Apt 205
Urbana IL 61801

Call Sign: W9YH
Synton ARC
1406 W Green St Everitt Lab
Urbana IL 61801

Call Sign: W9KVF
Kenneth M Broga
205 W Indiana Ave
Urbana IL 61801

Call Sign: W9QS
Kenneth M Broga
205 W Indiana Ave
Urbana IL 61801

Call Sign: KB9KGV
Brian Foote
209 W Iowa St
Urbana IL 61801

Call Sign: K9XE
Ray F Boehmer
210 W Iowa St
Urbana IL 61801

Call Sign: KC9GIX
Purvesh B Thakker
1004 W Main St Apt 103
Urbana IL 61801

Call Sign: W9SB
Wayne E Otey
906.5 W Nevada St Apt 5
Urbana IL 61801

Call Sign: KB9SJA
Mark D Ginsberg
608 W Pennsylvania
Urbana IL 61801

Call Sign: KB9LRZ
University High School ARC
1212 W Springfield Ave
Urbana IL 61801

Call Sign: N9ZCP
Herry Sutanto
1109 W Stoughton 14
Urbana IL 61801

Call Sign: KB9PKE
Brian T Sleight
1004 W Stoughton 4
Urbana IL 61801

Call Sign: KC9CHT
Paul A Cziko
506 W Vermont
Urbana IL 61801

Call Sign: N9MJZ
Gary A Cziko
506 W Vermont Ave
Urbana IL 61801

Call Sign: KC9CVO
Eddy Tiner
402 W Washington
Urbana IL 61801

Call Sign: N9VOS
Henry K Mayer
711 W Washington
Urbana IL 61801

Call Sign: KB9IRJ
David N Griffiths
206 W Washington 12
Urbana IL 61801

Call Sign: W9IVB
Jack V Washburn
2 Weaver Pl
Urbana IL 61801

Call Sign: KB9DUY
Mark B Czarnowski
1709 B Willow Ct
Urbana IL 61801

Call Sign: W9MBC
Mark B Czarnowski
1709 b Willow Ct
Urbana IL 61801

Call Sign: KA9GKR
Gary G Swearingen
1817 Willow View Dr
Urbana IL 61801

Call Sign: N9NDG
Donald L Catherman II
1717 Wilson Rd
Urbana IL 61801

Call Sign: WD9IHM
Thomas W Johnson
Lot 8 Wilson Trailer Park

Urbana IL 61801

Call Sign: N9MNS
Will J Worley
2106 Zuppke
Urbana IL 61801

Call Sign: KA1YDI
Blair F Goodlin Jr
Urbana IL 61803

Call Sign: KC9AZV
Joseph W Hamilton
Urbana IL 618030476

Call Sign: AB9FJ
Joseph W Hamilton
Urbana IL 618030476

Call Sign: KC9KBE
Charles A Friedmann
Urbana IL 618030602

Call Sign: KB9TOO
Joseph P Shectman
Urbana IL 618030974

FCC Amateur Radio Licenses in Ursa

Call Sign: KC9KZU
David P Valeu
2574 E 603rd Ln
Ursa IL 62376

Call Sign: W9DPV
David P Valeu
2574 E 603rd Ln
Ursa IL 62376

Call Sign: KB9YN
Ron A Eberle
102 East St
Ursa IL 62376

Call Sign: KC9NER
Paul H Shriver
809 N 2000th Ave
Ursa IL 62376

Call Sign: KC9EQV
Kimberly K Swiderski
200 Sycamore
Ursa IL 62376

Call Sign: KB9HMC
John W Bates Sr
Ursa IL 62376

FCC Amateur Radio Licenses in Utica

Call Sign: KC9CIN
Mark E Mackay
130 Armstrong St
Utica IL 61373

Call Sign: KC9ROK
Jason R Corneglio
3021 E 10th Rd
Utica IL 61373

Call Sign: N9LCI
Edward W Rogers
3037 E 11th Rd
Utica IL 61373

Call Sign: N9RER
Karen A Rogers
3037 E 11th Rd
Utica IL 61373

Call Sign: KC9CIO
Paul A Bottomley
2871 E 752nd Rd
Utica IL 61373

Call Sign: KC9CVP
Brian A Shofner
309 E Church
Utica IL 61373

Call Sign: WB9ZJK
Craig E Wagner
1090 N 2803 Rd
Utica IL 61373

Call Sign: K9ZJK

Craig E Wagner
1090 N 2803 Rd
Utica IL 61373

Call Sign: KB9WKA
Patricia J Wagner
1090 N 2803 Rd
Utica IL 61373

Call Sign: N9YMB
Dustin L Spray
509 S Clark
Utica IL 61373

Call Sign: KC9IDH
David P Mateika
407 W Washington St
Utica IL 61373

Call Sign: KC9IZV
Mark L Connell
Utica IL 61373

Call Sign: K9MLC
Mark L Connell
Utica IL 61373

Call Sign: KC9CFU
Tri County ARS
Utica IL 61373

FCC Amateur Radio Licenses in Valier

Call Sign: K5QED
Charles A Kaross
111 E Burley St
Valier IL 628910065

Call Sign: N9MKW
Robert J Tindall
Box 361 Hayes St
Valier IL 62891

Call Sign: N9OUD
Dean G Mercer
101 Rea St
Valier IL 62891

Call Sign: K9AFV
Martin H Buchanan
503 S Jefferson
Valier IL 628910376

Call Sign: KC9CKO
David Patton
Valier IL 628910120

Call Sign: KC9CKP
Stephen L Patton
Valier IL 628910120

FCC Amateur Radio Licenses in Valmeyer

Call Sign: N0HOZ
Jeffrey P Schwartz
211 E Harrisonville
Valmeyer IL 62295

Call Sign: W0JPS
Jeffrey P Schwartz
211 E Harrisonville
Valmeyer IL 62295

FCC Amateur Radio Licenses in Vandalia

Call Sign: N9PVK
Robert D Dugan
Rr 2 Box 186
Vandalia IL 62471

Call Sign: KA9VPZ
Karen S Casner
Rt 1 Box 410
Vandalia IL 62471

Call Sign: KE9DW
William R Casner
Rt 1 Box 410
Vandalia IL 62471

Call Sign: AA8OS
Derek A Stewart
Rr 3 Box 739
Vandalia IL 62471

Call Sign: KB8PLO
Sharla J Stewart
Rr 3 Box 739
Vandalia IL 62471

Call Sign: W9VUZ
George H Huber
Rt 3 Box 769
Vandalia IL 62471

Call Sign: KB9WEV
Ryan A Cunningham
Rr3 Box 771
Vandalia IL 62471

Call Sign: WD9CTG
Robert D Ritter Jr
Imco Dr
Vandalia IL 62471

Call Sign: KC9IYP
Theodore B Miller
1006 N 2nd St
Vandalia IL 62471

Call Sign: KF9UC
Charles W Evans Jr
504 N 6th St
Vandalia IL 62471

Call Sign: K9CNG
Albert Hourigan Jr
839 N 6th St
Vandalia IL 62471

Call Sign: KA9ONJ
Norman L Lankow
116 N Elm St
Vandalia IL 62471

Call Sign: WA9OPW
Charles W Barenfanger Jr
129 N Kennedy Blvd
Vandalia IL 62471

Call Sign: KC9ISQ
Old Capital ARC
221 S 7th St
Vandalia IL 62471

Call Sign: KA9EZB
Hugh L O Dell
1405 St Louis Ave
Vandalia IL 62471

Call Sign: KB9AFH
Nancy J Campbell
2110 W Jefferson
Vandalia IL 62471

Call Sign: N9LKC
Howard W White
318 W Madison St
Vandalia IL 62471

Call Sign: N9PVL
Mary C White
318 W Madison St
Vandalia IL 62471

Call Sign: KC9IYN
Mark L Devall
425 W Main
Vandalia IL 62471

Call Sign: KC9IYO
Brian C Donnals
Vandalia IL 62471

Call Sign: KC9AHJ
George A Huber
Vandalia IL 62471

FCC Amateur Radio Licenses in Varna

Call Sign: KB9RKS
Steven J Brent
100 Chestnut
Varna IL 61375

Call Sign: WD9HZK
Dwight E Aussieker
771 CR 2350E
Varna IL 61375

Call Sign: KC9AWC
Jessica L Miller

Varna IL 61375

Call Sign: KB9PUT
Nick G Sotiriou
Varna IL 61378

FCC Amateur Radio Licenses in Venedy

Call Sign: KA0ROG
Richard E Stout
13321 CR 12
Venedy IL 62214

Call Sign: KB9OGK
Donald W Allen
159 Elkhorn Rd
Venedy IL 62214

Call Sign: KB9SCS
Glen Stewart
8662 SR 153
Venedy IL 622141832

Call Sign: KB9RZU
Clinton G Tull
22 W Church
Venedy IL 62214

FCC Amateur Radio Licenses in Vergennes

Call Sign: KA9RGA
Curtis E Terry
475 Holt
Vergennes IL 62994

FCC Amateur Radio Licenses in Vermilion

Call Sign: KB9RMU
William D Brown
Vermilion IL 61955

FCC Amateur Radio Licenses in Vermont

Call Sign: KA9AID

Steven C Young
1st W S St
Vermont IL 61484

Call Sign: N9AKS
Susan C Young
Rr 1 Box 72
Vermont IL 61484

Call Sign: KB9HRM
Harold L Mc Curdy
Rr 1 Box 93
Vermont IL 61484

Call Sign: K9OKO
James I Mc Gaughey
201 E 6th St
Vermont IL 61484

Call Sign: KB9PPY
Christopher M Wilson
300 S Walnut Rr 1 Box 35
Vermont IL 61484

Call Sign: N9MZT
Mary E Wilson
101 W 3rd
Vermont IL 61484

Call Sign: KC9OVI
Rachel B Haines
609 W 5th St
Vermont IL 61484

Call Sign: W9OER
Frederick B Haines
609 W 5th St
Vermont IL 61484

Call Sign: KC9NTU
Kevin S Haines
609 W 5th St
Vermont IL 61484

Call Sign: KC9OYN
Rebecca C Haines
609 W 5th St
Vermont IL 61484

Call Sign: KA5IWM
Marilyn R Haines
609 W 5th St
Vermont IL 61484

Call Sign: W9CPI
Stephen M Haines
609 W 5th St
Vermont IL 61484

Call Sign: K9EWK
O D Kost
Vermont IL 61484

Call Sign: KB9OH
Donald K Mc Carty
Vermont IL 61484

Call Sign: WA9BTT
Robert A Young
Vermont IL 61484

FCC Amateur Radio Licenses in Vernon

Call Sign: KB9WLE
John D Paulding
8761 Seven Hills Rd
Vernon IL 62892

Call Sign: KB9WLG
Michael L Paulding
8761 Seven Hills Rd
Vernon IL 62892

FCC Amateur Radio Licenses in Verona

Call Sign: N0ZTG
Finis H Naylor
420 Clark St
Verona IL 60479

Call Sign: N9YZA
Peter M Clarke
5520 W Indian Trl Rd
Verona IL 60479

FCC Amateur Radio Licenses in Versailles

Call Sign: KA9PHT
Roger L Luthy
Rr 1 Box 154
Versailles IL 62378

Call Sign: KB9JVU
Randall S Hester
210 E 1st
Versailles IL 62378

Call Sign: KB9QEF
Randall T Hester
314 N Lindsey
Versailles IL 62378

FCC Amateur Radio Licenses in Vienna

Call Sign: WW9F
James E Monroe
Rr 1 Box 1374
Vienna IL 62995

Call Sign: N9TSK
Patricia A Mighell
Rr 3 Box 288
Vienna IL 62995

Call Sign: KF9CO
Dannie L Waters
Rr 3 Box 507
Vienna IL 62995

Call Sign: N9DPA
Tilford Sanders
800 Galeener
Vienna IL 62995

Call Sign: WB9WJW
Jack Shelton
405 Galeener St
Vienna IL 62995

Call Sign: KA9JSD
Emil R Chambers
4045 Hwy 45 W

Vienna IL 62995

Call Sign: W9WG
James R Gray
701 Locust St
Vienna IL 62995

Call Sign: KA9UUQ
Jim F Miller
1007 Locust St
Vienna IL 62995

Call Sign: AA9PD
Frank C Workman
4200 Mt Shelter Care Rd
Vienna IL 62995

Call Sign: KC9TVH
Virgil D Miles
1560 Mt Shelter Rd
Vienna IL 62995

Call Sign: WB9KYW
Robert A Iwasyk
5550 Old Metropolis Rd
Vienna IL 629953724

Call Sign: KA9TXG
Kenneth R Hall
11650 Pleasant Ridge Rd
Vienna IL 62995

Call Sign: WB9WIY
Charles R Casper
150 Tulip Ln
Vienna IL 62995

Call Sign: KA9GDZ
Mary J Casper
150 Tulip Ln
Vienna IL 62995

Call Sign: KC9UXE
Jamie L Simmons
703 W Vine St
Vienna IL 62995

Call Sign: KB9EGY
Gene R Bishop

Vienna IL 62995

Call Sign: KA9OCL
Jane M Monroe
Vienna IL 62995

Call Sign: N9TSJ
John W Hand
Vienna IL 62995

FCC Amateur Radio Licenses in Villa Grove

Call Sign: N9HNG
Charles G Keith
402 Front St
Villa Grove IL 61956

Call Sign: KA9FCM
Joel E Lasswell
1353 N CR 1550 E
Villa Grove IL 61956

Call Sign: K9GTN
William J Jones
1 S Main St
Villa Grove IL 61956

Call Sign: N9XPK
Shirley K Fancher
504 S Spruce
Villa Grove IL 61956

Call Sign: KB9KBW
William H Olehy
201 Vine St
Villa Grove IL 61956

Call Sign: KA9LEU
James D Osborne
206 W Vine St
Villa Grove IL 61956

FCC Amateur Radio Licenses in Villa Ridge

Call Sign: N9WHD
Timothy D Mize
Rt 1 Box 1040 Meridian Rd

Villa Ridge IL 62996

Call Sign: KB9JLY
John D Mathis
Rr 1 Box 1830
Villa Ridge IL 62996

Call Sign: WA9BCN
Charles D Garrett
3022 Olmsted Rd
Villa Ridge IL 62996

Call Sign: WB1FFD
Raymond J Nottage
Box 1405 Rt 1
Villa Ridge IL 62996

FCC Amateur Radio Licenses in Viola

Call Sign: KB9WGW
Joseph J Welsh
1814 16th Ave
Viola IL 61486

Call Sign: KC9EHE
Mercer County Amater Radio
Group
1814 16th Ave
Viola IL 61486

Call Sign: N9RXM
Allen E Bloomfield
1508 16th St And 20th Ave
Viola IL 61486

Call Sign: KA9VZW
Gerald M Young
Viola IL 61486

Call Sign: N7PGP
Lynda E Raniero
Viola IL 614860051

Call Sign: W7DLE
Ralph J Raniero
Viola IL 614860051

FCC Amateur Radio Licenses in Virden

Call Sign: W9JXW
Walter E Weffenstette
35168 E 5th Rd
Virden IL 626904015

Call Sign: N9MCO
Robert A Ribley
1022 Noble St
Virden IL 62690

Call Sign: KC9GLY
Mark W Firehammer Jr
534 S Church St
Virden IL 62690

Call Sign: N9REW
James R Gerrity
565 W Jackson
Virden IL 62690

Call Sign: K9OLF
Charles E Jones
169 W Jackson St
Virden IL 62690

Call Sign: N9UNX
Jean O Marye
221 Wrightsman
Virden IL 62690

Call Sign: WS9V
James J Riba
Virden IL 62690

FCC Amateur Radio Licenses in Virginia

Call Sign: AA9DV
Donald W Riley
221 E Liberty
Virginia IL 62691

Call Sign: KB9EZY
Donna M Riley
221 E Liberty
Virginia IL 62691

Call Sign: N9RCO
Paul C Riley
221 E Liberty
Virginia IL 62691

Call Sign: KC9IDX
Frank E Anderson
432 E Union
Virginia IL 62691

Call Sign: KB2VKM
Kendra L Higgins
143 Illnois Rt 78
Virginia IL 62691

Call Sign: W9FIF
Robert A Daniel
860 Maple
Virginia IL 62691

Call Sign: N9QOH
Sean M Daniel
860 Maple St
Virginia IL 62691

Call Sign: KB9MGX
Michael E Lowe
231 N Front
Virginia IL 62691

Call Sign: WA9UQC
Ernest E Launer
502 S Cass St
Virginia IL 62691

Call Sign: KC9VCQ
Shirley A Bell
271 S Job
Virginia IL 62691

Call Sign: KC9VCP
Ronald L Bell
271 S Job St
Virginia IL 62691

Call Sign: N9XSU
Beverly K Bencher
302 S Main
Virginia IL 62691

Call Sign: N9QOI
James A Daniel
102 W Union St
Virginia IL 62691

FCC Amateur Radio Licenses in Walnut

Call Sign: N4GTX
Charles R Chadwick Jr
29604 1050E St
Walnut IL 61376

Call Sign: WA9RRB
Charles H Meisenheimer
14658 2400 N Ave
Walnut IL 613769801

Call Sign: KA9QFF
Sharon L Meisenheimer
14702 2400 N Ave
Walnut IL 613769748

Call Sign: K9WHW
Kenneth F Hardesty
9491 2775 N Ave
Walnut IL 613769178

Call Sign: WD9INW
Lester L Meisenheimer
R 1 Box 127A
Walnut IL 613769748

Call Sign: N9LVN
Malcolm C Willis
112 Clark St
Walnut IL 61376

Call Sign: KA9FZT
Robert K Neahring
114 Clark St
Walnut IL 61376

Call Sign: KB9NFV
Ryan T Atherton
404 Red Oak Rd
Walnut IL 61376

Call Sign: KC9PZR
Edward R Thompson
407 Whitver St
Walnut IL 61376

Call Sign: KC9PZM
Larry A Dewaele
Walnut IL 61376

FCC Amateur Radio Licenses in Walnut Hill

Call Sign: KC9EKL
Tammy J Landes
469 Myers Rd
Walnut Hill IL 62893

Call Sign: N9VQG
Frederick W Jones
20299 N Springer Church Ln
Walnut Hill IL 62893

FCC Amateur Radio Licenses in Walsh

Call Sign: WA9QOK
Charles R Heuman
7832 Main St
Walsh IL 62297

FCC Amateur Radio Licenses in Walshville

Call Sign: KB9MPM
Harold A Laurent
7105 Elm Tr
Walshville IL 62091

FCC Amateur Radio Licenses in Waltonville

Call Sign: WY9I
Roger A Marcum
218 Cole St
Waltonville IL 62894

Call Sign: KB9HOE

Carol J Cole
109 Dodds
Waltonville IL 62894

Call Sign: KB9HOB
Lyndell R Cole
109 Dodds
Waltonville IL 62894

Call Sign: KB9RWR
Melvin L Delaney
6998 N Spruce Ln
Waltonville IL 62894

Call Sign: KB9HEM
Rachael M Shurtz
Waltonville IL 62894

FCC Amateur Radio Licenses in Warren

Call Sign: KB9HDK
Robert D Sutter
506 Tisdell Ave
Warren IL 61087

Call Sign: KB9LEZ
Todd S Schwalbe
118 W Main St
Warren IL 61087

Call Sign: KF9SD
Patrick T Bottensek
Warren IL 61087

FCC Amateur Radio Licenses in Warrensburg

Call Sign: KC9BOK
Aaron R Thomas
Rr 1 Box 220A
Warrensburg IL 62573

Call Sign: K9TTZ
Robert W Kimmons
11242 N Kenney Rd
Warrensburg IL 62573

Call Sign: KC9ALT

Jack E Pugh
Warrensburg IL 62573

FCC Amateur Radio Licenses in Warsaw

Call Sign: W9NVG
George W Vradenburg
530 Clark St
Warsaw IL 62379

Call Sign: WB0ZHB
Charles P Porter II
330 Crawford St
Warsaw IL 623791233

Call Sign: KC9PL
John E Hobart
554 E Co Rd 1000
Warsaw IL 62379

Call Sign: K9BD
James L Cate
1177 N CR 630
Warsaw IL 62379

Call Sign: KA9AVO
Joseph L Bartholomew
620 Spruce
Warsaw IL 62379

FCC Amateur Radio Licenses in Washburn

Call Sign: KC9JVG
Jeremy D Degenhart
2022 CR 1400 E
Washburn IL 61570

Call Sign: KC9DHM
Kyle R Patterson
1840 CR 2100 N
Washburn IL 61570

Call Sign: N9WSS
Jerroll W Meinders
301 W Walnut
Washburn IL 61570

Call Sign: N9BBV
Robert C Heuermann Jr
408 Almond Dr
Washington IL 61571

Call Sign: KB9TVW
Douglas J Cecil
1501 Aspen Dr
Washington IL 61571

Call Sign: N9RFT
Andrew N Braun
1720 Autumn Rdg
Washington IL 61571

Call Sign: KB9JKY
James M Fisher
603 Avon Ct
Washington IL 61571

Call Sign: AA9XZ
James M Fisher
603 Avon Ct
Washington IL 61571

Call Sign: WD9FQM
William C Hatfield
304 Barbara Pkwy
Washington IL 61571

Call Sign: N9IPB
Michael B Miller
304 Belaire Dr
Washington IL 61571

Call Sign: N9GZP
Marc A Heuermann
403 Belaire Dr
Washington IL 615713368

Call Sign: W9AGS
Ronnie E Crebo
206 Bess St
Washington IL 61571

Call Sign: N9MZV

Robert J Petzing
120 Briar Ln
Washington IL 61571

Call Sign: KC9UCM
Shawn M Seibert
148 Camelin Dr
Washington IL 61571

Call Sign: KB9TBR
Robert J Warburton
1934 Canterbury Dr Apt 1A
Washington IL 61571

Call Sign: KC9QCS
Nicholas N De Stefano
303 Carlock Ct
Washington IL 61571

Call Sign: KB9GVB
Henry G Mc Cann
211 Central
Washington IL 61571

Call Sign: WA9SKV
William L Tripp
1004 Chelsea Pl
Washington IL 61571

Call Sign: KA9UKJ
Carl M Volz
117 Danforth
Washington IL 61571

Call Sign: N9XJX
Robert D Warner
206 Daniel Pkwy
Washington IL 61571

Call Sign: N9YUV
Adrian M Tubbs
1102 Devon Ln
Washington IL 61571

Call Sign: KC9LNJ
David M Thompson
902 Devonshire Rd
Washington IL 61571

Call Sign: KC9UCR
Joshua W Kramer
211 E Adams
Washington IL 61571

Call Sign: KB9CUR
Ryan D Cooper
1001 E Adams
Washington IL 61571

Call Sign: WA9LHK
Thomas M Berry
1012 E Adams
Washington IL 61571

Call Sign: W9TMB
Thomas M Berry
1012 E Adams
Washington IL 61571

Call Sign: KA9UYV
Robert L Roman
103 E Almond Dr
Washington IL 61571

Call Sign: N9GCA
Joanne L Heuermann
408 E Almond Dr
Washington IL 61571

Call Sign: WB9FEF
Clara Grenzebach
Rr2 E Cooper Rd
Washington IL 61571

Call Sign: KD0WW
John A Turnbull
109 E Holland
Washington IL 61571

Call Sign: KA9YCO
Earl A Riley
102 E Lancaster
Washington IL 61571

Call Sign: N9YUS
James R Jordan
2228 E Linnhill Ln
Washington IL 61571

Call Sign: N9ZQY
Andrew J Farraher
1500 Eagle Ave Apt 8
Washington IL 61571

Call Sign: WA9ADC
Francis J Andrews
904 Eldridge
Washington IL 615712822

Call Sign: AA9TY
Dale G Miller
702 Eldridge St
Washington IL 61571

Call Sign: KC9LTP
Christopher J Gavin
307 Elmhurst Dr
Washington IL 61571

Call Sign: N9WMJ
William B Shelander
283 Fairview
Washington IL 61571

Call Sign: N9KTZ
Philip J Irwin
203 Grandyle
Washington IL 61571

Call Sign: KB9IGH
Steve M Mc Candless
1615 Greenfield Dr
Washington IL 61571

Call Sign: K9SOI
Gary L Mc Candless
1615 Greenfield Dr
Washington IL 61571

Call Sign: WB9WMS
Fred L Block
22227 Grosenbach Rd
Washington IL 61571

Call Sign: WB9TPV
Jon I Gullett
22252 Grosenbach Rd

Washington IL 61571

Call Sign: KC9UCU
Larry M Broadfield
315 Hale St
Washington IL 61571

Call Sign: KB9ATO
De Wayne C Barton
1878 Hickory
Washington IL 61571

Call Sign: N9OJO
Bernard L Ingle
1994 Inglewood Dr
Washington IL 61571

Call Sign: W9JLS
Richard J Scott
1201 Kingsbury Rd
Washington IL 61571

Call Sign: KB9KCB
Robert R Mc Pheeters
2217 Knollaire Dr
Washington IL 615713320

Call Sign: WX9JC
Jarrod J Cook
409 Lexington Dr
Washington IL 61571

Call Sign: KA9JHL
Alan C Rodney
26415 Liberty Ln
Washington IL 61571

Call Sign: AA9JL
Richard E Dilts
306 Lynn Haven
Washington IL 61571

Call Sign: WD9IBM
James F Turner
302 Lynnhaven Dr
Washington IL 61571

Call Sign: N9YVJ
Steve J Stringfellow

315 Madison St
Washington IL 61571

Call Sign: N9XHL
David F Armstrong
1002 Mallard Way
Washington IL 61571

Call Sign: KB9TOA
Douglas S Meiner
2234 Mar Vista Dr
Washington IL 61571

Call Sign: KC9KSF
Mark P Riggio
306 Meadowlark Ln
Washington IL 615713331

Call Sign: K9MPR
Mark P Riggio
306 Meadowlark Ln
Washington IL 615713331

Call Sign: N9ZAA
John H Schmidt
815 Morris St
Washington IL 61571

Call Sign: WD9ILQ
R C Phillips
116 N Behrends
Washington IL 61571

Call Sign: KB9ZMS
Michael W Hediger
211 N Linnhill Ln
Washington IL 615711951

Call Sign: KB9WXY
Denise J Magnuson
610 N Main
Washington IL 61571

Call Sign: KB9THJ
Frank A Magnuson
610 N Main
Washington IL 61571

Call Sign: KB9WXZ

Jesse B Magnuson
610 N Main
Washington IL 61571

Call Sign: N9KGV
Cale E Eilers
502 N Main Apt I
Washington IL 61571

Call Sign: KC9CZK
David A Lucas
404 N Main St
Washington IL 61571

Call Sign: N9GYI
Todd J Heuermann
606 N Main St
Washington IL 61571

Call Sign: KA0UTE
Jean A Turnbull
502 N Main St P
Washington IL 61571

Call Sign: N9LFE
Thomas L Hunt
2222 Northridge Ln
Washington IL 61571

Call Sign: KB9PAA
Herbert A Paul
210 Oakwood Cir
Washington IL 61571

Call Sign: KA9VFA
Michael L Brashers
107 Oriental Dr
Washington IL 61571

Call Sign: KB9VVQ
Bryan D Kolb
106 Osage Dr
Washington IL 61571

Call Sign: KC9AHK
Thomas E Hyde
607 Peoria St
Washington IL 61571

Call Sign: KC9QVV
Thomas H Jefford
2269 Robin Rd
Washington IL 61571

Call Sign: KC9DHL
Deon M Miller
500 S Main
Washington IL 61571

Call Sign: KB9IAA
Nicholas A Poehlman
404 S Main St
Washington IL 61571

Call Sign: WA9CRT
Larry R Reed
604 S Main St
Washington IL 615712522

Call Sign: KC9MSD
Denise M Clothier
707 S Main St
Washington IL 615712566

Call Sign: KB9UMW
Danny E Crebo
406 S Summit Dr
Washington IL 61571

Call Sign: W9FYR
Steven A Tennant
607 S Summit Dr
Washington IL 61571

Call Sign: KC9OTU
James D Ashton
1412 Santa Fe Rd
Washington IL 61571

Call Sign: KC9TXD
William E Munstedt
1432 Santa Fe Rd
Washington IL 61571

Call Sign: WA9RGQ
Neely F Ragan Jr
272 School St
Washington IL 61571

Call Sign: WB9BDK
Jerome A Thies
1401 Shellbark Ct
Washington IL 61571

Call Sign: W9RRW
Louise O Lecocq
610 Spring
Washington IL 61571

Call Sign: W9FEM
Paul F Lecocq
610 Spring
Washington IL 61571

Call Sign: KC9UCX
Kevin A Wallisa
22082 Spring Creek Rd
Washington IL 61571

Call Sign: KB9PRJ
Robert C Keller
22432 Spring Creek Rd
Washington IL 61571

Call Sign: KC9PUO
Arthur Wild
22746 Spring Creek Rd
Washington IL 61571

Call Sign: KB9MJD
Andrew W Isbell
24875 Spring Creek Rd
Washington IL 61571

Call Sign: N9RPJ
Ronald W Burtsfield
24383 Springcreek Rd
Washington IL 61571

Call Sign: KE9CH
Joseph P Reames
306 Sterling
Washington IL 61571

Call Sign: KA9JFL
Denise M Reames
306 Sterling

Washington IL 615712106

Call Sign: KC9KAH
Steven R Bergstrom
1700 Sycamore
Washington IL 61571

Call Sign: N9UQN
Robert L Blaisdell
602 Terrace Ct
Washington IL 61571

Call Sign: KA9KJJ
Alfred W Dunham
510 W Adam St
Washington IL 61571

Call Sign: W9EZA
Danny L Hoover
407 W Adams St
Washington IL 61571

Call Sign: W9LBP
Diane M Hoover
407 W Adams St
Washington IL 61571

Call Sign: KC9TCP
Steven C Lawson
511 W Adams St
Washington IL 61571

Call Sign: WB9GRF
Wilburn W Watts
115 W Almond Dr
Washington IL 61571

Call Sign: KC9LNK
Gregory J Mc Candless
1407 W Jefferson St
Washington IL 61571

Call Sign: KC9UTN
Frank E Douglas IV
1609 W Jefferson St Apt A
Washington IL 61571

Call Sign: KC9UCL
William A Strickland

207 W Lawndale Ave
Washington IL 61571

Call Sign: K4BCM
Brian C Mendell
111 W Rio Dr
Washington IL 61571

Call Sign: K9EWF
Edwin W Fron
1402 Westgate Rd
Washington IL 60571

Call Sign: WD9DHB
Carl G Johnson
500 Whippoorwill Dr
Washington IL 61571

Call Sign: N1INP
Douglas S Allan
9 White Oat Ct
Washington IL 61571

Call Sign: KC9MKH
Michael W Burns
611 Wilshire Dr
Washington IL 61571

Call Sign: KC9SBZ
Ronald L Brautigan
603 Yorkshire Dr
Washington IL 61571

Call Sign: KF9XK
James B Degenhart
Washington IL 61571

Call Sign: KB9ZRG
Michael L Thorne
Washington IL 61571

FCC Amateur Radio Licenses in Washington Park

Call Sign: KC9BYR
Robert G Smith Sr
1400 N 53rd St
Washington Park IL
622042741

Call Sign: KB9RMW
Arthur R Aubuchon
5700 Warren
Washington Park IL 62204

FCC Amateur Radio Licenses in Wataga

Call Sign: WB9WER
Phyllis G Wallace
Rr 1 Box 56
Wataga IL 61488

Call Sign: WB9WEQ
Reba E Wallace Jr
Rr 1 Box 56
Wataga IL 61488

Call Sign: N9YVI
Bruce A Hagge
205 E Burch St
Wataga IL 61488

FCC Amateur Radio Licenses in Waterloo

Call Sign: W0RF
Francis X Davis
419 Adams Dr
Waterloo IL 62298

Call Sign: KG9CF
Dennis M Allscheid
8116 Andy Rd
Waterloo IL 62298

Call Sign: KC9ELX
Barbara A Maschmeyer
4832 Bohleysville R
Waterloo IL 62298

Call Sign: KL7MU
Carl E Maschmeyer
4832 Bohleysville Rd
Waterloo IL 622984638

Call Sign: N9WSH
Barbara A Boedges

311 Briarwood Dr
Waterloo IL 62298

Call Sign: KC9RUZ
Karen S Mccann
6 Country Lakes Ln
Waterloo IL 62298

Call Sign: KC9RUY
James P Mccann
6 Country Ln
Waterloo IL 62298

Call Sign: N9GQV
Rodney O Boker
7309 Covered Bridge Dr
Waterloo IL 62298

Call Sign: N9OMD
Billie R Hasty
7447 Covered Bridge Dr
Waterloo IL 62298

Call Sign: N9PBE
Gretchen E Hasty
7447 Covered Bridge Dr
Waterloo IL 62298

Call Sign: KC9RAY
Richard D Calvert
8479 D Rd
Waterloo IL 62298

Call Sign: KC9FHR
Barbara K Whitehouse
8731 D Rd
Waterloo IL 62298

Call Sign: N9ZNF
Gerald L Winschel
312 E 4th St
Waterloo IL 62298

Call Sign: KB9QKP
Alexander Y Fischer
628 E 4th St
Waterloo IL 62298

Call Sign: KB9JBP

Donovan J Fischer
628 E 4th St
Waterloo IL 62298

Call Sign: WY9X
Lewis Fischer
628 E 4th St
Waterloo IL 62298

Call Sign: KB9QBH
Linda K Fischer
628 E 4th St
Waterloo IL 62298

Call Sign: KB9YWO
Kevin D Sweet
4552 Fountain Brook Dr
Waterloo IL 62298

Call Sign: K9KDS
Kevin D Sweet
4552 Fountain Brook Dr
Waterloo IL 62298

Call Sign: KC9RUL
Frank R Buckholz
6851 Fountain Oaks Ln
Waterloo IL 62298

Call Sign: W9RUL
Frank R Buckholz
6851 Fountain Oaks Ln
Waterloo IL 62298

Call Sign: KC9RUM
Tamula C Buckholz
6851 Fountain Oaks Ln
Waterloo IL 62298

Call Sign: WA9RJP
Roy L Himmer
6941 Goeddeltown Rd
Waterloo IL 62298

Call Sign: KC9UEP
Jeff A Wyrick
817 Grand Prairie
Waterloo IL 62298

Call Sign: WA9ERT
Ervin W Sweet
3058 Hh Rd
Waterloo IL 62298

Call Sign: KB9MOK
Melanie B Walker
404 Hillcrest
Waterloo IL 62298

Call Sign: AA9UC
David D Walker
404 Hillcrest Dr
Waterloo IL 62298

Call Sign: N9PPK
Billy C King
208 Hoener
Waterloo IL 62298

Call Sign: WB0OSA
Ethel L Taylor
20 Judith Ln
Waterloo IL 62298

Call Sign: WA9TYY
Kenneth R Shreve
6802 K Rd
Waterloo IL 62298

Call Sign: K9KWL
Louis E Gerardi
5437 Konarcik Rd
Waterloo IL 62298

Call Sign: KR9G
Jim J Louvier
5710 Konarcik Rd
Waterloo IL 62298

Call Sign: KC9JCY
Donna R Bergmann
6754 Konarcik Rd
Waterloo IL 62298

Call Sign: KC9JCX
Louis A Bergmann
6754 Konarcik Rd
Waterloo IL 62298

Call Sign: WB4OJM
Felix E Pfeiffer
407 Lakeview Dr
Waterloo IL 62298

Call Sign: N9QNO
Grace K Miller
407 Lakeview Dr
Waterloo IL 62298

Call Sign: WD9DIO
Kenneth D Kloepper
5320 Lemen Rd
Waterloo IL 62298

Call Sign: KC9UJK
Jeff C Davis
1108 Maplewood Ln
Waterloo IL 62298

Call Sign: N9MQW
Gregory A Hoeffken
628 Mark Dr
Waterloo IL 62298

Call Sign: KB9VUI
Lynn V Dunlap
511 Mobile St
Waterloo IL 62298

Call Sign: N7NBS
Charles N Badger Jr
408 Mockingbird Ln
Waterloo IL 62298

Call Sign: WB6TRI
Roger E Larsson
713 Morrison Ave
Waterloo IL 62298

Call Sign: KC9TQU
Gerald E Nungesser
225 B N Main
Waterloo IL 62298

Call Sign: N9UCR
Kevin D Henke
241 N Main St

Waterloo IL 62298

Call Sign: KA0TGO
David J Muzilla
607 N Market St
Waterloo IL 62298

Call Sign: KC9FZM
Brad S Notheisen
1157 N Moore Rd
Waterloo IL 62298

Call Sign: N9MSR
Kathleen A Young
601 Park St
Waterloo IL 62298

Call Sign: N9MSS
Robert J Young
601 Park St
Waterloo IL 62298

Call Sign: KC9FZN
Andrew D Buettner
524 Paul Dr
Waterloo IL 62298

Call Sign: KF9XY
Edward J Warhover
1427 Rachael Ln
Waterloo IL 62298

Call Sign: KG0EG
Phillip L Kitchen
802 Ridge Rd
Waterloo IL 62298

Call Sign: KC9TYT
Donald K Burden
206 Rogers St
Waterloo IL 62298

Call Sign: KA9CJY
Virgil W Baker
703 S Library
Waterloo IL 62298

Call Sign: KB9BGE
Joseph L Tucker

715 S Market Box 143
Waterloo IL 62298

Call Sign: KC9FAT
Jeffrey D Hargiss
6401 S Ronnie Dr
Waterloo IL 62298

Call Sign: KA9LWE
Linda S Simmons
430 Sandalwood Dr
Waterloo IL 62298

Call Sign: N0KX
Rex M Pottorf
7063 SR 156
Waterloo IL 62298

Call Sign: KB9TTG
Stephen R Carmickle
5900 SR 3
Waterloo IL 62298

Call Sign: KC9FHM
Raymond A Weakly
6300 SR 3
Waterloo IL 62298

Call Sign: KB9NDQ
Hugh C Burris
1330 Stonefield Dr
Waterloo IL 62298

Call Sign: KC9RQD
Joseph E Flanagan
701 Sunset Ln
Waterloo IL 62298

Call Sign: N9USW
Joseph E Flanagan
701 Sunset Ln
Waterloo IL 62298

Call Sign: KB9LOE
Steven C Muench
305 W 3rd
Waterloo IL 62298

Call Sign: K9SCM

Steven C Muench
305 W 3rd
Waterloo IL 62298

Call Sign: AB9FO
Richard C Smith
224 W Rose Ln
Waterloo IL 62298

Call Sign: KC9JLI
John J Kessler
610 Willow Ln
Waterloo IL 62298

Call Sign: KC9HOO
Brian H Wright
5715 Winding Path Ln
Waterloo IL 62298

FCC Amateur Radio Licenses in Watseka

Call Sign: W9LIZ
Christine C Schroeder
1505N 2000E Rd
Watseka IL 609709555

Call Sign: N9UOW
Newell J Van Wormer
Rr 2 Box 170
Watseka IL 60970

Call Sign: N9TPP
Justin R Nedza
Rr 2 Box 222
Watseka IL 60970

Call Sign: WB9JHI
Lester Merhley Sr
Rr 3 Box 31
Watseka IL 60970

Call Sign: KC9BEC
Theodore A Nicoson
1654 E 2400 N Rd
Watseka IL 609707662

Call Sign: W9QKF
Sam R Ripple

420 E Locust St
Watseka IL 60970

Call Sign: KC9AVF
Iroquois County ARC
420 E Locust St
Watseka IL 60970

Call Sign: KC9RCD
Chris D Jaworski
535 E Mulberry St
Watseka IL 60970

Call Sign: KB9MHO
William J Ahlgren
707 E Sycamore
Watseka IL 60970

Call Sign: KB9MUN
Howard D Ralph
418 E Walnut
Watseka IL 60970

Call Sign: KC9LBZ
Janet L Focken
103 E Washington
Watseka IL 60970

Call Sign: KC9FON
Timothy R Focken
103 E Washington Ave
Watseka IL 60970

Call Sign: W9TRF
Timothy R Focken
103 E Washington Ave
Watseka IL 60970

Call Sign: WD9AYJ
Maurice H Dowling
100 Loveridge Ln
Watseka IL 60970

Call Sign: KC9LUV
Wendal K Ralph
408 Mulberry St
Watseka IL 60970

Call Sign: AD9L

Iroquois County ARC
1505 N 2000 E Rd
Watseka IL 60970

Call Sign: W9RWX
Iroquois County ARC
1505 N 2000 E Rd
Watseka IL 60970

Call Sign: K9CS
Carl F Schroeder
1505 N 2000 E Rd
Watseka IL 609709555

Call Sign: KC9PWZ
Melissa A Meredith
411 N 8th St
Watseka IL 60970

Call Sign: W9CJM
Chris J Meredith
411 N 8th St
Watseka IL 60970

Call Sign: KC9OQM
Christopher J Meredith
411 N 8th St
Watseka IL 60970

Call Sign: KC9MCA
Troy J Simpson
704 S 2nd St
Watseka IL 60970

Call Sign: W9KVR
Troy J Simpson
704 S 2nd St
Watseka IL 60970

Call Sign: KC9HHT
Michael J Marcier
319 S 3rd St
Watseka IL 60970

Call Sign: KC9GWD
Benny J Marcier
434 S 4th St
Watseka IL 60970

Call Sign: KC9PGB
Billy Perce
519 S 5th St
Watseka IL 60970

Call Sign: KC9OQN
Jakob W Anderson
135 S Belmont Ave
Watseka IL 60970

Call Sign: KC9OQO
John S Anderson
135 S Belmont Ave
Watseka IL 60970

Call Sign: WB9QKE
Donald M Wene
108 W Jackson
Watseka IL 60970

Call Sign: KC9NEW
Glenn Raymond School
Science Club
101 W Mulberry St
Watseka IL 60970

Call Sign: W9GRS
Glenn Raymond School
Science Club
101 W Mulberry St
Watseka IL 60970

Call Sign: W9RWX
Clark M Wockner
1200 W Smith St
Watseka IL 60970

FCC Amateur Radio Licenses in Watson

Call Sign: KB9VKO
Brian A Becker
14547 E 500th Ave
Watson IL 62473

Call Sign: KF9HS
Randall E Becker
14547 E 500th Ave
Watson IL 62473

Call Sign: KB9SSP
Mark A Percival
14162 E 650 Ave
Watson IL 62473

Call Sign: KB9VKP
John E Percival
14162 E 650th Ave
Watson IL 62473

Call Sign: KB9UVK
Sheila S Percival
14162 E 650th Ave
Watson IL 62473

Call Sign: KC9HHP
Jeremy J Hubbard
9454 N 1115th Rd
Watson IL 62473

Call Sign: KC9JIT
Susan J Barnett
301 S East St
Watson IL 62473

Call Sign: KB9SSN
Donald G Davis
305 W Main St
Watson IL 62473

Call Sign: KB9HUX
James A Moake Jr
Watson IL 62473

Call Sign: KB9SSL
James P Faber
Watson IL 62473

Call Sign: KY9X
Stanley E Wilber
Watson IL 62473

FCC Amateur Radio Licenses in Waverly

Call Sign: K9BSY
Meryl E Newberry
395 Kimber St

Waverly IL 62692

Call Sign: N9AYF
Dwight F Homann
149 S Brooks St
Waverly IL 626921035

Call Sign: KD4EUL
Gary L Roth
503 S Miller
Waverly IL 62692

Call Sign: KC9MLH
Phyllis M Osborne
288 W Tanner 5
Waverly IL 62692

FCC Amateur Radio Licenses in Wayne City

Call Sign: KZ9E
Clifford H Clark
R 1 Box 213A
Wayne City IL 62895

Call Sign: KB9LBL
Rosemary E Clark
Rt 1 Box 213A
Wayne City IL 62895

Call Sign: AA9WK
Clyde L Cross
Rr 1 Box 245
Wayne City IL 628959522

Call Sign: KB9KSL
Judith A Harvey
R 1 Box 252
Wayne City IL 62895

Call Sign: KB9POM
Wesley E Cline
22 Sectionline Rd
Wayne City IL 62895

Call Sign: WB9WZC
Glenda A Wood
Valley St
Wayne City IL 62895

Call Sign: WB9KWD
Berl F Hickey
410 W Washington St
Wayne City IL 62895

Call Sign: WB9DEH
Verdon L Wood
Wayne City IL 62895

Call Sign: WB9QJJ
Roger G Hertenstein
Wayne City IL 62895

Call Sign: K9KNX
Albert L Beasley
Wayne City IL 62895

Call Sign: KB9PVL
Mary B Cline
Wayne City IL 62895

Call Sign: AA9QX
John G Clark
Wayne City IL 628950106

FCC Amateur Radio Licenses in Waynesville

Call Sign: KC9PIP
Justin S Aldred
14930 Fairview Rd
Waynesville IL 61778

Call Sign: KC9PIO
Justine L Aldred
14930 Fairview Rd
Waynesville IL 61778

FCC Amateur Radio Licenses in Weldon

Call Sign: KC9FYN
Barbara A Stafford
215 Grove St Box 135
Weldon IL 618820135

Call Sign: KB9GIG
John O Stafford

215 Grove St Box 135
Weldon IL 618820135

Call Sign: K9ISZ
Eddie C Lane
58 Oak St
Weldon IL 618820387

Call Sign: N9VIT
Carolyn A Houston
Weldon IL 61882

FCC Amateur Radio Licenses in Wellington

Call Sign: KC9URK
Andrew A Austin
300 E Main
Wellington IL 60973

Call Sign: AB9LD
Michael P Poole
105 S Donovan St
Wellington IL 60973

FCC Amateur Radio Licenses in Wenona

Call Sign: KC9CIQ
Matt G Gula
957 CR 3100 E
Wenona IL 613779696

Call Sign: K9VWX
Donald W Hoge
827 E Il 17
Wenona IL 61377

Call Sign: KA9HYG
Edward J Divora
653 N 8th Rd
Wenona IL 61377

Call Sign: WA9SNM
Walter J Wenzlaff
205 N Spruce St
Wenona IL 61377

Call Sign: WA9BRH

Howard A Engler
202 S Locust
Wenona IL 61377

Call Sign: KC9TGV
Joshua D Mckean
405 S Locust St
Wenona IL 61377

Call Sign: WB9IMN
William R Marston
401 S Oak St
Wenona IL 61377

Call Sign: KC9IZY
Luke A Meyers
2980 Wenona Rd
Wenona IL 61377

Call Sign: N9QYN
Thomas E Destri
Wenona IL 61377

FCC Amateur Radio Licenses in West Brooklyn

Call Sign: WD9IVE
Daniel J Colangelo
2403 Shady Oaks Rd
West Brooklyn IL 613789711

FCC Amateur Radio Licenses in West Frankfort

Call Sign: N9NMO
Bettyann B Edwards
2172 Antioch Rd
West Frankfort IL 628965807

Call Sign: KB9ZM
James C Couture
2172 Antioch Rd
West Frankfort IL 628965807

Call Sign: KB9FYA
Rebecca A Couture
2172 Antioch Rd
West Frankfort IL 628965807

Call Sign: KC9SWP
John L Holleman
1800 B St
West Frankfort IL 62896

Call Sign: KB9CHU
Corey D Julian
3074 Baseline Rd
West Frankfort IL 62896

Call Sign: WI9U
Danny P Julian
3074 Baseline Rd
West Frankfort IL 62896

Call Sign: KC9RYK
Kyle A Nicholson
17979 Biehl Rd
West Frankfort IL 62896

Call Sign: KC9THM
Tim J Nicholson
17979 Biehl Rd
West Frankfort IL 62896

Call Sign: W9EKX
Francis M Wright
R 4 Box 263
West Frankfort IL 62896

Call Sign: KC5LDR
Barbara A Baker
309 E 8th Apt A
West Frankfort IL 62896

Call Sign: WB9ZFE
Jay M Bussler
1407 E 9th St
West Frankfort IL 62896

Call Sign: KG9LC
John J Zortz
906 E Clark
West Frankfort IL 62896

Call Sign: WD9JEB
John T Walley
809 E Clark St
West Frankfort IL 62896

Call Sign: KC9MCM
Dennis A Davis
1914 E Cleveland St
West Frankfort IL 62896

Call Sign: KE9ZN
Lewis G Russell
713 E Elm St
West Frankfort IL 62896

Call Sign: N9ZDZ
Darren D Braggs
1408 E Elm St
West Frankfort IL 62896

Call Sign: KB9JEC
Gina M Braggs
1408 E Elm St
West Frankfort IL 62896

Call Sign: KB9SHY
Don J Webb
310 E Garland St
West Frankfort IL 62896

Call Sign: N9BJG
Cliff J Kellam
1703 E Garland St
West Frankfort IL 62896

Call Sign: W9BDA
George W Cotter
803 E Main St
West Frankfort IL 62896

Call Sign: WC9AAZ
Franklin Co Emerg Srv &
Disaster Agcy
1403 E Main St
West Frankfort IL 628961508

Call Sign: K9IEY
William L Stalions
1403 E Main St
West Frankfort IL 628961508

Call Sign: KA9QWQ
Irvin E Odum

1737 E Main St
West Frankfort IL 62896

Call Sign: K9OXQ
Olen L Ramsey
2206 E Main St
West Frankfort IL 62896

Call Sign: KF9LX
Jason C Majdich
1405 E Main St Apt 603
West Frankfort IL 62896

Call Sign: N9AZZ
Richard E Minton
904 E Poplar
West Frankfort IL 62896

Call Sign: KC9ADH
Richard L Minton
904 E Poplar
West Frankfort IL 62896

Call Sign: W9AZZ
Richard L Minton
904 E Poplar
West Frankfort IL 62896

Call Sign: KA9TEZ
Paul W Wyant
1704 E St Louis
West Frankfort IL 62896

Call Sign: KC9SZN
Chad A Johnson
1605 E St Louis St
West Frankfort IL 62896

Call Sign: KC9UFX
Robert D Elimon
2305 E St Louis St
West Frankfort IL 62896

Call Sign: KB9KCW
Robert E Hall
113 Elmwood
West Frankfort IL 62896

Call Sign: KB9YAE

Carl N Hall
116 Elmwood
West Frankfort IL 62896

Call Sign: K9MGN
Dwight K Mandrell
12003 Foxcroft Dr
West Frankfort IL 62896

Call Sign: AC9AV
Christopher L Pugh
36 Frankfort Dr
West Frankfort IL 62896

Call Sign: KC9SCZ
Paul L Mullins
8774 Freeman Spur Blacktop
West Frankfort IL 62896

Call Sign: AA9RF
Sid Smilanich
508 Hughes
West Frankfort IL 62896

Call Sign: WB9JIP
Arvie G Dorris
16024 Mine 25 Rd
West Frankfort IL 62896

Call Sign: WB9JIO
Margaret L Dorris
16024 Mine 25 Rd
West Frankfort IL 62896

Call Sign: N9WFI
Robert A Van Zandt
410 N Crawford St
West Frankfort IL 62896

Call Sign: K9THA
Wilbur E Lauer
404 N Gardner St
West Frankfort IL 62896

Call Sign: WA9BOT
Thomas N Little
311 N Horrell
West Frankfort IL 62896

Call Sign: AA9RM
Donna G Smilanich
508 N Hughes
West Frankfort IL 62896

Call Sign: N9PBH
Bennie D Manion III
605 N Parkhill
West Frankfort IL 62896

Call Sign: N9RZQ
Larry M Pfister
7571 Parrish Cir
West Frankfort IL 62896

Call Sign: KA9PGI
Thomas H Gunter
7732 Parrish Cir
West Frankfort IL 62896

Call Sign: KC9NWC
David W Batts
17202 Parrish Rd
West Frankfort IL 62896

Call Sign: AB9ST
David W Batts
17202 Parrish Rd
West Frankfort IL 62896

Call Sign: K9JJE
Frances J Nicholson
21 Razer Dr
West Frankfort IL 628961935

Call Sign: KC9PCG
Gary A Little
100 Razer Dr Apt 11
West Frankfort IL 62896

Call Sign: K9LLW
Don J Webb
114 S Emma
West Frankfort IL 62896

Call Sign: WA9DOO
John L Russell
805 S Emma St
West Frankfort IL 62896

Call Sign: W9NFV
Ralph L Williams
610 S Jackson St
West Frankfort IL 628963239

Call Sign: KC9AHF
John D Gross
602 S Locust
West Frankfort IL 62896

Call Sign: KB9NDW
Mark F Rundle
18704 State Hwy 149
West Frankfort IL 62896

Call Sign: KB9MST
Frank P Rundle
18704 State Hwy 149
West Frankfort IL 62896

Call Sign: KB9OTH
John G Rundle
18704 State Hwy 149
West Frankfort IL 62896

Call Sign: KB9MTP
Kathryn F Rundle
18704 State Hwy 149
West Frankfort IL 62896

Call Sign: KC9STL
H F Blackbirds 1st Air Wing
17019 State Hwy 149 E
West Frankfort IL 62896

Call Sign: AA9MC
H F Blackbirds 1st Air Wing
17019 State Hwy 149 E
West Frankfort IL 62896

Call Sign: AG4WO
Jay B Fuller
999 State Hwy 37
West Frankfort IL 62896

Call Sign: KB9TMQ
Wayne M Seagle
201.5 W 9th St

West Frankfort IL 628961114

Call Sign: WA9TSI
Peter W Barbera
213 W Lindell
West Frankfort IL 628962017

Call Sign: N9PGK
Rick D Lewis
217 W Lindell
West Frankfort IL 62896

Call Sign: KC9RZB
David R Williams
801 W Lindell
West Frankfort IL 62896

Call Sign: KM4UA
Bill W Craig
501 W Oak
West Frankfort IL 62896

Call Sign: KB9MFW
Ralph T Perry
1206 W Oak
West Frankfort IL 62896

Call Sign: KC9RTP
Judy L Craig
501 W Oak St
West Frankfort IL 62896

Call Sign: W9PHH
Nancy D Bundy
209 W St Louis St
West Frankfort IL 62896

Call Sign: KV5A
Kenneth D Brown
806 W St Louis St
West Frankfort IL 62896

Call Sign: KB9EZC
Alfred P Hosick
14592 Wilburn Rd
West Frankfort IL 62896

FCC Amateur Radio Licenses in West Liberty

Call Sign: KF9NM
Roger D Hart
West Liberty IL 62475

FCC Amateur Radio Licenses in West Peoria

Call Sign: KC9RZS
Eugene R Buffard
3200 Alice Ave
West Peoria IL 61604

Call Sign: W8QGE
David W Barker
652 Coolidge Ct
West Peoria IL 61604

Call Sign: W9EKG
Brandon M Cutright
2110 W Ayres Ave
West Peoria IL 616045506

Call Sign: KB9KBD
Donnadee Pearsall
2122 W Barker
West Peoria IL 616045512

Call Sign: N9YVE
Richard D Stoneburner
2623 W Kenwood Ave
West Peoria IL 61604

Call Sign: N9PSS
Patrick A Jeschke
2305 W Laura Ave
West Peoria IL 61604

Call Sign: KC9NWD
Robert R Archer
2215 W Moss Ave
West Peoria IL 61604

Call Sign: KC9QMZ
Scot P Guariglia
2615 W Rohmann Ave
West Peoria IL 61604

FCC Amateur Radio Licenses in West Point

Call Sign: KA9WWU
David F Hale
West Point IL 62380

FCC Amateur Radio Licenses in West Salem

Call Sign: KB9KLE
Bob D Morris
Rr 1 Box 187
West Salem IL 62476

Call Sign: N9XEH
James L Marks
Rr 1 Box 251
West Salem IL 62476

Call Sign: KA9CYC
Martin W Greatline
Rt 1 Box 322
West Salem IL 62476

Call Sign: AG4IA
Amos J Chenoweth
1020 CR 1750 N
West Salem IL 62476

Call Sign: KB9KOM
Debra S Goldsmith
201 E North St
West Salem IL 62476

Call Sign: KB9KKF
Eric T Goldsmith
201 E North St
West Salem IL 62476

Call Sign: KB9KLF
Donny L Knackmus
206 S Prairie
West Salem IL 62476

Call Sign: KB9LFM
Ella M Knackmus
206 S Prairie St
West Salem IL 62476

West Union IL 624770043

FCC Amateur Radio Licenses in West Union

Call Sign: N9VNQ
Wade A Jackson
Rr 2 Box 5
West Union IL 62477

Call Sign: N9GIK
Michael W Bumpus
18134 E Angling Rd
West Union IL 62477

Call Sign: N9GMN
Carl R Robinson Jr
214 E Washington St
West Union IL 62477

Call Sign: N9LKW
Reta M Bumpus
5966 N 2100th St
West Union IL 624772602

Call Sign: KB9IOF
Jean H Kilmer
8020 N Darand Rd
West Union IL 62477

Call Sign: KF9OY
Carl L Kilmer
8020 N Darand Rd
West Union IL 624779650

Call Sign: K9HHS
William P Crumrin
109 S Walnut St
West Union IL 62477

Call Sign: KB9GLY
Karen M Cork
West Union IL 62477

Call Sign: WA9WKK
Roy D Cork
West Union IL 62477

Call Sign: WA9DCO
Clay Cork Jr

FCC Amateur Radio Licenses in West York

Call Sign: KC9NCX
Charles E Morrison
21219 N 1050 St
West York IL 62478

FCC Amateur Radio Licenses in Westfield

Call Sign: WD9JDQ
Daniel L Cohen
2255N CR 2420E
Westfield IL 62474

Call Sign: KA7EXH
Ronny L Young
305 E Walnut
Westfield IL 62474

Call Sign: AB9GI
Ronny L Young
305 E Walnut
Westfield IL 62474

Call Sign: KA9YAJ
Michelle L Cohen
2255 N CR 2420E
Westfield IL 62474

Call Sign: KC9GWT
Bette A Young
Westfield IL 62474

FCC Amateur Radio Licenses in Westville

Call Sign: KA9DTK
Jimmy L Torbit
120 Clark St
Westville IL 61883

Call Sign: KC9USH
Stuart L Winland
16177 E Clingan Ln
Westville IL 61883

Call Sign: WB9TUG
John Falletti
510 E Kelly
Westville IL 61883

Call Sign: KB9GS
Jan J Mayer
613 E Kelly
Westville IL 61883

Call Sign: KA9KAM
Roberta M Mayer
701 E Kelly Ave
Westville IL 61883

Call Sign: N9UWE
Dan J Lehnen
309 E Williams
Westville IL 61883

Call Sign: W9OGQ
Carl L Merlie
1214 English St
Westville IL 61883

Call Sign: KC9RMX
Ronald J Delva
15 James
Westville IL 61883

Call Sign: W9VPR
Jerry D Smith
212 Market St
Westville IL 61883

Call Sign: W4VIO
Franklin D Ritter
223 N Jefferson St
Westville IL 61883

Call Sign: W9CR
Carl G Davis
121 N Scott St
Westville IL 61883

Call Sign: W9OIL
Henry L Falconio Jr
135 N State St

Westville IL 61883

Call Sign: W9IUH
John E Urbas
220 N State St
Westville IL 61883

Call Sign: K9JHV
Victor D Latoz
125 N West St
Westville IL 61883

Call Sign: W9PAO
Roy H Hanson
721 S State St
Westville IL 61883

Call Sign: K9PVM
Ben M Lattuada
904 S State St
Westville IL 61883

Call Sign: KC9AFM
John A Karl
1602 S State St
Westville IL 61883

Call Sign: KC9JAK
John A Karl
1602 S State St
Westville IL 618836011

Call Sign: WB9QWP
Charles D Mc Carty
123 Sunset Dr
Westville IL 61883

Call Sign: KC9FPT
Alfred A Carle
201 Virginia Ave
Westville IL 61883

Call Sign: KC9VQK
Mike R Bertelli
128 Washington Ave
Westville IL 61883

Call Sign: N9XLI
John D Lugoski Sr

Westville IL 61883

FCC Amateur Radio Licenses in Wheeler

Call Sign: KA9RCG
Wesley G Salyers
Rr 1 Box 304
Wheeler IL 62479

FCC Amateur Radio Licenses in White Hall

Call Sign: KC9VPR
William C Hoesman
530 Edgewood Dr
White Hall IL 62092

Call Sign: KC9OXT
Kate J Johnson
215 W Lincoln
White Hall IL 62092

Call Sign: KC9OPI
Samuel L Collins
215 W Lincoln
White Hall IL 62092

Call Sign: W9OCC
Samuel L Collins
215 W Lincoln
White Hall IL 62092

Call Sign: W8VMT
James L Telzrow
White Hall IL 62092

FCC Amateur Radio Licenses in White Heath

Call Sign: N9IXS
John Avelis III
R 1 Box 102
White Heath IL 61884

Call Sign: KB9DDI
Mary M Avelis
R 1 Box 102
White Heath IL 61884

Call Sign: KB9WCI
Robert S Trusty
103 Commercial St
White Heath IL 61884

Call Sign: WE9E
John Avelis Jr
1456 E 2275 N Rd
White Heath IL 61884

Call Sign: KC9PCR
Tony R Benson
103 E High St
White Heath IL 61884

Call Sign: KB9WEW
Charles E Morris
1134 E Old Rt 47
White Heath IL 61884

Call Sign: KA9UOU
Pamela J O Connor
1913 N 1400 E Rd
White Heath IL 61884

Call Sign: KA9SZY
Timothy M O Connor
1913 N 1400 E Rd
White Heath IL 618840096

Call Sign: W9TBB
Fred R Ore
1352 Treasure Ln
White Heath IL 618849316

Call Sign: KC9JRY
Ronald W Rochyby
White Heath IL 61884

FCC Amateur Radio Licenses in Whittington

Call Sign: N9UQC
David P Lingle
Rr 1 Box 24
Whittington IL 62897

Call Sign: N9WLE

James B Reeves
12586 Golf Course Dr 723
Whittington IL 62897

FCC Amateur Radio Licenses in Williamsville

Call Sign: KM5BC
Carl L Cosand
143 800th Ave
Williamsville IL 62693

Call Sign: WD9GGS
Jesse L Harris
333 E Conray Box 172
Williamsville IL 62693

FCC Amateur Radio Licenses in Willisville

Call Sign: WB9YUM
Jesse L Woolsey
104 Kings Hwy
Willisville IL 62997

Call Sign: KC9DQ
Dennis D Welty
415 Russell St
Willisville IL 62997

Call Sign: KF9NW
Robert E Franklin
Willisville IL 62997

FCC Amateur Radio Licenses in Willow Hill

Call Sign: KC9TVC
William E Leffler
19344A E 1050 Ave
Willow Hill IL 62480

FCC Amateur Radio Licenses in Winchester

Call Sign: WD9GBV
Reta L Killebrew
R 1 Box 105

Winchester IL 62694

Call Sign: KC9MLJ
Greggory K Lewis
234 N Commercial St
Winchester IL 62694

Call Sign: K9GKL
Greggory K Lewis
234 N Commercial St
Winchester IL 62694

Call Sign: W9OAF
Ronald F Robinson
245 Pearl
Winchester IL 62694

Call Sign: KB9LYR
Kenneth C Roundcount
170 S Hill
Winchester IL 62694

Call Sign: WA9RTA
Roland L Wallis
1438 Wallis Rd
Winchester IL 62694

FCC Amateur Radio Licenses in Windsor

Call Sign: KB9YCC
Chris W Demkov
813 Maine St
Windsor IL 61957

Call Sign: WX9D
Jerry H Van Matre
503 N Chestnut
Windsor IL 61957

Call Sign: KB9SUD
Steven W Shirley
415 S Maple Ave
Windsor IL 61957

FCC Amateur Radio Licenses in Winnebago

Call Sign: KE9ZK

Kevin M Sandager
208 Bluff St
Winnebago IL 61088

Call Sign: N9ISL
David J Klepitch
9820 Bridgeland Rd
Winnebago IL 61088

Call Sign: KC9ROV
Patrick L D Amato Sr
9820 Bridgeland Rd
Winnebago IL 61088

Call Sign: N9GFS
Sam D D Amato
9820 Bridgeland Rd
Winnebago IL 61088

Call Sign: KB9JRU
Scott R Remer
9019 Cunningham Rd
Winnebago IL 61088

Call Sign: KC9CJY
Jarrod J Cook
617 David Dr
Winnebago IL 61088

Call Sign: W9KG
Ambrose A Kopp
1243 E Montague Rd
Winnebago IL 61088

Call Sign: KB9IW
Steven E Makulec
8041 Hilltop Ct E
Winnebago IL 610889652

Call Sign: KB9RSH
Michael R Luna
606 Jarvis Dr
Winnebago IL 61088

Call Sign: KB9TPE
Sue L Luna
606 Jarvis Dr
Winnebago IL 61088

Call Sign: KB9TQ
William A Smith
4805 Kendall Rd
Winnebago IL 61088

Call Sign: KA9MCX
Mary E Weltzer
1306 Lamson Dr
Winnebago IL 61088

Call Sign: WD9HSH
Thomas M Weltzer
1306 Lamson Dr
Winnebago IL 61088

Call Sign: W9TMW
Thomas M Weltzer
1306 Lamson Dr
Winnebago IL 61088

Call Sign: KB9FRX
Vail R Cordell IV
403 Mallard Rd
Winnebago IL 610889783

Call Sign: KC9BPV
Carl G Trank
227 Mathew Ct
Winnebago IL 61088

Call Sign: W5MHZ
Randy C Trank
227 Mathew Ct
Winnebago IL 61088

Call Sign: W9KOK
Dick B Mitchell
10776 Montague Rd
Winnebago IL 61088

Call Sign: WF9J
Richard L Tidberg
3751 N Hoisington Rd
Winnebago IL 61088

Call Sign: KC9DGA
Benjamin E Vassmer
2010 N Welson Rd
Winnebago IL 61088

Call Sign: WD9CHD
Delbert A West
621 S Goodling St
Winnebago IL 610889217

Call Sign: KB9CLE
Daniel B Visel
3861 S Weldon Rd
Winnebago IL 61088

Call Sign: KB9ERO
Jeana M Visel
3861 S Weldon Rd
Winnebago IL 61088

Call Sign: KC9UAX
David S Dunn
412 W McNair Rd
Winnebago IL 61088

Call Sign: W9DSD
David S Dunn
412 W McNair Rd
Winnebago IL 61088

Call Sign: K9KCX
Robert F Schmoock
12142 W SR
Winnebago IL 61088

Call Sign: KC9RMJ
Jerry A Horn
405 Zearl Ct
Winnebago IL 61088

Call Sign: KV9E
Jerry A Horn
405 Zearl Ct
Winnebago IL 61088

FCC Amateur Radio Licenses in Winslow

Call Sign: KC9TXC
Richard J Prien
11750 N Damascus Rd
Winslow IL 61089

Call Sign: N9TJC
Robert M Curran
15127 W Nora Rd
Winslow IL 61089

Call Sign: KC9JNC
Larry R Fulfs
7202 W Winslow Rd
Winslow IL 61089

FCC Amateur Radio Licenses in Witt

Call Sign: KB9TZV
Rebecca L Styron
17178 N 17th Ave
Witt IL 62094

Call Sign: KG9KE
Dorothy A Mc Daniel
616 N SR 1 Box 147B
Witt IL 62094

Call Sign: KB9BAJ
John E Mc Daniel
616 North St
Witt IL 62094

Call Sign: KB9UJR
Jeromy L Miller
15218 Paisley Rd
Witt IL 62094

Call Sign: N9SYO
John C Livesay
134 S 7th St
Witt IL 62094

Call Sign: KC9ITX
Evan M Fifer
Witt IL 62094

Call Sign: K9TCB
Evan M Fifer
Witt IL 62094

FCC Amateur Radio Licenses in Wood River

Call Sign: KA9MCR
Edward E Turnbeaugh
653 1st St
Wood River IL 62095

Call Sign: KB9EXC
Andrew G E Carr
655 1st St
Wood River IL 62095

Call Sign: WA9ETR
William G Burney
502 7th St
Wood River IL 62095

Call Sign: W9OJN
Grover E Sparks
944 Cedar
Wood River IL 62095

Call Sign: KC9SLH
Maurice E Jones
667 Colonial Dr
Wood River IL 62095

Call Sign: W9WDD
Charles L Vannoy
413 Crestview Dr
Wood River IL 620954060

Call Sign: KB9BYK
Andrew S Auer
103 E Acton
Wood River IL 62095

Call Sign: N9VFR
David S Duncan
635 E Acton
Wood River IL 62095

Call Sign: N9DVV
Caleb O Bost
395 E Edwardsville Rd Apt
332
Wood River IL 62095

Call Sign: N9PFH
Robert D Pearson
865 E Penning Ave

Wood River IL 620952139

Call Sign: K9IQE
Boris E Kusmanoff
829 E Penning Ave
Wood River IL 62095

Call Sign: WB9LXM
Francis R Droit
69 Eckhard Ave
Wood River IL 62095

Call Sign: KB9PAI
Roger N Weiss
608 George
Wood River IL 62095

Call Sign: KA9EKS
Ralph C Richter
205 Greenbriar Dr
Wood River IL 62095

Call Sign: N9JWZ
Norma L Richter
205 Greenbriar Dr
Wood River IL 62095

Call Sign: N9GYU
Michael D Mc Kinney Sr
630 Halloran Ave
Wood River IL 62095

Call Sign: KB9UCE
Mark A Frields
67 Kendall Dr
Wood River IL 62095

Call Sign: KB9MTG
Robbie A Nooner
849 Lewis Ave
Wood River IL 62095

Call Sign: KC9STT
Neil A Sherman
560 N 1st St
Wood River IL 62095

Call Sign: K9HWT
Jerry L Manis

12 N 6th St
Wood River IL 62095

Call Sign: KB9JET
Mark A Manis
12 N 6th St
Wood River IL 62095

Call Sign: N9WHH
Christopher D Holland
965 N Wood River Ave
Wood River IL 62095

Call Sign: K9THU
Robert W Keefe
644 Penning Ave
Wood River IL 62095

Call Sign: KB9IMF
Douglas D Davis
224 Picker Ave
Wood River IL 62095

Call Sign: K9DYF
Donald C Keber
726 Rice St
Wood River IL 62095

Call Sign: N9YYR
Jerry A Robins
454 Roosevelt Ave
Wood River IL 62095

Call Sign: KA9PPE
Larry E Bruhn
210 S 13th St
Wood River IL 62095

Call Sign: N9SIH
Steven M Ambo
137 S 7th St
Wood River IL 62095

Call Sign: KB9GZA
Steven M Ambo
137 S 7th St
Wood River IL 62095

Call Sign: KB9ZVL

Alan S Howard
224 S 7th St
Wood River IL 62095

Call Sign: N9YNQ
Mark E Brown
163 S 8th St
Wood River IL 62095

Call Sign: KB9WGM
Richard C Grant
133 Thompson 8
Wood River IL 62095

Call Sign: KC9SYZ
Stephen C Bond
216 Whitelaw
Wood River IL 62095

Call Sign: N9XKK
Michael O Shea
932 Whitelaw
Wood River IL 62095

Call Sign: KB9VUV
Shawn C Lynch
978 Wood Rivers Ave
Wood River IL 62095

Call Sign: W9FD
Walter W Johler
Wood River IL 62095

FCC Amateur Radio Licenses in Woodhull

Call Sign: KB9LDB
Greg H Bloomberg
Rr 1 Box 105
Woodhull IL 61490

FCC Amateur Radio Licenses in Woodlawn

Call Sign: KB9DBP
Ernest A Carpenter
Rr 2 Box 86
Woodlawn IL 62898

Call Sign: KB9RNN
Robert A Kinison
Rt 1 Box 92
Woodlawn IL 62898

Call Sign: KB9QXT
David P Kinison
Rt1 Box 92
Woodlawn IL 62898

Call Sign: KC9UQU
Kevin R Wilson
13044 Dayton Dr
Woodlawn IL 62898

Call Sign: WD9ALL
Kevin R Wilson
13044 Dayton Dr
Woodlawn IL 62898

Call Sign: KB9UEP
Daniel J Meadows
4986 E Richview Rd
Woodlawn IL 628982204

Call Sign: KB9LVI
Quintin L Kimmel
5339 E Richview Rd
Woodlawn IL 62898

Call Sign: WA9GYU
Leroy R Burke Sr
Woodlawn IL 62898

FCC Amateur Radio Licenses in Woodson

Call Sign: WA9YTQ
Ronald E Luttrell
Main St
Woodson IL 62695

Call Sign: KB9ANR
Paula J Luttrell
Woodson IL 62695

FCC Amateur Radio Licenses in Woosung

Call Sign: WA9MTL
Edwin D Yingling
Woosung IL 61091

FCC Amateur Radio Licenses in Worden

Call Sign: KB9MAL
Kimberly J Pomatto
9308 Barenfenger Rd
Worden IL 62097

Call Sign: KB9MAM
Michael S Pomatto
9308 Barenfenger Rd
Worden IL 62097

Call Sign: KA9WDY
Terry L Pomatto
Rr 1 Box 479
Worden IL 62097

Call Sign: N9NYC
Dwight G Yaw
7771 Brickyard Rd
Worden IL 62097

Call Sign: N9BVJ
Robert E Travis
1791 Commodore Walk
Worden IL 62097

Call Sign: KB9BDY
Matthew T Dooly
7674 E Frontage Rd
Worden IL 62097

Call Sign: N9MYM
Rick L Burgess
1755 Fountainbleu Dr
Worden IL 62097

Call Sign: KC9UZQ
Rick L Burgess
1755 Fountainbleu Dr
Worden IL 62097

Call Sign: AC9AW
Rick L Burgess

1755 Fountainbleu Dr
Worden IL 62097

Call Sign: KU9T
Rick L Burgess
1755 Fountainbleu Dr
Worden IL 62097

Call Sign: KA9KHS
Roger D Quarton
223 N Lincoln St
Worden IL 62097

Call Sign: W8FEX
Curtis A Smith
1846 Sextant Dr
Worden IL 62097

Call Sign: KC9UPV
Michael D Gale
9823 SR 140
Worden IL 62097

Call Sign: WX9F
Dawn M Skapinski
1674 Sutwan Dr
Worden IL 62097

Call Sign: KC9MYO
Devon R Bledsoe
109 W Kell St
Worden IL 62097

Call Sign: KC9TVV
Wendy H Bledsoe
109 W Kell St
Worden IL 62097

Call Sign: KC9MYP
Jeremy A Bledsoe
109 W Kell St
Worden IL 62097

Call Sign: WJ6B
Jeremy A Bledsoe
109 W Kell St
Worden IL 62097

Call Sign: KC9TVU

Samuel D Bledsoe
109 W Kell St
Worden IL 62097

FCC Amateur Radio Licenses in Wyanet

Call Sign: N9FGT
Denny L Taylor
406 S Maple Box 172
Wyanet IL 61379

FCC Amateur Radio Licenses in Wyoming

Call Sign: N9RLU
Randy L Irwin
Rr 2 Box 76
Wyoming IL 614919522

FCC Amateur Radio Licenses in Xenia

Call Sign: KB9TRI
Louis G Moses
6329 Beard
Xenia IL 62899

Call Sign: KC9ESV
Daniel B Staat
Rr1 Box 179W
Xenia IL 62899

Call Sign: KB9SRQ
Dale E Hillyer
Rt 1 Box 195 D
Xenia IL 62899

Call Sign: KB9USK
Gregory E Ashley
Rt 1 Box 195 D
Xenia IL 62899

Call Sign: N9SPS
Walter J Johnson
Rr 2 Box 37
Xenia IL 62899

Call Sign: KB9UXA

Hazel M Hillyer
1027 Church St
Xenia IL 62899

Call Sign: KC9BUL
James E Krutsinger
656 Popeberry Ln
Xenia IL 628992285

Call Sign: W9WF
Gary W Bright
960 Shortleaf Rd
Xenia IL 62899

Call Sign: W9EIN
Clyde W Miller
Xenia IL 62899

FCC Amateur Radio Licenses in Yale

Call Sign: KC9FMP
Jerald B Andrews
403 N Range St
Yale IL 62481

FCC Amateur Radio Licenses in Yates City

Call Sign: W9GSA
Paul D Gibb
215 Main
Yates City IL 61572

Call Sign: KA9VQP
Kim M Frakes
Yates City IL 61572

Call Sign: KA9QMT
Steven W Frakes
Yates City IL 61572

FCC Amateur Radio Licenses in Zeigler

Call Sign: KC9RCE
Dale E Martin Sr
106 Elm St
Zeigler IL 62999

Call Sign: AB9VR
Dale E Martin Sr
106 Elm St
Zeigler IL 62999

Call Sign: KC9RCF
Lisa M Martin
106 Elm St
Zeigler IL 62999

Call Sign: AB9VQ
Lisa M Martin
106 Elm St
Zeigler IL 62999

Call Sign: KB9BVA
James O Trepanier
109 Mongoose St
Zeigler IL 62999

Call Sign: KB9GJC
Michael R Land
214 N Main St
Zeigler IL 62999

Call Sign: N9YWT
Marion S Martin
5 North St
Zeigler IL 62999

Call Sign: KC9OFJ
Michael D Jarvis
134 Prairie St
Zeigler IL 62999

Call Sign: KC9KWN
Ryan M Buckingham
304 S Main St
Zeigler IL 62999

Call Sign: KC9KWH
Daivd L Grear
302 S Pine
Zeigler IL 62999

Call Sign: KB9MLB
Randall D Bush
106 School St

Zeigler IL 62999

Call Sign: N1ER
Randall D Bush
106 School St
Zeigler IL 62999

Call Sign: KC9CVT
James A Mcclure
305 Walnut
Zeigler IL 62999

www.ingramcontent.com/pod-product-compliance
Lightning Source LLC
Chambersburg PA
CBHW081049280326
41928CB00053B/2890